A BASIC MUSIC
LIBRARY

A BASIC MUSIC LIBRARY

Essential Scores and Sound Recordings

FOURTH EDITION

COMPILED BY THE MUSIC LIBRARY ASSOCIATION

DANIEL F. BOOMHOWER, *Editor*

VOLUME 1: POPULAR MUSIC

Edited by

EDWARD KOMARA

AMERICAN LIBRARY ASSOCIATION

CHICAGO   2017

While extensive effort has gone into ensuring the reliability of the information in this book, the publisher makes no warranty, express or implied, with respect to the material contained herein.

ISBN: 978-0-8389-1039-9 (print)

Library of Congress Cataloging-in-Publication Data

Names: Boomhower, Daniel F., 1976– | Komara, Edward M., 1966– | Maple, Amanda, 1956– | Vick, Liza. | Music Library Association.

Title: A basic music library : essential scores and sound recordings / compiled by the Music Library Association ; Daniel F. Boomhower, editor ; Edward Komara, Amanda Maple, and Liza Vick, associate editors.

Description: Fourth edition. | Chicago : American Library Association, 2017. | Includes bibliographical references and index.

Identifiers: LCCN 2013020223 | ISBN 9780838910399 (v. 1 ; alk. paper) | ISBN 9780838915301 (v. 2 ; alk. paper) | ISBN 9780838915318 (v. 3 ; alk. paper)

Subjects: LCSH: Music—Bibliography. | Music libraries—Collection development.

Classification: LCC ML113 .B3 2017 | DDC 016.78—dc23 LC record available at https://lccn.loc.gov/2013020223

Composition by Dianne M. Rooney in Charis SIL typeface.

♾ This paper meets the requirements of ANSI/NISO Z39.48-1992 (Permanence of Paper)

Printed in the United States of America

21 20 19 18 17   5 4 3 2 1

CONTENTS

GENERAL INTRODUCTION
by Daniel F. Boomhower   vii

VOLUME 1: POPULAR MUSIC   1

INTRODUCTION *by Edward Komara*

1   Music of Colonial North America and
    the United States to about 1900   5

2   Blues   15

3   Jazz   33

4   Mainstream Popular and New Age   65

5   Country and Western   85

6   Rock   101

7   Rhythm and Blues and Soul   125

8   Rap and Hip-Hop   153

9   Gospel Music and Other Popular
    Christian Music   165

10   Children's Music   179

11   Holidays, Special Occasions, Patriotic
     Music, and Miscellaneous   185

ABOUT THE EDITORS AND CONTRIBUTORS   191

INDEX   195

GENERAL INTRODUCTION

by DANIEL F. BOOMHOWER

This volume is intended to offer suggestions for anyone, regardless of musical training or experience, who is seeking to develop music collections in libraries of all kinds. While containing the thoughtful advice of librarians and scholars, these suggestions must be matched to real-world circumstances. It seems entirely unlikely that a library would need to include in its collection every item listed in this volume. Only some of the lists in this volume may be useful for one library; other institutions may need much more in a particular area than could possibly be included in this publication.

The fluid nature of the market of music materials, especially sound recordings, will make it unlikely that every item in the volume or even in a single list could be acquired at any given time. Likewise, important new publications will continue to appear that find their way into library collections through routine collection development processes. Through the listing of individual items here, the contributors and editors of this volume have strived to offer *representative* lists that might provide an indication of the nature of the various kinds of music available. Additionally, we have provided introductory information that gives an overview

of particular concepts and issues relevant to the various styles of music treated here. Through these introductions, it is hoped that the reader will become confident in extending the scope of his collection-building efforts to include content not cited here.

Library collections must serve a specific community. Identifying and acquiring the materials that are most useful to that community should remain the focus of library collecting. This volume offers generalized guidance. A "basic" music collection is not a "perfect" music collection. Indeed, the "perfect" music collection may emerge from helpful suggestions, but it is something that has to be carefully developed to be useful to real readers and listeners. With that in mind, I hope this volume is useful, and that it also serves as a point of departure.

A Basic Music Library, published in three previous editions (1978, 1983, and 1997), was originally conceived to offer collecting guidance to library selectors without a music background who often worked in public libraries and smaller academic libraries. However, with the dramatic expansion in the amount of music available and the amount of music sought by patrons in libraries of all kinds, the audience for *A Basic Music*

Library may now be considered to be much larger. This would include a greater number of library selectors with training in some musical tradition, but with unequal command of all styles of music.

Reflecting the changing nature of available music and the diversity of patron interests that libraries seek to serve, *A Basic Music Library* has evolved with each successive edition. Initially, the focus was on printed materials: books and scores. In the third edition, books were no longer included and sound recordings became a dominant component of the publication. In all three of these editions, the better portion of the publication treated music in the Western art music tradition, or what is typically called "classical music." The shift from books to sound recordings in the third edition reflected both the changing nature of libraries' needs and the appearance of publications that provided suitable guidance for developing collections of music books.

This fourth edition has also adapted to changing circumstances in libraries, whether a given library seeks to sustain existing collections or to establish new music collections. Most significantly, the fourth edition will comprise three separate volumes that treat "popular music," "world music," and "classical music," respectively. This flexible format will enable users of *A Basic Music Library* to focus attention on the materials of greatest interest. To meet changing library needs, the fourth edition also incorporates:

- expanded coverage of world music, including CDs and DVDs;
- updated coverage of popular music, including CDs, DVDs, and songbooks;
- integrated coverage of classical music, combining printed music with CDs and DVDs; and
- citations that have been carefully balanced in order to offer a culturally, geographically, and stylistically diverse representation of music throughout the world.

Library collecting is the process of employing limited resources to bring together the best materials, drawn from a variety of available sources, that will serve the needs of library users at a particular time and place. The present volume was compiled in exactly the same way. There is not sufficient space to include items some may consider "basic," and some may imagine the nature of the lists included here as greatly expanding the notion of "basic." A fine line must be tread. On the one hand, too short a list begins to assume a prescriptive nature. On the other hand, too long a list can obscure what is of greatest importance. Similarly, the perception of what it might cost to build an appropriate collection in a particular musical area greatly depends on the number of items that seem necessary. The goal of the lists in this publication is to offer a representative snapshot of the scope of music from different regions of the world, in different genres, and for different instruments. From these lists, and with the guidance of the introductory essays, it should become possible to determine what is most suitable for meeting the needs of one's library and community.

Bringing this volume to completion involved significant effort on the part of many individuals and institutions. First and foremost, the contributors whose work fills these pages deserve the greatest thanks. Without their time and expertise this volume would not have been possible. Likewise, the associate editors gave enormously of their time to organize the contributions and to see that each contribution reached the page in the best and clearest form, reflective of the high standards evident in each chapter. As work on this fourth edition got underway, the editors sought counsel from a range of authorities on the nature of musical canons, and their thoughts were published in the Music Library Association's journal *Notes,* volume 64, no. 2, pages 209–247. These essays served as a counterpoise to the nitty-gritty work of defining a core selection of titles that represents as much of the world's music as possible. We are also deeply indebted to the contributors and editors of the previous editions of *A Basic Music Library,* upon whose excellent work this edition is grounded. In particular, William E. Anderson provided a significant amount of material that served as the basis of revisions for many popular and world music chapters.

VOLUME

POPULAR MUSIC

1

Introduction by **EDWARD KOMARA**

For many people, popular music is the only music they know. Despite what its critics often think, popular music has its achievements, its longevity, its adventures, its history, and, most important, its appeal. Many librarians with music training come from classical backgrounds, so they may not be familiar with some individual kinds of popular music—the very kinds that today's patrons ask for in public libraries and, increasingly, in academic libraries.

Over the last 110 years, the creative drives and the business of American popular music have evolved. In 1900, music was sold in print form, whether sheet music or scores, for performance at home or local functions. The styles emerging in the United States to or about 1900—whether religious music and spirituals, band music, popular vocal and instrumental music, or ragtime—would be transformed into the kinds of popular music we know today. Much of what we call mainstream pop was created by composers—among them George M. Cohan, Irving Berlin, Jerome Kern, George Gershwin, and Cole Porter—not for records, but for singers featured in musical shows and revues, and later in the movies.

When sound recording playback was improved in the early 1900s to convey human voices and recognizable musical instruments, it would only be a matter of some time before styles of music would become prominent not through the composers, but through the performers. Jazz was the first to achieve more recognition through records than through printed publications, and by the end of the 1930s its swing style was a favorite form of American popular music. Blues from the South and Chicago, and country music from Texas to the Carolinas, appeared initially in regional records markets, but by 1942 both styles engendered artists of national popularity. Because of the distinctive, indelible nature of recorded sound, in contrast to the notated music open to any number of interpretations, jazz, blues, and country were important in gradually steering the public identification of music from eye to ear. Popular religious music before World War II developed independently from the classical and spiritual forms, and gospel music appeared in the 1930s largely through the compositions of Thomas A. Dorsey.

After World War II, popular music reached a peak, and then passed into a transitional era. Christmas music

was introducing many new secular songs, often more about Santa Claus than the baby Jesus. The musical theater of Rodgers and Hammerstein and of Frank Loesser provided many new songs for nightclub singers and recording artists. The development of the vinyl LP disc, playing for 20 minutes or more per side, led to concept collections and overviews, notably the Capitol LPs of Frank Sinatra (1953–1960) and the Verve label Songbook series by Ella Fitzgerald. Jazz musicians were improvising to chromatic scales and the show tunes of Gershwin and Porter, and the resulting style became known as bebop, and later as modern jazz. Rhythm and blues was an entertaining style by and for postwar African American dancers and listeners. Blues and country adopted from jazz and rhythm and blues the concept of the piano-bass-drums rhythm section, which enabled some cross-pollination of musical characteristics, and eventually in the mid-1950s led to the early rock and roll of Elvis Presley, Bill Haley, Little Richard, and Buddy Holly.

If jazz was America's popular music in the 1940s, and mainstream pop, including show music, in the 1950s and early 1960s, then rock (initially known as rock and roll) succeeded them in the 1960s, especially with the British Invasion of English rock groups to America beginning with the Beatles in 1964. The mix of folk music with rock in the mid- to late-1960s helped to deepen the expressive power of rock beyond that of its historic antecedents. As the white baby-boomer consumer audience swelled from the late 1960s through the 1970s, so did the business of rock music. Some jazz musicians explored free jazz, a new territory of group improvisation beyond the bebop scales and standard song structures. With the influence of postwar gospel music, some forms of rhythm and blues were transformed into soul, providing a musical response of the visual and social impacts of civil rights reforms and black pride.

The later 1970s and 1980s may be seen as a period of ferment. New age music from the West Coast, and the rap and hip hop from the Brooklyn projects quickly spread from their immediate cultures through recordings. Rock had its brash punk and new wave periods, and later techno and metal styles. Country music increasingly sounded like it came more from the sidewalks than from the fields. The jazz tradition in concerts and clinics took on the appearance of "America's classical music," although many young jazz mavericks kept their styles burbling in lofts and weekend clubs.

Digital means of recording new music, and of restoring older recordings, have lent a freshness/sterility/sameness to music recorded over the last 50 years. The introduction of the compact disc in the United States in 1983, and the emergence of the Web (and the downloading and audiostreaming technologies) have made music more widely and more freely available than ever. Furthermore, the "postmodern" way of thinking that any artifact can have an immediate impact (regardless of the intent behind the artifact's creation) has resulted in a broad receptivity to all kinds of recorded music (including world music, too). When a digital playback of a deceased recording artist is played, the question "does this artist tour?" is as likely to be asked by a recording industry executive as by a teenager. What music our children listen to tomorrow, depends in part on what they listen to today.

The librarian need not be concerned with history, but rather with the immediate requests from patrons. If what is initially acquired gets much use, then more of the same should be acquired. One way to use this guide is to consult the index to see in which chapter section the previously acquired artists are located, and then buy other material listed in that section. For further development in a kind of music, explore the other sections in the same chapter.

The contents of the popular music chapters, along with those of the rest of *A Basic Music Library,* are too plentiful to be canonical in function; moreover, the interests and needs of most library patrons (especially the younger ones) are too varied to expect such canonicity from the library. The citations in each chapter were selected to be representative of major styles, artist, genres, and eras. They are not meant to be used in isolation, but rather as recommended beginning purchases, and they may be considered along with material listed in other expert sources. By the time this volume is in print, some of the listings may be outdated. As world music editor Liza Vick notes in her introduction to part II, the fluidity of the popular music data in this volume cannot be stressed enough.

Citation details, including name order, name and title wording, diacritics, and spelling are largely taken from OCLC and LC authority records, or from the packaging of the physical recordings. Due to the limitations on printed page space and preparation time, in some cases not every performer in an anthology is listed; furthermore, the birth and death years for the individual members of recording acts are omitted. Directors, producers, and editors are only included when they are the creative authorities for a CD or DVD. Dates listed refer to original releases and reissues; those for recording

sessions may be included in order to distinguish multiple recordings by the same recording artist. Titles of major series are included in parentheses.

In each chapter, up to 10 percent of the listed items have a star (★) indicating a high priority for library acquisitions. The compiler(s) of these chapters recommended stars for items that they deemed exemplary. For some chapters, however, the final distribution of these stars was done by the Jazz/Pop section editor in order to stay within 10 percent; this editorial reduction may emphasize the artist as exemplary, not an individual CD. Credit for the helpfulness of the stars is due to the contributing compilers, blame for apparent omissions for some items is due to the section editor. Users of this guide may feel more or different entries deserve stars. To the extent that this is true, we believe our readers will find that arranging the purchase of these other items for their libraries will provide the most meaningful demonstration of valuable and legitimate alternatives to our recommendations.

MP3 availability and out-of-print (OP) statuses for sound recordings can change very quickly in today's recorded music marketplace. Some items listed as available in MP3 format may be out-of-print in CD format, and vice versa. Many recommendations may now be available as MP3 downloads on free websites and through iTunes, others via streaming services such as eMusic and Napster. Out-of-print items are included because a significant number of such recordings are reissued at short notice. It is also important to note that a few labels, such as Smithsonian Folkways, reissue some older recordings on custom CDs, on demand or in emerging formats (such as DRM-free digital downloads). These citations are noted as CD on demand or custom CD series.

SELECTIVE LIST OF REFERENCE SOURCES AND ADVANCED READINGS

Barry Kernfeld, editor, *New Grove Dictionary of Jazz* (London: Macmillan, 2002).

Edward Komara, editor, *Encyclopedia of the Blues* (New York: Routledge Press, 2006).

Colin Larkin, editor, *Encyclopedia of Popular Music* (New York; Oxford: Oxford University Press, 2006).

Steven Suskin, *Show Tunes: The Songs, Shows, and Careers of Broadway's Major Composers* (New York: Oxford University Press, 2000).

Russell Sanjek and David Sanjek, *Pennies from Heaven: The American Popular Music Business in the Twentieth Century* (New York: Da Capo Press, 1996).

Charles Hiroshi Garrett, *The Grove Dictionary of American Music,* second edition (New York: Oxford University Press, 2013).

All Music (www.allmusic.com)

SUGGESTED PERIODICALS FOR UP-TO-DATE CD NOTICES AND REVIEWS

U.S. to 1900—*American Music*

Jazz—*Downbeat, Cadence*

Blues—*Living Blues, Blues Revue*

Country—*Country Standard Time, Bluegrass Unlimited,* and *Dirty Linen*

Popular Religious—*Black Grooves* (Archives of African American Music and Culture; http://blackgrooves .org)

Rock—*Rolling Stone, Spin*

Rhythm and Blues/Soul—*Living Blues, Black Grooves* (Archives of African American Music and Culture; http://blackgrooves.org)

Music of Colonial North America and the United States to about 1900

Compiled by **MARK McKNIGHT**

RELIGIOUS MUSIC   *6*
SPIRITUALS   *7*
POLITICAL MUSIC   *8*
   Revolutionary War Period   *8*
   Civil War Period   *9*
BAND MUSIC   *9*
POPULAR VOCAL AND INSTRUMENTAL MUSIC   *10*
RAGTIME   *12*

Extending from the colonial era to the brink of commercial sound recording, the pieces listed in this chapter were, for the most part, written in notated form and distributed in prints, broadsides, scores and parts, and sheet music. Therefore, most of the selected recordings are performances from printed primary sources, reflecting music composition rather than improvisation. (For selections exhibiting improvisation or reflective of an oral culture, see Volume 2: World Music, chapter 1, "Folk and Traditional Music of North America.")

While the present chapter cannot claim to be comprehensive, it does provide recommendations for several distinctive early American musical genres, with the sections appearing in approximate historical order. Religious music constitutes some of the earliest notated American music, including hymnody, psalmody, fuguing tunes, the sacred music of the Moravians and the

Shakers, and the repertory found in the nineteenth-century collections *The Sacred Harp* (edited by B. F. White, 1859) and *The Social Harp* (1855). Although African American spirituals did not see print until the publication *Slave Songs of the United States* (1867), their provenance in oral traditions likely goes back to the early nineteenth century, and their preservation was ensured with the first "jubilee" performing groups, especially the Fisk Jubilee Singers. The political music from the American Revolution and the Federal era ranged from songs and ballads to fife-and-drum music to political campaign songs. Much of the recorded Civil War music is of songs that may have been heard at campfires and in battle, while the songs popular in domestic parlors have been reprinted in song collections. Band music of the mid- to late-nineteenth century features much brass band repertory, chief among which are the marches of John Philip Sousa, as well as the boisterous, crowd-gathering

music of the circus. The section on popular vocal and instrumental music covers the antecedents of what would become American pop, including dance, minstrel shows, parlor songs, Stephen Collins Foster hits, and vaudeville. Ragtime caps the chapter, popular not only in its heyday of the 1890s through 1910s, but also during its revival in the 1960s and the 1970s, especially after it was used in the film soundtrack for *The Sting*, winner of the 1973 Academy Award for Best Picture.

In addition to music to be enjoyed in its own right, each section includes music that served as precursors to later kinds of music listed elsewhere in this book. All sections contain primarily sound recordings, with related scores added whenever available.

Libraries wishing to have online access to music of 1750 through 1900 America should look into subscribing to the DRAM audio stream web resource (www.dramonline.org), which includes among its labels the content of the important New World Records recordings, many of which are listed here.

RELIGIOUS MUSIC

COLLECTIONS

1   *Awake, My Soul: The Story of "The Sacred Harp."* Awake Productions: AP-002. 2007. 2 DVDs.

2   *Early Shaker Spirituals.* Rounder: CD0078. 1996. CD.

3   *Fasola: Fifty-Three Shape Note Folk Hymns.* Smithsonian Folkways: AHM 4151 (F-4151). 1970, [200–?] (custom issue). 2 CDs.

4   *Glory to Him Who Is the Resurrection: A Moravian Music Sampler.* Moravian Music Foundation: MUJ0572. 2010. CD.

5   ★*Ten Sacred Songs for Soprano, Strings, and Organ: Music of the Moravians in America from the Archives of the Moravian Church at Bethlehem, Pennsylvania.* C. F. Peters: 6084. 1954. Score.

INDIVIDUALS AND GROUPS

6   Anonymous 4
   6.1   *American Angels.* Harmonia Mundi: HMU 907326. 2003. CD.
   6.2   *Gloryland* [Darol Anger, Mike Marshall]. Harmonia Mundi: HMU 907400. 2006. CD.

7   Billings, William
   7.1   *The Complete Works of William Billings.* American Musicological Society / Colonial Society of Massachusetts. 1977–1990. 4 vol. score.

7.2   *The Continental Harmonist: Hymns and Fuging Tunes* [Gregg Smith Singers]. Premier: PRCD 1008. 1991. CD.

7.3   *A Land of Pure Delight: Anthems and Fuging Tunes* [His Majestie's Clerkes; Paul Hillier, dir.]. Harmonia Mundi: HMU 907048. 1991, 1992. CD.

7.4   *Wake Ev'ry Breath* [William Appling Singers and Orchestra]. New World Records: 80539-2. 1996, 1998. CD.

8   Boston Camerata
   8.1   *The American Vocalist: Spirituals and Folk Hymns, 1850–1870* [Joel Cohen, dir.]. Erato: 2292-45818-2. 2009. CD.
   8.2   *Lost Music of Early America: Music of the Moravians* [Joel Cohen, dir.]. Telarc: CD-80482. 1997, 1998. CD.
   8.3   *Simple Gifts: Shaker Chants and Spirituals* [Joel Cohen, Schola Cantorum of Boston, Shaker Community of Sabbathday Lake, Maine]. Apex: 2564603672. 2011. CD.
   8.4   *Trav'ling Home: American Spirituals, 1770–1870* [Joel Cohen, dir.]. Erato: 0630-12711-2. 1992, 1996. CD.

9   Chanticleer
   9.1   *Our American Journey* [Joseph Jennings, dir.]. Teldec Classics: 0927-48556-2. 2002. CD.
   9.2   *Where the Sun Will Never Go Down* [Joseph Jennings, dir.]. Teldec Classics: 4509-90878-2. 1990, 1994. CD.

10 Enfield Shaker Singers. *I Am Filled with Heavenly Treasures* [Mary Ann Haagen, dir.]. New World Records: 80617-2. 2003, 2004. CD.

11 Ensemble Phoenix Munich. *Rose of Sharon: 100 Years of American Music, 1770–1870* [Joel Frederiksen, dir.]. Harmonia Mundi: HMC 902085. 2011. CD.

12 Erbsen, Wayne. *Old-Time Gospel Favorites: 14 Gospel Classics with Harmony and Old-Time Instruments.* Native Ground Music: 95033. 2011. CD.

13 Gregg Smith Singers. *Southern Harmony* [1854] [William Duckworth, arr.]. Lovely Music: LCD 2033. 1994. CD.

14 His Majestie's Clerkes
   14.1 *Early American Choral Music* [Paul Hillier, dir.]. Harmonia Mundi: HCX 3957048, HCX 3957128. 2001–2002. 2 CDs.

14.2 *Home to Thanksgiving: Songs of Thanks and Praise* [Paul Hillier, dir.]. Harmonia Mundi: 2907264. 1999. CD.

15 Kansas City Chorale. *Alleluia: An American Hymnal* [1620–1800]. Nimbus: 5568. 1998, 1999. CD.

16 ★Marrocco, W. Thomas, and Harold Gleason, eds. *Music in America: An Anthology from the Landing of the Pilgrims to the Close of the Civil War, 1620–1865.* W. W. Norton. 1964, 1981. Score.

17 ★McCurry, John G. *The Social Harp* [1855]. University of Georgia Press. 1973, 2006. Score.

18 McGraw, Hugh. *The Social Harp: Early American Shape-Note Songs* [1855] [Vocal ensemble of Southern traditional singers]. Rounder: CD0094. 1994. CD.

19 New England Voices. *The River of Love: Music of the Shakers and Based on Shaker Themes.* Albany Records: TROY 988. 2007. CD.

20 Norumbega Harmony. *Sweet Seraphic Fire: New England Singing-School Music from the Norumbega Harmony* [Stephen Marini, dir.]. New World Records: 80640-2. 2005. CD.

21 Oregon State University Choir. *Make a Joyful Noise: Mainstreams and Backstreams of American Psalmody, 1770–1840.* New World Records: 80255-2. 1978, 1996. CD.

22 Rose Ensemble. *And Glory Shone Around* [Jordan Sramek, artistic dir.]. Rose Ensemble: Rose 00009. 2008. CD.

23 Smith College Glee Club. *Music of the Shakers* [Amherst College Glee Club]. Smithsonian Folkways: FH 5378. 1976 (custom issue). CD.

24 Sturbridge Singers. *The New England Harmony: A Collection of American Choral Music.* Smithsonian Folkways: FW 32377. 1964 (custom issue). CD.

25 Tudor Choir [Seattle]
　25.1 *Gentle Words: Shaker Songs* [Doug Fullington, dir.]. Loft Recordings: LRCD 1041. 2000, 2001. CD.
　25.2 *The Shapenote Album* [Doug Fullington, dir.]. Loft Recordings: LRCD 1042. 1995, [2001]. CD.

26 Walker, William, compiler
　26.1 ★*The Southern Harmony* [1854]. Promusicamericana. 1966. Score.
　26.2 *Southern Harmony, Excerpts* [William Duckworth, arr.]. Henmar / Peters.

1993, 2000. Score (12 separate octavo publications: Windham, Nashville, Leander, Turtle Dove, Sardina, Social Band, Primrose, Consolation, Hebrew Children, Wondrous Love, Solemn Thought, Rock of Ages).

27 Waverly Consort. *An American Journey: Bound for the Promised Land.* [1750–1855] [Michael Jaffee, dir.]. Angel: 55533. 1995, 1996. CD.

28 ★Western Wind. *I Am the Rose of Sharon: Early American Vocal Music.* Western Wind: WW1776. 1973, [2002?]. CD.

29 White, B. F. (Benjamin Franklin), compiler. *The Sacred Harp* [1859, 1860]. Broadman Press. 1968. Score.

30 Wiregrass Sacred Harp Singers. *Desire for Piety: Songs from the B. F. White "Sacred Harp."* New World Records: 80519-2. 1993, 1997. CD.

31 Word of Mouth Chorus. *Rivers of Delight: American Folk Hymns from the Sacred Harp Tradition.* Nonesuch: 71360-2. 1979, 1989. CD.

SPIRITUALS

COLLECTION

32 *A First-Time Buyer's Guide to American Negro Spirituals* [1922–1945] [Paul Robeson, Marian Anderson, Roland Hayes, Dorothy Maynor, Mahalia Jackson, Thomas A. Dorsey, Gary Davis, Blind Willie Johnson, Ellabelle Davis, A. W. Nix, Jules Bledsoe, Bessie Smith, Cally Fancy, Georgia Peach, J. C. Burnett, Washington Phillips, Jubilee Singers, and others]. Primo Collection: PRMCD6038. 2006. 2 CDs.

INDIVIDUALS AND GROUPS

33 Allen, William Francis. *Slave Songs of the United States: The Complete 1867 Collection of Slave Songs.* Hal Leonard. 2007, 1965. Score.

34 Althouse, Jay, compiler. *Spirituals for Solo Singers: 11 Spirituals Arranged for Solo Voice and Piano; for Recitals, Concerts and Contests.* Alfred Music Publishing. 1994. Score with CD.

35 Anderson, Marian. *Spirituals* [1932–1952]. RCA: 09026-63306-2. 1999. CD.

36 Beck, Andy, compiler. *Spirituals for Solo Singers, Vol. 2: 10 Spirituals Arranged for Solo Voice and Piano; for Recitals, Concerts, and Contests.* Alfred Music Publishing. 2006. Score with CD.

37   Counterpoint. *Let Me Fly: Music of Struggle, Solace and Survival in Black America* [Jonita Lattimore; Robert de Cormier, dir.]. Albany Records: TROY 896. 2006. CD.

38   Harlem Spiritual Ensemble. *Sisters of Freedom.* Arts Music: 49002. 1999, 2000. CD.

39   Hendricks, Barbara. *Give Me Jesus: Spirituals* [Moses Hogan Singers; Moses Hogan, dir.]. EMI Classics: 7243 5 56788 2. 1998. CD.

40   Larue, Michel. *Songs of the American Negro Slaves.* Smithsonian Folkways: FD 5252. 1960, [2007]. CD.

41   Moses, Oral. *Songs of America* [Rosalyn Floyd, Timothy Holley]. Albany Records: TROY 1011. 2007, 2008. CD.

42   Norman, Jessye. *Spirituals in Concert* [Kathleen Battle; James Levine, dir.]. Deutsche Grammophon: 429 790-2. 1990, 1991. CD.

43   Ragin, Derek Lee. *Negro Spirituals* [Moses Hogan Chorale, Bridget Bazile, Cheryl Clansy; Moses Hogan, dir.]. Virgin Classics: 0946 363305 2 5. 2006. CD.

POLITICAL MUSIC
Revolutionary War Period

COLLECTIONS

44   *American Songs of Revolutionary Times and the Civil War Era.* Collectables: COL-CD-0905. 2006. CD.

45   *Authentic Songs of the American Revolution and the Civil War Era.* Grammercy Records. 2007. CD.

46   *Music of the American Revolution: The Birth of Liberty* [Sherrill Milnes, Seth McCoy, Neely Bruce]. New World Records: 80276-2. 1976, 1996. CD.

47   *Songs and Ballads of American History and of the Assassination of Presidents.* Rounder: CD 1509. 1998. CD.

INDIVIDUALS AND GROUPS

48   Boston Camerata. *The Liberty Tree: Early American Music, 1776–1861* [Joel Cohen, dir.]. Erato: 256469212-0, 3984-21668-2. 1998, 2009. CD.

49   Brand, Oscar. *Presidential Campaign Songs, 1789–1996.* Smithsonian Folkways: SFW CD 45051. 1998, 1999. CD.

50   Federal Music Society. *Music of the Federal Era* [John Baldon, dir.]. New World Records: 80299-2. 1978, 1994. CD.

51   Fifes and Drums of Williamsburg. *The World Turned Upside Down: Music from the Yorktown Battlefield.* Colonial Williamsburg Foundation: WSCD-18. 2003. CD (video enhanced).

52   Hedge, Christopher. *Andrew Jackson: The Atrocious Saint* [David Grisman and R. Carlos Nakai]. That's That: 302935. 2008. CD.

53   House, Wallace
   53.1 *Ballads of the Revolution* [1767–1781]. Smithsonian Folkways: FW 5001. 1953, [199–?] (custom issue). CD.
   53.2 *Ballads of the War of 1812* [1791–1836]. Smithsonian Folkways: FW 5002. 1954, [199–?]. CD.

54   Janovsky, Peter. *Winners and Losers: Campaign Songs from the Critical Elections in American History, Vols. 1 and 2* [1800–1976]. Smithsonian Folkways: F37260-37261. 1978, 1980, [200–?] (custom issue). 2 CDs.

55   Jyväskylä Sinfonia. *The 18th Century American Overture* [Patrick Gallois, cond.]. Naxos: 8.559654. 2011. CD.

56   Keane, Brian. *The War That Made America.* Soundtrack to the PBS television special "The War That Made America: The Story of the French and Indian War." Valley Entertainment: VLT-15202. [2005]. CD.

57   Nathan Hale Ancient Fifes and Drums. *Music of the American Revolution: The Sounds of Ancient Fifes and Drums.* Nathan Hale Ancient Fifes and Drums. 2003. CD.

58   O'Connor, Mark. *Liberty* [Yo-Yo Ma, violoncello; Wynton Marsalis, trumpet; James Taylor, vocals and guitar; Jerry Douglas, dobro; John Jarvis, harpsichord, keyboards, and piano; Russ Barenberg, guitar; John Mock, pennywhistle, low whistle, recorder, and bodhrán; Mark Schatz, bass and banjo; Glen Worf, bass; Nashville Symphony Orchestra; and Kenneth Schermerhorn, cond.]. Sony: 88697 52307 2/61. 2009 (1997). CD.

Civil War Period

COLLECTIONS

59 *Bloody War: Songs, 1924–1939*. Tompkins Square: TSQ 2479. 2010. CD.

60 *Blue and Gray: Songs of the Civil War*. Altissimo Records: 5574. 2003. CD.

61 *The Civil War Music Collector's Edition* [Hutchinson Family Singers, Morning Sun Singers, Doug Green, James Bryan, Jerry Perkins, Princely Players]. Time-Life Music: R103-12. 1991. 3 CDs.

62 *Songs of the Civil War*. Sony: 48607. 1991. CD.

63 ★*Songs of the Civil War: First Recordings from Original Editions*. New World: 80202-2. 1976, [1987?]. CD

INDIVIDUALS AND GROUPS

64 American Brass Quintet Brass Band
    64.1 *Music of the 26th N.C. Regimental Band, CSA, Vol. 1: A Storm in the Land*. New World Records: 80608-2. 2002. CD.
    64.2 *Music of the 26th N.C. Regimental Band, CSA, Vol. 2: Cheer, Boys, Cheer!* New World Records: 80652-2. 2006. CD.

65 Americus Brass Band. *Music of the Civil War*. Summit: DCD 126. 1991. CD.

66 Battlefield Balladeers. *For the Old Folks at Home* [David Corbett, vocals and instruments; Eileen Corbett, vocals; and Boston Corbett, banjo]. S&N. 2009. CD.

67 Cook, Judy
    67.1 *Lincoln's America*. Creative Engineering: CEI-J05-0909. 2009. CD.
    67.2 *Tenting Tonight*. Creative Engineering: CEI-JC03-0708. 2008. CD.

68 Crawford, Richard, compiler. *Civil War Songbook*. Dover. 1977. Score.

69 D. C. Hall's New Concert and Quadrille Band. *Union and Liberty! Music Heard on the Northern Homefront during the Civil War*. Dorian: DOR 90197. 1993, 1994. CD.

70 Davis, Charles. *Civil War Piano: Parlor Memories*. Star Line: 9015. 2002. CD.

71 Eastman Wind Ensemble. *The Civil War: Its Music and Its Sounds* [Frederick Fennell, dir.]. Mercury: 432591-2. 1960, 1962, 1990. 2 CDs.

72 52nd Regimental String Band. *The Civil War Grand Military Ball*. Greg Todd. 2008. CD.

73 Foster, Stephen Collins
    73.1 *Civil War Songs* [Linda Russell, Abby Newton, Robert Leidhecker, Rudolph Palmer]. Helicon Records: 1002. 1997. CD.
    73.2 *Dear Friends and Gentle Hearts: The Songs of Stephen Foster and the Civil War* [Bob Welch, vocals and instrumentals; and additional performers]. Snowflakes in June Pub. 2008. CD.

74 Jimerson, Douglas
    74.1 *The Civil War*. Amerimusic: 21005. 2000. 4 CDs.
    74.2 *Civil War* [Federal City Brass Band]. Amerimusic: 21007. 2007. CD.

75 Mormon Tabernacle Choir. *Songs of the Civil War and Stephen Foster Favorites*. Sony: 48297. 1992. CD.

76 97th Regimental String Band. *Songs of the Civil War: Battlefields and Campfires*. 97th Regimental String Band. 1995. CD.

77 Nye, Hermes. *Ballads of the Civil War, 1831–1865*. Smithsonian Folkways: F-5004. 1954, [200–?] (custom issue). CD.

78 2nd South Carolina String Band.
    78.1 *Dulcem Melodies: Favorite Campfire Songs of the Civil War Era*. Palmetto Productions. 2006. CD.
    78.2 *Far, Far from Home*. Lion Heart Film Works. 2008. DVD.
    78.3 *In High Cotton: Favorite Camp Songs of the Civil War*. Palmetto Productions. 2002. CD.
    78.4 *Lightning in a Jar: An Evening of Civil War Music*. Palmetto Productions. 2008. CD.

79 Silber, Irwin, and Jerry Silverman. *Score of the Civil War*. Dover. 1960, 1995. Score.

80 Trillium. *Crossing the Stream*. Little Miracles. 2009. CD.

BAND MUSIC

81 American Brass Quintet Brass Band. *The Yankee Brass Band: Music from Mid-Nineteenth Century America*. New World: 80312-2. 1981, [1988?]. CD.

82 American Serenade Band. *The Golden Age of Brass, Vols. 1–3* [David Hickman, Mark H. Lawrence,

Michael J. Colburn; Henry Charles Smith, dir.].
Summit: DCD 114, DCD 121, DCD 150. 1990–
1993. 3 CDs.

83   Eastman Wind Ensemble. *Screamers: March Time*
[Frederick Fennell, dir.]. Mercury: 432 019 2.
1991. CD.

84   Edwin Franko Goldman Band. *The Golden Age
of the American March.* New World: 80266-2.
1992. CD.

85   Grafulla, C. S. *Grafulla's Favorites* [Dodworth
Saxhorn Band]. New World Records: 80556-2.
1999. CD.

86   Great American Main Street Band. *Under the
Big Top: 100 Years of Circus Music* [Sam Pilafian,
Mark Gould]. Angel: CDC 54728. 1992,
1993. CD.

87   Marsalis, Wynton. *Carnaval* [Eastman Wind
Ensemble; Donald Hunsberger, dir.]. CBS
Masterworks MK 42137. 1987.

88   Pryor, Arthur. *Arthur Pryor: Trombone Soloist of
the Sousa Band* [1901–1911] [Pryor Band, Sousa
Band]. Crystal: CD451. 1997. CD.

89   Schwartz, Gerard. *Cornet Favorites; Highlights from
Cousins* [William Bolcom, Ronald Barron, Kenneth
Cooper]. Nonesuch: 79157-2. 1973, 1987. CD.

90   Sousa, John Philip
   90.1   *A Grand Sousa Concert* [Nonpareil Wind
      Band; Timothy Foley, dir.]. Angel / EMI:
      CDC 54130. 1990, 1991. CD.
   90.2   *Music for Wind Band, Vols. 1–15.* Naxos:
      8.559058 (vol. 1); 8.559059 (vol. 2);
      8.559092 (vol. 3); 8.559093 (vol. 4);
      8.559131 (vol. 5); 8.559132 (vol. 6);
      8.559247 (vol. 7); 8.559248 (vol. 8);
      8.559396 (vol. 9); 8.559397 (vol. 10)
      8.559690 (vol. 11); 8.559691 (vol. 12);
      8.559729 (vol. 13); 8.559730 (vol. 14);
      8.559745 (vol. 15). 2001–2015. 15 CDs.
   90.3   *The Original All-American Sousa!* [Keith
      Brion, New Sousa Band]. Delos: DE 3102.
      1990. CD.
   90.4   *Sousa Marches Recorded by the Sousa Band*
      [Sousa Band]. Crystal: CD461-CD463. 2000.
      3 CDs.
   90.5   *Sousa's Great Marches in Piano Transcription:
      Original Sheet Music of 23 Works.* Dover.
      1975. Score.

90.6   *The United States Marine Band Performs Sousa
      Marches* [United States Marine Band]. Arts
      Music: 49009. 2003. CD.

POPULAR VOCAL
AND INSTRUMENTAL MUSIC

COLLECTIONS

91   *The 1890s, Vol.1: Wipe Him Off the Land.* [1890–
1902]. Archeophone: ARCH 9004. 2000. CD.

92   *The 1890s, Vol. 2: Wear Yer Bran' New Gown.*
[1892–1900]. Archeophone: ARCH 9006.
2002. CD.

93   *Angels' Visits and Other Vocal Gems of Victorian
America* [Kathleen Battle, Rose Taylor, Raymond
Murcell, Harmoneion Singers]. New World
Records: 80220-2. 1977, [1993]. CD.

94   *Come and Trip It: Instrumental Dance Music,
1780s–1920s* [Federal Music Society, Dick
Hyman, Gerard Schwarz]. New World Records:
80293-2. 1978, [1994]. CD.

95   *Coney Island Baby: The Society for the Preservation
and Encouragement of Barber Shop Quartet Singing
in America; 1990 Top Twenty Barber Shop Quartets.*
Compendia: CDD 559. 2002. CD.

96   *The Early Minstrel Show* [Robert Winans, David
Van Keersbilck, Peter DiSante, Brian Mark, Roger
Smith, Vincent Tufo, Percy Danforth, Matthew
Heumann]. New World Records: 80338-2. 1980,
1998. CD.

97   *English Country Dances: From Playford's Dancing
Master, 1651–1703* [Broadside Band]. Saydisc:
CD-SDL 393. 1991. CD.

98   *Lost Sounds: Blacks and the Birth of the Recording Industry, 1891–1922.* Archeophone: ARCH
1005. 2005. 2 CDs; accompanies book of
same title.

99   *Music of the Gilded Age.* Music from the Met. Classical Communications: 14-013320. 2004. CD.

100   *Over the Hills and Far Away: Being a Collection of
Music from 18th-Century Annapolis* [David and
Ginger Hildebrand]. Albany Records: H-103.
1990. CD.

101   *Songs: Foster, Griffes, Copland* [Thomas Hampson,
baritone and with piano or instrumental ensemble; Deborah Voigt, soprano; Brian Zeger, piano

(Griffes); Barbara Hendricks, soprano; London Symphony Orchestra; and Michael Tilson Thomas, cond. (Copland)]. EMI Classics: 50999 2 34479 2 9. 2008. CD.

INDIVIDUALS AND GROUPS

102   ★Aler, John. *Where Home Is: Life in Nineteenth-Century Cincinnati, Crossroads of the East and West* [Clifford Jackson, Harmoneion Singers]. New World Records: 80251-2. 1977, [1995]. CD.

103   Broadside Band. *John Playford's Popular Tunes.* Amon Ra: CD-SAR 28. 1986. CD.

104   Caine, Uri. *The Sidewalks of New York: Tin Pan Alley* [1890–1915]. Winter and Winter: 910 038-2. 1999. CD.

105   Cincinnati's University Singers
      105.1   *The Hand That Holds the Bread: Progress and Protest in the Gilded Age (Songs from the Civil War to the Columbian Exposition).* New World Records: 80267-2. 1976, 1997. CD.
      105.2   *"I Wants to Be a Actor Lady" and Other Hits from Early Musical Comedies* [Earl Rivers]. New World Records: 80221-2. 1978, 1995. CD.

106   Cohen, Shelly. *The Gateway West* [New Horizon Singers and Pacific "Pops" Orchestra]. Stagecoach Inn Museum Foundation. 2008. CD.

107   Danton, Jean. *American Dreamer: Heart Songs.* Albany Records: TROY 319. 1998. CD.

108   Eastman Wind Ensemble. *Homespun America: Music for Brass Band, Social Orchestra and Choral Groups from the Mid-19th Century* [Manchester Cornet Band]. Vox Box: CDX-5088 (SVBX-5309). 1976, 1993. 2 CDs.

109   Erbsen, Wayne. *Love Songs of the Civil War.* Native Ground: NG-CD 009. 1999. CD.

110   Flesher, Bob. *Minstrel Banjo Style* [Joe Ayers, Clarke Buehling, Bob Carlin, Tony Trischka, Bob Winans]. Rounder. 2009 (1994). CD.

111   Foster, Stephen Collins
      111.1   *American Dreamer* [Thomas Hampson, Jay Ungar, Molly Mason, David Alpher]. Angel: CDC 54621. 1992. CD.
      111.2   *Beautiful Dreamer: Robert White Sings Stephen Foster* [National Philharmonic, Charles Gerhardt]. RCA: RCD1-5853. 1986. CD.
      111.3   *Songs of Stephen Foster* [Jan DeGaetani, Leslie Guinn, Gilbert Kalish]. Nonesuch: 79158-2 (71268). 1972, 1987. CD.
      111.4   *Songs of Stephen Foster* [Richard Conrad, baritone; and Ellen Chickering and Beverly Orlove, piano and in part with chorus]. Arsis Audio: CD 167. 2008. CD.
      111.5   *Songs of Stephen Foster.* H. Leonard: HL00313094. 1999. Score.
      111.6   *Sons of the Pioneers Sing the Stephen Foster Songbook* [Sons of the Pioneers]. Varèse Sarabande: 302 067 022 2. 2010. CD.
      111.7   *The Stephen Foster Collection: Stephen Foster in Contrast* [Bing Crosby, The Robert Farnon Octet, Sammy Kaye and His Orchestra, Al Jolson, and Andre Kostelanetz and His Orchestra]. Jasmine: JASCD 454. 2007. 2 CDs.
      111.8   *Stephen Foster Song Book: Original Sheet Music of 40 Songs.* Dover. 1974. Score.
      111.9   *Stephen Foster Songs* [Julianne Baird, Linda Russell, Frederick Urrey, Ridley Enslow]. Albany Records: TROY 119. 1994. CD.
      111.10 *The Voices That Are Gone* [Matt Turner, cello; Peg Carrothers, vocals; Bill Carrothers, vocals and piano]. Illusions: ILL 313003. 2008. CD.

112   Fremont, Robert A., compiler. *Favorite Songs of the Nineties; Complete Original Sheet Music for 89 Songs.* Dover. 1973. Score.

113   ★Gale, Priscilla. *Dream Faces* [Andrej Mentschukoff]. Centaur Records: CRC 2389. 1997, 1998. CD.

114   Gardner, Mark L. *Songs of the Santa Fe Trail and the Far West.* Native Ground: NG-CD 003. [1996]. CD.

115   Hesperus. *Colonial America.* Maggie's Music: MD 20764 (MM227). 2003. CD.

116   Ingalls, Charles. *Pa's Fiddle* [Pa's Fiddle Band]. Pa's Fiddle: PFR 0169-2. 2011. CD.

117   Jacobs-Bond, Carrie. *Songs My Grandmother Taught Me* [Peggy Balensuela, William Hughes]. Albany Records: TROY 438. 2000, 2001. CD.

118   McCabe, Daniel. *An American Idyll: American Songs from 1800–1860.* Fleur de Son Classics: FDS 57924. 1997. CD

119   Mesney, Dorothy. *The Parlour Piano: American Popular Songs of the 1800s* [Myron McPherson].

Smithsonian Folkways: F-32321. 1978, [200–?]. CD.

120   Morris, Joan
   120.1   *After the Ball: A Treasury of Turn-of-the-Century Popular Songs; Highlights from Vaudeville* [William Bolcom]. Nonesuch: 79148-2. 1974, 1976, 1987. CD.
   120.2   *Moonlight Bay: Songs as Is and Songs as Was* [William Bolcom]. Albany Records: TROY 318. 1998. CD.

121   Nashville Mandolin Ensemble. *All the Rage: Mandolin Ensemble Music from 1897–1924*. New World Records: 80544-2. 1998. CD.

122   Raph, Theodore, compiler. *The American Song Treasury: 100 Favorites*. Dover. 1964, 1986. Score.

123   Shirley, George. *Battle Pieces* [William Bolcom]. Albany Records: TROY 606. 2003. CD.

RAGTIME

COLLECTIONS

124   *Early Syncopated Dance Music: Cakewalks, Two-Steps, Trots and Glides* [James Reese Europe, Sousa Band, Columbia Symphony Orchestra, Zonophone Concert Band, Pryor Band, Walter B. Rogers Band, Ladd's Black Aces]. Smithsonian Folkways: FWRBF37. 1978, [200–?] (custom issue). CD.

125   *The Greatest Ragtime of the Century* [1915–1931] [Eubie Blake, Jimmy Blythe, James P. Johnson, Scott Joplin, Jelly Roll Morton, Fats Waller]. Shout! Factory: DK 30160. 1987, 2003. CD.

INDIVIDUALS AND GROUPS

126   Appleby, Amy, and Peter Pickow, compilers. *The Library of Ragtime and Early Blues Piano*. Amsco. 1995. Score.

127   Appling, William. *William Appling Plays Scott Joplin & J. S. Bach*. Albany: TROY1163. 2010. CD.

128   Avatar Brass Quintet. *Magnetic Rags: Ragtime for Brass*. Klavier: K-77029. 1997, 2000. CD.

129   Blake, Eubie
   129.1   *Memories of You* [1917–1921, 1973 (mostly piano rolls)]. Shout! Factory: 30146. 2003. CD.
   129.2   *Sincerely, Eubie Blake: Nine Original Compositions for Piano Solo*. Hal Leonard: HL9313. 1975. Score.

   129.3   *That's Ragtime!* AEI: AEI-CD 606. 1985, 2000. CD.

130   ★Blesh, Rudi, compiler. *Classic Piano Rags: Complete Original Music for 81 Rags*. Dover. 1973. Score.

131   Cohan, George M., composer. *You're a Grand Old Rag* [Bernadette Boerckel and Colin Pritchard, vocals]. New World: 80685-2. 2008. CD.

132   Dowling, Richard. *World's Greatest Piano Rags* [Joseph C. Northrup, Artie Matthews, Joseph F. Lamb, James Scott, Jay Roberts, Scott Joplin, William Bolcom, Eubie Blake, George Gershwin, Zez Confrey]. Klavier: K77035. 1998, 2004. CD.

133   Europe, James, Victor Minstrels, Sousa's Band, Arthur Collins, Conway's Orchestra, and Six Brown Brothers. *I'll Dance Till de Sun Breaks Through: Ragtime, Cakewalks and Stomps* [1898–1923]. Saydisc: CD-SDL-336. 1985. CD.

134   Hyman, Dick. *Dick Hyman's Century of Jazz Piano*. Arbors: ARCD 19348. 2009. 5 CDs + DVD.

135   Joplin, Scott
   135.1   *Classic Ragtime from Rare Piano Rolls*. MicroWerks: 813411010694. 2010. 3 CDs.
   135.2   *Complete Piano Rags*. Dover. 1988. Score.
   135.3   *The Complete Rags, Marches and Waltzes*. Nimbus: NI 2546-2548. 2009. 3 CDs.
   135.4   *Elite Syncopations: Classic Ragtime from Rare Piano Rolls 1899–1918*. MicroWerks: MW 069-B. 2010. CD.
   135.5   *Elite Syncopations: Classic Ragtime from Rare Piano Rolls, 1899–1917* [Hal Boulware]. Shout! Factory: DK 30156. 1987, 2003. CD.
   135.6   *Euphonic Sounds: The Music of Scott Joplin* [William Bolcom, piano]. Musical Heritage Society: 5189442. 2008 (1988). CD.
   135.7   *Greatest Hits* [Dick Hyman, James Levine]. RCA Victor: 60842-2-RG. 1991. CD.
   135.8   *Piano Rags* [Joshua Rifkin]. Nonesuch: 79159-2. 1969–72, 1987. CD.
   135.9   *Piano Works, 1899–1904* [Dick Hyman]. RCA: 7993-2-RG. 1975, 1988. CD.
   135.10   *Rags and Waltzes* [Joshua Rifkin and Ralph Grierson, piano; Southland Singers; and George Spoonhaltz, cond.]. EMI Classics: 50999 2 34477 2 1. 2008 (1974, 1980). CD.

135.11 *Rags to Riches: The Essential Hits* [Robert Strickland]. Intersound: 5970. 2005. CD.

135.12 *Ragtime: The Music of Scott Joplin.* Madacy: TC2 53829. 2008. 3 CDs.

135.13 *Rag-Time Music* [Itzhak Perlman, violin; and Andre Previn, piano]. EMI Classics: 50999 2 35726 2 1. 2009 (1974). CD.

135.14 *The Red Back Book: Elite Syncopations* [New England Conservatory Ragtime Ensemble; Gunther Schuller, dir.]. Angel: CDC 74193 (36060). 1973–1974, 1985. CD.

135.15 *Scott Joplin: His Complete Works* [Richard Zimmerman]. LaserLight Digital: 15 945. 1993. 5 CDs.

135.16 *Scott Joplin: King of Ragtime Writers from Classic Piano Rolls.* MicroWerks. 2010. CD.

136 Lamb, Joseph

136.1 *American Beauties: The Rags of Joseph Lamb* [Virginia Eskin]. Koch International Classics: 7495. 1995, 2000. CD.

136.2 *A Study in Classic Ragtime* [1959]. Smithsonian Folkways: FG 3562. 1960, [200–?] (custom issue). CD.

137 Morath, Max

137.1 *Max Morath Plays the Best of Scott Joplin and Other Rag Classics* [Original Rag Quartet]. Vanguard: 39/40. 1967, 1990. CD.

137.2 *Ragtime Women* [Morath Ragtime Quintet]. Vanguard: 79402-2. 1977, 1994. CD.

138 New England Ragtime Ensemble. *The Art of the Rag* [Gunther Schuller, dir.]. GM: 3018. 1990. CD.

139 Old 78's. *Old Time Fiddle Rags, Classic and Minstrel Banjo.* theold78s.com. 2008. CD.

140 Paragon Ragtime Orchestra

140.1 *Black Manhattan: Theater and Dance Music of James Reese Europe, Will Marion Cook, and Members of the Legendary Clef Club.* New World Records: 80611-2. 2003. CD.

140.2 *Knockout Drops: American Popular Music from the Ragtime Era.* Paragon Ragtime Orchestra. 1995, 1997. CD.

140.3 *The Paragon Orchestra (Finally) Plays "The Entertainer."* Rialto Recording Co.: 6005. 2004. CD.

140.4 *That Demon Rag: American Popular Music from the Ragtime Era.* Paragon Ragtime Orchestra: PRO-6001. 1992, 1998. CD.

141 Scott, James. *Classic Ragtime from Rare Piano Rolls.* Collectables Records. 1997, 2008. CD.

142 Smart, Gary. *American Beauty: A Ragtime Bouquet.* Albany Records: TROY 1029. 2008. CD.

143 Swanson, Adam. *On a Circular Staircase* [Luckey Roberts, Zez Confrey, Arthur Marshall, Maceo Pinkard, W. C. Handy, Tom Turpin, Joseph Lamb, and others]. Rivermont: BSW-2209. 2008. CD.

144 Wright, Bryan Sheldon. *Breakin' Notes* [Scott Joplin, Joseph Lamb, James Scott, Arthur Marshall, Willie Anderson, and others]. Rivermont: BSW-2212. 2010. CD.

Blues

Compiled by **WILLIAM E. ANDERSON** *with* **EDWARD KOMARA**

GENERAL COLLECTIONS   *16*
ROOTS   *18*
SONGSTERS, STRING BANDS, AND JUG BANDS   *19*
VAUDEVILLE OR CLASSIC BLUES   *20*
MISSISSIPPI DELTA BLUES   *20*
MEMPHIS AND ST. LOUIS BLUES   *21*
TEXAS, ARKANSAS, AND LOUISIANA BLUES   *22*
GEORGIA, ALABAMA, AND THE EAST COAST BLUES   *22*
PIANO BLUES   *22*
BLUES IN THE CITIES: 1920s–1940s   *23*
POSTWAR MIDWESTERN BLUES   *24*
TEXAS AND WEST COAST BLUES   *26*
LOUISIANA BLUES   *27*
MODERN BLUES   *27*
BLUES AND ROCK   *29*
BLUES REVIVAL AND FOLK BLUES   *30*
CONTEMPORARY BLUES AND SOUL   *30*

A secular African American music, the blues originated at the beginning of the twentieth century
across the southern United States from Texas to
the Carolinas. What began as a folk music within oral
cultures soon became "popular" through sheet music,
recordings, and performances by touring blues singers
in clubs and theaters. Blues has a distinct (although
sometimes overlapping) audience and history from that
of jazz and rhythm and blues. Recommendations from
those genres are covered in chapters 3 and 7. African
American antecedents to the blues may be found in
chapter 1, and additional early blues recordings may be
found in chapter 12.

Many early southern blues singers were known as
songsters, and they recorded other material as well,
including blues ballads, religious songs, minstrel tunes,

and even pop songs. Appearing a little later, jug bands and string bands also performed a wide repertoire and often used homemade instruments. The first recorded blues, however, were by women vaudeville performers in the early 1920s. These performers could be heard in theaters before the age of the microphone, and learned blues songs while touring the South. Their records, often called classic blues, usually featured jazz-like bands or pianists for accompaniment.

Before the development of mass media (radio and records), individual regions of the South developed blues with distinguishing characteristics, especially the Carolinas ("Piedmont"), Atlanta, and west Tennessee (including Memphis). Most striking of the pre-World War II styles were those of the Mississippi Delta between Vicksburg and Memphis. Delta blues is characterized by intense vocal styles and strongly rhythmic guitar accompaniments, which may be heard in the early work of Charley Patton, Son House, Tommy Johnson, Bukka White, Skip James, and Robert Johnson. Their successors Muddy Waters, Howlin' Wolf, and Elmore James recorded in Chicago in the amplified urban styles of the 1940s and 1950s, thus sustaining the Delta style for adoption by today's musicians.

Most of the previously cited blues artists were accompanied by guitar. There was also a piano blues tradition that developed in the lumber camps and towns of the South, and in such cities as Indianapolis and St. Louis. Among the many piano styles was the popular boogie woogie style with its characteristic eight-to-the-bar left hand figures. With the wartime migrations of African Americans into the cities, rural styles began to be adapted to the new performance settings, whether crowded noisy clubs or recording studios with improved microphones. As a result, the 1930s and 1940s saw the rise of transplanted southern musicians in northern cities, beginning with Big Bill Broonzy, Lonnie Johnson, Memphis Minnie, Tampa Red, and John Lee "Sonny Boy" Williamson.

Many bluesmen from Texas migrated to the West Coast. Their postwar sound, featuring melodic single-note guitar styles and laid-back singing, was introduced by T-Bone Walker and Lowell Fulson, among others. Back in Texas, the music of Lightnin' Hopkins retained the "down home" rural flavor. However, to the east, the swamp blues of rural Louisiana and the blues styles of New Orleans shared a regional similarity, while absorbing some of the trends introduced through modern blues.

Modern blues is a synthesis of many earlier developments—Delta blues and gospel vocals, West Coast guitar styles, big band horns—that brought about music that was national in appeal. The popularity of the style developed by B. B. King in Memphis was the catalyst for other guitarists and singers, including a number from the Chicago west side, Texas, and the Memphis / north Mississippi area. In the 1960s rock bands (initially British groups) like the Rolling Stones, the Yardbirds, John Mayall, Eric Clapton, Led Zeppelin, Paul Butterfield, and Michael Bloomfield took up the songs being played by electrically amplified bands in Chicago, later discovering for themselves the related, antecedent Delta styles. Meanwhile, during and after the 1960s folk music revival, there was a discovery of blues by the mainstream folk and rock audiences. Many older performers were "rediscovered" at folk festivals and recorded for the first time in years. Others, like Mance Lipscomb, had been playing blues since its beginnings but had not recorded before their discoveries in the 1960s.

During the 1970s and 1980s, some bluesmen were performing for the older blues audience, others to the fans of 1960s soul music acts, and still others tapped into rock audiences. Through the 1990s, veteran blues singers like Bobby Bland, Charles Brown, and Koko Taylor maintained their careers, and Robert Ward and Snooks Eaglin gained listener attention denied in their youth. Begun in 1971, Alligator Records was one of the first labels to develop a contemporary audience for blues. Other current imprints include Malaco, which has presented today's southern blues and soul/blues styles, Blind Pig for urban blues and rock blues tastes, and Fat Possum for postmodern, younger, sometimes rap and punk listeners.

GENERAL COLLECTIONS

COLLECTIONS

145   ★*The Blues: A Smithsonian Collection of Classic Blues Singers* [1923–1985] (Blind Lemon Jefferson, Papa Charlie Jackson, Ma Rainey, Robert Johnson, Bessie Smith, Sippie Wallace, Barbecue Bob, Texas Alexander, Furry Lewis, Blind Willie Johnson, Gus Cannon, Tommy Johnson, Henry Thomas, Leroy Carr, Frank Stokes, Mississippi John Hurt, Lonnie Johnson, Charley Patton, Roosevelt Sykes, Memphis Minnie, Sleepy John Estes, Blind Boy Fuller, Memphis Jug Band, Mississippi Sheiks, Walter Davis, Son House, Skip James, Bumble Bee Slim, Blind Willie McTell, Bill Broonzy, Kokomo Arnold, Big Joe Williams, Little Brother Montgomery, Peetie Wheatstraw, Sonny Boy Williamson, Jimmy Rushing, Joe Turner, Bukka White, Tampa Red, Big Maceo, Washboard

Sam, T-Bone Walker, Tommy McClennan, Louis Jordan, Eddie "Cleanhead" Vinson, Charles Brown, Wynonie Harris, John Lee Hooker, Lightnin' Hopkins, Jimmy Witherspoon, Muddy Waters, Howlin' Wolf, Lowell Fulson, Jimmy Yancey, Big Mama Thornton, Junior Parker, Junior Wells, Elmore James, Memphis Slim, Bobby Bland, Buddy Guy, Lightnin' Slim, Otis Rush, Jimmy Reed, Ray Charles, Latimore, and others). Smithsonian: 2550 (RD 101). 1993. 4 CDs.

146 ★*Blues Classics* [1927–1969] (Furry Lewis, Jim Jackson, Leroy Carr, Cow Cow Davenport, Tampa Red, Georgia Tom, Chippie Hill, Robert Wilkins, Memphis Minnie, Kokomo Arnold, Roosevelt Sykes, Peetie Wheatstraw, Blind Boy Fuller, Sleepy John Estes, Lonnie Johnson, Georgia White, Rosetta Tharpe, Robert Lee McCoy, Joe Turner, Louis Jordan, Dinah Washington, Muddy Waters, Robert Nighthawk, Memphis Slim, Cecil Gant, Jimmy Rogers, Little Walter, Big Mama Thornton, Eddie Boyd, Gatemouth Brown, Lowell Fulson, Sonny Boy Williamson, Howlin' Wolf, Fenton Robinson, Buddy Guy, Junior Parker, Bobby Bland, Albert Colins, B. B. King, Koko Taylor, and others). MCA: MCAD3-11441. 1996. 3 CDs.

147 *Blues Standards*. Hal Leonard: HL00311199. 2000. Score.

148 *Conversation with the Blues* [1960] (Boogie Woogie Red, Lil Son Jackson, J. B. Lenoir, Otis Spann, Lightnin' Hopkins, Mance Lipscomb, Roosevelt Sykes, John Lee Hooker, Henry Townsend, Little Brother Montgomery, and others). Cambridge University Press. 1997. CD supplement with book of same name by Paul Oliver.

149 ★*I Can't Be Satisfied: Early American Women Blues Singers, Vol. 1: Country* [1927–1934] (Lottie Kimbrough, Memphis Minnie, Bessie Tucker, and others). Yazoo: 2026. 1997. CD.

150 ★*Legends of the Blues, Vol. 1* [1925–1965] (Bessie Smith, Blind Lemon Jefferson, Mississippi John Hurt, Blind Willie McTell, Lonnie Johnson, Charley Patton, Leroy Carr, Peetie Wheatstraw, Robert Johnson, Blind Boy Fuller, Bill Broonzy, Memphis Minnie, Bukka White, Big Joe Williams, Son House, and others). Columbia: CK 46215. 1990. CD.

151 ★*Legends of the Blues, Vol. 2* [1929–1941] (Roosevelt Sykes, Texas Alexander, Barbecue Bob,

Tampa Red, Walter Roland, Bumble Bee Slim, Robert Wilkins, Victoria Spivey, Charlie Spand, Champion Jack Dupree, Brownie McGhee). Columbia: CK 47467. 1991. CD.

152 ★*Let's Get Loose: Folk and Popular Blues Styles from the Beginning to the Early 1940s* [1916–1942] (Yank Rachell, Pillie Bolling, Hattie Hudson, Clara Smith, Leroy Carr, Walter Roland, Joe McCoy, Tommy McClennan, Sonny Boy Williamson, Five Breezes, and others). New World: 80290. 2003. CD. Notes available online.

153 *Martin Scorsese Presents: The Blues, a Musical Journey*. Sony Music Entertainment / Columbia Music Video: C7D55808. 2003. 6 DVDs.

154 ★*Mean Old World: The Blues from 1940–1994* (Louis Jordan, Arthur Crudup, Leadbelly, Dinah Washington, T-Bone Walker, Big Maceo, Sonny Boy Williamson, Roy Brown, Amos Milburn, Charles Brown, John Lee Hooker, Tampa Red, Professor Longhair, Muddy Waters, Percy Mayfield, Elmore James, Little Walter, Joe Turner, Otis Rush, Jimmy Witherspoon, Fred McDowell, Freddie King, Lightnin' Hopkins, Jimmy Reed, Bobby Bland, B. B. Kng, Junior Wells, Albert King, Magic Sam, Little Milton, Junior Kimbrough, Taj Mahal, Buddy Guy, and others). Smithsonian: RB0007 (RD 110). 1996. 4 CDs.

155 *Meaning in the Blues*. JSP: JSP 77141. 2011. 4 CDs.

156 *News and the Blues: Telling It Like It Is* [1927–1947] (Bessie Smith, Victoria Spivey, Blind Willie McTell, Mississippi John Hurt, Charley Patton, Blind Boy Fuller, Bukka White, Memphis Minnie, and others). Columbia: CK 46217. 1990. CD.

157 *The Roots of Rap: Classic Recordings of the 1920's and 30's* (Blind Willie Johnson, Luke Jordan, Allen Brothers, Memphis Jug Band, Speckled Red, Butterbeans and Susie, Jimmie Davis, Leroy Carr, Blind Willie McTell, Memphis Minnie, and others). Yazoo: 2018. 1996. CD.

158 ★*The Story of the Blues* [1928–1968] (Mississippi John Hurt, Blind Willie McTell, Charley Patton, Blind Lemon Jefferson, Peg Leg Howell, Leadbelly, Barbecue Bob, Memphis Jug Band, Bessie Smith, Leroy Carr, Peetie Wheatstraw, Bo Carter, Robert Johnson, Bukka White, Memphis Minnie, Blind Boy Fuller, Brownie McGhee, Bill Broonzy, Joe Turner, Otis Spann, Elmore James,

Johnny Shines, and others). Columbia: C2K 86334 (30008). 2003. 2 CDs.

159   *When the Sun Goes Down 1: Walk Right In* [1926–1941] (Big Joe Williams, Leadbelly, Bill Broonzy, Milton Brown, Bukka White, Tommy Johnson, Carter Family, Alberta Hunter, Cannon's Jug Stompers, DeFord Bailey, Frank Crummit, Paul Robeson, and others). RCA Bluebird: 63986. 2002. CD.

160   *When the Sun Goes Down 2: The First Time I Met the Blues* [1927–1936] (Victoria Spivey, Cannon's Jug Stompers, Jim Jackson, Tommy Johnson, Blind Willie McTell, Memphis Jug Band, Furry Lewis, Sippie Wallace, Jimmie Rodgers, Sleepy John Estes, Jimmie Davis, Bo Carter, Little Brother Montgomery, Mississippi Sheiks, Frank Stokes, and others). RCA Bluebird: 63987. 2002. CD.

INDIVIDUALS AND GROUPS

161   Grossman, Stefan
    161.1   *Country Blues Guitar.* Mel Bay. 2002.
    161.2   *Fingerpicking Blues Guitar Instrumentals.* Mel Bay. 2002.
    161.3   *Fingerpicking Guitar Solos in Open Tunings.* Mel Bay. 2002. Score.

162   Grossman, Stefan, Stephen Calt, and Hal Grossman. *Country Blues Songbook.* Oak Publications. 1973.

163   Handy, W. C., Abbe Niles, and Miguel Covarrubias. *Blues: An Anthology.* Applewood Books. 2001; reprint of 1926 publication. Score.

164   Koch, Greg. *Blues Guitar: Learn to Play Blues Guitar with Step-by-Step Lessons and 20 Great Blues Songs.* Hal Leonard: HL00697344. 2002. Score.

165   Mann, Woody. *The Basics: Building a Foundation of Repertoire and Technique for Acoustic Fingerstyle Blues.* Oak Publications. 2003. Score.

166   Mann, Woody, and David Gahr. *The Blues Fakebook.* Oak Publications. 1995. Score.

167   Rubin, Dave
    167.1   *Beginning Blues Guitar: A Guide to the Essential Chords, Licks, Techniques, and Concepts.* Hal Leonard: HL00695916. 2007. Score.
    167.2   *Open Tunings for Blues Guitar.* Hal Leonard: HL 00695412 2001. Score.

    167.3   *Solo Blues Guitar.* Hal Leonard: HL00699719. 2006. Score.

168   Rubin, Dave, Mark Freed, and Rick Plunkett. *12-Bar Blues.* Hal Leonard: HL00695187. 1999. Score.

ROOTS

169   *Afro-American Blues and Game Songs* [1933–1941] (Vera Hall, Muddy Waters, Sonny Terry, and others). Rounder: 1513 (Library of Congress AFS L4). 1998. CD.

170   *Afro-American Folk Music from Tate and Panola Counties, Mississippi* [1942, 1969–1971]. Rounder: 1515 (Library of Congress AFS L 67). 2000. CD.

171   *Afro-American Spirituals, Work Songs, and Ballads* [1933–1939]. Rounder: 1510 (Library of Congress AFS L3). 1998. CD.

172   *American Primitive, Vol. 1: Raw Pre-War Gospel* [1926–1936]. Revenant: 206. 1997. CD.

173   *American Primitive, Vol. 2: Pre-War Revenants* [1897–1939]. Revenant: 214. 2005. 2 CDs.

174   *Big Brazos (Deep River of Song)* [1933–1934]. Rounder: 1826. 2000. CD.

175   Charters, Samuel, ed. *Blues Masters, Vol. 10: Blues Roots* [1950–1976] (Robert Pete Williams, Lightnin' Hopkins, Mandingo Griots, Jali Nyama Suso, Furry Lewis, and others). Rhino: 71135. 1993. CD.

176   Jackson, Bruce, ed. *Wake Up Dead Man: Black Convict Worksongs from Texas Prisons* [1965–1966]. Rounder: 2013. 1994. CD.

177   ★Lomax, Alan, ed. *The Roots of the Blues* [1959] (Fred McDowell, Lonnie Young, Bessie Jones, and others). New World: 80252-2. 1992. CD. Liner notes online.

178   ★*Negro Blues and Hollers* [1941–1942] (Son House, Willie Brown, David Edwards, and others). Rounder: 1501 (Library of Congress AFS L59). 1997. CD.

179   *Negro Prison Camp Worksongs* [1951]. Smithsonian Folkways: 4475. 2001. CD. CD-R.

180   *Negro Work Songs and Calls* [1933–1940]. Rounder: 1517 (Library of Congress AFS L8). 1999. CD.

181 *Prison Songs, Vol. 1: Murderous Home* [1947–1948]. The Alan Lomax Collection. Rounder: 1714. 1997. CD.

182 Turner, Othar. *Everybody Hollerin' Goat* [1992–1997]. Birdman: BMR 018. 1997. CD.

SONGSTERS, STRING BANDS, AND JUG BANDS

COLLECTIONS

183 *Before the Blues: The Early American Black Music Scene; Classic Recordings from the 1920's and 30's, Vols. 1–3* (Cannon's Jug Stompers, Charley Patton, Eck Robertson, Blind Lemon Jefferson, Mississippi John Hurt, Memphis Jug Band, Cow Cow Davenport, Robert Wilkins, B. F. Shelton, Blind Willie Johnson, and others). Yazoo: 2015-2017. 1996. 3 CDs.

184 *Good for What Ails You: Music of the Medicine Shows* [1926–1937] (Daddy Stovepipe, Gid Tanner, Dallas String Band, Pink Anderson, Jim Jackson, Allen Brothers, Carolina Tarheels, Henry Thomas, Chris Bouchillon, Cannon's Jug Stompers, Uncle Dave Macon, Frank Stokes, Papa Charlie Jackson, Frank Hutchison, Charlie Poole, Emmett Miller, and others). Old Hat: 1005. 2005. 2 CDs.

185 *Harmonica Blues: Great Harmonica Performances of the 1920s and '30s* [1928–1936] (Jaybird Coleman, DeFord Bailey, Jazz Gillum). Yazoo: 1053. 1991. CD.

186 *Memphis Shakedown: More Jug Band Classics* [1929–1941] (Memphis Jug Band, Jack Kelley, Jed Davenport, and others). JSP: 7752. 2005. 4 CDs.

187 *A Richer Tradition: Country Blues and String Band Music* [1923–1942] (Daddy Stovepipe, Richard "Rabbit" Brown, Papa Charlie Jackson, Hambone Willie Newbern, Sylvester Weaver, Pink Anderson, Ed Bell, and others). JSP: 7798. 2007. 4 CDs.

188 *Ruckus Juice and Chittlins: The Great Jug Bands—Classic Recordings of the 1920s and '30s, Vol. 1* (Memphis Jug Band, Cincinnati Jug Band, Cannon's Jug Stompers, Jed Davenport, Jack Kelly, Birmingham Jug Band, Earl McDonald, and others). Yazoo: 2032. 1998. CD.

189 *Ruckus Juice and Chittlins: The Great Jug Bands—Classic Recordings of the 1920s and '30s, Vol. 2* (Memphis Jug Band, Cincinnati Jug Band, Cannon's Jug Stompers, Jed Davenport, Jack Kelly, Birmingham Jug Band, Earl McDonald, and others). Yazoo: 2033. 1998. CD.

190 *Songsters and Saints: Vocal Traditions on Race Records, Vol. 1* [1927–1931] (Peg Leg Howell, Pink Anderson, Charley Patton, Bo Chatmon, Washington Phillips, Roosevelt Graves, Rev. A. W. Nix, and others). Matchbox / UK: 2001/2002. 1984. 2 LPs.

191 *Songsters and Saints: Vocal Traditions on Race Records, Vol. 2* [1925–1930] (Papa Charlie Jackson, Gus Cannon, Jim Jackson, Frank Stokes, Henry Thomas, Luke Jordan, Blind Blake, Rev. J. M. Gates, Arizona Dranes, Blind Joe Taggart, Blind Willie Johnson, and others). Matchbox / UK: 2003/2004. 1984. 2 LPs.

192 *Violin, Sing the Blues for Me: African-American Fiddlers* [1926–1949] (Lonnie Johnson, Peg Leg Howell, Whistler, Frank Stokes, Bo Chatmon, Memphis Jug Band, Tommie Bradley, Andrew and Jim Baxter, Mississippi Sheiks, Jack Kelly, and others). Old Hat: 1002. 1999. CD

INDIVIDUALS AND GROUPS

193 Cannon's Jug Stompers. *The Best of Cannon's Jug Stompers* [1927–1930]. Yazoo: 2060. 2001. CD.

194 Davis, Reverend Gary. *Gospel, Blues, and Street Songs* [1950, 1956] (Pink Anderson). Original Blues Classics / Fantasy: OBCCD-524-2. 1991. CD.

195 Grossman, Stefan. *Ragtime Blues*. Oak Publications. 1984. Score.

196 ★Hurt, Mississippi John. *Avalon Blues* [1928]. Sbme Special Mkts.: 64986. 2008. CD.

197 Leadbelly
   197.1 *Huddie Ledbetter's Best* [1944]. Beat Goes On (Capitol): BGOCD 403. 1989. CD.
   197.2 *King of the 12-String Guitar* [1935]. Columbia: 46776. 1991. CD.
   197.3 *Lead Belly's Last Sessions* [1948]. Smithsonian Folkways: 40068-40071 (241/242). 1994. 4 CDs.
   197.4 ★*The Library of Congress Recordings, Vols. 1–3* [1934–1940]. Rounder: 1044-1046. 1991. 3 CDs.
   197.5 *The Library of Congress Recordings, Vols. 4–6* [1934–1940]. Rounder: 1097-1099. 1994. 3 CDs.

198 Memphis Jug Band
    198.1 *The Best Of . . .* [1927–1934]. Yazoo:
       2059. 2001. CD.
    198.2 *Memphis Jug Band with Cannon's Jug
       Stompers* [1927–1930]. JSP: 7745. 2005.
       4 CDs.

199 Mississippi Sheiks
    199.1 *Honey Babe Let the Deal Go Down: Best
       of the Mississippi Sheiks* [1930–1931].
       Columbia: CK 65709. 2004. CD.
    199.2 *Stop and Listen* [1930–1934]. Yazoo:
       2006. 1992. CD.

200 Stokes, Frank. *Best Of . . .* [1927–1929]. Yazoo:
    2072. 2005. CD.

201 ★Thomas, Henry. *Texas Worried Blues: Complete
    Recorded Works* [1927–1929]. Yazoo: 1080.
    1989. CD.

VAUDEVILLE OR CLASSIC BLUES

COLLECTIONS

202 *Better Boot That Thing: Great Women Blues Singers
    of the 1920's* [1927–1930] (Alberta Hunter,
    Victoria Spivey, Bessie Tucker, Ida May Mack,
    and others). RCA Bluebird: 07863-66065-2.
    1992. CD.

203 *Blues Masters, Vol. 11: Classic Blues Women*
    [1921–1954] (Mamie Smith, Trixie Smith, Ma
    Rainey, Sippie Wallace, Ida Cox, Bessie Smith,
    Victoria Spivey, Alberta Hunter, Billie Pierce, and
    others). Rhino: 71134. 1993. CD.

204 ★*I Can't Be Satisfied: Early American Women Blues
    Singers, Vol. 2: Town* [1923–1929] (Victoria
    Spivey, Clara Smith, Martha Copeland, Sara
    Martin, Sippie Wallace, Ma Rainey, Bertha
    "Chippie" Hill, and others). Yazoo: 2027.
    1997. CD.

205 *Mean Mothers: Independent Womens' Blues,
    Vol. 1* [1926–1949] (Martha Copeland, Ida Cox,
    Lil Green, and others). Rosetta: RRCD-1300.
    1991. CD.

INDIVIDUALS AND GROUPS

206 Butterbeans and Susie. *Complete Recorded Works,
    Vol. 1* [1924–1925]. Document: DOCD-5544.
    1997. CD.

207 Cox, Ida. *The Uncrowned Queen of the Blues*
    [1923–1924]. Black Swan: BSCD-7. 1996. CD.

208 Hunter, Alberta. *Young Alberta Hunter* [1922–
    1940]. Mojo: 310. 1996. CD.

209 Rainey, Ma
    209.1 *Ma Rainey's Black Bottom* [1924–1928].
       Yazoo: 1071. 1990. CD.
    209.2 *Mother of the Blues* [1924–1928]. JSP:
       7793. 2007. CD.

210 Smith, Bessie
    210.1 *Bessie Smith Songbook*. Hal Leonard:
       HL00308232. 1994. Score.
    210.2 *The Complete Recordings, Vols. 1–5* [1923–
       1933]. Columbia: C2K-47091, -47471,
       -47474, -52838, -57546. 1991–1994.
       5 2-CD sets.
    210.3 *The Complete Recordings, Vols. 1–8*
       [1923–1933]. Frog / UK: DGF 40-DGF 47.
       2001. 8 CDs.
    210.4 *Empress of the Blues, Vol. 2* [1926–1933].
       JSP: 930. 2006. 4 CDs.
    210.5 ★*The Essential Bessie Smith* [1923–1933].
       Columbia: C2K 64922. 1997. 2 CDs.
    210.6 *Queen of the Blues, Vol. 1* [1923–1926].
       JSP: 929. 2006. 4 CDs.

MISSISSIPPI DELTA BLUES

COLLECTIONS

211 *Acoustic Country Blues Guitar: Delta Blues before
    Robert Johnson,* Dave Rubin, editor (Skip James,
    Blind Blake, Son House, Peetie Wheatstraw,
    Johnny Temple, Bukka White, Hambone Willie
    Newbern, Lonnie Johnson, Charley Patton,
    Calvin Frazier, Robert Johnson). Hal Leonard:
    HL00695139. 2000. Score.

212 *Back to the Crossroads: The Roots of Robert
    Johnson* [1927–1937] (Skip James, Kokomo
    Arnold, Leroy Carr, Son House, Lonnie Johnson,
    Charley Patton, Mississippi Sheiks, Scrapper
    Blackwell, Peetie Wheatstraw, Bumble Bee Slim,
    Harlem Hamfats, and others). Yazoo: 2070.
    2004. CD.

213 *Big Joe Williams and the Stars of Mississippi
    Blues* [1935–1951] (Tommy McClennan, Henry
    Townsend, David "Honeyboy" Edwards, Robert
    Petway, and others). JSP: 7719. 2003. 5 CDs.

214 *Blues in the Mississippi Night* [1946]. Rounder:
    1860. 2003. CD. Alan Lomax interviews Big Bill
    Broonzy, Sonny Boy Williamson, and Memphis
    Slim.

215   *Blues Masters, Vol. 8: Mississippi Delta Blues* [1928–1968] (Charley Patton, Robert Johnson, B. B. King, Willie Brown, Tommy Johnson, Son House, Muddy Waters, Howlin' Wolf, Elmore James, and others). Rhino: 71130. 1993. CD.

216   *Canned Heat Blues: Masters of Delta Blues* [1928] (Furry Lewis, Tommy Johnson, Ishman Bracey). RCA Bluebird: 017863-61047-2. 1992. CD.

217   *Deep Blues* [Original Soundtrack] (R. L. Burnside, Big John Jackson, Frank Frost, Jack Owens, and others). Anxious / Atlantic: 82450-2. 1992. CD.

218   *Legends of Country Blues* [1928–1941] (Skip James, Son House, Bukka White, Tommy Johnson, Ishmon Bracey). JSP: 7715. 2003. CD.

219   *Masters of the Country Blues: Son House and Bukka White.* Yazoo Home Video: 500. 2000. DVD.

220   ★*Masters of the Delta Blues: The Friends of Charlie Patton* [1928–1934] (Son House, Willie Brown, Tommy Johnson, Bukka White, Louise Johnson, and others). Yazoo: 2002. 2002, 1991. CD.

221   *The Road to Robert Johnson and Beyond* [1926–1951] (Robert Johnson, Son House, Blind Blake, Skip James, Blind Lemon Jefferson, Charley Patton, Ma Rainey, Lonnie Johnson, Kokomo Arnold, Peetie Wheatstraw, Henry Thomas, Muddy Waters, Robert Lockwood, Johnny Shines, Elmore James). JSP: 7795. 2007. 4 CDs.

INDIVIDUALS AND GROUPS

222   Grossman, Stefan
   222.1   *Country Blues Guitar in Open Tunings.* Mel Bay. 2002. Score.
   222.2   *Delta Blues.* Oak Publications. 1988. Score.
   222.3   *Delta Blues Guitar.* Mel Bay. 2002. Score.

223   House, Son. *Delta Blues: The Original Library of Congress Sessions* [1941–1942]. Shout! Factory: 30170. 2003. CD.

224   James, Skip
   224.1   *Complete Early Recordings* [1931]. Yazoo: 2009. 1994. CD.
   224.2   *The Skip James Collection.* Hal Leonard: HL00690167. 1999. Score.

225   Johnson, Robert
   225.1   ★*The Centennial Collection* [1936–1937]. Columbia/Legacy: 88697 85907 2. 2011. 2 CDs.
   225.2   *King of the Delta Blues Singers* [1936–1937]. Columbia: CK 65746. 1998. CD.

225.3   *The New Transcriptions.* Hal Leonard: HL00690271. 1999. Score.
225.4   *Robert Johnson, King of the Delta Blues.* Hal Leonard: HL00660066. 2000. Score.
225.5   *The Search for Robert Johnson.* Sony Music Entertainment: CVD49113. 1992, 2001. DVD.

226   Patton, Charley
   226.1   ★*The Best of Charlie Patton* [1929–1934]. Yazoo: 2069. 2003. CD.
   226.2   *Complete Recordings, 1929–1934.* JSP: 7702. 2002. 5 CDs.

227   Waters, Muddy. *The Complete Plantation Recordings: The Historic 1941–42 Library of Congress Field Recordings.* MCA Chess: CHD-9344. 1993. CD.

228   White, Bukka. *The Complete Bukka White* [1937–1940]. Columbia / Legacy: CK 52782. 1994. CD.

MEMPHIS AND ST. LOUIS BLUES

COLLECTIONS

229   *Blues Masters, Vol. 12: Memphis Blues* [1927–1954] (Frank Stokes, Memphis Jug Band, Gus Cannon, Jim Jackson, Furry Lewis, Memphis Minnie, Sleepy John Estes, Jack Kelly, Joe Hill Louis, B. B. King, Willie Nix, Howlin' Wolf, James Cotton, Junior Parker, Rufus Thomas, Roscoe Gordon, Bobby Bland, and others). Rhino: 71129. 1993. CD.

230   *Masters of Memphis Blues* (Gus Cannon, Beale Street Sheiks, Little Buddy Doyle, Furry Lewis, Frank Stokes, Robert Wilkins, and others). JSP: 7725. 2004. 4 CDs.

231   ★*Memphis Masters: Early American Blues Classics* [1927–1934] (Furry Lewis, Joe McCoy, Frank Stokes, Memphis Minnie, Gus Cannon, Memphis Jug Band, and others). Yazoo: 2008. 1994. CD.

232   *St. Louis Blues: The Depression* [1929–1935] (Henry Townsend, Charlie Jordan, Hi Henry Brown, Peetie Wheatstraw, and others). Yazoo: 1030. 1991. CD.

233   *Wild About My Lovin': Beale Street Blues, 1928–30* (Memphis Jug Band, Cannon's Jug Stompers, Jim Jackson, Frank Stokes). RCA: 2461-2-R. 1991. CD.

INDIVIDUALS AND GROUPS

234 Estes, Sleepy John. *I Ain't Gonna Be Worried No More* [1929–1941]. Yazoo: 2004. 1992. CD.

235 Wilkins, Robert. *The Original Rolling Stone* [1928–1935]. Yazoo: 1077. 1989. CD.

TEXAS, ARKANSAS, AND LOUISIANA BLUES

COLLECTIONS

236 *The Blues of Texas, Arkansas, and Louisiana* [1927–1932] (Little Hat Jones, Texas Alexander, Henry Thomas, Blind Lemon Jefferson, King Solomon Hill, Six Cylinder Smith, Buddy Boy Hawkins, and others). Yazoo: 1004. 1991. CD. ALT TITLE: *Don't Leave Me Here.*

237 *Texas Blues: Early Blues Masters from the Lone Star State* [1927–1939] (Henry Thomas, Ramblin' Thomas, Oscar Woods, Coley Jones, Little Hat Jones, Black Ace, and others). JSP: 7730. 2004. CD.

INDIVIDUALS AND GROUPS

238 Grossman, Stefan. *Texas Blues*. Oak Publications. 1984. Score.

239 Jefferson, Blind Lemon
  239.1 *All the Classic Sides* [1926–1929]. JSP: 7706. 2003. 4 CDs.
  239.2 *Best of Blind Lemon Jefferson* [1926–1929]. Yazoo: 2057. 2000. CD.

GEORGIA, ALABAMA, AND THE EAST COAST BLUES

COLLECTIONS

240 *Alabama Blues* [1927–1931] (Ed Bell, Barefoot Bill, Jaybird Coleman, and others). Yazoo: 1006. 1991. CD.

241 *Atlanta Blues: Big City Blues from the Heartland* [1926–1949] (Julius Daniels, Curley Weaver, Peg Leg Howell, and others). JSP: 7754. 2005. 4 CDs.

242 *The Georgia Blues* [1927–1933] (Peg Leg Howell, Barbecue Bob, Sylvester Weaver, Charlie Lincoln, Bumble Bee Slim, Blind Blake, and others). Yazoo: 1012. 1991. CD.

243 ★*Guitar Wizards* [1926–1935] (Carl Martin, Blind Blake, Tampa Red, William Moore, and others). Yazoo: 1016. 1991. CD.

244 *Play My Juke-Box: East Coast Blues* [1943–1954] (Curley Weaver, Guitar Shorty, Big Chief Ellis, Guitar Slim and Jelly Belly, Tarheel Slim, and others). Flyright: 45. 1992. CD.

INDIVIDUALS AND GROUPS

245 Barbecue Bob. *Chocolate to the Bone* [1927–1930]. Yazoo: 2005. 1992. CD.

246 Blind Blake
  246.1 *All the Published Sides* [1926–1930]. JSP: 7714. 2003. 5 CDs.
  246.2 ★*Best of Blind Blake* [1926–1930]. Yazoo: 2058. 2000. CD.

247 Fuller, Blind Boy
  247.1 *Blind Boy Fuller, 1935–1938*. JSP: 7735. 2004. 4 CDs.
  247.2 *Blind Boy Fuller, Vol. 2* [1935–1949]. JSP: 7772. 2004. 4 CDs.
  247.3 *East Coast Piedmont Style* [1935–1939]. Columbia: CK 46777. 1991. CD.

248 Hovington, Frank. *Gone with the Wind* [1975]. Flyright: CD66. 2000. CD.

249 McTell, Blind Willie
  249.1 *The Classic Years, 1927–1940*. JSP: 7711. 2003. 4 CDs.
  249.2 *The Definitive Blind Willie McTell* [1929–1933]. Columbia / Legacy: C2K 53234. 2002. 2 CDs.
  249.3 *Statesboro Blues* [1927–1932]. RCA: 55157. 2003. CD.

PIANO BLUES

COLLECTIONS

250 *Barrelhouse Boogie* [1936–1941] (Jimmy Yancey, Meade Lux Lewis, Pete Johnson, Albert Ammons). RCA Bluebird: 8334-2-RB. 1989. CD.

251 ★*Cuttin' the Boogie: Piano Blues and Boogie Woogie* [1926–1941] (Meade Lux Lewis, Pete Johnson, Albert Ammons, Jimmy Blythe, and others). New World: 259. 1977. LP.

252 *Grinder Man Blues: Masters of the Blues Piano* [1935–1945] (Big Maceo Merriweather, Little Brother Montgomery, Memphis Slim). RCA: 2098-2-R. 1990. CD.

253 Harrison, Mark. *Blues Piano: The Complete Guide with CD*. Hal Leonard: HL00311007. 2003. Score.

254 *Hey! Piano Man* [1935–1940] (Jimmy Yancey, Meade Lux Lewis, Pete Johnson, Albert Ammons). JSP: 7747. 2005. 4 CDs.

255 ★*Juke Joint Saturday Night: Piano Blues, Rags and Stomps; Classic Recordings from the 1920s and '30s* (Jabo Williams, Louise Johnson, Little Brother Montgomery, Skip James, James Wiggins, Roosevelt Sykes, and others). Yazoo: 2053. 2000. CD.

256 *Mama Don't Allow No Easy Riders Here: Strutting the Dozens; Classic Piano Rags, Blues, and Stomps* [1928–1935] (Cow Cow Davenport, Will Ezell, Speckled Red, Blind Leroy Garnett, and others). Yazoo: 2034. 1998. CD.

257 *Rockin' This House: Chicago Blues Piano* [1946–1953] (Memphis Slim, Eddie Boyd, Roosevelt Sykes). JSP: 7762. 2006. 4 CDs.

258 *Shake Your Wicked Knees: Rent Parties and Good Times* [1928–1943] (Pine Top Smith, Cow Cow Davenport, Meade Lux Lewis, Romeo Nelson, Montana Taylor, Jimmy Yancey, and others). Yazoo: 2035. 1998. CD.

259 *Twenty First Street Stomp: Piano Blues of St. Louis* (Stump Johnson, Henry Brown, Effie Miller, Roosevelt Sykes, Sparks Brothers, and others). Yazoo: 2061. 2002. CD.

INDIVIDUALS AND GROUPS

260 Dupree, Champion Jack
  260.1 *Blues from the Gutter* [1958]. Atlantic: 82434-2. 1992. CD.
  260.2 *New Orleans Barrelhouse Boogie* [1940–1941]. Columbia: CK 52834. 1993. CD.

261 Lowry, Todd, Warren Wiegratz, Doug Boduch, Tom McGirr, and Scott Schroedl. *Best of Blues Piano*. Hal Leonard: HL00695841. 2005. Score.

262 Merriweather, Big Maceo. *The Bluebird Recordings, Vol. 1: Chicago, 1941–1942*. RCA Bluebird: 07863-66715-2. 1997. CD.

263 Shaw, Robert. *The Ma Grinder* [1963–1977]. Arhoolie: 377. 1992. CD.

264 Spann, Otis
  264.1 *Otis Spann Is the Blues* [1960]. Candid: CCD-79001. 1999. CD.
  264.2 *Walking the Blues* [1960]. Candid: CCD-79025. 2008. CD.

265 Sykes, Roosevelt. *Roosevelt Sykes, 1929–1942*. Best of Blues: 15. 1996. CD.

BLUES IN THE CITIES:
1920s–1940s

COLLECTIONS

266 *Bottleneck Trendsetters of the 1930s* [1934–1937] (Casey Bill Weldon, Kokomo Arnold). Yazoo: 1049. 1992. CD.

267 *Favorite Country Blues: Guitar-Piano Duets* [1929–1937] (Roosevelt Sykes, Blind Blake, Walter Davis, Leroy Carr, Cripple Clarence Lofton, Bumble Bee Slim, Charlie Spand, and others). Yazoo: 1015. 1992. CD.

268 *Good Time Blues: Harmonicas, Kazoos, Washboards, and Cow-Bells* [1930–1941] (Memphis Jug Band, Roosevelt Graves, Charlie Burse, Bernice Edwards, Sonny Terry, Curley Weaver, Joe McCoy, Buddy Moss, and others). Columbia: CK 46780. 1991. CD.

269 *Raunchy Business: Hot Nuts and Lollypops* [1928–1939] (Lil Johnson, Lonnie Johnson, Lucille Bogan, Bo Carter, Mississippi Sheiks, and others). Columbia: CK 46783. 1991. CD. Import available.

270 *When the Sun Goes Down 3: That's Chicago's South Side* [1931–1942] (Peetie Wheatstraw, Roosevelt Sykes, Lil Johnson, Bill Broonzy, Leroy Carr, Walter Davis, Meade Lux Lewis, Robert Lee McCoy, Sonny Boy Williamson, Speckled Red, Washboard Sam, Tommy McClennan, Jazz Gillum, Tampa Red, Lonnie Johnson, and others). RCA Bluebird: 63988. 2002. CD.

271 *When the Sun Goes Down 4: That's All Right* [1939–1955] (Doctor Clayton, Big Maceo, Cats and a Fiddle, Memphis Slim, Pete Johnson, Albert Ammons, Lil Green, Robert Lockwood, Sunnyland Slim, Eddie Boyd, Arthur Crudup, Roosevelt Sykes, Tampa Red, Piano Red, Sonny Terry, Little Richard, and others). RCA Bluebird: 63989. 2002. CD. Import.

INDIVIDUALS AND GROUPS

272 Broonzy, Big Bill
  272.1 *All the Classic Sides* [1928–1937]. JSP: 7718. 2003. 5 CDs.
  272.2 *Big Bill Broonzy, Vol. 2* [1937–1940]. JSP: 7750. 2005. 4 CDs.

273   Carter, Bo. *Banana in Your Fruit Basket.* Yazoo: CD 1064. 1992. CD.

274   Crudup, Arthur "Big Boy." *Rock Me Mama* [1941–1954]. RCA Bluebird: 55155. 2003. CD.

275   Johnson, Lonnie
    275.1   *A Life In Music.* JSP: 77117. 2009. 4 CDs.
    275.2   ★*Steppin' on the Blues* [1925–1932]. Columbia: CK 46221. 1990. CD.

276   *Leroy Carr and Scrapper Blackwell, Vol. 1, 1928–1934.* JSP 77104. 2008. 4 CDs

277   Memphis Minnie
    277.1   ★*Hoodoo Lady* [1933–1937]. Columbia: CK 46775. 1991. CD.
    277.2   *Queen of the Country Blues* [1929–1937]. JSP: 7716. 2003. 5 CDs.

278   Tampa Red
    278.1   *The Bluebird Recordings, 1936–1938.* RCA: 0783-66722-2. 1997. 2 CDs.
    278.2   *The Complete Bluebird Recordings, Vol. 1* [1934–1936]. RCA Bluebird: 07863-66721-2. 1997. 2 CDs.
    278.3   *The Guitar Wizard* [1932–1934]. Columbia / Legacy: CK 53235. 1994. CD.

279   Terry, Sonny
    279.1   *Hometown Blues* [1948–1952] (Brownie McGhee). Mainstream / Legacy: JK 53625. 1991. CD.
    279.2   *Sonny Terry's Country Blues Harmonica.* Oak Publications. 1975. Score.

280   Terry, Sonny, and Brownie McGhee. *Country Blues Troubadours, 1938–1948.* JSP: 7721. 2003. 5 CDs.

281   Turner, Joe
    281.1   *I've Been to Kansas City, Vol. 1* [1940–1941]. Decca Jazz: MCAD-42351. 1990. CD.
    281.2   *Shout, Rattle, and Roll* [1938–1954]. Proper Box: 89. 2005. 4 CDs.

282   Washboard Sam
    282.1   *Rockin' My Blues Away* [1941–1947]. RCA Bluebird: 07863-61042-2. 1992. CD.
    282.2   *Washboard Sam 1936–1947.* Best of Blues / Wolf: 1. 1992. CD.

283   Wheatstraw, Peetie. *The Devil's Son in Law* [1930–1941]. Story of Blues: 3541-2. 1988. CD.

284   Williamson, John Lee "Sonny Boy"
    284.1   *The Original Sonny Boy Williamson, Vol. 1* [1937–1939]. JSP: 7797. 2007. 4 CDs.

    284.2   *The Original Sonny Boy Williamson.* JSP: 77101. 2009. 4 CDs.

POSTWAR MIDWESTERN BLUES

COLLECTIONS

285   *Blues Masters, Vol. 2: Postwar Chicago Blues* [1950–1962] (Muddy Waters, Howlin' Wolf, Buddy Guy, Little Walter, Sonny Boy Williamson, Jimmy Reed, Otis Rush, Magic Sam, and others). Rhino: 71122. 1992. CD.

286   *Blues Masters, Vol. 4: Harmonica Classics* [1952–1981] (Little Walter, Walter Horton, Junior Wells, James Cotton, Paul Butterfield, Sonny Boy Williamson, and others). Rhino: 71124. 1992. CD.

287   ★*Chess Blues* [1947–1967] (Muddy Waters, Little Johnny Jones, Robert Nighthawk, Jimmy Rogers, Howlin' Wolf, Memphis Minnie, Little Walter, Eddie Boyd, John Brim, Lowell Fulson, Sonny Boy Williamson, Buddy Guy, Elmore James, Little Milton, and others). MCA Chess: CHD4-9340. 1992. 4 CDs.

288   *Chicago Blues: 15 Electric Blues Guitar Classics . . . Plus the Story Behind Five Generations of Blues in the Windy City.* Hal Leonard: HL00690326. 2000. Score.

289   *Chicago Is Just That Way* [1945–1953] (Tampa Red, Big Maceo, Johnny Shines, Muddy Waters, Jazz Gillum, Sunnyland Slim, Roosevelt Sykes, Floyd Jones, Snooky Pryor, Little Walter, Eddie Boyd, Bill Broonzy, Willie Mabon, Jimmy Rogers, Robert Lockwood, and others). JSP: 7744. 2005. 4 CDs.

290   ★*Chicago: The Blues Today!* [1965] (Junior Wells, J. B. Hutto, Otis Rush, James Cotton, Johnny Shines, Walter Horton). Vanguard: 172/174-2. 1999. 3 CDs.

291   *Detroit Blues: Blues from the Motor City* [1938–1954] (John Lee Hooker, Eddie Kirkland, Baby Boy Warren, Eddie Burns, Louisiana Red, Big Maceo, and others). JSP: 7736. 2004. 4 CDs.

292   *Drop Down Mama* [1949–1953] (Robert Nighthawk, Johnny Shines, Floyd Jones, Arthur "Big Boy" Spires, David "Honeyboy" Edwards, and others). MCA Chess: CHD-93002. 1990. CD.

INDIVIDUALS AND GROUPS

293 Anderson, Little Willie. *Swinging the Blues* [1979]. Earwig: CD4930. 1994. CD.

294 Cotton, James. *Deep in the Blues*. Verve: 314 529 849-2. 1996. CD.

295 Dixon, Willie
    295.1 *The Chess Box* [1951–1968] (Little Walter, Eddie Boyd, Willie Mabon, Muddy Waters, Howlin' Wolf, Lowell Fulson, Willie Dixon, Bo Diddley, Sonny Boy Williamson, Koko Taylor, Little Milton, and others). MCA Chess: CHD2-16500. 1988. 2 CDs.
    295.2 *Willie Dixon: The Master Blues Composer, 1915–1992*. Hal Leonard: HL00660178. 1992. Score.

296 Hooker, John Lee.
    296.1 *Classic Early Years* [1948–1951]. JSP: 7703. 2002. 4 CDs.
    296.2 *Don't Turn Me from Your Door* [1953–1961]. Atlantic: 82365-2. 1992. CD.
    296.3 *John Lee Hooker: A Blues Legend*. Goodman Group / Hal Leonard: HL00660169. 1991. Score.
    296.4 *The Legendary Modern Recordings* [1948–1954]. Ace: 315. 1993. CD. import.
    296.5 ★*The Ultimate Collection* [1948–1990]. Rhino: 70572. 1991. 2 CDs.

297 Howlin' Wolf.
    297.1 *The Chess Box* [1951–1963]. MCA Chess: CHD3-9332. 1991. 3 CDs.
    297.2 ★*His Best* [1951–1961]. MCA Chess: 9375. 1997. CD.
    297.3 *Howlin' Wolf Featuring Hubert Sumlin on Guitar* (Kenn Chipkin, John Garwood, Fred Sokolow). Hal Leonard: HL00694905. 1996. Score.
    297.4 *The Howlin' Wolf Story*. Blue Sea Productions / BMG Distribution: 8.28766E+11. 2003. DVD.

298 James, Elmore
    298.1 *Elmore James: Master of the Electric Slide Guitar*. Hal Leonard: HL00694938. 1996. Score.
    298.2 *The Sky Is Crying: The History of Elmore James* [1951–1961]. Rhino: 71190. 1993. CD.

299 Lenoir, J. B. *J. B. Lenoir* [1954–1958]. Martin Scorsese Presents the Blues. MCA Chess: B0000617-02. 2003. CD.

300 Little Walter.
    300.1 *The Blues World of Little Walter* [1950–1951]. Delmark: 648. 1993. CD.
    300.2 *The Essential Little Walter* [1952–1963]. MCA Chess: CHD2-9342. 1993. 2 CDs.
    300.3 ★*His Best*. MCA Chess: CHD-9384. 1997. CD.

301 Memphis Slim. *Messin' Around with the Blues: The Very Best of Memphis Slim* [1946–1948]. Collectables: 2892. 2004. CD.

302 Nighthawk, Robert. *Bricks in My Pillow* [1951–1952]. Delmark: 711. 1998. CD.

303 Perkins, Pinetop. *Sweet Black Angel*. Verve. 1998. CD.

304 Pryor, Snooky. *An Introduction to Snooky Pryor* [1948–1960s]. Fuel 2000: 302 061 605 2. 2007. CD.

305 Robinson, Fenton. *Somebody Loan Me a Dime* [1974]. Alligator: ALCD 4705. 1990. CD.

306 *Rockin' This House: Chicago Blues Piano* [1946–1953] (Memphis Slim, Roosevelt Sykes, and Eddie Boyd). JSP: 7762. 2006. 4 CDs.

307 Shines, Johnny
    307.1 *Dust My Broom* [1951–1955]. Paula: 14. 1994. CD.
    307.2 *Sweet Home Chicago: The J.O.B. Sessions* [1951–1955]. P-Vine: PCD-24051. 2001. CD.

308 Waters, Muddy
    308.1 ★*The Anthology* [1947–1972]. MCA: 088 112 649. 2001. CD.
    308.2 *The Chess Box* [1947–1972]. MCA Chess: CHD3-80002. 1989. 3 CDs.
    308.3 *Deep Blues*. Hal Leonard: HL00694789. 1995. Score.
    308.4 Muddy Waters. *The Definitive Collection*. Geffen: B0006273-02. 2006. CD.
    308.5 *Muddy "Mississippi" Waters Live* [1979]. Epic / Legacy: E2K 86559. 2003. 2 CDs.

309 Wells, Junior
    309.1 *Blues Hit Big Town* [1953–1954]. Delmark: 640. 1998. CD.
    309.2 ★*Hoodoo Man Blues* [1965]. Delmark: 612. 1990. CD.

310 Williamson, Aleck Miller "Sonny Boy"
    310.1 *The Essential Sonny Boy Williamson* [1955–1964]. MCA Chess: CHD2-9343. 1993. 2 CDs.

310.2   *His Best* [1955–1964]. MCA Chess: CHD-9377. 1997. CD.

310.3   *King Biscuit Time* [1951, 1965]. Arhoolie: 310. 1989. CD.

TEXAS AND WEST COAST BLUES

COLLECTIONS

311   *Blues Masters, Vol. 3: Texas Blues* [1927–1987] (Blind Lemon Jefferson, Charles Brown, T-Bone Walker, Percy Mayfield, Gatemouth Brown, Freddie King, Lightnin' Hopkins, Big Mama Thornton, Stevie Ray Vaughan, Albert Collins, Johnny Copeland, and others). Rhino: 71123. 1992. CD.

312   *Boogie Uproar: Texas Blues and R&B* [1947–1954] (Clarence "Gatemouth" Brown, ZuZu Bollin, Goree Carter, Lester Williams, and others). JSP: 7758. 2006. 4 CDs.

313   *The Swingtime Records Story: R&B, Blues, and Gospel* [1946–1952] (Lowell Fulson, Floyd Dixon, Jimmy Witherspoon, Pete Johnson, Ray Charles, Lloyd Glenn, Jimmy McCracklin, Joe Turner, and others). Capricorn: 42024-2. 1994. 2 CDs.

314   *Texas Blues: Bill Quinn's Gold Star Recordings* [1947–1951] (Lil' Son Jackson, L. C. Williams, Thunder Smith, and others). Arhoolie: 352. 1992. CD.

315   *Texas Blues: Oak Anthology of Blues Guitar.* Oak Publications. 1984. Score.

316   *Texas Music, Vol. 1: Postwar Blues Combos* [1947–1970] (T-Bone Walker, Charles Brown, Frankie Lee Sims, Albert Collins, Gatemouth Brown, Johnny Copeland, Pee Wee Crayton, Amos Milburn, Ivory Joe Hunter, Freddie King, Goree Carter, Lester Williams, and others). Rhino: 71781. 1994. CD.

INDIVIDUALS AND GROUPS

317   Brown, Clarence "Gatemouth." *The Original Peacock Recordings* [1952–1959]. Rounder: 2039. 1990. CD.

318   Collins, Albert. *Truckin' with Albert Collins* [1962–1963]. MCA: MCAD-10423. 1990. CD.

319   Fuller, Jesse. *San Francisco Bay Blues* [1963]. Prestige / Good Time Jazz: OBCCD-537-2. 1991. CD.

320   Fulson, Lowell
320.1   *Hung Down Head* [1954–1961]. MCA Chess: CHD-9325. 1991. CD.

320.2   *Lowell Fulson, 1946 to 1953.* JSP: 7728. 2004. 4 CDs.

320.3   *Tramp / Soul* [1964–1966]. Ace: 339. 2001. CD. Import.

321   Hopkins, Lightnin'
321.1   *All the Classics, 1946–1951* [1946–1951]. JSP: 7705. 2003. 5 CDs.

321.2   *Complete Aladdin Recordings* [1946–1948]. EMI: 96843. 1991. 2 CDs.

321.3   *Gold Star Sessions, Vols. 1 and 2* [1947–1950]. Arhoolie: 330, 337. 1990. 2 CDs.

321.4   *Mojo Hand: The Lightnin' Hopkins Anthology* [1946–1972]. Rhino: 71226. 1993. 2 CDs.

321.5   *Very Best of Lightnin' Hopkins* [1946–1961]. Rhino: 79860. 2000. CD.

322   Jackson, Melvin "Lil' Son." *Lil' Son Jackson, Vols. 1 and 2* [1948–1952]. Document: DOCD 5680-81. 2008. 2 CDs.

323   Mercy Dee
323.1   *One Room Country Shack* [1952–1953]. Specialty: SPCD-7036-2. 1993. CD.

323.2   *Troublesome Mind* [1961]. Arhoolie: 369. 1991. CD.

324   Thornton, Big Mama
324.1   *Ball 'n' Chain* [1965–1968]. Arhoolie: 305. 1989. CD.

324.2   *Hound Dog: The Peacock Recordings* [1952–1957]. Peacock / MCA: MCAD-10668. 1992. CD.

325   Walker, T-Bone
325.1   *The Complete Capitol / Black and White Recordings* [1940–1949]. Capitol: 29379. 1995. 3 CDs.

325.2   *The Complete Imperial Recordings* [1950–1954]. EMI: 96737. 1991. 2 CDs.

325.3   *The Original Source* [1929–1951]. Proper Box: 38. 2002. 4 CDs.

325.4   *T-Bone Blues* [1955–1957]. Atlantic: 8020-2. 1989. CD.

325.5   *The T-Bone Walker Collection: 20 Great Tunes from a Blues Legend.* Bug Music / Hal Leonard: HL00690132. 1999. Score.

325.6   *Very Best of T-Bone Walker* [1945–1972]. Rhino: 79894. 2000. CD.

326   Watson, Johnny "Guitar"
326.1   *Very Best of Johnny "Guitar" Watson* [1952–1963]. Rhino: 75702. 1999. CD.

326.2 *The Very Best of Johnny "Guitar" Watson: In Loving Memory [1953–1963]. Collectables: COL-5807. 1996. CD.*

LOUISIANA BLUES

COLLECTIONS

327 *The Best of Excello Records* [1950s–1960s] (Gladiolas, Jerry McCain, Arthur Gunter, Lillian Offit, Louis Brooks, King Crooners, Lonesome Sundown, Guitar Gable, Lazy Lester, Lightnin' Slim, Slim Harpo, Carol Fran, and others). Excello: 3001. 1994. CD.

328 *Dark Clouds Rollin': Excello Swamp Blues Classics* [1955–1966] (Slim Harpo, Lazy Lester, Silas Hogan, Lonesome Sundown, Lightnin' Slim, and others). Excello / AVI: 4210. 1995. CD.

329 *House Rockin' and Hip Shakin': The Best of Excello Blues* [1955–1966] (Jerry McCain, Arthur Gunter, Lonesome Sundown, Guitar Gable, Lazy Lester, Lightnin' Slim, Slim Harpo, Silas Hogan, and others). Hip-O: 40071. 1997. CD.

330 *New Orleans Guitar* [1947–1955] (Smiley Lewis, Guitar Slim, Pee Wee Crayton, T-Bone Walker, and others). JSP: 7773. 2006. 4 CDs.

INDIVIDUALS AND GROUPS

331 Adams, Johnny. *I Won't Cry: Original Ron Recordings* [1959–1963]. Rounder: 2083. 1991. CD.

332 Eaglin, Snooks. *Country Boy Down in New Orleans* [1959–1960]. Arhoolie: 348. 1991. CD.

333 Guitar Slim. *Suffering Mind* [1953–1955]. Specialty: SPCD-7007-2. 1991. CD.

334 Lewis, Smiley. *I Hear You Knockin': The Best of Smiley Lewis* [1950–1960]. Collectables: COL-5630. 1995. CD.

335 Slim Harpo. *The Best of Slim Harpo* [1957–1970]. Hip-O: 40072. 1997. CD.

MODERN BLUES

COLLECTIONS

336 ★*The Best of Duke-Peacock Blues* [1949–1962] (Gatemouth Brown, Big Mama Thornton, Johnny Ace, Larry Davis, Junior Parker, Otis Rush, Bobby Bland, and others). Duke-Peacock: MCAD-10667. 1992. CD.

337 *Blue Flames: A Sun Blues Collection* [1951–1955] (Jackie Brenston, Howlin' Wolf, Rufus Thomas, Little Milton, James Cotton, Little Junior Parker, Doctor Ross, B. B. King, Roscoe Gordon, and others). Rhino: 70962. 1990. CD.

338 *Blues Masters, Vol. 1: Urban Blues* [1940–1966] (Guitar Slim, Pee Wee Crayton, Otis Rush, Lowell Fulson, Bobby Bland, T-Bone Walker, Junior Parker, Little Johnny Taylor, Albert King, Erskine Hawkins, Jimmy Witherspoon, Johnny Otis, Charles Brown, Eddie "Cleanhead" Vinson, Dinah Washington, Joe Turner, and others). Rhino: 71121. 1992. CD.

339 *The Cobra Records Story: Chicago Rock and Blues* [1956–1958] (Otis Rush, Buddy Guy, Magic Sam, Ike Turner, Walter Horton, Sunnyland Slim, and others). Capricorn: 42012-2. 1993. 2 CDs.

340 *The Jewel / Paula Records Story: The Blues, Rhythm and Blues, and Soul Recordings* [1965–1989] (Little Johnny Taylor, Lightnin' Hopkins, Ted Taylor, Toussaint McCall, Frank Frost, Carter Brothers, Little Joe Blue, Buster Benton, and others). Capricorn: 42014-2. 1993. 2 CDs.

341 *Memphis Blues: Important Postwar Recordings* [1951–1955] (Joe Hill Louis, Doctor Ross, Sleepy John Estes, Pinetop Perkins, Howlin' Wolf, Earl Hooker, Walter Horton, Little Milton, Rufus Thomas, Junior Parker, Bobby Bland, Roscoe Gordon, Ike Turner, and others). JSP: 7777. 2006. 4 CDs.

342 *The Modern Records Blues Story* [1949–1956] (John Lee Hooker, Jimmy Witherspoon, Lightnin' Hopkins, Howlin' Wolf, Bobby Bland, B. B. King, Roscoe Gordon, Ike Turner, Elmore James, Etta James, Little Milton, Lowell Fulson, and others). Fuel 2000: 302 061 345-2. 2003. CD.

343 *Soul Shots, Vol. 4: Urban Blues* [1960–1971] (T-Bone Walker, Bobby Bland, B. B. King, Otis Rush, Buddy Guy, Junior Parker, Little Milton, Lowell Fulson, Buddy Guy, Albert Collins, Z. Z. Hill, and others). Rhino: 75758. 1989. CD.

344 *The Sun Blues Years* [1952–1955] (Little Milton, Billy Love, Billy Emerson, Joe Hill Louis, Junior Parker, Roscoe Gordon, Rufus Thomas, Walter Horton, Pinetop Perkins, James Cotton, and others). Original Sun: 41010. 2000. CD.

345 *Sun Records: The Ultimate Blues Collection.* Varèse Sarabande: 302 066 478 2. 2003. 2 CDs.

346   *Sun Records Harmonica Classics* [1953–1955]
      (Dr. Ross, Walter Horton, Joe Hill Louis, Hot Shot
      Love, and others). Rounder: SS 29. 1989. CD.

347   *Superblues: All-Time Classic Blues Hits, Vol. 1*
      [1957–1981] (B. B. King, Z. Z. Hill, Albert King,
      Howlin' Wolf, Jimmy Reed, Koko Taylor, Bobby
      Bland, Little Johnny Taylor, Little Milton, and
      others). Stax: SCD-8551-2. 1990. CD.

INDIVIDUALS AND GROUPS

348   Ace, Johnny. *Johnny Ace Memorial Album* [1952–
      1954]. MCA: MCAD-31183. 1988. CD.

349   Bland, Bobby
      349.1   *★Bobby "Blue" Bland: The Anthology*
              [1952–1977]. MCA: 088 112 596-2. 2001.
              2 CDs.
      349.2   *Greatest Hits, Vol. 1* [1957–1966]. MCA:
              11783. 1998. CD.
      349.3   *Two Steps from the Blues* [1957–1961].
              MCA: 088 112 516-2. 2001. CD.

350   Brown, Charles. *All My Life*. Rounder: BB CD
      9501. 1990. CD.

351   ★Guy, Buddy. *The Very Best of Buddy Guy* [1958–
      1981]. Rhino: 70280. 1992. CD.

352   Hooker, Earl
      352.1   *Blue Guitar: The Chief and Age Sessions*
              [1959–1963]. Paula: PCD-18 [1991]. CD.
      352.2   *An Introduction to Earl Hooker*
              [1950s–1960s]. Fuel 2000: 302 061 554
              2. 2006. CD.
      352.3   *Two Bugs and a Roach* [1952–1953,
              1968–1969]. Arhoolie: 324. 1990. CD.

353   King, Albert
      353.1   *The Best of Albert King* [1968–1973]. Stax:
              FCD-60-005. 1988. CD.
      353.2   *The Complete King and Bobbin Recordings*
              [1959–1963]. Collectables: 2887.
              2004. CD.
      353.3   *★King of the Blues Guitar* [1966–1968].
              Atlantic: 8213-2. 1989. CD.
      353.4   *Live Wire / Blues Power* [1968]. Stax: SCD-
              4128-2. 2003. CD.
      353.5   *More Big Blues* [1959–1963]. Ace: 827.
              2001. CD.
      353.6   *The Ultimate Collection* [1953–1984].
              Rhino: 71268. 1993. 2 CDs.
      353.7   *The Very Best of Albert King* [1960–1975].
              Rhino: 75703. 1999. CD.
      353.8   *The Very Best of Albert King*. Hal Leonard:
              HL00690504. 2002. Score.

354   King, B. B
      354.1   *Anthology* [1962–1998]. MCA: 088 112
              411. 2000. 2 CDs.
      354.2   *B. B. King: The King of the Blues* [1949–
              1991]. MCA: MCAD4-10677. 1992. 4 CDs.
      354.3   *B. B. King Anthology*. Hal Leonard:
              HL00690492. 2001. Score.
      354.4   *Gold* [1963–1999]. Geffen: B0006587-02.
              2006. 2 CDs.
      354.5   *How Blue Can You Get? Classic Live
              Performances* [1964–1994]. MCA: MCAD2-
              11443. 1996. 2 CDs.
      354.6   *★Live at the Regal* [1964]. MCA: 11646.
              1997. CD.
      354.7   *Original Greatest Hits* [1949–1960]. Virgin:
              11654. 2005. 2 CDs.
      354.8   *The Ultimate Collection* [1951–2000].
              Geffen: 0003854-02. 2005. CD.

355   King, Freddy
      355.1   *The Freddie King Collection*. Hal Leonard:
              HL00690134. 1999. Score.
      355.2   *Ultimate Collection* [1960–1975]. Hip-O:
              314 520 909-2. 1993. CD.
      355.3   *The Very Best of Freddy King, Vol. 1.* [1960–
              1961] Collectables: 2824. 2002. CD.

356   Little Milton (Campbell)
      356.1   *Anthology, 1953–1961*. Varese: 66359.
              2002. CD.
      356.2   *Greatest Hits* [1961–1969]. MCA Chess:
              CHD-9386. 1997. CD.
      356.3   *Welcome to the Club: The Essential Chess
              Recordings* [1961–1970]. MCA Chess:
              CHD2-9350. 1994. 2 CDs.

357   Magic Sam (Maghett)
      357.1   *★West Side Soul* [1967]. Delmark: 615.
              1990. CD.
      357.2   *. . . With a Feeling!* [1957–1966].
              Westside: 890. 2001. CD.

358   McCain, Jerry. *Good Stuff*. Varese Sarabande:
      VSD-6022. 1999. CD.

359   Parker, Junior
      359.1   *The Collection*. Umvd Import: UNIP68910.
              2003. CD.
      359.2   *Junior's Blues: The Duke Recordings,
              Vol. 1* [1954–1964]. Duke / MCA:
              MCAD- 10669. 1992. CD.

360   Rubin, Dave
      360.1   *Art of the Shuffle, for Guitar: An Exploration
              of Shuffle, Boogie, and Swing Rhythms*. Hal
              Leonard. 1995. Score.

360.2 *Inside the Blues, 1942–1982.* Hal Leonard: HL00696558. 1995. Score.

361 ★Rush, Otis. *The Essential Otis Rush: Classic Cobra Recordings* [1956–1958]. Fuel 2000: 061 077. 2000. CD.

362 Sokolow, Fred, and Ronny S. Schiff. *Electric Blues Guitar Giants.* Goodman Group / Hal Leonard: HL00694915. 1994. Score.

363 Taylor, Little Johnny. *Greatest Hits* [1963–1968]. Fantasy: FCD-4510-2. 1991. CD.

364 Walker, Philip. *Bottom of the Top* [1973]. Hightone: HCD 8020. 1989. CD.

365 Wilson, U. P. *Attack of the Atomic Guitar* [1992]. Red Lightnin': RLCD 0094 [1998]. CD.

366 Young, Mighty Joe. *Mighty Man.* Blind Pig: BPCD 5040. 1997. CD.

BLUES AND ROCK

COLLECTIONS

367 *Blues Masters, Vol. 6: Blues Originals* [1928–1965] (Sonny Boy Williamson, Howlin' Wolf, Otis Rush, Elmore James, Muddy Waters, Ann Cole, Robert Johnson, Henry Thomas, Slim Harpo, and others). Rhino: 71127. 1993. CD.

368 *The Roots of Rock* [1928–1931] (Memphis Minnie, Charley Patton, Bukka White, Skip James, Bo Carter, Blind Blake, Blind Willie McTell, Henry Thomas, Tommy Johnson, Robert Wilkins, Gus Cannon, and others). Yazoo: 1063. 1991. CD.

369 *Stroll On: An Immediate Blues Collection* [1964–1966] (Yardbirds, Rod Stewart, Cyril Davies, Jeff Beck, John Mayall, Albert Lee, Savoy Brown, Eric Clapton, Jimmy Page, and others). Immediate / Sony Music Special Products: AK 47348. 1991. CD.

INDIVIDUALS AND GROUPS

370 Bishop, Elvin. *Struttin' My Stuff* [1975]. Capricorn: 314 536 135-2. 1997. CD.

371 Butterfield, Paul
371.1 *An Anthology: The Elektra Years* [1965–1971] (Michael Bloomfield, Elvin Bishop). Elektra: 62124. 1997. 2 CDs.
371.2 *East West* [1966] (Michael Bloomfield, Elvin Bishop). Elektra: 7315-2. 1988. CD.

371.3 *Paul Butterfield Teaches Blues Harmonica Master Class: Sessions with a Legendary Player.* Homespun Tapes / Hal Leonard: HL00699089. 1997. Score.

372 Canned Heat. *The Very Best of Canned Heat* [1967–1973]. Capitol: 60146. 2005. CD.

373 Fabulous Thunderbirds
373.1 *The Essential Fabulous Thunderbirds* [1979–1982]. Chrysalis: 21851. 1991. CD.
373.2 *Hot Stuff: The Greatest Hits* [1986–1992]. Epic: 53007. 1992. CD.

374 ★Mahal, Taj. *Giant Step / Ole Folks at Home* [1969]. Columbia: CKG 18. 1989. CD.

375 Mayall, John
375.1 ★*Blues Breakers* [1965]. London: 800 086 2. 2001. CD.
375.2 *Blues Breakers.* Hal Leonard: HL00694896. 1993. Score.
375.3 *London Blues* [1964–1969]. Deram: 844 302-2. 1992. 2 CDs.

376 Musselwhite, Charlie
376.1 *The Harmonica according to Charlie Musselwhite* [1979]. Blind Pig: 5016. 1994. CD.
376.2 *Stand Back! Here Comes Charley Musselwhite's South Side Band* [1967]. Vanguard: 79232. 1991. CD.

377 North Mississippi All-Stars. *Polaris.* Tone-Cool: 79102-21513-2. 2003. CD.

378 Robillard, Duke. *Living with the Blues.* Stony Plain. 2002. CD.

379 Shepherd, Kenny Wayne. *Ledbetter Heights.* Giant: 9 24621-2. 1995. CD.

380 Tedeschi, Susan. *Just Won't Burn.* Tone-Cool: TC 1164. 1998. CD.

381 Thorogood, George. *Anthology.* Capitol / EMI: 72435-27573-2-9. 2000. CD.

382 Trucks, Derek. *Joyful Noise.* Columbia: CK86507. 2002. CD.

383 Vaughan, Stevie Ray, John Tapella, Fred Sokolow, and Ronny S. Schiff. *Stevie Ray Vaughan, Lightnin' Blues, 1983–1987.* Hal Leonard: HL00660058. 1990. Score.

384 Winter, Johnny
384.1 *Best of Johnny Winter* [1969–1979]. Columbia / Legacy: 85926. 2002. CD.

384.2 *Scorchin' Blues* [1968–1979]. Columbia: CK 52466. 1992. CD.

385 Yardbirds. *Five Live Yardbirds* [1964]. Rhino: 70189. 1988. CD.

BLUES REVIVAL AND FOLK BLUES

COLLECTIONS

386 *The American Folk Blues Festival, 1962–1966, Vol. 1*. Hip-O Records: B0000750-09. 2003. 2 DVDs.

387 *The American Folk Blues Festival, 1962–1966, Vol. 2*. Hip-O Records: B0000751-09. 2003. 2 DVDs.

388 *The American Folk Blues Festival, 1962–1966, Vol. 3*. Hip-O Records: B0002937-09. 2004. 2 DVDs.

389 *The American Folk Blues Festival: The British Tours, 1963–1966*. Hip-O Records: B000835309. 2007. 2 DVDs.

390 *Blues Masters, Vol. 7: Blues Revival* [1959–1969] (Mississippi John Hurt, Son House, Fred McDowell, John Lee Hooker, John Mayall, Albert King, Paul Butterfield, Canned Heat, and others). Rhino: 71128. 1993. CD.

391 *Masters of the Country Blues: Fred McDowell and Big Joe Williams*. Yazoo Home Video: 504. 2002. DVD.

392 *Newport Folk Festival: Best of the Blues, 1959–68* (Mississippi John Hurt, Skip James, Son House, Bukka White, Fred McDowell, Muddy Waters, Mance Lipscomb, Gary Davis, Brownie McGhee, Sonny Terry, Sleepy John Estes, Lightnin' Hopkins, John Lee Hooker, and others). Vanguard: 193–195. 2001. 3 CDs.

INDIVIDUALS AND GROUPS

393 Bonner, Weldon "Juke Boy." *Life Gave Me a Dirty Deal* [1967–1968]. Arhoolie: 375. 1993. CD.

394 Hopkins, Lightnin'. *Texas Blues* [1961–1969]. Arhoolie: 302. 1989. CD.

395 House, Son. *Father of the Delta Blues* [1965]. Columbia: C2K 48867. 1992. 2 CDs.

396 Hunter, Alberta. *Amtrak Blues* [1979]. Columbia: CK 36430. 1988. CD.

397 Hurt, Mississippi John. *Mississippi John Hurt Today* [1964]. Vanguard: 79220. 1987. CD.

398 Jackson, John. *Don't Let Your Deal Go Down* [1965–1969]. Arhoolie: 378. 1992. CD.

399 ★James, Skip. *Skip James Today* [1966]. Vanguard: 79219. 1988. CD.

400 ★Lipscomb, Mance. *Texas Songster* [1960–1964]. Arhoolie: 306. 1989. CD.

401 Martin, Bogan, and Armstrong. *Martin, Bogan, and Armstrong / That Old Gang of Mine* [1974, 1978] (Carl Martin, Ted Bogan, Howard Armstrong). Flying Fish: 70003. 1992. CD. CD-R.

402 ★McDowell, Fred. *You Gotta Move* [1964–1965]. Arhoolie: 304. 1993. CD.

403 Memphis Slim and Sonny Boy Williamson. *Memphis Slim and Sonny Boy Williamson: Live in Europe*. Hip-O Records: B0003135-09. 2004. DVD.

404 ★Terry, Sonny, and Brownie McGhee. *Brownie McGhee and Sonny Terry Sing* [1957] (Brownie McGhee). Smithsonian / Folkways: SF 40011. 1990. CD.

405 Wallace, Sippie. *Women Be Wise* [1966]. Storyville: 8024. 2011. CD.

406 Williams, Big Joe. *Shake Your Boogie* [1960, 1969]. Arhoolie: 315. 1990. CD.

407 Williams, Robert Pete. *I'm Blue as a Man Can Be* [1959–1960]. Arhoolie: 394. 1994. CD.

CONTEMPORARY BLUES AND SOUL

COLLECTIONS

408 *Blues Fest: Modern Blues of the '70s* [1970–1979] (Albert King, Hound Dog Taylor, Son Seals, Koko Taylor, Carey Bell, Paul Butterfield, Allman Brothers, Ann Peebles, B. B. King, Fabulous Thunderbirds, Roomful of Blues, Luther Allison, Jimmy Dawkins, Jimmy Johnson, Eddie Shaw, Bobby Rush, and others). Rhino: 72191. 1995. CD.

409 *Blues Fest: Modern Blues of the '80s* [1982–1989] (Stevie Ray Vaughan, James Cotton, Lonnie Brooks, Magic Slim, Robert Cray, Lil' Ed, Kenny Neal, Roy Rogers, John Lee Hooker, Jeannie Cheatham, Ted Hawkins, Katie Webster, Kinsey

Report, Ronnie Earl, and others). Rhino: 72192. 1995. CD.

410   *Blues Fest: Modern Blues of the '90s* [1990–1995] (Buddy Guy, Lucky Peterson, William Clarke, Etta James, Charles Brown, Robert Ward, Angela Strehli, Billy Boy Arnold, Taj Mahal, R. L. Burnside, Lonnie Pitchford, and others). Rhino: 72193. 1995. CD.

411   *The Blues Is Alright, Vol. 1* [1976–1985] (Z. Z. Hill, Little Milton, Denise LaSalle, Bobby Bland, Latimore, Johnny Taylor, and others). Malaco: 7430. 1993. CD.

412   *Blues Masters, Vol. 9: Postmodern Blues* [1968–1986] (Albert Collins, Robert Cray, Stevie Ray Vaughan, Earl Hooker, B. B. King, Bobby Bland, Son Seals, Magic Slim, Koko Taylor, Johnny Winter, Fabulous Thunderbirds, and others). Rhino: 71132. 1993. CD.

413   *Blues Routes* [1990–1995] (John Cephas, Phil Wiggins, Pinetop Perkins, Robert Lockwood Jr., Etta Baker, Claude Williams, Sammy Price, Boozoo Chavis, and others). Smithsonian Folkways: 40118. 1999. CD.

414   *Deep Blues: A Musical Pilgrimage to the Crossroads.* Shout! Factory: 30179. 2003. DVD.

415   *Living Chicago Blues, Vol. 1* [1978] (Jimmy Johnson, Eddie Shaw, Carey Bell, Left Hand Frank). Alligator: 7701. 1991. CD.

416   *Living Chicago Blues, Vol. 2* [1978] (Lonnie Brooks, Magic Slim, Pinetop Perkins, Johnny "Big Moose" Walker). Alligator: 7702. 1991. CD.

417   *Living Chicago Blues, Vol. 3* [1980] (A. C. Reed, Sons of Blues, Lovie Lee, Lacey Gibson, Scotty and the Rib Tips). Alligator: 7703. 1991. CD.

418   *Living Chicago Blues, Vol. 4* [1980] (Luther Johnson, Queen Sylvia Embry, Detroit Junior, Big Leon Brooks, Andrew Brown). Alligator: 7704. 1991. CD.

419   *The New Bluebloods* [1987] (Kinsey Report, Valerie Wellington, Sons of Blues, Gloria Hardman, Lil' Ed and the Blues Imperials, and others). Alligator: 7707. 1989. CD.

INDIVIDUALS AND GROUPS

420   Adams, Johnny. *Walking on a Tightrope: The Songs of Percy Mayfield.* Rounder: 2095. 1989. CD.

421   Barnes, Roosevelt "Booba." *Heartbroken Man.* Rooster Blues: R72623. 1990. CD.

422   Belfour, Robert. *What's Wrong with You.* Fat Possum: 80336-2. 2000. CD.

423   Branch, Billy. *Blues Keep Following Me Around.* Verve: 314 527 268-2. 1995. CD.

424   Brooks, Lonnie. *Bayou Lightning* [1979]. Alligator: 4714. 1997. CD.

425   Brown, Clarence "Gatemouth." *Alright Again!* [1981]. Rounder: 2028. 1991. CD.

426   Burke, Solomon. *Soul Alive!* [1981]. Rounder: 2167. 2002. 2 CDs.

427   Burnside, R. L. *Too Bad Jim.* Fat Possum / Epitaph: 80307. 1994. CD.

428   Campbell, Eddie C. *King of the Jungle* [1977]. Rooster Blues: R2602. 1996. CD.

429   Cephas, John. *Guitar Man* (Phil Wiggins). Flying Fish: 70470. 1989. CD.

430   Clay, Otis. *I'll Treat You Right.* Bullseye Blues: 9520. 1992. CD.

431   Collins, Albert
    431.1   ★*Ice Pickin'* [1978]. Alligator: 4713. 1987. CD.
    431.2   *Showdown!* (Robert Cray, Johnny Copeland). Alligator: 4743. 1986. CD.

432   ★Copeland, Johnny. *Texas Twister* [1977–1985]. Rounder: 11504. 1986. CD.

433   Copeland, Shemekiah. *Turn the Heat Up.* Alligator: ALCD 4857. 1998. CD.

434   Cray, Robert
    434.1   *False Accusations* [1985]. Hightone: HCD-8005. 1988. CD.
    434.2   ★*Strong Persuader.* Hightone / Mercury: 830 568-2. 1986. CD.

435   Davis, Guy. *Butt Naked Free.* Red House: RHR CD 142. 2000. CD.

436   Funderburgh, Anson. *The Best of Anson Funderburgh and the Rockets: Blast Off* [1981–2003]. Shout! Factory: 10060. 2006. CD.

437   Guy, Buddy
    437.1   *Damn Right, I've Got the Blues.* Silvertone / Jive: 1462-2-J. 1991. CD.
    437.2   *Sweet Tea.* Silvertone / Jive: 01241-41751-2. 2001. CD.

438 Harris, Corey. *Greens from the Garden*. Alligator: 4864. 1999. CD.

439 Heartsman, Johnny. *The Touch*. Alligator: 4800. 1991. CD.

440 ★Hill, Z. Z. *Greatest Hits* [1980–1984]. Malaco: 7437. 1990. CD.

441 Hooker, John Lee. *The Healer*. Razor and Tie: 7930185012-2. 1990. CD.

442 Horton, Big Walter. *Big Walter Horton with Carey Bell* [1972]. Alligator: 4702. 1989. CD.

443 James, Etta. *The Right Time*. Elektra: 61347-2. 1992. CD.

444 Johnson, Big Jack. *All the Way Back*. M.C. Records: MC0035. 1998. CD.

445 Johnson, Jimmy. *Johnson's Whacks* [1978]. Delmark: 644. 1991. CD.

446 Kimbrough, Junior. *All Night Long*. Fat Possum: 80308-2. 1992. CD.

447 King, Chris Thomas. *Cry of the Prophets*. Sire / Hightone: 9 26186-2. 1990. CD.

448 King, Little Jimmy. *Something inside of Me*. Bullseye: 9537. 1995. CD.

449 Kinsey Report. *Edge of the City*. Alligator: 4758. 1987. CD.

450 LaSalle, Denise. *Still Trapped*. Malaco: 7454. 1990. CD.

451 Lil' Ed and the Blues Imperials. *Chicken, Gravy, and Biscuits*. Alligator: ALCD 4772. 1989. CD.

452 Lockwood, Robert, Jr.
  452.1 *The Complete Trix Recordings* [1973–1975]. Savoy Jazz: 17312. 2003. 2 CDs.
  452.2 *Steady Rollin' Man* [1973]. Delmark: 630. 1992. CD.

453 Mooney, John. *Telephone King*. Blind Pig: POW 4101. 1991. CD.

454 Moore, Johnny B. *Live at Blue Chicago*. Delmark: 688. 1996. CD.

455 Neal, Kenny. *Walking on Fire*. Alligator: 4795. 1991. CD.

456 Rubin, Dave. *The Best of R&B: A Step-by-Step Breakdown of the Guitar Styles and Techniques*. Hal Leonard: HL00695288. 2000. Score.

457 Rush, Bobby. *Bobby Rush Live at Ground Zero Blues Club*. MVD Visual: DRDV 3001. 2007. DVD.

458 Rush, Otis
  458.1 *All Your Love I Miss Loving: Live at the Wise Fools Pub, Chicago* [1976]. Delmark: 781. 2005. CD.
  458.2 *Right Place, Wrong Time* [1971]. Hightone: 8007. 1985. CD.

459 Saffire—The Uppity Blues Women. *Cleaning House*. Alligator: ALCD 4840. 1996. CD.

460 ★Seals, Son. *Midnight Son* [1976]. Alligator: 4708. 1990. CD.

461 Seals, Son, and David Whitehill. *Bad Axe Blues*. Hal Leonard: HL00690150. 1999.

462 Taylor, Hound Dog. *Hound Dog Taylor and the Houserockers* [1971]. Alligator: 4701. 1989. CD.

463 ★Taylor, Koko. *I Got What It Takes* [1975]. Alligator: 4706. 1991. CD.

464 Taylor, Otis. *White African*. NorthernBlues: NB0002. 2001. CD.

465 Vaughan, Stevie Ray
  465.1 *The Essential Stevie Ray Vaughan and Double Trouble* [1980–1990]. Epic: E2K 86423. 2002. CD.
  465.2 *The Sky Is Crying* [1984–1989]. Epic: EK47390. 1991. CD.

466 Walker, Joe Louis
  466.1 *Blue Soul*. Hightone: HCD 8019. 1989. CD.
  466.2 *The Gift*. Hightone: HCD 8012. 1988. CD.

467 Ward, Robert. *Fear No Evil*. Black Top: 1063. 1991. CD.

468 Webster, Katie. *Swamp Boogie Queen*. Alligator: 4766. 1988. CD.

469 Wellington, Valerie. *Million Dollar Secret* [1984]. Rooster Blues: RB 2619. 1995. CD.

Jazz

Compiled by WILLIAM E. ANDERSON
with
ANDERS GRIFFEN *and* RICHARD MCRAE

GENERAL COLLECTIONS   35
EARLY JAZZ   37
NEW ORLEANS REVIVAL AND TRADITIONAL STYLES   38
LOUIS ARMSTRONG   38
OTHER EARLY SOLOISTS   38
EARLY JAZZ PIANO STYLES   39
BIG BANDS AND THE SWING ERA   39
KANSAS CITY AND OTHER TERRITORY BANDS   40
DUKE ELLINGTON   40
SWING SOLOISTS AND COMBOS   41
BEBOP   42
CHARLIE PARKER   43
THE 1950s AND 1960s: COOL JAZZ AND THE WEST COAST   43
HARD BOP AND RELATED EXTENSIONS OF BEBOP   44
POPULAR JAZZ OF THE 1950s AND 1960s   46
THELONIOUS MONK   46
CHARLES MINGUS   47
MILES DAVIS   47
JOHN COLTRANE   47
FREE JAZZ AND RELATED STYLES OF THE 1960s   48
PIANO IN THE 1960s   49
SWING MAINSTREAM SINCE 1950   50
BIG BANDS SINCE THE 1950s   51
JAZZ SINGERS   52
JAZZ AND POETRY, AND CONCEPT ALBUMS   55
FUSION   55
JAZZ AND THE WORLD   56

MODERN MAINSTREAM: 1970S   *57*
CROSSOVER JAZZ: 1970S–1990S   *58*
JAZZ OUTSIDE THE MAINSTREAM: THE AACM, BAG,
   AND THE LOFTS   *58*

CONTEMPORARY ARTISTS: 1970S THROUGH THE
   2000S   *59*
JAZZ AND THE CLASSICS: THIRD STREAM   *62*
JAZZ AND FILM   *63*

Jazz is a mostly instrumental music developed around the turn of the century in African American urban communities. It is usually characterized by a propulsive rhythm known as swing, the use of a rhythm section that includes a drum kit, personalized instrumental solos, and the use of twelve-bar blues or thirty-two-bar song forms as performance frameworks. Not all jazz reflects every characteristic, and there are differences among listeners and critics in defining the boundaries of jazz. For the purposes of collection development, we have taken a relatively broad view of what constitutes jazz. The main genres in jazz are New Orleans, Chicago, Dixieland, swing, bebop, cool, hard bop, free jazz, fusion, and third stream. While ragtime and blues both influenced jazz, neither is in itself jazz. Recommendations for ragtime and blues may be found in chapters 1, 2, and 12. Above all, jazz is improvisation; therefore, recordings are the primary documents of its history.

What is commonly referred to as early jazz developed mostly in New Orleans, even though the recordings of its pioneers were made in Chicago or New York. Later, in the 1940s, the New Orleans style enjoyed a surge of new interest, including the discovery of local musicians who had not recorded before. Louis Armstrong was the first great soloist of jazz, his trumpet and singing styles becoming very influential when jazz became of national interest. His earliest recordings show him beginning to break away from New Orleans jazz conventions with his swing virtuosity and sense of phrase development. Other early soloists in the 1920s were Sidney Bechet and Johnny Dodds, also from New Orleans, and Bix Beiderbecke from Iowa. The early piano styles of Jelly Roll Morton in New Orleans and James P. Johnson in New York grew out of ragtime; Duke Ellington and Fats Waller were among those who built upon Johnson's stride style.

The big bands emerged during the 1920s when band leaders enlarged their groups to meet the performance demands of floor shows and dancers. Arrangers began conceiving the big band as a combination of sections: brass, reeds, and rhythm. By arranging the reeds behind a trumpet solo or pitting the brass against the reeds in call and response, these arrangers blazed the big band concept that was later popularized by Benny Goodman and Tommy Dorsey. Key bands of the era were led by Fletcher Henderson, Duke Ellington, Jimmie Lunceford, William McKinney (McKinney's Cotton Pickers), and Chick Webb. The "territory" bands from Kansas City and the Midwest/Southwest led by Count Basie, Andy Kirk (aided with arrangements by Mary Lou Williams), and Jay McShann shared a sound based on the blues and exciting "head" arrangements.

Meanwhile, many small group recordings were featuring swing soloists who were identifiable by ear. The saxophone became more prominent, thanks to the solos of Coleman Hawkins and Lester Young. Other improvisers were trumpeter Roy Eldridge, pianists Nat King Cole and Art Tatum, and guitarists Charlie Christian and Django Reinhardt. From the leading big bands like those of Ellington, Goodman, and Artie Shaw, smaller groups were formed for recording sessions, sometimes with guest soloists.

Bebop evolved in the early 1940s from the small swing groups and the virtuosic techniques of Tatum and Christian. Dizzy Gillespie, Charlie Parker, and Thelonious Monk expanded the possibilities of jazz expression with their melodic, harmonic, and rhythmic innovations. While the focus was on small combos, there were also some bebop-oriented big bands. Fruitful collaborations between bebop and Latin musicians, especially Gillespie and Machito, were captured on disc. In the 1950s and 1960s bebop split into various subgenres. Although the association of "cool jazz" with white West Coast musicians and "hard bop" with black East Coast and midwestern players is an oversimplification (and therefore leads to some inconsistencies), it is a useful way of organizing a very active period in jazz history. The important contributions of Thelonious Monk, Charles Mingus, Miles Davis, and John Coltrane cross stylistic boundaries, so these artists are each given a section. Artists associated with the cool style include Chet Baker, Gerry Mulligan, Shelly Manne, and Shorty Rogers. The chamber jazz of the Modern Jazz Quartet, Lennie Tristano, and Chico Hamilton is sometimes associated with cool jazz. Saxophonists such as Stan Getz and Serge Chaloff are associated with cool jazz because they share the influence of the lighter-toned swing tenor

Lester Young. In contrast, Curtis Counce, Hampton Hawes, and Art Pepper are considered West Coast only because of their residency. Significant hard bop artists include Art Blakey, Horace Silver, Cannonball Adderley, and Clifford Brown. Those who sustained bebop into the 1950s and 1960s are Dexter Gordon, J. J. Johnson, and Sonny Rollins.

While Miles Davis remains best known for his performances with John Coltrane, his 1960s group with Wayne Shorter and Herbie Hancock and his albums with arranger Gil Evans merit close attention. Bill Evans influenced younger pianists such as Chick Corea, Herbie Hancock, and Keith Jarrett. Coltrane's classic quartet with McCoy Tyner, Jimmy Garrison, and Elvin Jones lasted from 1960 through 1965, with his efforts toward "free jazz" following until his 1967 death. Free jazz was a radical approach to improvisation demanding new interactions from all participating musicians. Although foreshadowed by Lennie Tristano in the late 1940s, the main period of free jazz was the 1960s, with Coltrane, Ornette Coleman, Albert Ayler, Cecil Taylor, Don Cherry, Archie Shepp, and Sun Ra.

Despite the musical experiments of the 1950s and 1960s, a swing mainstream audience supported musicians who developed their styles before 1940 and continued to play mostly mainstream jazz along with younger musicians who adopted or adapted swing mainstream styles. Some big bands since the 1950s, like those led by Basie and Ellington, continued the swing era traditions, but contemporary adaptations came from Toshiko Akiyoshi, Carla Bley, Gil Evans, Thad Jones and Mel Lewis, and Stan Kenton.

Jazz singers played with words and melodies alike; among the most celebrated are Billie Holiday, Sarah Vaughan, Ella Fitzgerald, Billy Eckstine, and Betty Carter. Popular singers who were influenced by jazz or worked with jazz musicians are Fred Astaire, Connie Boswell, Bing Crosby, and Ethel Waters. Jazz-influenced musicians after 1945 include Rosemary Clooney, Nat King Cole, Lena Horne, Nora Jones, Peggy Lee, Nina Simone, and Frank Sinatra. Sometimes jazz concentrated on the words themselves, as on jazz and poetry recordings in which spoken word is combined with jazz or on concept albums when (mostly) jazz musicians interpret the music of a particular composer or express a producer's concept.

The name "fusion" was applied to the mix of jazz with rock and rhythm and blues. The early innovations of Miles Davis's late 1960s and 1970s bands led to several groups composed of his former members, such as Wayne Shorter, Joe Zawinul, Herbie Hancock, Tony Williams, Chick Corea, Billy Cobham, and John McLaughlin. The work of Gary Burton with Larry Coryell and Pat Metheny is also noteworthy.

Jazz and the world have been mutually enriching. Musicians from outside the United States have embraced jazz; European jazz styles emerged from England, Western Europe, and Russia, as well as from South African expatriates. In turn, American jazz musicians have been strongly influenced by the music of other cultures. Many jazz musicians showed a strong interest in "world music," whether it was Ellington, Coltrane, and Randy Weston reaching outward or Asian American jazz musicians exploring their roots.

By the 1970s, the modern mainstream shifted from swing to bop, sustaining the careers of musicians who began in the 1940s through the 1960s. Their successors who have continued the traditions of bebop and related forms are found in the contemporary artists section. During the same time, what was being called crossover jazz was being marketed as "jazz," even though the jazz characteristics may have been minimal. On the other hand, jazz outside the mainstream developed in the 1970s in Chicago (the Association for the Advancement of Creative Musicians [AACM]), St. Louis (The Black Artists Group [BAG], including Hamiett Bluiett, Julius Hemphill, and Oliver Lake [of the World Saxophone Quartet]), and New York City (the informal "loft jazz" movement).

Since 1980, among the contemporary artists, there have been "neoclassicists" who carry on styles established before their lifetimes, finding new forms of expression or new twists. In contrast, there are older musicians who have continued to push their music in new directions.

Jazz and the classics have collaborated often, with jazz taking a formal approach to composition, utilizing "chamber music" conventions or blending as "third stream," the methods of "classical" and "jazz." Jazz and film have also been interdependent, whether with jazz as film subject matter or as effective and evocative soundtrack music.

GENERAL COLLECTIONS

COLLECTIONS

470 ★*At the Jazz Band Ball: Early Hot Jazz, Song, and Dance.* (Dorsey Brothers Band, Duke Ellington, Boswell Sisters, Louis Armstrong, Paul Whiteman with Bix Beiderbecke, Bill Robinson, Charlie Wellman, Bessie Smith, Tessie Maize, Tommy

Christian, Ben Burnie, Ruby Darby). Yazoo: 514. 2000. DVD.

471   ★*Central Avenue Sounds: Jazz in Los Angeles* [1921–1956] (Kid Ory, Jelly Roll Morton, Louis Armstrong, Lionel Hampton, Art Tatum, Lester Young, T-Bone Walker, Nat King Cole, Hadda Brooks, Slim Gaillard, Gerald Wilson, Charlie Parker, Howard McGhee, Dexter Gordon, Nellie Lutcher, Jimmie Witherspoon, Joe Liggins, Jimmy Liggins, Roy Milton, Johnny Otis, Buddy Collette, Charles Mingus, Roy Porter, Wardell Gray, Percy Mayfield, Johnny Moore, Big Jay McNeely, and others). Rhino: 75872. 1999. 4 CDs.

472   ★*Greatest Jazz Films Ever* (*Jammin' the Blues*, feat. Lester Young, Red Callender, and others, dir. Gjon Mili [1944]; *Be Bop's Nest*, feat. Charlie Parker, Dizzy Gillespie [*Stage Entrance* TV show, 1951 or 1952]; *Jazz at the Philharmonic*, feat. Ella Fitzgerald, Coleman Hawkins, Charlie Parker, dir. Gjon Mili; *The Sound of Miles Davis* [complete edition], feat. Miles Davis, John Coltrane, and Gil Evans, dir. Jack Smight; *The Sound of Jazz* [complete edition], feat. Billie Holiday, Count Basie, Thelonious Monk, Jimmy Giuffre, and many others, dir. Jack Smight; *Jazz from Studio 61*, feat. Ahmad Jamal and Ben Webster). Idem Home Video: IDVD 1059. 2003. 2 DVDs.

473   *The Hal Leonard Real Jazz Standards Fake Book*. Hal Leonard: HL00240161. 2011. Score.

474   *Jazz: A Film by Ken Burns*. PBS / Warner Home Video: B8262D–B8272D. 2000. 10 DVDs.

475   *Jazz: The Smithsonian Anthology* [1917–2003]. Smithsonian Folkways: SFW CD 40820. 2010. 6 CD set.

476   *Jazz Improv Basics: The All-Purpose Reference Guide*. Hal Leonard: HL00843195. 2011. Score with CD.

477   *Jazz Masters: Vintage Collection, 1958–1961*. (Miles Davis, John Coltrane, Billie Holiday, Ahmad Jamal, Lester Young, The Count Basie Orchestra, Gerry Mulligan, Thelonious Monk Trio, Coleman Hawkins, Ben Webster). Fred Baker Film and Video / Warner Vision: 2564600582. 1990. DVD.

478   ★*Ken Burns Jazz: The Story of America's Music* [1917–1992] (Jim Europe, ODJB, James P. Johnson, King Oliver, Bessie Smith, Jelly Roll Morton, Fletcher Henderson, Louis Armstrong, Duke Ellington, Bix Beiderbecke, Benny Moten, Jimmie Lunceford, Benny Goodman, Count Basie, Billie Holiday, Art Tatum, Pete Johnson, Chick Webb, Django Reinhardt, Coleman Hawkins, Artie Shaw, Tommy Dorsey, Gene Krupa, Dizzy Gillespie, Charlie Parker, Bud Powell, Thelonious Monk, Miles Davis, Sarah Vaughan, Chet Baker, Gerry Mulligan, Horace Silver, Clifford Brown/ Max Roach, Sonny Rollins, Modern Jazz Quartet, Dave Brubeck, John Coltrane, Cecil Taylor, Ornette Coleman, Charles Mingus, Stan Getz, Weather Report, Grover Washington, Herbie Hancock, Dexter Gordon, Cassandra Wilson, and others). Sony: 61432. 2000. 5 CDs.

479   *Lost Chords: White Musicians and Their Contributions to Jazz* [1920–1944] (Bix Beiderbecke, Connie Boswell, Tommy Dorsey, Bud Freeman, Benny Goodman, Eddie Lang, Pee Wee Russell, Jack Teagarden, Joe Venuti, and others). Retrieval: 79018. 1999. 2 CDs.

480   *Piano Legends*. (Jelly Roll Morton [audio only], Willie Smith, Meade Lux Lewis, Earl Hines, Mary Lou Williams, Fats Waller, Art Tatum, Oscar Peterson, Marian McPartland, Teddy Wilson, Bud Powell, Thelonius Monk, Horace Silver, Mal Waldron, John Lewis, Lennie Tristano, Dave Brubeck, Duke Ellington, Count Basie, McCoy Tyner, Bill Evans, Keith Jarrett, Cecil Taylor, Chick Corea). Video Artists International: 4209. 2001. DVD.

481   *Progressions: 100 Years of Jazz Guitar* [1906–2001] (Lonnie Johnson, Eddie Lang, Django Reinhardt, Charlie Christian, Tiny Grimes, Bill De Arrango, Barney Kessel, Jimmy Raney, Les Paul, Tal Farlow, Jim Hall, Kenny Burrell, Wes Montgomery, Herb Ellis, Grant Green, Joe Pass, George Benson, Pat Martino, Larry Coryell, Sonny Sharrock, John McLaughlin, John Abercrombie, Pat Metheny, James Blood Ulmer, Bill Frisell, John Scofield, and others). Columbia / Legacy: C4K 86462. 2005. 4 CDs.

482   *Real Book*. Hal Leonard: HL00240221 (vol. 1), HL00240293 (vol. 2), HL00240233 (vol. 3), HL00240296 (vol. 4). 2004–2010. 4 vol. score. Also editions for B-flat, E-flat, and bass clef instruments.

483   *Real Chord Changes and Substitutions*. Hal Leonard: HL00240001–HL00240004. 1992. 4 vol. score. Also edition for B-flat instruments.

484 ★*Real Jazz Classics Fake Book.* Hal Leonard: HL00240162. 2002. Score.

485 ★*Real Vocal Book.* Hal Leonard: HL00240230. 2006. 2 vol. score.

486 ★*The Smithsonian Collection of Classic Jazz* [1916–1981] (Bessie Smith, King Oliver, Sidney Bechet, James P. Johnson, Louis Armstrong, Earl Hines, Bix Beiderbecke, Jimmie Noone, Fletcher Henderson, Red Nichols, Bennie Moten, Fats Waller, Meade Lux Lewis, Benny Goodman, Coleman Hawkins, Billie Holiday, Ella Fitzgerald, Art Tatum, Jimmie Lunceford, Gene Krupa, Roy Eldridge, Benny Carter, Lionel Hampton, Django Reinhardt, Duke Ellington, Count Basie, Lester Young, Charlie Christian, Don Byas, Dizzy Gillespie, Charlie Parker, Erroll Garner, Bud Powell, Dexter Gordon, Tadd Dameron, Lennie Tristano, Red Norvo, Stan Getz, Sarah Vaughan, Thelonious Monk, Horace Silver, Miles Davis, Gil Evans, Charles Mingus, Modern Jazz Quartet, Sonny Rollins, Clifford Brown, Max Roach, Wes Montgomery, Bill Evans, Cecil Taylor, John Coltrane, Ornette Coleman, World Saxophone Quartet). Smithsonian: 2502. 1987. 5 CDs.

487 ★*Sound of Jazz* [1957] (Henry "Red" Allen, Count Basie, Lester Young, Coleman Hawkins, Ben Webster, Billie Holiday, Roy Eldridge, Thelonious Monk, Jimmy Giuffre). Idem Home Video: IDVD 1058. 2003. DVD.

INDIVIDUALS AND GROUPS

488 Aebersold, Jamey
    488.1 *How to Play Jazz and Improvise, 6th Ed.* Jamey Aebersold Jazz, vol. 1. J. Aebersold Jazz: JA 2025D. 1992. Score with CD.
    488.2 *Nothin' but Blues, 3rd Rev. Ed.* Jamey Aebersold Jazz, vol. 2. J. Aebersold Jazz: JA 1211D. 2000?. Score with CD.

489 Baker, David. *Jazz Improvisation: A Comprehensive Method of Study for All Players,* 2nd rev. ed. Frangipani Press. 1983. Score.

490 Chester, Gary. *The New Breed.* Modern Drummer / Hal Leonard: HL06620100. 2006. Score.

491 Fewell, Garrison. *Jazz Improvisation for Guitar: A Harmonic Approach.* Hal Leonard: HL50449594. 2010. Score with CD.

492 Green, Michael. *Essential Jazz Percussion: Drumming in the Style of Modern Jazz Masters.* Mel Bay: MB20948BCD. 2010. Score with CD.

493 Houghton, Steve, and Tom Warrington. *Essential Styles for the Drummer and Bassist: A Cross Section of Styles as Played by Today's Top Artists.* Alfred: 4300. 1990. Score.

494 Morello, Joe. *Rudimental Jazz: A Musical Application of Rudiments to the Drumset.* Modern Drummer Publications: HL00333126. 2010. Score with CD.

495 O'Mahoney, Terry. *Jazz Drumming Transitions.* Hal Leonard: HL06620140. 2010. Score with CD.

496 Weston, Ollie. *Exploring Jazz Clarinet.* Schott: ED 13350. 2010. Score.

EARLY JAZZ

COLLECTIONS

497 New Orleans Rhythm Kings. *The New Orleans Rhythm Kings and Jelly Roll Morton* [1922–1923]. Milestone: 47020. 1992. CD.

498 ★Oliver, Joe "King." *Off the Record: The Complete 1923 Jazz Band Recordings.* Off the Record / Archeophone: OTR-MM6-C2. 2007. 2 CDs.

499 *Riverside History of Classic Jazz* [c1900–1954] (Scott Joplin, Jelly Roll Morton, King Oliver, Louis Armstrong, Sidney Bechet, New Orleans Rhythm Kings, Bix Beiderbecke, James P. Johnson, Duke Ellington, Fletcher Henderson, and others). Riverside / Fantasy: 3RBCD-005-2. 1994. 3 CDs.

INDIVIDUALS AND GROUPS

500 Keppard, Freddie. *Freddie Keppard: The Complete Set* [1923–1927]. Retrieval: 709017. 1999. CD.

501 Morton, Jelly Roll
    501.1 *Birth of the Hot: The Classic Chicago "Red Hot Peppers" Sessions* [1926–1927]. RCA Bluebird: 66641. 1993. CD.
    501.2 *Collected Piano Music.* Smithsonian Institution Press / G. Schirmer: Ed. 3257. 1982. Score.
    501.3 ★*Jelly Roll Morton, 1926–1930.* JSP: 903 [1991]. 5 CDs.
    501.4 *Jelly Roll Morton: The Complete Library of Congress Recordings by Alan Lomax* [1938]. Rounder: 1888. 2005. 8 CDs and 2 vols.

502 Original Dixieland Jazz Band. *75th Anniversary* [1917–1921]. RCA Bluebird: 61098. 1992. CD.

NEW ORLEANS REVIVAL AND TRADITIONAL STYLES

COLLECTION

503   *New Orleans Jazz* [1959–1985] (Kid Thomas Valentine, Billie and Dede Pierce, New Orleans Rag Time Orchestra, Captain John Handy, George Lewis, Kid Howard, Punch Miller). Arhoolie: 346. 1990. CD.

INDIVIDUALS AND GROUPS

504   Baby Dodds. *Talking and Drum Solos/Country Brass Bands* [1946, 1954]. Atavistic: 241. 2003. CD.

505   Eureka Brass Band. *New Orleans Funeral and Parade* [1951]. American Music: 70. 1992. CD.

506   Gillock, William. *New Orleans Jazz Styles: Complete*. Willis Music: HL00416922. 2011. Score.

507   Johnson, Bunk. *The King of the Blues* [1944]. American Music: AMCD-1. 1989. CD.

508   Lewis, George. *George Lewis with Kid Shots* [1944–1945]. American Music: AMCD-2. 1990. CD.

509   ★Ory, Edward "Kid." *Kid Ory's Creole Jazz Band 1944–45*. Good Time Jazz: 12022. 1991. CD.

LOUIS ARMSTRONG

510   Louis Armstrong
    510.1   *The Big Band Recordings, 1930/32*. JSP: 4202. 2008. 2 CDs.
    510.2   *The Complete Hot Five and Hot Seven Recordings* [1925–1929]. Columbia: 68285. 2006. 4 CDs.
    510.3   ★*Ken Burns Jazz Collection: Louis Armstrong* [1923–1967]. Sony: 61440. 2000. CD.
    510.4   *Louis Armstrong Live in '59*. Jazz Icons. Reelin' in the Years: DVWW-JILA. 2006. DVD.
    510.5   *Rhythm Saved the World* [1935–1936]. Decca Jazz: GRD-602. 1991. CD.
    510.6   *Satchmo: Louis Armstrong*. Masters of American Music. S'more Entertainment: SMO-DV-7109. 2011. DVD.
    510.7   *Sugar: The Best of the Complete RCA Victor Recordings* [1932–1933, 1946–1947]. RCA Bluebird: 63851. 2001. CD.

OTHER EARLY SOLOISTS

COLLECTION

511   *Pioneers of the Jazz Guitar* [1928–1937] (Eddie Lang, Lonnie Johnson, Carl Kress, Dick McDonough, and others). Yazoo: 1057. 1997. CD.

INDIVIDUALS AND GROUPS

512   Bechet, Sidney
    512.1   *The Best of Sidney Bechet* [1939–1953]. Blue Note: 28891. 1994. CD.
    512.2   ★*Ken Burns Jazz Collection: Sidney Bechet* [1923–1947]. Sony / Legacy: 61441. 2000. CD.
    512.3   *The Legendary Sidney Bechet* [1932–1941]. RCA Bluebird: 6590-2-RB. 1989. CD.

513   Beiderbecke, Bix
    513.1   *Bix: Ain't None of Them Play Like Him Yet*. Playboy Jazz / Universal Music and Video: PBV 9043. 1994. DVD.
    513.2   *Bix Beiderbecke and the Chicago Cornets* [1924–1925]. Milestone: 47019. 1992. CD.
    513.3   ★*Bix Beiderbecke, Vol. 1: Singin' the Blues* [1927–1928]. Columbia: 45450. 1990. CD.
    513.4   *Bix Beiderbecke, Vol. 2: At the Jazz Band Ball* [1927–1928]. Columbia: 46175. 1990. CD.

514   Dodds, Johnny. *Definitive Dodds* [1926–1927]. Retrieval: 79056. 2008. CD.

515   Lang, Eddie. *New York Sessions* [1926-1935] (Joe Venuti). JSP: 916. 2003. 4 CD set.

516   Nichols, Red. *Red Nichols and Miff Mole, 1925–1927* (Miff Mole). Retrieval: 79010. 1998. CD.

517   Noone, Jimmie. *Chicago Rhythm, Apex Blues* [1923–1943]. JSP: 926. 2006. 4 CDs.

518   Smith, Jabbo. *Jabbo Smith, 1929–1938*. Retrieval: 79013. 1996. CD.

519   Teagarden, Jack. *King of the Blues Trombone* [1928–1940]. Collector's Choice: 279. 2002. 2 CDs.

520   Venuti, Joe. *Stringing the Blues* [1927–1932] (Eddie Lang). Koch Jazz: 7888. 2000. 2 CDs.

EARLY JAZZ PIANO STYLES

COLLECTION

521   *Barrelhouse Boogie* [1936–1941] (Jimmy Yancey, Meade Lux Lewis, Pete Johnson, Albert Ammons). RCA Bluebird: 8334-2-RB. 1989. CD.

INDIVIDUALS AND GROUPS

522   Hines, Earl

  522.1   *Earl Hines Collection: Piano Solos* [1928–1940]. Collector's Classics: COCD 11. 1993. CD.

  522.2   *Storyville Presents Earl Hines: The Complete Transcriptions.* Wise: AM1000043. 2010. Score with CD.

523   ★Johnson, James P. *Harlem Stride Piano* [1921–1929]. Hot 'n Sweet / EPM: 151032. 1992. CD.

524   Roberts, Luckey. *Luckey and the Lion* [1958] (Willie "The Lion" Smith). Good Time Jazz: 10035. 1991. CD.

525   Smith, Willie "The Lion." *The Lion and the Lamb* [1935–1944]. Topaz / Pearl: 1057. 1996. CD.

526   ★Waller, Fats. *Complete Victor Piano Solos* [1927–1941]. Definitive: 11297. 2006. 2 CDs.

527   Wilson, Teddy

  527.1   *Piano Solos* [1934–1937]. Affinity / Charly: CDAFS 1016. 1991. CD.

  527.2   *Storyville Presents Teddy Wilson: The Original Piano Transcriptions.* Wise: AM1000032. 2010. Score with CD.

BIG BANDS AND THE SWING ERA

COLLECTIONS

528   *An Anthology of Big Band Swing* [1930–1955] (Duke Ellington, Luis Russell, Fletcher Henderson, Mills Blue Rhythm Band, Don Redman, Dorsey Brothers, Earl Hines, Jimmie Lunceford, Claude Hopkins, Tiny Bradshaw, Count Basie, Casa Loma Orchestra, Bob Crosby, Andy Kirk, Louis Armstrong, Spud Murphy, Benny Carter, Jay McShann, Lucky Millinder, Jack Teagarden, Roy Eldridge, Woody Herman, Charlie Barnet, Lionel Hampton, Tommy Dorsey, Benny Goodman, and others). Decca Jazz: GRD2-629. 1993. 2 CDs.

529   ★*Big Band Jazz: From the Beginnings to the Fifties* [1924–1956] (Paul Whiteman, Fletcher Henderson, McKinney's Cotton Pickers, Luis Russell, Casa Loma Orchestra, Jesse Stone, Missourians, Bennie Moten, Earl Hines, Chick Webb, Jimmie Lunceford, Benny Goodman, Andy Kirk, Tommy Dorsey, Count Basie, Charlie Barnet, Artie Shaw, Glenn Miller, Harry James, Benny Carter, Erskine Hawkins, Duke Ellington, Lionel Hampton, Woody Herman, Billy Eckstine, Boyd Raeburn, Dizzy Gillespie, Claude Thornhill, Elliot Lawrence, Stan Kenton). Smithsonian: RD 030. 1983. 4 CDs.

530   *Torch Songs: A Collection of Sultry Jazz and Big Band Standards.* Hal Leonard: HL00490446. 2010. Score.

INDIVIDUALS AND GROUPS

531   ★Calloway, Cab. *Best of the Big Bands* [1932–1942]. Columbia: 45336. 1990. CD.

532   Carter, Benny. *The Music Master* [1930–1952]. Proper Box: 68. 2006. 4 CDs.

533   Crosby, Bob. *Big Band Dixieland* [1936-1940]. Jasmine: 2564. 2000. 2 CD set.

534   Dorsey Brothers. *Best of the Big Bands* [1928–1933]. Columbia: 48908. 1992. CD.

535   Dorsey, Jimmy. *Contrasts* [1936–1943]. Decca Jazz: GRD-626. 1993. CD.

536   Dorsey, Tommy. *Yes Indeed!* [1939–1945] (Sy Oliver, arr.). RCA Bluebird: 9987-2-RB. 1990. CD.

537   Goodman, Benny

  537.1   *Benny Goodman: Adventures in the Kingdom of Swing.* Columbia Music Video: CVD 49186. 1993. DVD.

  537.2   ★*Benny Goodman at Carnegie Hall: Complete* [1938]. Columbia: 65143. 1999. 2 CDs.

  537.3   ★*The Essential Benny Goodman* [1934–1946]. Columbia / Bluebird / Legacy: 88697 09491 2. 2007. 2 CDs.

  537.4   *Ken Burns Jazz Collection: Benny Goodman* [1927–1958]. Sony / Legacy: 61445. 2000. CD.

538   Gray, Glen. *Best of the Big Bands* [1931–1934] (Casa Loma Orchestra). Columbia: 45345. 1990. CD.

539   Hampton, Lionel. *The Lionel Hampton Story* [1937–1949]. Proper Box: 12. 2000. 4 CDs. Includes small group recordings as well as big band.

540 Hawkins, Erskine. *The Original Tuxedo Junction* [1938–1945]. RCA: 9682. 1989. CD.

541 Henderson, Fletcher
    541.1 ★*Ken Burns Jazz Collection: Fletcher Henderson* [1924–1940]. Sony / Legacy: 61477. 2000. CD.
    541.2 ★*A Study in Frustration* [1923–1938]. Columbia: C3K 57596. 1994. 3 CDs.

542 Herman, Woody
    542.1 ★*Blowin' Up a Storm!* [1945–1947]. Columbia / Legacy: C2K 65646. 2001. 2 CDs.
    542.2 *Keeper of the Flame* [1945–1947]. Capitol: 98453. 1992. CD.

543 Hines, Earl. *Piano Man* [1928–1944]. Definitive: 11290. 2007. CD.

544 Lunceford, Jimmie. *It's the Way That You Swing It* [1934-1945]. Jasmine: 391. 2002. 2 CD set.

545 McKinney's Cotton Pickers. *The Band Don Redman Built* [1928–1930]. RCA Bluebird: 2275-2-RB. 1990. CD.

546 Raeburn, Boyd. *Boyd Meets Stravinsky* [1946]. Savoy: 92984. 2000. CD.

547 Russell, Luis. *The Luis Russell Story* [1929–1934]. Challenge / Retrieval: 79023. 2005. 2 CDs.

548 ★Shaw, Artie. *The Essential Artie Shaw* [1936–1953]. Bluebird / Legacy: 82876 692392. 2005. 2 CDs.

549 Thornhill, Claude. *Best of the Big Bands* [1941–1947]. Columbia: 46152. 1990. CD.

550 ★Webb, Chick. *Spinnin' the Webb* [1929–1939]. Decca Jazz: GRD-635. 1994. CD.

KANSAS CITY AND OTHER TERRITORY BANDS

COLLECTIONS

551 *Last of the Blue Devils.* Kino Video: K168 DVD. 2001. DVD.

552 *The Real Kansas City of the '20s, '30s, and '40s* [1925–1941] (Bennie Moten, Jesse Stone, Julia Lee, George E. Lee, Walter Page, Andy Kirk, Count Basie, Lester Young, Don Albert, Pete Johnson, Harlan Leonard, Jay McShann, Mary Lou Williams, and others). Columbia / Legacy: 64855. 1996. CD.

INDIVIDUALS AND GROUPS

553 Basie, Count
    553.1 *America's #1 Band* [1936–1951]. Columbia / Legacy: 87110. 2003. 4 CDs.
    553.2 ★*The Complete Decca Recordings* [1937–1939]. Decca Jazz: GRD3-611. 1992. 3 CDs.
    553.3 *Count Basie: Swingin' the Blues.* Masters of American music. EuroArts: 2057148. 2010. DVD.
    553.4 *Kansas City Powerhouse* [1929–1932, 1947–1949] (Bennie Moten). RCA Bluebird: 63903. 2002. CD. Import available.
    553.5 ★*Ken Burns Jazz Collection: Count Basie* [1932–1957]. Verve: 549 090. 2000. CD.

554 ★Kirk, Andy. *Mary's Idea* [1936–1941] (Mary Lou Williams). Decca Jazz: GRD-622. 1993. CD.

555 Leonard, Harlan. *Harlan Leonard and His Rockets, 1940.* Classics: 670. 1992. CD.

556 McShann, Jay. *Blues from Kansas City* [1941–1943]. Decca Jazz: GRD-614. 1992. CD.

557 Moten, Bennie. *Bennie Moten's Kansas City Orchestra* [1929–1932]. RCA Bluebird: 9768-2-RB. 1989. CD.

DUKE ELLINGTON

558 Ellington, Duke
    558.1 *The Best of Early Ellington* [1926–1931]. Decca Jazz: GRD-660. 1996. CD.
    558.2 *The Best of the Complete RCA Victor Recordings, 1944–1946.* RCA Victor: 63462. 2000. CD.
    558.3 ★*The Duke* [1927–1962]. Columbia / Legacy: 65841. 1999. 3 CDs.
    558.4 *Duke Ellington.* Jamey Aebersold Jazz: JA 1221D. 1978. Score with CD.
    558.5 *Duke Ellington and His Orchestra, 1929–1943.* Storyville Films: 16033. 2003. DVD.
    558.6 ★*The Essential Duke Ellington* [1927–1960]. Columbia / Legacy: C2K 89281. 2005. 2 CDs.
    558.7 ★*Ken Burns Jazz Collection: Duke Ellington* [1927–1960]. Sony / Legacy: 61444. 2000. CD.
    558.8 *Never No Lament: The Blanton–Webster Band* [1940–1942]. RCA Bluebird: 50857. 2003. 3 CDs.

559 Strayhorn, Billy. *Lush Life.* Jamey Aebersold Jazz: V66DS. 1995. Score with 2 CDs.

SWING SOLOISTS AND COMBOS

COLLECTIONS

560 *After Hours: Charlie Christian, Jazz Immortal / Dizzy Gillespie, 1941.* Fantasy: OJCCD-1932-2. 2000. CD.

561 ★*The Commodore Story* [1938–1950] (Eddie Condon, Billie Holiday, Don Byas, Lester Young, Coleman Hawkins, Benny Carter, Lee Wiley, Jelly Roll Morton, Bunk Johnson, Bob Wilber, Wild Bill Davison, Bobby Hackett, Jack Teagarden, Pee Wee Russell, Bud Freeman, Chu Berry, Art Hodes, Joe Sullivan, Jess Stacy, Willie "The Lion" Smith, Ralph Sutton, and others). Commodore / GRP: CMD2-400. 1997. 2 CDs.

562 *The Duke's Men: Small Groups, Vol. 1* [1934–1938] (Rex Stewart, Barney Bigard, Johnny Hodges, Cootie Williams). Columbia: C2K 46995. 1991. 2 CDs.

563 *The Duke's Men: Small Groups, Vol. 2* [1938–1940] (Rex Stewart, Barney Bigard, Johnny Hodges, Cootie Williams). Columbia: C2K 48835. 1993. 2 CDs.

564 ★*From Spirituals to Swing: The Legendary 1938 and 1939 Carnegie Hall Concerts Produced by John Hammond* [1938–1939] (Count Basie, Lester Young, Charlie Christian, Benny Goodman, James P. Johnson, Sidney Bechet, Joe Turner, Pete Johnson, Meade Lux Lewis, Albert Ammons, Rosetta Tharpe, Bill Broonzy, Golden Gate Quartet, and others). Vanguard: 169/171. 1999. 3 CDs.

INDIVIDUALS AND GROUPS

565 Allen, Henry "Red." *Ride, Red, Ride* [1930–1946]. ASV: 5356. 2000. CD.

566 Ammons, Albert. *The First Day* [1939] (Meade Lux Lewis). Blue Note: 98450. 1992. CD.

567 Berigan, Bunny. *The Pied Piper* [1934–1940]. RCA Bluebird: 66615. 1995. CD.

568 Byas, Don
568.1 *Complete American Small Group Recordings* [1944–1946]. Definitive: 11213. 2001. 4 CDs.

568.2 *Complete 1946–1951 European Small Group Master Takes* [1946–1951]. Definitive: 11214. 2001. 3 CDs.

569 Christian, Charlie
569.1 ★*The Genius of the Electric Guitar* [1939–1941]. Columbia / Legacy: CSX 65564. 2002. 4 CDs. Import available.
569.2 *Original Guitar Hero* [1939–1941]. Columbia: 86834. 2002. CD.

570 Cole, Nat King. *Best of the Nat King Cole Trio: Instrumental Classics* [1944–1947]. Capitol: 98288. 1992. CD.

571 Condon, Eddie. *Chicago Style* [1927–1940]. ASV: 5192. 1996. CD.

572 Davison, Wild Bill. *The Commodore Master Takes* [1943–1946]. Commodore / GRP: CMD-405. 1997. CD.

573 ★Eldridge, Roy. *After You've Gone* [1936–1946]. Decca Jazz: GRD-605. 1991. CD.

574 Freeman, Bud. *Swingin' with "The Eel"* [1927–1945]. ASV: 5280. 1998. CD.

575 Garner, Erroll. *The Complete Savoy and Dial Master Takes* [1945–1949]. Definitive: 11154. 1999. 2 CDs.

576 Goodman, Benny
576.1 *Benny Goodman Sextet Featuring Charlie Christian* [1939–1941]. Columbia: 45144. 1989. CD.
576.2 *The Complete Capitol Trios* [1947–1954]. Capitol: 21225. 1999. CD.
576.3 *The Complete RCA Victor Small Group Recordings* [1935–1939]. RCA Victor: 09026-68764-2. 1997. 2 CDs.

577 Grappelli, Stéphane. *Stéphane Grappelli.* Hal Leonard. 2010. Score with enhanced CD.

578 Hampton, Lionel. *Ring Dem Bells* [1937–1940]. Bluebird's Best. RCA Bluebird: 63966. 2002. CD.

579 Hawkins, Coleman
579.1 *Body and Soul* [1939–1956]. RCA Bluebird: 68515. 1996. CD.
579.2 *Classic Tenors* [1943] (Lester Young). Signature / CBS: 38446. 1983. CD. import-Japan.
579.3 ★*Ken Burns Jazz Collection: Coleman Hawkins* [1926–1963]. Verve: 549 085. 2000. CD.

580 Kirby, John. *Complete Columbia and RCA Victor Recordings* [1939–1942]. Definitive: 11168. 2000. 2 CDs.

581 Norvo, Red. *Dance of the Octopus* [1933–1936]. Hep: 1044. 1995. CD.

582 Reinhardt, Django
  582.1 ★*The Best of Django Reinhardt* [1936–1948]. Blue Note: 37138. 1996. CD.
  582.2 *Django Reinhardt: Gypsy Jazz*. Jamey Aebersold Jazz. 2010. Score with CD.

583 Russell, Pee Wee. *The Land of Jazz* [1927–1944]. Topaz Jazz: 1018. 1995. CD.

584 Shaw, Artie. *The Complete Gramercy Five Sessions* [1940, 1945]. RCA Bluebird: 7637-2-RB. 1989. CD.

585 Spanier, Muggsy. *Ragtime Band Sessions* [1939]. RCA Bluebird: 66550. 1995. CD.

586 Stacy, Jess. *Ec-Stacy: 25 Great Piano Performances* [1935–1945]. ASV: 5172. 1995. CD.

587 Tatum, Art
  587.1 ★*The Best of the Complete Pablo Solo Masterpieces* [1953–1955]. Pablo: 2405-442. 2003. CD.
  587.2 ★*Classic Early Solos* [1934–1936]. Decca Jazz: GRD-607. 1991. CD. Import available.
  587.3 *Genius of Art Tatum*. Columbia Pictures Pub.: TPF0077. 1988. Score.
  587.4 *Piano Starts Here* [1933, 1949]. Sbme Special Markets: 64690. 2008. CD.
  587.5 *Solos (1940)*. Decca Jazz: 42327. 1989. CD.

588 Waller, Fats
  588.1 *The Complete Recorded Works, Vol. 2: A Handful of Keys* [1929–1934] (6 vols. available in this JSP series). JSP: 928. 2006. 4 CDs.
  588.2 ★*Handful of Keys* [1938–1942]. Sony/BMG: 886972481227. 2008. CD.

589 Williams, Mary Lou. *Zodiac Suite* [1945]. Smithsonian Folkways: 40810. 1995. CD.

590 Wilson, Teddy. *The Noble Art of Teddy Wilson* [1933–1946]. ASV: 5450. 2002. CD.

591 Young, Lester
  591.1 *The Complete Aladdin Sessions* [1942–1948]. Blue Note: 32787. 1995. 2 CDs.
  591.2 *The "Kansas City" Sessions* [1938, 1944]. Commodore / GRP: GRD-402. 1997. CD.
  591.3 ★*Ken Burns Jazz Collection: Lester Young* [1936–1957]. Verve: 549 082. 2000. CD.
  591.4 *Timeless* [1944, 1949]. Savoy Jazz: 17162. 2003. CD.

BEBOP

COLLECTION

592 ★*The Original Mambo Kings: An Afro-Cubop Anthology* [1948–1954] (Machito, Charlie Parker, Flip Phillips, Dizzy Gillespie, Chico O'Farrell). Verve: 314 513 876-2. 1992. CD.

INDIVIDUALS AND GROUPS

593 Eckstine, Billy. *The Legendary Big Band* [1944–1947]. Savoy Jazz: 17125. 2002. 2 CDs.

594 Gillespie, Dizzy
  594.1 ★*The Complete RCA Victor Recordings* [1937–1949]. RCA Bluebird: 66528. 1995. 2 CDs.
  594.2 *Dizzy Gillespie Collection*. Hal Leonard: HL00672479. 2002. Score.
  594.3 ★*Ken Burns Jazz Collection: Dizzy Gillespie* [1940–1967]. Verve: 549 086. 2000. CD.
  594.4 *A Night in Tunisia: The Very Best of Dizzy Gillespie* [1944–1949]. RCA: 84866. 2006. CD.

595 Gordon, Dexter. *Settin' the Pace* [1945–1947]. Savoy Jazz: 17027. 1998. CD.

596 Gray, Wardell. *Memorial, Vol. 1* [1949–1953]. Fantasy: OJCCD-050-2. 1992. CD.

597 Haig, Al. *Al Haig Trio: Jazz Will-O'-the-Wisp* [1954]. Fresh Sound: 38. 1991. CD.

598 Johnson, J. J. *Origins: The Savoy Sessions* [1946–1949]. Savoy Jazz: 17127. 2002. CD.

599 Navarro, Fats
  599.1 *The Complete Blue Note and Capitol Recordings of Fats Navarro and Tadd Dameron* [1947–1949]. Blue Note: 33373. 1995. 2 CDs.
  599.2 *Goin' to Minton's* [1946–1947]. Savoy Jazz: 92861. 1999. CD.

600 Powell, Bud
  600.1 ★*The Amazing Bud Powell, Vol. 1* [1949–1951]. Blue Note: 32136. 2001. CD.
  600.2 ★*The Amazing Bud Powell, Vol. 2* [1951–1953]. Blue Note: 32137. 2001. CD.

600.3 *Bud Powell Real Book.* Hal Leonard: HL00240331. 2010. Score.

600.4 *Jazz Giant* [1949–1950]. Verve: 543 832-2. 2001. CD.

601 Stitt, Sonny. *Sonny Stitt / Bud Powell / J. J. Johnson* [1949–1950]. Fantasy: OJCCD-009-2. 1989. CD.

602 Wallington, George. *The George Wallington Trios* [1952–1953]. Fantasy: OJCCD-1754-2. 1990. CD.

CHARLIE PARKER

603 Parker, Charlie

603.1 *All "Bird."* Jamey Aebersold Jazz: JA 1215D. 1976. Score with CD.

603.2 ★*Best of the Complete Savoy and Dial Studio Recordings* [1944–1948]. Savoy Jazz: 17120. 2002. CD.

603.3 *Celebrating Bird: The Triumph of Charlie Parker.* Pioneer Artists: PA-99-605-D. 1999. DVD.

603.4 *Charlie Parker Omnibook.* Atlantic Music: NLGGC. 1978. Score.

603.5 *The Complete Savoy and Dial Studio Recordings* [1944–1948]. Savoy Jazz: 92911. 2000. 8 CDs.

603.6 ★*Confirmation: Best of the Verve Years* [1946–1954]. Verve: 314 527 815-2. 1995. 2 CDs.

603.7 *Diz 'n' Bird at Carnegie Hall* [1947]. Roost / Blue Note: 57061. 1997. CD.

603.8 ★*Jazz at Massey Hall* [1953]. Fantasy: OJCCD-044-2. 1989. CD.

603.9 *Ken Burns Jazz Collection: Charlie Parker* [1941–1954]. Verve: 549 084. 2000. CD.

603.10 *Town Hall, New York City, June 22, 1945* (Dizzy Gillespie). Uptown: 27.51. 2005. CD.

THE 1950s AND 1960s: COOL JAZZ AND THE WEST COAST

COLLECTION

604 *The Birth of the Cool, Vol. 2* [1951–1953] (Shorty Rogers, Gerry Mulligan, Miles Davis, and others). Capitol: 98935. 1992. CD.

INDIVIDUALS AND GROUPS

605 Almeida, Laurindo. *Brazilliance, Vol. 1* [1953] (Bud Shank). Pacific Jazz: 96339. 1991. CD.

606 Baker, Chet

606.1 *The Best of Chet Baker Plays* [1953–1957]. Pacific Jazz: 97161. 1992. CD.

606.2 *Chet Baker Live in '64 and '79.* Jazz Icons. Reelin' in the Years: DVWW-JICHB. 2006. DVD.

607 Brubeck, Dave

607.1 *Dave Brubeck Live in '64 and '66.* Jazz Icons. Reelin' in the Years; Naxos: 2.119005. 2007. DVD.

607.2 *Jazz at Oberlin* [1953]. Fantasy: 31991. 2010. CD.

608 Chaloff, Serge. *Blue Serge* [1956]. Capitol: 94505. 1998. CD.

609 Counce, Curtis. *You Get More Bounce with Curtis Counce* [1956–1957]. Fantasy: OJCCD-159-2. 1988. CD.

610 ★Davis, Miles. *Complete Birth of the Cool* [1949–1950]. Capitol: 94550. 1998. CD.

611 Getz, Stan

611.1 *Best of the West Coast Sessions* [1955–1957]. Verve: 314 537 084-2. 1997. CD.

611.2 *The Complete Roost Recordings* [1950–1954]. Roulette: 59622. 1997. 3 CDs.

611.3 *Focus* [1961]. Verve: 314 521 419-2. 1997. CD.

611.4 *Quartets* [1949–1950]. Fantasy: OJCCD-121-2. 1991. CD.

611.5 *Stan Getz and J. J. Johnson at the Opera House* [1957]. Verve: 831 272-2. 1986. CD.

612 Hamilton, Chico

612.1 *Gongs East / Three Faces of Chico* [1958–1959]. Collectables: 7801. 2005. CD.

612.2 *Three Classic Albums Plus* [1953–1956]. Avid Entertainment: 949. 2008. 2 CDs.

613 Hawes, Hampton. *The Trio, Vol. 1* [1955]. Fantasy: OJCCD-316-2. 1987. CD.

614 Kessel, Barney. *The Poll Winners* [1957] (Shelly Manne, Ray Brown). Fantasy: OJCCD-156-2. 1988. CD.

615 Konitz, Lee

615.1 ★*Konitz Meets Mulligan* [1953] (Gerry Mulligan). Pacific Jazz: 46847. 1988. CD. Import available.

615.2 *Subconscious Lee* [1949–1950]. Fantasy: OJCCD-186-2. 1991. CD.

616   Lewis, John. *2 Degrees East, 3 Degrees West* [1956] (Bill Perkins). Pacific Jazz: 46859. 1988. CD. Import available (Japan).

617   Manne, Shelly
    617.1   *Shelly Manne and His Men, Vol. 1: The West Coast Sound* [1953, 1955]. Fantasy: OJCCD-152-2. 1988. CD.
    617.2   *"The Three" and "The Two"* [1954]. Fantasy: OJCCD-172-2. 1992. CD.

618   Modern Jazz Quartet
    618.1   *Concorde* [1955]. Fantasy: OJCCD-00202. 1987. CD.
    618.2   *Dedicated to Connie* [1960]. Atlantic: 82763. 1995. 2 CDs.
    618.3   ★*Django* [1953–1954]. Prestige: 8110. 2 006. CD.
    618.4   *No Sun in Venice* [1957]. Atlantic: 1284. 1975. CD. Import available.

619   Mulligan, Gerry
    619.1   ★*The Best of the Gerry Mulligan Quartet with Chet Baker* [1952–1953]. Pacific Jazz: 95481. 1991. CD.
    619.2   *The Original Sextet: Complete Studio Masters* [1955–1956]. Lone Hill Jazz: 10242. 2006. 2 CDs.

620   Norvo, Red. *The Modern Red Norvo* [1945, 1950–1951]. Savoy Jazz: 17113. 2002. 2 CDs.

621   Pepper, Art
    621.1   ★*Art Pepper Meets the Rhythm Section* [1957]. Contemporary: 31992. 2010. CD.
    621.2   *Art Pepper Plus Eleven: Modern Jazz Classics* [1959]. Fantasy: OJCCD-341-2. 1988. CD.

622   Rogers, Shorty. *Shorty Rogers, Vol. 1: West Coast Trumpet* [1946–1954]. JSP: 944. 2008. 4 CDs.

623   Smith, Johnny. *Moonlight in Vermont* [1952–1953]. Blue Note: 93091. 2004. CD.

624   Tjader, Cal. *Monterey Concerts* [1959]. Prestige: 24026. 1973. CD.

625   Tristano, Lennie
    625.1   ★*Intuition* [1949, 1956] (Warne Marsh). Capitol: 52771. 1996. CD.

HARD BOP AND RELATED EXTENSIONS OF BEBOP

COLLECTIONS

626   *Blue Note: A Story of Modern Jazz.* EuroArts Entertainment: 2005678. 2007. DVD.

627   *Four Tenors: John Coltrane, Charles Lloyd, Sonny Rollins and Ben Webster.* Idem Home Video: IDVD 1116. 2001. DVD.

INDIVIDUALS AND GROUPS

628   Adderley, Cannonball
    628.1   *Cannonball Adderley Sextet: Live in Los Angeles, Tokyo and Lugano, 1962–63.* Jazz Shots: 2869086. 2009. DVD.
    628.2   *Quintet in Chicago* [1959] (John Coltrane). EmArcy: 314 559 770-2. 1999. CD. Import available (Japan).
    628.3   *Them Dirty Blues* [1960]. Capitol Jazz: 95447. 2000. CD.

629   Ammons, Gene. *Boss Tenor* [1960]. Prestige: 8102. 2006. CD.

630   Blakey, Art
    630.1   *Art Blakey and the Jazz Messengers Live in '58.* Jazz Icons. Reelin' in the Years: DVWW-JIAB. 2006. DVD.
    630.2   *Free for All* [1964]. Blue Note: 92426. 2004. CD.
    630.3   ★*Ken Burns Jazz Collection: Art Blakey* [1954–1981]. Verve: 549 089. 2000. CD.
    630.4   ★*A Night at Birdland, Vols. 1 and 2* [1954]. Blue Note: 32146/32147. 2001. 2 CDs.
    630.5   *A Night in Tunisia* [1960]. Blue Note: 64474. 2005. CD.

631   Brooks, Tina. *True Blue* [1960]. Blue Note: 64473. 2005. CD.

632   Brown, Clifford
    632.1   *Brown and Roach, Inc* [1954]. EmArcy: 814 644-2. 1987. CD.
    632.2   *Clifford Brown Memorial Album* [1953] (Tadd Dameron). Fantasy: OJCCD-017-2. 1987. CD.
    632.3   *Jazz Style of Clifford Brown* (David Baker). Studio P/R / Warner Bros.: SB104. 1982. Score.

633   ★Burrell, Kenny. *Guitar Forms* [1964–1965]. Verve: 314 521 403-2. 1997. CD.

634 Byrd, Donald. *At the Half-Note Cafe, Vols. 1 and 2* [1960]. Blue Note: 90881. 2004. 2 CDs.

635 Clark, Sonny
   635.1 *Cool Struttin'* [1958]. Blue Note: 95327. 1999. CD.
   635.2 *Leapin' and Lopin'* [1961]. Blue Note: 15366. 2008. CD.

636 Davis, Eddie "Lockjaw." *Cookbook, Vol. 1* [1958]. Prestige: 30009. 2006. CD.

637 Dorham, Kenny. *Whistle Stop* [1961]. Blue Note: 25646. 2000. CD.

638 Farlow, Tal. *Swinging Guitar of . . .* [1956]. Verve: 314 559 515-2. 1999. CD.

639 Farmer, Art
   639.1 *Art Farmer Live in '64*. Jazz Icons. Reelin' in the Years: 2.119019. 2009. DVD.
   639.2 *Meet the Jazztet* [1960]. Chess: 91550. 1990. CD.

640 Gordon, Dexter
   640.1 *Dexter Gordon Live in '63 and '64*. Jazz Icons. Reelin' in the Years; Naxos: 2.119002. 2007. DVD.
   640.2 *Dexter Gordon: Swingin' Hard Bop*. Jamey Aebersold Jazz: JA 1312D. 1998. Score with CD.
   640.3 *Doin' Allright* [1960]. Blue Note: 96503. 2004. CD.

   640.4 ★*Go!* [1962]. Blue Note: 98794. 1999. CD.
   640.5 *Our Man in Paris* [1963]. Blue Note: 80914. 2003. CD.

641 Green, Grant. *The Complete Quartets with Sonny Clark* [1961–1962]. Blue Note: 57194. 1997. 2 CDs.

642 Griffin, Johnny. *Introducing Johnny Griffin* [1956]. Blue Note: 74218. 2007. CD.

643 Henderson, Joe. *Inner Urge*. Jamey Aebersold Jazz. Jamey Aebersold Jazz: V108DS. 2004. Score with CD.

644 Hope, Elmo. *Trio* [1959]. Fantasy: OJCCD-477-2. 1990. CD.

645 Hubbard, Freddie
   645.1 *Breaking Point* [1964]. Blue Note: 90845. 2004. CD.
   645.2 *Freddie Hubbard*. Jamey Aebersold Jazz: JA 1288D. 1993. Score with CD.

646 Johnson, J. J.
   646.1 ★*The Eminent J. J. Johnson, Vols. 1 and 2* [1953–1955]. Blue Note: 32143/32144. 2001. 2 CDs.
   646.2 *13 Original Songs*. Jamey Aebersold Jazz: V111DS. 2005. Score with CD.
   646.3 *Trombone Master* [1957–1960]. Columbia: 44443. 1989. CD.

647 McLean, Jackie. *Bluesnik* [1961]. Blue Note: 65145. 2009. CD.

648 Mingus, Charles. *Charles Mingus*. Jazz Icons. Reelin' in the Years; Naxos: 2.119006. 2007. DVD.

649 Mitchell, Blue. *The Thing to Do* [1964]. Blue Note: 94319. 2004. CD.

650 Mobley, Hank. *Soul Station* [1960]. Blue Note: 95343. 1999. CD.

651 Montgomery, Wes
   651.1 *Impressions: The Verve Jazz Sides* [1964–1966]. Verve: 314 521 690-2. 1995. 2 CDs.
   651.2 ★*The Incredible Jazz Guitar of Wes Montgomery* [1960]. Fantasy: OJCCD-036-2. 1992. CD.
   651.3 *Wes Montgomery Live in '65*. Jazz Icons. Reelin' in the Years; Naxos: 2.119003. 2007. DVD.

652 Moody, James. *Moody's Mood for Blues* [1954–1955]. Fantasy: OJCCD-1837-2. 1994. CD.

653 Morgan, Lee
   653.1 ★*Best of Lee Morgan* [1957–1965]. Blue Note: 91138. 1988. CD.
   653.2 *Sidewinder* [1963]. Blue Note: 95332. 1999. CD.
   653.3 *Sidewinder*. Jamey Aebersold Jazz: V106DS. 2003. Score with CD.

654 Nelson, Oliver. *Blues and the Abstract Truth* [1961]. Impulse!: B0009781-02. 2007. CD.

655 Newborn, Phineas, Jr. *A World of Piano* [1961]. Fantasy: JCCD-175-2. 1991. CD.

656 Nichols, Herbie. *Complete Blue Note Recordings* [1955–1956]. Blue Note: 59352. 1997. 3 CDs.

657 Rollins, Sonny
   657.1 *The Bridge* [1962]. RCA: 52472. 2003. CD. Import available.
   657.2 *Jazz Style of Sonny Rollins* (David Baker). Studio 224: B-99. 1980. Score.

657.3 *Ken Burns Jazz Collection: Sonny Rollins* [1954–1966]. Verve: 549 091. 2000. CD.

657.4 *A Night at the Village Vanguard* [1957]. Blue Note: 99795. 1999. 2 CDs.

657.5 *Saxophone Colossus* [1956]. Prestige: 8105. 2006. CD.

657.6 *Saxophone Colossus.* Winstar Home Entertainment: WHE73025. 1998. DVD.

657.7 *Sonny Rollins.* New approach to jazz improvisation. Jamey Aebersold Jazz: JA 1217D. 1976. Score with CD.

657.8 *Way Out West* [1957]. Contemporary: 31993. 2010. CD.

658 Shorter, Wayne. *Wayne Shorter: Jazz Classics.* Jamey Aebersold Jazz: V33DS. 1985. Score with CD.

659 Silver, Horace
659.1 *The Best of Horace Silver, Vol. 1* [1954–1964]. Blue Note: 91143. 1988. CD.

659.2 *The Best of Horace Silver, Vol. 2* [1964–1972]. Blue Note: 93206. 1989. CD.

659.3 *Horace Silver.* Jamey Aebersold Jazz: JA 1228D. 1992. Score with CD.

660 Smith, Jimmy
660.1 *Best of the Blue Note Years* [1956–1986]. Blue Note: 91140. 1988. CD.

660.2 *Jimmy Smith Live in '69.* Jazz Icons. Reelin' in the Years: 2.119018. 2009. DVD.

660.3 *Walk on the Wild Side: Best of the Verve Years* [1962–1966]. Verve: 527 950-2. 1995. 2 CDs.

661 Turrentine, Stanley. *The Best of Stanley Turrentine* [1960–1966]. Blue Note: 93201. 1989. CD.

662 Weston, Randy. *African Cookbook* [1964]. Collectables: 6759. 2006. CD.

663 Woods, Phil. *Phil Woods.* Jamey Aebersold Jazz: V121DS. 2008. Score with CD.

POPULAR JAZZ OF THE 1950s AND 1960s

COLLECTION

664 *Jazz on a Summer's Day* [1958] (Louis Armstrong, Mahalia Jackson, Chuck Berry, Dinah Washington, Thelonious Monk, Gerry Mulligan, Jimmy Giuffre, Anita O'Day, Jack Teagarden, Chico Hamilton, Sonny Stitt, George Shearing, Big Maybelle, and others). New Yorker Video: DVD 16500. 2000. DVD.

INDIVIDUALS AND GROUPS

665 Brubeck, Dave
665.1 *Dave Brubeck: In Your Own Sweet Way.* Jamey Aebersold Jazz. Jamey Aebersold Jazz: V105DS. 2003. Score with CD.

665.2 *Time Out* [1959]. Columbia: 65122. 1997. CD.

666 Garner, Erroll. *The Original Misty* [1954–1955]. Mercury: 834 910-2. 1988. CD.

667 Getz, Stan. *Getz / Gilberto* [1963] (Joao Gilberto). Verve: 314 521 414-2. 1997. CD.

668 Guaraldi, Vince. *Greatest Hits* [1962–1966]. Fantasy: 7706. 1989. CD.

669 *Jamal, Ahmad. *But Not for Me: Live at the Pershing* [1958]. Chess: 9108. 1988. CD.

670 Lewis, Ramsey. *Ramsey Lewis' Finest Hour* [1961–1967]. Verve: 314 543 763-2. 2000. CD.

671 Mann, Herbie. *The Best of Herbie Mann* [1961–1968]. Atlantic: 1544. 1970. CD.

672 McCann, Les. *Swiss Movement* [1969] (Eddie Harris). Rhino: 72452. 1996. CD.

673 Shearing, George. *George Shearing* [1949–1954]. Verve: 314 529 900-2. 1996. CD.

THELONIOUS MONK

674 Monk, Thelonious
674.1 *At the Five Spot* [1958]. Milestone: 47043. 2007. CD.

674.2 *Best of Thelonious Monk.* Hal Leonard: HL00672388. 2004? Score.

674.3 *Brilliant Corners* [1956]. Riverside: 30501. 2008. CD.

674.4 *The Complete Blue Note Recordings of Thelonious Monk* [1947–1952, 1957]. Blue Note: 306363. 1994. 4 CDs.

674.5 *Ken Burns Jazz Collection: Thelonious Monk* [1947–1971]. Sony: 61449. 2000. CD.

674.6 *Monk's Dream* [1962]. Columbia / Legacy: 63536. 2002. CD.

674.7 *Monk's Music* [1957]. Fantasy: 32689. 2011. CD.

674.8 *Thelonious Monk.* Jamey Aebersold Jazz: V56DS. 1993. Score with CD.

674.9 *Thelonious Monk: American Composer.* Medici Arts: 2057118. 2009. DVD.

674.10 ★*Thelonious Monk Orchestra at Town Hall* [1959]. Riverside: 30190. 2007. CD.

674.11 ★*Thelonious Monk Quartet with John Coltrane at Carnegie Hall* [1957]. Blue Note: 35173. 2005. CD.

674.12 *Thelonious Monk with John Coltrane* [1957]. Concord Music Group: 31989. 1987. CD.

CHARLES MINGUS

675   Mingus, Charles

675.1 *The Black Saint and the Sinner Lady* [1963]. Impulse!: IMPD-174. 1995. CD.

675.2 *Charles "Baron" Mingus: West Coast, 1945–1949*. Uptown: 27.48. 2000. CD.

675.3 *Charles Mingus: Live in '64*. Reelin' in the Years Prod. / Naxos: 2.119006. 2007. DVD.

675.4 *Charles Mingus: More Than a Fake Book*. Jazz Workshop; Hal Leonard: HL00673220. 1991. Score.

675.5 *Charles Mingus: Triumph of the Underdog*. Shanachie: 6315. 1999. DVD.

675.6 *The Great Concert of Charles Mingus* [1964]. Verve: B0002680-02. 2003. 2 CDs.

675.7 ★*Ken Burns Jazz Collection: Charles Mingus* [1957–1972]. Sony: 61448. 2000. CD.

675.8 *Let My Children Hear Music* [1972]. Columbia: 48910. 1992. CD.

675.9 ★*Mingus Ah Um* [1959]. Columbia: 65512. 1998. CD.

675.10 *Mingus Dynasty* [1959]. Columbia: 65513. 1998. CD.

675.11 ★*Pithecanthropus Erectus* [1956]. Atlantic: 8809. 1987. CD.

675.12 *Tijuana Moods* [1957]. RCA: 88697 05533 2. 2007. CD.

MILES DAVIS

676   Davis, Miles

676.1 *Cookin'* [1956]. Prestige: 30157. 2007. CD.

676.2 *E.S.P.* [1965]. Columbia: 65683. 1998. CD.

676.3 *Filles de Kilimanjaro* [1968]. Columbia: 9750. 2009. CD.

676.4 *Jazz Style of Miles Davis* (David Baker). Studio 222 / CPP Belwin. 1980. Score.

676.5 ★*Ken Burns Jazz Collection* [1947–1986]. Sony / Legacy: 61443. 2000. CD.

676.6 ★*Kind of Blue* [1959]. Columbia: 64935. 1997. CD.

676.7 *Live in Europe '67*. Columbia; Legacy: 88697524922-53. 2009. DVD.

676.8 *The Magic of Miles Davis*. Jamey Aebersold Jazz: JA 1272/73D. 1994. Score with CD.

676.9 ★*Miles Ahead* [1957] (Gil Evans, arr.). Columbia: 65121. 1997. CD. Import available.

676.10 *Miles Davis Story*. Columbia Music Video: CVD54040. 2002. DVD.

676.11 *Miles Electric: A Different Kind of Blue*. Eagle Eye Media: EE39020-9. 2004. DVD.

676.12 *Miles Smiles* [1966]. Columbia: 65682. 1998. CD. Import available.

676.13 *Milestones* [1958]. Columbia: 85203. 2001. CD. Import available.

676.14 ★*Porgy and Bess* [1958] (Gil Evans, arr.). Columbia: 65141. 1997. CD.

676.15 *Relaxin'* [1956]. Prestige: 8104. 2006. CD.

676.16 ★*Round about Midnight* [1955–1956]. Columbia: 85201. 2001. CD.

676.17 ★*Sketches of Spain* [1959–1960] (Gil Evans, arr.). Columbia: 65142. 1997. CD.

676.18 *Someday My Prince Will Come* [1961]. Columbia: 65919. 1999. CD.

676.19 *Workin'* [1956]. Prestige: 30080. 2006. CD.

JOHN COLTRANE

677   Coltrane, John

677.1 *Ascension* [1965]. Impulse!: 543 413. 2000. CD.

677.2 ★*Blue Train* [1957]. Blue Note: 95326. 2003. CD.

677.3 *Coltrane* [1962]. Impulse!: 589 567. 2002. CD.

677.4 *The Complete Africa / Brass Sessions* [1961]. Impulse!: IMPD-2-168. 1995. 2 CDs.

677.5 *Crescent* [1964]. Impulse!: B0010969-02. 2008. CD.

677.6 ★*Giant Steps* [1959]. Rhino: 75204. 1998. CD.

677.7 *Impressions* [1961–1963]. Impulse!: B0010967-02. 2008. CD.

677.8 *Interstellar Space* [1967]. Impulse!: 543 415. 2000. CD.

677.9 ★*John Coltrane and Johnny Hartman* [1963]. Impulse!: B0010966-02. 2008. CD.

677.10 *John Coltrane: Live in '60, '61, and '65*. Reelin' in the Years: 2.119007. 2007. DVD.

677.11 ★*Ken Burns Jazz Collection: John Coltrane* [1956–1967]. Verve: 549 083. 2000. CD.

677.12 *Live at Birdland* [1963]. Impulse!: B0010968-02. 2008. CD.

677.13 *Live at the Village Vanguard* [1961]. Impulse!: B0010117-02. 2007. CD.

677.14 ★*A Love Supreme* [1964]. Impulse!: B0000610-02. 2003. CD.

677.15 *Meditations* [1965]. Impulse!: B0012405-02. 2009. CD.

677.16 *Music of John Coltrane*. Hal Leonard: HL00660165. 1991. Score.

677.17 *My Favorite Things* [1960]. Rhino: 75204. 1998. CD.

677.18 *Soultrane* [1958]. Prestige: 30006. 2006. CD.

677.19 *The World according to John Coltrane*. Masters of American Music. Medici Arts: 2057108. 2010. DVD.

FREE JAZZ AND RELATED STYLES OF THE 1960s

COLLECTION

678 *Ornette Coleman Trio / Sound?* [1966] (Ornette Coleman Trio [1st film]; Roland Kirk and John Cage [2nd film]. Efor Films: 2869045. 2004. DVD.

INDIVIDUALS AND GROUPS

679 Ayler, Albert

679.1 *Bells / Prophecy* [1964–1965]. ESP-DISK: 4006. 2005. CD.

679.2 *Spirits* [1964]. Breathless / Get Back: 52006. 2005. CD. Alternate title: *Witches and Devils*.

679.3 *Spiritual Unity* [1964]. ESP-DISK: 1002. 2005. CD.

680 Cherry, Don. *Complete Communion* [1965]. Blue Note: 22673. 2000. CD.

681 Coleman, Ornette

681.1 *At the Golden Circle, Vols. 1 and 2* [1965]. Blue Note: 35518/35519. 2002. 2 CDs.

681.2 ★*Free Jazz* [1960]. Atlantic: 1364. 1988. CD.

681.3 ★*Ken Burns Jazz Collection: Ornette Coleman* [1958–1976]. Sony / Legacy: 61450. 2000. CD.

681.4 ★*The Shape of Jazz to Come* [1959]. Atlantic: 1317. 1992. CD.

681.5 *This Is Our Music* [1960]. Atlantic: 1353. 2005. CD. Import.

682 Dolphy, Eric

682.1 *Eric Dolphy at the Five Spot, Vol. 1* [1961]. Prestige: 30656. 2008. CD.

682.2 *Far Cry* [1961] (Booker Little). Fantasy: OJCCD-400-2. 1989. CD.

682.3 *Outward Bound* [1960]. Prestige: 30083. 2006. CD.

683 Giuffre, Jimmy. *Jimmy Giuffre 3, 1961* [1961]. ECM: 1438/1439. 1992. 2 CDs.

684 Haden, Charlie. *Liberation Music Orchestra* [1969]. Impulse!: IMPD-188. 1996. CD.

685 ★Henderson, Joe. *Page One* [1963]. Blue Note: 98795. 1999. CD.

686 Hill, Andrew. *Point of Departure* [1964]. Blue Note: 99007. 1999. CD.

687 Hutcherson, Bobby. *Dialogue* [1965]. Blue Note: 35586. 2002. CD.

688 Kirk, Rahsaan Roland

688.1 *Does Your House Have Lions: The Rahsaan Roland Kirk Anthology* [1966–1975]. Rhino: 71406. 1993. 2 CDs.

688.2 *Rahsaan Roland Kirk Live in '63 and '67*. Jazz Icons. Reelin' in the Years; Naxos: 2.119008. 2008. DVD.

688.3 ★*Rip, Rig, and Panic / Now Please Don't You Cry, Beautiful Edith* [1965, 1967]. EmArcy: 832 164-2. 1990. CD.

689 Lacy, Steve

689.1 *Evidence* [1961] (Don Cherry). Fantasy: OJCCD-1755-2. 1990. CD.

689.2 *The Straight Horn of Steve Lacy* [1960]. Candid: 79007. 1989. CD.

690 Lateef, Yusef. *Eastern Sounds* [1961]. Prestige: 30012. 2006. CD.

691 Little, Booker

691.1 *Booker Little and Friend* [1961] (import available). Rhino: 79855. 2000. CD.

691.2 *Out Front* [1960]. Candid: 79027. 2000. CD.

692 McLean, Jackie

692.1 *Destination Out* [1963]. Blue Note: 92424. 2004. CD.

692.2 *Let Freedom Ring* [1962]. Blue Note: 80908. 2003. CD.

693 Moncur, Grachan, III. *Evolution* [1963]. Blue Note: 15365. 2008. CD.

694 New York Art Quartet. *New York Art Quartet* [1964] (John Tchicai, Roswell Rudd, Lewis Worrell, Milford Graves). ESP-DISK: 1004. 2008. CD.

695 Ra, Sun
  695.1 *Cosmic Tones for Mental Therapy / Art Forms of Dimensions Tomorrow* [1961–1963]. Evidence: 22036. 1992. CD.
  695.2 ★*Heliocentric Worlds* [1965]. ESP-DISK: 4062. 2010. 3 CDs.
  695.3 *Sun Ra: A Joyful Noise.* Winstar Home Entertainment: 2WHE73021. 1998. DVD.

696 Roach, Max
  696.1 ★*Percussion Bitter Suite* [1961]. Impulse!: GRD-122. 1993. CD.
  696.2 *We Insist: Freedom Now Suite* [1960]. Candid: 79002. 1990. CD.

697 Rollins, Sonny
  697.1 *East Broadway Rundown* [1966]. Impulse!: GRD-161. 1995. CD. Import available.
  697.2 *Our Man in Jazz* [1962]. RCA: 74321851602. 2001. CD. Import available (Europe or Japan).

698 Sanders, Pharoah
  698.1 *Karma* [1969]. Impulse!: GRD-153. 1995. CD.
  698.2 *Tauhid* [1966]. Impulse!: GRD-129. 1993. CD.

699 Shepp, Archie
  699.1 *Four for Trane* [1964]. Impulse!: IMPD-218. 1997. CD.
  699.2 *The New York Contemporary Five* [1963] (Don Cherry, John Tchicai). Delmark: 409. 2010. CD.
  699.3 *On This Night* [1965]. Impulse!: GRD-125. 1993. CD.

700 Shorter, Wayne
  700.1 *Adam's Apple* [1966]. Blue Note: 80912. 2003. CD.
  700.2 *Night Dreamer* [1964]. Blue Note: 64467. 2005. CD.

PIANO IN THE 1960s

701 Bley, Paul. *Closer* [1965]. ESP-DISK: 1021. 2008. CD.

702 Byard, Jaki
  702.1 *Blues for Smoke* [1960]. Candid: 79018. 1988. CD.
  702.2 *Solo / Strings* [1968–1969]. Prestige: 24246. 2000. CD.

703 Corea, Chick. *Now He Sings, Now He Sobs* [1968]. Blue Note: 38265. 2002. CD.

704 Evans, Bill
  704.1 *Bill Evans* (Andy LaVerne). TRO / Hal Leonard: HL00000116. 2001? Score.
  704.2 *Bill Evans at Town Hall, Vol. 1* [1966]. Verve: 831 271-2. 1986. CD.
  704.3 *Bill Evans Live, '64–'75.* Jazz Icons. Reelin' in the Years; Naxos: 2.119013. 2008. DVD.
  704.4 *Conversations with Myself* [1963]. Verve: 314 521 409-2. 1997. CD.
  704.5 *Everybody Digs Bill Evans* [1958]. Riverside: 30182. 2007. CD.
  704.6 *Portrait in Jazz* [1959]. Riverside: 30678. 2008. CD.
  704.7 ★*Sunday at the Village Vanguard* [1961]. Riverside: 30509. 2008. CD.
  704.8 ★*Waltz for Debby* [1961]. Riverside: 32326. 2010. CD.

705 Garner, Erroll. *Erroll Garner Live in '63 and '64.* Jazz Icons. Reelin' in the Years; Naxos: 2.119021. 2009. DVD.

706 Hancock, Herbie
  706.1 *Empyrean Isles* [1964]. Blue Note: 98796. 1998. CD.
  706.2 ★*Ken Burns Jazz Collection: Herbie Hancock* [1962–1995]. Sony / Legacy: 61446. 2000. CD.
  706.3 *Maiden Voyage* [1965]. Blue Note: 95331. 1999. CD.

707 Harris, Barry. *Magnificent!* [1969]. Fantasy: OJCCD-1026-2. 1999. CD.

708 Peterson, Oscar. *Oscar Peterson: The Life of a Legend.* View Video: 2352. 2010. DVD.

709 Taylor, Cecil
  709.1 *Cecil Taylor: All the Notes.* MVD Visual: MVD5101D. 2010. DVD.
  709.2 *Cecil Taylor Unit / Roswell Rudd Sextet: Mixed* [1961, 1966]. Impulse!: IMPD-270. 1998. CD.
  709.3 *Conquistador!* [1966]. Blue Note: 90840. 2004. CD.

709.4   *Nefertiti, the Beautiful One Has Come* [1962]. Revenant: 202. 1997. 2 CDs.

709.5   ★*Unit Structures* [1966]. Blue Note: 84237. 1987. CD.

709.6   *The World of Cecil Taylor* [1960]. Candid: 79006. 2001. CD.

710   Tyner, McCoy. *The Real McCoy* [1967]. Blue Note: 97807. 1999. CD.

SWING MAINSTREAM SINCE 1950

INDIVIDUALS AND GROUPS

711   Alden, Howard. *Take Your Pick* [1996]. Concord Jazz: 4743. 1997. CD.

712   Armstrong, Louis

712.1   *The Great Summit: Master Takes* [1961] (Duke Ellington). Roulette: 24547. 2000. CD.

712.2   *Louis Armstrong Plays W. C. Handy* [1954]. Columbia: 64925. 1997. CD.

712.3   *Satch Plays Fats* [1955]. Columbia: 64927. 2000. CD.

712.4   *Satchmo: A Musical Autobiography* [1947–1957]. Verve: 314 543 822-2. 2001. 3 CDs.

713   Basie, Count

713.1   *Count Basie Jam: Montreux '77* (Roy Eldridge, Benny Carter, Zoot Sims, Vic Dickenson, Al Grey, and others). Fantasy: OJCCD-379-2. 1989. CD.

713.2   *For the First Time* [1974]. Pablo: 2310-712-2. 1987. CD.

714   Braff, Ruby. *A Sailboat in the Moonlight* [1985]. Concord Jazz: 4296. 1986. CD.

715   Carter, Benny

715.1   *Further Definitions* [1961]. Impulse!: 229. 1997. CD.

715.2   *Montreux '77*. Pablo: 374. 1989. CD. Also on DVD.

715.3   *Over the Rainbow* [1988]. MusicMasters: 5015. 1989. CD.

716   Cheatham, Doc. *Duets and Solos* [1976–1979] (Sammy Price). Sackville: 5002. [199-?]. 2 CDs.

717   Clayton, Buck. *Complete Legendary Jam Sessions Master Takes* [1953–1956]. Lone Hill Jazz: 10115. 2004. 3 CDs.

718   Cole, Nat King. *After Midnight: The Complete Session* [1956]. Capitol Jazz: 20087. 1999. CD.

719   Eldridge, Roy

719.1   *Little Jazz: The Best of the Verve Years* [1951–1960]. Verve: 314 523 338-2. 1994. CD.

719.2   *Roy and Diz* [1954] (Dizzy Gillespie). Verve: 521 647. 1994. CD.

720   Ellington, Duke

720.1   *Back to Back* [1959] (Johnny Hodges). Verve: 314 521 404-2. 1997. CD.

720.2   *Money Jungle* [1962] (Charles Mingus, Max Roach). Blue Note: 38227. 2002. CD.

721   Garner, Erroll. *Concert by the Sea* [1955]. Columbia: 40589. 1985. CD.

722   Grappelli, Stéphane

722.1   *Jazz in Paris: Improvisations* [1956]. Verve: 314 549 242-2. 2000. CD.

722.2   *Jazz Masters, Vol. 11: Stephane Grappelli* [1966–1992]. Verve: 314 516 758-2. 1994. CD.

723   Hackett, Bobby. *Two Classic Albums from Bobby Hackett and Jack Teagarden: Jazz Ultimate / Coast Concert* [1955, 1957] (Jack Teagarden). Collectors' Choice: 165-2. 2000. CD.

724   Hampton, Lionel. *Lionel Hampton with Oscar Peterson* [1953–1954]. Verve: 314 521 853-2. 1994. CD.

725   Hawkins, Coleman. *The High and Mighty Hawk* [1955–1958]. Poll Winners: 27235. 2010. CD.

726   Hines, Earl. *Earl Hines Plays Duke Ellington* [1971–1975]. New World: 80361. 1988. 2 CDs.

727   Hodes, Art. *Tribute to the Greats* [1976–1978]. Delmark: 238. 2001. CD.

728   McKenna, Dave. *Dancing in the Dark* [1985]. Concord Jazz: 4292. 1986. CD.

729   Paul, Les. *Les Paul Live in New York*. Questar: QD3943. 2010. DVD.

730   Peterson, Oscar

730.1   ★*At the Stratford Shakespeare Festival* [1956]. Verve: 314 513 72-2. 1993. CD.

730.2   *Oscar Peterson Live in '63, '64, and '65*. Jazz Icons. Reelin' in the Years; Naxos: 2.11901. 2008. DVD.

730.3   *Trio Plus One* [1964] (Clark Terry). Verve: 6.02517Ewith11. 2007. CD.

731   Quebec, Ike. *Blue and Sentimental* [1961]. Blue Note: 93184. 2008. CD.

732 Russell, Pee Wee

    732.1 *Jazz Reunion* [1961] (Coleman Hawkins). Candid: 79020. 1990. CD.

    732.2 ★*Swingin' with Pee Wee* [1958, 1960]. Prestige: 24213. 1999. CD.

733 Sutton, Ralph. *At Cafe des Copains* [1983–1987]. Sackville: 2019. 1991. CD.

734 Terry, Clark. *Complete Studio Recordings* [1964–1966] (Bob Brookmeyer). Lone Hill Jazz: 10199. 2005. 2 CDs.

735 Thompson, Lucky

    735.1 *Lucky Strikes* [1964]. Fantasy: OJCCD-194-2. 1987. CD.

    735.2 *Lucky Thompson Meets Oscar Pettiford* [1956] (Oscar Pettiford). Fresh Sound: 424. 2006. CD. Alternate title: *Tricotism*.

736 Webster, Ben

    736.1 ★*Soulville* [1959]. Verve: 314 521 449-2. 2003. CD.

    736.2 *Tenor Sax Legend: Live and Intimate.* Shanachie: 6333. 2009. DVD.

737 Williams, Mary Lou. *Free Spirits* [1975]. Steeplechase: 31043. 1987. CD.

738 Young, Lester. *Pres and Teddy* [1952, 1956] (Teddy Wilson). Verve: 831 270-2. 1986. CD.

BIG BANDS SINCE THE 1950S

COLLECTION

739 *Big Band Renaissance: The Evolution of the Jazz Orchestra* [1941–1989] (Jay McShann, Boyd Raeburn, Duke Ellington, Benny Goodman, Charlie Barnet, Artie Shaw, Count Basie, Woody Herman, Stan Kenton, Sauter-Finegan, Ted Heath, Harry James, Maynard Ferguson, Buddy Rich, Herb Pomeroy, Johnny Richards, Dizzy Gillespie, Terry Gibbs, Gerry Mulligan, Quincy Jones, Gerald Wilson, Thad Jones, Mel Lewis, Duke Pearson, Clare Fischer, John Dankworth, Kenny Clarke, Francy Boland, Don Ellis, Toshiko Akiyoshi, Rob McConnell, Gil Evans, George Russell, Benny Carter, Manny Albam, Henry Mancini, Oliver Nelson, Muhal Richard Abrams, Sun Ra, Charlie Haden, and others). Smithsonian: RD 108. 1995. 5 CDs.

INDIVIDUALS AND GROUPS

740 Akiyoshi, Toshiko. *The Toshiko Akiyoshi Jazz Orchestra: Strive for Jive* (Lew Tabackin). View Video: 2336. 2009. DVD.

741 Basie, Count

    741.1 *April in Paris* [1955–1956]. Verve: 521 402-2. 1997. CD.

    741.2 *Chairman of the Board* [1959]. Roulette: 81664. 2003. CD.

742 Bellson, Louie. *Inferno* [1974, 1979]. Concord Jazz: 2158. 2002. 2 CDs.

743 Bley, Carla

    743.1 *European Tour* [1977]. Watt / ECM: 8. 1988. CD.

    743.2 *Social Studies* [1980]. Watt / ECM: 11. 1988. CD.

744 Carter, Benny. *Central City Sketches* [1987]. Nimbus: 2716. 2009. CD.

745 Criss, Sonny. *Sonny's Dream* [1968] (Horace Tapscott, arr.). Fantasy: OJCCD-707-2. 1992. CD.

746 Dameron, Tadd

    746.1 *Fontainebleau* [1956]. Fantasy: OJCCD-055-2. 1987. CD.

    746.2 *The Magic Touch* [1962]. Fantasy: OJCCD-143-2. 1992. CD.

747 Either/Orchestra. *The Brunt* [1993]. Accurate: 3262. 1994. CD.

748 Ellington, Duke

    748.1 *Afro-Eurasian Eclipse* [1971]. Fantasy: OJCCD-645-2. 1975. CD.

    748.2 ★*Ellington at Newport (Complete)* [1956]. Columbia: C2K 64932. 1999. 2 CDs.

    748.3 ★*The Far East Suite* [1966]. RCA Bluebird: 55614. 2003. CD.

    748.4 *New Orleans Suite* [1970]. Atlantic: 1580. 1987. CD. Available as import.

    748.5 *Such Sweet Thunder* [1957]. Columbia: 65568. 1999. CD.

749 Ellis, Don

    749.1 *Electric Bath* [1967]. Columbia: 65522. 1998. CD.

    749.2 *Electric Heart, Don Ellis: The Man, His Time, His Music.* Sights & Sounds Films: SNRDVD002. 2008. DVD.

750 Evans, Gil

    750.1 *The Complete Pacific Jazz Sessions* [1958–1959]. Blue Note: 58300. 2006. CD.

750.2 *Gil Evans and Ten* [1957]. Fantasy: OJCCD-346-2. 1989. CD.

750.3 *Individualism of Gil Evans* [1964]. Verve: 833 804-2. 1988. CD. Import.

750.4 *Out of the Cool* [1960]. Impulse!: B0009783-02. 2007. CD.

751 Ferguson, Maynard. *The Essential Maynard Ferguson* [1954–1998]. Columbia / Legacy: 88697 05164 2. 2007. 2 CDs.

752 Gibbs, Terry. *Dream Band* [1959]. Contemporary: 7647. 1986. CD.

753 Gillespie, Dizzy. *Birk's Works: The Verve Big Band Sessions* [1956–1957]. Verve: 314 527 900-2. 1995. 2 CDs.

754 Hampton, Lionel. *Lionel Hampton Live in '58*. Jazz Icons. Reelin' in the Years; Naxos: 2.119012. 2008. DVD.

755 Herman, Woody

755.1 *Giant Steps* [1973]. Fantasy: OJCCD-344-2. 1994. CD.

755.2 *Woody Herman Live in '64*. Jazz Icons. Reelin' in the Years: 2.119016. 2009. DVD.

756 Jones, Quincy. *Quincy Jones Live in '60*. Jazz Icons. Reelin' in the Years: DVWW-JIQJ. 2006. DVD.

757 Jones, Thad. *Live at the Village Vanguard* [1967] (Mel Lewis). Blue Note: 60438. 2005. CD.

758 Kenton, Stan

758.1 *The Best of Stan Kenton* [1943–1961]. Capitol Jazz: 31504. 1995. CD.

758.2 ★*New Concepts of Artistry in Rhythm* [1956]. Capitol: 92865. 1989. CD.

759 Mingus Big Band. *Live in Time*. Dreyfus Jazz: 365832. 1996. 2 CDs.

760 Pettiford, Oscar. *The Complete Big Band Studio Recordings* [1956–1957]. Lonehill Jazz: 10168. 2005. CD.

761 Rich, Buddy

761.1 *Buddy Rich: Holland 1978*. Jazz Icons. Reelin' in the Years: DVWW-JIBR. 2006. DVD.

761.2 *Swingin' New Big Band* [1966]. Pacific Jazz: 35232. 1995. CD.

762 Rivers, Sam. *Sam Rivers' Rivbea All-Star Orchestra: Inspiration* [1998]. RCA: 64717. 1999. CD.

763 Schneider, Maria. *Evanescence* [1992]. Artists Share: 6. 2005. CD.

764 Wilson, Gerald. *Moment of Truth* [1962]. Pacific Jazz: 92928. 1989. CD.

JAZZ SINGERS

COLLECTIONS

765 *The Bebop Singers* [1950–1973] (King Pleasure, Dizzy Gillespie, Eddie Jefferson, Annie Ross, Jon Hendricks, Joe Carroll). Prestige: 24216. 1999. CD.

766 ★*The Jazz Singers: A Smithsonian Collection of Jazz Vocals from 1919–1994* (Bessie Smith; Louis Armstrong; Jimmy Rushing; Billie Holiday; Helen Humes; Hot Lips Page; Billy Eckstine; Jimmy Witherspoon; Joe Williams; Lambert, Hendricks, and Ross; Ernestine Anderson; Lorez Alexandria; Cassandra Wilson; Ivie Anderson; Cab Calloway; Anita O'Day; Louis Jordan; Ethel Waters; Mildred Bailey; Al Hibbler; Joe Turner; Ella Fitzgerald; Frank Sinatra; Sarah Vaughan; Dinah Washington; Nat King Cole; Dakota Staton; Nina Simone; Aretha Franklin; Marvin Gaye; Etta Jones; Fats Waller; June Christy; Chris Connor; Nancy Wilson; Shirley Horn; Johnny Hartman; Carmen McRae; and others). Smithsonian: RD 113. 1998. 5 CDs.

767 *Legendary Big Band Singers* [1931–1951] (Cab Calloway, Louis Armstrong, Sy Oliver, Pha Terrell, June Richmond, Jimmy Rushing, Helen Humes, Jack Teagarden, Helen O'Connell, Bob Eberly, Walter Brown, Rosetta Tharpe, Ella Fitzgerald, Kay Starr, Dinah Washington, Ella Johnson, Arthur Prysock). Decca Jazz: GRD-642. 1994. CD.

INDIVIDUALS AND GROUPS

768 Allison, Mose. *Greatest Hits* [1957–1959]. Fantasy: OJCCD-6004-2. 1988. CD.

769 Allyson, Karrin. *Ballads: Remembering John Coltrane*. Concord Jazz: 4950. 2001. CD.

770 Anderson, Ernestine. *Never Make Your Move Too Soon*. Concord Jazz: 4147. 1981. CD.

771 Armstrong, Louis

771.1 *The Definitive Collection* [1938–1967]. Hip-O: B0004893-02. 2006. CD.

771.2 ★*Ella Fitzgerald and Louis Armstrong*
[1956]. Verve: 543 304-2. 2000. CD.

772 Bailey, Mildred. *The Rockin' Chair Lady* [1931–1950]. Decca Jazz: GRD-644. 1994. CD.

773 Bey, Andy. *Ain't Necessarily So* [1997]. 12th Street Records: 9292982-2. 2007. CD.

774 Carter, Betty
   774.1 *The Audience with Betty Carter* [1979]. Verve: 835 684-2. 1988. 2 CDs.
   774.2 *I Can't Help It* [1958–1959]. Impulse!: GRD-114. 1992. CD.

775 Christy, June. *Something Cool* [1953–1955]. Capitol: 34069. 2001. CD.

776 Clayton, Jay. *Circle Dancing*. Sunnyside: 1076. 1997. CD.

777 Connor, Chris. *Warm Cool: The Atlantic Years* [1956–1963]. 32 Jazz: 32108. 1999. 2 CDs.

778 Elling, Kurt. *The Messenger* [1994–1996]. Blue Note: 52727. 1997. CD.

779 Fitzgerald, Ella
   779.1 *Ella and Oscar* [1975] (Oscar Peterson). Original Jazz Classics: 32693. 2011. CD.
   779.2 *Ella Fitzgerald Live in '57 and '63*. Jazz Icons. Reelin' in the Years: DVWW-JIEF. 2006. DVD.
   779.3 *Ellington Songbook* [1956–1957]. Verve: 559 248-2. 1999. 3 CDs.
   779.4 ★*George and Ira Gershwin Songbook* [1959]. Verve: 539 759-2. 1998. 4 CDs. Import available.
   779.5 *Harold Arlen Songbook* [1960–1961]. Verve: 314 589 108-2. 2001. 2 CDs.
   779.6 *Mack the Knife: The Complete Ella in Berlin Concert* [1960]. Verve: 314 519 564-2. 1993. CD.
   779.7 *Pure Ella (Ella Sings Gershwin)* [1950, 1954]. Decca Jazz: GRD-636. 1994. CD.
   779.8 *75th Birthday Celebration: Greatest Hits* [1935–1955]. Decca Jazz: GRD2-619. 1993. 2 CDs.
   779.9 *Sings the Cole Porter Songbook, Vols. 1 and 2* [1956]. Verve: 314 537 257-2. 1997. 2 CDs.
   779.10 *Sings the Rodgers and Hart Songbook, Vols. 1 and 2* [1956]. Verve: 314 537 258-2. 1997. 2 CDs.

780 Frishberg, Dave. *Classics* [1982–1983]. Concord Jazz: 4462. 1991. CD.

781 Holiday, Billie
   781.1 *Billie Holiday / Lester Young: A Musical Romance* [1937–1941, 1958]. Columbia / Legacy: 86635. 2002. CD.
   781.2 *Billie's Blues: Her Best Performances on Film*. Jazz Shots: 2869097. 2010. DVD.
   781.3 ★*The Commodore Master Takes* [1939, 1944]. Commodore: 543 272-2. 2000. CD.
   781.4 *The Complete Verve Studio Master Takes* [1952–1959]. Verve: B0004291-02. 2005. 6 CDs.
   781.5 ★*Ken Burns Jazz Collection: Billie Holiday* [1935–1958]. Verve: 549 081-2. 2000. CD.
   781.6 ★*Lady Day: The Best of Billie Holiday* [1935–1942]. Columbia / Legacy: C2K 85979. 2001. 2 CDs.
   781.7 *Lady Day: The Many Faces of Billie Holiday*. Masters of American Music. Medici Arts: 2057098. 2009. DVD.
   781.8 *Lady Day: The Master Takes and Singles* [1935–1942]. Columbia / Legacy: 88697 10955 2. 2007. 4 CDs.
   781.9 *Original Decca Recordings* [1944–1950]. Decca Jazz: GRD2-601. 1991. 2 CDs.

782 Horn, Shirley
   782.1 *Close Enough for Love*. Verve: 837 933-2. 1989. CD.
   782.2 *Here's to Life*. Verve: 314 511 879-2. 1992. CD.

783 Humes, Helen. *Songs I Like to Sing* [1960]. Fantasy: OJCCD-171-2. 1988. CD.

784 Jarreau, Al. *Look to the Rainbow: Al Jarreau Live in Europe* [1977]. Warner Bros.: 3052 [198-?]. CD.

785 Jefferson, Eddie. *Body and Soul* [1968]. Fantasy: OJCCD-396-2. 1989. CD.

786 Jones, Etta. *Don't Go to Strangers* [1960]. Prestige: 30007. 2006. CD.

787 Jordan, Sheila. *Portrait of Sheila* [1962]. Blue Note: 89002. 1989. CD.

788 Krall, Diana. *The Very Best of Diana Krall* [1996–2006]. Verve: B000941202. 2007. CD.

789 Lambert, Hendricks, and Ross
  789.1 *The Hottest New Group in Jazz* [1959–1961]. Columbia / Legacy: C2K 64933. 1996. 2 CDs.
  789.2 *Sing a Song of Basie* [1957]. Impulse!: 543 827-2. 2001. CD. Import available.

790 Lincoln, Abbey
  790.1 *Abbey Is Blue* [1959]. Fantasy: OJCCD-069-2. 1987. CD.
  790.2 *You Gotta Pay the Band.* Verve: 314 511 110-2. 1991. CD.

791 Mahogany, Kevin. *Pride and Joy.* Telarc: 83542. 2002. CD.

792 McCorkle, Susannah. *No More Blues.* Concord Jazz: 4370. 1989. CD.

793 McFerrin, Bobby. *The Voice.* Elektra / Musician: 60366. 1984. CD.

794 McRae, Carmen
  794.1 *Carmen Sings Monk* [1988]. Bluebird: 63841. 2001. CD.
  794.2 *The Great American Songbook* [1972]. Atlantic: 904. 1988. CD.
  794.3 *Sings Lover Man* [1961]. Columbia / Legacy: 65115. 1997. CD.

795 Merrill, Helen. *Helen Merrill* [1954] (Clifford Brown). Verve: 814 643-2. 1989. CD.

796 Murphy, Mark
  796.1 *Rah* [1961]. Fantasy: OJCCD-141-2. 1994. CD.
  796.2 *Timeless* [1978–1991]. Savoy: 17212. 2003. CD.

797 O'Day, Anita
  797.1 *Anita O'Day* [1952–1962]. Verve Jazz Masters 49. Verve: 527 653-2. 1995. CD.
  797.2 *Anita O'Day Live in '63 and '70.* Jazz Icons. Reelin' in the Years; Naxos: 2.108003. 2008. DVD.

798 Reeves, Dianne. *Best of Dianne Reeves.* Blue Note: 35867. 2002. CD.

799 Rushing, Jimmy. *The Essential Jimmy Rushing* [1954–1957]. Vanguard: 65/66. 1990. CD.

800 Scott, Jimmy
  800.1 *All the Way.* Sire: 26955. 1992. CD.
  800.2 *Falling in Love Is Wonderful* [1962]. Rhino: 781423. 2002. CD.

801 Simone, Nina. *Nina Simone Live in '65 and '68.* Jazz Icons. Reelin' in the Years; Naxos: 2.119014. 2008. DVD.

802 Sullivan, Maxine. *Close as Pages in a Book* [1969]. Audiophile: 203. 1987. CD.

803 Torme, Mel
  803.1 *Mel Torme: The Best of the Concord Years* [1983–1996]. Concord Jazz: 4871. 1999. 2 CDs.
  803.2 *Mel Torme Swings Shubert Alley* [1960]. Verve: 821 581-2. 1984. CD. Import available.

804 Vaughan, Sarah
  804.1 *How Long Has This Been Going On?* [1978]. Pablo: 2310-821-2. 1987. CD.
  804.2 ★*Ken Burns Jazz Collection: Sarah Vaughan* [1944–1974]. Verve: 549 088-2. 2000. CD.
  804.3 *Sarah Vaughan* [1954] (Clifford Brown). EmArcy: 314 543 305-2. 2000. CD.
  804.4 *Sarah Vaughan: The Divine One.* Masters of American Music. Medici Arts: 2057128. 2010. DVD.
  804.5 *Sarah Vaughan Live in '58 and '64.* Jazz Icons. Reelin' in the Years; Naxos: 2.119004. 2007. DVD.
  804.6 *Sings the George Gershwin Songbook* [1957]. Max Cat. 2010. 2 CDs.
  804.7 *Swingin' Easy* [1954, 1957]. EmArcy: 314 514 072-2. 1992. CD.

805 Wiley, Lee. *Lee Wiley Sings the Songs of Rodgers and Hart and Harold Arlen* [1940, 1943]. Audiophile: ACD-10. 1992. CD.

806 Williams, Joe
  806.1 *Every Day: The Best of the Verve Years* [1955–1957, 1987–1990]. Verve: 314 519 813-2. 1993. 2 CDs.
  806.2 *Nothin' but the Blues.* Delos: 4001. 1984. CD.

807 ★Wilson, Cassandra. *Blue Light 'til Dawn.* Blue Note: 81357. 1993. CD.

808 Wilson, Nancy. *Nancy Wilson / Cannonball Adderley* [1961]. Capitol: 81204. 1993. CD.

JAZZ AND POETRY, AND CONCEPT ALBUMS

COLLECTIONS

809 *Amarcord Nino Rota.* (Hal Wilner, Jaki Byard, Carla Bley, Bill Frisell, Muhal Richard Abrams, David Amram, Steve Lacy, Sharon Freeman, and others). Hannibal: 9301. 1982. CD.

810 *Conjure: Music for the Texts of Ishmael Reed* [1983] (Kip Hanrahan, David Murray, Carla Bley, Olu Dara, Lester Bowie, Milton Cardona, Steve Swallow, Billy Hart, Taj Mahal, Allen Toussaint, and others). American Clave: 1006. 2009. CD.

811 *Harlem in Vogue: The Poetry and Jazz of Langston Hughes* [1958] (Langston Hughes, Charles Mingus, Leonard Feather, Bob Dorough, and others). Fingertips: CD01. 2011. CD.

812 *The Jack Kerouac Collection* [1958–1959] (Al Cohn, Zoot Sims, Steve Allen). Rhino: 70939. 1990. 3 CDs.

INDIVIDUALS AND GROUPS

813 Last Poets. *The Last Poets* [1970]. Fuel 2000: 302 061 226 2. 2002. CD.

814 Nordine, Ken. *You're Getting Better: The Word Jazz Dot Masters* [1957–1960]. Geffen: B0005171-02. 2005. CD.

815 Scott-Heron, Gil. *The Revolution Will Not Be Televised* [1970–1972]. RCA Bluebird: 6994. 1988. CD.

FUSION

INDIVIDUALS AND GROUPS

816 Abercrombie, John
  816.1 *Gateway* [1975] (Dave Holland, Jack DeJohnette). ECM: 1061. 2008. CD.
  816.2 *John Abercrombie.* MVD Visual: MVD5010D. 2010. DVD.

817 Brecker Brothers
  817.1 *Brecker Brothers: Electro Jazz-Fusion.* Jamey Aebersold Jazz: JA 1313D. 1998. Score with CD.
  817.2 *Sneakin' Up Behind You: The Very Best of the Brecker Brothers* [1975–1981]. Arista / Legacy: 84865. 2006. CD. CD-R.

818 Burton, Gary
  818.1 *Crystal Silence* [1972] (Chick Corea). ECM: 1024. 1987. CD.
  818.2 *Dreams So Real* [1975]. ECM: 1072. 1988. CD. compositions of Carla Bley.

819 Cobham, Billy. *Best of Billy Cobham* [1973–1976]. Atlantic: 19238. 1987. CD.

820 Corea, Chick
  820.1 *The Anthology* [1973–1975]. Concord: 30847-02. 2008. 2 CDs.
  820.2 ★*Return to Forever* [1971]. ECM: 1022. 1999. CD.

821 Coryell, Larry. *The Essential Larry Coryell* [1968–1972]. Vanguard: 75/76. 1988. CD.

822 Davis, Miles
  822.1 ★*Bitches Brew* [1969]. Columbia: 54519. 2010. 2 CDs, DVD. DVD is live recording from Copenhagen, 1969.
  822.2 *In a Silent Way* [1969]. Columbia: 86556. 2002. CD.
  822.3 *Live Evil* [1970]. Columbia: C2K 65135. 1997. 2 CDs.
  822.4 *A Tribute to Jack Johnson* [1970]. Columbia: 93599. 2005. CD.
  822.5 *Tutu.* Warner Bros.: 25490. 1986. CD.

823 Fleck, Bela. *Flight of the Cosmic Hippo.* Warner Bros.: 26562. 1991. CD.

824 Hancock, Herbie
  824.1 *Future Shock* [1983]. Columbia: 65962. 1999. CD.
  824.2 ★*Head Hunters* [1973]. Columbia: 65123. 1997. CD.

825 Hunter, Charlie. *Steady Groovin'* [1995–2001]. Blue Note: 84146. 2005. CD.

826 Mahavishnu Orchestra
  826.1 *Birds of Fire* [1972]. Columbia: 66081. 2000. CD.
  826.2 *Inner Mounting Flame* [1971]. Columbia: 65523. 1998. CD.

827 ★McLaughlin, John. *The Essential John McLaughlin* [1963–2006]. Columbia / Legacy: 88697 06831 2. 2007. 2 CDs.

828 Medeski, Martin, and Wood. *Combustication* (John Medeski, Billy Martin, Chris Wood). Blue Note: 93011. 1998. CD.

829   Metheny, Pat
    829.1   *80/81* [1980]. ECM: 1180. 1990. CD.
    829.2   *Offramp* [1981]. ECM: 1216. 1992. CD.
    829.3   *Pat Metheny Group* [1978]. ECM: 1114. 1986. CD.

830   Pastorius, Jaco
    830.1   *Jaco Pastorius* [1976]. Epic: 64977. 2000. CD.
    830.2   *Jaco Pastorius.* Hal Leonard: HL00843165. 2010. Score with CD.

831   Sanborn, David. *Songs.* Jamey Aebersold Jazz: V103DS. 2002. Score with CD.

832   Weather Report
    832.1   ★*I Sing the Body Electric* [1971–1972]. Columbia: 46107. 1990. CD.
    832.2   *Mysterious Traveller* [1974]. Columbia: 65112. 2002. CD.

833   Zawinul, Joe
    833.1   *Joe Zawinul.* Hal Leonard: HL00843202. 2011. Score with CD.
    833.2   *Zawinul* [1970]. Mosaic Contemporary: 5006. 2007. CD.

JAZZ AND THE WORLD

INDIVIDUALS AND GROUPS

834   Bailey, Derek. *Figuring* [1987–1988] (Barre Phillips). Incus: CD 05. 1990. CD.

835   Braam, Michiel. *Het Xyz Der Bik Bent Braam.* BVHAAST: 9610-11 [1996]. 2 CDs.

836   Breuker, Willem
    836.1   *Bob's Gallery* [1987]. BVHAAST: 8801. 1993. CD.
    836.2   *In Holland* [1981]. BVHAAST: 101. 2002. CD.

837   Brotzmann, Peter
    837.1   *The Chicago Octet/Tentet* [1997]. OkkaDisk: 12022. 1998. 3 CDs.
    837.2   *The Complete Machine Gun Sessions* [1967–1968]. Atavistic: 262. 2007. CD.

838   Clusone 3. *Soft Lights and Sweet Music* [1993] (Michael Moore, Ernst Reijseger, Han Bennink). hatOLOGY: 657. 2008. CD.

839   Company. *Company 6 and 7* [1977] (Derek Bailey, Leo Smith, Anthony Braxton, Steve Lacy, Evan Parker, Tristan Honsinger, Lol Coxhill, Han Bennink, and others). Incus: CD 07. 1994. CD.

840   Dorge, Pierre. *Brikama* [1984]. Steeplechase: 31188. 1992. CD.

841   Dyani, Johnny. *Song for Biko* [1978]. Steeplechase: 31109. 1994. CD.

842   Ganelin Trio. *Ancora Da Capo* [1980]. Leo: 108. 1997. CD.

843   Garbarek, Jan. *Witchi-Tai-To.* ECM: 1041. 1974. CD.

844   Globe Unity. *Rumbling* [1975]. FMP: CD 40. 1991. CD.

845   Gratkowski, Frank. *Kollaps.* Red Toucan: 9317. 2001. CD.

846   Houn, Fred. *We Refuse to Be Used and Abused.* SoulNote: 121167-2. 1988. CD. Also known as Fred Ho.

847   Ibrahim, Abdullah. *Dollar Brand: African Piano* [1969]. JAPO / ECM: 60002. 1989. CD.

848   Italian Instabile Orchestra. *Skies of Europe.* ECM: 1543. 1995. CD.

849   Iyer, Vijay. *Historicity.* ACT: 9489. 2009. CD.

850   Jang, Jon. *Self Defense!* (Pan-Asian Arkestra). SoulNote: 121203-2. 1992. CD. CD-R.

851   Komeda, Krzysztof. *Astigmatic* [1965] (Tomasz Stanko). Muza: 536. 2001. CD.

852   Mangelsdorff, Albert. *Three Originals: The Wide Point / Trilogue / Albert Live in Montreux* [1975–1976, 1980]. Verve: 314 519 213-2. 1993. 2 CDs. Import available.

853   McGregor, Chris. *Chris McGregor's Brotherhood of Breath* [1971]. Repertoire: 4468. 1994. CD.

854   Mengelberg, Misha
    854.1   *Four in One* (Dave Douglas). Songlines: 1535-5. 2001. CD.
    854.2   *ICP Orchestra: Oh My Dog* (Instant Composers Pool). ICP: 40. 2001. CD.

855   Minton, Phil. *Doughnut in One Hand* [1996]. FMP: 91. 1998. CD.

856   Montoliu, Tete. *Tete!* [1974]. Steeplechase: 31029. 1987. CD.

857   Parker, Evan. *Process and Reality.* FMP: CD 37. 1991. CD.

858   Rypdal, Terje. *Odyssey* [1975]. ECM: 1067/1068. 2002. 2 CD set.

859 Saluzzi, Dino. *Cité de la Musique* [1996]. ECM: 1616. 1998. CD.

860 Schweizer, Irene. *Piano Solo, Vol. 1*. Intakt: CD 020. 1991. CD.

861 Shakti. *Shakti with John Mclaughlin* [1975] (John McLaughlin, L.Shankar, Zakir Hussain). Columbia: 46868. 1991. CD.

862 Solal, Martial. *Bluesine*. SoulNote: 121060-2. 1983. CD. CD-R.

863 Stanko, Tomasz. *Balladyna* [1975]. ECM: 1071. 2008. CD.

864 Surman, John. *The Amazing Adventures of Simon Simon* [1981]. ECM: 1193. 2001. CD.

865 Valdes, Chucho. *Bele Bele en la Habana*. Blue Note: 23082. 1998. CD.

866 von Schlippenbach, Alexander
     866.1 *Elf Bagatellen* [1972–1990]. FMP: CD 27. 1990. CD.
     866.2 *Monk's Casino* [2003–2004]. Intakt: 100. 2005. 3 CD set.

867 Walcott, Collin. *Codona* [1978] (Don Cherry, Nana Vasconcelos). ECM: 1132. 1989. CD.

868 Weber, Eberhard. *The Colors of Chloe* [1973]. ECM: 1042. 1988. CD.

MODERN MAINSTREAM: 1970s

INDIVIDUALS AND GROUPS

869 Adams, Pepper. *Conjuration: Fat Tuesday's Session* [1983]. Reservoir: 113. 1990. CD.

870 Bartz, Gary. *Harlem Bush Music* [1970–1971]. Milestone: 47101. 2004. CD.

871 Blakey, Art. *Coast to Coast* [1984–1985]. Concord Jazz: 4926. 2000. 2 CDs. Includes *New York Scene* and *Live at Kimball's*.

872 Byard, Jaki. *Sunshine of My Soul: Live at the Keystone Korner* [1978]. HighNote: 7169. 2007. CD.

873 Cohn, Al. *Body and Soul* [1973] (Zoot Sims). 32 Jazz: 32017. 1997. CD. Import-Japan.

874 Evans, Bill
     874.1 *Intuition* [1974] (Eddie Gomez). Fantasy: OJCCD-470-2. 1990. CD.
     874.2 *The Paris Concert: Edition One* [1979]. Blue Note: 28672. 2001. CD.

875 Farmer, Art. *Something to Live For: The Music of Billy Strayhorn*. Contemporary: 14029. 1987. CD.

876 Flanagan, Tommy
     876.1 *Nights at the Vanguard*. Uptown: 27.29. 1987. CD.
     876.2 *Tommy Flanagan Trio '77*. Eagle Eye Media: EE 39068-9. 2005. DVD.

877 Getz, Stan. *Pure Getz* [1982]. Concord Jazz: 4188. 1985. CD.

878 Gillespie, Dizzy. *Dizzy Gillespie's Big 4* [1974]. Fantasy: OJCCD-443-2. 1990. CD.

879 Gordon, Dexter. *Homecoming: Live at the Village Vanguard* [1976]. Columbia: C2K 46824. 1990. 2 CDs.

880 Griffin, Johnny. *Return of the Griffin* [1978]. Fantasy: OJCCD-1888-2. 1996. CD.

881 Hall, Jim. *Alone Together* [1972] (Ron Carter). Fantasy: OJCCD-467-2. 1990. CD.

882 Heath, Jimmy. *You or Me*. Steeplechase: 31370. 1995. CD.

883 Jones, Hank. *Live at Maybeck Recital Hall, Vol. 16*. Concord Jazz: 4502. 1992. CD.

884 McPartland, Marian. *In My Life*. Concord Jazz: 4561. 1993. CD.

885 Moody, James. *Moody's Party: Live at the Blue Note*. Telarc: 83382. 1995. CD.

886 Morgan, Frank. *Reflections* [1989]. Fantasy: OJCCD-1046-2. 2000. CD.

887 Pass, Joe. *Virtuoso* [1973]. Pablo: 31990. 2010. CD.

888 Pepper, Art
     888.1 *Art Pepper: Notes from a Jazz Survivor*. Shanachie: 8316. 1999. DVD.
     888.2 *Landscape* [1979]. Fantasy: OJCCD-676-2. 1991. CD.

889 Roach, Max. *Live at Blues Alley*. MVD Visual: MVD5168D. 2011. DVD.

890 Rodney, Red. *Then and Now*. Chesky: 79. 1992. CD.

891 Rollins, Sonny
     891.1 *Don't Stop the Carnival* [1978]. Milestone: 55005. 1989. CD.
     891.2 *Road Shows, Vol. 1* [1980–2007]. Doxy / EmArcy: B0012165-02. 2008. CD.

892   Rowles, Jimmy. *Jimmy Rowles / Ray Brown: The Duo Sessions* [1977, 1979]. Concord Jazz: 4938. 2000. 2 CDs.

893   Shaw, Woody
    893.1   *Rosewood* [1977]. Columbia: 65519. 1998. CD.
    893.2   *Solid* [1986]. Savoy Jazz: 17298. 2003. CD.

894   Shorter, Wayne. *Wayne Shorter Live at Montreux 1996.* Eagle Eye Media: EE 39178-9. 2009 DVD.

895   Sims, Zoot. *If I'm Lucky* [1977]. Fantasy: OJCCD-683-2. 1992. CD.

896   Stitt, Sonny. *Endgame Brilliance: Constellation & Tune Up* [1971–1972]. 32 Jazz: 32009. 1997. CD.

897   Tyner, McCoy
    897.1   *Echoes of a Friend* [1972]. Fantasy: OJCCD-650-2. 1991. CD.
    897.2   *Enlightenment* [1973]. Milestone: 55001. 1990. CD.

898   V.S.O.P. *The Quintet: V.S.O.P.* [1976] (Herbie Hancock, Wayne Shorter, Freddie Hubbard, Ron Carter, Tony Williams). Columbia: 34976. 1988. CD.

899   Weston, Randy
    899.1   *Blues to Africa.* Freedom: 741014. 1975. CD.
    899.2   *Spirits of Our Ancestors.* Antilles: 511 896-2. 1992. 2 CDs.

900   Woods, Phil
    900.1   *Here's to My Lady* [1988]. Chesky: 3. 1994. CD.
    900.2   ★*Three for All* [1981] (Tommy Flanagan, Red Mitchell). Enja: 3081. 1989. CD.

CROSSOVER JAZZ: 1970s–1990s

INDIVIDUALS AND GROUPS

901   ★Benson, George. *George Benson Anthology* [1964–1999]. Warner Archives: 79934. 2000. 2 CDs.

902   The Crusaders. *The Crusaders' Finest Hour* [1971–1981]. GRP: 543 762-2. 2000. CD.

903   Hubbard, Freddie. *Freddie Hubbard Live in France 1973.* Jazz Icons. Reelin' in the Years; Naxos: DVBX-6001. 2011. DVD.

904   Jones, Quincy. *Quincy Jones' Finest Hour* [1956–1978]. Verve: 069 490 667-2. 2000. CD.

905   Lewis, Ramsey. *Sun Goddess* [1974]. Columbia: 33194. 1984. CD.

906   Mangione, Chuck
    906.1   *Chuck Mangione.* Hal Leonard: HL00843188. 2011. Score with CD.
    906.2   *Feels So Good* [1977]. AANDM: 3219. 1990. CD.

907   Ponty, Jean-Luc. *Le Voyage: The Jean-Luc Ponty Anthology* [1975–1993]. Rhino: 72155. 1996. 2 CDs.

908   Sanborn, David. *The Best of David Sanborn* [1978–1988]. Warner Bros.: 45768. 1994. CD.

909   Spyro Gyra. *The Very Best of Spyro Gyra.* Universal: 314 543 595-2. 2002. CD.

910   Washington, Grover
    910.1   *Mister Magic* [1975]. Motown: 530 103-2. 1995. CD.
    910.2   *Winelight.* Elektra: 305. 1980. CD.

911   Yellowjackets. *Best of the Yellowjackets.* Warner Bros.: 47585. 1999. CD.

JAZZ OUTSIDE THE MAINSTREAM: THE AACM, BAG, AND THE LOFTS

INDIVIDUALS AND GROUPS

912   Abrams, Muhal Richard. *Young at Heart, Wise in Time* [1968]. Delmark: 423. 1996. CD.

913   Air. *Air Mail* (Henry Threadgill, Fred Hopkins, Steve McCall). Black Saint: 120049-2. 1981. CD. CD-R.

914   Anderson, Fred. *Dark Day: Live at the Museum of Contemporary Art / Live in Verona* [1979]. Atavistic: 218. 2001. 2 CDs.

915   Art Ensemble of Chicago
    915.1   *Americans Swinging in Paris: The Pathe Sessions* [1969–1970]. EMI: 539667. 2002. CD. Includes *People in Sorrow* and *Les Stances à Sophie*; import.
    915.2   *Full Force* [1980]. ECM: 1167. 2008. CD.
    915.3   ★*Urban Bushmen* [1980]. ECM: 1211/1212. 1982. 2 CDs.

916   Bang, Billy. *Rainbow Gladiator.* SoulNote: 121016-2. 1981. CD. CD-R.

917 Bluiett, Hamiet. *Resolution.* Black Saint: 120014-2. 1978. CD.

918 Bowie, Lester. *The Great Pretender* [1981]. ECM: 1209. 2008. CD.

919 Braxton, Anthony
  919.1 *For Alto* [1969]. Delmark: 420. 2000. CD.
  919.2 *3 Compositions of New Jazz* [1968]. Delmark: 415. 1991. CD.
  919.3 *Willisau (Quartet) 1991.* hat ART: 4-6100. 1992. 4 CDs.

920 Circle. *Paris Concert* [1971] (Chick Corea, Anthony Braxton, Dave Holland, Barry Altschul). ECM: 1018/1019. 2001. 2 CDs.

921 Freeman, Chico. *Destiny's Dance* [1981]. Fantasy: OJCCD-799-2. 1993. CD.

922 Harper, Billy. *Black Saint.* Black Saint: 120001. 1975. CD. CD-R.

923 Hemphill, Julius
  923.1 *Raw Materials and Residuals* [1977]. Black Saint: 120015-2. 1993. CD.
  923.2 *Reflections ('Coon Bid'ness)* [1972, 1975]. Freedom: 741012. 1991. CD.

924 Jenkins, Leroy. *Mixed Quintet* [1979]. Black Saint: 120060-2. 1983. CD.

925 Lake, Oliver. *Prophet.* Black Saint: 120044-2. 1981. CD. CD-R.

926 Lowe, Frank. *Decision in Paradise.* SoulNote: 121082-2. 1985. CD. CD-R.

927 Mitchell, Roscoe
  927.1 *Sound* [1966]. Delmark: 408. 1996. CD.

928 Murray, David
  928.1 *Deep River.* DIW: 830. 1989. CD.
  928.2 *3D Family* [1978]. hatOLOGY: 608. 2006. CD.

929 Revolutionary Ensemble. *Vietnam* [1972] (Leroy Jenkins, Sirone, Jerome Cooper). ESP-DISK: 3007. 2009. CD.

930 Rivers, Sam. *Sam Rivers / Dave Holland, Vols. 1 and 2.* Improvising Artists: 123843-2/123848-2. 1976. 2 CDs.

931 Smith, (Wadada) Leo. *Kabell Years* [1971–1979]. Tzadik: 7610-4. 2004. 4 CDs.

932 Threadgill, Henry
  932.1 *Just the Facts and Pass the Bucket.* About Time: 1005. 1983. CD.
  932.2 *Up Popped the Two Lips.* Pi: 2. 2001. CD.
  932.3 *Where's Your Cup?* Columbia: 67617. 1997. CD.
  932.4 *You Know the Number* [1986]. Novus: 3013-2-N. 1987. CD.

933 World Saxophone Quartet
  933.1 *Revue* [1980]. Black Saint: 120056-2. 1982. CD. CD-R.
  933.2 ★*Steppin' with the World Saxophone Quartet* (Julius Hemphill, Oliver Lake, David Murray, Hamiet Bluiett). Black Saint: 120027-2. 1979. CD. CD-R.
  933.3 *W.S.Q.* Black Saint: 120046-2. 1981. CD. CD-R.

CONTEMPORARY ARTISTS: 1970s THROUGH THE 2000s

COLLECTIONS

934 *Icons among Us.* (Marco Benevento, Terence Blanchard, Anat Cohen, Avishai Cohen Trio, Ravi Coltrane, daKAH, Bill Frisell, Robert Glasper, Russell Gunn, Herbie Hancock, Wynton Marsalis, Medeski Martin and Wood, Nicholas Payton, Tineke Postma, Dianne Reeves, Roy Hargrove, John Scofield, Wayne Shorter, Skerik, Esperanza Spalding, the Bad Plus, Brian Blade, Charlie Hunter, Danilo Perez, Donald Harrison). Indiepix Films: IP3939. 2010. 4 DVDs with CD-ROM.

935 *Live from the Village Vanguard* (Freddie Hubbard Quartet; Michel Petrucciani Trio with Jim Hall; John Abercrombie Quartet; Mal Waldron Quintet; Lee Konitz Quartet; David Murray Quartet).Unicorn Video: 96110-96115. 2003. 6 DVDs.

INDIVIDUALS AND GROUPS

936 AALY Trio. *Stumble* (Ken Vandermark). Wobbly Rail: 2. 1998. CD.

937 Adams, George. *Decisions* [1984] (Don Pullen). Timeless: SJP 205. 1990. CD.

938 Allen, Geri. *Segments* (Charlie Haden, Paul Motian). DIW: 833. 1989. CD.

939 Allison, Ben. *Riding the Nuclear Tiger.* Palmetto: 2067. 2000. CD.

940 Barron, Kenny. *Wanton Spirit.* Verve: 314 522 364-2. 1994. CD.

941   Berne, Tim
   941.1   *Sanctified Dreams* [1987]. Koch Jazz:
       7825. 1996. CD.
   941.2   *The Sublime And.* Thirsty Ear: 57139.2.
       2003. 2 CDs.

942   Blanchard, Terence. *Wandering Moon.* Sony
   Classical: 89111. 2000. CD.

943   Bloom, Jane Ira. *Mental Weather* [2007]. Outline:
   139. 1989. CD.

944   Brackeen, Charles. *Worshippers Come Nigh*
   [1987]. Silkheart: 111. 1989. CD.

945   Brackeen, Joanne. *Turnaround* [1992]. Evidence:
   22123. 1995. CD.

946   Bradford, Bobby. *Comin' On* (John Carter).
   hatOLOGY: 693. 2011. CD.

947   ★Brecker, Michael. *Michael Brecker.* MCA: 5980.
   1987. CD.

948   Byron, Don. *Tuskegee Experiments* [1990–1991].
   Elektra / Nonesuch: 79280. 1992. CD.

949   Caine, Uri. *Solitaire.* Winter and Winter: 910 075-
   2. 2001. CD.

950   Carter, James. *Real Quietstorm.* Atlantic: 82742.
   1995. CD.

951   Carter, John. *Castles of Ghana.* Gramavision:
   79423. 1986. CD.

952   Carter, Regina. *Motor City Moments* (Kenny
   Barron). Verve: 314 543 927-2. 2000. CD.

953   Chapin, Thomas. *You Don't Know Me* [1994].
   Arabesque: 115. 2009. CD.

954   Charlap, Bill. *Written in the Stars.* Blue Note:
   27291. 2000. CD.

955   Cline, Nels. *New Monastery: The Music of Andrew
   Hill.* Cryptogramophone: 130. 2006. CD.

956   Coleman, Ornette
   956.1   *The Complete Science Fiction Sessions* [1971–
       1972]. Columbia: 63569. 2000. 2 CDs.
   956.2   *Sound Grammar.* Sound Grammar / Phrase
       Text: 11593. 2006. CD.

957   Coleman, Steve
   957.1   *Curves of Life.* RCA Victor: 31693.
       1995. CD.
   957.2   *Mancy of Sound* [2007]. Pi: 38. 2011. CD.

958   Corea, Chick. *Trio Music* [1981]. ECM: 2-1232.
   2001. 2 CDs.

959   Cowell, Stanley. *Angel Eyes.* Steeplechase: 31339.
   1994. CD.

960   Crispell, Marilyn
   960.1   *For Coltrane* [1987]. Leo: 195. 1993. CD.
   960.2   *The Storyteller* (music of Annette Peacock).
       ECM: 1847. 2004. CD.

961   Davis, Anthony. *Of Blues and Dreams* [1978].
   Sackville: 3020. 2001. CD.

962   DeJohnette, Jack
   962.1   ★*Album Album.* ECM: 1280. 1984. CD.
   962.2   *Special Edition* [1979]. ECM: 1152.
       2008. CD.

963   Dickerson, Walt. *Dialogue* [1977] (Richard Davis).
   Steeplechase: 37029/30. 1996. 2 CDs.

964   Dirty Dozen Brass Band. *Live: Mardi Gras in
   Montreux.* Rounder: 2052. 1986. CD.

965   Douglas, Dave
   965.1   *In Our Lifetime.* New World: 80471.
       1995. CD.
   965.2   *Tiny Bell Trio: Constellations* [1995].
       hatOLOGY: 666. 2009. CD.

966   Ehrlich, Marty
   966.1   *Malinke's Dance.* Omnitone: 12003.
       2000. CD.
   966.2   *News on the Rail.* Palmetto: 2113.
       2005. CD.

967   Eskelin, Ellery. *One Great Day* [1996]. hatOLOGY:
   691. 2011. CD.

968   Eubanks, Kevin. *Guitarist* [1982]. Wounded Bird:
   213. 2004. CD.

969   Frisell, Bill
   969.1   *Before We Were Born.* Elektra / Musician:
       60843. 1989. CD.
   969.2   ★*Lookout for Hope* [1987]. ECM: 1350.
       2008. CD.

970   Garrett, Kenny. *Standard of Language* [2001–
   2002]. Warner Bros.: 48404. 2003. CD.

971   Gonzalez, Dennis. *Stefan* [1986]. Silkheart: 101.
   1989. CD.

972   Gress, Drew. *7 Black Butterflies.* Premonition /
   Koch: 5809. 2005. CD.

973   Haden, Charlie
   973.1   *The Ballad of the Fallen* (Liberation
       Music Orchestra). ECM: 1248. 1983. CD.
   973.2   *Quartet West: Always Say Goodbye.* Verve:
       314 521 501-2. 1994. CD.

974 Hargrove, Roy. *Roy Hargrove Quintet with the Tenors of Our Time* (Johnny Griffin, Joe Henderson, Branford Marsalis, Joshua Redman, Stanley Turrentine). Verve: 314 523 019-2. 1994. CD.

975 Harrell, Tom
    975.1 *Sail Away* [1989]. Fantasy: OJCCD-1095-2. 2003. CD.
    975.2 *Tom Harrell.* Jamey Aebersold Jazz: JA 1291. 1994. Score with CD.

976 Harris, Craig. *Black Bone.* SoulNote: 121055-2. 1984. CD. CD-R.

977 Hemingway, Gerry. *Devils Paradise* [1999]. Clean Feed: 10. 2003. CD.

978 Herbie Nichols Project. *Strange City.* (Frank Kimbrough, Ben Allison, Ron Horton, Ted Nash, Michael Blake, Wycliffe Gordon, Matt Wilson). Palmetto: 2077. 2001. CD.

979 Hersch, Fred
    979.1 *Let Yourself Go: The Lives of Jazz Pianist Fred Hersch.* Aha!DVD: 300026311X. 2009. DVD.
    979.2 *Thelonious: Fred Hersch Plays Monk.* Nonesuch: 79456. 1998. CD.

980 Holland, Dave
    980.1 ★*Conference of the Birds* [1972]. ECM: 1027. 1987. CD.
    980.2 *Jumpin' In.* ECM: 1269. 1984. CD.
    980.3 *Prime Directive.* ECM: 1698. 1999. CD.

981 Jackson, Ronald Shannon. *Eye on You.* About Time: 1003. 1980. LP.

982 Jarrett, Keith
    982.1 *Belonging* [1974] (Jan Garbarek). ECM: 1050. 1988. CD.
    982.2 *Koln Concert* [1975]. ECM: 1064/65. 2000. 2 CDs.
    982.3 *Silence* [1977]. Impulse!: GRD-117. 1992. CD.
    982.4 *Whisper Not.* ECM: 1724/25. 2000. 2 CDs.

983 Jewels and Binoculars. *Floater* (Michael Moore, Lindsey Horner, Michael Vatcher). Ramboy: 20. 2004. CD.

984 Johnson, Marc. *Bass Desires* [1985]. ECM: 1299. 2008. CD.

985 Julius Hemphill Sextet. *Hard Blues* (Marty Ehrlich). Clean Feed: 27. 2004. CD.

986 Lacy, Steve
    986.1 *The Holy la* [1998]. Sunnyside: 1120. 2003. CD.
    986.2 *Morning Joy (Live at Sunset Paris)* [1986]. hatOLOGY: 556. 2001. CD.
    986.3 *Steve Lacy–Roswell Rudd Quartet: Early and Late* [1962, 1999] (Roswell Rudd). 2901Cuneiform: 250/251. 2007. 2 CDs.

987 Lloyd, Charles. *Voice in the Night.* ECM: 1674. 1999. CD.

988 Lovano, Joe
    988.1 *From the Soul.* Blue Note: 98636. 1992. CD.
    988.2 *Kids* (Hank Jones). Blue Note: 70281. 2007. CD.

989 Malone, Russell. *Playground.* MaxJazz: 601. 2004. CD.

990 Marsalis, Branford. *Renaissance.* Columbia: 40711. 1987. CD.

991 Marsalis, Wynton
    991.1 *Black Codes (from the Underground).* Columbia: 40009. 1985. CD.
    991.2 *Blood on the Fields* [1995]. Columbia: CXK 57694. 1997. 3 CDs.
    991.3 *The Majesty of the Blues* [1988]. Wounded Bird: 5091. 2007. CD.

992 Mays, Bill. *Live at Jazz Standard.* Palmetto: 2112. 2005. CD.

993 McBride, Christian. *Fingerpainting: The Music of Herbie Hancock.* Verve: 314 537 856-2. 1997. CD.

994 Mehldau, Brad. *Art of the Trio, Vol. 1.* Warner Bros.: 46260. 1997. CD.

995 Melford, Myra. *Even the Sounds Shine* [1994]. hatOLOGY: 597. 2003. CD.

996 Microscopic Septet. *Seven Men in Neckties: History of the Micros, Vol. 1* [1983–1990]. Cuneiform: 236/237. 2006. 2 CDs.

997 Monk, T. S. *Monk on Monk.* N-Coded Music: 10017. 1997. CD.

998 Moran, Jason
    998.1 *Jason Moran Presents the Bandwagon.* Blue Note: 80917. 2003. CD.
    998.2 *Modernistic.* Blue Note: 39838. 2002. CD.

999   Motian, Paul. *It Should Have Happened a Long Time Ago*. ECM: 1283. 1985. CD.

1000   Newton, James. *African Flower* [1985]. Blue Note: 46292. 1997. CD.

1001   Old and New Dreams. *Playing* [1980] (Don Cherry, Dewey Redman, Charlie Haden, Ed Blackwell). ECM: 1205. 1994. CD.

1002   Osby, Greg. *Channel Three*. Blue Note: 60671. 2005. CD.

1003   Peplowski, Ken. *Noir Blue*. Capri: 74098. 2010. CD.

1004   Peterson, Ralph, Jr. *Fo'tet Plays Monk* [1995]. Evidence: 22174. 1997. CD.

1005   Pope, Odean. *Locked and Loaded: Live at the Blue Note* [2004] (Saxophone Choir). HalfNote: 4526. 2006. CD.

1006   Pullen, Don. *New Beginnings*. Blue Note: 91785. 1989. CD.

1007   Rebirth Brass Band. *Kickin' It Live: The Glass House*. Rounder: 2106. 1991. CD.

1008   Redman, Joshua
    1008.1   *Back East*. Nonesuch: 104252. 2007. CD.
    1008.2   *Wish*. Warner Bros.: 45365. 1993. CD.

1009   Ribot, Marc. *Spiritual Unity*. Pi: 15. 2005. CD.

1010   Roney, Wallace. *No Room for Argument*. Stretch: 9033. 1999. CD.

1011   Rosnes, Renee. *As We Are Now*. Blue Note: 56810. 1997. CD.

1012   Rova Saxophone Quartet. *Beat Kennel*. Black Saint: 120126-2. 1987. CD. CD-R.

1013   Rudd, Roswell. *Regeneration*. SoulNote: 121054-2. 1983. CD. CD-R.

1014   Scofield, John
    1014.1   *Enroute: John Scofield Trio Live*. Verve: B0001699-02. 2004. CD.
    1014.2   *Time on My Hands*. Blue Note: 92894. 1990. CD.

1015   Spalding, Esperanza. *Radio Music Society*. Heads Up International: HUI-33626-00. 2012. CD.

1016   Tapscott, Horace. *The Dark Tree* [1989]. hatOLOGY: 630. 2009. 2 CDs.

1017   Taylor, Cecil
    1017.1   *Silent Tongues* [1974]. Freedom / Black Lion: 877633. 2000. CD.
    1017.2   *3 Phasis* [1978]. New World: 80303. 1988. CD.
    1017.3   *Willisau Concert* [2000]. Intakt: CD 072. 2002. CD.

1018   29th Street Saxophone Quartet. *The Real Deal*. Antilles: 314 510 942-2. 1987. CD.

1019   Ulmer, James "Blood." *Are You Glad to Be in America?* [1980]. DIW: 400. 1995. CD. Import.

1020   Vandermark, Ken
    1020.1   *School Days: Crossing Division*. OkkaDisk: 12037. 2000. CD.
    1020.2   *Vandermark 5: Simpatico*. Atavistic: 107. 1999. CD.

1021   Varner, Tom. *Second Communion*. Omnitone: 12102. 2001. CD.

1022   Waldron, Mal. *Sempre Amore* (Steve Lacy). SoulNote: 121170-2. 1987. CD. CD-R.

1023   Wallace, Bennie. *Bennie Wallace Plays Monk* [1981]. ENJA: 3091. 1994. CD.

1024   Ware, David S. *Wisdom of Uncertainty*. Aum Fidelity: AUM001. 1997. CD.

1025   Watson, Bobby. *Love Remains* [1986]. Red: 123212-2. 1993. CD.

1026   Wheeler, Kenny. *Deer Wan* [1977]. ECM: 1102. 1989. CD.

1027   Williams, Jessica. *The Best of Jessica Williams on Jazz Focus, Vol. 1* [1993–1996]. Jazz Focus: 40. 2007. CD.

1028   Wilson, Matt. *Smile*. Palmetto: 2049. 1999. CD.

1029   Zorn, John
    1029.1   *★Masada: Live at Tonic*. Tzadik: 7334. 2001. 2 CDs.
    1029.2   *News for Lulu* [1987]. hatOLOGY: 650. 2008. CD.

JAZZ AND THE CLASSICS: THIRD STREAM

COLLECTION

1030   *★The Birth of the Third Stream* [1956–1957] (Charles Mingus, George Russell, John Lewis, J. J. Johnson, Gunther Schuller, and others). Columbia / Legacy: 64929. 1996. CD.

INDIVIDUALS AND GROUPS

1031 Blake, Ran
    1031.1 *All That Is Tied.* Tompkins Square: 1965. 2006. CD.
    1031.2 *Short Life of Barbara Monk.* SoulNote: 121127-2. 1987. CD. CD-R.

1032 Bley, Carla. *Escalator over the Hill* [1968–1971]. Watt / ECM: 1802. 1998. 2 CDs.

1033 Brooks, John Benson. *Alabama Concerto* [1958]. Fantasy: OJCCD-1779-2. 1991. CD.

1034 Burton, Gary. *A Genuine Tong Funeral / Lofty Fake Anagram* [1968] (Carla Bley). Beat Goes On: 723. 2006. 2 CDs. Import.

1035 Charles, Teddy
    1035.1 *Collaboration: West* [1953] (Shorty Rogers). Fantasy: OJCCD-122-2. 1992. CD.
    1035.2 *The Teddy Charles Tentet* [1956]. Collectables: 6161. 2001. CD.

1036 Coleman, Ornette. *Skies of America* [1972]. Columbia / Legacy: 63568. 2000. CD.

1037 Ellis, Don. *How Time Passes* [1960]. Candid: 79004. 1987. CD.

1038 ★Giuffre, Jimmy. *The Jimmy Giuffre 3 / Trav'lin' Light* [1956]. Poll Winners: 27215. 2010. CD. Import.

1039 Kronos Quartet. *Monk Suite* [1984]. Savoy Jazz: 17404. 2004. CD.

1040 Legrand, Michel. *Legrand Jazz* [1957–1958]. Philips: 830 074-2. 1986. CD.

1041 Lewis, John. *Golden Striker / Jazz Abstractions* [1960] (Gunther Schuller, Eric Dolphy, Ornette Coleman, Jim Hall, and others). Collectables: 6252. 1999. CD.

1042 Modern Jazz Qartet. *Third Stream Music* [1960]. Wounded Bird: 1345. 2002. CD.

1043 Russell, George
    1043.1 *Ezz-Thetics* [1961]. Riverside: 30188. 2007. CD.
    1043.2 *The 80th Birthday Concert* [2003]. Concept Publishing. 2005. 2 CDs.
    1043.3 *Jazz in the Space Age* [1960]. Chessmates / GRP: GRD-826. 1998. CD. Import available.
    1043.4 *The Jazz Workshop* [1956]. Koch Jazz: 7850. 1998. CD.

JAZZ AND FILM

1044 *Alfie* [1966] (Sonny Rollins, Oliver Nelson)
    1044.1 Impulse!: IMPD-224. 1997. CD.
    1044.2 Paramount: 6604. 2000. DVD.

1045 *Anatomy of a Murder* [1959] (Duke Ellington)
    1045.1 Columbia / Legacy: 65569. 1999. CD. Import available.
    1045.2 Columbia TriStar HomeVideo: 7019. 2000. DVD.

1046 *Ascenseur Pour L'echafaud [Lift to the Scaffold]* [1957] (Miles Davis)
    1046.1 Criterion Collection: CC1627D. 2006. DVD.
    1046.2 Verve: B0009398-02. 2007. CD.

1047 *The Benny Goodman Story* [1955]
    1047.1 Capitol: 33569. 1995. CD.
    1047.2 Universal: 22636. 2003. DVD.

1048 *Bird* (Charlie Parker). Warner Home Video: 11820. 2010. DVD.

1049 *Blow Up* [1966] (Herbie Hancock)
    1049.1 Rhino: 72527. 1996. CD. Import available.
    1049.2 Warner Home Video: 65135. 2004. DVD. Import available.

1050 *The Cotton Club* [1984]
    1050.1 Geffen: 24062. 1984. CD. Import available.
    1050.2 MGM Home Entertainment: 1002205. 2001. DVD.

1051 *Inside Man* (Terence Blanchard)
    1051.1 Universal Studios Home Entertainment: 28847. 2006. DVD.
    1051.2 Varese Sarabande: 3020667222. 2006. CD.

1052 *Mo' Better Blues* [1990] (Branford Marsalis)
    1052.1 Columbia: 46792. 1990. CD.
    1052.2 Universal: 20536. 2000. DVD.

1053 *Naked Lunch* [1991] (Ornette Coleman, Howard Shore)
    1053.1 Criterion Collection: CC1599D. 2003. DVD.
    1053.2 Milan: 36110. 2005. CD.

1054 *New York, New York* [1977] (Ralph Burns, Georgie Auld)
    1054.1 EMI-Manhattan: 46090. 1985. CD.
    1054.2 MGM Home Entertainment: 1007430. 2004. DVD.

1055 *Odds against Tomorrow* [1959] (John Lewis, Moden Jazz Quartet)

    1055.1 Blue Note: 93415. 1990. CD.

    1055.2 MGM Home Entertainment: 1005697. 2003. DVD.

1056 *Round Midnight* [1986] (Dexter Gordon, Herbie Hancock, and others)

    1056.1 ★Columbia / Legacy: 85811. 2002. CD.

    1056.2 ★Warner Home Video: 11603. 2001. DVD.

1057 *Stormy Weather* [1943] (Fats Waller, Cab Calloway, Lena Horne, and others)

    1057.1 Soundtrack Factory: 33505. 1999. CD.

    1057.2 Twentieth Century Fox Home Entertainment. 2005. DVD.

1058 *Young Man with a Horn* [1949] (Harry James)

    1058.1 Soundtrack Factory: 33556. 2001. CD.

    1058.2 Warner Home Video: 4325. 2005. DVD.

4

Mainstream Popular and New Age

Compiled by SUSANNAH CLEVELAND *and* GROVER BAKER

MAINSTREAM POPULAR   66
  Pre-World War II   66
  Post-World War II through 1967   74
  Post–1967   78
NEW AGE   81
  East/West   81
  Electronic/Computer   81
  Ambient   81
  New Acoustic   82
  Jazz/Fusion   82
  Meditation Music   82
  Native American   82
  Progressive   82
  Solo Instrumental   82
  Sound Health Music   83
  Space Music   83
  World Music   83
  Samplers and Concept Albums   83

The following selections from American mainstream popular music in the twentieth century continue forward from the pre-1900 selections listed in chapter 1. In examining popular music from 1900 to the present, one sees a change from sheet music to recordings as the primary means of publication and sales. As a result of this change, pop music gradually became less composer-initiated and more performer-initiated. Many of the selections listed here are by composers known not so much for their own performances but rather for works created for or in collaboration with leading vocal performers. Eventually, American popular music came to be dominated by styles such as rock, country, and jazz, in which the performer and composer are one and the same (or at least work closely together as part of a distinct recording group). These styles are treated individually in separate chapters, though a few of the best pop-parodists, such

as Spike Jones and Weird Al Yankovic, are included here.

The section on songwriter anthologies focuses on the major American popular songwriters of the twentieth century, from Jerome Kern and George Gershwin to Burt Bacharach. Each recorded item features interpretations by a variety of singers. Several composers are also represented by a print collection of their songs.

The Pre–World War II section covers popular music from early recordings just after 1900 through 1945. This music originated more often from the stage (whether musical revues or shows), nightclubs, and movies than from radio and records. Chief performers of this era were Al Jolson and Bing Crosby. Artists who established themselves during this period but whose careers extended further, such as Ethel Merman and Judy Garland, are also listed here.

The styles of the artists featured in the post–World War II to 1967 section (sometimes marketed today as "easy listening" music) derive fundamentally from the prerock period, but they may show influences of rock, rhythm and blues, and other vernacular idioms. Prime examples include Frank Sinatra, Nat King Cole, Doris Day, Rosemary Clooney, and Johnny Mathis.

Cultural changes followed the rise of rock and roll and the coming of age of the baby boomer generation and their children. These changes are marked in popular music by a move away from jazz and big band idioms toward "soft rock" with fewer jazz influences. Many of these artists, including Barbra Streisand, Neil Diamond, and Joni Mitchell, have been presented as "adult contemporary."

Rounding out this chapter is a section covering the plurality of styles (whether ambient, new acoustic, "space age," digitally sampled electronic, Native American, jazz fusion, or world-music-derived) marketed since the late 1970s as New Age. Windham Hill and Narada have been leading labels for this relaxing, often meditative genre of music.

MAINSTREAM POPULAR

Pre–World War II

GENERAL COLLECTIONS

1059   ★*American Popular Song: Six Decades of Songwriters and Singers* [1911–1980] (Sophie Tucker, Bessie Smith, Billy Murray, Al Jolson, Marion Harris, Fred Astaire, Ethel Waters, Gene Austin, Helen Morgan, Bing Crosby, Russ Columbo, Mildred Bailey, Louis Armstrong, Billie Holiday, Helen Forrest, Judy Garland, Connee

Boswell, Lena Horne, Nat King Cole, Dinah Shore, Jo Stafford, Frank Sinatra, Billy Eckstine, Dick Haymes, Perry Como, Margaret Whiting, Mabel Mercer, Peggy Lee, Rosemary Clooney, Sarah Vaughan, Ella Fitzgerald, Carmen McRae, Joe Williams, Mel Torme, Teddi King, Barbara Cook, Tony Bennett, Barbra Streisand, and others). Smithsonian: RD031. 1984. 5 CDs.

1060   *Black Manhattan: Theater and Dance Music of James Reese Europe, Will Marion Cook, and Members of the Legendary Clef Club* (Edward Pleasant, Awert Andemicael, Paragon Ragtime Orchestra). New World: 80611. 2003. CD.

1061   ★*Brother, Can You Spare a Dime? American Song during the Great Depression* [1931–1941] (Woody Guthrie, Shirley Temple, Rudy Vallee, Bing Crosby, Glen Gray, Dick Powell, Glenn Miller, Bill Broonzy, Uncle Dave Macon, Delmore Brothers, Gene Autry, Almanac Singers, and others). New World: 80270. 2001. CD.

1062   ★*The Crooners* [1926–1941] (Willard Robison, Gene Austin, Seger Ellis, Smith Ballew, Bing Crosby, Harlan Lattimore, Russ Columbo, Red McKenzie, Cliff Edwards, Pinky Tomlin, Chick Bullock, Jack Teagarden, Harold Arlen, Buddy Clark, Eddy Howard, Frank Sinatra, Dick Haymes, and others). Art Deco Series. Columbia / Legacy: C2K 52942. 1993. 2 CDs.

1063   *Don't Give the Name a Bad Place: Types and Stereotypes in American Musical Theater, 1870–1900* (Max Morath, Bobby Floyd, Clifford Jackson, Danny Barker, Lois Winter, Rose Marie Jun, Phil Olson, Charles Magruder, Ralph Fields, Bernard Knee, Alan Sokoloff, Dick Hyman). New World: 80265. 1996. CD. MP3 album available.

1064   *The Flapper Box* [1930s–1940s] (George Formby, Andrews Sisters, Fred Astaire, Bing Crosby, Marlene Dietrich, Ethel Merman, Jo Stafford, Count Basie, and others). Pavilion: Past CDS 7010. 1992. 5 CDs.

1065   *Flappers, Vamps, and Sweet Young Things* [1924–1931] (Libby Holman, Kate Smith, Sophie Tucker, Marion Harris, Blossom Seeley, Annette Hanshaw, Ruth Etting, Greta Keller, Helen Morgan, Helen Kane, Gertrude Lawrence, and others). ASV Living Era: 5015-2. 1992. CD.

1066   *The Great Depression: American Music in the '30s* [1927–1941] (Rudy Vallee, Louis Armstrong, Duke Ellington, Victoria Spivey, Barbecue Bob,

Blind Willie Johnson, Casa Loma Orchestra, Ted Lewis, Red Norvo, Billie Holiday, Bill Cox, Chick Bullock, Memphis Minnie, Hal Kemp, Artie Shaw, Horace Heidt, and others). Columbia (Sony): CK 57589. 1993. CD. MP3 album available.

1067 *"I Wants to Be a Actor Lady" and Other Hits from Early Musical Comedies* [1860–1900] (Cincinnati's University Singers and Theater Orchestra; Earl Rivers, con.). New World: 80221. 1993. CD.

1068 ★*It Had to Be You: Popular Keyboard from the Days of the Speakeasy to the Television Era* (Zez Confrey, Eddy Duchin, Roger Williams, Frankie Carle, Liberace, and others). New World: 80298. 2002. LP.

1069 *Joe Franklin Presents . . . The Roaring '20s Roar Again* (Louis Armstrong, Al Jolson, Eddie Cantor, Adelaide Hall, Bing Crosby, Ruth Etting, Blossom Seeley, and others). Legacy (Sony): 64642. 1995. CD.

1070 ★*The Music Goes Round and Around: The Golden Years of Tin Pan Alley, 1930–1939* (Russ Columbo, Bing Crosby, Louis Armstrong, Mildred Bailey, Connee Boswell, Pha Terrell, Martha Raye, Ella Fitzgerald, Bea Wain, Jimmie Lunceford, and others). New World: 80248. 1977. LP.

1071 ★*Nipper's Greatest Hits: The 20's* [1920–1929] (Gene Austin, Fred Waring, Nat Shilkret, Paul Whiteman, Eddie Cantor, Vernon Dalhart, Jean Goldkette, Fanny Brice, Duke Ellington, Johnny Hamp, George Gershwin, and others). RCA: 2258-2-R. 1990. CD.

1072 ★*Nipper's Greatest Hits: The 30's, Vol. 1* [1929–1939] (Leo Reisman, Fanny Brice, Bing Crosby, Maurice Chevalier, Fred Astaire, Cab Calloway, Mae West, Tommy Dorsey, Wayne King, Fats Waller, Benny Goodman, Guy Lombardo, Larry Clinton, Glenn Miller, Kate Smith, and others). RCA: 9971-2-R. 1990. CD.

1073 ★*Nipper's Greatest Hits: The 40's, Vol. 1* [1938–1944] (Artie Shaw, Duke Ellington, David Rose, Sammy Kaye, Glenn Miller, Tommy Dorsey, Frank Sinatra, King Sisters, Freddy Martin, Dinah Shore, Charlie Barnet, Spike Jones, Vaughn Monroe, Lena Horne, and others). RCA: 9855-2-R. 1989. CD.

1074 *Phono-Cylinders, Vols. 1 and 2* [1904–1916] (Len Spencer, Edison Military Band, Kerry Mills, Arthur Collins, Ada Jones, Billy Murray, George W. Johnson, and others). Folkways: FW03886 (vol. 1); FW03887 (vol. 2). 2003. 2 CDs. Digital download or custom CD available from Smithsonian Folkways website.

1075 *The Phonographic Yearbook, 1907: Dear Old Golden Rule Days* (Enrico Caruso, Arthur Collins, May Irwin, Ada Jones, Billy Murray, Harry Lauder, Bert Williams, and others). Archeophone: 9008. 2003. CD.

1076 *The Phonographic Yearbook, 1908: Take Me Out with the Crowd* (Haydn Quartet, Ada Jones, Billy Murray, Peerless Quartet, Henry Burr, Arthur Collins, and others). Archeophone: 9009. 2004. CD.

1077 *The Phonographic Yearbook, 1912: Waitin' on the Levee* (Bob Roberts, American Quartet, Harry McDonough, Al Jolson, Billy Murray, Arthur Collins, Ada Jones, Fred Van Eps, Harry Lauder, Enrico Caruso, and others). Archeophone: 9003. 2001. CD.

1078 *The Phonographic Yearbook, 1922: An Angel's Voice I Hear* (Paul Whiteman, Al Jolson, Isham Jones, Marion Harrsi, Peerless Quartet, American Quartet, and others). Archeophone: 9007. 2002. CD.

1079 ★*Praise the Lord and Pass the Ammunition: Songs of World Wars I and II* [1915–1946] (Spike Jones, Kay Kyser, Al Jolson, Helen Forrest, American Quartet, Nora Bayes, Peerless Quartet, Dick Robertson, Kenny Baker, and others). New World: 80222. 1977. LP.

1080 *The Roaring 'Twenties* (Al Jolson, Irving Aaronson, Paul Whiteman, Fred Waring and His Pennsylvanians, Gertrude Lawrence, Helen Kane, Fred Astaire, Claude Hulbert, Whispering Jack Smith, Noel Coward, and others). Pavilion: PAST CD 7845. 2000. CD.

1081 ★*Sentimental Journey: Pop Vocal Classics, Vol. 1* [1942–1946] (Les Brown, Doris Day, Bing Crosby, Dick Haymes, Dinah Shore, Mills Brothers, Betty Hutton, Woody Herman, Billy Eckstine, Judy Garland, Harry James, Helen Forrest, Vaughn Monroe, Margaret Whiting, Martha Tilton, Johnny Mercer, Jo Stafford, Paul Weston, Andy Russell, Lena Horne, Frank

Sinatra, Nat King Cole). Rhino: R2-71249. 1993. CD.

1082 *16 Most Requested Songs of the 1940s, Vol. 1* [1941–1949] (Les Brown, Doris Day, Xavier Cugat, Harry James, Benny Goodman, Kay Kyser, Dinah Shore, and others). Columbia (Sony): CK 45108. 1989. CD. MP3 downloads album available.

1083 *16 Most Requested Songs of the 1940s, Vol. 2* [1939–1949] (Harry James, Benny Goodman, Xavier Cugat, Frankie Carle, Les Brown, Kay Kyser, Dinah Shore, Buddy Clark, and others). Columbia (Sony): CK 45109. 1989. CD. MP3 downloads album available.

1084 *Songs of WWI: From Original Recordings 1914–1926.* Take Two: TT201. 1997. 2 CDs.

1085 *Songs That Got Us through World War II* [1941–1945] (Andrews Sisters, Tommy Dorsey, Frank Sinatra, Mills Brothers, Harry James, Jo Stafford, Ink Spots, Jimmy Dorsey, Les Brown, Vaughn Monroe, Louis Armstrong, and others). Rhino: 70960. 1990. CD.

1086 *Songs That Got Us through World War II, Vol. 2* [1942–1951] (Glenn Miller, Louis Jordan, Vaughn Monroe, Duke Ellington, Freddy Slack, Marlene Dietrich, Bing Crosby, Andrews Sisters, Woody Herman, Dinah Shore, Benny Goodman, Lucky Millinder, Buddy Johnson, Pied Pipers, Billie Holiday, Roy Rogers, Jo Stafford). Rhino: 71718. 1994. CD.

1087 ★*Sophisticated Ladies* [1929–1940] (Ruth Etting, Helen Morgan, Greta Keller, Annette Hanshaw, Ethel Waters, Connee Boswell, Boswell Sisters, Frances Langford, Alice Faye, Lee Wiley, Helen Ward, Ella Logan, Maxine Sullivan, Mildred Bailey, Nan Wynn, Ginny Simms, and others). Art Deco Series. Sony: 52943. 1993. 2 CDs.

1088 *Stomp and Swerve: American Music Gets Hot* [1897–1925]. Archeophone: 1003. 2003. CD.

1089 ★*Swing Time! The Fabulous Big Band Era* [1925–1955] (Harry James, Claude Thornhill, Bunny Berigan, Benny Goodman, Woody Herman, Will Bradley, Ray Noble, Louis Prima, Don Albert, Cab Calloway, Duke Ellington, Charlie Barnet, Jimmy Dorsey, Paul Whiteman, Glenn Miller, Ben Pollack, Les Brown, Gene Krupa, Tommy Dorsey, Count Basie, Ted Lewis, Casa Loma Orchestra, Jan Savitt, Bob Crosby, Fletcher Henderson, Chick Webb, Jimmie Lunceford, and

others). Columbia (Sony): C3K 52862. 1993. 3 CDs. MP3 download available.

1090 *This Is Art Deco* [1913–1982] (Bert Williams, Al Jolson, Cliff Edwards, Gertrude Lawrence, Sophie Tucker, Bing Crosby, Eddie Cantor, Guy Lombardo, Boswell Sisters, Mills Brothers, Mae West, Ethel Merman, Fred Astaire, Marlene Dietrich, Dean Martin, Judy Garland, Helen Humes, Alberta Hunter, and others). Sony: 57111. 1993. CD.

1091 *Times Ain't What They Used to Be: Early Rural and Popular Music from Rare Original Film Masters* [1928–1935] (Jimmie Rodgers, Bob Wills' Texas Playboys, Eddie Thomas and Carl Scott, Uncle John Scruggs, and others). Yazoo: 512. 2000. DVD.

1092 *25 Sweethearts of Yesteryear* [1927–1945] (Bing Crosby, Johnny Marvin, Gene Austin, Maurice Chevalier, Al Jolson, Mills Brothers, Fats Waller, Dinah Shore, Nat King Cole, Eddie Cantor, Frank Sinatra, and others). ASV: CD AJA 5243. 1997. CD.

1093 *With My Little Ukulele in My Hand* [1916–1957] (George Formby, Sol Hoopii, Cliff "Ukulele Ike" Edwards, Jimmie Rodgers, Roy Smeck, and others). Proper: Properbox 140. 2008. 4 CDs.

1094 ★*Yes, Sir, That's My Baby: The Golden Years of Tin Pan Alley* [1920–1929] (Paul Whiteman, Al Jolson, Fred Waring, Ethel Waters, Ted Lewis, Jack Smith, Ruth Etting, Sophie Tucker, Cliff Edwards, Blossom Seeley, Gene Austin, Rudy Vallee, Louis Armstrong). New World: 80279. 2002. CD.

SONGWRITER COLLECTIONS

1095 Arlen, Harold

1095.1 *Harold Arlen* [1933–1985] (Judy Garland, Jack Teagarden, Ethel Merman, Lena Horne, Nat King Cole, Margaret Whiting, Bing Crosby, Andrews Sisters, Frances Wayne, Pearl Bailey, Bobby Short, Joe Williams, Mabel Mercer, Fred Astaire, Ella Fitzgerald, Tony Bennett, Oscar Peterson, Maureen McGovern, Mel Torme, and others). American Songbook Series, Vol. 5. Smithsonian: RD 048-5. 1992. CD.

1095.2 *Harold Arlen Songbook.* G. Schirmer: HL00359080. 1985. Score.

1096 Berlin, Irving

1096.1 *Irving Berlin* [1930–1987] (Al Jolson, Connee Boswell, Ella Fitzgerald, Kate Smith, Bing Crosby, Judy Garland, Fred Astaire, Dinah Shore, Mary Martin, Teddi King, Ethel Merman, Johnny Mathis, Mel Torme, Eileen Farrell, Max Morath, Dorothy Loudon, Tony Bennett, Barbara Cook, and others). American Songbook Series, Vol. 1. Smithsonian: RD 048-1. 1988. CD.

1096.2 *Irving Berlin Anthology.* Hal Leonard: HL00312493. 1994. Score.

1096.3 *Irving Berlin: A Hundred Years* [1930–1958] (Ben Selvin, Jan Garber, Connee Boswell, Victor Young, Eddie Cantor, Ethel Waters, Fred Astaire, Bunny Berigan, Billie Holiday, Mildred Bailey, Peggy Lee, Dinah Shore, Tony Bennett, Rosemary Clooney, Judy Holiday, Andre Kostelanetz, and others). Columbia: CGK 40035. 1988. CD. MP3 download available from Amazon.com.

1097 Carmichael, Hoagy

1097.1 *The Classic Hoagy Carmichael* [1927–1984] (Bix Beiderbecke, Paul Whiteman, Louis Armstrong, Boswell Sisters, Hoagy Carmichael, Mills Brothers, Bing Crosby, Benny Goodman, Mildred Bailey, Ethel Waters, Shirley Ross, Kate Smith, Billie Holiday, Frank Sinatra, Betty Hutton, Jo Stafford, Ella Fitzgerald, Ray Charles, Sarah Vaughan, Margaret Whiting, and others). Indiana Historical Society / Smithsonian Collection of Recordings: RD-038. 1988. 3 CDs. Available from the Indiana Historical Society website.

1097.2 *Hoagy Carmichael* [1932–1964] (Frank Sinatra, Mildred Bailey, Bing Crosby, Ethel Waters, Mills Brothers, Billy Eckstine, Ray Eberle, Dick Haymes, Sarah Vaughan, Johnny Mercer, Marilyn Monroe, Teddi King, Four Aces, Barbara Lea, Carmen McRae, Tony Bennett, Rosemary Clooney, and others). American Songbook Series, Vol. 9. Smithsonian: RD 048-9. 1993. CD.

1097.3 *Hoagy Carmichael Centennial Collection.* Hal Leonard: HL00306189. 1999. Score.

1098 Coleman, Cy

1098.1 *Big Spender, Witchcraft, and Other Cy Coleman Favorites.* Hal Leonard: HL00100231. 2007. Score.

1098.2 *Cy Coleman* [1958–1990] (Mabel Mercer, Johnny Mathis, Liza Minnelli, Peggy Lee, Jack Jones, Barbra Streisand, Gwen Verdon, Morgana King, Shirley MacLaine, Rosemary Clooney, Tony Bennett, Sarah Vaughan, Lainie Kazan, Sylvia Syms, Jackie and Roy, Mel Torme, and others). American Songbook Series, Vol. 19. Smithsonian: RD 048-19. 1994. CD.

1099 Ellington, Duke

1099.1 *Duke Ellington* [1938–1971] (Frank Sinatra, Rosemary Clooney, Billie Holiday, Billy Eckstine, Mildred Bailey, Carmen McRae, Tony Bennett, Peggy Lee, Dinah Shore, Jo Stafford, Joe Williams, Nat King Cole, Kitty Kallen, Lena Horne, Ella Fitzgerald, Mel Torme, and others). American Songbook Series, Vol. 10. Smithsonian: RD 048-10. 1993. CD.

1099.2 *Duke Ellington Anthology.* Hal Leonard: HL00313400. 2008. Score.

1100 Fields, Dorothy. *Dorothy Fields* [1932–1987] (Louis Armstrong, Mills Brothers, Adelaide Hall, Frances Langford, Fred Astaire, Billie Holiday, Ethel Merman, Bing Crosby, Nat King Cole, Pearl Bailey, Shirley Booth, Mae Barnes, Joe Williams, Judy Garland, Margaret Whiting, Tony Bennett, Mabel Mercer, Maureen McGovern, Aretha Franklin, Peggy Lee, Sylvia Syms, Gwen Verdon). American Songbook Series, Vol. 13. Smithsonian: RD 048-13. 1993. CD.

1101 Gershwin, George

1101.1 *The Definitive Collection* (Ernestine Anderson, Hal Mooney's Orchestra, Billie Holiday, Oscar Peterson, Fred Astaire, Diane Schuur, Helen Merrill, the Art Farmer–Benny Golson Jazztet, Carmen McRae, Ella Fitzgerald, Louis Armstrong, Dinah Washington, Quincy Jones and His Orchestra, Betty Carter, Joe Williams, Count Basie and His Orchestra, Shirley Horn, Sarah Vaughan, Judy Garland, Victor Young and His Orchestra, Blossom Dearie, Ellis Larkins, Bill Henderson and the Oscar

Peterson Trio, and others). Universal International: 84089. 2006. CD.

1101.2 *Fascinating Rhythm: George Gershwin* [1925–1951] (Al Jolson, Jane Russell, Fred and Adele Astaire, Hazel Scott, Dinah Shore, Bing Crosby, and others). Avid Records: AMSC 639. 1998. CD.

1101.3 *George Gershwin* [1920–1988] (Al Jolson, Paul Whiteman, Gertrude Lawrence, Lee Wiley, Nat King Cole, Judy Garland, Mel Torme, Mary Martin, Ella Fitzgerald, Fred Astaire, Chris Connor, Nancy Walker, Kaye Ballard, Sarah Vaughan, Mabel Mercer, Cab Calloway, Bobby Short, Lena Horne, Michael Feinstein, Maureen McGovern, and others). American Songbook Series, Vol. 2. Smithsonian: RD048-2. 1992. CD.

1101.4 *Just Gershwin Real Book.* Alfred Publishing: FBM0006. 2004. Score.

1102 Hammerstein, Oscar, II. *Oscar Hammerstein II* [1943–1965] (Alfred Drake, Joan Roberts, John Raitt, Billie Holiday, Margaret Whiting, Dick Haymes, Judy Garland, Jo Stafford, Ezio Pinza, Mary Martin, Louis Armstrong, Perry Como, Teddi King, David Allyn, Judy Holliday, Mabel Mercer, Marilyn Horne, Barbara Cook, Mel Torme, Julie Andrews, and others). American Songbook Series, Vol. 7. Smithsonian: RD 048-07. 1992. CD.

1103 Harburg, E. Y. *E. Y. Harburg* [1932–1990] (Bing Crosby, Judy Garland, Groucho Marx, Tommy Dorsey, Frank Sinatra, Deanna Durbin, Billie Holiday, Ella Logan, David Wayne, Barbara Cook, Sarah Vaughan, Dinah Washington, Rosemary Clooney, Carmen McRae, Doris Day, Bobby Short, Lena Horne, Jeri Southern, Tony Bennett, Susannah McCorkle, Margaret Whiting, and others). American Songbook Series, Vol. 16. Smithsonian: RD 048-16. 1994. CD.

1104 Kern, Jerome
1104.1 *Jerome Kern* [1932–1964] (Frank Sinatra, Paul Robeson, Helen Morgan, Billie Holiday, Kate Smith, Margaret Whiting, Helen Forrest, Dick Haymes, Judy Garland, Lena Horne, Mabel Mercer, Bobby Short, Teddi King, Sarah Vaughan, David Allyn, Ella Fitzgerald, Eileen Farrell, Nat King Cole, and others). American Songbook Series,

Vol. 4. Smithsonian: RD 048-04. 1992. CD.

1104.2 *Jerome Kern Collection.* Hal Leonard: HL01128012. 1988. Score.

1105 Lerner, Alan
1105.1 *Alan Jay Lerner* [1950–1987] (Robert Goulet, Fred Astaire, Hi-Los, Julie Andrews, Vic Damone, Louis Jourdan, Gogi Grant, John Raitt, Andy Williams, Richard Burton, Felicia Sanders, Nat King Cole, Barbara Harris, Marilyn Maye, Alfred Drake, Jackie and Roy, Barbra Streisand, and others). American Songbook Series, Vol. 8. Smithsonian: RD048-8. 1992. CD.

1105.2 *Best of Lerner and Loewe.* Hal Leonard: HL 00312240. 1997. Score.

1106 Loesser, Frank
1106.1 *Frank Loesser* [1938–1967] (Billie Holiday, Marlene Dietrich, Dick Haymes, Betty Hutton, Bing Crosby, Andrews Sisters, Ray Bolger, Margaret Whiting, Kay Kyser, Doris Day, Sarah Vaughan, Dinah Shore, Mabel Mercer, Four Lads, Peggy Lee, Dinah Washington, Johnny Mathis, Robert Morse, and others). American Songbook Series, Vol. 15. Smithsonian: RD048-15. 1994. CD.

1106.2 *Frank Loesser Songbook.* Hal Leonard: HL00444442. 1994. Score.

1106.3 *Heart and Soul: The Life and Music of Frank Loesser.* Final Cut Productions: 6.89077E+11. 2006. DVD.

1107 Mercer, Johnny
1107.1 *Johnny Mercer* [1937–1986] (Frances Langford, Louis Armstrong, Helen Ward, Mildred Bailey, Dinah Shore, Jo Stafford, Helen O'Connell, Bob Eberly, Bing Crosby, Mary Martin, Billie Holiday, Woody Herman, Mills Brothers, Judy Garland, Gordon MacRae, Margaret Whiting, Tony Bennett, Mel Torme, Johnny Mathis, Andy Williams, and others). American Songbook Series, Vol. 11. Smithsonian: RD048-11. 1993. CD.

1107.2 *Johnny Mercer Centennial Sheet Music Collection.* Alfred: 36571. 2011. Score.

1107.3 *Too Marvelous for Words: Capitol Sings Johnny Mercer* [1943–1968]. Capitol: CDP 7 96791 2. 1991. CD.

1108 Porter, Cole

    1108.1 *Cole Porter* [1932–1971] (Ethel Merman, Fred Astaire, Ethel Waters, Artie Shaw, Mary Martin, Billie Holiday, Lee Wiley, Bing Crosby, Andrews Sisters, Judy Garland, Gene Kelly, Peggy Lee, Mabel Mercer, Lena Horne, Ella Fitzgerald, Jeri Southern, Eileen Farrell, Bobby Short, Marlene Dietrich, and others). American Songbook Series, Vol. 3. Smithsonian: RD 048-3. 1991. CD.

    1108.2 *A Musical Anthology.* Hal Leonard: HL00312332. 1988. Score.

    1108.3 *The Very Best of Cole Porter* [1952–2003] (Ella Fitzgerald, Peggy Lee, Tony Bennett, Sarah Vaughan, Jeri Southern, Dean Martin, Shirley Horn, Helen Merrill, Louis Armstrong, Eartha Kitt, Billie Holiday, Mel Torme, Anita O'Day with Billy May and His Orchestra, Dinah Washington, Aaron Neville, Carmen McRae, Fred Astaire, and others). Hip-O: B0001780-02. 2004. CD.

1109 Rodgers, Richard

    1109.1 *Rodgers / Hart* [1932–1987] (Lee Wiley, Bing Crosby, Maurice Chevalier, Margaret Whiting, Dick Haymes, Judy Garland, Lena Horne, Mel Torme, Mary Martin, Peggy Lee, Bobby Short, Doris Day, Ella Fitzgerald, Sarah Vaughan, Elaine Strich, Carmen McRae, Joe Williams, Billie Holiday, Tony Bennett, Maureen McGovern, Nat King Cole, and others). American Songbook Series, Vol. 6. Smithsonian: RD 048-6. 1992. CD.

    1109.2 *Rodgers and Hammerstein Collection.* Hal Leonard: HL 00313207. 2002. Score.

    1109.3 *Rodgers and Hart: A Musical Anthology.* Hal Leonard: HL 00307940. 1995. Score.

1110 Schwartz, Arthur

    1110.1 *All Time Favorite Dietz and Schwartz Songs.* Alfred Publishing: MF9615. 1996. Score.

    1110.2 *Arthur Schwartz* [1931–1992] (Bing Crosby, Boswell Sisters, Ethel Waters, Mildred Bailey, Tony Martin, Margaret Whiting, Dinah Shore, Buddy Clark, Pearl Bailey, Mary Martin, Fred Astaire, Dick Haymes, Helen Merrill, Mel Torme, Judy Holliday, Judy Garland, Barbara Cook, Weslia Whitfield, and others).

American Songbook Series, Vol. 23. Smithsonian: RD 048-23. 1995. CD.

1111 Styne, Jule

    1111.1 *Jule Styne* [1942–1986] (Helen Forrest, Dinah Shore, Kitty Kallen, Frank Sinatra, Glenn Miller, Tex Beneke, Jo Stafford, Doris Day, Carol Channing, Tony Bennett, Judy Holliday, Ethel Merman, Johnny Mathis, June Christy, Judy Garland, Lena Horne, Barbra Streisand, Maxine Sullivan, and others). American Songbook Series, Vol. 12. Smithsonian: RD 048-12. 1993. CD.

    1111.2 Hal Leonard: HL00361198. 1989. Score.

1112 Van Heusen, Jimmy

    1112.1 *James Van Heusen* [1938–1991] (Paul Whiteman, Cab Calloway, Ray Eberle, Frank Sinatra, Bing Crosby, Chris Connor, Margaret Whiting, Dick Haymes, Dinah Shore, Doris Day, Hi-Los, June Christy, Lena Horne, Tony Bennett, Sarah Vaughan, Jack Jones, Joe Williams, Peggy Lee, Julie Andrews, Mary Cleere Haran, and others). American Songbook Series, Vol. 18. Smithsonian: RD 048-18. 1994. CD.

    1112.2 *Songs of Burke and Van Heusen* (Johnny Burke). Bourne Co.: 419841. 1994. Score.

1113 Waller, Fats

    1113.1 *The Genius of Thomas "Fats" Waller.* Alfred Publishing: TPF0120. 1990. Score.

    1113.2 *Waller / Razaf* [1928–1994] (Ted Lewis, Bing Crosby, Ethel Waters, Andy Razaf, Annette Hanshaw, Benny Goodman, Jack Teagarden, Mildred Bailey, Joe Haymes, Fats Waller, Boswell Sisters, Phil Harris, Judy Garland, Ray Noble, Lena Horne, Frankie Laine, Vaughn Monroe, Sarah Vaughan, Maxine Sullivan, Louis Armstrong, Dinah Washington, Lee Wiley, Sammy Davis, Jr., Helen Merrill). American Songbook Series, Vol. 21. Smithsonian: RD 048-21. 1994. CD.

1114 Warren, Harry. *Harry Warren* [1932–1987] (Ginger Rogers, Dick Powell, Glenn Miller, Harry James, Helen Forrest, Ray Eberle, Dick Haymes, Maxine Sullivan, Judy Garland, Fred Astaire, Nat

King Cole, Jo Stafford, Tony Bennett, Rosemary Clooney, Teddi King, Vic Damone, Jackie and Roy, David Allyn, Hi-Los, Mel Torme, Maureen McGovern, and others). American Songbook Series, Vol. 14. Smithsonian: RD 048-14. 1993. CD.

1115   Weill, Kurt
    1115.1   *Broadway and Hollywood.* Hal Leonard: HL00313063. 1997. Score.
    1115.2   *From Berlin to Broadway: A Selection* [1928–1945] (Harald Paulsen, Lotte Lenya, Bertolt Brecht, Walter Huston, David Brooks, Gertrude Lawrence, Danny Kaye, Mary Martin, Lewis Ruth Band, and others). Pearl: GEMM 0108. 2000. CD.

1116   Whiting, Richard. *Richard Whiting* [1929–1988] (Margaret Whiting, Maurice Chevalier, Jeanette MacDonald, Rudy Vallee, Ethel Merman, Boswell Sisters, Alice Faye, Shirley Temple, Lee Wiley, Tony Martin, Billie Holiday, Dick Powell, Kate Smith, Mel Torme, Bing Crosby, Carmen McRae, Nat King Cole, Tony Bennett, Doris Day, Jeri Southern, Susannah McCorkle, and others). American Songbook Series, Vol. 22. Smithsonian: RD 048-22. 1994. CD.

1117   Wilder, Alec
    1117.1   *Alec Wilder* (Mills Brothers, Mildred Bailey, Benny Goodman, Lena Horne, Sarah Vaughan, Frank Sinatra, Dinah Washington, Jeri Southern, Nat King Cole, Peggy Lee, Rosemary Clooney, Jo Stafford, Lee Wiley, Helen Merrill, Mabel Mercer, Dick Haymes, Eileen Farrell, Jackie and Roy, and others). American Songbook Series, Vol. 24. Smithsonian: AD048-24. 1995. CD.
    1117.2   *Alec Wilder Song Collection.* Hal Leonard: HL00378814. 2008. Score.

1118   Youmans, Vincent. *Vincent Youmans* [1926–1974] (Frank Sinatra, Beatrice Lillie, Fred Astaire, Rudy Vallee, Al Bowlly, Mildred Bailey, Andrews Sisters, Dinah Shore, Mary Martin, John Raitt, Lee Wiley, Doris Day, Elaine Strich, Roy Hamilton, Judy Garland, Liza Minnelli, and others). American Songbook Series, Vol. 20. Smithsonian: RD 048-20. 1994. CD.

INDIVIDUALS AND GROUPS

1119   ★Andrews Sisters. *50th Anniversary Collection, Vol. 1* [1937–1950]. MCA: MCAD-42044. 1987. CD.

1120   Astaire, Fred
    1120.1   *Essential Fred Astaire.* Columbia / Legacy: CK 87141. 2004. CD. Reissue: Sony 87141.
    1120.2   *Great American Songbook.* Columbia / Legacy: 82796 94492 2. 2006. CD. MP3 album available.
    1120.3   *Top Hat: Hits from Hollywood* [1935–1937]. Columbia: CK 64172. 1994. CD. MP3 album available.

1121   ★Boswell Sisters. *That's How Rhythm Was Born.* [1931–1935] (MP3 album available from Amazon.com). Columbia / Legacy: CK 66977. 1995. CD. Import and MP3 album available.

1122   Bradley, Will. *Best of Will Bradley with Ray McKinley: Eight to the Bar* (Ray McKinley). Collectables: 7618. 2005. CD.

1123   Cantor, Eddie
    1123.1   *The Best of Eddie Cantor: A Centennial Celebration* [1917–1957]. RCA: 07863-66033-2. 1992. CD.
    1123.2   *The Columbia Years* [1922–1940]. Columbia: C2K 57148. 1994. 2 CDs. MP3 album available.
    1123.3   *Makin' Whoopee with "Banjo Eyes"* [1922–1940]. ASV Living Era: 5357. 2000. CD. MP3 album available.

1124   Carmichael, Hoagy. *The First of the Singer Songwriters: Key Cuts* [1924–1946] (Bix Beiderbecke, Red Nichols, Paul Whiteman, Louis Armstrong, Fats Waller, Mildred Bailey, Ethel Waters, Dorsey Bros., Boswell Sisters, and others). JSP: 918. 2003. 4 CDs. MP3 album available. Box set reissued in 2009.

1125   Crosby, Bing
    1125.1   *Bing: His Legendary Years* [1931–1957]. MCA: MCAD4-10887. 1993. 4 CDs. MP3 album available.
    1125.2   *Bing Crosby and Some Jazz Friends* [1937–1951] (Paul Whiteman, Louis Armstrong, Louis Jordan, Eddie Condon, Connee Boswell, Lionel Hampton, Lee Wiley, Woody Herman, Bob Crosby, Jack Teagarden). Decca: GRD-603. 1991. CD. MP3 album available.

1125.3 *Bing's Gold Records* [1936–1950]. MCA: MCAD-11719. 1997. CD. MP3 album available.

1125.4 *Centennial Anthology* [1931]. Master Classics: 8.81163E+11 8070. 2006. CD, DVD.

1125.5 ★*A Centennial Anthology of His Decca Recordings* [1934–1956]. MCA: 113222. 2003. 2 CDs. MP3 album available.

1125.6 *It's Easy to Remember* [1926–1950] (Paul Whiteman, Duke Ellington, Lennie Hayton, George Stoll, Victor Young, John Scott Trotter, Xavier Cugat, and others). Proper Box: PROPERBOX 34. 2001. 4 CDs.

1125.7 *16 Most Requested Songs* [1931–1934]. Columbia: CK 48974. 1992. CD. Reissue: SBME Special Mkts: 749637. 2009.

1126 Crumit, Frank. *Gay Caballero* [1925–1935]. Sanctuary Classics: CD AJA 5457. 2002. CD. Available via Naxos Music Library (8.120502).

1127 Cugat, Xavier. *The Original Latin Dance King* [1940–1957]. SBME: 750645. 2002. CD.

1128 Dorsey, Jimmy

1128.1 *Greatest Hits* [c1940–1957]. Curb: D2-77411. 1991. CD.

1128.2 *Jimmy Dorsey and His Orchestra Play: 22 Original Recordings* [1940–1950] (Helen O'Connell and Bob Eberly). Hindsight Records: HCD-415. 1988. CD.

1129 Dorsey, Tommy

1129.1 *Greatest Hits* [1940–1942] (Frank Sinatra). RCA: 09026-68492-2. 1996. CD. MP3 album download.

1129.2 *Stop, Look, and Listen* [c.1935–1942]. ASV Living Era: CD AJA 5105. 1993. CD.

1130 Duchin, Eddy. *The Eddy Duchin Story: 24 Vintage Tracks* [1933–1938]. ASV: AJA 5205. 1996. CD.

1131 Etting, Ruth. *Ten Cents a Dance* [1926–1930]. ASV; Living Era: 5008. 1981. CD.

1132 Europe, James Reese. *James Reese Europe Featuring Noble Sissle* [1919]. IAJRC: 1012. 1996. CD.

1133 Fats Waller. *If You Got to Ask, You Ain't Got It!* [1926–1943]. Bluebird; RCA Victor; Legacy: 82876 81125 2. 2006. 3 CDs.

1134 Garland, Judy

1134.1 ★*Classic Judy Garland: The Capitol Years, 1955–1965.* Capitol: CDP 7243 5 39281 2 4. 2002. 2 CDs.

1134.2 *The Judy Garland Collection.* White Star. 2002. 4 DVDs.

1134.3 *20th Century Masters: The Best of Judy Garland* [1937–1945]. MCA: 11952. 1999. CD.

1135 ★Ink Spots. *Instant Classics.* [1933–1946]. El Records: ACMEM91CD. 2006. CD.

1136 James, Harry

1136.1 ★*Best of the Big Bands* [1939–1945]. SBME Special Markets: 72422. 2008. CD.

1136.2 *The Complete Recordings Nineteen Thirty-Nine: Featuring Frank Sinatra.* SBME Special Markets: 724762. 2008. CD.

1137 Jolson, Al

1137.1 ★*The Best of Al Jolson* [1945–1947]. 20th Century Masters—The Millennium Collection. MCA: 088 112 692-2. 2001. CD.

1137.2 *The Jazz Singer* [1926]. Warner Home Video: 79889. 2007. 3 DVDs.

1138 Kemp, Hal

1138.1 *The Best of Hal Kemp and His Orchestra* [1934–1937]. Collector's Choice: CCM 125-2. 2000. CD.

1138.2 *Got a Date with an Angel* [1933–1937]. ASV: 5399. 2003. CD.

1139 Kyser, Kay

1139.1 *Kollege of Musical Knowledge* [1941–1943]. ASV: 5332. 2005. CD.

1139.2 *Strict Education in Music: 50 of the Best* [1938–1947]. Jasmine: CD JAS 398. 2002. 2 CDs.

1140 ★Lombardo, Guy. *Sweetest Music This Side of Heaven* [c1925–1935]. ASV: AJA 5156. 1995. CD.

1141 Marlborough Singers and Chamber Players, tenor John English, and piano Rob Carriker. *Over There! Songs from America's Wars.* Newport Classic: NPD 85662. 2002. CD.

1142 Merman, Ethel

1142.1 *American Music Icon.* Allegro American Legends: ALE 100106. 2003. CD.

1142.2 ★*An Earful of Music* [1932–1950]. Sanctuary: CD AJA 5510. 2004. CD.

1142.3 *Mary Martin and Ethel Merman: Their Legendary Appearance on the Ford 50th Anniversary Show.* Video Artists International: 4292. 2004. DVD.

1143 Miller, Emmett. *The Minstrel Man from Georgia* [1938–1939]. Columbia Legacy: CK66999. 1996. CD. MP3 album available.

1144 ★Miller, Glenn. *Essential Glenn Miller* [1939–1942]. RCA Bluebird: 82876692412. 2005. 2 CDs.

1145 Mills Brothers. *The Anthology.* [1931–1968]. MCA: MCAD2-11279. 1995. 2 CDs.

1146 Morgan, Russ. *Russ Morgan and His Orchestra Play: 22 Original Big Band Recordings* [1937–1940]. Hindsight Records: HCD-404. 1987. CD.

1147 Murray, Billy. *The Billy Murray Anthology: The Denver Nightingale* [1903–1943]. Archeophone: 5501. 2002. CD.

1148 Scott, Raymond. *Reckless Nights and Turkish Twilights: The Music of Raymond Scott* [1937–1940]. SBME Special Markets: 724294. 2008. CD.

1149 Smith, Kate. *Essential Collection: God Bless America* [1929–1939]. Dynamic Entertainment: 3548. 2008. 3 CDs.

1150 Vallee, Rudy
  1150.1 *Life Is Just a Bowl of Cherries* [1928–1930]. Submarine: DSOY615. 2003. CD.
  1150.2 *Vagabond Lover* [1928–1939]. ASV Living Era: CD AJA 5562. 2005. CD. MP3 album available.

1151 Waters, Ethel
  1151.1 ★*Favourite Songs of Ethel Waters.* Sepia Recordings: 1079. 2006. CD.
  1151.2 *The Incomparable Ethel Waters.* Columbia / Legacy: CK 65852. 2003. CD. MP3 album available.
  1151.3 *1929–1939* (Benny Goodman, Duke Ellington). Timeless Records: CBC1-007. 1992. CD. MP3 album available.
  1151.4 ★*On Stage and Screen* [1925–1940]. Sony Music Columbia Special Products: 75018. 1995. CD.

1152 Weill, Kurt. *Kurt Weill: American Songbook Series* [1941–1987]. Smithsonian Folkways: RD 048-17. 1994. CD.

1153 Whiteman, Paul
  1153.1 *If I Had a Talking Picture of You, Vol. 1* [1925–1938]. Vocalion: CDEA 6129. 2007. CD.
  1153.2 *Makin' Whoopee, Vol. 2.* Vocalion: DUT 6137. 2008. CD.
  1153.3 *Whiteman Stomp* [1923–1936]. Submarine: DSOY711. 2006. CD.

1154 Williams, Bert. *The Middle Years* [1910–1918]. Archeophone: 5003. 2002. CD.

Post–World War II through 1967

GENERAL COLLECTIONS

1155 *Casey Kasem Presents America's Top Ten through the Years: The Doo-Wop Years, 1950s* (Impalas, Silhouettes, Four Preps, Coasters, Drifters, Chordettes, and others). Top Sail: OPCD-2825. 2002. CD.

1156 *Casey Kasem Presents America's Top Ten through the Years: The Sixties* (Supremes, Monkees, Box Tops, Rascals, Turtles, Yardbirds, Mamas and the Papas, Aretha Franklin, Sonny and Cher, and others). Top Sail: TSP-71887. 2000. CD.

1157 *Hit Parade, 1943* (Tommy Dorsey, Mills Brothers, Xavier Cugat, Judy Garland, Gene Kelly, Benny Goodman, Dinah Shore, Dick Haymes, Ink Spots, Paul Weston, Vaughn Moore, and others). Dynamic Entertainment: DYN 2904. 2007. CD. The Hit Parade series includes other vols. covering 1939–1957.

1158 *Hit Parade, 1956* (Elvis Presley, Carl Perkins, Patti Page, Nelson Riddle Orchestra, Doris Day, Kay Starr, Four Lads, Jim Lowe, Dean Martin, and others). Dynamic Entertainment: DYN 2917. 2007. CD. The Hit Parade series includes other vols. covering 1939–1957.

1159 *Incredibly Strange Music, Vol. 1* [c1941–1980]. Caroline: 1746-2. 1993. CD.

1160 *Incredibly Strange Music, Vol. 2* [c1941–1980]. Asphodel / RE / Search: 951. 1995. CD.

1161 *The Look of Love: The Burt Bacharach Collection* [1957–1996] (Drifters, Chuck Jackson, Gene McDaniels, Shirelles, Gene Pitney, Dionne Warwick, Tom Jones, Jackie DeShannon, Brook Benton, Dusty Springfield, Lou Johnson, Herb Alpert, B. J. Thomas, Carpenters, 5th Dimension, Elvis Costello, and others). Rhino: R2 75339. 1998. 3 CDs.

1162 *Moments to Remember: The Golden Hits of the '50s and '60s Live* (Patti Page, Roger Williams, Frankie Laine, Rosemary Clooney, Four Lads, Four Aces, Four Freshmen, Platters, and others). Shout! Factory: 826663-10196. 2006. DVD.

1163 ★*Nipper's Greatest Hits: The 50's, Vol. 1* (Dinah Shore, Mario Lanza, Pee Wee King, Eartha Kitt, Eddie Fisher, Kay Starr, Elvis Presley, Harry Belafonte, Ames Brothers, Perry Como, Browns, Neil Sedaka, Jim Reeves, and others). RCA: 8466-2-R. 1988. CD.

1164 *Nipper's Greatest Hits: The 50's, Vol. 2* (Phil Harris, Mario Lanza, Eddie Fisher, Ames Brothers, Perry Como, Elvis Presley, Harry Belafonte, Jim Reeves, Perez Prado, Neil Sedaka, Della Reese, Isley Brothers, and others). RCA: 8467-2-R. 1988. CD.

1165 *Pure 60's: The #1 Hits* (Dion, Del Shannon, Marvelettes, Lesley Gore, Martha and the Vandellas, Supremes, Troggs, Turtles, Monkees, Marvin Gaye, and others). UTV: 440 069 119-2. 2002. CD.

1166 *Sentimental Journey: Capitol's Great Ladies of Song* [1942–1963] (Dinah Shore, Helen Forrest, Andrews Sisters, Peggy Lee, June Christy, Billie Holiday, Anita O'Day, Helen O'Connell, and others). Capitol: CDP 798014 2. 1992. CD.

1167 *Sentimental Journey: Pop Vocal Classics, Vol. 1* [1942–1946] (Les Brown, Bing Crosby, Dinah Shore, Mills Brothers, Betty Hutton, Woody Herman, Billy Eckstine, Lena Horne, Frank Sinatra, and others). Rhino: R71249. 1993. CD.

1168 ★*Sentimental Journey: Pop Vocal Classics, Vol. 2* [1947–1950] (Bing Crosby, Peggy Lee, Doris Day, Buddy Clark, Dinah Shore, Vaughn Monroe, Patti Page, Billy Eckstine, Frankie Laine, Evelyn Knight, Mel Torme, Eileen Barton, Dick Haymes, Margaret Whiting, Teresa Brewer, Art Lund). Rhino: R71250. 1993. CD.

1169 ★*Sentimental Journey: Pop Vocal Classics, Vol. 3* [1950–1954] (Tony Bennett, Johnny Ray, Peggy Lee, Rosemary Clooney, Georgia Gibbs, Billy Eckstine, Percy Faith, Jo Stafford, Kay Starr, Tony Martin, Kitty Kallen, Dean Martin, Al Martino, Les Paul and Mary Ford, Don Cornell, Doris Day, Guy Mitchell, Eddie Fisher). Rhino: R71251. 1993. CD.

1170 *Sentimental Journey: Pop Vocal Classics, Vol. 4* (Bobby Darin, Peggy Lee, Debbie Reynolds, Joan Weber, Dinah Washington, Vic Damone, Johnny Mathis, Dean Martin, Patti Page, Judy Garland, Tony Bennett, Sammy Davis Jr., and others). Rhino: R2 71252. 1993. CD.

1171 *16 Most Requested Songs: The 1950s, Vol. 1* [1950–1957] (Guy Mitchell, Tony Bennett, Frankie Laine, Johnny Ray, Percy Faith, Four Lads, Doris Day, Rosemary Clooney, Mitch Miller, Ray Conniff, Johnny Mathis, and others). Columbia: CK 45110. 1989. CD.

1172 *Sweet and Lovely: Capitol's Great Ladies of Song* [1944–1965] (Judy Garland, Dakota Staton, Lena Horne, Kay Starr, Peggy Lee, Keely Smith, Margaret Whiting, Nancy Wilson, and others). Capitol: CDP 7 97802 2. 1992. CD.

SONGWRITER COLLECTIONS

1173 Anderson, Leroy. *The Leroy Anderson Songbook: A Centennial Celebration*. Alfred Publishing: 29154. 2008. Score.

1174 Bacharach, Burt. *The Songs of Bacharach and David*. Hal Leonard: HL00313112. 1999. Score.

1175 Diamond, Neil. *Neil Diamond Anthology*. Hal Leonard: HL00699690. 1984. Score.

INDIVIDUALS AND GROUPS

1176 Anderson, Leroy. *The Leroy Anderson Collection* [1950–1962]. MCA: MCAD2-9815A. 1998. 2 CDs.

1177 Anka, Paul. *30th Anniversary Collection: His All Time Greatest Hits* [1957–1978]. Rhino: R2 71489. 1989. CD.

1178 Belafonte, Harry
    1178.1 *Calypso* [1956]. RCA: 53801-2 (LPM 1248). 1992. CD.
    1178.2 *An Evening with Harry Belafonte and Friends*. Island. 2003. DVD.
    1178.3 *Very Best of Harry Belafonte* [1952–1961]. RCA: 07863 68097-2. 2001. CD.

1179 Bennett, Tony
    1179.1 *American Classic*. Sony: 88697028349. 2006. DVD.
    1179.2 *50 Years: The Artistry of Tony Bennett* (Ray Charles, Percy Faith, B. B. King, Diana Krall, and others). Sony: C5K 92784. 2004. 5 CDs.
    1179.3 *16 Most Requested Songs* [1950–1964]. Sony Australia: CK 40215. 2005. CD.

1180   Boone, Pat. *Pat Boone* [1955–1962]. 20th Century Masters. MCA: 088 112 394-2. 2000. CD.

1181   Brewer, Teresa. *The Best of Teresa Brewer* [1950–1957]. MCA: MCAD-1545 (Coral). 1989. CD.

1182   Clark, Buddy. *Here's to Romance* [1934–1949]. Sanctuary: CD AJA 5563. 2005. CD.

1183   Clooney, Rosemary
  1183.1   *Blue Rose* [1956] (Duke Ellington). SBME Special Markets: 724182. 2008. CD.
  1183.2   *16 Biggest Hits* [1951–1954]. Columbia / Legacy: CK 63553. 2000. CD.
  1183.3   *Songs from the Girl Singer: A Musical Autobiography* [1946–1998]. Concord Jazz: CCD2-4870-2. 1999. 2 CDs.

1184   Cole, Nat King
  1184.1   *After Midnight: Complete Session* [1956]. Capitol: 7243 5 20087 2 8. 1999. CD.
  1184.2   ★*Jumpin' at Capitol* [1942]. Rhino: R2 71009. 1990. CD.
  1184.3   *The Very Best of Nat King Cole* [1943–1964]. Capitol: 09463 59324 2 3. 2006. CD.
  1184.4   *The World of Nat King Cole*. Capitol: 72435-44226-9-0. 2006. DVD.

1185   ★Como, Perry. *Greatest Hits* [1945–1970]. RCA: 674362. 1999. CD.

1186   Conniff, Ray. *The Essential Ray Conniff* [1957]. Columbia / Legacy: C2K 89170. 2004. 2 CDs.

1187   Davis, Sammy, Jr.
  1187.1   *The Best of Sammy Davis, Jr. Live* [1985]. Eagle Rock Entertainment: EVC 33.39-9. 2007. DVD.
  1187.2   *The Definitive Collection* [1954–1976]. Hip-O: B0005378-02. 2006. CD.

1188   Day, Doris
  1188.1   *Daydreaming: The Very Best of Doris Day*. Columbia: 487361 2. 2002. CD.
  1188.2   *Golden Girl: Columbia Recordings 1944–1966* [1944–1966]. Columbia: C2K 65505. 1999. 2 CDs.

1189   Denny, Martin. *The Best of Martin Denny's Exotica* [late 1950s–early 1960s]. Capitol: CAP30935. 2006. CD.

1190   Esquivel. *Esquivel! Space Age Bachelor Pad Music* [1958–1967]. Bar / None: AHAON-043. 1994. CD.

1191   Faith, Percy. *Greatest Hits* [1958–1967]. Sony BMG: 723795. 2008. CD.

1192   Fisher, Eddie. *The Hits*. Golden Stars Holland: 5393. 2007. CD.

1193   Flanders, Michael and Donald Swann
  1193.1   *The Complete Flanders and Swann.* (1959–1967). EMI: CDFSB 1 / CDS 7974642. 3 CDs.
  1193.2   *The Songs of Michael Flanders and Donald Swann.* London: International/Faber, 1977, 1996, 2007. Score.

1194   Four Aces. *The Four Aces Greatest Hits* [1951–1955]. MCA: MCAD-10886. 1993. CD.

1195   ★Four Freshmen. *The Four Freshmen* [1951–1963]. Capitol Collector's Series. Capitol: 93197. 1991. CD.

1196   Four Lads. *16 Most Requested Songs* [1952–1958]. SBME Special Markets: 723251. 2008. CD.

1197   Garland, Judy. *Judy at Carnegie Hall* [1961]. Capitol: 72435-27876-2-3. 2001. 2 CDs.

1198   Gleason, Jackie. *The Best of Jackie Gleason.* EMI Special Products: 72434-99279-2-6. 2000. CD.

1199   Haymes, Dick. *Golden Years of Dick Haymes* [1941–1952]. Jasmine: JASBOX 9-4. 2003. 4 CDs.

1200   Hibbler, Al. *After the Lights Go Down Low* [1950–1951]. Collectables: COL-CD-6326. 2002. CD.

1201   ★Horne, Lena. *Best of Lena Horne* [1941–1958]. MSI Music Corp: 397388. 2007. CD.

1202   Jones, Spike
  1202.1   *At His Very Best* [1942–1949]. Rex: 302. 2006. 2 CDs.
  1202.2   *The Spike Jones Story* [1988]. Storyville Films: 26024. 2007. DVD.

1203   King, Teddi. *In the Beginning: The Complete Recordings, 1949–1954.* Baldwin Street Music: BJH-307. 2000. CD.

1204   Laine, Frankie. *Golden Greats*. Goldies: 25421. 2004. 3 CDs.

1205   Lanza, Mario
  1205.1   *American Caruso*. Kultur Video: D1295. 1999. DVD.
  1205.2   *The Essential Mario Lanza* [1949–1959]. RCA Red Seal: 88697 07409 2. 2007. CD.

1206 Lee, Peggy
    1206.1 *The Best of Miss Peggy Lee* [1941–1970]. Capitol: 72434-97308-2-3. 2001. CD.
    1206.2 *Fever: The Music of Peggy Lee.* Capitol: 72435 99365 9 8. 2004. DVD.

1207 *The Legendary Crooners: Frank Sinatra, Dean Martin, Bing Crosby, Nat King Cole, Perry Como.* Standing Room Only: D4241. 2006. DVD.

1208 Lehrer, Tom
    1208.1 *The Remains of Tom Lehrer.* 1953–1999. Warner Archives/Rhino: R2 79831. 2000. 3 CDs.
    1208.2 *Too Many Songs by Tom Lehrer.* New York: Pantheon, 1981. Score.

1209 London, Julie. *The Very Best of Julie London.* Capitol: CAP12129B. 2006. 2 CDs.

1210 Mancini, Henry. *Midnight, Moonlight, and Magic: The Very Best of Henry Mancini.* RCA: 82876 59226 2. 2004. CD.

1211 Martin, Dean
    1211.1 *Dean Martin* [1948–1960]. Capitol Collector's Series. Capitol: 91633. 1989. CD.
    1211.2 ★*That's Amore.* Capitol: 72434 77904 9 2. 2001. DVD.

1212 Mathis, Johnny
    1212.1 *Essential Johnny Mathis* [1951–1980]. Sony: C2K 63562. 2004. 2 CDs.
    1212.2 *Heavenly* [1959]. SBME Special Markets: 723881. 2008. CD.

1213 McGuire Sisters. *Greatest Hits* [1954–1961]. MCA: MCAD-31341. 1989. CD.

1214 Mercer, Johnny. *Johnny Mercer* [1942–1952]. Capitol Collector's Series. Capitol: CDP-7 92125 2. 1989. CD.

1215 Mercer, Mabel. *Mabel Mercer Sings Cole Porter* [1954]. Collectables: COL-CD-7786. 2006. CD.

1216 Miller, Mitch. *Sing Along with Mitch* [1958]. SBME Special Markets: 723791. 2008. CD.

1217 Morse, Ella Mae. *Ella Mae Morse* [1942–1957]. Capitol Collector's Series. Capitol: CDP 7 95288 2. 1992. CD.

1218 Page, Patti. *16 Most Requested Songs* [1950–1968]. Sony: CK 444401. 1989. CD.

1219 Paul, Les
    1219.1 *The Best of the Capitol Masters: 90th Birthday Edition* [1947–1955]. Capitol: 09463-11411-2-6. 2005. CD.
    1219.2 *Chasing Sound.* Koch Vision: KOC-DV-6432. 2007. DVD.
    1219.3 *The Legend and the Legacy* [1940–1959]. Capitol: C2-97654. 1991. 4 CDs.

1220 Prima, Louis
    1220.1 *Jump, Jive, an' Wail: The Essential Louis Prima* [1947–1962] (Keely Smith, Gia Maione, Phil Harris). Capitol: 09463-95266-2-8. 2007. CD.
    1220.2 *The Wildest.* Image Entertainment: ID0535BUDVD. 2001. DVD.

1221 Rodgers, Jimmie. *The Best of Jimmie Rodgers* [1957–1967]. Rhino: R2 70942. 1990. CD.

1222 Shore, Dinah. *The Ultimate Dinah Shore* [1959–1961]. EMI: 7243 5 35930 2 5. 2001. CD.

1223 Short, Bobby. *Live at the Café Carlyle* [1973]. Collectables: COL-CD-7771. 2006. CD.

1224 Sinatra, Frank
    1224.1 ★*Best of the Capitol Years* [1953–1960]. Capitol: CDP 0777 7 99225 29. 1992. CD.
    1224.2 *Come Fly with Me* [1957]. Capitol: 72434 96087 2 6. 1998. CD.
    1224.3 *Frank Sinatra: Concert Collection* (Nancy Sinatra, Ella Fitzgerald, Antonio Carlos Jobim, Count Basie Orchestra, Gene Kelly, Diahann Carroll, 5th Dimension, Don Costa, Dean Martin, Tony Bennett, Natalie Cole, Loretta Lynn, John Denver, Bing Crosby, Buddy Rich, and Tony Mottola). Shout! Factory: 826663-12220. 2010. 7 DVDs.
    1224.4 *Frank Sinatra Sings for Only the Lonely* [1958]. Capitol: 72434 94756 2 5. 1998. CD.
    1224.5 *In the Wee Small Hours* [1955]. Capitol: 72434 94755 2 6. 1998. CD.
    1224.6 *A Man and His Music* [1965]. Shout! Factory: 826663122213. 2011. DVD.
    1224.7 *Nice 'n' Easy* [1960]. Capitol: 72435-33745-2-5. 2002. CD.
    1224.8 ★*Songs for Swingin' Lovers* [1956]. Capitol: 72434 96226 2 3. 1998. CD.

1224.9 *Songs for Young Lovers / Swing Easy* [1954–1955]. Capitol: 72434 96089 2 4. 1998. CD.

1224.10 ★*The Very Good Years* [1960–1980]. Reprise: 9 26501-2. 1991. CD.

1224.11 *The Voice in Time: 1939–1952*. Legacy: 88697 09669 2. 2007. 4 CDs.

1225 ★Stafford, Jo. *Jo Stafford* [1943–1950]. Capitol Collector's Series. Capitol: CDP 7 91638 2. 1991. CD.

1226 Starr, Kay. *Kay Starr* [1947–1963]. Capitol Collector's Series. Capitol: CDP 7 94080 2. 1991. CD.

1227 Vaughn, Billy. *The Billy Vaughn Collection* [1954–1965]. Varèse Sarabande: 302 066 315 2. 2002. CD.

1228 Vinton, Bobby. *All-Time Greatest Hits*. Varèse Sarabande: 302 066 512 2. 2003. CD.

1229 Warwick, Dionne

1229.1 ★*Dionne Warwick Collection* [1962–1969]. Rhino: R2 71100. 1989. CD.

1229.2 *Live in Concert*. Image Entertainment: ID3864WIDVD. 2007. DVD.

1230 ★Washington, Dinah. *The Very Best of Dinah Washington*. EMI: 0946 3 68352 2 8. 2006. 3 CDs.

1231 Welk, Lawrence. *Biggest Hits*. MCA: MCAD 20854. 1995. CD.

1232 Williams, Andy

1232.1 *An Evening with Andy Williams: Live from the Royal Albert Hall, 1978*. Cherry Red: RPMDVD3. 2007. DVD.

1232.2 *16 Biggest Hits*. Columbia; Legacy: CK 63563. 2000. CD.

1232.3 *16 Most Requested Songs* [1956–1967]. Columbia: CK 40213. 1986. CD.

1233 Williams, Roger. *The Best of Roger Williams*. 20th Century Masters—the Millennium Collection. Geffen: B0001893-02. 2004. CD.

1234 Wilson, Nancy. *Yesterday's Love Songs, Today's Blues* [1963–1964]. Blue Note: CDP 7 96265 2. 1991. CD.

Post-1967

GENERAL COLLECTIONS

1235 *Billboard #1s: The '70s* (Doobie Brothers, Elton John, Carly Simon, Marvin Gaye, Peaches and Herb, Bread, Chic, Donna Summer, Al Green, Chicago, Blondie, and others). Rhino: R2 77776. 2006. 2 CDs.

1236 *Billboard #1s: The '80s* (Queen, Yes, Billy Idol, Genesis, Foreigner, Mick Jagger, ZZ Top, B-52s, Tubes, Rod Stewart, and others). Rhino: R2 78084. 2004. 2 CDs.

1237 *Complete Introduction to Disco* [1970–1980] (The Temptations, Isaac Hayes, Sly and the Family Stone, Sister Sledge, Commodores, KC and the Sunshine Band, Gloria Gaynor, Jackson 5, Kool and the Gang, Diana Ross, Thelma Houston, Cher, Donna Summer, and others). Universal Music Group: 5328514. 2010. 4 CDs.

1238 *80's Pop Hits* (Phil Collins, Toto, Clarence Clemons, Jackson Browne, Lisa Lisa and the Cult Jam, REO Speedwagon, Bonnie Tyler, Marvin Gaye, Wham!, Romantics, 'Til Tuesday, Luther Vandross, Basia, Cheap Trick, Bad English, New Kids on the Block, Bangles, Michael Bolton, Men at Work, Psychedelic Furs, and others). Sony: A3K 53495. 2001. 3 CDs.

1239 *Glee: The Music—Journey to Regionals*. Sony: 88697 72878 2. 2010. CD.

1240 *Have a Nice Decade: The '70s Pop Culture Box* (Edison Lighthouse, the Shocking Blue, Lynn Anderson, Guess Who, Sugarloaf, Norman Greenbaum, Murray Head, Delfonics, Jackson 5, James Taylor, Ocean, Lobo, Cat Stevens, Al Green, Rod Stewart, Melanie, Alice Cooper, Gilbert O'Sullivan, Wayne Newton, Gary Glitter, Dr. Hook and the Medicine Show, Carly Simon, Curtis Mayfield, Isley Brothers, Styx, James Brown, Jefferson Starship, Neil Sedaka, War, and others). Rhino: R2 72919. 1998. 7 CDs.

1241 *Like Omigod! The 80s Pop Culture Box (Totally)* (Devo, Buggles, Queen, Kool and the Gang, Pete Townsend, Blondie, the Vapors, Air Supply, Dolly Parton, Eddie Rabbitt, Christopher Cross, Gary Numan, Cars, Billy Squier, Rick Springfield, .38 Special, Tommy Tutone, Alan Parsons Project, Laura Branigan, Frank Zappa, Duran Duran, Missing Persons, Human League, Toni Basil, Bow Wow Wow, Thomas Dolby, Eddy Grant, Eurythmics, Culture Club, Cure, Pointer Sisters, Nena, Bryan Adams, Tears for Fears, Mr. Mister, and others). Rhino: R2 78239. 2002. 7 CDs.

1242 *90's Pop Hits* (Will Smith, Eagle Eye Cherry, Des'ree, Toad the Wet Sprocket, Groove Theory, U2, Lauryn Hill, Spin Doctors, General Public, Presidents of the United States of America, C + C Music Factory, Mandy Moore, Big Audio Dynamite II, and others). Sony: A3K 61005. 2002. 3 CDs.

1243 *70s Greatest Hits* (Bay City Rollers, Tony Orlando, Melanie, Daryl Hall, Jefferson Starship, Guess Who, Gladys Knight and the Pips, Pointer Sisters, and others). BMG Special Products: 47574. 2004. 3 CDs.

1244 *Whatever: The '90s Pop and Culture Box* [1990–1999] (M. C. Hammer, Social Distortion, They Might Be Giants, Sundays, Ice-T, Black Crowes, Matthew Sweet, Soul Asylum, Spin Doctors, Gin Blossoms, Ween, Tori Amos, R.E.M., Weezer, Oasis, Jewel, Sublime, Cardigans, Chumbawumba, and others). Rhino: R2 79716. 2005. 7 CDs.

SONGWRITER COLLECTIONS

1245 Joel, Billy. *My Lives*. Hal Leonard: HL00306790. 2006. Score.

1246 Manilow, Barry. *The Barry Manilow Anthology*. Hal Leonard: HL00306256. 2000. Score.

1247 Mitchell, Joni. *Hits*. Alfred Publishing: PG9666. 1997. Score.

INDIVIDUALS AND GROUPS

1248 ABBA. *Gold: Greatest Hits* [1974–1983]. Polydor: 314-517 007-2. 1993. CD.

1249 Adele
    1249.1 *19*. XL: 88697 31859 2. 2008. CD.
    1249.2 *21*. XL: 88697 44699 2. 2011. CD.
    1249.3 *25*. XL: 888751 75952. 2015. CD.

1250 Alpert, Herb. *Definitive Hits* [1962–1987]. Interscope: 069 490 886-2. 2001. CD.

1251 Bennett, Tony
    1251.1 *Duets: An American Classic* (Barbra Streisand, James Taylor, Paul McCartney, Elton John, Billy Joel, Stevie Wonder, Elvis Costello, Bono, Dixie Chicks, and others). RPM Records / Columbia: 82876809792. 2006. CD.
    1251.2 *The Tony Bennett / Bill Evans Album* [1975]. Fantasy: FCD-30177-2. 2006. CD.

1252 Bieber, Justin. *My World 2.0*. Island: B0014063-02. 2010. CD.

1253 Bread. *Best of Bread* [1969–1976]. Rhino: R2 74311. 2001. CD.

1254 Bublé, Michael. *Michael Bublé*. Reprise: 48376-2. 2003. CD.

1255 Captain and Tennille. *Ultimate Collection: The Complete Hits*. Hip-O: 520 901-2. 2001. CD.

1256 Carey, Mariah
    1256.1 *The Emancipation of Mimi* (Snoop Dogg, Jermaine Dupri, Twista, Nelly, and others). Island: B000578402. 2005. CD.
    1256.2 *#1s* [1990–1998] (JD, Whitney Houston, Brian McKnight, Boyz II Men, O.D.B., Trey Lorenz). Columbia: CK 69670. 1998. CD.

1257 ★Carpenters. *The Singles* [1969–1981]. Interscope: 490456-2. 2000. CD.

1258 Clark, Petula. *The Ultimate Petula Clark* [1964–1971]. BMG Heritage: 82876 51038-2. 2003. CD.

1259 Clooney, Rosemary
    1259.1 *Girl Singer*. Concord Jazz: CCD-4496. 1992. CD.
    1259.2 *Sings the Lyrics of Johnny Mercer*. Concord Jazz: CCD-4333. 1987. CD.

1260 Connick, Harry, Jr.
    1260.1 *Only You: In Concert*. Sony: CVD 58515. 2004. DVD.
    1260.2 *25* [1992]. SBME Special Markets: 723242. 2008. CD.

1261 Cook, Barbara. *Barbara Cook at Carnegie Hall* [1975]. Sony Classical: SMK 62017. 1996. CD.

1262 Costello, Elvis. *Painted from Memory* (Burt Bacharach). Mercury: 314 538 002-2. 1998. CD.

1263 Denver, John
    1263.1 *Country Roads Collection* [1971–1977]. RCA: 07863 67437 2. 1997. 4 CDs.
    1263.2 *Greatest Hits* [1971–1973]. RCA / Legacy: 82876 69376 2. 2005. CD.

1264 Diamond, Neil. *Essential Neil Diamond* [1966–2001]. Columbia: C2K 85681. 2001. 2 CDs.

1265 Dion, Céline
    1265.1 *All the Way: A Decade of Song and Video*. Sony / Epic: BVD 50229. 2001. DVD.

1265.2 *My Love: Ultimate Essential Collection.* Sony BMG: 88697 37452 2. 2008. 2 CDs.

1266 Duran Duran. *The Greatest* [1981-1997]. Capitol: 7243 4 96239 2 7. 1998. CD.

1267 Easton, Sheena. *Greatest Hits* [1980–1984]. Collectables: S21 18291. 1995. CD.

1268 Farrell, Eileen. *My Very Best* [1988]. Reference: RR60-CD. 1994. CD.

1269 5th Dimension. *Greatest Hits on Earth* [1967–1972]. Arista: ARCD 8335. 1990. CD.

1270 Fogelberg, Dan. *Greatest Hits* [1975–1981]. Full Moon / Epic: EK 38308. 1990. CD.

1271 G, Kenny. *The Ultimate Kenny G* [c1988–2000]. Arista: 736839. 2003. CD.

1272 Holland, Jolie. *Escondida.* Anti: 86692-2. 2004. CD.

1273 Houston, Whitney
   1273.1 *The Greatest Hits.* Arista. 2000. DVD.
   1273.2 *Whitney Houston* [1985]. Arista: ARCD-8212. 1990. CD.

1274 INXS. *The Best of INXS.* Rhino: R2 78251. 2002. CD.

1275 Isaak, Chris. *Best of Chris Isaak.* Mailboat: 3028. 2011. CD.

1276 Jewel. *Pieces of You.* Atlantic: 82700-2. 1994. CD.

1277 Joel, Billy
   1277.1 *The Essential Video Collection.* Sony: CVD 54094. 2001. DVD.
   1277.2 ★*Greatest Hits, Vols. 1 and 2* [1973–1985]. Columbia: 69391. 1998. 2 CDs.

1278 Jones, Norah. *Come Away with Me.* Blue Note: 7243 5 32088 2 0. 2002. CD.

1279 Jones, Tom. *Reloaded: Greatest Hits* [late 1960s–1999] (Art of Noise, Sterophonics, Van Morrison, Portishead, Cardigans). Universal: B0001 421-02. 2003. CD.

1280 Krall, Diana. *When I Look in Your Eyes* [1998]. Verve: IMPD-304. 1999. CD.

1281 Lady Gaga. *The Fame.* Interscope: B0011805-02. 2008. CD.

1282 Laine, Cleo. *Cleo's Choice.* GNP Crescendo: 9024. 1993. CD.

1283 MacColl, Kirsty. *The Best of Kirsty MacColl* [1979–2000]. Virgin: CDV 3008. 2005. CD.

1284 Manhattan Transfer
   1284.1 *Swing.* Atlantic: 83012. 1997. CD.
   1284.2 *The Very Best of Manhattan Transfer* [1975–1987]. Rhino: R2 71560. 1994. CD.

1285 Manilow, Barry. *Ultimate Manilow* [1973–1990]. Arista: 07822-10600-2. 2002. CD.

1286 Mantovani. *Golden Hits* [1967]. London: 800 085-2. 1990. CD.

1287 McKay, Nellie. *Get Away from Me.* Columbia: C2K 90664. 2004. 2 CDs.

1288 McLachlan, Sarah. *Closer: The Best of Sarah McLachlan.* Arista: 88697-30263-2. 2008. 2 CDs.

1289 Midler, Bette
   1289.1 *The Divine Bette Midler.* Shout! Factory: 32975. 2005. DVD.
   1289.2 *Experience the Divine: Greatest Hits* [1972–1991]. Atlantic: 7567-80667-2. 2000. CD.

1290 Minnelli, Liza. *Liza Minnelli at Carnegie Hall (Highlights)* [1987]. Telarc: CD-85502. 1990. CD.

1291 Mitchell, Joni
   1291.1 *Blue* [1971]. Rhino: 74795. 2007. CD.
   1291.2 *Court and Spark* [1974]. Asylum: 1001-2. 1990. CD.
   1291.3 *Hits* [1967–1991]. Reprise: 9 46326-2. 1996. CD.
   1291.4 *Ladies of the Canyon* [1970]. Reprise: CD 6376-2. 1990. CD.

1292 Monae, Janelle. *ArchAndroid.* Bad Boy Entertainment / Wondaland: 512256-2. 2010. CD.

1293 Newton-John, Olivia. *Back to Basics: The Essential Collection* [1971–1992]. Geffen: GEFD-24470. 1992. CD.

1294 Nilsson, Harry. *Personal Best: The Harry Nilsson Anthology* [1967–1977]. RCA: 07863-66354-2. 1995. 2 CDs.

1295 Perry, Katy. *Teenage Dream.* Capitol: 5.09997E + 12 085093. 2010. CD.

1296 Peyroux, Madeleine. *Careless Love.* Rounder: 11661-3192-2. 2004. CD.

1297 Pink Martini. *Hang on Little Tomato* [c2001]. Heinz Records: HNZ002. 2004. CD.

1298 Raitt, Bonnie
    1298.1 *The Best of Bonnie Raitt on Capitol, 1989–2003* [1989–2003]. Capitol: CDP 7243 5 90491 2 0. 2003. CD.
    1298.2 *Nick of Time.* Capitol: 91268. 1989. CD.

1299 Reddy, Helen. *The Woman I Am: The Definitive Collection* [1971–1980]. Capitol: 09463-57613-2-0. 2006. CD.

1300 Rihanna. *Good Girl Gone Bad* (Jay-Z and Ne-Yo). Def Jam: B0008968-02. 2007. CD.

1301 Schuur, Diane. *The Best of Diane Schuur.* GRP: GRP-9888. 1997. CD.

1302 Simone, Nina. *Anthology* [1957–1993]. RCA / BMG Heritage: 82876 530152. 2003. 2 CDs.

1303 Smith, Sam. *In the Lonely Hour.* Capitol: B002061102. 2014. CD

1304 Spears, Britney. *Oops! . . . I Did It Again.* Jive: 01241-41704-2. 2000. CD.

1305 Springfield, Dusty. *Dusty in Memphis* [1968–1971]. Rhino: R2 75580. 1999. CD.

1306 Sting. *Brand New Day.* Interscope: 694904432. 1999. CD.

1307 Streisand, Barbra
    1307.1 *The Concerts.* Hip-O: B0012832-09. 2009. 3 DVDs.
    1307.2 ★*Greatest Hits* [c1960–1969]. SBME Special Markets: 722968. 2008. CD.
    1307.3 ★*Greatest Hits, Vol. 2* [1973–1978]. Columbia: CK 35679. 1984. CD.
    1307.4 *Highlights from "Just for the Record"* [1955–1988]. SBME Special Markets: 724287. 2008. CD.

1308 Swift, Taylor
    1308.1 *Fearless.* Big Machine Records: BMRATS0200. 2008. CD.
    1308.2 *1989.* Big Machine Records: BMRBD0500A. 2014. CD.

1309 Timberlake, Justin
    1309.1 *Futuresex/Lovesounds.* Jive: 82876-87068-2. 2006. CD.
    1309.2 *Justified.* Jive: 01241-41823-2. 2002. CD.

1310 Wainwright, Rufus. *Want One.* Dreamworks: B0000896-12. 2003. CD.

1311 Winehouse, Amy. *Back to Black.* Republic: B0008428-02. 2007. CD.

1312 Yankovic, Weird Al
    1312.1 *The Ultimate Video Collection.* Volcano: 82876-53727-9. 2003. DVD.
    1312.2 *"Weird Al" Yankovic's Greatest Hits.* SBME Special Markets: 791777. 1999. CD.

NEW AGE
East/West

1313 Kitajima, Osamu. *Osamu* [1977]. East Quest: 1837787. 2010. LP.
1314 Kitaro
    1314.1 *Silk Road, Vol. 1* [1981]. New World: 150030. 2002. CD.
    1314.2 *Silk Road, Vol. 2* [1981]. New World: 150031. 2002. CD.
1315 Yoshizawa, Masakazu. *Kyori (Innervisions)* [1987]. Fortuna: 17052. 1991. CD.

Electronic/Computer

1316 Arkenstone, David. *Valley in the Clouds / In the Wake of the Wind* [1987, 1991]. Narada: 72435-90938-2-6. 2003. 2 CDs.
1317 Carlos, Wendy. (Walter Carlos). *Switched on Bach* [1968]. East Side Digital: ESD81602. 2001. CD.
1318 Jarre, Jean-Michel. *Oxygene* [1976]. Dreyfus: FDM 36140-2. 1993. CD.
1319 Vangelis
    1319.1 *Antarctica: Music from the Soundtrack* [1983]. Polydor: 815 732-2. 1990. CD.
    1319.2 ★*China* [1979]. Polydor: 813 653-2. 1990. CD.
    1319.3 *Opera Sauvage* [1978–1979]. Polydor: 829 663-2. 1990. CD.

Ambient

1320 Budd, Harold
    1320.1 *Ambient 2: The Plateaux of Mirror* [1980] (Brian Eno). Virgin: 7243 8 66497 2 0. 2004. CD.
    1320.2 *Pavilion of Dreams* [1976]. Editions EG: EEGCD 30. 1992. CD.
1321 DeJohnette, Jack. *Peace Time.* Kindred Rhythm: 1139. 2007. CD.
1322 Eno, Brian. *Ambient 1: Music for Airports* [1978]. Virgin: 7243 8 66495 2 2. 2004. CD.

1323 Penguin Cafe Orchestra. *Penguin Cafe Orchestra* [1981]. Caroline: 127342C. 2008. CD.

New Acoustic

1324 Ackerman, William
  1324.1 *Passage* [1981]. Windham Hill: 2-VWH-21003. 2009. CD.
  1324.2 *The William Ackerman Collection.* Hal Leonard: HL00690016. 1999. Score.

1325 Kottke, Leo
  1325.1 *The Music of Leo Kottke.* Accent on Music: ISBN-13: 978-0936799186. 1991. Score with CD.
  1325.2 ★*A Shout toward Noon.* Private Music: 2007-2-P. 1986. CD.

Jazz/Fusion

1326 Hassell, Jon. *Last Night the Moon Came Dropping Its Clothes in the Street.* ECM: ECM 2077. 2009. CD.

1327 Oregon. *The Essential Oregon* [1972–1976]. Vanguard: VCD-109/110. 1990. CD.

1328 Shadowfax. *Shadowfax* [1982]. Windham Hill: CD-1022. 1997. CD.

1329 Winter, Paul
  1329.1 *Canyon* [1980–1985]. Living Music: LD-0006. 1985. CD.
  1329.2 *Icarus* [1974]. Living Music: LD-0004. 1988. CD.
  1329.3 *Wolf Eyes: A Retrospective* [1980–1988]. Living Music: LD-0018. 1988. CD.

Meditation Music

1330 Deuter, C. H. *Nirvana Road* [1984]. Kuckuck: 11068-2. 1992. CD.

1331 ★Horn, Paul. *Inside the Taj Mahal, I and II* [1968]. Transparent Music: 500082. 2001. CD.

1332 ★Scott, Tony. *Music for Zen Meditation* [1964]. Verve: 314 521 444-2. 1997. CD.

1333 Wolff, Henry. *Tibetan Bells II* [1978] (Nancy Hennings). Celestial Harmonies: 13005. 1991. CD.

Native American

1334 Coyote Oldman. *In Medicine River* [1994]. Coyote Oldman: 5. 2008. CD.

1335 Nakai, R. Carlos. *Sundance Season* [1987]. Celestial Harmonies: 13024-2. 1992. CD.

Progressive

1336 Ciani, Suzanne
  1336.1 *New Age Piano.* Hal Leonard: HL00490470. 1991. Score with CD.
  1336.2 *The Velocity of Love* [1985]. Seventh Wave: SWP7003-2. 1995. CD.

1337 Isham, Mark. *Vapor Drawings* [1983]. Windham Hill: WD-1027. 1997. CD.

1338 Liebert, Ottmar. *Nouveau Flamenco.* Higher Octave: 77520. 1990. CD.

1339 ★Mannheim Steamroller. *Fresh Aire* [1974–1975]. American Gramaphone: AG5001-2. 2000. CD.

1340 ★Oldfield, Mike. *Tubular Bells* [1973]. Virgin: 849388. 2000. CD.

1341 Popol Vuh
  1341.1 *In Den Gärten Pharoas* [1972–1982]. SPV: 085 70112 CD. 2004. CD.
  1341.2 *Tantric Songs/Hosianna Mantra* [1981]. Celestial Harmonies: 13006-2. 1991. CD.

1342 Rypdal, Terje. *Selected Recordings* [1971–1981]. ECM / Universal Japan: 4009. 2002. CD.

1343 Tibbetts, Steve. *Yr* [1980]. ECM: 21355. 1994. CD.

1344 Vollenweider, Andreas
  1344.1 *Behind the Gardens, behind the Wall, under the Tree* [1981]. SLG: KIN 17543. 2005. CD.
  1344.2 *Caverna Magica* [1982]. SLG: KIN 17529. 2005. CD.

1345 Yanni. *The Very Best of Yanni.* Private Music: 01934-11568-2. 2000. CD.

Solo Instrumental

1346 Aaberg, Philip. *High Plains.* Windham Hill: CD-1037. 1985. CD.

1347 De Grassi, Alex. *Alex de Grassi: A Windham Hill Retrospective* [1992]. Windham Hill: 21011. 2010. CD.

1348 ★Hedges, Michael. *Aerial Boundaries.* Windham Hill: CD-1032. 1984. CD.

1349 Jones, Michael
    1349.1 *Pianoscapes: Deluxe Edition* [1985].
        Narada: 72438-12495-2-9. 2002. 2 CDs.
    1349.2 *Solos and Sketches for New Age Piano.*
        Hal Leonard: HL00490413. 1991. Score.

1350 Lanz, David. *Cristofori's Dream* [1987–1988].
    Narada: 72438-46963-2-0. 1999. CD.

1351 Newton, James. *Echo Canyon* [1984]. Celestial
    Harmonies: 13012-2. 1991. CD.

1352 Tingstad, Eric
    1352.1 *Narada Guitar Sampler.* Hal Leonard:
        HL00699349. 1992. Score.
    1352.2 *Pastorale: Music of Nature and Grace*
        (Nancy Rumbel). Narada / Sona Gaia:
        ND-61061. 1997. CD.

1353 Winston, George
    1353.1 ★*Autumn: 20th Anniversary Edition*
        [1980]. Windham Hill: 01934-11610-2.
        2001. CD.
    1353.2 *Piano Solos.* Hal Leonard: HL00306822.
        2007. Score.
    1353.3 *December: 20th Anniversary Edition*
        [1982]. Windham Hill: 01934-11611-2.
        2001. CD.

Sound Health Music

1354 Halpern, Steven. *Chakra Suite* [1975, 2001].
    Steven Halpern's Inner Peace Music: IPM 8000.
    2002. CD.

Space Music

1355 Demby, Constance. *Novus Magnificat* [1986].
    Hearts of Space: HS-11003-2. 1991. CD.

1356 Lynch, Ray. *Deep Breakfast* [1986]. Ray Lynch
    Productions: 3537 11118-2. 2001. CD.

1357 Roach, Steve. *Dreamtime Return* [1988]. Project
    Records: Projekt 175. 2005. 2 CDs.

1358 ★Tangerine Dream. *Stratosfear* [1976]. Virgin:
    86092. 1992. CD.

World Music

1359 Ancient Future. *Natural Rhythms* [1981]. Philo:
    CD PH 9006. 1994. CD.

1360 Clannad. *Celtic Themes: Very Best of Clannad.*
    Sony BMG Europe: 728115. 2008. CD.

1361 ★Enya. *Watermark*. Warner Brothers: 9 26774-2.
    1988. CD.

1362 McKennitt, Loreena
    1362.1 *The Mask and the Mirror* [1994].
        Quinlan Road Unlimited: B0007954-02.
        2006. CD.
    1362.2 *The Visit* [1992]. Quinlan Road Limited:
        B0007955-02. 2006. CD.

1363 Micus, Stephen. *On the Wing*. ECM: ECM 1987.
    2007. CD.

1364 Spheeris, Chris. *The Best of Chris Spheeris, 1990–
    2000*. Essence Records: ES-1006-2. 2001. CD.

1365 Stivell, Alan. *Renaissance of the Celtic Harp*.
    Mercury France: 8180072. 1987. CD.

Samplers and Concept Albums

1366 *Magnum Mysterium: A Special 2-1/2 Hour
    Collection of Sacred Music Classics*. Celestial
    Harmonies: 14060-2. 1994. 2 CDs.

1367 *Narada Decade: The Anniversary Collection* [1983–
    1993] (Michael Jones, Peter Buffett, Spencer
    Brewer, Ancient Future, David Arkenstone,
    David Lanz, Michael Gettel, and others). Narada:
    ND2-63911. 1993. 2 CDs.

1368 *Narada Wilderness Collection* [1990] (David
    Arkenstone, Spencer Brewer, Tingstad and
    Rumbel, Peter Buffett, David Lanz, and others).
    Narada: ND-63905. 1990. CD.

1369 *New Age Piano Sampler* (Yanni, Jim Chappell,
    Eddie Jobson, John Jarvis, Suzanne Cianni). Hal
    Leonard: HL0036090. 1988. Score.

1370 *Piano Solos: Narada Artists* (Michael Jones, Ira
    Stein, Wayne Gratz, Spencer Brewer, Kostia,
    Nancy Rumbel, Sheldon Mirowitz, Michael
    Gettel, Brian Mann, Bob Read). Hal Leonard:
    HL00292008. 1992. Score.

1371 *Pioneers of the New Age* [1972–1980] (Weather
    Report, Wendy Carlos, Jean-Pierre Rampal,
    Claude Bolling, Baden Powell, Carlos Santana,
    John McLaughlin, Paul Winter, Dave Brubeck
    Quartet, Terry Riley, Shakti, and Paul Horn).
    Columbia: CK 44314. 1991. CD.

1372 *A Quiet Revolution: 30 Years of Windham Hill*
    [1978–2005] (Will Ackerman, Liz Story, George
    Winston, David Arkenstone, and others).
    Windham Hill / Legacy: 82876695572. 2005.
    4 CDs.

1373   *Solace: A Windham Hill Collection* (Montreux, Michael Hedges, Alex de Grassi, George Winston, Will Ackerman, Liz Story, Nightnoise, Shadowfax, Tuck and Patti, Jim Brickman with Collin Raye and Susan Ashton, David Arkenstone, Yanni). Windham Hill: 01934-11470-9. 1999. DVD.

1374   *Starflight 1* (Kevin Braheny, Steve Roach, Tim Clark, Michael Amerian, and others). Hearts of Space Radio Program Series. Hearts of Space: HS100-2. 1986. CD.

1375   *Sunday Morning Coffee* (Chip Davis, Richard Burmer, Jackson Berkey, Doug Smith, and others). American Gramaphone: AGCD 100. 1991. CD.

1376   *Ultimate New Age* (Shadowfax, William Ackerman, John Tesh, Jim Chapell, George Winston, Ray Lynch, Vangelis, David Lanz, Enya, Philip Aaberg, Steven Halpern, Kitaro, and others). Hal Leonard: HL00311160. 2004. Score.

1377   *Windham Hill: The First Ten Years* [1977–1987] (William Ackerman, Alex De Grassi, George Winston, Shadowfax, Liz Story, Michael Hedges, Scott Cossu, Montreux, Mark Isham, Philip Aaberg, Nightnoise, and others). Windham Hill: WD-1095. 1990. 2 CDs.

1378   *The World of Private Music* (Yanni, Patrick O'Hearn, Lucia Hwong, Ancient Dreams, and others). Private Music: 2009-2-P. 1990. CD.

5

Country and Western

Compiled by GARY R. BOYE

GENERAL COLLECTIONS *86*
PRE–WORLD WAR II *86*
WESTERN SWING *88*
MAINSTREAM COUNTRY MUSIC: 1940s–1970s *89*
BLUEGRASS *94*
CONTEMPORARY: 1980s–PRESENT *97*
ALT-COUNTRY/AMERICANA *99*

The first generation of country artists recorded during the 1920s through 1930s; country historians call this period "pre–World War II" (or simply "prewar"). It includes the so-called hillbilly styles of predominately southeastern performers and, in the 1930s, a growing number of artists in western or "cowboy" styles. The combination of these two styles set the stage for the commercial success of what was generally called country and western music during and after the war. Artists who established themselves in this period but whose careers extended further are listed here.

Western swing developed in the Southwest during the 1930s when Milton Brown, Bob Wills, and others fused hillbilly fiddle styles with blues and big band swing. Western Swing was also popular on the West Coast and influenced the development of the electric guitar, the steel guitar, and the honky-tonk style. From the 1940s through the 1970s, mainstream country music competed with and continually crossed over into popular music. This era saw the establishment of Nashville as the performing and recording capital of country music. Individual styles of this time include the honky-tonk style of the 1940s (Hank Williams Sr., Lefty Frizzell, Ernest Tubb), the increasingly pop-oriented Nashville sound of the 1950s, the Bakersfield sound of the 1960s (especially Buck Owens and his lead guitarist, Don Rich), and the outlaws of the 1970s (especially Waylon Jennings and Willie Nelson). Bluegrass originated with Bill Monroe and His Blue Grass Boys from the late 1930s and 1940s. More than any other style of country music, bluegrass can be defined primarily by its use of acoustic string instruments including the fiddle, mandolin, five-string banjo, guitar, and upright bass. As mainstream country music moved toward electric instruments and larger venues calling for more amplification in the 1960s, bluegrass musicians found themselves aligned

with the folk revival and more conservative country styles, creating an audience different from that of mainstream country music.

The contemporary section (1980s to the present) covers many artists who are still performing today and marks the period when country music became a national and then international industry, competing with and, in many cases, becoming virtually identical to mainstream popular music, especially with the absorption of rock music styles and attitudes into the Nashville mainstream. Since the 1980s, television has been replacing radio as the primary marketing tool for young artists. More recently, as an alternative to the commercialized country music mainstream, alt-country/Americana has become a niche for artists who are often difficult to categorize but who have found varying degrees of commercial success—although rarely on the level of the mainstream superstars. Interestingly, they have audiences who often value the earlier artists of country music or styles not closely associated with traditional country music, such as punk rock.

Because much of the earlier country music recordings were originally released in a singles format, rather than on LP or CD, the collector is faced with a wider variety of anthologies than in most types of popular music. Some of these anthologies are ideal for the beginning listener but are, in many cases, long out-of-print. The best currently available anthologies have been preferred here. In cases where the original release was in LP or CD format, the original album titles are included in the hope that the entire contents will be re-released in their original format. Print publications are of two types: (1) songbooks presenting the words, melodies, and chords of individual songs; or (2) transcriptions in music staff notation or tablature that follow exactly a particular recording of a song. Finally, there has been a growing number of DVDs released in recent years covering early national and especially syndicated country music television shows. These recordings are especially valuable in giving a complete picture of the music and how it was performed, as well as keys to the wide variety of instrumental techniques being used.

GENERAL COLLECTIONS

1379   ★*American Roots Music* [1920–2001] (James Cotton, Earl Scruggs, Jimmie Rodgers, Carter Family, Uncle Dave Macon, Roy Acuff, and others). Palm Pictures: 2075. 2001. 4 CDs.

1380   *American Roots Music* (Bob Wills, Earl Scruggs, Doc Watson, and others). Palm Pictures: 3039. 2001. 2 DVDs.

1381   *Classic Country: Kings of Country* [1941–1980] (Ernest Tubb, Hank Snow, Lefty Frizzell, Hank Williams, Tennessee Ernie Ford, Webb Pierce, Porter Wagoner, Johnny Cash, Ray Price, Don Gibson, Jim Reeves, Marty Robbins, Faron Young, George Jones, Buck Owens, Eddy Arnold, Conway Twitty, Charlie Rich, Waylon Jennings, Willie Nelson.). Time Life: 192382. 2005. CD.

1382   *Classic Country Music: A Smithsonian Collection* [1924–1986] (Gid Tanner, Uncle Dave Macon, Vernon Dalhart, Carter Family, Jimmie Rodgers, Gene Autry, Milton Brown, Roy Acuff, Patsy Montana, Sons of the Pioneers, Bob Wills, Ernest Tubb, Eddy Arnold, Hank Williams, Loretta Lynn, Lefty Frizzell, Goerge Jones, Gram Parsons, Willie Nelson, Emmylou Harris, Alabama, Dolly Parton, Judds, and others). Smithsonian: 42. 1990. 4 CDs.

1383   *Country Guitar Bible*. Hal Leonard: 634025597. c2000.

1384   Phillips, Stacy. *The Dobro Book*. Oak Publications: 825601835. 1977.

1385   *16 Down Home Country Classics* (Rose Maddox, Hazel Dickens and Alice Gerrard, J. E. Mainer, Snuffy Jenkins, Armstrong Twins, Del McCoury, Sam McGee, Louisiana Honey Dippers, Toni Brown, Suzi and Eric Thompson, Maddox Brothers and Rose, Kenny Baker, Bill Neely, Any Old Time String Band, A. P. Carter, Hodges Brothers). Arhoolie: 110. 1998. CD.

PRE–WORLD WAR II

COLLECTIONS

1386   ★*Anthology of American Folk Music, Vols. 1–3* [1927–1932] (Dick Justice, Nelstone's Hawaiians, Clarence Ashley, Coley Jones, Bill and Belle Reed, Buell Kazee, Chubby Parker, Uncle Eck Dunford, Richard Burnett and Leonard Rutherford, Buster Carter and Preston Young, Carolina Tar Heels, G. B. Grayson, Edward L. Crain, Kelly Harrel, Carter Family, Williamson Brothers and Curry, Frank Hutchison, and others). Smithsonian Folkways: 40090. 1997. 6 CDs.

1387   ★*Anthology of American Folk Music, Vol. 4* [1928–1940] (Monroe Brothers, Carter Family,

Uncle Dave Macon, Blue Sky Boys, and others). Revenant Records: 211. 2000. CD.

1388 Cicchetti, Stephen, and Fly Bredenberg. *Old-Time Country Guitar: An Instruction Guide to Old-Timey Solo Fingerpicking Guitar.* Oak Publications: 825601673. 1976. Score.

1389 Kaufman, Alan. *Beginning Old-Time Fiddle.* Oak Publications: 825601886. 1977. Score.

1390 *Old-Time Mountain Ballads* [1926–1929] (G. B. Grayson, B. F. Shelton, Buell Kazee, Clarence Ashley, Uncle Dave Macon, Ernest Stoneman, Blind Alfred Reed, and others). County: 3504. 1995. CD.

1391 *Old-Time Mountain Guitar* [1926–1931] (Sam McGee, Frank Hutchinson, South Georgia Highballers, Roy Harvey, and others). County: 3512. 1998. CD.

INDIVIDUALS AND GROUPS

1392 Acuff, Roy
 1392.1 ★*The Essential Roy Acuff* [1938–1949]. Columbia/Legacy: 90906. 2004. CD.
 1392.2 *King of the Hillbillies, Vol. 1: The First 100 Commercial Sides, Some Never before Reissued* [1936–1942]. JSP: 7799. 2007. 4 CDs.

1393 Allen Brothers. *The Chattanooga Boys: Complete Recorded Works in Chronological Order, Vol. 1, 1927–1930* (Austin and Lee Allen). Document: 8033. 2000. CD.

1394 *Altamont: Black Stringband Music* [1942–1949] (Nathan Frazier, Frank Patterson, Murph Gribble, John Lusk). Rounder Select: CD 0238. 1992. CD.

1395 Ashley, Clarence. *Greenback Dollar, 1929–1933.* County: 3520. 2002. CD.

1396 Autry, Gene
 1396.1 ★*The Essential Gene Autry* [1933–1946]. Columbia: 48957. c1992. CD.
 1396.2 *That Silver Haired Daddy of Mine* [1929–1933]. Bear Family: 15944. 2006. 9 CDs.

1397 Bailey, DeFord. *The Legendary DeFord Bailey: Country Music's First Black Star* [1974–1976]. Tennessee Folklore Society: 122. 1998. CD.

1398 Blue Sky Boys
 1398.1 *The Blue Sky Boys* [1936–1950]. JSP: 7782. 2007. 5 CDs.
 1398.2 *In Concert, 1964.* Rounder: 11536. 1989. CD.
 1398.3 *The Sunny Side of Life* [1936–1950]. Bear Family: 15951. 2003. 5 CDs.

1399 Boggs, Dock. *His Twelve Original Recordings* [1927–1929]. Smithsonian Folkways: 654. 2001. CD.

1400 Britt, Elton. *RCA Years* [1937–1942]. Collector's Choice: 1486. 1998. CD.

1401 Carlisle, Cliff. *Blues Yodeler and Steel Guitar Wizard.* Arhoolie: 7039. 1996. CD.

1402 Carson, Fiddlin' John. *The Complete Recorded Works, Vol. 1* [1923–1924]. Document: 8014. 1997. CD.

1403 Carter Family
 1403.1 ★*The Carter Family: Country Music Hall of Fame* [1936–1938]. MCA: 10088. 1991. CD.
 1403.2 *The Carter Family, 1927–1934: A. P., Sara, Maybelle* [1927–1934]. JSP: 7701. 2001. 5 CDs.
 1403.3 *The Carter Family, 1935–1941, Vol. 2* [1935–1941]. JSP: 7708. 2003. 5 CDs.
 1403.4 *The Carter Family on Border Radio, Vol. 1* [1939]. Arhoolie: 411. 1995. CD.
 1403.5 *In the Shadow of Clinch Mountain* [1927–1941]. Bear Family: 15865. 2000. 12 CDs.

1404 Dalhart, Vernon. *Inducted into the Hall of Fame, 1981* [1920s–1930s]. King: 3820. 1999. CD.

1405 Darby, Tom, and Jimmie Tarlton. *Darby and Tarlton: Complete Recordings* [1927–1933]. Bear Family: 15764. 1995. 3 CDs.

1406 Davis, Jimmie. *Greatest Hits, Finest Performances.* Sun Records: 7014. 1995. CD.

1407 Delmore Brothers
 1407.1 *Brown's Ferry Blues* [1933–1940]. County: 116. 1995. CD.
 1407.2 *Classic Cuts* [1933–1941]. JSP: 7727. 2004. 4 CDs.

1408 Grayson, G. B., and Henry Whitter. *Recordings of Grayson and Whitter, 1928–1930.* County: 3517. 1999. CD.

1409 Griffin, Rex. *Last Letter* [1935–1946]. Bear Family: 15911. 1996. 3 CDs.

1410 Hoosier Hot Shots. *Definitive Hoosier Hotshots Collection* [1935–1942]. Collector's Choice: 378. 2003. 2 CDs.

1411 King, Pee Wee. *Biggest Hits/Country Barn Dance.* Collectables: 7322. 2004. CD.

1412 Lulu Belle and Scotty. *Sweethearts of Country Music.* Gusto: 821. 2008. CD.

1413 Macon, Uncle Dave
  1413.1 *Classic Sides* [1924–1938]. JSP: 7729. 2004. 4 CDs.
  1413.2 ★*Go Long Mule* [1926–1938]. County: 3505. 1994. CD.
  1413.3 *Keep My Skillet Good and Greasy* [1924–1950]. Bear Family: 15978. 2004. 9 CDs.

1414 Mainer, J. E. *1935–1939: The Early Years.* JSP: 77118. 2009. 4 CDs.

1415 ★McGee, Sam. *Complete Recorded Works, 1926–1934, in Chronological Order.* Document: 8036. 1999. CD.

1416 Miller, Polk. *Polk Miller and His Old South Quartette* [1909–1928]. Tompkins Square: 2028. 2008. CD.

1417 ★Montana, Patsy. *Best of Patsy Montana.* Collectors' Choice: 185. 2001. CD.

1418 ★Poole, Charlie. *Old-Time Songs* [1925–1930]. County: 3501. 1993. CD.

1419 Robertson, Eck. *Old-Time Texas Fiddler* [1922–1929]. County: 3515. 1998. CD.

1420 Robison, Carson. *Home, Sweet Home on the Prairie: 25 Cowboy Classics* [1928–1936]. ASV Living Era: 5187. 1996. CD.

1421 Rodgers, Jimmie
  1421.1 ★*The Essential Jimmie Rodgers* [1927–1933]. RCA: 07863-67500. 1997. CD.
  1421.2 *Recordings, 1927–1933.* JSP: 7704. 2002. 5 CDs.
  1421.3 *The Singing Brakeman* [1927–1955]. Bear Family: 15540. 1994. 6 CDs.

1422 Rogers, Roy. *Happy Trails: The Roy Rogers Collection, 1937–1990.* Rhino: 75722. 1999. CD.

1423 Smith, Fiddlin' Arthur. *Fiddlin' Arthur Smith and His Dixieliners* [1937–1940]. County: 3526. 2002. CD.

1424 Sons of the Pioneers
  1424.1 *Sons of the Pioneers: Country Music Hall of Fame.* MCA Nashville: 10090. 1991. CD.
  1424.2 *Ultimate Collection* [1934–1954]. Hip-O: 088 112 815. 2002. CD.

1425 Stoneman, Ernest. *Ernest V. Stoneman: The Unsung Father of Country Music* [1925–1934]. 5-String Productions: 5SPH 001. 2008. 2 CDs.

1426 Tanner, Gid, and the Skillet Lickers. *Old-Time Fiddle Tunes and Songs from North Georgia* [1927–1931]. County: 3509. 1996. CD.

1427 *White Country Blues: A Lighter Shade of Blues* [1926–1938] (Frank Hutchison, Charlie Poole, Darby and Tarlton, Riley Puckett, Roy Acuff, Cliff Carlisle, Callahan Brothers, Allen Brothers, and others). Columbia: 47466. 1993. 2 CDs.

WESTERN SWING

COLLECTIONS

1428 *Doughboys, Playboys, and Cowboys: The Golden Years of Western Swing* [1932–1948] (Milton Brown, Bob Wills, Bill Boyd, Tune Wranglers, Cliff Bruner, Light Crust Doughboys, Adolph Hofner, Hank Penny, Spade Cooley, Tex Williams, Hank Thompson, and others). Proper: 6. 1999. 4 CDs.

1429 *Heroes of Country Music, Vol. 1: Legends of Western Swing* [1932–1957] (Milton Brown, Light Crust Doughboys, Bob Wills, Tex Williams, Leon McAuliffe, Hank Thompson, Cliff Bruner, Hank Penny, Johnnie Lee Wills, Spade Cooley, and others). Rhino: 72440. 1996. CD.

1430 *Legends of Western Swing Guitar* [c1940–c1990] (Billy Dozier, Bob Kiser, Muriel "Zeke" Campbell, Benny Garcia, Cameron Hill, Jimmy Wyble, Junior Barnard). Vestapol: 13062. 2003. DVD.

1431 *Swingbillies: Hillbilly and Western Swing on Modern/Colonial/Flair, 1947–1952* (Jimmie Dolan and His Texas Ramblers, Homer Clemons and His Texas Swingbillies, Rocky Morgan and His Triple R Boys, Tommy Little and the Sunrise Rangers, Jimmy Bryant and the Sons of the Saddle, Bill Woods and His Orange Blossom Playboys, Jody Webb and His Round Up Boys, Papa Cairo and His Boys, Joe Bean and His San

Antonians, Chuck Guillory and His Rhythm Boys, Jack Tucker and Dusty Rhodes, Louie Hooks and His Rhythm Five, Ted Shelton and His Bryan County Boys, Cliff Bruner and His Texas Wanderers). Ace Records: 893. 2003. CD.

1432 *Texas Music, Vol. 2: Western Swing and Honky Tonk*. [1935–1975] (Bob Wills, Light Crust Doughboys, Milton Brown, Cliff Bruner, Ernest Tubb, Floyd Tillman, Harry Choates, Lefty Frizzell, Hank Thompson, Johnny Gimble, Asleep at the Wheel, Ted Daffan, Al Dexter, and others). Rhino: 71782. 1994. CD.

1433 *Western Swing: 40 Bootstompers from the Golden Age*. (Milton Brown and His Musical Brownies, Bob Wills and His Texas Playboys, Bill Boyd and His Cowboy Ramblers, Patsy Montana, Tune Wranglers, Jimmie Revard and His Oklahoma Playboys, Cliff Bruner's Texas Wanderers, W. Lee O'Daniel and His Hillbilly Boys, Nite Owls, Shelly Lee Alley and His Alley Cats, Adolph Hofner, Light Crust Doughboys, Hank Penny and His Radio Cowboys, Al Dexter and His Troopers, Johnnie Lee Wills, Spade Cooley and His Orchestra, and others). Primo: 6008. 2007. 2 CDs.

INDIVIDUALS AND GROUPS

1434 Asleep at the Wheel
    1434.1 *Comin' Right at Ya / Texas Gold* [1972]. Koch: 8172. 2000. CD.
    1434.2 ★*The Swingin' Best of Asleep at the Wheel* [1971–1988]. Sony BMG Music Entertainment: 724000. 2008. CD.

1435 Boyd, Bill [Bill Boyd's Cowboy Ramblers]. *Saturday Night Rag* [1934–1936]. Acrobat: 132. 2004. CD.

1436 Brown, Milton
    1436.1 ★*Complete Recordings of the Father of Western Swing, 1932–1937*. Texas Rose: TXRCD1–TXRCD5. 1996. 5 CDs.
    1436.2 *Western Swing Chronicles, Vol. 1* [1932–1936]. Origin Jazz: 1000. 2001. CD.

1437 Bruner, Cliff. *Cliff Bruner and His Texas Wanderers* [1937–1950]. Bear Family: 15932. 1997. 5 CDs.

1438 Commander Cody and His Lost Planet Airmen. *Lost in the Ozone* [1971]. MCA: 31185. 1990. CD.

1439 Cooley, Spade. *Shame on You*. Collectables: 9582. 2004. CD.

1440 Duncan, Tommy. *Texas Moon*. Bear Family: 15907. 1996. CD.

1441 Hofner, Adolph. *South Texas Swing*. Arhoolie: 7029. 1994. CD.

1442 Light Crust Doughboys. *Light Crust Doughboys, 1936–1941*. Krazy Kat: 37. 2007. CD.

1443 McAuliffe, Leon. *Take It Away the Leon Way!* [1950–1959]. Jasmine Music: 3514. 2001. CD.

1444 Penny, Hank. *Flamin' Mamie, 1938–1941*. Krazy Kat: 31. 2004. CD.

1445 Riders in the Sky. *Best of the West* [1980–1983]. Rounder: 11517. 1988. CD.

1446 ★Thompson, Hank. *Hank Thompson* [1947–1961]. Capitol Nashville: 36901. 1996. CD.

1447 Williams, Tex. *Smoke! Smoke! Smoke!* Country Stars: 55493. 2007. CD.

1448 Wills, Bob
    1448.1 *Anthology* [1935–1973]. Rhino: 70744. 1991. 2 CDs.
    1448.2 ★*The Essential Bob Wills* [1935–1947]. Columbia: 48958. 1992. CD.
    1448.3 ★*San Antonio Rose* [1932–1947]. Bear Family: 15933. 2000. 11 CDs.

MAINSTREAM COUNTRY MUSIC: 1940s–1970s

COLLECTIONS

1449 *All-Time Country and Western Hits* [1946–1953] (Cowboy Copas, Moon Mullican, Bonnie Lou, Grandpa Jones, Delmore Brothers, Reno and Smiley, Wayne Raney, and others). King: 710. 1987. CD.

1450 *Hank Williams Songbook* [1946–1960] (Molly O'Day, Jimmy Dickens, Ray Price, Anita Carter, Marty Robbins, Johnny Cash, and others). Varese Sarabande: 302 066 461 2. 2003. CD.

1451 *The Hee Haw Collection, Vol. 3* [1970s] (Tammy Wynette, George Jones, Faron Young). WEA: M18973. 2005. DVD.

1452 ★*Will the Circle Be Unbroken?* [1972] (Nitty Gritty Dirt Band, Doc Watson, Roy Acuff, Maybelle Carter, Merle Travis, Earl Scruggs, and others). Capitol: 35148. 2002. 2 CDs.

INDIVIDUALS AND GROUPS

1453   Amazing Rhythm Aces. *Stacked Deck.* Sony Music Entertainment: 15120. 2000. CD.

1454   Anderson, Bill. *Definitive Collection* [1960–1978]. MCA Nashville: 6123. 2006. CD.

1455   Anderson, Lynn. *Greatest Hits.* Collector's Choice: 482. 2005. CD.

1456   Arnold, Eddy
   1456.1   *Seven Decades of Hits/Greatest Songs.* Curb: 79108. 2008. 2 CDs.
   1456.2   ★*Ultimate Eddy Arnold* [1946–1967]. BMG Heritage: 56329. 2003. CD.

1457   Atkins, Chet
   1457.1   *Essential Chet Atkins.* RCA: 707677. 2007. 2 CDs.
   1457.2   *Guitar Legend: The RCA Years.* Buddha: 99673. 2000. 2 CDs.

1458   Bandy, Moe. *Honky Tonk Amnesia: The Hard Country Sound of Moe Bandy.* Razor and Tie: 82096. 1996. CD.

1459   Bare, Bobby. *The Best of Bobby Bare* [1958–1969]. Razor and Tie: 2043. 1994. CD.

1460   Brown's Ferry Four. *16 Greatest Hits* [1946–1952]. Starday: 3017. 1998. CD.

1461   Bryant, Jimmy. *Frettin' Fingers: The Lightning Guitar of Jimmy Bryant.* Sundazed: 11134. 2003. 3 CDs.

1462   Byrds. *Sweetheart of the Rodeo* [1968]. Columbia: 65150. 1997. CD.

1463   Campbell, Glen
   1463.1   *All the Best* [1967–1977]. Capitol: 41816. 2003. CD.
   1463.2   *Gentle on My Mind* [1967]. Capitol Nashville: 35230. 2001. CD.

1464   Cash, Johnny
   1464.1   *American Recordings* [1994]. Sony: 717707. 2007. CD.
   1464.2   *Come Along and Ride This Train.* Bear Family: 15563. 1994. 4 CDs.
   1464.3   *Johnny Cash at Folsom Prison and San Quentin* [1968–1969]. Columbia / Legacy: 82876766582. 2006. CD.
   1464.4   *Johnny Cash at "Town Hall Party"* [1958–1959]. Bear Family: BVD20001AT. 2002. DVD.
   1464.5   *Man in Black, 1954–1958* [1954–1958]. Bear Family: 15517. 1994. 5 CDs.
   1464.6   *Man in Black, 1959–1962* [1959–1962]. Bear Family: 15562. 1994. 5 CDs.
   1464.7   ★*Sun Years* [1955–1958]. Rhino: 70950. 1990. CD.

1465   Clark, Guy
   1465.1   *The Essential Guy Clark* [1975–1978]. RCA: 67404. 1997. CD.
   1465.2   *Old No. 1* [1975]. Sony BMG Music Entertainment: 359. 2008. CD.

1466   Clark, Roy. *Greatest Hits* [1963–1976]. Varese Fontana: 5608. 1995. CD.

1467   Cline, Patsy
   1467.1   *Gold.* MCA Nashville: 4119. 2005. 2 CDs.
   1467.2   *Patsy Cline: Sweet Dreams Still* [1950s–1963] (Director: Gregory Hall). MPI Home Video: MPI7738. 2005. DVD.
   1467.3   ★*The Patsy Cline Collection* [1954–1963]. MCA: 10421. 1991. 4 CDs.

1468   Coe, David Allan. *For the Record: The First 10 Years.* Sony: 39585. 1990. CD.

1469   Cooper, Wilma Lee and Stoney. *Very Best of Wilma Lee and Stoney Cooper and the Clinch Mountain Clan* [1956–1963]. Varèse Sarabande: 302066323. 2002. CD.

1470   Copas, Cowboy. *Best of the Best.* King: 502. 2004. CD.

1471   *Country Music Classics with Marty Robbins and Ernest Tubb* [1954–1956] (Albert Gannaway, dir.). Shanachie: 602. 1991. DVD.

1472   *Country Music Classics with Webb Pierce and Chet Atkins* [1954–1957] (Albert Gannaway, dir.). Shanachie: 601. 1998. DVD.

1473   *Country Style, U.S.A.* [1950s] (Jim Reeves, Faron Young, Little Jimmy Dickens, Ernest Tubb, Webb Pierce, and others). Bear Family: BVD 20111-20114. 2007. DVD.

1474   Cramer, Floyd. *Essential Floyd Cramer* [1957–1966]. RCA: 66591. 1995. CD.

1475   Curless, Dick. *Tombstone Every Mile.* Sundazed: 9001. 2004. CD.

1476   Daffan, Ted, and His Texans. *Born to Lose.* Jasmine Music: 3547. 2004. CD.

1477   Davis, Skeeter. *Skeeter Davis* [1954–1973]. RCA Country Legends. Buddha: 99829. 2001. CD.

1478   Dean, Jimmy. *The Complete Columbia Hits and More* [1957–1965]. Collector's Choice: 459. 2004. CD.

1479   Delmore Brothers. *Freight Train Boogie* [1946–1952]. Ace Records: 455. 1993. CD.

1480   Dickens, Little Jimmy. *I'm Little but I'm Loud: The Little Jimmy Dickens Collection* [1949–1969]. Razor and Tie: 2107. 1996. CD.

1481   Dudley, Dave. *The Best of Dave Dudley*. Mercury: 170284. 2002. CD.

1482   Dylan, Bob. *Nashville Skyline*. Sony: 92394. 2004. CD.

1483   Fargo, Donna. *The Best of Donna Fargo*. MCA Nashville: 170243. 2002. CD.

1484   Fender, Freddy. *The Best of Freddy Fender*. MCA Nashville: 844302. 2007. CD.

1485   Flatlanders. *More a Legend Than a Band* [1972] (Joe Ely, Jimmy Dale Gilmore, Butch Hancock). Rounder: SS 34. 1990. CD.

1486   Flying Burrito Brothers. *Hot Burritos! The Flying Burrito Brothers Anthology, 1969–1972*. Interscope Records: 490610. 2000. CD.

1487   ★Foley, Red. *Red Foley: Country Music Hall of Fame* [1944–1953]. MCA: 10084. 1991. CD.

1488   Ford, Tennessee Ernie
    1488.1   *Greatest Hits*. Collectables: 9373. 2003. CD.
    1488.2   *Proper Introduction to Tennessee Ernie Ford: Rock City Boogie*. Proper: 2032. 2004. CD.

1489   Frizzell, Lefty
    1489.1   *Life's Like Poetry*. Bear Family: 15550. 1994. 12 CDs.
    1489.2   *Look What Thoughts Will Do* [1950–1965]. Columbia: C2K 64880. 1997. 2 CDs.
    1489.3   ★*That's the Way Life Goes: The Hit Songs, 1950–1975*. Raven: 195. 2004. CD.

1490   Garland, Hank. *Hank Garland and His Sugar Footers* [1949–1957]. Bear Family: 15551. 1994. CD.

1491   Gayle, Crystal. *The Best of Crystal Gayle* [1977–1995]. Rhino: 78282. 2002. CD.

1492   Gibson, Don. *Don Gibson*. RCA Country Legends. RCA Victor: 97912. 2001. CD.

1493   Gilley, Mickey. *Room Full of Roses / Gilley's Smokin'* [1974–1976]. Audium Entertainment: 8182. 2003. CD.

1494   Glaser, Tompall
    1494.1   *Hillbilly Central #1: My Notorious Youth* [1973–1974]. Bear Family: 16187. 2006. CD.
    1494.2   *Hillbilly Central #2: Another Log on the Fire* [1974–1975]. Bear Family: 16520. 2006. CD.

1495   Haggard, Merle.
    1495.1   *Down Every Road*. Capitol: 35711. 1996. 4 CDs.
    1495.2   ★*Hag: The Best of Merle Haggard* [1962–1994]. Capitol: 62704. 2006. CD.
    1495.3   *Rainbow Stew: Live at Anaheim Stadium*. MCA: 31101. 2003. CD.

1496   Hall, Tom T.
    1496.1   *Definitive Collection*. Hip-O: 5943. 2006. CD.
    1496.2   *The Essential Tom T. Hall: The Story Songs* [1967–1988]. Mercury: 422 834 529. 1998. 2 CDs.

1497   Hazlewood, Lee. *These Boots Are Made for Walkin': The Complete MGM Recordings* [1965–1967]. Ace Records: 860. 2002. CD.

1498   Homer and Jethro. *America's Song Butchers: The Weird World of Homer and Jethro* [1949–1965]. Razor and Tie: 2130. 1997. CD.

1499   Horton, Johnny. *The Essential Johnny Horton: Honky Tonk Man* [1956–1960]. Columbia: 64761. 1996. 2 CDs.

1500   Husky, Ferlin. *Greatest Hits*. Curb: 77341. 1990. CD.

1501   Jackson, Stonewall. *Best of Stonewall Jackson* [1950s–1970s]. Collectors' Choice: 346. 2003. CD.

1502   James, Sonny. *Greatest Hits*. Curb: 77359. 1990. CD.

1503   Jennings, Waylon
    1503.1   *Dreaming My Dreams* [1975]. Buddha: 99826. 2001. CD. Three albums in one.
    1503.2   ★*Essential Waylon Jennings* [1964–2001]. RCA: 88697 07615 2. 2007. CD.
    1503.3   *Honky Tonk Heroes* [1973]. Buddha: 99619. 1999. CD. Three albums in one.
    1503.4   *Ramblin' Man* [1974]. Buddha: 99699. 2000. CD. Three albums in one.

1504   Johnnie and Jack. *Best of Johnnie and Jack.* Koch: 9882. 2005. CD.

1505   Jones, George
    1505.1   *Anniversary: Ten Years of Hits* [1972–1982]. Epic: 38323. 1982. CD.
    1505.2   *The Best of George Jones* [1955–1967]. Rhino: 70531. 1991. CD.
    1505.3   ★*The Essential George Jones: The Spirit of Country* [1955–1987]. Sony / Legacy: 65718. 1998. 2 CDs.
    1505.4   *George Jones: Live Recordings from Church Street Station!* [1950s] (George Jones, Johnny Rodriguez, Mark Gray). MVD Visual: MVD6689. 2007. DVD.
    1505.5   *She Thinks I Still Care: The Complete United Artists Recordings, 1962–1964.* Bear Family: 16818. 2008. 5 CDs.

1506   Jones, Grandpa. *28 Greatest Hits.* King: 5102. 1998. CD.

1507   Kristofferson, Kris. *Essential Kris Kristofferson* [1969–1999]. Sony: 64992. 2004. CD.

1508   Lee, Brenda. *Anthology* [1956–1980]. MCA: 10384. 1991. 2 CDs.

1509   Lewis, Jerry Lee. *The Best of Jerry Lee Lewis* [1957–1980]. Mercury Nashville: 546736. 1999. CD.

1510   Louvin Brothers
    1510.1   *Close Harmony* [1947–1963]. Bear Family: 15561. 1994. 8 CDs.
    1510.2   *Satan Is Real* [1959]. Capitol: 37378. 1996. CD.
    1510.3   ★*When I Stop Dreaming: The Best of the Louvin Brothers* [1952–1962]. Razor and Tie: 2068. 1995. CD.

1511   Lynn, Loretta
    1511.1   *Coal Miner's Daughter* [1980] (Loretta Lynn story; Michael Apted, dir.). Universal: 26753. 2005. DVD.
    1511.2   ★*Definitive Collection* [1964–1978]. MCA Nashville: 453702. 2005. CD.
    1511.3   *Honky Tonk Girl: The Loretta Lynn Collection* [1960–1988]. MCA Nashville: 11070. 1994. 3 CDs.
    1511.4   *Loretta Lynn* [1961–1976]. MCA: 10083. 1991. CD.
    1511.5   *Loretta Lynn: Honky Tonk Girl* [1990] (Mark Hall, dir.). White Star: D3088. 2002. DVD.

1512   Lynn, Loretta, and Conway Twitty. *The Best of Conway Twitty and Loretta Lynn* [1971–1981]. MCA Nashville: 112251. 2000. CD.

1513   Maddox Brothers and Rose. *America's Most Colorful Hillbilly Band* [1946–1951]. Arhoolie: 391. 1993. CD.

1514   Mandrell, Barbara. *The Best of Barbara Mandrell.* MCA Nashville: 170160. 2000. CD.

1515   Maphis, Joe. *Flying Fingers* [1955–1960]. Bear Family: 16103. 1997. CD.

1516   Miller, Roger
    1516.1   ★*All Time Greatest Hits.* Mercury Nashville: B0000233-02. 2003. CD.
    1516.2   *King of the Road: The Genius of Roger Miller* [1957–1985]. Mercury Nashville: 526993. 1995. 3 CDs.

1517   Mullican, Moon. *Moonshine Jamboree.* Ace Records: 458. 1994. CD.

1518   Nelson, Willie
    1518.1   *Nite Life: Greatest Hits and Rare Tracks, 1959–1971.* Rhino: 70987. 1990. CD.
    1518.2   *Phases and Stages* [1974]. Rhino Flashback: 82192. 2008. CD.
    1518.3   ★*Red Headed Stranger* [1975]. Columbia: 63589. 2000. CD.

1519   O'Day, Molly. *Molly O'Day and the Cumberland Mountain Folks* [1946–1951]. Bear Family: 15565. 1992. 2 CDs.

1520   Outlaws. *Wanted: The Outlaws* [1976] (Waylon Jennings, Willie Nelson, Jessi Colter, Tompall Glaser). RCA: 66841. 1996. CD.

1521   Owens, Buck
    1521.1   ★*The Buck Owens Collection, 1959–1990.* Rhino: 71016. 1992. 3 CDs.
    1521.2   *Very Best of Buck Owens, Vol. 1* [1959–1972]. Rhino: 71816. 1994. CD.

1522   Parsons, Gram. *G. P. / Grievous Angel* [1973–1974]. Reprise: 26108. 1990. CD.

1523   Parton, Dolly. *Dolly Parton Live and Well* (Russell Hall, dir.). Sugar Hill: SUG-DVD-3998. 2003. DVD.

1524   Paycheck, Johnny. *16 Biggest Hits* [1972–1980]. Epic: 69968. 1999. CD.

1525   Payne, Leon. *I Love You Because.* Bear Family: 16195. 1999. CD.

1526 Pierce, Webb. *King of the Honky-Tonk* [1952–1959]. Direct Source: 32542. 1994. CD.

1527 Price, Ray. *The Essential Ray Price* [1951–1962]. Columbia / Legacy: 48532. 1991. CD.

1528 Pride, Charley
    1528.1 *Charley Pride*. RCA Country Legends: 99760. 2000. CD.
    1528.2 ★*Essential Charley Pride* [1966–1978]. RCA: 67428. 1997. CD.

1529 Reed, Jerry. *Essential Jerry Reed* [1966–1982]. RCA: 66592. 1995. CD.

1530 Reeves, Jim. *Essential Jim Reeves* [1953–1970]. RCA Nashville / Legacy: 814302. 2006. 2 CDs.

1531 Rich, Charlie
    1531.1 *Feel Like Going Home: The Essential Charlie Rich* [1959–1993]. Epic: 64762. 1997. 2 CDs.
    1531.2 *Ultimate Collection* [1959–1991]. Hip-O: 012 157 597. 2000. CD.

1532 Ritter, Tex
    1532.1 *High Noon* [1942–1957]. Bear Family: 15634. 1994. CD.
    1532.2 *High Noon*. Bear Family: 16356. 2000. 4 CDs.

1533 Robbins, Marty. *The Essential Marty Robbins* [1951–1982]. Sony: 92569. 2005. 2 CDs.

1534 Ronstadt, Linda. *Very Best of Linda Ronstadt* [1967–1993]. Elektra: 76109. 2002. CD.

1535 Shaver, Billy Joe. *Old Five and Dimers Like Me* [1973]. Koch: 7938. 1996. CD.

1536 Shepard, Jean
    1536.1 *Jean Shepard, Honky–Tonk Heroine: Classic Capitol Recordings, 1952–1964*. Country Music Foundation: CMF-021D. 1995. CD.
    1536.2 *Melody Ranch Girl* [1952–1964]. Bear Family: 15905. 1996. 5 CDs.

1537 Smith, Arthur "Guitar Boogie." *Here Comes the Boogie Man* [1940s]. Jasmine Music: 3502. 2000. CD.

1538 Smith, Carl. *The Essential Carl Smith* [1950–1956]. Columbia: 47996. 1991. CD.

1539 Smith, Connie. *The Essential Connie Smith* [1964–1972]. RCA: 66824. 1996. CD.

1540 Snow, Hank. *The Essential Hank Snow* [1950–1973]. RCA: 66931. 1997. CD.

1541 Statler Brothers
    1541.1 *Best of the Statler Brothers, Vol. 1* [1970–1975]. Mercury: 822 524. 1985. CD.
    1541.2 *Definitive Collection*. Mercury Nashville: 3075. 2005. CD.

1542 Stewart, Wynn. *Very Best of Wynn Stewart 1958–1962* [1958–1962]. Varèse Sarabande: 302 066 231 2. 2001. CD.

1543 Tillis, Mel. *Hitsides! 1970–1980*. UMG Recordings: 205. 2006. CD.

1544 Tillman, Floyd. *The Best of Floyd Tillman* [1946–1954]. Collector's Choice: 34707. 1998. CD.

1545 Travis, Merle
    1545.1 *Best of Merle Travis: Sweet Temptation 1946–1953*. Razor and Tie: 25684. 2000. CD.
    1545.2 *Guitar Rags and a Too Fast Past* [1943–1955]. Bear Family: 15637. 1994. 5 CDs.

1546 Tubb, Ernest
    1546.1 *The Complete Live 1965 Show* [1965]. Lost Gold / Camelot: 5018. 1998. 2 CDs.
    1546.2 ★*The Texas Troubadour* [1936–1952]. Proper: 54. 2003. 4 CDs.

1547 Tucker, Tanya. *Greatest Hits* [1972–1975]. Sony BMG Music Entertainment: 724830. 2008. CD.

1548 Twitty, Conway
    1548.1 *Gold*. MCA Nashville: B0005199-02. 2006. CD.
    1548.2 *Silver Anniversary Collection* [1965–1989]. MCA: 8035. 1990. CD.

1549 Wagoner, Porter, and Dolly Parton. *The Essential Porter and Dolly* [1967–1973]. RCA: 66858. 1996. CD.

1550 *Walk the Line* (James Mangold, dir.). 20th Century Fox Home Entertainment: 2232422. 2006. DVD. Johnny Cash story.

1551 Walker, Jerry Jeff
    1551.1 *Ultimate Collection*. UMG Recordings: 112563. 2001. CD.
    1551.2 *Viva Terlingua!* [1973]. MCA: 919. 1990. CD.

1552 Watson, Doc, and Merle Watson
    1552.1 *Black Mountain Rag* [1980]. Rounder: 11620. 2006. CD.
    1552.2 *Doc and the Boys/Live and Pickin'* [1976, 1979]. Southern Music: 1976. 2003. CD.

1552.3 *Essential Doc Watson* [1963–1964]. Vanguard: 45/46. 1990. CD.

1552.4 *Southbound* [1966]. Vanguard: 79213. 1990. CD.

1553 Wells, Kitty. *Essential Recordings* [1950-1959]. Primo: PRMP 6121. 2011. 2 CDs.

1554 West, Dottie. *Dottie West* [1963–1973]. BMG Entertainment: 99828. 2001. CD.

1555 West, Wesley W. "Speedy," and Ivy J. "Jimmy" Bryant. *Stratosphere Boogie: The Flaming Guitars of Speedy West and Jimmy Bryant* [1952–1956]. Razor and Tie: 2067. 1995. CD.

1556 Williams, Hank, [Sr.]

1556.1 ★*Complete Hank Williams* [1946–1952]. Mercury Nashville: 536077. 1998. 10 CDs.

1556.2 *40 Greatest Hits* [1947–1953]. Polydor: 821 233. 1988. 2 CDs.

1556.3 *Hank Williams: Honky Tonk Blues* (Morgan Neville, dir.). PBS American Masters Series. Universal Music and Video Distribution: B0002723-09. 2004. DVD.

1556.4 *The Original Singles Collection—Plus* [1947–1953]. Polydor: 847 194. 1990. 3 CDs.

1557 Wynette, Tammy. *Anniversary, 20 Years of Hits: The First Lady of Country Music* [1966–1980]. Epic: 40625. 1987. CD.

1558 Young, Faron

1558.1 *The Best of Faron Young.* Mercury Nashville: 170205. 2001. CD.

1558.2 *Live Fast, Love Hard: Original Capitol Recordings 1952–1962.* Country Music Foundation: CMF-020D. 1995. CD.

BLUEGRASS

COLLECTIONS

1559 *Angels Are Singing: A Women's Bluegrass Gospel Collection* [1973–2001] (Cox Family, Ginny Hawker, Dry Branch Fire Squad, Kathy Kallick, Laurie Lewis, Rhonda Vincent, and others). Rounder: 11661-0485-2. 2002. CD.

1560 *Appalachian Stomp: Bluegrass Classics* [1949–1989] (Bill Monroe, Flatt and Scruggs, Jimmy Martin, Country Gentlemen, Del McCoury, Alison Krauss, and others). Rhino: 71870. 1995. CD.

1561 *The Best of Bluegrass, Vol. 1: Standards* [1948–1963] (Stanley Brothers, Carl Story, Flatt and Scruggs, Country Gentlemen, Red Allen, Osborne Brothers, and others). Mercury: 848 979. 1991. CD.

1562 *The Bluegrass Album, Vol. 1* [1980] (J.D. Crowe, Bobby Hicks, Doyle Lawson, Todd Phillips, Tony Rice). Rounder: CD 0140. 1991. CD.

1563 *Blue Ribbon Bluegrass* (Cox Family, Nashville Bluegrass Band, Alison Krauss, Ricky Skaggs, Johnson Mountain Boys, Laurie Lewis, Tony Rice, J. D. Crowe, and others). Rounder: 11. 1993. CD.

1564 *Hand-Picked: 25 Years of Bluegrass on Rounder Records* [1970–1995] (J.D. Crowe, Del McCoury, Dry Branch Fire Squad, David Grisman, Tony Rice, Johnson Mountain Boys, Tony Trischka, Allison Krauss, Nashville Bluegrass Band, Bela Fleck, Cox Family, Ricky Skaggs, and others). Rounder: 25. 1995. 2 CDs.

1565 *High Lonesome: The Story of Bluegrass Music* (Rachel Liebling, writer, dir.). Shanachie: SH 604. 1991. DVD.

1566 *Mountain Music Bluegrass Style* [1958–1959] (Tex Logan, Mike Seeger, John Cohen, Don Stover, B. Lilly, Chubby Anthony, Earl Taylor and the Stoney Mountain Boys, Bob Baker and the Pike County Boys, Smiley Hobbs, Bob Yellin, Elmer Pegdon, Earl Taylor, Walter Hensley, Sam Hutchins, Jimmie Grier, Jerry Stuart, Pete Kuykendall). Smithsonian Folkways: 40038. 1991. CD.

1567 *Top of the Hill Bluegrass* (Peter Rowan, Nashville Bluegrass Band, Doc Watson, Lonesome River Band, Seldom Scene, Tim O'Brien, Jerry Douglas, New Grass Revival, Doyle Lawson, Hot Rize, Ricky Skaggs, and others). Sugar Hill: 9201. 1995. CD.

INDIVIDUALS AND GROUPS

1568 Allen, Red, and Frank Wakefield. *Folkways Years, 1964–1983.* Smithsonian Folkways: 40127. 2001. CD.

1569 Auldridge, Mike. *Dobro / Blues and Bluegrass* [1972]. Takoma: 8914. 2002. CD.

1570 Baker, Kenny. *Master Fiddler* [1968–1983]. County: 2705. 1993. CD.

1571 Blake, Norman. *Whiskey before Breakfast* [1976]. Rounder Select: CD 0063. 1994. CD.

1572 Blue Highway. *Blue Highway* [1999]. Ceili Music: 2002. 2001. CD.

1573 Brody, David. *Kenny Baker Fiddle.* Oak Publications: 825602246. 1979. Score.

1574 Bush, Sam. *Glamour and Grits.* Sugar Hill: 3849. 1996. CD.

1575 Clements, Vassar. *Hillbilly Jazz* [1974]. Flying Fish: 70101. 1992. CD.

1576 Clifton, Bill. *Bill Clifton: The Early Years, 1957–1958.* Rounder: 1021. 1992. CD.

1577 Country Gazette. *Hello Operator . . . This Is Country Gazette* [1976–1987]. Flying Fish: 70112. 1992. CD.

1578 Country Gentlemen
   1578.1 *Complete Vanguard Recordings.* Vanguard: 79711. 2002. CD.
   1578.2 *Country Songs, Old and New* [1959]. Smithsonian Folkways: 40004. 1990. CD.
   1578.3 *Early Rebel Recordings, 1962–1971.* Rebel: 4002. 1998. 4 CDs.

1579 Cox Family. *Beyond the City.* Rounder: CD 0327. 1995. CD.

1580 ★Crowe, J. D. *J. D. Crowe and the New South* [1975]. Rounder: CD 0044. 1986. CD.

1581 Dillards
   1581.1 *There Is a Time, 1963–1970.* Vanguard: 131/132. 1991. CD.
   1581.2 *Wheatstraw Suite* [1968]. Collector's Choice: 280. 2002. CD.

1582 Douglas, Jerry. *Slide Rule.* Sugar Hill: 3797. 1992. CD.

1583 Flatt, Lester, Earl Scruggs, and the Foggy Mountain Boys
   1583.1 *Best of the Flatt and Scruggs TV Show: Classic Bluegrass from 1956 to 1962.* Shanachie: SH 611 and 612. 2007. 2 DVDs.
   1583.2 ★*The Complete Mercury Sessions* [1948–1950]. Mercury Nashville: 0000070-02. 2003. CD.
   1583.3 ★*The Essential Flatt and Scruggs: 'Tis Sweet to Be Remembered* [1950–1967]. Columbia: 64877. 1997. 2 CDs.

1583.4 *Flatt and Scruggs, 1948–1959.* Bear Family: 15472. 1994. 4 CDs.
1583.5 *Flatt and Scruggs, 1959–1963.* Bear Family: 15559. 1994. 4 CDs.

1584 Fleck, Béla. *Bluegrass Sessions: Tales from the Acoustic Planet, Vol. 2.* Warner Bros.: 47332. 1999. CD.

1585 Graves, Josh. *Josh Graves.* Rebel: 1747. 1998. CD.

1586 Grisman, David. *The David Grisman Rounder Compact Disc.* Rounder: CD 0069. 1990. CD.

1587 Hartford, John
   1587.1 ★*Aereo Plain* [1971]. Rounder: CD 0366. 1997. CD.
   1587.2 *Me Oh My, How the Time Does Fly* [1976–1987]. Flying Fish: 70440. 1992. CD.

1588 Jim and Jesse
   1588.1 *Bluegrass and More* [1960–1969]. Bear Family: 15716. 1994. 5 CDs.
   1588.2 *Jim and Jesse, 1952–1955.* Bear Family: 15635. 1994. CD.
   1588.3 *Jim and Jesse Story: 24 Greatest Hits.* CMH Records: 9454. 2007. CD.

1589 Johnson Mountain Boys
   1589.1 *At the Old Schoolhouse.* Rounder: 0260/0261. 1989. 2 CDs.
   1589.2 *Blue Diamond.* Rounder: 293. 1993. CD.

1590 Kentucky Colonels. *Appalachian Swing!* [1964]. SANDP: 717. 2005. CD.

1591 Krauss, Alison
   1591.1 *Every Time You Say Goodbye.* Rounder: CD 0285. 1992. CD.
   1591.2 ★*Now That I've Found You: A Collection* [1987–1994]. Rounder: CD 0325. 1995. CD.

1592 Lawson, Doyle. *Rock My Soul* [1981]. Sugar Hill: 3717. 1990. CD.

1593 Lewis, Laurie. *The Oak and the Laurel* [1987]. Rounder: CD 0340. 1995. CD.

1594 Martin, Jimmy
   1594.1 *Don't Cry to Me.* Thrill Jockey: 145. 2004. CD.
   1594.2 *Greatest Hits.* Gusto: 603. 2006. CD.
   1594.3 *Jimmy Martin and the Sunny Mountain Boys* [1954–1974]. Bear Family: 15705. 1994. 5 CDs.

1595 McCoury, Del
   1595.1 *The Cold Hard Facts.* Rounder: CD 0363. 1996. CD.
   1595.2 *Del and the Boys* [2001]. McCoury Music: 10. 2007. CD.
   1595.3 *Don't Stop the Music.* Rounder: CD 0245. 1990. CD.

1596 Monroe, Bill
   1596.1 ★*Blue Grass, 1950–1958.* Bear Family: 15423. 1994. 5 CDs.
   1596.2 *Blue Grass, 1959–1969.* Bear Family: 15529. 1994. 4 CDs.
   1596.3 *Blue Grass, 1970–1979.* Bear Family: 15606. 1995. 4 CDs.
   1596.4 ★*Blue Moon of Kentucky, 1936–1949.* Bear Family: 16399. 2003. 6 CDs.
   1596.5 *The Music of Bill Monroe from 1936 to 1994.* MCA: 11048. 1994. 4 CDs.
   1596.6 *My Last Days on Earth, Blue Grass, 1981–1994.* Bear Family: 16637. 2006. 6 CDs.
   1596.7 ★*16 Gems* [1945–1949]. Columbia: 53908. 1996. CD.

1597 Nashville Bluegrass Band. *The Boys Are Back in Town.* Sugar Hill: 3778. 1990. CD.

1598 New Grass Revival
   1598.1 *Fly through the Country / When the Storm Is Over* [1975, 1977]. Flying Fish: 70032. 1992. CD.
   1598.2 *Live* [1983]. Sugar Hill: 3771. 1989. CD.

1599 O'Brien, Tim. *Red on Blonde.* Sugar Hill: 3853. 1996. CD.

1600 Old and in the Way. *Old and in the Way* [1973]. Grateful Dead: 40222. 1996. CD.

1601 Osborne Brothers
   1601.1 *Country Bluegrass* [1965–1975]. Universal Special Markets: 20976. 1996. CD.
   1601.2 *The Osborne Brothers, 1956–1968.* Bear Family: 15598. 1995. 4 CDs.
   1601.3 *The Osborne Brothers, 1968–1974.* Bear Family: 15748. 1995. 4 CDs.

1602 Reno, Don, and Red Smiley
   1602.1 *Don Reno and Red Smiley and the Tennessee Cut–Ups, 1959–1963.* Gusto: GT4-0955-2. 2006. 4 CDs.
   1602.2 *Sweethearts in Heaven: The Complete Dot Recordings 1957–1964.* Bear Family: 16728. 2005. CD.

1603 Rice, Tony
   1603.1 *58957: The Bluegrass Guitar Collection.* Rounder: 11622. 2003. CD.
   1603.2 *Manzanita (Tony Rice Unit)* [1979]. Rounder: CD 0092. 1998. CD.

1604 Rowan, Peter. *All on a Rising Day.* Sugar Hill: 3791. 1991. CD.

1605 Scruggs, Earl
   1605.1 *Earl Scruggs and the 5-String Banjo.* Hal Leonard. 2005. Score with CD.
   1605.2 *Essential Earl Scruggs* [1946–1980s]. Sony: 90858. 2004. 2 CDs.

1606 Seeger, Pete. *Pete Seeger's Rainbow Quest* [1960s] (The Stanley Brothers and the Clinch Mountain Boys with Cousin Emmy; Doc Watson with Clint Howard and Fred Price). Shanachie: 605. 2005. DVD.

1607 Seldom Scene
   1607.1 *Act 3* [1973]. Rebel: 1528. 1994. CD.
   1607.2 *Old Train* [1974]. Rebel: 1536. 1994. CD.
   1607.3 *Recorded Live at the Cellar Door* [1974]. Rebel: 1103. 1997. CD.

1608 Sparks, Larry
   1608.1 *Classic Bluegrass.* Rebel: 1107. 1989. CD.
   1608.2 *Last Suit You Wear.* McCoury Music: 4. 2007. CD.

1609 Stanley Brothers
   1609.1 ★*The Complete Columbia Stanley Brothers* [1949–1952]. Columbia: 53798. 1996. CD.
   1609.2 ★*The Complete Mercury Recordings* [1953–1958]. Mercury: B0000534-02. 2003. 2 CDs.
   1609.3 *Earliest Recordings: The Complete Rich-R-Tone 78s* [1947–1952]. Revenant: 203. 1997. CD.
   1609.4 *The Early Starday-King Years, 1958–1961.* Starday / King Records: 7000. 1993. 4 CDs.
   1609.5 *Riding That Midnight Train: The Starday-King Years, 1958–1961.* Westside: 820. 1999. CD.

1610 Stanley, Ralph
   1610.1 *Clinch Mountain Country.* Rebel: 5001. 1997. 2 CDs.
   1610.2 *Saturday Night; Sunday Morning.* Freeland: 9001. 1992. 2 CDs.

1611 Story, Carl. *Bluegrass Gospel Collection* [1976]. CMH Records: 8788. 2004. CD.

1612 Strength in Numbers. *The Telluride Sessions* [1989] (Sam Bush, Béla Fleck, Jerry Douglas, Mark O'Connor, Edgar Meyer). MCA: 70033. 1998. CD.

1613 Traum, Happy. *Bluegrass Guitar*. Oak Publications: 825601533. 1974. Score.

1614 Vincent, Rhonda. *One Step Ahead*. Rounder: 610497. 2003. CD.

1615 Watson, Doc. *The Songs of Doc Watson*. Oak Publications: 9825601207. 1971. Score.

1616 Wernick, Peter
    1616.1 *Bluegrass Banjo*. Oak Publications: 0825601487. 1974. Score with CD.
    1616.2 *Bluegrass Songbook*. Oak Publications: OK 63198. 1976. Score.

1617 Wiseman, Mac
    1617.1 *Early Dot Recordings, Vol. 3* [1952–1954]. County: 113. 1992. CD.
    1617.2 *Mac Wiseman Story* [1976]. CMH Records: 9001. 1996. CD.

CONTEMPORARY: 1980s–PRESENT

COLLECTIONS

1618 *Big Book of Country Rock*. Hal Leonard: HL00311748. 2008. Score.

1619 *Grand Ole Opry at Carnegie Hall* (Trace Adkins, Vince Gill, Little Jimmy Dickens, Trisha Yearwood, Charley Pride, Alison Krauss and Union Station, Ricky Skaggs, and others). Sony BMG Music Entertainment: 82876-81116-9. 2006. DVD.

1620 *O Brother, Where Art Thou?* (Joel Coen, dir.). Touchstone Home Video: 21654. 2001. DVD.

INDIVIDUALS AND GROUPS

1621 Adkins, Trace. *Greatest Hits Collection, Vol. 1*. Capitol: 81512. 2003. CD.

1622 Alabama. *Essential Alabama* [1980–1998]. RCA: 68635. 2005. CD.

1623 Anderson, John. *Greatest Hits*. Warner Bros.: 25169. 2009. CD.

1624 Bellamy Brothers. *Best of Bellamy Brothers* [1976–1987]. Curb: 77554. 1992. CD.

1625 Black, Clint
    1625.1 ★*Greatest Hits* [1989–1994]. RCA: 66671. 1996. CD.
    1625.2 *Killin' Time* [1989]. Sony BMG Music Entertainment: 700034. 2006. CD.

1626 Bogguss, Suzy. *20 Greatest Hits*. Capitol: 40691. 2002. CD.

1627 Brooks, Garth
    1627.1 *Garth Brooks* [1989]. Pearl: 107. 2007. CD.
    1627.2 *No Fences* [1990]. Pearl: 114. 2007. CD.
    1627.3 *Ropin' the Wind* [1991]. Pearl: 145. 2007. CD.
    1627.4 ★*Ultimate Hits*. Pearl: 213. 2007. CD.

1628 ★Brooks and Dunn. *Greatest Hits Collection* [1991–1997]. Arista: 18852. 1997. CD.

1629 Brown, Junior. *12 Shades of Brown* [1990]. Curb: 77635. 1993. CD.

1630 Byrd, Tracy. *Definitive Collection*. MCA Nashville: 8135. 2007. CD.

1631 Carpenter, Mary-Chapin. *Come On Come On*. Columbia: 48881. 1992. CD.

1632 Cash, Rosanne
    1632.1 ★*Seven Year Ache* [1981]. Sony: 77637. 2005. CD.
    1632.2 *Very Best of Rosanne Cash*. Sony: 86996. 2005. CD.

1633 Chesney, Kenny. *Greatest Hits*. BNA Records: 67976. 2000. CD.

1634 Chesnutt, Mark. *Longnecks and Short Stories*. MCA: 10530. 1992. CD.

1635 Crowell, Rodney. *Diamonds and Dirt* [1988]. Sony BMG Music Entertainment: 61612 2008. CD.

1636 Cyrus, Billy Ray. *The Best of Billy Ray Cyrus* [1992–1998]. Mercury Nashville: 170165. 2003. CD.

1637 Dalton, Lacy J. *Anthology*. Renaissance: RMED00228. 2000. CD.

1638 Daniels, Charlie. *Decade of Hits*. Sony: 65694. 1999. CD.

1639 Davies, Gail. *Gail Davies* [1978]. Varèse Sarabande: 66348. 2002. CD.

1640 Desert Rose Band. *A Dozen Roses: Greatest Hits* [1987–1990]. Curb: 77571. 1991. CD.

1641   Dixie Chicks
    1641.1   *Fly.* Monument: 69678. 1999. CD.
    1641.2   *Home.* Columbia: 86840. 2002. CD.
    1641.3   *Wide Open Spaces.* Monument: 68195. 1998. CD.

1642   Ely, Joe
    1642.1   *The Best of Joe Ely* [1977–1995]. MCA: 088 170 151. 2000. CD.
    1642.2   *Honky Tonk Masquerade* [1978]. Universal Music Special Markets: CBUJ 0743. 2007. CD.

1643   Evans, Sara. *Born to Fly / Restless* [2000, 2003]. Sony: 36844. 2008. CD.

1644   Fricke, Janie. *Anthology.* Renaissance: RMED00206. 1999. CD.

1645   Gatlin Brothers. *Best of the Gatlins: All the Gold in California* [1975–1988]. Sony BMG Custom Marketing Group: 723655. 2008. CD.

1646   Gatton, Danny. *88 Elmira St.* Elektra: 61032. 1991. CD.

1647   Gill, Vince
    1647.1   ★*The Best of Vince Gill.* MCA Nashville: 92302. 2007. CD.
    1647.2   *When I Call Your Name.* MCA: 42321. 1989. CD.

1648   Gilmore, Jimmie Dale
    1648.1   *After Awhile.* Nonesuch: 61148. 1991. CD.
    1648.2   *Fair and Square.* Hightone: 8011. 1988. CD.

1649   Gosdin, Vern. *Chiseled in Stone* [1987]. Sony BMG Music Entertainment: 40982. 2008. CD.

1650   Greenwood, Lee. *The Best of Lee Greenwood.* 20th Century Masters—the Millennium Collection. MCA Nashville: 170264. 2002. CD.

1651   Griffith, Nanci. *The Best of Nanci Griffith.* MCA Nashville: 170191. 2001. CD.

1652   Harris, Emmylou
    1652.1   ★*Anthology: The Warner/Reprise Years* [1975–1990]. Warner Archives / Rhino: 76705. 2001. 2 CDs.
    1652.2   *At the Ryman.* Reprise: 26664. 1992. CD.

1653   Highwaymen. *The Highwaymen* [1985]. Sony BMG Music Entertainment: 722888. 2008. CD.

1654   Hill, Faith. *Breathe.* Warner Bros.: 47373. 1999. CD.

1655   Hodgson, Lee. *Hot Country: A Comprehensive Guide to Lead and Rhythm Country Guitar Playing.* Sanctuary: 186074138X. 1997. Score with CD.

1656   Jackson, Alan
    1656.1   *Greatest Hits Collection* [1989–1994]. Arista: 18801. 1995. CD.
    1656.2   *Here in the Real World* [1989]. BMG Special Products: 46537. 2001. CD.

1657   Judds. *Number One Hits.* Curb: 77965. 2000. CD.

1658   Keith, Toby. *The Best of Toby Keith* [1993–1998]. Mercury Nashville: B000770702. 2007. CD.

1659   lang, k.d. *Shadowland.* Sire: 25724. 1988. CD.

1660   Lee, Albert. *Speechless / Gagged but Not Bound* [1987, 1988]. Raven: 276. 2008. CD.

1661   Lee, Johnny. *Greatest Hits.* Rhino: 236348. 2007. CD.

1662   Loveless, Patty. *Definitive Collection.* MCA Nashville: 334402. 2005. CD.

1663   Lovett, Lyle. *Lyle Lovett.* Curb / MCA: 31307. 1986. CD.

1664   Mavericks. *Definitive Collection* [1992–1999]. MCA Nashville: 2501. 2004. CD.

1665   McBride, Martina. *The Way That I Am* [1993]. Collectables: 8400. 2004. CD.

1666   McEntire, Reba
    1666.1   ★*Greatest Hits* [1984–1987]. MCA: 5979. 1987. CD.
    1666.2   *Reba #1's* [1982–2003]. MCA Nashville: B0005366-02. 2005. CD.

1667   McGraw, Tim. *Greatest Hits.* Curb: 77978. 2000. CD.

1668   Milsap, Ronnie. *Ultimate Ronnie Milsap.* RCA Nashville: 58517. 2004. CD.

1669   Murphey, Michael Martin. *Cowboy Songs.* Warner Bros.: 26308. 1990. CD.

1670   Oak Ridge Boys. *Gold* [1973–1988]. MCA Nashville: B0008142-02. 2007. 2 CDs.

1671   Paisley, Brad
    1671.1   *Time Well Wasted.* Arista: 69642. 2005. CD.
    1671.2   *Who Needs Pictures.* Arista: 18871. 1999. CD.

1672   Parton, Dolly
    1672.1   ★*Essential Dolly Parton* [1966–2000].
        RCA: 69240. 2005. CD.
    1672.2   *Mission Chapel Memories 1971–1975*
        [1971–1975]. Raven: 121. 2001. CD.
    1672.3   *Ultimate Dolly Parton.* RCA: 52008.
        2003. CD.

1673   Parton, Dolly, Linda Ronstadt, and Emmylou
    Harris. *Trio.* Warner Bros.: 25491. 1986. CD.

1674   Rimes, LeAnn. *Blue.* Curb: 77821. 1996. CD.

1675   Rogers, Kenny. *Ten Years of Gold.* EMI Special
    Products: 18080. 1995. CD.

1676   Skaggs, Ricky. *Waitin' for the Sun to Shine /
    Highways and Heartaches* [1981, 1982]. Gott
    Discs: GOTTCD025. 2000. CD.

1677   Stewart, Gary. *Out of Hand; Your Place or Mine*
    [1975–1977]. Koch: 8249. 2001. CD.

1678   ★Strait, George. *Greatest Hits* [1981–1984].
    MCA: 5567. 1985. CD.

1679   Stuart, Marty. *Let There Be Country.* Sony: 59965.
    2003. CD.

1680   Texas Tornados. *Texas Tornados* (Freddie Fender,
    Flaco Jimenez, Augie Meyer, Doug Sahm).
    Reprise: 26251. 1990. CD.

1681   Travis, Randy
    1681.1   *I Told You So—the Ultimate Hits of Randy
        Travis* [1985-2009]. Warner Bros.:
        518189-2. 2009. 2 CDs.
    1681.2   ★*Storms of Life* [1986]. Rhino Flashback:
        384892. 2008. CD.

1682   Tritt, Travis. *Very Best of Travis Tritt* [1990–
    2000]. Rhino: 74817. 2007. CD.

1683   Twain, Shania. *Greatest Hits* [1995–2002].
    Mercury Nashville: B0003072-02. 2004. CD.

1684   *Urban Cowboy* (directed by James Bridges).
    Paramount: 12854. 2002. DVD.

1685   Van Shelton, Ricky. *16 Biggest Hits* [1987–1993].
    Sony: 41336. 2009. CD.

1686   Watson, Gene. *Greatest Hits* [1975–1980]. Curb:
    77393. 1990. CD.

1687   White, Bryan. *Greatest Hits.* Asylum / Warner
    Bros.: 237308. 2007. CD.

1688   Whitley, Keith. *Keith Whitley.* BMG Heritage:
    65103. 2002. CD.

1689   Williams, Don. *The Best of Don Williams, Vol. 1*
    [1975–1982]. MCA Nashville: 112250. 2000. CD.

1690   Williams, Hank, Jr.
    1690.1   ★*Hank Williams Jr.'s Greatest Hits.* Curb:
        77638. 1993. CD.
    1690.2   *Whiskey Bent and Hell Bound* [1979].
        Curb: 77724. 1995. CD.

1691   Yearwood, Trisha. *Hearts in Armor.* MCA Special
    Products: 924502. 2007. CD.

1692   Yoakam, Dwight
    1692.1   *Guitars, Cadillacs, Etc., Etc.* Reprise:
        25372. 1986. CD.
    1692.2   *This Time.* Reprise: 45241. 1993. CD.

ALT-COUNTRY/AMERICANA

1693   Adams, Ryan. *Heartbreaker.* Bloodshot: BS 071.
    2000. CD.

1694   Allen, Terry. *Lubbock (on Everything)* [1979].
    Sugar Hill: 1047. 1995. CD.

1695   Alvin, Dave. *Interstate City.* Hightone: 8074.
    1996. CD.

1696   BR5-49. *BR5-49.* BMG: 45922. 2003. CD.

1697   Contenders. *Contenders* [1977]. Gadfly: 283.
    2002. CD.

1698   Cowboy Junkies. *Trinity Session* [1987]. RCA:
    8568. 1990. CD.

1699   Cowboy Nation. *We Do as We Please.* Paras:
    6004. 2001. CD.

1700   Dement, Iris. *Infamous Angel.* Warner Bros.:
    45238. 1993. CD.

1701   Earle, Steve
    1701.1   *Ain't Ever Satisfied: The Steve Earle
        Collection* [1985–1991]. Hip-O: 40006.
        1996. 2 CDs.
    1701.2   ★*Guitar Town* [1986]. MCA Nashville:
        170265. 2002. CD.
    1701.3   *I Feel Alright.* Warner Bros.: 46201.
        1996. CD.

1702   Earle, Steve, and Del McCoury. *The Mountain.*
    E Squared: 1064. 1999. CD.

1703   Freakwater. *Old Paint.* Thrill Jockey: 22. 1995. CD.

1704   Fulks, Robbie. *Country Love Songs.* Bloodshot:
    BS 011. 1996. CD.

1705   Jayhawks. *Tomorrow the Green Grass*. American Recordings: 72732. 2011. 2 CDs. Includes bonus tracks.

1706   Keen, Robert Earl, Jr. *Best* [1992–1995]. Koch: 4114. 2007. CD.

1707   Miller, Buddy. *Best of the Hightone Years* [1995–2002]. Shout! Factory: 10973. 2008. CD.

1708   Scott, Darrell. *Aloha from Nashville*. Sugar Hill: 3864. 1997. CD.

1709   Uncle Tupelo
    1709.1   *89/93: An Anthology* [1989–1993]. Sony: 62223. 2002. CD.
    1709.2   ★Uncle Tupelo. *No Depression* [1990]. Sony: 86427. 2003. CD.

1710   Van Zandt, Townes. *Anthology 1968–1979*. Fuel: 128. 2001. CD.

1711   Watson, Dale. *Cheatin' Heart Attack*. Hightone: 8061. 1995. CD.

1712   Welch, Gillian. *Revival* [1996]. Acony Records: ACNY-0101. 2001. CD.

1713   Whiskeytown
    1713.1   *Faithless Street*. Outpost Records: 30002. 1998. CD.
    1713.2   *Strangers Almanac* [1997]. Geffen Records: 30005. 2008. CD.

1714   Williams, Lucinda
    1714.1   *Car Wheels on a Gravel Road*. Island / Mercury: 558338. 1998. CD.
    1714.2   *Sweet Old World*. Chameleon / WEA: 61351. 1992. CD.

6

Rock

Compiled by **THOMAS BELL** *and* **JOE C. CLARK**

GENERAL COLLECTIONS   *103*
ELVIS PRESLEY AND ROCKABILLY   *103*
EARLY ROCK 'N' ROLL   *104*
TEEN IDOLS, INSTRUMENTALS, AND DANCE HITS   *105*
BRITISH INVASION   *105*
THE U.S. ROCK SCENE IN THE SIXTIES   *107*
   Surf, Bubblegum, Garage Bands, and Pop   *107*
   Folk-Rock   *107*
   The West Coast and Texas   *108*
BRITISH FOLK-ROCK   *109*
GUITAR HEROES   *110*
INFLUENCES ON THE 1980s: 1960s AND 1970s BANDS   *110*
THE 1970s   *111*
   Singer-Songwriters   *111*
   Los Angeles   *112*
   U.S. Hitmakers   *112*
   British Superstars   *113*
   Southern Rock   *113*
   Heavy Metal/Hard Rock   *113*
   Art Rock and Rock Theater   *114*
   Early Rappers   *115*
   Punk and New Wave: U.S.   *115*
   Punk and New Wave: U.K.   *116*
POST-PUNK   *117*
WOMEN IN ROCK SINCE THE 1970s   *117*
ROCK: THE 1980s AND BEYOND   *118*
   Mainstream   *118*
   Alternative   *119*
DANCE MUSIC, ELECTRONICA, ETC.   *123*
POST-ROCK   *124*

The deepest roots of "rock" may be traced to African American spirituals and Anglo-American folk music. In the 1950s, rock emerged as a style distinct from its diverse influences and elements that include, but are not limited to, gospel, jazz, blues, soul, rhythm and blues, folk, and country. It is characterized by its core performing unit, the rock band, which often consists of a rhythm section of bass and drums, with singers and electric guitarists as featured virtuosos.

The history of rock has seen many movements and developments. Early rock and roll included several seminal figures such as Bill Haley, Chuck Berry, and Little Richard, but none enjoyed the initial attention accorded to Elvis Presley. From 1959 through 1963, "teen idols," instrumentals, and dance hits prevailed in the music marketed to young record buyers. The British Invasion spearheaded by the Beatles in February 1964 brought a wave of young British rock acts to America, reaffirming through imitation the music of the 1950s rock pioneers and their blues and country models. That is not to say that young American musicians were not developing their own new music for their peers. The U.S. rock scene in the 1960s produced distinctive subgenres such as surf music, bubblegum, garage bands, and pop. Folk rock as developed by Bob Dylan adopted the kinds of traditional American folk music to deepen the emotional range of rock, and it led to the British folk rock of Donovan and Richard Thompson. Music being made in the West Coast cities of San Francisco and Los Angeles and in Texas brought forth new styles (the Jefferson Airplane, Frank Zappa) and new legends (the Doors, the Grateful Dead, Janis Joplin). The period spanning the late 1960s and the 1970s was the heyday of guitar heroes like Jimi Hendrix, Eric Clapton, and Jimmy Page, yet it was also the time of then-little-known bands like Big Star and the Velvet Underground that were influences on 1980s bands.

As the 1970s unfolded, many subgenres of rock bloomed, among them singer-songwriters, Los Angeles singers, hitmakers, and superstars (some of them British superstars at that). A classy, at times self-conscious brand of music was the art rock and "rock theater." Heavier sounds emerged through gritty timbres and louder amplification heard most forcefully in southern rock, hard rock, and heavy metal. As loud were the American and British forms of punk rock and new wave, which were initially brash but later came to have lyrics of considerable wit and irony. Rock in the 1980s and since has evolved to include styles alternative to and even beyond the prevailing "pop" and "classic" radio mainstreams; punk, new wave, and no wave would come to be called postpunk, shoegaze, house, and electronica. At the same time, women in rock since the 1970s have written and recorded an enduring, at times self-referential stream of work.

The wide availability of many kinds of rock music records past and present has allowed many listeners to explore and choose without care for who came first or whether the recording act was popular or even well-known at the time of recording. This kind of postmodern openness to any recording is one factor in the continued presence of seemingly outdated genres such as psychedelic, experimental (Beefheart, Zappa), guitar rock (Clapton, Hendrix), and underground bands (some of whom would become ubiquitous shortly after their demise). Long after their breakups, bands who were virtually unknown to general audiences (like the Velvet Underground, the Silver Apples, Can, and the Contortions, to name a few) have proven powerfully influential over time through their records. Whatever the permutation and currency, rock in these styles can be found vacillating between order and chaos, returning to its roots (as U2 with Johnny Cash and B. B. King) or taking pages from experimental, boundary-pushing formal composers (as Can with Stockhausen, or Sonic Youth with Cage).

Albums are frequently reissued, usually with new label numbers and occasionally on a different label. While some reissues are identical to the original release, older titles are often rereleased (and often remastered) as "special editions" or commemorative editions that include extra tracks, additional printed material. Some bands boast multiple greatest hits collections, with some organized by time period and others by label.

For the librarian new to collecting rock music, reviews of the recordings abound. Good places to start are the All Music Guide (www.allmusic.com) and the CD hotlist (http://cdhotlist.btol.com). Metacritic (www.metacritic.com/music) gives albums a cumulative score based on reviews from both mainstream and independent publications with links to reviews that appear online. Other sources of reviews include National Public Radio (www.npr.org/music), *Billboard* (www.billboard.com), and the magazines *Mojo*, *Under the Radar*, *Spin*, and *Rolling Stone*.

To aid study and imitation of famous rock performances, especially those with fast and extensive guitar solos, notated transcription books are sometimes available as companions to the records. Hal Leonard and Warner Brothers publish transcription books of all rock genres and for most mainstream rock artists. For easy-to-read notation that accurately reflects the guitar parts, guitarists should seek those publications issued as "authentic tablature," "guitar recorded versions,"

"note-for-note transcriptions," "guitar tablature edition," and "guitar play- along" series with CDs. Similar editions are also available for keyboard, drums, and bass, with transcriptions of single artists or genre collections. Avoid "easy guitar" and piano/guitar books, as they generally provide watered down arrangements for piano with guitar chords added as an afterthought.

GENERAL COLLECTIONS

1715 *Acoustic Guitar Bible.* Hal Leonard: HL00690432. 2000. Score.

1716 *Acoustic Guitar Tab White Pages.* Hal Leonard: HL00699590. 2003. Score.

1717 *Acoustic Rock Guitar Bible.* Hal Leonard: HL00690625. 2003. Score.

1718 *Bass Tab White Pages.* Hal Leonard: HL00690508. 2001. Score.

1719 *Classic Rock Guitar Bible.* Hal Leonard: HL00690662. 2004. Score.

1720 *The Colossal Guitar Songbook.* Hal Leonard: HL00690454. 2001. Score.

1721 *Disco Guitar Bible.* Hal Leonard: HL00690627. 2003. Score.

1722 *Folk-Rock Guitar Bible.* Hal Leonard: HL00690464. 2000. Score.

1723 *Grunge Guitar Bible.* Hal Leonard: HL00690649. 2003. Score.

1724 *Guitar Tab White Pages.* Hal Leonard: HL00690471. 2001. Score.

1725 *Guitar Tab White Pages, Vol. 2.* Hal Leonard: HL00699557. 2003. Score.

1726 *Guitar Tab White Pages, Vol. 3.* Hal Leonard: HL00690791. 2005. Score.

1727 *Hard Rock Bass Bible.* Hal Leonard: HL00690746. 2004. Score.

1728 *Hard Rock Guitar Bible.* Hal Leonard: HL00690453. 2001. Score.

1729 *Pop/Rock Bass Bible.* Hal Leonard: HL00690747. 2005. Score.

1730 *Pop/Rock Guitar Bible.* Hal Leonard: HL00690517. 2002. Score.

1731 *Rock Bass Bible.* Hal Leonard: HL00690446. 2000. Score.

1732 *Rock-Blues Guitar Bible.* Hal Leonard: HL00690450. 2000. Score.

1733 *Rock Guitar Bible.* Hal Leonard: HL00690313. 1998. Score.

1734 *Southern Rock Guitar Bible.* Hal Leonard: HL00690723. 2004. Score.

ELVIS PRESLEY AND ROCKABILLY

1735 Lewis, Jerry Lee
   1735.1 *The Definitive Collection.* Hip-O: B0004259-02. 2005. CD.
   1735.2 ★*18 Original Greatest Hits* [1956–1963]. Rhino: 70255. 1984. CD.

1736 ★Perkins, Carl. *Original Sun Greatest Hits* [1955–1957]. Rhino: 75890. 1986. CD.

1737 Presley, Elvis
   1737.1 ★*Elvis: 30 #1 Hits* [1956–1976]. RCA: 68079. 2002. CD.
   1737.2 *Elvis, from Nashville to Memphis* [1960–1969]. RCA: 07863 66160-2. 1993. 5 CDs.
   1737.3 *Elvis Presley* [1956]. RCA: 88697907952. 2011. 2 CDs.
   1737.4 *Elvis '68 Comeback* [1968]. Sony BMG Music Entertainment: 82876 70505-9. 2006. DVD.
   1737.5 *The Guitars of Elvis* (Scotty Moore, Hank Garland, James Burton). Hal Leonard: HL00696507. 1993.
   1737.6 *The King of Rock 'n' Roll: The Complete 50's Masters* [1953–1958]. RCA: 07863-66050-2. 1992. 5 CDs.

1738 *Rockabilly Riot.* Sanctuary: 06076-84632-2. 2003. CD.

1739 *Rockin' Bones: 1950s Punk and Rockabilly.* Rhino: R2 73346. 2006. 4 CDs.

1740 *Sun Records: 50th Anniversary.* Varèse Sarabande: 302 066 386 2. 2002. 3 CDs.

1741 ★*Sun Records' Greatest Hits* [1952–1958] (Elvis Presley, Carl Perkins, Jerry Lee Lewis, Billy Lee Riley, Johnny Cash, Roy Orbison, Howlin' Wolf, and Rufus Thomas). Curb: D2-07029. 2010. CD.

1742 *Sun Rockabilly: The Classic Recordings* [1955–1959] (Billy Lee Riley, Warren Smith, Malcolm Yellvington, and others). Rounder: SS 37. 1990. CD.

EARLY ROCK 'N' ROLL

COLLECTIONS

1743 *Best of Doo Wop Ballads* [1954–1961] (Dion and the Belmonts, Five Satins, Dells, Moonglows, Penguins, Flamingos, Spaniels, and others). Rhino: 75763. 1989. CD.

1744 *Best of Doo Wop Uptempo* [1954–1963] (Del-Vikings, El Dorados, Silhouettes, Crows, Cadillacs, Dion and the Belmonts, Frankie Lymon and the Teenagers, and others). Rhino: 75764. 1989. CD.

1745 ★*The Doo Wop Box: 101 Vocal Group Gems from the Golden Age of Rock 'n' Roll* [1948–1987] (Orioles, Ravens, Five Keys, Crows, Drifters, Spaniels, Chords, Penguins, Moonglows, Turbans, Platters, Cadillacs, Teenagers, Flamingos, Clovers, Five Satins, Dells, Del-Vikings, Silhouettes, Chantels, Impressions, Elegants, Imperials, Dion and the Belmonts, Skyliners, Impalas, Zodiacs, Jive Five, Randy and the Rainbows, and others). Rhino: 71463. 1993. 4 CDs.

1746 *Early Rock Guitar Bible*. Hal Leonard: HL00690680. 2004. Score.

1747 *Genuine Rockabilly Guitar Hits*. Hal Leonard: HL00694848. 1993. Score.

1748 *The Golden Era of Rock 'n' Roll* [1954–1963] (Bill Haley, Crows, Joe Turner, Moonglows, Chuck Berry, Monotones, Rick Nelson, Eddie Cochran, and others). Hip-O: 225102. 2004. 3 CDs.

1749 ★*Legends of Guitar: Rock—The '50s, Vol. 1* (Chuck Berry, Bo Diddley, Bill Haley, Duane Eddy, Les Paul, Eddie Cochran, Link Wray, Gene Vincent, Buddy Holly, Carl Perkins, and others). Rhino: 70719. 1990. CD.

1750 ★*Legends of Guitar: Rock—The '50s, Vol. 2* (Rick Nelson, Billy Riley, Ike Turner, Mickey Baker, Buddy Holly, Scotty Moore, Johnny Burnette, Gene Vincent, Santo and Johnny, Bill Haley, Eddie Cochran, Chuck Berry, Duane Eddy, Ritchie Valens, and others). Rhino: 70561. 1991. CD.

1751 *Let There Be Drums, Vol. 1: The '50s* [1949–1961] (Sandy Nelson, Bill Haley, Bo Diddley, Little Richard, Preston Epps, Fats Domino, Buddy Holly, Chuck Berry, Cozy Cole, Jerry Lee Lewis, Johnny and the Hurricanes, Coasters, Dion, Ray Charles, and others). Rhino (Max Weinberg): 71547. 1994. CD.

1752 *Rock and Roll: The Early Days* [1948–1957] (Chords, Wynonie Harris, Big Mama Thornton, Muddy Waters, Joe Turner, Buddy Holly, Elvis Presley, Carl Perkins, Chuck Berry, Bo Diddley, Little Richard, Jerry Lee Lewis). RCA: PCD1-5463. 1985. CD.

1753 *Rockabilly Guitar Bible*. Hal Leonard: HL00690570. 2003. Score.

1754 *Roots of Rock: 1945–1956*. Time-Life: 2RNR-30. 1990. CD.

1755 *The Roots of Rock 'n' Roll, 1946–1954* (Johnny Ace, Hank Ballard, Tiny Bradshaw, Jackie Brenston, Roy Brown, Ruth Brown, Professor Longhair, Clovers, Delmore Brothers, Fats Domino, Drifters, Five Royales, Tennessee Ernie Ford, Roscoe Gordon, Guitar Slim, Bill Haley, Lionel Hampton, Wynonie Harris, Howlin' Wolf, Ivory Joe Hunter, Louis Jordan, B. B. King, Little Richard, Percy Mayfield, Amos Milburn, Roy Milton, Orioles, Lloyd Price, Ravens, Johnnie Ray, Rosetta Tharpe, Big Mama Thornton, Merle Travis, Joe Turner, T-Bone Walker, Muddy Waters, Hank Williams, Chuck Willis, and others). Hip-O: 2252. 2004. 3 CDs.

1756 *Street Corner Serenade: The Greatest Doo-Wop Hits of the '50s and '60s* (Teenagers, Del-Vikings, Cadillacs, Penguins, Elegants, Dion and the Belmonts, Moonglows, Platters, Drifters, Flamingos, Crests, Dells, Marcels, Silhouettes, Five Satins, and others). Rhino: 75835. 1999. CD.

1757 *25 Classic Doo-Wop Ballads*. Varèse Sarabande: 3020665552. 2004. CD.

1758 *Ultimate Rock and Roll Collection: The 50s*. Collectables: COL-2514. 1997. CD.

INDIVIDUALS AND GROUPS

1759 Berry, Chuck
    1759.1 *Chuck Berry*. Hal Leonard: HL00692385. 1999. Score.
    1759.2 *Chuck Berry: The Chess Box* [1955–1973]. Chess: CHD3-80001. 1988. 3 CDs.
    1759.3 ★*The Definitive Collection*. Chess: B0004417-02. 2006. CD.

1760 ★Cochran, Eddie. *Somethin' Else: The Fine Lookin' Hits of Eddie Cochran* [1956–1960]. Razor and Tie: 2162. 1998. CD.

1761 ★Diddley, Bo. *The Chess Box* [1955–1968].
      Chess: CHD2-19502. 1988. 2 CDs.

1762 Everly Brothers
      1762.1 ★*Cadence Classics: Their 20 Greatest Hits*
                  [1957–1960]. Rhino: 5258. 1985. CD.
      1762.2 *Golden Hits* [1960–1962]. Warner Bros.:
                  1471-2. 1988. CD.
      1762.3 *Walk Right Back: The Everly Brothers on
                  Warner Brothers* [1960–1969]. Warner
                  Archives: 45164. 1993. 2 CDs.

1763 Haley, Bill
      1763.1 *The Best of Bill Haley and His Comets,
                  1951–1954*. MCA: MCAD-5539. 2004. CD.
      1763.2 *Rock around the Clock*. Decca:
                  B0001705-02. 2004. CD.

1764 Hawkins, Ronnie. *The Best of Ronnie Hawkins and
      the Hawks* [1959–1963]. Rhino: 70966. 1990. CD.

1765 Holly, Buddy. *The Buddy Holly Collection* [1957–
      1958]. MCA: MCAD2-10883. 1993. 2 CDs.

1766 Little Richard
      1766.1 *The Essential Little Richard*. Specialty:
                  SPCD 2154. 1985. CD.
      1766.2 ★*The Georgia Peach* [1955–1957].
                  Specialty: SPCD-7012-2. 1991. CD.

1767 Lymon, Frankie. *The Best of Frankie Lymon and
      the Teenagers* [1956–1960]. Rhino: 70918.
      1989. CD.

1768 Platters
      1768.1 *All-Time Greatest Hits*. Mercury:
                  B0001755-02. 2004. CD.
      1768.2 *The Magic Touch: An Anthology* [1955–
                  1961]. Mercury: 314 510 314-2. 1991.
                  2 CDs.

1769 Valens, Ritchie. *La Bamba and Other Hits*.
      Flashback: R2 78172. 2004. CD.

1770 Vincent, Gene. *Gene Vincent* [1956–1958].
      Capitol Collector's Series. Capitol: 94074.
      1990. CD.

TEEN IDOLS, INSTRUMENTALS, AND DANCE HITS

COLLECTIONS

1771 *Rock Instrumental Classics, Vol. 2: The 60s* [1959–
      1968] (Ventures, Lonnie Mack, Tornadoes,
      Duane Eddy, Mason Williams, and others).
      Rhino: 71602. 1994. CD.

1772 *25 Rockin Instrumentals*. Varèse Sarabande: 302
      066 484 2. 2003. CD.

INDIVIDUALS AND GROUPS

1773 Darin, Bobby. *The Ultimate Bobby Darin* [1958–
      1966]. Warner: 9-27606-2. 1986. CD.

1774 Dion. *Greatest Hits* (Belmonts). Repertoire: 4745-
      WG. 1999. CD.

1775 Eddy, Duane. *Twang Thang: The Duane Eddy
      Anthology* [1957–1986]. Rhino: 71223. 1993.
      2 CDs.

1776 Four Seasons
      1776.1 *In Season: Frankie Valli and the Four
                  Seasons Anthology* [1962–1976]. Rhino:
                  72466. 2001. 2 CDs.
      1776.2 *The Very Best of Frankie Valli and the
                  Four Seasons*. Rhino: R2 74494.
                  1998. CD.

1777 Francis, Connie. *Gold*. Polydor / Universal:
      B0004022-02. 2005. 2 CDs.

1778 Nelson, Rick. *Greatest Hits*. Capitol: 09463-
      12262-2-9. 2005. CD.

1779 Orbison, Roy. *16 Biggest Hits*. Sony: 741335.
      2009. CD.

1780 Pitney, Gene. *Anthology* [1961–1968]. Rhino:
      75896 (Musicor). 1986. CD.

1781 Sedaka, Neil. *All Time Greatest Hits* [1958–
      1963]. RCA: 6876-2-R. 1988. CD.

1782 Shannon, Del
      1782.1 *Greatest Hits* [1961–1965]. Rhino:
                  70977. 1990. CD.
      1782.2 *25 All-Time Greatest Hits* [1961–1965].
                  Varèse: 302 066 270 2. 2001. CD.

1783 Vee, Bobby. *The Very Best of Bobby Vee*. EMI;
      Capitol; Collectables: 2744. 1999. CD.

1784 Ventures. *Walk Don't Run: The Best of the
      Ventures* [1960–1968]. EMI: 93451. 1990. CD.

1785 Wray, Link. *Rumble! The Best of Link Wray*
      [1958–1976]. Rhino: 71222. 1993. CD.

BRITISH INVASION

COLLECTIONS

1786 *The American Roots of the British Invasion*
      (Shirelles, Isley Brothers, Little Willie John,

Larry Williams, John Lee Hooker, Little Richard, Carl Perkins, Buck Owens, Bobby Day, Gene Pitney, and others). Varèse Sarabande: 302 066 334 2. 2002. CD.

1787   *The British Beat: The Best of the 60s.* Shout! Factory: 826663-10355. 2007. 3 CDs.

1788   *The British Invasion* [1963–1967] (Dusty Springfield, Who, Small Faces, and others). Hip-O: 184102. 2004. 3 CDs.

1789   *British Invasion.* Hip-O: B0007082-02. 2006. 2 CDs.

1790   *British Invasion: Guitar Classics.* Hal Leonard: HL00690213. 1998. Score.

1791   ★*Nuggets II: Original Artifacts from the British Empire and Beyond* [1964–1969] (Creation, Move, Action, Easybeats, Pretty Things, Marmalade, Small Faces, Los Bravos, Van Morrison, Troggs, Golden Earing, Davy Jones [David Bowie], Love Sculpture, Cuby and the Blizzards, Guess Who, Status Quo, Os Mutantes, and others). Rhino: 76787. 1998. 4 CDs.

1792   *25 Hits from the British Invasion* (Zombies, Chad and Jeremy, Donovan, Dave Clark Five, Petula Clark, Animals, Tornadoes, Yardbirds, Searchers, Ian Whitcomb, Hollies, Lulu, Easybeats, Small Faces, and others). Varèse Sarabande: 302 066 333 2. 2002. CD.

INDIVIDUALS AND GROUPS

1793   Animals. *Best of the Animals* [1964–1965]. Abkco: 4324 2 (MGM). 1987. CD.

1794   Beatles

   1794.1   ★*Abbey Road* [1969]. Capitol: 0946 3 82468 2 4. 2009. CD.

   1794.2   *The Beatles* [White Album] [1968]. Capitol: 0946 3 82466 2 6. 2009. 2 CDs.

   1794.3   *The Beatles: Complete Scores.* Hal Leonard: HL00673228. 1993. Score.

   1794.4   *The Beatles: Past Masters.* Capitol: 50999 6 96764 2 0. 2009. 2 CDs.

   1794.5   *Beatles for Sale.* Capitol: 0946 3 82414 2 3. 2009. CD.

   1794.6   *A Hard Day's Night* [1964]

       a)   Capitol: 0946 3 82413 2 4. 2009. CD.

       b)   Miramax Home Entertainment: 18301. 2002. 2 DVDs.

   1794.7   *Help!* Capitol: 0946 3 82415 2 2. 2009. CD.

   1794.8   ★*Please Please Me.* Capitol: 0946 3 82416 2 1. 2009. CD.

   1794.9   ★*Revolver.* Capitol: 0946 3 82417 2 0. 2009. CD.

   1794.10   ★*Rubber Soul.* Capitol: 0946 3 82418 2 9. 2009. CD.

   1794.11   ★*Sgt. Pepper's Lonely Hearts Club Band* [1967]. Capitol: 0946 3 82419 2 8. 2009. CD.

   1794.12   ★*With the Beatles.* Capitol: 0946 3 82420 2 4. 2009. CD.

1795   Bee Gees. *Bee Gees Greatest.* Polydor: 800 071-2. 1986. 2 CDs.

1796   Dave Clark Five. *The Hits.* Universal TV UK: 1781774 2008. CD.

1797   Hollies. *The Hollies' Greatest Hits.* Epic / Legacy: EK 86463. 2002. CD.

1798   Kinks

   1798.1   *The Kink Kronikles* [1966–1970]. Reprise: 6454-2. 1989. 2 CDs.

   1798.2   ★*The Ultimate Collection.* Sanctuary: SANDD 109. 2002. 2 CDs.

1799   Move. *The Best of the Move.* Repertoire. 1997. CD.

1800   Pink Floyd

   1800.1   *Saucerful of Secrets* [1968]. Capitol: CDP 0777 7 46383 2 6. 1994. CD.

   1800.2   *Works* [1967–1973]. Capitol: 46478 (12276). 1983. CD.

1801   Procol Harum. *Greatest Hits.* A&M: 31454 0523 2. 1996. CD.

1802   Rolling Stones

   1802.1   *Aftermath* [1966]. Abkco: 9476-2 (London 476). 2002. CD.

   1802.2   ★*Beggars Banquet* [1968]. Abkco: 9539-2 (London 539). 2002. CD.

   1802.3   ★*Hot Rocks* [1964–1971]. Abkco: 9667-2 (London 606/7). 1986. 2 CDs.

   1802.4   *Let It Bleed* [1969]. Abkco: 9004-2 (London 4). 2002. CD.

   1802.5   *Out of Our Heads* [1965]. Abkco: 94292. 2002. CD.

   1802.6   *The Rolling Stones Guitar Anthology.* Hal Leonard: HL00690631. 2003.

   1802.7   *The Rolling Stones, Now!* [1964]. Abkco: 9420-2 (London 420). 2002. CD.

   1802.8   *Singles Collection: The London Years* [1963–1969]. Abkco: 9231-2. 1989. 3 CDs.

1803 Spencer Davis Group. *The Best of the Spencer Davis Group* [1964–1967] (Stevie Winwood). EMI: 46598 (United Artists). 1987. CD.

1804 Traffic
   1804.1 ★*Mr. Fantasy* [1967]. Island: 314 542 823-2. 2000. CD.
   1804.2 *Smiling Phases* [1967–1974]. Island: 314 510 553-2. 1991. 2 CDs.
   1804.3 *Traffic* [1968]. Island: 314 542 852-2 (UA 6676). 2001. CD.

1805 The Who
   1805.1 *Best of the Who*. Hal Leonard: HL00690447. 2001. Score.
   1805.2 *The Kids Are Alright* [1979]. Pioneer Entertainment: 12103. 2003. 2 DVDs.
   1805.3 *Live at Leeds* [1970]. MCA: MCAD-11215. 1995. CD.
   1805.4 *30 Years of Maximum R&B* [1964–1989]. MCA: MCAD4-11020. 1994. 4 CDs.
   1805.5 *Tommy* [1969]. MCA: MCAD11417. 1996. CD.
   1805.6 *Who's Next* [1971]. MCA: MCAD-37217. 1984. CD.
   1805.7 ★*Who's Next*. Deluxe ed. [1971]. MCA: 088 113 056-2. 2003. 2 CDs.

1806 ★Yardbirds. *Ultimate!* Rhino: R2 79825. 2001. 2 CDs.

1807 ★Zombies. *Odyssey and Oracle* [1968]. Big Beat: 181. 1998. CD.

THE U.S. ROCK SCENE IN THE SIXTIES
Surf, Bubblegum, Garage Bands, and Pop

COLLECTIONS

1808 ★*Nuggets: Artifacts of the First Psychedelic Era* [1964–1969] (Standells, Seeds, Count Five, Easybeats, Syndicate of Sound, Monkees, Troggs, Amboy Dukes, Blues Magoos, Castaways, Music Machine, Five Americans, Nightcrawlers, Electric Prunes, Shadows of Knight, Strawberry Alarm Clock, Barbarians, Cyrkle, Choir, and others). Rhino: R2 75466. 1998. 4 CDs.

1809 *Nuggets: A Classic Collection from the Psychedelic Sixties* [1964–1969] (Standells, Seeds, Count Five, Easybeats, Syndicate of Sound, Monkees, Troggs, Amboy Dukes, and others). Rhino: 75892. 1986. CD.

1810 ★*Surfin' Hits* [1962–1965] (Beach Boys, Jan and Dean, Surfaris, Chantays, Dick Dale, Marketts, and others). Rhino: 70089. 1989. CD.

1811 *25 All-Time Greatest Bubblegum Hits* [1967–1973] (Tommy Roe, Tommy James, Ohio Express, Monkees, 1910 Fruitgum Co., Dawn, Archies, and others). Varèse Sarabande: 302 066 132 2. 2000. CD.

INDIVIDUALS AND GROUPS

1812 Beach Boys
   1812.1 ★*Pet Sounds* [1966]. Capitol: 26266 (T-2458). 2001. CD.
   1812.2 ★*The Sounds of Summer: The Very Best of the Beach Boys*. Capitol: 82710. 2003. CD.

1813 James, Tommy. *Anthology* (Shondells). Rhino: R2 70920. 1989. CD.

1814 Jan and Dean. *Surf City: The Best of Jan and Dean* [1961–1966]. EMI: 92772. 1990. CD.

1815 Monkees. *Greatest Hits* [1966–1968]. Rhino: 72190. 1995. CD.

1816 Rascals. *The Very Best of the Rascals* [1965–1971]. Rhino / Atlantic: 71277. 1993. CD.

1817 Revere, Paul. *Greatest Hits* [1963–1967] (Raiders). Columbia: CK66009. 2000. CD.

1818 Righteous Brothers. *The Very Best of the Righteous Brothers: Unchained Melody* [1964–1968]. Verve: 847248-2. 1990. CD.

1819 Ryder, Mitch. *Rev Up: The Best of Mitch Ryder and the Detroit Wheels* [1966–1971]. Rhino: 70941. 1989. CD.

Folk-Rock

COLLECTION

1820 *Songs of Protest* [1962–1971] (Barry McGuire, Sonny Bono, Turtles, Country Joe, Rascals, Eric Burdon, Janis Ian, Temptations, Edwin Starr, Phil Ochs, Donovan, and others). Rhino: 70734. 1991. CD.

INDIVIDUALS AND GROUPS

1821 The Band
   1821.1 ★*The Band* [1969]. Capitol: 25389 (132). 2000. CD.
   1821.2 *Greatest Hits*. Capitol: 24941. 2000. CD.

1821.3 *The Last Waltz* [1976] (Robbie Roberston; Martin Scorsese, dir.). MGM Home Entertainment: 1003426. 2002. DVD.

1821.4 *Music from Big Pink* [1968]. Capitol: 25390 (2955). 2000. CD.

1822 Byrds

1822.1 *Sweetheart of the Rodeo.* Columbia: 87189. 2003. 2 CDs.

1822.2 ★*20 Essential Tracks from the Boxed Set* [1965–1990]. Columbia: CK 47884. 1992. CD.

1823 Dylan, Bob

1823.1 ★*Blonde on Blonde* [1966]. Columbia: 92400. 2004. CD.

1823.2 *Blood on the Tracks* [1974]. Columbia: 92398. 2004. CD.

1823.3 *Bob Dylan: Don't Look Back* [1965] (Joan Baez, Donovan). New Video Group: NVG-9824. 2007. 2 DVDs, companion book, and flipbook.

1823.4 ★*Bringing It All Back Home* [1964]. Columbia: 92401. 2003. CD.

1823.5 Dylan, Bob, and the Band. *The Basement Tapes* [1967]. Columbia: 08229. 2009. 2 CDs.

1823.6 ★*Highway 61 Revisited* [1965]. Columbia: 92399. 2004. CD.

1823.7 *John Wesley Harding* [1967]. Columbia: 92395. 2004. CD.

1823.8 *Live 1966: The "Royal Albert Hall" Concert.* Bootleg Series 4. Columbia: C2K 65759. 1998. 2 CDs.

1823.9 *Nashville Skyline* [1969]. Columbia: 92394. 2003. CD.

1823.10 *No Direction Home* (Joan Baez, Allan Ginsberg, Maria Muldaur, Pete Seeger, Liam Clancy, Mavis Staples). Paramount: 3105. 2005. 2 DVDs.

1823.11 *Time out of Mind.* Columbia: 68556. 1997. CD.

1824 Lovin' Spoonful. *Greatest Hits* [1965–1968]. Buddha: 74465-99716-2. 2000. CD.

1825 Mamas and the Papas. *Greatest Hits.* MCA: 11740. 1998. CD.

1826 Simon and Garfunkel

1826.1 *Bridge over Troubled Water* [1970]. Columbia: 66004. 2001. CD.

1826.2 ★*Greatest Hits* [1965–1970]. Columbia: CK 31350. 1985. CD.

1827 Sonny and Cher. *The Beat Goes On: The Best of Sonny and Cher* [1965–1967]. Atco: 91762-2. 1991. CD.

1828 Turtles. *Save the Turtles: The Turtles Greatest Hits.* FloEdCo: 48002. 2009. CD.

The West Coast and Texas

COLLECTIONS

1829 *San Francisco Nights* [1965–1968] (Beau Brummels, Youngbloods, Sly and the Family Stone, Quicksilver Messenger Service, Country Joe and the Fish, Blue Cheer, and others). Rhino: 70536. 1991. CD.

1830 *Texas Music, Vol. 3: Garage Bands and Psychedelia* [1960s] (Roy Head, Bobby Fuller, Sam the Sham, Sir Douglas, Steve Miller, 13th Floor Elevators, Johnny Winter, and others). Rhino: 71783. 1994. CD.

INDIVIDUALS AND GROUPS

1831 ★Big Brother and the Holding Company. *Cheap Thrills* [1968] (Janis Joplin). Columbia: CK 65784 (9700). 1999. CD.

1832 Buffalo Springfield

1832.1 *Buffalo Springfield Again* [1967]. Atco: 33-226-2. 1990. CD.

1832.2 ★*Retrospective: The Best of Buffalo Springfield* [1966–1968]. Atco: 38-105-2. 1988. CD.

1833 Country Joe and the Fish. *The Collected Country Joe and the Fish* [1965–1970]. Vanguard: VCD-111. 1987. CD.

1834 ★Creedence Clearwater Revival. *Chronicle* [1968–1972]. Fantasy: CCR2. 1991. CD.

1835 Doors

1835.1 ★*The Doors* [1967]. Elektra / Rhino: R2 101184. 2007. CD.

1835.2 *The Doors Essential Guitar Collection.* Hal Leonard: HL00690348. 2000. Score.

1835.3 *The Doors Legacy: The Absolute Best* [1967–1971]. Rhino: 73889. 2003. 2 CDs.

1835.4 *The Very Best of the Doors* [1967–1971]. Elektra / Rhino: R2 277180. 2007. 2 CDs.

1836 Flying Burrito Brothers. *Hot Burritos! The Flying Burrito Brothers Anthology* [1969–1972]. A&M: 069 490 610-2. 2000. 2 CDs.

1837 Grateful Dead

    1837.1 *American Beauty* [1970]. Rhino: 74397. 2003. CD.

    1837.2 *Ladies and Gentlemen . . . The Grateful Dead: Fillmore East, April 1971.* Arista: 14075. 2000. 4 CDs.

    1837.3 ★*Live Dead* [1969]. Rhino: 74395. 2003. CD.

    1837.4 *Workingman's Dead* [1970]. Rhino: 74396. 2003. CD.

1838 Jefferson Airplane

    1838.1 *Jefferson Airplane Loves You* [1962–1974]. RCA: 07863-61110-2. 1992. 3 CDs.

    1838.2 ★*Surrealistic Pillow* [1967]. RCA: 82876 5035102. 2003. CD.

1839 Joplin, Janis. *Pearl* [1971]. Columbia: CK 65786 (30322). 1999. CD.

1840 Miller, Steve. *The Best of Steve Miller, 1968–1973.* Capitol: 95271. 1990. CD.

1841 Moby Grape. *Vintage: The Very Best of Moby Grape* [1967–1970]. Columbia: C2K 53041. 1993. 2 CDs.

1842 Nelson, Tracy. *The Best of Tracy Nelson / Mother Earth* [1968–1972]. Reprise Archives: 46232. 1996. CD.

1843 Quicksilver Messenger Service

    1843.1 *Happy Trails* [1968–1969]. Capitol: 91215 (120). 1988. CD.

    1843.2 *Quicksilver Messenger Service* [1968]. Capitol: 91146 (2904). 1988. CD.

    1843.3 *Sons of Mercury* [1968–1975]. Rhino: 70747. 1991. 2 CDs.

1844 Sahm, Doug. *The Best of Doug Sahm and the Sir Douglas Quintet* [1968–1975]. Mercury: 846 586-2. 1990. CD.

1845 Santana

    1845.1 *Abraxas* [1970]. Columbia: CK 65490 (30130). 1998. CD.

    1845.2 ★*Santana* [1969]. Columbia: C2K 90272. 2004. 2 CDs.

    1845.3 *Santana's Greatest Hits.* Hal Leonard: HL00690031. 1996. Score.

    1845.4 *Viva Santana!* [1967–1986]. Columbia: C2K 44344. 1988. 2 CDs.

1846 Sly and the Family Stone

    1846.1 *The Essential Sly and the Family Stone* [1968–1973]. Epic: E2K 86867. 2002. 2 CDs.

    1846.2 ★*Greatest Hits* [1968–1973]. Epic: 75910 2. 2007. CD.

1847 Spirit. *Time Circle* [1968–1972]. Epic: E2K 47363. 1991. 2 CDs.

1848 Steppenwolf. *All Time Greatest Hits* [1968–1970]. MCA: 088 112 063-2. 1999. CD.

1849 13th Floor Elevators. *Easter Everywhere* [1967]. Collectables: COL-CD-0553. 1993. CD.

1850 Zappa, Frank

    1850.1 *Absolutely Free* [1967] (Mothers of Invention). Rykodisc: RCD-10502. 1995. CD.

    1850.2 *Freak Out!* [1966] (Mothers of Invention). Rykodisc: 10501. 1995. CD.

    1850.3 *Hot Rats* [1969]. Rykodisc: RCD-10508. 1995. CD.

    1850.4 *Strictly Commercial: The Best of Frank Zappa* [1966–1988]. Rykodisc: RCD-40500. 1995. CD.

    1850.5 ★*We're Only in It for the Money* [1968] (Mothers of Invention). Rykodisc: RCD-10503. 1995. CD.

BRITISH FOLK-ROCK

1851 Donovan

    1851.1 *Greatest Hits* [1966–1968]. Epic: EK 65730 (26439). 1999. CD.

    1851.2 *Troubadour: The Definitive Collection* [1964–1976]. Epic: E2K 46986. 1992. 2 CDs.

1852 Drake, Nick

    1852.1 *Five Leaves Left* [1969]. Island: 842915. 2000. CD.

    1852.2 *Way to Blue: An Introduction to Nick Drake* [1969–1972]. Hannibal: HNCD 1386. 1994. CD.

1853 Fairport Convention

    1853.1 *Liege and Lief* [1969]. A&M: 75021-4257-2. 1990. CD.

    1853.2 ★*Unhalfbricking* [1969]. Island: IMCD 293. 2003. CD.

    1853.3 *What We Did on Our Holidays* [1968]. Universal Island: 063597. 2003. CD.

1854 Incredible String Band. *The Hangman's Beautiful Daughter* [1967]. Fledg'ling: 3078. 2010. CD.

1855 Martyn, John. *Sweet Little Mysteries: The Island Anthology* [1971–1987]. Island: 314 522245-2. 1994. 2 CDs.

1856 Pentangle
 1856.1 *Early Classics* [1968–1972]. Shanachie: 79078. 1992. CD.
 1856.2 *Light Flight: The Anthology* [1968–1971]. Sanctuary / Castle: 81163. 2002. 2 CDs.
 1856.3 *Sweet Child* [1968]. Sanctuary / Castle: 81121. 2001. 2 CDs.

1857 Steeleye Span. *Spanning the Years*. Chrysalis / EMI: F2 32236. 1995. 2 CDs.

1858 Thompson, Richard. *Shoot Out the Lights* [1982] (Linda Thompson). Hannibal: 571303. 1992. CD.

1859 Thompson, Richard. *Walking on a Wire: 1968–2009*. Shout! Factory: 311087. 2009. 4 CDs.

GUITAR HEROES

COLLECTIONS

1860 *Legends of Guitar: Rock—The '60s, Vol. 1* [1959–1969] (Ventures, Yardbirds, Lonnie Mack, Jimi Hendrix, Chet Atkins, Frank Zappa, Steve Cropper, Dick Dale, Shadows, Byrds, Kinks, and others). Rhino: 70720. 1990. CD.

1861 *Legends of Guitar: Rock—The '60s, Vol. 2* [1960–1970] (Jeff Beck, Jerry Garcia, Cream, John Mayall, Allman Brothers, and others). Rhino: 70562. 1991. CD.

INDIVIDUALS AND GROUPS

1862 Beck, Jeff
 1862.1 *Blow by Blow* [1975]. Epic: EK 85440 (33409). 2001. CD.
 1862.2 *Truth* [1968]. Epic: 77352 2. 2006. CD.

1863 Clapton, Eric
 1863.1 *Crossroads* [1963–1987]. Polydor: 835 261-2. 1988. 4 CDs.
 1863.2 *Eric Clapton Anthology*. Hal Leonard: HL00690590. 2003. Score.
 1863.3 *461 Ocean Boulevard* [1974]. Polydor: 314 531 821-2. 1995. CD.
 1863.4 *Slowhand* [1977]. Polydor: 314 531 825-2. 1997. CD.

1864 Cream
 1864.1 *Disraeli Gears* [1967]. Polygram: 314 531 811-2. 1997. CD.
 1864.2 *Fresh Cream* [1966]. Polygram: 314 531 810. 1997. CD.
 1864.3 ★*The Very Best of Cream* [1966–1968]. Polydor: 314 523 752-2. 1995. CD.
 1864.4 *Wheels of Fire* [1968]. Polydor: 314 531 812-2. 1997. 2 CDs.

1865 ★Derek and the Dominos. *Layla and Other Assorted Love Songs* [1970]. RSO / Polydor: 314 531 820-2. 1996. CD.

1866 Hendrix, Jimi
 1866.1 *Axis: Bold As Love* [1967]. Sony Legacy: 762163. 2010. CD, DVD.
 1866.2 ★*Are You Experienced?* [1967]. Sony Legacy: 762162. 2010. CD, DVD.
 1866.3 *BBC Sessions* [1967]. Sony Legacy: 774519. 2010. 2 CDs, DVD.
 1866.4 ★*Electric Ladyland* [1968]. Sony Legacy: 762164. 2010. CD, DVD.
 1866.5 *Experience Hendrix: The Best of Jimi Hendrix* [1966–1970]. MCA: 11671. 1997. CD.
 1866.6 *Live at Monterey* [1967]. Experience Hendrix: 984302. 2007. CD.
 1866.7 *Voodoo Child: The Jimi Hendrix Collection* [1966–1970]. MCA: 112 603-2. 2001. 2 CDs.

1867 Led Zeppelin
 1867.1 *Led Zeppelin* [1969]. Atlantic: 82632 (8216). 1994. CD.
 1867.2 ★*Led Zeppelin II* [1969]. Atlantic: 82633-2 (8236). 1994. CD.
 1867.3 ★*Led Zeppelin IV [Zo-So]* [1971]. Atlantic: 82638 (7208). 1994. CD.
 1867.4 *Led Zeppelin Classics*. Warner Bros. Publications: GF0585. 1993. Score.

1868 Mayall, John. *Bluesbreakers* [1966] (Eric Clapton). Deram: 422 882 967-2. 2001. CD.

1869 Ten Years After. *The Essential Ten Years After* [1968–1970]. Chrysalis: 21857. 1991. CD.

INFLUENCES ON THE 1980s: 1960s AND 1970s BANDS

INDIVIDUALS AND GROUPS

1870 Barrett, Syd
 1870.1 *Barrett* [1970]. EMI: CDP 7 46606 2. 1990. CD.
 1870.2 *The Madcap Laughs* [1970]. EMI: CDP 7 46607 2. 1990. CD.

1871 Big Star. *#1 Record / Radio City* [1972, 1973]. Fantasy: FAN-31457. 2009. CD.

1872   Captain Beefheart
 1872.1   *Shiny Beast (Bat Chain Puller)* [1978].
          Virgin: 00946 365517 22. 2006. CD.
 1872.2   *Trout Mask Replica* [1969]. Bizarre /
          Straight / Reprise: 2027-2. 1989. CD.

1873   DNA. *DNA on DNA* [1978–1982]. No More
       Records: NO 012CD. 2004. CD.

1874   Half Japanese
 1874.1   *Half Japanese: The Band That Would Be
          King* (Jad and David Fair, Moe Tucker,
          Penn Jillette, Byron Coley). Vanguard:
          1892649292 (ISBN). 2000. DVD.
 1874.2   *Loud and Horrible* [1981 and 1983].
          Drag City: DC270. 2004. CD.

1875   Johnston, Daniel
 1875.1   *The Devil and Daniel Johnston.* Sony
          Pictures Home Entertainment: 15493.
          2006. DVD.
 1875.2   *Fun.* Atlantic: 82659-2. 1994. CD.

1876   MC5
 1876.1   *Back in the USA* [1970]. Rhino: 71033.
          1992. CD.
 1876.2   *Kick out the Jams* [1968]. Elektra:
          9 60894-2. 1991. CD.

1877   Mott the Hoople. *Old Records Never Die* [1969–
       1974] (Ian Hunter). Shout! Factory: 826663-
       10970. 2008. 2 CDs.

1878   New York Dolls. *New York Dolls* [1973].
       Mercury: 832 752-2. 1988. CD.

1879   NRBQ. *Peek-a-Boo: The Best of NRBQ* [1969–
       1989]. Rhino: 70770. 1990. 2 CDs.

1880   Parsons, Gram. *GP / Grievous Angel* [1973, 1974]
       (Emmylou Harris). Reprise: 9 26108-2. 1990. CD.

1881   ★Pop, Iggy. *Raw Power* [1973] (Stooges).
       Columbia: 88697 56149 2. 2010. 2 CDs.

1882   Raspberries. *The Raspberries* [1972–1974].
       Capitol Collector's Series. Capitol: 92126.
       1991. CD.

1883   Richman, Jonathan. *The Modern Lovers* [1976].
       Sanctuary / Castle: 02182-36294-2. 2007. CD.

1884   Rundgren, Todd. *The Very Best of Todd Rundgren*
       [1968–1985]. Rhino: R2 72811. 1997. CD.

1885   Shaggs. *Philosophy of the World* [1969]. RCA
       Victor: 90926 63371-2. 1999. CD.

1886   Silver Apples. *Silver Apples* [1968]. Phoenix:
       ASH3003. 2008. CD.

1887   Stooges
 1887.1   *Fun House* [1970]. Rhino: R2 73175.
          2005. 2 CDs.
 1887.2   *The Stooges* [1969]. Rhino: R2 73176.
          2005. 2 CDs.

1888   *Straight Outta Cleveland* (Raspberries, Michael
       Stanley, James Gang, Devo, Pere Ubu, Dead
       Boys, Rachel Sweet, and others). Oglio: 81573-2.
       1995. CD.

1889   Velvet Underground
 1889.1   *Loaded* [1970]. Warner Special Products:
          27613-2. 1987. CD.
 1889.2   *Peel Slowly and See* [1965–1970]. Verve:
          314 527 887-2. 1995. 5 CDs.
 1889.3   *The Velvet Underground* [1969]. Verve:
          314 531 525-2 1996. CD.
 1889.4   ★*The Velvet Underground and Nico* [1967].
          Verve: 314 531 520-2. 1996. CD.

1890   Young Marble Giants. *Colossal Youth* [1980].
       Domino: DNO 135. 2007. 3 CDs.

THE 1970s

Singer-Songwriters

1891   Jeffreys, Garland. *Ghost Writer / American Boy
       and Girl.* Raven: RVCD-334. 1977, 1979. 2 CDs.

1892   ★King, Carole. *Tapestry* [1971]. Ode / Epic: EK
       65850 (77009). 1999. CD.

1893   Mitchell, Joni
 1893.1   *Blue* [1971]. Reprise: 2038-2. 1999. CD.
 1893.2   ★*Court and Spark* [1974]. Asylum: 1001-
          2. 1985. CD.
 1893.3   *Hijera* [1976]. Asylum: 1087. 1987. CD.

1894   Morrison, Van
 1894.1   ★*Astral Weeks* [1968]. Warner Bros.:
          1768-2. 1987. CD.
 1894.2   *Moondance* [1970]. Warner Bros.: 3103-
          2 (1835). 1985. CD.
 1894.3   *Van Morrison Guitar Songbook.* Alfred:
          739051164. 2008. Score.

1895   Nyro, Laura. *Stoned Soul Picnic: The Best of
       Laura Nyro* [1966–1994]. Columbia: C2K 48880.
       1997. CD.

1896   Simon, Carly. *The Best of Carly Simon* [1971–
       1975]. Elektra: 109-2. 1984. CD.

1897 Simon, Paul
    1897.1 *The Essential Paul Simon.* Warner Bros.: 159420-2. 2007. 2 CDs.
    1897.2 *Negotiations and Love Songs* [1971–1986]. Warner Bros.: 25789-2. 1988. CD.

1898 Snow, Phoebe. *The Very Best of Phoebe Snow.* Sony: CK 62241. 2001. CD.

1899 Stevens, Cat (Yusuf Islam). *Greatest Hits* [1970–1975]. A&M: 314 546 889-2 (4519). 2000. CD.

1900 Taylor, James
    1900.1 *James Taylor's Greatest Hits.* Warner Bros.: 3113-2. 1988. CD.
    1900.2 ★*Sweet Baby James* [1969]. Warner Bros.: 1843-2. 1987. CD.

Los Angeles

1901 Browne, Jackson
    1901.1 *The Pretender* [1976]. Elektra: 107-2. 1987. CD.
    1901.2 *The Very Best of Jackson Browne.* Elektra: R2 78091. 2004. 2 CDs.

1902 Cooder, Ry
    1902.1 *Into the Purple Valley* [1972]. Reprise: 2052-2. 1988. CD.
    1902.2 *Paradise and Lunch* [1974]. Reprise: 2179-2. 1988. CD.

1903 Crosby, Stills and Nash
    1903.1 *The Best of Crosby, Stills and Nash.* Hal Leonard: HL00690613. 2005. Score.
    1903.2 *Crosby, Stills and Nash* [1969]. Atlantic / Rhino: R2 73290. 2006. CD.

1904 Doobie Brothers. *The Very Best of the Doobie Brothers.* Warner Bros. / Rhino: R2 73384. 2007. 2 CDs.

1905 Eagles
    1905.1 ★*Greatest Hits, 1971–1975.* Asylum: 105-2. 1985. CD.
    1905.2 *Greatest Hits, Vol. 2* [1976–1982]. Asylum: 60205-2. 1986. CD.
    1905.3 *Hotel California* [1976]. Elektra: 103-2 (Asylum 1084). 1990. CD.

1906 Fleetwood Mac
    1906.1 *Fleetwood Mac* [1975]. Reprise: R2 73881. 2004. CD.
    1906.2 ★*Rumours* [1977]. Warner Bros.: 3010-2. 1985. CD.

1907 Little Feat. *Waiting for Columbus* [1977]. Rhino: R2 78274. 2001. 2 CDs.

1908 Newman, Randy
    1908.1 *The Best of Randy Newman.* Warner Archives; Rhino: R2 74364. 2001. CD.
    1908.2 *Sail Away* [1972]. Reprise / Rhino: R2 78244. 2002. CD.

1909 Ronstadt, Linda
    1909.1 *Greatest Hits I and II* [1967–1975]. Rhino: 8122 79984 6. 2007. CD.
    1909.2 *Heart Like a Wheel* [1974]. Capitol: 46073 (11358). 1987. CD.
    1909.3 *The Very Best of Linda Ronstadt* [1967–1993]. Rhino: 76109. 2002. CD.

1910 Steely Dan. *The Definitive Collection.* Geffen: 675202. 2006. CD.

1911 Young, Neil
    1911.1 ★*Decade* [1966–1976]. Reprise: 2257-2. 1988. 2 CDs.
    1911.2 *Ragged Glory.* Reprise: 26315-2. 1990. CD.
    1911.3 *Rust Never Sleeps* [1979]. Reprise: 2295-2. 1987. CD.
    1911.4 *Tonight's the Night* [1975]. Reprise: 2221. 1987. CD.

1912 Zevon, Warren. *A Quiet Normal Life: The Best of Warren Zevon* [1976–1982]. Asylum: 60503-2. 1986. CD.

U.S. Hitmakers

1913 Blood, Sweat, and Tears
    1913.1 *Child Is Father to the Man* [1968]. Columbia: CK 63987 (9619). 2000. CD.
    1913.2 *What Goes Up: Best of Blood, Sweat, and Tears.* Legacy; Columbia: C2K 64166. 1995. 2 CDs.

1914 Chicago. *Chicago IX: Greatest Hits* [1969–1975, 1976]. Rhino: R2 73229. 2005. CD.

1915 Hall and Oates. *The Very Best of Daryl Hall and John Oates.* RCA / BMG: 07863 69319-2. 2001. CD.

1916 Miller, Steve. *Greatest Hits, 1974–1978.* Capitol: 46101. 1987. CD.

1917 Scaggs, Boz. *Silk Degrees* [1976]. Columbia: 82876 86715 2. 2007. CD.

1918 Seger, Bob
    1918.1 *Greatest Hits* [1975–1994]. Capitol: 30334. 1994. CD.
    1918.2 *Live Bullet* [1975]. Capitol: 509990 98330 2 9. 2011. CD.

1919 ★Springsteen, Bruce. *Born to Run* [1975]. Columbia: CK 33795. 1985. CD.

1920 Three Dog Night. *The Complete Hit Singles* [1969–1975]. Geffen: B0001779-02. 2004. CD.

British Superstars

1921 Cocker, Joe. *Greatest Hits* [1969–1974]. A&M: 75021-3257-2. 1987. CD.

1922 Electric Light Orchestra. *ELO's Greatest Hits* [1973–1978]. Jet / CBS: ZK 36310. 1986. CD.

1923 Harrison, George. *All Things Must Pass* [1970]. Capitol: 30474. 2001. CD.

1924 Jethro Tull
  1924.1 *The Best of Acoustic.* Capitol: 09463-88896-2-5. 2007. CD.
  1924.2 *The Very Best of Jethro Tull.* Chrysalis: 32614. 2001. CD.

1925 John, Elton
  1925.1 ★*Greatest Hits, Vol. 1* [1970–1974]. Rocket / Polydor: 314 512 532-2. 1992. CD.
  1925.2 *Greatest Hits, Vol. 2* [1974–1976]. Rocket / Polydor: 314 512 533-2. 1992. CD.

1926 Lennon, John
  1926.1 *Imagine* [1971]. Capitol: 24858. 2000. CD.
  1926.2 ★*Lennon Legend* [1969–1980]. Parlophone / EMI: 21954. 1997. CD.
  1926.3 *Plastic Ono Band.* Capitol: 28740. 2010. CD.
  1926.4 *Shaved Fish* [1969–1975]. Capitol: 46642. 1988. CD.

1927 McCartney, Paul. *All the Best* [1970–1986]. Capitol: 48287. 1987. CD.

1928 Moody Blues. *The Best of the Moody Blues.* Polydor: 31453 5800-2. 1996. CD.

1929 Pink Floyd
  1929.1 ★*Dark Side of the Moon.* EMI; Capitol: 28955. 2011. CD.
  1929.2 *The Wall* [1979]. Capitol: 31243. 2000. 2 CDs.

1930 Queen. *Greatest Hits* [1974–1981]. Hollywood: 2061 61265-2 (Elektra). 1992. CD.

1931 Rolling Stones
  1931.1 ★*Exile on Main St.* Universal Music Group: B0014131-02. 2010. CD.
  1931.2 *Jump Back: The Best of the Rolling Stones, '71–'93* [1971–1989. Virgin: 39321. 1993. CD.
  1931.3 *Some Girls.* Universal Music Group: B0012837-02. 2009. CD.
  1931.4 *Sticky Fingers.* Universal Music Group: B0012799-02. 2009. CD.
  1931.5 *Sucking in the Seventies.* Virgin: 72438-73339-2-5. 2005. CD.

1932 Stewart, Rod
  1932.1 *Downtown Train: Selections from the Storyteller Anthology* [1976–1989]. Warner Bros.: 26158-2. 1990. CD.
  1932.2 *Every Picture Tells a Story* [1971]. Mercury: 314 558 060-2 (609). 1988. CD.

1933 T Rex. *Electric Warrior* [1971]. Rhino: 76111. 2003. CD.

Southern Rock

COLLECTION

1934 *Southern Rock Gold.* Hip-O: B0005515-02. 2005. 2 CDs.

INDIVIDUALS AND GROUPS

1935 Allman Brothers
  1935.1 *Dreams* [1968–1985]. Polydor: 839 417-2. 1989. 4 CDs.
  1935.2 ★*Live at Fillmore East* [1971]. Capricorn: 314 531 260-2 (802). 1998. CD.

1936 Lynyrd Skynyrd. *All Time Greatest Hits* [1973–1977]. MCA: 088 112 229-2. 2000. CD.

1937 Marshall Tucker Band. *Anthology: The First 30 Years* [1973–2004]. Sony: D2K 34097. 2005. 2 CDs.

Heavy Metal/Hard Rock

COLLECTION

1938 *Heavy Metal: The First 20 Years* (Judas Priest, Rainbow, Scorpions, Alice Cooper, Ronnie James Dio, Blue Oyster Cult, and Queensryche). Time Life: M19182. 2006. CD.

INDIVIDUALS AND GROUPS

1939 Aerosmith
  1939.1 *Greatest Hits* [1974–1982]. Columbia: CK 57367 (36865). 1993. CD.

1939.2 *O, Yeah! Ultimate Aerosmith Hits* [1973–2002]. Columbia: CK 86700. 2002. 2 CDs.

1939.3 *O, Yeah! Ultimate Aerosmith Hits*. Hal Leonard: HL00690603. 2006. Score.

1940   Black Sabbath. *Paranoid* [1970]. Warner Bros.: 3104-2 (1887). 1989. CD.

1941   Blue Oyster Cult. *Don't Fear the Reaper: Best of Blue Oyster Cult*. Columbia: 65918. 2000. CD.

1942   Boston. *Boston* [1976]. Epic: 69699 86322 2. 2006. CD.

1943   Cheap Trick. *Cheap Trick at Budokan* [1978]. Epic: EK 86448 (35795). 2002. CD.

1944   Cooper, Alice. *Mascara and Monsters: The Best of Alice Cooper*. Warner Archives; Rhino: R2 75806. 2001. CD.

1945   Deep Purple. *Machine Head* [1972]. Warner Bros.: 3100-2 (2607). 1987. CD.

1946   Grand Funk Railroad. *Greatest Hits*. Capitol: 72438-63707-2-3. 2006. CD.

1947   Judas Priest. *Metal Works* [1973–1993]. Columbia: C2K 53932. 1993. 2 CDs.

1948   Kiss. *The Very Best of Kiss*. Mercury: 440 063 122-2. 2002. CD.

1949   *Monsters of Rock*. Razor & Tie: 89004-2. 1998. CD.

1950   Nugent, Ted. *Great Gonzos: The Best of Ted Nugent* [1975–1981]. Epic: EK 65704 (37667). 1999. CD.

1951   ZZ Top. *Greatest Hits* [1970–1990]. Warner Bros.: 26846-2. 1992. CD.

Art Rock and Rock Theater

1952   Bowie, David

1952.1 *Best of Bowie* [1969–2002]. Virgin: 41929. 2002. 2 CDs.

1952.2 *Best of Bowie* [1971–2000]. Virgin: 07243 4 90106 9 7. 2002. 2 DVDs.

1952.3 ★*The Rise and Fall of Ziggy Stardust* [1972]. Virgin: 21900. 1999. CD.

1953   Cabaret Voltaire. *Original Sound of Sheffield '78/'82*. Mute: 9190-2. 2002. CD.

1954   Cale, John. *Paris 1919* [1973]. Reprise: 2131-2. 1994. CD.

1955   Can

1955.1 *Can*. Spoon: 047. 2003. CD, 2 DVDs.

1955.2 *Ege Bamyasi* [1972]. Spoon: 008. 2004. CD.

1955.3 *Tago Mago* [1971]. Mute: 9054. 2004. CD.

1956   Cow, Henry. *Unrest* [1974]. Rer USA: 752725010221. 2005. CD.

1957   Eno, Brian

1957.1 *Another Green World* [1975]. Virgin: 7243 5 77291 2 3. 2004. CD.

1957.2 *Before and after Science* [1977]. Virgin: 7243 5 77292 2 2. 2004. CD.

1958   Faust. *Faust / So Far* [1971, 1972]. Collectors' Choice / Universal: WWCCM01792. 2000. CD.

1959   Ferry, Brian

1959.1 *Best of Roxy Music* [1972–1982]. Virgin: 10395. 2001. CD.

1959.2 *For Your Pleasure: The Second Roxy Music Album* [1973] (Roxy Music). Virgin: 47449. 1999. CD.

1960   Genesis. *The Lamb Lies Down on Broadway* [1974]. Atco: 82677-2 (401-2). 1994. 2 CDs.

1961   King Crimson. *The Condensed 21st Century Guide to King Crimson, 1969–2003*. Discipline Global Mobile: DGM0604. 2006. 2 CDs.

1962   Kraftwerk

1962.1 *Autobahn* [1975]. Astralwerks: 50999 3 08300 2 8. 2009. CD.

1962.2 *Minimum-Maximum*. Astralwerks: 60611. 2005. 2 CDs.

1962.3 *Trans-Europe Express* [1977]. Astralwerks: 50999 3 08303 2 5. 2009. CD.

1963   Neu! *Neu!* [1972]. Grönland Records: 00854882200719. 2008. CD.

1964   Red Krayola. *God Bless the Red Krayola and All Who Sail with It* [1968]. Sunspots: SPOT 512. 2003. CD.

1965   Reed, Lou

1965.1 *Animal Serenade*. Sire / Reprise: 48678. 2004. 2 CDs.

1965.2 *NYC Man: The Collections* [1967–2002]. BMG Heritage: 50564. 2003. 2 CDs.

1965.3 *Walk on the Wild Side: The Best of Lou Reed* [1972–1976]. RCA: 3753-2-R. 2008. CD.

1966   Residents

1966.1 *Eskimo* [1979]. Mute: 5099952190926. 2008. CD.

1966.2 *Icky Flix*. East Side Digital: ESD 81562. 2001. DVD.

1966.3 *The Residents' Commercial Album* [1980]. Mute: MUE9275. 2004. CD.

1967 Soft Machine
1967.1 *Man in a Deaf Corner: Anthology, 1963–1970*. Mooncrest: 62. 2001. 2 CDs.
1967.2 *Third*. Sony BMG: 82876872932. 2007. 2 CDs.

1968 Van Dyke Parks. *Song Cycle* [1968]. Warner Bros.: 9 25856-2. 1990. CD.

1969 Walker, Scott. *Scott 4* [1969]. Mercury: 510 882-2. 2000. CD.

1970 Wyatt, Robert. *Rock Bottom* [1974]. Thirsty Ear: 57045.2. 1998. CD.

1971 Yes. *Fragile* [1972]. Rhino: 73789. 2003. CD. Remastered / Bonus Tracks.

Early Rappers

1972 Iceberg Slim. *Reflections* [1976]. Uproar: UP12862. 2008. CD.

1973 Last Poets. *The Last Poets* [1970]. Fuel: 302 061 226 2. 2002. CD.

1974 Scott-Heron, Gil. *Small Talk at 125th and Lenox* [1970]. Flying Dutchman: 66611-2. 1993. CD.

1975 U-Roy. *Dread in Babylon* [1975]. Virgin: CDFL2007. 2004. CD.

1976 Watts Prophets. *Things Gonna Get Greater* [1969]. Water: 157. 2005. CD.

Punk and New Wave: U.S.

COLLECTIONS

1977 *American Hardcore* [1981–1986] (Black Flag, Minor Threat, Bad Brains, SSD, MDC, DOA, DRI, Adolescents, 7 Seconds, Henry Rollins, Ian MacKaye, Keith Morris). Sony Pictures Home Entertainment: 17096. 2007. DVD.

1978 *D.I.Y. Blank Generation: The New York Scene* [1975–1978] (Dictators Ramones, Patti Smith Group, Mink, Tuff Darts, DeVille, Blondie, Back Street Boys, Blondie, Momps, Voidoids, Television, Dead Boys, Heartbreakers [Johnny Thunders], Suicide). Rhino: 71175. 1993. CD.

1979 *No New York* [1978] (Contortions, Teenage Jesus and the Jerks, Mars, DNA; Brian Eno, prod.). Lilith: LR102. 2006. CD.

1980 *Punk: Attitude* (Black Flag, New York Dolls, MC5, Stooges, Clash, Sex Pistols, Ramones, Slits, X-Ray Spex, Dead Kennedys, Siouxsie and the Banshees, Patty Smith; Don Letts, dir.). Capital Entertainment: CEE0008. 2005. 2 DVDs. Includes U.S. and U.K. artists.

1981 *The Tomorrow Show with Tom Snyder: Punk and New Wave* (Elvis Costello and the Attractions, Jam, John Lydon, Joan Jett, Plasmatics, Iggy Pop, Ramones, Patti Smith, Paul Weller). Shout! Factory: D20 38145. 2006. 2 DVDs.

INDIVIDUALS AND GROUPS

1982 Black Flag. *Damaged* [1981]. SST: SST CD 007. 1990. CD.

1983 Blondie. *Greatest Hits*. Capitol: 42068. 2002. CD.

1984 Cars
1984.1 *Complete Greatest Hits* [1978–1987]. Rhino: 78288. 2002. CD.
1984.2 *Greatest Hits* [1978–1984]. Elektra: 60464-2. 1990. CD.

1985 Dead Boys. *Young, Loud and Snotty* [1977]. Sire: 26981 (6038). 1992. CD.

1986 Dead Kennedys. *Fresh Fruit for Rotting Vegetables* [1980]. Cherry Red / Manifesto: MFO 42907. 2010. CD.

1987 Devo. *Q: Are We Not Men? A: We Are Devo* [1978]. Warner Bros.: 3239-2. 1988. CD.

1988 Germs. *MIA: The Complete Anthology* [1977–1980]. Slash: R2 79954. 1993. CD.

1989 Hell, Richard, and the Voidoids. *Blank Generation* [1977]. Sire: 9026137-2. 1990. CD.

1990 Johnny Thunders and the Heartbreakers. *L.A.M.F.* [1977]. Jungle / Cargo: 044. 2003. CD.

1991 Lunch, Lydia. *Queen of Siam* [1979]. Atavistic: ALP77CD. 2009. CD.

1992 Minor Threat. *Complete Discography* [1981]. Dischord: Dischord 40. 2003. CD.

1993 Mission of Burma. *Vs (the Definitive Edition plus Bonus DVD)* [1982]. Special edition. Matador: OLE 731-9. 1997. CD.

1994 Pere Ubu
1994.1 *The Modern Dance* [1976–1977]. DGC: 25206. 1998. CD.

1994.2 *The Tenement Year [Remastered & Expanded].* Mercury: 9846251. 2007. CD.

1994.3 *Terminal Tower: An Archival Collection* [1975–1980]. DGC: 25207. 1998. CD.

1995 Ramones

1995.1 ★*Ramones* [1976]. Rhino: R2 74306. 2001. CD.

1995.2 *Rocket to Russia* [1977]. Rhino: 74309. 2001. CD.

1996 Rezillos. *Can't Stand the Rezillos: The (Almost) Complete Rezillos* [1978]. Sire: 26942. 1993. CD.

1997 ★Smith, Patti. *Horses* [1975]. Arista: 18827 (8362). 1996. CD.

1998 Suicide. *Suicide: The First Album* [1977]. Mute: 9104 (Red Star 7001). 2000. 2 CDs.

1999 Talking Heads

1999.1 *Fear of Music* [1979]. Warner Bros.; Reprise; Maverick: 6076. 1990. CD.

1999.2 *Remain in Light* [1980]. Sire: R2 76452. 2005. CD.

1999.3 *Stop Making Sense* [1983]. Warner Bros.: 47489 (25186). 1999. CD.

1999.4 *Stop Making Sense* [1984] (Tina Weymouth, Jerry Harrison, Chris Frantz, David Byrne; Jonathan Demme, dir. Palm Pictures: 3013-2. 1999. DVD.

2000 Television. *Marquee Moon* [1977]. Rhino: 73920. 2003. CD.

2001 Weirdos. *Weird World, Vol.1: 1977–1981.* Frontier: 31040. 1991. CD.

2002 Wipers. *Wipers Box Set: Is This Real?/Youth of America/Over the Edge* [1980, 1981, and 1983]. Zeno Records: Z-005. 2001. 3 CDs.

Punk and New Wave: U.K.

COLLECTIONS

2003 *No Thanks! The '70s Punk Rebellion* [1972–1979] (Ramones, Clash, Nick Lowe, Buzzcocks, Saints, Damned, Jam, Pere Ubu, Modern Lovers, Television, Adverts, Heartbreakers, Iggy and the Stooges, Mink DeVille, X-Ray Spex, Wire, Richard Hell and the Voidoids, Stranglers, Runaways, New York Dolls, Dictators, Patti Smith, Generation X, Ultravox!, Blondie, Boomtown Rats, Fall, Stiff Little Fingers, Wire, Vibrators, Dead Boys, Magazine, Elvis Costello, Undertones, Ian Dury, Suicide, Devo, Mekons, Germs, Rezillos, Pretenders, Alternative TV, Tom Robinson Band, Black Flag, Siouxsie and the Banshees, X, Dead Kennedys, Soft Boys, Slits, Cramps, Talking Heads, Sham 69, Cure, Joe Jackson, Gang of Four, Johnny Thunders, Joy Division, and others). Rhino: 73926. 2003. 4 CDs.

2004 *Stiff, Stiffer, Stiffest: A Stiff Records Collection.* Metro: 42. 2001. CD.

2005 *Too Much Two Tone.* EMI Gold Imports: 523772 2004. CD.

INDIVIDUALS AND GROUPS

2006 Adverts. *Crossing the Red Sea with the Adverts* [1978]. Fire Records / Redeye: 143. 2011. CD.

2007 Alternative TV. *The Image Has Cracked* [1978]. Anagram UK / Zoom: 24. 2003. CD.

2008 Buzzcocks. *Singles Going Steady* [1977–1979]. Capitol: 13153. 1992. CD.

2009 Clash

2009.1 ★*The Clash* [1977]. Columbia Records/ Sony 63883. 2000. CD.

2009.2 *London Calling* [1979]. Columbia Records/Sony 63885. 2000. CD.

2010 Costello, Elvis

2010.1 *The Best of Elvis Costello: The First 10 Years* [1977–1987]. Hip-O: B0008640-02. 2007. CD.

2010.2 ★*My Aim Is True* [1976–1977]. Universal: 863502. 2007. 2 CDs. Remastered and reissued.

2010.3 *This Year's Model* [1978]. Hip-O: 10681-02. 2008. 2 CDs.

2011 Crass. *Feeding of the 5000* [1978]. Crass: CC01. 2011. CD.

2012 Dexys Midnight Runners. *Searching for the Young Soul Rebels* [1980]. EMI America: 25600. 2000. CD.

2013 English Beat. *Beat This! The Best of the English Beat.* Sire: 40735-2. 2000. CD.

2014 Generation X. *Generation X* [1978]. EMI Gold: 52957. 2002. CD.

2015 Germs. *MIA: The Complete Anthology* [1977–1980]. Slash: R2 79954. 2000. CD.

2016 Jam

    2016.1 *In the City* [1977]. Ume Imports: 537 417-2 (6110). 2004. CD.

    2016.2 *The Sound of the Jam.* Interscope: 440 065 635-2. 2003. CD.

2017 LiLiPUT/Kleenex. *LiLiPUT.* Kill Rock Stars: KRS 373. 2001. 2 CDs.

2018 Lowe, Nick. *Basher: The Best of Nick Lowe* [1978–1988]. Columbia: CK 45313. 1989. CD.

2019 Parker, Graham. *Heat Treatment* [1976]. Mercury: 548 682. 2001. CD.

2020 ★Police. *Every Breath You Take: The Classics* [1978–1983]. Universal: 3765-02. 2005. CD. Remastered and reissued.

2021 Raincoats. *The Raincoats* [1979]. Phantom Sound & Vision: 1574359. 2009. CD.

2022 Saints. *I'm Stranded* [1977]. Emi Aus / Zoom: 5003712. 1997. CD.

2023 Sex Pistols

    2023.1 *The Filth and the Fury.* New Line Home Video: N5086. 2000. DVD.

    2023.2 ★*Never Mind the Bollocks Here's the Sex Pistols* [1977]. Warner Bros.: 3147-2. 1990. CD.

2024 Sham 69. *Tell Us the Truth* [1978]. Captain Oi! Uk / Zoom: CPTOAHOYDPX611. 2005. CD.

2025 Siouxsie and the Banshees. *Once upon a Time: The Singles.* Ume Imports. 2006. CD.

2026 Slits. *Cut* [1979]. Island: 548 186-2. 1990. CD.

2027 Specials. *The Specials.* Capitol: 7243 5 37697 0 3. 2002. CD.

2028 Stiff Little Fingers. *Inflammable Material* [1979]. Restless: 773788. 2005. CD.

2029 Undertones. *The Undertones* [1978–1979]. Salvo Uk / Zoomn: SALVOCD017. 2009. CD.

2030 X-Ray Specs. *Let's Submerge: The Anthology.* Castle: 02182-36271-2. 2006. 2 CDs.

POST-PUNK

2031 Birthday Party

    2031.1 *Junkyard* [1981–1982]. 2.13.61 / BMG: 99694. 2000. CD.

    2031.2 *Pleasure Heads Must Burn* [1982] (Nick Cave, Mick Harvey, and Rowland S. Howard). Cherry Red Films: CRDVD20. 2003. DVD.

    2031.3 *Prayers on Fire* [1980-1981] (Nick Cave, Mick Harvey, and Rowland S. Howard). Sony; BMG; Buddah; SBME: BUDD99691. 2000. CD.

2032 The Fall

    2032.1 *Grotesque (after Gramme)* [1980]. Essential / Castle: 640. 1998. CD.

    2032.2 *Live at the Witch Trials* [1977–1979]. Sanctuary: 81236. 2004. CD.

    2032.3 *This Nation's Saving Grace* [1985]. Beggars Banquet: BBL 67 CD. 1988. CD.

2033 Gang of Four

    2033.1 *A Brief History of the Twentieth Century* [1978–1983]. Warner Bros.: 26448-2. 1990. CD.

    2033.2 *Entertainment!* [1979]. Warner Bros.: R2-78428. 2005. CD.

2034 Human League. *The Very Best of the Human League.* Caroline: CAR 92645. 2003. CD.

2035 Joy Division

    2035.1 *Closer* [1980]. Quest / Warner Bros: 25841. 1989. CD.

    2035.2 ★*Unknown Pleasures* [1979]. Quest / Warner Bros.: 25840-2. 1990. CD.

2036 Public Image Ltd. *Second Edition (Metal Box)* [1979]. Warner Bros.: 3288-2. 1989. CD.

2037 Slits. *Cut* [1979]. Island: BECDUMG 5321250. 2010. CD.

2038 Throwing Muses

    2038.1 *House Tornado / the Fat Skier* [1988]. 4AD: GAD802CD. 2007. CD.

    2038.2 *In a Doghouse* [1985–1987]. Rykodisc (USA): RYKS 10377. 1998. 2 CDs.

2039 Wire

    2039.1 *Chairs Missing* [1978]. Pink Flag: PF12. 2006. CD.

    2039.2 *Pink Flag* [1977–1978]. Pink Flag: PFLG11. 2006. CD.

WOMEN IN ROCK SINCE THE 1970s

2040 Armatrading, Joan. *Greatest Hits.* A&M: 31454 0525 2. 1996. CD.

2041 Bangles. *Greatest Hits* [1984–1988]. Legacy: 11886973178829. 2008. CD.

2042   Benatar, Pat. *Ultimate Collection*. Capitol: 17330. 2008. 2 CDs.

2043   Bush, Kate. *The Whole Story* [1978–1985]. EMI America: 46414. 1986. CD.

2044   Cherry, Neneh. *Raw Like Sushi*. Virgin: 86116 (91252). 1989. CD.

2045   Cibo Matto. *Viva! La Woman*. Warner Bros.: 45989. 1996. CD.

2046   Faithfull, Marianne. *Broken English* [1979]. Island: 422 842 355-2. 1993. CD.

2047   Fanny. *Fanny* [1970]. Reprise: 6416. LP.

2048   Go-Go's. *Return to the Valley of the Go-Go's* [1981–1984, 1994]. I.R.S. / A&M: 7243 8 29694 26. 1994. CD.

2049   Heart
   2049.1   *Greatest Hits* [1975–1983]. Epic: EK 69015. 1998. CD.
   2049.2   *Greatest Hits, 1985–1995*. Capitol: 26803. 2000. CD.

2050   Jett, Joan
   2050.1   *Fit to Be Tied: Great Hits by Joan Jett and the Blackhearts*. Blackheart: 314 536 440-2. 1997. CD.
   2050.2   *I Love Rock 'N' Roll* [1981]. Blackheart: 4833752962. 2006. CD.

2051   Jones, Rickie Lee. *Rickie Lee Jones* [1979]. Warner Bros.: 3296. 1990. CD.

2052   Lauper, Cyndi. *She's So Unusual* [1983]. Epic: EK 62169. 2000. CD.

2053   ★Madonna. *The Immaculate Collection* [1984–1992]. Sire: 26440-2. 1992. CD.

2054   Muldaur, Maria. *Maria Muldaur* [1974]. Rhino Flashback: 2148-2. 2009. CD.

2055   O'Connor, Sinead. *I Do Not Want What I Haven't Got*. Chrysalis: 21759. 1990. CD.

2056   Ono, Yoko
   2056.1   *A Story* [1974–1986]. Rykodisc: 10420. 1997. CD.
   2056.2   *Walking on Thin Ice* [1971–1986]. Rykodisc: 20230. 1992. CD.

2057   Raitt, Bonnie
   2057.1   *Give It Up* [1972]. Rhino: 78378. 2002. CD.
   2057.2   *Nick of Time*. Capitol: 91268. 1989. CD.

2058   Runaways. *The Best of the Runaways* [1976–1977]. Island Def Jam: 0004609-02. 2005. CD.

2059   Shocked, Michelle. *Mercury Poise: 1988–1995*. Mercury: 314 532 960-2. 1996. CD.

2060   Siberry, Jane. *When I Was a Boy* [1991–1993]. Reprise: 26824. 1993. CD.

2061   Springfield, Dusty. *Dusty in Memphis* [1968–1971]. Rhino: 75580. 1999. CD.

2062   Turner, Tina. *Private Dancer* [1984]. Capitol: 55833 (12330). 1997. CD.

2063   Williams, Lucinda
   2063.1   *Car Wheels on a Gravel Road*. Mercury: 314 558 338-2. 1998. CD.
   2063.2   *Sweet Old World*. Chameleon: 61351-2. 1992. CD.

ROCK: THE 1980s AND BEYOND

Mainstream

2064   AC/DC. *Back in Black* [1980]. Epic: EK 80207. 2003. CD.

2065   Bon Jovi. *Slippery When Wet* [1986]. Mercury: 314 538 089-2 (830 264). 1998. CD.

2066   Coldplay. *A Rush of Blood to the Head*. Capitol: 40504. 2002. CD.

2067   Collins, Phil. *No Jacket Required*. Atlantic: 81240-2. 1985. CD.

2068   Def Leppard. *Hysteria: Deluxe Edition*. Mercury: 060249843047(7). 2006. CD.

2069   Dire Straits. *Sultans of Swing: The Very Best of Dire Straits*. Warner Bros.: 9 47130-2. 1998. CD.

2070   Duran Duran. *Greatest*. Capitol: 7243 4 96239 2 7. 1998. CD.

2071   Eurythmics. *Ultimate Collection*. Arista: 82876737992. 1999. CD.

2072   Foreigner. *No End in Sight: The Very Best of Foreigner*. Rhino: R2 512130. 2008. 2 CDs.

2073   Gabriel, Peter
   2073.1   *Shaking the Tree: 16 Golden Greats* [1977–1990]. Geffen: 35256095. 2002. CD.
   2073.2   *So*. Geffen: 069 493 272-2 (24088). 1986. CD.
   2073.3   *Us*. Geffen: 069 493 275-2 (Virgin) 24473. 1992. CD.

2074 Genesis. *Invisible Touch*. Atlantic / Rhino R2 301244. 2007. CD, DVD.

2075 Guns 'n' Roses. *Appetite for Destruction*. Geffen: 24148-2. 1987. CD.

2076 Henley, Don
    2076.1 *Building the Perfect Beast*. Geffen: 24026-2. 1984. CD.
    2076.2 *The End of the Innocence*. Geffen: 24217. 1989. CD.

2077 Huey Lewis and the News. *Sports [Exp. Ed.]* [1983]. Chrysalis / Capitol: 72435-20669-2-6. 1999. CD.

2078 Iron Maiden
    2078.1 *Best of the Beast*. Emi Argent/Zoom: BECDEMIT00853184. 1996. CD.
    2078.2 *Somewhere Back in Time: Best of 1980–1989* [1980–1989]. Sanctuary / Universal: 8697304782. 2008. CD.

2079 Journey. *Escape* [1981]. Legacy: 82876858972. 2006. CD.

2080 Mellencamp, John. *Scarecrow* [1985]. Mercury / Island: 422 824 865-2. 2005. CD.

2081 Metallica
    2081.1 *Master of Puppets*. Elektra: 60439. 1986. CD.
    2081.2 *Metallica* [1986]. Elektra: 6113-2. 1991. CD.

2082 REO Speedwagon. *The Hits* [1977–1988]. Columbia Records / Sony: 86518. 2002. CD.

2083 Rush. *Chronicles Deluxe Ed* [1974–1989]. Mercury: B0003420-00. 1990. CD, DVD.

2084 Simon, Paul. *Graceland*. Columbia Records / Sony: 84250. 2011. CD.

2085 Springsteen, Bruce
    2085.1 ★*Born in the USA*. Columbia: CK 38653. 1984. CD.
    2085.2 *The Essential Bruce Springsteen* [1972–2002]. Columbia: C2K 90773. 2003. 3 CDs.

2086 Tom Petty and the Heartbreakers. *Greatest Hits* [1976–1993] (Heartbreakers). MCA: 10813. 1993. CD.

2087 U2
    2087.1 *Achtung Baby*. Island: 510 347. 1991. CD.
    2087.2 *Elevation 2001: U2 Live from Boston*. Universal Music: 3145865439. 2001. 2 DVDs.
    2087.3 ★*The Joshua Tree*. Universal / Island: B0010285-02. 1987. CD.
    2087.4 *U218 Singles*. Hal Leonard: HL00690894. 2007. Score.
    2087.5 *War* [1983]. Island: 422 811 148-2. 1991. CD.

2088 Van Halen
    2088.1 *The Best of Van Halen, Vol. 1*. Warner Bros.: PG9665. 1996. Score.
    2088.2 *1984* [1983]. Warner / Reprise / Maverick 47741. 2000. CD.
    2088.3 ★*Van Halen* [1978]. Warner Bros.: 3075-2. 1990. CD.

2089 Wham. *Make It Big*. Columbia: CK 39595. 1984. CD.

2090 Winwood, Steve. *Chronicles* [1977–1986]. Island: 422 842 364-2. 1991. CD.

Alternative

COLLECTIONS

2091 *American Hardcore: The History of American Punk Rock*. Rhino: RHI2-74192. 2006. CD.

2092 *Dig!* (Anton Newcombe and the Brian Jonestown Massacre [Joel Gion, Matt Hollywood, Dean Taylor, Jeff Davies, Peter Hayes, Dave Deresinski], Courtney Taylor and the Dandy Warhols [Peter Holmstrom, Eric Hedford, Zia McCabe]). Palm Pictures: PALMDV 3104. 2005. 2 DVDs.

INDIVIDUALS AND GROUPS

2093 Amos, Tori. *Little Earthquakes*. Atlantic: 82358. 1992. CD.

2094 Angels of Light. *How I Loved You*. Young God; Revolver: YNGG16. 2001. CD.

2095 Anthrax. *Among the Living*. Island: 422 842 447-2 (90584). 1990. CD.

2096 B-52s
    2096.1 *The B-52s* [1979]. Warner Bros.: 3355-2. 1990. CD.
    2096.2 *Time Capsule: Songs for a Future Generation* [1979–1992]. Reprise: 46920. 1998. CD.

2097 Bad Brains
    2097.1 *Bad Brains* [1981]. ROIR: 8223. 1996. CD.
    2097.2 *Rock for Light* [1982]. Caroline: 1613. 1991. CD.

2098 Bauhaus. *Crackle* [1979–1985]. Beggars Banquet: BEGL 2018 CD. 1998. CD.

2099 ★Beck. *Odelay*. DGC: 24823. 1996. CD.

2100 Bedhead. *What Fun Life Was* [1993]. Touch & Go: 20924. 2001. CD.

2101 Big Black. *The Rich Man's Eight Track Tape* [1987]. Touch & Go: TG94CD. 1992. CD.

2102 Bikini Kill
      2102.1 *The First Two Records* [1991–1992]. Kill Rock Stars: 204. 1994. CD.
      2102.2 *The Singles* [1993–1995]. Kill Rock Stars: 298. 1998. CD.

2103 Björk
      2103.1 *Debut*. Elektra: 61468. 1993. CD.
      2103.2 ★*Post*. Elektra: 61740. 1995. CD.

2104 Black Flag. *Damaged* [1980–1981]. SST: SSTCD-007. 1993. CD.

2105 Blasters. *Live: Going Home* (Sonny Burgess, Billy Boy Arnold). Shout! Factory: DK 30244. 2004. CD.

2106 Boredoms. *Super Are*. Birdman: 19. 1998. CD.

2107 Breeders. *Last Splash*. 4AD / Elektra: 61508. 1993. CD.

2108 Buckley, Jeff
      2108.1 *Grace*. Columbia: CK 57528. 1994. CD.
      2108.2 *Jeff Buckley: Live in Chicago* [1995]. Columbia Music Video: CVD 50216. 2000. DVD.

2109 Built to Spill. *There's Nothing Wrong with Love*. UP: 6. 1994. CD.

2110 Butthole Surfers. *Locust Abortion Technician* [1987]. Latino Bugger Veil: 5. 1999. CD.

2111 Chrome. *Half Machine Lip Moves* [1978, 1979]. Cleopatra: CLEO7142. 2011. CD.

2112 Cocteau Twins
      2112.1 *Head over Heels* [1983]. 4AD: 70313. 2003. CD.
      2112.2 *Treasure* [1984]. 4AD: 70412. 2003. CD.

2113 Codeine. *Frigid Stars*. Subpop: SP 107B. 1991. CD.

2114 Cramps. *Songs the Lord Taught Us* [1980]. I.R.S. / A&M: 44797 00072. 1990. CD.

2115 Cure. *Staring at the Sea: The Singles [Import]* [1979–1985]. Universal: 60477. 1986. CD.

2116 Depeche Mode. *Violator*. Warner Bros.: 26081. 1990. CD.

2117 Difranco, Ani
      2117.1 *Knuckle Down*. Righteous Babe: RBR042-D. 2005. CD.
      2117.2 *Not a Pretty Girl*. Righteous Babe: RBR007-D. 1995. CD.

2118 Dinosaur Jr. *You're Living All over Me* [1987]. Merge: MRG244. 2005. CD.

2119 Discharge. *Hear Nothing See Nothing* [1982]. Castle: 72319. 2003. CD.

2120 Drive-By Truckers. *Decoration Day*. New West: 6047. 2003. CD.

2121 Echo and the Bunnymen. *Heaven up Here* [1981]. Rhino: 2564-61162-2. 2003. CD.

2122 Electrelane. *The Power Out* [2003]. Beggars Banquet. 2004. CD.

2123 Everything but the Girl. *Walking Wounded*. Atlantic: 82912. 1996. CD.

2124 Exploited. *Totally Exploited*. Taang! Records: 155. 2001. CD.

2125 Feelies
      2125.1 *Crazy Rhythms*. Bar None: BRN-CD-196 2009. CD.
      2125.2 *Only Life*. Water: WATER225. 2008. CD.

2126 Flaming Lips
      2126.1 *The Fearless Freaks: The Wondrously Improbable Story of the Flaming Lips*. Shout! Factory: D2D 32634. 2005. 2 DVDs.
      2126.2 *The Soft Bulletin*. Warner Bros.: 9 46876-2. 1999. CD.

2127 Flipper. *The Generic Album* [1980–1981]. Water: Water231. 2008. CD.

2128 Fountains of Wayne. *Welcome Interstate Managers*. Virgin: 90875. 2003. CD.

2129 Frith, Fred, and Henry Kaiser. *Friends and Enemies*. Cuneiform: 117. 2003. 2 CDs.

2130 Fugazi. *Repeater + 3 Songs*. Dischord: 45. 1992. CD.

2131 Germano, Lisa. *Lullaby for Liquid Pig*. Young God: 36. 2007. 2 CDs.

2132 Go-Betweens
      2132.1 *Bellavista Terrace: Best of the Go-Betweens* [1982–1988]. Beggars Banquet: 2020. 1999. CD.

2132.2   *16 Lovers Lane* [1988]. EMI Imports. 2006. 2 CDs.

2133   Golden Palominos. *Pure*. Restless: 72761-2. 1994. CD.

2134   Green Day. *Dookie*. Reprise: 45529. 1994. CD.

2135   Gun Club. *Fire of Love* [1981]. Last Call. 2003. CD. Import.

2136   Happy Mondays. *Pills 'n' Thrills and Bellyaches*. Elektra: 60986. 1990. CD.

2137   Harvey, P. J.
    2137.1   *Dry*. Indigo: 162 555001-2. 1992. CD.
    2137.2   *Rid of Me*. Island: 514 696. 1993. CD.
    2137.3   *To Bring You My Love*. Island: 524 085. 1995. CD.

2138   Hersh, Kristin
    2138.1   *The Grotto* (Howe Gelb, Andrew Bird). 4AD: CAD2302CD. 2003. CD.
    2138.2   *Hips and Makers* [1994]. Sire: 45413. 2009. CD.

2139   Hiatt, John. *Bring the Family* [1987]. A&M: 7502-19158 (5158). 1991. CD.

2140   Hole. *Live through This*. DGC: 24631. 1994. CD.

2141   Hüsker Dü
    2141.1   *New Day Rising* [1984]. SST: SSTCD-031. 1991. CD.
    2141.2   *Zen Arcade* [1983]. SST: 27. 1991. CD.

2142   Jane's Addiction. *Nothing's Shocking* [1988]. Warner Bros.: 25727-2. 1991. CD.

2143   Jesus and Mary Chain
    2143.1   *Psychocandy* [1985]. Rhino: 436348. 2008. CD.
    2143.2   *Psychocandy* [1985]. Expanded Edition. Edsel EDSG 806. 2011. 2 CDs.

2144   Leftfield. *Leftism*. Hard Hands / Sony: CK 67231. 1995. CD.

2145   ★Living Colour. *Vivid* [1988]. Sony / BMG Custom Marketing: 70356. 2002. CD.

2146   ★Los Lobos. *How Will the Wolf Survive?* [1984]. Slash: 25177-2. 1991. CD.

2147   Low. *Secret Name*. Kranky: 35. 1998. CD.

2148   Massive Attack. *Blue Lines*. Virgin: 86228. 1991. CD.

2149   Meat Puppets. *Meat Puppets II* [1983]. Rykodisc: 10467 (SST 019). 1999. CD.

2150   Megadeth. *Peace Sells . . . But Who's Buying?* 25th anniversary special ed. [1986]. Capitol: 293452. 2011. CD.

2151   Midnight Oil. *Diesel and Dust*. Columbia: CK 40967. 1988. CD.

2152   Ministry. *The Land of Rape and Honey* [1988]. Wounded Bird / Phantom: 64145799. 2007. CD.

2153   Minutemen
    2153.1   *Double Nickels on the Dime* [1983–1984]. SST: SSTCD-028. 1989. CD.
    2153.2   *We Jam Econo*. Plexifilm: 28. 2006. 2 DVDs.

2154   Morissette, Alanis. *Jagged Little Pill*. Maverick / Reprise: 45901. 1995. CD.

2155   Motorhead. *No Remorse* [1979–1982]. Metal-Is / Sanctuary: 85208. 2001. 2 CDs.

2156   My Bloody Valentine
    2156.1   *Isn't Anything* [1988]. Sire: 9 45231-2. 1993. CD.
    2156.2   *Loveless*. Sire: 26759-2. 1991. CD.

2157   Napalm Death. *Scum* [1987]. Earache / EMI: BECDERCH3. 1999. CD.

2158   New Order. *International*. Warner: 81227383527. 2002. CD.

2159   New Pornographers. *Electric Version*. Matador: 551. 2003. CD.

2160   Nine Inch Nails
    2160.1   *And All That Could Have Been*. Universal: 4400609659. 2002. 2 DVDs.
    2160.2   *The Downward Spiral*. Nothing / Interscope: 92346. 1994. CD.

2161   Nirvana
    2161.1   *In Utero*. DGC: CD 24607. 1993. CD.
    2161.2   *Live! Tonight! Sold Out!!* Geffen: B0007914-09. 2006. DVD.
    2161.3   ★*Nevermind*. DGC / Geffen: DGCD-24425. 1991. CD.

2162   No Doubt. *Rock Steady*. Interscope: 069 493 158-2. 2001. CD.

2163   Oasis
    2163.1   *Definitely Maybe* [1994]. Reprise: 516149. 2009. CD.
    2163.2   *(What's the Story) Morning Glory?* Big Brother / Reprise: 517125-2. 2008. CD.

2164   Pavement
    2164.1 *Brighten the Corners*. Matador / Capitol: 55226. 1997. CD.
    2164.2 *Crooked Rain, Crooked Rain*. Matador: 79. 1994. CD.
    2164.3 *Slanted and Enchanted*. Matador: OLE 038-2. 1992. CD.
    2164.4 *Slow Century* [1999–2002]. Matador: OLE 388-9. 2002. 2 DVDs.

2165   Pearl Jam
    2165.1 *Pearl Jam: Touring Band 2000*. Epic Music Video: EVD 54010. 2001. DVD.
    2165.2 *Ten*. Epic Associated: ZK 47857. 1991. CD.

2166   Pet Shop Boys. *Discography: The Complete Singles Collection* [1985–1991]. EMI: 97097. 1991. CD.

2167   Pixies
    2167.1 *Doolittle* [1989]. 4AD / Ada: 60856-2. 2003. CD. Can't find OCLC for the 2003 version.
    2167.2 *Surfer Rosa* [1987]. 4AD / Elektra: 78030. 2003. CD.

2168   Pogues
    2168.1 *If I Should Fall from Grace with God Remastered* [1988]. Rhino: 74069. 1991. CD.
    2168.2 *Rum, Sodomy, and the Lash* [1985]. Rhino: 74072. 2006. CD.

2169   Portishead. *Dummy*. Polygram: 828 553. 1994. CD.

2170   ★Pretenders. *The Singles* [1979–1986]. Rhino: 511067. 2008. CD.

2171   Primal Scream. *Screamadelica*. Sire: 26714. 1991. CD.

2172   Prodigy
    2172.1 *The Fat of the Land*. Maverick: 46606. 1997. CD.
    2172.2 *Music for the Jilted Generation*. XL / Mute: 9003. 1995. CD.

2173   Psychedelic Furs. *All of This and Nothing* [1980–1988]. Sony / BMG: 723980. 2008. CD.

2174   Pulp. *Different Class*. Poly Tone: 524165. 1996. CD.

2175   R.E.M.
    2175.1 *Automatic for the People*. Warner: 45055-2. 1992. CD.
    2175.2 *Document* [1987]. I.R.S.: 72434-93480-2-8. 1998. CD.

    2175.3 ★*Eponymous* [1981–1987]. I.R.S.: 72434-93457-2-0. 1998. CD.
    2175.4 *Murmur* [1983]. I.R.S. / A&M: 4479700142. 1990. CD.

2176   Radiohead
    2176.1 *The Bends*. Capitol: 29626. 1995. CD.
    2176.2 *Hail to the Thief*. Capitol: 84543. 2003. CD.
    2176.3 *Meeting People Is Easy*. Capitol Records: 77860. 1998. DVD.
    2176.4 ★*OK Computer*. Capitol: 55229. 1997. CD.

2177   Rage against the Machine. *Rage against the Machine*. Epic: 52959. 1992. CD.

2178   Red Hot Chili Peppers. *Bloodsugarsexmagik*. Warner Bros.: 26681. 1991. CD.

2179   Replacements. *Let It Be* [1984]. Rhino: 438844. 2008. CD.

2180   Ride. *Nowhere*. Warner Bros.: 26462. 1990. CD.

2181   Rollins Band. *End of Silence*. Imago: 21006-2. 1992. CD.

2182   Shellac. *At Action Park*. Touch & Go: 20841. 1994. CD.

2183   Shins. *Chutes Too Narrow*. Sub Pop: 625. 2003. CD.

2184   Slayer. *Reign in Blood* [1986]. American: 88697 12882 2. 2007. CD.

2185   Sleater-Kinney
    2185.1 *Call the Doctor*. Chainsaw: 13. 1996. CD.
    2185.2 *Dig Me Out*. Kill Rock Stars: 279. 1997. CD.
    2185.3 *The Hot Rock*. Kill Rock Stars: KRS 321. 1999. CD.

2186   Slint
    2186.1 *Spiderland* (Brian McMahan, David Pajo, Britt Walford). Touch and Go: 64. 1991. CD.
    2186.2 *Tweez* [1989] (Brian McMahan, David Pajo, Britt Walford). Touch and Go: TG138CD. 1993. CD.

2187   Smashing Pumpkins. *Siamese Dream*. Virgin: 88267. 1993. CD.

2188   Smith, Elliott
    2188.1 *Either/Or*. Kill Rock Stars: 269. 1997. CD.
    2188.2 *Elliott Smith*. Kill Rock Stars: KRS 246. 1995. CD.

2189 ★Smiths. *Best, Vol. 1* [1984–1988]. Warner: 45042-2. 1992. CD.

2190 Sonic Youth
    2190.1 *Bad Moon Rising* [1984–1985]. Geffen: 24512. 1995. CD.
    2190.2 *Corporate Ghost: The Videos, 1990–2002.* Geffen / Universal: B000075409. 2004. DVD.
    2190.3 *Daydream Nation* [1988]. DGC: DGCD-25415. 1993. CD.
    2190.4 *Sister* [1987]. DGC: DGCD-24514 (SST-134). 2003. CD.

2191 Soundgarden. *Superunknown.* A&M: 314 540198-2. 1994. CD.

2192 Spiritualized. *Ladies and Gentlemen We Are Floating in Space.* Arista: 18974. 1997. CD.

2193 Spoon. *Girls Can Tell.* Merge: MRG195. 2001. CD.

2194 Squeeze. *Singles: 45s and under Remastered* [1978–1982]. A&M: 75021-3338-2. 1995. CD.

2195 Stereolab. *Emperor Tomato Ketchup.* Elektra; Asylum: 61840. 1996. CD.

2196 Stone Roses. *The Stone Roses.* 20th anniversary ed. Silvertone / Legacy: 88697560632. 2009. CD.

2197 Sublime. *Sublime.* Gasoline Alley / MCA: 11413. 1996. CD.

2198 Swans. *Children of God / World of Skin* [1987]. Young God Records: YG02. 2003. CD.

2199 Swell Maps. *Jane from Occupied Europe* [1980]. Secretly Canadian: SC109. 2004. CD.

2200 Throbbing Gristle
    2200.1 *The Second Annual Report of Throbbing Gristle* [1977]. Forced Exposure: 001. 2011. CD.
    2200.2 *Throbbing Gristle Bring You 20 Jazz Funk Greats* [1979]. Forced Exposure: 003. 2011. CD.

2201 Throwing Muses. *Anthology* 4AD: 3150. 2011. CD.

2202 Tortoise. *Millions Now Living Will Never Die.* Thrill Jockey: 25. 1996. CD.

2203 Violent Femmes. *Violent Femmes* [1981–1983]. Rhino: R2 79951. 2000. CD.

2204 ★Waits, Tom. *Rain Dogs* [1985]. Poly Tone: 826382. 1990. CD.

2205 Was (Not Was). *Boo!* (Kris Kristofferson). Rykodisc: RCD 10943. 2008. CD.

2206 Weezer. *Weezer (Blue Album).* DGC: 24629. 1994. CD.

2207 White, Jack
    2207.1 *Blunderbuss.* Third Man Records: 88691 95993 2. 2012. CD.
    2207.2 *Lazaretto.* Third Man Records: 88843 06398 2. 2014. CD.

2208 White Stripes, The
    2208.1 *De Stijl.* Warner Bros.; Third Man Records: 512135. 2008. CD.
    2208.2 *Elephant.* V2 Records: VVR 1027452. 2003. CD.
    2208.3 *White Blood Cells* [2001]. Warner Bros.; Third Man Records: 512136. 2008. CD.

2209 Wilco
    2209.1 *Summer Teeth.* Reprise: 47282. 1999. CD.
    2209.2 *Yankee Hotel Foxtrot.* Nonesuch: 79669. 2002. CD.

2210 X
    2210.1 *Beyond and Back: The X Anthology.* Elektra: 62103-2. 1997. 2 CDs.
    2210.2 *X: The Unheard Music.* Image Entertainment: 2254. 2005. DVD.

2211 XTC. *Compact XTC: The Singles, 1978–1985.* EMI: 86476. 2005. CD.

2212 Yeah Yeah Yeahs. *Fever to Tell.* Interscope: B0000349-02. 2003. CD.

2213 Yo La Tengo
    2213.1 *Electr-O-Pura.* Matador: OLE 132. 1995. CD.
    2213.2 *I Can Hear the Heart Beating as One.* Matador: 222. 1997. CD.

DANCE MUSIC, ELECTRONICA, ETC.

COLLECTION

2214 *A Life Less Lived: The Gothic Box.* Rhino: R2 73374. 2006. 4 CDs.

INDIVIDUALS AND GROUPS

2215 Air. *Moon Safari.* 10th anniversary special ed. Astralwerks Records / EMI: 509992074801 8. 1998. 2 CDs, DVD.

2216 Aphex Twin
    2216.1 *Richard D. James Album.* Warp / Sire: 62010. 1996. CD.

2216.2 *Selected Ambient Works, 85–92.* Pias America: 4. 1993. CD.

2216.3 *Selected Ambient Works, Vol. II.* Warp / Sire: 45482. 1994. 2 CDs.

2217   Basement Jaxx
2217.1 *Kish Kash.* Astralwerks: 93878. 2003. CD.
2217.2 *Remedy.* Astralwerks: 6270. 1999. CD.

2218   Chemical Brothers
2218.1 *Dig Your Own Hole.* Freestyle Dust / Astralwerks: 6180. 1997. CD.
2218.2 *Exit Planet Dust.* Freestyle Dust / Astralwerks: 6157. 1995. CD.

2219   Daft Punk. *Homework.* Virgin: 42609. 1996. CD.

2220   Fatboy Slim. *You've Come a Long Way, Baby.* Astralwerks: 66247. 1998. CD.

2221   King Tubby. *Roots of Dub.* Traffic Entertainment Group: 50761. 2010. CD.

2222   Liquid Liquid. *Liquid Liquid* [1981–1983]. GR2: GR20009. 2008. CD.

2223   Luomo. *Present Lover.* Kinetic: 67728-54733-2. 2004. CD.

2224   Moby
2224.1 *Go: The Very Best of Moby, Deluxe Ed., Vol. 2.* Richard Hall Music: 63881-27347-2. 2006. 2 CDs.
2224.2 *Moby.* Instinct: 241. 1992. CD.
2224.3 *Play.* Mute: CDSTUMM172. 1999. CD.

2225   Neutral Milk Hotel. *In the Aeroplane over the Sea.* Merge: 136. 1998. CD.

2226   Orb. *The Orb's Adventures beyond the Ultraworld.* Universal I.S.: 162 535 005-2. 1991. 2 CDs.

2227   Perry, Lee "Scratch."
2227.1 *Essential Lee Perry: The Ultimate Upsetter* [1968–1978]. Metro Doubles: METRDCD562. 2005. 2 CDs.
2227.2 *The Ultimate Upsetter.* Video Music: MVD5289D. 2005. 2 CDs.

2228   Prefuse 73. *Vocal Studies + Uprock Narratives.* Warp: 83. 2001. CD.

2229   Sherwood, Adrian. *Never Trust a Hippy.* Real World: 52099631. 2003. CD.

2230   Size, Roni, and Reprazent. *New Forms.* UMGD—Fontana: 314 536 544-2. 1997. 2 CDs.

2231   Streets. *Original Pirate Material.* Vice / Ada: 93181. 2002. CD.

2232   Tricky. *Maxinquaye.* Island: 524 089. 1995. CD.

POST-ROCK

2233   Caballero, Don. *For Respect.* Touch & Go: 20820. 1993. CD.

2234   Clinic. *Internal Wrangler.* Domino; Ada: DOMUS01. 2000. CD.

2235   For Carnation. *The For Carnation* [2000]. Touch & Go: 20914. 2000. CD.

2236   Godspeed You Black Emperor. *Lift Your Skinny Fists Like Antennas to Heaven.* Kranky: 43. 2000. CD.

2237   Mogwai. *Young Team* [1997]. Chemikal Underground: CMKLCHUS016. 2008. 2 CDs.

2238   Silver Mt. Zion. *Born into Trouble as the Sparks Fly Upward.* Constellation: 18. 2001. CD.

7

Rhythm and Blues
and Soul

Compiled by **TERRY SIMPKINS** *and* **JEFFREY WANSER**

RHYTHM AND BLUES   *126*
   General Style   126
   Blues   130
   Jazz   130
   Jump Blues   130
   Vocal Groups   131
   Regional Styles   133
   Neo-Soul   135
   New Jack Swing   135
   Contemporary   136
   Label Overview   136
SOUL   *138*
   General Style   138
   Vocal Groups   145
   Regional Styles   146
   Instrumental and Soundtracks   147
   Gospel   147
   Contemporary   148
   Neo-Soul   148
   Blues   148
   Label Overview   148
FUNK   *150*
   General Style   150
DISCO   *152*
   General Style   152
   Label Overview   152
   Soundtrack   152

Rhythm and blues (R&B) is a blanket term describing a variety of styles of African American popular music from approximately 1945 to the present. It had its origins in the post–World War II period, following the demise of big band swing. Small combos came to the fore, with progenitors in the jump blues and boogie-woogie of artists such as Louis Jordan and Lucky Millinder. The term rhythm and blues first gained wide use in the late 1940s, and in 1949, Billboard magazine renamed its "race recordings" charts with this new, less offensive designation. While these charts included many styles of African American music, including blues, gospel, and jazz, R&B came to mean a style of popular dance music with an insistent backbeat. Fed by regional styles from New Orleans, Chicago, Los Angeles, and other cities, R&B developed along numerous lines and incorporated influences from gospel, pop music, and country. The jump blues tradition continued through singers such as Wynonie Harris, Ruth Brown, and LaVern Baker, while a smoother club blues gained popularity through artists such as Charles Brown and Ivory Joe Hunter. Vocal groups gained prominence in the early 1950s, leading to what would later be called doo-wop. R&B had a profound influence on the foundation and development of rock and roll through such artists as Fats Domino and Little Richard, and there has been significant cross-fertilization since.

By the late 1950s, many artists such as James Brown, Sam Cooke, and Ray Charles had combined musical elements of gospel with R&B, leading to the development of "soul" music, a term that eclipsed "R&B" for over a decade. Centers of music during this period shifted, and Detroit (Motown), Memphis (Stax/Volt), and Philadelphia (Philadelphia International) became vital to the development of soul music. The Motown sound, highly pop-oriented, competed with southern soul as well as other urban styles for the consumer dollar. In the 1970s, musical styles fragmented, and disco and funk became highly popular outgrowths of soul music, with their emphasis on beat or instrumentation over vocals.

The term *R&B* came back into vogue in the 1980s to describe a variety of styles in the postdisco/postfunk musical environment. While rap music became popular, soul singing made a comeback in the form of neosoul, new jack swing, and contemporary (sometimes referred to as *urban contemporary* or *quiet storm*). Current artists mix older and newer styles in a kaleidoscope of sounds that continue to fascinate fans.

Subgenres identified here include R&B generally, soul music, funk, and disco. While many others might be considered, the number of categories was limited for simplicity's sake. R&B is not defined by time or place so much as by continuity of sound, including the use of blues chords with a backbeat for dancing, and includes some of the earliest and most recent music in the section. Soul music (Otis Redding, Curtis Mayfield) refers mostly to 1960s and 1970s styles that combine R&B with gospel music to create unique sounds. Funk (Parliament, Rick James) is a style that incorporates extended jams and polyrhythmic complexity, and disco (Donna Summer, Chic) emphasizes dance beats over other aspects. These four subgenres are necessarily somewhat fluid, as artists changed their styles to accommodate changing tastes, and crossovers and combinations of styles have been common. For example, James Brown was instrumental in both soul and funk, and groups such as the Isley Brothers evolved from R&B doo-wop to soul to disco. Not all artists listed are African American, as categories refer to style rather than ethnicity.

Sub-subgenres both break down the four subgenres down and cut across them. The vocal groups sub-subgenre appears in both the soul and R&B genres and simply refers to the presence of multiple singers. Stylistically, this includes R&B-oriented doo-wop (the Moonglows, Frankie Lymon and the Teenagers), Motown groups (the Temptations, Diana Ross and the Supremes), Philadelphia soul groups, and "girl groups" (the Shirelles, the Crystals). Other sub-subgenres include jump blues (Louis Jordan, Lucky Millinder), contemporary (Toni Braxton, R. Kelly), new jack swing (Keith Sweat, Boyz II Men), and neosoul (Anita Baker, Alicia Keyes). In addition, regional categories are differentiated, including New Orleans (Professor Longhair, Fats Domino) and Philadelphia (the Stylistics, the O'Jays). A few jazz and blues artists have also been listed when considered important to R&B or soul.

In addition to stylistic considerations, other categories have been used to designate recordings. For sound recordings these include label overviews (Atlantic, Motown, Stax/Volt), best-of compilations in either single or multidisc formats, and individual releases. For video recordings, distinctions are made among concert films, documentaries, and best-of compilations, and for scores, categories include anthologies and best-of compilations.

RHYTHM AND BLUES
General Style
COLLECTIONS

2239 ★*The R&B Box* [1943–1972] (Louis Jordan, Buddy Johnson, Illinois Jacquet, Joe Liggins, Lionel Hampton, Jimmy Liggins, Johnny Moore, Charles Brown, Ravens, Roy Milton, Julia Lee,

Nellie Lutcher, Mabel Scott, Amos Milburn, Paul Williams, Big Jay McNeely, Dinah Washington, Johnny Otis, Percy Mayfield, Jackie Brenston, Five Keys, Lloyd Price, Ruth Brown, Orioles, Joe Turner, Professor Longhair, Clovers, Spaniels, Penguins, LaVern Baker, Moonglows, Ray Charles, Johnny Ace, Clyde McPhatter, Drifters, Shirley and Lee, Cadillacs, James Brown, Fats Domino, Big Maybelle, Chuck Willis, Dells, Jesse Belvin, Coasters, Jackie Wilson, Chantels, Huey Smith, Impressions, Wilbert Harrison, Flamingos, Dee Clark, Etta James, Bobby Bland, Solomon Burke, Mary Wells, Chuck Jackson, Booker T. and the MGs, Marvin Gaye, Miracles, Joe Tex, Little Milton, Four Tops, Isley Brothers, Wilson Pickett, Percy Sledge, Temptations, Eddie Floyd, Aaron Neville, Otis Redding, James Carr, Aretha Franklin, Sam and Dave, B. B. King, Brook Benton, Ike and Tina Turner, and others). Rhino: R2 71806. 1994. 6 CDs.

2240 *Stars of the Apollo* [1927–1965] (Bessie Smith with Buck and His Band, Buck and Bubbles and Their Buckets, Mamie Smith, Butterbeans and Susie, Claude Hopkins, Mills Brothers, Cab Calloway, Baron Lee, Jimmy Johnson, Bill "Bojangles" Robinson, Don Redman, Earl Hines, Ruby Smith, Ella Fitzgerald, Teddy Wilson, Ella Logan, Eddie "Cleanhead" Vinson, Cootie Williams, "Hot Lips" Page, Slim Gaillard, Ida Cox, Billie Holiday, Count Basie, Jimmy Rushing, Claude Thornhill, Maxine Sullivan, Pearl Bailey, Jackie "Moms" Mabley, Big Maybelle, Leroy Kirkland, Duke Ellington, Sarah Vaughan, Bobby Brown Quartet, Screamin' Jay Hawkins, Aretha Franklin). Columbia: C2K 53407. 1992. 2 CDs.

INDIVIDUALS AND GROUPS

2241 Adams, Faye. *The Herald Recordings* [1953–1957]. Collectables: COL-CD-5122. 1992. CD.

2242 Ashford and Simpson. *The Very Best of Ashford and Simpson* [1973–1984]. Rhino: R2 79804. 2002. CD.

2243 Atlantic Starr. *Ultimate Collection* [1978–1992]. Hip-O: 4906552. 2000. CD.

2244 Baker, Anita. *Rapture*. Elektra: 9 60444-2. 1986. CD.

2245 Baker, LaVern. *Soul on Fire: The Best of Lavern Baker* [1953–1962]. Atlantic: 82311-2. 1991. CD.

2246 Baker, Mickey. *In the '50s: Hit, Git, and Split* [1952–1956] (Sylvia Robinson). Rev-Ola: CRBAND 29. 2007. CD.

2247 Ballard, Hank. *Sexy Ways: The Best of Hank Ballard and the Midnighters* [1953–1961]. Rhino: R2 71512. 1993. CD.

2248 ★Brown, Charles. *The Complete Aladdin Recordings of Charles Brown* [1945–1956]. Mosaic: MD5-153. 1994. 5 CDs.

2249 Brown, Roy. *Good Rocking Tonight: The Best of Roy Brown* [1947–1957]. Rhino: R2 71545. 1994. CD.

2250 Brown, Ruth. *Miss Rhythm: Greatest Hits and More* [1949–1960]. Atlantic: 82061-2. 1989. 2 CDs.

2251 Dixon, Floyd. *Marshall, Texas Is My Home* [1953–1957]. Specialty: SPCD-7011-2. 1991. CD.

2252 Doggett, Bill
   2252.1 *The EP Collection* [1954-1960]. See for Miles: SEECD 689. 1999. CD.
   2252.2 *The Very Best of Bill Doggett: Honky Tonk* [1952–1953]. Collectables: COL-CD-2876. 2005. CD.

2253 Gant, Cecil. *1944–1945*. Fly: 61. 1997. CD.

2254 Gayten, Paul. *Chess King of New Orleans: The Chess Years* [1954–1959]. Chess: CHD-9294. 1989. CD.

2255 Gordon, Roscoe. *I'm Gonna Shake It!* [1951–1957]. Varèse Sarabande / Sun: 302 066 385 2. 2002. CD.

2256 Griffin Brothers. *Blues with a Beat* [early 1950s] (Margie Day). Acrobat: 209. 2003. CD.

2257 Grimes, Tiny
   2257.1 *Tiny Grimes, 1944–1949*. Classics Records: 5048. 2002. CD.
   2257.2 *Tiny Grimes, 1949–1951*. Classics Records: 5106. 2004. CD.
   2257.3 *Tiny Grimes, 1951–1954*. Classics Records: 5146. 2005. CD.

2258 Hamilton, Roy. *Anthology*. Collectables: COL-CD-8823. 1995. 2 CDs.

2259 Harris, Wynonie
   2259.1 *Bloodshot Eyes: The Best of Wynonie Harris* [1947–1955]. Rhino: R2 71544. 1994. CD.

2259.2 ★*The Very Best of Wynonie Harris: Good Rockin' Tonight* [1947–1954]. Collectables: COL-CD-2872. 2003. CD.

2260 Hawkins, Screamin' Jay. *Cow Fingers and Mosquito Pie* [mid–1950s]. SPV: SPV 91662 CD. 2008. CD.

2261 Hunter, Ivory Joe
2261.1 *Since I Met You Baby: The Best of Ivory Joe Hunter* [1949–1958]. Razor and Tie: RE 2052. 1994. CD.
2261.2 *Woo Wee!: The King and Deluxe Acetate Series* [1945–1949]. Ace: 1092. 2006. CD.

2262 Jackson, Bull Moose. *The Very Best of Bull Moose Jackson: Big Ten-Inch Record* [1945–1955]. Collectables: COL-CD-2890. 2004. CD.

2263 Jackson, Janet
2263.1 *Control.* A&M: CD-3905. 1986. CD.
2263.2 *Design of a Decade, 1986/1996.* A&M: 31454 0399 2. 1995. CD.
2263.3 *From Janet to Damita Jo: The Videos.* Virgin Records America: 7243 5 99508 9 1. 2004. DVD.
2263.4 *Janet Jackon's Rhythm Nation 1814.* A&M: CD 3920. 1989. CD.
2263.5 *The Velvet Rope Tour Live in Concert / Live in Hawaii.* Eagle Vision: EV30106-9. 2004. 2 DVDs.

2264 Jackson, Michael
2264.1 *The Essential Michael Jackson* [1969–1995]. MJJ Productions / Epic / Legacy: E2K 94287. 2005. 2 CDs.
2264.2 *Greatest Hits: History, Vol. 1* [1979–1995]. Epic: EK 85250. 2001. CD.
2264.3 *Michael Jackson Live in Bucharest: The Dangerous Tour* [1992]. Epic Music Video: EVD 53497. 2004. DVD.
2264.4 *Off the Wall* [1979]. Epic / MJJ Productions: EK 66070. 2001. CD.
2264.5 ★*Thriller* [1982] (Paul McCartney). Epic: EK 66073. 2001. CD.
2264.6 *Video Greatest Hits: History.* Epic Music Video: EVD 50123. 2000. DVD.

2265 Jackson, Millie
2265.1 *Totally Unrestricted: The Millie Jackson Anthology* [1971–1983]. Rhino: R2 72863. 1997. 2 CDs.
2265.2 *21 of the Best, 1971–1983.* Southbound: CDSEWM 100. 1994. CD.

2265.3 *The Very Best of Millie Jackson* [1986–1994]. Jive: 01241-41540-2. 1994. CD.

2266 James, Etta
2266.1 *At Last!* [1960]. Chess / MCA: CHD-12017. 1999. CD.
2266.2 ★*The Chess Box* [1960–1974]. Chess / MCA: 088 112 288-2. 2000. 3 CDs.
2266.3 *The Essential Etta James* [1960–1975]. Chess / MCA: CHD2-9341. 1993. 2 CDs.
2266.4 *Etta James Rocks the House* [1963]. Chess / MCA: CHD 9184. 1992. CD.
2266.5 *Tell Mama: The Complete Muscle Shoals Sessions* [1967–1968]. Chess / MCA: 088 112 518-2. 2001. CD.

2267 James, Etta, and the Roots Band. *Burnin' Down the House.* Eagle Eye Media: EE 19016. 2001. DVD.

2268 Jamiroquai. *High Times: Singles, 1992–2006*

2269 John, Little Willie
2269.1 ★*Fever: The Best of Little Willie John* [1955–1963]. Rhino: R2 71511. 1993. CD.
2269.2 *The Very Best of Little Willie John* [1955–1962]. Collectables: COL-CD-2822. 2001. CD.

2270 Johnson, Buddy
2270.1 *Buddy and Ella Johnson: 1953–1964* [1953-1964] (Ella Johnson). Bear Family: BCD 15479 DH. 1992. 4 CDs.
2270.2 *Walk 'Em: The Decca Sessions* [1941–1953]. Ace: CDCHD 623. 1996. CD.

2271 Johnson, Marv. *The Best of Marv Johnson: You've Got What It Takes* [1958–1963]. EMI: E2-98895. 1992. CD.

2272 Kenner, Chris. *I Like It Like That: Golden Classics.* Collectables: COL-CD-5166. 1994. CD.

2273 Lance, Major. *The Very Best of Major Lance* [1963–1967]. Epic: EK 62243. 2000. CD.

2274 Lattisaw, Stacy. *The Very Best of Stacy Lattisaw* [1979–1988]. Rhino: R2 72945. 1998. CD.

2275 LeVert. *The Best of LeVert* [1985–1997]. Rhino: R2 76781. 2001. CD.

2276 Lewis, Barbara. *Hello Stranger: The Best of Barbara Lewis* [1962–1968]. Rhino / Atlantic: R2 71619. 1994. CD.

2277 Lutcher, Nellie
2277.1 *The Best of Nellie Lutcher* [1947–1951].

Capitol Jazz: CDP 7243 8 35039 2 6. 1995. CD.

2277.2 *Nellie Lutcher and Her Rhythm* [1947-1963]. Bear Family: BCD 15910 DI. 1996. 4 CDs.

2278 Maze

2278.1 *Anthology* (Frankie Beverly). Right Stuff: 7243-8-35885-2-7. 1996. 2 CDs.

2278.2 *Greatest Hits* (Frankie Beverly). Right Stuff: 72435-79856-2-8. 2004. CD.

2279 McPhatter, Clyde

2279.1 *Deep Sea Ball: The Best of Clyde McPhatter.* Atlantic: 82314-2. 1991. CD.

2279.2 *Lover Please: The Complete MGM and Mercury Singles* [1959-1965]. Hip-O Select: B0014233-02. 2010. 2 CDs.

2280 Milburn, Amos

2280.1 *The Complete Aladdin Recordings of Amos Milburn* [1946-1957]. Mosaic: MD7-155. 1994. 7 CDs.

2280.2 *Let's Have a Party: The Aladdin Recordings* [1946–1957]. Rev-Ola: CR BAND 27. 2007. CD.

2281 Mills, Stephanie

2281.1 *Gold.* Hip-O: B0005899-02. 2006. 2 CDs.

2281.2 *The Ultimate Collection.* Hip-O: HIPD-40146. 1999. CD.

2282 Milton, Roy. *Roy Milton and His Solid Senders* [1945–1952]. Specialty: SPCD 7004. 1989. CD.

2283 Mitchell, Willie. *Poppa Willie: The Hi Years, 1962–74.* Hi Records: HEXD 48. 2001. 2 CDs.

2284 Moore, Melba. *This Is It: The Best of Melba Moore* [1975–1987]. Razor and Tie: RE2062. 1995. CD.

2285 New Edition

2285.1 *Gold* [1984–1996] (Bobby Brown, Johnny Gill). Hip-O: B0005330-02. 2005. 2 CDs.

2285.2 *Hits* (Bobby Brown, Johnny Gill). Geffen: B0001728-02. 2004. CD.

2286 Ocean, Billy. *Ultimate Collection.* Jive: 82876623802. 2004. CD.

2287 Osborne, Jeffrey. *Ultimate Collection* [1976–1990]. Hip-O: 069 490 421 2. 1999. CD.

2288 Otis, Johnny

2288.1 *The Capitol Years* [late 1950s] (Marie Adams, Ernie Freeman, Earl Palmer). EMI-Capitol / Collectables: COL-CD-2773. 2000. CD.

2288.2 *The Johnny Otis Rhythm and Blues Caravan* (Little Esther Phillips). Savoy Jazz: 92859-2. 2002. 3 CDs.

2288.3 *Rock Me Baby: The Mercury and Peacock Sides 1951–55* [1951-1955]. Rev-Ola Bandstand: CD BAND 9. 2007. CD.

2289 Parker, Ray, Jr. *Greatest Hits.* Arista: 07822-18732-2. 1993. CD.

2290 Pendergrass, Teddy. *Teddy, Live in '79.* Shout! Factory: DVD 10025. 2006. DVD.

2291 Phillips, Esther. *Esther: The Best of Esther Phillips* [1962–1970]. Rhino: R2 72624. 1997. 2 CDs.

2292 Price, Lloyd

2292.1 *Lawdy!* [1952–1956]. Specialty: SPCD-7010-2. 1991. CD.

2292.2 *Lloyd Price, Vol. 2: Heavy Dreams* [1952–1956]. Specialty: SPCD 7047-DJ. 1993. CD.

2293 Prince. *The Hits Collection* [1970s–1990s]. Warner Reprise: 38371-2. 1993. DVD.

2294 Rhodes, Todd. *Blues for the Red Boy: The Early Sensation Recordings* [1947–1951]. Ace: CDCHD 856. 2002. CD.

2295 Richie, Lionel. *Lionel Richie Collection* [1970s–1980s]. Motown / Universal. 2003. DVD.

2296 Rushen, Patrice. *Haven't You Heard: The Best of Patrice Rushen* [1978–1987]

2296.1 Elektra Traditions: R2 73513. 1996. CD.

2296.2 Sony / BMG: 88697 02224 9. 2006 DVD.

2297 Thomas, Rufus. *His R&B Recordings 1949–1956: The Sun Years, Plus.* Bear Family: BCD 16695 AH. 2008. CD.

2298 Turner, Ike. *The Sun Sessions* [1951–1958] (Kings of Rhythm, Johnny O'Neal, Billy Emerson, Raymond Hill, Bonnie Turner). Varèse Sarabande: 302 066 232 2. 2001. CD.

2299 Turner, Ike, and Tina Turner. *The Legends Ike and Tina Turner Live in '71.* Eagle Vision: EV 30085-9. 2004. DVD.

2300 Turner, Tina

2300.1 *One Last Time Live in Concert* [2000]. Eagle Vision: EV300059. 2000. DVD.

2300.2 *Tina: All the Best—The Live Collection.* Capitol: C9 7243 5 44345 9 4. 2005. DVD.

2301   Williams, Larry. *Bad Boy* [1957–1959].
       Specialty: SPCD 7002. 1989. CD.

2302   Willis, Chuck
       2302.1   *I Remember Chuck Willis/the King of the*
                Stroll [1956–1958]. Collectables: COL-
                CD6889. 2001. CD.
       2302.2   *Let's Jump Tonight!: The Best of Chuck*
                Willis from 1951-56 [1951–1956]. Epic /
                Okeh / Legacy: EK 53619. 1994. CD.
       2302.3   *Stroll On: The Chuck Willis Collection.*
                Razor and Tie: RE 2055. 1994. CD.

Blues

2303   Big Maybelle. *I've Got a Feelin': Okeh and Savoy*
       Recordings, 1952–56. Rev-Ola Bandstand: 20.
       2008. CD.

2304   Guitar Slim. *Sufferin' Mind* [1953–1955].
       Specialty: SPCD-7007-2. 1991. CD.

2305   Lee, Julia
       2305.1   *Kansas City Star* [1927–1957]. Bear
                Family: BCD 15770 EI. 1995. 5 CDs.
       2305.2   *Kansas City's First Lady of the Blues*
                [1944–1947]. JSP: JSPCD3405. 2011.
                2 CDs.

2306   Liggins, Jimmy. *Jimmy Liggins and His Drops*
       of Joy [1947–1953]. Specialty: SPCD 7005.
       1989. CD.

2307   Liggins, Joe. *Joe Liggins and the Honeydrippers*
       [1950–1954]. Specialty: SPCD 7006. 1989. CD.

2308   Mayfield, Percy
       2308.1   ★*His Tangerine and Atlantic Sides*
                [1962–1974]. Rhino Handmade: RHM2
                7828. 2004. CD.
       2308.2   *Percy Mayfield: Poet of the Blues* [1950–
                1954]. Specialty: SPCD 7001. 1989. CD.

2309   Turner, Ike. *Rhythm Rockin' Blues: The Legendary*
       Modern Recordings [1950–1955]. Ace: CDCHD
       553. 1995. CD.

2310   Turner, Joe
       2310.1   *Big, Bad, and Blue: The Big Joe Turner*
                Anthology [1938–1983]. Rhino: R2
                71550. 1994. 3 CDs.
       2310.2   ★*Jumpin' with Joe: The Complete Aladdin*
                and Imperial Recordings [1947–1950].
                EMI: E2 99293. 1993. CD.
       2310.3   *The Very Best of Big Joe Turner* [1951–
                1959]. Rhino: R2 72968. 1998. CD.

2311   Witherspoon, Jimmy
       2311.1   *The Best of Jimmy Witherspoon: Jazz Me*
                Blues [1956–1969]. Fantasy: PRCD-
                11008-2. 1998. CD.
       2311.2   *Blowin' in from Kansas City* [1940s–
                1950s]. Ace: CDCHD 279. 1991. CD.
       2311.3   *Live at the 1972 Monterey Jazz Festival.*
                Monterey Jazz Festival: MJFR-30638.
                2008. CD.
       2311.4   *The 'Spoon Concerts* [1959]. Fantasy:
                FCD-24701-2. 1989. CD.
       2311.5   *Urban Blues Singing Legend* [1945–1963].
                JSP: JSP7778. 2006. 4 CDs.

Jazz

2312   Humes, Helen. *Knockin' Myself Out* [1927–1951].
       Jazz Legends: JAZ 2012. 2005. CD.

2313   Washington, Dinah
       2313.1   *After Hours with Miss "D"* [1953].
                Verve: B0000094-02. 2004. CD.
       2313.2   *Back to the Blues* [early 1960s]. Roulette
                Jazz: CDP 7243 8 54334 2 9. 1997. CD.
       2313.3   *The Complete Roulette Dinah Washington*
                Sessions [1962–1963]. Mosaic: MD5-
                227. 2004. 5 CDs.
       2313.4   *The Definitive Dinah Washington*
                [1943–1962]. Verve: 314 589 839-2.
                2002. CD.
       2313.5   *Dinah Jams* [1954]. EmArcy: 814 639-
                2. 1990. CD.
       2313.6   *Dinah Sings Bessie Smith* [1957–1958].
                Verve: 314 538 635-2. 1999. CD.
       2313.7   ★*The Fabulous Miss D! The Keynote,*
                Decca, and Mercury Singles 1943–1953.
                Hip-O Select: B0014668-02. 2010. 4
                CDs.
       2313.8   *First Issue: The Dinah Washington Story:*
                The Original Recordings [1943–1961].
                PolyGram: 314 514 841-2. 1993. 2 CDs.
       2313.9   *Gold.* Verve: B0009453-02. 2007. 2 CDs.
       2313.10 *What a Diff'rence a Day Makes* [1959].
                Mercury / Polygram: 818 815-2.
                1984. CD.

Jump Blues

COLLECTION

2314   *The Big Horn: The History of the Honkin' and*
       Screamin' Saxophone [1942–1952] (Illinois
       Jacquet, Big Jim Wynn, Pazuzza Simon, Arnett
       Cobb, Morris Lane, Dick Davis, Wild Bill Moore,

Paul Williams, Jack McVea, Weasel Parker, Hal Singer, Tom Archia, John Hardee, Little Willie Jackson, Eddie Chamblee, Red Prysock, Benny Golson, Earl Bostic, Joe Thomas, Harold Land, Big Jay McNeely, Frank "Floorshow" Culley, Eddie "Lockjaw" Davis, Freddie Mitchell, Lee Allen, Leroy "Batman" Rankin, Herb Hardesty, Birdie Davis, Margaret Backstrom, Sam "The Man" Taylor, Cecil Payne, Ray Abrams, James von Streeter, Earl Johnson, Maxwell Davis, Willis Jackson, Charlie Singleton, Fred Jackson, Lynn Hope, Julian Dash, Buddy Tate, Plas Johnson, Al Sears, Fats Noel, Jimmy Jackson, Paul Bascomb, Joe Houston, Jimmy Forrest, David Brooks). Proper: PROPERBOX 61. 2003. 4 CDs.

INDIVIDUALS AND GROUPS

2315   Bostic, Earl
   2315.1   *The Earl Bostic Story* [1945–1955]. Proper: PPER211. 2006. 4 CDs.
   2315.2   *The EP Collection* [1950-1958]. See for Miles: SEECD 688. 1999. CD.

2316   Bradshaw, Tiny
   2316.1   *Breakin' Up the House* [1934–1951]. Proper: PVCD101. 2002. 2 CDs.
   2316.2   *The EP Collection–Plus* [1949-1955]. See for Miles: SEECD 703. 1999. CD.

2317   Carr, Wynona. *Jump Jack Jump!* [1955–1959]. Specialty: SPCD-7048-DJ. 1993. CD.

2318   Jordan, Louis
   2318.1   *The Best of Louis Jordan* [1941–1954]. MCA: MCAD-4079. 1989. CD.
   2318.2   *Let the Good Times Roll: The Anthology, 1938–1953*. MCA / Decca: MCAD2-11907. 1999. 2 CDs.
   2318.3   ★*Let the Good Times Roll: The Complete Decca Recordings 1938–1954*. Bear Family: BCD 15557. 1999. 9 CDs.
   2318.4   *Louis Jordan and His Tympany 5* [1938–1950]. JSP: JSPCD905A/ JSPCD905E. 2001. 5 CDs.
   2318.5   *Louis Jordan and His Tympany Five* [1930s–1940s] (Louis Armstrong, Cab Calloway, Nat King Cole Trio, Sammy Davis Jr.). BMG: 72333-80008-9. 2000. DVD.

2319   Millinder, Lucky
   2319.1   *Apollo Jump* (Rosetta Tharp, Wynonie Harris, Bull Moose Jackson). Proper: PVCD 115. 2002. 2 CDs.
   2319.2   *The Very Best of Lucky Millinder*. Collectables: COL-CD-2898. 2005. CD.

Vocal Groups

COLLECTIONS

2320   ★*Atlantic Vocal Groups, 1951–1963* (Clovers, Drifters, Carmen Taylor and the Boleros, Chords, Playboys, Regals, Playboys, Sheiks, Sh-Booms, Royal Jokers, Cardinals, Diamonds, Chordcats, Sensations, Pearls, Bobbettes, Castelles, Crescendos, Flyers, Clyde McPhatter, Ospreys, Penguins, Glowtones, King Bees, Del-Larks, Coasters, Vibraharps, Superiors, Romeos, Versatones, Skyliners, Billy Storm, Top Notes, and Time Tones). Rhino Handmade: RHM2 07738. 2008. 4 CDs.

2321   *The Best of the Girl Groups, Vols. 1 and 2* [1958–1966] (Shangri Las, Chiffons, Dixie Cups, Shirelles, Betty Everett, Angels, Little Eva, Cookies, Essex, Exciters, and others). Rhino: R2 70988; R2 70989. 1990. 2 CDs.

2322   ★*The Doo-Wop Box* [1948–1957] (Orioles, Ravens, Five Keys, Crows, Drifters, Flamingos, Harp-Tones, Velvets, Spaniels, Chords, Cadillacs, Jewels, Penguins, Moonglows, Rainbows, Wrens, Nutmegs, Platters, Jacks, Turbans, El Dorados, Valentines, Frankie Lymon and the Teenagers, Clovers, Willows, Cleftones, Five Satins, Channels, Dells, Heartbeats, Schoolboys, Del-Vikings, Lewis Lymon and the Teenchords, Solitaires, Gladiolas, Dubs, Paragons, Mello-Kings, Hearts, Shells, Rob-Roys, Silhouettes, Monotones, Dion and the Belmonts, Danleers, Impressions, Elegants, Little Anthony and the Imperials, Crests, Fiestas, Skyliners, Impalas, Mystics, Eternals, Passions, Jesters, Maurice Williams and the Zodiacs, Capris, Marcels, Tokens, Shep and the Limelites, Regents, Edsels, Jive Five, Halos, Earls, Quotations, Excellents, Five Discs, Randy and the Rainbows, Vito and the Salutations, and others). Rhino: R2 71463. 1993. 4 CDs.

2323   *The Doo-Wop Box II* [1951–1963] (Larks, Clovers, Mello-Moods, Vocaleers, Crows, Spaniels, Four Tunes, Five Keys, Rivileers, Counts, Moonglows, Scarlets, Penguins, Mellows, Cardinals, Hearts, Don Julian and the Meadowlarks, Danderliers, Harptones, Four Fellows, Robins, Heartbeats, El Dorados, Cleftones, Teen Queens, Drifters, Cadillacs,

Valentines, Magnificents, Flamingos, Platters,
Bop-Chords, Solitaires, Monarchs, Frankie
Lymon and the Teenagers, Chips, Spaniels,
Cufflinks, Johnnie and Joe, Velvetones, Cellos,
Five Satins, Bobbettes, Velours, Paragons,
Channels, Dubs, Collegians, Fidelitys, Kodaks,
Imperials, Spaniels, Falcons, Shirelles,
Skyliners, Sheppards, Miracles, Royal Teens,
Impacts, Eternals, Dion and the Belmonts,
Desires, Passions, Temptations, Crests, Desires,
Paradons, Chimes, Starlites, Pentagons, Little
Caesar and the Romans, Blue Jays, Curtis
Lee, Dreamlovers, Regents, Chantels, Stereos,
Marcels, Gene Chandler, Devotions, Don and
Juan, Volumes, Duprees, Jive Five, Anthony and
the Sophomores, Penguins, Camelots, Classics,
and others). Rhino: R2 72507. 1996. 4 CDs.

2324   *Old Town Doo-Wop, Vols.1–3* [1953–1962]
(Capris, Bonnevilles, Keytones, Solitaires,
Harptones, Royaltones, Vocaleers, Five Crowns,
Laurels, Co-Eds, Fiestas, Symbols, Earls,
Valentines, Tru-Tones, Esquires, and others).
Ace: CDCHD 433, 470, 471. 1993. 3 CDs.

INDIVIDUALS AND GROUPS

2325   Cadillacs
2325.1   *The Best of the Cadillacs* [1954–1959].
          Rhino: R2 70955. 1990. CD.
2325.2   *The Complete Josie Sessions* [1954–1963].
          Bear Family: BCD 15648 DI. 1995. 4 CDs.

2326   Chantels. *The Best of the Chantels* [1957–1961].
        Rhino: R2 70954. 1990. CD.

2327   Cleftones. *The Ultimate Collection* [late 1950s–
        early 1960s]. Collectables: COL-CD-7864.
        2007. CD.

2328   Clovers. *Your Cash Ain't Nothin But Trash: Their
        Greatest Hits, 1951–55* [1951]. Rev-Ola: CR REV
        146. 2006. CD.

2329   ★Coasters. *There's a Riot Goin' On: The Coasters
        on ATCO* [1955–1966]. Rhino Handmade:
        0349777402. 2008. 4 CDs.

2330   Commodores. *Anthology* [1973–1985]. Motown:
        314 585 088-2. 2001. 2 CDs.

2331   Crystals. *The Best of the Crystals* [1961–1964].
        Abkco: 72142. 1992. CD.

2332   Dells. *Anthology* [1954–1991]. Hip-O: 314 545
        106 2. 1999. 2 CDs.

2333   Destiny's Child. *#1's* [1999–2004]. Sony Urban
        Music / Columbia: CK 97765. 2005. CD.

2334   Dominoes. *The Very Best of Billy Ward and
        Dominoes* [1951–1954]. Collectables: COL-CD-
        2827. 2002. CD.

2335   Drifters
2335.1   ★*All Time Greatest Hits and More* [1959–
          1965]. Atlantic: 81931-2. 1988. CD.
2335.2   *Rockin' and Driftin'* [1953–1976]. Rhino:
          R2 72417. 1996. 3 CDs.

2336   Emotions. *The Best of the Emotions: Best of My
        Love* [1976–1981]. Columbia / Legacy: CK
        64832. 1996. CD.

2337   Five Keys. *Rocking and Crying the Blues, 1951–
        1957.* Rev-Ola: 22. 2008. CD.

2338   Five Royales
2338.1   *It's Hard but It's Fair: King Hits and
          Rarities* [1954–1960]. Ace: CDCHD
          1038. 2005. CD.
2338.2   ★*Monkey Hips and Rice: The "5" Royales
          Anthology* [1952–1965]. Rhino: R2
          71546. 1991. 2 CDs.

2339   Five Satins
2339.1   *The Original Master Tapes Collection,
          Vol. 1* [1956–1961]. Collectables: COL-
          CD-7508. 2002. CD.
2339.2   *The Original Master Tapes Collection, Vol.
          2* [1957–1961]. Collectables: COL-CD-
          7509. 2002. CD.

2340   Flamingos
2340.1   *The Best of the Flamingos* [1953–1961].
          Rhino: R2 70967. 1990. CD.
2340.2   *Complete Chess Masters Plus* [1955–1956].
          Chess / MCA: CHD-9378. 1997. CD.

2341   Four Tops
2341.1   *Anthology: 50th Anniversary* [1964–
          1988]. Hip-O: B0000488-02. 2004.
          2 CDs.
2341.2   *50th Anniversary: The Singles Collection,
          1961–1971.* Hip-O Select: B0015942-02.
          2011. 3 CDs.
2341.3   *Fourever* [1956–1992]. Hip-O: 314 556
          225-2. 2001. 4 CDs.
2341.4   *Lost and Found: Lost without You 1963–
          1970.* Hip-O Select. 2007. 2 CDs.

2342   Isley Brothers. *Summer Breeze: Greatest Hits,
        Live.* Eagle Rock Entertainment: EV30136-9.
        2005. DVD.

2343   Jackson 5
   2343.1 *Gold* [1969–1976]. Motown: B0004196-02. 2005. CD.
   2343.2 *Live at the Forum* [1970–1972]. Hip-O Select: B0014405-02. 2010. 2 CDs.
   2343.3 *The Ultimate Collection* [1969–1975]. Motown: 314530558-2. 1996. CD.

2344   Julian, Don, and the Meadowlarks. *Heaven and Paradise* [1954–1958]. Ace: CDCHD 552. 1995. CD.

2345   Lewis, Earl, and the Channels. *The Best of Earl Lewis and the Channels: New York's Finest* [1956–1961]. Collectables: COL-CD-5012. 1991. CD.

2346   *Life Could Be a Dream: The Doo-Wop Sound* [1950s–1960s] (Teenagers, Cadillacs, Chantels, Spaniels, Bobbettes, Diamonds, and others). White Star: D3094. 2002. DVD.

2347   Little Anthony and the Imperials. *The Best of Little Anthony and the Imperials* [1950s–1960s]. Rhino: R2 70919. 1989. CD.

2348   Lymon, Frankie, and the Teenagers. *The Very Best of Frankie Lymon and the Teenagers* [1955–1958]. Rhino: R2 75507. 1998. CD.

2349   Moonglows
   2349.1 *Blue Velvet: The Ultimate Collection* [1953–1959]. Chess: CHD2-9345. 1993. 2 CDs.
   2349.2 *The Moonglows* [1954–1957]. 20th Century Masters, Millennium Collection. MCA: 088 112 882-2. 2002. CD.

2350   Olympics
   2350.1 *Doin' the Hully Gully / Dance by the Light of the Moon / Party Time* [1959–1961]. Ace: CDCHD 324. 1991. CD.
   2350.2 *The Very Best of the Olympics* [1958–1974]. Varèse Sarabande / Demon: 302 066 362 2. 2002. CD.

2351   Orioles
   2351.1 *Jubilee Recordings* [1948–1960] (Sonny Til). Bear Family: BCD 15682 FI. 1993. 5 CDs.
   2351.2 *The Orioles Sing Their Greatest Hits* (Sonny Til). Collectables: COL-CD-5408. 1991. CD.

2352   Persuasions
   2352.1 *Chirpin'* [1977]. Elektra: 1099-2. 1990. CD.
   2352.2 *Street Corner Symphony* [1971]. Collectables: COL-CD-5235. 1991. CD.

2353   Ravens. *Their Complete National Recordings, 1947–1950* [1947–1950]. Savoy Jazz: SVY 17307. 2003. 2 CDs.

2354   Robins. *I Must Be Dreamin': The Robins on RCA, Crown, and Spark, 1953–55*. El Toro: 111. 2008. CD.

2355   Ronettes. *The Best of the Ronettes* [1963–1969]. Abkco / Phil Spector Records: 72122. 1992. CD.

2356   Ross, Diana. *50th Anniversary: The Singles Collection, 1961–1969* (Supremes). Hip-O Select: B0015943-02. 2011. 3 CDs.

2357   ★Shirelles. *The Shirelles 25 All-Time Greatest Hits* [1958–1964]. Varèse Sarabande: VSD-6029. 1999. CD.

2358   Spaniels. *40th Anniversary, 1953–1993*. Collectables: COL-CD-5584. 1995. CD.

Regional Styles

New Orleans

COLLECTIONS

2359   *Finger Poppin' and Stompin' Feet: 20 Classic Allen Toussaint Productions for Minit Records, 1960–1962* (Showmen, Ernie K-Doe, Aaron Neville, Jessie Hill, Irma Thomas, Benny Spellman, Del Royals, and others). EMI / Capitol: 72435-37450-2-8. 2002. CD.

2360   *Make It Funky!* (Allen Toussaint, Bonnie Raitt, Dirty Dozen Brass Band, Earl Palmer, Funky Meters, Irma Thomas, Neville Brothers, and others). Sony: 11952. 2005. DVD

2361   *The Mercury New Orleans Sessions 1950 and 1953* (Alma Mondy, Professor Longhair, Theard Johnson, George Miller, Joe Gaines, Dwine Craven, Silvertone Singers, Pat Valdelar, Ray Johnson, Herbert Moore). Bear Family: BCD 16804 BH. 2007. 2 CDs.

INDIVIDUALS AND GROUPS

2362   Domino, Fats
   2362.1 ★*Out of New Orleans* [1949–1962]. Bear Family: BCD 15541 HI. 1993. 8 CDs.
   2362.2 *The Legends of New Orleans: The Music of Fats Domino* [2001]. Shout! Factory: DVD 32001. 2003. DVD. DVD and VHS may have different titles.

2362.3 *Walking to New Orleans* [1949–1962]. Capitol: 72435-37374-2-9. 2002. 4 CDs.

2363 Dorsey, Lee. *Wheelin' and Dealin': The Definitive Collection* [1961–1969]. Arista: 07822-18980-2. 1997. CD.

2364 Dr. John
    2364.1 ★*Dr. John's Gumbo* [1972]. Atco: 7006-2. 1986. CD.
    2364.2 *Gris-Gris* [1968]. Collectables: CCM-131-2. 2000. CD.
    2364.3 *Mos' Scocious: The Dr. John Anthology* [1959–1989]. Rhino: R2 71450. 1993. 2 CDs.

2365 King, Earl
    2365.1 *Come On: The Complete Imperial Recordings* [1960–1962]. EMI: OKR-CD-4970. 2003. CD.
    2365.2 *Earl's Pearls: The Very Best of Earl King* [1955–1960]. Westside: WESM 520. 1997. CD.

2366 Meters. *The Meters Anthology: Funkify Your Life.* Rhino: R2 71869. 1995. 2 CDs.

2367 Neville, Aaron. *Ultimate Collection* [1960–1997]. Universal Music: 314 520 192-2. 2001. CD.

2368 Neville, Art. *Art Neville: His Specialty Recordings, 1956-58* [1956–1958]. Specialty: SPCD-7023-2. 1992. CD.

2369 Neville Brothers
    2369.1 *Fiyo on the Bayou* [1981]. A&M: CD 4866. 1987. CD.
    2369.2 *Gold* [1954–2004]. Hip-O: B0004539-02. 2005. 2 CDs.
    2369.3 *Tell It Like It Is* [1989] (Gregg Allman, Jimmy Buffett, Bonnie Raitt, Buckwheat Zydeco, and others). Image Entertainment: ID2077EBDVD. 2004. DVD.
    2369.4 *Uptown Rulin': The Best of the Neville Brothers* [1990s]. A&M: 069 490 403 2. 1999. CD.
    2369.5 *The Very Best of the Neville Brothers* [1960–1987]. Rhino: R2 72626. 1997. CD.
    2369.6 *Yellow Moon.* A&M: CD 5240. 1989. CD.

2370 Professor Longhair
    2370.1 ★*Crawfish Fiesta* [1979] (Dr. John). Alligator: ALCD 4718. 1988. CD.
    2370.2 *Fess: The Professor Longhair Anthology* [1949–1980]. Rhino: R2 71502. 1993. 2 CDs.
    2370.3 *New Orleans Piano* [1949, 1953]. Atlantic: 7225-2. 2003. CD.
    2370.4 *Rock 'n' Roll Gumbo* [1974] (Clarence "Gatemouth" Brown). Sunny Side: SYS3049. 2006. CD.

2371 Shirley and Lee
    2371.1 *Shirley and Lee (Legendary Masters Series, Vol. 1)* [1952–1958]. Collectables: COL-5637. 1995. CD.
    2371.2 *The Sweethearts of the Blues* [1952–1963]. Bear Family: BCD 15960 DI. 1997. 4 CDs.

2372 Smith, Huey "Piano." *Having a Good Time with Huey "Piano" Smith and His Clowns* [1956–1962]. Westside: WESM 516. 1997. CD. Import.

2373 Thomas, Irma
    2373.1 *Simply the Best: Live.* Rounder: CD 2110. 1991. CD.
    2373.2 *Sweet Soul Queen of New Orleans: The Irma Thomas Collection* [1961–1965]. Razor and Tie: RE 2097-2. 1996. CD.

2374 Toussaint, Allen
    2374.1 *The Allen Toussaint Collection* [1970–1978]. Reprise: 9 26549-2. 1991. CD.
    2374.2 *What Is Success? The Scepter and Bell Recordings* [late 1960s–early 1970s]. Kent Soul: CDKEND 286. 2007. CD. Import.

2375 Wild Tchoupitoulas. *The Wild Tchoupitoulas* [1976]. Mango / Island: 162-539 908-2. 1993. CD.

Nashville

2376 ★*Nashville Jumps: Blues and Rhythm on Nashville Independent Labels 1945–1955* [1945-1955] (Wynonie Harris, Walter Davis, Walter "Tang" Smith, Vivian Verson, Tuff Green, Tucker Coles, Tommy McGhee, Tommy Brooks, Tom Douglas, The Fat Man, The BlueJacks, Ted Jarrett, Sunnyland Slim, St. Louis Jimmy, Smokey Hogg, Slim Hunt, Shy Guy Douglas, Sherman Williams, Sherman Johnson, Rudy Green, Roosevelt Sykes, Roosevelt Lee, Robert Gill, Richard Armstrong, Red Miller, Red Calhoun, Mr. Swing, Max Blues Bailey, Marigolds, Louis Campbell, Louis Brooks, Little Maxie Bailey, Little Eddie, Leap Frogs, Larry Birdsong, Kid King's Combo, Julius King, Joe Williams, Jimmy Sweeney, Jerry McCain, Jack Cooley, Helen Foster, Good Rocking Beasley, Good Rockin' Sam, Gay Crosse, Eddie

Jones, Earl Gaines, Dusty Brooks, Don Q and his Q Tones, Doc Wiley, Dixie Doodlers, Del Thorne, Daddy Dean, Crown Prince Waterford, Christine Kittrell, Charles Ruckles, Cecil Gant, Bobby Prince, Bobby Plater, Blues Rockers, Blue Flamers, Billie McAllister, Big Three Trio, Beulah Bryant, Bernard Hardison, B. B. King, and Arthur Gunter). Bear Family: BCD 15864 HL. 2000. 8 CDs.

2377 *Night Train to Nashville: Music City Rhythm and Blues, 1945–1970, Vol. 1* (Cecil Gant, Rudy Green, Kid King's Combo, Christine Kittrell, Prisoners, Varieteers, Arthur Gunter, Hank Crawford, Louis Brooks, Marigolds, Gene Allison, Esquerita, Audrey Bryant, Roscoe Shelton, Larry Birdsong, Jimmy Beck, Earl Gaines, Shy Guy Douglas, Etta James, Johnny Jones, Frank Howard, Arthur Alexander, Ruth Brown, Sam Baker, Bobby Hebb, Joe Tex, Hytones, Avons, Joe Simon, Clifford Curry, Valentines, Johnny Adams, Robert Knight, and others). Country Music Foundation / Lost Highway: B0002100-02. 2004. 2 CDs.

2378 *Night Train to Nashville: Music City Rhythm and Blues, 1945–1970, Vol. 2* (Jimmy Sweeney, Richard Armstrong, Ivory Joe Hunter, Charlie Dowell, Billie McAllister, Gay Crosse, Good Humor Six, Helen Foster, Bernard Hardison, Gene Allison, Ted Jarrett, Lillian Offitt, Gladiolas, Charles "Wigg" Walker and the Daffodils, Kinglets, Little Ike, Neptunes, Hal and Jean, Freddie North, Jimmy Bell aka Jimmy Sweeney, Dr. Feelgood, Piano Red, Christine Kittrell, Herbert Hunter, Clyde McPhatter, Esther Phillips, Arthur Alexander, Earl Gaines, Marion James, Roscoe Shelton, Johnny Jones, King Casuals, Jimmy Church, Frank Howard, Sandra King, Spidells, Johnny Bragg, Fabulettes, Joe Simon, Imperials, and others). Country Music Foundation / Lost Highway: B0005228-02. 2005. 2 CDs.

Neo-Soul

2379 Arie, India. *See* India. Arie

2380 Badu, Erykah
 - 2380.1 *Mama's Gun.* Motown: 012 153 259-2. 2000. CD.
 - 2380.2 *New Amerykah, Part One: 4th World War.* Universal Motown Records: B0010800-02. 2007. CD.

2381 Baker, Anita. *A Night of Rapture* [1987]. Cine-Vu International: NSVD9920-9. 2007. DVD.

2382 ★Hill, Lauryn. *The Miseducation of Lauryn Hill.* Ruff House / Columbia: CK69035. 1998. CD.

2383 India. Arie
 - 2383.1 *Acoustic Soul.* Motown: 440 013 770-2. 2001. CD.
 - 2383.2 *Voyage to India.* Motown: 440 064 755-2. 2002. CD.

2384 Keys, Alicia
 - 2384.1 *Alicia Keys Unplugged.* J Records: 82876-72906-9. 2005. DVD.
 - 2384.2 *Songs in A Minor.* J Records: 80813-20002-2. 2001. CD.

2385 Musiq Soulchild. *Juslisen.* Def Soul: 314 586 772-2. 2002. CD.

2386 Patterson, Rahsaan. *After Hours.* Artistry Music: ART 7001. 2004. CD.

2387 Scott, Jill
 - 2387.1 *Beautifully Human: Words and Sounds, Vol. 2.* Hidden Beach Recordings: EK 92773. 2004. CD.
 - 2387.2 *Live in Paris.* Hidden Beach Recordings: HBRDVD 0020. 2008. DVD.
 - 2387.3 *Who Is Jill Scott? Words and Sounds, Vol. 1.* Hidden Beach Recordings / Epic: EK 62137. 2000. CD.

New Jack Swing

2388 Boyz II Men. *Legacy: The Greatest Hits Collection, Deluxe ed.* [1991–2002]. Universal: B0001884-02. 2004. 2 CDs.

2389 Gill, Johnny. *Ultimate Collection* [1990–1996]. Universal Music Group / Hip-O: 314 584 274-2. 2002. CD.

2390 Guy. *Groove Me: The Very Best of Guy* [1988–1990]. MCA: 088 112 980-2. 2002. CD.

2391 Mint Condition. *The Collection, 1991–1998.* Perspective: 31454 9039 2. 1998. CD.

2392 Sweat, Keith
 - 2392.1 *The Best of Keith Sweat: Make You Sweat* [1987–1997]. Elektra / Rhino: R2 73954. 2004. CD.
 - 2392.2 *Sweat Hotel Live.* Shout! Factory: 9.78074E + 12. 2007. DVD.

Contemporary

2393   Adams, Oleta. *The Very Best of Oleta Adams* [1989–1995]. Mercury: 314 558 844-2. 1998. CD.

2394   Babyface. *The Essential Babyface* [1989–1996]. Epic: EK 89172. 2003. CD.

2395   Belle, Regina. *Baby Come to Me: The Best of Regina Belle* [1987–1995]. Columbia / Legacy: CK 65430. 1997. CD.

2396   Beyoncé
 2396.1   *B'day.* Sony Urban Music: 82876 88132 2. 2006. CD.
 2396.1   *Beyoncé.* Parkwood Entertainment: 88843032512. 2013. CD.
 2396.2   *I Am . . . Sasha Fierce.* Music World Music. 2008. 2 CDs.
 2396.3   *Lemonade.* Parkwood Entertainment: 88985336822. 2016. CD.

2397   Blige, Mary J.
 2397.1   ★*The Breakthrough.* Geffen: B0005722-02. 2005. CD.
 2397.2   *What's the 411?* Uptown Records / MCA: UPTD-10681. 1992. CD.

2398   Braxton, Toni. *The Essential Toni Braxton.* La Face: 88697055362. 2007. 2 CDs.

2399   Brown, Bobby. *Don't Be Cruel.* MCA: MCAD-42185. 1988. CD.

2400   Bryson, Peabo. *Anthology* [1976–1983]. Capitol: 72435-29673-2-2. 2001. 2 CDs.

2401   Cole, Natalie. *The Anthology* [1975–1981]. Capitol: 72435-81057-2-8. 1987. 2 CDs.

2402   D'Angelo. *Brown Sugar.* EMI: E2-32629. 1995. CD.

2403   D'Arby, Terence Trent. *Do You Love Me Like You Say: The Very Best of Terence Trent D'Arby* [1987–1995]. Columbia: 69699 85217 2. 2006. CD.

2404   En Vogue. *The Very Best of En Vogue* [1990–1997]. Rhino: R2 74348. 2001. CD.

2405   Gray, Macy
 2405.1   *Covered.* 429 Records: FTN 17854. 2012. CD.
 2405.2   *The Very Best of Macy Gray* [1999–2004]. Epic: EK 92944. 2004. CD.

2406   Jackson, Freddie. *Greatest Hits* [1985–1992]. Capitol: 09463-85737-2-2. 2007. CD.

2407   James, Leela. *My Soul.* Stax: STX-31641-02. 2010. CD.

2408   Kelly, R.
 2408.1   *R. Kelly as Mr. Showbiz: The Light It Up Tour.* Image Entertainment: ID3616ZBDVD. 2007. DVD. Alternate Title: *Live: The Light It Up Tour.*
 2408.2   ★*The R in R&B Collection, Vol. 1* [1991–2003]. Jive: 82876-53706-2. 2003. CD.

2409   LaBelle, Patti
 2409.1   *The Essential Patti Labelle.* Sony: 88697 21092 2. 2008. 2 CDs.
 2409.2   *Gold* [1963–2004]. Hip-O: B0004118-02. 2005. 2 CDs.
 2409.3   *Live! One Night Only* (Mariah Carey, Luther Vandross). MCA: 440 053 288-9. 2000. DVD.

2410   LaBelle, Patti, and the Bluebelles. *The Early Years* [1962–1964]. Ace: CDCHD441. 1993. CD.

2411   Legend, John. *Love in the Future.* G.O.O.D. Music: 88725 43994 2. 2013. CD.

2412   Maxwell. *Maxwell's Urban Hang Suite.* Columbia: CK 66434. 1996. CD.

2413   Mvula, Laura. *The Dreaming Room.* Sony Music: 88875165682. 2016. CD.

2414   Ocean, Frank. *Channel Orange.* Island Def Jam: B0015788-02. 2012. CD.

2415   TLC. *Now and Forever: The Hits* [1992–2003]. Arista: 82876-50208-2. 2003. CD.

2416   Vandross, Luther
 2416.1   *Any Love.* Epic: EK 44308. 1988. CD.
 2416.2   ★*The Essential Luther Vandross.* Epic / Legacy: E2K 89167. 2003. 2 CDs.
 2416.3   *Love, Luther.* Epic / J Records / Legacy: 88697 16780 2. 2007. 4 CDs.
 2416.4   *Luther Vandross Live at Radio City Music Hall, 2003.* J Records: 82876-55711-2. 2003. CD.

2417   Williams, Pharrell. *GIRL.* Sony/Columbia: 88843 05507 2. 2014. CD.

Label Overview

2418   ★*Atlantic R&B, 1947–1974* (Joe Morris, Tiny Grimes, Ruth Brown, Professor Longhair, Clovers, Cardinals, Joe Turner, Willis Jackson, Ray Charles, LaVern Baker, Drifters, Clyde McPhatter, Robins, Cookies, Chuck Willis, Ivory Joe Hunter, Ben E. King, Solomon Burke,

William Bell, Mar-Keys, Otis Redding, Rufus Thomas, Esther Phillips, Joe Tex, Wilson Pickett, Don Covay, Sam and Dave, Eddie Floyd, Arthur Conley, Aretha Franklin, Roberta Flack, Donny Hathaway, Spinners, and others). Atlantic: 8122-74755-2. 2006. 8 CDs.

2419 *Best of Ace Records, Vol. 2: The R&B Hits* [1955–1960] (Huey "Piano" Smith, Bobby Marchan, Earl King, Alvin "Red" Tyler, Al Collins, and others). Scotti Bros.: 75406-2. 1992. CD.

2420 *Best of Chess R&B, Vols. 1 and 2* [1956–1969] (Moonglows, Miracles, Jimmy McCracklin, Corsairs, Vibrations, Sugar Pie DeSanto, Etta James, Clarence "Frogman" Henry, Bobby Moore and the Rhythm Aces, Jan Bradley, Billy Stewart, Little Milton, Billy Stewart, Tony Clarke, Mitty Collier, Radiants, Dells, Laura Lee, Fontella Bass, Ramsey Lewis Trio, Jackie Ross, Etta James). Chess: CHD-31317; CHD-31318. 1987. 2 CDs.

2421 *Duke-Peacock's Greatest Hits* [1952–1973] (Big Mama Thornton, Junior Parker, Bobby Bland, Marie Adams, James Booker, Joe Hinton, Johnny Ace, O. V. Wright, Carl Carlton, and others). MCA: MCAD-10666. 1992. CD.

2422 *The Fire / Fury Records Story* [1957–1962] (Tarheel Slim, Wilbert Harrison, Buster Brown, Little Ann, Arthur "Big Boy" Crudup, Elmore James, Bobby Marchan, Mighty Joe Young, Willis Jackson, Lightnin' Hopkins, Sam Myers, Jay Cees, Upsetters, Gladys Knight and the Pips, Lee Dorsey, King Curtis and the Noble Knights, Titus Turner, Ronnie Miller (and the Pips), Don Gardner, Dee Dee Ford, Mary "B," Noble "Thin Man" Watts, Dr. Horse, June Bateman, Wild Jimmy Spruill, Marshall Jones, Lewis Jones, Kip Anderson, Les Cooper and the Soul Rockers, Bobby Porter, Joe Haywood). Capricorn: 9 42009-2. 1993. 2 CDs.

2423 *The Hi Records Story* [1959–1977] (Bill Black, Ace Cannon, Murray Kellum, Willie Mitchell, Gene Simmons, Charlie Rich, Al Green, Ann Peebles, Otis Clay, Syl Johnson, O. V. Wright, and others). Hi Records: Hi UK CD 101. 1989. CD.

2424 *King R&B Box Set* [1945–1966] (Wynonie Harris, Roy Brown, Bull Moose Jackson, Ivory Joe Hunter, Billy Ward, Midnighters, Little Willie John, James Brown, Syd Nathan, and others). King: KBSCD-7002. 1995. 4 CDs.

2425 ★*The Okeh Rhythm and Blues Story* [1949–1957] (Chris Powell, Red Saunders, Big Maybelle, Chuck Willis, Ravens, Larry Darnell, Treniers, Annie Laurie, Paul Gayten, Hadda Brooks, Titus Turner, Screamin' Jay Hawkins, Andre Williams, and others). Epic / Legacy: E3K 48912. 1993. 3 CDs.

2426 *The Scepter Records Story* [1959–1972] (Shirelles, Maxine Brown, Isley Brothers, Tommy Hunt, Dionne Warwick, Kingsmen, Chuck Jackson, Ronnie Milsap, Roy Head, B. J. Thomas, and others). Capricorn: 9 42003-2. 1992. 3 CDs.

2427 *Southern Rhythm 'n' Rock: The Best of Excello Records, Vol. 2* [1954–1966] (Gladiolas, Ruby Green, Louis Brooks and His Hi-Toppers, Ray Batts, Robert Garrett, Marigolds, Jerry McCain and His Upstarts, Arthur Gunter, King Crooners, Blues Rockers, Lillian Offitt, Surf Riders, Crescendos, Hooks Coleman, Roy Teo, Shy Guy Douglas, Meloairs). Excello / Rhino: R2 70897. 1990. CD.

2428 ★*The Specialty Story* [1944–1964] (Roy Milton, Joe Lutcher, Jimmy Liggins, Camille Howard, Percy Mayfield, Lloyd Price, Floyd Dixon, Jessie Belvin, Soul Stirrers, Little Richard, Larry Williams, Don and Dewey, and others). Specialty / Fantasy: 5SPCD-4412-2. 1994. 5 CDs.

2429 ★*Stompin' at the Savoy: The Original Indie Label, 1944–1961* (Hot Lips Page, Big Joe Turner, Gatemouth Moore, Billy Eckstine, Johnny Otis, Slim Gaillard, Pete Johnson, Tiny Bradshaw, Ravens, Doc Pomus, Hal Singer, Brownie McGhee, Ravens, Deacon McNeely, Robins, Marilyn Scott, Helen Humes, Four Buddies, Billy Wright, Little Esther, Varetta Dillard, Eddie Mack, Earl Johnson, Sticks McGhee, Nappy Brown, Little Jimmy Scott, Big Maybelle, Sammy Price, and others). Savoy Jazz: SVY 17446. 2004. 4 CDs.

2430 *The Swing Time Records Story: R&B, Blues, and Gospel, 1946–1952* (Lowell Fulson, Floyd Dixon, Eddie Williams, Jimmy Witherspoon, Joe Swift, Johnny Otis Band, Charles Brown, Nightingale Jubalaires, Pete Johnson, Big Joe Turner, Lloyd Glenn, Maxin Trio, Ray Charles, Earl Jackson, Edgar Hayes, Stardusters, Stars of Harmony, Percy Mayfield, Monroe Tucker Band, Clifford "Fat Man" Blivens, Jessie Thomas, Jimmy McCracklin, Joe Pullum, Earl Brown, Red Callender Combo, Three Musketeers, Playboy

Thomas, Hollywood Flames). Capricorn: 9 42024-2. 1994. 2 CDs.

2431 ★*The Vee-Jay Story: Celebrating 40 Years of Classic Hits* [1953–1965] (Spaniels, Jimmy Reed, El Dorados, Hazel McCollum, 5 Echoes, Jay McShann, Priscilla Brown, Kool Gents, Billy Emerson, Eddie Taylor, Magnificents, John Lee Hooker, Dells, Pee Wee Crayton, Delegates, Elmore James, Gene Allison, Billy Boy Arnold, Jerry Butler and the Impressions, Dee Clark, Hank Ballard and the Midnighters, Wade Flemons, Jimmy Witherspoon, Roscoe Gordon, J. B. Lenoir, Eddie Harris, Sheriff and the Ravels, Pips with Gladys Knight, Gene Chandler, Pearlettes, Shephards, Betty Everett, Rubies, Joe Simon, Little Richard, Fred Hughes). Vee-Jay: NVS2-3-400. 1993. 3 CDs.

SOUL

General Style

COLLECTIONS

2432 *Atlantic Soul Classics.* Warner Bros. 1987.

2433 *Beg, Scream, and Shout! The Big Ol' Box of '60s Soul* [1961–1969] (Ben E. King, O. V. Wright, Brenda Holloway, Toussaint McCall, Judy Clay, William Bell, Mad Lads, Jackson 5, Garnet Mimms, Barbara Mason, Smokey Robinson, Sam and Dave, Otis Clay, Sweet Inspirations, Barbara Lewis, Percy Sledge, Al Green, Impressions, Otis Redding, Aaron Neville, Tony Clarke, Leon Haywood, Tyrone Davis, Dionne Warwick, Maxine Brown, Bobby Womack, Billy Stewart, Esther Phillips, Gene Chandler, Jay Wiggins, Irma Thomas, Ray Charles, Lorraine Ellison, King Curtis, Dobie Gray, Barbara Acklin, O'Jays, Bettye Swann, Betty Everett, Four Tops, Aretha Franklin, Young-Holt Trio, Solomon Burke, Martha and the Vandellas, James Carr, Fontella Bass, Joe Tex, Gladys Knight and the Pips, Clarence Carter, Lou Rawls, James Brown, Jerry Butler, Willie Tee, Erma Franklin, Chuck Jackson, Stevie Wonder, Carla Thomas, Wilson Pickett, Bobby Moore and the Rhythm Aces, Joe Simon, Don Covay, Ike and Tina Turner, Mary Wells, Brenton Wood, Doris Troy, Booker T. and the MGs, Arthur Conley, Meters, Archie Bell, Freddie Scott, Howard Tate, Major Lance, Supremes, Gloria Jones, Marvin Gaye, Lee Rogers, Shirley Ellis, Johnnie Taylor, Bobby Patterson, Little Milton, Isley Brothers, Dyke and

the Blazers, Jackie Wilson, Edwin Starr, Robert Parker, Capitols, J. J. Jackson, Etta James, Temptations, Rufus Thomas, Mar-Keys, Eddie Floyd, Junior Walker and the All-Stars, Bar-Kays, Kim Weston, Eddie Holland, David Ruffin, and others). Rhino: R2 72815. 1997. 6 CDs.

2434 *Birth of Soul, 4 Vols.* [1959–1964] (Caravans, Ray Charles, Benny Spellman, Solomon Burke, Willie Tee, Betty Harris, Kenny Gamble, Johnny Nash, Maxine Brown, Jimmy Ruffin, Falcons, Ike and Tina Turner, Chuck Jackson, 5 Royales, Betty Willis, Harold Burrage, Billy Bland, Della Reese, Ernestine Anderson, Bobby Bland, Otis Redding, Garnet Mimms, Gloria Lynn, Jerry Butler, Etta James, Sam Cooke, Little Anthony and the Imperials, Freddie Scott, Little Johnny Taylor, William Bell, Impressions, and others). Kent Soul: CDKEND 123, 147, 189, 275. 1996. 4 CDs.

2435 *Dave Godin's Deep Soul Treasures, Vols. 1–4* [1961–1983] [1961–1963]. (Knight Brothers, Irma Thomas, Jean Wells, Dori Grayson, Reuben Bell, Incredibles, Untouchables, Bessie Banks, Lee Moses, Doris Duke, Eddie Holman, Ben E. King, Nat Phillips, Arthur Conley, Johnny Adams, Otis Redding, Eddy Giles, Bessie Banks, Carla Thomas, Toussaint McCall, Eddie and Ernie, James Brown, Bobby Womack, Maxine Brown, Syl Johnson, Bettye Lavette, Rick James, Bobby Bland, Impressions, Loretta Williams, Knight Brothers, Eddie and Ernie, Chuck Edwards, Gladys Knight and the Pips, Miracles, Garnet Mimms, and others). Kent Soul: CDKEND 143, 158, 200, 230. 1997. 4 CDs.

2436 *Heaven Must Have Sent You: The Holland/ Dozier/Holland Story* [1963–1989] (Eddie Holland, Marvelettes, Martha and the Vandellas, Mary Wells, Marvin Gaye, Dusty Springfield, Supremes, Four Tops, Kim Weston, Elgins, Isley Brothers, Jr. Walker and the All Stars, Chris Clark, Smokey Robinson and the Miracles, Chairmen of the Board, Freda Payne, Flaming Ember, Politicians, Band, Holland-Dozier, Holland-Dozier-Holland, Lamont Dozier, Michael Jackson, Originals, Jackson 5, Eddie Kendricks, Sugar Pie Shalamar, Doobie Brothers, Simply Red). Hip-O: B0004845-02. 2005. 3 CDs.

2437 *Motown around the World* [1963–1981] (Supremes, Four Tops, Temptations, Stevie Wonder, Miracles, Jimmy Ruffin, Edwin Starr, Marvin Gaye, Velvelettes, Martha Reeves and

Vandellas, Jermaine Jackson, and Smokey Robinson). Hip-O Select; Motown: B0013187-02. 2010. 2 CDs.

2438 *Motown 45th Anniversary Songbook.* Hal Leonard: HL00311156. 2004.

2439 *Motown's First: The Ultimate Selection of Soul.* Tamala / Jobette: AF 09 90 06 64. 2005.

2440 *Respect: Aretha's Influences and Inspiration* [1948–1972] (Otis Redding, Thelma Jones, Don Covay, Jean Wells, Ben E. King, Brenda Holloway, Dinah Washington, Big Maybelle, Bobby Bland, Helen Humes, Johnny Ace, Little Miss Cornshucks, Jackie Wilson, Percy Mayfield, Ray Charles, James Carr, Mary Wheeler, Wilson Pickett, Howard Tate, Nina Simone, Bill Withers, Bobby Womack, Dionne Warwick, and Clara Ward). Ace: CDCHD 1214. 2009. CD.

2441 *Respect Yourself: The Stax Records Story.* Concord Music Publishing: 7032. 2007. DVD.

2442 *Soul Classics.* Hal Leonard: HL00310668. 2000.

2443 *Soul Shots: A Collection of Sixties Soul Classics* [1962–1969] (J. J. Jackson, James Brown and the Famous Flames, Dyke and the Blazers, Billy Stewart, Fontella Bass, James and Bobby Purify, Intruders, Checkmates Ltd., Lou Rawls, Ramsey Lewis Trio, Patti Drew, Larry Williams, Johnny Watson, Joe Jeffrey Group, Delfonics, King Curtis, Lorraine Ellison). Rhino: R2 75774. 1988. CD.

2444 *Soul to Soul* [1971] (Ike and Tina Turner, Voices of East Harlem, Santana, Wilson Pickett, Eddie Harris and Les McCann, Staple Singers). Rhino Home Video: R2 970327. 2004. DVD.

2445 *Standing in the Shadows of Motown* (Joan Osborne; Me'Shell NdegéOcello; Bootsy Collins; Gerald Levert; Ben Harper; The Funk Brothers; Chaka Khan; Montell Jordan; Earl Van Dyke). Artisan Entertainment: 13780. 2003. DVD.

2446 *Stax/Volt Revue: Live in Norway 1967* [1967] (Booker T. and the MGs, Mar-Keys, Arthur Conley, Eddie Floyd, Sam and Dave, Otis Redding). Reelin' in the Years: DVD 7030. 2007. DVD.

2447 *The Sweetest Feeling: A Van McCoy Songbook* [1962–1976] (Erma Franklin, Jackie Wilson, The Spellbinders, Betty Everett, Ruby and The Romantics, Nina Simone, Barbara Lewis, Chuck Jackson, Esther Phillips, Jerry Butler, Billy "T"

Soul, Teri Thornton, Gladys Knight and the Pips, Irma Thomas, Nancy Wilson, Oscar Weathers, Ilana, Aretha Franklin, Donny Hathaway, G. C. Cameron, The Ad Libs, Sharon Ridley, Brenda and the Tabulation, and Melba Moore). Kent Soul: CKDEND 334. 2010. CD.

INDIVIDUALS AND GROUPS

2448 Alexander, Arthur
    2448.1 *Lonely Just Like Me: The Final Chapter* [1993]. HackTone: R2 271932. 2007. CD.
    2448.2 *Rainbow Road: The Warner Brothers Recordings* [1972]. Warner Bros.: 2-45581. 1994. CD.
    2448.3 *The Ultimate Arthur Alexander* [1961–1964, 1975]. Razor and Tie: 2014. 1993. CD.

2449 Austin, Patti. *The Very Best of Patti Austin: The Singles, 1969–1986.* Warner Archives / Rhino: R2 74369. 2008. CD.

2450 Bar-Kays. *The Best of the Bar-Kays* [1968–1975]. Stax: SCD-8542-2. 1992. CD.

2451 Bass, Fontella. *Rescued: The Best of Fontella Bass* [1964–1968]. Chess / MCA: CHD 9335. 1992. CD.

2452 Bell, William
    2452.1 *The Best of William Bell* [1968–1974]. Stax: SCD-8541-2. 1988. CD.
    2452.2 *The Soul of a Bell* [1961–1967]. Stax: SCD-8607-2. 2002. CD.

2453 Benton, Brook. *Forty Greatest Hits* [1959–1970]. Mercury: 836 755-2. 1989. 2 CDs.

2454 *The Best Soul Songs Ever.* Hal Leonard: HL00311427. 2008. Score.

2455 *The Big Book of Motown.* Hal Leonard: HL00311061. 2004. Score.

2456 *The Big Book of Soul.* Hal Leonard: HLE90001146. 2004. Score.

2457 Brown, James
    2457.1 ★*Live at the Apollo* [1962]. Polydor: B0001715-02. 2004. CD.
    2457.2 *Live at the Apollo, Vol. 2* [1967]. Polydor: 314 549 864-2. 2001. 2 CDs.
    2457.3 *Live at the Garden* [1967] (Famous Flames). Hip-O Select: B0012928-02. 2009. 2 CDs.

2457.4 *★Roots of a Revolution* [1956–1964]. Polydor: 817 304-2. 1989. 2 CDs.

2457.5 *The Singles, Vol. 1: The Federal Years, 1956–1960.* Hip-O Select: B0007029-02. 2006. 2 CDs.

2457.6 *The Singles, Vol. 2: 1960–1963.* Hip-O Select: B0008510-02. 2007. 2 CDs.

2457.7 *The Singles, Vol. 3: 1964–1965.* Hip-O Select: B0008804-02. 2007. 2 CDs.

2457.8 *The Singles, Vol. 4: 1966–1967.* Hip-O Select: B0009472-02. 2007. 2 CDs.

2457.9 *The Singles, Vol. 5: 1967–1969.* Hip-O Select: B0010411-02. 2007. 2 CDs.

2457.10 *The Singles, Vol. 6: 1969–1970.* Hip-O Select: B0012204-02. 2008. 2 CDs.

2457.11 *The Singles, Vol. 7: 1970–1972.* Hip-O Select: B0012728-02. 2009. 2 CDs.

2457.12 *The Singles, Vol. 8: 1972–1973.* Hip-O Select: B0013349-02. 2009. 2 CDs.

2457.13 *The Singles, Vol. 9: 1973–1975.* Hip-O Select: B0014259-02. 2010. 2 CDs.

2457.14 *The Singles, Vol. 10: 1975–1979.* Hip-O Select: B0015279-02. 2011. 2 CDs.

2457.15 *The Singles, Vol. 11: 1979–1981.* Hip-O Select: B0016037-02. 2011. 2 CDs.

2457.16 *Star Time* [1956–1984]. Polydor: 849 108-2. 1991. 4 CDs.

2458 Brown, Maxine. *25 All-Time Greatest Hits* [1960s]. Varèse Sarabande: 302 066 378 2. 2002. CD.

2459 Burke, Solomon

2459.1 *A Change Is Gonna Come* [1985]. Rounder: CD 2053. 1994. CD.

2459.2 *Don't Give Up on Me.* Fat Possum: 80358-2. 2002. CD.

2459.3 *★Home in Your Heart: The Best of Solomon Burke* [1960–1968]. Rhino / Atlantic: R2 70284. 1992. 2 CDs.

2459.4 *Nashville.* Shout! Factory: 826663-10179. 2006. CD.

2459.5 *Soul Alive!* [1981]. Rounder: 11661-2167-2. 2002. 2 CDs.

2459.6 *You Can Run but You Can't Hide* [1955–1959]. Mr. R&B Records: RBD 108. 1991. CD.

2460 Butler, Jerry

2460.1 *The Best of Jerry Butler* [1958–1969]. Rhino: R2 75881. 1987. CD.

2460.2 *Iceman: The Mercury Years* [1966–1972]. Mercury: 314 510 968-2. 1992. 2 CDs.

2461 Carr, James. *The Complete Goldwax Singles* [1964–1970]. Kent Soul: CDKEND 202. 2001. CD.

2462 Carter, Clarence

2462.1 *The Best of Clarence Carter: The Dr.'s Greatest Prescriptions* [1977–1992]. Koch: KOC-CD-8093. 2001. CD.

2462.2 *Snatchin' It Back: The Best of Clarence Carter* [1963–1971]. Rhino: R2 70286. 1992. CD.

2463 Charles, Ray

2463.1 *The Complete Country and Western Recordings,* 1959–1986. Rhino: R2 75328. 1998. 4 CDs.

2463.2 *His Greatest Hits, Vols. 1 and 2* [1959–1972]. DCC Compact Classics: DZS-036 [v. 1]; DZS-037 [v. 2]. 1987. 2 CDs.

2463.3 *Live at the Montreux Jazz Festival* [1997]. Pioneer Artists: PA-11676. 2002. CD, DVD.

2463.4 *A Man and His Soul.* Warner Bros. 2004.

2463.5 *O-Genio Ray Charles, 1963: Live in Brazil.* Warner / Rhino Home Video: R2 970389. 2004. DVD.

2463.6 *★Pure Genius: The Complete Atlantic Recordings, 1952–1959.* Atlantic / Rhino: R2 74731. 2005. 7 CDs, 1 DVD.

2463.7 *Singular Genius: The Complete ABC Singles* [1960–1973]. Concord: CRE-33258. 2011. 5 CDs.

2464 Chi-Lites. *20 Greatest Hits* [1969–1974]. Brunswick: BRC 33009-2. 2001. CD.

2465 Clark, Dee. *You're Looking Good / Hold On, It's Dee Clark* [1960–1961]. Collectables: COL-CD-7265. 2000. CD.

2466 Clay, Otis. *Complete Otis Clay on Hi Records* [1971–1977]. Hi Records: HEXD 49. 1999. 2 CDs.

2467 Conley, Arthur. *The Platinum Collection* [1967–1969]. Warner Platinum: 9122-79994-6. 2007. CD.

2468 Cooke, Sam

2468.1 *★The Man Who Invented Soul* [1957–1964]. RCA: RCA 07863 67911-2. 2000. 4 CDs. Includes *Night Beat.*

2468.2 *One Night Stand: Sam Cooke Live at the Harlem Square Club, 1963.* RCA / Legacy: 82876 69552 2. 2005. CD.

2468.3 *Portrait of a Legend.* Warner Bros.: PFM 0316. 2004.

2468.4 *Sam Cooke, Legend.* WinStar: 10049. 2003. DVD.

2469 Covay, Don. *Mercy, Mercy! The Definitive Don Covay* [1957–1975]. Razor and Tie: RE 2053. 1994. CD.

2470 Davis, Tyrone. *20 Greatest Hits* [1968–1976]. Brunswick: BRC 33008-2. 2001. CD.

2471 Father's Children. *Who's Gonna Save the World* [1972]. Numero: 037. 2011. CD.

2472 Flack, Roberta
    2472.1 *First Take* [1969]. Atlantic: 82792-2. 1995. CD.
    2472.2 *The Very Best of Roberta Flack* [1970–1991]. Rhino: R2 73332. 2006. CD.

2473 Franklin, Aretha
    2473.1 *Aretha Franklin: Queen of Soul* [1967–1976]. Rhino: R2 71063. 1992. 4 CDs.
    2473.2 *Aretha, the Queen of Soul.* Creative Concepts: 07-1097. 1994.
    2473.3 ★*I Never Loved a Man the Way I Loved You* [1967]. Rhino: R2 71934. 1995. CD.
    2473.4 ★*Lady Soul* [1967]. Rhino: R2 71933. 1995. CD.
    2473.5 *Live at Fillmore West* [1971]. Atlantic / Rhino: R2 77629. 2006. 2 CDs.
    2473.6 *Spirit in the Dark* [1969–1970]. Rhino: 8122-71525-2. 1993. CD.
    2473.7 *Take a Look: Complete on Columbia* [1960-1968]. Columbia; Legacy: 88697792792. 2011. CD, DVD.
    2473.8 *Unforgettable: A Tribute to Dinah Washington* [1964]. Columbia / Legacy: CK 66201. 1995. CD.
    2473.9 *Young, Gifted, and Black* [1970–1971]. Rhino: 8122-71527-2. 1993. CD.

2474 Franklin, Erma. *Piece of Her Heart: The Epic and Shout Years* [1961-1968]. Shout! Factory: SHOUT 50. 2009. CD.

2475 Friends of Distinction. *Best of the Friends of Distinction* [1968–1972]. RCA: 07863. 1996. CD.

2476 Gaye, Marvin
    2476.1 *Gold* [1961–1984] (Kim Weston, Tammi Terrell). Motown: B0003119-02. 2005. 2 CDs.
    2476.2 *Let's Get It On* [1973]. Tamla: 440 064 021-2. 2002. CD.
    2476.3 *Marvin Gaye: Behind the Legend.* Eagle Rock Entertainment: EREDV555. 2004. DVD.
    2476.4 *Marvin Gaye—The Real Thing: In Performance, 1964–1981.* Universal Music Group / Hip-O: B0006453-09. 2006. DVD.
    2476.5 ★*The Master, 1961–1984* (Mary Wells, Kim Weston, Tammi Terrell, Diana Ross, Gladys Knight). Motown: 31453 0492-2. 1995. 4 CDs.
    2476.6 ★*What's Going On* [1971]. Motown: 440 064 022-2. 2002. CD.

2477 Green, Al
    2477.1 *The Best of Al Green.* Hal Leonard: HL00306476. 2002.
    2477.2 *Call Me* [1973]. Right Stuff: 72435-93747-2-7. 2004. CD.
    2477.3 *The Definitive Greatest Hits* [1970s]. Capitol: 094638204022. 2007. CD.
    2477.4 ★*The Immortal Soul of Al Green* [1967–1978]. Hi Records / Right Stuff: 72435-90551-2-1. 2004. 4 CDs.
    2477.5 *Let's Stay Together* [1972]. Right Stuff: 72435-42678-2-6. 2003. CD.

2478 Hathaway, Donny
    2478.1 *A Donny Hathaway Collection* [1970s]. Atlantic: 82092-2. 1990. CD.
    2478.2 ★*Everything Is Everything* [1970]. Atco: R2 72216. 1995. CD.
    2478.3 *Extensions of a Man* [1973]. Rhino: R2 71520. 1993. CD.
    2478.4 *These Songs for You, Live!* [1971–1973]. Atlantic / Rhino: R2 78075. 2004. CD.

2479 Hayes, Isaac
    2479.1 ★*Hot Buttered Soul* [1969] (Bar-Kays). Stax / Universal: STX-31458. 2009. CD.
    2479.2 *Isaac Hayes: Live at Montreux, 2005.* Eagle Eye Media: EE 39155-9. 2007. DVD.
    2479.3 *Shaft* [1971]. Stax: SCD-88002-2. 1988. CD.
    2479.4 *The Ultimate Isaac Hayes: Can You Dig It?* Stax: 3SCD-88043-2. 2005. 2 CDs, DVD.
    2479.5 *The Very Best of Isaac Hayes.* Stax: STXCD-30294. 2007. CD.

2480 Hill, Z. Z. *The Down Home Soul of Z. Z. Hill* [1960s]. Ace / Kent: CDKEN 099. 1992. CD.

2481 Hinton, Eddie. *Very Extremely Dangerous* [1978]. Shout! Factory: SHOUT 59. 2009. CD.

2482 Holloway, Brenda. *Brenda Holloway—Greatest Hits and Rare Classics* [1960s]. Motown: MOTD-5485. 1991. CD.

2483 Houston, Thelma. *The Best of Thelma Houston* [1972–1979]. Motown: 374635492-2. 1991. CD.

2484 Hughes, Jimmy
    2484.1 *Best of Jimmy Hughes* [1964–1970s]. Fame: 000103. 2008. CD.
    2484.2 *Something Extra Special: The Complete Volt Recordings 1968–1971* [1968-1971]. Kent Soul: CDKEND 341. 2010. CD.
    2484.3 *Steal Away: The Early Fame Recordings, Vol. 1* [1962-1965]. Kent Soul: CDKEND 324. 2009. CD.
    2484.4 *Why Not Tonight? The Fame Recordings, Vol. 2* [1965-1967]. Kent Soul: CDKEND 331. 2010. CD.

2485 Ingram, Luther. *If Loving You Is Wrong, I Don't Want to Be Right: The Best of Luther Ingram* [1966–1978]. Airline: AR-CD-0205. 2007. CD.

2486 Intruders. *Cowboys to Girls: The Best of the Intruders* [1966–1974]. Epic / Legacy: ZK 66688. 1995. CD.

2487 Jackson, George. *In Memphis, 1972–77: The Sounds of Memphis and Xl Recordings* [1972-1977]. Kent Soul: CDKEND 329. 2009. CD.

2488 Johnson, Syl
    2488.1 ★*Complete Mythology* [1959-1977]. Numero: 032-CD. 2010. 4 CDs, 6 LPs.
    2488.2 *The Complete Syl Johnson on Hi Records* [1973–1979]. Hi Records: HEXD 51. 2000. 2 CDs.

2489 Jones, Sharon. *100 Days, 100 Nights* (Dap-Kings). Daptone: DAP-012. 2007. CD.

2490 Kendricks, Eddie
    2490.1 *The Motown Solo Albums, Vol. 1: Keep on Truckin'* [1971–1974]. Hip-O Select: B0005132-02. 2005. 2 CDs.
    2490.2 *The Motown Solo Albums, Vol. 2: The Thin Man* [1973–1976]. Hip-O Select: B0007397-02. 2005. 3 CDs.
    2490.3 *The Ultimate Collection* [1970s]. Motown: 314530958-2. 1998. CD.

2491 King, Ben E. *The Very Best of Ben E. King* [1959–1975]. Rhino / Atlantic: R2-72970. 1998. CD.

2492 Kirkland, Mike James. *Don't Sell Your Soul: The Complete Story of Mike* [1966-1973]. Luv n' Haight: LHCD064. 2011. 2 CDs.

2493 Latham, Rick. *Advanced Funk Studies*. R. Latham; dist. Carl Fischer: RLP1. 2002. Score.

2494 Lavette, Bettye
    2494.1 *Do Your Duty* [1969-1971]. Sundazed: SC 6262. 2009. CD.
    2494.2 *I've Got My Own Hell to Raise* [2005]. Anti: 86772-2. 2005. CD.

2495 Main Ingredient. *Everybody Plays the Fool: The Best of Main Ingredient* [1970s]. RCA / Legacy: 82876 692132. 2005. CD.

2496 Marvelettes. *Ultimate Collection*. Motown: 314530856-2. 1998. CD.

2497 Mayfield, Curtis
    2497.1 ★*The Anthology* [1961–1977] (Impressions). MCA: MCAD2 10664. 1992. 2 CDs.*Curtis Live!* [1971, 1973]. Rhino: R2 79933. 2000. CD.
    2497.2 *The Curtis Mayfield Guitar Songbook*. Alfred: 28425. 2007. Score.
    2497.3 *Curtis Mayfield Live at Montreux, 1987* (Ray Charles). Eagle Eye Media: EE 39041-9. 2004. DVD.
    2497.4 *The Very Best of Curtis Mayfield* [1970–1979]. Rhino: R2 72584. 1997. CD.

2498 Mimms, Garnet. *Cry Baby: The Best of Garnet Mimms* [1960s] (Enchanters). Collectables: COL-CD-5248. 1991. CD.

2499 Padgett, Betty. *Betty Padgett* [1975]. Luv n' Haight: LHCD058. 2009. CD.

2500 Peebles, Ann. *The Complete Ann Peebles on Hi Records, Vols. 1 and 2* [1969–1981]. Hi Records: HEXD 55, HEXD 56. 2003. 2 CDs.

2501 Pendergrass, Teddy
    2501.1 *The Essential Teddy Pendergrass* [1972–1984]. Philadelphia International: 88697 17476 2. 2007. 2 CDs.
    2501.2 *The Very Best of Teddy Pendergrass*. Goldenlane: CLP 1025-2. 2001. CD.

2502 Penn, Dan. *Do Right Man*. Warner Bros.: 9 45519-2. 1994. CD.

2503 Pickett, Wilson
    2503.1 ★*Funky Midnight Mover: The Atlantic Studio Recordings* [1962-1978]. Rhino Handmade: RHM2 07753. 2009. 6 CDs.
    2503.2 *A Man and a Half: The Best of Wilson Pickett* [1962–1972]. Atlantic / Rhino: R2 70287. 1992. 2 CDs.
    2503.3 *The Very Best of Wilson Pickett* [1965–1971]. Rhino: R2 71212. 1993. CD.

2504 Preston, Billy
  2504.1 *Encouraging Words* [1970]. Apple: 5099990823923. 2010. CD.
  2504.2 *Ultimate Collection* [1972–1982]. Hip-O: 314 541 231-2. 2000. CD.

2505 Rawls, Lou
  2505.1 *The Essential Lou Rawls* [1962–1981]. Philadelphia International: 88697 17475 2. 2007. 2 CDs.
  2505.2 *The Jazz Channel Presents Lou Rawls.* BET on Jazz / Image Entertainment: ID9640BJDVD. 2000. DVD.

2506 Redding, Otis
  2506.1 *The Dock of the Bay* [1968]. Atco: 80254-2. 1991. CD.
  2506.2 *Dreams to Remember: The Legacy of Otis Redding* [1960s]. Stax / Reelin' in the Years: DVD-7031. 2007. DVD.
  2506.3 *Dreams to Remember: The Otis Redding Anthology* [1962–1968]. Rhino: R2 75471. 1998. 2 CDs.
  2506.4 *Greatest Hits.* Hal Leonard: HL00306423. 2000.
  2506.5 *Live on the Sunset Strip* [1966]. Stax: STX-32046. 2010. 2 CDs.
  2506.6 ★*Otis! The Definitive Otis Redding* [1960–1970]. Rhino: R2 71439. 1993. 4 CDs.
  2506.7 *Otis Blue: Otis Redding Sings Soul* [1965]. Atco / Rhino: R2 422140. 2008. 2 CDs.
  2506.8 *The Otis Redding Dictionary of Soul: Complete and Unbelievable* [1966]. Atco: 91707-2. 1991. CD.

2507 Richie, Lionel. *The Definitive Collection* [1982–2001]. Motown: 440 068 140-2. 2003. CD.

2508 Robinson, Smokey
  2508.1 *The Solo Albums, Vol. 2* [1975-1976]. Hip-O Select: B0014571-02. 2010. CD.
  2508.2 *Solo Anthology.* Motown: 440 014 986-2. 2001. 2 CDs.

2509 Ross, Diana
  2509.1 *Diana Ross Live: Stolen Moments—The Lady Sings . . . Jazz and Blues* [1992]. Motown: 440 016 892-9. 2002. DVD.
  2509.2 *The Definitive Collection* [1970–2006]. Hip-O: B0006088-02. 2006. CD.
  2509.3 *The Motown Anthology* [1970–1995]. Motown: 440 013 583-2. 2001. 2 CDs.

2510 Ruffin, David
  2510.1 *The Great David Ruffin: The Motown Solo Albums, Vol. 1* [1969–1974]. Hip-O Select: B0005168-02. 2005. 2 CDs.
  2510.2 *The Great David Ruffin: The Motown Solo Albums, Vol. 2 (+ More)* [1975–1977]. Hip-O Select: B0005140-02. 2006. 2 CDs.
  2510.3 *The Ultimate Collection* [1969–1976]. Motown: 314530959-2. 1998. CD.

2511 Ruffin, Jimmy. *The Ultimate Motown Collection* [1964–1971]. Motown / Universal: 981 200-6. 2003. 2 CDs.

2512 Rufus. *The Very Best of Rufus, Featuring Chaka Khan* [1974–1979]. MCA: MCAD-11543. 1996. CD.

2513 Saadiq, Raphael
  2513.1 *Stone Rollin'* [2011]. Columbia: 88697 60560 2. 2011. CD.
  2513.2 *The Way I See It* [2008]. Columbia. 2008. CD.

2514 Sam and Dave
  2514.1 ★*The Definitive Soul Collection* [1965–1971]. Atlantic / Rhino: 36412538. 2006. 2 CDs.
  2514.2 *The Original Soul Men* [1967–1980]. Hip-O. 2008. DVD.
  2514.3 *The Very Best of Sam and Dave* [1965–1968]. Rhino: R2 71871. 1995. CD.

2515 Simon, Joe
  2515.1 *The Chokin' Kind: Golden Classics* [1960s]. Collectables: COL-CD-5114. 1992. CD.
  2515.2 *Greatest Hits: The Spring Years, 1970–1977* [1970–1977]. Southbound: CDSEWD 102. 1997. CD.

2516 Sledge, Percy
  2516.1 ★*The Atlantic Recordings* [1966-1973]. Rhino Handmade: RHM2 526138. 2010. 4 CDs.
  2516.2 *It Tears Me Up: The Best of Percy Sledge* [1966–1971]. Atlantic: R 270285. 1992. CD.

2517 Smith, O. C. *The Very Best of O. C. Smith* [1965–1977]. Taragon: TARCD-1099. 2003. CD.

2518 Stewart, Billy. *One More Time: The Chess Years* [1956–1969]. Chess: CHD 6027. 1988. CD.

2519 Tate, Howard. *Get It While You Can: The Complete Legendary Verve Sessions* [1966–1969]. Hip-O Select: 2210. 2004. CD.

2520 Taylor, Ted. *Keep What You Get: The Rare & Unissued Ronn Recordings* [1971-1977]. Kent Soul: KENDCD 348. 2011. CD.

2521 Terrell, Tammi. *Come On and See Me: The Complete Solo Collection* [1961-1967]. Hip-O Select; Motown: B0014792-02. 2010. 2 CDs.

2522 Tex, Joe
    2522.1 *Singles A's and B's, Vol. 1: 1960–1964.* Shout! Factory: 64. 2010. CD.
    2522.2 *Singles A's and B's, Vol. 2: 1967–1968.* Shout! Factory: 67. 2010. CD.
    2522.3 *Singles A's and B's, Vol. 3: 1969–1972.* Shout! Factory: 72. 2011. CD.
    2522.4 *Singles A's and B's, Vol. 4: 1973–1976.* Shout! Factory: 76. 2011. CD.

2523 Turner. Ike, and Tina Turner
    2523.1 *Proud Mary: The Best of Ike and Tina Turner.* Sue / EMI: CDP-7-95846-2. 1991. CD.
    2523.2 *The Ike and Tina Turner Story, 1960–1975.* Time Life / EMI: M19300DIGI. 2004. 3 CDs.

2524 Turner, Tina. *Simply the Best.* Capitol: 72435-90433-0-2. 2002. CD, DVD. Also released as a single CD.

2525 *Ultimate Soul Guitar Collection.* Warner Bros.: GFM0312. 2003. Score.

2526 Warwick, Dionne
    2526.1 *The Dionne Warwick Collection: Her All-Time Greatest Hits* [1962–1970]. Rhino: R2 71100. 1989. CD.
    2526.2 *In Concert Classics Featuring Dionne Warwick* [1970s]. DPTV: DPT-DV 234. 1977. DVD.

2527 *Wattstax: 30th Anniversary Special Edition* [1972] (Isaac Hayes, Luther Ingram, Staple Singers, Johnnie Taylor, Emotions, and others). Warner: 34997. 2004. DVD.

2528 Wells, Mary. *The Ultimate Collection.* Motown: 314530859-2. 1998. CD.

2529 White, Barry
    2529.1 *All-Time Greatest Hits* [1973–1977]. Mercury: 314 522 459-2. 1994. CD.
    2529.2 ★*Just for You* [1973–1992]. Mercury: 314 514 143-2. 1992. 3 CDs.

    2529.3 *Let the Music Play: The Barry White Story.* Isis Productions: EV 30211-9. 2006. DVD.

2530 Wiggins, Spencer. *The Goldwax Years* [1965–1969, 1990]. Kent Soul: CDKEND 262. 2006. CD.

2531 Wilson, Jackie
    2531.1 ★*Mr. Excitement!* [1957–1975]. Rhino: R2 70775. 1992. 3 CDs.
    2531.2 *The Very Best of Jackie Wilson.* Ace: CDCH 913. 1987. CD.

2532 Withers, Bill. *The Very Best of Bill Withers* [1971–1986]. Sony: 5201462. 2005. CD.

2533 Womack, Bobby
    2533.1 *Anthology* [1967–1975]. Right Stuff: 72435-90299-2-4. 2003. 2 CDs.
    2533.2 *The Best of Bobby Womack: The Soul Years* [late 1960s–early 1970s]. Capitol: 509995 09491 20. 2008. CD.
    2533.3 *The Bravest Man in the Universe.* XL: XLCD561. 2012. CD.
    2533.4 *The Jazz Channel Presents Bobby Womack.* BET on Jazz / Image Entertainment: ID9641BJDVD. 2000. DVD.

2534 Wonder, Stevie
    2534.1 *At the Close of a Century* [1963–1998]. Motown: 012 153 992-2. 1999. 4 CDs.
    2534.2 *The Definitive Collection* [1963–1980s]. UTV / Motown: 440 066 164-2. 2002. CD.
    2534.3 ★*Innervisions* [1973]. Motown: 012 157 355-2. 2000. CD.
    2534.4 *The Original Musiquarium I* [1972–1982]. Motown: 3746360022. 1990. 2 CDs.
    2534.5 ★*Songs in the Key of Life* [1976]. Motown: 012 157 357-2. 2000. 2 CDs.
    2534.6 *Stevie Wonder Anthology.* Hal Leonard: HL00306447. 2003.
    2534.7 *Talking Book* [1972]. Motown: 012 157 354-2. 2000. CD.

2535 Wright, Betty. *The Platinum Collection* [1968–1973]. Warner Platinum / Rhino: 8122-79994-1. 2007. CD.

2536 Wright, O. V.
    2536.1 *The Complete O. V. Wright on Hi Records, Vol. 1: In the Studio* [1976-1979]. Hi: HEXD 47. 1999. 2 CDs.

2536.2 *The Complete O. V. Wright on Hi Records, Vol. 2: On Stage (Live in Japan)* [1979]. Hi: HILO 169. 1999. CD.

2536.3 *The Soul of O. V. Wright* [1964–1973]. MCA: MCAD-10670. 1992. CD.

2537 Wright, Willie. *Telling the Truth* [1977]. Numero: 038. 2011. 2 CDs.

Vocal Groups

2538 Curtis Mayfield and the Impressions. *Movin' On Up: The Music and Message of Curtis Mayfield and the Impressions* [1965–1973]. Reelin' in the Years / Universal Music Group: B0010887-09. 2008. DVD.

2539 ★Four Tops. *50th Anniversary: The Singles Collection, 1961–1971* [1961-1971]. Hip-O Select: B0015942-02. 2011. 3 CDs.

2540 Four Tops. *Reach Out* [1960s–1970s]. Motown: 1178709. 2008. DVD.

2541 Knight, Gladys, and the Pips

2541.1 *Essential Collection*. Hip-O: 314 545 029 2. 1999. CD.

2541.2 *Gladys Knight and the Pips and Ray Charles Live at the Greek Theatre* [1977]. Cine-Vu International: HSVD9913-9. 2006. DVD.

2541.3 *Gold* [1961–1991]. Hip-O: B0006781-02. 2006. 2 CDs.

2542 Isley Brothers

2542.1 *Best of the Isley Brothers*. Hal Leonard: HL00306762. 2006. Score.

2542.2 *The Isleys Live* [1973]. Rhino: R2 72284. 1996. CD.

2542.3 ★*It's Your Thing: The Story of the Isley Brothers* [1957–1996]. Sony: Z3K 65547. 1999. 3 CDs.

2542.4 *3 + 3* [1973]. Epic / Legacy: EK 85798. 2003. CD.

2542.5 *The Ultimate Isley Brothers* [1959–1985]. Epic / Legacy: ZK 62196. 2000. CD.

2543 Reeves, Martha, and the Vandellas

2543.1 *Gold*. Universal Music Enterprises / Hip-O / Motown: B0005226-02. 2006. 2 CDs.

2543.2 *The Ultimate Collection* [1963–1972]. Motown: 314530858-2. 1998. CD.

2544 Pointer Sisters

2544.1 *The Best of the Pointer Sisters* [1979–1987]. RCA: 07863 67909-2. 2000. CD.

2544.2 *Yes We Can Can: The Best of the Blue Thumb Recordings* [1973–1977]. Hip-O: HIPD-40052. 1997. CD.

2545 Robinson, Smokey, and the Miracles

2545.1 *Definitive Performances, 1963–1987*. Universal Music: B0007976-09. 2006. DVD.

2545.2 *35th Anniversary Collection* [1957–1986]. Motown: 37463-6334-2. 1994. 4 CDs.

2545.3 ★*The Ultimate Collection* [1959–1972]. Motown: 314530857-2. 1998. CD.

2546 Ross, Diana. *50th Anniversary: The Singles Collection, 1961–1969* [1961-1969] (Supremes). Hip-O Select: B0015943-02. 2011. 3 CDs.

2547 Ross, Diana, and the Supremes

2547.1 ★*Gold*. Motown: B0004515-02. 2005. 2 CDs.

2547.2 *The No. 1's* [1963–1969]. Motown: B0001368-02. 2003. CD.

2548 Soul Children. *Chronicle* [1968–1974]. Stax: SCD-4120-2. 1979. CD.

2549 Spinners

2549.1 *The Definitive Soul Collection* [1973–1980]. Atlantic / Rhino: R2 77667. 2006. 2 CDs.

2549.2 *The Very Best of the Spinners* [1970–1980]. Rhino: R2 71213. 1993. CD.

2550 Supremes

2550.1 *Magnificent: The Complete Studio Duets* [1970–1971] (Four Tops). Hip-O Select: B0013119-02. 2009. 2 CDs.

2550.2 *Meet the Supremes* [1962–1965]. Hip-O Select: B0013788-02. 2010. 2 CDs.

2550.3 *Reflections: Definitive Performances, 1964–1969*. Universal Music: B0007961-09. 2006. DVD.

2551 Temptations

2551.1 ★*Anthology* [1964–1986]. Motown: 31453 0524-2. 1995. 2 CDs.

2551.2 *Emperors of Soul* [1964–1984]. Motown: 31453-0338-2. 1994. 5 CDs.

2551.3 *Get Ready: Definitive Performances, 1965–1972*. Universal Music Group / Hip-O. 2006. DVD.

2551.4 *The Ultimate Collection* [1964–1975]. Motown: 31453-0562-2. 1997. CD.

Regional Styles

Philadelphia

COLLECTION

2552 ★*Love Train: The Sound of Philadelphia*
[1960s–1970s] (Soul Survivors, Delfonics,
Intruders, Jerry Butler, Wilson Pickett, Joe
Simon, Stylistics, Harold Melvin and the
Bluenotes, O'Jays, Spinners, Manhattans, Billy
Paul, MFSB, Three Degrees, Lou Rawls, Teddy
Pendergrass, Deniece Williams, Patti Labelle,
and others). Legacy: 88697352792. 2008.
4 CDs.

INDIVIDUALS AND GROUPS

2553 Delfonics. *La-la Means I Love You: The Definitive
Collection* [1968–1973]. Arista: 07822-18979-2.
1997. CD.

2554 Manhattans. *Sweet Talking Soul, 1965–1990*.
Shout! Factory: 826663 10942/3. 2008. 3 CDs.

2555 Melvin, Harold, and the Blue Notes. *The Essential
Harold Melvin and the Blue Notes*. Sony: EK
90627. 2004. CD.

2556 MFSB. *Love Is the Message: The Best of MFSB*.
Epic / Legacy / Philadelphia International: ZK
66689. 1995. CD.

2557 O'Jays. *The Ultimate O'Jays* [1972–1975]. Sony:
ZK 85100. 2001. CD.

2558 Stylistics. *The Best of the Stylistics* [1971–1974].
Amherst: AMH-9743. 1985. CD.

Detroit

2559 Dramatics
    2559.1 *Ultimate Collection* [1971–1980]. Hip-O:
314 560 196-2. 2000. CD.
    2559.2 *The Very Best of the Dramatics* [1969–
1989]. Stax: STXCD-30304. 2007. CD.

Memphis

2560 Thomas, Carla. *Gee Whiz: The Best of Carla
Thomas* [1960–1968]. Rhino: R2 71633.
1994. CD.

2561 Thomas, Rufus. *The Best of Rufus Thomas: Do the
Funky Somethin'* [1953–1971, 1994]. Rhino: R2
72410. 1996. CD.

East St. Louis, Illinois

2562 *Eccentric Soul: The Young Disciples* [1960s]
(LaVel Moore, Young Disciples Co., Third Flight,
Debonettes, Ames Harris Desert Water, Sharon
Clark and the Product of Time, DeDe Turner
Happening, Dauphin Williams, Georgettes,
Bobby McNutt, Eddie Fisher and Allan "Death"
Merry). Numero: 023. 2008. CD.

Phoenix

2563 *Eccentric Soul: Mighty Mike Lenaburg* [1962–
1980] (Lon Rogers & the Soul Blenders, Michael
Liggins, Sheila Jack, Ronnie Whitehead,
Soulsations, We the People, Soul Blenders, Small
Paul, Newlyweds). Numero: 011. 2006. CD.

New Orleans

2564 *Crescent City Soul: The Sound of New Orleans,
1947–1974* (Professor Longhair, Fats Domino,
Roy Brown, Dave Bartholomew, Huey "Piano"
Smith, Ernie K-Doe, Irma Thomas, Lee Dorsey,
Aaron Neville, Smiley Lewis, Shirley and Lee,
Lee Allen, Amos Milburne, Chris Kenner, Jessie
Hill, Earl King, Benny Spellman, and others).
EMI: 7243 8 37350 2 0. 1996. 4 CDs.

Miami

2565 *Eccentric Soul: The Outskirts of Deep City*
[1960s–1970s] (Rollers, Clarence Reid, Helene
Smith, Betty Wright, James Knight and the
Butlers, Lynn Williams, Rising Sun, Perk Badger,
Frank Williams and the Rocketeers, Deep City
Band, Nasty Dog Catchers, Snoopy Dean).
Numero: 017. 2007. CD.

Chicago

2566 *Birth of Soul: Special Chicago Edition* [1957-1964]
(Jerry Butler, The Impressions, Major Lance,
Betty Everett, Don and Bob, Etta and Harvey,
Jan Bradley, Rosco Gordon, The Accents, The
Radiants, The Sheppards, Wade Flemons, Etta
James, The Chanteurs, The Kavetts, Gerald Sims,
The Daylighters, Barbara Lewis, the Dells, the
Drew-Vels, Dee Clark, Sugar Pie DeSanto, and
Gene Chandler). Kent Soul: CDKEND 322.
2009. CD.

2567 *Eccentric Soul: The Nickel and Penny Labels*
[1967–1973] (Jerry Townes; Little Ben and
Cheers; Matta Baby; Norvells; Extentions;

Hallelujah Chorus; South Shore Commission; Richard Terry; Joyce Williams; Brothers and Sisters; Sidney Pinchback; South Suburban Electric Strings; Sidney Barnes; and Tel Fi Demo). Numero: 039. 2011. CD.

2568 *Eccentric Soul: Twinight's Lunar Rotation* [1967–1970] (Stormy, Annette Poindexter and the Pieces of Peace, Dynamic Tints, Nate Evans, Krystal Generation, Velma Perkins, Renaldo Domino, George McGregor and the Bonzettes, Mystiques, Sidney Pinchback and Schiller Street Gang, Perfections, Harrison and the Majestic Kind, Josephine Taylor, Notations, Kaldirons, Radiants, Chuck and Me, Elvin Spencer, Johnny Williams, Mist, Krystal Generation, Jo Ann Garrett, Jimmy Jones). Numero: 013. 2007. 2 CDs.

Wichita

2569 *Boddie Recording Company Cleveland, Ohio* [1958–1993] (Creations Unlimited, Ricky Hodges, Funky People, Frankie Pighee, Soulettes, Chantells, Jackie Russell, Angela Alexander, J. D. Saddler, Inter-Circle, Eddie and Ant Hill Mob, Bo and Metros, King James Version, A. C. Jones, Atomic Aces, Harvey Hall, Headlines, J. C. Akins, Modern Detergents, Harvey and Phenomenals, Little Anthony Mitchell, Penny North, Dukes, Rev. R. L. Hubbard, Brother Bill, Guiding Lights, Wings Of Faith Juniors Of Grand Rapids, MI, Seven Revelators, Victory 5, Sound Of Soul, Corinthian Singers, Fantastic Lightning Ares, Golden Harmonizers, Gospel Hebrews, Gospel Fabulators, Spiritual Believers, Silver Kings, Cleveland Golden Echos, Royal Kings, Swanee Nightingales, North Wind Of Cleveland, OH, Gospel Ensemble, and Juanita Ellis). Numero: 035. 2011. 3 CDs or 5 LPs.

Cleveland

2570 *Boddie Recording Company Cleveland, Ohio* [1958–1993] (Creations Unlimited, Ricky Hodges, Funky People, Frankie Pighee, Soulettes, Chantells, Jackie Russell, Angela Alexander, J. D. Saddler, Inter-Circle, Eddie and Ant Hill Mob, Bo and Metros, King James Version, A. C. Jones, Atomic Aces, Harvey Hall, Headlines, J. C. Akins, Modern Detergents, Harvey and Phenomenals, Little Anthony Mitchell, Penny North, Dukes, Rev. R. L. Hubbard, Brother Bill, Guiding Lights, Wings Of Faith Juniors Of

Grand Rapids, MI, Seven Revelators, Victory 5, Sound Of Soul, Corinthian Singers, Fantastic Lightning Ares, Golden Harmonizers, Gospel Hebrews, Gospel Fabulators, Spiritual Believers, Silver Kings, Cleveland Golden Echos, Royal Kings, Swanee Nightingales, North Wind Of Cleveland, OH, Gospel Ensemble, and Juanita Ellis). Numero: 035. 2011. 3 CDs or 5 LPs.

Instrumental and Soundtracks

2571 Booker T. and the MGs
   2571.1 *Potato Hole* (Drive-By Truckers). Anti: 86948-2. 2009. CD.
   2571.2 *Time Is Tight* [1962–1971; 1992–1994]. Stax: 3SCD-4424-2. 1998. 3 CDs.

2572 Hutch, Willie. *The Mack* [1973]. Motown: 31453-0389-2. 1996. CD.

2573 King Curtis. *Blow Man, Blow!* [1962–1965]. Bear Family: BCD 15670 CI. 1992. 3 CDs.

2574 King Curtis. *Live at Fillmore West* [1971]. Rhino: R2 77632. 2006. CD.

2575 *Music from the Wattstax Festival and Film* [1972] (Staple Singers, William Bell, Little Sonny, Lee Sain, Louise McCord, Deborah Manning, Kim Weston, Temprees, Frederick Knight, Newcomers, Eddie Floyd, Emotions, Golden Gate Quartet, Rance Allen Group, Bar-Kays, David Porter, Richard Pryor, Little Milton, Mel and Tim, Albert King, Johnnie Taylor, Carla Thomas, Rufus Thomas, Soul Children, Isaac Hayes, and others). Stax: STX3-30315. 2007. 3 CDs.

2576 Mayfield, Curtis. *Superfly* [1972]. Rhino: R2 75803. 1999. CD.

2577 Walker, Jr., and the All Stars. *The Ultimate Collection* [1962–1966]. Motown: 314530828-2. 1997. CD.

Gospel

2578 Cooke, Sam. *Sam Cooke with the Soul Stirrers: The Complete Specialty Recordings* [1951–1957]. Specialty: 3SPCD-4437-2. 2002. 3 CDs.

2579 Franklin, Aretha. *Amazing Grace: The Complete Recordings* [1972]. Rhino: R2 75627. 1999. 2 CDs.

2580 Staple Singers. *The Best of the Staple Singers* [1968–1974]. Stax / Fantasy: FCD-60-007. 1986. CD.

2581   Staples, Mavis. *You Are Not Alone* [2010]. Anti:
       87076-2. 2010. CD.

Contemporary

2582   Earth, Wind, and Fire
  2582.1   *The Eternal Dance* [1971–1989].
           Columbia / Legacy: C3K 52439. 1992.
           3 CDs.
  2582.2   *Gratitude* [1975]. Columbia / Legacy: CK
           65737. 1999. CD.
  2582.3   *Spirit* [1976]. Columbia / Legacy: CK
           65739. 2001. CD.
  2582.4   *That's the Way of the World* [1975].
           Columbia / Legacy: CK 65920.
           1999. CD.

2583   Turner, Tina. *Private Dancer* [1984]. Capitol:
       7243 8 55833 22. 1997. CD.

2584   Vandross, Luther
  2584.1   *From Luther, with Love: The Videos*. Sony
           / Epic: EVD 56961. 2004. DVD.
  2584.2   *Luther Vandross Live at Wembley* [1989].
           Sony: EVD 49023. 2000. DVD.

Neo-Soul

2585   Stone, Joss. *The Soul Sessions*. S-Curve: 7243 5
       42234 2 6. 2003. CD.

2586   Winehouse, Amy
  2586.1   *Back to Black*. Universal Republic:
           B0008555-02. 2006. CD.
  2586.2   *I Told You I Was Trouble: Live in London*.
           Island: B0010249-09. 2007. DVD.

Blues

2587   Taylor, Johnnie
  2587.1   *Chronicle: The 20 Greatest Hits* [1966–
           1975]. Stax / Fantasy: FCD 60-006.
           1991. CD.
  2587.2   *Rated X-Traordinaire: The Best of Johnnie
           Taylor* [1976–1980]. Columbia / Legacy:
           CK 64818. 1996. CD.

Label Overview

2588   *Action Speaks Louder Than Words: The Best of SSS
       International* [1967–1970] (Clarence Murray,
       Sam Dees, Robert Parker, Reuben Bell, Bettye
       LaVette, Betty Harris, Gloria Taylor, Johnny
       Adams, Big Al Downing, and others). VampiSoul
       Records: VAMPI CD 071. 2006. CD.

2589   ★*Atlantic Soul, 1959–1975* (Ray Charles,
       LaVern Baker, Ben E. King, Isley Brothers,
       Ikettes, Jimmy Ricks, Falcons, Solomon Burke,
       Bettye Lavette, Doris Troy, Untouchables,
       Nat Kendricks, Vibrations, Esther Phillips,
       Mack Rice, Wilson Pickett, Carla Thomas, Don
       Covay, Jo Ann and Troy, Tami Lynn, Tommy
       Hunt, Willie Tee, Coasters, Patti LaBelle, Mary
       Wells, Barbara Lewis, Soul Brothers Six, Sweet
       Inspirations, Billy Vera, Judy Clay, Jimmy
       Hughes, Aretha Franklin, Harvey Scales,
       Clarence Carter, Alvin Robinson, Otis Redding,
       Sam and Dave, Dynamics, C and the Shells,
       Percy Sledge, Baby Washington, Walter Jackson,
       Jackie Moore, King Floyd, Garland Green, James
       Carr, Persuaders, Donny Hathaway, Howard
       Tate, Bettye Swann, Spinners, Valentinos,
       Daryl Hall and John Oates, Trammps). Rhino
       Handmade: RHM2 7739. 2007. 4 CDs.

2590   *The Best of Loma Records: The Rise and Fall
       of a 1960's Soul Label* [1964–1968] (Ike and
       Tina Turner, Little Jerry Williams, Enchanters,
       Invincibles, Olympics, Walter Foster, Baby
       Lloyd, Bobby Bennett and the Dynamics,
       Apollas, Marvellos, Mary Lee Whitney, Lorraine
       Ellison, J. J. Jackson, Lukas Lollipop, Ben Aiken,
       Teen Turbans, Roy Redmond, Linda Jones,
       Ben Aiken, Carl Hall, Mighty Hannibal, Lonnie
       Youngblood, Three Degrees). Warner Archives:
       2-45711. 1995. 2 CDs.

2591   *The Complete Goldwax Singles, Vol. 1* [1962–
       1966] (Jon Kennedy; Bobby McDowell; Jeb
       Stewart; O. V. Wright; Eddie Bond; James Carr;
       Phillip and Faithfuls; Playboy Five, Ovations;
       Gene "Bowlegs" Miller, merits; Big Lucky Carter;
       Prince Gabe; Millionaires; Dorothy Williams;
       Al Vance; Spencer Wiggins; Lamars; and Vel
       Tones). Ace: CDCH2 1226. 2009. 2 CDs.

2592   *The Complete Goldwax Singles, Vol. 2* [1966–
       1967] (James Carr; Yo Yo's; Leroy Daniel; Gene
       "Bowlegs" Miller, Ovations; Ivory Joe Hunter;
       Jeanne Newman; Spencer Wiggins; George and
       Greer; Percy Milem; Eddie Jefferson; Barbara
       Perry; Terry's; Timmy Thomas; Kathy Davis; and
       Carmol Taylor). Ace: CDCH2 1236. 2009. 2 CDs.

2593   *The Complete Goldwax Singles, Vol. 3* [1967–
       1977] (Ben Atkins; Nomads; Spencer Wiggins;
       Kathy Davis; Carmol Taylor; James Carr; Willie
       Walker, Ovations; and Percy Milem). Ace:
       CDCH2 1248. 2010. 2 CDs.

2594 *The Complete Stax/Volt Singles 1959–1968* (Carla Thomas, Mar-Keys, William Bell, Del-Rios, Booker T. and the MGs, Eddie Kirk, Otis Redding, Sam and Dave, Mad Lads, Johnnie Taylor, Albert King, Jeanne and the Darlings, and others). Atlantic: 82218-2. 1991. 9 CDs.

2595 *The Complete Stax/Volt Soul Singles, Vol. 2: 1968–1971* (Isaac Hayes, Staple Singers, Rufus Thomas, Carla Thomas, Eddie Floyd, Bar-Kays, William Bell, Albert King, Mar-Keys, Booker T. and the MGs, Johnnie Taylor, Emotions, Margie Joseph, and others). Stax: 9SCD-4411-2. 1993. 9 CDs.

2596 *Crash of Thunder: Boss Soul, Funk, and R&B Sides from the Vaults of the King, Federal, and Deluxe Labels* [1965–1975] (Wayne Cochran, Presidents, Mickey Murray, Jeb Stuart, Charles Spurling, James Duncan, Robert Moore, Swinging Seven, and others). VampiSoul Records: VAMPI CD 083. 2007. CD.

2597 *Eccentric Soul: The Bandit Label* [1969–1974] (Majestic Arrows, Arrows, Altyrone Deno Brown, Johnny Davis, Linda Balintine). Numero: 003. 2004. CD.

2598 *Eccentric Soul: The Big Mack Label* [1962–1972] (L. Hollis and the Mackadoos, Edd Henry, Bob and Fred, Soul President, Performers, Mae Young, Grand Prix's, Manhattens, Ms. Tyree "Sugar" Jones, Essence, Mae Young, Sleepwalkers, Essence). Numero: 009. 2006. CD.

2599 *Eccentric Soul: The Capsoul Label* [1970–1974] (Johnson, Hawkins, Tatum and Durr; Marion Black; Kool Blues; Bill Moss; Four Mints; Ronnie Taylor; Elijah and the Ebonites, Smith). Numero: 001. 2004. CD.

2600 *Eccentric Soul: The Deep City Label* [1964–1968] (Them Two, Moovers, Helene Smith, Johnny K Killens and the Dynamics, Freda Gray and the Rocketeers, Betty Wright, Paul Kelly, Frank Williams and the Rocketeers). Numero: 007. 2006. CD.

2601 *Eccentric Soul: The Prix Label* [1969–1973] (Eddie Ray, OFS Unlimited, Mitchell Mitchell and Gene King, Joe King, Royal Esquires, Chip Willis and Double Exposure, Soul Ensemble, Marion Black, Harmonic Sounds Band, Penny and the Quarters). Numero: 015. 2007. CD.

2602 *Eccentric Soul: The Tragar and Note Labels* [1960s] (Tee Fletcher, Bill Wright, Eula Cooper, Chuck Wilder, Nathan Wilkes, L. Daniels, Franciene Thomas, Frankie and Robert, Tokay Lewis, Richard Cook, Langston and French, Knights, Sonia Ross, Sandy Gaye, Bobby Owens and the Diplomats, Young Divines, Four Tracks, Cherry Blend, Alice Swoboda, Andrea Williams, J. J. Jones). Numero: 020. 2008. 2 CDs.

2603 *Hitsville USA: The Motown Singles Collection* [1959–1971] (Contours, Four Tops, Marvin Gaye, Isley Brothers, Jackson 5, Gladys Knight, Martha and the Vandellas, Marvelettes, Miracles, Edwin Starr, Supremes, Temptations, Jr. Walker and the All Stars, Mary Wells, Stevie Wonder, Kim Weston, Brenda Holloway, and others). Motown: 37463-6312-2. 1992. 4 CDs.

2604 *Hitsville USA: The Motown Singles Collection, Vol. 2* [1972–1992] (Lionel Richie, Michael Jackson, Jackson 5, Supremes, Four Tops, Temptations, Stevie Wonder, Gladys Knight, Diana Ross, Marvin Gaye, Eddie Kendricks, Smokey Robinson, Thelma Houston, Commodores, Switch, Rick James, Teena Marie, Dazz Band, DeBarge, and others). Motown: 37463-6358-2. 1993. 4 CDs.

2605 *Muscle Shoals Sound* [1961–1972] (Arthur Alexander, Clarence Carter, Percy Sledge, Otis Redding, Wilson Pickett, Aretha Franklin, Arthur Conley, Etta James, Laura Lee, R. B. Greaves, Staple Singers, Mel and Tim). Rhino: R2 71517. 1993. CD.

2606 *Sam Cooke's SAR Records Story* [1959–1965] (Soul Stirrers, R. H. Harris, Womack Brothers, Valentinos, Simms Twins, Johnnie Morisette, and others). Abkco: 3122-2. 1994. 2 CDs.

2607 *Sam Cooke's SAR Records Story, 1959–1965.* CPP / Belwin: P1081SMX. 1994. Score.

2608 *The Spring Story: Essential 70s Soul* [1967–1983] (Act I, Millie Jackson, Joe Simon, Mayberry Movement, Jocelyn Brown, Fatback Band, Ray Godfrey, Garland Green, Flower Shoppe, Street People, Busta Jones, Winfield Parker, Little Eva Harris, Mainstreeters, Bobby Newsome, Phillip Mitchell, Joe Simon, Ronnie Walker, Joneses, Boys in the Band, Determinations). Southbound: CDSEWD 103. 1995. CD.

2609 *Stax/Volt Revue: Live in London, Vols. 1 and 2*
[1967] (Booker T. and the MGs, Mar-Keys, Eddie
Floyd, Otis Redding, Carla Thomas, Sam and
Dave). Atlantic: 82341-2 [v. 1], 82342-2 [v. 2].
1991. 2 CDs.

2610 *The Story of Brunswick: The Classic Sound
of Chicago Soul* (Jackie Wilson, Young-Holt
Trio, LaVern Baker, Gene Chandler, Artistics,
Marvin Smith, Count Basie, Billy Butler, Little
Richard, Barbara Acklin, Erma Franklin,
Major Lance, Fred Hughes, Otis Leavill, Lost
Generation, Tyrone Davis, Lionel Hampton,
Willie Henderson, Soul Expressions, Chi-Lites,
Hamilton Bohannon). Metro: METRCD511.
2002. 2 CDs. Import.

2611 *Top of the Stax, Vol. 1: Twenty Greatest Hits*
[1966–1974] (Sam and Dave, Eddie Floyd,
Staple Singers, Carla Thomas, Shirley Brown,
Soul Children, Johnnie Taylor, Little Milton,
William Bell, Jean Knight, Rufus Thomas,
Booker T. and the MGs, Mel and Tim, Dramatics,
Emotions, Otis Redding, Frederick Knight, Isaac
Hayes). Stax: SCD-88005-2. 1988. CD.

2612 *Top of the Stax, Vol. 2: Twenty Greatest Hits*
[1960s–1970s] (Mar-Keys, Staple Singers, Soul
Children, Otis Redding, Judy Clay, William Bell,
Booker T. and the MGs, Johnnie Taylor, Carla
Thomas, Little Milton, Rufus Thomas, Bar-Kays,
Temprees, Dramatics, Eddie Floyd, Emotions,
Albert King). Stax: SCD-880082. 1991. CD.

FUNK

General Style

COLLECTIONS

2613 *Gimme Your Hand, J-B!* [1972–1975] (Lee
Austin, Lyn Collins, Sly Slick and Wounded,
Hank Ballard, Shirley Jean and the Relations).
Polydor P Vine: PCD-1363. 2008. CD.

2614 *Good God! Born Again Funk* [1969-1980s]
(Pastor T. L. Barrett; Youth for Christ Choir;
Ada Richards; Gospel Comforters; Golden
Echoes; Lucy "Sister Soul" Rodgers; Gospel Soul
Revivals; Brother Samuel Cheatham; Victory
Travelers; Jordan Travelers; Inspirational Gospel
Singers; Sacred Four; Andrew Wartts; Gospel
Storytellers; Holy Disciples of Chicago, IL;
Sensational Five Singing Sons; Little Chris and
Righteous Singers; Sensational Five; Chicago

Travelers; James Austin; and St. Luke COGIC
Youth Choir). Numero: 030. 2010. CD.

2615 ★*What It Is! Funky Soul and Rare Grooves*
[1967–1977] (Watts 103rd St. Rhythm Band,
Bar-Kays, Rufus Thomas, Grassella Oliphant,
Eddie Harris, Clarence Carter, Commodores,
Johnny Cameron, Cyril Neville, Ananda
Shankar, Don Covay, Mongo Santamaria, Wilson
Pickett, Gene McDaniels, Junior Mance, Young-
Holt Unlimited, Allen Toussaint, Charles Wright,
Howard Tate, Clarence Reid, Seatrain, Meters,
Dr. John, Oscar Brown, Jr., Fred Wesley, Eddie
Hazel). Rhino: R2 77635. 2006. 4 CDs.

INDIVIDUALS AND GROUPS

2616 Average White Band. *Pickin' up the Pieces:
The Best of Average White Band* [1974–1980].
Atlantic / Rhino: R2 71054. 1992. CD.

2617 Bar-Kays. *The Best of the Bar-Kays* [1976–1989].
Mercury: 314 514 823-2. 1993. CD.

2618 Brothers Johnson. *Strawberry Letter 23: The Very
Best of the Brothers Johnson* [1975–1984]. A&M:
B00003850-2. 2003. CD.

2619 Brown, Chuck. *Bustin' Loose* [1979]. Valley Vue:
53903. 1993. CD.

2620 Brown, James
       2620.1 *Foundations of Funk: A Brand New Bag,
               1964–1969.* Polydor: 314 531 165-2.
               1996. 2 CDs.
       2620.2 *Funk Power 1970: A Brand New Thang*
               [1970–1971]. Polydor: 314 531 684-2.
               1996. CD.
       2620.3 *I Got the Feelin': James Brown in the '60s*
               [1968]. Shout! Factory: 826663-10879.
               2008. 3 DVDs.
       2620.4 *Say It Live and Loud: Live in Dallas
               08.26.68.* Polydor: 31455 7668-2.
               1998. CD.

2621 Cameo. *Gold* [1977–1990]. Mercury: B0004823-
02. 2005. 2 CDs.

2622 Chambers Brothers. *Time Has Come: The Best of
the Chambers Brothers* [1966–1970]. Columbia /
Legacy: CK 65036. 1996. CD.

2623 Clinton, George
       2623.1 *Computer Games* [1982]. Capitol: CDP 7
               96266 2. 1991. CD.
       2623.2 *The Mothership Connection* [1998].
               Gravity Ltd. / Pioneer Artists: PA-11664.
               2001. DVD.

2624 Collins, Bootsy. *The Bootsy Collins Anthology: Glory B Da' Funks on Me* [1976–1982]. Rhino: R2 74276. 2001. 2 CDs.

2625 Con Funk Shun. *The Best of Con Funk Shun* [1976–1985]. Mercury: 314 510 275-2. 1993. CD.

2626 Dazz Band. *Funkology: The Definitive Dazz Band* [1981–1985]. Motown: 314 530 418-2. 1994. CD.

2627 Earth, Wind, and Fire. *Earth, Wind and Fire in Concert* [1981]. Eagle Rock / Pioneer Artists: 30249. 2000. DVD.

2628 Fatback Band. *The Fattest of Fatback* [1974–1983]. Rhino: R2 72211. 1997. CD.

2629 Gap Band. *Ultimate Collection* [1979–1990]. Hip-O: 314 548 098-2. 2000. CD.

2630 Graham, Larry. *The Jam: The Larry Graham and Graham Central Station Anthology* [1970s–1990s]. Warner Archives / Rhino: R2 78388. 2001. 2 CDs.

2631 Hot Chocolate. *Every 1's a Winner: The Very Best of Hot Chocolate* [1970s]. EMI: E2 89068. 1993. CD.

2632 James, Rick
  2632.1 *The Definitive Collection* [1978–1988]. Motown: B0004099-02. 2006. CD.
  2632.2 *Gold.* Motown: B0003608-02. 2005. 2 CDs.
  2632.3 *Street Songs, Del. Ed* [1980–1981]. Motown: 440 014 696-2. 2001. 2 CDs.
  2632.4 *Super Freak Live 1982.* Eagle Vision: EV30127-9. 2005. DVD.

2633 Kool and the Gang
  2633.1 *The Best of Kool and the Gang, 1969–1976.* Mercury: 314 514 822-2. 1993. CD.
  2633.2 *Celebration: The Best of Kool and the Gang, 1979–1987.* Mercury: 314 522 458-2. 1994. CD.
  2633.3 *Videology* [1970s–1980s]. Island Def Jam: B0009505-09. 2007. DVD.

2634 L.T.D. *Greatest Hits* [1976–1981]. A&M: 3145405202. 1996. CD.

2635 Love Unlimited. *The Best of Love Unlimited* [1972–1980]. Mercury: 314 532 408-2. 1997. CD.

2636 New Birth. *The Very Best of New Birth, Inc* [1971–1975] (Nite-Liters; Love, Peace and Happiness). RCA: 07863 66732-2. 1995. CD.

2637 Ohio Players. *Funk on Fire: The Mercury Anthology* [1974–1978]. Mercury: 440 063 041-2. 2002. 2 CDs.

2638 Parliament
  2638.1 *The Best of Parliament: Give up the Funk* [1974–1980] (George Clinton, Bootsy Collins). Chronicles / Casablanca: 314 526 995-2. 1995. CD.
  2638.2 *The Clones of Dr. Funkenstein* [1976] (George Clinton, Bootsy Collins). Casablanca: 842 620-2. 1990. CD.
  2638.3 *Funkentelechy vs. the Placebo Syndrome* [1977] (George Clinton, Bootsy Collins). Casablanca: 824 501-2. 1990. CD.
  2638.4 *Gold* [1974–1980] (George Clinton, Bootsy Collins). Mercury: B0004197-02. 2005. 2 CDs.
  2638.5 ★*Mothership Connection* [1975] (George Clinton, Bootsy Collins). Mercury: 440 077 032-2. 2003. CD.
  2638.6 *The Mothership Connection—Live 1976* (Clinton, George). Shout! Factory: 826663. 1998. DVD.

2639 Prince
  2639.1 ★*1999.* Warner Bros.: 9 23720-2. 1982. CD.
  2639.2 *Dirty Mind.* Warner Bros.: 3478-2. 1980. CD.
  2639.3 *The Hits / the B-Sides.* Paisley Park / Warner Bros.: 31180396. 1993. 3 CDs.
  2639.4 *Prince: Live in Las Vegas* (Maceo Parker, Sheila E., and others). Universal Music Enterprises: B000099509. 2003. DVD.
  2639.5 ★*Purple Rain: Music from the Motion Picture.* Warner Bros.: 9 25110-2. 1984. CD.
  2639.6 *Sign "O" the Times.* Paisley Park / Warner Bros.: 9 25577-2. 1987. 2 CDs.
  2639.7 *The Very Best of Prince.* Warner Bros.: R2 74272. 2001. CD.

2640 Sly and the Family Stone
  2640.1 *The Essential Sly and the Family Stone* (Sly Stone). Sony / Epic: E2K 86867. 2002. 2 CDs.
  2640.2 *Greatest Hits* [1967–1969] (Sly Stone). Epic: 82876 75910 2. 2007. CD.
  2640.3 ★*Stand!* [1970] (Sly Stone). Epic: EK 26456. 1987. CD.
  2640.4 *There's a Riot Goin' On* [1971] (Sly Stone). Epic / Legacy: 82876 75911 2. 2007. CD.

2641   Tower of Power. *The Very Best of Tower of Power: The Warner Years* [1972–1975]. Warner Archives / Rhino: R2 74345. 2001. CD.

2642   War
   2642.1   *All Day Music* [1971]. Avenue Records / Rhino: R2 71042. 1992. CD.
   2642.2   *Anthology, 1970–1994*. Avenue Records / Rhino: R2 71774. 1994. 2 CDs.
   2642.3   *The World Is a Ghetto* [1972]. Avenue Records / Rhino: R2 71043. 1992. CD.

2643   Wright, Charles, and the Watts 103rd St. Rhythm Band. *Express Yourself* [1970]. Collectables: COL-CD-6561. 2005. CD.

DISCO
General Style

COLLECTION

2644   *Disco Box* [1973–1984] (Love Unlimited Orchestra, Jackson 5, Hues Corporation, Gloria Gaynor, Carol Douglas, Disco Tex and the Sex-O-Lettes, Shirley and Company, Gloria Gaynor, KC and the Sunshine Band, Van McCoy and the Soul City Symphony, Tavares, Silver Convention, 5000 Volts, Miracles, Hot Chocolate, Sylvers, Andrea True Connection, Candi Staton, Vicki Sue Robinson, Walter Murphy and the Big Apple Band, Wild Cherry, Rose Royce, Thelma Houston, Ritchie Family, Trammps, Heatwave, Donna Summer, Peter Brown, Chic, Evelyn "Champagne" King, Taste of Honey, Foxy, Alicia Bridges, Musique, Karen Young, Cheryl Lynn, Peaches and Herb, Village People, Chic, Gloria Gaynor, Bell and James, Dan Hartman, Sylvester, Amii Stewart, G.Q., Arpeggio, Sister Sledge, McFadden and Whitehead, Anita Ward, Donna Summer, Patrick Hernandez, Debbie Jacobs, Edwin Starr, Narada Michael Walden, Blondie, Inner Life, Lipps Inc., Kool and the Gang, Change, Young and Company, Boystown Gang, B.B.&Q. Band, Patrice Rushen, Weather Girls, Indeep, Freeez). Rhino: R2 75595. 1999. 4 CDs.

INDIVIDUALS AND GROUPS

2645   Chic. *The Very Best of Chic* [1977–1981]. Rhino: R2 79821. 2000. CD.

2646   Gaynor, Gloria. *I Will Survive: The Anthology* [1980s–1990s]. Polydor: 31455 7236-2. 1998. 2 CDs.

2647   Heatwave. *The Best of Heatwave: Always and Forever* [1977–1982]. Epic / Legacy: EK 64914. 1996. CD.

2648   Jones, Grace. *Nightclubbing* [1981]. Island: 422 842 368-2. 1991. CD.

2649   Kid Creole. *Going Places: The August Darnell Years 1976–1983*. Strut: STRUT034CD. 2008. CD.

2650   King, Evelyn "Champagne." *Evelyn "Champagne" King Greatest Hits* [1978–1986]. RCA: 07863693562. 2001. CD.

2651   Rose Royce. *The Very Best of Rose Royce*. Warner Archives / Rhino: R2 74294. 2001. CD.

2652   Sister Sledge. *The Best of Sister Sledge (1973–1985)*. Rhino: R2 71060. 1992. CD.

2653   Staton, Candi. *The Best of Candi Staton* [1974–1980]. Warner Archives: 2-45730. 1995. CD.

2654   Summer, Donna
   2654.1   *Bad Girls* [1979]. Island Def Jam: B0000683-02. 2003. 2 CDs.
   2654.2   *Donna Summer Live and More Encore!* Epic: EVD 50202. 1999. DVD.
   2654.3   *The Journey: The Very Best of Donna Summer* [1975–1989]. UTV: B0001009-02. 2003. 2 CDs.

2655   Sylvester. *The Original Hits* [1978–1981]. Fantasy: FCD-7710-2. 1989. CD.

Label Overview

2656   *The Best of T. K. Disco* [1974–1979] (USA European Connection, Beautiful Bend, Amant, Paul Lewis, Kat Mandu, Margaret Reynolds, Gregg Diamond's Star Cruiser, KC and the Sunshine Band, Joe Thomas, Tempest Trio, Uncle Louie, Quartz, Johnny Harris, Herman Kelly and Life). Hot Productions: 17. 1995. CD.

2657   *Don't Stop: Recording Tap* [1981–1983] (Arnie Love and the Lovettes, Jackie Stoudemire, Missy Dee and the Melody Crew, Annette Denvil, Fabulous 3 MCs, Magnetism, Bonnie Freeman). Numero: 019. 2008. CD.

Soundtrack

2658   ★*Saturday Night Fever* [1977] (Bee Gees, Tavares, Kool and the Gang, KC and the Sunshine Band, MFSB, Trammps). Polydor: 42282 5389 2. 1995. CD.

Rap and Hip-Hop

Compiled by **ANDREW LEACH**

COLLECTIONS *153*
INDIVIDUALS AND GROUPS *155*
SOUNDTRACKS *163*

H ip-hop culture, including rap music, emerged as a cultural movement by and for African Americans in the South Bronx in New York City during the 1970s. Rap, or to use the proactive term, *MCing* (rapping), is generally considered to be one of hip-hop's four primary elements; DJing (turntablism), breaking (breakdancing), and graffiti art (aerosol art) constitute the other three. Rap music has become the best known expression of hip-hop, largely because it has been easiest to market to a commercial audience. Hip-hop and rap gained widespread popularity during the 1980s and 1990s through radio, television, records, films, and magazines, growing beyond the early city beginnings to become a national presence in culture and music.

Although more recent than most of musical genres represented in *A Basic Music Library,* rap and hip-hop are increasingly regarded as subjects worthy of exploration and research. For further reading, the following texts are recommended: Jeff Chang, *Can't Stop Won't Stop: A History of the Hip-Hop Generation* (St. Martin's Press, 2005); Andrew Leach, "One Day It'll All Make Sense: Hip Hop and Rap Resources for Music Librarians," *Notes: Quarterly Journal of the Music Library Association,* vol. 65, no. 1 (September 2008): 9–37; and Tricia Rose,

Black Noise: Rap Music and Black Culture in Contemporary America (University Press of New England, 1994).

This chapter lists essential CDs and DVDs of rap music and hip-hop culture from the 1970s to the present. An attempt has been made to represent a broad array of musical styles within the genre, including old school rap, gangsta rap, southern rap, underground rap, and turntablism. Also represented are materials focusing on the history of significant record labels (among them Sugar Hill, Def Jam, and Tommy Boy), rap outside the United States (including Africa and Brazil), and hip-hop's nonmusical elements. For sacred expressions in rap music, see chapter 9.

COLLECTIONS

2659 *Africa Raps.* Trikont: US-0294. 2001. CD.

2660 *African Rap.* Rough Guide series. World Music Network: RGNET1126CD. 2004. CD.

2661 *Anticon Presents Music for the Advancement of Hip Hop.* Anticon: ABR002. 1999. CD.

2662 *Beef.* QD3 / Image: QDE1967DVD. 2003. DVD.

2663   *The Best of Enjoy! Records* (Fearless Four, Spoonie Gee, Treacherous Three). Hot: HTCD 5. 1989. CD.

2664   *Brazilian Hip-Hop*. Rough Guide Series. World Music Network: RGNET1141CD. 2004. CD.

2665   *The Breakin' DVD Collection* [1984]. MGM: 64665243. 2005. 4 DVDs. Includes *Beat Street, Breakin', Breakin' 2: Electric Boogaloo*.

2666   ★*Def Jam Music Group, Inc.: 10th Year Anniversary*. Def Jam: 314 523 848-2. 1995. 4 CDs.

2667   *Def Jux Presents* . . . Def Jux: DJX005. 2001. CD.

2668   *Definitive Jux Presents II*. Definitive Jux: DJX22. 2002. CD.

2669   *East Side's Most Wanted, Vol. 1*. East Side: ESR-3000. 1999. CD.

2670   *East Side's Most Wanted, Vol. 2*. East Side: ESR-3001. 1999. CD.

2671   *15 Years on Death Row*. Death Row: DRR-CD-63077. 2006. 2 CDs.

2672   *Freestyle: The Art of Rhyme*. Palm: 3107 WR02. 2004. DVD.

2673   *Graffiti Rock* [1984]. Music Video: DRB-1337. 2002. DVD.

2674   *The Hip Hop Box* [1978–2003] (Treacherous Three). Hip-O: 440 069 588-2. 2004. 4 CDs.

2675   *Hip Hop Essentials, 1979–1991* (Busy Bee, Cold Crush Brothers, Fearless Four, Funky Four + 1, MC Shan, Roxanne Shante, Sequence, Treacherous Three). Tommy Boy: TB 1634-2–TB 1645-2. 2005–2006. 8 CDs.

2676   ★*Hip Hop Greats [Classic Raps]*. Rhino: R2 70957. 1986. CD.

2677   *Hip Hop Immortals: We Got Your Kids*. Image: ID0716NRDVD. 2004. DVD.

2678   *House Party* [1990]. New Line: N4854. 2000. DVD.

2679   *Kurtis Blow Presents the History of Rap, Vol. 1: The Genesis*. Rhino: R2 72851. 1997. CD. OP.

2680   *Kurtis Blow Presents the History of Rap, Vol. 2: The Birth of the Rap Record* (Davy DMX, Funky 4 + 1, Lovebug Starski, Sequence, Spoonie Gee, Treacherous Three). Rhino: R2 72852. 1997. CD. OP.

2681   *Kurtis Blow Presents the History of Rap, Vol. 3: The Golden Age* (MC Shan). Rhino: R2 72853. 1997. CD. OP.

2682   *Lyricist Lounge, Vol. 1*. Open Mic / Rawkus: RWK-1129-2. 1998. 2 CDs.

2683   *Lyricist Lounge: Dirty States of America*. MIC / Image: ID9416LGDVD. 2004. DVD.

2684   *Return of the DJ, Vol. 1*. Bomb Hip-Hop: BOMB 2002. 1997. CD. OP.

2685   *Return of the DJ, Vol. 2*. Bomb Hip-Hop: BOMB 2003. 1997. CD.

2686   *Rhyme and Reason* [1997]. Miramax: 22306. 2000. DVD. OP.

2687   *Solesides: Greatest Bumps* [1992–1997]. Quannum: QP 022-2. 2000. 2 CDs.

2688   *Soundbombing: The Ultimate Guide to Underground Hip-Hop*. Rawkus: 088 112 907-2. 1997. CD. OP.

2689   *Stones Throw 101*. Stones Throw: STH2102. 2004. CD.

2690   *Street Jams: Hip-Hop from the Top, Part 1* [1979–1985] (Davy DMX). Rhino: R2 70577. 1992. CD. OP.

2691   *Street Jams: Hip-Hop from the Top, Part 2* [1981–1985]. Rhino: R2 70578. 1992. CD. OP.

2692   *Street Jams: Hip-Hop from the Top, Part 3* [1984–1985] (Real Roxanne, Roxanne Shante, MC Shan). Rhino: R2 71555. 1994. CD. OP.

2693   *Street Jams: Hip-Hop from the Top, Part 4* [1985] (Roxanne Shante). Rhino: R2 71556. 1994. CD. OP.

2694   *Style Wars* [1983]. Public Art. 2004. 2 DVDs.

2695   ★*The Sugar Hill Records Story* (Busy Bee, Sequence, Spoonie Gee, Treacherous Three). Rhino: R2 75841. 1997. 5 CDs.

2696   ★*Tommy Boy Greatest Beats: The First Fifteen Years, 1981–1996*. Tommy Boy: TBCD 1115, TBCD 1165, TBCD 1117, TBCD 1166, TBCD 1312. 1998. 5 CDs.

2697   ★*Wild Style* [1982]. Rhino: R2 2367. 2002. DVD.

INDIVIDUALS AND GROUPS

2698 Above the Law
  2698.1 *Black Mafia Life.* Ruthless: 9 24477-2. 1992. CD.
  2698.2 *Livin' Like Hustlers.* Ruthless: EK 46041. 1990. CD.

2699 Aceyalone
  2699.1 *All Balls Don't Bounce, Revisited* [1995]. Decon / Project Blowed: DC 008. 2004. 2 CDs.
  2699.2 *A Book of Human Language.* Project Blowed: PBR002-2. 1998. CD. OP.

2700 Aesop Rock
  2700.1 *Float* [1999]. Mush: MH-202. 2004. CD.
  2700.2 *Labor Days.* Def Jux: DJX13. 2001. CD.

2701 Tha Alkaholiks. *21 and Over.* BMG: 07863-66280-2. 1993. CD.

2702 Antipop Consortium. *Arrhythmia.* Warp: WARPCD94. 2002. CD.

2703 Arrested Development. *3 Years, 5 Months, and 2 Days in the Life of . . .* Chrysalis: CDP-21. 1992. CD.

2704 Atmosphere
  2704.1 *Godlovesugly.* Fat Beats: 6591235001-2. 2002. CD. OP.
  2704.2 *Headshots: Se7en.* Rhymesayers: 0053-2. 2005. 2 CDs.

2705 ★Bambaataa, Afrika *Looking for the Perfect Beat, 1980–1985.* Tommy Boy: TBCD 1457. 2001. CD.

2706 Banner, David. *Certified.* SRC / Universal: B0004975-02. 2005. CD.

2707 Barkley, Gnarls. *St. Elsewhere.* Downtown / Atlantic: 8 7803-70003-2 0. 2006. CD.

2708 Base, Rob, and DJ E-Z Rock. *It Takes Two.* Profile: PCD-1267. 1988. CD. OP.

2709 Beastie Boys
  2709.1 *Check Your Head.* Grand Royal: CDP 7 98938 2. 1992. CD.
  2709.2 *Hot Sauce Committee Part Two.* Capitol: 5099950563920. 2011. CD.
  2709.3 *Ill Communication.* Grand Royal: CDP 7243 8 28599 2 5. 1994. CD.
  2709.4 *Licensed to Ill.* Def Jam: 314 527 351-2. 1986. CD.
  2709.5 ★*Paul's Boutique.* Capitol: CDP 7 91743 2. 1989. CD.

2710 Beat Junkies
  2710.1 *The World Famous Beat Junkies, Vol. 1.* P.R.: 54280. 1997. 2 CDs. OP.
  2710.2 *The World Famous Beat Junkies, Vol. 2.* Blackberry: BLK005. 1999. 2 CDs.

2711 Beatnuts. *The Beatnuts [Street Level].* Relativity / Violator: 88561-1179-2. 1994. CD.

2712 Big L. *Lifestylez ov da Poor and Dangerous.* Columbia: CK 53795. 1995. CD.

2713 Big Punisher. *Capital Punishment.* Loud: 1815-2. 1998. CD.

2714 Binary Star. *Masters of the Universe* [2000]. L.A. Underground: LUG1002. 2004. CD. OP.

2715 Biz Markie. *The Best of Cold Chillin': Goin' Off + The Biz Never Sleeps* [1988–1989]. LandSpeed: LSR 8808. 2001. 2 CDs. OP.

2716 Black Eyed Peas. *Behind the Front.* Interscope: INTD-90152. 1998. CD.

2717 Black Moon. *Enta da Stage.* Wreck: NRV 9101-02002-2. 1993. CD.

2718 Black Sheep. *A Wolf in Sheep's Clothing.* Mercury: 422 848 368-2. 1991. CD.

2719 Blackalicious
  2719.1 *Blazing Arrow.* MCA: 088 112 806-2. 2002. CD.
  2719.2 *Nia.* Quannum: QP-020-2. 2000. CD.

2720 Blige, Mary J. *What's the 411?* Uptown / MCA: UPTD-10681. 1992. CD.

2721 Blow, Kurtis
  2721.1 *The Best of Kurtis Blow.* Mercury: 314 522 456-2. 1994. CD.
  2721.2 *Kurtis Blow* [1980]. Mercury: 314 558 200-2. 1998. CD.

2722 Body Count. *Body Count.* Sire: 9 26878-2. 1992. CD.

2723 Bone Thugs-n-Harmony
  2723.1 *The Collection, Vol. 1* [1994–1998]. Ruthless: EK 69715. 1998. CD.
  2723.2 *E. 1999 Eternal.* Ruthless: EK 69443. 1995. CD.

2724 Boogie Down Productions
  2724.1 *By All Means Necessary.* Jive: 1097-2-J. 1988. CD.
  2724.2 ★*Criminal Minded* [1987]. B-Boy: BB4787. 1997. CD.

2724.3 *Edutainment.* Jive: 1358-2-J. 1990. CD.

2724.4 *Ghetto Music: The Blueprint of Hip Hop.* Jive: 1187-2-J. 1989. CD.

2725   Boot Camp Clik. *The Chosen Few.* Duck Down: DDM-CD-2000. 2002. CD.

2726   Brand Nubian

2726.1 *In God We Trust.* Elektra: 9-61381-2. 1992. CD.

2726.2 *One for All.* Elektra: 9 60946-2. 1990. CD.

2727   Brother Ali. *Shadows on the Sun.* Rhymesayers: RS0034-2. 2003. CD.

2728   Brown, Foxy. *Ill Na Na.* Violator / Def Jam: 314 533 684-2. 1996. CD.

2729   Da Bush Babees. *Gravity.* Warner Bros.: 9 46229-2. 1996. CD.

2730   Cage. *Hell's Winter.* Definitive Jux: DJX123. 2005. CD.

2731   Camp Lo. *Uptown Saturday Night* [1997]. Profile / Arista: 07822-16413-2. 1999. CD.

2732   Canibus. *Can-I-Bus.* Universal: UD 53136. 1998. CD.

2733   Cannibal Ox. *The Cold Vein.* Def Jux: DJX07-2. 2001. CD.

2734   Capone-n-Noreaga. *The War Report.* Penalty: PENCD 3041-2. 1997. CD.

2735   Cappadonna. *The Pillage.* Razor Sharp: EK 67947. 1998. CD.

2736   Casual. *Fear Itself.* Jive: 01241-41520-2. 1994. CD.

2737   Chamillionaire. *Ultimate Victory.* Universal / Motown: B0008812-02. 2007. CD.

2738   Clipse. *Hell Hath No Fury.* Re-Up Gang / Star Trak / Zomba: 82876-52119-2. 2006. CD.

2739   Cold Crush Brothers. *Fresh, Wild, Fly, and Bold.* Tuff City / Ol' Skool Flava: OSFCD4006. 1995. CD.

2740   Common Sense. *Resurrection.* Relativity: 88561-1208-2. 1994. CD.

2741   Common

2741.1 *Like Water for Chocolate.* MCA: 088 111 970-2. 2000. CD.

2741.2 *One Day It'll All Make Sense.* Relativity: 88561-1640-2. 1997. CD.

2742   Company Flow. *Funcrusherplus.* Rawkus: RWK 1134-2. 1997. CD. OP.

2743   Compton's Most Wanted. *Music to Driveby* [1992]. Sony / BMG: 723636. 2008. CD.

2744   Coolio. *Gangsta's Paradise.* Tommy Boy: TBCD 1157. 1995. CD.

2745   Cormega. *The Realness.* Legal Hustle: LSR 9203. 2001. CD. OP.

2746   Coup

2746.1 *Genocide and Juice* [1994]. Wild Pitch: 4200052. 2008. CD.

2746.2 *Steal This Double Album* [1998]. FOAD: FOAD-4600. 2002. 2 CDs.

2747   Cypress Hill

2747.1 *Black Sunday.* Ruffhouse: CK 53931. 1993. CD.

2747.2 *Cypress Hill.* Columbia: CK 47889. 1991. CD.

2748   D.O.C. *No One Can Do It Better.* Ruthless: 91275-2. 1989. CD.

2749   Dan the Automator. *A Much Better Tomorrow.* 75 Ark: CAT 75006. 2000. CD. OP.

2750   Danger Doom. *The Mouse and the Mask.* Epitaph: 86775-2. 2005. CD.

2751   Das EFX. *Dead Serious.* EastWest: 91827-2. 1992. CD.

2752   Das Racist. *Relax.* Greedhead: 160298. 2011. CD.

2753   Daz Dillinger. *Retaliation, Revenge and Get Back* [1998]. Death Row: DRR 63020-2. 2001. CD.

2754   De La Soul

2754.1 *Buhloone Mindstate.* Tommy Boy: TBCD 1063. 1993. CD.

2754.2 *De La Soul Is Dead.* Tommy Boy: TBCD 1029. 1991. CD.

2754.3 *The Grind Date.* Sanctuary Urban: 06076-87512-2. 2004. CD.

2754.4 *Stakes Is High.* Tommy Boy: TBCD 1149. 1996. CD.

2754.5 ★*3 Feet High and Rising.* Tommy Boy: TBCD 1019. 1989. CD.

2755   Dead Prez

2755.1 *Let's Get Free.* Loud: 1867-2. 2000. CD.

2755.2 *RBG: Revolutionary but Gangsta.* Sony Urban Music / Columbia: CK 89050. 2004. CD.

2756 Dee, Kool Moe. *Greatest Hits*. Jive: 01241-41493-2. 1993. CD.

2757 Del Tha Funkee Homosapien
    2757.1 *Both Sides of the Brain*. Hieroglyphics: 2301032. 2000. CD.
    2757.2 *I Wish My Brother George Was Here*. Elektra: 61133-2. 1991. CD.

2758 Deltron 3030. *Deltron 3030*. 75 Ark: 75033. 2000. CD.

2759 Diamond and the Psychotic Neurotics. *Stunts, Blunts, and Hip Hop*. Mercury: 314 513 934-2. 1992. CD.

2760 Digable Planets
    2760.1 *Blowout Comb*. Pendulum: E2-30654. 1994. CD.
    2760.2 *Reachin' (A New Refutation of Time and Space)*. Pendulum: 9 61414-2. 1993. CD.

2761 Digital Underground. *Sex Packets*. Tommy Boy: TBCD 1026. 1990. CD.

2762 Dilated Peoples. *The Platform*. Capitol: CDP 7243 5 233102 4. 2000. CD.

2763 Disposable Heroes of Hiphoprisy. *Hypocrisy Is the Greatest Luxury*. 4th and B'way: 162-444 043-2. 1992. CD.

2764 Diverse. *One A.M.* Chocolate Industries: CHLT039CD. 2003. CD. OP.

2765 Dizzee Rascal. *Boy in Da Corner*. Matador: OLE 600-2. 2004. CD.

2766 DJ Faust. *Man or Myth?* Bomb Hip-Hop: BOMB 2007. 1998. CD.

2767 DJ Jazzy Jeff and the Fresh Prince. *He's the DJ, I'm the Rapper*. Jive: 1091-2-J. 1988. CD.

2768 DJ Qbert. *Wave Twisters: Episode 7 Million—Sonic Wars within the Protons*. Galactic Butt Hair: GBH0007-2. 1998. CD.

2769 DJ Quik
    2769.1 *Quik Is the Name*. Profile: 07822-19056-2. 1998. CD.
    2769.2 *Safe + Sound*. Profile: PRO-1462-2. 1995. CD.

2770 DJ Shadow. *Endtroducing . . . .* Mowax: 697-124-123-2. 1996. CD.

2771 DMX
    2771.1 *Flesh of My Flesh, Blood of My Blood*. Def Jam: 314 538 640-2. 1998. CD.

2771.2 *It's Dark and Hell Is Hot*. Def Jam: 314 558 227-2. 1998. CD.

2772 Tha Dogg Pound. *Dogg Food* [1995]. Death Row: DRR 63007-2. 2001. CD.

2773 Dr. Dre
    2773.1 *2001*. Aftermath / Interscope: 069490486-2. 1999. CD.
    2773.2 ★*The Chronic* [1992]. Death Row: 728706300025. 2001. CD.

2774 Dr. Octagon. *Dr. Octagonecologyst*. Dreamworks: DRMD-50021. 1996. CD.

2775 Drake. *Thank Me Later*. Universal Motown: 2743307. 2010. CD.

2776 Dream Warriors. *And Now the Legacy Begins*. 4th and B'way: 162-444-037-2. 1991. CD. OP.

2777 Dupri, Jermaine. *Jermaine Dupri Presents Life in 1472: The Original Soundtrack*. Sony / SoSoDef: CK 69087. 1998. CD. OP.

2778 Eazy-E
    2778.1 *Eazy-Duz-It* [1988]. Priority: 72435-41041-2-1. 2002. CD.
    2778.2 *Eternal E: Gangsta Memorial Edition*. Priority: 72435-60682-0-9. 2005. 2 CDs.

2779 *Ego Trip's the Big Playback* (Grandmaster Caz). Rawkus: P2 25608. 2000. CD.

2780 Eightball and MJG
    2780.1 *Comin' out Hard*. Suave: SR-0001. 1993. CD.
    2780.2 *In Our Lifetime*. Suave House: UD-53251. 1999. CD.

2781 Elliott, Missy. *Supa Dupa Fly*. Gold Mind / Eastwest: 62062-2. 1997. CD.

2782 El-P. *I'll Sleep When You're Dead*. Definitive Jux: DJX137. 2007. CD.

2783 Eminem
    2783.1 *The Eminem Show*. Aftermath: 694932902. 2002. CD.
    2783.2 *The Marshall Mathers LP*. Aftermath / Interscope: 069490629-2. 2000. CD.
    2783.3 *The Slim Shady LP*. Interscope: INTD-90287. 1999. CD.

2784 EPMD
    2784.1 *Business as Usual*. Columbia: CK 47067. 1990. CD.
    2784.2 *Business Never Personal*. Rush: OK 52848. 1992. CD. OP.

2784.3 *★Strictly Business.* Priority: CDL 57135. 1988. CD.

2784.4 *Unfinished Business.* Priority: CDL 57136. 1989. CD.

2785 Eric B. and Rakim

2785.1 *Follow the Leader* [1988]. Geffen: B0004324-02. 2005. CD.

2785.2 *★Paid in Full* [1987]. Island: B0004323-02. 2005. CD.

2786 Esham. *Kkkill the Fetus: The Album.* Reel Life: RLP1013CD. 1993. CD.

2787 Eve. *Ruff Ryder's First Lady.* Interscope: 694904532. 1999. CD.

2788 Fat Boys

2788.1 *All Meat No Filler! The Best of Fat Boys.* Rhino: R2 72632. 1997. CD. OP.

2788.2 *Fat Boys.* Sutra: SCD 1015. 1984. CD.

2789 Fat Joe. *Don Cartagena.* Mystic: 92805-2. 1998. CD.

2790 Fiasco, Lupe. *Food and Liquor.* Atlantic: 83959-2. 2006. CD.

2791 50 Cent

2791.1 *Get Rich or Die Tryin'.* Shady / Aftermath / Interscope: 694935442. 2003. CD.

2791.2 *The Massacre.* Shady / Aftermath / Interscope: B0004092-02. 2005. CD.

2792 Flying Lotus. *Cosmogramma.* Warp: WARPCD195. 2010. CD.

2793 Foreign Exchange. *Connected.* Barely Breaking Even: BBECD047. 2004. CD.

2794 Francis, Sage. *Personal Journals.* Anticon: abr0021. 2002. CD.

2795 Freestyle Fellowship

2795.1 *Innercity Griots.* 4th and B'way: 162-444 050-2. 1993. CD.

2795.2 *To Whom It May Concern . . .* Basement: 825994112320. 2002. CD.

2796 Fresh, Doug E., and the Get Fresh Crew. *The World's Greatest Entertainer* [1988]. SPV / BCM: 076-555632. 2005. CD.

2797 *The Freshest Kids.* Image: ID1647QDDVD. 2002. DVD.

2798 ★Fugees. *The Score.* Ruff House / Columbia: CK 67147. 1996. CD.

2799 Game. *The Documentary.* Aftermath / G Unit / Interscope: B0003562-02. 2005. CD.

2800 Gang Starr

2800.1 *Daily Operation.* Chrysalis: CDP-21910. 1992. CD.

2800.2 *★Step in the Arena.* Chrysalis: F2 21798. 1990. CD.

2800.3 *The Ownerz.* Virgin: 7243 5 80251 2 5. 2003. CD.

2801 Genius

2801.1 *Beneath the Surface.* MCA: MCADE-11969. 1999. CD.

2801.2 *Liquid Swords.* Geffen: GEFD-24813. 1995. CD.

2802 Geto Boys

2802.1 *The Geto Boys.* Def American: 9 24306-2. 1990. CD.

2802.2 *We Can't Be Stopped.* Rap-A-Lot: CDL 57161. 1991. CD.

2803 Ghostface Killah

2803.1 *Ironman.* Razor Sharp / Epic: EK 67729. 1996. CD.

2803.2 *Supreme Clientele.* Razor Sharp / Epic: EK 69325. 2000. CD.

2804 *Global Hip Hop.* Manteca: MANTCD048. 2004. CD.

2805 Goodie Mob

2805.1 *Soul Food.* LaFace: 73008-26018-2. 1995. CD.

2805.2 *Still Standing.* LaFace: 73008-26047-2. 1998. CD.

2806 Gorillaz. *Demon Days.* Virgin: 7243 8 73838 2 1. 2005. CD.

2807 Grae, Jean. *Attack of the Attacking Things: The Dirty Mixes.* Third Earth: 3EM008. 2002. CD. OP.

2808 Grand Puba. *Reel to Reel.* Elektra: 61314-2. 1992. CD.

2809 ★Grandmaster Flash and Melle Mel. *The Best of Grandmaster Flash, Melle Mel, and the Furious Five: Message from Beat Street.* Rhino: R2 71606. 1994. CD.

2810 Gravediggaz. *6 Feet Deep.* Island: 314-524 016-2. 1994. CD.

2811 Green, Cee-Lo

2811.1 *Cee-Lo Green and His Perfect Imperfections.* Arista: 07822-14682-2. 2002. CD.

2811.2 *Cee-Lo Green . . . Is the Soul Machine.* Arista: 82876-52111-2. 2004. CD.

2811.3 *The Lady Killer.* Elektra: 7567889289. 2010. CD.

2812 Guru. *Jazzmatazz, Vol. 1.* Chrysalis: F2-21998. 1993. CD.

2813 Handsome Boy Modeling School. *So . . . How's Your Girl?* Tommy Boy: TBCD 1258. 1999. CD.

2814 Heavy D and the Boyz
2814.1 *Big Tyme.* MCA: MCAD-42302. 1989. CD.
2814.2 *Heavy Hitz.* MCA: 088 T12 382-2. 2000. CD.

2815 Heltah Skeltah. *Nocturnal.* Priority: 0 4992 50532 2 7. 1996. CD.

2816 Hieroglyphics
2816.1 *Full Circle.* Hieroglyphics Imperium: 2301092. 2003. CD.
2816.2 *3rd Eye Vision.* Hieroglyphics Imperium: HI8473. 1998. CD. OP.

2817 ★Hill, Lauryn. *The Miseducation of Lauryn Hill.* Ruff House / Columbia: CK69035. 1998. CD.

2818 House of Pain. *House of Pain.* Tommy Boy: TBCD 1056. 1992. CD.

2819 Ice Cube
2819.1 ★*Amerikkka's Most Wanted* [1990]. Priority: 72435-37601-2-0. 2003. CD.
2819.2 *Death Certificate* [1991]. Priority: 72435-43341-2-2. 2002. CD.
2819.3 *The Predator* [1992]. Priority: 72435-43339-2-7. 2003. CD.

2820 Ice-T
2820.1 ★*The Iceberg: Freedom of Speech . . . Just Watch What You Say.* Sire: 9 26028-2. 1989. CD.
2820.2 *O.G.: Original Gangster.* Sire: 9 26492-2. 1991. CD.
2820.3 *Power.* Sire: 9 25765-2. 1988. CD.

2821 Invisibl Skratch Piklz
2821.1 *The Shiggar Fraggar Show! Vol. 1.* Hip Hop Slam: 15. 1998. CD. OP.
2821.2 *The Shiggar Fraggar Show! Vol. 2.* Hip Hop Slam: 9. 2000. CD. OP.

2822 J Dilla. *Donuts.* Stones Throw: STH2126. 2006. CD.

2823 Jay-Z
2823.1 *The Black Album.* Roc-A-Fella: B0001528-02. 2003. CD.
2823.2 ★*The Blueprint.* Roc-A-Fella: 314 586 396-2. 2001. CD.
2823.3 *Hard Knock Life, Vol. 2.* Roc-A-Fella: 314 558 902-2. 1998. CD.
2823.4 *Reasonable Doubt* [1996]. Roc-A-Fella: P2 50040. 1998. CD.

2824 Jean, Wyclef. *The Carnival.* Ruffhouse / Columbia: CK 68201. 1997. CD.

2825 Jeru the Damaja
2825.1 *The Sun Rises in the East.* PayDay / FFRR: 697 124 011-2. 1994. CD.
2825.2 *Wrath of the Math.* PayDay / FFRR: 697 124 119-2. 1996. CD.

2826 Jungle Brothers
2826.1 *Done by the Forces of Nature.* Warner Bros.: 9 26072-2. 1989. CD.
2826.2 ★*Straight out the Jungle.* Warlock: WARCD-2704. 1988. CD.

2827 Jurassic 5
2827.1 *Power in Numbers.* Interscope: 694934372. 2002. CD.
2827.2 *Quality Control.* Interscope: 069490664 2. 2000. CD.

2828 Juvenile. *400 Degreez.* Cash Money: UD-53162. 1998. CD.

2829 Kam. *Neva Again.* Street Knowledge / Eastwest: 92208-2. 1993. CD. OP.

2830 Kane, Big Daddy
2830.1 *It's a Big Daddy Thing.* Cold Chillin': 9 25941-2. 1989. CD.
2830.2 *Long Live the Kane.* Cold Chillin': 9 25731-2. 1988. CD.

2831 Kid 'n' Play. *2 Hype.* Select: SED 21628. 1988. CD.

2832 Kid Cudi. *Man on the Moon: The End of the Day.* Universal Music Group: B001332101. 2009. CD.

2833 Kid Frost. *Hispanic Causing Panic.* Virgin: 2-91377. 1990. CD.

2834 Kid Koala. *Carpal Tunnel Syndrome.* Ninja Tune: ZEN CD34. 2000. CD.

2835 Kool G Rap and DJ Polo. *The Best of Cold Chillin'* [1984–1992]. LandSpeed: LSR 8803 CD. 2000. 2 CDs. OP.

2836 Kool Keith. *Black Elvis/Lost in Space.* Ruffhouse: WK52000. 1999. CD. OP.

2837 *Krush Groove* [1985]. Warner: 11529. 2003. DVD.

2838   Kweli, Talib. *Quality*. Rawkus: 088 113 048-2. 2002. CD.

2839   Kweli, Talib, and Hi Tek. *Reflection Eternal [Train of Thought]*. Rawkus: P2 26143. 2000. CD.

2840   Latyrx. *The Album* [1997]. Quannum / Solesides: QP 033. 2002. CD.

2841   Leaders of the New School. *A Future without a Past*. Elektra: 9 60976-2. 1991. CD.

2842   Da Lench Mob. *Guerillas in Tha Mist*. Street Knowledge: 7 92206-2. 1992. CD.

2843   Lil Wayne. *Tha Carter*. Cash Money: B0001537-02. 2004. CD.

2844   Lil' Jon and the East Side Boyz. *Kings of Crunk*. TVT / BME: TV-2370-2. 2002. CD.

2845   Lil' Kim. *Hard Core*. Big Beat: 92733-2. 1996. CD.

2846   Little Brother. *The Minstrel Show*. Atlantic: 83783-2. 2005. CD.

2847   LL Cool J
    2847.1   *Mama Said Knock You Out*. Def Jam: 314 523 477-2. 1990. CD.
    2847.2   *Radio*. Def Jam: 314 527 352-2. 1985. CD.

2848   Lootpack. *Soundpieces: Da Antidote!* Stones Throw: STH2019. 1999. CD.

2849   Lord Finesse and DJ Mike Smooth. *Funky Technician* [1990]. Wild Pitch: WPD-2003. 2007. CD.

2850   Ludacris. *Word of Mouf*. Def Jam South: 314 586 446-2. 2001. CD.

2851   Lyrics Born. *Same !@#$ Different Day*. Quannum: 45778070329. 2005. CD.

2852   M.O.P. *Warriorz*. Loud: 1778-2. 2000. CD.

2853   Mack 10. *Based on a True Story*. Priority: P2 50675. 1997. CD.

2854   Madlib. *Beat Konducta, Vols. 1 and 2*. Stones Throw: STNT2133. 2006. CD.

2855   Madvillain. *Madvillainy*. Stones Throw: STH2065. 2004. CD.

2856   Main Source. *Breaking Atoms*. Wild Pitch: WPD 2004. 1991. CD.

2857   Makaveli. *The Don Killuminati: The 7 Day Theory* [1996] (File under Tupac Shakur). Koch / Death Row: KOC-CD-5810. 2005. CD.

2858   Mantronix. *The Album* [1985]. Warlock: WR-8707-2. 1999. CD.

2859   Marley Marl. *Marley Marl's House of Hits* [1987–1993]. Cold Chillin': CCCD 6005-2. 1995. CD. OP.

2860   Masta Ace. *The Best of Cold Chillin'*. LandSpeed: LSR 8804. 2001. CD. OP.

2861   Master P. *Ghetto D*. No Limit / Priority: P2 50659. 1997. CD.

2862   MC Hammer. *Please Hammer, Don't Hurt 'Em*. Capitol: CDP 7 92857 2. 1990. CD.

2863   MC Lyte
    2863.1   *Eyes on This*. First Priority: 91304-2. 1989. CD.
    2863.2   *Lyte as a Rock*. First Priority: 90905-2. 1988. CD.

2864   MC Ren. *Shock of the Hour*. Ruthless: 88561-5505-2. 1993. CD. OP.

2865   MC Solaar. *Prose Combat*. Cohiba: 697-124 013-2. 1994. CD. OP.

2866   Mellow Man Ace. *Escape from Havana*. Capitol: CDP 7 91295 2. 1989. CD. OP.

2867   Method Man. *Tical*. Def Jam: 314 523 839-2. 1994. CD.

2868   MF Doom
    2868.1   *Born Like This*. Lex: LEX069CD. 2009. CD.
    2868.2   *Mm . . . Food?* Rhymesayers: RSE0051-2. 2004. CD.

2869   Mix Master Mike. *Anti-Theft Device*. Asphodel: 985. 1998. CD.

2870   Mobb Deep
    2870.1   *Hell on Earth*. RCA / Loud: 78636699226. 1996. CD.
    2870.2   *The Infamous . . . .* RCA: 07863 66480-2. 1995. CD.

2871   Mos Def
    2871.1   *Black on Both Sides*. Rawkus: 088 112 905-2. 1999. CD.
    2871.2   *The Ecstatic*. Downtown: VVR706844. 2009. CD.

2872   ★Mos Def and Talib Kweli. *Mos Def and Talib Kweli Are Black Star* [1998]. Rawkus: 088 112 897-2. 2002. CD.

2873   Mr. Lif. *I Phantom*. Definitive Jux: DJX37. 2002. CD.

2874   *Murder Was the Case: The Soundtrack* [1994]. Death Row: DRR 63005-2. 2001. CD.

2875 Murs. *Murs 3:16: The 9th Edition*. Definitive Jux: DJX80. 2004. CD.

2876 N.E.R.D. *In Search of . . .* Virgin: 7243 8 11521 2 6. 2001. CD.

2877 N.W.A.
    2877.1 *Efil4zaggin [Niggaz4life]*. Priority: CDL 57126. 1991. CD.
    2877.2 ★*Straight Outta Compton*. Priority / Ruthless: 4XL57102. 1988. CD.

2878 Nas
    2878.1 *God's Son*. Columbia: CK 86930. 2002. 2 CDs.
    2878.2 ★*Illmatic*. Columbia: CK 57684. 1994. CD.
    2878.3 *It Was Written*. Columbia: CK 67015. 1996. CD.
    2878.4 *Stillmatic*. Sony / Columbia / Ill Will: CK 85736. 2001. CD.

2879 Naughty by Nature. *Naughty by Nature*. Tommy Boy: TBCD 1044. 1991. CD.

2880 Nelly. *Nellyville*. Universal: 440 017 747-2. 2002. CD.

2881 Notorious B.I.G.
    2881.1 *Life after Death*. Bad Boy: 78612-73011-2. 1997. 2 CDs.
    2881.2 ★*Ready to Die: The Remaster* [1994]. Bad Boy: 602498628010. 2004. CD.

2882 O. C. *Word . . . Life*. EMI: E2-30928. 1994. CD.

2883 Ol' Dirty Bastard. *Return to the 36 Chambers: The Dirty Version*. Elektra: 61659-2. 1995. CD.

2884 Onyx. *Bacdafucup*. Columbia: OK 53302. 1993. CD.

2885 Organized Konfusion
    2885.1 *Organized Konfusion*. Hollywood Basic: HB-61212-2. 1991. CD.
    2885.2 *Stress: The Extinction Agenda*. Hollywood Basic: HB-61406-2. 1994. CD.

2886 Orishas. *A Lo Cubano*. Universal / Surco: 012 159 571-2. 2000. CD.

2887 OutKast
    2887.1 *Aquemini*. LaFace: 73008-26053-2. 1998. CD.
    2887.2 *Atliens*. LaFace: 73008-26029-2. 1996. CD.
    2887.3 *Southernplayalisticadillacmuzik*. LaFace: 73008-26010-2. 1994. CD.
    2887.4 *Speakerboxxx. The Love Below*. Arista: 82876-50133-2. 2003. 2 CDs.
    2887.5 *Stankonia*. LaFace / Arista: 73008-26072-2. 2000. CD.

2888 Ozomatli. *Ozomatli*. Almo Sounds: AMSD-80020. 1998. CD.

2889 P. M. Dawn. *Of the Heart, of the Soul, and of the Cross: The Utopian Experience* [1991]. Gee Street: 63881-32509-2. 1997. CD.

2890 Paris. *Sleeping with the Enemy*. Scarface: SCR007-100-2. 1992. CD. OP.

2891 Peanut Butter Wolf
    2891.1 *My Vinyl Weighs a Ton*. Copasetik: COPA004CD. 1999. CD. OP.
    2891.2 *[Peanut Butter Wolf Presents] Stones Throw Ten Years*. Stones Throw: STH2142. 2006. 2 CDs.

2892 Perceptionists. *Black Dialogue*. Definitive Jux: DJX103. 2005. CD.

2893 Pharcyde. *Bizarre Ride II the Pharcyde*. Delicious Vinyl: R2 76783. 1992. CD.

2894 Pharoahe Monch
    2894.1 *Desire*. Universal: B0008096-02. 2007. CD.
    2894.2 *Internal Affairs*. Rawkus / Priority: P2 50137. 1999. CD. OP.

2895 Poor Righteous Teachers. *Holy Intellect*. Profile: PCD-1289. 1990. CD. OP.

2896 Prefuse 73. *Vocal Studies + Uprock Narratives*. Warp: WARPCD83. 2001. CD.

2897 Prince Paul. *A Prince among Thieves*. Tommy Boy: TBCD 1210. 1999. CD.

2898 Public Enemy
    2898.1 *Apocalypse 91 . . . The Enemy Strikes Black*. Def Jam: 314 523 479-2. 1991. CD.
    2898.2 ★*Fear of a Black Planet*. Def Jam: 314 523 446-2. 1990. CD.
    2898.3 ★*It Takes a Nation of Millions to Hold Us Back*. Def Jam: 314 527 358-2. 1988. CD.
    2898.4 *Yo! Bum Rush the Show*. Def Jam: 314 527 357-2. 1987. CD.

2899 Puff Daddy and the Family. *No Way Out*. Bad Boy: 78612-73012-2. 1997. CD.

2900 Quasimoto. *The Unseen*. Stones Throw: STH2025-2. 2000. CD.

2901 Queen Latifah. *All Hail the Queen*. Tommy Boy: TBCD 1022. 1989. CD.

2902 Raekwon. *Only Built 4 Cuban Linx*. RCA: 66663-2 07863. 1995. CD.

2903 Rah Digga. *Dirty Harriet*. Elektra: 62386-2. 2000. CD.

2904 Rakim. *The 18th Letter*. Universal: UD-53113. 1997. CD.

2905 *Rawkus Presents Soundbombing II*. Rawkus: 0 4992-50069-2 6. 1999. CD.

2906 Redman
      2906.1 *Muddy Waters*. Def Jam: 314 533 470-2. 1996. CD.
      2906.2 *Whut? Thee Album*. Rush: 314 523 518-2. 1992. CD.

2907 Rhymes, Busta
      2907.1 *Extinction Level Event: The Final World Front*. Elektra: 62211-2. 1998. CD.
      2907.2 *When Disaster Strikes . . .* Elektra: 62064-2. 1997. CD.

2908 rjd2. *Deadringer*. Definitive Jux: DJX35. 2002. CD.

2909 Rock, Pete. *Petestrumentals*. BBE: BBEBGCD002. 2001. CD.

2910 Rock, Pete, and C. L. Smooth
      2910.1 *The Main Ingredient*. Elektra: 61661-2. 1994. CD.
      2910.2 ★*Mecca and the Soul Brother*. Elektra: 60948-2. 1992. CD.

2911 Roots
      2911.1 *Game Theory*. Def Jam: B0007222-02. 2006. CD.
      2911.2 *Illadelph Halflife*. DGC: DGCD-24972. 1996. CD.
      2911.3 *Phrenology*. MCA: 1129962. 2002. CD.
      2911.4 ★*Things Fall Apart*. MCA: MCAD-11948. 1999. CD.
      2911.5 *Undun*. Def Jam: 602527869636. 2011. CD.

2912 Rule, Ja. *Venni Vetti Vecci*. Def Jam: 314 538 920-2. 1999. CD.

2913 Run-D.M.C.
      2913.1 *King of Rock* [1985]. Arista / Legacy / Profile: 82876695582. 2005. CD.
      2913.2 ★*Raising Hell* [1986]. Profile: 07822-16408-2. 1999. CD.

2913.3 *Run-D.M.C* [1984]. Profile / Arista: 07822-16406-2. 1999. CD.
2913.4 *Tougher Than Leather* [1988]. Arista / Legacy / Profile: 82876695592. 2005. CD.

2914 RZA. *The RZA Hits* [1993–1996]. Razor Sharp: EK 69610. 1999. CD.

2915 Salt-n-Pepa
      2915.1 *Blacks' Magic*. London / Next Plateau: 828 362-2. 1990. CD. OP.
      2915.2 *Hot, Cool and Vicious* [1986]. London / Next Plateau: 422 828 363-2. 1988. CD.

2916 Scarface
      2916.1 *Mr. Scarface Is Back*. Rap-A-Lot: 7243 8 40365 2 2. 1991. CD.
      2916.2 *The Diary*. Rap-A-Lot: 7243 8 39946 25. 1994. CD.

2917 Schooly D. *The Jive Collection, Vol. 3*. Jive: 01241-41567-2. 1995. CD. OP.

2918 *Scratch*. Palm: palmdvd3046-2. 2002. 2 DVDs.

2919 ★Slick Rick. *The Great Adventures of Slick Rick* [1988]. Def Jam: 314 527 359-2. 1995. CD.

2920 Smif-n-Wessun. *Dah Shinin'*. Wreck: NRV 2005-2. 1995. CD.

2921 Smith, Will. *Big Willie Style*. Columbia: CTDP 000282. 1997. CD.

2922 Snoop Dogg
      2922.1 *Tha Doggfather* [1996]. Death Row: 728706301121. 2001. CD.
      2922.2 ★*Doggystyle* [1993]. Death Row: 728706300223. 2001. CD.

2923 Souls of Mischief. *93 'til Infinity*. Zomba / Jive: 01241-41514-2. 1993. CD.

2924 Spearhead. *Home*. Capitol: CDP 7243 8 29113 2 6. 1994. CD.

2925 Stetsasonic. *In Full Gear* [1988]. Tommy Boy: TBCD 1459. 2001. CD.

2926 Sugarhill Gang. *Best of the Sugarhill Gang* [1979–1985]. Rhino: R2 71986. 1996. CD.

2927 Supernatural. *The Lost Freestyle Files*. Babygrande: BBG-CD-3. 2003. CD.

2928 Swift, Rob. *The Ablist*. Asphodel: 0993-2. 1999. CD.

2929 T. I. *King*. Grand Hustle / Atlantic: 83800-2. 2006. CD.

2930 3rd Bass. *The Cactus Album*. Def Jam: 314 527 361-2. 1989. CD. OP.

2931 Tone-Loc. *Loc-Ed after Dark*. Delicious Vinyl: 61044-71813-2. 1989. CD.

2932 Too Short
 2932.1 *Born to Mack*. Jive: 1100-2-J. 1988. CD.
 2932.2 *Life Is . . . Too Short*. Jive: 1149-2-J. 1988. CD.

2933 A Tribe Called Quest
 2933.1 ★*The Low End Theory*. Jive: 1418-2-J. 1991. CD.
 2933.2 *Midnight Marauders*. Jive: 01241-41490-2. 1993. CD.
 2933.3 *People's Instinctive Travels and the Paths of Rhythm*. Zomba: 1331-2-J. 1990. CD.

2934 2 Live Crew
 2934.1 *As Nasty as They Wanna Be*. Lil' Joe: XR 107-2. 1989. CD.
 2934.2 *Banned in the USA*. Luke: 91424-2. 1990. CD.

2935 2Pac
 2935.1 ★*All Eyez on Me* [1995]. Koch / Death Row: KOC-CD-5800. 2004. 2 CDs.
 2935.2 *Better Dayz*. Amaru / Tha Row / Interscope: 694970702. 2002. 2 CDs.
 2935.3 *Me against the World*. Amaru / Jive: 01241-41636-2. 1995. CD.
 2935.4 *Strictly 4 My N.I.G.G.A.Z*. Interscope: 01241-41634-2. 1993. CD.
 2935.5 *2pacalypse Now*. Amaru / Jive: 01241-41633-2. 1991. CD.

2936 UGK. *Ridin' Dirty*. Jive: 01241-41586-2. 1996. CD.

2937 Ultramagnetic MC's. *Critical Beatdown*. Next Plateau: NPE 5496-2. 1988. CD.

2938 UTFO. *Utfo*. Select: SEL-21614-2. 1985. CD.

2939 Vanilla Ice. *To the Extreme*. SBK: K2-95325. 1990. CD.

2940 Vaughn, Viktor *Vaudeville Villain*. Sound-Ink: TEG 2409. 2003. CD.

2941 Warren G. *Regulate . . . G Funk Era*. Violator / Rush: 314 523 335-2. 1994. CD.

2942 West, Kanye
 2942.1 *The College Dropout*. Roc-A-Fella: B0002030-02. 2004. CD.
 2942.2 *Late Registration*. Roc-A-Fella: B0004813-02. 2005. CD.
 2942.3 *My Beautiful Dark Twisted Fantasy*. Def Jam: 6025278910. 2010. CD.

2943 Westside Connection. *Bow Down*. Priority: 04992 50583 21. 1996. CD.

2944 Whodini. *Funky Beat: The Best of Whodini*. Jive: 82876 81596 2. 2006. CD.

2945 *Wild Style: Original Motion Picture Soundtrack* [1982] (Busy Bee, Grand Wizard Theodore, Grandmaster Caz). Rhino: R2 72892. 1997. CD.

2946 Wu-Tang Clan
 2946.1 ★*Enter the Wu-Tang: 36 Chambers*. Loud / RCA: 66336-2. 1993. CD.
 2946.2 *Wu-Tang Forever*. RCA / Loud: 07863 66905-2. 1997. 2 CDs.

2947 X-Clan. *To the East, Blackwards*. 4th and B'way: 444 019-2. 1990. CD.

2948 Xzibit. *40 Dayz and 40 Nightz*. Loud: 1840-2. 1998. CD.

2949 Young Jeezy. *Let's Get It: Thug Motivation 101*. Def Jam: B0004421-02. 2005. CD.

2950 Young MC. *Stone Cold Rhymin'*. Delicious Vinyl / Island: 91309-2. 1989. CD.

2951 Zion I. *Mind over Matter*. Ground Control: GCR 7015-2. 2000. CD.

SOUNDTRACKS

2952 *Above the Rim: The Soundtrack*. Death Row / Interscope: 92359-2. 1994. CD.

2953 *Wild Style: Original Motion Picture Soundtrack* [1982] (Busy Bee, Grand Wizard Theodore, Grandmaster Caz). Rhino: R2 72892. 1997. CD.

9

Gospel Music and Other Popular Christian Music

Compiled by **BRENDA NELSON-STRAUSS**

GENERAL COLLECTIONS *166*
AFRICAN AMERICAN GENERAL COLLECTIONS *166*
EVANGELISTS AND OTHER TRADITIONAL PERFORMERS *168*
AFRICAN AMERICAN GOSPEL SOLO PERSONALITIES *168*
AFRICAN AMERICAN GOSPEL QUARTETS *169*
AFRICAN AMERICAN GOSPEL COLLECTIONS: 1940s–1960s *170*
AFRICAN AMERICAN GOSPEL GROUPS *171*
AFRICAN AMERICAN GOSPEL CHOIRS *172*
CONTEMPORARY AFRICAN AMERICAN GOSPEL *173*
SOUTHERN WHITE RELIGIOUS STYLES *174*
INSPIRATIONAL, CONTEMPORARY CHRISTIAN, AND CHRISTIAN ROCK *175*
CHRISTIAN RAP *177*

The earliest recordings of African American religious music (evangelists and other traditional performers) range from folk spirituals and jubilee quartets to singing preachers and street corner evangelists who were influenced by rural blues musicians. Gospel quartets (often featuring five or six singers) were extremely popular in the 1930s and 1940s, while soloists and gospel groups of the 1940s to the 1960s, such as the Caravans, helped to spread the new gospel songs of Thomas A. Dorsey. The era of contemporary African African gospel music was ushered in by the Edwin Hawkins Singers in 1969 with "Oh Happy Day" and was further developed by Andraé Crouch, while James Cleveland pioneered the African American gospel choir movement (including mass choirs). Contemporary gospel of the twenty-first century frequently fuses elements of hip hop, R&B, and jazz, while Christian rap (also known as gospel rap or holy hip hop) blends the aesthetics of rap and hip hop with overtly Christian lyrics.

Popular religious music in the United States covers a broad range of styles and traditions with roots in both Africa and Europe. Southern white religious styles, sometimes referred to as southern gospel, grew out of the old shape-note singing of hymns and spirituals from the *Sacred Harp* and other songbooks (for performances from the *Sacred Harp*, see chapter 1) and was later influenced by country and bluegrass music. Through the 1970s and 1980s Christian rock and inspirational

pop music gained wide acceptance among the younger members of the rapidly growing evangelical community. By the end of the twentieth century, contemporary Christian music (CCM) became the broader term for rock and pop by white Christian artists, though recently CCM has increasingly been applied to music by black artists. However, most CCM discographies, such as the Billboard Guide, do not yet reflect this trend.

Libraries wishing to build collections of gospel and popular religious music should be aware that for the most part the recording sessions have been held and distributed by small labels, thus the CD issues tend to go out of print rather quickly. Often the only source for pre-2000 recordings are online stores that sell gently used recordings, such as Amazon Marketplace. Many early recordings not subject to U.S. copyright terms have recently been reissued by European companies (Document, Proper). The past decade has seen an explosion in the CCM and gospel markets, resulting in large record companies taking over many of the smaller independent labels and a corresponding increase in reissues and compilations. Reviews can still be difficult to find, with sources such as All Music Guide covering only the major artists, while coverage of tradition black gospel and emerging genres such as Christian rap are very spotty. Other sources of reviews include GOSPELflava (www.gospelflava.com), host of the annual Stellar Awards.

GENERAL COLLECTIONS

2954 ★*Goodbye Babylon* [1902–1960] (Alabama Sacred Harp Singers, Blind Lemon Jefferson, Chuck Wagon Gang, Golden Gate Jubilee Quartet, Ernest V. Stoneman's Dixie Mountaineers, Arizona Dranes, Carter Family, Holy Ghost Sanctified Singers, Kentucky Ramblers, Uncle Dave Macon, Dinwiddie Colored Quartet, Rosetta Tharpe, Thomas A. Dorsey, and others). Dust to Digital: DTD-01. 2003. 6 CDs with book.

2955 *The Gospel Tradition: The Roots and the Branches, Vol. 1* [1927–1956] (Blind Willie Johnson, Washington Phillips, Carter Family, Mitchell's Christian Singers, Humbard Family, Charioteers, Chuck Wagon Gang, and others). Columbia: CK 47333. 1991. CD.

2956 *The Half Ain't Never Been Told, Vols. 1 and 2* [1920s–1930s] (Fa Sol La Singers, Virginia Dandies, Washington Phillips, Uncle Dave Macon, Alabama Sacred Harp Singers, Ernest

Phipps and His Holiness Singers, Pace Jubilee Singers, Jones Brothers Trio, Kentucky Mountain Chorusters, Blind Willie Johnson, Bryant's Jubilee Quartette, Biddleville Quintette, Kentucky Ramblers, Megginson Female Quartette, Charlie Patton, Blind Joe Taggart, Bascom Lamar Lunsford, Utica Institute Jubilee Singers, Allison's Sacred Harp Singers, and others). Yazoo: 2049-2050. 1999. 2 CDs.

2957 *How Can I Keep from Singing: Early American Religious Music and Song, Vols. 1 and 2* [1920s–1930s] (Elder Burch and Congregation, Tennessee Mountaineers, Carolina Ladies Quartette, Allison's Sacred Harp Singers, Slim Ducket and Pig Norwood, Mountain Singers Male Quartette, and others). Yazoo: 2020-2021. 1996. 2 CDs.

AFRICAN AMERICAN GENERAL COLLECTIONS

2958 *All of My Appointed Time: Forty Years of a Cappella Gospel Singing* [1936–1976] (Golden Gate Jubilee Quartet, Kings of Harmony, Blue Jay Singers, Soul Stirrers, Georgia Peach, Bessie Griffin, Golden Harps, Marion Williams, Delta Rhythm Boys, Charioteers). Mojo / Jass: MOJO-308 (Jass 64). 1996. CD.

2959 *Classic African American Gospel from Smithsonian Folkways* [1948–1998] (Horace Sprott, Starlight Gospel Singers, Fisk Jubilee Singers, Little Brother Montgomery, Thrasher Wonders, Rev. Willie Gresham, Missionary Quartet, Sister Ernestine Washington, Bunk Johnson, Sonny Terry, Two Gospel Keys, Elder Charles Beck, Rev. Gary Davis, Elizabeth Cotten, Lead Belly, and others). Smithsonian Folkways: SFW40194. 2008. CD.

2960 *Fire in My Bones: Raw, Rare and Otherworldy African-American Gospel* [1944-2007] (Elder Beck, Two Gospel Keys, Snooks Eaglin, Louis Overstreet, Utah Smith, Ebenezer Baptist Church Choir, Straight Street Holiness Group, Hickory Bottom Harmoneers, and others). Tompkins Square: TSQ 2271. 2009. 3 CDs.

2961 ★*Good News: 100 Gospel Greats* [1926–1951] (Famous Blue Jay Singers, Mitchell's Christian Singers, Heavenly Gospel Singers, Golden Gate Jubilee Quartet, Charioteers, Trumpeteers, Dixie Hummingbirds, Sister Rosetta Tharpe, Mahalia

Jackson, Sister Ernestine Washington, Original Gospel Harmonettes, Soul Stirrers, Pilgrim Travelers, Five Blind Boys of Alabama, Five Blind Boys of Mississippi, and others). Proper: Properbox 42. 2002. 4 CDs.

2962   *Gospel* [1982] (James Cleveland, Shirley Caesar, Walter Hawkins and The Hawkins Family, Mighty Clouds of Joy, and Clark Sisters). Monterey Home Video: 319452. 2002. DVD.

2963   *Gospel: Negro Spirituals / Gospel Songs, 1926–1942* (Blind Willie Johnson, Arizona Dranes, Rev. J. M. Gates, Mitchell's Christian Singers, Washington Phillips, Norfolk Jubilee Quartet, Thomas A. Dorsey, Heavenly Gospel Singers, Mahalia Jackson, Selah Jubilee Singers, Gary Davis, Blind Joe Taggart, Louis Armstrong, Golden Gate Quartet, Georgia Peach, Rosetta Tharpe, Southern Sons, Charioteers, and others). Fremeaux: FA 008. 1993. 2 CDs.

2964   ★*The Gospel Sound* [1926–1968] (Blind Willie Johnson, Golden Gate Quartet, Arizona Dranes, Mitchell's Christian Singers, Rev. J. M. Gates, Dorothy Love Coates, Mahalia Jackson, Marion Williams, Staple Singers, Abyssinian Baptist Choir, Dixie Hummingbirds, Angelic Gospel Singers). Columbia / Legacy: C2K 57160 (31086). 1994. 2 CDs.

2965   ★*The Gospel Sound of Spirit Feel* [1947–1986] (Rosetta Tharpe, Mahalia Jackson, Soul Stirrers, Robert Anderson, Ernestine Washington, Roberta Martin, Spirit of Memphis, Jessie Mae Renfro, Dixie Hummingbirds, Clara Ward, Sensational Nightingales, Fairfield Four, Consolers, Marion Williams, and others). Spirit Feel: 1012. 1991. CD.

2966   ★*Jubilation! Great Gospel Performances, Vol. 1: Black Gospel* [1937–1975] (Mahalia Jackson, Roberta Martin, Angelic Gospel Singers, Golden Gate Quartet, Georgia Peach, Soul Stirrers, Clara Ward, Swan Silvertones, James Cleveland, Dixie Hummingbirds, Shirley Caesar, Pilgrim Travelers, Edwin Hawkins, and others). Rhino: 70288. 1992. CD.

2967   ★*Jubilation! Great Gospel Performances, Vol. 2: More Black Gospel* [1938–1964] (Soul Stirrers, Mahalia Jackson, Davis Sisters, Caravans, Alex Bradford, Staple Singers, Five Blind Boys of Mississippi, Swan Silvertones, Gospel Harmonettes, and others). Rhino: 70289. 1992. CD.

2968   ★*Precious Lord: Recordings of the Great Gospel Songs of Thomas A. Dorsey* [1973] (Bessie Griffin, Marion Williams, Alex Bradford, Delois Barrett Campbell, R. H. Harris, Sallie Martin, Thomas A. Dorsey). Columbia: CK 57164 (CG 32151). 1994. CD.

2969   *Rejoice and Shout* [1920-2000] (Smokey Robinson, Andraé Crouch, Mavis Staples, Ira Tucker Sr., Marie Knight, and others). Magnolia Home Entertainment: 10145. 2011. DVD.

2970   *The Rough Guide to Gospel* [1940s–1970s] (Dixie Hummingbirds, Albertina Walker, Dorothy Norwood, Shirley Caesar, Mahalia Jackson, Caravans, Inez Andrews, Fairfield Four, Staple Singers, Blind Boys of Alabama, and others). World Music Network: 1090. 2002. CD.

2971   ★*Say Amen, Somebody*. 25th ann. del. ed. [1982] (Thomas A. Dorsey, Sallie Martin, Willie Mae Ford Smith, Delois Barrett Campbell, Barrett Sisters, O'Neal Twins, Zella Jackson Price). Ryko Filmworks: 10891. 2007. CD, DVD.

2972   *Spreading the Word: Early Gospel Recordings* [1926–1950] (Arizona Dranes, Holy Ghost Sanctified Singers, Louisville Sanctified Singers, Washington Phillips, Texas Jubilee Singers, Southern Sanctified Singers, and others). JSP: JSP7733. 2004. 4 CDs.

2973   *Story of Gospel Music* (Mahalia Jackson, Shirley Caesar, Tramaine Hawkins, Fisk University Jubilee Singers, Cissy Houston, Rance Allen, Thomas A. Dorsey, Fairfield Four, Sister Rosetta Tharpe, Aretha Franklin, Clara Ward Singers, Dixie Hummingbirds, James Cleveland, Vanessa Bell Armstrong, Edwin Hawkins Singers, Clark Sisters, John P. Kee, Danny Eason and Abundant Life). BBC Video: E2108. 2004. DVD.

2974   *Testify! The Gospel Box* [1942–1997] (Southern Sons, Golden Gate Quartet, Fairfield Four, Trumpeteers, Dorothy Love Coates, Sallie Martin, Five Blind Boys, Dixie Hummingbirds, Maceo Woods, Highway QC's, Staple Singers, Mahalia Jackson, James Cleveland, Alex Bradford, Swan Silvertones, Mighty Clouds of Joy, Edwin Hawkins, Inez Andrews, Aretha Franklin, O'Neal Twins, Walter Hawkins, Shirley Caesar, Marion Williams, Clara Ward, Caravans, Andrae Crouch, John P. Kee, Winans, F. C. Barnes, Sounds of Blackness, Williams Brothers, and others). Rhino: 75734. 1999. 3 CDs.

2975 ★*Wade in the Water: African American Sacred Music Traditions, Vols. 1–4* [1989–1992]. Smithsonian Folkways: SFW 40076. 1994. 4 CDs. CDs also issued separately.

EVANGELISTS AND OTHER TRADITIONAL PERFORMERS

COLLECTIONS

2976 *American Primitive, Vol. 1: Raw Pre-War Gospel (1926–36)* (Blind Willie Davis, Blind Mamie Forehand, Jaybird Coleman, Charley Patton, Blind Joe Taggart, Bukka White, Elder Otis Jones, Blind Roosevelt Graves, and others). Revenant: 206. 1997. CD.

2977 *Negro Religious Songs and Services* [1936–1942] (Reverend Sin Killer Griffin, Blind Jimmie Strothers, Joe Lee, Turner Junior Johnson, Dock Reed, Bozie Sturdivant, and others). Rounder: 1514 (Library of Congress L 10). 1999. CD. Field recordings collected by John and Alan Lomax, and others.

2978 *On One Accord: Singing and Praying Bands of Tidewater, Maryland, and Delaware* [1986–1991]. Global Village Music: CD 225. 1992. CD.

2979 *Preachin' the Gospel: Holy Blues* [1927–1953] (Blind Willie Johnson, Arizona Dranes, Washington Phillips, Josh White, Sister O. M. Terrell, and others). Columbia / Legacy: CK 46779. 1991. CD.

2980 ★*Sacred Steel: The Steel Guitar Tradition of the House of God Churches* (Elder Maurice Ted Beard, Campbell Brothers with Katie Jackson, Calvin Cooke, Willie Eason, Elder Aubrey Ghent, Rev. Glenn Lee, Robert Randolph, Henry Nelson). Arhoolie Foundation: AFV-203. 2001. DVD.

2981 *Saints' Paradise: Trombone Shout Bands from the United House of Prayer* [1990–1996]. Smithsonian Folkways: 40117. 1999. CD.

2982 *This May Be My Last Time Singing: Raw African-American Gospel on 45rpm* [1957-1982] (Sam Williams and the Harris Singers, Silver Harpes, Fantastic Angels, Gospel Keys, Prophet G. Lusk, Carolina Kings, Rev. George Oliver, Elder Robert McMurray, Missionary Mamie Sample, and others). Tompkins Square: TSQ 2639. 2011. 3 CDs.

INDIVIDUALS AND GROUPS

2983 Davis, Gary. *The Complete Early Recordings of Rev. Gary Davis* [1935–1949]. Yazoo: 2011. 1994. CD.

2984 Johnson, Blind Willie. *The Complete Blind Willie Johnson* [1927–1930]. Columbia: C2K 52835. 1993. 2 CDs.

2985 Phillips, Washington. *I Am Born to Preach the Gospel* [1927–1929]. Yazoo: 2003. 1991. CD.

2986 Wiregrass Sacred Harp Singers. *The Colored Sacred Harp*. New World: 80433-2. 1993. CD.

AFRICAN AMERICAN GOSPEL SOLO PERSONALITIES

COLLECTIONS

2987 *Gospel Warriors: Over 50 Years of Great Solo Performances* [1931–1982] (Rosetta Tharpe, Georgia Peach, Clara Ward, Marion Williams, Bessie Griffin, Frances Steadman, Sister Jessie Mae Renfro, and Mary Johnson Davis.). Spirit Feel: SFD-1003. 1990. CD.

2988 *The Great Gospel Men* [1947–1986] (Brother Joe May, Norsalus McKissick, Robert Anderson, J. Robert Bradley, Alex Bradford, J. Earle Hines, Eugene Smith, James Cleveland, R. L. Knowles). Spirit Feel / Shanachie: 6005. 1993. CD.

2989 ★*The Great Gospel Women* [1939–1991] (Mahalia Jackson, Willie Mae Ford Smith, Rosetta Tharpe, Marion Williams, Clara Ward, Cora Martin, Dorothy Love Coates, Roberta Martin, Marie Knight, Frances Steadman, and others). Spirit Feel / Shanachie: 6004. 1993. CD.

2990 *The Great Gospel Women, Vol. 2* [1942–1992] (Mahalia Jackson, Rosetta Tharpe, Ernestine B. Washington, Edna Gallmon Cooke, Marie Knight, Clara Ward, Marion Williams, Bessie Griffin, and others). Spirit Feel / Shanachie: 6017. 1995. CD.

2991 *Mother Smith and Her Children* [1950–1987] (Willie Mae Ford Smith, Martha Bass, Joe May, Edna Gallmon Cooke). Spirit Feel: SFD-1010. 1989. CD.

INDIVIDUALS AND GROUPS

2992   Andrews, Inez. *Headline News* [1970s]. MCA (Peacock Gospel Classics): MCAD-12003. 1999. CD.

2993   Bradford, Alex. *Too Close* [1953–1958] (Sallie Martin, Bessie Griffin, Princess Stewart, Bradford Specials, Men of Song). Specialty: 7042. 1993. CD.

2994   Caesar, Shirley
    2994.1   ★*First Lady of Gospel* [1970s–1980s]. Liquid 8: LIQ 12013. 2003. 2 CDs.
    2994.2   *Live in Chicago* (Milton Brunson and the Thompson Community Singers). Word / Epic: EK 47743. 1988. CD.

2995   Carr, Wynona. *Dragnet for Jesus* [1949–1954] (R. H. Harris, Joe May, C. L. Franklin, and New Bethel Baptist Church Choir). Legends of gospel. Specialty: SPCD-7016-2. 1992. CD.

2996   Cleveland, James
    2996.1   *Down Memory Lane* [1980] (Inez Andrews, Barrett Sisters, Albertina Walker, Metro Mass Choir, Rev. Isaac Whitman). Savoy: SDVD 9500. 1987. DVD. Recorded live at the Mt. Pisgah Baptist Church, Chicago, IL.
    2996.2   ★*Peace Be Still* [1963] (Angelic Choir). Savoy: 14076. 1998. CD.

2997   Franklin, Aretha
    2997.1   ★*Amazing Grace: The Complete Recordings* [1972–1999] (James Cleveland, Southern California Community Choir). Rhino: 75627. 1999. 2 CDs.
    2997.2   *Aretha Gospel* [1956]. Chess / MCA: 91521. 1991. CD.

2998   Griffin, Bessie. *Even Me: Four Decades of Bessie Griffin* [1948–1987]. Spirit Feel / Shanachie: 6038. 2000. CD.

2999   Jackson, Mahalia
    2999.1   *Best of Mahalia Jackson* [1954–1963]. Columbia: 66911. 1995. CD.
    2999.2   ★*Gospels, Spirituals and Hymns; Vols. 1 and 2* [1954–1969]. Columbia: 65594-65598. 1998. 4 CDs.
    2999.3   ★*How I Got Over: The Apollo Records Sessions* [1946–1954]. Westside: 303. 1998. 3 CDs.
    2999.4   *Mahalia Jackson* [1957–1962]. VAI: 4413. 2007. DVD.

3000   Little Richard. *God Is Real* [1959]. Peacock Gospel Classics series. MCA (Coral): MCAD 12005. 1999. CD.

3001   May, Brother Joe. *Thunderbolt of the Middle West* [1952–1955] (Sallie Martin Singers, Sister Wynona Carr, Pilgrim Travelers, Annette May). Specialty: 7033-2. 1992. CD.

3002   Robinson, Cleophus. *Someone to Care: The Battle Sessions* [1962–1963]. Specialty: 7055. 1994. CD.

3003   ★Tharpe, Rosetta. *Original Soul Sister* [1938–1949]. Proper: 51. 2002. 4 CDs.

3004   Walker, Albertina. *Please Be Patient with Me* [1979] (James Cleveland). Savoy: SCD 14527. 2004. CD.

3005   ★Williams, Marion. *My Soul Looks Back: The Genius of Marion Williams* [1962–1992]. Spirit Feel / Shanachie: 6011. 1994. CD.

AFRICAN AMERICAN GOSPEL QUARTETS

COLLECTIONS

3006   *The Earliest Negro Vocal Quartets, 1894–1928* (Dinwiddie Colored Quartet, Old South Quartette, Apollo Male Quartette, and others). Document: 5061. 1991. CD.

3007   *Happy in the Service of the Lord: Memphis Gospel Quartet Heritage, the 1980s, Vols. 1 and 2* [1982–1983] (Gospel Writers, Holy Ghost Spirituals, Harmonizers, Harps of Melody, Pattersonaires, Spirit of Memphis). High Water: 6516-6517. 2000.

3008   *I Hear Music in the Air: A Treasury of Gospel Music* [1926–1942] (Golden Gate Quartet, Heavenly Gospel Singers, Southern Sons, Morris Brown Quartet, Wright Brothers Gospel Singers, and others). RCA: 2099-2-R. 1990. CD.

3009   *Kings of the Gospel Highway: The Golden Age of Gospel Quartets* [1939–1958] (R. H. Harris, Soul Stirrers, Pilgrim Travelers, Swan Silvertones, Spirit of Memphis, Five Blind Boys of Mississippi, Sensational Nightingales). Shanachie: 6039. 2000. CD.

3010   *Living Legends of Gospel: The Quartets, Vols. 1 and 2* (Mighty Clouds of Joy, Soul Stirrers, Tommy Ellison and the Singing Stars, Troy Ramey and the Soul Searchers, Swanee Quintet, Luther

Barnes and the Sunset Jubilaires, Lou Rawls, Fairfield Four, Racy Brothers, and others). Good Times Video: 05-81872, 05-81884. 2004. DVD.

3011   *A Warrior on the Battlefield: A Cappella Trail Blazers [1927–1942] (Golden Gate Quartet, Norfolk Jubilee Quartet, Silver Leaf Quartet, Heavenly Gospel Singers, T.C.I. Women's Four, Pullman Porters Quartette, Bethel Quartet, Davis Bible Singers, and others). Rounder: 1137. 1997. CD.

INDIVIDUALS AND GROUPS

3012   Blind Boys of Alabama. *Retrospective* [1970s–1990s]. Sheridan Square Records: 7616. 2007. 3 CDs.

3013   Canton Spirituals. *Living the Dream: Live in Washington, D.C.* [1997]. Verity: 01241-43021-9. 2006. DVD.

3014   Dixie Hummingbirds
   3014.1   *The Best of the Dixie Hummingbirds* [1953–1966]. MCA Special Products: MCAD-22043 (Peacock 138). 1991. CD.
   3014.2   *Jesus Has Traveled This Road Before* [1939–1952]. Gospel Friend: PN-1503. 2000. CD.

3015   Fairfield Four
   3015.1   *Standing in the Safety Zone* [1991–1992]. Warner Bros: 26945. 1992. CD.
   3015.2   *Standing on the Rock* [1950–1953]. Nashboro Golden Gospel series. Nashboro: 4003. 1994. CD.

3016   Five Blind Boys of Alabama. *Oh Lord Stand by Me / Marching up to Zion* [1953–1958]. Specialty: 7203. 1991. CD.

3017   Five Blind Boys of Mississippi. *The Five Blind Boys of Mississippi* [1947–1954]. Acrobat: ADDCD 3003. 2006. 2 CDs.

3018   Golden Gate Quartet
   3018.1   *Swing Down Chariot* [1941–1950]. Columbia: CK 47131. 1991. CD.
   3018.2   *Travelin' Shoes* [1937–1939]. RCA heritage series. Bluebird: 66063-2. 1992. CD.

3019   Harmonizing Four
   3019.1   *The Harmonizing Four, 1943–1954.* Acrobat: 3005. 2006. 2 CDs.
   3019.2   *When Day Is Done: Very Best of the Harmonizing Four* [1957–1965]. Collectables: 6106 (VeeJay). 1998. CD.

3020   Highway Q. C.'s. *Very Best of the Highway Q. C.'s: Nearer My God* [1955–1964]. Collectables Gospel Classics: COL-6107. 1998. CD.

3021   Lee Williams and the Spiritual QC's. *Tell the Angels: Live in Memphis*. MCG: 7034. 2005. DVD.

3022   Mighty Clouds of Joy. *The Best of Mighty Clouds of Joy* [1960–1966]. 20th century masters. MCA: 088 112 865-2. 2002. CD.

3023   Pilgrim Travelers. *The Best of the Pilgrim Travelers* [1948–1956]. Specialty: 7204. 1991. CD.

3024   Sensational Nightingales. *The Best of the Sensational Nightingales* [1956–1966]. MCA Special Products: MCAD-22044. 1991. CD.

3025   Soul Stirrers
   3025.1   *Sam Cooke with the Soul Stirrers: The Complete Specialty Records Recordings [1951–1957] (Sam Cooke). Specialty: 3SPCD-4437-2. 2002. 3 CDs.
   3025.2   Shine on Me [1950] (R.H. Harris). Specialty: 7013. 1992. CD.

3026   Sterling Jubilee Singers. *Jesus Hits Like the Atom Bomb* [1993–1994] (John Alexander). New World: 80513. 1997. CD.

3027   Swan Silvertones
   3027.1   *Love Lifted Me / My Rock* [1952–1953]. Specialty: 7202. 1991. CD.
   3027.2   *Pray for Me / Let's Go to Church Together* [1956–1961]. Collectables: 7234. 2000. CD.
   3027.3   *Swan Silvertones, 1946–1951.* Acrobat: 3004. 2005. 2 CDs.

3028   Swanee Quintet. *The Best of Swanee Quintet* [1953–1966]. Nashboro: NASH4503-2. 1995. CD.

3029   Williams Brothers. *Greatest Hits, Vol. 1* [1980s–1991]. Malaco: 4451. 1991. CD.

AFRICAN AMERICAN GOSPEL COLLECTIONS, 1940s–1960s

3030   *All God's Sons and Daughters: Chicago's Gospel Legends [1940s–1950s] (Delois Barrett Campbell, Eugene Smith, Robert Anderson, Norsalus McKissick, Roberta Martin, Bessie Folk, Myrtle Scott, and others). Shanachie: 6037. 1999. CD.

3031 *The Best of King Gospel* [1949–1953] (Spirit of Memphis, Swan Silvertones, Trumpeteers, Cumberland River Singers, Nightingales, Four Interns). Ace: 873. 2003. CD.

3032 *The Best of Nashboro Gospel* [1951–1968] (Angelic Gospel Singers, Consolers, Edna Gallmon Cooke, Swanee Quintet, Fairfield Four, Supreme Angels, Jordan River Singers, Brother Joe May, Famous Skylarks, Radio Four, Brooklyn All Stars, and others). Nashboro / AVI: 4001. 1994. CD.

3033 *Good News: 22 Gospel Greats* [1955–1963] (Caravans, Five Blind Boys of Mississippi, Harmonizing Four, Highway QCs, Staple Singers, Swan Silvertones). Charly: CHARLY 98. 1987. CD.

3034 *The Great 1955 Shrine Concert* (Pilgrim Travelers, Caravans, Joe May, Soul Stirrers, Dorothy Love Coates and the Original Gospel Harmonettes, and others). Specialty: 7045. 1993. CD.

3035 *Greatest Gospel Gems* [1948–1958] (Soul Stirrers, Alex Bradford, Swan Silvertones, Chosen Gospel Singers, Gospel Harmonettes, Five Blind Boys of Alabama, Joe May, Pilgrim Travelers, Robert Anderson, Wynona Carr, and others). Specialty: 7206. 1991. CD.

3036 *Jesus Put a Song in My Soul* [1948–1958] (Clara Ward Singers, Selah Jubilee Singers, Friendly Brothers, Zion Harmonizers, Five Gospel Stirrers, and others). Gospel Heritage: HT CD 10. 1992. CD.

3037 *None but the Righteous: Chess Gospel Greats* [1951–1972] (Aretha Franklin, Soul Stirrers, Violinaires, Martha Bass, Rev. C. L. Franklin, Windy City Four, Elder Beck, Alex Bradford, and others). Chess: 9336. 1992. CD.

3038 *Powerhouse Gospel on Independent Labels* [1946–1959] (Pilgrim Singers, Silvertone Quintet, Spiritualaires of Columbia, Soul Satisfiers of Philadelphia, Kansas City Soul Revivers, Sister Rosa Shaw, Deacon Tom Foger, Jackson Gospel Singers, and others). JSP: JSP77135. 2010. 4 CDs.

3039 ★*Working the Road: The Golden Age of Chicago Gospel* [1951–1956] (Robert Anderson/ Caravans, Robert Ballinger, Lucy Smith Singers, Singing Sammy Lewis). Delmark: 702. 1997. CD.

AFRICAN AMERICAN GOSPEL GROUPS

3040 Angelic Gospel Singers. *Touch Me Lord Jesus* [1949–1955]. Malaco: 4381. 1982. CD.

3041 Caravans
    3041.1 ★*The Best of the Caravans* [1956–1962] (Albertina Walker, Shirley Caesar, Inez Andrews, Delores Washington, Cassietta George, Josephine Howard, Eddie Williams, James Herndon). Savoy: 7012. 2004.
    3041.2 *The Best of Shirley Caesar with the Caravans* [1958–1962] (Albertina Walker, Cassietta George, Dorothy Norwood, Inez Andrews, Shirley Caesar, and others). Savoy Gospel: 14202. 1995. CD.
    3041.3 *Jesus and Me: The Very Best of the Caravans with Albertina Walker* [1962–1964] (Albertina Walker, Cassietta George, Dorothy Norwood, Inez Andrews, Shirley Caesar, and others). Collectables: COL-6101 (VeeJay). 1998. CD.

3042 ★Clara Ward Singers. *I Feel the Holy Spirit* [1949–1952] (Ward, Clara, 1924-1973.). Gospel Friend: 1502. 2005. CD.

3043 Consolers. *Lord Bring Me Down* [1950s–1970s]. MCA: 21102. 1998. CD.

3044 Davis Sisters
    3044.1 *The Best of the Famous Davis Sisters of Philadelphia, PA* [1955–1968]. Savoy: 70587. 2001. CD.
    3044.2 *Davis Sisters 1949–1952* [1949–1952]. Heritage: 47 (Gotham). 2003. CD.

3045 Gospel Harmonettes. *The Best of Dorothy Love Coates and the Original Gospel Harmonettes* [1951–1956] (Coates, Dorothy Love. Specialty: 7205. 1991. CD.

3046 Meditation Singers. *Good News* [1953–1959]. Specialty: 7032. 1992. CD.

3047 Roberta Martin Singers. *The Best of the Roberta Martin Singers* [1957–1966] (Archie Dennis, Narsalus McKissick, Gloria Griffin, Delores Barrett, Eugene Smith, Bessie Folk, Lucy Smith Collier). Savoy: 7018. 1990. CD.

3048 Sallie Martin Singers. *Throw out the Lifeline* [1950–1952] (Cora Martin, Sallie Martin). Specialty: 7043. 1993. CD.

3049 Staple Singers
3049.1 *Freedom Highway* [1964–1966]. Columbia: CK 47334. 1991. CD.
3049.2 *The Best of the Vee-Jay Years* [1956-1961]. Shout! Factory: 826663-10641. 2007. CD.

3050 Stars of Faith. *God and Me* [1962–1963] (Williams, Marion). Collectables: 7230 (Vee-Jay 5024/5031). 2002. CD.

AFRICAN AMERICAN GOSPEL CHOIRS

COLLECTIONS

3051 *Going Up Yonder: The Best of the Gospel Choirs* (Walter Hawkins and the Love Center Choir, Walt Whitman and the Soul Children of Chicago, Andraé Crouch, Eddie James and the Phoenix Mass Choir, L.A. Mass Choir, Dallas Fort Worth Mass Choir, Bishop Paul S. Morton, and others). Time Life / WEA: 22126-2. 2008. CD.

3052 *Greatest Gospel Choirs* [1986–1994] (Chicago Mass Choir, North Carolina Mass Choir, L.A. Mass Choir, New Jersey Mass Choir). MCA: 20959. 1996. CD.

3053 *Stand Up: A Collection of America's Great Gospel Choirs* [1980s–1990s] (Rev. Milton Brunson and the Thompson Community Singers, O'Landa Draper and the Associates Choir, New Life Community Choir, Rev. James Cleveland and the Angelic Choir, and others). Word / Epic: EK66555. 1994. CD.

INDIVIDUALS AND GROUPS

3054 Abyssinian Baptist Gospel Choir. *Shakin' the Rafters* [1960] (Alex Bradford, con.). Columbia: CK 49335 (CS 8348). 1991. CD.

3055 Brunson, Milton. *Great Gospel Moments* [1982–1997] (Thompson Community Singers). Word: 86195. 2000. CD.

3056 Chicago Mass Choir. *Just Having Church Live*. New Haven Films: 8073-9. 2007. DVD.

3057 Clark, Mattie Moss. *I Don't Know What I Would Do without the Lord* [1974] (Southwest Michigan

State Choir). Sound of Gospel: SOGCD 3012. 2005. CD.

3058 Cleveland, James
3058.1 ★*The Best of Rev. James Cleveland and the G.M.W.A* (Gospel Music Workshop of America Mass Choir). Savoy: SCD 7111. 1993. CD.
3058.2 *It's a New Day* [1979] (Southern California Community Choir). Savoy: SCD7035. 2007. CD.
3058.3 *James Cleveland Sings with the World's Greatest Choirs* [1980]. Savoy: 7059. 1995. CD.

3059 Dallas Fort Worth Mass Choir. *I Will Let Nothing Separate Me*. Savoy: SAV 7101. 1991. CD.

3060 Edwin Hawkins Singers
3060.1 ★*Oh Happy Day* [1969]. Encore Collection. Buddah: 44513. 1997. CD.
3060.2 *Oh Happy Day: The Best of the Edwin Hawkins Singers* [1969–1970s]. Buddah: 99727. 2001. CD.

3061 Florida Mass Choir. *Now, I Can See* (V. Michael McKay, Arthur T. Jones). Malaco: 6011. 1992. CD.

3062 Georgia Mass Choir. *Georgia Mass Choir* (Kirk Franklin, Dorothy Anderson, La Shun Pace, Rev. Milton Biggham, Rev. Timothy Wright, and others). 601 Music: SXDVD 9909. 2006. DVD.

3063 God's Property. *God's Property from Kirk Franklin's Nu Nation* (Kirk Franklin). B-Rite Music: INTD-90093. 1997. CD.

3064 Gospel Music Workshop of America National Mass Choir. 25th anniversary ed. [1992]. Verity: 0124143077-2. 1997. CD.

3065 Jakes, Bishop T. D. *Woman, Thou Art Loosed*. Word / Epic: EK 67931. 1997. CD.

3066 Kee, John P. *Essential John P. Kee* [1987–2000s] (New Life Community Choir). Verity / Legacy: 88697159082. 2007. 2 CDs.

3067 L.A. Mass Choir. *Best of L.A. Mass Choir* [1989–1995]. Platinum Ent.: 51416 12112. 1996. CD.

3068 Lawrence, Donald. *Best of Donald Lawrence and the Tri-City Singers: Restoring the Years* [1993–2000s] (Tri-City Singers). EMI Gospel: 91802. 2003. CD.

3069 Mississippi Mass Choir
   3069.1 *The First Twenty Years* [1988–2008].
      Malaco: MDVD 9054. 2008. DVD.
   3069.2 *It Remains to Be Seen . . .* Malaco: MCD
      6013. 1993. CD.

3070 Morton, Bishop Paul. *We Offer Christ* (Greater St.
   Stephen Mass Choir). Blackberry; Malaco: BBD-
   1603. 1993. CD.

3071 Norwood, Dorothy. *Live* (Northern California
   G.M.W.A. Mass Choir). Malaco: 4450. 1991. CD.

3072 Walker, Hezekiah. *The Essential Hezekiah Walker*
   [1990s–2000s] (Love Fellowship Crusade Choir).
   Legacy / Verity: 88697153892. 2007. 2 CDs.

3073 West Angeles Church of God in Christ Mass
   Choir and Congregation. *Saints in Praise: Their
   Very Best* [1989–1992]. Sparrow: SPD 1572.
   1996. CD.

CONTEMPORARY AFRICAN AMERICAN GOSPEL

COLLECTION

3074 *Wow Gospel #1s* [2000–2007] (God's Property,
   Mary Mary, Kierra Kiki Sheard, Myron Butler
   and Levi, Tye Tribbett and G.A., Dietrick
   Haddon, Fred Hammond and Radical for Christ,
   Smokie Norful, Yolanda Adams, Kirk Franklin,
   and others). Zomba: 88697087642. 2007. 2 CDs.

INDIVIDUALS AND GROUPS

3075 Adams, Yolanda. *Mountain High, Valley Low*.
   Elektra: 62439-2. 1999. CD.

3076 Allen, Rance. *Best of the Rance Allen Group*
   [1971–1979] (Rance Allen Group). Stax: SCD-
   8540-2. 1988. CD.

3077 Armstrong, Vanessa Bell. *Best of Vanessa Bell
   Armstrong* [1987–1999]. Verity: 01241-43138-2.
   1999. CD.

3078 Baylor, Helen. *Greatest Hits* [1990s]. Word:
   80688592622. 1999. CD.

3079 Carr, Kurt. *One Church* [2004] (Kurt Carr
   Project). Gospo-Centric: 75751-70058-2.
   2005. CD.

3080 Clark Sisters. *Is My Living in Vain* [1980] (Mattie
   Moss Clark). Sony Music Special Products: A
   22145. 1991. CD.

3081 Clark-Sheard, Karen. *Finally* (Faith Evans,
   Donald Lawrence, Kierra Sheard, Clark Sisters).
   Island: 314 524 397-2. 1997. CD.

3082 Commissioned. *Best of Commissioned* [1985–
   1996] (Fred Hammond, Marvin Sapp). Verity:
   01241-43126-2. 1999. CD.

3083 Crouch, Andraé
   3083.1 ★*15 Songs That Redefined Gospel Music
      in the 1970s* (Disciples). History makers.
      Sparrow: SPD 80663. 2003. CD.
   3083.2 *Mighty Wind* [2004] (Lawrence Beamen,
      Karen Clark-Sheard, Marcus Cole,
      Tachina Danielle, Lauren Evans, Fred
      Hammond, Daniel Johnson, Crystal
      Lewis, Ingrid Rosario, Tata Vega, Marvin
      Winans). Zomba: 82876-73645-2.
      2006. CD.
   3083.3 *This Is Another Day* [1976] (Disciples).
      Light: 4875 (5683). 1993. CD.

3084 Dillard, Ricky. *The 7th Episode: Live in Toronto*
   (New Generation Chorale). NuSpring; EMI:
   2678. 2008. CD, DVD.

3085 Franklin, Kirk
   3085.1 *Kirk Franklin and the Family*. Gospo-
      Centric: GCD 2119. 1993. CD.
   3085.2 ★*Nu Nation Project* [1998] (Rodney
      Jenkins, Mary J. Blige, Bill Withers,
      R. Kelly, Bono). Gospo-Centric: INTD-
      90178. 2001. CD.

3086 Green, Al. *The Lord Will Make a Way / Higher
   Plane* [1980, 1981]. Hi / Cream: 189. 2002. CD.

3087 Haddon, Deitrick. *Anthology: The Writer and
   His Music* [2004–2006]. Tyscot: TYS 984192 2.
   2011. CD, DVD. Deluxe Ed.

3088 Hammond, Fred. *Purpose by Design* (Radical for
   Christ). Verity; Face to Face: 01241-43140-2.
   2000. CD.

3089 Hawkins, Tremaine. *All My Best to You*. Sparrow:
   1429. 1994. CD.

3090 ★Hawkins, Walter. *Love Alive* [1975] (Love
   Center Choir). Classic gold. Light: 5677.
   2004. CD.

3091 Houghton, Israel. *Live from Another Level* (New
   Breed). Integrity: E2K 91263. 2004. 2 CDs.

3092 Mary Mary. *Thankful*. Columbia: CK 63740.
   2000. CD.

3093   Moss, J. *J Moss Project*. Gospo-Centric: 75751-70068-2. 2004. CD.

3094   Norful, Smokie. *Life Changing*. EMI Gospel: 0946 3 33347 2 4. 2006. CD.

3095   Peoples, Dottie. *On Time God* (People's Choice Chorale). Atlanta International Record: AIR 10200. 1994. CD.

3096   Sapp, Marvin. *Here I Am*. Verity: 88697-53156-2. 2010. CD.

3097   Smallwood, Richard. *The Praise and Worship Songs of Richard Smallwood* (Vision). Verity: 82876-53710-2. 2003. CD.

3098   Take 6. *Take 6*. Reprise: 9 25670-2. 1988. CD.

3099   Tonéx. *Out the Box* (Peculiar People). Zomba: 82876-53713-2. 2003. 2 CDs.

3100   Tribbett, Tye. *Victory Live!* (Greater Anointing [G.A.]). Sony Urban: 82876 77526 2. 2005. CD.

3101   Trin-I-Tee 5:7. *Holla: The Best of Trin-I-Tee 5:7* (Kirk Franklin, Tramaine Hawkins). Gospo-Centric / Legacy: 88697 11291 2. 2007. CD.

3102   Winans. *The Definitive Original Greatest Hits* [1981–2001] (West Angeles COGIC Mass Choir). Artemis Gospel: 51706. 2005. 2 CDs.

3103   Winans, BeBe. *Heaven* (CeCe Winans). Capitol: 90959. 1988. CD.

3104   Winans, CeCe
    3104.1 *Everlasting Love*. Pioneer: 92793-2. 1998. CD.
    3104.2 *Purified*. Sony / PureSprings Gospel: EK 93997. 2005. CD.

3105   Winans, Vickie
    3105.1 *Be Encouraged* [1985]. Light: 51416 1049 2. 1987. CD.
    3105.2 *How I Got Over* (Tye Tribbett, Tim Bowman). Destiny Joy: 829569812028. 2009. CD.

SOUTHERN WHITE RELIGIOUS STYLES

COLLECTIONS

3106   *Awake My Soul: The Story of the Sacred Harp*. Sp. ed. [1998–2006]. Awake Productions: AP-002. 2007. 2 DVDs.

3107   *Children of the Heav'nly King: Religious Expression in the Central Blue Ridge* [1978–1979]. Rounder: 1506/07 (Library of Congress L69/L70). 1981. 2 CDs. Library of Congress Archive of Folk Culture.

3108   *Close Harmony: A History of Southern Gospel Music, Vol. 1* [1920–1955] (Golden Gate Quartet, LeFevres, Chuck Wagon Gang, Stamps-Baxter Quartet, Speer Family, Blackwood Brothers, and others). Dualtone: 80302-01190-2. 2003. CD.

3109   *Favorite Sacred Songs* [1940s–1950s] (Delmore Brothers, Grandpa Jones, Wayne Raney, Swanee River Boys, Brother Claude Ely, and others). King: 556. 1988. CD.

3110   ★*The Gospel Ship: Baptist Hymns and White Spirituals from the Southern Mountains* [1977]. New World: 80294-2. 1994. CD. Field recordings made by Alan Lomax in Kentucky, Virginia, and Arkansas.

3111   *I Belong to This Band: Eighty-Five Years of Sacred Harp Recordings* [1922–2006] (Roswell Sacred Harp Singers, Alabama Sacred Harp Singers, Denson's Sacred Harp Singers, Henagar-Union Sacred Harp Convention, and others). Dust to Digital: DTD-06. 2006. CD. Companion to the film *Awake My Soul: The Story of "The Sacred Harp."*

3112   *Jubilation! Great Gospel Performances, Vol. 3: Country Gospel* [1929–1981] (Hank Williams, Flatt and Scruggs, Kitty Wells, Louvin Brothers, Carter Family, Roy Acuff, Martha Carson, Bill Monroe, Ernest Tubb, Doyle Lawson, Ricky Scaggs, and others). Rhino: 70290. 1992. CD.

3113   *Mountain Gospel: The Sacred Roots of Country Music* [1926–1941] (Phipps Singers, Alfred G. Karnes, Laurel Firemen, Virginia Dandies, Roswell Sacred Harp, Ernest Stoneman, Carolina Ramblers, Deal Family, Ernest Phipps and His Holiness Quartet, McCravy Brothers, and others). JSP: JSP7755. 2005. 4 CDs.

3114   ★*Something Got a Hold of Me: A Treasury of Sacred Music* [1927–1941] (Carter Family, Monroe Brothers, Blue Sky Boys, Dixon Brothers, Blind Alfred Reed, Wade Mainer, Uncle Dave Macon, and others). RCA: 2100-2-R. 1990. CD.

3115   *Songs of the Old Regular Baptists: Lined-out Hymnody from Southeastern Kentucky* [1992–

1993] (Field recordings by Jeff Todd Titon). Smithsonian Folkways: 40106. 1997. CD.

3116 *Southern Gospel's Top 20 Songs of the Century* (Cathedrals, Statesmen, Oak Ridge Boys, Bill Gaither Trio, Chuck Wagon Gang, Florida Boys, Speers, Hinsons, Inspirations, Rambos, LeFevres, and others). New Haven: 8010-2. 2000. CD.

INDIVIDUALS AND GROUPS

3117 Alabama Sacred Harp Convention. *White Spirituals from the Sacred Harp: The Alabama Sacred Harp Convention* [1959] (Field recordings by Alan Lomax). New World: 80205-2. 1992. CD.

3118 ★Blackwood Brothers Quartet. *The Blackwoods* [1950s]. Gaither gospel series. Spring House: SHD4905. 1997. CD.

3119 Cash, Johnny. *The Gospel Music of Johnny Cash* [1970s–1990s?]. EMI Christian Music Group: 617884273224. 2008. 2 CDs.

3120 Cathedral Quartet. *Cathedral Classics* [1970s–1980s]. New Haven: 8052-2. 2005. CD.

3121 Chuck Wagon Gang. *I'll Fly Away* [1942–1966]. Music Mill / Sony: MME-71014-2. 2004. CD.

3122 Florida Boys. *45 Songs of Faith* [1960s–1990s]. Gospel Music Hall of Fame Series. Songs of Faith: SOF401. 2006. 2 CDs.

3123 Ford, Tennessee Ernie. *Country Gospel Classics, Vol. 1* [1950s–1960s]. Capitol: 95849. 1991. CD.

3124 Gaithers. *The Early Works* [1974–1983] (Bill Gaither, Gloria Gaither). Benson: 84418-2893-2. 1992. CD.

3125 Happy Goodman Family. *The Goodmans Greatest Hits* [1960s–1970s]. Gospel Legacy Series. New Haven: 8037-2. 2003. CD.

3126 Isaacs. *Songs of the Faith*. Horizon: HR09752. 2003. CD.

3127 Kingsmen. *All Time Favorites*. Gospel Legacy Series. New Haven: 8044-2. 2004. CD.

3128 Oak Ridge Boys. *The Gospel Sessions* [1970s]. New Haven: 8076-2. 2008. CD.

3129 Old Harp Singers of Eastern Tennessee
   3129.1 *Old Harp Singing* [1951] Smithsonian Folkways: FA 2356. 2001. CD.
   3129.2 *Old Harp Singing* [1951]. Smithsonian Folkways: 2356. 2001. CD.

3130 Presley, Elvis
   3130.1 *Elvis Gospel 1957–1971: Known Only to Him* [1957–1971] (Jordanaires, Imperials). RCA: 9586-2-R. 1989. CD.
   3130.2 *I Believe: The Gospel Masters* [1956–1974] (Jordanaires, Imperials Quartet). RCA / Legacy: 8869745884. 2009. 4 CDs.

3131 Speer Family. *First Family of Gospel* [1970–1986]. Gospel Legacy Series. New Haven: 8074-2. 2007. CD.

3132 Statesmen Quartet. *Hovie Lister and the Statesmen* [1950s]. Gaither Gospel Series. Spring House: SHD4904. 1997. CD.

3133 Travis, Randy. *Three Wooden Crosses: The Inspirational Hits of Randy Travis* (John Anderson, Mac Powell, and Blind Boys of Alabama). Word; Curb; Warner Bros.: WD2-887820. 2009. CD.

3134 West, Harry. *Favorite Gospel Songs* [1957] (Jeanie West). Smithsonian Folkways: FA 2357. 2001. CD.

INSPIRATIONAL, CONTEMPORARY CHRISTIAN, AND CHRISTIAN ROCK

COLLECTIONS

3135 *Best of Christian Rock (1970–1986), Vol. 1* (Mylon LeFevre, Larry Norman, Glass Harp, Love Song, Petra, The Way, Parable, Daniel Amos, DeGarmo and Key, Resurrection Band, Steve Taylor, and Whiteheart). History makers. Sparrow: SPD 80649. 2003. CD.

3136 *CCM Top 100: Greatest Songs in Christian Music, Vol. 1* [1970s–2000s] (Rich Mullins, Avalon, Crystal Lewis, Imperials, Third Day, Amy Grant, 4him, Twila Paris, Charlie Peacock, White Heart, Steven Curtis Chapman, Petra, Sandi Patty, Michael W. Smith, DC Talk, Warren Barfield, and others). Creative Trust Workshop: CTW 1742. 2004. 2 CDs.

3137 *First Love: A Historic Gathering of Jesus Music Pioneers* (Barry McGuire, Jamie Owens Collins, Terry Clark, Chuck Girard, Annie Herring, Randy Stonehill, Darrell Mansfield, John Fischer, Randy Matthews, Matthew Ward, Paul Clark, Andráe Crouch). Reel Productions: 6.7857E+11. 1998. 2 CDs, 2 DVDs.

INDIVIDUALS AND GROUPS

3138   Ashton, Susan. *Angels of Mercy*. Sparrow: SPD-1327. 1992. CD.

3139   Becker, Margaret. *Steps of Faith* [1987–1991]. Sparrow: SPD-1354. 1992. CD.

3140   Boone, Debby. *You Light up My Life: Greatest Inspirational Songs* [1976–1987]. Curb: D2-77959. 2001. CD.

3141   Caedmon's Call. *Caedmon's Call*. Warner Alliance: 9 46463-2. 1997. CD.

3142   Carman. *The Absolute Best* [1988–1990s]. Sparrow: SPD-1339. 1993. CD.

3143   Casting Crowns. *Lifesong*. Beach Street; Provident: 83061-0770-2. 2005. CD.

3144   Chapman, Steven Curtis
    3144.1   *Now and Then* [1990s–2004]. Sparrow: 94637651223. 2006. 2 CDs.
    3144.2   *Speechless*. Sparrow: SPD 1695. 1999.CD.
    3144.3   *This Moment*. Sparrow: SPD 86393. 2007. CD.

3145   DC Talk. *Jesus Freak*. 10th annual special edition. [1995]. ForeFront: 11571. 2006. 2 CDs.

3146   Dylan, Bob
    3146.1   *Saved* [1980]. Columbia: CK 36553. 1990. CD.
    3146.2   *Slow Train Coming* [1979]. Columbia: CK 92397. 2004. CD.

3147   Glad. *Acapella Project*. Benson: CD02445. 1988. CD.

3148   Grant, Amy
    3148.1   ★*The Collection* [1979–1985]. RCA: 66258-2. 1986. CD.
    3148.2   *Greatest Hits* [1986–2004] (Vince Gill, Keb' Mo', Peter Cetera). A&M: B0003415-02. 2004. 2 CDs.
    3148.3   *Heart in Motion*. A&M: 75021 5321 2. 1991. CD.

3149   Green, Keith. *Ministry Years, Vol. 1* [1977–1979]. Sparrow: SPD-1568—SPD-1569. 1999. 2 CDs. Enhanced CD.

3150   Imperials. *The Imperials* [1964–1976]. Gospel music hall of fame series. Benson / BMG: 82342. 1998. 2 CDs.

3151   Jars of Clay
    3151.1   *The Long Fall Back to Earth*. Essential: 8306109032. 2009. CD.
    3151.2   *Triple Feature* [1995–1999]. Provident / Sony: EPCD 5573. 2010. 3 CDs. Includes 3 albums: *Jars of Clay*; *Much Afraid*; *If I Left the Zoo*.

3152   Keaggy, Phil. *Phil Keaggy and Sunday's Child* (Sunday's Child). Myrrh / Word: 701 6876 616. 1988. CD.

3153   Love Song. *Love Song* [1972]. Calvary classics collection series. Calvary / Word: 7018167698. 2011. CD.

3154   Munizzi, Martha. *No Limits—Live*. Integrity; Columbia: C2K 677093. 2006. 2 CDs.

3155   Norman, Larry
    3155.1   *Rebel Poet, Jukebox Balladeer: The Anthology* [1968–1981]. Arena Rock: ARE 059. 2008. CD.
    3155.2   *Upon This Rock, Coll. Ed* [1969]. Solid Rock: SRD 969. 2002. 2 CDs.

3156   Omartian, Michael. *White Horse / Adam Again* [1974, 1975]. Myrrh / Word: 701 6894 614. 1991. CD.

3157   Patty (Patti), Sandi. *Finest Moments* [1978–1986]. Word / Epic: EK 47739. 1989. CD.

3158   Peacock, Charlie. *Love Life*. Sparrow: SPD-1303. 1991. CD.

3159   Petra
    3159.1   *Farewell*. Inpop: PODVD1376. 2006. DVD.
    3159.2   *Petra* [1974]. Word / Epic: EK 48802. 1992. CD.
    3159.3   *Ultimate Collection* [1974–2003]. EMI: 50666. 2006. 2 CDs.

3160   2nd Chapter of Acts. *20* [1972–1992]. Sparrow: SPD-1332. 1992. 2 CDs.

3161   Smith, Michael W.
    3161.1   *The First Decade* [1983–1993]. Reunion: 701 0086 729. 1993. CD.
    3161.2   *The Second Decade* [1993–2003]. Reunion: 02341-0080-2. 2003. CD.

3162   Switchfoot. *The Beautiful Letdown*. Sparrow: SPD 51976. 2003. CD.

3163 Taff, Russ

    3163.1 *The Best of Russ Taff* [1990s–2003]. Gaither gospel series. Spring House: SHD2456. 2003. CD.

    3163.2 *The Way Home*. Word / A&M: 8440. 1989. CD.

3164 Third Day. *Chronology, Vol. 1* [1996–2000]. Provident / Essential: 083061-0838-2. 2007. CD, DVD.

3165 Third Day. *Chronology, Vol. 2*. Provident / Essential: 83061-0839-2. 2008. CD, DVD.

3166 Velasquez, Jaci. *Mi Corazón*. Sony: LAK-84289/2-475233. 2001. CD. Latin CCM, sung in Spanish.

CHRISTIAN RAP

COLLECTION

3167 *Holy Hip Hop: Taking the Gospel to the Streets, Vols. 1-12* [2004–2011]. EMI. 2009. CD. Ongoing series, released as single CDs.

INDIVIDUALS AND GROUPS

3168 Ambassador. *Stop the Funeral* (Sean Simmonds, Charmaine, Canton Jones, Melissa T, Jessica Reedy, Ryan Stevenson, KJ52, Michelle Bonilla, GOD'S sERVANT, J.A.Z., Shai Linne, C-Lite, Cruz Cordero, and DJ Wade-o). Xist Music; Black Fuel: XST001. 2011. CD.

3169 Baraka, Sho. *Lions and Liars* (Erica Cumbo, Lecrae, J.R., Chinua Hawk, Trip Lee, Tedashii, and others). Reach: 829569814626. 2010. CD.

3170 Cross Movement. *History: Our Place in His Story*. Cross Movement: 88141300242. 2007. CD.

3171 Cross Movement. *Holy Culture*. BEC: BED82654. 2003. CD.

3172 da' T.R.U.T.H. *Moment of Truth*. Cross Movement: 881412-0000-29. 2004. CD.

3173 Flame

    3173.1 *Our World Fallen*. Cross Movement: 881413-0026-2. 2007. CD.

    3173.2 *Our World Redeemed*. Cross Movement: 881413-00302-0. 2008. CD.

3174 Gospel Gangstaz

    3174.1 *Gang Affiliated*. MYX / Holy Terra: FLD9460. 1994. CD.

    3174.2 *I Can See Clearly Now*. B-Rite: 606949025328. 1999. CD.

3175 Grits

    3175.1 *The Art of Translation*. Gotee: GTD2871R. 2002. CD.

    3175.2 *Grammatical Revolution*. Gotee: GTD2805. 1999. CD.

3176 Jones, Canton. *Dominionaire* (D-Maub, Messenja, James Fortune, Ramona Estell, Keith Johnson, KJ52, Richie Righteous, Erica Cumbo, Edna Jones, Deitrick Haddon, DPB, Mr. Del, and Jonathan Phillips). CAJO: 829569818228. 2011. 2 CDs.

3177 Lecrae. *Rehab*. Reach: 8295698161125. 2010. CD.

3178 Lee, Trip. *Between Two Worlds*. Reach: 8153. 2010. CD.

3179 116 Clique. *The Compilation Album* (Lecrae, Sho Baraka, Tedashii, Thi'Sl, and Json). Reach: 733792589827. 2005. CD.

3180 P.I.D. *The Chosen Ones*. Frontline: FLD9215. 1991. CD.

3181 T-Bone

    3181.1 *Bone-a-Fide*. Flicker / EMI: FLD2660. 2005. CD.

    3181.2 *Tha Life of a Hoodlum*. Metro One: 74948813329. 1995. CD.

3182 Tedashii. *Blacklight*. Reach: RCHR8184. 2011. CD.

3183 TobyMac

    3183.1 *Momentum*. ForeFront: FFD5294. 2001. CD.

    3183.2 *Welcome to Diverse City*. ForeFront: FED66417. 2004. Enhanced CD.

Children's Music

Compiled by **SUSANNAH CLEVELAND**

BABIES AND TODDLERS   *180*
PRESCHOOL   *180*
SCHOOL AGE OR ALL AGES   *181*
MULTICULTURAL MUSIC   *181*
RELIGIOUS AND HOLIDAY MUSIC   *182*
CLASSICAL MUSIC FOR CHILDREN   *182*
LULLABIES   *183*

This chapter contains sections for materials aimed at specific age groups (babies and toddlers, preschool, school age, and all ages) and sections for materials based around specific styles and purposes (multicultural music, religious and holiday music, classical music for children, and lullabies). Selections cover activities and sing-alongs, education, cultural awareness, and entertainment.

Music has long been a vehicle for teaching children about other cultures, but in recent decades the "world music" genre (labeled here as "multicultural music") has expanded in the children's music realm just as it has in the adult sector. Standard recordings in this genre from Smithsonian Folkways and similar labels persist in their popularity, but the growth of this market is emphasized by the development of labels such as Putomayo Kids, which specifically target young audiences.

Certain standby artists—Raffi and *Sesame Street*'s Bob McGrath, for example—remain popular and are still staples in the repertoire, with staying power well beyond many of their popular culture parallels. Similarly, classical works with particular appeal to children (Prokofiev's *Peter and the Wolf* and Poulenc's *Babar the Elephant*) maintain their appeal while being supplemented by a greater variety of video content aimed at enticing young listeners with the lives and works of the great composers.

Materials that will appeal to parents as well as youngsters receive special emphasis. Selections along this vein include several children's albums recorded by pop or rock musicians (such as the Barenaked Ladies' *Snack Time!*) and lullaby interpretations of popular artists' works (the Rockabye Baby! series).

BABIES AND TODDLERS

COLLECTION

3184 *Kidsongs: I'd Like to Teach the World to Sing* [1986]. Image Entertainment: ID1660TODVD. 2002. DVD.

INDIVIDUALS AND GROUPS

3185 Baby Loves Jazz Band. *Baby Loves Jazz: Go Baby Go!* Verve: B0007025-02. 2006. CD.

3186 Bartels, Joanie
    3186.1 *Dancin' Magic* [1991]. BMG Special Product: 146824. 2003. CD.
    3186.2 *Sillytime Magic*. Discovery Music: 146826. 1989. CD.

3187 Hickman, Sarah. *Toddler*. Sleeveless: 8.08275E+11. 2001. CD.

3188 McGrath, Bob, and Katharine Smithrim. *Songs and Games for Toddlers* [1985]. Bob's Kids Music: 4101603. 2000. CD.

3189 Old Town School of Folk Music. *Wiggleworms Love You*. Old Town School Recordings: OTS001. 2005. CD.

3190 Palmer, Hap. *Baby Songs Original*. Twentieth Century Fox Home Entertainment: 24543078609. 2003. DVD.

PRESCHOOL

COLLECTIONS

3191 *The Bottle Let Me Down: Songs for Bumpy Wagon Rides*. (Alejandro Escovedo, Handsome Family, Asylum Street Spankers, Rex Hobart and the Misery Boys, Jon Rauhouse, Waco Brothers, Kelly Hogan, and others). Bloodshot Records: BS078. 2002. CD.

3192 *Children's Songs*. Hal Leonard: HL00311054. 2000. Score.

3193 *Colours Are Brighter: Songs for Children and Grown Ups Too* (Four Tet, Rasputina, Franz Ferdinand, Snow Patrol, Divine Comedy, Kooks, Half Man Half Biscuit, Barcelona Pavillion, Jonathan Richman, Belle and Sebastian, Ivor Cutler Trio, Flaming Lips, Kathryn Williams). Rough Trade: RTRADCD358. 2006. CD.

3194 *100 Kids' Songs*. Hal Leonard: HL00310572. 1999. Score.

INDIVIDUALS AND GROUPS

3195 Asylum Street Spankers. *Mommy Says No!* Yellow Dog Records: YDR1471. 2007. CD.

3196 ★Barenaked Ladies. *Snack Time!* [2008]. Raisin Records: 100207. 2011. CD.

3197 Berkner, Laurie. *Whaddaya Think of That?* Two Tomatoes: CMCD1. 2001. CD.

3198 ★Fitzgerald, Ella. *Miss Ella's Playhouse* [1936–1966]. Verve: B0008345-02. 2008. CD.

3199 *High Five*. Rockinmama. 2010. CD.

3200 Jenkins, Ella. *Early, Early Childhood Songs* [1972]. Smithsonian Folkways: CD SF 45015. 1996. CD.

3201 Knight, Tom. *The Library Boogie* [2001]. Orchard Kids: OK2101. 2010. CD.

3202 McGrath, Bob
    3202.1 ★*Bob's Favorite Street Songs* [1991]. Bob's Kids Music: 96003. 2000. CD.
    3202.2 *Sing Me a Story* [1997]. Bob's Kids Music: 5002. 2003. CD.

3203 Palmer, Hap
    3203.1 *Sally the Swinging Snake* [1986]. Educational Activities: CD 617. 2001. CD.
    3203.2 ★*Walter the Waltzing Worm*. Educational Activities: CD 555. 1992. CD.

3204 Raffi
    3204.1 *More Singable Songs* [1977]. Rounder: CD 8052. 1996. CD.
    3204.2 *Raffi in Concert* [1984]. Rounder: 11661-8116-9. 2002. DVD.
    3204.3 *Rise and Shine* [1982]. Rounder: CD 8055. 1996. CD.
    3204.4 *Singable Songs for the Very Young* [1976]. Rounder: CD 8051. 1996. CD.

3205 Seeger, Pete. *Stories and Songs for Little Children* [198?]. High Windy Audio: HW 1207. 2000. CD.

3206 ★They Might Be Giants. *No!* Rounder: 11661-8113-2. 2002. CD.

3207 ★Wee Hairy Beasties. *Animal Crackers*. Bloodshot Records: BS136. 2006. CD.

SCHOOL AGE OR ALL AGES

COLLECTIONS

3208 *Disney's Greatest Hits, Vol. 1.* Walt Disney Records: 60693-7. 2001. CD. This volume is the first in the series of greatest hits from Disney films, old and new.

3209 *For the Kids Three!* (Moby, Jolie Holland, Damien Jurado, Of Montreal, Over the Rhine, Barenaked Ladies, Mates of State, and others). Nettwerk Records: 0 6700 30748 2 7. 2007. CD.

3210 *Greasy Kid Stuff* (Dandy Lions, Phantom Surfers, Nutley Brass, Happiest Guys in the World, Michael Shelley, Tony Burrello, T. Lance and the Coctails, James Kochalka Superstar with the Zambonis, Fastbacks, Mr. T Experience, Go-Nuts, Hoppin' Haole Brothers, Waco Brothers, S. F. Seals, Yo La Tengo). Confidential Recordings: CON 3002-2. 2002. CD.

3211 *Vintage Children's Favorites* [1926–1950] (Vernon Dalhart, Henry Hall, Hill Billies, Bing Crosby, Danny Kaye, Paul Robeson, and others). ASV Living Era: CD AJA 5274. 1999. CD.

INDIVIDUALS AND GROUPS

3212 Boydston, John. *Eat Every Bean and Pea on Your Plate.* Boyd's Tone Records: 3669. 2006. CD.

3213 Boynton, Sandra. *Rhinoceros Tap* (Adam Bryant, Michael Ford). Rounder: 11661-8121-2. 2004. CD.

3214 Dawson, Kimya. *Alphabutt.* K Records: KLP193. 2008. CD.

3215 Dorough, Bob. *Schoolhouse Rock!* Sp. 30th ann. ed. [1973–1996]. Buena Vista Home Entertainment: 23048. 2002. 2 DVDs.

3216 England, Frances. *Fascinating Creatures.* Frances England: UPC:837101219549. 2006. CD.

3217 Garcia, Jerry, and David Grisman. *Not for Kids Only.* Acoustic Disc: ACD-9. 1993. CD.

3218 ★Gothic Archies. *The Tragic Treasury: Songs from a Series of Unfortunate Events.* (Stephin Merritt, Lemony Snicket, John Woo). Nonesuch: 79951-2. 2006. CD.

3219 ★Jenkins, Ella. *You'll Sing a Song and I'll Sing a Song* [1966]. Smithsonian Folkways: CD SF 45010. 1989. CD.

3220 Johnson, Jack. *Sing-a-Longs and Lullabies for the Film Curious George* (G. Love, Ben Harper, and others). Brushfire Records: B0006116-02. 2005. CD.

3221 Lithgow, John. *The Sunny Side of the Street.* Razor and Tie: 7930182959-2. 2006. CD.

3222 Mitchell, Elizabeth. *You Are My Little Bird.* Smithsonian / Folkways: SFW CD 45063. 2006. CD.

3223 Thomas, Marlo, and Friends. *Free to Be . . . You and Me* [1972]. Arista: ARCD-8325. 1983. CD.

3224 Trout Fishing in America. *Mine!* Trout Records: TRT-9. 1994. CD.

3225 Zanes, Dan, and Friends

    3225.1 *All around the Kitchen! Crazy Videos and Concert Songs!* Festival Five Records: FFR008. 2005. DVD.

    3225.2 *Family Dance* (Barbara Brousal, Roseanne Cash, Rubi Theatre Co., Loudon Wainwright III, Sandra Bernhard, Father Goose, Donald Saaf, Lyris Hung). Festival Five Records: 2. 2001. CD.

MULTICULTURAL MUSIC

COLLECTIONS

3226 *Animal Playground* (Wee Hairy Beasties, Quartetto Cetra, Be Good Tanyas, P'tits Loups du Jazz, Samba Salad, Ladysmith Black Mambazo, and others). Putumayo: PUT 264-2. 2007. CD.

3227 *Baby Loves Salsa Presents Salsa for Kittens and Puppies.* Baby Loves Music: 3. 2008. CD.

3228 *The Planet Sleeps* [1997]. Work Group: OK 6777. 2008. CD.

3229 *Sesame Street Playground.* Putumayo: PUT 283-2. 2008. CD, DVD.

3230 *World Playground: A Musical Adventure for Kids* (Toure Kunda, Colibri, Cedella Marley Booker and Taj Mahal, Trevor Adamson, Teresa Doyle, Buckwheat Zydeco, Glykeria, Manu Chao, and others). Putumayo: PUTU 154-2. 1999. CD.

INDIVIDUALS AND GROUPS

3231 African Children's Choir. *It Takes the Whole Village* [1998]. African Children's Choir. 2005. CD.

3232 Casey, Karan. *Seal Maiden: A Celtic Musical*. Music for Little People: R2 79858. 2000. CD.

3233 Doucet, Michael. *Le Hoogie Boogie: Louisiana French Music for Children*. Rounder: CD 8022. 1992. CD.

3234 Jenkins, Ella

  3234.1 *African American Folk Songs and Rhythms* [1960]. Smithsonian Folkways: SFW CD 45003. 1998. CD.

  3234.2 *Multi-Cultural Children's Songs*. Smithsonian Folkways: SF 45045. 1995. CD.

3235 Skiera-Zucek, Lois. *Songs about Native Americans*. Kimbo Educational: KIM 9132CD. 1994. CD.

3236 Vernay, Lucienne. *Songs in French for Children* [1956]. Sony Music Special Products: A 24299. 2001. CD.

RELIGIOUS AND HOLIDAY MUSIC

COLLECTIONS

3237 *All Aboard the Holiday Express*. Hal Leonard: HL09970917. 2000. Score.

3238 *Chanukah at Home* [1988] (Dan Crow, Marcia Berman, Uncle Ruthie Buell, J. P. Nightingale, Fred Sokolow). Rounder: CD 8017. 2009. CD.

3239 *Festive Songs for the Jewish Holidays*. Hal Leonard: HL00296195. 2002. Score.

3240 *Hanukkah and Chinese New Year*. Kimbo Educational: KIM 12CD. 2002. CD.

3241 *Holiday Fun*. Hal Leonard: HL 00310893. 2002. Score.

INDIVIDUALS AND GROUPS

3242 Bonna, Geanora, Vaughn Fuller, and Charles Mims. *Kwanzaa for Young People (and Everyone Else!)*. Charphelia: CH 70002. 2002. CD.

3243 Buchman, Rachel. *Jewish Holiday Songs for Children*. Rounder: CD 8028. 1993. CD.

3244 Guaraldi, Vince. *Charlie Brown's Holiday Hits* [1965–1998]. Fantasy: FCD-9682-2. 1998. CD.

3245 Jenkins, Ella. *Holiday Times: Songs, Stories, Rhymes and Chants for Christmas, Kwanza, Hanukkah, Chinese New Year, and St. Patrick's Day*. Smithsonian / Folkways: SF 45041. 1996. CD.

3246 McGrath, Bob. *Christmas Sing Along*. Bob's Kids Music: 4101803. 2006. CD.

3247 Palmer, Hap. *Hap Palmer's Holiday Magic* [1990]. Hap-Pal: HP108. 1996. CD.

3248 Penner, Fred. *Christmastime*. Casablanca Kids: CAS-CD-42017. 2007. CD.

3249 Raffi. *Raffi's Christmas Album* [1983]. Rounder: 11661-8114-2. 2002. CD.

3250 Scelsa, Greg, and Steve Millang. *Holidays and Special Times* [1989]. Youngheart: 009CD. 2000. CD.

3251 Scruggs, Joe. *Merry Christmas* [1989]. Shadow Play / Education Graphics Press: 9562. 1997. CD.

CLASSICAL MUSIC FOR CHILDREN

COLLECTIONS

3252 ★New York Philharmonic / Leonard Bernstein. *Bernstein Favorites: Children's Classics*. [1960]. Sony Classical: SFK 46712. 1991. CD. Contains Prokofiev's *Peter and Wolf*, Saint-Saen's *Carnival of the Animals*, and Britten's *Young Person's Guide to the Orchestra*.

3253 *Daydreams and Lullabies: A Celebration of Poetry, Songs, and Classical Music*. (Music by Bach, Beethoven, Mozart, Schubert, Brahms, Tchaikovsky, and others). Classical Kids / BMG Music: 068478-4239-2. 1992. CD.

3254 Royal Philharmonic Orchestra. *The Runaway Bunny, Paddington Bear's First Concert, Tubby the Tuba*. (Brooke Shields and Stephen Fry, narrs.). Sony Classical: 88697-22855-2. 2008. CD.

INDIVIDUALS AND GROUPS

3255 Bach, Johann Sebastian. *Mr. Bach Comes to Call*. Classical Kids: 84425-9. 2007. DVD.

3256 Beethoven, Ludwig van. *Beethoven Lives Upstairs* [1989]. Classical Kids: CGD 4200. 2002. DVD.

3257 Kleinsinger, George. *Tubby the Tuba* [1994] (Manhattan Transfer, Tommy Johnson, Naples Philharmonic [Timothy Russell, dir.]). d'Note Records: DND 3001. 2001. CD.

3258 Louchard, Ric

  3258.1 *G'night Wolfgang: Classical Piano Solos for Bedtime* [1989]. Music for Little People: 9 42500-2. 1993. CD.

3258.2 *Hey Ludwig! Classical Piano Solos for Playful Times.* Music for Little People: 9 42537-2. 1993. CD.

3259 Mozart, Wolfgang Amadeus

3259.1 *Baby Mozart Music Festival* [2000]. Buena Vista Home Entertainment: 25941. 2004. DVD.

3259.2 *The Magic Flute Story: An Opera Fantasy* (Horst Gebhardt, Magdalen Falewicz, Heidrun Halk, Dieter Schole, Inge Uibel, Hermann Christian Polster, Guntfried Speck, Gewandhaus Orchestra [Gert Bahner, con.]). V.I.E.W. Video: 2422. 2001. DVD.

3260 Poulenc, Francis. *Babar the Elephant* (Meryl Streep, Mona and Renee Golabek, New Zealand Symphony Orchestra [JoAnn Falletta, con.]). Koch International Classics: 3-7368-2 HI. 1996. CD. Also contains Ravel's Mother Goose Suite.

3261 Vivaldi, Antonio. *Vivaldi's Ring of Mystery* (Adelle Armin, Studio Arts Orchestra [Walter Babiak, con.]). Classical Kids: 06847-84206-2. 1991. CD.

LULLABIES

COLLECTIONS

3262 *Baby Einstein: Lullaby Classics.* Buena Vista: 861085. 2004. CD.

3263 *Dreamland: World Lullabies and Soothing Songs.* (Angelique Kidjo with Carlos Santana, Erick Manana, Teresa Doyle, Sibongile Khumalo, Claudia Martinez, Letterstick Band, and others). Putumayo World Music: PUT 212-2. 2003. CD.

3264 *Jazz Lullaby.* (Singers Unlimited, Mel Tormé, Ella Fitzgerald, Johnny Hodges, Bill Evans, Ben Webster, Ray Bryant, Acoustic Alchemy, Wes Montgomery, Abbey Lincoln). Verve: B0009761-02. 2008. CD.

INDIVIDUALS AND GROUPS

3265 Armstrong, Michael

3265.1 *Lullaby Renditions of the Cure.* Rockabye Baby! series. Baby Bock Records: CD 9813. 2006. CD. The Rockabye Baby! series includes soothing arrangements of music and includes several entries, from groups as diverse as Metallica and Coldplay.

3265.2 *Lullaby Renditions of Radiohead.* Baby Bock Records: CD 9800. 2006. CD.

3266 Bartels, Joanie. *Lullaby Magic* [1985]. Discovery Music: 02184-94400-2. 2005. CD.

11

Holidays, Special Occasions, Patriotic Music, and Miscellaneous

Compiled by **EDWARD KOMARA**

HOLIDAYS   *186*
   Christmas   186
   Halloween   188
   Kwanzaa   188
SPECIAL OCCASIONS   *188*
   Weddings   188
   Sport and College Songs   189
NATIONAL ANTHEMS AND PATRIOTIC MUSIC   *189*
SOUND EFFECTS   *189*

This chapter lists CDs, songbooks, and scores for holidays and special occasions in American life. Unlike most of the printed music listed in *A Basic Music Library,* the print selections included here are not for study but rather for practical performances by family, friends, and sometimes musicians hired for an occasion. Much the same could be said for the sound recordings, as many (especially the Christmas ones) may be heard during festivities, although others have become highly regarded, indeed favorite, to be enjoyed as solitary listening during the appropriate season.

The bulk of the holiday music listed here is for Christmas, including sacred music for use during church services, carols relating the Christmas story, classical music treatments ranging from selections from Handel's *Messiah* (1742) to Menotti's *Amahl and the Night Visitors* (1951), and secular pop favorites heard

annually on radio and television. Listings for Halloween and Kwanzaa are also included. Additional holiday music for children may be found in chapter 10. Jewish music for Hanukkah and other occasions may be found in chapters 10 and 17.

During the warmer months, when many weddings are held, sheet music for the service organist or pianist is in high demand; acquiring multiple copies of the more representative collections is recommended.

Collections of college songs (including team fight songs), special effects, and national anthems may seem low priority, but they do supply several musical needs and even help to answer the occasional nonmusic reference question. Marches usually heard during the Fourth of July (especially those by John Phillip Sousa) may be found in the "Bands" section of chapter 1.

HOLIDAYS

Christmas

Traditional

COLLECTIONS

3267 *Big Book of Christmas Songs.* Hal Leonard: HL00102235. 1991. Score.

3268 *Christmas for Two.* Alfred Publishing. 2003.

3269 *Classical Singer's Christmas Album.* Hal Leonard: HL00740062 (high voice). 1992. Score.

3270 *★An Old World Christmas: Holiday Favorites from Europe.* Deutsche Grammophon: 413 657-2. 1980. CD. Score.

3271 *100 Great Christmas Songs.* Alfred Publishing. 1998.

3272 *12 Christmas Favorites.* Hal Leonard. 2005. Score.

INDIVIDUALS AND GROUPS

3273 Althouse, Jay, arr. *Christmas for Solo Singers.* Alfred Publishing. 1995. Score.

3274 Best, Martin. *Thys Yool: A Medieval Christmas.* Nimbus: NI 5137. 1988. CD.

3275 Boston Camerata (Joel Cohen)
  3275.1 *Noel, Noel! French Christmas Music, 1200–1600.* Erato: 45420-2. 1990. CD.
  3275.2 *★Sing We Noel: Christmas Music from England and Early America* [1978]. Nonesuch: 71354-2. 1978. CD.

3276 Boytim, Joan Frey. *Christmas Solos for All Ages.* Hal Leonard: HL00740168, HL00740169, HL00740170. 2001. Score.

3277 Cuellar, Carol, compiler. *170 Christmas Songs and Carols.* Alfred Publishing. 1998. Score.

3278 Ehret, Walter, and George Evans. *International Book of Christmas Carols.* Walton Music Corp.: [1963] 1980. Score.

3279 King's Singers. *A Little Christmas Music.* EMI: 49909. 1989. CD.

3280 Lerch, Louise. *Christmas Solos for Kids.* Hal Leonard. 2001. Score.

3281 Mormon Tabernacle Choir / Leonard Bernstein. *The Joy of Christmas* [1960]. CBS: XMT 6499. 1997. CD.

3282 Pavarotti, Luciano. *O Holy Night* [1976]. London: 414044-2. 1984. CD.

3283 Philadelphia Brass Ensemble. *A Festival of Carols in Brass* [1967]. CBS: MK 7033. 2012. CD.

3284 Quink. *Carols around the World.* Telarc: CD-80202. 1989. CD.

3285 Revels Company / John Langstaff. *Christmas Day in the Morning: A Revels Celebration of the Winter Solstice* [1987]. Revels: CD 1087. 1990. CD.

3286 Robert Shaw Chorale. *A Festival of Carols* [1957–1963]. RCA: 6429-2-RG. 1987. CD.

3287 Shafferman, Jean Anne. *Carols for Two.* Alfred Publishing. 1996. Score.

3288 Tadlock, Cheryl G., compiler. *Classics for Christmas.* Carl Fischer: VF12. 2005. Score.

3289 Vienna Boys Choir. *Christmas with the Vienna Boys Choir* [1975–1979] (Hermann Prey, Placido Domingo). RCA: 7930-2-RG. 1988. CD.

3290 Walters, Richard, arr.
  3290.1 *The Christmas Collection.* Hal Leonard: HL00740153. 2002. Score.
  3290.2 *Classical Carols.* Hal Leonard: HL00747024 (high voice); HL00747025 (low voice). 1992. Score.

Popular

COLLECTIONS

3291 *Best Christmas Songs Ever.* Hal Leonard: HL00359130. 1986. Score.

3292 *Best in Christmas Sheet Music.* Alfred Publishing [1997] 2005.

3293 *★Billboard Greatest Christmas Hits, 1935–1954* (Bing Crosby, gene Autry, Nat King Cole, Spike Jones, Jimmy Boyd, Eartha Kitt, and others). Rhino: 70637. 1989. CD.

3294 *★Billboard Greatest Christmas Hits, 1955–1983* (Bobby Helms, Brenda Lee, Chipmunks, Harry Simeone Chorale, Elvis Presley, Charles Brown, Drifters, Harry Belafonte, and others). Rhino: 70636. 1989. CD.

3295 *Blue Yule: Christmas Blues and R&B Classics* [1950–1990] (Charles Brown, Lightnin' Hopkins, Roy Milton, Canned Heat, Sonny Boy Williamson, John Lee Hooker, Louis Jordan, Jimmy Liggins, and others). Rhino: 70568. 1991. CD.

3296 *Christian Christmas Hits.* Hal Leonard: HL00311140. 2004. Score.

3297 *Christian Christmas Songbook.* Hal Leonard: HL00310901. 2002. Score.

3298 *The Christmas Caroling Songbook.* Hal Leonard: HL00240283. 2006. Score.

3299 *Christmas Carols from around the World: A Celebration of International Carols and Regional Traditions.* Alfred Publishing: 28390. 2007. Score.

3300 *A Christmas Gift for You from Phil Spector* [1963] (Crystals, Ronettes, Darlene Love, Bob B. Soxx and the Blue Jeans). Abkco: 4005-2. 1989. CD.

3301 *Christmas Hits Sheet Music Playlist.* Alfred Publishing: 31407. 2008. Score.

3302 *Christmas Sheet Music Hits.* Alfred Publishing: MFM0416. 2004. Score.

3303 *The Christmas Songs Big Book.* Alfred Publishing: 28069. 2007. Score.

3304 *Christmas Time Is Here.* Hal Leonard: HL00310761. 2001. Score.

3305 *The Complete Christmas Music Collection.* Alfred Publishing: F3350SMD. 2005. Score.

3306 *The Definitive Christmas Collection.* Hal Leonard: HL00311602. 2004. Score.

3307 *Dr. Demento Presents: The Greatest Christmas Novelty CD of All Time* [1947–1980s] (Chipmunks, Spike Jones, Singing Dogs, Stan Freburg, Elmo and Patsy, Yogi Yorgesson, Allan Sherman, and others). Rhino: 75755. 1989. CD.

3308 *Enchanted Carols: A Feast of Christmas Music with Victorian Music Boxes, Handbells, Church Bells, Barrel Organs, Street Pianos, Handbell Choirs, and Brass Bands.* Saydisc: CD-SDL-327. 1981. CD.

3309 *Essential Songs: Christmas.* Hal Leonard: HL00311241. 2005. Score.

3310 *Genuine Houserockin' Christmas.* Alligator. 2003. CD.

3311 *Handel's Messiah: A Soulful Celebration* (Dianne Reeves, Patti Austin, Stevie Wonder, George Duke, Take 6, Al Jarreau). Word Entertainment. 1992. CD.

3312 *The Hilarious Holiday Songbook.* Alfred Publishing: 28391. 2007. Score.

3313 *Hipsters' Holiday: Vocal Jazz and R&B Classics* [1946–1989] (Louis Armstrong; Eartha Kitt; Lambert, Hendricks and Ross; Miles Davis; Mabel Scott; Babs Gonzales; Lena Horne; and others). Rhino: 70910. 1989. CD.

3314 *Jingle Bell Jazz* [1961–1969, 1985] (Duke Ellington, Lionel Hampton, Carmen McRae, Dave Brubeck, Herbie Hancock, Miles Davis, Dexter Gordon, McCoy Tyner, Heath Brothers, Wynton Marsalis, Paquito D'Rivera, and others). Columbia: CK 40166. 1985. CD.

3315 *Love That Christmas Music: Over 60 of the Best-Loved Christmas Songs.* Alfred Publishing: MFM0519. 2005. Score.

3316 *120 Best-Known Christmas Songs.* Alfred Publishing: VF1854A. 2000. Score.

3317 *The Original Soul Christmas* [1963–1978] (Clarence Carter, King Curtis, Otis Redding, Joe Tex, Booker T. and the MGs, Carla Thomas, Solomon Burke, William Bell, Ray Charles). Rhino: R2 71788. 1994. CD.

3318 *A Romantic Christmas.* Hal Leonard: HL00310759. 2001. Score.

3319 *Santa's Greatest Hits.* Hal Leonard: HL00311139. 2004. Score.

3320 *Songs of Christmas.* Alfred Publishing: MFM0523. 2005.

3321 *A Winter's Solstice* (William Ackerman, Philip Aaberg, Liz Story, Mark Isham, and others). Windham Hill: WD-1045. 1985. CD.

3322 *The World's Most Beloved Christmas Songs.* Alfred Publishing: 31406. 2008.

3323 *Yule Struttin': A Blue Note Christmas* [1953–1990] (Bobby Watson, Lou Rawls, Chet Baker, Dexter Gordon, and others). Blue Note: 94857. 1990. CD.

INDIVIDUALS AND GROUPS

3324 ★Beach Boys. *Christmas with the Beach Boys* [1963–1977]. Capitol: 72435 79765-2-7. 2004. CD.

3325 Brown, James. *The Best of James Brown: The Christmas Collection* [1966]. 20th Century Masters series. Polydor. 2003. CD.

3326 Cole, Nat King. *The Christmas Song* [1963]. Capitol: 46318. 1992. CD.

3327 Edison, Roger, compiler. *The World's Greatest Christmas Songs for Piano and Voice: 73 Best-*

Loved Christmas Songs and Seasonal Favorites. Alfred Publishing: 22506. 2004. Score.

3328 Fitzgerald, Ella. *Ella Wishes You a Swinging Christmas* [1960]. Verve: 827150-2. 1988. CD.

3329 ★Guaraldi, Vince. *A Charlie Brown Christmas* [1965]. Fantasy: FCD-8431-2. 1988. CD.

3330 Harris, Emmylou. *Light of the Stable: The Christmas Album* [1975–1979]. Warner Brothers: 3484-2. 1992. CD.

3331 Inman, Bryce, compiler. *25 Contemporary Christmas Hits.* Hal Leonard: 080689 482281. 2004. Score.

3332 Jackson 5. *Jackson 5 Christmas Album* [1970]. Motown: 37463-5250-2. 1986. CD.

3333 ★Jackson, Mahalia. *Silent Night* [1955]. Columbia: CK 38304 (CL 702). 1987. CD.

3334 Jones, Spike. *It's a Spike Jones Christmas* [1956]. Rhino: 70196. 1988. CD.

3335 Mannheim Steamroller. *Mannheim Steamroller Christmas.* American Gramophone: AGCD-1984. 1984. CD.

3336 Nelson, Willie. *Pretty Paper* [1979]. Columbia: CK 36189. 1986. CD.

3337 Roches. *We Three Kings.* MCA / Paradox: MCAD-10020. 1990. CD.

3338 Seeger, Mike. *American Folk Songs for Christmas* (Peggy Seeger, Penny Seeger). Rounder: CD 0268/0269. 1989. 2 CDs.

3339 Seeger, Pete. *Traditional Christmas Carols* [1967]. Smithsonian Folkways: SF 40024. 1989. CD.

3340 ★Sinatra, Frank. *The Sinatra Christmas Album* [1957]. Capitol: 48329. 1988. CD.

3341 Staple Singers. *The 25th Day of December* [1962]. Riverside. 2007. CD.

3342 Streisand, Barbra. *A Christmas Album* [1967]. Columbia: CK 9557. 1989. CD.

3343 Supremes. *Merry Christmas* [1965]. Motown. 1999. CD.

3344 Temptations
    3344.1 *Give Love at Christmas* [1980]. MCA. 1987. CD.
    3344.2 *The Temptations Christmas Card* [1970]. Motown: 37463-5251-1. 1986. CD.

3345 Winter, Paul. *Wintersong.* Living Music: LD0012. 1986. CD.

Halloween

COLLECTIONS

3346 *Fright Night: Music That Goes Bump in the Night.* CBS: MDK 45530. 1989. CD.

3347 ★*Halloween Hits* [1955–1969] (Bobby Boris Pickett, Jumpin' Gene Simmons, Ray Parker Jr., Sheb Wooley, Ran-Dells, Screamin' Jay Hawkins, and others). Rhino: 70535. 1991. CD.

3348 *Halloween Hootenanny* (John Zacherle, Rob Zombie, Horton Heat, Davie Allan, and others). Zombie A Go-Go Records: DGCD-25214. 1998. CD.

INDIVIDUALS AND GROUPS

3349 Cincinnati Pops / Erich Kunzel. *Chiller.* Telarc: CD-80189. 1989. CD.

3350 Gold, Andrew. *Andrew Gold's Halloween Howls* (Linda Ronstadt, David Cassidy, Karla Bonoff, Stephen Bishop, Nicolette Larson). Kid Rhino: R2 723532. 1996. CD.

3351 Sonic Realm. *Halloween Horrorscape.* Sonic Realm: 5678. 2007. CD.

Kwanzaa

3352 Mims, Charles, and Patsy Moore. *Kwanzaa for Young People (and Everyone Else!)* (Vaughn Fuller). Charphelia: CH 70001. 1999. CD.

3353 Summers, Bill. *The Essence of Kwanzaa.* Monkey Hill Records: MON 8137-2. 1997. CD.

3354 Women of the Calabash. *The Kwanzaa Album.* Bermuda Reefs Records: 1823-2. 1998. CD.

SPECIAL OCCASIONS
Weddings

3355 *Amazing Wedding Songs.* Brentwood-Benson Music Pub: 45757-0544-7. 2003. Score.

3356 *The Best Wedding Songs Ever.* Hal Leonard: HL00311096. 2004. Score.

3357 *The Bride's Guide to Wedding Music: A Complete Resource including 65 Musical Selections in All Styles Plus an Article on Planning the Music for*

Your Wedding Ceremony. Hal Leonard: HL00310615. 2000. Score.

3358 *The Collection of Wedding Music.* Warner Brothers: MFM0401. 2004. Score.

3359 *Essential Songs: Wedding.* Hal Leonard: HL00311309. 2005. Score.

3360 Inman, Bryce, compiler. *Contemporary Wedding Favorites.* Hal Leonard: 080689 507281. 2006. Score.

3361 *The Knot Collection of Ceremony and Wedding Music Selected by the Knot's Carley Roney* [2003]. Sony Classical: Sk 92826. 2005. CD.

3362 Okun, Milton, compiler. *Great Songs . . . For Weddings.* Hal Leonard: 250100. 2007. Score.

3363 *Rockin' and Rollin' Wedding Songs, Vol. 1* [1950–1975] (Paul Anka, Beach Boys, Dixie Cups, Captain and Tennille, 5th Dimension, Little Esther, Willows, Paul and Paula, and others). Rhino: 70588. 1992. CD.

3364 *Rockin' and Rollin' Wedding Songs, Vol. 2* [1958–1974] (Platters, Al Green, Jimmy Soul, Big Bopper, Lloyd Price, and others). Rhino: 70589. 1992. CD.

3365 *Songs for a Christian Wedding.* Hal Leonard: HL00310960. 1999. Score.

3366 *Traditional and Popular Wedding Music.* Warner Brothers: MF9720. 1997. Score.

3367 *25 Wedding Favorites.* SPJ Music: ACD 8848. 2000. CD.

3368 *Wedding Songs Big Book.* Alfred Publishing: 28070. 2007. Score.

Sport and College Songs

COLLECTION

3369 *34 Hit Parade Extras: College Songs.* Hal Leonard: Hl00384961. 1976. Score.

INDIVIDUALS AND GROUPS

3370 Marching Chiefs. *The Best of College Football Fight Songs* [1997]. Sheridan Square Records: 7644. 2007. CD.

3371 Studwell, W., and B. Schueneman. *College Fight Songs: An Anthology.* Haworth Press. 1998–2001. Score.

3372 University of Michigan Band / William D. Revelli. *41 Great College Victory Songs* [1971]. Vanguard Records: 29/30-2. 1987. 2 CDs.

NATIONAL ANTHEMS AND PATRIOTIC MUSIC

COLLECTION

3373 *National Anthems from around the World.* Hal Leonard: HL00311633. 1996. Score.

INDIVIDUALS AND GROUPS

3374 ★Breiner, Peter. *Complete National Anthems of the World* [1996]. Marco Polo: 8.208009. 2005. 8 CDs.

3375 Guthrie, Kari. *National Anthems, Vols. 1–4.* Hi I.Que Publishing. 1992–1993. Score.

3376 Hang, Xing. *Encyclopedia of National Anthems.* Scarecrow Press. 2011. Score.

3377 Mormon Tabernacle Choir. *God Bless America* [1973–1976]. Sony: MDK 48295. 1992. CD.

3378 Reed, W. L., and Bristow, M. J. *National Anthems of the World.* Sterling Publishing Company. 1985. Score.

3379 Regimental Band of the Coldstream Guards
    3379.1 ★*Collections of National Anthems, Vol. 1* [1988]. Denon: 4500-2. 1990. CD.
    3379.2 ★*Collections of National Anthems, Vol. 2* [1988]. Denon: 4501-2. 1990. CD.

3380 Robert Shaw Chorale. *Battle Cry of Freedom* [1962]. RCA: 60814-2-RG. 1991. CD.

3381 Vienna State Opera Orchestra. *National Anthems of the World* [1960s]. Legacy: CD 301. 1988. CD.

SOUND EFFECTS

3382 *Authentic Sound Effects, Vols. 1–3.* Elektra: 60731-2/60733-2. 1987. CD.

3383 *1000 Sound Effects.* Madacy: IML2 51818. 2005. CD.

CONTRIBUTORS

VOLUME EDITOR

EDWARD KOMARA (Popular Music; Blues; Holidays, Special Occasions, Patriotic Music, and Misc.) is the Crane (Music) Librarian at the State University of New York at Potsdam. Previously, he was Music Librarian/Blues Archivist at the University of Mississippi (1993–2001). He earned his degrees at St. John's College, Annapolis (BA, 1988) and SUNY Buffalo (MLS, 1991; MA, 1992). His books include *ZaFTIG: The Zappa Family Trust Issues Guide* (Scott Parker Books, 2015), *100 Books Every Blues Fan Should Own* (with Greg Johnson; Rowman and Littlefield, 2014), *The Road to Robert Johnson* (Hal Leonard, 2007), *The Encyclopedia of the Blues* (as editor; Routledge Press, 2006), and *The Dial Recordings of Charlie Parker* (Greenwood Press, 1998). He has also contributed articles to *The Grove Dictionary of American Music*, 2nd ed. (Oxford University Press, 2013) and to the two-part series *The Rise and Fall of Paramount Records* (Third Man Records and Revenant Records, 2013–2014). A member of the Music Library Association at the national and chapter levels, he is a frequent reviewer of jazz and blues publications for *Notes* and the *Association of Recorded Sound Collections Journal.* He has also published in *Black Music Research Journal* and *Living Blues.*

■ ■ ■

WILLIAM E. ANDERSON (deceased) (Jazz; Blues) was a Senior Department Subject Specialist in the Fine Arts & Special Collections Department at Cleveland Public Library. For many years he hosted radio programs at WRUW-FM 91.1, featuring jazz on *Bird Calls* and *Walking Dr. Bill's Rhythm & Blues Survey.* He contributed an article on Cleveland jazz clubs to *The New Grove Dictionary of Jazz* (2nd ed., 2002). He served along with Kent Underwood as sound recordings editor for *A Basic Music Library,* 3rd ed.

GROVER BAKER (Mainstream Popular and New Age) is Visual and Performing Arts Librarian at the James E. Walker Library, Middle Tennessee State University. Previously, he served as Librarian at the Center for Popular Music, also at MTSU. He holds an MS in Information Sciences from the University of Tennessee at Knoxville (2006). He also holds a Master of Church Music, with a second major in Conducting, from The

Southern Baptist Theological Seminary (1995), and a BM in Church Music from Belmont University (1992). Prior to arriving at MTSU in 2006, he worked as Music/Education Assistant in the Lila D. Bunch Library of Belmont University (1995–2005). Additionally, he has served as Music Director and Pianist for churches in Tennessee and Kentucky. He is a member of the Music Library Association and its Southeast Chapter (SEMLA) and also maintains membership in the American Library Association. He has been a contributor to *Music Reference Services Quarterly* and serves as a music reference instructor with MLA's Educational Outreach Program. He is an active participant in the music ministries of his church where he sings baritone in the choir, plays trumpet in the brass ensemble, and provides service music on piano.

THOMAS BELL (Rock) is Performing Arts Librarian at the Hale Library, Kansas State University. He holds the BFA degree in Music from Stephens College (1985), an MA in Music from the University of California Santa Barbara (1989), and an MLIS from The University of Texas at Austin (2001). He also studied music and gave recitals at the Britten-Pears School in Aldeburgh, England (1988 and 1989). He has done freelance writing about indie music, especially experimental and avant rock, for the webzine Spacelab: Reinventing the Future, and is a regular writer for CD Hotlist: New Releases for Libraries. He has also contributed reviews to *Notes*. He has been a performer of early music since 1986, when he began working with Alejandro Planchart, and he currently directs the Collegium Musicum at Kansas State University. He sometimes collaborates on experimental electro-chamber rock projects as well as teaches a course he created, The Underground Architects of Modern Pop Music.

GARY R. BOYE (Country) is Professor and Music Librarian for the Erneston Music Library at Appalachian State University in Boone, North Carolina, where he has worked since 2000. He holds degrees in musicology (PhD, Duke University, 1995), library science (MSLS, University of North Carolina at Chapel Hill, 2000), and guitar literature and performance (MA, BM, University of Georgia, 1988 and 1986). He has published articles in *Playing the Lute, Guitar, and Vihuela: Essays on Historical Practice and Modern Interpretation* (Cambridge: Cambridge University Press, 1997) and *The New Grove Dictionary of Music and Musicians* (New York: Macmillan, 2000), as well as several journals, including the *Journal of Seventeenth-Century Music* and the *Lute Society Quarterly*. A member of the Music Library Association since 1999, he has served as Chair of the MLA Jazz & Popular

Music Round Table (2002–2006) and as editor of the Members Publications column for the MLA Newsletter (2002–present).

JOE C. CLARK (Rock) is Head of the Performing Arts Library at Kent State University. Previously, he was Head of Library Media and the Slide Library at the University of Maryland, Baltimore County. He holds a BA in Music from the University of Utah, an MA in Information Resources and Library Science from the University of Arizona, and an MA in Ethnomusicology from Arizona State University. He has contributed to *The Encyclopedia of the Blues* (Routledge Press, 2006) and *The Encyclopedia of American Gospel Music* (Routledge Press, 2005), as well as to *Notes* and *Percussive Notes*. Before becoming a librarian, he enjoyed life as a professional guitarist and music educator.

SUSANNAH CLEVELAND (Children's Music; Mainstream Popular and New Age) has been the Head of the Music Library and Sound Recordings Archives at Bowling Green State University since 2006—the largest collection of popular music recordings at an academic institution in North America. Previously, she was the Music Recordings and Digital Resources Librarian at the University of North Texas Music Library where she planned and oversaw digital projects, special collections processing, and circulating sound recording collections. She holds a BM in Music History from Baylor University (1994) and an MM in Musicology (2001), as well as an MS in Library and Information Science (1997) from the University of North Texas in Denton. Her scholarship includes work with non-textual searching and classification of music and music librarian personnel and career issues.

ANDERS GRIFFEN (Jazz) is a freelance drummer, performer, and recording artist in New York City, working in a range of contexts, including jazz, folk, rock, and modern dance theater. He holds a BFA in Music Composition from the Conservatory of Music at SUNY-Purchase College (1996) and an MLIS from UCLA (2007). Previously, he was the Head Catalog Librarian at the Peter Jay Sharp Library at the Manhattan School of Music and an archivist for the Music Division at New York Public Library.

ANDREW LEACH (Rap and Hip-Hop) is the Director of Library and Archives at the Rock and Roll Hall of Fame and Museum in Cleveland. Previously, he served as Librarian and Archivist at the Center for Black Music Research at Columbia College Chicago (2000–2008). He

earned his degrees in music and library science from the University of Illinois at Urbana-Champaign and has worked in music libraries and archives since 1993. As a member of the Music Library Association, Leach has served as Coordinator of the Black Music Collections Roundtable and Chair of the Dena Epstein Award Committee. He has presented papers to the Music Library Association, the Society for American Music, and the American Library Association, and he has contributed articles and reviews to publications including *Notes, ARSC Journal,* and *The Encyclopedia of the Blues* (Routledge, 2006). His bibliographical essay on hip-hop and rap entitled, "One Day It'll All Make Sense: Hip-Hop and Rap Resources for Music Librarians," appeared in the September 2008 issue of *Notes.* Leach is also an active performing and recording musician.

MARK McKNIGHT (Music of Colonial North America and the United States to about 1900) is the Head of the Music Library at the University of North Texas, where he also teaches courses in music history and research in the UNT College of Music. He holds a BA in Music from the University of Central Arkansas, an MA and PhD in Music History from Louisiana State University, and an MS in Library and Information Science from the University of Illinois. He is active in a number of professional and scholarly organizations, including the American Musicological Society, the Society for American Music, the American Library Association, and the Music Library Association, in which he has held a number of offices. He has written and lectured extensively on 19th-century American music criticism, early American sheet music, and the music of Louisiana and New Orleans. Publications include articles and reviews in *Notes, American Music, Black Music Research Journal, ARSC Journal, Music Publishing and Collecting: Essays in Honor of Donald W. Krummel,* and *A Basic Music Library,* 3rd ed. He is also author of *Music Classification Systems* (Lanham, MD: Scarecrow Press, 2002) and a contributor to *The New Grove Dictionary of Music and Musicians,* 2nd ed.

RICHARD McRAE (Jazz) is a Catalog Librarian at Sibley Music Library, Eastman School of Music. He holds a BMus degree from the University of Massachusetts (1980) and an MLS (1989) and MA in Music History (1993) from the University at Buffalo. He worked as a cataloger for the American Music Center in 1989, and was a faculty member at the University at Buffalo Music Library from 1990 to 2007. He is a member of the Music Library Association and its New York State/Ontario Chapter and has contributed to *Notes.* As a freelance trombonist he has performed in orchestral, chamber, jazz, klezmer, salsa, pop, blues, rock, African/Latin, and Baltic ensembles.

BRENDA NELSON-STRAUSS (Gospel Music and Other Popular Christian Music) is currently Head of Collections at the Archives of African American Music and Culture at Indiana University. She serves as editor for the music review website Black Grooves and has served as Director of the Library of Congress National Sound Recording Preservation Plan. She holds a BMus from Western Washington University, an MLS from Indiana University with a Music Specialization, and completed coursework for an MA in Folklore and Ethnomusicology at IU. She was the Director of the Chicago Symphony Orchestra's Rosenthal Archives from 1989–2002, and worked as a catalog librarian at IU's Archives of Traditional Music from 1985–1989. She currently chairs MLA's Black Music Roundtable, was chair of the Preservation Committee from 1994–2001, and is a past president of the Association for Recorded Sound Collections.

TERRY SIMPKINS (Rhythm and Blues and Soul) is Director of Discovery and Access Services at Middlebury College, Middlebury, Vermont. Previously, he was Director of Collection Management and a music cataloger for Middlebury. Other institutions where he has worked include the Sibley Music Library at the Eastman School of Music in Rochester, NY, and St. Olaf College in Northfield, Minnesota. He holds degrees from MIT (BS, 1987), Westminster Choir College (MM, 1992), and the University of Illinois (MLS, 1996). He has published an article on cataloging popular music for *Cataloging & Classification Quarterly;* has served on various bibliographic control committees for the Music Library Association; and reviews recordings for Black Grooves, a music review site hosted by the Archives of African American Music & Culture (AAAMC) at Indiana University.

JEFFREY WANSER (Rhythm and Blues and Soul) is Collection Development Librarian and is in charge of the music collections at the Hiram College Library, Hiram, Ohio, where he has worked since 1984. He holds a BA in Anthropology from Adelphi University, an MA in Anthropology from SUNY-Binghamton, and an MLS from the University of Pittsburgh. Before becoming a librarian, he worked as a research archaeologist in New York and in Maryland. His research interests include early American industry, material culture, and American popular music; he also teaches anthropology for Hiram College. A relatively new member of the Music Library Association, his music-related articles have appeared in *The Encyclopedia of the Blues* (Routledge Press,

2006) and the *Encyclopedia of Alabama* (online, 2007). He is currently a contributor of jazz and folk music reviews to CD Hotlist and frequently writes book reviews for *Choice* and *Material Culture*.

EDITOR

DANIEL F. BOOMHOWER is director of the library at Dumbarton Oaks, a research center in Washington, DC, affiliated with Harvard University. Previously, he served as the Head of the Reader Services Section of the Music Division at the Library of Congress, as Head of the Performing Arts Library at Kent State University, and as Assistant Music Librarian at Princeton University. He studied music and library science at Case Western Reserve University in Cleveland, Ohio, the University of Illinois at Urbana-Champaign, and Wittenberg University in Springfield, Ohio. His study of music began with the violin and continues with research on the sources and methods used in music scholarship and on the reception of the music of Johann Sebastian Bach.

INDEX

Stars (★) are used to denote high-priority items.

A

Aaberg, Philip
  High Plains, 1346
  Ultimate New Age (collection), 1376
  Windham Hill: The First Ten Years (collection), 1377
  A Winter's Solstice (collection), 3321
AACM (Association for the Advancement of Creative Musicians). *See* jazz outside the mainstream: the AACM, BAG, and the lofts
AALY Trio. *Stumble,* 936
Aaronson, Irving. *The Roaring 'Twenties* (collection), 1080
ABBA. *Gold: Greatest Hits,* 1248
Abercrombie, John
  Gateway, 816.1
  John Abercrombie, 816.2
  Progressions: 100 Years of Jazz Guitar (collection), 481
Above the Law
  Black Mafia Life, 2698.1
  Livin' Like Hustlers, 2698.2
Abrams, Muhal Richard
  Amarcord Nino Rota (collection), 809

Big Band Renaissance: The Evolution of the Jazz Orchestra (collection), 739
Young at Heart, Wise in Time, 912
Abrams, Ray. *The Big Horn: The History of the Honkin' and Screamin' Saxophone* (collection), 2314
Abundant Life. *Story of Gospel Music* (collection), 2973
Abyssinian Baptist Choir
  ★*The Gospel Sound* (collection), 2964
  Shakin' the Rafters, 3054
Accents. *Birth of Soul: Special Chicago Edition* (collection), 2566
AC/DC. *Back in Black,* 2064
Ace, Johnny
  ★*The Best of Duke-Peacock Blues* (collection), 336
  Duke-Peacock's Greatest Hits (collection), 2421
  Johnny Ace Memorial Album, 348
  Respect: Aretha's Influences and Inspiration (collection), 2440
  ★*The R&B Box* (collection), 2239
  The Roots of Rock 'n' Roll, 1946–1954 (collection), 1755
Aceyalone
  All Balls Don't Bounce, Revisited, 2699.1

A Book of Human Language, 2699.2
Ackerman, William
  Passage, 1324.1
  A Quiet Revolution: 30 Years of Windham Hill (collection), 1372
  Solace: A Windham Hill Collection (collection), 1373
  Ultimate New Age (collection), 1376
  The William Ackerman Collection, 1324.2
  Windham Hill: The First Ten Years (collection), 1377
  A Winter's Solstice (collection), 3321
Acklin, Barbara
  Beg, Scream, and Shout! The Big Ol' Box of '60s Soul (collection), 2433
  The Story of Brunswick: The Classic Sound of Chicago Soul (collection), 2610
Acoustic Academy. *Jazz Lullaby* (collection), 3264
Act I. *The Spring Story: Essential 70s Soul* (collection), 2608
★Action. *Nuggets II: Original Artifacts from the British Empire and Beyond* (collection), 1791

Acuff, Roy
  ★*American Roots Music* (collection),
    1379
  *Classic Country Music: A Smithsonian
    Collection* (collection), 1382
  ★*The Essential Roy Acuff*, 1392.1
  *Jubilation! Great Gospel Performances,
    Vol. 3: Country Gospel* (collection),
    3112
  *King of the Hillbillies, Vol. 1: The First
    100 Commercial Sides, Some Never
    before Reissued* (Acuff), 1392.2
  *White Country Blues: A Lighter Shade of
    Blues*, 1427
  ★*Will the Circle Be Unbroken?*
    (collection), 1452
The Ad Libs. *The Sweetest Feeling: A Van
    McCoy Songbook* (collection), 2447
Adams, Bryan. *Like Omigod! The 80s Pop
    Culture Box (Totally)* (collection),
    1241
Adams, Faye. *The Herald Recordings*, 2241
Adams, George. *Decisions*, 937
Adams, Johnny
  *Action Speaks Louder Than Words:
    The Best of SSS International*
    (collection), 2588
  *Dave Godin's Deep Soul Treasures, Vols.
    1–4* (collection), 2435
  I Won't Cry: Original Ron Recordings,
    331
  *Night Train to Nashville: Music City
    Rhythm and Blues, 1945–1970,
    Vol. 1* (collection), 2377
  *Walking on a Tightrope: The Songs of
    Percy Mayfield*, 420
Adams, Marie. *Duke-Peacock's Greatest
    Hits* (collection), 2421
Adams, Oleta. *The Very Best of Oleta
    Adams*, 2393
Adams, Pepper. *Conjuration: Fat Tuesday's
    Session*, 869
Adams, Ryan. *Heartbreaker*, 1693
Adams, Yolanda
  Mountain High, Valley Low, 3075
  Wow Gospel #1s (collection), 3074
Adamson, Trevor. *World Playground:
    A Musical Adventure for Kids*
    (collection), 3230
Adderley, Cannonball
  *Cannonball Adderley Sextet: Live in
    Los Angeles, Tokyo and Lugano,
    1962–63*, 628.1
  Quintet in Chicago, 628.2
  Them Dirty Blues, 628.3
Adele
  19, 1249.1
  21, 1249.2
  25, 1249.3
Adkins, Trace
  Grand Ole Opry at Carnegie Hall
    (collection), 1619
  Greatest Hits Collection, Vol. 1, 1621

Adolescents. *American Hardcore*
    (collection), 1977
Adverts
  Crossing the Red Sea with the Adverts,
    2006
  No Thanks! The '70s Punk Rebellion
    (collection), 2003
Aebersold, Jamey
  *How to Play Jazz and Improvise, 6th
    Ed.*, 488.1
  Nothin' but Blues, 3rd Rev. Ed., 488.2
Aerosmith
  Greatest Hits, 1939.1
  O, Yeah! Ultimate Aerosmith Hits,
    1939.2, 1939.3
Aesop Rock
  Float, 2700.1
  Labor Days, 2700.2
African American general gospel
    collections, 2958–2975
African American gospel choirs, 3051–
    3073
  *Going Up Yonder: The Best of the
    Gospel Choirs* (collection), 3051
  Greatest Gospel Choirs (collection),
    3052
  *Stand Up: A Collection of America's
    Great Gospel Choirs* (collection),
    3053
African American gospel collections,
    1940s–1960s, 3030–3039
  ★*All God's Sons and Daughters:
    Chicago's Gospel Legends*
    (collection), 3030
  The Best of King Gospel (collection),
    3031
  The Best of Nashboro Gospel
    (collection), 3032
  Good News: 22 Gospel Greats
    (collection), 3033
  Greatest Gospel Gems (collection),
    3035
  The Great 1955 Shrine Concert
    (collection), 3034
  Jesus Put a Song in My Soul
    (collection), 3036
  *None but the Righteous: Chess Gospel
    Greats* (collection), 3037
  *Powerhouse Gospel on Independent
    Labels* (collection), 3038
  ★*Working the Road: The Golden Age of
    Chicago Gospel* (collection), 3039
African American gospel, contemporary.
    See contemporary African
    American gospel
African American gospel groups, 3040–
    3050
  *Best of Donald Lawrence and the Tri-
    City Singers: Restoring the Years*,
    3068
  Best of L.A. Mass Choir, 3067
  *The Best of Dorothy Love Coates and the
    Original Gospel Harmonettes*, 3045

★*The Best of Rev. James Cleveland and
    the G.M.W.A.*, 3058.1
*The Best of Shirley Caesar with the
    Caravans*, 3041.2
★*The Best of the Caravans*, 3041.1
*The Best of the Famous Davis Sisters of
    Philadelphia, PA*, 3044.1
The Best of the Roberta Martin Singers,
    3047
The Best of the Vee-Jay Years (Staple
    Singers), 3049.2
Davis Sisters 1949–1952, 3044.2
Essential John P. Kee, 3066
The Essential Hezekiah Walker, 3072
The First Twenty Years (Mississippi
    Mass Choir), 3069.1
Freedom Highway (Staple Singers),
    3049.1
Georgia Mass Choir, 3062
God and Me (Stars of Faith), 3050
*God's Property from Kirk Franklin's Nu
    Nation*, 3063
Good News (Meditation Singers),
    3046
Great Gospel Moments (Brunson), 3055
*I Don't Know What I Would Do without
    the Lord* (Clark), 3057
★*I Feel the Holy Spirit* (Clara Ward
    Singers), 3042
I Will Let Nothing Separate Me (Dallas
    Fort Worth Mass Choir), 3059
It Remains to Be Seen . . . (Mississippi
    Mass Choir), 3069.2
It's a New Day (Cleveland), 3058.2
*James Cleveland Sings with the World's
    Greatest Choirs*, 3058.3
*Jesus and Me: The Very Best of the
    Caravans with Albertina Walker*,
    3041.3
Just Having Church Live (Chicago Mass
    Choir), 3056
Live (Norwood), 3071
Lord Bring Me Down (Consolers),
    3043
Now, I Can See (Florida Mass Choir),
    3061
*Oh Happy Day: The Best of the Edwin
    Hawkins Singers*, 3060.2
★*Oh Happy Day* (Edwin Hawkins
    Singers), 3060.1
Saints in Praise: Their Very Best (West
    Angeles Church of God in Christ
    Mass Choir and Congregation),
    3073
Shakin' the Rafters (Abyssinian
    Baptist Gospel Choir), 3054
Throw out the Lifeline (Sallie Martin
    Singers), 3048
Touch Me Lord Jesus (Angelic Gospel
    Singers), 3040
We Offer Christ (Morton), 3070
Woman, Thou Art Loosed (Jakes),
    3065

African American gospel quartets, 3006–3029
  ★*A Warrior on the Battlefield: A Cappella Trail Blazers* (collection), 3011
  The Best of Mighty Clouds of Joy, 3022
  The Best of Swanee Quintet, 3028
  ★*The Best of the Dixie Hummingbirds*, 3014.1
  The Best of the Pilgrim Travelers, 3023
  The Best of the Sensational Nightingales, 3024
  The Earliest Negro Vocal Quartets, 1894–1928 (collection), 3006
  The Five Blind Boys of Mississippi, 3017
  Greatest Hits, Vol 1 (Williams Brothers), 3029
  Happy in the Service of the Lord: Memphis Gospel Quartet Heritage, the 1980s, Vols. 1 and 2 (collection), 3007
  The Harmonizing Four, 1943–1954, 3019.1
  I Hear Music in the Air: A Treasury of Gospel Music (collection), 3008
  Jesus Has Traveled This Road Before (Dixie Hummingbirds), 3014.2
  Jesus Hits Like the Atom Bomb (Sterling Jubilee Singers), 3026
  Kings of the Gospel Highway: The Golden Age of Gospel Quartets (collection), 3009
  Living Legends of Gospel: The Quartets, Vols. 1 and 2 (collection), 3010
  Living the Dream: Live in Washington, D.C. (Canton Spirituals), 3013
  Love Lifted Me / My Rock (Swan Silvertones), 3027.1
  Oh Lord Stand by Me / Marching up to Zion (Five Blind Boys of Alabama), 3016
  Pray for Me / Let's Go to Church Together (Swan Silvertones), 3027.2
  Retrospective (Blind Boys of Alabama), 3012
  ★*Sam Cooke with the Soul Stirrers: The Complete Specialty Records Recordings*, 3025.1
  Shine on Me (Soul Stirrers), 3025.2
  Standing in the Safety Zone (Fairfield Four), 3015.1
  Standing on the Rock (Fairfield Four), 3015.2
  Swan Silvertones, 1946–1951, 3027.3
  Swing Down Chariot (Golden Gate Quartet), 3018.1
  Tell the Angels: Live in Memphis (Lee Williams and the Spiritual QC's), 3021
  Travelin' Shoes (Golden Gate Quartet), 3018.2

  Very Best of the Highway Q. C.'S: Nearer My God, 3020
  When Day Is Done: Very Best of the Harmonizing Four, 3019.2
African American gospel solo personalities, 2987–3005
  ★*Amazing Grace: The Complete Recordings* (Franklin), 2997.1
  Aretha Gospel (Franklin), 2997.2
  Best of Mahalia Jackson, 2999.1
  Down Memory Lane (Cleveland), 2996.1
  Dragnet for Jesus (Carr), 2995
  Even Me: Four Decades of Bessie Griffin, 2998
  ★*First Lady of Gospel* (Caesar), 2994.1
  God Is Real (Little Richard), 3000
  Gospel Warriors: Over 50 Years of Great Solo Performances (collection), 2987
  ★*Gospels, Spirituals and Hymns; Vols. 1 and 2* (Jackson), 2999.2
  The Great Gospel Men (collection), 2988
  ★*The Great Gospel Women* (collection), 2989
  The Great Gospel Women, Vol. 2 (collection), 2990
  Headline News (Andrews), 2992
  ★*How I Got Over: The Apollo Records Sessions* (Jackson), 2999.3
  Live in Chicago (Caesar), 2994.2
  Mahalia Jackson, 2999.4
  Mother Smith and Her Children (collection), 2991
  ★*My Soul Looks Back: The Genius of Marion Williams*, 3005
  ★*Original Soul Sister* (Tharpe), 3003
  ★*Peace Be Still* (Cleveland), 2996.2
  Please Be Patient with Me (Walker), 3004
  Someone to Care: The Battle Sessions (Robinson), 3002
  Thunderbolt of the Middle West (May), 3001
  Too Close (Bradford), 2993
African Children's Choir. *It Takes the Whole Village*, 3231
African-American spirituals. *See* spirituals
Aiken, Ben. *The Best of Loma Records: The Rise and Fall of a 1960's Soul Label* (collection), 2590
Air
  Air Mail, 913
  Moon Safari, 2215
Air Supply. *Like Omigod! The 80s Pop Culture Box (Totally)* (collection), 1241
Akins, J. C. *Boddie Recording Company Cleveland, Ohio* (collection), 2569, 2570

Akiyoshi, Toshiko
  Big Band Renaissance: The Evolution of the Jazz Orchestra (collection), 739
  The Toshiko Akiyoshi Jazz Orchestra: Strive for Jive, 740
Alabama
  Classic Country Music: A Smithsonian Collection (collection), 1382
  Essential Alabama, 1622
Alabama blues. *See* Georgia, Alabama, and the East Coast blues
Alabama Sacred Harp Convention. *White Spirituals from the Sacred Harp: The Alabama Sacred Harp Convention*, 3117
Alabama Sacred Harp Singers
  ★*Goodbye Babylon* (collection), 2954
  I Belong to This Band: Eighty-Five Years of Sacred Harp Recordings (collection), 3111
  The Half Ain't Never Been Told, Vols. 1 and 2 (collection), 2956
Alan Parsons Project. *Like Omigod! The 80s Pop Culture Box (Totally)* (collection), 1241
Albam, Manny. *Big Band Renaissance: The Evolution of the Jazz Orchestra* (collection), 739
Albert, Don
  The Real Kansas City of the '20s, '30s, and '40s (collection), 552
  ★*Swing Time! The Fabulous Big Band Era* (collection), 1089
Alden, Howard. *Take Your Pick*, 711
Aler, John. *Where Home Is: Life in Nineteenth-Century Cincinnati, Crossroads of the East and West*, 102
Alexander, Angela. *Boddie Recording Company Cleveland, Ohio* (collection), 2569
Alexander, Arthur
  Boddie Recording Company Cleveland, Ohio (collection), 2570
  Lonely Just Like Me: The Final Chapter, 2448.1
  Muscle Shoals Sound (collection), 2605
  Night Train to Nashville: Music City Rhythm and Blues, 1945–1970, Vol. 1 (collection), 2377
  Night Train to Nashville: Music City Rhythm and Blues, 1945–1970, Vol. 2 (collection), 2378
  Rainbow Road: The Warner Brothers Recordings, 2448.2
  The Ultimate Arthur Alexander, 2448.3
Alexander, Texas
  ★*The Blues: A Smithsonian Collection of Classic Blues Singers* (collection), 145

Alexander, Texas (cont.)
   The Blues of Texas, Arkansas, and Louisiana (collection), 236
   ★*Legends of the Blues, Vol. 2* (collection), 151
Alexandria, Lorez. ★*The Jazz Singers: A Smithsonian Collection of Jazz Vocals from 1919–1994* (collection), 766
Alkaholiks, Tha. *21 and Over,* 2701
All Music (website), p3
Allan, Davie. *Halloween Hootenanny* (collection), 3348
Allen Brothers
   The Chattanooga Boys: Complete Recorded Works in Chronological Order, Vol. 1, 1927–1930, 1393
   Good for What Ails You: Music of the Medicine Shows (collection), 184
   The Roots of Rap: Classic Recordings of the 1920's and 30's (collection), 157
   White Country Blues: A Lighter Shade of Blues, 1427
Allen, Geri. *Segments,* 938
Allen, Henry "Red"
   Ride, Red, Ride, 565
   ★*Sound of Jazz* (collection), 487
Allen, Lee
   The Big Horn: The History of the Honkin' and Screamin' Saxophone (collection), 2314
   Crescent City Soul: The Sound of New Orleans, 1947–1974 (collection), 2564
Allen, Rance
   Best of the Rance Allen Group, 3076
   Story of Gospel Music (collection), 2973
Allen, Red
   The Best of Bluegrass, Vol. 1: Standards (collection), 1561
   Folkways Years, 1964–1983, 1568
Allen, Steve. *The Jack Kerouac Collection* (collection), 812
Allen, Terry. *Lubbock (on Everything),* 1694
Allen, William Francis. *Slave Songs of the United States: The Complete 1867 Collection of Slave Songs,* 33
Alley, Shelly Lee, and His Alley Cats. *Western Swing: 40 Bootstompers from the Golden Age* (collection), 1433
Allison, Ben. *Riding the Nuclear Tiger,* 939
Allison, Gene
   Night Train to Nashville: Music City Rhythm and Blues, 1945–1970, Vol. 1 (collection), 2377
   Night Train to Nashville: Music City Rhythm and Blues, 1945–1970, Vol. 2 (collection), 2378
   ★*The Vee-Jay Story: Celebrating 40 Years of Classic Hits* (collection), 2431

Allison, Luther. *Blues Fest: Modern Blues of the '70s* (collection), 408
Allison, Mose. *Greatest Hits,* 768
Allison's Sacred Harp Singers
   The Half Ain't Never Been Told, Vols. 1 and 2 (collection), 2956
   How Can I Keep from Singing: Early American Religious Music and Song, Vols. 1 and 2 (collection), 2957
The Allman Brothers
   Blues Fest: Modern Blues of the '70s (collection), 408
   Dreams, 1935.1
   Legends of Guitar: Rock–The '60s, Vol. 2 (collection), 1861
   ★*Live at Fillmore East,* 1935.2
Allyn, David
   Harry Warren (songwriter collection), 1114
   Jerome Kern (songwriter collection), 1104.1
   Oscar Hammerstein II (songwriter collection), 1102
Allyson, Karrin. *Ballads: Remembering John Coltrane* (Allyson), 769
Almanac Singers. ★*Brother, Can You Spare a Dime? American Song during the Great Depression* (collection), 1061
Almeida, Laurindo. *Brazilliance, Vol. 1,* 605
Alpert, Herb
   Definitive Hits, 1250
   The Look of Love: The Burt Bacharach Collection (collection), 1161
alt-country/Americana, 1693–1714
   Ain't Ever Satisfied: The Steve Earle Collection, 1701.1
   Aloha from Nashville (Scott), 1708
   Anthology 1968–1979 (Van Zandt), 1710
   Best (Keen), 1706
   Best of the Hightone Years (Miller), 1707
   BR5-49, 1696
   Car Wheels on a Gravel Road (Williams), 1714.1
   Cheatin' Heart Attack (Watson), 1711
   Contenders, 1697
   Country Love Songs (Fulks), 1704
   89/93: An Anthology (Uncle Tupelo), 1709.1
   Faithless Street (Whiskeytown), 1713.1
   ★*Guitar Town* (Earle), 1701.2
   Heartbreaker (Adams), 1693
   I Feel Alright (Earle), 1701.3
   Infamous Angel (Dement), 1700
   Interstate City (Alvin), 1695
   Lubbock (on Everything) (Allen), 1694
   No Depression (Uncle Tupelo), 1709.2
   Old Paint (Freakwater), 1703
   Revival (Welch), 1712

   Strangers Almanac (Whiskeytown), 1713.2
   Sweet Old World (Williams), 1714.2
   The Mountain (Earle and McCoury), 1702
   Tomorrow the Green Grass (Jayhawks), 1705
   Trinity Session (Cowboy Junkies), 1698
   We Do as We Please (Cowboy Nation), 1699
alternative rock
   All of This and Nothing (Psychedelic Furs), 2173
   American Hardcore: The History of American Punk Rock (collection), 2091
   Among the Living (Anthrax), 2095
   And All That Could Have Been (Nine Inch Nails), 2160.1
   Anthology (Throwing Muses), 2201
   At Action Park (Shellac), 2182
   Automatic for the People (R.E.M.), 2175.1
   Bad Brains, 2097.1
   Bad Moon Rising (Sonic Youth), 2190.1
   Bellavista Terrace: Best of the Go-Betweens, 2132.1
   The Bends (Radiohead), 2176.1
   ★*Best, Vol. 1* (Smiths), 2189
   Beyond and Back: The X Anthology, 2210.1
   The B-52s, 2096.1
   Bloodsugarsexmagik (Red Hot Chili Peppers), 2178
   Blue Lines (Massive Attack), 2148
   Blunderbuss (White), 2207.1
   Boo! (Was [Not Was]), 2205
   Brighten the Corners (Pavement), 2164.1
   Bring the Family (Hiatt), 2139
   Call the Doctor (Sleater-Kinney), 2185.1
   Children of God / World of Skin (Swans), 2198
   Chutes Too Narrow (Shins), 2183
   Compact XTC: The Singles, 1978–1985, 2211
   Corporate Ghost: The Videos, 1990–2002 (Sonic Youth), 2190.2
   Crackle (Bauhaus), 2098
   Crazy Rhythms (Feelies), 2125.1
   Crooked Rain, Crooked Rain (Pavement), 2164.2
   Damaged (Black Flag), 2104
   Daydream Nation (Sonic Youth), 2190.3
   De Stijl (The White Stripes), 2208.1
   Debut (Björk), 2103.1
   Decoration Day (Drive-By Truckers), 2120
   Definitely Maybe (Oasis), 2163.1

Diesel and Dust (Midnight Oil), 2151
Different Class (Pulp), 2174
Dig! (collection), 2092
Dig Me Out (Sleater-Kinney), 2185.2
Discography: The Complete Singles Collection (Pearl Jam), 2166
Document (R.E.M.), 2175.2
Dookie (Green Day), 2134
Doolittle (Pixies), 2167.1
Double Nickels on the Dime (Minutemen), 2153.1
The Downward Spiral (Nine Inch Nails), 2160.2
Dry (Harvey), 2137.1
Dummy (Portishead), 2169
Either/Or (Smith), 2188.1
Electric Version (New Pornographers), 2159
Electr-O-Pura (Yo La Tengo), 2213.1
Elephant (The White Stripes), 2208.2
Elliott Smith, 2188.2
Emperor Tomato Ketchup (Stereolab), 2195
End of Silence (Rollins Band), 2181
★*Eponymous* (R.E.M.), 2175.3
The Fat of the Land (Prodigy), 2172.1
The Fearless Freaks: The Wondrously Improbable Story of the Flaming Lips, 2126.1
Fever to Tell (Yeah Yeah Yeahs), 2212
Fire of Love (Gun Club), 2135
The First Two Records (Bikini Kill), 2102.1
Friends and Enemies (Frith and Kaiser), 2129
Frigid Stars (Codeine), 2113
The Generic Album (Flipper), 2127
Girls Can Tell (Spoon), 2193
Grace (Buckley), 2108.1
The Grotto (Hersh), 2138.1
Hail to the Thief (Radiohead), 2176.2
Half Machine Lip Moves (Chrome), 2111
Head over Heels (Cocteau Twins), 2112.1
Hear Nothing See Nothing (Discharge), 2119
Heaven up Here (Echo and the Bunnymen), 2121
Hips and Makers (Hersh), 2138.2
The Hot Rock (Sleater-Kinney), 2185.3
How I Loved You (Angels of Light), 2094
★*How Will the Wolf Survive?* (Los Lobos), 2146
I Can Hear the Heart Beating as One (Yo La Tengo), 2213.2
If I Should Fall from Grace with God Remastered (Pogues), 2168.1
In Utero (Nirvana), 2161.1
International (New Order), 2158

Isn't Anything (My Bloody Valentine), 2156.1
Jagged Little Pill (Morissette), 2154
Jane from Occupied Europe (Swell Maps), 2199
Jeff Buckley: Live in Chicago, 2108.2
Knuckle Down (Difranco), 2117.1
Ladies and Gentlemen We Are Floating in Space (Spiritualized), 2192
The Land of Rape and Honey (Ministry), 2152
Last Splash (Breeders), 2107
Lazaretto (White), 2207.2
Leftism (Leftfield), 2144
Let It Be (Replacements), 2179
Little Earthquakes (Amos), 2093
Live: Going Home (Blasters), 2105
Live through This (Hole), 2140
Live! Tonight! Sold Out!! (Nirvana), 2161.2
Locust Abortion Technician (Butthole Surfers), 2110
Loveless (My Bloody Valentine), 2156.2
Lullaby for Liquid Pig (Germano), 2131
Meat Puppets II, 2149
Meeting People Is Easy (Radiohead), 2176.3
Millions Now Living Will Never Die (Tortoise), 2202
Murmur (R.E.M.), 2175.4
Music for the Jilted Generation (Prodigy), 2172.2
★*Nevermind* (Nirvana), 2161.3
New Day Rising (Hüsker Dü), 2141.1
No Remorse (Motorhead), 2155
Not a Pretty Girl (Difranco), 2117.2
Nothing's Shocking (Jane's Addiction), 2142
Nowhere (Ride), 2180
★*Odelay* (Beck), 2099
★*OK Computer* (Radiohead), 2176.4
Only Life (Feelies), 2125.2
Peace Sells . . . But Who's Buying? (Megadeth), 2150
Pearl Jam: Touring Band 2000, 2165.1
Pills 'n' Thrills and Bellyaches (Happy Mondays), 2136
★*Post* (Björk), 2103.2
The Power Out (Electrelane), 2122
Psychocandy (Jesus and Mary Chain), 2143.1, 2143.2
Pure (Golden Palominos), 2133
Rage against the Machine (Rage against the Machine), 2177
Rain Dogs (Waits), 2204
Reign in Blood (Slayer), 2184
Repeater + 3 Songs (Fugazi), 2130
The Rich Man's Eight Track Tape (Big Black), 2101
Rid of Me (Harvey), 2137.2
Rock for Light (Bad Brains), 2097.2
Rock Steady (No Doubt), 2162

Rum, Sodomy, and the Lash (Pogues), 2168.2
Screamadelica (Primal Scream), 2171
Scum (Napalm Death), 2157
The Second Annual Report of Throbbing Gristle, 2200.1
Secret Name (Low), 2147
Siamese Dream (Smashing Pumpkins), 2187
Singles: 45s and under Remastered (Squeeze), 2194
The Singles (Bikini Kill), 2102.2
★*The Singles* (Pretenders), 2170
Sister (Sonic Youth), 2190.4
16 Lovers Lane (Go-Betweens), 2132.2
Slanted and Enchanted (Pavement), 2164.3
Slow Century (Pavement), 2164.4
The Soft Bulletin (Flaming Lips), 2126.2
Songs the Lord Taught Us (Cramps), 2114
Spiderland (Slint), 2186.1
Staring at the Sea: The Singles [Import] (Cure), 2115
The Stone Roses, 2196
Sublime, 2197
Summer Teeth (Wilco), 2209.1
Super Are (Boredoms), 2106
Superunknown (Soundgarden), 2191
Surfer Rosa (Pixies), 2167.2
Ten (Pearl Jam), 2165.2
There's Nothing Wrong with Love (Built to Spill), 2109
Throbbing Gristle Bring You 20 Jazz Funk Greats, 2200.2
Time Capsule: Songs for a Future Generation (B-52s), 2096.2
To Bring You My Love (Harvey), 2137.3
Totally Exploited, 2124
Treasure (Cocteau Twins), 2112.2
Tweez (Slint), 2186.2
Violator (Depeche Mode), 2116
Violent Femmes, 2203
★*Vivid* (Living Colour), 2145
Walking Wounded (Everything but the Girl), 2123
We Jam Econo (Minutemen), 2153.2
Weezer, 2206
Welcome Interstate Managers (Fountains of Wayne), 2128
What Fun Life Was (Bedhead), 2100
(What's the Story) Morning Glory? (Oasis), 2163.2
White Blood Cells (The White Stripes), 2208.3
X: The Unheard Music, 2210.2
Yankee Hotel Foxtrot (Wilco), 2209.2
You're Living All over Me (Dinosaur Jr.), 2118
Zen Arcade (Hüsker Dü), 2141.2

Alternative TV
    The Image Has Cracked, 2007
    No Thanks! The '70s Punk Rebellion
        (collection), 2003
Althouse, Jay
    Christmas for Solo Singers, 3273
    Spirituals for Solo Singers: 11 Spirituals
        Arranged for Solo Voice and Piano;
        for Recitals, Concerts and
        Contests, 34
Alvin, Dave. *Interstate City,* 1695
Amant. *The Best of T. K. Disco*
        (collection), 2656
Amazing Rhythm Aces. *Stacked Deck,*
        1453
Ambassador. *Stop the Funeral,* 3168
ambient new age, 1320–1323
    Ambient 1: Music for Airports (Eno),
        1322
    Ambient 2: The Plateaux of Mirror
        (Budd), 1320.1
    Pavilion of Dreams (Budd), 1320.2
    Peace Time (DeJohnette), 1321
    Penguin Cafe Orchestra (Penguin Cafe
        Orchestra), 1323
Amboy Dukes
    Nuggets: A Classic Collection from the
        Psychedelic Sixties (collection),
        1809
    ★*Nuggets: Artifacts of the First*
        Psychedelic Era (collection), 1808
Amerian, Michael. *Starflight 1*
        (collection), 1374
American Brass Quintet Brass Band
    Music of the 26th N.C. Regimental
        Band, CSA, Vol. 1: A Storm in the
        Land, 64.1
    Music of the 26th N.C. Regimental
        Band, CSA, Vol. 2: Cheer, Boys,
        Cheer!, 64.2
    The Yankee Brass Band: Music from
        Mid-Nineteenth Century America, 81
American Quartet
    The Phonographic Yearbook, 1912:
        Waitin' on the Levee (collection),
        1077
    The Phonographic Yearbook, 1922: An
        Angel's Voice I Hear (collection),
        1078
    ★*Praise the Lord and Pass the*
        Ammunition: Songs of World Wars I
        and II (collection), 1079
American Serenade Band. *The Golden Age*
        of Brass, Vols. 1–3, 82
Americus Brass Band. *Music of the Civil*
        War, 65
Ames Brothers
    ★*Nipper's Greatest Hits: The 50's, Vol. 1*
        (collection), 1163
    Nipper's Greatest Hits: The 50's, Vol. 2
        (collection), 1164
Ames Harris Desert Water. *Eccentric Soul:*
        The Young Disciples (collection),
        2562

Ammons, Albert
    Barrelhouse Boogie (collection), 250,
        521
    ★*Cuttin' the Boogie: Piano Blues and*
        Boogie Woogie (collection), 251
    The First Day, 566
    ★*From Spirituals to Swing: The*
        Legendary 1938 and 1939 Carnegie
        Hall Concerts Produced by John
        Hammond (collection), 564
    Hey! Piano Man (collection), 254
    When the Sun Goes Down 4: That's All
        Right (collection), 271
Ammons, Gene. *Boss Tenor,* 629
Amos, Daniel. *Best of Christian Rock*
        (1970–1986), Vol. 1 (collection),
        3135
Amos, Tori
    Little Earthquakes, 2093
    Whatever: The '90s Pop and Culture
        Box (collection), 1244
Amram, David. *Amarcord Nino Rota*
        (collection), 809
Ancient Dreams. *The World of Private*
        Music (collection), 1378
Ancient Future
    Narada Decade: The Anniversary
        Collection (collection), 1367
    Natural Rhythms, 1359
Andemicael, Awert. *Black Manhattan:*
        Theater and Dance Music of James
        Reese Europe, Will Marion Cook,
        and Members of the Legendary Clef
        Club (collection), 1060
Anderson, Bill. *Definitive Collection,* 1454
Anderson, Ernestine
    Birth of Soul, 4 Vols. (collection), 2434
    The Definitive Collection (songwriter
        collection), 1101.1
    ★*The Jazz Singers: A Smithsonian*
        Collection of Jazz Vocals from
        1919–1994 (collection), 766
    Never Make Your Move Too Soon, 770
Anderson, Fred. *Dark Day: Live at the*
        Museum of Contemporary Art / Live
        in Verona, 914
★Anderson, Ivie. *The Jazz Singers:*
        A Smithsonian Collection of
        Jazz Vocals from 1919–1994
        (collection), 766
Anderson, John. *Greatest Hits,* 1623
Anderson, Kip. *The Fire / Fury Records*
        Story (collection), 2422
Anderson, Leroy
    The Leroy Anderson Collection, 1176
    The Leroy Anderson Songbook: A
        Centennial Celebration (songwriter
        collection), 1173
Anderson, Little Willie. *Swinging the Blues*
        (Anderson), 293
Anderson, Lynn
    Greatest Hits, 1455
    Have a Nice Decade: The '70s Pop
        Culture Box (collection),

Anderson, Marian
    A First-Time Buyer's Guide to American
        Negro Spirituals (collection), 32
    Spirituals, 35
Anderson, Pink
    Good for What Ails You: Music of the
        Medicine Shows (collection), 184
    A Richer Tradition: Country Blues and
        String Band Music (collection), 187
    Songsters and Saints: Vocal Traditions
        on Race Records, Vol. 1 (collection),
        190
Anderson, Robert
    ★*All God's Sons and Daughters:*
        Chicago's Gospel Legends
        (collection), 3030
    ★*The Gospel Sound of Spirit Feel*
        (collection), 2965
    Greatest Gospel Gems (collection), 3035
    The Great Gospel Men (collection), 2988
    ★*Working the Road: The Golden Age of*
        Chicago Gospel (collection), 3039
Anderson, William E., pvii–viii
Andrea True Connection. *Disco Box*
        (collection), 2644
Andrews, Inez
    Headline News, 2992
    Testify! The Gospel Box (collection),
        2974
    The Rough Guide to Gospel (collection),
        2970
Andrews, Julie
    Alan Jay Lerner (songwriter
        collection), 1105.1
    James Van Heusen (songwriter
        collection), 1112.1
    Oscar Hammerstein II (songwriter
        collection), 1102
The Andrews Sisters
    Cole Porter (songwriter collection),
        1108.1
    ★*50th Anniversary Collection, Vol. 1,*
        1119
    The Flapper Box (collection), 1064
    Frank Loesser (songwriter collection),
        1106.1
    Harold Arlen (songwriter collection),
        1095.1
    Sentimental Journey: Capitol's Great
        Ladies of Song (collection), 1166
    Songs That Got Us through World
        War II (collection), 1085
    Songs That Got Us through World
        War II, Vol. 2 (collection), 1086
    Vincent Youmans (songwriter
        collection), 1118
Angelic Gospel Singers
    The Best of Nashboro Gospel
        (collection), 3032
    ★*The Gospel Sound* (collection), 2964
    ★*Jubilation! Great Gospel Performances,*
        Vol. 1: Black Gospel (collection),
        2966
    Touch Me Lord Jesus, 3040

Angels. *The Best of the Girl Groups, Vols. 1 and 2* (collection), 2321

Angels of Light. *How I Loved You,* 2094

Animals
   Best of the Animals, 1793
   25 Hits from the British Invasion (collection), 1792

Anka, Paul. *30th Anniversary Collection: His All Time Greatest Hits,* 1177

Anonymous
   American Angels, 6.1
   Gloryland, 6.2

Anthony and the Sophomores. *The Doo-Wop Box II* (collection), 2323

Anthony, Chubby. *Mountain Music Bluegrass Style* (collection), 1566

Anthrax. *Among the Living,* 2095

Antipop Consortium. *Arrhythmia,* 2702

Any Old Time String Band. *16 Down Home Country Classics* (collection), 1385

Aphex Twin
   Richard D. James Album, 2216.1
   Selected Ambient Works, 85–92, 2216.2
   Selected Ambient Works, Vol. II, 2216.3

Apollas. *The Best of Loma Records: The Rise and Fall of a 1960's Soul Label* (collection), 2590

Apollo Male Quartette. *The Earliest Negro Vocal Quartets, 1894–1928* (collection), 3006

Appleby, Amy. *The Library of Ragtime and Early Blues Piano,* 126

Appling, William. *William Appling Plays Scott Joplin & J. S. Bach,* 127

Archia, Tom. *The Big Horn: The History of the Honkin' and Screamin' Saxophone* (collection), 2314

Archies. *25 All-Time Greatest Bubblegum Hits* (collection), 1811

Argeggio. *Disco Box* (collection), 2644

Arie, India. *See* India.Arie

Arkenstone, David
   Narada Decade: The Anniversary Collection (collection), 1367
   Narada Wilderness Collection (collection), 1368
   A Quiet Revolution: 30 Years of Windham Hill (collection), 1372
   Solace: A Windham Hill Collection (collection), 1373
   Valley in the Clouds / In the Wake of the Wind, 1316

Arlen, Harold
   ★*The Crooners* (collection), 1062
   Harold Arlen Songbook (songwriter collection), 1095.2
   Harold Arlen (songwriter collection), 1095.1

Armatrading, Joan. *Greatest Hits,* 2040

Armstrong, Howard. *Martin, Bogan, and Armstrong / That Old Gang of Mine* (Martin, Bogan, and Armstrong), 401

Armstrong, Louis, 510.1–510.7
   ★*American Popular Song: Six Decades of Songwriters and Singers* (collection), 1059
   An Anthology of Big Band Swing (collection), 528
   ★*At the Jazz Band Ball: Early Hot Jazz, Song, and Dance* (collection), 470
   The Big Band Recordings, 510.1
   Bing Crosby and Some Jazz Friends (Crosby), 1125.2
   ★*Central Avenue Sounds: Jazz in Los Angeles* (collection), 471
   The Classic Hoagy Carmichael (songwriter collection), 1097.1
   The Complete Hot Five and Hot Seven Recordings, 510.2
   The Definitive Collection, 771.1
   The Definitive Collection (songwriter collection), 1101.1
   Dorothy Fields (songwriter collection), 1100
   ★*Ella Fitzgerald and Louis Armstrong,* 771.2
   The First of the Singer Songwriters: Key Cuts (Carmichael), 1124
   Gospel: Negro Spirituals / Gospel Songs, 1926–1942 (collection), 2963
   The Great Depression: American Music in the '30s (collection), 1066
   The Great Summit: Master Takes, 712.1
   Hipsters' Holiday: Vocal Jazz and R&B Classics (collection), 3313
   ★*Jazz on a Summer's Day* (collection), 664
   ★*The Jazz Singers: A Smithsonian Collection of Jazz Vocals from 1919–1994* (collection), 766
   Joe Franklin Presents . . . The Roaring '20s Roar Again (collection), 1069
   Johnny Mercer (songwriter collection), 1107.1
   ★*Ken Burns Jazz Collection: Louis Armstrong,* 510.3
   ★*Ken Burns Jazz: The Story of America's Music* (collection), 478
   Legendary Big Band Singers (collection), 767
   Louis Armstrong Live in '59, 510.4
   Louis Armstrong Plays W. C. Handy, 712.2
   ★*The Music Goes Round and Around: The Golden Years of Tin Pan Alley, 1930–1939* (collection), 1070
   Oscar Hammerstein II (songwriter collection), 1102
   Rhythm Saved the World, 510.5
   Riverside History of Classic Jazz (collection), 499
   Satch Plays Fats, 712.3
   Satchmo: A Musical Autobiography, 712.4
   Satchmo: Louis Armstrong, 510.6
   ★*The Smithsonian Collection of Classic Jazz* (collection), 486
   Songs That Got Us through World War II (collection), 1085
   Sugar: The Best of the Complete RCA Victor Recordings, 510.7
   The Very Best of Cole Porter (songwriter collection), 1108.3
   Waller / Razaf (songwriter collection), 1113.2
   ★*Yes, Sir, That's My Baby: The Golden Years of Tin Pan Alley* (collection), 1094

Armstrong, Michael
   Lullaby Renditions of Radiohead, 3265.2
   Lullaby Renditions of the Cure, 3265.1

Armstrong, Richard
   ★*Nashville Jumps: Blues and Rhythm on Nashville Independent Labels 1945–1955* (collection), 2376
   Night Train to Nashville: Music City Rhythm and Blues, 1945–1970, Vol. 2 (collection), 2378

Armstrong Twins. *16 Down Home Country Classics* (collection), 1385

Armstrong, Vanessa Bell
   Best of Vanessa Bell Armstrong, 3077
   Story of Gospel Music (collection), 2973

Arnold, Billy Boy
   Blues Fest: Modern Blues of the '90s (collection), 410
   ★*The Vee-Jay Story: Celebrating 40 Years of Classic Hits* (collection), 2431

Arnold, Eddy
   Classic Country: Kings of Country (collection), 1381
   Classic Country Music: A Smithsonian Collection (collection), 1382
   Seven Decades of Hits/Greatest Songs, 1456.1
   ★*Ultimate Eddy Arnold,* 1456.2

Arnold, James "Kokomo"
   Back to the Crossroads: The Roots of Robert Johnson (collection), 212
   ★*Blues Classics* (collection), 146
   ★*The Blues: A Smithsonian Collection of Classic Blues Singers* (collection), 145
   Bottleneck Trendsetters of the 1930s (collection), 266
   The Road to Robert Johnson and Beyond (collection), 221

Arrested Development. *3 Years, 5 Months, and 2 Days in the Life of . . .,* 2703

Arrows. *Eccentric Soul: The Bandit Label* (collection), 2597

Art Ensemble of Chicago
   Americans Swinging in Paris: The Pathe Sessions, 915.1
   Full Force, 915.2
   ★*Urban Bushmen,* 915.3

art rock and rock theater, 1952–1971
    Animal Serenade (Reed), 1965.1
    Another Green World (Eno), 1957.1
    Autobahn (Kraftwerk), 1962.1
    Before and after Science (Eno), 1957.2
    Best of Bowie, 1952.1, 1952.2
    Best of Roxy Music (Ferry), 1959.1
    Can, 1955.1
    The Condensed 21st Century Guide to King Crimson, 1969–2003, 1961
    Ege Bamyas (Can), 1955.2
    Eskimo (Residents), 1966.1
    Faust / So Far, 1958
    For Your Pleasure: The Second Roxy Music Album (Ferry), 1959.2
    Fragile (Yes), 1971
    God Bless the Red Krayola and All Who Sail with It, 1964
    Icky Flix (Residents), 1966.2
    The Lamb Lies Down on Broadway (Genesis), 1960
    Man in a Deaf Corner: Anthology, 1963–1970 (Soft Machine), 1967.1
    Minimum-Maximum (Kraftwerk), 1962.2
    Neu!, 1963
    NYC Man: The Collections (Reed), 1965.2
    Original Sound of Sheffield '78/'82 (Cabaret Voltaire), 1953
    Paris 1919 (Cale), 1954
    The Residents' Commercial Album, 1966.3
    ★*The Rise and Fall of Ziggy Stardust* (Bowie), 1952.3
    Rock Bottom (Wyatt), 1970
    Scott 4, 1969
    Song Cycle (Parks), 1968
    Tago Mago (Can), 1955.3
    Third (Soft Machine), 1967.2
    Trans-Europe Express (Kraftwerk), 1962.3
    Unrest (Cow), 1956
    Walk on the Wild Side: The Best of Lou Reed, 1965.3
Artistics. *The Story of Brunswick: The Classic Sound of Chicago Soul* (collection), 2610
Ashford and Simpson. *The Very Best of Ashford and Simpson,* 2242
Ashley, Clarence
    ★*Anthology of American Folk Music, Vols. 1–3* (collection), 1386
    Greenback Dollar, 1395
    Old-Time Mountain Ballads (collection), 1390
Ashton, Susan. *Angels of Mercy,* 3138
Asleep at the Wheel
    Coming' Right at Ya / Texas Gold, 1434.1
    Texas Music, Vol. 2: Western Swing and Honky Tonk (collection), 1432
    Western Swing: 40 Bootstompers from the Golden Age, 1434.2

Association for the Advancement of Creative Musicians (AACM). *See* jazz outside the mainstream: the AACM, BAG, and the lofts
Astaire, Adele. *Fascinating Rhythm: George Gershwin* (songwriter collection), 1101.2
Astaire, Fred
    Alan Jay Lerner (songwriter collection), 1105.1
    ★*American Popular Song: Six Decades of Songwriters and Singers* (collection), 1059
    Arthur Schwartz (songwriter collection), 1110.2
    Cole Porter (songwriter collection), 1108.1
    The Definitive Collection (songwriter collection), 1101.1
    Dorothy Fields (songwriter collection), 1100
    Essential Fred Astaire, 1120.1
    Fascinating Rhythm: George Gershwin (songwriter collection), 1101.2
    The Flapper Box (collection), 1064
    George Gershwin (songwriter collection), 1101.3
    Great American Songbook, 1120.2
    Harold Arlen (songwriter collection), 1095.1
    Harry Warren (songwriter collection), 1114
    Irving Berlin: A Hundred Years (songwriter collection), 1096.3
    Irving Berlin (songwriter collection), 1096.1
    ★*Nipper's Greatest Hits: The 30's, Vol. 1* (collection), 1072
    The Roaring 'Twenties (collection), 1080
    This Is Art Deco (collection), 1090
    Top Hat: Hits from Hollywood, 1120.3
    The Very Best of Cole Porter (songwriter collection), 1108.3
    Vincent Youmans (songwriter collection), 1118
Asylum Street Spankers
    The Bottle Let Me Down: Songs for Bumpy Wagon Rides (collection), 3191
    Mommy Says No!, 3195
Atkins, Ben. *The Complete Goldwax Singles, Vol. 3* (collection), 2593
Atkins, Chet
    Essential Chet Atkins, 1457.1
    Guitar Legend: The RCA Years, 1457.2
    Legends of Guitar: Rock–The '60s, Vol. 1 (collection), 1860
Atlantic Starr. *Ultimate Collection,* 2243
Atmosphere
    Godlovesugly, 2704.1
    Headshots: Se7en, 2704.2

Atomic Aces. *Boddie Recording Company Cleveland, Ohio* (collection), 2569, 2570
Auld, Georgie
    New York, New York [1985] (Burns and Auld), 1054.1
    New York, New York [2004] (Burns and Auld), 1054.2
Auldridge, Mike. *Dobro / Blues and Bluegrass,* 1569
Austin, Gene
    ★*American Popular Song: Six Decades of Songwriters and Singers* (collection), 1059
    ★*The Crooners* (collection), 1062
    ★*Nipper's Greatest Hits: The 20's* (collection), 1071
    25 Sweethearts of Yesteryear (collection), 1092
    ★*Yes, Sir, That's My Baby: The Golden Years of Tin Pan Alley* (collection), 1094
Austin, James. *Good God! Born Again Funk* (collection), 2614
Austin, Lee. *Gimme Your Hand, J-B!* (collection), 2613
Austin, Patti. *The Very Best of Patti Austin: The Singles, 1969–1986,* 2449
Autry, Gene
    ★*Billboard Greatest Christmas Hits, 1935–1954* (collection), 3293
    ★*Brother, Can You Spare a Dime? American Song during the Great Depression* (collection), 1061
    Classic Country Music: A Smithsonian Collection (collection), 1382
    ★*The Essential Gene Autry,* 1396.1
    That Silver Haired Daddy of Mine, 1396.2
Avalon. *CCM Top 100: Greatest Songs in Christian Music, Vol. 1* (collection), 3136
avant garde jazz. *See* jazz outside the mainstream: the AACM, BAG, and the lofts
Avatar Brass Quintet. *Magnetic Rags: Ragtime for Brass,* 128
Average White Band. *Pickin' up the Pieces: The Best of Average White Band,* 2616
Avishai Cohen Trio. *Icons among Us* (collection), 934
Avons. *Night Train to Nashville: Music City Rhythm and Blues, 1945–1970, Vol. 1* (collection), 2377
Ayler, Albert
    Bells / Prophecy, 679.1
    Spirits, 679.2
    Spiritual Unity, 679.3

B

babies' and toddlers' music, 3184–3190
    Baby Loves Jazz: Go Baby Go!, 3185
    Baby Songs Original (Palmer), 3190

Dancin' Magic (Bartels), 3186.1

Kidsongs: I'd Like to Teach the World to Sing (collection), 3184

Sillytime Magic (Bartels), 3186.2

Songs and Games for Toddlers (McGrath and Smithrim), 3188

Toddler (Hickman), 3187

Wiggleworms Love You (Old Town School of Folk Music), 3189

Baby Dodds. *Talking and Drum Solos / Country Brass Bands,* 504

Baby Lloyd. *The Best of Loma Records: The Rise and Fall of a 1960's Soul Label* (collection), 2590

Baby Loves Jazz Band. *Baby Loves Jazz: Go Baby Go!,* 3185

Babyface. *The Essential Babyface,* 2394

Bach, Johann Sebastian. *Mr. Bach Comes to Call,* 3255

Bacharach, Burt. *The Songs of Bacharach and David* (songwriter collection), 1174

Back Street Boys. *D.I.Y. Blank Generation: The New York Scene* (collection), 1978

Backstrom, Margaret. *The Big Horn: The History of the Honkin' and Screamin' Saxophone* (collection), 2314

Bad Brains
American Hardcore (collection), 1977
Bad Brains, 2097.1
Rock for Light, 2097.2

Bad English. *80's Pop Hits* (collection), 1238

The Bad Plus. *Icons among Us* (collection), 934

Badger, Perk. *Eccentric Soul: The Outskirts of Deep City* (collection), 2565

Badu, Erykah
Mama's Gun, 2380.1
New Amerykah, Part One: 4th World War, 2380.2

BAG (Black Artists Group). *See* jazz outside the mainstream: the AACM, BAG, and the lofts

Bailey, DeFord
Harmonica Blues: Great Harmonica Performances of the 1920s and '30s (collection), 185
The Legendary DeFord Bailey: Country Music's First Black Star, 1397
When the Sun Goes Down 1: Walk Right In (collection), 159

Bailey, Derek. *Figuring,* 834

★Bailey, Little Maxie. *Nashville Jumps: Blues and Rhythm on Nashville Independent Labels 1945–1955* (collection), 2376

★Bailey, Max Blues. *Nashville Jumps: Blues and Rhythm on Nashville Independent Labels 1945–1955* (collection), 2376

Bailey, Mildred
Alec Wilder (songwriter collection), 1117.1
★*American Popular Song: Six Decades of Songwriters and Singers* (collection), 1059
Arthur Schwartz (songwriter collection), 1110.2
The Classic Hoagy Carmichael (songwriter collection), 1097.1
Duke Ellington (songwriter collection), 1099.1
The First of the Singer Songwriters: Key Cuts (Carmichael), 1124
Hoagy Carmichael (songwriter collection), 1097.2
Irving Berlin: A Hundred Years (songwriter collection), 1096.3
★*The Jazz Singers: A Smithsonian Collection of Jazz Vocals from 1919–1994* (collection), 766
Johnny Mercer (songwriter collection), 1107.1
★*The Music Goes Round and Around: The Golden Years of Tin Pan Alley, 1930–1939* (collection), 1070
The Rockin' Chair Lady, 772
★*Sophisticated Ladies* (collection), 1087
Vincent Youmans (songwriter collection), 1118
Waller / Razaf (songwriter collection), 1113.2

Bailey, Pearl
Arthur Schwartz (songwriter collection), 1110.2
Dorothy Fields (songwriter collection), 1100
Harold Arlen (songwriter collection), 1095.1
Stars of the Apollo (collection), 2240

Baker, Anita
A Night of Rapture, 2381
Rapture, 2244

Baker, Bob and the Pike County Boys. *Mountain Music Bluegrass Style* (collection), 1566

Baker, Chet
The Best of Chet Baker Plays, 606.1
Chet Baker Live in '64 and '79, 606.2
★*Ken Burns Jazz: The Story of America's Music* (collection), 478
Yule Struttin': A Blue Note Christmas (collection), 3323

Baker, David. *Jazz Improvisation: A Comprehensive Method of Study for All Players,* 489

Baker, Etta. *Blues Routes* (collection), 413

Baker, Kenny
Master Fiddler, 1570
★*Praise the Lord and Pass the Ammunition: Songs of World Wars I and II* (collection), 1079
16 Down Home Country Classics (collection), 1385

Baker, LaVern
★*Atlantic R&B, 1947–1974* (collection), 2418
★*Atlantic Soul, 1959–1975* (collection), 2589
★*The R&B Box* (collection), 2239
Soul on Fire: The Best of LaVern Baker, 2245
The Story of Brunswick: The Classic Sound of Chicago Soul (collection), 2610

Baker, Mickey
In the '50s: Hit, Git, and Split, 2246
★*Legends of Guitar: Rock–The '50s, Vol. 2* (collection), 1750

Baker, Sam. *Night Train to Nashville: Music City Rhythm and Blues, 1945–1970, Vol. 1* (collection), 2377

Balintine, Linda. *Eccentric Soul: The Bandit Label* (collection), 2597

Ballard, Hank
Gimme Your Hand, J-B! (collection), 2613
The Roots of Rock 'n' Roll, 1946–1954 (collection), 1755
Sexy Ways: The Best of Hank Ballard and the Midnighters, 2247
★*The Vee-Jay Story: Celebrating 40 Years of Classic Hits* (collection), 2431

Ballard, Kaye. *George Gershwin* (songwriter collection), 1101.3

★Ballew, Smith. *The Crooners* (collection), 1062

★Ballinger, Robert. *Working the Road: The Golden Age of Chicago Gospel* (collection), 3039

★Bambaataa, Afrika. *Looking for the Perfect Beat, 1980–1985,* 2705

The Band
★*The Band,* 1821.1
The Basement Tapes, 1823.5
Greatest Hits, 1821.2
Heaven Must Have Sent You: The Holland/Dozier/Holland Story (collection), 2436
The Last Waltz, 1821.3
Music from Big Pink, 1821.4

band music, 81–90.6
Arthur Pryor: Trombone Soloist of the Sousa Band, 88
Carnaval (Marsalis), 87
Cornet Favorites; Highlights from Cousins (Schwartz), 89
The Golden Age of Brass, Vols. 1–3 (American Serenade Band), 82
The Golden Age of the American March (Edwin Franko Goldman Band), 84
Grafulla's Favorites, 85
A Grand Sousa Concert (Sousa), 90.1
Music for Wind Band, Vols. 1–15 (Sousa), 90.2
The Original All-American Sousa!, 90.3

band music (cont.)
    Screamers: March Time (Eastman Wind
        Ensemble), 83
    *Sousa Marches Recorded by the Sousa
        Band,* 90.4
    *Sousa's Great Marches in Piano
        Transcription: Original Sheet Music
        of 23 Works* (Sousa), 90.5
    *Under the Big Top: 100 Years of Circus
        Music* (Great American Main Street
        Band), 86
    *The United States Marine Band
        Performs Sousa Marches,* 90.6
    *The Yankee Brass Band: Music from
        Mid-Nineteenth Century America*
        (American Brass Quintet Brass
        Band), 81
Bandy, Moe. *Honky Tonk Amnesia: The
        Hard Country Sound of Moe Bandy,*
        1458
Bang, Billy. *Rainbow Gladiator,* 916
The Bangles
    80's Pop Hits (collection), 1238
    Greatest Hits, 2041
Banks, Bessie. *Dave Godin's Deep Soul
        Treasures, Vols. 1–4* (collection),
        2435
Banner, David. *Certified,* 2706
Baraka, Sho. *Lions and Liars,* 3169
★Barbarians. *Nuggets: Artifacts of the First
        Psychedelic Era* (collection), 1808
Barbecue Bob
    ★*The Blues: A Smithsonian
        Collection of Classic Blues Singers*
        (collection), 145
    Chocolate to the Bone, 245
    The Georgia Blues (collection), 242
    *The Great Depression: American Music
        in the '30s* (collection), 1066
    ★*Legends of the Blues, Vol. 2*
        (collection), 151
    ★*The Story of the Blues* (collection),
        158
Barcelona Pavilion. *Colours Are Brighter:
        Songs for Children and Grown Ups
        Too* (collection), 3193
Bare, Bobby. *The Best of Bobby Bare,*
        1459
Barefoot Bill. *Alabama Blues* (collection),
        240
Barenaked Ladies
    For the Kids Three! (collection), 3209
    ★*Snack Time!,* 3196
Barfield, Warren. *CCM Top 100: Greatest
        Songs in Christian Music, Vol. 1*
        (collection), 3136
The Bar-Kays
    *Beg, Scream, and Shout! The Big Ol'
        Box of '60s Soul* (collection), 2433
    The Best of the Bar-Kays, 2450, 2617
    *The Complete Stax/Volt Soul Singles,
        Vol. 2: 1968–1971* (collection),
        2595

*Top of the Stax, Vol. 2: Twenty Greatest
        Hits* (collection), 2612
    ★*What It Is! Funky Soul and Rare
        Grooves* (collection), 2615
Barker, Danny. *Don't Give the Name a
        Bad Place: Types and Stereotypes in
        American Musical Theater, 1870–
        1900* (collection), 1063
Barkley, Gnarls. *St. Elsewhere,* 2707
Barnard, Junior. *Legends of Western Swing
        Guitar* (collection), 1430
Barnes, F. C. *Testify! The Gospel Box*
        (collection), 2974
Barnes, Luther and the Sunset Jubilaires.
        *Living Legends of Gospel: The Quar-
        tets, Vols. 1 and 2* (collection), 3010
Barnes, Mae. *Dorothy Fields* (songwriter
        collection), 1100
Barnes, Roosevelt "Booba." *Heartbroken
        Man,* 421
Barnes, Sidney. *Eccentric Soul: The Nickel
        and Penny Labels* (collection), 2567
Barnet, Charlie
    An Anthology of Big Band Swing
        (collection), 528
    ★*Big Band Jazz: From the Beginnings to
        the Fifties* (collection), 529
    *Big Band Renaissance: The Evolution of
        the Jazz Orchestra* (collection), 739
    ★*Nipper's Greatest Hits: The 40's, Vol. 1*
        (collection), 1073
    ★*Swing Time! The Fabulous Big Band
        Era* (collection), 1089
Barrett, Pastor T. L. *Good God! Born
        Again Funk* (collection), 2614
Barrett Sisters. ★*Say Amen, Somebody*
        (collection), 2971
Barrett, Syd
    Barrett, 1870.1
    The Madcap Laughs, 1870.2
Barron, Kenny. *Wanton Spirit,* 940
Bartels, Joanie
    Dancin' Magic, 3186.1
    Lullaby Magic, 3266
    Sillytime Magic, 3186.2
Bartholomew, Dave. *Crescent City Soul:
        The Sound of New Orleans, 1947–
        1974* (collection), 2564
★Barton, Eileen. *Sentimental Journey: Pop
        Vocal Classics, Vol. 2* (collection),
        1168
Bartz, Gary. *Harlem Bush Music,* 870
Bascomb, Paul. *The Big Horn: The History
        of the Honkin' and Screamin'
        Saxophone* (collection), 2314
Base, Rob. *It Takes Two,* 2708
Basement Jaxx
    Kish Kash, 2217.1
    Remedy, 2217.2
Basia. *80's Pop Hits* (collection), 1238
Basic Music Library
    changes in this edition, pvii–viii
    overview, pvii–viii

Basie, Count
    America's #1 Band, 553.1
    An Anthology of Big Band Swing
        (collection), 528
    April in Paris, 741.1
    ★*Big Band Jazz: From the Beginnings to
        the Fifties* (collection), 529
    *Big Band Renaissance: The Evolution of
        the Jazz Orchestra* (collection), 739
    Chairman of the Board, 741.2
    ★*The Complete Decca Recordings,* 553.2
    Count Basie Jam: Montreux '77, 713.1
    Count Basie: Swingin' the Blues, 553.3
    The Definitive Collection (songwriter
        collection), 1101.1
    The Flapper Box (collection), 1064
    For the First Time, 713.2
    Frank Sinatra: Concert Collection, 1224.3
    ★*From Spirituals to Swing: The
        Legendary 1938 and 1939 Carnegie
        Hall Concerts Produced by John
        Hammond* (collection), 564
    *Jazz Masters: Vintage Collection, 1958–
        1961* (collection), 477
    Kansas City Powerhouse, 553.4
    ★*Ken Burns Jazz Collection: Count
        Basie,* 553.5
    ★*Ken Burns Jazz: The Story of
        America's Music* (collection), 478
    Piano Legends (collection), 480
    *The Real Kansas City of the '20s, '30s,
        and '40s* (collection), 552
    ★*The Smithsonian Collection of Classic
        Jazz* (collection), 486
    ★*Sound of Jazz* (collection), 487
    Stars of the Apollo (collection), 2240
    *The Story of Brunswick: The Classic
        Sound of Chicago Soul* (collection),
        2610
    ★*Swing Time! The Fabulous Big Band
        Era* (collection), 1089
Basil, Toni. *Like Omigod! The 80s Pop
        Culture Box (Totally)* (collection),
        1241
Bass, Fontella
    *Beg, Scream, and Shout! The Big Ol'
        Box of '60s Soul* (collection), 2433
    Best of Chess R&B, Vols. 1 and 2
        (collection), 2420
    Rescued: The Best of Fontella Bass,
        2451
    *Soul Shots: A Collection of Sixties Soul
        Classics* (collection), 2443
Bass, Martha
    Mother Smith and Her Children
        (collection), 2991
    *None but the Righteous: Chess Gospel
        Greats* (collection), 3037
Bateman, June. *The Fire / Fury Records
        Story* (collection), 2422
Battle, Kathleen. *Angels' Visits and Other
        Vocal Gems of Victorian America*
        (collection), 93

Battlefield Balladeers. *For the Old Folks at Home,* 66

Batts, Ray. *Southern Rhythm 'n' Rock: The Best of Excello Records, Vol. 22* (collection), 2427

Bauhaus. *Crackle,* 2098

Baxter, Andrew. *Violin, Sing the Blues for Me: African-American Fiddlers* (collection), 192

Baxter, Jim. *Violin, Sing the Blues for Me: African-American Fiddlers* (collection), 192

Bay City Rollers. *70s Greatest Hits* (collection), 1243

★Bayes, Nora. *Praise the Lord and Pass the Ammunition: Songs of World Wars I and II* (collection), 1079

Baylor, Helen. *Greatest Hits,* 3078

B. B. & Q. Band. *Disco Box* (collection), 2644

Be Good Tanyas. *Animal Playground* (collection), 3226

The Beach Boys
Christmas with the Beach Boys, 3324
★*Pet Sounds,* 1812.1
★*The Sounds of Summer: The Very Best of the Beach Boys,* 1812.2
★*Surfin' Hits* (collection), 1810

Beale Street Sheiks. *Masters of Memphis Blues* (collection), 230

Bean, Joe, and His San Antonians. *Swingbillies: Hillbilly and Western Swing on Modern/Colonial/Flair, 1947–1952* (collection), 1431

★Beard, Eler Maurice Ted. *Sacred Steel: The Steel Guitar Tradition of the House of God Churches* (collection), 2980

★Beasley, Good Rockin' Sam. *Nashville Jumps: Blues and Rhythm on Nashville Independent Labels 1945–1955* (collection), 2376

Beastie Boys
Check Your Head, 2709.1
Hot Sauce Committee Part Two, 2709.2
Ill Communication, 2709.3
Licensed to Ill, 2709.4
★*Paul's Boutique,* 2709.5

Beat Junkies
The World Famous Beat Junkies, Vol. 1, 2710.1
The World Famous Beat Junkies, Vol. 2, 2710.2

The Beatles
★*Abbey Road,* 1794.1
Beatles for Sale, 1794.5
The Beatles, 1794.2
The Beatles: Complete Scores, 1794.3
The Beatles: Past Masters, 1794.4
A Hard Day's Night, 1794.6
Help!, 1794.7
★*Please Please Me,* 1794.8
★*Revolver,* 1794.9

★*Rubber Soul,* 1794.10
★*Sgt. Pepper's Lonely Hearts Club Band,* 1794.11
★*With the Beatles,* 1794.12

Beatnuts. *The Beatnuts [Street Level],* 2711

Beautiful Bend. *The Best of T. K. Disco* (collection), 2656

bebop, 592–602. *See also* hard bop and related extensions of bebop
Al Haig Trio: Jazz Will-O'-the-Wisp (Haig), 597
★*The Amazing Bud Powell, Vol. 1* (Powell), 600.1
★*The Amazing Bud Powell, Vol. 2* (Powell), 600.2
Bud Powell Real Book (Powell), 600.3
collections, 592
The Complete Blue Note and Capitol Recordings of Fats Navarro and Tadd Dameron (Navarro), 599.1
★*The Complete RCA Victor Recordings* (Gillespie), 594.1
Dizzy Gillespie Collection (Gillespie), 594.2
The George Wallington Trios (Wallington), 602
Goin' to Minton's (Navarro), 599.2
Jazz Giant (Powell), 600.4
★*Ken Burns Jazz Collection: Dizzy Gillespie* (Gillespie), 594.3
The Legendary Big Band (Eckstine), 593
Memorial, Vol. 1 (Gray), 596
A Night in Tunisia: The Very Best of Dizzy Gillespie (Gillespie), 594.4
★*The Original Mambo Kings: An Afro-Cubop Anthology* (collection), 592
Origins: The Savoy Sessions (Johnson), 598
Settin' the Pace (Gordon), 595
Sonny Stitt / Bud Powell / J. J. Johnson (Stitt), 601

Bechet, Sidney
The Best of Sidney Bechet, 512.1
★*From Spirituals to Swing: The Legendary 1938 and 1939 Carnegie Hall Concerts Produced by John Hammond* (collection), 564
★*Ken Burns Jazz Collection: Sidney Bechet,* 512.2
The Legendary Sidney Bechet, 512.3
Riverside History of Classic Jazz (collection), 499
★*The Smithsonian Collection of Classic Jazz* (collection), 486

Beck, Andy. *Spirituals for Solo Singers, Vol. 2: 10 Spirituals Arranged for Solo Voice and Piano; for Recitals, Concerts, and Contests,* 36

Beck, Elder Charles
Classic African American Gospel from Smithsonian Folkways (collection), 2959

Fire in My Bones: Raw, Rare and Otherworldy African-American Gospel (collection), 2960
None but the Righteous: Chess Gospel Greats (collection), 3037

Beck, Jeff
Blow by Blow, 1862.1
Legends of Guitar: Rock–The '60s, Vol. 2 (collection), 1861
Stroll On: An Immediate Blues Collection (collection), 369
Truth, 1862.2

Beck, Jimmy. *Night Train to Nashville: Music City Rhythm and Blues, 1945–1970, Vol. 1* (collection), 2377

★Beck. *Odelay,* 2099

Becker, Margaret. *Steps of Faith,* 3139

Bedhead. *What Fun Life Was,* 2100

Bee Gees
Bee Gees Greatest, 1795
★*Saturday Night Fever,* 2658

Beethoven, Ludwig van. *Beethoven Lives Upstairs,* 3256

Beiderbecke, Bix
★*At the Jazz Band Ball: Early Hot Jazz, Song, and Dance* (collection), 470
Bix: Ain't None of Them Play Like Him Yet, 513.1
Bix Beiderbecke and the Chicago Cornets, 513.2
★*Bix Beiderbecke, Vol. 1: Singin' the Blues,* 513.3
Bix Beiderbecke, Vol. 2: At the Jazz Band Ball, 513.4
The Classic Hoagy Carmichael (songwriter collection), 1097.1
The First of the Singer Songwriters: Key Cuts (Carmichael), 1124
★*Ken Burns Jazz: The Story of America's Music* (collection), 478
Lost Chords: White Musicians and Their Contributions to Jazz (collection), 479
Riverside History of Classic Jazz (collection), 499
★*The Smithsonian Collection of Classic Jazz* (collection), 486

Belafonte, Harry
★*Billboard Greatest Christmas Hits, 1955–1983* (collection), 3294
Calypso, 1178.1
An Evening with Harry Belafonte and Friends, 1178.2
★*Nipper's Greatest Hits: The 50's, Vol. 1* (collection), 1163
Nipper's Greatest Hits: The 50's, Vol. 2 (collection), 1164
Very Best of Harry Belafonte, 1178.3

Belfour, Robert. *What's Wrong with You,* 422

Bell and James. *Disco Box* (collection), 2644

Bell, Archie. *Beg, Scream, and Shout! The Big Ol' Box of '60s Soul* (collection), 2433

Bell, Carey
Blues Fest: Modern Blues of the '70s (collection), 408
Living Chicago Blues, Vol. 1 (collection), 415

Bell, Ed
Alabama Blues (collection), 240
A Richer Tradition: Country Blues and String Band Music (collection), 187

Bell, Jimmy, aka Jimmy Sweeney. *Night Train to Nashville: Music City Rhythm and Blues, 1945–1970, Vol. 2* (collection), 2378

Bell, Reuben
Action Speaks Louder Than Words: The Best of SSS International (collection), 2588
Dave Godin's Deep Soul Treasures, Vols. 1–4 (collection), 2435

Bell, William
★*Atlantic R&B, 1947–1974* (collection), 2418
Beg, Scream, and Shout! The Big Ol' Box of '60s Soul (collection), 2433
The Best of William Bell, 2452.1
Birth of Soul, 4 Vols. (collection), 2434
The Complete Stax/Volt Singles 1959–1968 (collection), 2594
The Complete Stax/Volt Soul Singles, Vol. 2: 1968–1971 (collection), 2595
The Soul of a Bell, 2452.2
Top of the Stax, Vol. 1: Twenty Greatest Hits (collection), 2611
Top of the Stax, Vol. 2: Twenty Greatest Hits (collection), 2612

Bellamy Brothers. *Best of Bellamy Brothers,* 1624

Belle and Sebastian. *Colours Are Brighter: Songs for Children and Grown Ups Too* (collection), 3193

Belle, Regina. *Baby Come to Me: The Best of Regina Belle,* 2395

Bellson, Louie. *Inferno,* 742

Belvin, Jesse
★*The R&B Box* (collection), 2239
★*The Specialty Story* (collection), 2428

Benatar, Pat. *Ultimate Collection,* 2042

Beneke, Tex. *Jule Styne* (songwriter collection), 1111.1

Benevento, Marco. *Icons among Us* (collection), 934

Bennett, Bobby and the Dynamics. *The Best of Loma Records: The Rise and Fall of a 1960's Soul Label* (collection), 2590

Bennett, Tony
American Classic, 1179.1
★*American Popular Song: Six Decades of Songwriters and Singers* (collection), 1059

Cy Coleman (songwriter collection), 1098.2
Dorothy Fields (songwriter collection), 1100
Duets: An American Classic, 1251.1
Duke Ellington (songwriter collection), 1099.1
E. Y. Harburg (songwriter collection), 1103
50 Years: The Artistry of Tony Bennett, 1179.2
Frank Sinatra: Concert Collection, 1224.3
Harold Arlen (songwriter collection), 1095.1
Harry Warren (songwriter collection), 1114
Hoagy Carmichael (songwriter collection), 1097.2
Irving Berlin: A Hundred Years (songwriter collection), 1096.3
Irving Berlin (songwriter collection), 1096.1
James Van Heusen (songwriter collection), 1112.1
Johnny Mercer (songwriter collection), 1107.1
Jule Styne (songwriter collection), 1111.1
Richard Whiting (songwriter collection), 1116
Rodgers / Hart (songwriter collection), 1109.1
Sentimental Journey: Pop Vocal Classics, Vol. 4 (collection), 1170
★*Sentimental Journey: Pop Vocal Classics, Vol. 3* (collection), 1169
16 Most Requested Songs, 1179.3
16 Most Requested Songs: The 1950s, Vol. 1 (collection), 1171
The Tony Bennett / Bill Evans Album, 1251.2
The Very Best of Cole Porter (songwriter collection), 1108.3

Benson, George
★*George Benson Anthology,* 901
Progressions: 100 Years of Jazz Guitar (collection), 481

Benton, Brook
Forty Greatest Hits, 2453
The Look of Love: The Burt Bacharach Collection (collection), 1161
★*The R&B Box* (collection), 2239

Berigan, Bunny
Irving Berlin: A Hundred Years (songwriter collection), 1096.3
The Pied Piper, 567
★*Swing Time! The Fabulous Big Band Era* (collection), 1089

Berkey, Jackson. *Sunday Morning Coffee* (collection), 1375

Berkner, Laurie. *Whaddaya Think of That?,* 3197

Berlin, Irving
Irving Berlin (songwriter collection), 1096.1
Irving Berlin: A Hundred Years (songwriter collection), 1096.3
Irving Berlin Anthology (songwriter collection), 1096.2

Berman, Marcia. *Chanukah at Home* (collection), 3238

Berne, Tim
Sanctified Dreams, 941.1
The Sublime And, 941.2

Bernstein, Leonard
★*Bernstein Favorites: Children's Classics* (collection), 3252
The Joy of Christmas, 3281

Berry, Chu. ★*The Commodore Story* (collection), 561

Berry, Chuck
Chuck Berry, 1759.1
Chuck Berry: The Chess Box, 1759.2
★*The Definitive Collection,* 1759.3
The Golden Era of Rock 'n' Roll (collection), 1748
★*Jazz on a Summer's Day* (collection), 664
★*Legends of Guitar: Rock–The '50s, Vol. 1* (collection), 1749
★*Legends of Guitar: Rock–The '50s, Vol. 2* (collection), 1750
Let There Be Drums, Vol. 1: The '50s (collection), 1751
Rock and Roll: The Early Days (collection), 1752

Best, Martin. *Thys Yool: A Medieval Christmas,* 3274

★Bethel Quartet. *A Warrior on the Battlefield: A Cappella Trail Blazers* (collection), 3011

Bey, Andy. *Ain't Necessarily So,* 773

Beyoncé
B'day, 2396.1
Beyoncé, 2396.2
I Am . . . Sasha Fierce, 2396.3
Lemonade, 2396.3

The B-52s
The B-52s, 2096.1
Billboard #1s: The '80s (collection), 1236
Time Capsule: Songs for a Future Generation, 2096.2

Biddleville Quintette. *The Half Ain't Never Been Told, Vols. 1 and 2* (collection), 2956

Bieber, Justin. *My World 2.0,* 1252

Big Audio Dynamite II. *90's Pop Hits* (collection), 1242

big bands and the swing era, 528–550
An Anthology of Big Band Swing (collection), 528
The Band Don Redman Built (McKinney's Cotton Pickers), 545
Benny Goodman: Adventures in the Kingdom of Swing (Goodman), 537.1

★*Benny Goodman at Carnegie Hall: Complete* (Goodman), 537.2

★*Best of the Big Bands* (Calloway), 531

Best of the Big Bands (Dorsey Brothers), 534

Best of the Big Bands (Gray), 538

Best of the Big Bands (Thornhill), 549

Big Band Dixieland (Crosby), 533

★*Big Band Jazz: From the Beginnings to the Fifties* (collection), 529

★*Blowin' Up a Storm!* (Herman), 542.1

Boyd Meets Stravinsky (Raeburn), 546

collections, 528–530

Contrasts (Dorsey), 535

★*The Essential Artie Shaw* (Shaw), 548

★*The Essential Benny Goodman* (Goodman), 537.3

It's the Way That You Swing It (Lunceford), 544

Keeper of the Flame (Herman), 542.2

Ken Burns Jazz Collection: Benny Goodman (Goodman), 537.4

★*Ken Burns Jazz Collection: Fletcher Henderson* (Henderson), 541.1

The Lionel Hampton Story (Hampton), 539

The Luis Russell Story (Russell), 547

The Music Master (Carter), 532

The Original Tuxedo Junction (Hawkins), 540

Piano Man (Hines), 543

★*Spinnin' the Webb* (Webb), 550

★*A Study in Frustration* (Henderson), 541.2

Torch Songs: A Collection of Sultry Jazz and Big Band Standards (collection), 530

Yes Indeed! (Dorsey), 536

big bands since the 1950s, 739–764

Afro-Eurasian Eclipse (Ellington), 748.1

April in Paris (Basie), 741.1

The Best of Stan Kenton (Kenton), 758.1

Big Band Renaissance: The Evolution of the Jazz Orchestra (collection), 739

Birk's Works: The Verve Big Band Sessions (Gillespie), 753

The Brunt (Either/Orchestra), 747

Buddy Rich: Holland 1978 (Rich), 761.1

Central City Sketches (Carter), 744

Chairman of the Board (Basie), 741.2

collections, 739

The Complete Big Band Studio Recordings (Pettiford), 760

The Complete Pacific Jazz Sessions (Evans), 750.1

Dream Band (Gibbs), 752

Electric Bath (Ellis), 749.1

Electric Heart, Don Ellis: The Man, His Time, His Music (Ellis), 749.2

★*Ellington at Newport* (Ellington), 748.2

The Essential Maynard Ferguson (Ferguson), 751

European Tour (Bley), 743.1

Evanescence (Schneider), 763

★*The Far East Suite* (Ellington), 748.3

Fontainebleau (Dameron), 746.1

Giant Steps (Herman), 755.1

Gil Evans and Ten (Evans), 750.2

Individualism of Gil Evans (Evans), 750.3

Inferno (Bellson), 742

Lionel Hampton Live in '58 (Hampton), 754

Live at the Village Vanguard (Jones), 757

Live in Time (Mingus Big Band), 759

The Magic Touch (Dameron), 746.2

Moment of Truth (Wilson), 764

★*New Concepts of Artistry in Rhythm* (Kenton), 758.2

New Orleans Suite (Ellington), 748.4

Out of the Cool (Evans), 750.4

Quincy Jones Live in '60 (Jones), 756

Sam Rivers' Rivbea All-Star Orchestra: Inspiration (Rivers), 762

Social Studies (Bley), 743.2

Sonny's Dream (Criss), 745

Such Sweet Thunder (Ellington), 748.5

Swingin' New Big Band (Rich), 761.2

The Toshiko Akiyoshi Jazz Orchestra: Strive for Jive (Akiyoshi), 740

Woody Herman Live in '64 (Herman), 755.2

Big Black. *The Rich Man's Eight Track Tape,* 2101

Big Brother and the Holding Company. *Cheap Thrills,* 1831

Big L. *Lifestylez ov da Poor and Dangerous,* 2712

Big Maceo. *See* Merriweather, Big Maceo

Big Maybelle

I've Got a Feelin': Okeh and Savoy Recordings, 1952–56, 2303

★*Jazz on a Summer's Day* (collection), 664

★*The Okeh Rhythm and Blues Story* (collection), 2425

★*The R&B Box* (collection), 2239

Respect: Aretha's Influences and Inspiration (collection), 2440

Stars of the Apollo (collection), 2240

★*Stompin' at the Savoy: The Original Indie Label, 1944–1961* (collection), 2429

Big Punisher. *Capital Punishment,* 2713

Big Star. *#1 Record / Radio City,* 1871

★Big Three Trio. *Nashville Jumps: Blues and Rhythm on Nashville Independent Labels 1945–1955* (collection), 2376

Bigard, Barney

The Duke's Men: Small Groups, Vol. 1 (collection), 562

The Duke's Men: Small Groups, Vol. 2 (collection), 563

Bikini Kill

The First Two Records, 2102.1

The Singles, 2102.2

Bill, Brother. *Boddie Recording Company Cleveland, Ohio* (collection), 2569, 2570

Billings, William

The Complete Works of William Billings, 7.1

The Continental Harmonist: Hymns and Fuging Tunes, 7.2

A Land of Pure Delight: Anthems and Fuging Tunes, 7.3

Wake Ev'ry Breath, 7.4

Binary Star. *Masters of the Universe,* 2714

Birdsong, Larry

★*Nashville Jumps: Blues and Rhythm on Nashville Independent Labels 1945–1955* (collection), 2376

Night Train to Nashville: Music City Rhythm and Blues, 1945–1970, Vol. 1 (collection), 2377

Birmingham Jug Band

Ruckus Juice and Chittlins: The Great Jug Bands—Classic Recordings of the 1920s and '30s, Vol. 1 (collection), 188

Ruckus Juice and Chittlins: The Great Jug Bands—Classic Recordings of the 1920s and '30s, Vol. 2 (collection), 189

Birthday Party

Junkyard, 2031.1

Pleasure Heads Must Burn, 2031.2

Prayers on Fire, 2031.3

Bishop, Elvin. *Struttin' My Stuff,* 370

Biz Markie. *The Best of Cold Chillin': Goin' Off + The Biz Never Sleeps,* 2715

Björk

Debut, 2103.1

★*Post,* 2103.2

Black Ace. *Texas Blues: Early Blues Masters from the Lone Star State* (collection), 237

Black Artists Group (BAG). *See* jazz outside the mainstream: the AACM, BAG, and the lofts

Black, Bill. *The Hi Records Story* (collection), 2423

Black, Clint

★*Greatest Hits,* 1625.1

Killin' Time, 1625.2

Black Crowes. *Whatever: The '90s Pop and Culture Box* (collection), 1244

Black Eyed Peas. *Behind the Front,* 2716

Black Flag

American Hardcore (collection), 1977

Damaged, 1982, 2104

No Thanks! The '70s Punk Rebellion (collection), 2003

Punk: Attitude (collection), 1980

Black, Marion
    Eccentric Soul: The Capsoul Label
        (collection), 2599
    Eccentric Soul: The Prix Label
        (collection), 2601
Black Moon. *Enta da Stage*, 2717
Black Sabbath. *Paranoid*, 1940
Black Sheep. *A Wolf in Sheep's* Clothing,
    2718
Blackalicious
    Blazing Arrow, 2719.1
    Nia, 2719.2
Blackwell, Scrapper
    *Back to the Crossroads: The Roots of
        Robert Johnson* (collection), 212
    *Leroy Carr and Scrapper Blackwell,
        Volume 1, 1928–1934*, 276
The Blackwood Brothers
    ★*The Blackwoods*, 3118
    *Close Harmony: A History of Southern
        Gospel Music, Vol. 1* (collection),
        3108
Blade, Brian. *Icons among Us* (collection),
    934
Blake, Blind
    *Acoustic Country Blues Guitar: Delta
        Blues before Robert Johnson*
        (collection), 211
    All the Published Sides, 246.1
    ★*Best of Blind Blake*, 246.2
    *Favorite Country Blues: Guitar-Piano
        Duets* (collection), 267
    The Georgia Blues (collection), 242
    ★*Guitar Wizards* (collection), 243
    *The Road to Robert Johnson and
        Beyond* (collection), 221
    The Roots of Rock (collection), 368
    *Songsters and Saints: Vocal Traditions
        on Race Records, Vol. 2*, 191
Blake, Eubie
    The Greatest Ragtime of the Century
        (collection), 125
    Memories of You, 129.1
    *Sincerely, Eubie Blake: Nine Original
        Compositions for Piano Solo*, 129.2
    That's Ragtime!, 129.3
Blake, Norman. *Whiskey before Breakfast*,
    1571
Blake, Ran
    All That Is Tied, 1031.1
    Short Life of Barbara Monk, 1031.2
Blakemore, Amos Wells, Jr. *See* Wells,
    Junior
Blakey, Art
    *Art Blakey and the Jazz Messengers Live
        in '58*, 630.1
    Coast to Coast, 871
    Free for All, 630.2
    ★*Ken Burns Jazz Collection: Art Blakey*,
        630.3
    ★*A Night at Birdland, Vols. 1 and 2*,
        630.4
    A Night in Tunisia, 630.5

Blanchard, Terence
    Icons among Us (collection), 934
    Inside Man [2006] [CD], 1051.2
    Inside Man [2006] [DVD], 1051.1
    Wandering Moon, 942
Bland, Billy. *Birth of Soul, 4 Vols.*
    (collection), 2434
Bland, Bobby
    ★*The Best of Duke-Peacock Blues*
        (collection), 336
    Birth of Soul, 4 Vols. (collection), 2434
    ★*Blues Classics* (collection), 146
    Blues Masters, Vol. 1: Urban Blues
        (collection), 338
    Blues Masters, Vol. 9: Postmodern Blues
        (collection), 412
    Blues Masters, Vol. 12: Memphis Blues
        (collection), 229
    ★*The Blues: A Smithsonian Collection
        of Classic Blues Singers* (collection),
        145
    The Blues Is Alright, Vol. 1 (collection),
        411
    ★*Bobby "Blue" Bland: The Anthology*,
        349.1
    *Dave Godin's Deep Soul Treasures, Vols.
        1–4* (collection), 2435
    Duke-Peacock's Greatest Hits
        (collection), 2421
    Greatest Hits, Vol. 1, 349.2
    ★*Mean Old World: The Blues from
        1940–1994* (collection), 154
    *Memphis Blues: Important Postwar
        Recordings* (collection), 341
    The Modern Records Blues Story
        (collection), 342
    ★*The R&B Box* (collection), 2239
    *Respect: Aretha's Influences and
        Inspiration* (collection), 2440
    Soul Shots, Vol. 4: Urban Blues
        (collection), 343
    *Superblues: All-Time Classic Blues Hits,
        Vol. 1* (collection), 347
    Two Steps from the Blues, 349.3
Blasters. *Live: Going Home*, 2105
Bledsoe, Jules. *A First-Time Buyer's
    Guide to American Negro Spirituals*
    (collection), 32
★Blesh, Rudi. *Classic Piano Rags: Complete
    Original Music for 81 Rags*, 130
Bley, Carla
    Amarcord Nino Rota (collection), 809
    *Conjure: Music for the Texts of Ishmael
        Reed* (collection), 810
    Escalator over the Hill, 1032
    European Tour, 743.1
    Social Studies, 743.2
Bley, Paul. *Closer*, 701
Blige, Mary J.
    ★*The Breakthrough*, 2397.1
    What's the 411?, 2397.2, 2720
Blind Boys of Alabama
    Retrospective, 3012

The Rough Guide to Gospel (collection),
    2970
Blivens, Clifford "Fat Man." *The
    Swing Time Records Story: R&B,
    Blues, and Gospel, 1946–1952*
    (collection), 2430
Blondie
    Billboard #1s: The '70s (collection),
        1235
    Disco Box (collection), 2644
    *D.I.Y. Blank Generation: The New York
        Scene* (collection), 1978
    Greatest Hits, 1983
    *Like Omigod! The 80s Pop Culture Box
        (Totally)* (collection), 1241
    No Thanks! The '70s Punk Rebellion
        (collection), 2003
Blood, Sweat, and Tears
    Child Is Father to the Man, 1913.1
    *What Goes Up: Best of Blood, Sweat,
        and Tears*, 1913.2
Bloom, Jane Ira. *Mental Weather*, 943
Blount, Herman Poole. *See* Sun Ra
Blow, Kurtis
    The Best of Kurtis Blow, 2721.1
    Kurtis Blow, 2721.2
Blue Cheer. *San Francisco Nights*
    (collection), 1829
★Blue Flamers. *Nashville Jumps: Blues and
    Rhythm on Nashville Independent
    Labels 1945–1955* (collection),
    2376
Blue Highway. *Blue Highway*, 1572
Blue Jay Singers. *All of My Appointed
    Time: Forty Years of a Cappella
    Gospel Singing* (collection),
    2958
Blue Jays. *The Doo-Wop Box II*
    (collection), 2323
Blue Oyster Cult
    *Don't Fear the Reaper: Best of Blue
        Oyster Cult*, 1941
    Heavy Metal: The First 20 Years
        (collection), 1938
The Blue Sky Boys
    ★*Anthology of American Folk Music,
        Vol. 4* (collection), 1387
    The Blue Sky Boys, 1398.1
    In Concert, 1964, 1398.2
    ★*Something Got a Hold of Me:
        A Treasury of Sacred Music*
        (collection), 3114
    The Sunny Side of Life, 1398.3
bluegrass, 1559–1617
    Act 3 (Seldom Scene), 1607.1
    ★*Aereo-Plain* (Hartford), 1587.1
    All on a Rising Day (Rowan), 1604
    *Angels Are Singing: A Women's
        Bluegrass Gospel Collection*, 1559
    Appalachian Stomp: Bluegrass Classics
        (collection), 1560
    Appalachian Swing! (Kentucky
        Colonels), 1590

At the Old Schoolhouse (Johnson Mountain Boys), 1589.1

Best of the Flatt and Scruggs TV Show: Classic Bluegrass from 1956 to 1962, 1583.1

The Best of Bluegrass, Vol. 1: Standards (collection), 1561

Beyond the City (Cox Family), 1579

Bill Clifton: The Early Years, 1957–1958, 1576

Blue Diamond (Johnson Mountain Boys), 1589.2

Blue Grass, 1959–1969 (Monroe), 1596.2

Blue Grass, 1970–1979 (Monroe), 1596.3

★*Blue Grass, 1950–1958* (Monroe), 1596.1

Blue Highway, 1572

★*Blue Moon of Kentucky, 1936–1949* (Monroe), 1596.4

Blue Ribbon Bluegrass (collection), 1563

Bluegrass and More (Jim and Jesse), 1588.1

Bluegrass Banjo (Wernick), 1616.1

Bluegrass Gospel Collection (Story), 1611

Bluegrass Guitar (Traum), 1613

Bluegrass Sessions: Tales from the Acoustic Planet, Vol. 2 (Fleck), 1584

Bluegrass Songbook (Wernick), 1616.2

The Bluegrass Album, Vol. 1 (collection), 1562

The Boys Are Back in Town (Nashville Bluegrass Band), 1597

Classic Bluegrass (Sparks), 1608.1

Clinch Mountain Country (Stanley), 1610.1

The Cold Hard Facts (McCoury), 1595.1

Complete Vanguard Recordings (Country Gentlemen), 1578.1

★*The Complete Columbia Stanley Brothers*, 1609.1

★*The Complete Mercury Recordings* (Stanley Brothers), 1609.2

★*The Complete Mercury Sessions* (Flatt and Scruggs), 1583.2

Country Bluegrass (Osbourne Brothers), 1601.1

Country Songs, Old and New (Country Gentlemen), 1578.2

The David Grisman Rounder Compact Disc, 1586

Del and the Boys (McCoury), 1595.2

Dobro / Blues and Bluegrass (Auldridge), 1569

Don Reno and Red Smiley and the Tennessee Cut–Ups, 1959–1963, 1602.1

Don't Cry to Me (Martin), 1594.1

Don't Stop the Music (McCoury), 1595.3

Earl Scruggs and the 5-String Banjo, 1605.1

Earliest Recordings: The Complete Rich-RTone 78s (Stanley Brothers), 1609.3

Early Dot Recordings, Vol. 3 (Wiseman), 1617.1

Early Rebel Recordings, 1962–1971 (Country Gentlemen), 1578.3

The Early Starday-King Years, 1958–1961 (Stanley Brothers), 1609.4

Essential Earl Scruggs, 1605.2

★*The Essential Flatt and Scruggs: 'Tis Sweet to Be Remembered*, 1583.3

Every Time You Say Goodbye (Krauss), 1591.1

58957: The Bluegrass Guitar Collection (Rice), 1603.1

Flatt and Scruggs, 1948–1959, 1583.4

Flatt and Scruggs, 1959–1963, 1583.5

Fly through the Country / When the Storm Is Over (New Grass Revival), 1598.1

Folkways Years, 1964–1983 (Allen and Wakefield), 1568

Glamour and Grits (Bush), 1574

Greatest Hits (Martin), 1594.2

Hand-Picked: 25 Years of Bluegrass on Rounder Records (collection), 1564

Hello Operator . . . This Is Country Gazette, 1577

High Lonesome: The Story of Bluegrass Music (collection), 1565

Hillbilly Jazz (Clements), 1575

★*J. D. Crowe and the New South*, 1580

Jim and Jesse, 1952–1955, 1588.2

Jim and Jesse Story: 24 Greatest Hits, 1588.3

Jimmy Martin and the Sunny Mountain Boys, 1594.3

Josh Graves, 1585

Kenny Baker Fiddle (Brody), 1573

Last Suit You Wear (Sparks), 1608.1

Live (New Grass Revival), 1598.2

Mac Wiseman Story, 1617.2

Manzanita (Rice), 1603.2

Master Fiddler (Baker), 1570

Me Oh My, How the Time Does Fly (Hartford), 1587.2

Mountain Music Bluegrass Style (collection), 1566

The Music of Bill Monroe from 1936 to 1994 (Monroe), 1596.5

My Last Days on Earth, Blue Grass, 1981–1994 (Monroe), 1596.6

★*Now That I've Found You: A Collection* (Krauss), 1591.2

The Oak and the Laurel (Lewis), 1593

Old and in the Way, 1600

Old Train2 (Seldom Scene), 1607.2

One Step Ahead (Vincent), 1614

The Osborne Brothers, 1956–1968, 1601.2

The Osborne Brothers, 1968–1974, 1601.3

Pete Seeger's Rainbow Quest, 1606

Recorded Live at the Cellar Door (Seldom Scene), 1607.3

Red on Blonde (O'Brien), 1599

Riding That Midnight Train: The Starday-King Years, 1958–1961 (Stanley Brothers), 1609.5

Rock My Soul (Lawson), 1592

Saturday Night; Sunday Morning (Stanley), 1610.2

★*16 Gems* (Monroe), 1596.7

Slide Rule (Douglas), 1582

The Songs of Doc Watson, 1615

Sweethearts in Heaven: The Complete Dot Recordings 1957–1964 (Reno and Smiley), 1602.2

The Telluride Sessions (Strength in Numbers), 1612

There Is a Time, 1963–1970 (Dillards), 1581.1

Top of the Hill Bluegrass (collection), 1567

Wheatstraw Suite (Dillards), 1581.2

Whiskey before Breakfast (Blake), 1571

★*The BlueJacks. Nashville Jumps: Blues and Rhythm on Nashville Independent Labels 1945–1955* (collection), 2376

blues, 145–168, 2303–2311. See also rhythm and blues

The Basics: Building a Foundation of Repertoire and Technique for Acoustic Fingerstyle Blues (Mann), 165

Beginning Blues Guitar: A Guide to the Essential Chords, Licks, Techniques, and Concepts (Rubin), 167.1

The Best of Jimmy Witherspoon: Jazz Me Blues, 2311.1

Big, Bad, and Blue: The Big Joe Turner Anthology, 2310.1, 2310.2

Blowin' in from Kansas City (Witherspoon), 2311.2

Blues: An Anthology (Handy, Niles and Covarrubias), 163

blues and rock, 367–385

★*Blues Classics* (collection), 146

Blues Guitar: Learn to Play Blues Guitar with Step-by-Step Lessons and 20 Great Blues Songs (Koch), 164

blues revival and folk blues, 386–407

Blues Standards (collection), 147

★*The Blues: A Smithsonian Collection of Classic Blues Singers* (collection), 145

The Blues Fakebook (Mann and Gahr), 166

contemporary blues and soul, 408–469

blues (cont.)

Conversation with the Blues (collection), 148

Country Blues Guitar (Grossman), 161.1

Country Blues Songbook (Grossman, Calt and Grossman), V.162

Fingerpicking Blues Guitar Instrumentals (Grossman), 161.2

Fingerpicking Guitar Solos in Open Tunings (Grossman), 161.3

general collections, 145–168

★His Tangerine and Atlantic Sides (Mayfield), 2308.1

★I Can't Be Satisfied: Early American Women Blues Singers, Vol. 1: Country (collection), 149

I've Got a Feelin': Okeh and Savoy Recordings, 1952–56 (Big Maybelle), 2303

Jimmy Liggins and His Drops of Joy, 2306

Joe Liggins and the Honeydrippers, 2307

Kansas City Star (Lee), 2305.1

Kansas City's First Lady of the Blues (Lee), 2305.2

★Legends of the Blues, Vol. 1 (collection), 150

★Legends of the Blues, Vol. 2 (collection), 151

★Let's Get Loose: Folk and Popular Blues Styles from the Beginning to the Early 1940s (collection), 152

Live at the 1972 Monterey Jazz Festival (Witherspoon), 2311.3

Louisiana blues, 327–335

Martin Scorsese Presents: The Blues, a Musical Journey (collection), 153

★Mean Old World: The Blues from 1940–1994 (collection), 154

Meaning in the Blues (collection), 155

Memphis and St. Louis blues, 229–235

Mississippi Delta blues, 211–228

modern blues. See modern blues

News and the Blues: Telling It Like It Is (collection), 156

Open Tunings for Blues Guitar (Rubin), 167.2

overview, p15–16

Percy Mayfield: Poet of the Blues, 2308.2

periodicals for up-to-date CD notices and reviews, suggested, p3

piano blues, 250–265

postwar midwestern blues, 285–310

Rhythm Rockin' Blues: The Legendary Modern Recordings (Turner), 2309

roots, 169–182

The Roots of Rap: Classic Recordings of the 1920's and 30's (collection), 157

Solo Blues Guitar (Rubin), 167.3

songsters, string bands, and jug bands, 183–201

soul, 2587

★The Story of the Blues (collection), 158

Sufferin' Mind (Guitar Slim), 2304

Texas and West coast blues, 311–326

Texas, Arkansas, and Louisiana blues, 236–239

The 'Spoon Concerts (Witherspoon), 2311.4

The Very Best of Big Joe Turner, 2310.3

12-Bar Blues (Rubin, Freed and Plunkett), 168

Urban Blues Singing Legend (Witherspoon), 2311.5

vaudeville or classic blues, 202–210.6

When the Sun Goes Down 2: The First Time I Met the Blues (collection), 160

When the Sun Goes Down 1: Walk Right In (collection), 159

blues and rock, 367–385

Anthology (Thorogood), 381

An Anthology: The Elektra Years (Butterfield), 371.1

Best of Johnny Winter (Winter), 384.1

Blues Breakers [1993] (Mayall), 375.2

★Blues Breakers [1965] (Mayall), 375.1

Blues Masters, Vol. 6: Blues Originals (collection), 367

collections, 367–369

East West (Butterfield), 371.2

The Essential Fabulous Thunderbirds (Fabulous Thunderbirds), 373.1

Five Live Yardbirds (Yardbirds), 385

★Giant Step / Ole Folks at Home (Mahal), 374

The Harmonica according to Charlie Musselwhite (Musselwhite), 376.1

Hot Stuff: The Greatest Hits (Fabulous Thunderbirds), 373.2

Joyful Noise (Trucks), 382

Just Won't Burn (Tedeschi), 380

Ledbetter Heights (Shepherd), 379

Living with the Blues (Robillard), 378

London Blues (Mayall), 375.3

Paul Butterfield Teaches Blues Harmonica Master Class: Sessions with a Legendary Player (Butterfield), 371.3

Polaris (North Mississippi All-Stars), 377

The Roots of Rock (collection), 368

Scorchin' Blues (Winter), 384.2

Stand Back! Here Comes Charley Musselwhite's South Side Band (Musselwhite), 376.2

Stevie Ray Vaughan, Lightnin' Blues, 1983–1987 (Vaughan, Tapella, Sokolow and Schiff), 383

Stroll On: An Immediate Blues Collection (collection), 369

Struttin' My Stuff (Bishop), 370

The Very Best of Canned Heat (Canned Heat), 372

blues and soul, contemporary. See contemporary blues and soul

blues in the cities: 1920s–1940s, 266–284

All the Classic Sides (Broonzy), 272.1

Banana in Your Fruit Basket (Carter), 273

Big Bill Broonzy, Vol. 2 (Broonzy), 272.2

The Bluebird Recordings, 1936–1938 (Tampa Red), 278.1

Bottleneck Trendsetters of the 1930s (collection), 266

collections, 266–271

The Complete Bluebird Recordings, Vol. 1 (Tampa Red), 278.2

Country Blues Troubadours, 1938–1948 (Terry and McGhee), 280

The Devil's Son in Law (Wheatstraw), 283

Favorite Country Blues: Guitar-Piano Duets (collection), 267

Good Time Blues: Harmonicas, Kazoos, Washboards, and Cow-Bells (collection), 268

The Guitar Wizard (Tampa Red), 278.3

Hometown Blues (Terry), 279.1

★Hoodoo Lady (Memphis Minnie), 277.1

I've Been to Kansas City, Vol. 1 (Turner), 281.1

Leroy Carr and Scrapper Blackwell, Volume 1, 1928–1934, 276

A Life in Music (Johnson), 275.1

The Original Sonny Boy Williamson, Vol. 1 (Williamson), 284.1

The Original Sonny Boy Williamson (Williamson), 284.2

Queen of the Country Blues (Memphis Minnie), 277.2

Raunchy Business: Hot Nuts and Lollypops (collection), 269

Rock Me Mama (Crudup), 274

Rockin' My Blues Away (Washboard Sam), 282.1

Shout, Rattle, and Roll (Turner), 281.2

Sonny Terry's Country Blues Harmonica (Terry), 279.2

★Steppin' on the Blues (Johnson), 275.2

Washboard Sam 1936–1947 (Washboard Sam), 282.2

When the Sun Goes Down 4: That's All Right (collection), 271

When the Sun Goes Down 3: That's Chicago's South Side (collection), 270

★Blues Magoos. *Nuggets: Artifacts of the First Psychedelic Era* (collection), 1808

blues revival and folk blues, 386–407

The American Folk Blues Festival: The British Tours, 1963–1966 (collection), 389

The American Folk Blues Festival, 1962–1966, Vol. 1 (collection), 386

The American Folk Blues Festival, 1962–1966, Vol. 2 (collection), 387

The American Folk Blues Festival, 1962–1966, Vol. 3 (collection), 388

Amtrak Blues (Hunter), 396

Blues Masters, Vol. 7: Blues Revival (collection), 390

★*Brownie McGhee and Sonny Terry Sing* (Terry and McGhee), 404

collections, 386–392

Don't Let Your Deal Go Down (Jackson), 398

Father of the Delta Blues (House), 395

I'm Blue as a Man Can Be (Williams), 407

Life Gave Me a Dirty Deal (Bonner), 393

Martin, Bogan, and Armstrong / That Old Gang of Mine (Martin, Bogan, and Armstrong), 401

Masters of the Country Blues: Fred McDowell and Big Joe Williams (collection), 391

Memphis Slim and Sonny Boy Williamson: Live in Europe (Memphis Slim and Sonny Boy Williamson), 403

Mississippi John Hurt Today (Hurt), 397

Newport Folk Festival: Best of the Blues, 1959–68 (collection), 392

Shake Your Boogie (Williams), 406

★*Skip James Today* (James), 399

Texas Blues (Hopkins), 394

★*Texas Songster* (Lipscomb), 400

Women Be Wise (Wallace), 405

★*You Gotta Move* (McDowell), 402

Blues Rockers

★*Nashville Jumps: Blues and Rhythm on Nashville Independent Labels 1945–1955* (collection), 2376

Southern Rhythm 'n' Rock: The Best of Excello Records, Vol. 22 (collection), 2427

blues soul, 2587

Chronicle: The 20 Greatest Hits (Taylor), 2587.1

Rated X-Traordinaire: The Best of Johnnie Taylor, 2587.2

Bluiett, Hamlet. *Resolution*, 917

Blythe, Jimmy

★*Cuttin' the Boogie: Piano Blues and Boogie Woogie* (collection), 251

The Greatest Ragtime of the Century (collection), 125

Bo and Metros. *Boddie Recording Company Cleveland, Ohio* (collection), 2569, 2570

Bob and Fred. *Eccentric Soul: The Big Mack Label* (collection), 2598

Bobby Brown Quartet. *Stars of the Apollo* (collection), 2240

The Bobbettes

★*Atlantic Vocal Groups, 1951–1963* (collection), 2320

The Doo-Wop Box II (collection), 2323

Life Could Be a Dream: The Doo-Wop Sound, 2346

Boduch, Doug. *Best of Blues Piano* (Lowry, Wiegratz, Boduch, McGirr and Schroedl), 261

Body Count. *Body Count*, 2722

Bogan, Lucille. *Raunchy Business: Hot Nuts and Lollypops* (collection), 269

Bogan, Ted. *Martin, Bogan, and Armstrong / That Old Gang of Mine* (Martin, Bogan, and Armstrong), 401

Boggs, Dock. *His Twelve Original Recordings*, 1399

Bogguss, Suzy. *20 Greatest Hits*, 1626

Bohannon, Hamilton. *The Story of Brunswick: The Classic Sound of Chicago Soul* (collection), 2610

Boland, Francy. *Big Band Renaissance: The Evolution of the Jazz Orchestra* (collection), 739

Bolger, Ray. *Frank Loesser* (songwriter collection), 1106.1

Bollin, ZuZu. *Boogie Uproar: Texas Blues and R&B* (collection), 312

Bolling, Claude. *Pioneers of the New Age* (collection), 1371

Bolling, Pillie. ★*Let's Get Loose: Folk and Popular Blues Styles from the Beginning to the Early 1940s* (collection), 152

Bolton, Michael. *80's Pop Hits* (collection), 1238

Bon Jovi. *Slippery When Wet*, 2065

Bond, Eddie. *The Complete Goldwax Singles, Vol. 1* (collection), 2591

Bone Thugs-n-Harmony

The Collection, Vol. 1, 2723.1

E. 1999 Eternal, 2723.2

Bonna, Geanora. *Kwanzaa for Young People (and Everyone Else!)*, 3242

Bonner, Weldon "Juke Boy." *Life Gave Me a Dirty Deal*, 393

Bonnevilles. *Old Town Doo-Wop, Vols. 1–3* (collection), 2324

Bono. *Duets: An American Classic* (Bennett), 1251.1

Bono, Sonny. *Songs of Protest* (collection), 1820

Boogie Down Productions

By All Means Necessary, 2724.1

★*Criminal Minded*, 2724.2

Edutainment, 2724.3

Ghetto Music: The Blueprint of Hip Hop, 2724.4

Booker, Cedella Marley. *World Playground: A Musical Adventure for Kids* (collection), 3230

Booker, James. *Duke-Peacock's Greatest Hits* (collection), 2421

Booker T. and the MGs

Beg, Scream, and Shout! The Big Ol' Box of '60s Soul (collection), 2433

The Complete Stax/Volt Singles 1959–1968 (collection), 2594

The Complete Stax/Volt Soul Singles, Vol. 2: 1968–1971 (collection), 2595

Potato Hole, 2571.1

★*The R&B Box* (collection), 2239

Stax/Volt Revue: Live in London, Vols. 1 and 2 (collection), 2609

Stax/Volt Revue: Live in Norway 1967 (collection), 2446

Time Is Tight, 2571.2

Top of the Stax, Vol. 1: Twenty Greatest Hits (collection), 2611

Top of the Stax, Vol. 2: Twenty Greatest Hits (collection), 2612

The Boomtown Rats. *No Thanks! The '70s Punk Rebellion* (collection), 2003

Boone, Debby. *You Light up My Life: Greatest Inspirational Songs*, 3140

Boone, Pat. *Pat Boone*, 1180

Boot Camp Clik. *The Chosen Few*, 2725

Booth, Shirley. *Dorothy Fields* (songwriter collection), 1100

Bop-Chords. *The Doo-Wop Box II* (collection), 2323

Boredoms. *Super Are*, 2106

Bostic, Earl

The Big Horn: The History of the Honkin' and Screamin' Saxophone (collection), 2314

The Earl Bostic Story, 2315.1

The EP Collection, 2315.2

Boston. *Boston*, 1942

Boston Camerata

The American Vocalist: Spirituals and Folk Hymns, 1850-1870, 8.1

The Liberty Tree: Early American Music, 48

Lost Music of Early America: Music of the Moravians, 8.2

Noel, Noel! French Christmas Music, 1200–1600, 3275.1

Simple Gifts: Shaker Chants and Spirituals, 8.3

★*Sing We Noel: Christmas Music from England and Early America*, 3275.2

Boston Camerata (cont.)
  *Trav'ling Home: American Spirituals,
    1770–1870,* 8.4
Boswell, Connee
  ★*American Popular Song: Six Decades
    of Songwriters and Singers*
    (collection), 1059
  Bing Crosby and Some Jazz Friends
    (Crosby), 1125.2
  Irving Berlin: A Hundred Years
    (songwriter collection), 1096.3
  Irving Berlin (songwriter collection),
    1096.1
  *Lost Chords: White Musicians and Their
    Contributions to Jazz* (collection),
    479
  ★*The Music Goes Round and Around:
    The Golden Years of Tin Pan Alley,
    1930–1939* (collection), 1070
  ★*Sophisticated Ladies* (collection), 1087
The Boswell Sisters
  Arthur Schwartz (songwriter
    collection), 1110.2
  ★*At the Jazz Band Ball: Early Hot Jazz,
    Song, and Dance* (collection), 470
  The Classic Hoagy Carmichael
    (songwriter collection), 1097.1
  *The First of the Singer Songwriters: Key
    Cuts* (Carmichael), 1124
  Richard Whiting (songwriter
    collection), 1116
  ★*Sophisticated Ladies* (collection), 1087
  ★*That's How Rhythm Was Born,* 1121
  This Is Art Deco (collection), 1090
  Waller / Razaf (songwriter collection),
    1113.2
Bouchillon, Chris. *Good for What Ails
    You: Music of the Medicine Shows*
    (collection), 184
Bow Wow Wow. *Like Omigod! The
    80s Pop Culture Box (Totally)*
    (collection), 1241
Bowie, David
  Best of Bowie, 1952.1, 1952.2
  ★*Nuggets II: Original Artifacts from
    the British Empire and Beyond*
    (collection), 1791
  ★*The Rise and Fall of Ziggy Stardust,*
    1952.3
Bowie, Lester
  *Conjure: Music for the Texts of Ishmael
    Reed* (collection), 810
  The Great Pretender, 918
Bowlly, Al. *Vincent Youmans* (songwriter
    collection), 1118
The Box Tops. *Casey Kasem Presents
    America's Top Ten through the
    Years: The Sixties* (collection),
    1156
Boyd, Bill, and His Cowboy Ramblers
  Saturday Night Rag, 1435
  *Western Swing: 40 Bootstompers from
    the Golden Age* (collection), 1433

Boyd, Bill. *Doughboys, Playboys, and
    Cowboys: The Golden Years of
    Western Swing* (collection), 1428
Boyd, Eddie
  ★*Blues Classics* (collection), 146
  ★*Chess Blues* (collection), 287
  Chicago Is Just That Way (collection),
    289
  *Rockin' This House: Chicago Blues
    Piano* (collection), 257, 306
  *When the Sun Goes Down 4: That's All
    Right* (collection), 271
★Boyd, Jimmie. *Billboard Greatest
    Christmas Hits, 1935–1954*
    (collection), 3293
Boydston, John. *Eat Every Bean and Pea
    on Your Plate,* 3212
Boynton, Sandra. *Rhinoceros Tap,* 3213
Boys in the Band. *The Spring Story:
    Essential 70s Soul* (collection),
    2608
Boystown Gang. *Disco Box* (collection),
    2644
Boytim, Joan Frey. *Christmas Solos for All
    Ages,* 3276
Boyz II Men
  *Legacy: The Greatest Hits Collection,
    Deluxe ed.,* 2388
  #1s, 1256.2
BR5-49. *BR5-49,* 1696
Braam, Michiel. *Het Xyz Der Bik Bent
    Braam,* 835
Bracey, Ishmon
  *Canned Heat Blues: Masters of Delta
    Blues* (collection), 216
  Legends of Country Blues (collection),
    218
Brackeen, Charles. *Worshippers Come
    Nigh,* 944
Brackeen, Joanne. *Turnaround,* 945
Bradford, Alex
  Greatest Gospel Gems (collection), 3035
  ★*Jubilation! Great Gospel Performances,
    Vol. 2: More Black Gospel*
    (collection), 2967
  *None but the Righteous: Chess Gospel
    Greats* (collection), 3037
  ★*Precious Lord: Recordings of the Great
    Gospel Songs of Thomas A. Dorsey*
    (collection), 2968
  Testify! The Gospel Box (collection),
    2974
  The Great Gospel Men (collection),
    2988
  Too Close, 2993
Bradford, Bobby. *Comin' On,* 946
Bradley, J. Robert. *The Great Gospel Men*
    (collection), 2988
Bradley, Jan
  Best of Chess R&B, Vols. 1 and 2
    (collection), 2420
  Birth of Soul: Special Chicago Edition
    (collection), 2566

Bradley, Tommie. *Violin, Sing the Blues
    for Me: African-American Fiddlers*
    (collection), 192
Bradley, Will
  *Best of Will Bradley with Ray McKinley:
    Eight to the Bar,* 1122
  ★*Swing Time! The Fabulous Big Band
    Era* (collection), 1089
Bradshaw, Tiny
  An Anthology of Big Band Swing
    (collection), 528
  Breakin' Up the House, 2316.1
  The EP Collection–Plus, 2316.2
  The Roots of Rock 'n' Roll, 1946–1954
    (collection), 1755
  ★*Stompin' at the Savoy: The
    Original Indie Label, 1944–1961*
    (collection), 2429
Braff, Ruby. *A Sailboat in the Moonlight,*
    714
Bragg, Johnny. *Night Train to Nashville:
    Music City Rhythm and Blues,
    1945–1970, Vol. 2* (collection),
    2378
Braheny, Kevin. *Starflight 1* (collection),
    1374
Branch, Billy. *Blues Keep Following Me
    Around,* 423
Brand Nubian
  In God We Trust, 2726.1
  One for All, 2726.2
Brand, Oscar. *Presidential Campaign
    Songs, 1789–1996,* 49
Branigan, Laura. *Like Omigod! The
    80s Pop Culture Box (Totally)*
    (collection), 1241
Braxton, Anthony
  For Alto, 919.1
  3 Compositions of New Jazz, 919.2
  Willisau (Quartet) 1991, 919.3
Braxton, Toni. *The Essential Toni Braxton,*
    2398
Bread
  Best of Bread, 1253
  Billboard #1s: The '70s (collection),
    1235
Brecht, Bertolt. *From Berlin to Broadway:
    A Selection* (songwriter collection),
    1115.2
Brecker Brothers
  Brecker Brothers: Electro Jazz-Fusion,
    817.1
  *Sneakin' Up Behind You: The Very
    Best of the Brecker Brothers,*
    817.2
★Brecker, Michael. *Michael Brecker,* 947
Bredenberg, Fly. *Old-Time Country Guitar:
    An Instruction Guide to Old-Timey
    Solo Fingerpicking Guitar* (Cicchetti
    and Bredenberg), 1388
The Breeders. *Last Splash,* 2107
★Breiner, Peter. *Complete National
    Anthems of the World,* 3374

Brenda and the Tabulation. *The Sweetest Feeling: A Van McCoy Songbook* (collection), 2447
Brenston, Jackie
  Blue Flames: A Sun Blues Collection (collection), 337
  ★*The R&B Box* (collection), 2239
  The Roots of Rock 'n' Roll, 1946–1954 (collection), 1755
Breuker, Willem
  Bob's Gallery, 836.1
  In Holland, 836.2
Brewer, Spencer
  Narada Decade: The Anniversary Collection (collection), 1367
  Narada Wilderness Collection (collection), 1368
  Piano Solos: Narada Artists (collection), 1370
Brewer, Teresa
  The Best of Teresa Brewer, 1181
  ★*Sentimental Journey: Pop Vocal Classics, Vol. 2* (collection), 1168
Brice, Fanny
  ★*Nipper's Greatest Hits: The 20's* (collection), 1071
  ★*Nipper's Greatest Hits: The 30's, Vol. 1* (collection), 1072
Brickman, Jim. *Solace: A Windham Hill Collection* (collection), 1373
Bridges, Alicia. *Disco Box* (collection), 2644
★Brim, John. *Chess Blues* (collection), 287
Bristow, M. J. *National Anthems of the World,* 3378
British folk-rock, 1851–1859
  Early Classics (Pentangle), 1856.1
  Five Leaves Left (Drake), 1852.1
  Greatest Hits (Donovan), 1851.1
  Liege and Lief (Fairport Convention), 1853.1
  Light Flight: The Anthology (Pentangle), 1856.2
  Shoot Out the Lights (Thompson), 1858
  Spanning the Years (Steeleye Span), 1857
  Sweet Child (Pentangle), 1856.3
  Sweet Little Mysteries: The Island Anthology (Martyn), 1855
  The Hangman's Beautiful Daughter (Incredible String Band), 1854
  Troubadour: The Definitive Collection (Donovan), 1851.2
  ★*Unhalfbricking* (Fairport Convention), 1853.2
  Walking on a Wire: 1968–2009 (Thompson), 1859
  Way to Blue: An Introduction to Nick Drake, 1852.2
  What We Did on Our Holidays (Fairport Convention), 1853.3
British invasion, 1786–1807
  ★*Abbey Road* (Beatles), 1794.1

Aftermath (Rolling Stones), 1802.1
The American Roots of the British Invasion (collection), 1786
Beatles for Sale, 1794.5
The Beatles, 1794.2
The Beatles: Complete Scores, 1794.3
The Beatles: Past Masters, 1794.4
Bee Gees Greatest, 1795
★*Beggars Banquet* (Rolling Stones), 1802.2
Best of the Animals, 1793
Best of the Who, 1805.1
The Best of the Move, 1799
The Best of the Spencer Davis Group, 1803
British Invasion (collection), 1789
British Invasion: Guitar Classics (collection), 1790
The British Beat: The Best of the 60s (collection), 1787
The British Invasion (collection), 1788
Greatest Hits (Procol Harum), 1801
A Hard Day's Night (Beatles), 1794.6
Help! (Beatles), 1794.7
The Hits (Dave Clark Five), 1796
The Hollies' Greatest Hits, 1797
★*Hot Rocks* (Rolling Stones), 1802.3
The Kids Are Alright (The Who), 1805.2
The Kink Kronikles (Kinks), 1798.1
Let It Bleed (Rolling Stones), 1802.4
Live at Leeds (The Who), 1805.3
★*Mr. Fantasy* (Traffic), 1804.1
★*Nuggets II: Original Artifacts from the British Empire and Beyond* (collection), 1791
★*Odyssey and Oracle* (Zombies), 1807
Out of Our Heads (Rolling Stones), 1802.5
★*Please Please Me* (Beatles), 1794.8
★*Revolver* (Beatles), 1794.9
The Rolling Stones Guitar Anthology, 1802.6
The Rolling Stones, Now!, 1802.7
★*Rubber Soul* (Beatles), 1794.10
Saucerful of Secrets (Pink Floyd), 1800.1
★*Sgt. Pepper's* Lonely Hearts Club Band (Beatles), 1794.11
Singles Collection: The London Years (Rolling Stones), 1802.8
Smiling Phases (Traffic), 1804.2
30 Years of Maximum R&B (The Who), 1805.4
Tommy (The Who), 1805.5
Traffic, 1804.3
25 Hits from the British Invasion (collection), 1792
★*Ultimate!* (Yardbirds), 1806
★*The Ultimate Collection* (Kinks), 1798.2
★*Who's Next. Deluxe Ed.* (The Who), 1805.7

Who's Next (The Who), 1805.6
★*With the Beatles,* 1794.12
Works (Pink Floyd), 1800.2
British superstars, 1921–1933
  All the Best (McCartney), 1927
  All Things Must Pass (Harrison), 1923
  The Best of Acoustic (Jethro Hull), 1924.1
  The Best of the Moody Blues, 1928
  ★*Dark Side of the Moon* (Pink Floyd), 1929.1
  Downtown Train: Selections from the Storyteller Anthology (Stewart), 1932.1
  Electric Warrior (T Rex), 1933
  ELO's Greatest Hits, 1922
  Every Picture Tells a Story (Stewart), 1932.2
  ★*Exile on Main St.* (Rolling Stones), 1931.1
  Greatest Hits (Cocker), 1921
  Greatest Hits (Queen), 1930
  Greatest Hits, Vol. 2 (John), 1925.2
  ★*Greatest Hits, Vol. 1* (John), 1925.1
  Imagine (Lennon), 1926.1
  Jump Back: The Best of the Rolling Stones, '71–'93, 1931.2
  ★*Lennon Legend,* 1926.2
  Plastic Ono Band (Lennon), 1926.3
  Shaved Fish (Lennon), 1926.4
  Some Girls (Rolling Stones), 1931.3
  Sticky Fingers (Rolling Stones), 1931.4
  Sucking in the Seventies (Rolling Stones), 1931.5
  The Very Best of Jethro Tull, 1924.2
  The Wall (Pink Floyd), 1929.2
Britt, Elton. *RCA Years,* 1400
Broadside Band. *John Playford's Popular Tunes* (Broadside Band), 103
Broadus, Cordozar Calvin, Jr. *See* Snoop Dogg
Brody, David. *Kenny Baker Fiddle,* 1573
Brooklyn All Stars. *The Best of Nashboro Gospel* (collection), 3032
★Brooks and Dunn. *Greatest Hits Collection,* 1628
Brooks, Big Leon. *Living Chicago Blues, Vol. 4* (collection), 418
Brooks, David
  From Berlin to Broadway: A Selection (songwriter collection), 1115.2
  The Big Horn: The History of the Honkin' and Screamin' Saxophone (collection), 2314
★Brooks, Dusty. *Nashville Jumps: Blues and Rhythm on Nashville Independent Labels 1945–1955* (collection), 2376
Brooks, Garth
  Garth Brooks, 1627.1
  No Fences, 1627.2
  Ropin' the Wind, 1627.3
  ★*Ultimate Hits,* 1627.4

Brooks, Hadda
  ★*Central Avenue Sounds: Jazz in Los
    Angeles* (collection), 471
  ★*The Okeh Rhythm and Blues Story*
    (collection), 2425
Brooks, John Benson. *Alabama Concerto,*
  1033
Brooks, Lonnie
  Bayou Lightning, 424
  Blues Fest: Modern Blues of the '80s
    (collection), 409
  Living Chicago Blues, Vol. 2 (collection),
    416
Brooks, Louis
  The Best of Excello Records
    (collection), 327
  ★*Nashville Jumps: Blues and Rhythm
    on Nashville Independent Labels
    1945–1955* (collection), 2376
  *Night Train to Nashville: Music City
    Rhythm and Blues, 1945–1970,
    Vol. 1* (collection), 2377
  *Southern Rhythm 'n' Rock: The
    Best of Excello Records, Vol. 22*
    (collection), 2427
Brooks, Tina. *True Blue,* 631
★Brooks, Tommy. *Nashville Jumps:
  Blues and Rhythm on Nashville
  Independent Labels 1945–1955*
  (collection), 2376
Broonzy, Big Bill
  All the Classic Sides, 272.1
  Big Bill Broonzy, Vol. 2, 272.2
  Blues in the Mississippi Night
    (collection), 214
  ★*The Blues: A Smithsonian Collection
    of Classic Blues Singers* (collection),
    145
  ★*Brother, Can You Spare a Dime?
    American Song during the Great
    Depression* (collection), 1061
  Chicago Is Just That Way (collection),
    289
  ★*From Spirituals to Swing: The
    Legendary 1938 and 1939 Carnegie
    Hall Concerts Produced by John
    Hammond* (collection), 564
  ★*Legends of the Blues, Vol. 1*
    (collection), 150
  ★*The Story of the Blues* (collection),
    158
  *When the Sun Goes Down 3: That's
    Chicago's South Side* (collection),
    270
  *When the Sun Goes Down 1: Walk Right
    In* (collection), 159
Brother Ali. *Shadows on the Sun,* 2727
Brothers and Sisters. *Eccentric Soul:
  The Nickel and Penny Labels*
  (collection), 2567
Brothers Johnson. *Strawberry Letter
  23: The Very Best of the Brothers
  Johnson,* 2618

Brotzmann, Peter
  The Chicago Octet/Tentet, 837.1
  The Complete Machine Gun Sessions,
    837.2
Brown, Altyrone Deno. *Eccentric Soul: The
  Bandit Label* (collection), 2597
Brown, Andrew. *Living Chicago Blues,
  Vol. 4* (collection), 418
Brown, Bobby. *Don't Be Cruel,* 2399
Brown, Buster. *The Fire / Fury Records
  Story* (collection), 2422
Brown, Charles
  All My Life, 350
  ★*Billboard Greatest Christmas Hits,
    1955–1983* (collection), 3294
  *Blue Yule: Christmas Blues and R&B
    Classics* (collection), 3295
  Blues Fest: Modern Blues of the '90s
    (collection), 410
  Blues Masters, Vol. 3: Texas Blues
    (collection), 311
  Blues Masters, Vol. 1: Urban Blues
    (collection), 338
  ★*The Blues: A Smithsonian Collection
    of Classic Blues Singers* (collection),
    145
  ★*The Complete Aladdin Recordings of
    Charles Brown,* 2248
  ★*Mean Old World: The Blues from
    1940–1994* (collection), 154
  ★*The R&B Box* (collection), 2239
  *The Swing Time Records Story: R&B,
    Blues, and Gospel, 1946–1952*
    (collection), 2430
  ★*Texas Music, Vol. 1: Postwar Blues
    Combos* (collection), 316
Brown, Chuck. *Bustin' Loose,* 2619
Brown, Clarence "Gatemouth"
  Alright Again!, 425
  ★*The Best of Duke-Peacock Blues*
    (collection), 336
  ★*Blues Classics* (collection), 146
  Blues Masters, Vol. 3: Texas Blues
    (collection), 311
  Boogie Uproar: Texas Blues and R&B
    (collection), 312
  The Original Peacock Recordings, 317
  ★*Texas Music, Vol. 1: Postwar Blues
    Combos* (collection), 316
Brown, Clifford
  Brown and Roach Incorporated, 632.1
  Clifford Brown Memorial Album,
    632.2
  Jazz Style of Clifford Brown, 632.3
  ★*Ken Burns Jazz: The Story of
    America's Music* (collection), 478
Brown, Earl. *The Swing Time Records
  Story: R&B, Blues, and Gospel,
  1946–1952* (collection), 2430
Brown, Foxy. *Ill Na Na,* 2728
Brown, Henry. *Twenty First Street Stomp:
  Piano Blues of St. Louis* (collection),
  259

Brown, Hi Henry. *St. Louis Blues: The
  Depression* (collection), 232
Brown, James
  *Beg, Scream, and Shout! The Big Ol'
    Box of '60s Soul* (collection), 2433
  *The Best of James Brown: The
    Christmas Collection,* 3325
  *Dave Godin's Deep Soul Treasures,
    Vols. 1–4* (collection), 2435
  *Foundations of Funk: A Brand New Bag,
    1964–1969,* 2620.1
  Funk Power 1970: A Brand New Thang,
    2620.2
  *Have a Nice Decade: The '70s Pop
    Culture Box* (collection), 1240
  *I Got the Feelin': James Brown in the
    60s,* 2620.3
  King R&B Box Set (collection), 2424
  ★*Live at the Apollo,* 2457.1
  Live at the Apollo, Vol. 2, 2457.2
  Live at the Garden, 2457.3
  ★*The R&B Box* (collection), 2239
  ★*Roots of a Revolution,* 2457.4
  Say It Live and Loud: Live in Dallas,
    2620.4
  The Singles, Vol. 2: 1960–1963, 2457.6
  The Singles, Vol. 3: 1964–1965, 2457.7
  The Singles, Vol. 4: 1966–1967, 2457.8
  The Singles, Vol. 5: 1967–1969, 2457.9
  The Singles, Vol. 6: 1969–1970,
    2457.10
  The Singles, Vol. 7: 1970–1972,
    2457.11
  The Singles, Vol. 8: 1972–1973,
    2457.12
  The Singles, Vol. 9: 1973–1975,
    2457.13
  The Singles, Vol. 10: 1975–1979,
    2457.14
  The Singles, Vol. 11: 1979–1981,
    2457.15
  *The Singles, Vol. 1: The Federal Years,
    1956–1960,* 2457.5
  *Soul Shots: A Collection of Sixties Soul
    Classics* (collection), 2443
  Star Time, 2457.16
Brown, Jocelyn. *The Spring Story:
  Essential 70s Soul* (collection),
  2608
Brown, Junior. *12 Shades of Brown,*
  1629
Brown, Les
  *Sentimental Journey: Pop Vocal
    Classics, Vol. 1* (collection), 1081,
    1167
  *16 Most Requested Songs of the 1940s,
    Vol. 1* (collection), 1082
  *16 Most Requested Songs of the 1940s,
    Vol. 2* (collection), 1083
  *Songs That Got Us through World War
    II* (collection), 1085
  ★*Swing Time! The Fabulous Big Band
    Era* (collection), 1089

Brown, Maxine
  *Beg, Scream, and Shout! The Big Ol'
    Box of '60s Soul* (collection), 2433
  Birth of Soul, 4 Vols. (collection), 2434
  *Dave Godin's Deep Soul Treasures,
    Vols. 1–4* (collection), 2435
  The Scepter Records Story (collection),
    2426
  25 All-Time Greatest Hits, 2458
Brown, Milton
  *Classic Country Music: A Smithsonian
    Collection* (collection), 1382
  ★*Complete Recordings of the Father
    of Western Swing, 1932–1937,*
    1436.1
  *Doughboys, Playboys, and Cowboys:
    The Golden Years of Western Swing*
    (collection), 1428
  *Heroes of Country Music, Vol. 1: Legends
    of Western Swing*(collection), 1429
  *Texas Music, Vol. 2: Western Swing and
    Honky Tonk* (collection), 1432
  *Western Swing: 40 Bootstompers from
    the Golden Age* (collection), 1433
  Western Swing Chronicles, Vol. 1,
    1436.2
  *When the Sun Goes Down 1: Walk Right
    In* (collection), 159
★Brown, Nappy. *Stompin' at the Savoy:
    The Original Indie Label, 1944–
    1961* (collection), 2429
★Brown, Oscar, Jr. *What It Is! Funky Soul
    and Rare Grooves* (collection),
    2615
Brown, Peter. *Disco Box* (collection),
    2644
★Brown, Priscilla. *The Vee-Jay Story:
    Celebrating 40 Years of Classic Hits*
    (collection), 2431
Brown, Richard "Rabbit." *A Richer
    Tradition: Country Blues and String
    Band Music* (collection), 187
Brown, Robert Clifford. *See* Washboard
    Sam
Brown, Roy
  *Crescent City Soul: The Sound of New
    Orleans, 1947–1974* (collection),
    2564
  Good Rocking Tonight: The Best of Roy
    Brown, 2249
  King R&B Box Set (collection), 2424
  ★*Mean Old World: The Blues from
    1940–1994* (collection), 154
  The Roots of Rock 'n' Roll, 1946–1954
    (collection), 1755
Brown, Ruth
  ★*Atlantic R&B, 1947–1974*
    (collection), 2418
  Miss Rhythm: Greatest Hits and More,
    2250
  *Night Train to Nashville: Music City
    Rhythm and Blues, 1945–1970,
    Vol. 1* (collection), 2377

★*The R&B Box* (collection), 2239
The Roots of Rock 'n' Roll, 1946–1954
    (collection), 1755
Brown, Savoy. *Stroll On: An Immediate
    Blues Collection* (collection), 369
Brown, Shirley. *Top of the Stax, Vol. 1:
    Twenty Greatest Hits* (collection),
    2611
Brown, Toni. *16 Down Home Country
    Classics* (collection), 1385
Brown, Walter. *Legendary Big Band
    Singers* (collection), 767
Brown, Willie
  *Blues Masters, Vol. 8: Mississippi Delta
    Blues* (collection), 215
  ★*Masters of the Delta Blues: The Friends
    of Charlie Patton* (collection), 220
  ★*Negro Blues and Hollers* (collection),
    178
Browne, Jackson
  80's Pop Hits (collection), 1238
  The Pretender, 1901.1
  The Very Best of Jackson Browne,
    1901.2
Brown's Ferry Four. *16 Greatest Hits,*
    1460
★Browns. *Nipper's Greatest Hits: The 50's,
    Vol. 1* (collection), 1163
Brubeck, Dave
  Dave Brubeck: In Your Own Sweet Way,
    665.1
  Dave Brubeck Live in '64 and '66,
    607.1
  Jazz at Oberlin, 607.2
  Jingle Bell Jazz (collection), 3314
  ★*Ken Burns Jazz: The Story of
    America's Music* (collection), 478
  Piano Legends (collection), 480
  Pioneers of the New Age (collection),
    1371
  ★*Time Out,* 665.2
Bruce, Neely. *Music of the American
    Revolution: The Birth of Liberty*
    (collection), 46
Brummels, Beau. *San Francisco Nights*
    (collection), 1829
Bruner, Cliff
  Cliff Bruner and His Texas Wanderers,
    1437
  *Doughboys, Playboys, and Cowboys:
    The Golden Years of Western Swing*
    (collection), 1428
  *Heroes of Country Music, Vol. 1:
    Legends of Western Swing*
    (collection), 1429
  *Swingbillies: Hillbilly and Western
    Swing on Modern/Colonial/Flair,
    1947–1952* (collection), 1431
  *Texas Music, Vol. 2: Western Swing
    and Honky Tonk* (collection),
    1432
Brunson, Milton
  Great Gospel Moments, 3055

*Stand Up: A Collection of America's
    Great Gospel Choirs* (collection),
    3053
Bryan, James. *The Civil War Music
    Collector's Edition* (collection), 61
Bryant, Audrey. *Night Train to Nashville:
    Music City Rhythm and Blues,
    1945–1970, Vol. 1* (collection),
    2377
★Bryant, Beulah. *Nashville Jumps:
    Blues and Rhythm on Nashville
    Independent Labels 1945–1955*
    (collection), 2376
Bryant, Jimmy
  *Frettin' Fingers: The Lightning Guitar of
    Jimmy Bryant,* 1461
  *Stratosphere Boogie: The Flaming
    Guitars of Speedy West and Jimmy
    Bryant,* 1555
Bryant, Jimmy and the Sons of the
    Saddle. *Swingbillies: Hillbilly and
    Western Swing on Modern/Colonial/
    Flair, 1947–1952* (collection),
    1431
Bryant, Ray. *Jazz Lullaby* (collection),
    3264
Bryant's Jubilee Quartette. *The Half Ain't
    Never Been Told, Vols. 1 and 2*
    (collection), 2956
Bryson, Peabo. *Anthology,* 2400
bubblegum. *See* surf, bubblegum, garage
    bands, and pop
Bublé, Michael. *Michael Bublé,* 1254
Buchman, Rachel. *Jewish Holiday Songs
    for Children,* 3243
Buck and Bubbles and Their Buckets.
    Stars of the Apollo (collection),
    2240
Buck and His Band. *Stars of the Apollo*
    (collection), 2240
Buckley, Jeff
  Grace, 2108.1
  Jeff Buckley: Live in Chicago, 2108.2
Buckwheat Zydeco. *World Playground:
    A Musical Adventure for Kids*
    (collection), 3230
Budd, Harold
  Ambient 2: The Plateaux of Mirror,
    1320.1
  Pavilion of Dreams, 1320.2
Buell, Uncle Ruthie. *Chanukah at Home*
    (collection), 3238
Buffalo Springfield
  Buffalo Springfield Again, 1832.1
  ★*Retrospective: The Best of Buffalo
    Springfield,* 1832.2
Buffett, Peter
  *Narada Decade: The Anniversary
    Collection* (collection), 1367
  Narada Wilderness Collection
    (collection), 1368
Buggles. *Like Omigod! The 80s Pop Culture
    Box (Totally)* (collection), 1241

Built to Spill. *There's Nothing Wrong with Love,* 2109

Bullock, Chick
★*The Crooners* (collection), 1062
The Great Depression: American Music in the '30s (collection), 1066

Bumble Bee Slim
Back to the Crossroads: The Roots of Robert Johnson (collection), 212
★*The Blues: A Smithsonian Collection of Classic Blues Singers* (collection), 145
Favorite Country Blues: Guitar-Piano Duets (collection), 267
The Georgia Blues (collection), 242
★*Legends of the Blues, Vol. 2* (collection), 151

Bunn, Alden. *See* Slim, Tarheel

Bunn, Allen Rathel. *See* Slim, Tarheel

Burch, Elder, and Congregation. *How Can I Keep from Singing: Early American Religious Music and Song, Vols. 1 and 2* (collection), 2957

Burdon, Eric. *Songs of Protest* (collection), 1820

Burke, Solomon
★*Atlantic R&B, 1947–1974* (collection), 2418
★*Atlantic Soul, 1959–1975* (collection), 2589
Beg, Scream, and Shout! The Big Ol' Box of '60s Soul (collection), 2433
Birth of Soul, 4 Vols. (collection), 2434
A Change Is Gonna Come, 2459.1
Don't Give Up on Me, 2459.2
★*Home in Your Heart: The Best of Solomon Burke,* 2459.3
Nashville, 2459.4
★*The R&B Box* (collection), 2239
Soul Alive!, 2459.5
Soul Alive! (Burke), 426
You Can Run but You Can't Hide, 2459.6

Burmer, Richard. *Sunday Morning Coffee* (collection), 1375

Burnett, Chester Arthur. *See* Howlin' Wolf

Burnett, J. C. *A First-Time Buyer's Guide to American Negro Spirituals* (collection), 32

★Burnett, Richard. *Anthology of American Folk Music, Vols. 1–3* (collection), 1386

★Burnette, Johnny. *Legends of Guitar: Rock The '50s, Vol. 2* (collection), 1750

★Burnie, Ben. *At the Jazz Band Ball: Early Hot Jazz, Song, and Dance* (collection), 470

Burns, Eddie. *Detroit Blues: Blues from the Motor City* (collection), 291

Burns, Ralph
New York, New York [1985] (Burns and Auld), 1054.1

New York, New York [2004] (Burns and Auld), 1054.2

Burnside, R. L.
Blues Fest: Modern Blues of the '90s (collection), 410
Deep Blues (collection), 217
Too Bad Jim, 427

Burr, Henry. *The Phonographic Yearbook, 1908: Take Me Out with the Crowd* (collection), 1076

Burrage, Harold. *Birth of Soul, 4 Vols.* (collection), 2434

Burrell, Kenny
★*Guitar Forms,* 633
Progressions: 100 Years of Jazz Guitar (collection), 481

Burrello, Tony. *Greasy Kid Stuff* (collection), 3210

Burse, Charlie. *Good Time Blues: Harmonicas, Kazoos, Washboards, and Cow-Bells* (collection), 268

Burton, Gary
Crystal Silence, 818.1
Dreams So Real, 818.2
A Genuine Tong Funeral / Lofty Fake Anagram, 1034

Burton, Richard. *Alan Jay Lerner* (songwriter collection), 1105.1

Bush, Kate. *The Whole Story,* 2043

Bush, Sam. *Glamour and Grits,* 1574

Busta Jones. *The Spring Story: Essential 70s Soul* (collection), 2608

Busta Rhymes
Extinction Level Event: The Final World Front, 2907.1
When Disaster Strikes . . ., 2907.2

Busy Bee. *Hip Hop Essentials, 1979–1991* (collection), 2675

Butler, Billy. *The Story of Brunswick: The Classic Sound of Chicago Soul* (collection), 2610

Butler, Jerry
Beg, Scream, and Shout! The Big Ol' Box of '60s Soul (collection), 2433
The Best of Jerry Butler, 2460.1
Birth of Soul: Special Chicago Edition (collection), 2566
Birth of Soul, 4 Vols. (collection), 2434
Iceman: The Mercury Years, 2460.2
★*Love Train: The Sound of Philadelphia* (collection), 2552
The Sweetest Feeling: A Van McCoy Songbook (collection), 2447
★Butler, Jerry and the Impressions. *The Vee-Jay Story: Celebrating 40 Years of Classic Hits* (collection), 2431

Butler, Myron, and Levi. *Wow Gospel #1s* (collection), 3074

Butterbeans and Susie
Complete Recorded Works, Vol. 1, 206
The Roots of Rap: Classic Recordings of the 1920's and 30's (collection), 157

Stars of the Apollo (collection), 2240

Butterfield, Paul
An Anthology: The Elektra Years, 371.1
Blues Fest: Modern Blues of the '70s (collection), 408
Blues Masters, Vol. 7: Blues Revival (collection), 390
Blues Masters, Vol. 4: Harmonica Classics (collection), 286
East West, 371.2
Paul Butterfield Teaches Blues Harmonica Master Class: Sessions with a Legendary Player, 371.3

Butthole Surfers. *Locust Abortion Technician,* 2110

Buzzcocks
No Thanks! The '70s Punk Rebellion (collection), 2003
Singles Going Steady, 2008

Byard, Jaki
Amarcord Nino Rota (collection), 809
Blues for Smoke, 702.1
Solo / Strings, 702.2
Sunshine of My Soul: Live at the Keystone Korner, 872

Byas, Don
★*The Commodore Story* (collection), 561
Complete American Small Group Recordings, 568.1
Complete 1946–1951 European Small Group Master Takes, 568.2
★*The Smithsonian Collection of Classic Jazz* (collection), 486

Byrd, Donald. *At the Half-Note Cafe, Vols. 1 and 2,* 634

Byrd, Henry Roeland "Roy." *See* Longhair, Professor

Byrd, Tracy. *Definitive Collection,* 1630

The Byrds
Legends of Guitar: Rock–The '60s, Vol. 1 (collection), 1860
Sweetheart of the Rodeo, 1462, 1822.1
★*20 Essential Tracks from the Boxed Set,* 1822.2

Byron, Don. *Tuskegee Experiments,* 948

C

★C and the Shells. *Atlantic Soul, 1959–1975* (collection), 2589

C + C Music Factory. *90's Pop Hits* (collection), 1242

Caballero, Don. *For Respect,* 2233

Cabaret Voltaire. *Original Sound of Sheffield '78/'82,* 1953

The Cadillacs
Best of Doo Wop Uptempo (collection), 1744
The Best of the Cadillacs, 2325.1
The Complete Josie Sessions, 2325.2
★*The Doo Wop Box: 101 Vocal Group Gems from the Golden Age of Rock 'n' Roll* (collection), 1745

★*The Doo-Wop Box* (collection), 2322
The Doo-Wop Box II (collection), 2323
Life Could Be a Dream: The Doo-Wop Sound, 2346
★*The R&B Box* (collection), 2239
Street Corner Serenade: The Greatest Doo-Wop Hits of the '50s and '60s (collection), 1756
Caedmon's Call. *Caedmon's Call,* 3141
Caesar, Shirley
   ★*First Lady of Gospel,* 2994.1
   Gospel (collection), 2962
   ★*Jubilation! Great Gospel Performances, Vol. 1: Black Gospel* (collection), 2966
   Live in Chicago, 2994.2
   The Rough Guide to Gospel (collection), 2970
   Story of Gospel Music (collection), 2973
   Testify! The Gospel Box (collection), 2974
Cage. *Hell's Winter,* 2730
Caine, Uri
   The Sidewalks of New York: Tin Pan Alley, 104
   Solitaire, 949
Cairo, Pap, and His Boys. *Swingbillies: Hillbilly and Western Swing on Modern/Colonial/Flair, 1947–1952* (collection), 1431
Cale, John. *Paris 1919,* 1954
★Calhoun, Red. *Nashville Jumps: Blues and Rhythm on Nashville Independent Labels 1945–1955* (collection), 2376
Callahan Brothers. *White Country Blues: A Lighter Shade of Blues,* 1427
Calloway, Cab
   ★*Best of the Big Bands,* 531
   George Gershwin (songwriter collection), 1101.3
   James Van Heusen (songwriter collection), 1112.1
   ★*The Jazz Singers: A Smithsonian Collection of Jazz Vocals from 1919–1994* (collection), 766
   Legendary Big Band Singers (collection), 767
   ★*Nipper's Greatest Hits: The 30's, Vol. 1* (collection), 1072
   Stars of the Apollo (collection), 2240
   Stormy Weather [1999] (Waller, Calloway, Horn, and others), 1057.1
   Stormy Weather [2005] (Waller, Calloway, Horn, and others), 1057.2
   ★*Swing Time! The Fabulous Big Band Era* (collection), 1089
Calt, Stephen. *Country Blues Songbook,* 162
Camelots. *The Doo-Wop Box II* (collection), 2323

Cameo. *Gold,* 2621
Cameron, G. C. *The Sweetest Feeling: A Van McCoy Songbook* (collection), 2447
★Cameron, Johnny. *What It Is! Funky Soul and Rare Grooves* (collection), 2615
Camp Lo. *Uptown Saturday Night,* 2731
★Campbell Brothers with Katie Jackson. *Sacred Steel: The Steel Guitar Tradition of the House of God Churches* (collection), 2980
Campbell, Delois Barrett
   ★*All God's Sons and Daughters: Chicago's Gospel Legends* (collection), 3030
   ★*Precious Lord: Recordings of the Great Gospel Songs of Thomas A. Dorsey* (collection), 2968
   ★*Say Amen, Somebody* (collection), 2971
Campbell, Eddie C. *King of the Jungle,* 428
Campbell, Glen
   All the Best, 1463.1
   Gentle on My Mind, 1463.2
Campbell, James Milton, Jr. *See* Little Milton
★Campbell, Louis. *Nashville Jumps: Blues and Rhythm on Nashville Independent Labels 1945–1955* (collection), 2376
Campbell, Muriel "Zeke." *Legends of Western Swing Guitar* (collection), 1430
Can
   Can, 1955.1
   Ege Bamyasi, 1955.2
   Tago Mago, 1955.3
Caniubs. *Can-I-Bus,* 2732
Canned Heat
   Blue Yule: Christmas Blues and R&B Classics (collection), 3295
   Blues Masters, Vol. 7: Blues Revival (collection), 390
   The Very Best of Canned Heat, 372
Cannibal Ox. *The Cold Vein,* 2733
Cannon, Ace. *The Hi Records Story* (collection), 2423
Cannon, Gus
   Blues Masters, Vol. 12: Memphis Blues (collection), 229
   ★*The Blues: A Smithsonian Collection of Classic Blues Singers* (collection), 145
   Masters of Memphis Blues (collection), 230
   ★*Memphis Masters: Early American Blues Classics* (collection), 231
   The Roots of Rock (collection), 368
   Songsters and Saints: Vocal Traditions on Race Records, Vol. 2 (collection), 191

Cannon's Jug Stompers
   Before the Blues: The Early American Black Music Scene; Classic Recordings from the 1920's and 30's, Vols. 1–3 (collection), 183
   The Best of Cannon's Jug Stompers, 193
   Good for What Ails You: Music of the Medicine Shows (collection), 184
   Ruckus Juice and Chittlins: The Great Jug Bands—Classic Recordings of the 1920s and '30s, Vol. 1 (collection), 188
   Ruckus Juice and Chittlins: The Great Jug Bands—Classic Recordings of the 1920s and '30s, Vol. 2 (collection), 189
   When the Sun Goes Down 2: The First Time I Met the Blues (collection), 160
   When the Sun Goes Down 1: Walk Right In (collection), 159
   Wild About My Lovin': Beale Street Blues, 1928–30 (collection), 233
Cantor, Eddie
   The Best of Eddie Cantor: A Centennial Celebration, 1123.1
   The Columbia Years, 1123.2
   Irving Berlin: A Hundred Years (songwriter collection), 1096.3
   Joe Franklin Presents . . . The Roaring '20s Roar Again (collection), 1069
   Makin' Whoopee with "Banjo Eyes," 1123.3
   ★*Nipper's Greatest Hits: The 20's* (collection), 1071
   This Is Art Deco (collection), 1090
   25 Sweethearts of Yesteryear (collection), 1092
Canton Spirituals. *Living the Dream: Live in Washington, D.C.,* 3013
Capitols. *Beg, Scream, and Shout! The Big Ol' Box of '60s Soul* (collection), 2433
Capone-n-Noreaga. *The War Report,* 2734
Cappadonna. *The Pillage,* 2735
The Capris
   ★*The Doo-Wop Box* (collection), 2322
   Old Town Doo-Wop, Vols. 1–3 (collection), 2324
Captain and Tennille. *Ultimate Collection: The Complete Hits,* 1255
Captain Beefheart
   Shiny Beast (Bat Chain Puller), 1872.1
   Trout Mask Replica, 1872.2
The Caravans
   The Best of Shirley Caesar with the Caravans, 3041.2
   ★*The Best of the Caravans,* 3041.1
   Birth of Soul, 4 Vols. (collection), 2434
   Good News: 22 Gospel Greats (collection), 3033

The Caravans (cont.)
    The Great 1955 Shrine Concert
        (collection), 3034
    *Jesus and Me: The Very Best of the
        Caravans with Albertina Walker,*
        3041.3
    ★*Jubilation! Great Gospel Performances,
        Vol. 2: More Black Gospel*
        (collection), 2967
    The Rough Guide to Gospel (collection),
        2970
    Testify! The Gospel Box (collection),
        2974
    ★*Working the Road: The Golden Age of
        Chicago Gospel* (collection), 3039
The Cardigans. *Whatever: The '90s Pop
        and Culture Box* (collection), 1244
The Cardinals
    ★*Atlantic R&B, 1947–1974*
        (collection), 2418
    ★*Atlantic Vocal Groups, 1951–1963*
        (collection), 2320
    The Doo-Wop Box II (collection), 2323
Cardona, Milton. *Conjure: Music for the
        Texts of Ishmael Reed* (collection),
        810
Carey, Mariah
    The Emancipation of Mimi, 1256.1
    #1s, 1256.2
Carle, Frankie
    ★*It Had to Be You: Popular Keyboard
        from the Days of the Speakeasy
        to the Television Era* (collection),
        1068
    *16 Most Requested Songs of the 1940s,
        Vol. 2* (collection), 1083
Carlisle, Cliff
    Blues Yodeler and Steel Guitar Wizard,
        1401
    *White Country Blues: A Lighter Shade of
        Blues,* 1427
Carlos, Wendy
    Pioneers of the New Age (collection),
        1371
    Switched on Bach, 1317
Carlton, Carl. *Duke-Peacock's Greatest Hits*
        (collection), 2421
Carman. *The Absolute Best,* 3142
Carmichael, Hoagy
    The Classic Hoagy Carmichael
        (songwriter collection), 1097.1
    *The First of the Singer Songwriters: Key
        Cuts,* 1124
    Hoagy Carmichael Centennial Collection
        (songwriter collection), 1097.3
    Hoagy Carmichael (songwriter
        collection), 1097.2
Carolina Kings. *This May Be My Last
        Time Singing: Raw African-
        American Gospel on 45rpm*
        (collection), 2982
Carolina Ladies Quartette. *How Can I
        Keep from Singing: Early American*

*Religious Music and Song, Vols. 1
        and 2* (collection), 2957
Carolina Ramblers. *Mountain Gospel:
        The Sacred Roots of Country Music*
        (collection), 3113
Carolina Tar Heels
    ★*Anthology of American Folk Music,
        Vols. 1–3* (collection), 1386
    *Good for What Ails You: Music of the
        Medicine Shows* (collection), 184
Carpenter, Mary Chapin. *Come On Come
        On,* 1631
Carpenters
    *The Look of Love: The Burt Bacharach
        Collection* (collection), 1161
    ★*The Singles,* 1257
Carr, James
    ★*Atlantic Soul, 1959–1975*
        (collection), 2589
    *Beg, Scream, and Shout! The Big Ol'
        Box of '60s Soul* (collection), 2433
    The Complete Goldwax Singles, 2461
    The Complete Goldwax Singles, Vol. 1
        (collection), 2591
    The Complete Goldwax Singles, Vol. 2
        (collection), 2592
    The Complete Goldwax Singles, Vol. 3
        (collection), 2593
    ★*The R&B Box* (collection), 2239
    *Respect: Aretha's Influences and
        Inspiration* (collection), 2440
Carr, Kurt. *One Church,* 3079
Carr, Leroy
    *Back to the Crossroads: The Roots of
        Robert Johnson* (collection), 212
    ★*Blues Classics* (collection), 146
    ★*The Blues: A Smithsonian Collection
        of Classic Blues Singers* (collection),
        145
    *Favorite Country Blues: Guitar-Piano
        Duets* (collection), 267
    ★*Legends of the Blues, Vol. 1*
        (collection), 150
    *Leroy Carr and Scrapper Blackwell,
        Volume 1, 1928–1934,* 276
    ★*Let's Get Loose: Folk and Popular
        Blues Styles from the Beginning to
        the Early 1940s* (collection), 152
    *The Roots of Rap: Classic Recordings
        of the 1920's and 30's* (collection),
        157
    ★*The Story of the Blues* (collection),
        158
    *When the Sun Goes Down 3: That's
        Chicago's South Side* (collection),
        270
Carr, Wynona
    Dragnet for Jesus, 2995
    Greatest Gospel Gems (collection),
        3035
    Jump Jack Jump!, 2317
Carriker, Rob. *Over There! Songs from
        America's Wars* (Marlborough

Singers and Chamber Players,
        tenor John English, and piano Rob
        Carriker), 1141
Carroll, Diahann. *Frank Sinatra: Concert
        Collection,* 1224.3
Carroll, Joe. *The Bebop Singers*
        (collection), 765
Carson, Fiddlin' John. *The Complete
        Recorded Works, Vol. 1,* 1402
Carson, Martha. *Jubilation! Great Gospel
        Performances, Vol. 3: Country
        Gospel* (collection), 3112
The Cars
    Complete Greatest Hits, 1984.1
    Greatest Hits, 1984.2
    *Like Omigod! The 80s Pop Culture Box
        (Totally)* (collection), 1241
Carter, A. P. *16 Down Home Country
        Classics* (collection), 1385
Carter, Anita. *Hank Williams Songbook*
        (collection), 1450
Carter, Benny
    An Anthology of Big Band Swing
        (collection), 528
    ★*Big Band Jazz: From the Beginnings to
        the Fifties* (collection), 529
    *Big Band Renaissance: The Evolution
        of the Jazz Orchestra* (collection),
        739
    Central City Sketches, 744
    ★*The Commodore Story* (collection),
        561
    Further Definitions, 715.1
    Montreux '77, 715.2
    The Music Master, 532
    Over the Rainbow, 715.3
    ★*The Smithsonian Collection of Classic
        Jazz* (collection), 486
Carter, Betty
    The Audience with Betty Carter, 774.1
    The Definitive Collection (songwriter
        collection), 1101.1
    I Can't Help It, 774.2
Carter, Big Lucky. *The Complete Goldwax
        Singles, Vol. 1* (collection), 2591
Carter, Bo
    Banana in Your Fruit Basket, 273
    *Raunchy Business: Hot Nuts and
        Lollypops* (collection), 269
    The Roots of Rock (collection), 368
    ★*The Story of the Blues* (collection),
        158
    *When the Sun Goes Down 2: The First
        Time I Met the Blues* (collection),
        160
★Carter, Buster. *Anthology of American
        Folk Music, Vols. 1–3* (collection),
        1386
Carter, Clarence
    ★*Atlantic Soul, 1959–1975*
        (collection), 2589
    *Beg, Scream, and Shout! The Big Ol'
        Box of '60s Soul* (collection), 2433

The Best of Clarence Carter: The Dr.'s Greatest Prescriptions, 2462.1
Muscle Shoals Sound (collection), 2605
Snatchin' It Back: The Best of Clarence Carter, 2462.2
★*What It Is! Funky Soul and Rare Grooves* (collection), 2615
The Carter Family
  ★*American Roots Music* (collection), 1379
  ★*Anthology of American Folk Music, Vol. 4* (collection), 1387
  ★*Anthology of American Folk Music, Vols. 1–3* (collection), 1386
  The Carter Family, 1927–1934: A. P., Sara, Maybelle, 1403.2
  ★*The Carter Family: Country Music Hall of Fame*, 1403.1
  The Carter Family on Border Radio, Vol. 1, 1403.4
  The Carter Family, 1935–1941, Vol. 2, 1403.3
  Classic Country Music: A Smithsonian Collection (collection), 1382
  ★*Goodbye Babylon* (collection), 2954
  The Gospel Tradition: The Roots and the Branches, Vol. 1 (collection), 2955
  In the Shadow of Clinch Mountain, 1403.5
  Jubilation! Great Gospel Performances, Vol. 3: Country Gospel (collection), 3112
  ★*Something Got a Hold of Me: A Treasury of Sacred Music* (collection), 3114
  When the Sun Goes Down 1: Walk Right In (collection), 159
Carter, Goree
  Boogie Uproar: Texas Blues and R&B (collection), 312
  ★*Texas Music, Vol. 1: Postwar Blues Combos* (collection), 316
Carter, James. *Real Quietstorm*, 950
Carter, John. *Castles of Ghana*, 951
★Carter, Maybelle. *Will the Circle Be Unbroken?* (collection), 1452
Carter, Regina. *Motor City Moments*, 952
Carter, Shawn Corey. *See* Jay Z
Caruso, Enrico
  The Phonographic Yearbook, 1907: Dear Old Golden Rule Days (collection), 1075
  The Phonographic Yearbook, 1912: Waitin' on the Levee (collection), 1077
Casa Loma Orchestra
  An Anthology of Big Band Swing (collection), 528
  ★*Big Band Jazz: From the Beginnings to the Fifties* (collection), 529
  The Great Depression: American Music in the '30s (collection), 1066

★*Swing Time! The Fabulous Big Band Era* (collection), 1089
Casey, Karan. *Seal Maiden: A Celtic Musical*, 3232
Cash, Johnny
  American Recordings, 1464.1
  Classic Country: Kings of Country (collection), 1381
  Come Along and Ride This Train, 1464.2
  The Gospel Music of Johnny Cash, 3119
  Hank Williams Songbook (collection), 1450
  Johnny Cash at Folsom Prison and San Quentin, 1464.3
  Johnny Cash at Town Hall Party, 1464.4
  Man in Black, 1954–1958, 1464.5
  Man in Black, 1959–1962, 1464.6
  ★*Sun Records' Greatest Hits* (collection), 1741
  ★*Sun Years*, 1464.7
Cash, Rosanne
  ★*Seven Year Ache*, 1632.1
  Very Best of Rosanne Cash, 1632.2
★Castaways. *Nuggets: Artifacts of the First Psychedelic Era* (collection), 1808
★Castelles. *Atlantic Vocal Groups, 1951–1963* (collection), 2320
Casting Crowns. *Lifesong*, 3143
Casual. *Fear Itself*, 2736
Cathedral Quartet. *Cathedral Classics*, 3120
Cats and a Fiddle. *When the Sun Goes Down 4: That's All Right* (collection), 271
Cavoukian, Raffi. *See* Raffi
Cees, Jay. *The Fire / Fury Records Story* (collection), 2422
The Cellos. *The Doo-Wop Box II* (collection), 2323
Cephas, John
  Blues Routes (collection), 413
  Guitar Man, 429
Chad and Jeremy. *25 Hits from the British Invasion* (collection), 1792
Chairmen of the Board. *Heaven Must Have Sent You: The Holland/ Dozier/Holland Story* (collection), 2436
Chaloff, Serge. *Blue Serge*, 608
Chambers Brothers. *Time Has Come: The Best of the Chambers Brothers*, 2622
Chamblee, Eddie. *The Big Horn: The History of the Honkin' and Screamin' Saxophone* (collection), 2314
Chamillionaire. *Ultimate Victory*, 2737
Chandler, Gene
  Beg, Scream, and Shout! The Big Ol' Box of '60s Soul (collection), 2433
  Birth of Soul: Special Chicago Edition (collection), 2566

The Doo-Wop Box II (collection), 2323
The Story of Brunswick: The Classic Sound of Chicago Soul (collection), 2610
★*The Vee-Jay Story: Celebrating 40 Years of Classic Hits* (collection), 2431
Change. *Disco Box* (collection), 2644
Channels
  ★*The Doo-Wop Box* (collection), 2322
  The Doo-Wop Box II (collection), 2323
Channing, Carol. *Jule Styne* (songwriter collection), 1111.1
★Chantays. *Surfin' Hits* (collection), 1810
The Chantels
  The Best of the Chantels, 2326
  Boddie Recording Company Cleveland, Ohio (collection), 2569, 2570
  ★*The Doo Wop Box: 101 Vocal Group Gems from the Golden Age of Rock 'n' Roll* (collection), 1745
  The Doo-Wop Box II (collection), 2323
  Life Could Be a Dream: The Doo-Wop Sound, 2346
  ★*The R&B Box* (collection), 2239
Chanteurs. *Birth of Soul: Special Chicago Edition* (collection), 2566
Chanticleer
  Our American Journey, 9.1
  Where the Sun Will Never Go Down, 9.2
Chao, Manu. *World Playground: A Musical Adventure for Kids* (collection), 3230
Chapell, Jim. *Ultimate New Age* (collection), 1376
Chapin, Thomas. *You Don't Know Me*, 953
Chapman, Steven Curtis
  CCM Top 100: Greatest Songs in Christian Music, Vol. 1 (collection), 3136
  Now and Then, 3144.1
  Speechless, 3144.2
  This Moment, 3144.3
Chappell, Jim. *New Age Piano Sampler* (collection), 1369
Charioteers
  All of My Appointed Time: Forty Years of a Cappella Gospel Singing (collection), 2958
  ★*Good News: 100 Gospel Greats* (collection), 2961
  Gospel: Negro Spirituals / Gospel Songs, 1926–1942 (collection), 2963
  The Gospel Tradition: The Roots and the Branches, Vol. 1 (collection), 2955
Charlap, Bill. *Written in the Stars*, 954
Charles, Ray
  ★*Atlantic R&B, 1947–1974* (collection), 2418
  ★*Atlantic Soul, 1959–1975* (collection), 2589
  Beg, Scream, and Shout! The Big Ol' Box of '60s Soul (collection), 2433

Charles, Ray (cont.)
  Birth of Soul, 4 Vols. (collection), 2434
  ★*The Blues: A Smithsonian Collection of Classic Blues Singers* (collection), 145
  The Classic Hoagy Carmichael (songwriter collection), 1097.1
  The Complete Country and Western Recordings, 1959–1986, 2463.1
  50 Years: The Artistry of Tony Bennett (Bennett), 1179.2
  His Greatest Hits, Vols. 1 and 2, 2463.2
  Let There Be Drums, Vol. 1: The '50s (collection), 1751
  Live at the Montreux Jazz Festival, 2463.3
  A Man and His Soul, 2463.4
  O-Genio Ray Charles, 1963: Live in Brazil, 2463.5
  ★*Pure Genius: The Complete Atlantic Recordings, 1952–1959,* 2463.6
  ★*The R&B Box* (collection), 2239
  Respect: Aretha's Influences and Inspiration (collection), 2440
  Singular Genius: The Complete ABC Singles, 2463.7
  The Swing Time Records Story: R&B, Blues, and Gospel, 1946–1952 (collection), 2430
  The Swingtime Records Story: R&B, Blues, and Gospel (collection), 313
Charles, Teddy
  Collaboration: West, 1035.1
  The Teddy Charles Tentet, 1035.2
Charters, Samuel. *Blues Masters, Vol. 10: Blues Roots,* 175
Chatman, John Len. *See* Memphis Slim
Chatmon, Bo
  Songsters and Saints: Vocal Traditions on Race Records, Vol. 1 (collection), 190
  Violin, Sing the Blues for Me: African-American Fiddlers (collection), 192
Chavis, Boozoo. *Blues Routes* (collection), 413
Cheap Trick
  Cheap Trick at Budokan, 1943
  80's Pop Hits (collection), 1238
Cheatham, Brother Samuel. *Good God! Born Again Funk* (collection), 2614
Cheatham, Doc. *Duets and Solos,* 716
Cheatham, Jeannie. *Blues Fest: Modern Blues of the '80s* (collection), 409
Checkmates Ltd. *Soul Shots: A Collection of Sixties Soul Classics* (collection), 2443
The Chemical Brothers
  Dig Your Own Hole, 2218.1
  Exit Planet Dust, 2218.2
Cher. *Complete Introduction to Disco* (collection), 1237
Cherry Blend. *Eccentric Soul: The Tragar and Note Labels* (collection), 2602

Cherry, Don. *Complete Communion,* 680
Cherry, Eagle Eye. *90's Pop Hits* (collection), 1242
Cherry, Neneh. *Raw Like Sushi,* 2044
Chesney, Kenny. *Greatest Hits,* 1633
Chesnutt, Mark. *Longnecks and Short Stories,* 1634
Chester, Gary. *The New Breed,* 490
Chevalier, Maurice
  ★*Nipper's Greatest Hits: The 30's, Vol. 1* (collection), 1072
  Richard Whiting (songwriter collection), 1116
  Rodgers / Hart (songwriter collection), 1109.1
  25 Sweethearts of Yesteryear (collection), 1092
Chic
  Billboard #1s: The '70s (collection), 1235
  Disco Box (collection), 2644
  The Very Best of Chic, 2645
Chicago
  Billboard #1s: The '70s (collection), 1235
  Chicago IX: Greatest Hits, 1914
Chicago Mass Choir
  Greatest Gospel Choirs (collection), 3052
  Just Having Church Live, 3056
Chicago soul
  Birth of Soul: Special Chicago Edition (collection), 2566
  Eccentric Soul: The Nickel and Penny Labels (collection), 2567
  Eccentric Soul: Twinight's Lunar Rotation (collection), 2568
Chicago Travelers. *Good God! Born Again Funk* (collection), 2614
Chiffons. *The Best of the Girl Groups, Vols. 1 and 2* (collection), 2321
children's music
  babies and toddlers, 3184–3190
  classical music for children, 3252–3261
  lullabies, 3262–3266
  multicultural music, 3226–3236
  overview, p.179
  preschool, 3191–3207
  religious and holiday music, 3237–3251
  school age or all ages, 3208–3225
The Chi-Lites
  The Story of Brunswick: The Classic Sound of Chicago Soul (collection), 2610
  20 Greatest Hits, 2464
Chimes. *The Doo-Wop Box II* (collection), 2323
The Chipmunks
  ★*Billboard Greatest Christmas Hits, 1955–1983* (collection), 3294

Dr. Demento Presents: The Greatest Christmas Novelty CD of All Time (collection), 3307
Chips. *The Doo-Wop Box II* (collection), 2323
Choates, Harry. *Texas Music, Vol. 2: Western Swing and Honky Tonk* (collection), 1432
★Choir. *Nuggets: Artifacts of the First Psychedelic Era* (collection), 1808
★Chordcats. *Atlantic Vocal Groups, 1951–1963* (collection), 2320
Chordettes. *Casey Kasem Presents America's Top Ten through the Years: The Doo-Wop Years, 1950s* (collection), 1155
The Chords
  ★*Atlantic Vocal Groups, 1951–1963* (collection), 2320
  ★*The Doo Wop Box: 101 Vocal Group Gems from the Golden Age of Rock 'n' Roll* (collection), 1745
  ★*The Doo-Wop Box* (collection), 2322
  Rock and Roll: The Early Days (collection), 1752
Chosen Gospel Singers. *Greatest Gospel Gems* (collection), 3035
Christian, Charlie
  ★*From Spirituals to Swing: The Legendary 1938 and 1939 Carnegie Hall Concerts Produced by John Hammond* (collection), 564
  ★*The Genius of the Electric Guitar,* 569.1
  Original Guitar Hero, 569.2
  Progressions: 100 Years of Jazz Guitar (collection), 481
  ★*The Smithsonian Collection of Classic Jazz* (collection), 486
Christian music, popular. *See* gospel music and other popular Christian music
Christian rap, 3167–3183
  The Art of Translation (Grits), 3175.1
  Between Two Worlds (Lee), 3178
  Blacklight (Tedashii), 3182
  Bone-a-Fide (T-Bone), 3181.1
  The Chosen Ones (P.I.D.), 3180
  The Compilation Album (116 Clique), 3179
  Dominionaire (Jones), 3176
  Gang Affiliated (Gospel Gangstaz), 3174.1
  Grammatical Revolution (Grits), 3175.2
  History: Our Place in His Story (Cross Movement), 3170
  Holy Culture (Cross Movement), 3171
  Holy Hip Hop: Taking the Gospel to the Streets, Vols. 1-12 (collection), 3167
  I Can See Clearly Now (Gospel Gangstaz), 3174.2
  Tha Life of a Hoodlum (T-Bone), 3181.2

Lions and Liars (Baraka), 3169
Moment of Truth (da' T.R.U.T.H.), 3172
Momentum (TobyMac), 3183.1
Our World Fallen (Flame), 3173.1
Our World Redeemed (Flame), 3173.2
Rehab (Lecrae), 3177
Stop the Funeral (Ambassador), 3168
Welcome to Diverse City (TobyMac), 3183.2
Christian rock. *See* inspirational, contemporary Christian, and Christian Rock
★Christian, Tommy. *At the Jazz Band Ball: Early Hot Jazz, Song, and Dance* (collection), 470
Christmas music
    popular, 3291–3345
    traditional, 3267–3290
Christy, June
    James Van Heusen (songwriter collection), 1112.1
    ★*The Jazz Singers: A Smithsonian Collection of Jazz Vocals from 1919–1994* (collection), 766
    Jule Styne (songwriter collection), 1111.1
    Sentimental Journey: Capitol's Great Ladies of Song (collection), 1166
    Something Cool, 775
Chrome. *Half Machine Lip Moves*, 2111
Chryssomallis, Yiannis. *See* Yanni
Chuck and Me. *Eccentric Soul: Twinight's Lunar Rotation* (collection), 2568
Chuck Wagon Gang
    Close Harmony: A History of Southern Gospel Music, Vol. 1 (collection), 3108
    ★*Goodbye Babylon* (collection), 2954
    I'll Fly Away, 3121
    The Gospel Tradition: The Roots and the Branches, Vol. 1 (collection), 2955
Chumbawumba. *Whatever: The '90s Pop and Culture Box* (collection), 1244
Church, Jimmy. *Night Train to Nashville: Music City Rhythm and Blues, 1945–1970, Vol. 2* (collection), 2378
Ciani, Suzanne
    New Age Piano, 1336.1
    New Age Piano Sampler (collection), 1369
    The Velocity of Love, 1336.2
Cibo Matto. *Viva! La Woman*, 2045
Cicchetti, Stephen. *Old-Time Country Guitar: An Instruction Guide to Old-Timey Solo Fingerpicking Guitar* (Cicchetti and Bredenberg), 1388
Ciccone, Madonna Louise. *See* Madonna
Cincinnati Jug Band
    Ruckus Juice and Chittlins: The Great Jug Bands—Classic Recordings of the 1920s and '30s, Vol. 1 (collection), 188
    Ruckus Juice and Chittlins: The Great Jug Bands—Classic Recordings of the 1920s and '30s, Vol. 2 (collection), 189
Cincinnati Pops. *Chiller*, 3349
Cincinnati's University Singers
    The Hand That Holds the Bread: Progress and Protest in the Gilded Age (Songs from the Civil War to the Columbian Exposition), 105.1
    "I Wants to Be a Actor Lady" and Other Hits from Early Musical Comedies, 105.2, 1067
Circle. *Paris Concert*, 920
Civil War period political music, 59–80
    Ballads of the Civil War, 1831–1865 (Nye), 77
    Bloody War: Songs, 1924-1939 (collection), 59
    Blue and Gray: Songs of the Civil War (collection), 60
    Civil War (Jimerson), 74.2
    Civil War Piano: Parlor Memories (Davis), 70
    Civil War Songbook (Crawford), 68
    Civil War Songs (Foster), 73.1
    The Civil War Grand Military Ball (52nd Regimental String Band), 72
    The Civil War: Its Music and Its Sounds (Eastman Wind Ensemble), 71
    The Civil War (Jimerson), 74.1
    The Civil War Music Collector's Edition (collection), 61
    collections, 59–63
    Crossing the Stream (Trillium), 80
    Dear Friends and Gentle Hearts: The Songs of Stephen Foster and the Civil War (Foster), 73.2
    Dulcem Melodies: Favorite Campfire Songs of the Civil War Era (2nd South Carolina String Band), 78.1
    Far, Far from Home (2nd South Carolina String Band), 78.2
    For the Old Folks at Home (Battlefield Balladeers), 66
    In High Cotton: Favorite Camp Songs of the Civil War (2nd South Carolina String Band), 78.3
    Lightning in a Jar: An Evening of Civil War Music (2nd South Carolina String Band), 78.4
    Lincoln's America (Cook), 67.1
    Music of the Civil War (Americus Brass Band), 65
    Music of the 26th N.C. Regimental Band, CSA, Vol. 1: A Storm in the Land (American Brass Quintet Brass Band), 64.1
    Music of the 26th N.C. Regimental Band, CSA, Vol. 2: Cheer, Boys, Cheer! (American Brass Quintet Brass Band), 64.2
    Score of the Civil War (Silber and Silverman), 79
    Songs of the Civil War and Stephen Foster Favorites (Mormon Tabernacle Choir), 75
    Songs of the Civil War: Battlefields and Campfires (97th Regimental String Band), 76
    Songs of the Civil War (collection), 62
    ★*Songs of the Civil War: First Recordings from Original Editions* (collection), 63
    Tenting Tonight (Cook), 67.2
    Union and Liberty! Music Heard on the Northern Homefront during the Civil War (D. C. Hall's New Concert and Quadrille Band), 69
Clannad. *Celtic Themes: Very Best of Clannad*, 1360
Clapton, Eric
    Crossroads, 1863.1
    Eric Clapton Anthology, 1863.2
    461 Ocean Boulevard, 1863.3
    Slowhand, 1863.4
    Stroll On: An Immediate Blues Collection (collection), 369
Clara Ward Singers
    ★*I Feel the Holy Spirit*, 3042
    Jesus Put a Song in My Soul (collection), 3036
    Story of Gospel Music (collection), 2973
Clark, Buddy
    Arthur Schwartz (songwriter collection), 1110.2
    ★*The Crooners* (collection), 1062
    Here's to Romance, 1182
    ★*Sentimental Journey: Pop Vocal Classics, Vol. 2* (collection), 1168
    16 Most Requested Songs of the 1940s, Vol. 2 (collection), 1083
Clark, Chris. *Heaven Must Have Sent You: The Holland/Dozier/Holland Story* (collection), 2436
Clark, Dee
    Birth of Soul: Special Chicago Edition (collection), 2566
    ★*The R&B Box* (collection), 2239
    ★*The Vee-Jay Story: Celebrating 40 Years of Classic Hits* (collection), 2431
    You're Looking Good / Hold On, It's Dee Clark, 2465
Clark, Guy
    The Essential Guy Clark, 1465.1
    Old No. 1, 1465.2
Clark, Mattie Moss. *I Don't Know What I Would Do without the Lord*, 3057
Clark, Paul. *First Love: A Historic Gathering of Jesus Music Pioneers* (collection), 3137

Clark, Petula
  25 Hits from the British Invasion
    (collection), 1792
  The Ultimate Petula Clark, 1258
Clark, Roy. *Greatest Hits,* 1466
Clark, Sharon and the Product of Time.
    Eccentric Soul: The Young Disciples
    (collection), 2562
The Clark Sisters
  Gospel (collection), 2962
  Is My Living in Vain, 3080
  Story of Gospel Music (collection),
    2973
Clark, Sonny
  Cool Struttin', 635.1
  Leapin' and Lopin', 635.2
Clark, Terry. *First Love: A Historic
    Gathering of Jesus Music Pioneers*
    (collection), 3137
Clark, Tim. *Starflight 1* (collection), 1374
Clarke, Kenny. *Big Band Renaissance:
    The Evolution of the Jazz Orchestra*
    (collection), 739
Clarke, Tony
  *Beg, Scream, and Shout! The Big Ol'
    Box of '60s Soul* (collection),
    2433
  Best of Chess R&B, Vols. 1 and 2
    (collection), 2420
Clarke, William. *Blues Fest: Modern Blues
    of the '90s* (collection), 410
Clark-Sheard, Karen. *Finally,* 3081
The Clash
  ★*The Clash,* 2009.1
  London Calling, 2009.2
  No Thanks! The '70s Punk Rebellion
    (collection), 2003
  Punk: Attitude (collection), 1980
classic blues. vaudeville or. *See*
    vaudeville or classic blues
classical music for children, 3252–3261
  Babar the Elephant (Poulenc), 3260
  Baby Mozart Music Festival, 3259.1
  Beethoven Lives Upstairs, 3256
  ★*Bernstein Favorites: Children's Classics*
    (collection), 3252
  collections, 3252–3254
  *Daydreams and Lullabies: A Celebration
    of Poetry, Songs, and Classical
    Music* (collection), 3253
  *G'night Wolfgang: Classical Piano
    Solos for Bedtime* (Louchard),
    3258.1
  *Hey Ludwig! Classical Piano Solos for
    Playful Times* (Louchard), 3258.2
  Mr. Bach Comes to Call, 3255
  *The Magic Flute Story: An Opera
    Fantasy* (Mozart), 3259.2
  *The Runaway Bunny, Paddington
    Bear's First Concert, Tubby the Tuba*
    (collection), 3254
  Tubby the Tuba (Kleinsinger), 3257
  Vivaldi's Ring of Mystery, 3261

Classics. *The Doo-Wop Box II* (collection),
    2323
Clay, Judy
  ★*Atlantic Soul, 1959–1975*
    (collection), 2589
  *Beg, Scream, and Shout! The Big Ol'
    Box of '60s Soul* (collection), 2433
  *Top of the Stax, Vol. 2: Twenty Greatest
    Hits* (collection), 2612
Clay, Otis
  *Beg, Scream, and Shout! The Big Ol'
    Box of '60s Soul* (collection), 2433
  Complete Otis Clay on Hi Records, 2466
  I'll Treat You Right, 430
  The Hi Records Story (collection),
    2423
Clayton, Buck. *Complete Legendary Jam
    Sessions Master Takes,* 717
Clayton, Doctor. *When the Sun Goes Down
    4: That's All Right* (collection), 271
Clayton, Jay. *Circle Dancing,* 776
The Cleftones
  ★*The Doo-Wop Box* (collection), 2322
  The Doo-Wop Box II (collection), 2323
  The Ultimate Collection, 2327
Clements, Vassar. *Hillbilly Jazz,* 1575
Clemons, Clarence. *80's Pop Hits*
    (collection), 1238
Clemons, Homer, and His Texas
    Swingbillies. *Swingbillies: Hillbilly
    and Western Swing on Modern/
    Colonial/Flair, 1947–1952*
    (collection), 1431
Cleveland Golden Echos. *Boddie
    Recording Company Cleveland, Ohio*
    (collection), 2569, 2570
Cleveland, Rev. James
  ★*The Best of Rev. James Cleveland and
    the G.M.W.A.,* 3058.1
  Down Memory Lane, 2996.1
  Gospel (collection), 2962
  The Great Gospel Men (collection),
    2988
  It's a New Day, 3058.2
  *James Cleveland Sings with the World's
    Greatest Choirs,* 3058.3
  ★*Jubilation! Great Gospel Performances,
    Vol. 1: Black Gospel* (collection),
    2966
  ★*Peace Be Still,* 2996.2
  *Stand Up: A Collection of America's
    Great Gospel Choirs* (collection),
    3053
  Story of Gospel Music (collection),
    2973
  Testify! The Gospel Box (collection),
    2974
Cleveland soul. *Boddie Recording
    Company Cleveland, Ohio*
    (collection), 2570
Cliff Bruner's Texas Wanderers. *Western
    Swing: 40 Bootstompers from the
    Golden Age* (collection), 1433

Clifton, Bill. *Bill Clifton: The Early Years,
    1957–1958,* 1576
Cline, Nels. *New Monastery: The Music of
    Andrew Hill,* 955
Cline, Patsy
  Gold, 1467.1
  Patsy Cline: Sweet Dreams Still, 1467.2
  ★*The Patsy Cline Collection,* 1467.3
Clinic. *Internal Wrangler,* 2234
Clinton, George
  Computer Games, 2623.1
  The Mothership Connection, 2623.2
★Clinton, Larry. *Nipper's Greatest Hits:
    The 30's, Vol. 1* (collection), 1072
Clipse. *Hell Hath No Fury,* 2738
Clooney, Rosemary
  Alec Wilder (songwriter collection),
    1117.1
  ★*American Popular Song: Six Decades
    of Songwriters and Singers*
    (collection), 1059
  Blue Rose, 1183.1
  Cy Coleman (songwriter collection),
    1098.2
  Duke Ellington (songwriter collection),
    1099.1
  E. Y. Harburg (songwriter collection),
    1103
  Girl Singer, 1259.1
  Harry Warren (songwriter collection),
    1114
  Hoagy Carmichael (songwriter
    collection), 1097.2
  Irving Berlin: A Hundred Years
    (songwriter collection), 1096.3
  *Moments to Remember: The Golden
    Hits of the '50s and '60s Live*
    (collection), 1162
  ★*Sentimental Journey: Pop Vocal
    Classics, Vol. 3* (collection), 1169
  Sings the Lyrics of Johnny Mercer,
    1259.2
  16 Biggest Hits, 1183.2
  *16 Most Requested Songs: The 1950s,
    Vol. 1* (collection), 1171
  *Songs from the Girl Singer: A Musical
    Autobiography,* 1183.3
The Clovers
  ★*Atlantic R&B, 1947–1974*
    (collection), 2418
  ★*Atlantic Vocal Groups, 1951–1963*
    (collection), 2320
  ★*The Doo Wop Box: 101 Vocal Group
    Gems from the Golden Age of Rock
    'n' Roll* (collection), 1745
  ★*The Doo-Wop Box* (collection), 2322
  The Doo-Wop Box II (collection), 2323
  ★*The R&B Box* (collection), 2239
  The Roots of Rock 'n' Roll, 1946–1954
    (collection), 1755
  *Your Cash Ain't Nothin But Trash:
    Their Greatest Hits, 1951–55,*
    2328

Clusone 3. *Soft Lights and Sweet Music,* 838

The Coasters
  ★*Atlantic Soul, 1959–1975* (collection), 2589
  ★*Atlantic Vocal Groups, 1951–1963* (collection), 2320
  Casey Kasem Presents America's Top Ten through the Years: The Doo-Wop Years, 1950s (collection), 1155
  Let There Be Drums, Vol. 1: The '50s (collection), 1751
  ★*The R&B Box* (collection), 2239
  ★*There's a Riot Goin' On: The Coasters on ATCO,* 2329

Coates, Dorothy Love
  ★*The Gospel Sound* (collection), 2964
  ★*The Great Gospel Women* (collection), 2989
  The Great 1955 Shrine Concert (collection), 3034
  Testify! The Gospel Box (collection), 2974

Cobb, Arnett. *The Big Horn: The History of the Honkin' and Screamin' Saxophone* (collection), 2314

Cobham, Billy. *Best of Billy Cobham,* 819

Cochran, Eddie
  The Golden Era of Rock 'n' Roll (collection), 1748
  ★*Legends of Guitar: Rock–The '50s, Vol. 1* (collection), 1749
  ★*Legends of Guitar: Rock–The '50s, Vol. 2* (collection), 1750
  ★*Somethin' Else: The Fine Lookin' Hits of Eddie Cochran,* 1760

Cochran, Wayne. *Crash of Thunder: Boss Soul, Funk, and R&B Sides from the Vaults of the King, Federal, and Deluxe Labels* (collection), 2596

Cocker, Joe. *Greatest Hits,* 1921

Cocteau Twins
  Head over Heels, 2112.1
  Treasure, 2112.2

Codeine. *Frigid Stars,* 2113

Coe, David Allan. *For the Record: The First 10 Years,* 1468

Co-Eds. *Old Town Doo-Wop, Vols. 1–3* (collection), 2324

Cohan, George M. *You're a Grand Old Rag,* 131

Cohen, Anat. *Icons among Us* (collection), 934

Cohen, John. *Mountain Music Bluegrass Style* (collection), 1566

Cohen, Shelly. *The Gateway West,* 106

Cohn, Al
  Body and Soul, 873
  The Jack Kerouac Collection (collection), 812

Cold Crush Brothers
  Fresh, Wild, Fly, and Bold, 2739

Hip Hop Essentials, 1979–1991 (collection), 2675

Coldplay. *A Rush of Blood to the Head,* 2066

Cole, Ann. *Blues Masters, Vol. 6: Blues Originals* (collection), 367

Cole, Cozy. *Let There Be Drums, Vol. 1: The '50s* (collection), 1751

Cole, Nat King
  After Midnight: The Complete Session, 718, 1184.1
  Alan Jay Lerner (songwriter collection), 1105.1
  Alec Wilder (songwriter collection), 1117.1
  ★*American Popular Song: Six Decades of Songwriters and Singers* (collection), 1059
  Best of the Nat King Cole Trio: Instrumental Classics, 570
  ★*Billboard Greatest Christmas Hits, 1935–1954* (collection), 3293
  ★*Central Avenue Sounds: Jazz in Los Angeles* (collection), 471
  The Christmas Song, 3326
  Dorothy Fields (songwriter collection), 1100
  Duke Ellington (songwriter collection), 1099.1
  George Gershwin (songwriter collection), 1101.3
  Harold Arlen (songwriter collection), 1095.1
  Harry Warren (songwriter collection), 1114
  ★*The Jazz Singers: A Smithsonian Collection of Jazz Vocals from 1919–1994* (collection), 766
  Jerome Kern (songwriter collection), 1104.1
  ★*Jumpin' at Capitol,* 1184.2
  The Legendary Crooners: Frank Sinatra, Dean Martin, Bing Crosby, Nat King Cole, Perry Como (collection), 1207
  Richard Whiting (songwriter collection), 1116
  Rodgers / Hart (songwriter collection), 1109.1
  ★*Sentimental Journey: Pop Vocal Classics, Vol. 1* (collection), 1081
  25 Sweethearts of Yesteryear (collection), 1092
  The Very Best of Nat King Cole, 1184.3
  The World of Nat King Cole, 1184.4

Cole, Natalie
  The Anthology, 2401
  Frank Sinatra: Concert Collection, 1224.3

Coleman, Cy
  Big Spender, Witchcraft, and Other Cy Coleman Favorites (songwriter collection), 1098.1

Cy Coleman (songwriter collection), 1098.2

Coleman, Hooks. *Southern Rhythm 'n' Rock: The Best of Excello Records, Vol. 22* (collection), 2427

Coleman, Jaybird
  Alabama Blues (collection), 240
  American Primitive, Vol. 1: Raw Pre-War Gospel (collection), 2976
  Harmonica Blues: Great Harmonica Performances of the 1920s and '30s (collection), 185

Coleman, Lamont. *See* Big L

Coleman, Ornette
  At the Golden Circle, Vols. 1 and 2, 681.1
  The Complete Science Fiction Sessions, 956.1
  ★*Free Jazz,* 681.2
  ★*Ken Burns Jazz Collection: Ornette Coleman,* 681.3
  ★*Ken Burns Jazz: The Story of America's Music* (collection), 478
  Naked Lunch [2003] (Coleman and Shore), 1053.1
  Naked Lunch [2005] (Coleman and Shore), 1053.2
  ★*The Shape of Jazz to Come,* 681.4
  Skies of America, 1036
  ★*The Smithsonian Collection of Classic Jazz* (collection), 486
  Sound Grammar, 956.2
  This Is Our Music, 681.5

Coleman, Steve
  Curves of Life, 957.1
  Mancy of Sound, 957.2

Coles, Dennis. *See* Ghostface Killah

★Coles, Tucker. *Nashville Jumps: Blues and Rhythm on Nashville Independent Labels 1945–1955* (collection), 2376

Colibri. *World Playground: A Musical Adventure for Kids* (collection), 3230

collections
  African American gospel
    choirs, 3051–3053
    collections, 1940s–1960s, 3030–3039
    contemporary, 3074
    quartets, 3006–3011
    solo personalities, 2987–2991
  alternative rock, 2091–2092
  bebop, 592
  big bands
    and the swing era, 528–530
    since the 1950s, 739
  bluegrass, 1559–1567
  blues
    and rock, 367–369
    contemporary blues and soul, 408–419
    general collections, 145–160

collections (cont.)
in the cities: 1920s–1940s, 266–271
jump blues, 2314
revival and folk blues, 386–392
vocal rhythm and blues groups, 2320–2324
British invasion, 1786–1792
children's music
babies' and toddlers' music, 3184
classical music, 3252–3254
lullabies, 3262–3264
multicultural, 3226–3230
preschool, 3191–3194
religious and holiday, 3237–3241
school age or all ages, 3208–3211
Christian rap, 3167
contemporary country and western: 1980s–present, 1618–1620
country and western, 1379–1385
dance music, electronica, etc., 2214
disco, 2644
early rock 'n' roll, 1743–1758
early soloists, 511
evangelists and other traditional performers, 2976–2982
free jazz and related styles of the 1960s, 678
funk, 2613–2615
Georgia, Alabama, and the East Coast blues, 240–244
gospel music and other popular Christian music, 2954–2957
guitar heroes, 1860–1861
hard bop and related extensions of bebop, 626–627
heavy metal/hard rock, 1938
holidays
Christmas, popular, 3291–3323
Christmas, traditional, 3267–3272
Halloween, 3346–3348
inspirational, contemporary Christian, and Christian Rock, 3135–3137
jazz
and film, 1050
and poetry, and concept albums, 809–812
and the classics: third stream, 1030
early jazz, 497–499
early jazz piano styles, 521
general collection, 470–487
popular jazz of the 1950s and 1960s, 664
singers, 765–767
Kansas City and other territory bands, 551–552
Louisiana blues, 327–335
mainstream country music: 1940s–1970s, 1449–1452
mainstream popular post-1967, 1235–1247

post-World War II through 1967, 1155–1175
pre-World War II, 1059–1118
Memphis and St. Louis blues, 229–233
Mississippi Delta blues, 211–221
modern blues, 336–347
New Orleans revival and traditional styles, 503
The 1950s and 1960s: cool jazz and the West Coast, 604
piano blues, 250–259
political music
Civil War period, 59–63
Revolutionary War period, 44–47
popular vocal and instrumental music, 91–101
postwar midwestern blues, 285–292
pre–World War II country and western, 1386–1391
punk and new wave
U.K., 2003–2005
U.S., 1977–1981
ragtime, 124–125
rap and hip-hop, 2659–2697
regional rhythm and blues styles, 2359–2361
regional soul styles, 2552
religious music, 1–5
rhythm and blues, 2239–2240
rock, 1715–1734
roots, 169–181
samplers and concept albums new age, 1366–1378
songsters, string bands, and jug bands, 183–192
soul, 2432–2447
southern rock, 1934
southern white religious styles, 3106–3116
spirituals, 32
sport and college songs, 3369
swing soloists and combos, 560–564
teen idols, instrumentals, and dance hits, 1771–1772
Texas and West coast blues, 311–316
Texas, Arkansas, and Louisiana blues, 236–237
U.S. rock scene in the sixties
folk-rock, 1820
surf, bubblegum, garage bands, and pop, 1808–1811
West coast and Texas, 1829–1830
vaudeville or classic blues, 202–205
western swing, 1428–1433
college songs. See sport and college songs
Collegians. The Doo-Wop Box II (collection), 2323
★Collette, Buddy. Central Avenue Sounds: Jazz in Los Angeles (collection), 471
Collier, Mitty. Best of Chess R&B, Vols. 1 and 2 (collection), 2420

Collins, Al. Best of Ace Records, Vol. 2: The R&B Hits (collection), 2419
Collins, Albert
★Blues Classics (collection), 146
Blues Masters, Vol. 9: Postmodern Blues (collection), 412
Blues Masters, Vol. 3: Texas Blues (collection), 311
★Ice Pickin', 431.1
Showdown!, 431.2
Soul Shots, Vol. 4: Urban Blues (collection), 343
★Texas Music, Vol. 1: Postwar Blues Combos (collection), 316
Truckin' with Albert Collins, 318
Collins, Arthur
I'll Dance Till de Sun Breaks Through: Ragtime, Cakewalks and Stomps, 133
Phono-Cylinders, Vols. 1 and 2 (collection), 1074
The Phonographic Yearbook, 1907: Dear Old Golden Rule Days (collection), 1075
The Phonographic Yearbook, 1908: Take Me Out with the Crowd (collection), 1076
The Phonographic Yearbook, 1912: Waitin' on the Levee (collection), 1077
Collins, Bootsy
Standing in the Shadows of Motown (collection), 2445
The Bootsy Collins Anthology: Glory B Da' Funks on Me, 2624
Collins, Jamie Owens. First Love: A Historic Gathering of Jesus Music Pioneers (collection), 3137
Collins, Lyn. Gimme Your Hand, J-B! (collection), 2613
Collins, Phil
80's Pop Hits (collection), 1238
No Jacket Required, 2067
Colonial North America and the United States to 1900. See U.S. to 1900
Coltrane, John, 677
Ascension, 677.1
★Blue Train, 677.2
Coltrane, 677.3
The Complete Africa / Brass Sessions, 677.4
Crescent, 677.5
Four Tenors: John Coltrane, Charles Lloyd, Sonny Rollins and Ben Webster (collection), 627
★Giant Steps, 677.6
Impressions, 677.7
Interstellar Space, 677.8
Jazz Masters: Vintage Collection, 1958–1961 (collection), 477
★John Coltrane and Johnny Hartman, 677.9

John Coltrane: Live in '60, '61, and '65,
   677.10
★*Ken Burns Jazz Collection: John
   Coltrane,* 677.11
★*Ken Burns Jazz: The Story of
   America's Music* (collection), 478
Live at Birdland, 677.12
Live at Village Vanguard, 677.13
★*A Love Supreme,* 677.14
Meditations, 677.15
Music of John Coltrane, 677.16
My Favorite Things, 677.17
★*The Smithsonian Collection of Classic
   Jazz* (collection), 486
Soultrane, 677.18
The World According to John Coltrane,
   677.19
Coltrane, Ravi. *Icons among Us*
   (collection), 934
Columbia Symphony Orchestra.
   *Early Syncopated Dance Music:
   Cakewalks, Two-Steps, Trots and
   Glides* (collection), 124
Columbo, Russ
   ★*American Popular Song: Six Decades
      of Songwriters and Singers*
      (collection), 1059
   ★*The Crooners* (collection), 1062
   ★*The Music Goes Round and Around:
      The Golden Years of Tin Pan Alley,
      1930–1939* (collection), 1070
Commander Cody and His Lost Planet
   Airmen. *Lost in the Ozone,* 1438
Commissioned. *Best of Commissioned,*
   3082
Commodores
   Anthology, 2330
   Complete Introduction to Disco
      (collection), 1237
   *Hitsville USA: The Motown Singles
      Collection, Vol. 2* (collection), 2604
   ★*What It Is! Funky Soul and Rare
      Grooves* (collection), 2615
Common
   Like Water for Chocolate, 2741.1
   One Day It'll All Make Sense, 2741.2
Common Sense. *Resurrection,* 2740
Como, Perry
   ★*American Popular Song: Six Decades
      of Songwriters and Singers*
      (collection), 1059
   ★*Greatest Hits,* 1185
   *The Legendary Crooners: Frank Sinatra,
      Dean Martin, Bing Crosby, Nat King
      Cole, Perry Como* (collection),
      1207
   Nipper's Greatest Hits: The 50's, Vol. 2
      (collection), 1164
   ★*Nipper's Greatest Hits: The 50's, Vol. 1*
      (collection), 1163
   Oscar Hammerstein II (songwriter
      collection), 1102
Company. *Company 6 and 7,* 839

Company Flow. *Funcrusherplus,* 2742
Compton's Most Wanted. *Music to
   Driveby,* 2743
computer new age. *See* electronic/
   computer new age
Con Funk Shun. *The Best of* Con Funk
   Shun, 2625
concept albums. *See* samplers and
   concept albums (new age)
Condon, Eddie
   Bing Crosby and Some Jazz Friends
      (Crosby), 1125.2
   Chicago Style, 571
   ★*The Commodore Story* (collection),
      561
★Confrey, Zez. *It Had to Be You: Popular
   Keyboard from the Days of the
   Speakeasy to the Television Era*
   (collection), 1068
Conley, Arthur
   ★*Atlantic R&B, 1947–1974*
      (collection), 2418
   *Beg, Scream, and Shout! The Big Ol'
      Box of '60s Soul* (collection), 2433
   *Dave Godin's Deep Soul Treasures,
      Vols. 1–4* (collection), 2435
   Muscle Shoals Sound (collection), 2605
   Stax/Volt Revue: Live in Norway 1967
      (collection), 2446
   The Platinum Collection, 2467
Connick, Harry, Jr.
   Only You: In Concert, 1260.1
   25, 1260.2
Conniff, Ray
   The Essential Ray Conniff, 1186
   *16 Most Requested Songs: The 1950s,
      Vol. 1* (collection), 1171
Connor, Chris
   George Gershwin (songwriter
      collection), 1101.3
   James Van Heusen (songwriter
      collection), 1112.1
   ★*The Jazz Singers: A Smithsonian
      Collection of Jazz Vocals from
      1919–1994* (collection), 766
   Warm Cool: The Atlantic Years, 777
The Consolers
   The Best of Nashboro Gospel
      (collection), 3032
   ★*The Gospel Sound of Spirit Feel*
      (collection), 2965
   Lord Bring Me Down, 3043
contemporary African American gospel,
   3074–3105
   All My Best to You (Hawkins), 3089
   Anthology: The Writer and His Music
      (Haddon), 3087
   Be Encouraged (Winans), 3105.1
   Best of Commissioned, 3082
   Best of the Rance Allen Group, 3076
   Best of Vanessa Bell Armstrong, 3077
   The Definitive Original Greatest Hits
      (Winans), 3102

Everlasting Love (Winans), 3104.1
★*15 Songs That Redefined Gospel Music
   in the 1970s* (Crouch), 3083.1
Finally (Clark-Sheard), 3081
Greatest Hits (Baylor), 3078
Heaven (Winans), 3103
Here I Am (Saoo), 3096
Holla: The Best of Trin-I-Tee 5:7, 3101
How I Got Over (Winans), 3105.2
Is My Living in Vain (Clark Sisters),
   3080
J Moss Project, 3093
Kirk Franklin and the Family, 3085.1
Life Changing (Norful), 3094
Live from Another Level (Houghton),
   3091
*The Lord Will Make a Way / Higher
   Plane* (Green), 3086
★*Love Alive* (Hawkins), 3090
Mighty Wind (Crouch), 3083.2
Mountain High, Valley Low (Adams),
   3075
★*Nu Nation Project* (Franklin), 3085.2
On Time God (Peoples), 3095
One Church (Carr), 3079
Out the Box (Tonéx), 3099
*The Praise and Worship Songs of
   Richard Smallwood,* 3097
Purified (Winans), 3104.2
Purpose by Design (Hammond), 3088
The 7th Episode: Live in Toronto
   (Dillard), 3084
Take 6, 3098
Thankful (Mary Mary), 3092
This Is Another Day (Crouch), 3083.3
Victory Live! (Tribbett), 3100
Wow Gospel #1s (collection), 3074
contemporary artists: 1970s through the
   2000s, 934–1029
   African Flower (Newton), 1000
   ★*Album Album* (DeJohnette), 962.1
   Angel Eyes (Cowell), 959
   Are You Glad to Be in America?
      (Ulmer), 1019
   Art of the Trio, Vol. 1 (Mehldau), 994
   As We Are Now (Rosnes), 1011
   Back East (Redman), 1008.1
   The Ballad of the Fallen (Haden),
      973.1
   Bass Desires (Johnson), 984
   Beat Kennel (Rova Saxophone
      Quartet), 1012
   Before We Were Born (Frisell), 969.1
   Belonging (Jarrett), 982.1
   Bennie Wallace Plays Monk (Wallace),
      1023
   *The Best of Jessica Williams on Jazz
      Focus, Vol. 1,* 1027
   Black Bone (Harris), 976
   Black Codes (from the Underground)
      (Marsalis), 991.1
   Blood on the Fields (Marsalis), 991.2
   Castles of Ghana (Carter), 951

contemporary artists (cont.)
Channel Three (Osby), 1002
Comin' On (Bradford), 946
The Complete Science Fiction Sessions (Coleman), 956.1
★*Conference of the Birds* (Holland), 980.1
Curves of Life (Coleman), 957.1
The Dark Tree (Tapscott), 1016
Decisions (Adams), 937
Deer Wan (Wheeler), 1026
Devils Paradise (Hemingway), 977
Dialogue (Dickerson), 963
Enroute: John Scofield Trio Live (Scofield), 1014.1
Even the Sounds Shine (Melford), 995
Eye on You (Jackson), 981
Fingerpainting: The Music of Herbie Hancock (McBride), 993
Floater (Jewels and Binoculars), 983
For Coltrane (Crispell), 960.1
Fo'tet Plays Monk (Peterson), 1004
From the Soul (Lovano), 988.1
Guitarist (Eubanks), 968
Hard Blues (Julius Hemphill Sextet), 985
The Holy la (Lacy), 986.1
Icons among Us (collection), 934
In Our Lifetime (Douglas), 965.1
It Should Have Happened a Long Time Ago (Motian), 999
Jason Moran Presents the Bandwagon (Moran), 998.1
Jumpin' In (Holland), 980.2
Kickin' It Live: The Glass House (Rebirth Brass Band), 1007
Kids (Lovano), 988.2
Koln Concert (Jarrett), 982.2
Let Yourself Go: The Lives of Jazz Pianist Fred Hersch (Hersch), 979.1
Live at Jazz Standard (Mays), 992
Live from the Village Vanguard (collection), 935
Live: Mardi Gras in Montreux (Dirty Dozen Brass Band), 964
Locked and Loaded: Live at the Blue Note (Pope), 1005
★*Lookout for Hope* (Frisell), 969.2
Love Remains (Watson), 1025
The Majesty of the Blues (Marsalis), 991.3
Malinke's Dance (Ehrlich), 966.1
Mancy of Sound (Coleman), 957.2
★*Masada: Live at Tonic* (Zorn), 1029.1
Mental Weather (Bloom), 943
★*Michael Brecker* (Brecker), 947
Modernistic (Moran), 998.2
Monk on Monk, 997
Morning Joy (Live at Sunset Paris) (Lacy), 986.2
Motor City Moments (Carter), 952
New Beginnings (Pullen), 1006

New Monastery: The Music of Andrew Hill (Cline), 955
News for Lulu (Zorn), 1029.2
News on the Rail (Ehrlich), 966.2
No Room for Argument (Roney), 1010
Noir Blue (Peplowski), 1003
Of Blues and Dreams (Davis), 961
One Great Day (Eskelin), 967
Playground (Malone), 989
Playing (Old and New Dreams), 1001
Prime Directive (Holland), 980.3
Quartet West: Always Say Goodbye (Haden), 973.2
Radio Music Society (Spalding), 1015
Real Quietstorm (Carter), 950
The Real Deal (29th Street Saxophone Quartet), 1018
Regeneration (Rudd), 1013
Renaissance (Marsalis), 990
Riding the Nuclear Tiger (Allison), 939
Roy Hargrove Quintet with the Tenors of Our Time (Hargrove), 974
Sail Away (Harrell), 975.1
Sanctified Dreams (Berne), 941.1
School Days: Crossing Division (Vandermark), 1020.1
Second Communion (Varner), 1021
Segments (Allen), 938
Sempre Amore (Waldron), 1022
7 Black Butterflies (Gress), 972
Seven Men in Neckties: History of the Micros, Vol. 1 (Microscopic Septet), 996
Silence (Jarrett), 982.3
Silent Tongues (Taylor), 1017.1
Smile (Wilson), 1028
Solitaire (Caine), 949
Sound Grammar (Coleman), 956.2
Special Edition (DeJohnette), 962.2
Spiritual Unity (Ribot), 1009
Standard of Language (Garrett), 970
Stefan (Gonzalez), 971
Steve Lacy-Roswell Rudd Quartet: Early and Late (Lacy), 986.3
The Storyteller (Crispell), 960.2
Strange City (Herbie Nichols Project), 978
Stumble (AALY Trio), 936
The Sublime And (Berne), 941.2
Thelonious: Fred Hersch Plays Monk (Hersch), 979.2
3 Phasis (Taylor), 1017.2
Time on My Hands (Scofield), 1014.2
Tiny Bell Trio: Constellations (Douglas), 965.2
Tom Harrell (Harrell), 975.2
Trio Music (Corea), 958
Turnaround (Brackeen), 945
Tuskegee Experiments (Byron), 948
Vandermark 5: Simpatico (Vandermark), 1020.2
Voice in the Night (Lloyd), 987
Wandering Moon (Blanchard), 942

Wanton Spirit (Barron), 940
Whisper Not (Jarrett), 982.4
Willisau Concert (Taylor), 1017.3
Wisdom of Uncertainty (Ware), 1024
Wish (Redman), 1008.2
Worshippers Come Nigh (Brackeen), 944
Written in the Stars (Charlap), 954
You Don't Know Me (Chapin), 953
contemporary blues and soul, 408–469
All Night Long (Kimbrough), 446
All the Way Back (Johnson), 444
All Your Love I Miss Loving: Live at the Wise Fools Pub, Chicago (Rush), 458.1
Alright Again! (Brown), 425
Bad Axe Blues (Seals and Whitehill), 461
Bayou Lightning (Brooks), 424
The Best of Anson Funderburgh and the Rockets: Blast Off (Funderburgh), 436
The Best of R&B: A Step-by-Step Breakdown of the Guitar Styles and Techniques (Rubin), 456
Big Walter Horton with Carey Bell (Horton), 442
Blue Soul (Walker), 466.1
Blues Fest: Modern Blues of the '90s (collection), 410
Blues Fest: Modern Blues of the '70s (collection), 408
Blues Fest: Modern Blues of the '80s (collection), 409
Blues Keep Following Me Around (Branch), 423
Blues Masters, Vol. 9: Postmodern Blues (collection), 412
Blues Routes (collection), 413
The Blues Is Alright, Vol. 1 (collection), 411
Bobby Rush Live at Ground Zero Blues Club (Rush), 457
Butt Naked Free (Davis), 435
Chicken, Gravy, and Biscuits (Lil' Ed and the Blues Imperials), 451
Cleaning House (Saffire—The Uppity Blues Women), 459
collections, 408–419
The Complete Trix Recordings (Lockwood), 452.1
Cry of the Prophets (King), 447
Damn Right, I've Got the Blues (Guy), 437.1
Deep Blues: A Musical Pilgrimage to the Crossroads (collection), 414
Edge of the City (Kinsey Report), 449
The Essential Stevie Ray Vaughan and Double Trouble (Vaughan), 465.1
False Accusations (Cray), 434.1
Fear No Evil (Ward), 467
The Gift (Walker), 466.2
★*Greatest Hits* (Hill), 440

Greens from the Garden (Harris), 438
Guitar Man (Cephas), 429
The Healer (Hooker), 441
Heartbroken Man (Barnes), 421
Hound Dog Taylor and the Houserockers
    (Taylor), 462
★I Got What It Takes (Taylor), 463
★Ice Pickin' (Collins), 431.1
I'll Treat You Right (Clay), 430
Johnson's Whacks (Johnson), 445
King of the Jungle (Campbell), 428
Live at Blue Chicago (Moore), 454
Living Chicago Blues, Vol. 1 (collection),
    415
Living Chicago Blues, Vol. 2 (collection),
    416
Living Chicago Blues, Vol. 3 (collection),
    417
Living Chicago Blues, Vol. 4 (collection),
    418
★Midnight Son (Seals), 460
Million Dollar Secret (Wellington), 469
The New Bluebloods (collection), 419
Right Place, Wrong Time (Rush), 458.2
The Right Time (James), 443
Showdown! (Collins), 431.2
The Sky Is Crying (Vaughan), 465.2
Something Inside of Me (King), 448
Soul Alive! (Burke), 426
Steady Rollin' Man (Lockwood), 452.2
Still Trapped (LaSalle), 450
★Strong Persuader (Cray), 434.2
Swamp Boogie Queen (Webster), 468
Sweet Tea (Guy), 437.2
Telephone King (Mooney), 453
★Texas Twister (Copeland), 432
Too Bad Jim (Burnside), 427
The Touch (Heartsman), 439
Turn the Heat Up (Copeland), 433
Walking on a Tightrope: The Songs of
    Percy Mayfield (Adams), 420
Walking on Fire (Neal), 455
What's Wrong with You (Belfour), 422
White African (Taylor), 464
contemporary Christian. See
    inspirational, contemporary
    Christian, and Christian Rock
contemporary country and western:
    1980s–present, 1618–1692
After Awhile (Gilmore), 1648.1
Anthology (Dalton), 1637
Anthology (Fricke), 1644
★Anthology: The Warner/Reprise Years
    (Harris), 1652.1
At the Ryman (Harris), 1652.2
Best of Bellamy Brothers, 1624
Best of the Gatlins: All the Gold in
    California (Gatlin Brothers), 1645
The Best of Billy Ray Cyrus, 1636
The Best of Don Williams, Vol. 1, 1689
The Best of Joe Ely, 1642.1
The Best of Lee Greenwood, 1650
The Best of Nanci Griffith, 1651

The Best of Toby Keith, 1658
★The Best of Vince Gill, 1647.1
Big Book of Country Rock (Leonard),
    1618
Blue (Rimes), 1674
Born to Fly / Restless (Evans), 1643
Breathe (Hill), 1654
Chiseled in Stone (Gosdin), 1649
Come On Come On (Carpenter), 1631
Cowboy Songs (Murphey), 1669
Decade of Hits (Daniels), 1638
Definitive Collection (Byrd), 1630
Definitive Collection (Loveless), 1662
Definitive Collection (Mavericks), 1664
Diamonds and Dirt (Crowell), 1635
A Dozen Roses (Desert Rose Band),
    1640
88 Elira St. (Gatton), 1646
Essential Alabama, 1622
★Essential Dolly Parton, 1672.1
Fair and Square (Gilmore), 1648.2
Fly (Dixie Chicks), 1641.1
Gail Davies, 1639
Garth Brooks, 1627.1
Gold (Oak Ridge Boys), 1670
Grand Ole Opry at Carnegie Hall
    (collection), 1619
Greatest Hits (Anderson), 1623
★Greatest Hits (Black), 1625.1
Greatest Hits (Chesney), 1633
★Greatest Hits Collection (Brooks and
    Dunn), 1628
Greatest Hits Collection (Jackson),
    1656.1
Greatest Hits Collection, Vol. 1
    (Adkins), 1621
Greatest Hits (Lee), 1661
★Greatest Hits (McEntire), 1666.1
Greatest Hits (McGraw), 1667
★Greatest Hits (Strait), 1678
Greatest Hits (Twain), 1683
Greatest Hits (Watson), 1686
Greatest Hits (White), 1687
Guitars, Cadillacs, Etc., Etc. (Yoakam),
    1692.1
★Hank Williams Jr.'s Greatest Hits,
    1690.1
Hearts in Armor (Yearwood), 1691
Here in the Real World (Jackson),
    1656.2
Home (Dixie Chicks), 1641.2
Honky Tonk Masquerade (Ely), 1642.2
Hot Country: A Comprehensive Guide
    to Lead and Rhythm Country Guitar
    Playing (Hodgson), 1655
I Told You So: The Ultimate Hits of
    Randy Travis, 1681.1
Keith Whitley, 1688
Killin' Time (Black), 1625.2
Let There Be Country (Stuart), 1679
Longnecks and Short Stories (Chesnutt),
    1634
Lyle Lovett, 1663

Mission Chapel Memories 1971–1975
    (Parton), 1672.2
No Fences (Brooks), 1627.2
Number One Hits (Judds), 1657
O Brother, Where Art Thou?
    (collection), 1620
Out of Hand; Your Place or Mine
    (Stewart), 1677
Reba #1's (McEntire), 1666.2
Ropin' the Wind (Brooks), 1627.3
★Seven Year Ache (Cash), 1632.1
Shadowland (lang), 1659
16 Biggest Hits (Van Shelton), 1685
Speechless / Gagged but Not Bound
    (Lee), 1660
★Storms of Life (Travis), 1681.2
Ten Years of Gold (Rogers), 1675
Texas Tornadoes, 1680
The Highwaymen, 1653
The Way That I Am (McBride), 1665
This Time (Yoakam), 1692.2
Time Well Wasted (Paisley), 1671.1
Trio (Parton, Ronstadt, Harris), 1673
12 Shades of Brown (Brown), 1629
20 Greatest Hits (Bogguss), 1626
Ultimate Dolly Parton, 1672.3
★Ultimate Hits (Brooks), 1627.4
Ultimate Ronnie Milsap, 1668
Urban Cowboy (soundtrack), 1684
Very Best of Rosanne Cash, 1632.2
Very Best of Travis Tritt, 1682
Waitin' for the Sun to Shine / Highways
    and Heartaches (Skaggs), 1676
When I Call Your Name (Gill), 1647.2
Whiskey Bent and Hell Bound
    (Williams), 1690.2
Wide Open Spaces (Dixie Chicks),
    1641.3
contemporary rhythm and blues,
    2393–2417
Anthology (Bryson), 2400
The Anthology (Cole), 2401
Any Love (Vandross), 2416.1
Baby Come to Me: The Best of Regina
    Belle, 2395
B'day (Beyoncé), 2396.1
Beyoncé, 2396.2
★The Breakthrough (Blige), 2397.1
Brown Sugar (D'Angelo), 2402
Channel Orange (Ocean), 2414
Covered (Gray), 2405.1
Do You Love Me Like You Say: The
    Very Best of Terence Trent D'Arby,
    2403
Don't Be Cruel (Brown), 2399
The Dreaming Room (Mvula), 2413
The Early Years (Patti LaBelle and the
    Bluebelles), 2410
The Essential Babyface, 2394
★The Essential Luther Vandross, 2416.2
The Essential Patti LaBelle, 2409.1
The Essential Toni Braxton, 2398
GIRL (Williams), 2417

contemporary rhythm and blues (cont.)
  Gold (LaBelle), 2409.2
  Greatest Hits (Jackson), 2406
  I Am . . . Sasha Fierce (Beyoncé), 2396.3
  Lemonade (Beyoncé), 2396.4
  Live! One Night Only (LaBelle), 2409.3
  Love in the Future (Legend), 2411
  Love, Luther (Vandross), 2416.3
  Luther Vandross Live at Radio City Music Hall, 2003, 2416.4
  Maxwell's Urban Hang Suite, 2412
  My Soul (James), 2407
  Now and Forever: The Hits (TLC), 2415
  R. Kelly as Mr. Showbiz: The Light It Up Tour, 2408.1
  ★*The R in R&B Collection, Vol. 1* (Kelly), 2408.2
  The Very Best of En Vogue, 2404
  The Very Best of Macy Gray, 2405.2
  The Very Best of Oleta Adams, 2393
  What's the 411? (Blige), 2397.2
contemporary soul, 2582–2584
  The Eternal Dance (Earth, Wind, and Fire), 2582.1
  From Luther, with Love: The Videos (Vandross), 2584.1
  Gratitude (Earth, Wind, and Fire), 2582.2
  Luther Vandross Live at Wembley, 2584.2
  Private Dancer (Turner), 2583
  Spirit (Earth, Wind, and Fire), 2582.3
  That's the Way of the World (Earth, Wind, and Fire), 2582.4
Contenders. *Contenders,* 1697
Contortions. *No New York* (collection), 1979
Contours. *Hitsville USA: The Motown Singles Collection* (collection), 2603
Conway's Orchestra. *I'll Dance Till de Sun Breaks Through: Ragtime, Cakewalks and Stomps,* 133
Cooder, Ry
  Into the Purple Valley, 1902.1
  Paradise and Lunch, 1902.2
Cook, Barbara
  ★*American Popular Song: Six Decades of Songwriters and Singers* (collection), 1059
  Arthur Schwartz (songwriter collection), 1110.2
  Barbara Cook at Carnegie Hall, 1261
  E. Y. Harburg (songwriter collection), 1103
  Irving Berlin (songwriter collection), 1096.1
  Oscar Hammerstein II (songwriter collection), 1102
Cook, Judy
  Lincoln's America, 67.1
  Tenting Tonight, 67.2

Cook, Richard. *Eccentric Soul: The Tragar and Note Labels* (collection), 2602
★Cooke, Calvin. *Sacred Steel: The Steel Guitar Tradition of the House of God Churches* (collection), 2980
Cooke, Edna Gallmon
  The Best of Nashboro Gospel (collection), 3032
  The Great Gospel Women, Vol. 2 (collection), 2990
  Mother Smith and Her Children (collection), 2991
Cooke, Sam
  Birth of Soul, 4 Vols. (collection), 2434
  ★*The Man Who Invented Soul,* 2468.1
  One Night Stand: Sam Cooke Live at the Harlem Square Club, 1963, 2468.2
  Portrait of a Legend, 2468.3
  Sam Cooke, Legend, 2468.4
  Sam Cooke with the Soul Stirrers: The Complete Specialty Recordings, 2578
Cookies
  ★*Atlantic R&B, 1947–1974* (collection), 2418
  The Best of the Girl Groups, Vols. 1 and 2 (collection), 2321
Cooley, Jack. ★*Nashville Jumps: Blues and Rhythm on Nashville Independent Labels 1945–1955* (collection), 2376
Cooley, Spade
  Doughboys, Playboys, and Cowboys: The Golden Years of Western Swing (collection), 1428
  Heroes of Country Music, Vol. 1: Legends of Western Swing (collection), 1429
  Shame on You, 1439
Cooley, Spade, and His Orchestra. *Western Swing: 40 Bootstompers from the Golden Age* (collection), 1433
Coolio. *Gangsta's Paradise,* 2744
Cooper, Les and the Soul Rockers. *The Fire / Fury Records Story* (collection), 2422
Cooper, Alice
  Have a Nice Decade: The '70s Pop Culture Box (collection), 1240
  Heavy Metal: The First 20 Years (collection), 1938
  Mascara and Monsters: The Best of Alice Cooper, 1944
Cooper, Eula. *Eccentric Soul: The Tragar and Note Labels* (collection), 2602
Cooper, Wilma Lee and Stoney. *Very Best of Wilma Lee and Stoney Cooper and the Clinch Mountain Clan,* 1469
Copas, Cowboy
  All-Time Country and Western Hits (collection), 1449
  Best of the Best, 1470

Copeland, Johnny
  Blues Masters, Vol. 3: Texas Blues (collection), 311
  ★*Texas Music, Vol. 1: Postwar Blues Combos* (collection), 316
  ★*Texas Twister,* 432
Copeland, Martha
  ★*I Can't Be Satisfied: Early American Women Blues Singers, Vol. 2: Town* (collection), 204
  Mean Mothers: Independent Womens' Blues, Vol. 1 (collection), 205
Copeland, Shemekiah. *Turn the Heat Up,* 433
Corea, Chick
  The Anthology, 820.1
  Now He Sings, Now He Sobs, 703
  Piano Legends (collection), 480
  ★*Return to Forever,* 820.2
  Trio Music, 958
Corinthian Singers. *Boddie Recording Company Cleveland, Ohio* (collection), 2569, 2570
Cormega. *The Realness,* 2745
★Cornell, Don. *Sentimental Journey: Pop Vocal Classics, Vol. 3* (collection), 1169
Corsairs. *Best of Chess R&B, Vols. 1 and 2* (collection), 2420
Coryell, Larry
  The Essential Larry Coryell, 821
  Progressions: 100 Years of Jazz Guitar (collection), 481
Cossu, Scott. *Windham Hill: The First Ten Years* (collection), 1377
Costa, Don. *Frank Sinatra: Concert Collection,* 1224.3
Costello, Elvis
  The Best of Elvis Costello: The First 10 Years, 2010.1
  Duets: An American Classic (Bennett), 1251.1
  The Look of Love: The Burt Bacharach Collection (collection), 1161
  ★*My Aim Is True,* 2010.2
  No Thanks! The '70s Punk Rebellion (collection), 2003
  Painted from Memory, 1262
  The Tomorrow Show with Tom Snyder: Punk and New Wave (collection), 1981
  This Year's Model, 2010.3
Cotten, Elizabeth. *Classic African American Gospel from Smithsonian Folkways* (collection), 2959
Cotton, James
  ★*American Roots Music* (collection), 1379
  Blue Flames: A Sun Blues Collection (collection), 337
  Blues Fest: Modern Blues of the '80s (collection), 409

Blues Masters, Vol. 4: Harmonica Classics (collection), 286

Blues Masters, Vol. 12: Memphis Blues (collection), 229

★*Chicago: The Blues Today!* (collection), 290

Deep in the Blues, 294

The Sun Blues Years (collection), 344

Counce, Curtis. *You Get More Bounce with Curtis Counce,* 609

Count Five
Nuggets: A Classic Collection from the Psychedelic Sixties (collection), 1809

★*Nuggets: Artifacts of the First Psychedelic Era* (collection), 1808

Counterpoint. *Let Me Fly: Music of Struggle, Solace and Survival in Black America,* 37

country and western
alt-country/Americana, 1693–1714
★*American Roots Music* (CDs) (collection), 1379
American Roots Music (DVDs) (collection), 1380
bluegrass, 1559–1617
Classic Country: Kings of Country (collection), 1381
Classic Country Music: A Smithsonian Collection (collection), 1382
contemporary: 1980s–present, 1618–1692
Country Guitar Bible (collection), 1383
The Dobro Book (Phillips), 1384
general collections, 1379–1385
mainstream country music: 1940s–1970s, 1449–1558
overview, p85–86
periodicals for up-to-date CD notices and reviews, suggested, p3
pre–World War II, 1386–1427
16 Down Home Country Classics (collection), 1385
western swing, 1428–1448

Country Gazette. *Hello Operator . . . This Is Country Gazette,* 1577

Country Gentlemen
Appalachian Stomp: Bluegrass Classics (collection), 1560
The Best of Bluegrass, Vol. 1: Standards (collection), 1561
Complete Vanguard Recordings, 1578.1
Country Songs, Old and New, 1578.2
Early Rebel Recordings, 1962–1971, 1578.3

Country Joe and the Fish
San Francisco Nights (collection), 1829
The Collected Country Joe and the Fish, 1833

Country Joe. *Songs of Protest* (collection), 1820

Counts. *The Doo-Wop Box II* (collection), 2323

Coup
Genocide and Juice, 2746.1
Steal This Double Album, 2746.2

Covarrubias, Miguel. *Blues: An Anthology,* 163

Covay, Don
★*Atlantic R&B, 1947–1974* (collection), 2418
★*Atlantic Soul, 1959–1975* (collection), 2589
Beg, Scream, and Shout! The Big Ol' Box of '60s Soul (collection), 2433
Mercy, Mercy! The Definitive Don Covay, 2469
Respect: Aretha's Influences and Inspiration (collection), 2440
★*What It Is! Funky Soul and Rare Grooves* (collection), 2615

Cow, Henry. *Unrest,* 1956

Coward, Noel. *The Roaring 'Twenties* (collection), 1080

Cowboy Junkies. *Trinity Session,* 1698

Cowboy Nation. *We Do as We Please,* 1699

Cowell, Stanley. *Angel Eyes,* 959

Cox, Bill. *The Great Depression: American Music in the '30s* (collection), 1066

Cox Family
Angels Are Singing: A Women's Bluegrass Gospel Collection, 1559
Beyond the City, 1579
Blue Ribbon Bluegrass (collection), 1563
Hand-Picked: 25 Years of Bluegrass on Rounder Records (collection), 1564

Cox, Ida
Blues Masters, Vol. 11: Classic Blues Women (collection), 203
Mean Mothers: Independent Womens' Blues, Vol. 1 (collection), 205
Stars of the Apollo (collection), 2240
The Uncrowned Queen of the Blues, 207

★Crain, Edward L. *Anthology of American Folk Music, Vols. 1–3* (collection), 1386

Cramer, Floyd. *Essential Floyd Cramer,* 1474

The Cramps
No Thanks! The '70s Punk Rebellion (collection), 2003
Songs the Lord Taught Us, 2114

Crass. *Feeding of the 5000,* 2011

Craven, Dwine. *The Mercury New Orleans Sessions 1950 and 1953* (collection), 2361

Crawford, Hank. *Night Train to Nashville: Music City Rhythm and Blues, 1945–1970, Vol. 1* (collection), 2377

Crawford, Richard. *Civil War Songbook,* 68

Cray, Robert
Blues Fest: Modern Blues of the '80s (collection), 409
Blues Masters, Vol. 9: Postmodern Blues (collection), 412
False Accusations, 434.1
★*Strong Persuader,* 434.2

Crayton, Pee Wee
Blues Masters, Vol. 1: Urban Blues (collection), 338
New Orleans Guitar (collection), 330
★*Texas Music, Vol. 1: Postwar Blues Combos* (collection), 316
★*The Vee-Jay Story: Celebrating 40 Years of Classic Hits* (collection), 2431

Cream
Disraeli Gears, 1864.1
Fresh Cream, 1864.2
Legends of Guitar: Rock–The '60s, Vol. 2 (collection), 1861
★*The Very Best of Cream,* 1864.3
Wheels of Fire, 1864.4

★Creation. *Nuggets II: Original Artifacts from the British Empire and Beyond* (collection), 1791

Creations Unlimited. *Boddie Recording Company Cleveland, Ohio* (collection), 2569, 2570

★Creedence Clearwater Revival. *Chronicle,* 1834

The Crescendos
★*Atlantic Vocal Groups, 1951–1963* (collection), 2320
Southern Rhythm 'n' Rock: The Best of Excello Records, Vol. 22 (collection), 2427

The Crests
Street Corner Serenade: The Greatest Doo-Wop Hits of the '50s and '60s (collection), 1756
★*The Doo-Wop Box* (collection), 2322
The Doo-Wop Box II (collection), 2323

Crispell, Marilyn
For Coltrane, 960.1
The Storyteller, 960.2

Criss, Sonny. *Sonny's Dream,* 745

Cropper, Steve. *Legends of Guitar: Rock— The '60s, Vol. 1* (collection), 1860

Crosby, Bing
★*American Popular Song: Six Decades of Songwriters and Singers* (collection), 1059
Arthur Schwartz (songwriter collection), 1110.2
★*Billboard Greatest Christmas Hits, 1935–1954* (collection), 3293
Bing Crosby and Some Jazz Friends, 1125.2
Bing: His Legendary Years, 1125.1
Bing's Gold Records, 1125.3
★*Brother, Can You Spare a Dime? American Song during the Great Depression* (collection), 1061
Centennial Anthology, 1125.4
★*A Centennial Anthology of His Decca Recordings,* 1125.5

Crosby, Bing (cont.)
The Classic Hoagy Carmichael (songwriter collection), 1097.1
Cole Porter (songwriter collection), 1108.1
★The Crooners (collection), 1062
Dorothy Fields (songwriter collection), 1100
E. Y. Harburg (songwriter collection), 1103
Fascinating Rhythm: George Gershwin (songwriter collection), 1101.2
The Flapper Box (collection), 1064
Frank Loesser (songwriter collection), 1106.1
Frank Sinatra: Concert Collection, 1224.3
Harold Arlen (songwriter collection), 1095.1
Hoagy Carmichael (songwriter collection), 1097.2
Irving Berlin (songwriter collection), 1096.1
It's Easy to Remember, 1125.6
James Van Heusen (songwriter collection), 1112.1
Joe Franklin Presents . . . The Roaring '20s Roar Again (collection), 1069
Johnny Mercer (songwriter collection), 1107.1
The Legendary Crooners: Frank Sinatra, Dean Martin, Bing Crosby, Nat King Cole, Perry Como (collection), 1207
★The Music Goes Round and Around: The Golden Years of Tin Pan Alley, 1930–1939 (collection), 1070
★Nipper's Greatest Hits: The 30's, Vol. 1 (collection), 1072
Richard Whiting (songwriter collection), 1116
Rodgers / Hart (songwriter collection), 1109.1
Sentimental Journey: Pop Vocal Classics, Vol. 1 (collection), 1167
★Sentimental Journey: Pop Vocal Classics, Vol. 1 (collection), 1081
★Sentimental Journey: Pop Vocal Classics, Vol. 2 (collection), 1168
It's Easy to Remember, 1125.7
Songs That Got Us through World War II, Vol. 2 (collection), 1086
This Is Art Deco (collection), 1090
25 Sweethearts of Yesteryear (collection), 1092
Vintage Children's Favorites (collection), 3211
Waller / Razaf (songwriter collection), 1113.2
Crosby, Bob
An Anthology of Big Band Swing (collection), 528
Big Band Dixieland, 533

Bing Crosby and Some Jazz Friends (Crosby), 1125.2
★Swing Time! The Fabulous Big Band Era (collection), 1089
Crosby, Stills & Nash
The Best of Crosby, Stills & Nash, 1903.1
Crosby, Stills & Nash, 1903.2
Cross, Christopher. Like Omigod! The 80s Pop Culture Box (Totally) (collection), 1241
Cross Movement
History: Our Place in His Story, 3170
Holy Culture, 3171
Crosse, Gay
★Nashville Jumps: Blues and Rhythm on Nashville Independent Labels 1945–1955 (collection), 2376
Night Train to Nashville: Music City Rhythm and Blues, 1945–1970, Vol. 2 (collection), 2378
crossover jazz: 1970s–1990s, 901–911
Best of the Yellowjackets (Yellowjackets), 911
The Best of David Sanborn (Sanborn), 908
Chuck Mangione (Mangione), 906.1
The Crusaders' Finest Hour (The Crusaders), 902
Feels So Good (Mangione), 906.2
Freddie Hubbard Live in France 1973 (Hubbard), 903
★George Benson Anthology (Benson), 901
Le Voyage: The Jean-Luc Ponty Anthology (Ponty), 907
Mister Magic (Washington), 910.1
Quincy Jones' Finest Hour (Jones), 904
Sun Goddess (Lewis), 905
The Very Best of Spyro Gyra (Spyro Gyra), 909
Winelight (Washington), 910.2
Crouch, Andraé
★15 Songs That Redefined Gospel Music in the 1970s, 3083.1
First Love: A Historic Gathering of Jesus Music Pioneers (collection), 3137
Going Up Yonder: The Best of the Gospel Choirs (collection), 3051
Mighty Wind, 3083.2
Rejoice and Shout (collection), 2969
Testify! The Gospel Box (collection), 2974
This Is Another Day, 3083.3
Crow, Dan. Chanukah at Home (collection), 3238
Crowe, J. D.
Blue Ribbon Bluegrass (collection), 1563
Hand-Picked: 25 Years of Bluegrass on Rounder Records (collection), 1564
★J. D. Crowe and the New South, 1580

The Bluegrass Album, Vol. 1 (collection), 1562
Crowell, Rodney. Diamonds and Dirt, 1635
★Crown Prince Waterford. Nashville Jumps: Blues and Rhythm on Nashville Independent Labels 1945–1955 (collection), 2376
The Crows
Best of Doo Wop Uptempo (collection), 1744
★The Doo Wop Box: 101 Vocal Group Gems from the Golden Age of Rock 'n' Roll (collection), 1745
★The Doo-Wop Box (collection), 2322
The Doo-Wop Box II (collection), 2323
The Golden Era of Rock 'n' Roll (collection), 1748
Crudup, Arthur "Big Boy"
★Mean Old World: The Blues from 1940–1994 (collection), 154
Rock Me Mama (Crudup), 274
The Fire / Fury Records Story (collection), 2422
When the Sun Goes Down 4: That's All Right (collection), 271
Crumit, Frank
Gay Caballero, 1126
When the Sun Goes Down 1: Walk Right In (collection), 159
The Crusaders. The Crusaders' Finest Hour, 902
The Crystals
A Christmas Gift for You from Phil Spector (collection), 3300
The Best of the Crystals, 2331
★Cuby and the Blizzards. Nuggets II: Original Artifacts from the British Empire and Beyond (collection), 1791
Cuellar, Carol. 170 Christmas Songs and Carols, 3277
Cufflinks. The Doo-Wop Box II (collection), 2323
Cugat, Xavier
Hit Parade, 1943 (collection), 1157
It's Easy to Remember (Crosby), 1125.6
The Original Latin Dance King, 1127
16 Most Requested Songs of the 1940s, Vol. 1 (collection), 1082
16 Most Requested Songs of the 1940s, Vol. 2 (collection), 1083
Culley, Frank "Floorshow." The Big Horn: The History of the Honkin' and Screamin' Saxophone (collection), 2314
Culture Club. Like Omigod! The 80s Pop Culture Box (Totally) (collection), 1241
Cumberland River Singers. The Best of King Gospel (collection), 3031
The Cure
Like Omigod! The 80s Pop Culture Box (Totally) (collection), 1241

No Thanks! The '70s Punk Rebellion (collection), 2003

Staring at the Sea: The Singles [Import], 2115

Curless, Dick. *Tombstone Every Mile,* 1475

Curry, Clifford. *Night Train to Nashville: Music City Rhythm and Blues, 1945–1970, Vol. 1* (collection), 2377

Curtis, King
Beg, Scream, and Shout! The Big Ol' Box of '60s Soul (collection), 2433
Blow Man, Blow!, 2573
Live at Fillmore West, 2574
Soul Shots: A Collection of Sixties Soul Classics (collection), 2443

Cypress Hill
Black Sunday, 2747.1
Cypress Hill, 2747.2

★Cyrkle. *Nuggets: Artifacts of the First Psychedelic Era* (collection), 1808

Cyrus, Billy Ray. *The Best of* Billy Ray Cyrus, 1636

D

D. C. Hall's New Concert and Quadrille Band. *Union and Liberty! Music Heard on the Northern Homefront during the Civil War,* 69

Da Bush Babees. *Gravity,* 2729

Da Lench Mob. *Guerillas in Tha Mist,* 2842

da' T.R.U.T.H. *Moment of Truth,* 3172

★Daddy Dean. *Nashville Jumps: Blues and Rhythm on Nashville Independent Labels 1945–1955* (collection), 2376

Daffan, Ted
Born to Lose, 1476
Texas Music, Vol. 2: Western Swing and Honky Tonk (collection), 1432

Daft Punk. *Homework,* 2219

daKAH. *Icons among Us* (collection), 934

Dale, Dick
Legends of Guitar: Rock–The '60s, Vol. 1 (collection), 1860
★*Surfin' Hits* (collection), 1810

Dalhart, Vernon
Classic Country Music: A Smithsonian Collection (collection), 1382
Inducted into the Hall of Fame, 1981, 1404
★*Nipper's Greatest Hits: The 20's* (collection), 1071
Vintage Children's Favorites (collection), 3211

Dallas Fort Worth Mass Choir
Going Up Yonder: The Best of the Gospel Choirs (collection), 3051
I Will Let Nothing Separate Me, 3059

Dallas String Band. *Good for What Ails You: Music of the Medicine Shows* (collection), 184

Dalton, Lacy J. *Anthology,* 1637

Dameron, Tadd
Fontainebleau, 746.1
The Magic Touch, 746.2
★*The Smithsonian Collection of Classic Jazz* (collection), 486

Damned. *No Thanks! The '70s Punk Rebellion* (collection), 2003

Damone, Vic
Alan Jay Lerner (songwriter collection), 1105.1
Harry Warren (songwriter collection), 1114
Sentimental Journey: Pop Vocal Classics, Vol. 4 (collection), 1170

Dan the Automator. *A Much Better Tomorrow,* 2749

dance hits. *See* teen idols, instrumentals, and dance hits

dance music, electronica, etc., 2214–2232
Dig Your Own Hole (Chemical Brothers), 2218.1
Essential Lee Perry: The Ultimate Upsetter, 2227.1
Exit Planet Dust (Chemical Brothers), 2218.2
Go: The Very Best of Moby, Deluxe Ed., 2224.1
Homework (Daft Punk), 2219
In the Aeroplane over the Sea (Neutral Milk Hotel), 2225
Kish Kash (Basement Jaxx), 2217.1
A Life Less Lived: The Gothic Box (collection), 2214
Liquid Liquid, 2222
Maxinquaye (Tricky), 2232
Moby, 2224.2
Moon Safari (Air), 2215
Never Trust a Hippy (Sherwood), 2229
New Forms (Size and Reprazment), 2230
The Orb's Adventures beyond the Ultraworld, 2226
Original Pirate Material (Streets), 2231
Play (Moby), 2224.3
Present Lover (Luomo), 2223
Remedy (Basement Jaxx), 2217.2
Richard D. James Album (Aphex Twin), 2216.1
Roots of Dub (King Tubby), 2221
Selected Ambient Works, 85–92 (Aphex Twin), 2216.2
Selected Ambient Works, Vol. II (Aphex Twin), 2216.3
The Ultimate Upsetter (Perry), 2227.2
Vocal Studies + Uprock Narratives (Prefuse 73), 2228
You've Come a Long Way, Baby (Fatboy Slim), 2220

Danderliers. *The Doo-Wop Box II* (collection), 2323

Dandy Lions. *Greasy Kid Stuff* (collection), 3210

Danforth, Percy. *The Early Minstrel Show* (collection), 96

D'Angelo. *Brown Sugar,* 2402

Danger Doom. *The Mouse and the Mask,* 2750

Daniel, Leroy. *The Complete Goldwax Singles, Vol. 2* (collection), 2592

Daniels, Charlie. *Decade of Hits,* 1638

Daniels, Julius. *Atlanta Blues: Big City Blues from the Heartland* (collection), 241

Daniels, L. *Eccentric Soul: The Tragar and Note Labels* (collection), 2602

Dankworth, John. *Big Band Renaissance: The Evolution of the Jazz Orchestra* (collection), 739

★Danleers. *The Doo-Wop Box* (collection), 2322

Danton, Jean. *American Dreamer: Heart Songs,* 107

Dara, Olu. *Conjure: Music for the Texts of Ishmael Reed* (collection), 810

★Darby, Ruby. *At the Jazz Band Ball: Early Hot Jazz, Song, and Dance* (collection), 470

D'Arby, Terence Trent. *Do You Love Me Like You Say: The Very Best of Terence Trent D'Arby,* 2403

Darby, Tom
Darby and Tarlton: Complete Recordings, 1405
White Country Blues: A Lighter Shade of Blues, 1427

Darin, Bobby
Sentimental Journey: Pop Vocal Classics, Vol. 4 (collection), 1170
The Ultimate Bobby Darin, 1773

★Darnell, Larry. *The Okeh Rhythm and Blues Story* (collection), 2425

Das EFX. *Dead Serious,* 2751

Das Rascist. *Relax,* 2752

Dash, Julian. *The Big Horn: The History of the Honkin' and Screamin' Saxophone* (collection), 2314

Dave Clark Five
The Hits, 1796
25 Hits from the British Invasion (collection), 1792

Davenport, Cow Cow
Before the Blues: The Early American Black Music Scene; Classic Recordings from the 1920's and 30's, Vols. 1–3 (collection), 183
★*Blues Classics* (collection), 146
Mama Don't Allow No Easy Riders Here: Strutting the Dozens; Classic Piano Rags, Blues, and Stomps (collection), 256
Shake Your Wicked Knees: Rent Parties and Good Times (collection), 258

Davenport, Jed
   Memphis Shakedown: More Jug Band Classics (collection), 186
   Ruckus Juice and Chittlins: The Great Jug Bands—Classic Recordings of the 1920s and '30s, Vol. 1 (collection), 188
   Ruckus Juice and Chittlins: The Great Jug Bands—Classic Recordings of the 1920s and '30s, Vol. 2 (collection), 189
Davies, Cyril. *Stroll On: An Immediate Blues Collection* (collection), 369
Davies, Gail. *Gail Davies,* 1639
Davis, Anthony. *Of Blues and Dreams,* 961
Davis Bible Singers. ★*A Warrior on the Battlefield: A Cappella Trail Blazers* (collection), 3011
Davis, Birdie. *The Big Horn: The History of the Honkin' and Screamin' Saxophone* (collection), 2314
Davis, Blind Wilie. *American Primitive, Vol. 1: Raw Pre-War Gospel* (collection), 2976
Davis, Charles. *Civil War Piano: Parlor Memories,* 70
Davis, Chip. *Sunday Morning Coffee* (collection), 1375
Davis, Dick. *The Big Horn: The History of the Honkin' and Screamin' Saxophone* (collection), 2314
Davis, Eddie "Lockjaw"
   Cookbook, Vol. 1, 636
   The Big Horn: The History of the Honkin' and Screamin' Saxophone (collection), 2314
Davis, Ellabelle. *A First-Time Buyer's Guide to American Negro Spirituals* (collection), 32
Davis, Gary
   The Complete Early Recordings of Rev. Gary Davis, 2983
   A First-Time Buyer's Guide to American Negro Spirituals (collection), 32
   Gospel: Negro Spirituals / Gospel Songs, 1926–1942 (collection), 2963
   Newport Folk Festival: Best of the Blues, 1959–68 (collection), 392
Davis, Guy. *Butt Naked Free,* 435
Davis, Jimmie
   Greatest Hits, Finest Performances, 1406
   The Roots of Rap: Classic Recordings of the 1920's and 30's (collection), 157
   When the Sun Goes Down 2: The First Time I Met the Blues (collection), 160
Davis, Johnny. *Eccentric Soul: The Bandit Label* (collection), 2597
Davis, Kathy
   The Complete Goldwax Singles, Vol. 2 (collection), 2592

The Complete Goldwax Singles, Vol. 3 (collection), 2593
★Davis, Larry. *The Best of Duke-Peacock Blues* (collection), 336
Davis, Mary Johnson. *Gospel Warriors: Over 50 Years of Great Solo Performances* (collection), 2987
Davis, Maxwell. *The Big Horn: The History of the Honkin' and Screamin' Saxophone* (collection), 2314
Davis, Miles, 676
   Ascenseur Pour L'echafaud [Lift to the Scaffold] [2006], 1046.1
   Ascenseur Pour L'echafaud [Lift to the Scaffold] [2007], 1046.2
   The Birth of the Cool, Vol. 2 (collection), 604
   ★*Bitches Brew,* 822.1
   ★*Complete Birth of the Cool,* 610
   Cookin', 676.1
   E.S.P., 676.2
   Filles de Kilimanjaro, 676.3
   Hipsters' Holiday: Vocal Jazz and R&B Classics (collection), 3313
   In a Silent Way, 822.2
   Jazz Masters: Vintage Collection, 1958–1961 (collection), 477
   Jazz Style of Miles Davis, 676.4
   Jingle Bell Jazz (collection), 3314
   ★*Ken Burns Jazz Collection,* 676.5
   ★*Ken Burns Jazz: The Story of America's Music* (collection), 478
   ★*Kind of Blue,* 676.6
   Live Evil, 822.3
   Live in Europe '67, 676.7
   The Magic of Miles Davis, 676.8
   ★*Miles Ahead,* 676.9
   Miles Davis Story, 676.10
   Miles Electric: A Different Kind of Blue, 676.11
   Miles Smiles, 676.12
   Milestones, 676.13
   ★*Porgy and Bess,* 676.14
   Relaxin', 676.15
   ★*Round about Midnight,* 676.16
   ★*Sketches of Spain,* 676.17
   ★*The Smithsonian Collection of Classic Jazz* (collection), 486
   Someday My Prince Will Come, 676.18
   A Tribute to Jack Johnson, 822.4
   Tutu, 822.5
   Workin', 676.19
Davis, Reverend Gary
   Classic African American Gospel from Smithsonian Folkways (collection), 2959
   Gospel, Blues, and Street Songs (Davis), 194
Davis, Sammy, Jr.
   The Best of Sammy Davis, Jr. Live, 1187.1
   The Definitive Collection, 1187.2

Sentimental Journey: Pop Vocal Classics, Vol. 4 (collection), 1170
   Waller / Razaf (songwriter collection), 1113.2
Davis, Skeeter. *Skeeter Davis,* 1477
Davis, Tyrone
   Beg, Scream, and Shout! The Big Ol' Box of '60s Soul (collection), 2433
   The Story of Brunswick: The Classic Sound of Chicago Soul (collection), 2610
   20 Greatest Hits, 2470
Davis, Walter
   ★*The Blues: A Smithsonian Collection of Classic Blues Singers* (collection), 145
   Favorite Country Blues: Guitar-Piano Duets (collection), 267
   ★*Nashville Jumps: Blues and Rhythm on Nashville Independent Labels 1945–1955* (collection), 2376
   When the Sun Goes Down 3: That's Chicago's South Side (collection), 270
Davison, Wild Bill
   The Commodore Master Takes, 572
   ★*The Commodore Story* (collection), 561
The Davis Sisters
   The Best of the Famous Davis Sisters of Philadelphia, PA, 3044.1
   Davis Sisters 1949–1952, 3044.2
   ★*Jubilation! Great Gospel Performances, Vol. 2: More Black Gospel* (collection), 2967
Dawkins, Jimmy. *Blues Fest: Modern Blues of the '70s* (collection), 408
Dawn. *25 All-Time Greatest Bubblegum Hits* (collection), 1811
Dawson, Kimya. *Alphabutt,* 3214
Day, Bobby. *The American Roots of the British Invasion* (collection), 1786
Day, Doris
   Daydreaming: The Very Best of Doris Day, 1188.1
   E. Y. Harburg (songwriter collection), 1103
   Frank Loesser (songwriter collection), 1106.1
   Golden Girl: Columbia Recordings 1944–1966, 1188.2
   Hit Parade, 1956 (collection), 1158
   James Van Heusen (songwriter collection), 1112.1
   Jule Styne (songwriter collection), 1111.1
   Richard Whiting (songwriter collection), 1116
   Rodgers / Hart (songwriter collection), 1109.1
   ★*Sentimental Journey: Pop Vocal Classics, Vol. 1* (collection), 1081

★*Sentimental Journey: Pop Vocal Classics, Vol. 2* (collection), 1168

★*Sentimental Journey: Pop Vocal Classics, Vol. 3* (collection), 1169

16 Most Requested Songs of the 1940s, Vol. 1 (collection), 1082

16 Most Requested Songs: The 1950s, Vol. 1 (collection), 1171

Vincent Youmans (songwriter collection), 1118

Daylighters. *Birth of Soul: Special Chicago Edition* (collection), 2566

Daz Dillinger. *Retaliation, Revenge and Get Back,* 2753

Dazz Band
Funkology: The Definitive Dazz Band, 2626
Hitsville USA: The Motown Singles Collection, Vol. 2 (collection), 2604

DC Talk
CCM Top 100: Greatest Songs in Christian Music, Vol. 1 (collection), 3136
Jesus Freak, 3145

De Grassi, Alex
Alex de Grassi: A Windham Hill Retrospective, 1347
Solace: A Windham Hill Collection (collection), 1373
Windham Hill: The First Ten Years (collection), 1377

De La Soul
Buhloone Mindstate, 2754.1
De La Soul Is Dead, 2754.2
The Grind Date, 2754.3
Stakes Is High, 2754.4
★*3 Feet High and Rising,* 2754.4

Dead Boys
D.I.Y. Blank Generation: The New York Scene (collection), 1978
No Thanks! The '70s Punk Rebellion (collection), 2003
Straight Outta Cleveland (collection), 1888
Young, Loud and Snotty, 1985

Dead Kennedys
Fresh Fruit for Rotting Vegetables, 1986
No Thanks! The '70s Punk Rebellion (collection), 2003
Punk: Attitude (collection), 1980

Dead Prez
Let's Get Free, 2755.1
RBG: Revolutionary but Gangsta, 2755.2

Deal Family. *Mountain Gospel: The Sacred Roots of Country Music* (collection), 3113

Dean, Jimmy. *The Complete Columbia Hits and More,* 1478

Dean, Snoopy. *Eccentric Soul: The Outskirts of Deep City* (collection), 2565

DeArango, Bill. *Progressions: 100 Years of Jazz Guitar* (collection), 481

Dearie, Blossom. *The Definitive Collection* (songwriter collection), 1101.1

DeBarge. *Hitsville USA: The Motown Singles Collection, Vol. 2* (collection), 2604

Debonettes. *Eccentric Soul: The Young Disciples* (collection), 2562

DeDe Turner Happening. *Eccentric Soul: The Young Disciples* (collection), 2562

Dee, Kool Moe. *Greatest Hits,* 2756

Deep City Band. *Eccentric Soul: The Outskirts of Deep City* (collection), 2565

Deep Purple. *Machine Head,* 1945

Dees, Sam. *Action Speaks Louder Than Words: The Best of SSS International* (collection), 2588

Def Leppard. *Hysteria: Deluxe Edition,* 2068

DeGarmo and Key. *Best of Christian Rock (1970–1986), Vol. 1* (collection), 3135

DeJohnette, Jack
★*Album Album,* 962.1
Peace Time, 1321
Special Edition, 962.2

Del Royals. *Finger Poppin' and Stompin' Feet: 20 Classic Allen Toussaint Productions for Minit Records, 1960–1962* (collection), 2359

Del Tha Funkee Homosapien
Both Sides of the Brain, 2757.1
I Wish My Brother George Was Here, 2757.2

★Delegates. *The Vee-Jay Story: Celebrating 40 Years of Classic Hits* (collection), 2431

The Delfonics
Have a Nice Decade: The '70s Pop Culture Box (collection), 1240
La-la Means I Love You: The Definitive Collection, 2553
★*Love Train: The Sound of Philadelphia* (collection), 2552
Soul Shots: A Collection of Sixties Soul Classics (collection), 2443

★Del-Larks. *Atlantic Vocal Groups, 1951–1963* (collection), 2320

The Dells
Anthology, 2332
Best of Chess R&B, Vols. 1 and 2 (collection), 2420
Best of Doo Wop Ballads (collection), 1743
Birth of Soul: Special Chicago Edition (collection), 2566
★*The Doo Wop Box: 101 Vocal Group Gems from the Golden Age of Rock 'n' Roll* (collection), 1745
★*The Doo-Wop Box* (collection), 2322

★*The R&B Box* (collection), 2239
Street Corner Serenade: The Greatest Doo-Wop Hits of the '50s and '60s (collection), 1756
★*The Vee-Jay Story: Celebrating 40 Years of Classic Hits* (collection), 2431

The Delmore Brothers
All-Time Country and Western Hits (collection), 1449
★*Brother, Can You Spare a Dime? American Song during the Great Depression* (collection), 1061
Brown's Ferry Blues, 1407.1
Classic Cuts, 1407.2
Favorite Sacred Songs (collection), 3109
Freight Train Boogie, 1479
The Roots of Rock 'n' Roll, 1946–1954 (collection), 1755

Del-Rios. *The Complete Stax/Volt Singles 1959–1968* (collection), 2594

Delta Rhythm Boys. *All of My Appointed Time: Forty Years of a Cappella Gospel Singing* (collection), 2958

Deltron 3030. *Deltron 3030,* 2758

The Del-Vikings
Best of Doo Wop Uptempo (collection), 1744
★*The Doo Wop Box: 101 Vocal Group Gems from the Golden Age of Rock 'n' Roll* (collection), 1745
★*The Doo-Wop Box* (collection), 2322
Street Corner Serenade: The Greatest Doo-Wop Hits of the '50s and '60s (collection), 1756

Demby, Constance. *Novus Magnificat,* 1355

Dement, Iris. *Infamous Angel,* 1700

Denny, Martin. *The Best of Martin Denny's Exotica,* 1189

Denson's Sacred Harp Singers. *I Belong to This Band: Eighty-Five Years of Sacred Harp Recordings* (collection), 3111

Denver, John
Country Roads Collection, 1263.1
Frank Sinatra: Concert Collection, 1224.3
Greatest Hits, 1263.2

Denvil, Annette. *Don't Stop: Recording Tap* (collection), 2657

Depeche Mode. *Violator,* 2116

Derek and the Dominos. *Layla and Other Assorted Love Songs,* 1865

DeSanto, Sugar Pie
Best of Chess R&B, Vols. 1 and 2 (collection), 2420
Birth of Soul: Special Chicago Edition (collection), 2566

Desert Rose Band. *A Dozen Roses,* 1640

DeShannon, Jackie. *The Look of Love: The Burt Bacharach Collection* (collection), 1161

Desires. *The Doo-Wop Box II* (collection), 2323

Des'ree. *90's Pop Hits* (collection), 1242

Destiny's Child. *#1's*, 2333

Determinations. *The Spring Story: Essential 70s Soul* (collection), 2608

Detroit Junior. *Living Chicago Blues, Vol. 4* (collection), 418

Detroit soul
  The Very Best of the Dramatics, 2559.2
  Ultimate Collection (Dramatics), 2559.1

Deuter, C. H. *Nirvana Road*, 1330

DeVille
  D.I.Y. Blank Generation: The New York Scene (collection), 1978
  No Thanks! The '70s Punk Rebellion (collection), 2003

Devo
  Like Omigod! The 80s Pop Culture Box (Totally) (collection), 1241
  No Thanks! The '70s Punk Rebellion (collection), 2003
  Q: Are We Not Men? A: We Are Devo, 1987
  Straight Outta Cleveland (collection), 1888

Devotions. *The Doo-Wop Box II* (collection), 2323

Dexter, Al
  Texas Music, Vol. 2: Western Swing and Honky Tonk (collection), 1432
  Western Swing: 40 Bootstompers from the Golden Age (collection), 1433

Dexys Midnight Runners. *Searching for the Young Soul Rebels*, 2012

Diamond and the Psychotic Neurotics. *Stunts, Blunts, and Hip Hop*, 2759

Diamond, Neil
  Essential Neil Diamond, 1264
  Neil Diamond Anthology (songwriter collection), 1175

Diamonds
  ★*Atlantic Vocal Groups, 1951–1963* (collection), 2320
  Life Could Be a Dream: The Doo-Wop Sound, 2346

Dickens, Hazel. *16 Down Home Country Classics* (collection), 1385

Dickens, Little Jimmy
  Country Style, U.S.A. (collection), 1473
  Grand Ole Opry at Carnegie Hall (collection), 1619
  Hank Williams Songbook (collection), 1450
  I'm Little but I'm Loud: The Little Jimmy Dickens Collection, 1480

Dickerson, Walt. *Dialogue*, 963

The Dictators
  D.I.Y. Blank Generation: The New York Scene (collection), 1978

No Thanks! The '70s Punk Rebellion (collection), 2003

Diddley, Bo
  ★*The Chess Box*, 1761
  ★*Legends of Guitar: Rock–The '50s, Vol. 1* (collection), 1749
  Let There Be Drums, Vol. 1: The '50s (collection), 1751
  Rock and Roll: The Early Days (collection), 1752

Dietrich, Marlene
  Cole Porter (songwriter collection), 1108.1
  The Flapper Box (collection), 1064
  Frank Loesser (songwriter collection), 1106.1
  Songs That Got Us through World War II, Vol. 2 (collection), 1086
  This Is Art Deco (collection), 1090

Difranco, Ani
  Knuckle Down, 2117.1
  Not a Pretty Girl, 2117.2

Digable Planets
  Blowout Comb, 2760.1
  Reachin' (A New Refutation of Time and Space), 2760.2

Digital Underground. *Sex Packets*, 2761

Dilated Peoples. *The Platform*, 2762

Dillard, Ricky. *The 7th Episode: Live in Toronto*, 3084

★Dillard, Varetta. *Stompin' at the Savoy: The Original Indie Label, 1944–1961* (collection), 2429

Dillards
  There Is a Time, 1963–1970, 1581.1
  Wheatstraw Suite, 1581.2

Dinosaur Jr. *You're Living All over Me*, 2118

Dinwiddie Colored Quartet
  ★*Goodbye Babylon* (collection), 2954
  The Earliest Negro Vocal Quartets, 1894–1928 (collection), 3006

Dio, Ronnie James. *Heavy Metal: The First 20 Years* (collection), 1938

Dion and the Belmonts
  Best of Doo Wop Ballads (collection), 1743
  Best of Doo Wop Uptempo (collection), 1744
  ★*The Doo Wop Box: 101 Vocal Group Gems from the Golden Age of Rock 'n' Roll* (collection), 1745
  ★*The Doo-Wop Box* (collection), 2322
  The Doo-Wop Box II (collection), 2323
  Greatest Hits, 1774
  Let There Be Drums, Vol. 1: The '50s (collection), 1751
  Pure 60's: The #1 Hits (collection), 1165
  Street Corner Serenade: The Greatest Doo-Wop Hits of the '50s and '60s (collection), 1756

Dion, Céline
  All the Way: A Decade of Song and Video, 1265.1
  My Love: Ultimate Essential Collection, 1265.2

Dire Straits. *Sultans of Swing: The Very Best of Dire Straits*, 2069

Dirty Dozen Brass Band
  Live: Mardi Gras in Montreux, 964
  Make It Funky! (collection), 2360

DiSante, Peter. *The Early Minstrel Show* (collection), 96

Discharge. *Hear Nothing See Nothing*, 2119

disco
  Bad Girls (Summer), 2654.1
  The Best of Candi Staton, 2653
  The Best of Heatwave: Always and Forever, 2647
  The Best of Sister Sledge (1973–1985), 2652
  Disco Box (collection), 2644
  Donna Summer Live and More Encore!, 2654.2
  Evelyn "Champagne" King Greatest Hits, 2650
  general collection, 2644
  general style, 2644–2655
  Going Places: The August Darnell Years 1976–1983 (Kid Creole), 2649
  I Will Survive: The Anthology (Gaynor), 2646
  The Journey: The Very Best of Donna Summer, 2654.3
  label overview, 2656–2657
  Nightclubbing (Jones), 2648
  The Original Hits (Sylvester), 2655
  soundtrack, 2658
  The Very Best of Chic, 2645
  The Very Best of Rose Royce, 2651

disco label overview
  The Best of T. K. Disco (collection), 2656
  Don't Stop: Recording Tap (collection), 2657

★disco soundtrack. *Saturday Night Fever*, 2658

Disco Tex and the Sex-O-Lettes. *Disco Box* (collection), 2644

Disposable Heroes of Hiphoprisy. *Hypocrisy Is the Greatest Luxury*, 2763

Diverse. *One A.M.*, 2764

Divine Comedy. *Colours Are Brighter: Songs for Children and Grown Ups Too* (collection), 3193

Dixie Chicks
  Duets: An American Classic (Bennett), 1251.1
  Fly, 1641.1
  Home, 1641.2
  Wide Open Spaces, 1641.3

Dixie Cups. *The Best of the Girl Groups, Vols. 1 and 2* (collection), 2321

★Dixie Doodlers. *Nashville Jumps: Blues and Rhythm on Nashville Independent Labels 1945–1955* (collection), 2376
The Dixie Hummingbirds
    ★*The Best of the Dixie Hummingbirds*, 3014.1
    ★*Good News: 100 Gospel Greats* (collection), 2961
    ★*The Gospel Sound* (collection), 2964
    ★*The Gospel Sound of Spirit Feel* (collection), 2965
    Jesus Has Traveled This Road Before, 3014.2
    ★*Jubilation! Great Gospel Performances, Vol. 1: Black Gospel* (collection), 2966
    The Rough Guide to Gospel (collection), 2970
    Story of Gospel Music (collection), 2973
    Testify! The Gospel Box (collection), 2974
★Dixon Brothers. *Something Got a Hold of Me: A Treasury of Sacred Music* (collection), 3114
Dixon, Floyd
    Marshall, Texas Is My Home, 2251
    ★*The Specialty Story* (collection), 2428
    The Swing Time Records Story: R&B, Blues, and Gospel, 1946–1952 (collection), 2430
    The Swingtime Records Story: R&B, Blues, and Gospel (collection), 313
Dixon, Willie
    The Chess Box, 295.1
    Willie Dixon: The Master Blues Composer, 1915–1992, 295.2
Dizzee Rascal. *Boy in Da Corner*, 2765
DJ E-Z Rock. *It Takes Two*, 2708
DJ Faust. *Man or Myth?*, 2766
DJ Jazzy Jeff and the Fresh Prince. *He's the DJ, I'm the Rapper*, 2767
DJ Qbert. *Wave Twisters: Episode 7 Million—Sonic Wars within the Protons*, 2768
Dj Quik
    Quik Is the Name, 2769.1
    Safe + Sound, 2769.2
DJ Shadow. *Endtroducing . . . .*, 2770
DMX
    Flesh of My Flesh, Blood of My Blood, 2771.1
    It's Dark and Hell Is Hot, 2771.2
DNA
    DNA on DNA, 1873
    No New York (collection), 1979
DOA. *American Hardcore* (collection), 1977
D.O.C. *No One Can Do It Better*, 2748
Dodds, Baby (Warren, Jr.). *Talking and Drum Solos/Country Brass Bands*, 504

Dodds, Johnny. *Definitive Dodds*, 514
Dogg Pound, Tha. *Dogg Food*, 2772
Doggett, Bill
    The EP Collection, 2252.1
    The Very Best of Bill Doggett: Honky Tonk, 2252.2
Dolan, Jimmie, and His Texas Ramblers. *Swingbillies: Hillbilly and Western Swing on Modern/Colonial/Flair, 1947–1952* (collection), 1431
Dolby, Thomas. *Like Omigod! The 80s Pop Culture Box (Totally)* (collection), 1241
Dolphy, Eric
    Eric Dolphy at the Five Spot, Vol. 1, 682.1
    Far Cry, 682.2
    Outward Bound, 682.3
Domino, Fats
    Crescent City Soul: The Sound of New Orleans, 1947–1974 (collection), 2564
    The Legends of New Orleans: The Music of Fats Domino, 2362.2
    Let There Be Drums, Vol. 1: The '50s (collection), 1751
    ★*Out of New Orleans*, 2362.1
    ★*The R&B Box* (collection), 2239
    The Roots of Rock 'n' Roll, 1946–1954 (collection), 1755
    Walking to New Orleans, 2362.3
Domino, Renaldo. *Eccentric Soul: Twinight's Lunar Rotation* (collection), 2568
Dominoes. *The Very Best of Billy Ward and Dominoes*, 2334
Don and Bob. *Birth of Soul: Special Chicago Edition* (collection), 2566
★Don and Dewey. *The Specialty Story* (collection), 2428
Don and Juan. *The Doo-Wop Box II* (collection), 2323
★Don Q and his Q Tones. *Nashville Jumps: Blues and Rhythm on Nashville Independent Labels 1945–1955* (collection), 2376
Donovan
    Greatest Hits, 1851.1
    Songs of Protest (collection), 1820
    Troubadour: The Definitive Collection, 1851.2
    25 Hits from the British Invasion (collection), 1792
Doobie Brothers
    Billboard #1s: The '70s (collection), 1235
    Heaven Must Have Sent You: The Holland/Dozier/Holland Story (collection), 2436
    The Very Best of the Doobie Brothers, 1904
The Doors
    The Doors, 1835.1

The Doors Essential Guitar Collection, 1835.2
The Doors Legacy: The Absolute Best, 1835.3
The Very Best of the Doors, 1835.4
Dorge, Pierre. *Brikama*, 840
Dorham, Kenny. *Whistle Stop*, 637
Dorough, Bob
    Harlem in Vogue: The Poetry and Jazz of Langston Hughes (collection), 811
    Schoolhouse Rock!, 3215
The Dorsey Brothers
    An Anthology of Big Band Swing (collection), 528
    ★*At the Jazz Band Ball: Early Hot Jazz, Song, and Dance* (collection), 470
    Best of the Big Bands, 534
    The First of the Singer Songwriters: Key Cuts (Carmichael), 1124
Dorsey, Jimmy. *See also* The Dorsey Brothers
    Contrasts, 535
    Greatest Hits, 1128.1
    Jimmy Dorsey and His Orchestra Play: 22 Original Recordings, 1128.2
    Songs That Got Us through World War II (collection), 1085
    ★*Swing Time! The Fabulous Big Band Era* (collection), 1089
Dorsey, Lee
    Crescent City Soul: The Sound of New Orleans, 1947–1974 (collection), 2564
    The Fire / Fury Records Story (collection), 2422
    Wheelin' and Dealin': The Definitive Collection, 2363
Dorsey, Thomas A.
    A First-Time Buyer's Guide to American Negro Spirituals (collection), 32
    ★*Goodbye Babylon* (collection), 2954
    Gospel: Negro Spirituals / Gospel Songs, 1926–1942 (collection), 2963
    ★*Precious Lord: Recordings of the Great Gospel Songs of Thomas A. Dorsey* (collection), 2968
    ★*Say Amen, Somebody* (collection), 2971
    Story of Gospel Music (collection), 2973
Dorsey, Tommy. *See also* The Dorsey Brothers
    An Anthology of Big Band Swing (collection), 528
    ★*Big Band Jazz: From the Beginnings to the Fifties* (collection), 529
    E. Y. Harburg (songwriter collection), 1103
    Greatest Hits, 1129.1
    Hit Parade, 1943 (collection), 1157
    ★*Ken Burns Jazz: The Story of America's Music* (collection), 478

Dorsey, Tommy (cont.)
Lost Chords: White Musicians and Their Contributions to Jazz (collection), 479
★*Nipper's Greatest Hits: The 30's, Vol. 1* (collection), 1072
★*Nipper's Greatest Hits: The 40's, Vol. 1* (collection), 1073
Songs That Got Us through World War II (collection), 1085
Stop, Look, and Listen, 1129.2
★*Swing Time! The Fabulous Big Band Era* (collection), 1089
Yes Indeed!, 536
Doucet, Michael. *Le Hoogie Boogie: Louisiana French Music for Children,* 3233
Douglas, Carol. *Disco Box* (collection), 2644
Douglas, Dave
In Our Lifetime, 965.1
Tiny Bell Trio: Constellations, 965.2
Douglas, Jerry
Slide Rule, 1582
Top of the Hill Bluegrass (collection), 1567
Douglas, Lizzie. *See* Memphis Minnie
★Douglas, Tom. *Nashville Jumps: Blues and Rhythm on Nashville Independent Labels 1945–1955* (collection), 2376
Dowell, Charlie. *Night Train to Nashville: Music City Rhythm and Blues, 1945–1970, Vol. 2* (collection), 2378
Dowling, Richard. *World's Greatest Piano Rags,* 132
Downing, Big Al. *Action Speaks Louder Than Words: The Best of SSS International* (collection), 2588
Doyle, Little Buddy. *Masters of Memphis Blues* (collection), 230
Doyle, Teresa
Dreamland: World Lullabies and Soothing Songs (collection), 3263
World Playground: A Musical Adventure for Kids (collection), 3230
Dozier, Billy. *Legends of Western Swing Guitar* (collection), 1430
Dozier, Lamont. *Heaven Must Have Sent You: The Holland/Dozier/Holland Story* (collection), 2436
Dr. Feelgood. *Night Train to Nashville: Music City Rhythm and Blues, 1945–1970, Vol. 2* (collection), 2378
Dr. Hook. *Have a Nice Decade: The '70s Pop Culture Box* (collection), 1240
Dr. Horse. *The Fire / Fury Records Story* (collection), 2422
Dr. John
★*Dr. John's Gumbo,* 2364.1
Gris-Gris, 2364.2

Mos' Scocious: The Dr. John Anthology, 2364.3
★*What It Is! Funky Soul and Rare Grooves* (collection), 2615
Dr. Octagon. *Dr. Octagonecologyst,* 2774
Drake, Alfred
Alan Jay Lerner (songwriter collection), 1105.1
Oscar Hammerstein II (songwriter collection), 1102
Drake, Nick
Five Leaves Left, 1852.1
Way to Blue: An Introduction to Nick Drake, 1852.2
Drake. *Thank Me Later,* 2775
DRAM audio stream web resource, p6
Dramatics
The Very Best of the Dramatics, 2559.2
Top of the Stax, Vol. 1: Twenty Greatest Hits (collection), 2611
Top of the Stax, Vol. 2: Twenty Greatest Hits (collection), 2612
Ultimate Collection, 2559.1
Dranes, Arizona
★*Goodbye Babylon* (collection), 2954
Gospel: Negro Spirituals / Gospel Songs, 1926–1942 (collection), 2963
★*The Gospel Sound* (collection), 2964
Preachin' the Gospel: Holy Blues (collection), 2979
Songsters and Saints: Vocal Traditions on Race Records, Vol. 2 (collection), 191
Spreading the Word: Early Gospel Recordings (collection), 2972
Draper, O'Landa and the Associates Choir. *Stand Up: A Collection of America's Great Gospel Choirs* (collection), 3053
Dre, Dr.
★*The Chronic,* 2773.2
2001, 2773.1
Dream Warriors. *And Now the Legacy Begins,* 2776
Dreamlovers. *The Doo-Wop Box II* (collection), 2323
Drew, Pattie. *Soul Shots: A Collection of Sixties Soul Classics* (collection), 2443
Drew-Vels. *Birth of Soul: Special Chicago Edition* (collection), 2566
DRI. *American Hardcore* (collection), 1977
The Drifters
★*All Time Greatest Hits and More,* 2335.1
★*Atlantic R&B, 1947–1974* (collection), 2418
★*Atlantic Vocal Groups, 1951–1963* (collection), 2320
★*Billboard Greatest Christmas Hits, 1955–1983* (collection), 3294
Casey Kasem Presents America's Top Ten through the Years: The

Doo-Wop Years, 1950s (collection), 1155
★*The Doo Wop Box: 101 Vocal Group Gems from the Golden Age of Rock 'n' Roll* (collection), 1745
★*The Doo-Wop Box* (collection), 2322
The Doo-Wop Box II (collection), 2323
The Look of Love: The Burt Bacharach Collection (collection), 1161
★*The R&B Box* (collection), 2239
Rockin' and Driftin', 2335.2
The Roots of Rock 'n' Roll, 1946–1954 (collection), 1755
Street Corner Serenade: The Greatest Doo-Wop Hits of the '50s and '60s (collection), 1756
Drive-By Truckers. *Decoration Day,* 2120
D'Rivera, Paquito. *Jingle Bell Jazz* (collection), 3314
Dry Branch Fire Squad
Angels Are Singing: A Women's Bluegrass Gospel Collection, 1559
Hand-Picked: 25 Years of Bluegrass on Rounder Records (collection), 1564
Dubs
★*The Doo-Wop Box* (collection), 2322
The Doo-Wop Box II (collection), 2323
Duchin, Eddy
The Eddy Duchin Story: 24 Vintage Tracks, 1130
★*It Had to Be You: Popular Keyboard from the Days of the Speakeasy to the Television Era* (collection), 1068
Ducket, Slim, and Pig Norwood. *How Can I Keep from Singing: Early American Religious Music and Song, Vols. 1 and 2* (collection), 2957
Dudley, Dave. *The Best of* Dave Dudley, 1481
Duke, Doris. *Dave Godin's Deep Soul Treasures, Vols. 1–4* (collection), 2435
Dukes. *Boddie Recording Company Cleveland, Ohio* (collection), 2569, 2570
Duncan, James. *Crash of Thunder: Boss Soul, Funk, and R&B Sides from the Vaults of the King, Federal, and Deluxe Labels* (collection), 2596
Duncan, Tommy. *Texas Moon,* 1440
★Dunford, Uncle Eck. *Anthology of American Folk Music, Vols. 1–3* (collection), 1386
Dupree, Champion Jack
Blues from the Gutter, 260.1
★*Legends of the Blues, Vol. 2* (collection), 151
New Orleans Barrelhouse Boogie, 260.2
Duprees. *The Doo-Wop Box II* (collection), 2323

Dupri, Jermaine "JD"
  The Emancipation of Mimi (Carey),
    1256.1
  *Jermaine Dupri Presents Life in 1472:
    The Original Soundtrack,* 2777
  #1s (Carey), 1256.2
Duran Duran
  Greatest, 1266, 2070
  *Like Omigod! The 80s Pop Culture Box
    (Totally)* (collection), 1241
Durbin, Deanna. *E. Y. Harburg*
    (songwriter collection), 1103
Dury, Ian. *No Thanks! The '70s Punk
    Rebellion* (collection), 2003
Dyani, Johnny. *Song for Biko,* 841
Dyke and the Blazers
  *Beg, Scream, and Shout! The Big Ol'
    Box of '60s Soul* (collection), 2433
  *Soul Shots: A Collection of Sixties Soul
    Classics* (collection), 2443
Dyke, Earl Van. *Standing in the Shadows
    of Motown* (collection), 2445
Dylan, Bob
  The Basement Tapes, 1823.5
  ★*Blonde on Blonde,* 1823.1
  Blood on the Tracks, 1823.2
  Bob Dylan: Don't Look Back, 1823.3
  ★*Bringing It All Back Home,* 1823.4
  ★*Highway 61 Revisited,* 1823.6
  John Wesley Harding, 1823.7
  *Live 1966: The "Royal Albert Hall"
    Concert,* 1823.8
  Nashville Skyline, 1482, 1823.9
  No Direction Home, 1823.10
  Saved, 3146.1
  Slow Train Coming, 3146.2
  Time out of Mind, 1823.11
Dynamic Tints. *Eccentric Soul: Twinight's
    Lunar Rotation* (collection), 2568
★Dynamics. *Atlantic Soul, 1959–1975*
    (collection), 2589

E
The Eagles
  ★*Greatest Hits, 1971–1975,* 1905.1
  Greatest Hits, Vol. 2, 1905.2
  Hotel California, 1905.3
Eaglin, Snooks
  Country Boy Down in New Orleans, 332
  *Fire in My Bones: Raw, Rare and
    Otherworldy African-American
    Gospel* (collection), 2960
Earl, Ronnie. *Blues Fest: Modern Blues of
    the '80s* (collection), 409
Earle, Steve
  *Ain't Ever Satisfied: The Steve Earle
    Collection,* 1701.1
  ★*Guitar Town,* 1701.2
  I Feel Alright, 1701.3
  The Mountain, 1702
The Earls
  Old Town Doo-Wop, Vols. 1–3
    (collection), 2324

★*The Doo-Wop Box* (collection),
    2322
early American music. *See* U.S. to 1900
early jazz, 497–502
  *Birth of the Hot: The Classic Chicago
    "Red Hot Peppers" Sessions*
    (Morton), 501.1
  Collected Piano Music (Morton), 501.2
  collections, 497–499
  Freddie Keppard: The Complete Set
    (Keppard), 500
  ★*Jelly Roll Morton* (Morton), 501.3
  *Jelly Roll Morton: The Complete Library
    of Congress Recordings by Alan
    Lomax* (Morton), 501.4
  *The New Orleans Rhythm Kings and
    Jelly Roll Morton* (collection), 497
  ★*Off the Record: The Complete 1923
    Jazz Band Recordings* (collection),
    498
  Riverside History of Classic Jazz
    (collection), 499
  75th Anniversary (Original Dixieland
    Jazz Band), 502
early jazz piano styles, 521–527
  Barrelhouse Boogie (collection), 521
  collections, 521
  ★*Complete Victor Piano Solos* (Waller),
    526
  Earl Hines Collection: Piano Solos
    (Hines), 522.1
  ★*Harlem Stride Piano* (Johnson), 523
  The Lion and the Lamb (Smith), 525
  Luckey and the Lion (Roberts), 524
  Piano Solos (Wilson), 527.1
  *Storyville Presents Earl Hines: The
    Complete Transcriptions* (Hines),
    522.2
  *Storyville Presents Teddy Wilson:
    The Original Piano Transcriptions*
    (Wilson), 527.2
early jazz soloists, 511–520
  The Best of Sidney Bechet (Bechet),
    512.1
  *Bix: Ain't None of Them Play Like Him
    Yet* (Beiderbecke), 513.1
  *Bix Beiderbecke and the Chicago
    Cornets* (Beiderbecke), 513.2
  *Bix Beiderbecke, Vol. 2: At the Jazz
    Band Ball* (Beiderbecke), 513.4
  ★*Bix Beiderbecke, Vol. 1: Singin' the
    Blues* (Beiderbecke), 513.3
  Chicago Rhythm, Apex Blues (Noone),
    517
  collections, 511
  Definitive Dodds (Johnny Dodds), 514
  Jabbo Smith, 1929–1938 (Smith), 518
  ★*Ken Burns Jazz Collection: Sidney
    Bechet* (Bechet), 512.2
  King of the Blues Trombone
    (Teagarden), 519
  The Legendary Sidney Bechet (Bechet),
    512.3

New York Sessions (Lang), 515
Pioneers of the Jazz Guitar (collection),
    511
Red Nichols and Miff Mole, 1925–1927
    (Nichols), 516
Stringing the Blues (Venuti), 520
early rappers, 1972–1976
  Dread in Babylon (U-Roy), 1975
  The Last Poets, 1973
  Reflections (Iceberg Slim), 1972
  Small Talk at 125th and Lenox (Scott-
    Heron), 1974
  Things Gonna Get Greater (Watts
    Prophet), 1976
early rock 'n' roll, 1743–1770
  All-Time Greatest Hits (Platters), 1768.1
  Best of Doo Wop Ballads (collection),
    1743
  Best of Doo Wop Uptempo (collection),
    1744
  *The Best of Bill Haley and His Comets,
    1951–1954,* 1763.1
  *The Best of Frankie Lymon and the
    Teenagers,* 1767
  *The Best of Ronnie Hawkins and the
    Hawks,* 1764
  The Buddy Holly Collection, 1765
  ★*Cadence Classics: Their 20 Greatest
    Hits* (Everly Brothers), 1762.1
  ★*The Chess Box* (Diddley), 1761
  Chuck Berry, 1759.1
  Chuck Berry: The Chess Box, 1759.2
  ★*The Definitive Collection* (Berry),
    1759.3
  ★*The Doo Wop Box: 101 Vocal Group
    Gems from the Golden Age of Rock
    'n' Roll* (collection), 1745
  Early Rock Guitar Bible (collection),
    1746
  The Essential Little Richard, 1766.1
  Gene Vincent, 1770
  Genuine Rockabilly Guitar Hits
    (collection), 1747
  ★*The Georgia Peach* (Little Richard),
    1766.2
  Golden Hits (Everly Brothers), 1762.2
  The Golden Era of Rock 'n' Roll
    (collection), 1748
  La Bamba and Other Hits (Valens),
    1769
  ★*Legends of Guitar: Rock–The '50s,
    Vol. 1* (collection), 1749
  ★*Legends of Guitar: Rock–The '50s,
    Vol. 2* (collection), 1750
  Let There Be Drums, Vol. 1: The '50s
    (collection), 1751
  The Magic Touch: An Anthology
    (Platters), 1768.2
  Rock and Roll: The Early Days
    (collection), 1752
  Rock around the Clock (Haley), 1763.2
  Rockabilly Guitar Bible (collection),
    1753

early rock 'n' roll (cont.)

Roots of Rock: 1945–1956 (collection), 1754

The Roots of Rock 'n' Roll, 1946–1954 (collection), 1755

★Somethin' Else: The Fine Lookin' Hits of Eddie Cochran, 1760

Street Corner Serenade: The Greatest Doo-Wop Hits of the '50s and '60s (collection), 1756

25 Classic Doo-Wop Ballads (collection), 1757

Ultimate Rock and Roll Collection: The 50s (collection), 1758

Walk Right Back: The Everly Brothers on Warner Brothers, 1762.3

Earth, Wind, and Fire

Earth, Wind and Fire in Concert, 2627

Gratitude, 2582.2

Spirit, 2582.3

That's the Way of the World, 2582.4

The Eternal Dance, 2582.1

Eason, Danny. Story of Gospel Music (collection), 2973

★Eason, Willie. Sacred Steel: The Steel Guitar Tradition of the House of God Churches (collection), 2980

East coast blues. See Georgia, Alabama, and the East Coast blues

East St. Louis, Illinois, soul. Eccentric Soul: The Young Disciples (collection), 2562

Eastman Wind Ensemble

The Civil War: Its Music and Its Sounds, 71

Homespun America: Music for Brass Band, Social Orchestra and Choral Groups from the Mid-19th Century, 108

Screamers: March Time, 83

Easton, Admiral Amos. See Bumble Bee Slim

Easton, Sheena. Greatest Hits, 1267

East/West new age, 1313–1315

Kyori (Innervisions) (Yoshizawa), 1315

Osamu (Kitajima), 1313

Silk Road, Vol. 1 (Kitaro), 1314.1

Silk Road, Vol. 2 (Kitaro), 1314.2

The Easybeats

Nuggets: A Classic Collection from the Psychedelic Sixties (collection), 1809

★Nuggets: Artifacts of the First Psychedelic Era (collection), 1808

★Nuggets II: Original Artifacts from the British Empire and Beyond (collection), 1791

25 Hits from the British Invasion (collection), 1792

Eazy-E

Eazy-Duz-It, 2778.1

Eternal E: Gangsta Memorial Edition, 2778.2

Ebenezer Baptist Church Choir. Fire in My Bones: Raw, Rare and Otherworldy African-American Gospel (collection), 2960

Eberle, Ray

Harry Warren (songwriter collection), 1114

Hoagy Carmichael (songwriter collection), 1097.2

James Van Heusen (songwriter collection), 1112.1

Eberly, Bob

Johnny Mercer (songwriter collection), 1107.1

Legendary Big Band Singers (collection), 767

Echo and the Bunnymen. Heaven up Here, 2121

Eckstine, Billy

★American Popular Song: Six Decades of Songwriters and Singers (collection), 1059

★Big Band Jazz: From the Beginnings to the Fifties (collection), 529

Duke Ellington (songwriter collection), 1099.1

Hoagy Carmichael (songwriter collection), 1097.2

★The Jazz Singers: A Smithsonian Collection of Jazz Vocals from 1919–1994 (collection), 766

The Legendary Big Band, 593

Sentimental Journey: Pop Vocal Classics, Vol. 1 (collection), 1167

★Sentimental Journey: Pop Vocal Classics, Vol. 1 (collection), 1081

★Sentimental Journey: Pop Vocal Classics, Vol. 2 (collection), 1168

★Sentimental Journey: Pop Vocal Classics, Vol. 3 (collection), 1169

★Stompin' at the Savoy: The Original Indie Label, 1944–1961 (collection), 2429

Eddie and Ant Hill Mob. Boddie Recording Company Cleveland, Ohio (collection), 2569, 2570

Eddie and Ernie. Dave Godin's Deep Soul Treasures, Vols. 1–4 (collection), 2435

★Eddie, Little. Nashville Jumps: Blues and Rhythm on Nashville Independent Labels 1945–1955 (collection), 2376

Eddy, Duane

★Legends of Guitar: Rock–The '50s, Vol. 1 (collection), 1749

★Legends of Guitar: Rock–The '50s, Vol. 2 (collection), 1750

Rock Instrumental Classics, Vol. 2: The 60s (collection), 1771

Twang Thang: The Duane Eddy Anthology, 1775

Edison Lighthouse. Have a Nice Decade: The '70s Pop Culture Box (collection), 1240

Edison Military Band. Phono-Cylinders, Vols. 1 and 2 (collection), 1074

Edison, Roger. The World's Greatest Christmas Songs for Piano and Voice: 73 Best-Loved Christmas Songs and Seasonal Favorites, 3327

★Edsels. The Doo-Wop Box (collection), 2322

Edwards, Bernice. Good Time Blues: Harmonicas, Kazoos, Washboards, and Cow-Bells (collection), 268

Edwards, Chuck. Dave Godin's Deep Soul Treasures, Vols. 1–4 (collection), 2435

Edwards, Cliff "Ukulele Ike"

★The Crooners (collection), 1062

This Is Art Deco (collection), 1090

With My Little Ukulele in My Hand (collection), 1093

★Yes, Sir, That's My Baby: The Golden Years of Tin Pan Alley (collection), 1094

Edwards, David "Honeyboy"

Big Joe Williams and the Stars of Mississippi Blues (collection), 213

Drop Down Mama (collection), 292

★Negro Blues and Hollers (collection), 178

Edwin Hawkins Singers

★Oh Happy Day, 3060.1

Oh Happy Day: The Best of the Edwin Hawkins Singers, 3060.2

Story of Gospel Music (collection), 2973

Ehret, Walter. International Book of Christmas Carols, 3278

Ehrlich, Marty

Malinke's Dance, 966.1

News on the Rail, 966.2

Eightball and MJG

Comin' out Hard, 2780.1

In Our Lifetime, 2780.2

Either/Orchestra. The Brunt, 747

El Dorados

Best of Doo Wop Uptempo (collection), 1744

★The Doo-Wop Box (collection), 2322

The Doo-Wop Box II (collection), 2323

★The Vee-Jay Story: Celebrating 40 Years of Classic Hits (collection), 2431

Eldridge, Roy

★After You've Gone, 573

An Anthology of Big Band Swing (collection), 528

Little Jazz: The Best of the Verve Years, 719.1

Roy and Diz, 719.2

★The Smithsonian Collection of Classic Jazz (collection), 486

★Sound of Jazz (collection), 487

Electrelane. *The Power Out*, 2122

Electric Light Orchestra. *ELO's Greatest Hits*, 1922

★Electric Prunes. *Nuggets: Artifacts of the First Psychedelic Era* (collection), 1808

electronic/computer new age, 1316–1319

　Antarctica: Music from the Soundtrack (Vangelis), 1319.1

　★*China* (Vangelis), 1319.2

　Opera Sauvage (Vangelis), 1319.3

　Oxygene (Jarre), 1318

　Switched on Bach (Carlos), 1317

　Valley in the Clouds / In the Wake of the Wind (Arkenstone), 1316

The Elegants

　Street Corner Serenade: The Greatest Doo-Wop Hits of the '50s and '60s (collection), 1756

　★*The Doo Wop Box: 101 Vocal Group Gems from the Golden Age of Rock 'n' Roll* (collection), 1745

Elgins. *Heaven Must Have Sent You: The Holland/Dozier/Holland Story* (collection), 2436

Elijah and the Ebonites. *Eccentric Soul: The Capsoul Label* (collection), 2599

Elling, Kurt. *The Messenger*, 778

Ellington, Duke, 558–559

　Afro-Eurasian Eclipse, 748.1

　Anatomy of a Murder [1999], 1045.1

　Anatomy of a Murder [2000], 1045.2

　An Anthology of Big Band Swing (collection), 528

　★*At the Jazz Band Ball: Early Hot Jazz, Song, and Dance* (collection), 470

　Back to Back, 720.1

　The Best of Early Ellington, 558.1

　The Best of the Complete RCA Victor Recordings, 1944–1946, 558.2

　★*Big Band Jazz: From the Beginnings to the Fifties* (collection), 529

　Big Band Renaissance: The Evolution of the Jazz Orchestra (collection), 739

　Duke Ellington, 558.4

　Duke Ellington and His Orchestra, 1929–1943, 558.5

　Duke Ellington Anthology (songwriter collection), 1099.2

　Duke Ellington (songwriter collection), 1099.1

　★*The Duke*, 558.3

　★*Ellington at Newport*, 748.2

　★*The Essential Duke Ellington*, 558.6

　★*The Far East Suite*, 748.3

　The Great Depression: American Music in the '30s (collection), 1066

　It's Easy to Remember (Crosby), 1125.6

　Jingle Bell Jazz (collection), 3314

　★*Ken Burns Jazz Collection: Duke Ellington*, 558.7

　★*Ken Burns Jazz: The Story of America's Music* (collection), 478

　Money Jungle, 720.2

　Never No Lament: The Blanton–Webster Band, 558.8

　New Orleans Suite, 748.4

　★*Nipper's Greatest Hits: The 20's* (collection), 1071

　★*Nipper's Greatest Hits: The 40's, Vol. 1* (collection), 1073

　Piano Legends (collection), 480

　Riverside History of Classic Jazz (collection), 499

　★*The Smithsonian Collection of Classic Jazz* (collection), 486

　Songs That Got Us through World War II, Vol. 2 (collection), 1086

　Stars of the Apollo (collection), 2240

　Such Sweet Thunder, 748.5

　★*Swing Time! The Fabulous Big Band Era* (collection), 1089

Elliott, Missy. *Supa Dupa Fly*, 2781

Ellis, Big Chief. *Play My Juke-Box: East Coast Blues* (collection), 244

Ellis, Don

　Big Band Renaissance: The Evolution of the Jazz Orchestra (collection), 739

　Electric Bath, 749.1

　Electric Heart, Don Ellis: The Man, His Time, His Music, 749.2

　How Time Passes, 1037

Ellis, Herb. *Progressions: 100 Years of Jazz Guitar* (collection), 481

Ellis, Juanita. *Boddie Recording Company Cleveland, Ohio* (collection), 2569, 2570

★Ellis, Seger. *The Crooners* (collection), 1062

Ellis, Shirley. *Beg, Scream, and Shout! The Big Ol' Box of '60s Soul* (collection), 2433

Ellison, Lorraine

　Beg, Scream, and Shout! The Big Ol' Box of '60s Soul (collection), 2433

　The Best of Loma Records: The Rise and Fall of a 1960's Soul Label (collection), 2590

　Soul Shots: A Collection of Sixties Soul Classics (collection), 2443

Ellison, Tommy and the Singing Stars. *Living Legends of Gospel: The Quartets, Vols. 1 and 2* (collection), 3010

Elmo and Patsy. *Dr. Demento Presents: The Greatest Christmas Novelty CD of All Time* (collection), 3307

El-P. *I'll Sleep When You're Dead*, 2782

Elvis Presley and rockabilly, 1735–1742. *See also* Presley, Elvis

　The Definitive Collection (Lewis), 1735.1

　★*18 Original Greatest Hits* (Lewis), 1735.2

　Elvis '68 Comeback, 1737.4

　Elvis, from Nashville to Memphis, 1737.2

　★*Elvis: 30 #1 Hits* (Presley), 1737.1

　Elvis Presley, 1737.3

　The Guitars of Elvis, 1737.5

　The King of Rock 'n' Roll: The Complete 50's Masters, 1737.6

　★*Original Sun Greatest Hits* (Perkins), 1736

　Rockabilly Riot, 1738

　Rockin' Bones: 1950s Punk and Rockabilly, 1739

　★*Sun Records' Greatest Hits* (collection), 1741

　Sun Records: 50th Anniversary, 1740

　Sun Rockabilly: The Classic Recordings (collection), 1742

Ely, Brother Claude. *Favorite Sacred Songs* (collection), 3109

Ely, Joe

　The Best of Joe Ely, 1642.1

　Honky Tonk Masquerade, 1642.2

Embry, Queen Sylvia. *Living Chicago Blues, Vol. 4* (collection), 418

Emerson, Billy

　The Sun Blues Years (collection), 344

　★*The Vee-Jay Story: Celebrating 40 Years of Classic Hits* (collection), 2431

Eminem

　The Eminem Show, 2783.1

　The Marshall Mathers LP, 2783.2

　The Slim Shady LP, 2783.3

The Emotions

　The Best of the Emotions: Best of My Love, 2336

　The Complete Stax/Volt Soul Singles, Vol. 2: 1968–1971 (collection), 2595

　Top of the Stax, Vol. 1: Twenty Greatest Hits (collection), 2611

　Top of the Stax, Vol. 2: Twenty Greatest Hits (collection), 2612

En Vogue. *The Very Best of En Vogue*, 2404

Enchanters. *The Best of Loma Records: The Rise and Fall of a 1960's Soul Label* (collection), 2590

Encyclopedia of Popular Music (Larkin), p3

Encyclopedia of the Blues (Komara), p3

Enfield Shaker Singers. *I Am Filled with Heavenly Treasures*, 10

England, Frances. *Fascinating Creatures*, 3216

English Beat. *Beat This! The Best of the English Beat*, 2013

English, John. *Over There! Songs from America's Wars* (Marlborough Singers and Chamber Players, tenor John English, and piano Rob Carriker), 1141

Eno, Brian
    Ambient 1: Music for Airports, 1322
    Another Green World, 1957.1
    Before and after Science, 1957.2
Ensemble Phoenix Munich. *Rose of
    Sharon: 100 Years of American
    Music, 1770-1870* (Ensemble
    Phoenix Munich), 11
Enya
    Ultimate New Age (collection), 1376
    ★*Watermark,* 1361
EPMD
    Business as Usual, 2784.1
    Business Never Personal, 2784.2
    ★*Strictly Business,* 2784.3
    Unfinished Business, 2784.4
Epps, Preston. *Let There Be Drums, Vol. 1:
    The '50s* (collection), 1751
Eps, Fred Van. *The Phonographic
    Yearbook, 1912: Waitin' on the
    Levee* (collection), 1077
Erbsen, Wayne
    Love Songs of the Civil War, 109
    *Old-Time Gospel Favorites: 14 Gospel
    Classics with Harmony and Old-
    Time Instruments,* 12
Eric B. and Rakim
    Follow the Leader, 2785.1
    ★*Paid in Full,* 2785.2
★Ernest V. Stoneman's Dixie
    Mountaineers. *Goodbye Babylon*
    (collection), 2954
Escovedo, Alejandro. *The Bottle Let Me
    Down: Songs for Bumpy Wagon
    Rides* (collection), 3191
Esham. *Kkkill the Fetus: The Album,* 2786
Eskelin, Ellery. *One Great Day,* 967
Esquerita. *Night Train to Nashville: Music
    City Rhythm and Blues, 1945–1970,
    Vol. 1* (collection), 2377
Esquires. *Old Town Doo-Wop, Vols. 1–3*
    (collection), 2324
Esquivel, Juan Garcia. *Esquivel! Space Age
    Bachelor Pad Music,* 1190
Essence. *Eccentric Soul: The Big Mack
    Label* (collection), 2598
Essex. *The Best of the Girl Groups,
    Vols. 1 and 2* (collection), 2321
Estes, Sleepy John
    ★*Blues Classics* (collection), 146
    Blues Masters, Vol. 12: Memphis Blues
    (collection), 229
    ★*The Blues: A Smithsonian Collection
    of Classic Blues Singers* (collection),
    145
    I Ain't Gonna Be Worried No More, 234
    *Memphis Blues: Important Postwar
    Recordings* (collection), 341
    *Newport Folk Festival: Best of the Blues,
    1959–68* (collection), 392
    *When the Sun Goes Down 2: The First
    Time I Met the Blues* (collection),
    160

The Eternals
    ★*The Doo-Wop Box* (collection), 2322
    The Doo-Wop Box II (collection), 2323
Etta and Harvey. *Birth of Soul: Special
    Chicago Edition* (collection), 2566
Etting, Ruth
    *Flappers, Vamps, and Sweet Young
    Things* (collection), 1065
    *Joe Franklin Presents . . . The Roaring
    '20s Roar Again* (collection), 1069
    ★*Sophisticated Ladies* (collection),
    1087
    Ten Cents a Dance, 1131
    ★*Yes, Sir, That's My Baby: The Golden
    Years of Tin Pan Alley* (collection),
    1094
Eubanks, Kevin. *Guitarist,* 968
Eureka Brass Band. *New Orleans Funeral
    and Parade* (Eureka Brass Band),
    505
Europe, James Reese
    *Early Syncopated Dance Music:
    Cakewalks, Two-Steps, Trots and
    Glides* (collection), 124
    *I'll Dance Till de Sun Breaks Through:
    Ragtime, Cakewalks and Stomps,*
    133
    *James Reese Europe Featuring Noble
    Sissle,* 1132
    ★*Ken Burns Jazz: The Story of
    America's Music* (collection),
    478
Eurythmics
    *Like Omigod! The 80s Pop Culture Box
    (Totally)* (collection), 1241
    Ultimate Collection, 2071
Evan, George. *International Book of
    Christmas Carols,* 3278
evangelists and other traditional
    performers, 2976–2986
    *American Primitive, Vol. 1: Raw Pre-
    War Gospel* (collection), 2976
    The Colored Sacred Harp (Wiregrass
    Sacred Harp Singers), 2986
    The Complete Blind Willie Johnson,
    2984
    *The Complete Early Recordings of Rev.
    Gary Davis,* 2983
    I Am Born to Preach the Gospel
    (Washington), 2985
    Negro Religious Songs and Services
    (collection), 2977
    *On One Accord: Singing and Praying
    Bands of Tidewater, Maryland, and
    Delaware* (collection), 2978
    Preachin' the Gospel: Holy Blues
    (collection), 2979
    ★*Sacred Steel: The Steel Guitar
    Tradition of the House of God
    Churches* (collection), 2980
    *Saints' Paradise: Trombone Shout Bands
    from the United House of Prayer*
    (collection), 2981

    *This May Be My Last Time Singing: Raw
    African- American Gospel on 45rpm*
    (collection), 2982
Evans, Bill
    Bill Evans, 704.1
    Bill Evans at Town Hall, Vol. 1, 704.2
    Bill Evans Live, '64–'75, 704.3
    Conversations with Myself, 704.4
    Everybody Digs Bill Evans, 704.5
    Intuition, 874.1
    Jazz Lullaby (collection), 3264
    The Paris Concert: Edition One, 874.2
    Piano Legends (collection), 480
    Portrait in Jazz, 704.6
    ★*The Smithsonian Collection of Classic
    Jazz* (collection), 486
    ★*Sunday at the Village Vanguard,* 704.7
    The Tony Bennett / Bill Evans Album
    (Bennett), 1251.2
    ★*Waltz for Debby,* 704.8
Evans, Gil
    *Big Band Renaissance: The Evolution of
    the Jazz Orchestra* (collection), 739
    The Complete Pacific Jazz Sessions, 750.1
    Gil Evans and Ten, 750.2
    Individualism of Gil Evans, 750.3
    Out of the Cool, 750.4
Evans, Nate. *Eccentric Soul: Twinight's
    Lunar Rotation* (collection), 2568
Evans, Sara. *Born to Fly / Restless,* 1643
Eve. *Ruff Ryder's First Lady,* 2787
Everett, Betty
    *Beg, Scream, and Shout! The Big Ol'
    Box of '60s Soul* (collection), 2433
    *The Best of the Girl Groups, Vols. 1
    and 2* (collection), 2321
    Birth of Soul: Special Chicago Edition
    (collection), 2566
    *The Sweetest Feeling: A Van McCoy
    Songbook* (collection), 2447
    ★*The Vee-Jay Story: Celebrating 40
    Years of Classic Hits* (collection),
    2431
The Everly Brothers
    ★*Cadence Classics: Their 20 Greatest
    Hits,* 1762.1
    Golden Hits, 1762.2
    *Walk Right Back: The Everly Brothers
    on Warner Brothers,* 1762.3
Everything but the Girl. *Walking
    Wounded,* 2123
evolution of popular music, p1–3
★Excellents. *The Doo-Wop Box*
    (collection), 2322
Exciters. *The Best of the Girl Groups,
    Vols. 1 and 2* (collection), 2321
Exploited. *Totally Exploited,* 2124
Extentions. *Eccentric Soul: The Nickel and
    Penny Labels* (collection), 2567
Ezell, Will. *Mama Don't Allow No Easy
    Riders Here: Strutting the Dozens;
    Classic Piano Rags, Blues, and
    Stomps* (collection), 256

F

Fa Sol La Singers. *The Half Ain't Never Been Told, Vols. 1 and 2* (collection), 2956

Fabulettes. *Night Train to Nashville: Music City Rhythm and Blues, 1945–1970, Vol. 2* (collection), 2378

Fabulous 3 MCs. *Don't Stop: Recording Tap* (collection), 2657

The Fabulous Thunderbirds
    Blues Fest: Modern Blues of the '70s (collection), 408
    Blues Masters, Vol. 9: Postmodern Blues (collection), 412
    The Essential Fabulous Thunderbirds, 373.1
    Hot Stuff: The Greatest Hits, 373.2

The Fairfield Four
    The Best of Nashboro Gospel (collection), 3032
    ★*The Gospel Sound of Spirit Feel* (collection), 2965
    Living Legends of Gospel: The Quartets, Vols. 1 and 2 (collection), 3010
    The Rough Guide to Gospel (collection), 2970
    Standing in the Safety Zone, 3015.1
    Standing on the Rock, 3015.2
    Story of Gospel Music (collection), 2973
    Testify! The Gospel Box (collection), 2974

Fairport Convention
    Liege and Lief, 1853.1
    ★*Unhalfbricking,* 1853.2
    What We Did on Our Holidays, 1853.3

Faith, Percy
    50 Years: The Artistry of Tony Bennett (Bennett), 1179.2
    Greatest Hits, 1191
    ★*Sentimental Journey: Pop Vocal Classics, Vol. 3* (collection), 1169
    16 Most Requested Songs: The 1950s, Vol. 1 (collection), 1171

Faithfull, Marianne. *Broken English,* 2046

Falcons
    ★*Atlantic Soul, 1959–1975* (collection), 2589
    Birth of Soul, 4 Vols. (collection), 2434
    The Doo-Wop Box II (collection), 2323

The Fall
    Grotesque (after Gramme), 2032.1
    Live at the Witch Trials, 2032.2
    This Nation's Saving Grace, 2032.3

Fall. *No Thanks! The '70s Punk Rebellion* (collection), 2003

★Famous Blue Jay Singers. *Good News: 100 Gospel Greats* (collection), 2961

Famous Skylarks. *The Best of Nashboro Gospel* (collection), 3032

Fancy, Cally. *A First-Time Buyer's Guide to American Negro Spirituals* (collection), 32

Fanny. *Fanny,* 2047

Fantastic Angels. *This May Be My Last Time Singing: Raw African-American Gospel on 45rpm* (collection), 2982

Fantastic Lightning Ares. *Boddie Recording Company Cleveland, Ohio* (collection), 2569, 2570

Fargo, Donna. *The Best of Donna Fargo,* 1483

Farlow, Tal
    Progressions: 100 Years of Jazz Guitar (collection), 481
    Swinging Guitar of . . ., 638

Farmer, Art
    Art Farmer Live in '64, 639.1
    Meet the Jazztet, 639.2
    Something to Live For: The Music of Billy Strayhorn, 875

Farrell, Eileen
    Alec Wilder (songwriter collection), 1117.1
    Cole Porter (songwriter collection), 1108.1
    Irving Berlin (songwriter collection), 1096.1
    Jerome Kern (songwriter collection), 1104.1
    My Very Best, 1268

Fastbacks. *Greasy Kid Stuff* (collection), 3210

Fat Boys
    All Meat No Filler! The Best of Fat Boys, 2788.1
    Fat Boys, 2788.2

Fat Joe. *Don Cartagena,* 2789

★The Fat Man. *Nashville Jumps: Blues and Rhythm on Nashville Independent Labels 1945–1955* (collection), 2376

Fatback Band
    The Fattest of Fatback, 2628
    The Spring Story: Essential 70s Soul (collection), 2608

Fatboy Slim. *You've Come a Long Way, Baby,* 2220

Father's Children. *Who's Gonna Save the World,* 2471

Faust. *Faust / So Far,* 1958

Faye, Alice
    Richard Whiting (songwriter collection), 1116
    ★*Sophisticated Ladies* (collection), 1087

The Fearless Four
    The Best of Enjoy! Records (collection), 2663
    Hip Hop Essentials, 1979–1991 (collection), 2675

Feather, Leonard. *Harlem in Vogue: The Poetry and Jazz of Langston Hughes* (collection), 811

Federal Music Society
    Come and Trip It: Instrumental Dance Music, 1780s–1920s (collection), 94
    Music of the Federal Era, 50

The Feelies
    Crazy Rhythms, 2125.1
    Only Life, 2125.2

Feinstein, Michael. *George Gershwin* (songwriter collection), 1101.3

Fender, Freddy. *The Best of Freddy Fender,* 1484

Ferguson, Maynard
    Big Band Renaissance: The Evolution of the Jazz Orchestra (collection), 739
    The Essential Maynard Ferguson, 751

Ferry, Brian
    Best of Roxy Music, 1959.1
    For Your Pleasure: The Second Roxy Music Album, 1959.2

Fewell, Garrison. *Jazz Improvisation for Guitar: A Harmonic Approach,* 491

Fiasco, Lupe. *Food and Liquor,* 2790

Fidelitys. *The Doo-Wop Box II* (collection), 2323

Fields, Dorothy. *Dorothy Fields* (songwriter collection), 1100

Fields, Ralph. *Don't Give the Name a Bad Place: Types and Stereotypes in American Musical Theater, 1870–1900* (collection), 1063

The Fiestas
    ★*The Doo-Wop Box* (collection), 2322
    Old Town Doo-Wop, Vols. 1–3 (collection), 2324

Fifes and Drums of Williamsburg. *The World Turned Upside Down: Music from the Yorktown Battlefield,* 51

The 5th Dimension
    Frank Sinatra: Concert Collection, 1224.3
    Greatest Hits on Earth, 1269
    The Look of Love: The Burt Bacharach Collection (collection), 1161

50 Cent
    Get Rich or Die Tryin', 2791.1
    The Massacre, 2791.2

52nd Regimental String Band. *The Civil War Grand Military Ball,* 72

Firemen, Laurel. *Mountain Gospel: The Sacred Roots of Country Music* (collection), 3113

Fischer, Clare. *Big Band Renaissance: The Evolution of the Jazz Orchestra* (collection), 739

Fischer, John. *First Love: A Historic Gathering of Jesus Music Pioneers* (collection), 3137

Fisher, Eddie
    Eccentric Soul: The Young Disciples (collection), 2562
    The Hits, 1192
    Nipper's Greatest Hits: The 50's, Vol. 2 (collection), 1164

Fisher, Eddie (cont.)

★*Nipper's Greatest Hits: The 50's, Vol. 1* (collection), 1163

★*Sentimental Journey: Pop Vocal Classics, Vol. 3* (collection), 1169

Fisk Jubilee Singers. *Classic African American Gospel from Smithsonian Folkways* (collection), 2959

Fisk University Jubilee Singers. *Story of Gospel Music* (collection), 2973

Fitzgerald, Ella

★*American Popular Song: Six Decades of Songwriters and Singers* (collection), 1059

The Classic Hoagy Carmichael (songwriter collection), 1097.1

Cole Porter (songwriter collection), 1108.1

The Definitive Collection (songwriter collection), 1101.1

Duke Ellington (songwriter collection), 1099.1

Ella and Oscar, 779.1

Ella Fitzgerald Live in '57 and '63, 779.2

Ella Wishes You a Swinging Christmas, 3328

Ellington Songbook, 779.3

Frank Sinatra: Concert Collection, 1224.3

★*George and Ira Gershwin Songbook*, 779.4

George Gershwin (songwriter collection), 1101.3

Harold Arlen Songbook, 779.5

Harold Arlen (songwriter collection), 1095.1

Irving Berlin (songwriter collection), 1096.1

Jazz Lullaby (collection), 3264

★*The Jazz Singers: A Smithsonian Collection of Jazz Vocals from 1919–1994* (collection), 766

Jerome Kern (songwriter collection), 1104.1

Legendary Big Band Singers (collection), 767

Mack the Knife: The Complete Ella in Berlin Concert, 779.6

★*Miss Ella's* Playhouse, 3198

★*The Music Goes Round and Around: The Golden Years of Tin Pan Alley, 1930–1939* (collection), 1070

Pure Ella (Ella Sings Gershwin), 779.7

Rodgers / Hart (songwriter collection), 1109.1

75th Birthday Celebration: Greatest Hits, 779.8

Sings the Cole Porter Songbook, Vols. 1 and 2, 779.9

Sings the Rodgers and Hart Songbook, Vols. 1 and 2, 779.10

★*The Smithsonian Collection of Classic Jazz* (collection), 486

Stars of the Apollo (collection), 2240

The Very Best of Cole Porter (songwriter collection), 1108.3

★Five Americans. *Nuggets: Artifacts of the First Psychedelic Era* (collection), 1808

Five Blind Boys of Alabama

★*Good News: 100 Gospel Greats* (collection), 2961

Greatest Gospel Gems (collection), 3035

Oh Lord Stand by Me / Marching up to Zion, 3016

The Five Blind Boys of Mississippi

The Five Blind Boys of Mississippi, 3017

Good News: 22 Gospel Greats (collection), 3033

★*Jubilation! Great Gospel Performances, Vol. 2: More Black Gospel* (collection), 2967

Kings of the Gospel Highway: The Golden Age of Gospel Quartets (collection), 3009

★Five Breezes. *Let's Get Loose: Folk and Popular Blues Styles from the Beginning to the Early 1940s* (collection), 152

Five Crowns. *Old Town Doo-Wop, Vols. 1–3* (collection), 2324

★Five Discs. *The Doo-Wop Box* (collection), 2322

★5 Echoes. *The Vee-Jay Story: Celebrating 40 Years of Classic Hits* (collection), 2431

Five Gospel Stirrers. *Jesus Put a Song in My Soul* (collection), 3036

Five Keys

★*The Doo Wop Box: 101 Vocal Group Gems from the Golden Age of Rock 'n' Roll* (collection), 1745

★*The Doo-Wop Box* (collection), 2322

The Doo-Wop Box II (collection), 2323

★*The R&B Box* (collection), 2239

Rocking and Crying the Blues, 1951–1957, 2337

The "5" Royales

Birth of Soul, 4 Vols. (collection), 2434

It's Hard but It's Fair: King Hits and Rarities, 2338.1

★*Monkey Hips and Rice: The "5" Royales Anthology*, 2338.2

The Roots of Rock 'n' Roll, 1946–1954 (collection), 1755

The Five Satins

Best of Doo Wop Ballads (collection), 1743

Street Corner Serenade: The Greatest Doo-Wop Hits of the '50s and '60s (collection), 1756

★*The Doo Wop Box: 101 Vocal Group Gems from the Golden Age of Rock 'n' Roll* (collection), 1745

★*The Doo-Wop Box* (collection), 2322

The Doo-Wop Box II (collection), 2323

The Original Master Tapes Collection, Vol. 1, 2339.1

The Original Master Tapes Collection, Vol. 2, 2339.2

5000 Volts. *Disco Box* (collection), 2644

Flack, Roberta

★*Atlantic R&B, 1947–1974* (collection), 2418

First Take, 2472.1

The Very Best of Roberta Flack, 2472.2

Flame

Our World Fallen, 3173.1

Our World Redeemed, 3173.2

Flaming Ember. *Heaven Must Have Sent You: The Holland/Dozier/Holland Story* (collection), 2436

The Flaming Lips

Colours Are Brighter: Songs for Children and Grown Ups Too (collection), 3193

The Fearless Freaks: The Wondrously Improbable Story of the Flaming Lips, 2126.1

The Soft Bulletin, 2126.2

The Flamingos

Best of Doo Wop Ballads (collection), 1743

The Best of the Flamingos, 2340.1

Complete Chess Masters Plus, 2340.2

★*The Doo Wop Box: 101 Vocal Group Gems from the Golden Age of Rock 'n' Roll* (collection), 1745

★*The Doo-Wop Box* (collection), 2322

The Doo-Wop Box II (collection), 2323

★*The R&B Box* (collection), 2239

Street Corner Serenade: The Greatest Doo-Wop Hits of the '50s and '60s (collection), 1756

Flanagan, Tommy

Nights at the Vanguard, 876.1

Tommy Flanagan Trio '77, 876.2

Flanders, Michael

The Complete Flanders and Swann (Flanders and Swann), 1193.1

The Songs of Michael Flanders and Donald Swann (Flanders and Swann), 1193.2

Flatlanders. *More a Legend Than a Band*, 1485

Flatt, Lester and Scruggs, Earl

Appalachian Stomp: Bluegrass Classics (collection), 1560

The Best of Bluegrass, Vol. 1: Standards (collection), 1561

Best of the Flatt and Scruggs TV Show: Classic Bluegrass from 1956 to 1962, 1583.1

★*The Complete Mercury Sessions*, 1583.2

★*The Essential Flatt and Scruggs: 'Tis Sweet to Be Remembered*, 1583.3

Flatt and Scruggs, 1948–1959, 1583.4

Flatt and Scruggs, 1959–1963, 1583.5

Jubilation! Great Gospel Performances, Vol. 3: Country Gospel (collection), 3112

Fleck, Bela
 Bluegrass Sessions: Tales from the Acoustic Planet, Vol. 2, 1584
 Flight of the Cosmic Hippo, 823
 Hand-Picked: 25 Years of Bluegrass on Rounder Records (collection), 1564

Fleetwood Mac
 Fleetwood Mac, 1906.1
 ★*Rumours,* 1906.2

Flemons, Wade
 Birth of Soul: Special Chicago Edition (collection), 2566
 ★*The Vee-Jay Story: Celebrating 40 Years of Classic Hits* (collection), 2431

Flesher, Bob. *Minstrel Banjo Style,* 110

Fletcher, Tee. *Eccentric Soul: The Tragar and Note Labels* (collection), 2602

Flipper. *The Generic Album,* 2127

Florida Boys. *45 Songs of Faith,* 3122

Florida Mass Choir. *Now, I Can See,* 3061

Flower Shoppe. *The Spring Story: Essential 70s Soul* (collection), 2608

Floyd, Bobby. *Don't Give the Name a Bad Place: Types and Stereotypes in American Musical Theater, 1870–1900* (collection), 1063

Floyd, Eddie
 ★*Atlantic R&B, 1947–1974* (collection), 2418
 Beg, Scream, and Shout! The Big Ol' Box of '60s Soul (collection), 2433
 Stax/Volt Revue: Live in London, Vols. 1 and 2 (collection), 2609
 Stax/Volt Revue: Live in Norway 1967 (collection), 2446
 The Complete Stax/Volt Soul Singles, Vol. 2: 1968–1971 (collection), 2595
 ★*The R&B Box* (collection), 2239
 Top of the Stax, Vol. 1: Twenty Greatest Hits (collection), 2611
 Top of the Stax, Vol. 2: Twenty Greatest Hits (collection), 2612

★Floyd, King. *Atlantic Soul, 1959–1975* (collection), 2589

★Flyers. *Atlantic Vocal Groups, 1951–1963* (collection), 2320

Flying Burrito Brothers
 Hot Burritos! The Flying Burrito Brothers Anthology, 1836
 Hot Burritos! The Flying Burrito Brothers Anthology, 1969–1972, 1486

Flying Lotus. *Cosmogramma,* 2792

Fogelberg, Dan. *Greatest Hits,* 1270

Foger, Deacon Tom. *Powerhouse Gospel on Independent Labels* (collection), 3038

The Foggy Mountain Boys
 Best of the Flatt and Scruggs TV Show: Classic Bluegrass from 1956 to 1962, 1583.1
 ★*The Complete Mercury Sessions,* 1583.2
 ★*The Essential Flatt and Scruggs: 'Tis Sweet to Be Remembered,* 1583.3
 Flatt and Scruggs, 1948–1959, 1583.4
 Flatt and Scruggs, 1959–1963, 1583.5

★Foley, Red. *Red Foley: Country Music Hall of Fame,* 1487

★Folk, Bessie. *All God's Sons and Daughters: Chicago's Gospel Legends* (collection), 3030

folk blues. *See* blues revival and folk blues

folk-rock, 1820–1828. *See also* British folk-rock
 ★*The Band,* 1821.1
 The Basement Tapes (Dyland and the Band), 1823.5
 The Beat Goes On: The Best of Sonny and Cher, 1827
 ★*Blonde on Blonde* (Dylan), 1823.1
 Blood on the Tracks (Dylan), 1823.2
 Bob Dylan: Don't Look Back, 1823.3
 Bridge over Troubled Water (Simon and Garfunkel), 1826.1
 ★*Bringing It All Back Home* (Dylan), 1823.4
 Greatest Hits (Lovin' Spoonful), 1824
 Greatest Hits (Mamas and the Papas), 1825
 ★*Greatest Hits* (Simon and Garfunkel), 1826.2
 Greatest Hits (The Band), 1821.2
 ★*Highway 61 Revisited* (Dylan), 1823.6
 John Wesley Harding (Dylan), 1823.7
 The Last Waltz (The Band), 1821.3
 Live 1966: The "Royal Albert Hall" Concert (Dylan), 1823.8
 Music from Big Pink (The Band), 1821.4
 Nashville Skyline (Dylan), 1823.9
 No Direction Home (Dylan), 1823.10
 Save the Turtles: The Turtles Greatest Hits, 1828
 Songs of Protest (collection), 1820
 Sweetheart of the Rodeo (Byrds), 1822.1
 Time out of Mind (Dylan), 1823.11
 ★*20 Essential Tracks from the Boxed Set* (Byrds), 1822.2

For Carnation. *The For Carnation,* 2235

Ford, Dee Dee. *The Fire / Fury Records Story* (collection), 2422

★Ford, Mary. *Sentimental Journey: Pop Vocal Classics, Vol. 3* (collection), 1169

Ford, Tennessee Ernie
 Classic Country: Kings of Country (collection), 1381
 Country Gospel Classics, Vol. 1, 3123
 Greatest Hits, 1488.1
 Proper Introduction to Tennessee Ernie Ford: Rock City Boogie, 1488.2
 The Roots of Rock 'n' Roll, 1946–1954 (collection), 1755

Forehand, Blind Mamie. *American Primitive, Vol. 1: Raw Pre-War Gospel* (collection), 2976

Foreign Exchange. *Connected,* 2793

Foreigner
 Billboard #1s: The '80s (collection), 1236
 No End in Sight: The Very Best of Foreigner, 2072

Formby, George
 The Flapper Box (collection), 1064
 With My Little Ukulele in My Hand (collection), 1093

Forrest, Helen
 ★*American Popular Song: Six Decades of Songwriters and Singers* (collection), 1059
 Harry Warren (songwriter collection), 1114
 Jerome Kern (songwriter collection), 1104.1
 Jule Styne (songwriter collection), 1111.1
 ★*Praise the Lord and Pass the Ammunition: Songs of World Wars I and II* (collection), 1079
 Sentimental Journey: Capitol's Great Ladies of Song (collection), 1166
 ★*Sentimental Journey: Pop Vocal Classics, Vol. 1* (collection), 1081

Forrest, Jimmy. *The Big Horn: The History of the Honkin' and Screamin' Saxophone* (collection), 2314

Foster, Helen
 ★*Nashville Jumps: Blues and Rhythm on Nashville Independent Labels 1945–1955* (collection), 2376
 Night Train to Nashville: Music City Rhythm and Blues, 1945–1970, Vol. 2 (collection), 2378

Foster, Stephen Collins
 American Dreamer, 111.1
 Beautiful Dreamer: Robert White Sings Stephen Foster, 111.2
 Civil War Songs, 73.1
 Dear Friends and Gentle Hearts: The Songs of Stephen Foster and the Civil War, 73.2
 Songs of Stephen Foster (1972), 111.3
 Songs of Stephen Foster (1999), 111.5
 Songs of Stephen Foster (2008), 111.4
 Sons of the Pioneers Sing the Stephen Foster Songbook, 111.6
 Stephen Foster Song Book: Original Sheet Music of 40 Songs, 111.8
 Stephen Foster Songs, 111.9

Foster, Stephen Collins (cont.)
  The Stephen Foster Collection: Stephen Foster in Contrast, 111.7
  The Voices That Are Gone, 111.10
Foster, Walter. *The Best of Loma Records: The Rise and Fall of a 1960's Soul Label* (collection), 2590
Fountains of Wayne. *Welcome Interstate Managers*, 2128
The Four Aces
  The Four Aces Greatest Hits (Four Aces), 1194
  Hoagy Carmichael (songwriter collection), 1097.2
  Moments to Remember: The Golden Hits of the '50s and '60s Live (collection), 1162
★Four Buddies. *Stompin' at the Savoy: The Original Indie Label, 1944–1961* (collection), 2429
Four Fellows. *The Doo-Wop Box II* (collection), 2323
The Four Freshmen
  ★*The Four Freshmen*, 1195
  Moments to Remember: The Golden Hits of the '50s and '60s Live (collection), 1162
Four Interns. *The Best of King Gospel* (collection), 3031
The Four Lads
  Frank Loesser (songwriter collection), 1106.1
  Hit Parade, 1956 (collection), 1158
  Moments to Remember: The Golden Hits of the '50s and '60s Live (collection), 1162
  16 Most Requested Songs, 1196
  16 Most Requested Songs: The 1950s, Vol. 1 (collection), 1171
Four Mints. *Eccentric Soul: The Capsoul Label* (collection), 2599
The Four Preps. *Casey Kasem Presents America's Top Ten through the Years: The Doo-Wop Years, 1950s* (collection), 1155
The Four Seasons
  In Season: Frankie Valli and the Four Seasons Anthology, 1776.1
  The Very Best of Frankie Valli and the Four Seasons, 1776.2
Four Tet. *Colours Are Brighter: Songs for Children and Grown Ups Too* (collection), 3193
Four Tops
  Anthology: 50th Anniversary, 2341.1
  Beg, Scream, and Shout! The Big Ol' Box of '60s Soul (collection), 2433
  ★*50th Anniversary: The Singles Collection, 1961–1971*, 2341.2
  ★*50th Anniversary: The Singles Collection, 1961–1971*, 2539
  Fourever, 2341.3

  Heaven Must Have Sent You: The Holland/Dozier/Holland Story (collection), 2436
  Hitsville USA: The Motown Singles Collection (collection), 2603
  Hitsville USA: The Motown Singles Collection, Vol. 2 (collection), 2604
  Lost and Found: Lost without You 1963–1970, 2341.4
  Motown around the World (collection), 2437
  ★*The R&B Box* (collection), 2239
  Reach Out, 2540
Four Tracks. *Eccentric Soul: The Tragar and Note Labels* (collection), 2602
Four Tunes. *The Doo-Wop Box II* (collection), 2323
4Him. *CCM Top 100: Greatest Songs in Christian Music, Vol. 1* (collection), 3136
Foxy. *Disco Box* (collection), 2644
Fran, Carol. *The Best of Excello Records (collection)*, 327
Francis, Connie. *Gold*, 1777
Francis, Sage. *Personal Journals*, 2794
Frankie and Robert. *Eccentric Soul: The Tragar and Note Labels* (collection), 2602
Franklin, Aretha
  Amazing Grace: The Complete Recordings, 2579
  ★*Amazing Grace: The Complete Recordings*, 2997.1
  Aretha Franklin: Queen of Soul, 2473.1
  Aretha Gospel, 2997.2
  Aretha, the Queen of Soul, 2473.2
  ★*Atlantic R&B, 1947–1974* (collection), 2418
  ★*Atlantic Soul, 1959–1975* (collection), 2589
  Beg, Scream, and Shout! The Big Ol' Box of '60s Soul (collection), 2433
  Casey Kasem Presents America's Top Ten through the Years: The Sixties (collection), 1156
  Dorothy Fields (songwriter collection), 1100
  ★*I Never Loved a Man the Way I Loved You*, 2473.3
  ★*The Jazz Singers: A Smithsonian Collection of Jazz Vocals from 1919–1994* (collection), 766
  ★*Lady Soul*, 2473.4
  Live at Fillmore West, 2473.5
  Muscle Shoals Sound (collection), 2605
  None but the Righteous: Chess Gospel Greats (collection), 3037
  Spirit in the Dark, 2473.6
  Stars of the Apollo (collection), 2240
  Story of Gospel Music (collection), 2973
  Take a Look: Complete on Columbia, 2473.7

  Testify! The Gospel Box (collection), 2974
  ★*The R&B Box* (collection), 2239
  The Sweetest Feeling: A Van McCoy Songbook (collection), 2447
  Unforgettable: A Tribute to Dinah Washington, 2473.8
  Young, Gifted, and Black, 2473.9
Franklin, Erma
  Beg, Scream, and Shout! The Big Ol' Box of '60s Soul (collection), 2433
  Piece of Her Heart: The Epic and Shout Years, 2474
  The Story of Brunswick: The Classic Sound of Chicago Soul (collection), 2610
  The Sweetest Feeling: A Van McCoy Songbook (collection), 2447
Franklin, Kirk
  Kirk Franklin and the Family, 3085.1
  ★*Nu Nation Project*, 3085.2
  Wow Gospel #1s (collection), 3074
Franklin, Rev. C. L. *None but the Righteous: Chess Gospel Greats* (collection), 3037
Franz Ferdinand. *Colours Are Brighter: Songs for Children and Grown Ups Too* (collection), 3193
Frazier, Calvin. *Acoustic Country Blues Guitar: Delta Blues before Robert Johnson* (collection), 211
Freakwater. *Old Paint*, 1703
Freburg, Stan. *Dr. Demento Presents: The Greatest Christmas Novelty CD of All Time* (collection), 3307
Freddie Hubbard Quartet. *Live from the Village Vanguard* (collection), 935
Fredericks, Henry Saint Clair. See Mahal, Taj
free jazz and related styles of the 1960s, 678–700
  Adam's Apple (Shorter), 700.1
  At the Golden Circle, Vols. 1 and 2 (Coleman), 681.1
  Bells / Prophecy (Ayler), 679.1
  Booker Little and Friend (Little), 691.1
  collections, 678
  Complete Communion (Cherry), 680
  Cosmic Tones for Mental Therapy / Art Forms of Dimensions Tomorrow (Ra), 695.1
  Destination Out (McLean), 692.1
  Dialogue (Hutcherson), 687
  Does Your House Have Lions: The Rahsaan Roland Kirk Anthology (Kirk), 688.1
  East Broadway Rundown (Rollins), 697.1
  Eastern Sounds (Lateef), 690
  Eric Dolphy at the Five Spot, Vol. 1 (Dolphy), 682.1
  Evidence (Lacy), 689.1
  Evolution (Moncur), 693

Far Cry (Dolphy), 682.2

Four for Trane (Shepp), 699.1

★*Free Jazz* (Coleman), 681.2

★*Heliocentric Worlds* (Ra), 695.2

Jimmy Giuffre 3, 1961 (Giuffre), 683

Karma (Sanders), 698.1

★*Ken Burns Jazz Collection: Ornette Coleman* (Coleman), 681.3

Let Freedom Ring (McLean), 692.2

Liberation Music Orchestra (Haden), 684

New York Art Quartet (New York Art Quartet), 694

The New York Contemporary Five (Shepp), 699.2

Night Dreamer (Shorter), 700.2

On This Night (Shepp), 699.3

Ornette Coleman Trio / Sound? (collection), 678

Our Man in Jazz (Rollins), 697.2

Out Front (Little), 691.2

Outward Bound (Dolphy), 682.3

★*Page One* (Henderson), 685

★*Percussion Bitter Suite* (Roach), 696.1

Point of Departure (Hill), 686

Rahsaan Roland Kirk Live in '63 and '67 (Kirk), 688.2

★*Rip, Rig, and Panic / Now Please Don't You Cry, Beautiful Edith* (Kirk), 688.3

★*The Shape of Jazz to Come* (Coleman), 681.4

Spirits (Ayler), 679.2

Spiritual Unity (Ayler), 679.3

The Straight Horn of Steve Lacy (Lacy), 689.2

Sun Ra: A Joyful Noise (Ra), 695.3

Tauhid (Sanders), 698.2

This Is Our Music (Coleman), 681.5

We Insist: Freedom Now Suite (Roach), 696.2

Freed, Mark. *12-Bar Blues,* 168

Freeez. *Disco Box* (collection), 2644

Freeman, Bonnie. *Don't Stop: Recording Tap* (collection), 2657

Freeman, Bud

  ★*The Commodore Story* (collection), 561

  Lost Chords: White Musicians and Their Contributions to Jazz (collection), 479

  Swingin' with "The Eel," 574

Freeman, Chico. *Destiny's Dance,* 921

Freeman, Sharon. *Amarcord Nino Rota* (collection), 809

Freestyle Fellowship

  Innercity Griots, 2795.1

  To Whom It May Concern . . ., 2795.2

Fremont, Robert A. *Favorite Songs of the Nineties; Complete Original Sheet Music for 89 Songs,* 112

Fresh, Doug E., and the Get Fresh Crew. *The World's Greatest Entertainer,* 2796

Fricke, Janie. *Anthology,* 1644

Friendly Brothers. *Jesus Put a Song in My Soul* (collection), 3036

Friends of Distinction. *Best of the Friends of Distinction,* 2475

Frisell, Bill

  Amarcord Nino Rota (collection), 809

  Before We Were Born, 969.1

  Icons among Us (collection), 934

  ★*Lookout for Hope,* 969.2

  Progressions: 100 Years of Jazz Guitar (collection), 481

Frishberg, Dave. *Classics,* 780

Frith, Fred. *Friends and Enemies,* 2129

Frizzell, Lefty

  Classic Country: Kings of Country (collection), 1381

  Classic Country Music: A Smithsonian Collection (collection), 1382

  Life's Like Poetry, 1489.1

  Look What Thoughts Will Do, 1489.2

  Texas Music, Vol. 2: Western Swing and Honky Tonk (collection), 1432

  ★*That's the Way Life Goes: The Hit Songs, 1950–1975,* 1489.3

Frost, Frank. *Deep Blues* (collection), 217

Fugazi. *Repeater + 3 Songs,* 2130

★Fugees. *The Score,* 2798

Fulks, Robbie. *Country Love Songs,* 1704

Fuller, Blind Boy

  Blind Boy Fuller, 247.1

  Blind Boy Fuller, Vol. 2, 247.2

  ★*Blues Classics* (collection), 146

  ★*The Blues: A Smithsonian Collection of Classic Blues Singers* (collection), 145

  East Coast Piedmont Style (Fuller), 247.3

  ★*Legends of the Blues, Vol. 1* (collection), 150

  News and the Blues: Telling It Like It Is (collection), 156

  ★*The Story of the Blues* (collection), 158

Fuller, Bobby. *Texas Music, Vol. 3: Garage Bands and Psychedelia* (collection), 1830

Fuller, Jesse. *San Francisco Bay Blues,* 319

Fuller, Vaughn. *Kwanzaa for Young People (and Everyone Else!),* 3242

Fulson, Lowell

  ★*Blues Classics* (collection), 146

  Blues Masters, Vol. 1: Urban Blues (collection), 338

  ★*The Blues: A Smithsonian Collection of Classic Blues Singers* (collection), 145

  ★*Chess Blues* (collection), 287

  Hung Down Head, 320.1

  Lowell Fulson, 1946 to 1953, 320.2

The Modern Records Blues Story (collection), 342

Soul Shots, Vol. 4: Urban Blues (collection), 343

The Swing Time Records Story: R&B, Blues, and Gospel, 1946–1952 (collection), 313, 2430

Tramp / Soul, 320.3

Funderburgh, Anson. *The Best of Anson Funderburgh and the Rockets: Blast Off,* 436

funk

  All Day Music (War), 2642.1

  Anthology, 1970–1994 (War), 2642.2

  The Best of Con Funk Shun, 2625

  The Best of Kool and the Gang, 1969–1976, 2633.1

  The Best of Love Unlimited, 2635

  The Best of Parliament: Give up the Funk, 2638.1

  The Best of the Bar-Kays, 2617

  The Bootsy Collins Anthology: Glory B Da' Funks on Me, 2624

  Bustin' Loose (Brown), 2619

  Celebration: The Best of Kool and the Gang, 1979–1987, 2633.2

  The Clones of Dr. Funkenstein (Parliament), 2638.2

  Computer Games (Clinton), 2623.1

  The Definitive Collection (James), 2632.1

  Dirty Mind (Prince), 2639.2

  Earth, Wind and Fire in Concert, 2627

  The Essential Sly and the Family Stone, 2640.1

  Every 1's a Winner: The Very Best of Hot Chocolate, 2631

  Express Yourself (Charles Wright and the Watts 103rd St. Rhythm Band), 2643

  The Fattest of Fatback, 2628

  Foundations of Funk: A Brand New Bag, 1964–1969 (Brown), 2620.1

  Funk on Fire: The Mercury Anthology (Ohio Players), 2637

  Funk Power 1970: A Brand New Thang (Brown), 2620.2

  Funkentelechy vs. the Placebo Syndromei (Parliament), 2638.3

  Funkology: The Definitive Dazz Band, 2626

  general collections, 2613–2615

  general style, 2613–2643

  Gimme Your Hand, J-B! (collection), 2613

  Gold (Cameo), 2621

  Gold (James), 2632.2

  Gold (Parliament), 2638.4

  Good God! Born Again Funk (collection), 2614

  Greatest Hits (L.T.D.), 2634

  Greatest Hits (Sly and the Family Stone), 2640.2

funk (cont.)

The Hits / the B-Sides (Prince), 2639.3

I Got the Feelin': James Brown in the '60s, 2620.3

The Jam: The Larry Graham and Graham Central Station Anthology, 2630

★Mothership Connection (Parliament), 2638.5

The Mothership Connection (Clinton), 2623.2

The Mothership Connection: Live 1976 (Parliament), 2638.6

★1999 (Prince), 2639.1

Pickin' up the Pieces: The Best of Average White Band, 2616

Prince: Live in Las Vegas, 2639.4

★Purple Rain: Music from the Motion Picture (Prince), 2639.5

Say It Live and Loud: Live in Dallas (Brown), 2620.4

Sign "O" the Times (Prince), 2639.6

★Stand! (Sly and the Family Stone), 2640.3

Strawberry Letter 23: The Very Best of the Brothers Johnson, 2618

Street Songs, Del. Ed (James), 2632.3

Super Freak Live 1982 (James), 2632.4

There's a Riot Goin' On (Sly and the Family Stone), 2640.4

Time Has Come: The Best of the Chambers Brothers, 2622

Ultimate Collection (Gap Band), 2629

The Very Best of New Birth, Inc, 2636

The Very Best of Prince, 2639.7

The Very Best of Tower of Power: The Warner Years, 2641

Videology (Kool and the Gang), 2633.3

★What It Is! Funky Soul and Rare Grooves (collection), 2615

The World Is a Ghetto (War), 2642.3

The Funk Brothers. Standing in the Shadows of Motown (collection), 2445

Funky Four + 1. Hip Hop Essentials, 1979–1991 (collection), 2675

Funky Meters. Make It Funky! (collection), 2360

Funky People. Boddie Recording Company Cleveland, Ohio (collection), 2569, 2570

fusion, 816–833

The Anthology (Corea), 820.1

Best of Billy Cobham (Cobham), 819

Birds of Fire (Mahavishnu Orchestra), 826.1

★Bitches Brew (Davis), 822.1

Brecker Brothers: Electro Jazz-Fusion (Brecker Brothers), 817.1

Combustication (Medeski, Martin, and Wood), 828

Crystal Silence (Burton), 818.1

Dreams So Real (Burton), 818.2

80/81 (Metheny), 829.1

★The Essential John McLaughlin (McLaughlin), 827

The Essential Larry Coryell (Coryell), 821

Flight of the Cosmic Hippo (Fleck), 823

Future Shock (Hancock), 824.1

Gateway (Abercrombie), 816.1

★Head Hunters (Hancock), 824.2

★I Sing the Body Electric (Weather Report), 832.1

In a Silent Way (Davis), 822.2

Inner Mounting Flame (Mahavishnu Orchestra), 826.2

Jaco Pastorius [1976] (Pastorius), 830.1

Jaco Pastorius [2010] (Pastorius), 830.2

Joe Zawinul (Zawinul), 833.1

John Abercrombie (Abercrombie), 816.2

Live Evil (Davis), 822.3

Mysterious Traveller (Weather Report), 832.2

Offramp (Metheny), 829.2

Pat Metheny Group (Metheny), 829.3

★Return to Forever (Corea), 820.2

Sneakin' Up Behind You: The Very Best of the Brecker Brothers (Brecker Brothers), 817.2

Songs (Sanborn), 831

Steady Groovin' (Hunter), 825

A Tribute to Jack Johnson (Davis), 822.4

Tutu (Davis), 822.5

Zawinul (Zawinul), 833.2

G

Gabriel, Peter

Shaking the Tree: 16 Golden Greats, 2073.1

So, 2073.2

Us, 2073.3

Gahr, David. The Blues Fakebook, 166

Gaillard, Slim

★Central Avenue Sounds: Jazz in Los Angeles (collection), 471

Stars of the Apollo (collection), 2240

★Stompin' at the Savoy: The Original Indie Label, 1944–1961 (collection), 2429

Gaines, Earl

★Nashville Jumps: Blues and Rhythm on Nashville Independent Labels 1945–1955 (collection), 2376

Night Train to Nashville: Music City Rhythm and Blues, 1945–1970, Vol. 1 (collection), 2377

Night Train to Nashville: Music City Rhythm and Blues, 1945–1970, Vol. 2 (collection), 2378

Gaines, Joe. The Mercury New Orleans Sessions 1950 and 1953 (collection), 2361

Gaithers. The Early Works, 3124

★Gale, Priscilla. Dream Faces, 113

Gamble, Kenny. Birth of Soul, 4 Vols. (collection), 2434

Game. The Documentary, 2799

Ganelin Trio. Ancora Da Capo, 842

Gang of Four

A Brief History of the Twentieth Century, 2033.1

Entertainment!, 2033.2

No Thanks! The '70s Punk Rebellion (collection), 2003

Gang Starr

Daily Operation, 2800.1

The Ownerz, 2800.3

★Step in the Arena, 2800.2

Gant, Cecil

★Blues Classics (collection), 146

★Nashville Jumps: Blues and Rhythm on Nashville Independent Labels 1945–1955 (collection), 2376

Night Train to Nashville: Music City Rhythm and Blues, 1945–1970, Vol. 1 (collection), 2377

1944–1945, 2253

Gap Band. Ultimate Collection, 2629

garage bands. See surf, bubblegum, garage bands, and pop

Garbarek, Jan. Witchi-Tai-To, 843

Garber, Jan. Irving Berlin: A Hundred Years (songwriter collection), 1096.3

Garcia, Benny. Legends of Western Swing Guitar (collection), 1430

Garcia, Jerry

Legends of Guitar: Rock–The '60s, Vol. 2 (collection), 1861

Not for Kids Only, 3217

Gardner, Don. The Fire / Fury Records Story (collection), 2422

Gardner, Mark L. Songs of the Santa Fe Trail and the Far West, 114

Garland, Hank. Hank Garland and His Sugar Footers, 1490

Garland, Judy

★American Popular Song: Six Decades of Songwriters and Singers (collection), 1059

Arthur Schwartz (songwriter collection), 1110.2

★Classic Judy Garland: The Capitol Years, 1955–1965, 1134.1

Cole Porter (songwriter collection), 1108.1

The Definitive Collection (songwriter collection), 1101.1

Dorothy Fields (songwriter collection), 1100

E. Y. Harburg (songwriter collection), 1103

George Gershwin (songwriter collection), 1101.3

Harold Arlen (songwriter collection), 1095.1

Harry Warren (songwriter collection), 1114

Hit Parade, 1943 (collection), 1157

Irving Berlin (songwriter collection), 1096.1

Jerome Kern (songwriter collection), 1104.1

Johnny Mercer (songwriter collection), 1107.1

Judy at Carnegie Hall, 1197

The Judy Garland Collection, 1134.2

Jule Styne (songwriter collection), 1111.1

Oscar Hammerstein II (songwriter collection), 1102

Rodgers / Hart (songwriter collection), 1109.1

Sentimental Journey: Pop Vocal Classics, Vol. 4 (collection), 1170

★*Sentimental Journey: Pop Vocal Classics, Vol. 1* (collection), 1081

Sweet and Lovely: Capitol's Great Ladies of Song (collection), 1172

This Is Art Deco (collection), 1090

20th Century Masters: The Best of Judy Garland, 1134.3

Vincent Youmans (songwriter collection), 1118

Waller / Razaf (songwriter collection), 1113.2

Garner, Erroll

The Complete Savoy and Dial Master Takes, 575

Concert by the Sea, 721

Erroll Garner Live in '63 and '64, 705

The Original Misty, 666

★*The Smithsonian Collection of Classic Jazz* (collection), 486

Garnett, Blind Leroy. *Mama Don't Allow No Easy Riders Here: Strutting the Dozens; Classic Piano Rags, Blues, and Stomps* (collection), 256

Garrett, Jo Ann. *Eccentric Soul: Twinight's Lunar Rotation* (collection), 2568

Garrett, Kenny. *Standard of Language,* 970

Garrett, Robert. *Southern Rhythm 'n' Rock: The Best of Excello Records, Vol. 22* (collection), 2427

Gates, Rev. J. M.

Gospel: Negro Spirituals / Gospel Songs, 1926–1942 (collection), 2963

Songsters and Saints: Vocal Traditions on Race Records, Vol. 2 (collection), 191

★*The Gospel Sound* (collection), 2964

Gatlin Brothers. *Best of the Gatlins: All the Gold in California,* 1645

Gatton, Danny. *88 Elira St.,* 1646

Gaye, Marvin

Beg, Scream, and Shout! The Big Ol' Box of '60s Soul (collection), 2433

Billboard #1s: The '70s (collection), 1235

80's Pop Hits (collection), 1238

Gold, 2476.1

Heaven Must Have Sent You: The Holland/Dozier/Holland Story (collection), 2436

Hitsville USA: The Motown Singles Collection (collection), 2603

Hitsville USA: The Motown Singles Collection, Vol. 2 (collection), 2604

★*The Jazz Singers: A Smithsonian Collection of Jazz Vocals from 1919–1994* (collection), 766

Let's Get It On, 2476.2

Marvin Gaye: Behind the Legend, 2476.3

Marvin Gaye: The Real Thing: In Performance, 1964–1981, 2476.4

★*The Master, 1961–1984,* 2476.5

Motown around the World (collection), 2437

Pure 60's: The #1 Hits (collection), 1165

★*The R&B Box* (collection), 2239

★*What's Going On,* 2476.6

Gaye, Sandy. *Eccentric Soul: The Tragar and Note Labels* (collection), 2602

Gayle, Crystal. *The Best of* Crystal Gayle, 1491

Gaynor, Gloria

Complete Introduction to Disco (collection), 1237

Disco Box (collection), 2644

I Will Survive: The Anthology, 2646

Gayten, Paul

Chess King of New Orleans: The Chess Years, 2254

★*The Okeh Rhythm and Blues Story* (collection), 2425

General Public. *90's Pop Hits* (collection), 1242

Generation X

Generation X, 2014

No Thanks! The '70s Punk Rebellion (collection), 2003

Genesis

Billboard #1s: The '80s (collection), 1236

Invisible Touch, 2074

The Lamb Lies Down on Broadway, 1960

Genius

Beneath the Surface, 2801.1

Liquid Swords, 2801.2

George and Greer. *The Complete Goldwax Singles, Vol. 2* (collection), 2592

Georgettes. *Eccentric Soul: The Young Disciples* (collection), 2562

Georgia, Alabama, and the East Coast blues, 240–249

Alabama Blues (collection), 240

All the Published Sides (Blind Blake), 246.1

Atlanta Blues: Big City Blues from the Heartland (collection), 241

★*Best of Blind Blake* (Blind Blake), 246.2

Blind Boy Fuller (Fuller), 247.1

Blind Boy Fuller, Vol. 2 (Fuller), 247.2

Chocolate to the Bone (Barbecue Bob), 245

The Classic Years (McTell), 249.1

collections, 240–244

The Definitive Blind Willie McTell (McTell), 249.2

East Coast Piedmont Style (Fuller), 247.3

The Georgia Blues (collection), 242

Gone with the Wind (Hovington), 248

★*Guitar Wizards* (collection), 243

Play My Juke-Box: East Coast Blues (collection), 244

Statesboro Blues (McTell), 249.3

Georgia Mass Choir. *Georgia Mass Choir,* 3062

Georgia Peach

All of My Appointed Time: Forty Years of a Cappella Gospel Singing (collection), 2958

A First-Time Buyer's Guide to American Negro Spirituals (collection), 32

Gospel: Negro Spirituals / Gospel Songs, 1926–1942 (collection), 2963

Gospel Warriors: Over 50 Years of Great Solo Performances (collection), 2987

★*Jubilation! Great Gospel Performances, Vol. 1: Black Gospel* (collection), 2966

★Georgia Tom. *Blues Classics* (collection), 146. *See also* Dorsey, Thomas A.

Georgiou, Steven Demetre. *See* Stevens, Cat

Germano, Lisa. *Lullaby for Liquid Pig,* 2131

Germanotta, Stefani Joanne Angelina. *See* Lady Gaga

Germs

MIA: The Complete Anthology, 1988, 2015

No Thanks! The '70s Punk Rebellion (collection), 2003

Gerrard, Alice. *16 Down Home Country Classics* (collection), 1385

Gershwin, George

The Definitive Collection (songwriter collection), 1101.1

Fascinating Rhythm: George Gershwin (songwriter collection), 1101.2

George Gershwin (songwriter collection), 1101.3

Just Gershwin Real Book (songwriter collection), 1101.4

★*Nipper's Greatest Hits: The 20's* (collection), 1071

Geto Boys

The Geto Boys, 2802.1

We Can't Be Stopped, 2802.2

Gettel, Michael
   Narada Decade: The Anniversary Collection (collection), 1367
   Piano Solos: Narada Artists (collection), 1370
Getz, Stan
   Best of the West Coast Sessions, 611.1
   The Complete Roost Recordings, 611.2
   Focus, 611.3
   Getz / Gilberto, 667
   ★*Ken Burns Jazz: The Story of America's Music* (collection), 478
   Pure Getz, 877
   Quartets, 611.4
   ★*The Smithsonian Collection of Classic Jazz* (collection), 486
   Stan Getz and J. J. Johnson at the Opera House, 611.5
★Ghent, Rev. Aubrey. *Sacred Steel: The Steel Guitar Tradition of the House of God Churches* (collection), 2980
Ghostface Killah
   Ironman, 2803.1
   Supreme Clientele, 2803.2
★Gibbs, Georgia. *Sentimental Journey: Pop Vocal Classics, Vol. 3* (collection), 1169
Gibbs, Terry
   Big Band Renaissance: The Evolution of the Jazz Orchestra (collection), 739
   Dream Band, 752
Gibson, Don
   Classic Country: Kings of Country (collection), 1381
   Don Gibson, 1492
Gibson, Lacey. *Living Chicago Blues, Vol. 3* (collection), 417
Giles, Eddy. *Dave Godin's Deep Soul Treasures, Vols. 1–4* (collection), 2435
Gill, Johnny. *Ultimate Collection,* 2389
★Gill, Robert. *Nashville Jumps: Blues and Rhythm on Nashville Independent Labels 1945–1955* (collection), 2376
Gill, Vince
   ★*The Best of Vince Gill,* 1647.1
   Grand Ole Opry at Carnegie Hall (collection), 1619
   When I Call Your Name, 1647.2
Gillespie, Dizzy
   The Bebop Singers (collection), 765
   ★*Big Band Jazz: From the Beginnings to the Fifties* (collection), 529
   Big Band Renaissance: The Evolution of the Jazz Orchestra (collection), 739
   Birk's Works: The Verve Big Band Sessions, 753
   ★*The Complete RCA Victor Recordings,* 594.1
   Dizzy Gillespie Collection, 594.2
   Dizzy Gillespie's Big 4, 878

   ★*Ken Burns Jazz Collection: Dizzy Gillespie,* 594.3
   ★*Ken Burns Jazz: The Story of America's Music* (collection), 478
   A Night in Tunisia: The Very Best of Dizzy Gillespie, 594.4
   ★*The Original Mambo Kings: An Afro-Cubop Anthology* (collection), 592
   ★*The Smithsonian Collection of Classic Jazz* (collection), 486
Gilley Mickey. *Room Full of Roses / Gilley's Smokin',* 1493
Gillock, William. *New Orleans Jazz Styles: Complete* (Gillock), 506
Gillum, Jazz
   Chicago Is Just That Way (collection), 289
   Harmonica Blues: Great Harmonica Performances of the 1920s and '30s (collection), 185
   When the Sun Goes Down 3: That's Chicago's South Side (collection), 270
Gilmore, Jimmie Dale
   After Awhile, 1648.1
   Fair and Square, 1648.2
Gimble, Johnny. *Texas Music, Vol. 2: Western Swing and Honky Tonk* (collection), 1432
Gin Blossoms. *Whatever: The '90s Pop and Culture Box* (collection), 1244
Girard, Chuck. *First Love: A Historic Gathering of Jesus Music Pioneers* (collection), 3137
Giuffre, Jimmy
   ★*Jazz on a Summer's Day* (collection), 664
   Jimmy Giuffre 3, 1961, 683
   ★*The Jimmy Giuffre 3 / Trav'lin' Light,* 1038
   ★*Sound of Jazz* (collection), 487
Glad. *Acapella Project,* 3147
The Gladiolas
   The Best of Excello Records (collection), 327
   ★*The Doo-Wop Box* (collection), 2322
   Night Train to Nashville: Music City Rhythm and Blues, 1945–1970, Vol. 2 (collection), 2378
   Southern Rhythm 'n' Rock: The Best of Excello Records, Vol. 22 (collection), 2427
Glaser, Tompall
   Hillbilly Central #2: Another Log on the Fire, 1494.2
   Hillbilly Central #1: My Notorious Youth, 1494.1
Glasper, Robert. *Icons among Us* (collection), 934
Glass Harp. *Best of Christian Rock (1970–1986), Vol. 1* (collection), 3135
★Gleason, Harold. *Music in America: An Anthology from the Landing of the*

   Pilgrims to the Close of the Civil War, 1620–1865, 16
Gleason, Jackie. *The Best of Jackie Gleason,* 1198
Glenn, Lloyd. *The Swing Time Records Story: R&B, Blues, and Gospel, 1946–1952* (collection), 313, 2430
Glitter, Gary. *Have a Nice Decade: The '70s Pop Culture Box* (collection), 1240
Globe Unity. *Rumbling,* 844
★Glowtones. *Atlantic Vocal Groups, 1951–1963* (collection), 2320
Glykeria. *World Playground: A Musical Adventure for Kids* (collection), 3230
The Go-Betweens
   Bellavista Terrace: Best of the Go-Betweens, 2132.1
   16 Lovers Lane, 2132.2
Godfrey Ray. *The Spring Story: Essential 70s Soul* (collection), 2608
God's Property
   God's Property from Kirk Franklin's Nu Nation, 3063
   Wow Gospel #1s (collection), 3074
Godspeed You Black Emperor. *Lift Your Skinny Fists Like Antennas to Heaven,* 2236
Go-Go's. *Return to the Valley of the Go-Go's,* 2048
Gold, Andrew. *Andrew Gold's* Halloween Howls, 3350
★Golden Earing. *Nuggets II: Original Artifacts from the British Empire and Beyond* (collection), 1791
Golden Echoes. *Good God! Born Again Funk* (collection), 2614
Golden Gate Jubilee Quartet
   All of My Appointed Time: Forty Years of a Cappella Gospel Singing (collection), 2958
   ★*Good News: 100 Gospel Greats* (collection), 2961
   ★*Goodbye Babylon* (collection), 2954
Golden Gate Quartet
   Close Harmony: A History of Southern Gospel Music, Vol. 1 (collection), 3108
   ★*From Spirituals to Swing: The Legendary 1938 and 1939 Carnegie Hall Concerts Produced by John Hammond* (collection), 564
   Gospel: Negro Spirituals / Gospel Songs, 1926–1942 (collection), 2963
   ★*The Gospel Sound* (collection), 2964
   I Hear Music in the Air: A Treasury of Gospel Music (collection), 3008
   ★*Jubilation! Great Gospel Performances, Vol. 1: Black Gospel* (collection), 2966
   Swing Down Chariot, 3018.1

Testify! The Gospel Box (collection), 2974

Travelin' Shoes, 3018.2

★*A Warrior on the Battlefield: A Cappella Trail Blazers* (collection), 3011

Golden Harmonizers. *Boddie Recording Company Cleveland, Ohio* (collection), 2569, 2570

Golden Harps. *All of My Appointed Time: Forty Years of a Cappella Gospel Singing* (collection), 2958

Golden Palominos. *Pure,* 2133

★Goldkette, Jean. *Nipper's Greatest Hits: The 20's* (collection), 1071

Goldman, Edwin Franko. *The Golden Age of the American March,* 84

Golson, Benny. *The Big Horn: The History of the Honkin' and Screamin' Saxophone* (collection), 2314

Go-Nuts. *Greasy Kid Stuff* (collection), 3210

Gonzales, Babs. *Hipsters' Holiday: Vocal Jazz and R&B Classics* (collection), 3313

Gonzalez, Dennis. *Stefan,* 971

Good Humor Six. *Night Train to Nashville: Music City Rhythm and Blues, 1945–1970, Vol. 2* (collection), 2378

★Good Rockin' Sam. *Nashville Jumps: Blues and Rhythm on Nashville Independent Labels 1945–1955* (collection), 2376

Goodie Mob
  Soul Food, 2805.1
  Still Standing, 2805.2

Goodman, Benny
  Alec Wilder (songwriter collection), 1117.1
  An Anthology of Big Band Swing (collection), 528
  Benny Goodman: Adventures in the Kingdom of Swing, 537.1
  ★*Benny Goodman at Carnegie Hall: Complete,* 537.2
  Benny Goodman Sextet Featuring Charlie Christian, 576.1
  The Benny Goodman Story [1995], 1047.1
  The Benny Goodman Story [2003], 1047.2
  ★*Big Band Jazz: From the Beginnings to the Fifties* (collection), 529
  Big Band Renaissance: The Evolution of the Jazz Orchestra (collection), 739
  The Classic Hoagy Carmichael (songwriter collection), 1097.1
  The Complete Capitol Trios, 576.2
  The Complete RCA Victor Small Group Recordings, 576.3
  ★*The Essential Benny Goodman,* 537.3
  ★*From Spirituals to Swing: The Legendary 1938 and 1939 Carnegie Hall Concerts Produced by John Hammond* (collection), 564

Hit Parade, 1943 (collection), 1157

Ken Burns Jazz Collection: Benny Goodman, 537.4

★*Ken Burns Jazz: The Story of America's Music* (collection), 478

Lost Chords: White Musicians and Their Contributions to Jazz (collection), 479

★*Nipper's Greatest Hits: The 30's, Vol. 1* (collection), 1072

16 Most Requested Songs of the 1940s, Vol. 1 (collection), 1082

16 Most Requested Songs of the 1940s, Vol. 2 (collection), 1083

★*The Smithsonian Collection of Classic Jazz* (collection), 486

Songs That Got Us through World War II, Vol. 2 (collection), 1086

★*Swing Time! The Fabulous Big Band Era* (collection), 1089

Waller / Razaf (songwriter collection), 1113.2

Gordon, Dexter
  ★*Central Avenue Sounds: Jazz in Los Angeles* (collection), 471
  Dexter Gordon Live in '63 and '64, 640.1
  Dexter Gordon: Swingin' Hard Bop, 640.2
  Doin' Allright, 640.3
  ★*Go!,* 640.4
  Homecoming: Live at the Village Vanguard, 879
  Jingle Bell Jazz (collection), 3314
  ★*Ken Burns Jazz: The Story of America's Music* (collection), 478
  Our Man in Paris, 640.5
  ★*Round Midnight* [2001] (Gordon, Hancock, and others), 1056.2
  ★*Round Midnight* [2002] (Gordon, Hancock, and others), 1056.1
  Settin' the Pace, 595
  ★*The Smithsonian Collection of Classic Jazz* (collection), 486
  Yule Struttin': A Blue Note Christmas (collection), 3323

Gordon, Rosco
  Birth of Soul: Special Chicago Edition (collection), 2566
  Blue Flames: A Sun Blues Collection (collection), 337
  Blues Masters, Vol. 12: Memphis Blues (collection), 229
  I'm Gonna Shake It!, 2255
  Memphis Blues: Important Postwar Recordings (collection), 341
  The Modern Records Blues Story (collection), 342
  The Roots of Rock 'n' Roll, 1946–1954 (collection), 1755
  The Sun Blues Years (collection), 344

★*The Vee-Jay Story: Celebrating 40 Years of Classic Hits* (collection), 2431

Gore, Lesley. *Pure 60's: The #1 Hits* (collection), 1165

Gorelick, Kenneth Bruce. *See* Kenny G

Gorillaz. *Demon Days,* 2806

Gosdin, Vern. *Chiseled in Stone,* 1649

Gospel Comforters. *Good God! Born Again Funk* (collection), 2614

Gospel Ensemble. *Boddie Recording Company Cleveland, Ohio* (collection), 2569, 2570

Gospel Fabulators. *Boddie Recording Company Cleveland, Ohio* (collection), 2569, 2570

Gospel Gangstaz
  Gang Affiliated, 3174.1
  I Can See Clearly Now, 3174.2

Gospel Harmonettes
  The Best of Dorothy Love Coates and the Original Gospel Harmonettes, 3045
  Greatest Gospel Gems (collection), 3035
  ★*Jubilation! Great Gospel Performances, Vol. 2: More Black Gospel* (collection), 2967

Gospel Hebrews. *Boddie Recording Company Cleveland, Ohio* (collection), 2569, 2570

Gospel Keys. *This May Be My Last Time Singing: Raw African- American Gospel on 45rpm* (collection), 2982

gospel music and other popular Christian music
  African American general collections, 2958–2975
  African American gospel choirs, 3051–3073
  African American gospel collections, 1940s–1960s, 3030–3039
  African American gospel groups, 3040–3050
  African American gospel quartets, 3006–3029
  African American gospel solo personalities, 2987–3005
  All of My Appointed Time: Forty Years of a Cappella Gospel Singing (collection), 2958
  Christian rap, 3167–3183
  Classic African American Gospel from Smithsonian Folkways (collection), 2959
  contemporary African American gospel, 3074–3105
  evangelists and other traditional performers, 2976–2986
  Fire in My Bones: Raw, Rare and Otherworldy African-American Gospel (collection), 2960
  general collections, 2954–2957
  ★*Good News: 100 Gospel Greats* (collection), 2961

gospel music and other popular Christian
    music (cont.)
    ★Goodbye Babylon (collection), 2954
    Gospel (collection), 2962
    Gospel: Negro Spirituals / Gospel Songs,
        1926–1942 (collection), 2963
    ★The Gospel Sound (collection), 2964
    ★The Gospel Sound of Spirit Feel
        (collection), 2965
    The Gospel Tradition: The Roots and the
        Branches, Vol. 1 (collection), 2955
    The Half Ain't Never Been Told,
        Vols. 1 and 2 (collection), 2956
    How Can I Keep from Singing: Early
        American Religious Music and Song,
        Vols. 1 and 2 (collection), 2957
    inspirational, contemporary Christian,
        and Christian Rock, 3135–3166
    ★Jubilation! Great Gospel Performances,
        Vol. 1: Black Gospel (collection),
        2966
    ★Jubilation! Great Gospel Performances,
        Vol. 2: More Black Gospel
        (collection), 2967
    overview, p165–166
    ★Precious Lord: Recordings of the Great
        Gospel Songs of Thomas A. Dorsey
        (collection), 2968
    Rejoice and Shout (collection), 2969
    The Rough Guide to Gospel (collection),
        2970
    ★Say Amen, Somebody (collection),
        2971
    southern white religious styles,
        3106–3134
    Spreading the Word: Early Gospel
        Recordings (collection), 2972
    Story of Gospel Music (collection), 2973
    Testify! The Gospel Box (collection),
        2974
    ★Wade in the Water: African American
        Sacred Music Traditions, Vols. 1–4
        (collection), 2975
Gospel Music Workshop of America
    National Mass Choir, 3064
gospel soul, 2578–2581
    Amazing Grace: The Complete
        Recordings (Franklin), 2579
    The Best of the Staple Singers, 2580
    Sam Cooke with the Soul Stirrers: The
        Complete Specialty Recordings, 2578
    You Are Not Alone (Staple), 2581
Gospel Soul Revivals. Good God! Born
    Again Funk (collection), 2614
Gospel Storytellers. Good God! Born Again
    Funk (collection), 2614
Gospel Writers. Happy in the Service of
    the Lord: Memphis Gospel Quartet
    Heritage, the 1980s, Vols. 1 and 2
    (collection), 3007
★Gothic Archies. The Tragic Treasury:
    Songs from a Series of Unfortunate
    Events, 3218

Goulet, Robert. Alan Jay Lerner
    (songwriter collection), 1105.1
G.Q. Disco Box (collection), 2644
Grae, Jean. Attack of the Attacking Things:
    The Dirty Mixes, 2807
Grafulla, C. S. Grafulla's Favorites, 85
Graham, Larry. The Jam: The Larry
    Graham and Graham Central
    Station Anthology, 2630
Grand Funk Railroad. Greatest Hits, 1946
Grand Prix's. Eccentric Soul: The Big Mack
    Label (collection), 2598
Grand Puba. Reel to Reel, 2808
★Grandmaster Flash and Melle Mel. The
    Best of Grandmaster Flash, Melle
    Mel, and the Furious Five: Message
    from Beat Street, 2809
Grant, Amy
    CCM Top 100: Greatest Songs in
        Christian Music, Vol. 1 (collection),
        3136
    ★The Collection, 3148.1
    Greatest Hits, 3148.2
    Heart in Motion, 3148.3
Grant, Eddy. Like Omigod! The 80s Pop
    Culture Box (Totally) (collection),
    1241
Grant, Gogi. Alan Jay Lerner (songwriter
    collection), 1105.1
Grappelli, Stéphane
    Jazz in Paris: Improvisations, 722.1
    Jazz Masters, Vol. 11: Stephane
        Grappelli, 722.2
    Stéphane Grappelli, 577
Grateful Dead
    American Beauty, 1837.1
    Ladies and Gentlemen . . . The Grateful
        Dead: Fillmore East, April 1971,
        1837.2
    ★Live Dead, 1837.3
    Workingman's Dead, 1837.4
Gratkowski, Frank. Kollaps, 845
Gratz, Wayne. Piano Solos: Narada Artists
    (collection), 1370
Gravediggaz. 6 Feet Deep, 2810
Graves, Blind Roosevelt
    American Primitive, Vol. 1: Raw Pre-
        War Gospel (collection), 2976
    Good Time Blues: Harmonicas, Kazoos,
        Washboards, and Cow-Bells
        (collection), 268
    Songsters and Saints: Vocal Traditions
        on Race Records, Vol. 1
        (collection), 190
Graves, Josh. Josh Graves, 1585
Gray, Dobie. Beg, Scream, and Shout!
    The Big Ol' Box of '60s Soul
    (collection), 2433
Gray, Freda and the Rocketeers.
    Eccentric Soul: The Deep City Label
    (collection), 2600
Gray, Glen
    Best of the Big Bands, 538

★Brother, Can You Spare a Dime?
    American Song during the Great
    Depression (collection), 1061
Gray, Macy
    Covered, 2405.1
    The Very Best of Macy Gray, 2405.2
Gray, Wardell
    ★Central Avenue Sounds: Jazz in Los
        Angeles (collection), 471
    Memorial, Vol. 1, 596
Grayson, Dori. Dave Godin's Deep Soul
    Treasures, Vols. 1–4 (collection),
    2435
Grayson, G. B.
    ★Anthology of American Folk Music,
        Vols. 1–3 (collection), 1386
    Old-Time Mountain Ballads
        (collection), 1390
    Recordings of Grayson and Whitter,
        1408
The Great American Main Street Band.
    Under the Big Top: 100 Years of
    Circus Music, 86
Greaves, R. B. Muscle Shoals Sound
    (collection), 2605
Green, Al
    Beg, Scream, and Shout! The Big Ol'
        Box of '60s Soul (collection),
        2433
    The Best of Al Green, 2477.1
    Billboard #1s: The '70s (collection),
        1235
    Call Me, 2477.2
    The Definitive Greatest Hits, 2477.3
    Have a Nice Decade: The '70s Pop
        Culture Box (collection), 1240
    The Hi Records Story (collection),
        2423
    ★The Immortal Soul of Al Green,
        2477.4
    Let's Stay Together, 2477.5
    The Lord Will Make a Way / Higher
        Plane, 3086
Green, Cee-Lo
    Cee-Lo Green and His Perfect
        Imperfections, 2811.1
    Cee-Lo Green . . . Is the Soul Machine,
        2811.2
    The Lady Killer, 2811.3
Green Day. Dookie, 2134
Green, Doug. The Civil War Music
    Collector's Edition (collection), 61
Green, Garland
    ★Atlantic Soul, 1959–1975
        (collection), 2589
    The Spring Story: Essential 70s Soul
        (collection), 2608
Green, Grant
    The Complete Quartets with Sonny
        Clark, 641
    Progressions: 100 Years of Jazz Guitar
        (collection), 481
Green, Keith. Ministry Years, Vol. 1, 3149

Green, Lil
Mean Mothers: Independent Womens'
Blues, Vol. 1 (collection), 205
When the Sun Goes Down 4: That's All
Right (collection), 271
Green, Michael. Essential Jazz Percussion:
Drumming in the Style of Modern
Jazz Masters, 492
Green, Ruby. Southern Rhythm 'n' Rock:
The Best of Excello Records, Vol. 22
(collection), 2427
Green, Rudy
★Nashville Jumps: Blues and Rhythm
on Nashville Independent Labels
1945–1955 (collection), 2376
Night Train to Nashville: Music City
Rhythm and Blues, 1945–1970,
Vol. 1 (collection), 2377
★Green, Tuff. Nashville Jumps: Blues and
Rhythm on Nashville Independent
Labels 1945–1955 (collection),
2376
Greenbaum, Norman. Have a Nice
Decade: The '70s Pop Culture Box
(collection), 1240
Greenwood, Lee. The Best of Lee
Greenwood, 1650
Gregg Diamond's Star Cruiser. The Best of
T. K. Disco (collection), 2656
Gregg Smith Singers. Southern Harmony, 13
Gresham, Rev. Willie. Classic African
American Gospel from Smithsonian
Folkways (collection), 2959
Gress, Drew. 7 Black Butterflies, 972
Grier, Jimmie. Mountain Music Bluegrass
Style (collection), 1566
Griffin, Bessie
All of My Appointed Time: Forty
Years of a Cappella Gospel Singing
(collection), 2958
Even Me: Four Decades of Bessie Griffin,
2998
Gospel Warriors: Over 50 Years
of Great Solo Performances
(collection), 2987
The Great Gospel Women, Vol. 2
(collection), 2990
★Precious Lord: Recordings of the Great
Gospel Songs of Thomas A. Dorsey
(collection), 2968
Griffin Brothers. Blues with a Beat, 2256
Griffin, Johnny
Introducing Johnny Griffin, 642
Return of the Griffin, 880
Griffin, Reverend Sin Killer. Negro
Religious Songs and Services
(collection), 2977
Griffin, Rex. Last Letter, 1409
Griffith, Nanci. The Best of Nanci Griffith,
1651
Grimes, Tiny
★Atlantic R&B, 1947–1974 (collection),
2418

Progressions: 100 Years of Jazz Guitar
(collection), 481
Tiny Grimes, 1944–1949, 2257.1
Tiny Grimes, 1949–1951, 2257.2
Tiny Grimes, 1951–1954, 2257.3
Grisman, David
Hand-Picked: 25 Years of Bluegrass on
Rounder Records (collection), 1564
Not for Kids Only, 3217
The David Grisman Rounder Compact
Disc, 1586
Grits
The Art of Translation, 3175.1
Grammatical Revolution, 3175.2
★Gritty Dirt Band. Will the Circle Be
Unbroken? (collection), 1452
Groove Theory. 90's Pop Hits (collection),
1242
Grossman, Hal. Country Blues Songbook,
162
Grossman, Stefan
Country Blues Guitar, 161.1
Country Blues Guitar in Open Tunings,
222.1
Country Blues Songbook, 162
Delta Blues, 222.2
Delta Blues Guitar, 222.3
Fingerpicking Blues Guitar
Instrumentals, 161.2
Fingerpicking Guitar Solos in Open
Tunings, 161.3
Ragtime Blues, 195
Texas Blues, 238
The Grove Dictionary of American Music
(Garrett), p3
Guaraldi, Vince
A Charlie Brown Christmas, 3329
Charlie Brown's Holiday Hits, 3244
Greatest Hits, 668
The Guess Who
Have a Nice Decade: The '70s Pop
Culture Box (collection), 1240
★Nuggets II: Original Artifacts from
the British Empire and Beyond
(collection), 1791
70s Greatest Hits (collection), 1243
Guiding Lights. Boddie Recording
Company Cleveland, Ohio
(collection), 2569, 2570
Guillory, Chuck, and His Rhythm Boys.
Swingbillies: Hillbilly and Western
Swing on Modern/Colonial/Flair,
1947–1952 (collection), 1431
Guitar Gable
The Best of Excello Records (collection),
327
House Rockin' and Hip Shakin': The
Best of Excello Blues (collection),
329
guitar heroes, 1860–1869
★Are You Experienced? (Hendrix),
1866.2
Axis: Bold As Love (Hendrix), 1866.1

BBC Sessions (Hendrix), 1866.3
Blow by Blow (Beck), 1862.1
Bluesbreakers (Mayall), 1868
Crossroads (Clapton), 1863.1
Disraeli Gears (Cream), 1864.1
★Electric Ladyland (Hendrix), 1866.4
Eric Clapton Anthology, 1863.2
The Essential Ten Years After, 1869
Experience Hendrix: The Best of Jimi
Hendrix, 1866.5
461 Ocean Boulevard (Clapton), 1863.3
Fresh Cream, 1864.2
Layla and Other Assorted Love Songs
(Derek and the Dominos), 1865
Led Zeppelin, 1867.1
Led Zeppelin Classics, 1867.4
★Led Zeppelin II, 1867.2
★Led Zeppelin IV [Zo-So], 1867.3
Legends of Guitar: Rock–The '60s,
Vol. 1 (collection), 1860
Legends of Guitar: Rock–The '60s,
Vol. 2 (collection), 1861
Live at Monterey (Hendrix), 1866.6
Slowhand (Clapton), 1863.4
Truth (Beck), 1862.2
★The Very Best of Cream, 1864.3
Voodoo Child: The Jimi Hendrix
Collection, 1866.7
Wheels of Fire (Cream), 1864.4
Guitar Shorty. Play My Juke-Box: East
Coast Blues (collection), 244
Guitar Slim
Blues Masters, Vol. 1: Urban Blues
(collection), 338
★Nashville Jumps: Blues and Rhythm
on Nashville Independent Labels
1945–1955 (collection), 2376
New Orleans Guitar (collection), 330
Play My Juke-Box: East Coast Blues
(collection), 244
The Roots of Rock 'n' Roll, 1946–1954
(collection), 1755
Sufferin' Mind, 333, 2304
Gun Club. Fire of Love, 2135
Gunn, Russell. Icons among Us (collection),
934
Guns 'n' Roses. Appetite for Destruction,
2075
Gunter, Arthur
The Best of Excello Records (collection),
327
House Rockin' and Hip Shakin': The
Best of Excello Blues (collection),
329
★Nashville Jumps: Blues and Rhythm
on Nashville Independent Labels
1945–1955 (collection), 2376
Night Train to Nashville: Music City
Rhythm and Blues, 1945–1970,
Vol. 1 (collection), 2377
Southern Rhythm 'n' Rock: The
Best of Excello Records, Vol. 22
(collection), 2427

Guru. *Jazzmatazz, Vol. 1,* 2812

Guthrie, Kari. *National Anthems, Vols. 1–4,* 3375

★Guthrie, Woody. *Brother, Can You Spare a Dime? American Song during the Great Depression* (collection), 1061

Guy, Buddy

  ★*Blues Classics* (collection), 146

  Blues Fest: Modern Blues of the '90s (collection), 410

  Blues Masters, Vol. 2: Postwar Chicago Blues (collection), 285

  ★*The Blues: A Smithsonian Collection of Classic Blues Singers* (collection), 145

  ★*Chess Blues* (collection), 287

  The Cobra Records Story: Chicago Rock and Blues (collection), 339

  Damn Right, I've Got the Blues, 437.1

  ★*Mean Old World: The Blues from 1940–1994* (collection), 154

  Soul Shots, Vol. 4: Urban Blues (collection), 343

  Sweet Tea, 437.2

  ★*The Very Best of Buddy Guy,* 351

Guy. *Groove Me: The Very Best of Guy,* 2390

H

Hackett, Bobby

  ★*The Commodore Story* (collection), 561

  Two Classic Albums from Bobby Hackett and Jack Teagarden: Jazz Ultimate / Coast Concert, 723

Haddon, Dietrick

  Anthology: The Writer and His Music, 3087

  Wow Gospel #1s (collection), 3074

Haden, Charlie

  The Ballad of the Fallen, 973.1

  Big Band Renaissance: The Evolution of the Jazz Orchestra (collection), 739

  Liberation Music Orchestra, 684

  Quartet West: Always Say Goodbye, 973.2

Haggard, Merle

  Down Every Road, 1495.1

  ★*Hag: The Best of Merle Haggard,* 1495.2

  Rainbow Stew: Live at Anaheim Stadium, 1495.3

Haig, Al. *Al Haig Trio: Jazz Will-O'-the-Wisp,* 597

Hal and Jean. *Night Train to Nashville: Music City Rhythm and Blues, 1945–1970, Vol. 2* (collection), 2378

Haley, Bill

  The Best of Bill Haley and His Comets, 1951–1954, 1763.1

  The Golden Era of Rock 'n' Roll (collection), 1748

  ★*Legends of Guitar: Rock–The '50s, Vol. 1* (collection), 1749

  ★*Legends of Guitar: Rock–The '50s, Vol. 2* (collection), 1750

  Let There Be Drums, Vol. 1: The '50s (collection), 1751

  Rock around the Clock, 1763.2

  The Roots of Rock 'n' Roll, 1946–1954 (collection), 1755

Half Japanese

  Half Japanese: The Band That Would Be King, 1874.1

  Loud and Horrible, 1874.2

Half Man Half Biscuit. *Colours Are Brighter: Songs for Children and Grown Ups Too* (collection), 3193

Hall, Adelaide

  Dorothy Fields (songwriter collection), 1100

  Joe Franklin Presents . . . The Roaring '20s Roar Again (collection), 1069

Hall and Oates. *The Very Best of Daryl Hall and John Oates,* 1915

Hall, Carl. *The Best of Loma Records: The Rise and Fall of a 1960's Soul Label* (collection), 2590

Hall, Daryl

  ★*Atlantic Soul, 1959–1975* (collection), 2589

  70s Greatest Hits (collection), 1243

Hall, Harvey. *Boddie Recording Company Cleveland, Ohio* (collection), 2569, 2570

Hall, Henry. *Vintage Children's Favorites* (collection), 3211

Hall, Jim

  Alone Together, 881

  Progressions: 100 Years of Jazz Guitar (collection), 481

Hall, Richard Melville. *See* Moby

Hall, Tom T.

  Definitive Collection, 1496.1

  The Essential Tom T. Hall: The Story Songs, 1496.2

Hall, Vera. *Afro-American Blues and Game Songs* (collection), 169

Hallelujah Chorus. *Eccentric Soul: The Nickel and Penny Labels* (collection), 2567

Halloween music

  collections, 3346–3348

  Fright Night: Music That Goes Bump in the Night (collection), 3346

  ★*Halloween Hits* (collection), 3347

  Halloween Hootenanny (collection), 3348

★Halos. *The Doo-Wop Box* (collection), 2322

Halpern, Steven

  Chakra Suite, 1354

  Ultimate New Age (collection), 1376

Hamilton, Chico

  Gongs East / Three Faces of Chico, 612.1

  ★*Jazz on a Summer's Day* (collection), 664

  Three Classic Albums Plus, 612.2

Hamilton, Roy

  Anthology, 2258

  Vincent Youmans (songwriter collection), 1118

Hammer, M.C. [MC]

  Please Hammer, Don't Hurt 'Em, 2862

  Whatever: The '90s Pop and Culture Box (collection), 1244

Hammerstein, Oscar, II. *Oscar Hammerstein II* (songwriter collection), 1102

Hammond, Fred

  Purpose by Design, 3088

  Wow Gospel #1s (collection), 3074

★Hamp, Johnny. *Nipper's Greatest Hits: The 20's* (collection), 1071

Hampson, Thomas. *Songs: Foster, Griffes, Copland* (collection), 101

Hampton, Lionel

  An Anthology of Big Band Swing (collection), 528

  ★*Big Band Jazz: From the Beginnings to the Fifties* (collection), 529

  Bing Crosby and Some Jazz Friends (Crosby), 1125.2

  ★*Central Avenue Sounds: Jazz in Los Angeles* (collection), 471

  Jingle Bell Jazz (collection), 3314

  Lionel Hampton Live in '58, 754

  Lionel Hampton with Oscar Peterson, 724

  The Lionel Hampton Story, 539

  ★*The R&B Box* (collection), 2239

  Ring Dem Bells, 578

  The Roots of Rock 'n' Roll, 1946–1954 (collection), 1755

  ★*The Smithsonian Collection of Classic Jazz* (collection), 486

  The Story of Brunswick: The Classic Sound of Chicago Soul (collection), 2610

Hancock, Herbie

  Blow Up [1996], 1049.1

  Blow Up [2004], 1049.2

  Empyrean Isles, 706.1

  Future Shock, 824.1

  ★*Head Hunters,* 824.2

  Icons among Us (collection), 934

  Jingle Bell Jazz (collection), 3314

  ★*Ken Burns Jazz Collection: Herbie Hancock,* 706.2

  ★*Ken Burns Jazz: The Story of America's Music* (collection), 478

  Maiden Voyage, 706.3

  ★*Round Midnight* [2001] (Gordon, Hancock, and others), 1056.2

  ★*Round Midnight* [2002] (Gordon, Hancock, and others), 1056.1

Handsome Boy Modeling School. *So . . . How's Your Girl?,* 2813

Handsome Family. *The Bottle Let Me Down: Songs for Bumpy Wagon Rides* (collection), 3191

Handy, John. *New Orleans Jazz* (collection), 503

Handy, W. C. *Blues: An Anthology*, 163

Hang, Xing. *Encyclopedia of National Anthems*, 3376

Hanrahan, Kip. *Conjure: Music for the Texts of Ishmael Reed* (collection), 810

Hanshaw, Annette
  Flappers, Vamps, and Sweet Young Things (collection), 1065
  ★*Sophisticated Ladies* (collection), 1087
  Waller / Razaf (songwriter collection), 1113.2

Happiest Guys in the World. *Greasy Kid Stuff* (collection), 3210

Happy Goodman Family. *The Goodmans Greatest Hits*, 3125

Happy Mondays. *Pills 'n' Thrills and Bellyaches*, 2136

Haran, Mary Cleere. *James Van Heusen* (songwriter collection), 1112.1

Harburg, E. Y. *E. Y. Harburg* (songwriter collection), 1103

hard bop and related extensions of bebop, 626–663
  African Cookbook (Weston), 662
  Art Blakey and the Jazz Messengers Live in '58 (Blakey), 630.1
  Art Farmer Live in '64 (Farmer), 639.1
  At the Half-Note Cafe, Vols. 1 and 2 (Byrd), 634
  ★*Best of Lee Morgan* (Morgan), 653.1
  Best of the Blue Note Years (Smith), 660.1
  ★*The Best of Horace Silver, Vol. 1* (Silver), 659.1
  ★*The Best of Horace Silver, Vol. 2* (Silver), 659.2
  The Best of Stanley Turrentine (Turrentine), 661
  Blue Note: A Story of Modern Jazz (collection), 626
  Blues and the Abstract Truth (Nelson), 654
  Bluesnik (McLean), 647
  Boss Tenor (Ammons), 629
  Breaking Point (Hubbard), 645.1
  The Bridge (Rollins), 657.1
  Brown and Roach Incorporated (Brown), 632.1
  Cannonball Adderley Sextet: Live in Los Angeles, Tokyo and Lugano, 1962–63 (Adderley), 628.1
  Charles Mingus (Mingus), 648
  Clifford Brown Memorial Album (Brown), 632.2
  collections, 626–627
  Complete Blue Note Recordings (Nichols), 656

The Complete Quartets with Sonny Clark (Green), 641
Cookbook, Vol. 1 (Davis), 636
Cool Struttin' (Clark), 635.1
Dexter Gordon Live in '63 and '64 (Gordon), 640.1
Dexter Gordon: Swingin' Hard Bop (Gordon), 640.2
Doin' Allright (Gordon), 640.3
★*The Eminent J. J. Johnson, Vols. 1 and 2* (Johnson), 646.1
Four Tenors: John Coltrane, Charles Lloyd, Sonny Rollins and Ben Webster (collection), 627
Freddie Hubbard (Hubbard), 645.2
Free for All (Blakey), 630.2
★*Go!* (Gordon), 640.4
★*Guitar Forms* (Burrell), 633
Horace Silver (Silver), 659.3
Impressions: The Verve Jazz Sides (Montgomery), 651.1
★*The Incredible Jazz Guitar of Wes Montgomery* (Montgomery), 651.2
Inner Urge (Henderson), 643
Introducing Johnny Griffin (Griffin), 642
Jazz Style of Clifford Brown (Brown), 632.3
Jazz Style of Sonny Rollins (Rollins), 657.2
Jimmy Smith Live in '69 (Smith), 660.2
★*Ken Burns Jazz Collection: Art Blakey* (Blakey), 630.3
★*Ken Burns Jazz Collection: Sonny Rollins* (Rollins), 657.3
Leapin' and Lopin' (Clark), 635.2
Meet the Jazztet (Farmer), 639.2
Moody's Mood for Blues (Moody), 652
★*A Night at Birdland, Vols. 1 and 2* (Blakey), 630.4
★*A Night at the Village Vanguard* (Rollins), 657.4
A Night in Tunisia (Blakey), 630.5
Our Man in Paris (Gordon), 640.5
Phil Woods (Woods), 663
Quintet in Chicago (Adderley), 628.2
Saxophone Colossus [1956] (Rollins), 657.5
Saxophone Colossus [1998] (Rollins), 657.6
Sidewinder [1963] (Morgan), 653.2
Sidewinder [2003] (Morgan), 653.3
Sonny Rollins (Rollins), 657.7
Soul Station (Mobley), 650
Swinging Guitar of . . . (Farlow), 638
Them Dirty Blues (Adderley), 628.3
The Thing to Do (Mitchell), 649
13 Original Songs (Johnson), 646.2
Trio (Hope), 644
Trombone Master (Johnson), 646.3
True Blue (Brooks), 631
Walk on the Wild Side: Best of the Verve Years (Smith), 660.3

★*Way Out West* (Rollins), 657.8
Wayne Shorter: Jazz Classics (Shorter), 658
Wes Montgomery Live in '65 (Montgomery), 651.3
Whistle Stop (Dorham), 637
A World of Piano (Newborn), 655
hard rock. *See* heavy metal/hard rock
Hardee, John. *The Big Horn: The History of the Honkin' and Screamin' Saxophone* (collection), 2314
Hardesty, Herb. *The Big Horn: The History of the Honkin' and Screamin' Saxophone* (collection), 2314
Hardison, Bernard
  ★*Nashville Jumps: Blues and Rhythm on Nashville Independent Labels 1945–1955* (collection), 2376
  Night Train to Nashville: Music City Rhythm and Blues, 1945–1970, Vol. 2 (collection), 2378
Hardman, Gloria. *The New Bluebloods* (collection), 419
Hargrove, Roy
  Icons among Us (collection), 934
  Roy Hargrove Quintet with the Tenors of Our Time, 974
Harlem Hamfats. *Back to the Crossroads: The Roots of Robert Johnson* (collection), 212
Harlem Spiritual Ensemble. *Sisters of Freedom*, 38
Harmoneion Singers. *Angels' Visits and Other Vocal Gems of Victorian America* (collection), 93
Harmonic Sounds Band. *Eccentric Soul: The Prix Label* (collection), 2601
Harmonizers. *Happy in the Service of the Lord: Memphis Gospel Quartet Heritage, the 1980s, Vols. 1 and 2* (collection), 3007
The Harmonizing Four
  Good News: 22 Gospel Greats (collection), 3033
  The Harmonizing Four, 1943–1954, 3019.1
  When Day Is Done: Very Best of the Harmonizing Four, 3019.2
Harper, Ben. *Standing in the Shadows of Motown* (collection), 2445
Harper, Billy. *Black Saint*, 922
Harpo, Slim
  The Best of Excello Records (collection), 327
  The Best of Slim Harpo, 335
  Blues Masters, Vol. 6: Blues Originals (collection), 367
  Dark Clouds Rollin': Excello Swamp Blues Classics (collection), 328
  House Rockin' and Hip Shakin': The Best of Excello Blues (collection), 329

Harps of Melody. *Happy in the Service of the Lord: Memphis Gospel Quartet Heritage, the 1980s, Vols. 1 and 2* (collection), 3007

★Harp-Tones. *The Doo-Wop Box* (collection), 2322

The Harptones
 Old Town Doo-Wop, Vols. 1–3 (collection), 2324
 The Doo-Wop Box II (collection), 2323

★Harrell, Kelly. *Anthology of American Folk Music, Vols. 1–3* (collection), 1386

Harrell, Tom
 Sail Away, 975.1
 Tom Harrell, 975.2

Harris, Barbara. *Alan Jay Lerner* (songwriter collection), 1105.1

Harris, Barry. *Magnificent!*, 707

Harris, Betty
 Action Speaks Louder Than Words: The Best of SSS International (collection), 2588
 Birth of Soul, 4 Vols. (collection), 2434

Harris, Corey. *Greens from the Garden*, 438

Harris, Craig. *Black Bone*, 976

Harris, Eddie
 Soul to Soul (collection), 2444
 ★*The Vee-Jay Story: Celebrating 40 Years of Classic Hits* (collection), 2431
 ★*What It Is! Funky Soul and Rare Grooves* (collection), 2615

Harris, Emmylou
 ★*Anthology: The Warner/Reprise Years*, 1652.1
 At the Ryman, 1652.2
 Classic Country Music: A Smithsonian Collection (collection), 1382
 Light of the Stable: The Christmas Album, 3330
 Trio, 1673

Harris, Johnny. *The Best of T. K. Disco* (collection), 2656

Harris, Little Eva. *The Spring Story: Essential 70s Soul* (collection), 2608

Harris, Marion
 ★*American Popular Song: Six Decades of Songwriters and Singers* (collection), 1059
 Flappers, Vamps, and Sweet Young Things (collection), 1065

Harris, Phil
 Nipper's Greatest Hits: The 50's, Vol. 2 (collection), 1164
 Waller / Razaf (songwriter collection), 1113.2

Harris, R. H.
 Kings of the Gospel Highway: The Golden Age of Gospel Quartets (collection), 3009

★*Precious Lord: Recordings of the Great Gospel Songs of Thomas A. Dorsey* (collection), 2968

Sam Cooke's SAR Records Story (collection), 2606

Harris, Wynonie
 Bloodshot Eyes: The Best of Wynonie Harris, 2259.1
 ★*The Blues: A Smithsonian Collection of Classic Blues Singers* (collection), 145
 King R&B Box Set (collection), 2424
 ★*Nashville Jumps: Blues and Rhythm on Nashville Independent Labels 1945–1955* (collection), 2376
 Rock and Roll: The Early Days (collection), 1752
 The Roots of Rock 'n' Roll, 1946–1954 (collection), 1755
 ★*The Very Best of Wynonie Harris: Good Rockin' Tonight*, 2259.2

Harrison and the Majestic Kind. *Eccentric Soul: Twinight's Lunar Rotation* (collection), 2568

Harrison, Donald. *Icons among Us* (collection), 934

Harrison, George. *All Things Must Pass*, 1923

Harrison, Mark. *Blues Piano: The Complete Guide with CD* (collection), 253

Harrison, Wilbert
 The Fire / Fury Records Story (collection), 2422
 ★*The R&B Box* (collection), 2239

Harris, Marion. *The Phonographic Yearbook, 1922: An Angel's Voice I Hear* (collection), 1078

Harry Simeone Chorale. ★*Billboard Greatest Christmas Hits, 1955–1983* (collection), 3294

Hart, Billy. *Conjure: Music for the Texts of Ishmael Reed* (collection), 810

Hartford, John
 ★*Aereo-Plain*, 1587.1
 Me Oh My, How the Time Does Fly, 1587.2

Hartman, Dan. *Disco Box* (collection), 2644

Hartman, Johnny. ★*The Jazz Singers: A Smithsonian Collection of Jazz Vocals from 1919–1994* (collection), 766

Harvey and Phenomenals. *Boddie Recording Company Cleveland, Ohio* (collection), 2569, 2570

Harvey, P. J.
 Dry, 2137.1
 Rid of Me, 2137.2
 To Bring You My Love, 2137.3

Harvey, Roy. *Old-Time Mountain Guitar* (collection), 1391

Hassell, Jon. *Last Night the Moon Came Dropping Its Clothes in the Street*, 1326

Hathaway, Donny
 ★*Atlantic R&B, 1947–1974* (collection), 2418
 ★*Atlantic Soul, 1959–1975* (collection), 2589
 A Donny Hathaway Collection, 2478.1
 ★*Everything Is Everything*, 2478.2
 Extensions of a Man, 2478.3
 The Sweetest Feeling: A Van McCoy Songbook (collection), 2447
 These Songs for You, Live!, 2478.4

Hawes, Hampton. *The Trio, Vol. 1*, 613

Hawker, Ginny. *Angels Are Singing: A Women's Bluegrass Gospel Collection*, 1559

Hawkins, Buddy Boy. *The Blues of Texas, Arkansas, and Louisiana* (collection), 236

Hawkins, Coleman
 Body and Soul, 579.1
 Classic Tenors, 579.2
 ★*The Commodore Story* (collection), 561
 The High and Mighty Hawk, 725
 Jazz Masters: Vintage Collection, 1958–1961 (collection), 477
 ★*Ken Burns Jazz Collection: Coleman Hawkins*, 579.3
 ★*Ken Burns Jazz: The Story of America's Music* (collection), 478
 ★*The Smithsonian Collection of Classic Jazz* (collection), 486
 ★*Sound of Jazz* (collection), 487

Hawkins, Edwin
 ★*Jubilation! Great Gospel Performances, Vol. 1: Black Gospel* (collection), 2966
 Testify! The Gospel Box (collection), 2974

Hawkins, Erskine
 ★*Big Band Jazz: From the Beginnings to the Fifties* (collection), 529
 Blues Masters, Vol. 1: Urban Blues (collection), 338
 The Original Tuxedo Junction, 540

Hawkins, Ronnie. *The Best of Ronnie Hawkins and the Hawks*, 1764

Hawkins, Screamin' Jay
 Cow Fingers and Mosquito Pie, 2260
 ★*Halloween Hits* (collection), 3347
 ★*The Okeh Rhythm and Blues Story* (collection), 2425
 Stars of the Apollo (collection), 2240

Hawkins, Ted. *Blues Fest: Modern Blues of the '80s* (collection), 409

Hawkins, Tramaine. *Story of Gospel Music* (collection), 2973

Hawkins, Tremaine. *All My Best to You*, 3089

Hawkins, Walter
 Going Up Yonder: The Best of the Gospel Choirs (collection), 3051
 Gospel (collection), 2962

★*Love Alive,* 3090

Testify! The Gospel Box (collection), 2974

Haydn Quartet. *The Phonographic Yearbook, 1908: Take Me Out with the Crowd* (collection), 1076

Hayes, Edgar. *The Swing Time Records Story: R&B, Blues, and Gospel, 1946–1952* (collection), 2430

Hayes, Isaac
   Complete Introduction to Disco (collection), 1237
   The Complete Stax/Volt Soul Singles, Vol. 2: 1968–1971 (collection), 2595
   ★*Hot Buttered Soul,* 2479.1
   Isaac Hayes: Live at Montreux, 2005, 2479.2
   Shaft, 2479.3
   Top of the Stax, Vol. 1: Twenty Greatest Hits (collection), 2611
   The Ultimate Isaac Hayes: Can You Dig It?, 2479.4
   The Very Best of Isaac Hayes, 2479.5

Hayes, Roland. *A First-Time Buyer's Guide to American Negro Spirituals* (collection), 32

Haymes, Dick
   Alec Wilder (songwriter collection), 1117.1
   ★*American Popular Song: Six Decades of Songwriters and Singers* (collection), 1059
   Arthur Schwartz (songwriter collection), 1110.2
   ★*The Crooners* (collection), 1062
   Frank Loesser (songwriter collection), 1106.1
   Golden Years of Dick Haymes, 1199
   Harry Warren (songwriter collection), 1114
   Hit Parade, 1943 (collection), 1157
   Hoagy Carmichael (songwriter collection), 1097.2
   James Van Heusen (songwriter collection), 1112.1
   Jerome Kern (songwriter collection), 1104.1
   Oscar Hammerstein II (songwriter collection), 1102
   Rodgers / Hart (songwriter collection), 1109.1
   ★*Sentimental Journey: Pop Vocal Classics, Vol. 1* (collection), 1081
   ★*Sentimental Journey: Pop Vocal Classics, Vol. 2* (collection), 1168

Haymes, Joe. *Waller / Razaf* (songwriter collection), 1113.2

Haynes, Cornell Iral, Jr. *See* Nelly

Hayton, Lennie. *It's Easy to Remember* (Crosby), 1125.6

Haywood, Joe. *The Fire / Fury Records Story* (collection), 2422

Haywood, Leon. *Beg, Scream, and Shout! The Big Ol' Box of '60s Soul* (collection), 2433

Hazel, Eddie. ★*What It Is! Funky Soul and Rare Grooves* (collection), 2615

Hazlewood, Lee. *These Boots Are Made for Walkin':* The Complete MGM Recordings, 1497

Head, Murray. *Have a Nice Decade: The '70s Pop Culture Box* (collection), 1240

Head, Roy
   The Scepter Records Story (collection), 2426
   Texas Music, Vol. 3: Garage Bands and Psychedelia (collection), 1830

Headlines. *Boddie Recording Company Cleveland, Ohio* (collection), 2569, 2570

Heart
   Greatest Hits, 2049.1
   Greatest Hits, 1985–1995, 2049.2

Heartbeats
   ★*The Doo-Wop Box* (collection), 2322
   The Doo-Wop Box II (collection), 2323

The Heartbreakers
   D.I.Y. Blank Generation: The New York Scene (collection), 1978
   No Thanks! The '70s Punk Rebellion (collection), 2003

Hearts
   ★*The Doo-Wop Box* (collection), 2322
   The Doo-Wop Box II (collection), 2323

Heartsman, Johnny. *The Touch,* 439

Heat, Horton. *Halloween Hootenanny* (collection), 3348

Heath Brothers. *Jingle Bell Jazz* (collection), 3314

Heath, Jimmy. *You or Me,* 882

Heath, Ted. *Big Band Renaissance: The Evolution of the Jazz Orchestra* (collection), 739

Heatwave
   The Best of Heatwave: Always and Forever, 2647
   Disco Box (collection), 2644

Heavenly Gospel Singers
   ★*Good News: 100 Gospel Greats* (collection), 2961
   Gospel: Negro Spirituals / Gospel Songs, 1926–1942 (collection), 2963
   I Hear Music in the Air: A Treasury of Gospel Music (collection), 3008
   ★*A Warrior on the Battlefield: A Cappella Trail Blazers* (collection), 3011

Heavy D and the Boyz
   Big Tyme, 2814.1
   Heavy Hitz, 2814.2

heavy metal/hard rock, 1938–1951
   Boston, 1942
   Cheap Trick at Budokan, 1943
   Don't Fear the Reaper: Best of Blue Oyster Cult, 1941

Great Gonzos: The Best of Ted Nugent, 1950

Greatest Hits (Aerosmith), 1939.1

Greatest Hits (Grand Funk Railroad), 1946

Greatest Hits (ZZ Top), 1951

Heavy Metal: The First 20 Years (collection), 1938

Machine Head (Deep Purple), 1945

Mascara and Monsters: The Best of Alice Cooper, 1944

Metal Works (Judas Priest), 1947

Monsters of Rock, 1949

O, Yeah! Ultimate Aerosmith Hits (2002), 1939.2

O, Yeah! Ultimate Aerosmith Hits (2006), 1939.3

Paranoid (Black Sabbath), 1940

The Very Best of Kiss, 1948

Hebb, Bobby. *Night Train to Nashville: Music City Rhythm and Blues, 1945–1970, Vol. 1* (collection), 2377

Hedge, Christopher. *Andrew Jackson: The Atrocious Saint,* 52

Hedges, Michael
   ★*Aerial Boundaries,* 1348
   Solace: A Windham Hill Collection (collection), 1373
   Windham Hill: The First Ten Years (collection), 1377

Heidt, Horace. *The Great Depression: American Music in the '30s* (collection), 1066

Hell, Richard and the Voidoids
   Blank Generation, 1989
   No Thanks! The '70s Punk Rebellion (collection), 2003

★Helms, Bobby. *Billboard Greatest Christmas Hits, 1955–1983* (collection), 3294

Heltah Skeltah. *Nocturnal,* 2815

Hemingway, Gerry. *Devils Paradise,* 977

Hemphill, Julius
   Raw Materials and Residuals, 923.1
   Reflections ('Coon Bid'ness), 923.2

Henagar-Union Sacred Harp Convention. *I Belong to This Band: Eighty-Five Years of Sacred Harp Recordings* (collection), 3111

Henderson, Bill. *The Definitive Collection* (songwriter collection), 1101.1

Henderson, Fletcher
   An Anthology of Big Band Swing (collection), 528
   ★*Big Band Jazz: From the Beginnings to the Fifties* (collection), 529
   ★*Ken Burns Jazz Collection: Fletcher Henderson,* 541.1
   ★*Ken Burns Jazz: The Story of America's Music* (collection), 478
   Riverside History of Classic Jazz (collection), 499

Henderson, Fletcher (cont.)
    ★*The Smithsonian Collection of Classic
        Jazz* (collection), 486
    ★*A Study in Frustration,* 541.2
    ★*Swing Time! The Fabulous Big Band
        Era* (collection), 1089
Henderson, Joe
    Inner Urge, 643
    ★*Page One,* 685
Henderson, Willie. *The Story of
        Brunswick: The Classic Sound of
        Chicago Soul* (collection), 2610
Hendricks, Barbara
    Give Me Jesus: Spirituals, 39
    Songs: Foster, Griffes, Copland
        (collection), 101
Hendricks, Jon. *The Bebop Singers*
        (collection), 765
Hendrix, Jimi
    ★*Are You Experienced?,* 1866.2
    Axis: Bold As Love, 1866.1
    BBC Sessions, 1866.3
    ★*Electric Ladyland,* 1866.4
    *Experience Hendrix: The Best of Jimi
        Hendrix,* 1866.5
    *Legends of Guitar: Rock–The '60s,
        Vol. 1* (collection), 1860
    Live at Monterey, 1866.6
    *Voodoo Child: The Jimi Hendrix
        Collection,* 1866.7
Henley, Don
    Building the Perfect Beast, 2076.1
    The End of the Innocence, 2076.2
Henry, Clarence "Frogman." *Best of Chess
        R&B, Vols. 1 and 2* (collection), 2420
Henry, Edd. *Eccentric Soul: The Big Mack
        Label* (collection), 2598
Hensley, Walter. *Mountain Music
        Bluegrass Style* (collection), 1566
The Herbie Nichols Project. *Strange City,* 978
Herman, Woody
    An Anthology of Big Band Swing
        (collection), 528
    ★*Big Band Jazz: From the Beginnings to
        the Fifties* (collection), 529
    *Big Band Renaissance: The Evolution of
        the Jazz Orchestra* (collection), 739
    Bing Crosby and Some Jazz Friends
        (Crosby), 1125.2
    ★*Blowin' Up a Storm!,* 542.1
    Giant Steps, 755.1
    Johnny Mercer (songwriter collection),
        1107.1
    Keeper of the Flame, 542.2
    *Sentimental Journey: Pop Vocal
        Classics, Vol. 1* (collection), 1167
    ★*Sentimental Journey: Pop Vocal
        Classics, Vol. 1* (collection), 1081
    *Songs That Got Us through World War
        II, Vol. 2* (collection), 1086
    ★*Swing Time! The Fabulous Big Band
        Era* (collection), 1089
    Woody Herman Live in '64, 755.2

Hernandez, Patrick. *Disco Box* (collection),
        2644
Herring, Annie. *First Love: A Historic
        Gathering of Jesus Music Pioneers*
        (collection), 3137
Hersch, Fred
    *Let Yourself Go: The Lives of Jazz
        Pianist Fred Hersch,* 979.1
    Thelonious: Fred Hersch Plays Monk,
        979.2
Hersh, Kristin
    The Grotto, 2138.1
    Hips and Makers, 2138.2
Hesperus. *Colonial America,* 115
Heumann, Matthew. *The Early Minstrel
        Show* (collection), 96
Hiatt, John. *Bring the Family,* 2139
Hibbler, Al
    After the Lights Go Down Low, 1200
    ★*The Jazz Singers: A Smithsonian
        Collection of Jazz Vocals from
        1919–1994* (collection), 766
Hickman, Sarah. *Toddler,* 3187
Hickory Bottom Harmoneers. *Fire in My
        Bones: Raw, Rare and Otherworldy
        African-American Gospel*
        (collection), 2960
Hicks, Bobby. *The Bluegrass Album, Vol. 1*
        (collection), 1562
Hicks, Otis Verries. *See* Lightnin' Slim
Hieroglyphics
    Full Circle, 2816.1
    3rd Eye Vision, 2816.2
high-priority items
    African American gospel collections,
        1940s–1960s
        *All God's Sons and Daughters:
            Chicago's Gospel Legends*
            (collection), 3030
        *Working the Road: The Golden Age
            of Chicago Gospel* (collection),
            3039
    African American gospel groups
        *The Best of Rev. James Cleveland
            and the G.M.W.A.,* 3058.1
        The Best of the Caravans, 3041.1
        I Feel the Holy Spirit (Clara Ward
            Singers), 3042
        Oh Happy Day (Edwin Hawkins
            Singers), 3060.1
    African American gospel quartets
        *A Warrior on the Battlefield:
            A Cappella Trail Blazers*
            (collection), 3011
        The Best of the Dixie Hummingbirds,
            3014.1
        *Sam Cooke with the Soul Stirrers:
            The Complete Specialty Records
            Recordings,* 3025.1
    African American gospel solo
        personalities
        *Amazing Grace: The Complete
            Recordings* (Franklin), 2997.1

        First Lady of Gospel (Caesar),
            2994.1
        *Gospels, Spirituals and Hymns;
            Vols. 1 and 2* (Jackson), 2999.2
        *How I Got Over: The Apollo Records
            Sessions* (Jackson), 2999.3
        *My Soul Looks Back: The Genius of
            Marion Williams,* 3005
        Original Soul Sister (Tharpe), 3003
        Peace Be Still (Cleveland), 2996.2
        The Great Gospel Women
            (collection), 2989
alt-country/Americana. *Guitar Town*
        (Earle), 1701.2
alternative rock
    Best, Vol. 1 (Smiths), 2189
    Eponymous (R.E.M.), 2175.3
    How Will the Wolf Survive? (Los
        Lobos), 2146
    Nevermind (Nirvana), 2161.3
    Odelay (Beck), 2099
    OK Computer (Radiohead), 2176.4
    Post (Björk), 2103.2
    The Singles (Pretenders), 2170
    Vivid (Living Colour), 2145
art rock and rock theater. *The Rise
        and Fall of Ziggy Stardust* (Bowie),
        1952.3
bebop
    The Amazing Bud Powell, Vol. 1,
        600.1
    The Amazing Bud Powell, Vol. 2,
        600.2
    The Complete RCA Victor Recordings
        (Gillespie), 594.1
    *Ken Burns Jazz Collection: Dizzy
        Gillespie,* 594.3
    *The Original Mambo Kings: An Afro-
        Cubop Anthology* (collection),
        592
big bands and the swing era
    *Benny Goodman at Carnegie Hall:
        Complete,* 537.2
    Best of the Big Bands (Calloway),
        531
    *Big Band Jazz: From the Beginnings
        to the Fifties* (collection), 529
    Blowin' Up a Storm! (Herman),
        542.1
    The Essential Artie Shaw, 548
    The Essential Benny Goodman,
        537.3
    *Ken Burns Jazz Collection: Fletcher
        Henderson,* 541.1
    Spinnin' the Webb, 550
    A Study in Frustration (Henderson),
        541.2
big bands since the 1950s
    Ellington at Newport, 748.2
    The Far East Suite (Ellington),
        748.3
    New Concepts of Artistry in Rhythm
        (Kenton), 758.2

bluegrass
Aereo-Plain (Hartford), 1587.1
Blue Grass, 1950–1958 (Monroe), 1596.1
Blue Moon of Kentucky, 1936–1949 (Monroe), 1596.4
The Complete Columbia Stanley Brothers, 1609.1
The Complete Mercury Recordings (Stanley Brothers), 1609.2
The Complete Mercury Sessions (Flatt and Scruggs), 1583.2
The Essential Flatt and Scruggs: 'Tis Sweet to Be Remembered, 1583.3
J. D. Crowe and the New South, 1580
Now That I've Found You: A Collection (Krauss), 1591.2
16 Gems (Monroe), 1596.7
blues
Blues Classics (collection), 146
The Blues: A Smithsonian Collection of Classic Blues Singers (collection), 145
His Tangerine and Atlantic Sides (Mayfield), 2308.1
I Can't Be Satisfied: Early American Women Blues Singers, Vol. 1: Country (collection), 149
Legends of the Blues, Vol. 1 (collection), 150
Legends of the Blues, Vol. 2 (collection), 151
Let's Get Loose: Folk and Popular Blues Styles from the Beginning to the Early 1940s (collection), 152
Mean Old World: The Blues from 1940–1994 (collection), 154
The Story of the Blues (collection), 158
blues and rock
Blues Breakers [1965] (Mayall), 375.1
Giant Step / Ole Folks at Home (Mahal), 374
blues revival and folk blues
Brownie McGhee and Sonny Terry Sing, 404
Skip James Today, 399
Texas Songster (Lipscomb), 400
You Gotta Move (McDowell), 402
blues vocal groups. Atlantic Vocal Groups, 1951–1963 (collection), 2320
British folk-rock. Unhalfbricking (Fairport Convention), 1853.2
British invasion
Abbey Road (Beatles), 1794.1
Beggars Banquet (Rolling Stones), 1802.2
Hot Rocks (Rolling Stones), 1802.3

Mr. Fantasy (Traffic), 1804.1
Nuggets II: Original Artifacts from the British Empire and Beyond (collection), 1791
Odyssey and Oracle (Zombies), 1807
Please Please Me (Beatles), 1794.8
Revolver (Beatles), 1794.9
Rubber Soul (Beatles), 1794.10
Sgt. Pepper's Lonely Hearts Club Band (Beatles), 1794.11
The Ultimate Collection (Kinks), 1798.2
Ultimate! (Yardbirds), 1806
Who's Next (The Who), 1805.7
With the Beatles, 1794.12
British superstars
Dark Side of the Moon (Pink Floyd), 1929.1
Exile on Main St. (Rolling Stones), 1931.1
Greatest Hits, Vol. 1 (John), 1925.1
Lennon Legend, 1926.2
Charles Mingus
Ken Burns Jazz Collection: Charles Mingus, 675.7
Mingus Ah Um, 675.9
Pithecanthropus Erectus, 675.11
Charlie Parker
Best of the Complete Savoy and Dial Studio Recordings, 603.2
Confirmation: Best of the Verve Years, 603.6
Jazz at Massey Hall, 603.8
contemporary African American gospel
15 Songs That Redefined Gospel Music in the 1970s (Crouch), 3083.1
Love Alive (Hawkins), 3090
Nu Nation Project (Franklin), 3085.2
contemporary artists: 1970s through the 2000s
Album Album (DeJohnette), 962.1
Conference of the Birds (Holland), 980.1
Lookout for Hope (Frisell), 969.2
Masada: Live at Tonic (Zorn), 1029.1
Michael Brecker (Brecker), 947
contemporary blues and soul
Greatest Hits (Hill), 440
I Got What It Takes (Taylor), 463
Ice Pickin' (Collins), 431.1
Midnight Son (Seals), 460
Strong Persuader (Cray), 434.2
Texas Twister (Copeland), 432
contemporary country and western: 1980s–present
Anthology: The Warner/Reprise Years (Harris), 1652.1
The Best of Vince Gill, 1647.1

Essential Dolly Parton, 1672.1
Greatest Hits (Black), 1625.1
Greatest Hits Collection (Brooks and Dunn), 1628
Greatest Hits (McEntire), 1666.1
Greatest Hits (Strait), 1678
Hank Williams Jr.'s Greatest Hits, 1690.1
Seven Year Ache (Cash), 1632.1
Storms of Life (Travis), 1681.2
Ultimate Hits (Brooks), 1627.4
contemporary rhythm and blues
The Breakthrough (Blige), 2397.1
The Essential Luther Vandross, 2416.2
The R in R&B Collection, Vol. 1 (Kelly), 2408.2
country and western
American Roots Music (collection), 1379
Anthology of American Folk Music, Vol. 4 (collection), 1387
Anthology of American Folk Music, Vols. 1–3 (collection), 1386
crossover jazz: 1970s–1990s. George Benson Anthology, 901
disco soundtrack. Saturday Night Fever, 2658
Duke Ellington
The Duke, 558.3
The Essential Duke Ellington, 558.6
Ken Burns Jazz Collection: Duke Ellington, 558.7
early jazz
Jelly Roll Morton, 501.3
Off the Record: The Complete 1923 Jazz Band Recordings (collection), 498
early jazz piano styles
Complete Victor Piano Solos (Waller), 526
Harlem Stride Piano (Johnson), 523
early jazz soloists
Bix Beiderbecke, Vol. 1: Singin' the Blues, 513.3
Ken Burns Jazz Collection: Sidney Bechet, 512.2
early rock 'n' roll
Cadence Classics: Their 20 Greatest Hits (Everly Brothers), 1762.1
The Chess Box (Diddley), 1761
The Definitive Collection (Berry), 1759.3
The Doo Wop Box: 101 Vocal Group Gems from the Golden Age of Rock 'n' Roll (collection), 1745
The Georgia Peach (Little Richard), 1766.2
Legends of Guitar: Rock The '50s, Vol. 1 (collection), 1749
Legends of Guitar: Rock The '50s, Vol. 2 (collection), 1750

high-priority items (cont.)
    early rock 'n' roll (cont.)
        Somethin' Else: The Fine Lookin' Hits of Eddie Cochran, 1760
    electronic/computer new age. *China* (Vangelis), 1319.2
    Elvis Presley and rockabilly
        18 Original Greatest Hits (Lewis), 1735.2
        Elvis: 30 #1 Hits (Presley), 1737.1
        Original Sun Greatest Hits (Perkins), 1736
        Sun Records' Greatest Hits (collection), 1741
    evangelists and other traditional performers. *Sacred Steel: The Steel Guitar Tradition of the House of God Churches* (collection), 2980
    folk-rock
        Blonde on Blonde (Dylan), 1823.1
        Bringing It All Back Home (Dylan), 1823.4
        Greatest Hits (Simon and Garfunkel), 1826.2
        Highway 61 Revisited (Dylan), 1823.6
        The Band, 1821.1
        20 Essential Tracks from the Boxed Set (Byrds), 1822.2
    free jazz and related styles of the 1960s
        Free Jazz (Coleman), 681.2
        Heliocentric Worlds (Ra), 695.2
        Ken Burns Jazz Collection: Ornette Coleman, 681.3
        Page One (Henderson), 685
        Percussion Bitter Suite (Roach), 696.1
        Rip, Rig, and Panic / Now Please Don't You Cry, Beautiful Edith (Kirk), 688.3
        The Shape of Jazz to Come (Coleman), 681.4
    funk
        1999 (Prince), 2639.1
        Mothership Connection (Parliament), 2638.5
        Purple Rain: Music from the Motion Picture (Prince), 2639.5
        Stand! (Sly and the Family Stone), 2640.3
        What It Is! Funky Soul and Rare Grooves (collection), 2615
    fusion
        Bitches Brew (Davis), 822.1
        The Essential John McLaughlin, 827
        Head Hunters (Hancock), 824.2
        I Sing the Body Electric (Weather Report), 832.1
        Return to Forever (Corea), 820.2
    Georgia, Alabama, and the East Coast blues
        Best of Blind Blake, 246.2

Guitar Wizards (collection), 243
gospel music and other popular Christian music
    The Gospel Sound (collection), 2964
    The Gospel Sound of Spirit Feel (collection), 2965
    Jubilation! Great Gospel Performances, Vol. 1: Black Gospel (collection), 2966
    Jubilation! Great Gospel Performances, Vol. 2: More Black Gospel (collection), 2967
    Precious Lord: Recordings of the Great Gospel Songs of Thomas A. Dorsey (collection), 2968
    Say Amen, Somebody (collection), 2971
    Wade in the Water: African American Sacred Music Traditions, Vols. 1–4 (collection), 2975
guitar heroes
    Are You Experienced? (Hendrix), 1866.2
    Electric Ladyland (Hendrix), 1866.4
    Led Zeppelin II, 1867.2
    Led Zeppelin IV [Zo-So], 1867.3
    The Very Best of Cream, 1864.3
Halloween music. *Halloween Hits* (collection), 3347
hard bop and related extensions of bebop
    Best of Lee Morgan, 653.1
    The Best of Horace Silver, Vol. 1, 659.1
    The Best of Horace Silver, Vol. 2, 659.2
    The Eminent J. J. Johnson, Vols. 1 and 2, 646.1
    Go! (Gordon), 640.4
    Guitar Forms (Burrell), 633
    The Incredible Jazz Guitar of Wes Montgomery, 651.2
    Ken Burns Jazz Collection: Art Blakey, 630.3
    Ken Burns Jazz Collection: Sonny Rollins, 657.3
    A Night at Birdland, Vols. 1 and 2 (Blakey), 630.4
    A Night at the Village Vanguard (Rollins), 657.4
    Way Out West (Rollins), 657.8
influences on the 1980s: 1960s and 1970s bands
    Raw Power (Pop), 1881
    The Velvet Underground and Nico, 1889.4
inspirational, contemporary Christian, and Christian Rock. *The Collection* (Grant), 3148.1

jazz
    At the Jazz Band Ball: Early Hot Jazz, Song, and Dance (collection), 470
    Central Avenue Sounds: Jazz in Los Angeles (collection), 471
    The Fabulous Miss D! The Keynote, Decca, and Mercury Singles 1943–1953, 2313.7
    Greatest Jazz Films Ever (collection), 472
    Real Jazz Classics Fake Book (collection), 484
    Real Vocal Book (collection), 485
    The Smithsonian Collection of Classic Jazz (collection), 486
    Sound of Jazz (collection), 487
jazz and film
    Round Midnight [2001] (Gordon, Hancock, and others), 1056.2
    Round Midnight [2002] (Gordon, Hancock, and others), 1056.1
jazz and the classics: third stream. *The Jimmy Giuffre 3 / Trav'lin' Light* (Giuffre), 1038
jazz outside the mainstream: the AACM, BAG, and the lofts
    Steppin' with the World Saxophone Quartet (World Saxophone Quartet), 933.2
    Urban Bushmen (Art Ensemble of Chicago), 915.3
jazz singers
    Blue Light 'til Dawn (Wilson), 807
    The Commodore Master Takes (Holiday), 781.3
    Ella Fitzgerald and Louis Armstrong (Armstrong), 771.2
    George and Ira Gershwin Songbook (Fitzgerald), 779.4
    The Jazz Singers: A Smithsonian Collection of Jazz Vocals from 1919–1994 (collection), 766
    Ken Burns Jazz Collection: Billie Holiday, 781.5
    Ken Burns Jazz Collection: Sarah Vaughan, 804.2
    Lady Day: The Best of Billie Holiday, 781.6
John Coltrane
    Blue Train, 677.2
    Giant Steps, 677.6
    John Coltrane and Johnny Hartman, 677.9
    Ken Burns Jazz Collection: John Coltrane, 677.11
    A Love Supreme, 677.14
jump blues. *Let the Good Times Roll: The Complete Decca Recordings 1938–1954* (Jordan), 2318.3
Kansas City and other territory bands
    The Complete Decca Recordings (Basie), 553.2

Ken Burns Jazz Collection: Count Basie, 553.5
Mary's Idea (Kirk), 554
Los Angeles rock
  Decade (Young), 1911.1
  Greatest Hits, 1971–1975 (Eagles), 1905.1
  Rumours (Fleetwood Mac), 1906.2
Louis Armstrong. *Ken Burns Jazz Collection: Louis Armstrong,* 510.3
mainstream country music: 1940s–1970s
  All Time Greatest Hits (Miller), 1516.1
  The Buck Owens Collection, 1959–1990, 1521.1
  Complete Hank Williams, 1556.1
  Definitive Collection (Lynn), 1511.2
  Essential Charley Pride, 1528.2
  Essential Waylon Jennings, 1503.2
  The Essential George Jones: The Spirit of Country, 1505.3
  Hag: The Best of Merle Haggard, 1495.2
  The Patsy Cline Collection, 1467.3
  Red Foley: Country Music Hall of Fame, 1487
  Red Headed Stranger (Nelson), 1518.3
  Sun Years (Cash), 1464.7
  The Texas Troubadour (Tubb), 1546.2
  That's the Way Life Goes: The Hit Songs, 1950–1975 (Frizzell), 1489.3
  Ultimate Eddy Arnold, 1456.2
  When I Stop Dreaming: The Best of the Louvin Brothers, 1510.3
  Will the Circle Be Unbroken? (collection), 1452
mainstream rock
  Born in the USA (Springsteen), 2085.1
  The Joshua Tree (U2), 2087.3
  Van Halen, 2088.3
meditation music (new age)
  Inside the Taj Mahal, I and II (Horn), 1331
  Music for Zen Meditation (Scott), 1332
Memphis and St. Louis blues. *Memphis Masters: Early American Blues Classics* (collection), 231
Miles Davis
  Ken Burns Jazz Collection, 676.5
  Kind of Blue, 676.6
  Miles Ahead, 676.9
  Porgy and Bess, 676.14
  Round about Midnight, 676.16
  Sketches of Spain, 676.17
Mississippi Delta blues
  The Centennial Collection (Johnson), 225.1

Masters of the Delta Blues: The Friends of Charlie Patton (collection), 220
modern blues
  The Best of Duke-Peacock Blues (collection), 336
  Bobby "Blue" Bland: The Anthology, 349.1
  The Essential Otis Rush: Classic Cobra Recordings, 361
  King of the Blues Guitar (King), 353.3
  Live at the Regal (King), 354.6
  The Very Best of Buddy Guy, 351
  West Side Soul (Magic Sam), 357.1
modern mainstream: 1970s. *Three for All* (Woods), 900.2
national anthems and patriotic music
  Collections of National Anthems, Vol. 1 (Regimental Band of the Coldstream Guards), 3379.1
  Collections of National Anthems, Vol. 2 (Regimental Band of the Coldstream Guards), 3379.2
neo-soul. *The Miseducation of Lauryn Hill,* 2382
new acoustic (new age). *A Shout toward Noon* (Kottke), 1325.2
New Orleans revival and traditional styles. *Kid Ory's Creole Jazz Band 1944–45* (Ory), 509
New Orleans rhythm and blues
  Crawfish Fiesta (Professor Longhair), 2370.1
  Dr. John's Gumbo, 2364.1
  Out of New Orleans (Domino), 2362.1
The 1950s and 1960s: cool jazz and the West Coast
  Art Pepper Meets the Rhythm Section (Pepper), 621.1
  The Best of the Gerry Mulligan Quartet with Chet Baker (Mulligan), 619.1
  Complete Birth of the Cool (Davis), 610
  Django (Modern Jazz Quartet), 618.3
  Intuition (Tristano), 625.1
  Konitz Meets Mulligan (Konitz), 615.1
piano blues
  Cuttin' the Boogie: Piano Blues and Boogie Woogie (collection), 251
  Juke Joint Saturday Night: Piano Blues, Rags and Stomps; Classic Recordings from the 1920s and '30s (collection), 255
piano in the 1960s
  Ken Burns Jazz Collection: Herbie Hancock, 706.2
  Sunday at the Village Vanguard (Evans), 704.7

Unit Structures (Taylor), 709.5
Waltz for Debby (Evans), 704.8
political music—Civil War period. *Songs of the Civil War: First Recordings from Original Editions* (collection), 63
popular Christmas music. *Silent Night* (Jackson), 3333
popular jazz of the 1950s and 1960s
  But Not for Me: Live at the Pershing (Jamal), 669
  Jazz on a Summer's Day (collection), 664
  Time Out (Brubeck), 665.2
popular vocal and instrumental music. *Dream Faces* (Gale), 113
post-1967 mainstream popular
  Greatest Hits (Streisand), 1307.2
  Greatest Hits, Vol. 2 (Streisand), 1307.3
  Greatest Hits, Vols. 1 and 2 (Joel), 1277.2
  The Singles (Carpenters), 1257
post-punk rock. *Unknown Pleasures* (Joy Division), 2035.2
postwar midwestern blues
  The Anthology (Waters), 308.1
  Chess Blues (collection), 287
  Chicago: The Blues Today! (collection), 290
  His Best (Howlin' Wolf), 297.2
  His Best (Little Walter), 300.3
  His Best (Williamson), 310.2
  King Biscuit Time (Williamson), 310.3
  The Ultimate Collection (Hooker), 296.5
post-World War II through 1967 mainstream popular
  Best of Lena Horne, 1201
  Best of the Capitol Years (Sinatra), 1224.1
  Dionne Warwick Collection (Warwick), 1229.1
  The Four Freshmen, 1195
  Greatest Hits (Como), 1185
  Jo Stafford (Stafford), 1225
  Jumpin' at Capitol (Cole), 1184.2
  Nipper's Greatest Hits: The 50's, Vol. 1 (collection), 1163
  Sentimental Journey: Pop Vocal Classics, Vol. 2 (collection), 1168
  Sentimental Journey: Pop Vocal Classics, Vol. 3 (collection), 1169
  Songs for Swingin' Lovers (Sinatra), 1224.8
  That's Amore (Martin), 1211.2
  The Very Best of Dinah Washington, 1230
  The Very Good Years (Sinatra), 1224.10

high-priority items (cont.)
  preschool children's music
    Animal Crackers (Wee Hairy
      Beasties), 3207
    Bob's Favorite Street Songs
      (McGrath), 3202.1
    Miss Ella's Playhouse (Fitzgerald),
      3198
    No! (They Might Be Giants), 3206
    Snack Time! (Barenaked Ladies),
      3196
    Walter the Waltzing Worm
      (Palmer), 3203.2
  pre–World War II country and
    western
    Best of Patsy Montana, 1417
    *The Carter Family: Country Music
      Hall of Fame,* 1403.1
    *Complete Recorded Works, 1926–
      1934, in Chronological Order,*
      1415
    The Essential Gene Autry, 1396.1
    The Essential Jimmie Rodgers,
      1421.1
    The Essential Roy Acuff, 1392.1
    Go Long Mule (Macon), 1413.2
    Old-Time Songs (Poole), 1418
  pre-World War II mainstream popular
    *American Popular Song: Six Decades
      of Songwriters and Singers*
      (collection), 1059
    An Earful of Music (Merman),
      1142.2
    Best of the Big Bands (James),
      1136.1
    The Best of Al Jolson, 1137.1
    *Brother, Can You Spare a Dime?
      American Song during the Great
      Depression* (collection), 1061
    *A Centennial Anthology of His Decca
      Recordings* (Crosby), 1125.5
    *Classic Judy Garland: The Capitol
      Years, 1955–1965* (Garland),
      1134.1
    The Crooners (collection), 1062
    Essential Glenn Miller, 1144
    Favourite Songs of Ethel Waters,
      1151.1
    50th Anniversary Collection, Vol. 1
      (Andrews Sisters), 1119
    Instant Classics (Ink Spots), 1135
    *It Had to Be You: Popular
      Keyboard from the Days of the
      Speakeasy to the Television Era*
      (collection), 1068
    *The Music Goes Round and Around:
      The Golden Years of Tin Pan
      Alley, 1930–1939* (collection),
      1070
    Nipper's Greatest Hits: The 20's
      (collection), 1071
    *Nipper's Greatest Hits: The 30's,
      Vol. 1* (collection), 1072

    *Nipper's Greatest Hits: The 40's,
      Vol. 1* (collection), 1073
    On Stage and Screen (Waters),
      1151.4
    *Praise the Lord and Pass the
      Ammunition: Songs of World
      Wars I and II* (collection), 1079
    *Sentimental Journey: Pop Vocal
      Classics, Vol. 1* (collection),
      1081
    Sophisticated Ladies (collection),
      1087
    Sweetest Music This Side of Heaven
      (Lombardo), 1140
    *Swing Time! The Fabulous Big Band
      Era* (collection), 1089
    That's How Rhythm Was Born
      (Boswell Sisters), 1121
    *Yes, Sir, That's My Baby: The
      Golden Years of Tin Pan Alley*
      (collection), 1094
  progressive new age
    Fresh Aire (Mannheim
      Steamroller), 1339
    Tubular Bells (Oldfield), 1340
  punk and new wave: U.K.
    The Clash, 2009.1
    Every Breath You Take: The Classics
      (Police), 2020
    Horses (Smith), 1997
    My Aim Is True (Costello), 2010.2
    *Never Mind the Bollocks Here's the
      Sex Pistols,* 2023.2
    Ramones, 1995.1
  ragtime. *Classic Piano Rags: Complete
    Original Music for 81 Rags* (Blesh),
    130
  rap and hip-hop
    All Eyez on Me (2Pac), 2935.1
    Amerikkka's Most Wanted (Ice
      Cube), 2819.1
    The Best of Grandmaster Flash,
      Melle Mel, and the Furious Five:
      Message from Beat Street,
      2809
    The Blueprint (Jay Z), 2823.2
    The Chronic (Dr. Dre), 2773.2
    Criminal Minded (Boogie Down
      Productions), 2724.2
    *Def Jam Music Group, Inc.: 10th
      Year Anniversary* (collection),
      2666
    Doggystyle (Snoop Dogg), 2922.2
    Enter the Wu-Tang: 36 Chambers,
      2946.1
    Fear of a Black Planet (Public
      Enemy), 2898.2
    Hip Hop Greats [Classic Raps]
      (collection), 2676
    *The Iceberg: Freedom of Speech . . .
      Just Watch What You Say*
      (Ice-T), 2820.1
    Illmatic (Nas), 2878.2

    *It Takes a Nation of Millions to
      Hold Us Back* (Public Enemy),
      2898.3
    *Looking for the Perfect Beat,
      1980–1985* (Afrika
      Bambaataa), 2705
    The Low End Theory (A Tribe
      Called Quest), 2933.1
    Mecca and the Soul Brother (Rock
      and Smooth), 2910.2
    The Miseducation of Lauryn Hill,
      2817
    *Mos Def and Talib Kweli Are Black
      Star,* 2872
    Paid in Full (Eric B. and Rakim),
      2785.2
    Paul's Boutique (Beastie Boys),
      2709.5
    Raising Hell (Run-D.M.C.), 2913.2
    Ready to Die: The Remaster
      (Notorious B.I.G.), 2881.2
    The Score (Fugees), 2798
    Step in the Arena (Gang Starr),
      2800.2
    Straight out the Jungle (Jungle
      Brothers), 2826.2
    Straight Outta Compton (N.W.A.),
      2877.2
    Strictly Business (EPMD), 2784.3
    The Sugar Hill Records Story
      (collection), 2695
    Things Fall Apart (Roots), 2911.4
    3 Feet High and Rising (De La Soul),
      2754.4
    *Tommy Boy Greatest Beats: The
      First Fifteen Years, 1981–1996*
      (collection), 2696
    Wild Style (collection), 2697
  religious music
    *I Am the Rose of Sharon: Early
      American Vocal Music* (Western
      Wind), 28
    *Music in America: An Anthology
      from the Landing of the Pilgrims
      to the Close of the Civil War,
      1620–1865* (Marrocco and
      Gleason), 16
    The Social Harp (McCurry), 17
    The Southern Harmony (Walker),
      26.1
    *Ten Sacred Songs for Soprano,
      Strings, and Organ: Music of the
      Moravians in America from the
      Archives of the Moravian Church
      at Bethlehem, Pennsylvania,* 5
  rhythm and blues
    The Chess Box (James), 2266.2
    *The Complete Aladdin Recordings of
      Charles Brown,* 2248
    Fever: The Best of Little Willie John,
      2269.1
    The R&B Box (collection), 2239
    Thriller (Jackson), 2264.5

The Very Best of Wynonie Harris: Good Rockin' Tonight, 2259.2

rhythm and blues label overview

Atlantic R&B, 1947–1974 (collection), 2418

The Okeh Rhythm and Blues Story (collection), 2425

The Specialty Story (collection), 2428

Stompin' at the Savoy: The Original Indie Label, 1944–1961 (collection), 2429

The Vee-Jay Story: Celebrating 40 Years of Classic Hits (collection), 2431

rhythm and blues vocal groups

All Time Greatest Hits and More (Drifters), 2335.1

Monkey Hips and Rice: The "5" Royales Anthology, 2338.2

There's a Riot Goin' On: The Coasters on ATCO, 2329

roots

Avalon Blues (Hurt), 196

The Library of Congress Recordings, Vols. 1–3 (Leadbelly), 197.4

Negro Blues and Hollers (collection), 178

The Roots of the Blues (Lomax), 177

Texas Worried Blues: Complete Recorded Works (Thomas), 201

school age or all ages children's music

The Tragic Treasury: Songs from a Series of Unfortunate Events (Gothic Archies), 3218

You'll Sing a Song and I'll Sing a Song (Jenkins), 3219

singer-songwriters

Astral Weeks (Morrison), 1894.1

Court and Spark (Mitchell), 1893.2

Sweet Baby James (Taylor), 1900.2

Tapestry (King), 1892

solo instrumental new age

Aerial Boundaries (Hedges), 1348

Autumn: 20th Anniversary Edition (Winston), 1353.1

soul

The Anthology (Mayfield), 2497.1

The Atlantic Recordings (Sledge), 2516.1

Complete Mythology (Johnson), 2488.1

The Definitive Soul Collection (Sam and Dave), 2514.1

Everything Is Everything (Hathaway), 2478.2

Funky Midnight Mover: The Atlantic Studio Recordings (Pickett), 2503.1

Home in Your Heart: The Best of Solomon Burke, 2459.3

Hot Buttered Soul (Hayes), 2479.1

I Never Loved a Man the Way I Loved You (Franklin), 2473.3

The Immortal Soul of Al Green, 2477.4

Innervisions (Wonder), 2534.3

Just for You (White), 2529.2

Lady Soul (Franklin), 2473.4

Live at the Apollo (Brown), 2457.1

The Man Who Invented Soul (Cooke), 2468.1

The Master, 1961–1984 (Gaye), 2476.5

Mr. Excitement! (Wilson), 2531.1

Otis! The Definitive Otis Redding, 2506.6

Pure Genius: The Complete Atlantic Recordings, 1952–1959 (Charles), 2463.6

Roots of a Revolution (Brown), 2457.4

Songs in the Key of Life (Wonder), 2534.5

What's Going On (Gaye), 2476.6

soul label overview. *Atlantic Soul, 1959–1975* (collection), 2589

soul vocal groups

Anthology (Temptations), 2551.1

Gold (Ross), 2547.1

It's Your Thing: The Story of the Isley Brothers, 2542.3

50th Anniversary: The Singles Collection, 1961–1971 (Four Tops), 2539

The Ultimate Collection (Smokey Robinson and the Miracles), 2545.3

Southern rock. *Live at Fillmore East* (Allman Brothers), 1935.2

southern white religious styles. *The Blackwoods,* 3118

space music new age. *Stratosfear* (Tangerine Dream), 1358

surf, bubblegum, garage bands, and pop

Nuggets: Artifacts of the First Psychedelic Era (collection), 1808

Pet Sounds (Beach Boys), 1812.1

The Sounds of Summer: The Very Best of the Beach Boys, 1812.2

Surfin' Hits (collection), 1810

swing mainstream since 1950

At the Stratford Shakespeare Festival (Peterson), 730.1

Soulville (Webster), 736.1

Swingin' with Pee Wee (Russell), 732.2

swing soloists and combos

After You've Gone (Eldridge), 573

The Best of Django Reinhardt (Reinhardt), 582.1

The Best of the Complete Pablo Solo Masterpieces (Tatum), 587.1

Classic Early Solos (Tatum), 587.2

The Commodore Story (collection), 561

From Spirituals to Swing: The Legendary 1938 and 1939 Carnegie Hall Concerts Produced by John Hammond (collection), 564

The Genius of the Electric Guitar (Christian), 569.1

Handful of Keys (Waller), 588.2

Ken Burns Jazz Collection: Coleman Hawkins, 579.3

Ken Burns Jazz Collection: Lester Young, 591.3

Texas and West coast blues

Gold Star Sessions, Vols. 1 and 2 (Hopkins), 321.3

Texas Music, Vol. 1: Postwar Blues Combos (collection), 316

Very Best of T-Bone Walker, 325.6

Thelonious Monk

Ken Burns Jazz Collection: Thelonious Monk, 674.5

Thelonious Monk Orchestra at Town Hall, 674.10

Thelonious Monk Quartet with John Coltrane at Carnegie Hall, 674.11

traditional Christmas music. *Sing We Noel: Christmas Music from England and Early America* (Boston Camerata), 3275.2

U.S. hitmakers. *Born to Run* (Springsteen), 1919

vaudeville or classic blues. *The Essential Bessie Smith,* 210.5

West coast and Texas rock

Chronicle (Creedence Clearwater Revival), 1834

Greatest Hits (Sly and the Family Stone), 1846.2

Live Dead (Grateful Dead), 1837.3

Retrospective: The Best of Buffalo Springfield, 1832.2

Santana, 1845.2

Surrealistic Pillow (Jefferson Airplane), 1838.2

We're Only in It for the Money (Zappa), 1850.5

western swing

Complete Recordings of the Father of Western Swing, 1932–1937 (Brown), 1436.1

The Essential Bob Wills, 1448.2

Hank Thompson, 1446

San Antonio Rose (Wills), 1448.3

women in rock since in the 1970s. *The Immaculate Collection* (Madonna), 2053

world music new age. *Watermark* (Enya), 1361

Highway Q. C.'s
  Good News: 22 Gospel Greats
    (collection), 3033
  Testify! The Gospel Box (collection),
    2974
  Very Best of the Highway Q. C.'S:
    Nearer My God, 3020
Highwaymen. *The Highwaymen,* 1653
Hill, Andrew. *Point of Departure,* 686
Hill, Bertha "Chippie"
  ★*Blues Classics* (collection), 146
  ★*I Can't Be Satisfied: Early American*
    Women Blues Singers, Vol. 2: Town
    (collection), 204
Hill Billies. *Vintage Children's Favorites*
    (collection), 3211
Hill, Cameron. *Legends of Western Swing*
    Guitar (collection), 1430
Hill, Faith. *Breathe,* 1654
Hill, Jessie
  Crescent City Soul: The Sound of New
    Orleans, 1947–1974 (collection),
    2564
  Finger Poppin' and Stompin' Feet: 20
    Classic Allen Toussaint Productions
    for Minit Records, 1960–1962
    (collection), 2359
Hill, King Solomon. *The Blues of*
    Texas, Arkansas, and Louisiana
    (collection), 236
Hill, Lauryn
  ★*The Miseducation of Lauryn Hill,*
    2382, 2817
  90's Pop Hits (collection), 1242
Hill, Z. Z.
  The Blues Is Alright, Vol. 1 (collection),
    411
  The Down Home Soul of Z. Z. Hill,
    2480
  ★*Greatest Hits,* 440
  Soul Shots, Vol. 4: Urban Blues
    (collection), 343
  Superblues: All-Time Classic Blues Hits,
    Vol. 1 (collection), 347
The Hi-Los
  Alan Jay Lerner (songwriter
    collection), 1105.1
  Harry Warren (songwriter collection),
    1114
  James Van Heusen (songwriter
    collection), 1112.1
Hines, Earl
  An Anthology of Big Band Swing
    (collection), 528
  ★*Big Band Jazz: From the Beginnings to*
    the Fifties (collection), 529
  Earl Hines Collection: Piano Solos,
    522.1
  Earl Hines Plays Duke Ellington, 726
  Piano Legends (collection), 480
  Piano Man, 543
  ★*The Smithsonian Collection of Classic*
    Jazz (collection), 486

Stars of the Apollo (collection), 2240
Storyville Presents Earl Hines: The
  Complete Transcriptions, 522.2
Hines, J. Earl. *The Great Gospel Men*
  (collection), 2988
Hinton, Eddie. *Very Extremely Dangerous,*
  2481
Hinton, Joe. *Duke-Peacock's Greatest Hits*
  (collection), 2421
hip-hop. *See* rap and hip-hop
His Majestie's Clerkes
  Early American Choral Music, 14.1
  Home to Thanksgiving: Songs of Thanks
    and Praise, 14.2
hitmakers, U.S. *See* U.S. hitmakers
Hobart, Rex and the Misery Boys. *The*
  Bottle Let Me Down: Songs for
  Bumpy Wagon Rides (collection),
  3191
Hobbs, Smiley. *Mountain Music Bluegrass*
  Style (collection), 1566
Hodes, Art
  ★*The Commodore Story* (collection),
    561
  Tribute to the Greats, 727
Hodges Brothers. *16 Down Home Country*
  Classics (collection), 1385
Hodges, Johnny
  The Duke's Men: Small Groups, Vol. 1
    (collection), 562
  The Duke's Men: Small Groups, Vol. 2
    (collection), 563
  Jazz Lullaby (collection), 3264
Hodges, Ricky. *Boddie Recording Company*
  Cleveland, Ohio (collection), 2569,
  2570
Hodgson, Lee. *Hot Country: A*
  Comprehensive Guide to Lead and
  Rhythm Country Guitar Playing,
  1655
Hofner, Adolph
  Doughboys, Playboys, and Cowboys:
    The Golden Years of Western Swing
    (collection), 1428
  South Texas Swing, 1441
  Western Swing: 40 Bootstompers from
    the Golden Age (collection), 1433
Hogan, Kelly. *The Bottle Let Me Down:*
  Songs for Bumpy Wagon Rides
  (collection), 3191
Hogan, Silas
  Dark Clouds Rollin': Excello Swamp
    Blues Classics (collection), 328
  House Rockin' and Hip Shakin': The
    Best of Excello Blues (collection),
    329
Hole. *Live through This,* 2140
Holiday, Billie
  ★*American Popular Song: Six Decades*
    of Songwriters and Singers
    (collection), 1059
  Billie Holiday / Lester Young: A Musical
    Romance, 781.1

Billie's Blues: Her Best Performances on
  Film, 781.2
The Classic Hoagy Carmichael
  (songwriter collection), 1097.1
Cole Porter (songwriter collection),
  1108.1
★*The Commodore Master Takes,* 781.3
★*The Commodore Story* (collection), 561
The Complete Verve Studio Master
  Takes, 781.4
The Definitive Collection (songwriter
  collection), 1101.1
Dorothy Fields (songwriter collection),
  1100
Duke Ellington (songwriter collection),
  1099.1
E. Y. Harburg (songwriter collection),
  1103
Frank Loesser (songwriter collection),
  1106.1
The Great Depression: American Music
  in the '30s (collection), 1066
Irving Berlin: A Hundred Years
  (songwriter collection), 1096.3
Jazz Masters: Vintage Collection, 1958–
  1961 (collection), 477
★*The Jazz Singers: A Smithsonian*
  Collection of Jazz Vocals from
  1919–1994 (collection), 766
Jerome Kern (songwriter collection),
  1104.1
Johnny Mercer (songwriter collection),
  1107.1
★*Ken Burns Jazz Collection: Billie*
  Holiday, 781.5
★*Ken Burns Jazz: The Story of*
  America's Music (collection), 478
★*Lady Day: The Best of* Billie Holiday,
  781.6
Lady Day: The Many Faces of Billie
  Holiday, 781.7
Lady Day: The Master Takes and
  Singles, 781.8
Original Decca Recordings, 781.9
Oscar Hammerstein II (songwriter
  collection), 1102
Richard Whiting (songwriter
  collection), 1116
Rodgers / Hart (songwriter collection),
  1109.1
Sentimental Journey: Capitol's Great
  Ladies of Song (collection), 1166
★*The Smithsonian Collection of Classic*
  Jazz (collection), 486
Songs That Got Us through World
  War II, Vol. 2 (collection), 1086
★*Sound of Jazz* (collection), 487
Stars of the Apollo (collection), 2240
The Very Best of Cole Porter
  (songwriter collection), 1108.3
Holiday, Judy. *Irving Berlin: A Hundred*
  Years (songwriter collection),
  1096.3

holiday music, children's. *See* religious and holiday children's music
holidays
Christmas, 3267–3345
Halloween, 3346–3351
Kwanzaa, 3352–3354
overview, p185
Holland, Dave
★*Conference of the Birds,* 980.1
Jumpin' In, 980.2
Prime Directive, 980.3
Holland, Eddie
Beg, Scream, and Shout! The Big Ol' Box of '60s Soul (collection), 2433
Heaven Must Have Sent You: The Holland/Dozier/Holland Story (collection), 2436
Holland, Jolie
Escondida, 1272
For the Kids Three! (collection), 3209
Holland-Dozier. *Heaven Must Have Sent You: The Holland/Dozier/Holland Story* (collection), 2436
Holland-Dozier-Holland. *Heaven Must Have Sent You: The Holland/Dozier/Holland Story* (collection), 2436
Holliday, Judy
Arthur Schwartz (songwriter collection), 1110.2
Jule Styne (songwriter collection), 1111.1
Oscar Hammerstein II (songwriter collection), 1102
The Hollies
The Hollies' Greatest Hits, 1797
25 Hits from the British Invasion (collection), 1792
Hollis, L. and the Mackadoos. *Eccentric Soul: The Big Mack Label* (collection), 2598
Holloway, Brenda
Beg, Scream, and Shout! The Big Ol' Box of '60s Soul (collection), 2433
Brenda Holloway: Greatest Hits and Rare Classics, 2482
Hitsville USA: The Motown Singles Collection (collection), 2603
Hitsville USA: The Motown Singles Collection, Vol. 2 (collection), 2604
Respect: Aretha's Influences and Inspiration (collection), 2440
Holly, Buddy
The Buddy Holly Collection, 1765
★*Legends of Guitar: Rock–The '50s, Vol. 1* (collection), 1749
★*Legends of Guitar: Rock–The '50s, Vol. 2* (collection), 1750
Let There Be Drums, Vol. 1: The '50s (collection), 1751
Rock and Roll: The Early Days (collection), 1752

Hollywood Flames. *The Swing Time Records Story: R&B, Blues, and Gospel, 1946–1952* (collection), 2430
Holman, Eddie. *Dave Godin's Deep Soul Treasures, Vols. 1–4* (collection), 2435
Holman, Libby. *Flappers, Vamps, and Sweet Young Things* (collection), 1065
Holt, Morris. *See* Magic Slim
Holy Disciples of Chicago, IL. *Good God! Born Again Funk* (collection), 2614
Holy Ghost Sanctified Singers
★*Goodbye Babylon* (collection), 2954
Spreading the Word: Early Gospel Recordings (collection), 2972
Holy Ghost Spirituals. *Happy in the Service of the Lord: Memphis Gospel Quartet Heritage, the 1980s, Vols. 1 and 2* (collection), 3007
Homer and Jethro. *America's Song Butchers: The Weird World of Homer and Jethro,* 1498
Hooker, Earl
Blue Guitar: The Chief and Age Sessions, 352.1
Blues Masters, Vol. 9: Postmodern Blues (collection), 412
An Introduction to Earl Hooker, 352.2
Memphis Blues: Important Postwar Recordings (collection), 341
Two Bugs and a Roach, 352.3
Hooker, John Lee
The American Roots of the British Invasion (collection), 1786
Blue Yule: Christmas Blues and R&B Classics (collection), 3295
Blues Fest: Modern Blues of the '80s (collection), 409
Blues Masters, Vol. 7: Blues Revival (collection), 390
★*The Blues: A Smithsonian Collection of Classic Blues Singers* (collection), 145
Classic Early Years, 296.1
Conversation with the Blues (collection), 148
Detroit Blues: Blues from the Motor City (collection), 291
Don't Turn Me from Your Door, 296.2
The Healer, 441
John Lee Hooker: A Blues Legend, 296.3
The Legendary Modern Recordings, 296.4
★*Mean Old World: The Blues from 1940–1994* (collection), 154
The Modern Records Blues Story (collection), 342
Newport Folk Festival: Best of the Blues, 1959–68 (collection), 392
★*The Ultimate Collection,* 296.5

★*The Vee-Jay Story: Celebrating 40 Years of Classic Hits* (collection), 2431
Hooks, Louie, and His Rhythm Five. *Swingbillies: Hillbilly and Western Swing on Modern/Colonial/Flair, 1947–1952* (collection), 1431
Hoopii, Sol. *With My Little Ukulele in My Hand* (collection), 1093
Hoosier Hot Shots. *Definitive Hoosier Hotshots Collection,* 1410
Hope, Elmo. *Trio,* 644
Hope, Lynn. *The Big Horn: The History of the Honkin' and Screamin' Saxophone* (collection), 2314
Hopkins, Claude
An Anthology of Big Band Swing (collection), 528
Stars of the Apollo (collection), 2240
Hopkins, Lightnin'
All the Classics, 1946–1951, 321.1
Blue Yule: Christmas Blues and R&B Classics (collection), 3295
Blues Masters, Vol. 3: Texas Blues (collection), 311
★*The Blues: A Smithsonian Collection of Classic Blues Singers* (collection), 145
Complete Aladdin Recordings, 321.2
Conversation with the Blues (collection), 148
The Fire / Fury Records Story (collection), 2422
★*Gold Star Sessions, Vols. 1 and 2,* 321.3
★*Mean Old World: The Blues from 1940–1994* (collection), 154
The Modern Records Blues Story (collection), 342
Mojo Hand: The Lightnin' Hopkins Anthology, 321.4
Newport Folk Festival: Best of the Blues, 1959–68 (collection), 392
Texas Blues, 394
Very Best of Lightnin' Hopkins, 321.5
Hoppin' Haole Brothers. *Greasy Kid Stuff* (collection), 3210
Horn, Paul
★*Inside the Taj Mahal, I and II,* 1331
Pioneers of the New Age (collection), 1371
Horn, Shirley
Close Enough for Love, 782.1
The Definitive Collection (songwriter collection), 1101.1
Here's to Life, 782.2
★*The Jazz Singers: A Smithsonian Collection of Jazz Vocals from 1919–1994* (collection), 766
The Very Best of Cole Porter (songwriter collection), 1108.3

Horne, Lena
Alec Wilder (songwriter collection), 1117.1
★American Popular Song: Six Decades of Songwriters and Singers (collection), 1059
★Best of Lena Horne, 1201
Cole Porter (songwriter collection), 1108.1
Duke Ellington (songwriter collection), 1099.1
E. Y. Harburg (songwriter collection), 1103
George Gershwin (songwriter collection), 1101.3
Harold Arlen (songwriter collection), 1095.1
Hipsters' Holiday: Vocal Jazz and R&B Classics (collection), 3313
James Van Heusen (songwriter collection), 1112.1
Jerome Kern (songwriter collection), 1104.1
Jule Styne (songwriter collection), 1111.1
★Nipper's Greatest Hits: The 40's, Vol. 1 (collection), 1073
Rodgers / Hart (songwriter collection), 1109.1
Sentimental Journey: Pop Vocal Classics, Vol. 1 (collection), 1167
★Sentimental Journey: Pop Vocal Classics, Vol. 1 (collection), 1081
Stormy Weather [1999] (Waller, Calloway, Horn, and others), 1057.1
Stormy Weather [2005] (Waller, Calloway, Horn, and others), 1057.2
Sweet and Lovely: Capitol's Great Ladies of Song (collection), 1172
Waller / Razaf (songwriter collection), 1113.2
Horne, Marilyn. Oscar Hammerstein II (songwriter collection), 1102
Horton, Big Walter
Big Walter Horton with Carey Bell (Horton), 442
Blues Masters, Vol. 4: Harmonica Classics (collection), 286
★Chicago: The Blues Today! (collection), 290
The Cobra Records Story: Chicago Rock and Blues (collection), 339
Memphis Blues: Important Postwar Recordings (collection), 341
The Sun Blues Years (collection), 344
Sun Records Harmonica Classics (collection), 346
Horton, Johnny. The Essential Johnny Horton: Honky Tonk Man, 1499
Hot Chocolate
Disco Box (collection), 2644

Every 1's a Winner: The Very Best of Hot Chocolate, 2631
Hot Rize. Top of the Hill Bluegrass (collection), 1567
Hot Shot Love. Sun Records Harmonica Classics (collection), 346
Houghton, Israel. Live from Another Level, 3091
Houghton, Steve. Essential Styles for the Drummer and Bassist: A Cross Section of Styles as Played by Today's Top Artists (Houghton and Warrington), 493
Houn, Fred. We Refuse to Be Used and Abused, 846
House of Pain. House of Pain, 2818
House, Son
Acoustic Country Blues Guitar: Delta Blues before Robert Johnson (collection), 211
Back to the Crossroads: The Roots of Robert Johnson (collection), 212
Blues Masters, Vol. 7: Blues Revival (collection), 390
Blues Masters, Vol. 8: Mississippi Delta Blues (collection), 215
★The Blues: A Smithsonian Collection of Classic Blues Singers (collection), 145
Delta Blues: The Original Library of Congress Sessions, 223
Father of the Delta Blues, 395
Legends of Country Blues (collection), 218
★Legends of the Blues, Vol. 1 (collection), 150
Masters of the Country Blues: Son House and Bukka White (collection), 219
★Masters of the Delta Blues: The Friends of Charlie Patton (collection), 220
★Negro Blues and Hollers (collection), 178
Newport Folk Festival: Best of the Blues, 1959–68 (collection), 392
The Road to Robert Johnson and Beyond (collection), 221
House, Wallace
Ballads of the Revolution, 53.1
Ballads of the War of 1812, 53.2
Houston, Cissy. Story of Gospel Music (collection), 2973
Houston, Joe. The Big Horn: The History of the Honkin' and Screamin' Saxophone (collection), 2314
Houston, Thelma
The Best of Thelma Houston, 2483
Complete Introduction to Disco (collection), 1237
Disco Box (collection), 2644
Hitsville USA: The Motown Singles Collection, Vol. 2 (collection), 2604
Houston, Whitney
The Greatest Hits, 1273.1

#1s (Carey), 1256.2
Whitney Houston, 1273.2
Hovington, Frank. Gone with the Wind (Hovington), 248
★Howard, Camille. The Specialty Story (collection), 2428
★Howard, Eddy. The Crooners (collection), 1062
Howard, Frank
Night Train to Nashville: Music City Rhythm and Blues, 1945–1970, Vol. 1 (collection), 2377
Night Train to Nashville: Music City Rhythm and Blues, 1945–1970, Vol. 2 (collection), 2378
Howard, Kid. New Orleans Jazz (collection), 503
Howell, Peg Leg
Atlanta Blues: Big City Blues from the Heartland (collection), 241
The Georgia Blues (collection), 242
Songsters and Saints: Vocal Traditions on Race Records, Vol. 1 (collection), 190
★The Story of the Blues (collection), 158
Violin, Sing the Blues for Me: African-American Fiddlers (collection), 192
Howlin' Wolf
Blue Flames: A Sun Blues Collection (collection), 337
★Blues Classics (collection), 146
Blues Masters, Vol. 6: Blues Originals (collection), 367
Blues Masters, Vol. 12: Memphis Blues (collection), 229
Blues Masters, Vol. 8: Mississippi Delta Blues (collection), 215
Blues Masters, Vol. 2: Postwar Chicago Blues (collection), 285
★The Blues: A Smithsonian Collection of Classic Blues Singers (collection), 145
★Chess Blues (collection), 287
The Chess Box, 297.1
★His Best, 297.2
Howlin' Wolf Featuring Hubert Sumlin on Guitar, 297.3
The Howlin' Wolf Story, 297.4
Memphis Blues: Important Postwar Recordings (collection), 341
The Modern Records Blues Story (collection), 342
The Roots of Rock 'n' Roll, 1946–1954 (collection), 1755
★Sun Records' Greatest Hits (collection), 1741
Superblues: All-Time Classic Blues Hits, Vol. 1 (collection), 347
Hubbard, Freddie
Breaking Point, 645.1
Freddie Hubbard, 645.2

Freddie Hubbard Live in France 1973, 903

Hubbard, Rev. R. L. *Boddie Recording Company Cleveland, Ohio* (collection), 2569, 2570

Hudson, Hattie. ★*Let's Get Loose: Folk and Popular Blues Styles from the Beginning to the Early 1940s* (collection), 152

Hues Corporation. *Disco Box* (collection), 2644

Hughes, Fred
    The Story of Brunswick: The Classic Sound of Chicago Soul (collection), 2610
    ★*The Vee-Jay Story: Celebrating 40 Years of Classic Hits* (collection), 2431

Hughes, Jimmy
    ★*Atlantic Soul, 1959–1975* (collection), 2589
    Best of Jimmy Hughes, 2484.1
    Something Extra Special: The Complete Volt Recordings 1968–1971, 2484.2
    Steal Away: The Early Fame Recordings, Vol. 1, 2484.3
    Why Not Tonight? The Fame Recordings, Vol. 2, 2484.4

Hughes, Langston. *Harlem in Vogue: The Poetry and Jazz of Langston Hughes* (collection), 811

Hulbert, Claude. *The Roaring 'Twenties* (collection), 1080

The Human League
    Like Omigod! The 80s Pop Culture Box (Totally) (collection), 1241
    The Very Best of the Human League, 2034

Humbard Family. *The Gospel Tradition: The Roots and the Branches, Vol. 1* (collection), 2955

Humes, Helen
    ★*The Jazz Singers: A Smithsonian Collection of Jazz Vocals from 1919–1994* (collection), 766
    Knockin' Myself Out, 2312
    Legendary Big Band Singers (collection), 767
    Respect: Aretha's Influences and Inspiration (collection), 2440
    Songs I Like to Sing, 783
    ★*Stompin' at the Savoy: The Original Indie Label, 1944–1961* (collection), 2429
    This Is Art Deco (collection), 1090

★Hunt, Slim. *Nashville Jumps: Blues and Rhythm on Nashville Independent Labels 1945–1955* (collection), 2376

Hunt, Tommy
    ★*Atlantic Soul, 1959–1975* (collection), 2589

The Scepter Records Story (collection), 2426

Hunter, Alberta
    Amtrak Blues, 396
    Better Boot That Thing: Great Women Blues Singers of the 1920's (collection), 202
    Blues Masters, Vol. 11: Classic Blues Women (collection), 203
    This Is Art Deco (collection), 1090
    When the Sun Goes Down 1: Walk Right In (collection), 159
    Young Alberta Hunter, 208

Hunter, Charlie
    Icons among Us (collection), 934
    Steady Groovin', 825

Hunter, Herbert. *Night Train to Nashville: Music City Rhythm and Blues, 1945–1970, Vol. 2* (collection), 2378

Hunter, Ivory Joe
    ★*Atlantic R&B, 1947–1974* (collection), 2418
    The Complete Goldwax Singles, Vol. 2 (collection), 2592
    King R&B Box Set (collection), 2424
    Night Train to Nashville: Music City Rhythm and Blues, 1945–1970, Vol. 2 (collection), 2378
    The Roots of Rock 'n' Roll, 1946–1954 (collection), 1755
    Since I Met You Baby: The Best of Ivory Joe Hunter, 2261.1
    ★*Texas Music, Vol. 1: Postwar Blues Combos* (collection), 316
    Woo Wee!: The King and Deluxe Acetate Series, 2261.2

Hurt, Mississippi John
    ★*Avalon Blues*, 196
    Before the Blues: The Early American Black Music Scene; Classic Recordings from the 1920's and 30's, Vols. 1–3 (collection), 183
    Blues Masters, Vol. 7: Blues Revival (collection), 390
    ★*The Blues: A Smithsonian Collection of Classic Blues Singers* (collection), 145
    ★*Legends of the Blues, Vol. 1* (collection), 150
    Mississippi John Hurt Today, 397
    Newport Folk Festival: Best of the Blues, 1959–68 (collection), 392
    News and the Blues: Telling It Like It Is (collection), 156
    ★*The Story of the Blues* (collection), 158

Hüsker Dü
    New Day Rising, 2141.1
    Zen Arcade, 2141.2

Husky, Ferlin. *Greatest Hits*, 1500

Huston, Walter. *From Berlin to Broadway: A Selection* (songwriter collection), 1115.2

Hutch, Willie. *The Mack*, 2572

Hutcherson, Bobby. *Dialogue*, 687

Hutchins, Sam. *Mountain Music Bluegrass Style* (collection), 1566

Hutchinson Family Singers. *The Civil War Music Collector's Edition* (collection), 61

Hutchison, Frank
    ★*Anthology of American Folk Music, Vols. 1–3* (collection), 1386
    Good for What Ails You: Music of the Medicine Shows (collection), 184
    Old-Time Mountain Guitar (collection), 1391
    White Country Blues: A Lighter Shade of Blues, 1427

★Hutto, J. B. *Chicago: The Blues Today!* (collection), 290

Hutton, Betty
    The Classic Hoagy Carmichael (songwriter collection), 1097.1
    Frank Loesser (songwriter collection), 1106.1
    ★*Sentimental Journey: Pop Vocal Classics, Vol. 1* (collection), 1081, 1167

Hwong, Lucia. *The World of Private Music* (collection), 1378

Hyman, Dick
    Come and Trip It: Instrumental Dance Music, 1780s–1920s (collection), 94
    Dick Hyman's Century of Jazz Piano, 134
    Don't Give the Name a Bad Place: Types and Stereotypes in American Musical Theater, 1870–1900 (collection), 1063

Hytones. *Night Train to Nashville: Music City Rhythm and Blues, 1945–1970, Vol. 1* (collection), 2377

I

Ian, Janis. *Songs of Protest* (collection), 1820

Ibrahim, Abdullah. *Dollar Brand: African Piano*, 847

Ice Cube
    ★*Amerikkka's Most Wanted*, 2819.1
    Death Certificate, 2819.2
    The Predator, 2819.3

Iceberg Slim. *Reflections*, 1972

Ice-T
    O.G.: Original Gangster, 2820.2
    Power, 2820.3
    ★*The Iceberg: Freedom of Speech . . . Just Watch What You Say*, 2820.1
    Whatever: The '90s Pop and Culture Box (collection), 1244

Idol, Billy. *Billboard #1s: The '80s* (collection), 1236

Iggy and the Stooges. *No Thanks! The '70s Punk Rebellion* (collection), 2003. See also Pop, Iggy

★Ikettes. *Atlantic Soul, 1959–1975* (collection), 2589

Ilana. *The Sweetest Feeling: A Van McCoy Songbook* (collection), 2447

Impacts. *The Doo-Wop Box II* (collection), 2323

The Impalas

   Casey Kasem Presents America's Top Ten through the Years: The Doo-Wop Years, 1950s (collection), 1155

   ★*The Doo Wop Box: 101 Vocal Group Gems from the Golden Age of Rock 'n' Roll* (collection), 1745

   ★*The Doo-Wop Box* (collection), 2322

The Imperials

   CCM Top 100: Greatest Songs in Christian Music, Vol. 1 (collection), 3136

   ★*The Doo Wop Box: 101 Vocal Group Gems from the Golden Age of Rock 'n' Roll* (collection), 1745

   The Doo-Wop Box II (collection), 2323

   The Imperials, 3150

   Night Train to Nashville: Music City Rhythm and Blues, 1945–1970, Vol. 2 (collection), 2378

The Impressions

   Beg, Scream, and Shout! The Big Ol' Box of '60s Soul (collection), 2433

   Birth of Soul: Special Chicago Edition (collection), 2566

   Birth of Soul, 4 Vols. (collection), 2434

   Dave Godin's Deep Soul Treasures, Vols. 1–4 (collection), 2435

   ★*The Doo Wop Box: 101 Vocal Group Gems from the Golden Age of Rock 'n' Roll* (collection), 1745

   ★*The Doo-Wop Box* (collection), 2322

   ★*The R&B Box* (collection), 2239

Incredible String Band. *The Hangman's Beautiful Daughter,* 1854

Incredibles. *Dave Godin's Deep Soul Treasures, Vols. 1–4* (collection), 2435

Indeep. *Disco Box* (collection), 2644

India.Arie

   Acoustic Soul, 2383.1

   Voyage to India, 2383.2

influences on the 1980s: 1960s and 1970s bands, 1870–1890

   Back in the USA (MC5), 1876.1

   Barrett, 1870.1

   Colossal Youth (Young Marble Giants), 1890

   The Devil and Daniel Johnston, 1875.1

   DNA on DNA, 1873

   Fun House (Stooges), 1887.1

   Fun (Johnston), 1875.2

   GP / Grievous Angel (Parsons), 1880

   Half Japanese: The Band That Would Be King, 1874.1

   Kick out the Jams (MC5), 1876.2

Loaded (Velvet Underground), 1889.

Loud and Horrible (Half Japanese), 1874.2

The Madcap Laughs (Barrett), 1870.2

The Modern Lovers (Richman), 1883

New York Dolls, 1878

#1 Record / Radio City (Big Star), 1871

Old Records Never Die (Mott the Hoople), 1877

Peek-a-Boo: The Best of NRBQ, 1879

Peel Slowly and See (Velvet Underground), 1889.2

Philosophy of the World (Shaggs), 1885

The Raspberries, 1882

★*Raw Power* (Pop), 1881

Shiny Beast (Bat Chain Puller) (Captain Beefheart), 1872.1

Silver Apples, 1886

The Stooges, 1887.2

Straight Outta Cleveland (collection), 1888

Trout Mask Replica (Captain Beefheart), 1872.2

The Velvet Underground, 1889.3

★*The Velvet Underground and Nico,* 1889.4

The Very Best of Todd Rundgren, 1884

Ingalls, Charles. *Pa's Fiddle,* 116

Ingram, Luther. *If Loving You Is Wrong, I Don't Want to Be Right: The Best of Luther Ingram,* 2485

The Ink Spots

   Hit Parade, 1943 (collection), 1157

   ★*Instant Classics,* 1135

   Songs That Got Us through World War II (collection), 1085

Inman, Bryce

   Contemporary Wedding Favorites (collection), 3360

   25 Contemporary Christmas Hits, 3331

Inner Life. *Disco Box* (collection), 2644

inspirational, contemporary Christian, and Christian Rock, 3135–3166

   The Absolute Best (Carman), 3142

   Acapella Project (Glad), 3147

   Angels of Mercy (Ashton), 3138

   The Beautiful Letdown (Switchfoot), 3162

   Best of Christian Rock (1970–1986), Vol. 1 (collection), 3135

   The Best of Russ Taff, 3163.1

   Caedmon's Call, 3141

   CCM Top 100: Greatest Songs in Christian Music, Vol. 1 (collection), 3136

   Chronology, Vol. 1 (Third Day), 3164

   Chronology, Vol. 2 (Third Day), 3165

   ★*The Collection* (Grant), 3148.1

   Farewell (Petra), 3159.1

   Finest Moments (Patty), 3157

   First Love: A Historic Gathering of Jesus Music Pioneers (collection), 3137

The First Decade (Smith), 3161.1

Greatest Hits (Grant), 3148.2

Heart in Motion (Grant), 3148.3

The Imperials, 3150

Jesus Freak (DC Talk), 3145

Lifesong (Casting Crows), 3143

The Long Fall Back to Earth (Jars of Clay), 3151.1

Love Life (Peacock), 3158

Love Song, 3153

Mi Corazón (Valesquez), 3166

Ministry Years, Vol. 1 (Green), 3149

No Limits: Live (Munizzi), 3154

Now and Then (Chapman), 3144.1

Petra, 3159.2

Phil Keaggy and Sunday's Child, 3152

Rebel Poet, Jukebox Balladeer: The Anthology (Norman), 3155.1

Saved (Dylan), 3146.1

The Second Decade (Smith), 3161.2

Slow Train Coming (Dylan), 3146.2

Speechless (Chapman), 3144.2

Steps of Faith (Becker), 3139

This Moment (Chapman), 3144.3

Triple Feature (Jars of Clay), 3151.2

20 (2nd Chapter of Acts), 3160

Ultimate Collection (Petra), 3159.3

Upon This Rock, Coll. Ed (Norman), 3155.2

The Way Home (Taff), 3163

White Horse / Adam Again (Omartian), 3156

You Light up My Life: Greatest Inspirational Songs (Boone), 3140

inspirational Gospel Singers. *Good God! Born Again Funk* (collection), 2614

instrumental music and popular vocal music. *See* popular vocal and instrumental music

instrumental new age, solo. *See* solo instrumental (new age)

instrumental soul and soundtracks, 2571–2577

   Blow Man, Blow! (King Curtis), 2573

   Live at Fillmore West (King Curtis), 2574

   The Mack (Hutch), 2572

   Music from the Wattstax Festival and Film, 2575

   Potato Hole (Booker T. and the MGs), 2571.1

   Superfly (Mayfield), 2576

   The Ultimate Collection (Jr. Walker and the All Stars), 2577

   Time Is Tight (Booker T. and the MGs), 2571.2

instrumentals and dance hits. *See* teen idols, instrumentals, and dance hits

Inter-Circle. *Boddie Recording Company Cleveland, Ohio* (collection), 2569, 2570

The Intruders
    Cowboys to Girls: The Best of the
        Intruders, 2486
    ★Love Train: The Sound of Philadelphia
        (collection), 2552
    Soul Shots: A Collection of Sixties Soul
        Classics (collection), 2443
Invincibles. The Best of Loma Records: The
    Rise and Fall of a 1960's Soul Label
    (collection), 2590
Invisibl Skratch Pikla
    The Shiggar Fraggar Show! Vol. 1,
        2821.1
    The Shiggar Fraggar Show! Vol. 2,
        2821.2
INXS. The Best of INXS, 1274
Iron Maiden
    Best of the Beast, 2078.1
    Somewhere Back in Time: Best of
        1980–1989, 2078.2
Irwin, May. The Phonographic Yearbook,
    1907: Dear Old Golden Rule Days
    (collection), 1075
Isaacs. Songs of the Faith, 3126
Isaak, Chris. Best of Chris Isaak, 1275
Isham, Mark
    A Winter's Solstice (collection), 3321
    Vapor Drawings, 1337
    Windham Hill: The First Ten Years
        (collection), 1377
Islam, Yusuf. See Stevens, Cat
The Isley Brothers
    The American Roots of the British
        Invasion (collection), 1786
    ★Atlantic Soul, 1959–1975
        (collection), 2589
    Beg, Scream, and Shout! The Big Ol'
        Box of '60s Soul (collection), 2433
    Best of the Isley Brothers, 2542.1
    Have a Nice Decade: The '70s Pop
        Culture Box (collection), 1240
    Heaven Must Have Sent You: The
        Holland/Dozier/Holland Story
        (collection), 2436
    Hitsville USA: The Motown Singles
        Collection (collection), 2603
    The Isleys Live, 2542.2
    ★It's Your Thing: The Story of the Isley
        Brothers, 2542.3
    Nipper's Greatest Hits: The 50's, Vol. 2
        (collection), 1164
    ★The R&B Box (collection), 2239
    The Scepter Records Story (collection),
        2426
    Summer Breeze: Greatest Hits, Live, 2342
        3 + 3, 2542.4
    The Ultimate Isley Brothers, 2542.5
Italian Instabile Orchestra. Skies of
    Europe, 848
Ivor Cutler Trio. Colours Are Brighter:
    Songs for Children and Grown Ups
    Too (collection), 3193
Iyer, Vijay. Historicity, 849

J
J Dilla. Donuts, 2822
Jack, Sheila. Eccentric Soul: Mighty Mike
    Lenaburg (collection), 2563
Jackie and Roy
    Alan Jay Lerner (songwriter
        collection), 1105.1
    Alec Wilder (songwriter collection),
        1117.1
    Cy Coleman (songwriter collection),
        1098.2
    Harry Warren (songwriter collection),
        1114
★Jacks. The Doo-Wop Box (collection),
    2322
Jackson, Alan
    Greatest Hits Collection, 1656.1
    Here in the Real World, 1656.2
Jackson, Big John. Deep Blues
    (collection), 217
Jackson, Bruce. Wake Up Dead Man:
    Black Convict Worksongs from
    Texas Prisons (Jackson), 176
Jackson, Bull Moose
    King R&B Box Set (collection), 2424
    The Very Best of Bull Moose Jackson:
        Big Ten-Inch Record, 2262
Jackson, Chuck
    Beg, Scream, and Shout! The Big Ol'
        Box of '60s Soul (collection), 2433
    Birth of Soul, 4 Vols. (collection), 2434
    The Look of Love: The Burt Bacharach
        Collection (collection), 1161
    ★The R&B Box (collection), 2239
    The Scepter Records Story (collection),
        2426
    The Sweetest Feeling: A Van McCoy
        Songbook (collection), 2447
Jackson, Clifford. Don't Give the Name a
    Bad Place: Types and Stereotypes in
    American Musical Theater, 1870–
    1900 (collection), 1063
Jackson, Curtis James, III. See 50 Cent
Jackson, Earl. The Swing Time Records
    Story: R&B, Blues, and Gospel,
    1946–1952 (collection), 2430
The Jackson 5
    Beg, Scream, and Shout! The Big Ol'
        Box of '60s Soul (collection), 2433
    Complete Introduction to Disco
        (collection), 1237
    Disco Box (collection), 2644
    Gold, 2343.1
    Have a Nice Decade: The '70s Pop
        Culture Box (collection), 1240
    Heaven Must Have Sent You: The
        Holland/Dozier/Holland Story
        (collection), 2436
    Hitsville USA: The Motown Singles
        Collection (collection), 2603
    Hitsville USA: The Motown Singles
        Collection, Vol. 2 (collection), 2604
    Jackson 5 Christmas Album, 3332

    Live at the Forum, 2343.2
    The Ultimate Collection, 2343.3
Jackson, Fred. The Big Horn: The History
    of the Honkin' and Screamin'
    Saxophone (collection), 2314
Jackson, Freddie. Greatest Hits, 2406
Jackson, George. In Memphis, 1972–77:
    The Sounds of Memphis and Xl
    Recordings, 2487
Jackson Gospel Singers. Powerhouse
    Gospel on Independent Labels
    (collection), 3038
Jackson, J. J.
    Beg, Scream, and Shout! The Big Ol'
        Box of '60s Soul (collection),
        2433
    The Best of Loma Records: The Rise
        and Fall of a 1960's Soul Label
        (collection), 2590
    Soul Shots: A Collection of Sixties Soul
        Classics (collection), 2443
Jackson, Janet
    Control, 2263.1
    Design of a Decade, 1986/1996,
        2263.2
    From Janet to Damita Jo: The Videos,
        2263.3
    Janet Jackon's Rhythm Nation 1814,
        2263.4
    The Velvet Rope Tour Live in Concert /
        Live in Hawaii, 2263.5
Jackson, Jermaine. Motown around the
    World (collection), 2437
Jackson, Jim
    ★Blues Classics (collection), 146
    Blues Masters, Vol. 12: Memphis Blues
        (collection), 229
    Good for What Ails You: Music of the
        Medicine Shows (collection), 184
    Songsters and Saints: Vocal Traditions
        on Race Records, Vol. 2 (collection),
        191
    When the Sun Goes Down 2: The First
        Time I Met the Blues (collection),
        160
    Wild About My Lovin': Beale Street
        Blues, 1928–30 (collection), 233
Jackson, Jimmy. The Big Horn: The
    History of the Honkin' and
    Screamin' Saxophone (collection),
    2314
Jackson, Joe. No Thanks! The '70s Punk
    Rebellion (collection), 2003
Jackson, John. Don't Let Your Deal Go
    Down, 398
Jackson, Little Willie. The Big Horn:
    The History of the Honkin' and
    Screamin' Saxophone (collection),
    2314
Jackson, Mahalia
    Best of Mahalia Jackson, 2999.1
    A First-Time Buyer's Guide to American
        Negro Spirituals (collection), 32

★*Good News: 100 Gospel Greats* (collection), 2961

Gospel: Negro Spirituals / Gospel Songs, 1926–1942 (collection), 2963

★*Gospels, Spirituals and Hymns; Vols. 1 and 2,* 2999.2

★*The Gospel Sound* (collection), 2964

★*The Gospel Sound of Spirit Feel* (collection), 2965

★*The Great Gospel Women* (collection), 2989

The Great Gospel Women, Vol. 2 (collection), 2990

★*How I Got Over: The Apollo Records Sessions,* 2999.3

★*Jazz on a Summer's Day* (collection), 664

★*Jubilation! Great Gospel Performances, Vol. 1: Black Gospel* (collection), 2966

★*Jubilation! Great Gospel Performances, Vol. 2: More Black Gospel* (collection), 2967

Mahalia Jackson, 2999.4

The Rough Guide to Gospel (collection), 2970

★*Silent Night,* 3333

Story of Gospel Music (collection), 2973

Testify! The Gospel Box (collection), 2974

Jackson, Melvin "Lil' Son"
  Conversation with the Blues (collection), 148
  Lil' Son Jackson, Vols. 1 and 2, 322
  Texas Blues: Bill Quinn's Gold Star Recordings (collection), 314

Jackson, Michael
  The Essential Michael Jackson, 2264.1
  Greatest Hits: History, Vol. 1, 2264.2
  Heaven Must Have Sent You: The Holland/Dozier/Holland Story (collection), 2436
  Hitsville USA: The Motown Singles Collection, Vol. 2 (collection), 2604
  Michael Jackson Live in Bucharest: The Dangerous Tour, 2264.3
  Off the Wall, 2264.4
  ★*Thriller,* 2264.5
  Video Greatest Hits: History, 2264.6

Jackson, Millie
  The Spring Story: Essential 70s Soul (collection), 2608
  Totally Unrestricted: The Millie Jackson Anthology, 2265.1
  21 of the Best, 1971–1983, 2265.2
  The Very Best of Millie Jackson, 2265.3

Jackson, O'Shea, Sr. *See* Ice Cube

Jackson, Papa Charlie
  ★*The Blues: A Smithsonian Collection of Classic Blues Singers* (collection), 145

Good for What Ails You: Music of the Medicine Shows (collection), 184

A Richer Tradition: Country Blues and String Band Music (collection), 187

Songsters and Saints: Vocal Traditions on Race Records, Vol. 2 (collection), 191

Jackson, Ronald Shannon. *Eye on You,* 981

Jackson, Stonewall. *Best of Stonewall Jackson,* 1501

★Jackson, Walter. *Atlantic Soul, 1959–1975* (collection), 2589

Jackson, Willis
  ★*Atlantic R&B, 1947–1974* (collection), 2418
  The Big Horn: The History of the Honkin' and Screamin' Saxophone (collection), 2314
  The Fire / Fury Records Story (collection), 2422

Jacobs, Debbie. *Disco Box* (collection), 2644

Jacobs, Marion Walter. *See* Little Walter

Jacobs-Bond, Carrie. *Songs My Grandmother Taught Me,* 117

Jacquet, Illinois
  The Big Horn: The History of the Honkin' and Screamin' Saxophone (collection), 2314
  ★*The R&B Box* (collection), 2239

Jagger, Mick. *Billboard #1s: The '80s* (collection), 1236

Jakes, Bishop T. D. *Woman, Thou Art Loosed,* 3065

The Jam
  In the City, 2016.1
  No Thanks! The '70s Punk Rebellion (collection), 2003
  The Sound of the Jam, 2016.2
  The Tomorrow Show with Tom Snyder: Punk and New Wave (collection), 1981

Jamal, Ahmad
  ★*But Not for Me: Live at the Pershing* (Jamal), 669
  Jazz Masters: Vintage Collection, 1958–1961 (collection), 477

James, Eddie and the Phoenix Mass Choir. *Going Up Yonder: The Best of the Gospel Choirs* (collection), 3051

James, Elmore
  Blues Masters, Vol. 6: Blues Originals (collection), 367
  Blues Masters, Vol. 8: Mississippi Delta Blues (collection), 215
  ★*The Blues: A Smithsonian Collection of Classic Blues Singers* (collection), 145
  ★*Chess Blues* (collection), 287
  Elmore James: Master of the Electric Slide Guitar, 298.1

The Fire / Fury Records Story (collection), 2422

★*Mean Old World: The Blues from 1940–1994* (collection), 154

The Modern Records Blues Story (collection), 342

The Road to Robert Johnson and Beyond (collection), 221

The Sky Is Crying: The History of Elmore James, 298.2

★*The Story of the Blues* (collection), 158

★*The Vee-Jay Story: Celebrating 40 Years of Classic Hits* (collection), 2431

James, Etta
  At Last!, 2266.1
  Beg, Scream, and Shout! The Big Ol' Box of '60s Soul (collection), 2433
  Best of Chess R&B, Vols. 1 and 2 (collection), 2420
  Birth of Soul: Special Chicago Edition (collection), 2566
  Birth of Soul, 4 Vols. (collection), 2434
  Blues Fest: Modern Blues of the '90s (collection), 410
  Burnin' Down the House, 2267
  ★*The Chess Box,* 2266.2
  The Essential Etta James, 2266.3
  Etta James Rocks the House, 2266.4
  The Modern Records Blues Story (collection), 342
  Muscle Shoals Sound (collection), 2605
  Night Train to Nashville: Music City Rhythm and Blues, 1945–1970, Vol. 1 (collection), 2377
  ★*The R&B Box* (collection), 2239
  The Right Time, 443
  Tell Mama: The Complete Muscle Shoals Sessions, 2266.5

James Gang. *Straight Outta Cleveland* (collection), 1888

James, Harry
  ★*Best of the Big Bands,* 1136.1
  ★*Big Band Jazz: From the Beginnings to the Fifties* (collection), 529
  Big Band Renaissance: The Evolution of the Jazz Orchestra (collection), 739
  The Complete Recordings Nineteen Thirty-Nine: Featuring Frank Sinatra, 1136.2
  Harry Warren (songwriter collection), 1114
  ★*Sentimental Journey: Pop Vocal Classics, Vol. 1* (collection), 1081
  16 Most Requested Songs of the 1940s, Vol. 1 (collection), 1082
  16 Most Requested Songs of the 1940s, Vol. 2 (collection), 1083
  Songs That Got Us through World War II (collection), 1085
  ★*Swing Time! The Fabulous Big Band Era* (collection), 1089

Young Man with a Horn [2001], 1058.1

Young Man with a Horn [2005], 1058.2

James Kochalka Superstar with the Zambonis. *Greasy Kid Stuff* (collection), 3210

James, Leela. *My Soul,* 2407

James, Marion. *Night Train to Nashville: Music City Rhythm and Blues, 1945–1970, Vol. 2* (collection), 2378

James, Rick

  Dave Godin's Deep Soul Treasures, Vols. 1–4 (collection), 2435

  The Definitive Collection, 2632.1

  Gold, 2632.2

  Hitsville USA: The Motown Singles Collection, Vol. 2 (collection), 2604

  Street Songs, Del. Ed, 2632.3

  Super Freak Live 1982, 2632.4

James, Skip

  Acoustic Country Blues Guitar: Delta Blues before Robert Johnson (collection), 211

  Back to the Crossroads: The Roots of Robert Johnson (collection), 212

  ★*The Blues: A Smithsonian Collection of Classic Blues Singers* (collection), 145

  Complete Early Recordings, 224.1

  ★*Juke Joint Saturday Night: Piano Blues, Rags and Stomps; Classic Recordings from the 1920s and '30s* (collection), 255

  Legends of Country Blues (collection), 218

  Newport Folk Festival: Best of the Blues, 1959–68 (collection), 392

  The Road to Robert Johnson and Beyond (collection), 221

  The Roots of Rock (collection), 368

  The Skip James Collection, 224.2

  ★*Skip James Today,* 399

James, Sonny. *Greatest Hits,* 1502

James, Sylvester, Jr. *See* Sylvester

James, Tommy

  Anthology, 1813

  25 All-Time Greatest Bubblegum Hits (collection), 1811

Jamiroquai. *High Times: Singles, 1992–2006,* 2268

Jan and Dean

  Surf City: The Best of Jan and Dean, 1814

  ★*Surfin' Hits* (collection), 1810

Jane's Addiction. *Nothing's* Shocking, 2142

Jang, Jon. *Self Defense!,* 850

Janovsky, Peter. *Winners and Losers: Campaign Songs from the Critical Elections in American History, Vols. 1 and 2,* 54

Jarre, Jean-Michel. *Oxygene,* 1318

Jarreau, Al. *Look to the Rainbow: Al Jarreau Live in Europe,* 784

Jarrett, Keith

  Belonging, 982.1

  Koln Concert, 982.2

  Piano Legends (collection), 480

  Silence, 982.3

  Whisper Not, 982.4

Jarrett, Ted

  ★*Nashville Jumps: Blues and Rhythm on Nashville Independent Labels 1945–1955* (collection), 2376

  Night Train to Nashville: Music City Rhythm and Blues, 1945–1970, Vol. 2 (collection), 2378

Jars of Clay

  The Long Fall Back to Earth, 3151.1

  Triple Feature, 3151.2

Jarvis, John. *New Age Piano Sampler* (collection), 1369

Jay Z

  The Black Album, 2823.1

  ★*The Blueprint,* 2823.2

  Good Girl Gone Bad (Rihanna), 1300

  Hard Knock Life, Vol. 2, 2823.3

  Reasonable Doubt, 2823.4

Jayhawks. *Tomorrow the Green Grass,* 1705

jazz, 470–496, 2312–2313

  After Hours with Miss "D" (Washington), 2313.1

  ★*At the Jazz Band Ball: Early Hot Jazz, Song, and Dance* (collection), 470

  Back to the Blues (Washington), 2313.2

  bebop, 592–602

  big bands and the swing era, 528–550

  big bands since the 1950s, 739–764

  The New Breed (Chester), 490

  ★*Central Avenue Sounds: Jazz in Los Angeles* (collection), 471

  Charles Mingus, 675

  Charlie Parker, 603

  The Complete Roulette Dinah Washington Sessions, 2313.3

  contemporary artists: 1970s through the 2000s, 934–1029

  crossover jazz: 1970s–1990s, 901–911

  The Definitive Dinah Washington, 2313.4

  Dinah Jams (Washington), 2313.5

  Dinah Sings Bessie Smith (Washington), 2313.6

  Duke Ellington, 558–559

  early jazz, 497–502

  early jazz piano styles, 521–527

  early soloists, 511–520

  Essential Jazz Percussion: Drumming in the Style of Modern Jazz Masters (Green), 492

  Essential Styles for the Drummer and Bassist: A Cross Section of Styles

    as Played by Today's Top Artists (Houghton and Warrington), 493

  Exploring Jazz Clarinet (Weston), 496

  ★*The Fabulous Miss D! The Keynote, Decca, and Mercury Singles 1943–1953* (Washington), 2313.7

  First Issue: The Dinah Washington Story: The Original Recordings, 2313.8

  free jazz and related styles of the 1960s, 678–700

  fusion, 816–833

  general collections, 470–496

  Gold (Washington), 2313.9

  ★*Greatest Jazz Films Ever* (collection), 472

  The Hal Leonard Real Jazz Standards Fake Book (collection), 473

  hard bop and related extensions of bebop, 626–663

  How to Play Jazz and Improvise, 6th Ed. (Aebersold), 488.1

  Jazz: A Film by Ken Burns (collection), 474

  jazz and film, 1044–1058

  jazz and poetry, and concept albums, 809–815

  jazz and the classics: third stream, 1030–1043

  jazz and the world, 834–868

  Jazz Drumming Transitions (O'Mahoney), 495

  Jazz Improv Basics: The All-Purpose Reference Guide (collection), 476

  Jazz Improvisation: A Comprehensive Method of Study for All Players (Baker), 489

  Jazz Improvisation for Guitar: A Harmonic Approach (Fewell), 491

  Jazz Masters: Vintage Collection, 1958–1961 (collection), 477

  jazz outside the mainstream: the AACM, BAG, and the lofts, 912–933

  jazz singers, 765–808

  Jazz: The Smithsonian Anthology (collection), 475

  John Coltrane, 677

  Kansas City and other territory bands, 551–557

  ★*Ken Burns Jazz: The Story of America's Music* (collection), 478

  Lost Chords: White Musicians and Their Contributions to Jazz (collection), 479

  Louis Armstrong, 510.1–510.7

  Miles Davis, 676

  modern mainstream: 1970s, 869–900

  New Orleans revival and traditional styles, 503–509

  The 1950s and 1960s: cool jazz and the West Coast, 604–625

  Nothin' but Blues, 3rd Rev. Ed. (Aebersold), 488.2

jazz (cont.)

overview, p34–35

periodicals for up-to-date CD notices and reviews, suggested, p3

piano in the 1960s, 701–710

Piano Legends (collection), 480

popular jazz of the 1950s and 1960s, 664–673

Progressions: 100 Years of Jazz Guitar (collection), 481

Real Book (collection), 482

Real Chord Changes and Substitutions (collection), 483

★*Real Jazz Classics Fake Book* (collection), 484

★*Real Vocal Book* (collection), 485

Rudimental Jazz: A Musical Application of Rudiments to the Drumset (Morello), 494

★*The Smithsonian Collection of Classic Jazz* (collection), 486

★*Sound of Jazz* (collection), 487

swing mainstream since 1950, 711–738

swing soloists and combos, 560–591

Thelonious Monk, 674

What a Diff'rence a Day Makes (Washington), 2313.10

jazz and film, 1044–1058

Alfie [1997] (Rollins and Nelson), 1044.1

Alfie [2000] (Rollins and Nelson), 1044.2

Anatomy of a Murder [1999] (Ellington), 1045.1

Anatomy of a Murder [2000] (Ellington), 1045.2

Ascenseur Pour L'echafaud [Lift to the Scaffold] [2006] (Davis), 1046.1

Ascenseur Pour L'echafaud [Lift to the Scaffold] [2007] (Davis), 1046.2

The Benny Goodman Story [1995] (Goodman), 1047.1

The Benny Goodman Story [2003] (Goodman), 1047.2

Bird (Parker), 1048

Blow Up [1996] (Hancock), 1049.1

Blow Up [2004] (Hancock), 1049.2

The Cotton Club [1984] (collection), 1050.1

The Cotton Club [2001] (collection), 1050.2

★*Greatest Jazz Films Ever* (collection), 472

Inside Man [2006] [CD] (Blanchard), 1051.2

Inside Man [2006] [DVD] (Blanchard), 1051.1

Jazz: A Film by Ken Burns (collection), 474

Mo' Better Blues [1990] (Marsalis), 1052.1

Mo' Better Blues [2000] (Marsalis), 1052.2

Naked Lunch [2003] (Coleman and Shore), 1053.1

Naked Lunch [2005] (Coleman and Shore), 1053.2

New York, New York [1985] (Burns and Auld), 1054.1

New York, New York [2004] (Burns and Auld), 1054.2

Odds against Tomorrow [1990] (Lewis and Modern Jazz Quartet), 1055.1

Odds against Tomorrow [2003] (Lewis and Modern Jazz Quartet), 1055.2

★*Round Midnight* [2001] (Gordon, Hancock, and others), 1056.2

★*Round Midnight* [2002] (Gordon, Hancock, and others), 1056.1

Stormy Weather [1999] (Waller, Calloway, Horn, and others), 1057.1

Stormy Weather [2005] (Waller, Calloway, Horn, and others), 1057.2

Young Man with a Horn [2001] (James), 1058.1

Young Man with a Horn [2005] (James), 1058.2

jazz and poetry, and concept albums, 809–815

Amarcord Nino Rota (collection), 809

collections, 809–812

Conjure: Music for the Texts of Ishmael Reed (collection), 810

Harlem in Vogue: The Poetry and Jazz of Langston Hughes (collection), 811

The Jack Kerouac Collection (collection), 812

The Last Poets (Last Poets), 813

The Revolution Will Not Be Televised (Scott-Heron), 815

You're Getting Better: The Word Jazz Dot Masters (Nordine), 814

jazz and the classics: third stream, 1030–1043

Alabama Concerto (Brooks), 1033

All That Is Tied (Blake), 1031.1

★*The Birth of the Third Stream* (collection), 1030

Collaboration: West (Charles), 1035.1

collections, 1030

The 80th Birthday Concert (Russell), 1043.2

Escalator over the Hill (Bley), 1032

Ezz-Thetics (Russell), 1043.1

A Genuine Tong Funeral / Lofty Fake Anagram (Burton), 1034

Golden Striker / Jazz Abstractions (Lewis), 1041

How Time Passes (Ellis), 1037

Jazz in the Space Age (Russell), 1043.3

The Jazz Workshop (Russell), 1043.4

★*The Jimmy Giuffre 3 / Trav'lin' Light* (Giuffre), 1038

Legrand Jazz (Legrand), 1040

Monk Suite (Kronos Quartet), 1039

Short Life of Barbara Monk (Blake), 1031.2

Skies of America (Coleman), 1036

The Teddy Charles Tentet (Charles), 1035.2

Third Stream Music (Modern Jazz Quartet), 1042

jazz and the world, 834–868

The Amazing Adventures of Simon Simon (Surman), 864

Ancora Da Capo (Ganelin Trio), 842

Astigmatic (Komeda), 851

Balladyna (Stanko), 863

Bele Bele en la Habana (Valdes), 865

Bluesine (Solal), 862

Bob's Gallery (Breuker), 836.1

Brikama (Dorge), 840

The Chicago Octet/Tentet (Brotzmann), 837.1

Chris McGregor's Brotherhood of Breath (McGregor), 853

Cité de la Musique (Saluzzi), 859

Codona (Walcott), 867

The Colors of Chloe (Weber), 868

Company 6 and 7 (Company), 839

The Complete Machine Gun Sessions (Brotzmann), 837.2

Dollar Brand: African Piano (Ibrahim), 847

Doughnut in One Hand (Minton), 855

Elf Bagatellen (von Schlippenbach), 866.1

Figuring (Bailey), 834

Four in One (Mengelberg), 854.1

Het Xyz Der Bik Bent Braam (Braam), 835

Historicity (Iyer), 849

ICP Orchestra: Oh My Dog (Mengelberg), 854.2

In Holland (Breuker), 836.2

Kollaps (Gratkowski), 845

Monk's Casino (von Schlippenbach), 866.2

Odyssey (Rypdal), 858

Piano Solo, Vol. 1 (Schweizer), 860

Process and Reality (Parker), 857

Rumbling (Globe Unity), 844

Self Defense! (Jang), 850

Shakti with John McLaughlin (Shakti), 861

Skies of Europe (Italian Instabile Orchestra), 848

Soft Lights and Sweet Music (Clusone 3), 838

Song for Biko (Dyani), 841

Tete! (Montoliu), 856

Three Originals: The Wide Point / Trilogue / Albert Live in Montreux (Mangelsdorff), 852

We Refuse to Be Used and Abused
(Houn), 846
Witchi-Tai-To (Garbarek), 843
jazz outside the mainstream: the
AACM, BAG, and the lofts,
912–933
Air Mail (Air), 913
*Americans Swinging in Paris: The
Pathe Sessions* (Art Ensemble of
Chicago), 915.1
Black Saint (Harper), 922
*Dark Day: Live at the Museum of
Contemporary Art / Live in Verona*
(Anderson), 914
Decision in Paradise (Lowe), 926
Deep River (Murray), 928.1
Destiny's Dance (Freeman), 921
For Alto (Braxton), 919.1
Full Force (Art Ensemble of Chicago),
915.2
The Great Pretender (Bowie), 918
Just the Facts and Pass the Bucket
(Threadgill), 932.1
Kabell Years (Smith), 931
Mixed Quintet (Jenkins), 924
Paris Concert (Circle), 920
Prophet (Lake), 925
Rainbow Gladiator (Bang), 916
Raw Materials and Residuals
(Hemphill), 923.1
Reflections ('Coon Bid'ness)
(Hemphill), 923.2
Resolution (Bluiett), 917
Revue (World Saxophone Quartet),
933.1
*Sam Rivers / Dave Holland, Vols. 1
and 2* (Rivers), 930
Sound (Mitchell), 927.1
★*Steppin' with the World Saxophone
Quartet* (World Saxophone
Quartet), 933.2
3 Compositions of New Jazz (Braxton),
919.2
3D Family (Murray), 928.2
Up Popped the Two Lips (Threadgill),
932.2
★*Urban Bushmen* (Art Ensemble of
Chicago), 915.3
Vietnam (Revolutionary Ensemble),
929
Where's Your Cup? (Threadgill), 932.3
Willisau (Quartet) 1991 (Braxton),
919.3
W.S.Q. (World Saxophone Quartet),
933.3
You Know the Number (Threadgill),
932.4
Young at Heart, Wise in Time
(Abrams), 912
jazz singers, 765–808
Abbey Is Blue (Lincoln), 790.1
Ain't Necessarily So (Bey), 773
All the Way (Scott), 800.1

Anita O'Day Live in '63 and '70
(O'Day), 797.2
Anita O'Day (O'Day), 797.1
The Audience with Betty Carter
(Carter), 774.1
Ballads: Remembering John Coltrane
(Allyson), 769
The Bebop Singers (collection), 765
Best of Dianne Reeves (Reeves), 798
*Billie Holiday / Lester Young: A Musical
Romance* (Holiday), 781.1
*Billie's Blues: Her Best Performances on
Film* (Holiday), 781.2
★*Blue Light 'til Dawn* (Wilson), 807
Body and Soul (Jefferson), 785
Carmen Sings Monk (McRae), 794.1
Circle Dancing (Clayton), 776
Classics (Frishberg), 780
Close as Pages in a Book (Sullivan),
802
Close Enough for Love (Horn), 782.1
collections, 765–767
★*The Commodore Master Takes*
(Holiday), 781.3
*The Complete Verve Studio Master
Takes* (Holiday), 781.4
The Definitive Collection (Armstrong),
771.1
Don't Go to Strangers (Jones), 786
Ella and Oscar (Fitzgerald), 779.1
★*Ella Fitzgerald and Louis Armstrong*
(Armstrong), 771.2
Ella Fitzgerald Live in '57 and '63
(Fitzgerald), 779.2
Ellington Songbook (Fitzgerald), 779.3
The Essential Jimmy Rushing (Rushing),
799
Every Day: The Best of the Verve Years
(Williams), 806.1
Falling in Love Is Wonderful (Scott),
800.2
★*George and Ira Gershwin Songbook*
(Fitzgerald), 779.4
Greatest Hits (Allison), 768
The Great American Songbook
(McRae), 794.2
Harold Arlen Songbook (Fitzgerald),
779.5
Helen Merrill (Merrill), 795
Here's to Life (Horn), 782.2
The Hottest New Group in Jazz
(Lambert, Hendricks, and Ross),
789.1
How Long Has This Been Going On?
(Vaughan), 804.1
I Can't Help It (Carter), 774.2
★*The Jazz Singers: A Smithsonian
Collection of Jazz Vocals from
1919–1994* (collection), 766
★*Ken Burns Jazz Collection: Billie
Holiday* (Holiday), 781.5
★*Ken Burns Jazz Collection: Sarah
Vaughan* (Vaughan), 804.2

★*Lady Day: The Best of* Billie Holiday
(Holiday), 781.6
*Lady Day: The Many Faces of Billie
Holiday* (Holiday), 781.7
Lady Day: The Master Takes and Singles
(Holiday), 781.8
*Lee Wiley Sings the Songs of Rodgers
and Hart and Harold Arlen* (Wiley),
805
Legendary Big Band Singers
(collection), 767
*Look to the Rainbow: Al Jarreau Live in
Europe* (Jarreau), 784
*Mack the Knife: The Complete Ella in
Berlin Concert* (Fitzgerald), 779.6
Mel Torme: The Best of the Concord
Years (Torme), 803.1
Mel Torme Swings Shubert Alley
(Torme), 803.2
The Messenger (Elling), 778
Nancy Wilson / Cannonball Adderley
(Wilson), 808
Never Make Your Move Too Soon
(Anderson), 770
Nina Simone Live in '65 and '68
(Simone), 801
No More Blues (McCorkle), 792
Nothin' but the Blues (Williams), 806.2
Original Decca Recordings (Holiday),
781.9
Portrait of Sheila (Jordan), 787
Pride and Joy (Mahogany), 791
Pure Ella (Ella Sings Gershwin)
(Fitzgerald), 779.7
Rah (Murphy), 796.1
The Rockin' Chair Lady (Bailey), 772
Sarah Vaughan Live in '58 and '64
(Vaughan), 804.5
Sarah Vaughan: The Divine One
(Vaughan), 804.4
Sarah Vaughan (Vaughan), 804.3
75th Birthday Celebration: Greatest Hits
(Fitzgerald), 779.8
Sing a Song of Basie (Lambert,
Hendricks, and Ross), 789.2
Sings Lover Man (McRae), 794.3
*Sings the Cole Porter Songbook, Vols. 1
and 2* (Fitzgerald), 779.9
Sings the George Gershwin Songbook
(Vaughan), 804.6
*Sings the Rodgers and Hart Songbook,
Vols. 1 and 2* (Fitzgerald), 779.10
Something Cool (Christy), 775
Songs I Like to Sing (Humes), 783
Swingin' Easy (Vaughan), 804.7
Timeless (Murphy), 796.2
The Very Best of Diana Krall (Krall),
788
The Voice (McFerrin), 793
Warm Cool: The Atlantic Years
(Connor), 777
You Gotta Pay the Band (Lincoln),
790.2

jazz/fusion (new age), 1326–1329
    Canyon (Winter), 1329.1
    The Essential Oregon (Oregon), 1327
    Icarus (Winter), 1329.2
    Last Night the Moon Came Dropping Its
       Clothes in the Street (Hassell), 1326
    Shadowfax (Shadowfax), 1328
    Wolf Eyes: A Retrospective (Winter),
       1329.3
The Jazztet. *The Definitive Collection*
    (songwriter collection), 1101.1
Jean, Wyclef. *The Carnival*, 2824
Jeanne and the Darlings. *The Complete*
    Stax/Volt Singles 1959–1968
    (collection), 2594
Jefferson Airplane
    Jefferson Airplane Loves You, 1838.1
    ★*Surrealistic Pillow*, 1838.2
Jefferson, Blind Lemon
    All the Classic Sides, 239.1
    Before the Blues: The Early American
       Black Music Scene; Classic
       Recordings from the 1920's and
       30's, Vols. 1–3 (collection), 183
    Best of Blind Lemon Jefferson, 239.2
    Blues Masters, Vol. 3: Texas Blues
       (collection), 311
    ★*The Blues: A Smithsonian Collection*
       of Classic Blues Singers (collection),
       145
    The Blues of Texas, Arkansas, and
       Louisiana (collection), 236
    ★*Goodbye Babylon* (collection), 2954
    ★*Legends of the Blues, Vol. 1*
       (collection), 150
    The Road to Robert Johnson and
       Beyond (collection), 221
    ★*The Story of the Blues* (collection),
       158
Jefferson, Eddie
    The Bebop Singers (collection), 765
    Body and Soul, 785
    The Complete Goldwax Singles, Vol. 2
       (collection), 2592
Jefferson Starship
    Have a Nice Decade: The '70s Pop
       Culture Box (collection), 1240
    70s Greatest Hits (collection), 1243
Jeffreys, Garland. *Ghost Writer /*
    American Boy and Girl, 1891
Jelly Belly. *Play My Juke-Box: East Coast*
    Blues (collection), 244
Jenkins, Ella
    African American Folk Songs and
       Rhythms, 3234.1
    Early, Early Childhood Songs, 3200
    Holiday Times: Songs, Stories, Rhymes
       and Chants for Christmas, Kwanzaa,
       Hanukkah, Chinese New Year, and
       St. Patrick's Day, 3245
    Multi-Cultural Children's Songs, 3234.2
    ★*You'll Sing a Song and I'll Sing a Song*,
       3219

Jenkins, Leroy. *Mixed Quintet*, 924
Jenkins, Snuffy. *16 Down Home Country*
    Classics (collection), 1385
Jennings, Waylon
    Classic Country: Kings of Country
       (collection), 1381
    Dreaming My Dreams, 1503.1
    ★*Essential Waylon Jennings*, 1503.2
    Honky Tonk Heroes, 1503.3
    Ramblin' Man, 1503.4
Jeru the Damaja
    The Sun Rises in the East, 2825.1
    Wrath of the Math, 2825.2
★Jesters. *The Doo-Wop Box* (collection),
    2322
Jesus and Mary Chain. *Psychocandy*,
    2143.1, 2143.2
Jethro Tull
    The Best of Acoustic, 1924.1
    The Very Best of Jethro Tull, 1924.2
Jett, Joan
    Fit to Be Tied: Great Hits by Joan Jett
       and the Blackhearts, 2050.1
    I Love Rock 'N' Roll, 2050.2
    The Tomorrow Show with Tom Snyder:
       Punk and New Wave (collection),
       1981
Jewel
    Pieces of You, 1276
    Whatever: The '90s Pop and Culture
       Box (collection), 1244
Jewels and Binoculars. *Floater*, 983
★Jewels. *The Doo-Wop Box* (collection),
    2322
Jim and Jesse
    Bluegrass and More, 1588.1
    Jim and Jesse, 1952–1955, 1588.2
    Jim and Jesse Story: 24 Greatest Hits,
       1588.3
Jimerson, Douglas
    Civil War, 74.2
    The Civil War, 74.1
Jive Five
    ★*The Doo Wop Box: 101 Vocal Group*
       Gems from the Golden Age of Rock
       'n' Roll (collection), 1745
    ★*The Doo-Wop Box* (collection), 2322
    The Doo-Wop Box II (collection), 2323
★Jo Ann and Troy. *Atlantic Soul, 1959–*
    1975 (collection), 2589
Jobim, Antonio Carlos. *Frank Sinatra:*
    Concert Collection, 1224.3
Jobson, Eddie. *New Age Piano Sampler*
    (collection), 1369
Joe Jeffrey Group. *Soul Shots: A Collection*
    of Sixties Soul Classics (collection),
    2443
Joel, Billy
    Duets: An American Classic (Bennett),
       1251.1
    The Essential Video Collection, 1277.1
    ★*Greatest Hits, Vols. 1 and 2*, 1277.2
    My Lives, 1245

John Abercrombie Quartet. *Live from the*
    Village Vanguard (collection), 935
John, Elton
    Billboard #1s: The '70s (collection),
       1235
    Duets: An American Classic (Bennett),
       1251.1
    Greatest Hits, Vol. 2, 1925.2
    ★*Greatest Hits, Vol. 1*, 1925.1
John, Little Willie
    ★*Fever: The Best of* Little Willie John,
       2269.1
    The Very Best of Little Willie John,
       2269.2
Johnnie and Jack. *Best of Johnnie and*
    Jack, 1504
Johnnie and Joe. *The Doo-Wop Box II*
    (collection), 2323
Johnny and the Hurricanes. *Let There*
    Be Drums, Vol. 1: The '50s
    (collection), 1751
Johnny Otis Band. *The Swing Time*
    Records Story: R&B, Blues, and
    Gospel, 1946–1952 (collection),
    2430
Johnny Thunders and the Heartbreakers.
    L.A.M.F., 1990
Johnson, Big Jack. *All the Way Back*, 444
Johnson, Blind Willie
    Before the Blues: The Early American
       Black Music Scene; Classic
       Recordings from the 1920's and
       30's, Vols. 1–3 (collection), 183
    ★*The Blues: A Smithsonian Collection*
       of Classic Blues Singers (collection),
       145
    The Complete Blind Willie Johnson,
       2984
    A First-Time Buyer's Guide to American
       Negro Spirituals (collection), 32
    Gospel: Negro Spirituals / Gospel Songs,
       1926–1942 (collection), 2963
    ★*The Gospel Sound* (collection), 2964
    The Gospel Tradition: The Roots and the
       Branches, Vol. 1 (collection), 2955
    The Great Depression: American Music
       in the '30s (collection), 1066
    The Half Ain't Never Been Told, Vols. 1
       and 2 (collection), 2956
    Preachin' the Gospel: Holy Blues
       (collection), 2979
    The Roots of Rap: Classic Recordings
       of the 1920's and 30's (collection),
       157
    Songsters and Saints: Vocal Traditions
       on Race Records, Vol. 2
       (collection), 191
Johnson, Buddy
    Buddy and Ella Johnson: 1953–1964,
       2270.1
    Songs That Got Us through World
       War II, Vol. 2 (collection), 1086
    ★*The R&B Box* (collection), 2239

Walk 'Em: The Decca Sessions,
    2270.2
Johnson, Bunk
    *Classic African American Gospel from
        Smithsonian Folkways* (collection),
        2959
    ★*The Commodore Story* (collection), 561
    The King of the Blues, 507
Johnson, Earl
    *The Big Horn: The History of the
        Honkin' and Screamin' Saxophone*
        (collection), 2314
    ★*Stompin' at the Savoy: The
        Original Indie Label, 1944–1961*
        (collection), 2429
Johnson, Ella. *Legendary Big Band Singers*
    (collection), 767
Johnson, George W. *Phono-Cylinders,
    Vols. 1 and 2* (collection), 1074
Johnson, Hawkins, Tatum and Durr.
    Eccentric Soul: The Capsoul Label
    (collection), 2599
Johnson, J. J.
    ★*The Birth of the Third Stream*
        (collection), 1030
    ★*The Eminent J. J. Johnson, Vols. 1
        and 2,* 646.1
    Origins: The Savoy Sessions, 598
    13 Original Songs, 646.2
    Trombone Master, 646.3
Johnson, Jack. *Sing-a-Longs and Lullabies
    for the Film Curious George,* 3220
Johnson, James P.
    ★*From Spirituals to Swing: The
        Legendary 1938 and 1939 Carnegie
        Hall Concerts Produced by John
        Hammond* (collection), 564
    The Greatest Ragtime of the Century
        (collection), 125
    ★*Harlem Stride Piano,* 523
    ★*Ken Burns Jazz: The Story of
        America's Music* (collection), 478
    Riverside History of Classic Jazz
        (collection), 499
    ★*The Smithsonian Collection of Classic
        Jazz* (collection), 486
Johnson, Jimmy
    Blues Fest: Modern Blues of the '70s
        (collection), 408
    Johnson's Whacks, 445
    Living Chicago Blues, Vol. 1 (collection),
        415
    Stars of the Apollo (collection), 2240
Johnson, Leslie Carswell. *See* Lazy Lester
Johnson, Lil
    *Raunchy Business: Hot Nuts and
        Lollypops* (collection), 269
    *When the Sun Goes Down 3: That's
        Chicago's South Side* (collection), 270
Johnson, Lonnie
    *Acoustic Country Blues Guitar: Delta
        Blues before Robert Johnson*
        (collection), 211

*Back to the Crossroads: The Roots of
    Robert Johnson* (collection), 212
★*Blues Classics* (collection), 146
★*The Blues: A Smithsonian Collection
    of Classic Blues Singers* (collection),
    145
★*Legends of the Blues, Vol. 1*
    (collection), 150
A Life in Music, 275.1
Pioneers of the Jazz Guitar (collection),
    511
Progressions: 100 Years of Jazz Guitar
    (collection), 481
*Raunchy Business: Hot Nuts and
    Lollypops* (collection), 269
*The Road to Robert Johnson and
    Beyond* (collection), 221
★*Steppin' on the Blues,* 275.2
*Violin, Sing the Blues for Me: African-
    American Fiddlers* (collection), 192
*When the Sun Goes Down 3: That's
    Chicago's South Side* (collection),
    270
Johnson, Lou. *The Look of Love: The Burt
    Bacharach Collection* (collection),
    1161
Johnson, Louise
    ★*Juke Joint Saturday Night: Piano
        Blues, Rags and Stomps; Classic
        Recordings from the 1920s and '30s*
        (collection), 255
    ★*Masters of the Delta Blues: The Friends
        of Charlie Patton* (collection), 220
Johnson, Luther. *Living Chicago Blues,
    Vol. 4* (collection), 418
Johnson, Marc. *Bass Desires,* 984
Johnson, Marv. *The Best of* Marv
    Johnson: You've Got What It
    Takes, 2271
Johnson Mountain Boys
    At the Old Schoolhouse, 1589.1
    Blue Diamond, 1589.2
    Blue Ribbon Bluegrass (collection),
        1563
    *Hand-Picked: 25 Years of Bluegrass on
        Rounder Records* (collection), 1564
Johnson, Pete
    Barrelhouse Boogie (collection), 250,
        521
    ★*Cuttin' the Boogie: Piano Blues and
        Boogie Woogie* (collection), 251
    ★*From Spirituals to Swing: The
        Legendary 1938 and 1939 Carnegie
        Hall Concerts Produced by John
        Hammond* (collection), 564
    Hey! Piano Man (collection), 254
    ★*Ken Burns Jazz: The Story of
        America's Music* (collection), 478
    *The Real Kansas City of the '20s, '30s,
        and '40s* (collection), 552
    ★*Stompin' at the Savoy: The
        Original Indie Label, 1944–1961*
        (collection), 2429

*The Swing Time Records Story: R&B,
    Blues, and Gospel, 1946–1952*
    (collection), 313, 2430
*When the Sun Goes Down 4: That's All
    Right* (collection), 271
Johnson, Plas. *The Big Horn: The History
    of the Honkin' and Screamin'
    Saxophone* (collection), 2314
Johnson, Ray. *The Mercury New
    Orleans Sessions 1950 and 1953*
    (collection), 2361
Johnson, Robert
    *Acoustic Country Blues Guitar: Delta
        Blues before Robert Johnson*
        (collection), 211
    Blues Masters, Vol. 6: Blues Originals
        (collection), 367
    *Blues Masters, Vol. 8: Mississippi Delta
        Blues* (collection), 215
    ★*The Blues: A Smithsonian Collection
        of Classic Blues Singers* (collection),
        145
    ★*The Centennial Collection* (Johnson),
        225.1
    King of the Delta Blues Singers
        (Johnson), 225.2
    ★*Legends of the Blues, Vol. 1*
        (collection), 150
    The New Transcriptions, 225.3
    *The Road to Robert Johnson and
        Beyond* (collection), 221
    Robert Johnson, King of the Delta Blues,
        225.4
    The Search for Robert Johnson,
        225.5
    ★*The Story of the Blues* (collection),
        158
★Johnson, Sherman. *Nashville Jumps:
    Blues and Rhythm on Nashville
    Independent Labels 1945–1955*
    (collection), 2376
Johnson, Stump. *Twenty First Street
    Stomp: Piano Blues of St. Louis*
    (collection), 259
Johnson, Syl
    ★*Complete Mythology,* 2488.1
    *The Complete Syl Johnson on Hi
        Records,* 2488.2
    *Dave Godin's Deep Soul Treasures,
        Vols. 1–4* (collection), 2435
    The Hi Records Story (collection),
        2423
Johnson, Theard. *The Mercury New
    Orleans Sessions 1950 and 1953*
    (collection), 2361
Johnson, Tommy
    *Blues Masters, Vol. 8: Mississippi Delta
        Blues* (collection), 215
    ★*The Blues: A Smithsonian Collection
        of Classic Blues Singers* (collection),
        145
    *Canned Heat Blues: Masters of Delta
        Blues* (collection), 216

Johnson, Tommy (cont.)
Legends of Country Blues (collection), 218
★*Masters of the Delta Blues: The Friends of Charlie Patton* (collection), 220
The Roots of Rock (collection), 368
When the Sun Goes Down 2: The First Time I Met the Blues (collection), 160
When the Sun Goes Down 1: Walk Right In (collection), 159
Johnson, Turner Junior. *Negro Religious Songs and Services* (collection), 2977
Johnston, Daniel
Fun, 1875.2
The Devil and Daniel Johnston, 1875.1
Jolson, Al
★*American Popular Song: Six Decades of Songwriters and Singers* (collection), 1059
★*The Best of* Al Jolson, 1137.1
Fascinating Rhythm: George Gershwin (songwriter collection), 1101.2
George Gershwin (songwriter collection), 1101.3
Irving Berlin (songwriter collection), 1096.1
The Jazz Singer, 1137.2
Joe Franklin Presents . . . The Roaring '20s Roar Again (collection), 1069
The Phonographic Yearbook, 1922: An Angel's Voice I Hear (collection), 1078
The Phonographic Yearbook, 1912: Waitin' on the Levee (collection), 1077
★*Praise the Lord and Pass the Ammunition: Songs of World Wars I and II* (collection), 1079
The Roaring 'Twenties (collection), 1080
This Is Art Deco (collection), 1090
25 Sweethearts of Yesteryear (collection), 1092
★*Yes, Sir, That's My Baby: The Golden Years of Tin Pan Alley* (collection), 1094
Jones, A. C. *Boddie Recording Company Cleveland, Ohio* (collection), 2569, 2570
Jones, Ada
Phono-Cylinders, Vols. 1 and 2 (collection), 1074
The Phonographic Yearbook, 1907: Dear Old Golden Rule Days (collection), 1075
The Phonographic Yearbook, 1908: Take Me Out with the Crowd (collection), 1076
The Phonographic Yearbook, 1912: Waitin' on the Levee (collection), 1077

Jones Brothers Trio. *The Half Ain't Never Been Told, Vols. 1 and 2* (collection), 2956
Jones, Canton. *Dominionaire,* 3176
Jones, Coley
★*Anthology of American Folk Music, Vols. 1–3* (collection), 1386
Texas Blues: Early Blues Masters from the Lone Star State (collection), 237
★Jones, Davey. *Nuggets II: Original Artifacts from the British Empire and Beyond* (collection), 1791
Jones, Eddie. *See* Guitar Slim
Jones, Elder Otis. *American Primitive, Vol. 1: Raw Pre-War Gospel* (collection), 2976
Jones, Etta
Don't Go to Strangers, 786
★*The Jazz Singers: A Smithsonian Collection of Jazz Vocals from 1919–1994* (collection), 766
Jones, Floyd
Chicago Is Just That Way (collection), 289
Drop Down Mama (collection), 292
Jones, George
Anniversary: Ten Years of Hits, 1505.1
The Best of George Jones, 1505.2
Classic Country: Kings of Country (collection), 1381
Classic Country Music: A Smithsonian Collection (collection), 1382
★*The Essential George Jones: The Spirit of Country,* 1505.3
George Jones: Live Recordings from Church Street Station!, 1505.4
The Hee Haw Collection, Vol. 3 (collection), 1451
She Thinks I Still Care: The Complete United Artists Recordings, 1962–1964, 1505.5
Jones, Gloria. *Beg, Scream, and Shout! The Big Ol' Box of '60s Soul* (collection), 2433
Jones, Grace. *Nightclubbing,* 2648
Jones, Grandpa
All-Time Country and Western Hits (collection), 1449
Favorite Sacred Songs (collection), 3109
28 Greatest Hits, 1506
Jones, Hank. *Live at Maybeck Recital Hall, Vol. 16,* 883
Jones, Isham. *The Phonographic Yearbook, 1922: An Angel's Voice I Hear* (collection), 1078
Jones, Jack
Cy Coleman (songwriter collection), 1098.2
James Van Heusen (songwriter collection), 1112.1

Jones, Jimmy. *Eccentric Soul: Twinight's Lunar Rotation* (collection), 2568
Jones, Johnny
Night Train to Nashville: Music City Rhythm and Blues, 1945–1970, Vol. 1 (collection), 2377
Night Train to Nashville: Music City Rhythm and Blues, 1945–1970, Vol. 2 (collection), 2378
Jones, Lewis. *The Fire / Fury Records Story* (collection), 2422
Jones, Linda. *The Best of Loma Records: The Rise and Fall of a 1960's Soul Label* (collection), 2590
Jones, Little Hat
The Blues of Texas, Arkansas, and Louisiana (collection), 236
Texas Blues: Early Blues Masters from the Lone Star State (collection), 237
★Jones, Little Johnny. *Chess Blues* (collection), 287
Jones, Marshall. *The Fire / Fury Records Story* (collection), 2422
Jones, Michael
Narada Decade: The Anniversary Collection (collection), 1367
Piano Solos: Narada Artists (collection), 1370
Pianoscapes: Deluxe Edition, 1349.1
Solos and Sketches for New Age Piano, 1349.2
Jones, Ms. Tyree "Sugar." *Eccentric Soul: The Big Mack Label* (collection), 2598
Jones, Norah. *Come Away with Me,* 1278
Jones, Quincy
Big Band Renaissance: The Evolution of the Jazz Orchestra (collection), 739
The Definitive Collection (songwriter collection), 1101.1
Quincy Jones' Finest Hour, 904
Quincy Jones Live in '60, 756
Jones, Rickie Lee. *Rickie Lee Jones,* 2051
Jones, Russell Tyrone. *See* Ol' Dirty Bastard
Jones, Sharon. *100 Days, 100 Nights,* 2489
Jones, Spike
At His Very Best, 1202.1
★*Billboard Greatest Christmas Hits, 1935–1954* (collection), 3293
Dr. Demento Presents: The Greatest Christmas Novelty CD of All Time (collection), 3307
It's a Spike Jones Christmas, 3334
★*Nipper's Greatest Hits: The 40's, Vol. 1* (collection), 1073
★*Praise the Lord and Pass the Ammunition: Songs of World Wars I and II* (collection), 1079
The Spike Jones Story, 1202.2

Jones, Thad
    Big Band Renaissance: The Evolution of the Jazz Orchestra (collection), 739
    Live at the Village Vanguard, 757
Jones, Thelma. *Respect: Aretha's Influences and Inspiration* (collection), 2440
Jones, Tom
    The Look of Love: The Burt Bacharach Collection (collection), 1161
    Reloaded: Greatest Hits, 1279
Joneses. *The Spring Story: Essential 70s Soul* (collection), 2608
Joplin, Janis. *Pearl,* 1839
Joplin, Scott
    Classic Ragtime from Rare Piano Rolls, 135.1
    Complete Piano Rags, 135.2
    The Complete Rags, Marches and Waltzes, 135.3
    Elite Syncopations: Classic Ragtime from Rare Piano Rolls 1899–1918, 135.4
    Elite Syncopations: Classic Ragtime from Rare Piano Rolls, 1899–1917, 135.5
    Euphonic Sounds: The Music of Scott Joplin, 135.6
    Greatest Hits, 135.7
    The Greatest Ragtime of the Century (collection), 125
    Piano Rags, 135.8
    Piano Works, 1899–1904, 135.9
    Rags and Waltzes, 135.10
    Rags to Riches: The Essential Hits, 135.11
    Rag-Time Music, 135.13
    Ragtime: The Music of Scott Joplin, 135.12
    The Red Back Book: Elite Syncopations, 135.14
    Riverside History of Classic Jazz (collection), 499
    Scott Joplin: His Complete Works, 135.15
    Scott Joplin: King of Ragtime Writers from Classic Piano Rolls, 135.16
Jordan, Charlie. *St. Louis Blues: The Depression* (collection), 232
Jordan, Louis
    The Best of Louis Jordan, 2318.1
    Bing Crosby and Some Jazz Friends (Crosby), 1125.2
    Blue Yule: Christmas Blues and R&B Classics (collection), 3295
    ★*Blues Classics* (collection), 146
    ★*The Blues: A Smithsonian Collection of Classic Blues Singers* (collection), 145
    ★*The Jazz Singers: A Smithsonian Collection of Jazz Vocals from 1919–1994* (collection), 766
    Let the Good Times Roll: The Anthology, 1938–1953, 2318.2
    ★*Let the Good Times Roll: The Complete Decca Recordings 1938–1954,* 2318.3
    Louis Jordan and His Tympany 5, 2318.4
    Louis Jordan and His Tympany Five, 2318.5
    ★*Mean Old World: The Blues from 1940–1994* (collection), 154
    Songs That Got Us through World War II, Vol. 2 (collection), 1086
    ★*The R&B Box* (collection), 2239
    The Roots of Rock 'n' Roll, 1946–1954 (collection), 1755
Jordan, Luke
    The Roots of Rap: Classic Recordings of the 1920's and 30's (collection), 157
    Songsters and Saints: Vocal Traditions on Race Records, Vol. 2 (collection), 191
Jordan, Montell. *Standing in the Shadows of Motown* (collection), 2445
Jordan River Singers. *The Best of Nashboro Gospel* (collection), 3032
Jordan, Sheila. *Portrait of Sheila,* 787
Joseph, Margie. *The Complete Stax/Volt Soul Singles, Vol. 2: 1968–1971* (collection), 2595
Jourdan, Louis. *Alan Jay Lerner* (songwriter collection), 1105.1
Journey. *Escape,* 2079
Joy Division
    Closer, 2035.1
    No Thanks! The '70s Punk Rebellion (collection), 2003
    ★*Unknown Pleasures,* 2035.2
Jubilee Singers. *A First-Time Buyer's Guide to American Negro Spirituals* (collection), 32
Judas Priest
    Heavy Metal: The First 20 Years (collection), 1938
    Metal Works, 1947
The Judds
    Classic Country Music: A Smithsonian Collection (collection), 1382
    Number One Hits, 1657
jug bands. *See* songsters, string bands, and jug bands
Julian, Don and the Meadowlarks
    The Doo-Wop Box II (collection), 2323
    Heaven and Paradise, 2344
The Julius Hemphill Sextet. *Hard Blues,* 985
jump blues, 2314–2319
    Apollo Jump (Millinder), 2319.1
    The Best of Louis Jordan, 2318.1
    The Big Horn: The History of the Honkin' and Screamin' Saxophone (collection), 2314
    Breakin' Up the House (Bradshaw), 2316.1
    The Earl Bostic Story, 2315.1
    The EP Collection (Bostic), 2315.2
    The EP Collection–Plus (Bradshaw), 2316.2
    Jump Jack Jump! (Carr), 2317
    Let the Good Times Roll: The Anthology, 1938–1953 (Jordan), 2318.2
    ★*Let the Good Times Roll: The Complete Decca Recordings 1938–1954* (Jordan), 2318.3
    Louis Jordan and His Tympany 5, 2318.4
    Louis Jordan and His Tympany Five, 2318.5
    The Very Best of Lucky Millinder, 2319.2
Jun, Rose Marie. *Don't Give the Name a Bad Place: Types and Stereotypes in American Musical Theater, 1870–1900* (collection), 1063
Jungle Brothers
    Done by the Forces of Nature, 2826.1
    ★*Straight out the Jungle,* 2826.2
Jurado, Damien. *For the Kids Three!* (collection), 3209
Jurassic 5
    Power in Numbers, 2827.1
    Quality Control, 2827.2
★Justice, Dick. *Anthology of American Folk Music, Vols. 1–3* (collection), 1386
Juvenile. *400 Degreez,* 2828
Jyväskylä Sinfonia. *The 18th Century American Overture,* 55

K

Kaiser, Henry. *Friends and Enemies,* 2129
Kaldirons. *Eccentric Soul: Twinight's Lunar Rotation* (collection), 2568
Kallen, Kitty
    Duke Ellington (songwriter collection), 1099.1
    Jule Styne (songwriter collection), 1111.1
    ★*Sentimental Journey: Pop Vocal Classics, Vol. 3* (collection), 1169
Kallick, Kathy. *Angels Are Singing: A Women's Bluegrass Gospel Collection,* 1559
Kam. *Neva Again,* 2829
Kane, Big Daddy
    It's a Big Daddy Thing, 2830.1
    Long Live the Kane, 2830.2
Kane, Helen
    Flappers, Vamps, and Sweet Young Things (collection), 1065
    The Roaring 'Twenties (collection), 1080
Kansas City and other territory bands, 551–557
    America's #1 Band (Basie), 553.1
    Bennie Moten's Kansas City Orchestra (Moten), 557

Kansas City and other territory bands (cont.)
    Blues from Kansas City (McShann), 556
    collections, 551–552
    ★*The Complete Decca Recordings*
        (Basie), 553.2
    Count Basie: Swingin' the Blues (Basie),
        553.3
    Harlan Leonard and His Rockets
        (Leonard), 555
    Kansas City Powerhouse (Basie), 553.4
    ★*Ken Burns Jazz Collection: Count
        Basie* (Basie), 553.5
    Last of the Blue Devils (collection), 551
    ★*Mary's Idea* (Kirk), 554
    *The Real Kansas City of the '20s, '30s,
        and '40s* (collection), 552
Kansas City Chorale. *Alleluia: An
    American Hymnal,* 15
Kansas City Soul Revivers. *Powerhouse
    Gospel on Independent Labels*
    (collection), 3038
Karnes, Alfred G. *Mountain Gospel: The
    Sacred Roots of Country Music*
    (collection), 3113
Kat Mandu. *The Best of T. K. Disco*
    (collection), 2656
Kaufman, Alan. *Beginning Old-Time Fiddle,*
    1389
Kavetts. *Birth of Soul: Special Chicago
    Edition* (collection), 2566
Kaye, Danny
    From Berlin to Broadway: A Selection
        (songwriter collection), 1115.2
    Vintage Children's Favorites
        (collection), 3211
★Kaye, Sammy. *Nipper's Greatest Hits: The
    40's, Vol. 1* (collection), 1073
Kazan, Lainie. *Cy Coleman* (songwriter
    collection), 1098.2
Kazee, Buell
    ★*Anthology of American Folk Music,
        Vols. 1–3* (collection), 1386
    Old-Time Mountain Ballads
        (collection), 1390
KC and the Sunshine Band
    The Best of T. K. Disco (collection),
        2656
    Complete Introduction to Disco
        (collection), 1237
    Disco Box (collection), 2644
    ★*Saturday Night Fever,* 2658
K-Doe, Ernie
    *Crescent City Soul: The Sound of New
        Orleans, 1947–1974* (collection),
        2564
    *Finger Poppin' and Stompin' Feet: 20
        Classic Allen Toussaint Productions
        for Minit Records, 1960–1962*
        (collection), 2359
Keaggy, Phil. *Phil Keaggy and Sunday's
    Child,* 3152
Keane, Brian. *The War That Made
    America,* 56

Kee, John P.
    Essential John P. Kee, 3066
    Story of Gospel Music (collection),
        2973
    Testify! The Gospel Box (collection),
        2974
Keen, Robert Earl, Jr. *Best,* 1706
Keith, Toby. *The Best of* Toby Keith, 1658
Keller, Greta
    *Flappers, Vamps, and Sweet Young
        Things* (collection), 1065
    ★*Sophisticated Ladies* (collection), 1087
Kelley, Jack. *Memphis Shakedown: More
    Jug Band Classics* (collection), 186
Kellum, Murray. *The Hi Records Story*
    (collection), 2423
Kelly, Gene
    Cole Porter (songwriter collection),
        1108.1
    Frank Sinatra: Concert Collection,
        1224.3
    Hit Parade, 1943 (collection), 1157
Kelly, Herman, and Life. *The Best of T. K.
    Disco* (collection), 2656
Kelly, Jack
    Blues Masters, Vol. 12: Memphis Blues
        (collection), 229
    *Ruckus Juice and Chittlins: The Great
        Jug Bands—Classic Recordings
        of the 1920s and '30s, Vol. 1*
        (collection), 188
    *Ruckus Juice and Chittlins: The Great
        Jug Bands—Classic Recordings
        of the 1920s and '30s, Vol. 2*
        (collection), 189
    *Violin, Sing the Blues for Me: African-
        American Fiddlers* (collection), 192
Kelly, Paul. *Eccentric Soul: The Deep City
    Label* (collection), 2600
Kelly, R.
    *R. Kelly as Mr. Showbiz: The Light It Up
        Tour,* 2408.1
    ★*The R in R&B Collection, Vol. 1,*
        2408.2
Kemp, Hal
    *The Best of Hal Kemp and His
        Orchestra,* 1138.1
    Got a Date with an Angel, 1138.2
    *The Great Depression: American Music
        in the '30s* (collection), 1066
Kendricks, Eddie
    *Heaven Must Have Sent You: The
        Holland/Dozier/Holland Story*
        (collection), 2436
    *Hitsville USA: The Motown Singles
        Collection, Vol. 2* (collection), 2604
    *The Motown Solo Albums, Vol. 1: Keep
        on Truckin',* 2490.1
    *The Motown Solo Albums, Vol. 2: The
        Thin Man,* 2490.2
    The Ultimate Collection, 2490.3
★Kendricks, Nat. *Atlantic Soul,
    1959–1975* (collection), 2589

Kennedy, Jon. *The Complete Goldwax
    Singles, Vol. 1* (collection), 2591
Kenner, Chris
    *Crescent City Soul: The Sound of New
        Orleans, 1947–1974* (collection),
        2564
    I Like It Like That: Golden Classics, 2272
Kenny G. *The Ultimate Kenny G,* 1271
Kenton, Stan
    The Best of Stan Kenton, 758.1
    ★*Big Band Jazz: From the Beginnings to
        the Fifties* (collection), 529
    *Big Band Renaissance: The Evolution of
        the Jazz Orchestra* (collection), 739
    ★*New Concepts of Artistry in Rhythm,*
        758.2
Kentucky Colonels. *Appalachian Swing!,*
    1590
Kentucky Mountain Choristers. *The Half
    Ain't Never Been Told, Vols. 1 and 2*
    (collection), 2956
Kentucky Ramblers
    ★*Goodbye Babylon* (collection), 2954
    *The Half Ain't Never Been Told,
        Vols. 1 and 2* (collection), 2956
Keppard, Freddie. *Freddie Keppard: The
    Complete Set,* 500
Kern, Jerome
    Jerome Kern Collection (songwriter
        collection), 1104.2
    Jerome Kern (songwriter collection),
        1104.1
Kessel, Barney
    The Poll Winners, 614
    Progressions: 100 Years of Jazz Guitar
        (collection), 481
Keys, Alicia
    Alicia Keys Unplugged, 2384.1
    Songs in A Minor, 2384.2
Keytones. *Old Town Doo-Wop, Vols. 1–3*
    (collection), 2324
Khan, Chaka. *Standing in the Shadows of
    Motown* (collection), 2445
Khumalo, Sibongile. *Dreamland: World
    Lullabies and Soothing Songs*
    (collection), 3263
Kid Creole. *Going Places: The August
    Darnell Years 1976–1983,* 2649
Kid Cudi. *Man on the Moon: The End of
    the Day,* 2832
Kid Frost. *Hispanic Causing Panic,* 2833
Kid King's Combo
    ★*Nashville Jumps: Blues and Rhythm
        on Nashville Independent Labels
        1945–1955* (collection), 2376
    *Night Train to Nashville: Music City
        Rhythm and Blues, 1945–1970,
        Vol. 1* (collection), 2377
Kid Koala. *Carpal Tunnel Syndrome,* 2834
Kid 'n' Play. *2 Hype,* 2831
Kidjo, Angelique. *Dreamland: World
    Lullabies and Soothing Songs*
    (collection), 3263

Kilcher, Jewel. *See* Jewel

Killens, Johnny K and the Dynamics. *Eccentric Soul: The Deep City Label* (collection), 2600

Kimbrough, Junior
  All Night Long, 446
  ★*Mean Old World: The Blues from 1940–1994* (collection), 154

★Kimbrough, Lottie. *I Can't Be Satisfied: Early American Women Blues Singers, Vol. 1: Country* (collection), 149

King, Albert
  The Best *of* Albert King, 353.1
  Blues Fest: Modern Blues of the '70s (collection), 408
  Blues Masters, Vol. 7: Blues Revival (collection), 390
  Blues Masters, Vol. 1: Urban Blues (collection), 338
  The Complete King and Bobbin Recordings, 353.2
  The Complete Stax/Volt Singles 1959–1968 (collection), 2594
  The Complete Stax/Volt Soul Singles, Vol. 2: 1968–1971 (collection), 2595
  ★*King of the Blues Guitar,* 353.3
  Live Wire / Blues Power, 353.4
  ★*Mean Old World: The Blues from 1940–1994* (collection), 154
  More Big Blues, 353.5
  Superblues: All-Time Classic Blues Hits, Vol. 1 (collection), 347
  Top of the Stax, Vol. 2: Twenty Greatest Hits (collection), 2612
  The Ultimate Collection, 353.6
  The Very Best of Albert King [1999], 353.7
  The Very Best of Albert King [2002], 353.8

King, B. B.
  Anthology, 354.1
  B. B. King Anthology, 354.3
  B. B. King: The King of the Blues, 354.2
  Blue Flames: A Sun Blues Collection (collection), 337
  ★*Blues Classics* (collection), 146
  Blues Fest: Modern Blues of the '70s (collection), 408
  Blues Masters, Vol. 12: Memphis Blues (collection), 229
  Blues Masters, Vol. 8: Mississippi Delta Blues (collection), 215
  Blues Masters, Vol. 9: Postmodern Blues (collection), 412
  50 Years: The Artistry of Tony Bennett (Bennett), 1179.2
  Gold, 354.4
  How Blue Can You Get? Classic Live Performances, 354.5
  ★*Live at the Regal,* 354.6

★*Mean Old World: The Blues from 1940–1994* (collection), 154

The Modern Records Blues Story (collection), 342

★*Nashville Jumps: Blues and Rhythm on Nashville Independent Labels 1945–1955* (collection), 2376

Original Greatest Hits, 354.7

★*The R&B Box* (collection), 2239

The Roots of Rock 'n' Roll, 1946–1954 (collection), 1755

Soul Shots, Vol. 4: Urban Blues (collection), 343

Superblues: All-Time Classic Blues Hits, Vol. 1 (collection), 347

The Ultimate Collection, 354.8

★King Bees. *Atlantic Vocal Groups, 1951–1963* (collection), 2320

King, Ben E.
  ★*Atlantic R&B, 1947–1974* (collection), 2418
  ★*Atlantic Soul, 1959–1975* (collection), 2589
  Beg, Scream, and Shout! The Big Ol' Box of '60s Soul (collection), 2433
  Dave Godin's Deep Soul Treasures, Vols. 1–4 (collection), 2435
  Respect: Aretha's Influences and Inspiration (collection), 2440
  The Very Best of Ben E. King, 2491

★King, Carole. *Tapestry,* 1892

King Casuals. *Night Train to Nashville: Music City Rhythm and Blues, 1945–1970, Vol. 2* (collection), 2378

King, Chris Thomas. *Cry of the Prophets,* 447

King Crimson. *The Condensed 21st Century Guide to King Crimson, 1969–2003,* 1961

King Crooners
  The Best of Excello Records (collection), 327
  Southern Rhythm 'n' Rock: The Best of Excello Records, Vol. 22 (collection), 2427

King Curtis and the Noble Knights. *The Fire / Fury Records Story* (collection), 2422

King, Earl
  Best of Ace Records, Vol. 2: The R&B Hits (collection), 2419
  Come On: The Complete Imperial Recordings, 2365.1
  Crescent City Soul: The Sound of New Orleans, 1947–1974 (collection), 2564
  Earl's Pearls: The Very Best of Earl King, 2365.2

King, Evelyn "Champagne"
  Disco Box (collection), 2644
  Evelyn "Champagne" King Greatest Hits, 2650

King, Freddie
  Blues Masters, Vol. 3: Texas Blues (collection), 311
  The Freddie King Collection, 355.1
  ★*Mean Old World: The Blues from 1940–1994* (collection), 154
  ★*Texas Music, Vol. 1: Postwar Blues Combos* (collection), 316
  Ultimate Collection, 355.2
  The Very Best of Freddy King, Vol. 1, 355.3

King, Gene. *Eccentric Soul: The Prix Label* (collection), 2601

King James Version. *Boddie Recording Company Cleveland, Ohio* (collection), 2569, 2570

King, Joe. *Eccentric Soul: The Prix Label* (collection), 2601

★King, Julius. *Nashville Jumps: Blues and Rhythm on Nashville Independent Labels 1945–1955* (collection), 2376

King, Little Jimmy. *Something Inside of Me,* 448

King, Morgana. *Cy Coleman* (songwriter collection), 1098.2

King, Pee Wee
  Biggest Hits/Country Barn Dance, 1411
  ★*Nipper's Greatest Hits: The 50's, Vol. 1* (collection), 1163

King Pleasure. *The Bebop Singers* (collection), 765

King, Riley B. *See* King, B. B.

King, Sandra. *Night Train to Nashville: Music City Rhythm and Blues, 1945–1970, Vol. 2* (collection), 2378

★King Sisters. *Nipper's Greatest Hits: The 40's, Vol. 1* (collection), 1073

King, Teddi
  ★*American Popular Song: Six Decades of Songwriters and Singers* (collection), 1059
  Harry Warren (songwriter collection), 1114
  Hoagy Carmichael (songwriter collection), 1097.2
  In the Beginning: The Complete Recordings, 1949–1954, 1203
  Irving Berlin (songwriter collection), 1096.1
  Jerome Kern (songwriter collection), 1104.1
  Oscar Hammerstein II (songwriter collection), 1102

King Tubby. *Roots of Dub,* 2221

★King, Wayne. *Nipper's Greatest Hits: The 30's, Vol. 1* (collection), 1072

Kinglets. *Night Train to Nashville: Music City Rhythm and Blues, 1945–1970, Vol. 2* (collection), 2378

Kings of Harmony. *All of My Appointed Time: Forty Years of a Cappella Gospel Singing* (collection), 2958

King's Singers. *A Little Christmas Music,* 3279

The Kingsmen
All Time Favorites, 3127
The Scepter Records Story (collection), 2426

The Kinks
Legends of Guitar: Rock–The '60s, Vol. 1 (collection), 1860
The Kink Kronikles, 1798.1
★*The Ultimate Collection,* 1798.2

The Kinsey Report
Blues Fest: Modern Blues of the '80s (collection), 409
Edge of the City, 449
The New Bluebloods (collection), 419

Kirby, John. *Complete Columbia and RCA Victor Recordings,* 580

Kirk, Andy
An Anthology of Big Band Swing (collection), 528
★*Big Band Jazz: From the Beginnings to the Fifties* (collection), 529
★*Mary's Idea,* 554
The Real Kansas City of the '20s, '30s, and '40s (collection), 552

Kirk, Eddie. *The Complete Stax/Volt Singles 1959–1968* (collection), 2594

Kirk, Rahsaan Roland
Does Your House Have Lions: The Rahsaan Roland Kirk Anthology, 688.1
Rahsaan Roland Kirk Live in '63 and '67, 688.2
★*Rip, Rig, and Panic / Now Please Don't You Cry, Beautiful Edith,* 688.3

Kirkland, Eddie. *Detroit Blues: Blues from the Motor City* (collection), 291

Kirkland, Leroy. *Stars of the Apollo* (collection), 2240

Kirkland, Mike James. *Don't Sell Your Soul: The Complete Story of Mike,* 2492

Kiser, Bob. *Legends of Western Swing Guitar* (collection), 1430

Kiss. *The Very Best of Kiss,* 1948

Kitajima, Osamu. *Osamu,* 1313

Kitaro
Silk Road, Vol. 1, 1314.1
Silk Road, Vol. 2, 1314.2
Ultimate New Age (collection), 1376

Kitt, Eartha
★*Billboard Greatest Christmas Hits, 1935–1954* (collection), 3293
★*Billboard Greatest Christmas Hits, 1955–1983* (collection), 3294
Hipsters' Holiday: Vocal Jazz and R&B Classics (collection), 3313

★*Nipper's Greatest Hits: The 50's, Vol. 1* (collection), 1163
The Very Best of Cole Porter (songwriter collection), 1108.3

Kittrell, Christine
★*Nashville Jumps: Blues and Rhythm on Nashville Independent Labels 1945–1955* (collection), 2376
Night Train to Nashville: Music City Rhythm and Blues, 1945–1970, Vol. 1 (collection), 2377
Night Train to Nashville: Music City Rhythm and Blues, 1945–1970, Vol. 2 (collection), 2378

Kleinsinger, George. *Tubby the Tuba,* 3257

Knee, Bernard. *Don't Give the Name a Bad Place: Types and Stereotypes in American Musical Theater, 1870–1900* (collection), 1063

Knight Brothers. *Dave Godin's Deep Soul Treasures, Vols. 1–4* (collection), 2435

★Knight, Evelyn. *Sentimental Journey: Pop Vocal Classics, Vol. 2* (collection), 1168

Knight, Frederick. *Top of the Stax, Vol. 1: Twenty Greatest Hits* (collection), 2611

Knight, Gladys and the Pips
Beg, Scream, and Shout! The Big Ol' Box of '60s Soul (collection), 2433
Dave Godin's Deep Soul Treasures, Vols. 1–4 (collection), 2435
Essential Collection, 2541.1
The Fire / Fury Records Story (collection), 2422
Gladys Knight and the Pips and Ray Charles Live at the Greek Theatre, 2541.2
Gold, 2541.3
Hitsville USA: The Motown Singles Collection (collection), 2603
Hitsville USA: The Motown Singles Collection, Vol. 2 (collection), 2604
70s Greatest Hits (collection), 1243
The Sweetest Feeling: A Van McCoy Songbook (collection), 2447
★*The Vee-Jay Story: Celebrating 40 Years of Classic Hits* (collection), 2431

Knight, James and the Butlers. *Eccentric Soul: The Outskirts of Deep City* (collection), 2565

Knight, Jean. *Top of the Stax, Vol. 1: Twenty Greatest Hits* (collection), 2611

Knight, Marie
★*The Great Gospel Women* (collection), 2989
The Great Gospel Women, Vol. 2 (collection), 2990
Rejoice and Shout (collection), 2969

Knight, Robert. *Night Train to Nashville: Music City Rhythm and Blues, 1945–1970, Vol. 1* (collection), 2377

Knight, Tom. *The Library Boogie,* 3201

Knights. *Eccentric Soul: The Tragar and Note Labels* (collection), 2602

Knowles, R. L. *The Great Gospel Men* (collection), 2988

Koch, Greg. *Blues Guitar: Learn to Play Blues Guitar with Step-by-Step Lessons and 20 Great Blues Songs,* 164

Kodaks. *The Doo-Wop Box II* (collection), 2323

Komeda, Krzysztof. *Astigmatic,* 851

Konitz, Lee
★*Konitz Meets Mulligan,* 615.1
Subconscious Lee, 615.2

Kooks. *Colours Are Brighter: Songs for Children and Grown Ups Too* (collection), 3193

Kool and the Gang
The Best of Kool and the Gang, 1969–1976, 2633.1
Celebration: The Best of Kool and the Gang, 1979–1987, 2633.2
Complete Introduction to Disco (collection), 1237
Disco Box (collection), 2644
Like Omigod! The 80s Pop Culture Box (Totally) (collection), 1241
★*Saturday Night Fever,* 2658
Videology, 2633.3

Kool Blues. *Eccentric Soul: The Capsoul Label* (collection), 2599

Kool G Rap and DJ Polo. *The Best of Cold Chillin',* 2835

★Kool Gents. *The Vee-Jay Story: Celebrating 40 Years of Classic Hits* (collection), 2431

Kool Keith. *Black Elvis/Lost in Space,* 2836

Kostelanetz, Andre. *Irving Berlin: A Hundred Years* (songwriter collection), 1096.3

Kostia. *Piano Solos: Narada Artists* (collection), 1370

Kottke, Leo
The Music of Leo Kottke, 1325.1
★*A Shout toward Noon,* 1325.2

Kraftwerk
Autobahn, 1962.1
Minimum-Maximum, 1962.2
Trans-Europe Express, 1962.3

Krall, Diana
50 Years: The Artistry of Tony Bennett (Bennett), 1179.2
The Very Best of Diana Krall, 788
When I Look in Your Eyes, 1280

Krauss, Alison
Appalachian Stomp: Bluegrass Classics (collection), 1560

Blue Ribbon Bluegrass (collection), 1563

Every Time You Say Goodbye, 1591.1

Grand Ole Opry at Carnegie Hall (collection), 1619

Hand-Picked: 25 Years of Bluegrass on Rounder Records (collection), 1564

★*Now That I've Found You: A Collection,* 1591.2

Kress, Carl. *Pioneers of the Jazz Guitar* (collection), 511

Kristofferson, Kris. *Essential Kris Kristofferson,* 1507

Kronos Quartet. *Monk Suite,* 1039

Krupa, Gene
   ★*Ken Burns Jazz: The Story of America's Music* (collection), 478
   ★*The Smithsonian Collection of Classic Jazz* (collection), 486
   ★*Swing Time! The Fabulous Big Band Era* (collection), 1089

Krystal Generation. *Eccentric Soul: Twinight's Lunar Rotation* (collection), 2568

Kunda, Toure. *World Playground: A Musical Adventure for Kids* (collection), 3230

Kunzel, Erich. *Chiller,* 3349

Kuykendall, Pete. *Mountain Music Bluegrass Style* (collection), 1566

Kwanzaa music
   Kwanzaa for Young People (and Everyone Else!) (Mims and Moore), 3352
   The Essence of Kwanzaa (Summers), 3353
   The Kwanzaa Album (Women of the Calabash), 3354

Kweli, Talib, and Hi Tek. *Reflection Eternal [Train of Thought],* 2839

Kweli, Talib. *Quality,* 2838

Kyser, Kay
   Frank Loesser (songwriter collection), 1106.1
   Kollege of Musical Knowledge, 1139.1
   ★*Praise the Lord and Pass the Ammunition: Songs of World Wars I and II* (collection), 1079
   16 Most Requested Songs of the 1940s, Vol. 1 (collection), 1082
   16 Most Requested Songs of the 1940s, Vol. 2 (collection), 1083
   Strict Education in Music: 50 of the Best, 1139.2

L

L.A. Mass Choir
   Best of L.A. Mass Choir, 3067
   Going Up Yonder: The Best of the Gospel Choirs (collection), 3051
   Greatest Gospel Choirs (collection), 3052

label overviews
   disco, 2656–2657
   rhythm and blues, 2418–2431
   soul, 2588–2612

LaBelle, Patti
   ★*Atlantic Soul, 1959–1975* (collection), 2589
   The Early Years, 2410
   The Essential Patti LaBelle, 2409.1
   Gold, 2409.2
   Live! One Night Only, 2409.3
   ★*Love Train: The Sound of Philadelphia* (collection), 2552

Lacy, Steve
   Amarcord Nino Rota (collection), 809
   Evidence, 689.1
   The Holy la, 986.1
   Morning Joy (Live at Sunset Paris), 986.2
   Steve Lacy–Roswell Rudd Quartet: Early and Late, 986.3
   The Straight Horn of Steve Lacy, 689.2

Ladd's Black Aces. *Early Syncopated Dance Music: Cakewalks, Two-Steps, Trots and Glides* (collection), 124

Lady Gaga. *The Fame,* 1281

Ladysmith Black Mambazo. *Animal Playground* (collection), 3226

Laine, Cleo. *Cleo's Choice,* 1282

Laine, Frankie
   Golden Greats, 1204
   Moments to Remember: The Golden Hits of the '50s and '60s Live (collection), 1162
   ★*Sentimental Journey: Pop Vocal Classics, Vol. 2* (collection), 1168
   16 Most Requested Songs: The 1950s, Vol. 1 (collection), 1171
   Waller / Razaf (songwriter collection), 1113.2

Lake, Oliver. *Prophet,* 925

Lamars. *The Complete Goldwax Singles, Vol. 1* (collection), 2591

Lamb, Joseph
   American Beauties: The Rags of Joseph Lamb, 136.1
   A Study in Classic Ragtime, 136.2

Lambert, Hendricks, and Ross
   Hipsters' Holiday: Vocal Jazz and R&B Classics (collection), 3313
   The Hottest New Group in Jazz, 789.1
   ★*The Jazz Singers: A Smithsonian Collection of Jazz Vocals from 1919–1994* (collection), 766
   Sing a Song of Basie, 789.2

LaMothe, Ferdinand Joseph. *See* Morton, Jelly Roll

Lance, Major
   Beg, Scream, and Shout! The Big Ol' Box of '60s Soul (collection), 2433
   Birth of Soul: Special Chicago Edition (collection), 2566

The Story of Brunswick: The Classic Sound of Chicago Soul (collection), 2610

The Very Best of Major Lance, 2273

Lance, T., and the Coctails. *Greasy Kid Stuff* (collection), 3210

Land, Harold. *The Big Horn: The History of the Honkin' and Screamin' Saxophone* (collection), 2314

Lane, Morris. *The Big Horn: The History of the Honkin' and Screamin' Saxophone* (collection), 2314

Lang, Eddie
   Lost Chords: White Musicians and Their Contributions to Jazz (collection), 479
   New York Sessions, 515
   Pioneers of the Jazz Guitar (collection), 511
   Progressions: 100 Years of Jazz Guitar (collection), 481

lang, k.d. *Shadowland,* 1659

Langford, Frances
   Dorothy Fields (songwriter collection), 1100
   Johnny Mercer (songwriter collection), 1107.1
   ★*Sophisticated Ladies* (collection), 1087

Langstaff, John. *Christmas Day in the Morning: A Revels Celebration of the Winter Solstice,* 3285

Lanz, David
   Cristofori's Dream, 1350
   Narada Decade: The Anniversary Collection (collection), 1367
   Narada Wilderness Collection (collection), 1368
   Ultimate New Age (collection), 1376

Lanza, Mario
   American Caruso, 1205.1
   The Essential Mario Lanza, 1205.2
   Nipper's Greatest Hits: The 50's, Vol. 2 (collection), 1164
   ★*Nipper's Greatest Hits: The 50's, Vol. 1* (collection), 1163

Laongston and French. *Eccentric Soul: The Tragar and Note Labels* (collection), 2602

Larkins, Ellis. *The Definitive Collection* (songwriter collection), 1101.1

Larks. *The Doo-Wop Box II* (collection), 2323

Larue, Michel. *Songs of the American Negro Slaves,* 40

LaSalle, Denise
   The Blues Is Alright, Vol. 1 (collection), 411
   Still Trapped, 450

Last Poets. *The Last Poets,* 813, 1973

Lateef, Yusef. *Eastern Sounds,* 690

Latham, Rick. *Advanced Funk Studies,* 2493

Latimore
  ★The Blues: A Smithsonian Collection
    of Classic Blues Singers (collection),
    145
  The Blues Is Alright, Vol. 1 (collection),
    411
★Lattimore, Harlan. The Crooners
    (collection), 1062
Lattisaw, Stacy. The Very Best of Stacy
    Lattisaw, 2274
Latyrx. The Album, 2840
Lauder, Harry
  The Phonographic Yearbook, 1907:
    Dear Old Golden Rule Days
    (collection), 1075
  The Phonographic Yearbook, 1912:
    Waitin' on the Levee (collection),
    1077
Lauper, Cyndi. She's So Unusual, 2052
Laurels. Old Town Doo-Wop, Vols. 1–3
    (collection), 2324
★Laurie, Annie. The Okeh Rhythm and
    Blues Story (collection), 2425
LaVette, Bettye
  Action Speaks Louder Than Words:
    The Best of SSS International
    (collection), 2588
  ★Atlantic Soul, 1959–1975
    (collection), 2589
  Dave Godin's Deep Soul Treasures,
    Vols. 1–4 (collection), 2435
  Do Your Duty, 2494.1
  I've Got My Own Hell to Raise, 2494.2
Lawrence, Donald. Best of Donald
    Lawrence and the Tri-City Singers:
    Restoring the Years, 3068
★Lawrence, Elliot. Big Band Jazz:
    From the Beginnings to the Fifties
    (collection), 529
Lawrence, Gertrude
  Flappers, Vamps, and Sweet Young
    Things (collection), 1065
  From Berlin to Broadway: A Selection
    (songwriter collection), 1115.2
  George Gershwin (songwriter
    collection), 1101.3
  The Roaring 'Twenties (collection),
    1080
  This Is Art Deco (collection), 1090
Lawson, Doyle
  Jubilation! Great Gospel Performances,
    Vol. 3: Country Gospel (collection),
    3112
  Rock My Soul, 1592
  The Bluegrass Album, Vol. 1
    (collection), 1562
  Top of the Hill Bluegrass (collection),
    1567
Lazy Lester
  The Best of Excello Records (collection),
    327
  Dark Clouds Rollin': Excello Swamp
    Blues Classics (collection), 328

House Rockin' and Hip Shakin': The
    Best of Excello Blues (collection),
    329
Lea, Barbara. Hoagy Carmichael
    (songwriter collection), 1097.2
Lead Belly
  Classic African American Gospel from
    Smithsonian Folkways (collection),
    2959
  Huddie Ledbetter's Best, 197.1
  King of the 12-String Guitar, 197.2
  Lead Belly's Last Sessions, 197.3
  The Library of Congress Recordings,
    Vols. 4–6, 197.5
  ★The Library of Congress Recordings,
    Vols. 1–3, 197.4
  ★Mean Old World: The Blues from
    1940–1994 (collection), 154
  ★The Story of the Blues (collection),
    158
  When the Sun Goes Down 1: Walk Right
    In (collection), 159
Leaders of the New School. A Future
    without a Past, 2841
★Leap Frogs. Nashville Jumps: Blues and
    Rhythm on Nashville Independent
    Labels 1945–1955 (collection),
    2376
Leavill, Otis. The Story of Brunswick:
    The Classic Sound of Chicago Soul
    (collection), 2610
Lecrae. Rehab, 3177
Led Zeppelin
  Led Zeppelin, 1867.1
  Led Zeppelin Classics, 1867.4
  ★Led Zeppelin II, 1867.2
  ★Led Zeppelin IV [Zo-So], 1867.3
Lee, Albert
  Speechless / Gagged but Not Bound,
    1660
  Stroll On: An Immediate Blues
    Collection (collection), 369
Lee, Baron. Stars of the Apollo
    (collection), 2240
Lee, Brenda
  Anthology, 1508
  ★Billboard Greatest Christmas Hits,
    1955–1983 (collection), 3294
Lee, Curtis. The Doo-Wop Box II
    (collection), 2323
Lee, George E. The Real Kansas City of the
    '20s, '30s, and '40s (collection),
    552
Lee, Joe. Negro Religious Songs and
    Services (collection), 2977
Lee, Johnny. Greatest Hits, 1661
Lee, Julia
  Kansas City Star, 2305.1
  Kansas City's First Lady of the Blues,
    2305.2
  ★The R&B Box (collection), 2239
  The Real Kansas City of the '20s, '30s,
    and '40s (collection), 552

Lee Konitz Quartet. Live from the Village
    Vanguard (collection), 935
Lee, Laura
  Best of Chess R&B, Vols. 1 and 2
    (collection), 2420
  Muscle Shoals Sound (collection), 2605
Lee, Lovie. Living Chicago Blues, Vol. 3
    (collection), 417
Lee, Peggy
  Alec Wilder (songwriter collection),
    1117.1
  ★American Popular Song: Six Decades
    of Songwriters and Singers
    (collection), 1059
  The Best of Miss Peggy Lee, 1206.1
  Cole Porter (songwriter collection),
    1108.1
  Cy Coleman (songwriter collection),
    1098.2
  Dorothy Fields (songwriter collection),
    1100
  Duke Ellington (songwriter collection),
    1099.1
  Fever: The Music of Peggy Lee, 1206.2
  Frank Loesser (songwriter collection),
    1106.1
  Irving Berlin: A Hundred Years
    (songwriter collection), 1096.3
  James Van Heusen (songwriter
    collection), 1112.1
  Rodgers / Hart (songwriter collection),
    1109.1
  Sentimental Journey: Capitol's Great
    Ladies of Song (collection), 1166
  Sentimental Journey: Pop Vocal
    Classics, Vol. 4 (collection), 1170
  ★Sentimental Journey: Pop Vocal
    Classics, Vol. 2 (collection), 1168
  ★Sentimental Journey: Pop Vocal
    Classics, Vol. 3 (collection), 1169
  Sweet and Lovely: Capitol's Great Ladies
    of Song (collection), 1172
  The Very Best of Cole Porter
    (songwriter collection), 1108.3
★Lee, Rev, Glenn. Sacred Steel: The Steel
    Guitar Tradition of the House of God
    Churches (collection), 2980
★Lee, Roosevelt. Nashville Jumps:
    Blues and Rhythm on Nashville
    Independent Labels 1945–1955
    (collection), 2376
Lee, Trip. Between Two Worlds, 3178
LeFevre, Mylon. Best of Christian Rock
    (1970–1986), Vol. 1 (collection),
    3135
LeFevres. Close Harmony: A History of
    Southern Gospel Music, Vol. 1
    (collection), 3108
Left Hand Frank. Living Chicago Blues,
    Vol. 1 (collection), 415
Leftfield. Leftism, 2144
Legend, John. Love in the Future, 2411
Legrand, Michel. Legrand Jazz, 1040

Lehrer, Tom
  The Remains of Tom Lehrer, 1208.1
  Too Many Songs by Tom Lehrer, 1208.2
Lennon, John
  Imagine, 1926.1
  ★*Lennon Legend,* 1926.2
  Plastic Ono Band, 1926.3
  Shaved Fish, 1926.4
Lenoir, J. B.
  Conversation with the Blues
    (collection), 148
  J. B. Lenoir, 299
  ★*The Vee-Jay Story: Celebrating 40 Years
    of Classic Hits* (collection), 2431
Lenya, Lotte. *From Berlin to Broadway: A
    Selection* (songwriter collection),
    1115.2
Leonard, Hal
  Big Book of Country Rock, 1618
  Country Guitar Bible, 1383
  *The Hal Leonard Real Jazz Standards
    Fake Book* (collection), 473
Leonard, Harlan
  Harlan Leonard and His Rockets, 555
  *The Real Kansas City of the '20s, '30s,
    and '40s* (collection), 552
Lerch, Louise. *Christmas Solos for Kids,*
    3280
Lerner, Alan
  Alan Jay Lerner (songwriter
    collection), 1105.1
  Best of Lerner and Loewe (songwriter
    collection), 1105.2
Letterstick Band. *Dreamland: World
    Lullabies and Soothing Songs*
    (collection), 3263
LeVert. *The Best of LeVert,* 2275
Levert, Gerald. *Standing in the Shadows of
    Motown* (collection), 2445
Lewis, Barbara
  ★*Atlantic Soul, 1959–1975*
    (collection), 2589
  *Beg, Scream, and Shout! The Big Ol'
    Box of '60s Soul* (collection), 2433
  Birth of Soul: Special Chicago Edition
    (collection), 2566
  Hello Stranger: The Best of Barbara
    Lewis, 2276
  *The Sweetest Feeling: A Van McCoy
    Songbook* (collection), 2447
Lewis, Crystal. *CCM Top 100: Greatest
    Songs in Christian Music, Vol. 1*
    (collection), 3136
Lewis, Earl and the Channels. *The Best of*
    Earl Lewis and the Channels: New
    York's Finest, 2345
Lewis, Furry
  ★*Blues Classics* (collection), 146
  Blues Masters, Vol. 12: Memphis Blues
    (collection), 229
  ★*The Blues: A Smithsonian Collection
    of Classic Blues Singers* (collection),
    145

*Canned Heat Blues: Masters of Delta
    Blues* (collection), 216
Masters of Memphis Blues (collection),
    230
★*Memphis Masters: Early American
    Blues Classics* (collection), 231
*When the Sun Goes Down 2: The First
    Time I Met the Blues* (collection),
    160
Lewis, George
  George Lewis with Kid Shots, 508
  New Orleans Jazz (collection), 503
Lewis, Huey and the News. *Sports [Exp.
    Ed.],* 2077
Lewis, Jerry Lee
  The Best of Jerry Lee Lewis, 1509
  The Definitive Collection, 1735.1
  ★*18 Original Greatest Hits,* 1735.2
  Let There Be Drums, Vol. 1: The '50s
    (collection), 1751
  Rock and Roll: The Early Days
    (collection), 1752
  ★*Sun Records' Greatest Hits* (collection),
    1741
Lewis, John
  ★*The Birth of the Third Stream*
    (collection), 1030
  Golden Striker / Jazz Abstractions, 1041
  Odds against Tomorrow [1990] (Lewis
    and Modern Jazz Quartet), 1055.1
  Odds against Tomorrow [2003] (Lewis
    and Modern Jazz Quartet), 1055.2
  Piano Legends (collection), 480
  2 Degrees East, 3 Degrees West, 616
Lewis, Laurie
  *Angels Are Singing: A Women's
    Bluegrass Gospel Collection,* 1559
  Blue Ribbon Bluegrass (collection),
    1563
  The Oak and the Laurel, 1593
Lewis, Meade Lux
  Barrelhouse Boogie (collection), 250,
    521
  ★*Cuttin' the Boogie: Piano Blues and
    Boogie Woogie* (collection), 251
  ★*From Spirituals to Swing: The
    Legendary 1938 and 1939 Carnegie
    Hall Concerts Produced by John
    Hammond* (collection), 564
  Hey! Piano Man (collection), 254
  Piano Legends (collection), 480
  *Shake Your Wicked Knees: Rent Parties
    and Good Times* (collection), 258
  ★*The Smithsonian Collection of Classic
    Jazz* (collection), 486
  *When the Sun Goes Down 3: That's
    Chicago's South Side* (collection),
    270
Lewis, Mel. *Big Band Renaissance: The
    Evolution of the Jazz Orchestra*
    (collection), 739
Lewis, Paul. *The Best of T. K. Disco*
    (collection), 2656

Lewis, Ramsey
  Ramsey Lewis' Finest Hour, 670
  Sun Goddess, 905
Lewis Ruth Band. *From Berlin to
    Broadway: A Selection* (songwriter
    collection), 1115.2
Lewis, Singing Sammy. ★*Working the
    Road: The Golden Age of Chicago
    Gospel* (collection), 3039
Lewis, Smiley
  *Crescent City Soul: The Sound of New
    Orleans, 1947–1974* (collection),
    2564
  New Orleans Guitar (collection), 330
Lewis, Ted
  *The Great Depression: American Music
    in the '30s* (collection), 1066
  ★*Swing Time! The Fabulous Big Band
    Era* (collection), 1089
  Waller / Razaf (songwriter collection),
    1113.2
  ★*Yes, Sir, That's My Baby: The Golden
    Years of Tin Pan Alley* (collection),
    1094
Lewis, Tokay. *Eccentric Soul: The Tragar
    and Note Labels* (collection), 2602
★Liberace. *It Had to Be You: Popular
    Keyboard from the Days of the
    Speakeasy to the Television Era*
    (collection), 1068
Liebert, Ottmar. *Nouveau Flamenco,* 1338
Liggins, Jimmy
  *Blue Yule: Christmas Blues and R&B
    Classics* (collection), 3295
  ★*Central Avenue Sounds: Jazz in Los
    Angeles* (collection), 471
  Jimmy Liggins and His Drops of Joy,
    2306
  ★*The R&B Box* (collection), 2239
  ★*The Specialty Story* (collection), 2428
Liggins, Joe
  ★*Central Avenue Sounds: Jazz in Los
    Angeles* (collection), 471
  Joe Liggins and the Honeydrippers,
    2307
  ★*The R&B Box* (collection), 2239
Liggins, Michael. *Eccentric Soul: Mighty
    Mike Lenaburg* (collection), 2563
Light Crust Doughboys
  *Doughboys, Playboys, and Cowboys:
    The Golden Years of Western Swing*
    (collection), 1428
  *Heroes of Country Music, Vol. 1:
    Legends of Western Swing*
    (collection), 1429
  Light Crust Doughboys, 1936–1941, 1442
  *Texas Music, Vol. 2: Western Swing and
    Honky Tonk* (collection), 1432
  *Western Swing: 40 Bootstompers from
    the Golden Age* (collection), 1433
Lightnin' Slim
  The Best of Excello Records (collection),
    327

Lightnin' Slim (cont.)

★*The Blues: A Smithsonian Collection of Classic Blues Singers* (collection), 145

Dark Clouds Rollin': Excello Swamp Blues Classics (collection), 328

House Rockin' and Hip Shakin': The Best of Excello Blues (collection), 329

Lil' Ed and the Blues Imperials

Chicken, Gravy, and Biscuits, 451

The New Bluebloods (collection), 419

Lil' Jon and the East Side Boyz. *Kings of Crunk*, 2844

Lil' Kim. *Hard Core*, 2845

Lil Wayne. *Tha Carter*, 2843

LiLiPUT/Kleenex. *LiLiPUT*, 2017

Lillie, Beatrice. *Vincent Youmans* (songwriter collection), 1118

Lilly, B. *Mountain Music Bluegrass Style* (collection), 1566

Lincoln, Abbey

Abbey Is Blue, 790.1

Jazz Lullaby (collection), 3264

You Gotta Pay the Band, 790.2

Lincoln, Charlie. *The Georgia Blues* (collection), 242

Lipps Inc. *Disco Box* (collection), 2644

Lipscomb, Mance

Conversation with the Blues (collection), 148

Newport Folk Festival: Best of the Blues, 1959–68 (collection), 392

★*Texas Songster*, 400

Liquid Liquid. *Liquid Liquid*, 2222

Lisa Lisa and the Cult Jam. *80's Pop Hits* (collection), 1238

Lithgow, John. *The Sunny Side of the Street*, 3221

Little Ann. *The Fire / Fury Records Story* (collection), 2422

Little Anthony and the Imperials

The Best of Little Anthony and the Imperials, 2347

Birth of Soul, 4 Vols. (collection), 2434

Boddie Recording Company Cleveland, Ohio (collection), 2570

Little Ben and Cheers. *Eccentric Soul: The Nickel and Penny Labels* (collection), 2567

Little, Booker

Booker Little and Friend, 691.1

Out Front, 691.2

Little Brother. *The Minstrel Show*, 2846

Little Caesar and the Romans. *The Doo-Wop Box II* (collection), 2323

Little Chris and Righteous Singers. *Good God! Born Again Funk* (collection), 2614

★Little Esther. *Stompin' at the Savoy: The Original Indie Label, 1944–1961* (collection), 2429

Little Eva. *The Best of the Girl Groups, Vols. 1 and 2* (collection), 2321

Little Feat. *Waiting for Columbus*, 1907

Little Ike. *Night Train to Nashville: Music City Rhythm and Blues, 1945–1970, Vol. 2* (collection), 2378

Little Milton

Anthology, 356.1

Beg, Scream, and Shout! The Big Ol' Box of '60s Soul (collection), 2433

Best of Chess R&B, Vols. 1 and 2 (collection), 2420

Blue Flames: A Sun Blues Collection (collection), 337

The Blues Is Alright, Vol. 1 (collection), 411

★*Chess Blues* (collection), 287

Greatest Hits, 356.2

★*Mean Old World: The Blues from 1940–1994* (collection), 154

Memphis Blues: Important Postwar Recordings (collection), 341

The Modern Records Blues Story (collection), 342

Soul Shots, Vol. 4: Urban Blues (collection), 343

The Sun Blues Years (collection), 344

Superblues: All-Time Classic Blues Hits, Vol. 1 (collection), 347

★*The R&B Box* (collection), 2239

Top of the Stax, Vol. 1: Twenty Greatest Hits (collection), 2611

Top of the Stax, Vol. 2: Twenty Greatest Hits (collection), 2612

Welcome to the Club: The Essential Chess Recordings, 356.3

Little Miss Cornshucks. *Respect: Aretha's Influences and Inspiration* (collection), 2440

Little Richard

The American Roots of the British Invasion (collection), 1786

The Essential Little Richard, 1766.1

★*The Georgia Peach*, 1766.2

God Is Real, 3000

Let There Be Drums, Vol. 1: The '50s (collection), 1751

Rock and Roll: The Early Days (collection), 1752

The Roots of Rock 'n' Roll, 1946–1954 (collection), 1755

★*The Specialty Story* (collection), 2428

The Story of Brunswick: The Classic Sound of Chicago Soul (collection), 2610

★*The Vee-Jay Story: Celebrating 40 Years of Classic Hits* (collection), 2431

When the Sun Goes Down 4: That's All Right (collection), 271

Little, Tommy and the Sunrise Rangers. *Swingbillies: Hillbilly and Western Swing on Modern/Colonial/Flair, 1947–1952* (collection), 1431

Little Walter

★*Blues Classics* (collection), 146

Blues Masters, Vol. 4: Harmonica Classics (collection), 286

Blues Masters, Vol. 2: Postwar Chicago Blues (collection), 285

The Blues World of Little Walter (Little Walter), 300.1

★*Chess Blues* (collection), 287

Chicago Is Just That Way (collection), 289

The Essential Little Walter, 300.2

★*His Best*, 300.3

★*Mean Old World: The Blues from 1940–1994* (collection), 154

Little Willie John

King R&B Box Set (collection), 2424

The American Roots of the British Invasion (collection), 1786

★Living Colour. *Vivid*, 2145

LL Cool J

Mama Said Knock You Out, 2847.1

Radio, 2847.2

Lloyd, Charles

Four Tenors: John Coltrane, Charles Lloyd, Sonny Rollins and Ben Webster (collection), 627

Voice in the Night, 987

Lobo. *Have a Nice Decade: The '70s Pop Culture Box* (collection), 1240

Lockwood, Robert, Jr.

Blues Routes (collection), 413

Chicago Is Just That Way (collection), 289

The Complete Trix Recordings, 452.1

The Road to Robert Johnson and Beyond (collection), 221

Steady Rollin' Man, 452.2

When the Sun Goes Down 4: That's All Right (collection), 271

Loesser, Frank

Frank Loesser Songbook (songwriter collection), 1106.2

Frank Loesser (songwriter collection), 1106.1

Heart and Soul: The Life and Music of Frank Loesser (songwriter collection), 1106.3

loft jazz. *See* jazz outside the mainstream: the AACM, BAG, and the lofts

Lofton, Cripple Clarence. *Favorite Country Blues: Guitar-Piano Duets* (collection), 267

Logan, Ella

E. Y. Harburg (songwriter collection), 1103

★*Sophisticated Ladies* (collection), 1087

Stars of the Apollo (collection), 2240

Logan, Tex. *Mountain Music Bluegrass Style* (collection), 1566

Lollipop, Lukas. *The Best of Loma Records: The Rise and Fall of a 1960's Soul Label* (collection), 2590

★Lomax, Alan. *The Roots of the Blues,* 177
Lombardo, Guy
  ★*Nipper's Greatest Hits: The 30's,
    Vol. 1* (collection), 1072
  ★*Sweetest Music This Side of Heaven,*
    1140
  This Is Art Deco (collection), 1090
London, Julie. *The Very Best of Julie
  London,* 1209
London Symphony Orchestra. *Songs:
  Foster, Griffes, Copland* (collection),
  101
Lonesome River Band. *Top of the Hill
  Bluegrass* (collection), 1567
Lonesome Sundown
  The Best of Excello Records (collection),
    327
  *Dark Clouds Rollin': Excello Swamp
    Blues Classics* (collection), 328
  *House Rockin' and Hip Shakin': The
    Best of Excello Blues* (collection),
    329
Longhair, Professor
  ★*Atlantic R&B, 1947–1974*
    (collection), 2418
  ★*Crawfish Fiesta,* 2370.1
  *Crescent City Soul: The Sound of New
    Orleans, 1947–1974* (collection),
    2564
  Fess: The Professor Longhair Anthology,
    2370.2
  ★*Mean Old World: The Blues from
    1940–1994* (collection), 154
  *The Mercury New Orleans Sessions
    1950 and 1953* (collection), 2361
  New Orleans Piano, 2370.3
  ★*The R&B Box* (collection), 2239
  Rock 'n' Roll Gumbo, 2370.4
  The Roots of Rock 'n' Roll, 1946–1954
    (collection), 1755
Lootpack. *Soundpieces: Da Antidote!,* 2848
Lord Finesse and DJ Mike Smooth. *Funky
  Technician,* 2849
Lorenz, Trey. *#1s* (Carey), 1256.2
Los Angeles rock, 1901–1912
  The Best of Crosby, Stills & Nash,
    1903.1
  The Best of Randy Newman, 1908.1
  Crosby, Stills & Nash, 1903.2
  ★*Decade* (Young), 1911.1
  The Definitive Collection (Steely Dan),
    1910
  Fleetwood Mac, 1906.1
  ★*Greatest Hits, 1971–1975* (Eagles),
    1905.1
  Greatest Hits I and II (Ronstadt),
    1909.1
  Greatest Hits, Vol. 2 (Eagles), 1905.2
  Heart Like a Wheel (Ronstadt), 1909.2
  Hotel California (Eagles), 1905.3
  Into the Purple Valley (Cooder), 1902.1
  Paradise and Lunch (Cooder), 1902.2
  The Pretender (Browne), 1901.1

*A Quiet Normal Life: The Best of
  Warren Zevon,* 1912
Ragged Glory (Young), 1911.2
★*Rumours* (Fleetwood Mac), 1906.2
Rust Never Sleeps (Young), 1911.3
Sail Away (Newman), 1908.2
Tonight's the Night (Young), 1911.4
The Very Best of Jackson Browne, 1901.2
The Very Best of Linda Ronstadt, 1909.3
The Very Best of the Doobie Brothers,
  1904
Waiting for Columbus (Little Feat),
  1907
★Los Bravos. *Nuggets II: Original Artifacts
  from the British Empire and Beyond*
  (collection), 1791
★Los Lobos. *How Will the Wolf Survive?,*
  2146
Lost Generation. *The Story of Brunswick:
  The Classic Sound of Chicago Soul*
  (collection), 2610
Lou, Bonnie. *All-Time Country and
  Western Hits* (collection), 1449
Louchard, Ric
  *G'night Wolfgang: Classical Piano Solos
    for Bedtime,* 3258.1
  *Hey Ludwig! Classical Piano Solos for
    Playful Times,* 3258.2
Loudon, Dorothy. *Irving Berlin*
  (songwriter collection), 1096.1
Louis, Joe Hill
  Blues Masters, Vol. 12: Memphis Blues
    (collection), 229
  *Memphis Blues: Important Postwar
    Recordings* (collection), 341
  Sun Records Harmonica Classics
    (collection), 346
  The Sun Blues Years (collection), 344
Louisiana blues, 327–335
  The Best of Excello Records (collection),
    327
  The Best of Slim Harpo (Harpo), 335
  collections, 327–335
  Country Boy Down in New Orleans
    (Eaglin), 332
  *Dark Clouds Rollin': Excello Swamp
    Blues Classics* (collection), 328
  *House Rockin' and Hip Shakin': The
    Best of Excello Blues* (collection),
    329
  *I Hear You Knockin': The Best of
    Smiley Lewis* (Lewis), 334
  I Won't Cry: Original Ron Recordings
    (Adams), 331
  New Orleans Guitar (collection), 330
  Suffering Mind (Guitar Slim), 333
Louisiana Honey Dippers. *16 Down Home
  Country Classics* (collection), 1385
Louisiana Red. *Detroit Blues: Blues from
  the Motor City* (collection), 291
Louisville Sanctified Singers. *Spreading
  the Word: Early Gospel Recordings*
  (collection), 2972

The Louvin Brothers
  Close Harmony, 1510.1
  *Jubilation! Great Gospel Performances,
    Vol. 3: Country Gospel* (collection),
    3112
  Satan Is Real, 1510.2
  ★*When I Stop Dreaming: The Best of* the
    Louvin Brothers, 1510.3
Lovano, Joe
  From the Soul, 988.1
  Kids, 988.2
Love, Arnie and the Lovettes. *Don't Stop:
  Recording Tap* (collection), 2657
Love, Billy. *The Sun Blues Years*
  (collection), 344
Love, Darlene. *A Christmas Gift for You
  from Phil Spector* (collection), 3300
★Love Sculpture. *Nuggets II: Original
  Artifacts from the British Empire and
  Beyond* (collection), 1791
Love Song
  *Best of Christian Rock (1970–1986),
    Vol. 1* (collection), 3135
  Love Song, 3153
Love Unlimited Orchestra
  The Best of Love Unlimited, 2635
  Disco Box (collection), 2644
Loveless, Patty. *Definitive Collection,* 1662
Lovett, Lyle. *Lyle Lovett,* 1663
Lovin' Spoonful. *Greatest Hits,* 1824
Low. *Secret Name,* 2147
Lowe, Frank. *Decision in Paradise,* 926
Lowe, Jim. *Hit Parade, 1956* (collection),
  1158
Lowe, Nick
  Basher: The Best of Nick Lowe, 2018
  No Thanks! The '70s Punk Rebellion
    (collection), 2003
Lowry, Todd. *Best of Blues Piano* (Lowry,
  Wiegratz, Boduch, McGirr and
  Schroedl), 261
L.T.D. *Greatest Hits,* 2634
Luandrew, Albert. *See* Sunnyland Slim
★Lucy Smith Singers. *Working the Road:
  The Golden Age of Chicago Gospel*
  (collection), 3039
Ludacris. *Word of Mouf,* 2850
lullabies, 3262–3266
  Baby Einstein: Lullaby Classics
    (collection), 3262
  collections, 3262–3264
  *Dreamland: World Lullabies and
    Soothing Songs* (collection), 3263
  Jazz Lullaby (collection), 3264
  Lullaby Magic (Bartels), 3266
  Lullaby Renditions of Radiohead
    (Armstrong), 3265.2
  Lullaby Renditions of the Cure
    (Armstrong), 3265.1
Lulu Belle and Scotty. *Sweethearts of
  Country Music,* 1412
Lulu. *25 Hits from the British Invasion*
  (collection), 1792

Lunceford, Jimmie
   An Anthology of Big Band Swing
     (collection), 528
   ★*Big Band Jazz: From the Beginnings to
     the Fifties* (collection), 529
   It's the Way That You Swing It, 544
   ★*Ken Burns Jazz: The Story of
     America's Music* (collection), 478
   ★*The Music Goes Round and Around:
     The Golden Years of Tin Pan Alley,
     1930–1939* (collection), 1070
   ★*The Smithsonian Collection of Classic
     Jazz* (collection), 486
   ★*Swing Time! The Fabulous Big Band
     Era* (collection), 1089
Lunch, Lydia. *Queen of Siam,* 1991
★Lund, Art. *Sentimental Journey: Pop
   Vocal Classics, Vol. 2* (collection),
   1168
Lunsford, Bascom Lamar. *The Half Ain't
   Never Been Told, Vols. 1 and 2*
   (collection), 2956
Luomo. *Present Lover,* 2223
Lusk, Prophet G. *This May Be My
   Last Time Singing: Raw African-
   American Gospel on 45rpm*
   (collection), 2982
★Lutcher, Joe. *The Specialty Story*
   (collection), 2428
Lutcher, Nellie
   The Best of Nellie Lutcher, 2277.1
   ★*Central Avenue Sounds: Jazz in Los
     Angeles* (collection), 471
   Nellie Lutcher and Her Rhythm, 2277.2
   ★*The R&B Box* (collection), 2239
Lydon, John. *The Tomorrow Show with
   Tom Snyder: Punk and New Wave*
   (collection), 1981
Lymon, Frankie and the Teenagers
   Best of Doo Wop Uptempo (collection),
     1744
   *The Best of Frankie Lymon and the
     Teenagers,* 1767
   ★*The Doo-Wop Box* (collection), 2322
   The Doo-Wop Box II (collection), 2323
   *The Very Best of Frankie Lymon and the
     Teenagers,* 2348
★Lymon, Lewis and the Teenchords. *The
   Doo-Wop Box* (collection), 2322
Lynch, Ray
   Deep Breakfast, 1356
   Ultimate New Age (collection), 1376
Lynn, Cheryl. *Disco Box* (collection),
   2644
Lynn, Gloria. *Birth of Soul, 4 Vols.*
   (collection), 2434
Lynn, Loretta
   The Best of Conway Twitty and
     Loretta Lynn, 1512
   *Classic Country Music: A Smithsonian
     Collection* (collection), 1382
   Coal Miner's Daughter, 1511.1
   ★*Definitive Collection,* 1511.2

Frank Sinatra: Concert Collection,
   1224.3
*Honky Tonk Girl: The Loretta Lynn
   Collection,* 1511.3
Loretta Lynn, 1511.4
Loretta Lynn: Honky Tonk Girl, 1511.5
★Lynn, Tami. *Atlantic Soul, 1959–1975*
   (collection), 2589
Lynyrd Skynyrd. *All Time Greatest Hits,*
   1936
Lyrics Born. *Same !@#$ Different Day,*
   2851
Lyte, MC
   Eyes on This, 2863.1
   Lyte as a Rock, 2863.2

M

Mabley, Jackie "Moms." *Stars of the
   Apollo* (collection), 2240
Mabon, Willie. *Chicago Is Just That Way*
   (collection), 289
MacColl, Kirsty. *The Best of Kirsty
   MacColl,* 1283
MacDonald, Jeanette. *Richard Whiting*
   (songwriter collection), 1116
★Machito. *The Original Mambo Kings: An
   Afro-Cubop Anthology* (collection),
   592
Mack 10. *Based on a True Story,* 2853
★Mack, Eddie. *Stompin' at the Savoy: The
   Original Indie Label, 1944–1961*
   (collection), 2429
Mack, Ida May. *Better Boot That Thing:
   Great Women Blues Singers of the
   1920's* (collection), 202
Mack, Lonnie
   *Legends of Guitar: Rock–The '60s,
     Vol. 1* (collection), 1860
   *Rock Instrumental Classics, Vol. 2:
     The 60s* (collection), 1771
MacKaye, Ian. *American Hardcore*
   (collection), 1977
MacLaine, Shirley. *Cy Coleman*
   (songwriter collection), 1098.2
Macon, Uncle Dave
   ★*American Roots Music* (collection),
     1379
   ★*Anthology of American Folk Music,
     Vol. 4* (collection), 1387
   ★*Brother, Can You Spare a Dime?
     American Song during the Great
     Depression* (collection), 1061
   *Classic Country Music: A Smithsonian
     Collection* (collection), 1382
   Classic Sides, 1413.1
   ★*Go Long Mule,* 1413.2
   *Good for What Ails You: Music of the
     Medicine Shows* (collection), 184
   ★*Goodbye Babylon* (collection), 2954
   *The Half Ain't Never Been Told,
     Vols. 1 and 2* (collection), 2956
   Keep My Skillet Good and Greasy,
     1413.3

Old-Time Mountain Ballads
   (collection), 1390
   ★*Something Got a Hold of Me:
     A Treasury of Sacred Music*
     (collection), 3114
MacRae, Gordon. *Johnny Mercer*
   (songwriter collection), 1107.1
The Mad Lads
   *Beg, Scream, and Shout! The Big Ol'
     Box of '60s Soul* (collection), 2433
   *The Complete Stax/Volt Singles
     1959–1968* (collection), 2594
Maddox Brothers and Rose
   America's Most Colorful Hillbilly
     Band, 1513
   16 Down Home Country Classics
     (collection), 1385
Maddox, Rose. *16 Down Home Country
   Classics* (collection), 1385
Madlib. *Beat Konducta, Vols. 1 and 2,* 2854
★Madonna. *The Immaculate Collection,*
   2053
Madvillain. *Madvillainy,* 2855
Magazine. *No Thanks! The '70s Punk
   Rebellion* (collection), 2003
Maghett, Samuel Gene. *See* Magic Sam
Magic Sam
   . . . With a Feeling!, 357.2
   *Blues Masters, Vol. 2: Postwar Chicago
     Blues* (collection), 285
   *The Cobra Records Story: Chicago Rock
     and Blues* (collection), 339
   ★*Mean Old World: The Blues from
     1940–1994* (collection), 154
   ★*West Side Soul,* 357.1
Magic Slim
   Blues Fest: Modern Blues of the '80s
     (collection), 409
   Blues Masters, Vol. 9: Postmodern Blues
     (collection), 412
   Living Chicago Blues, Vol. 2
     (collection), 416
Magnetism. *Don't Stop: Recording Tap*
   (collection), 2657
The Magnificents
   The Doo-Wop Box II (collection), 2323
   ★*The Vee-Jay Story: Celebrating 40
     Years of Classic Hits* (collection),
     2431
Magruder, Charles. *Don't Give the Name
   a Bad Place: Types and Stereotypes
   in American Musical Theater,
   1870–1900* (collection), 1063
Mahal, Taj
   Blues Fest: Modern Blues of the '90s
     (collection), 410
   *Conjure: Music for the Texts of Ishmael
     Reed* (collection), 810
   ★*Giant Step / Ole Folks at Home,* 374
   ★*Mean Old World: The Blues from
     1940–1994* (collection), 154
   *World Playground: A Musical Adventure
     for Kids* (collection), 3230

Mahavishnu Orchestra
  Birds of Fire, 826.1
  Inner Mounting Flame, 826.2
Mahogany, Kevin. *Pride and Joy*, 791
Main Ingredient. *Everybody Plays the Fool: The Best of* Main Ingredient, 2495
Main Source. *Breaking Atoms*, 2856
Mainer, J. E.
  1935–1939: The Early Years, 1414
  16 Down Home Country Classics (collection), 1385
★Mainer, Wade. *Something Got a Hold of Me: A Treasury of Sacred Music* (collection), 3114
mainstream country music: 1940s–1970s, 1449–1558
  All the Best (Campbell), 1463.1
  ★*All Time Greatest Hits* (Miller), 1516.1
  All-Time Country and Western Hits (collection), 1449
  American Recordings (Cash), 1464.1
  America's Most Colorful Hillbilly Band (Maddox Brothers and Rose), 1513
  America's Song Butchers: The Weird World of Homer and Jethro, 1498
  Anniversary: Ten Years of Hits (Jones), 1505.1
  Anniversary, 20 Years of Hits: The First Lady of Country Music (Wynette), 1557
  Anthology (Lee), 1508
  Best of Johnnie and Jack, 1504
  Best of Merle Travis: Sweet Temptation 1946–1953, 1545.1
  Best of Stonewall Jackson, 1501
  Best of the Best (Copas), 1470
  Best of the Statler Brothers, Vol. 1, 1541.1
  The Best of Barbara Mandrell, 1514
  The Best of Bobby Bare, 1459
  The Best of Conway Twitty and Loretta Lynn, 1512
  The Best of Crystal Gayle, 1491
  The Best of Dave Dudley, 1481
  The Best of Donna Fargo, 1483
  The Best of Faron Young, 1558.1
  The Best of Floyd Tillman, 1544
  The Best of Freddy Fender, 1484
  The Best of George Jones, 1505.2
  The Best of Jerry Lee Lewis, 1509
  Black Mountain Rag (Watson), 1552.1
  Born to Lose (Daffan and His Texans), 1476
  ★*The Buck Owens Collection, 1959–1990*, 1521.1
  Charley Pride, 1528.1
  Close Harmony (Louvin Brothers), 1510.1
  Coal Miner's Daughter (Lynn), 1511.1
  Come Along and Ride This Train (Cash), 1464.2
  ★*Complete Hank Williams*, 1556.1

  The Complete Columbia Hits and More (Dean), 1478
  The Complete Live 1965 Show (Tubb), 1546.1
  Country Music Classics with Marty Robbins and Ernest Tubb, 1471
  Country Music Classics with Webb Pierce and Chet Atkins, 1472
  Country Style, U.S.A. (collection), 1473
  Definitive Collection (Anderson), 1454
  Definitive Collection (Hall), 1496.1
  ★*Definitive Collection* (Lynn), 1511.2
  Definitive Collection (Statler Brothers), 1541.2
  Doc and the Boys/Live and Pickin' (Watson), 1552.2
  Dolly Parton Live and Well, 1523
  Don Gibson, 1492
  Dottie West, 1554
  Down Every Road (Haggard), 1495.1
  Dreaming My Dreams (Jennings), 1503.1
  ★*Essential Charley Pride*, 1528.2
  Essential Chet Atkins, 1457.1
  Essential Doc Watson, 1552.3
  Essential Floyd Cramer, 1474
  Essential Jerry Reed, 1529
  Essential Jim Reeves, 1530
  Essential Kris Kristofferson, 1507
  Essential Recordings (Wells), 1553
  ★*Essential Waylon Jennings*, 1503.2
  The Essential Carl Smith, 1538
  The Essential Connie Smith, 1539
  ★*The Essential George Jones: The Spirit of Country*, 1505.3
  The Essential Guy Clark, 1465.1
  The Essential Hank Snow, 1540
  The Essential Johnny Horton: Honky Tonk Man, 1499
  The Essential Marty Robbins, 1533
  The Essential Porter and Dolly (Wagoner and Parton), 1549
  The Essential Ray Price, 1527
  The Essential Tom T. Hall: The Story Songs, 1496.2
  Feel Like Going Home: The Essential Charlie Rich, 1531.1
  Flying Fingers (Maphis), 1515
  For the Record: The First 10 Years (Coe), 1468
  40 Greatest Hits (Williams), 1556.2
  Freight Train Boogie (Delmore Brothers), 1479
  Frettin' Fingers: The Lightning Guitar of Jimmy Bryant, 1461
  G. P. / Grievous Angel (Parsons), 1522
  Gentle on My Mind (Campbell), 1463.2
  George Jones: Live Recordings from Church Street Station!, 1505.4
  Gold (Cline), 1467.1
  Gold (Twitty), 1548.1
  Greatest Hits (Anderson), 1455

  Greatest Hits (Clark), 1466
  Greatest Hits (Ferlin), 1500
  Greatest Hits (Ford), 1488.1
  Greatest Hits (James), 1502
  Greatest Hits (Tucker), 1547
  Guitar Legend: The RCA Years (Atkins), 1457.2
  Guitar Rags and a Too Fast Past (Travis), 1545.2
  ★*Hag: The Best of* Merle Haggard, 1495.2
  Hank Garland and His Sugar Footers, 1490
  Hank Williams: Honky Tonk Blues, 1556.3
  Hank Williams Songbook (collection), 1450
  The Hee Haw Collection, Vol. 3 (collection), 1451
  Here Comes the Boogie Man (Smith), 1537
  High Noon (Ritter), 1532.1, 1532.2
  Hillbilly Central #2: Another Log on the Fire (Glaser), 1494.2
  Hillbilly Central #1: My Notorious Youth (Glaser), 1494.1
  Hitsides! 1970–1980 (Tillis), 1543
  Honky Tonk Amnesia: The Hard Country Sound of Moe Bandy, 1458
  Honky Tonk Girl: The Loretta Lynn Collection, 1511.3
  Honky Tonk Heroes (Jennings), 1503.3
  Hot Burritos! The Flying Burrito Brothers Anthology, 1969–1972, 1486
  I Love You Because (Payne), 1525
  I'm Little but I'm Loud: The Little Jimmy Dickens Collection, 1480
  Jean Shepard, Honky–Tonk Heroine: Classic Capitol Recordings, 1952–1964, 1536.1
  Johnny Cash at Folsom Prison and San Quentin, 1464.3
  Johnny Cash at Town Hall Party, 1464.4
  King of the Honky-Tonk (Pierce), 1526
  King of the Road: The Genius of Roger Miller, 1516.2
  Life's Like Poetry (Frizzell), 1489.1
  Live Fast, Love Hard: Original Capitol Recordings 1952–1962 (Young), 1558.2
  Look What Thoughts Will Do (Frizzell), 1489.2
  Loretta Lynn, 1511.4
  Loretta Lynn: Honky Tonk Girl, 1511.5
  Man in Black, 1954–1958 (Cash), 1464.5
  Man in Black, 1959–1962 (Cash), 1464.6
  Melody Ranch Girl (Shepard), 1536.2
  Molly O'Day and the Cumberland Mountain Folks, 1519

mainstream country music (cont.)

Moonshine Jamboree (Mullican), 1517

More a Legend Than a Band (Flatlanders), 1485

Nashville Skyline (Dylan), 1482

Nite Life: Greatest Hits and Rare Tracks, 1959–1971 (Nelson), 1518.1

Old Five and Dimers Like Me (Shepard), 1535

Old No. 1 (Clark), 1465.2

The Original Singles Collection . . . Plus (Williams), 1556.4

Patsy Cline: Sweet Dreams Still, 1467.2

★*The Patsy Cline Collection,* 1467.3

Phases and Stages (Nelson), 1518.2

Proper Introduction to Tennessee Ernie Ford: Rock City Boogie, 1488.2

Rainbow Stew: Live at Anaheim Stadium (Haggard), 1495.3

Ramblin' Man (Jennings), 1503.4

★*Red Foley: Country Music Hall of Fame,* 1487

★*Red Headed Stranger* (Nelson), 1518.3

Room Full of Roses / Gilley's Smokin' (Gilley), 1493

Satan Is Real (Louvin Brothers), 1510.2

Seven Decades of Hits/Greatest Songs (Arnold), 1456.1

She Thinks I Still Care: The Complete United Artists Recordings, 1962–1964 (Jones), 1505.5

Silver Anniversary Collection (Twitty), 1548.2

16 Biggest Hits (Paycheck), 1524

16 Greatest Hits (Brown's Ferry Four), 1460

Skeeter Davis, 1477

Southbound (Watson), 1552.3

Stacked Deck (Amazing Rhythm Aces), 1453

Stratosphere Boogie: The Flaming Guitars of Speedy West and Jimmy Bryant, 1555

★*Sun Years* (Cash), 1464.7

Sweetheart of the Rodeo (Byrds), 1462

★*The Texas Troubadour* (Tubb), 1546.2

★*That's the Way Life Goes: The Hit Songs, 1950–1975* (Frizzell), 1489.3

These Boots Are Made for Walkin': The Complete MGM Recordings (Hazlewood), 1497

Tombstone Every Mile (Curless), 1475

28 Greatest Hits (Jones), 1506

Ultimate Collection (Rich), 1531.2

Ultimate Collection (Walker), 1551.1

★*Ultimate Eddy Arnold,* 1456.2

Very Best of Buck Owens, Vol. 1, 1521.2

Very Best of Linda Ronstadt, 1534

Very Best of Wilma Lee and Stoney Cooper and the Clinch Mountain Clan, 1469

Very Best of Wynn Stewart 1958–1962, 1542

Viva Terlingua! (Walker), 1551.2

Walk the Line, 1550

Wanted: The Outlaws, 1520

★*When I Stop Dreaming: The Best of the Louvin Brothers,* 1510.3

★*Will the Circle Be Unbroken?* (collection), 1452

mainstream popular

overview, p65–66

post-1967, 1235–1312

post-World War II through 1967, 1155–1234

pre-World War II, 1059–1154

mainstream rock, 2064–2090

Achtung Baby (U2), 2087.1

Appetite for Destruction (Guns 'n' Roses), 2075

Back in Black (AC/DC), 2064

Best of the Beast (Iron Maiden), 2078.1

The Best of Van Halen, Vol. 1, 2088.1

★*Born in the USA* (Springsteen), 2085.1

Building the Perfect Beast (Henley), 2076.1

Chronicles Deluxe Ed (Rush), 2083

Chronicles (Winwood), 2090

Elevation 2001: U2 Live from Boston, 2087.2

The End of the Innocence (Henley), 2076.2

Escape (Journey), 2079

The Essential Bruce Springsteen, 2085.2

Graceland (Simon), 2084

Greatest (Duran Duran), 2070

Greatest Hits (Tom Petty and the Heartbreakers), 2086

The Hits (REO Speedwagon), 2082

Hysteria: Deluxe Edition (Def Leppard), 2068

Invisible Touch (Genesis), 2074

★*The Joshua Tree* (U2), 2087.3

Make It Big (Wham), 2089

Master of Puppets (Metallica), 2081.1

1984 (Van Halen), 2088.2

No End in Sight: The Very Best of Foreigner, 2072

No Jacket Required (Collins), 2067

A Rush of Blood to the Head (Coldplay), 2066

Scarecrow (Mellencamp), 2080

Shaking the Tree: 16 Golden Greats (Gabriel), 2073.1

Slippery When Wet (Bon Jovi), 2065

So (Gabriel), 2073.2

Somewhere Back in Time: Best of 1980–1989 (Maiden), 2078.2

Sports [Exp. Ed.] (Huey Lewis and the News), 2077

Sultans of Swing: The Very Best of Dire Straits, 2069, 2081.2

U218 Singles, 2087.4

Ultimate Collection (Eurythmics), 2071

Us (Gabriel), 2073.3

★*Van Halen,* 2088.3

War (U2), 2087.5

Mainstreeters. *The Spring Story: Essential 70s Soul* (collection), 2608

★*Maize, Tessie. At the Jazz Band Ball: Early Hot Jazz, Song, and Dance* (collection), 470

Majestic Arrows. *Eccentric Soul: The Bandit Label* (collection), 2597

Makaveli. *The Don Killuminati: The 7 Day Theory,* 2857

Mal Waldron Quintet. *Live from the Village Vanguard* (collection), 935

Malone, Russell. *Playground,* 989

The Mamas and the Papas

Casey Kasem Presents America's Top Ten through the Years: The Sixties (collection), 1156

Greatest Hits, 1825

Manak, Chris. *See* Peanut Butter Wolf

Manana, Erick. *Dreamland: World Lullabies and Soothing Songs* (collection), 3263

★Mance, Junior. *What It Is! Funky Soul and Rare Grooves* (collection), 2615

Mancini, Henry

Big Band Renaissance: The Evolution of the Jazz Orchestra (collection), 739

Midnight, Moonlight, and Magic: The Very Best of Henry Mancini, 1210

Mandrell, Barbara. *The Best of Barbara Mandrell,* 1514

Mangelsdorff, Albert. *Three Originals: The Wide Point / Trilogue / Albert Live in Montreux,* 852

Mangione, Chuck

Chuck Mangione, 906.1

Feels So Good, 906.2

Manhattan Transfer

Swing, 1284.1

The Very Best of Manhattan Transfer, 1284.2

The Manhattans

Eccentric Soul: The Big Mack Label (collection), 2598

★*Love Train: The Sound of Philadelphia* (collection), 2552

Sweet Talking Soul, 1965–1990, 2554

Manilow, Barry

The Barry Manilow Anthology, 1246

Ultimate Manilow, 1285

Mann, Brian. *Piano Solos: Narada Artists* (collection), 1370

Mann, Herbie. *The Best of Herbie Mann,* 671

Mann, Woody
    *The Basics: Building a Foundation
        of Repertoire and Technique for
        Acoustic Fingerstyle Blues,* 165
    The Blues Fakebook, 166
Manne, Shelly
    *Shelly Manne and His Men, Vol. 1: The
        West Coast Sound,* 617.1
    "The Three" and "The Two," 617.2
Mannheim Steamroller
    ★*Fresh Aire,* 1339
    Mannheim Steamroller Christmas,
        3335
Mansfield, Darrell. *First Love: A Historic
    Gathering of Jesus Music Pioneers*
    (collection), 3137
Mantovani. *Golden Hits,* 1286
Mantronix. *The Album,* 2858
Maphis, Joe. *Flying Fingers,* 1515
The Marcels
    ★*The Doo-Wop Box* (collection), 2322
    The Doo-Wop Box II (collection), 2323
    *Street Corner Serenade: The Greatest
        Doo-Wop Hits of the '50s and '60s*
        (collection), 1756
Marchan, Bobby
    *Best of Ace Records, Vol. 2: The R&B
        Hits* (collection), 2419
    The Fire / Fury Records Story
        (collection), 2422
Marching Chiefs. *The Best of* College
    Football Fight Songs (collection),
    3370
Marie, Teena. *Hitsville USA: The
    Motown Singles Collection, Vol. 2*
    (collection), 2604
The Marigolds
    ★*Nashville Jumps: Blues and Rhythm
        on Nashville Independent Labels
        1945–1955* (collection), 2376
    *Night Train to Nashville: Music City
        Rhythm and Blues, 1945–1970,
        Vol. 1* (collection), 2377
    *Southern Rhythm 'n' Rock: The
        Best of Excello Records, Vol. 22*
        (collection), 2427
Mark, Brian. *The Early Minstrel Show*
    (collection), 96
★Marketts. *Surfin' Hits* (collection), 1810
The Mar-Keys
    ★*Atlantic R&B, 1947–1974* (collection),
        2418
    *Beg, Scream, and Shout! The Big Ol'
        Box of '60s Soul* (collection), 2433
    *Stax/Volt Revue: Live in London, Vols. 1
        and 2* (collection), 2609
    Stax/Volt Revue: Live in Norway 1967
        (collection), 2446
    *The Complete Stax/Volt Singles
        1959–1968* (collection), 2594
    *The Complete Stax/Volt Soul Singles,
        Vol. 2: 1968–1971* (collection),
        2595

*Top of the Stax, Vol. 2: Twenty Greatest
    Hits* (collection), 2612
Marlborough Singers and Chamber
    Players, tenor John English, and
    piano Rob Carrike. *Over There!
    Songs from America's Wars,* 1141
Marley Marl. *Marley Marl's House of Hits,*
    2859
★Marmalade. *Nuggets II: Original Artifacts
    from the British Empire and Beyond*
    (collection), 1791
★Marocco, W. Thomas. *Music in America:
    An Anthology from the Landing of
    the Pilgrims to the Close of the Civil
    War, 1620–1865,* 16
Marrow, Tracy Lauren. *See* Ice-T
Mars. *No New York* (collection), 1979
Marsalis, Branford
    Mo' Better Blues [1990], 1052.1
    Mo' Better Blues [2000], 1052.2
    Renaissance, 990
Marsalis, Wynton
    Black Codes (from the Underground),
        991.1
    Blood on the Fields, 991.2
    Carnaval, 87
    Icons among Us (collection), 934
    Jingle Bell Jazz (collection), 3314
    The Majesty of the Blues, 991.3
Marshall Tucker Band. *Anthology: The
    First 30 Years,* 1937
Martha and the Vandellas
    *Beg, Scream, and Shout! The Big Ol'
        Box of '60s Soul* (collection), 2433
    *Heaven Must Have Sent You: The
        Holland/Dozier/Holland Story*
        (collection), 2436
    *Hitsville USA: The Motown Singles
        Collection* (collection), 2603
    Pure 60's: The #1 Hits (collection),
        1165
Martin, Carl
    ★*Guitar Wizards* (collection), 243
    *Martin, Bogan, and Armstrong / That
        Old Gang of Mine* (Martin, Bogan,
        and Armstrong), 401
Martin, Cora. ★*The Great Gospel Women*
    (collection), 2989
Martin, Dean
    Dean Martin, 1211.1
    Frank Sinatra: Concert Collection,
        1224.3
    Hit Parade, 1956 (collection), 1158
    *The Legendary Crooners: Frank Sinatra,
        Dean Martin, Bing Crosby, Nat King
        Cole, Perry Como* (collection),
        1207
    *Sentimental Journey: Pop Vocal
        Classics, Vol. 4* (collection), 1170
    ★*Sentimental Journey: Pop Vocal
        Classics, Vol. 3* (collection), 1169
    ★*That's Amore,* 1211.2
    This Is Art Deco (collection), 1090

The Very Best of Cole Porter
    (songwriter collection), 1108.3
★Martin, Freddy. *Nipper's Greatest Hits:
    The 40's, Vol. 1* (collection), 1073
Martin, Jimmy
    Appalachian Stomp: Bluegrass Classics
        (collection), 1560
    Don't Cry to Me, 1594.1
    Greatest Hits, 1594.2
    *Jimmy Martin and the Sunny Mountain
        Boys,* 1594.3
Martin, Mary
    Arthur Schwartz (songwriter
        collection), 1110.2
    Cole Porter (songwriter collection),
        1108.1
    From Berlin to Broadway: A Selection
        (songwriter collection),
        1115.2
    George Gershwin (songwriter
        collection), 1101.3
    Irving Berlin (songwriter collection),
        1096.1
    Johnny Mercer (songwriter collection),
        1107.1
    Oscar Hammerstein II (songwriter
        collection), 1102
    Rodgers / Hart (songwriter collection),
        1109.1
    Vincent Youmans (songwriter
        collection), 1118
Martin, Roberta
    ★*All God's Sons and Daughters:
        Chicago's Gospel Legends*
        (collection), 3030
    ★*The Gospel Sound of Spirit Feel*
        (collection), 2965
    ★*The Great Gospel Women* (collection),
        2989
    ★*Jubilation! Great Gospel Performances,
        Vol. 1: Black Gospel* (collection),
        2966
Martin, Sallie
    ★*Precious Lord: Recordings of the Great
        Gospel Songs of Thomas A. Dorsey*
        (collection), 2968
    ★*Say Amen, Somebody* (collection),
        2971
    Testify! The Gospel Box (collection),
        2974
Martin, Sara. ★*I Can't Be Satisfied: Early
    American Women Blues Singers,
    Vol. 2: Town* (collection), 204
Martin, Tony
    Arthur Schwartz (songwriter
        collection), 1110.2
    Richard Whiting (songwriter
        collection), 1116
    ★*Sentimental Journey: Pop Vocal
        Classics, Vol. 3* (collection), 1169
Martinez, Claudia. *Dreamland: World
    Lullabies and Soothing Songs*
    (collection), 3263

★Martino, Al. *Sentimental Journey: Pop Vocal Classics, Vol. 3* (collection), 1169

Martino, Pat. *Progressions: 100 Years of Jazz Guitar* (collection), 481

Martyn, John. *Sweet Little Mysteries: The Island Anthology*, 1855

The Marvelettes
  Heaven Must Have Sent You: The Holland/Dozier/Holland Story (collection), 2436
  Hitsville USA: The Motown Singles Collection (collection), 2603
  Pure 60's: The #1 Hits (collection), 1165
  Ultimate Collection, 2496

Marvellos. *The Best of Loma Records: The Rise and Fall of a 1960's Soul Label* (collection), 2590

Marvin, Johnny. *25 Sweethearts of Yesteryear* (collection), 1092

Marx, Groucho. *E. Y. Harburg* (songwriter collection), 1103

Mary "B." *The Fire / Fury Records Story* (collection), 2422

Mary Mary
  Thankful, 3092
  Wow Gospel #1s (collection), 3074

Mason, Barbara. *Beg, Scream, and Shout! The Big Ol' Box of '60s Soul* (collection), 2433

Massive Attack. *Blue Lines*, 2148

Masta Ace. *The Best of* Cold Chillin', 2860

Master P. *Ghetto D*, 2861

Mates of State. *For the Kids Three!* (collection), 3209

Mathers, Marshall Bruce, III. *See* Eminem

Mathis, Johnny
  Cy Coleman (songwriter collection), 1098.2
  Essential Johnny Mathis, 1212.1
  Frank Loesser (songwriter collection), 1106.1
  Heavenly, 1212.2
  Irving Berlin (songwriter collection), 1096.1
  Johnny Mercer (songwriter collection), 1107.1
  Jule Styne (songwriter collection), 1111.1
  Sentimental Journey: Pop Vocal Classics, Vol. 4 (collection), 1170
  16 Most Requested Songs: The 1950s, Vol. 1 (collection), 1171

Matta Baby. *Eccentric Soul: The Nickel and Penny Labels* (collection), 2567

Matthews, Randy. *First Love: A Historic Gathering of Jesus Music Pioneers* (collection), 3137

Mavericks. *Definitive Collection*, 1664

Maxin Trio. *The Swing Time Records Story: R&B, Blues, and Gospel, 1946–1952* (collection), 2430

Maxwell. *Maxwell's Urban Hang Suite*, 2412

May, Brother Joe
  The Best of Nashboro Gospel (collection), 3032
  The Great Gospel Men (collection), 2988
  The Great 1955 Shrine Concert (collection), 3034
  Greatest Gospel Gems (collection), 3035
  Mother Smith and Her Children (collection), 2991
  Thunderbolt of the Middle West, 3001

Mayall, John
  Blues Breakers [1993], 375.2
  ★*Blues Breakers* [1965], 375.1
  Blues Masters, Vol. 7: Blues Revival (collection), 390
  Bluesbreakers, 1868
  Legends of Guitar: Rock–The '60s, Vol. 2 (collection), 1861
  London Blues, 375.3
  Stroll On: An Immediate Blues Collection (collection), 369

Mayberry Movement. *The Spring Story: Essential 70s Soul* (collection), 2608

Maye, Marilyn. *Alan Jay Lerner* (songwriter collection), 1105.1

Mayfield, Curtis
  ★*The Anthology*, 2497.1
  Curtis Mayfield Live at Montreux, 1987, 2497.3
  The Curtis Mayfield Guitar Songbook, 2497.2
  Have a Nice Decade: The '70s Pop Culture Box (collection), 1240
  Superfly, 2576
  The Very Best of Curtis Mayfield, 2497.4

Mayfield, Curtis and the Impressions. *Movin'* On Up: The Music and Message of Curtis Mayfield and the Impressions, 2538

Mayfield, Percy
  Blues Masters, Vol. 3: Texas Blues (collection), 311
  ★*Central Avenue Sounds: Jazz in Los Angeles* (collection), 471
  ★*His Tangerine and Atlantic Sides*, 2308.1
  ★*Mean Old World: The Blues from 1940–1994* (collection), 154
  Percy Mayfield: Poet of the Blues, 2308.2
  Respect: Aretha's Influences and Inspiration (collection), 2440
  ★*The R&B Box* (collection), 2239
  The Roots of Rock 'n' Roll, 1946–1954 (collection), 1755
  ★*The Specialty Story* (collection), 2428

The Swing Time Records Story: R&B, Blues, and Gospel, 1946–1952 (collection), 2430

Maynor, Dorothy. *A First-Time Buyer's Guide to American Negro Spirituals* (collection), 32

Mays, Bill. *Live at Jazz Standard*, 992

Maze
  Anthology, 2278.1
  Greatest Hits, 2278.2

MC5
  Back in the USA, 1876.1
  Kick out the Jams, 1876.2
  Punk: Attitude (collection), 1980

McAllister, Billie
  ★*Nashville Jumps: Blues and Rhythm on Nashville Independent Labels 1945–1955* (collection), 2376
  Night Train to Nashville: Music City Rhythm and Blues, 1945–1970, Vol. 2 (collection), 2378

McAuliffe, Leon
  Heroes of Country Music, Vol. 1: Legends of Western Swing (collection), 1429
  Take It Away the Leon Way!, 1443

McBride, Christian. *Fingerpainting: The Music of Herbie Hancock*, 993

McBride, Martina. *The Way That I Am*, 1665

McCabe, Daniel. *An American Idyll: American Songs from 1800–1860*, 118

McCain, Jerry
  The Best of Excello Records (collection), 327
  Good Stuff, 358
  House Rockin' and Hip Shakin': The Best of Excello Blues (collection), 329
  ★*Nashville Jumps: Blues and Rhythm on Nashville Independent Labels 1945–1955* (collection), 2376
  Southern Rhythm 'n' Rock: The Best of Excello Records, Vol. 22 (collection), 2427

McCall, Toussaint
  Beg, Scream, and Shout! The Big Ol' Box of '60s Soul (collection), 2433
  Dave Godin's Deep Soul Treasures, Vols. 1–4 (collection), 2435

McCann, Les
  Soul to Soul (collection), 2444
  Swiss Movement, 672

McCartney, Paul
  All the Best, 1927
  Duets: An American Classic (Bennett), 1251.1

McClennan, Tommy
  Big Joe Williams and the Stars of Mississippi Blues (collection), 213

★*The Blues: A Smithsonian Collection of Classic Blues Singers* (collection), 145

★*Let's Get Loose: Folk and Popular Blues Styles from the Beginning to the Early 1940s* (collection), 152

When the Sun Goes Down 3: That's Chicago's South Side (collection), 270

★McCollum, Hazel. *The Vee-Jay Story: Celebrating 40 Years of Classic Hits* (collection), 2431

McConnell, Rob. *Big Band Renaissance: The Evolution of the Jazz Orchestra* (collection), 739

McCorkle, Susannah
  E. Y. Harburg (songwriter collection), 1103
  No More Blues, 792
  Richard Whiting (songwriter collection), 1116

McCoury, Del
  Appalachian Stomp: Bluegrass Classics (collection), 1560
  The Cold Hard Facts, 1595.1
  Del and the Boys, 1595.2
  Don't Stop the Music, 1595.3
  Hand-Picked: 25 Years of Bluegrass on Rounder Records (collection), 1564
  The Mountain, 1702
  16 Down Home Country Classics (collection), 1385

McCoy, Joe
  Good Time Blues: Harmonicas, Kazoos, Washboards, and Cow-Bells (collection), 268
  ★*Let's Get Loose: Folk and Popular Blues Styles from the Beginning to the Early 1940s* (collection), 152
  ★*Memphis Masters: Early American Blues Classics* (collection), 231

McCoy, Robert Lee
  ★*Blues Classics* (collection), 146
  When the Sun Goes Down 3: That's Chicago's South Side (collection), 270

McCoy, Seth. *Music of the American Revolution: The Birth of Liberty* (collection), 46

McCoy, Van, and the Soul City Symphony. *Disco Box* (collection), 2644

McCracklin, Jimmy
  Best of Chess R&B, Vols. 1 and 2 (collection), 2420
  The Swing Time Records Story: R&B, Blues, and Gospel, 1946–1952 (collection), 313, 2430

McCravy Brothers. *Mountain Gospel: The Sacred Roots of Country Music* (collection), 3113

★McCurry, John G. *The Social Harp,* 17

McDaniels, Gene
  The Look of Love: The Burt Bacharach Collection (collection), 1161
  ★*What It Is! Funky Soul and Rare Grooves* (collection), 2615

McDonald, Earl
  Ruckus Juice and Chittlins: The Great Jug Bands—Classic Recordings of the 1920s and '30s, Vol. 1 (collection), 188
  Ruckus Juice and Chittlins: The Great Jug Bands—Classic Recordings of the 1920s and '30s, Vol. 2 (collection), 189

McDonough, Dick. *Pioneers of the Jazz Guitar* (collection), 511

McDonough, Harry. *The Phonographic Yearbook, 1912: Waitin' on the Levee* (collection), 1077

McDowell, Bobby. *The Complete Goldwax Singles, Vol. 1* (collection), 2591

McDowell, Fred
  Blues Masters, Vol. 7: Blues Revival (collection), 390
  Masters of the Country Blues: Fred McDowell and Big Joe Williams (collection), 391
  ★*Mean Old World: The Blues from 1940–1994* (collection), 154
  Newport Folk Festival: Best of the Blues, 1959–68 (collection), 392
  ★*You Gotta Move,* 402

McEntire, Reba
  ★*Greatest Hits,* 1666.1
  Reba #1s, 1666.2

McFadden and Whitehead. *Disco Box* (collection), 2644

McFerrin, Bobby. *The Voice,* 793

McGee, Sam
  ★*Complete Recorded Works, 1926–1934, in Chronological Order,* 1415
  Old-Time Mountain Guitar (collection), 1391
  16 Down Home Country Classics (collection), 1385

★McGee, Tommy. *Nashville Jumps: Blues and Rhythm on Nashville Independent Labels 1945–1955* (collection), 2376

McGhee, Brownie
  ★*Brownie McGhee and Sonny Terry Sing* (Terry and McGhee), 404
  Country Blues Troubadours, 1938–1948 (Terry and McGhee), 280
  ★*Legends of the Blues, Vol. 2* (collection), 151
  Newport Folk Festival: Best of the Blues, 1959–68 (collection), 392
  ★*Stompin' at the Savoy: The Original Indie Label, 1944–1961* (collection), 2429
  ★*The Story of the Blues* (collection), 158

★McGhee, Howard. *Central Avenue Sounds: Jazz in Los Angeles* (collection), 471

★McGhee, Sticks. *Stompin' at the Savoy: The Original Indie Label, 1944–1961* (collection), 2429

McGirr, Tom. *Best of Blues Piano* (Lowry, Wiegratz, Boduch, McGirr and Schroedl), 261

McGovern, Maureen
  Dorothy Fields (songwriter collection), 1100
  George Gershwin (songwriter collection), 1101.3
  Harold Arlen (songwriter collection), 1095.1
  Harry Warren (songwriter collection), 1114
  Rodgers / Hart (songwriter collection), 1109.1

McGrath, Bob
  ★*Bob's Favorite Street Songs,* 3202.1
  Christmas Sing Along, 3246
  Sing Me a Story, 3202.2
  Songs and Games for Toddlers, 3188

McGraw, Hugh. *The Social Harp: Early American Shape-Note Songs,* 18

McGraw, Tm. *Greatest Hits,* 1667

McGregor, Chris. *Chris McGregor's Brotherhood of Breath,* 853

McGregor, George and the Bonzettes. *Eccentric Soul: Twinight's Lunar Rotation* (collection), 2568

McGuire, Barry
  First Love: A Historic Gathering of Jesus Music Pioneers (collection), 3137
  Songs of Protest (collection), 1820

McGuire Sisters. *Greatest Hits,* 1213

McKay, Nellie. *Get Away from Me,* 1287

McKenna, Dave. *Dancing in the Dark,* 728

McKennitt, Loreena
  The Mask and the Mirror, 1362.1
  The Visit, 1362.2

★McKenzie, Red. *The Crooners* (collection), 1062

McKinney's Cotton Pickers
  The Band Don Redman Built, 545
  ★*Big Band Jazz: From the Beginnings to the Fifties* (collection), 529

McKissick, Norsalus
  ★*All God's Sons and Daughters: Chicago's Gospel Legends* (collection), 3030
  The Great Gospel Men (collection), 2988

McKnight, Brian. *#1s* (Carey), 1256.2

McLachlan, Sarah. *Closer: The Best of Sarah McLachlan,* 1288

McLaughlin, John
  ★*The Essential John McLaughlin,* 827
  Pioneers of the New Age (collection), 1371

McLaughlin, John (cont.)
  Progressions: 100 Years of Jazz Guitar (collection), 481
McLean, Jackie
  Bluesnik, 647
  Destination Out, 692.1
  Let Freedom Ring, 692.2
McMurray, Elder Robert. *This May Be My Last Time Singing: Raw African- American Gospel on 45rpm* (collection), 2982
McNeely, Big Jay
  ★*Central Avenue Sounds: Jazz in Los Angeles* (collection), 471
  The Big Horn: The History of the Honkin' and Screamin' Saxophone (collection), 2314
  ★*The R&B Box* (collection), 2239
★McNeely, Deacon. *Stompin' at the Savoy: The Original Indie Label, 1944–1961* (collection), 2429
McNutt, Bobby. *Eccentric Soul: The Young Disciples* (collection), 2562
McPartland, Marian
  In My Life, 884
  Piano Legends (collection), 480
McPhatter, Clyde
  ★*Atlantic R&B, 1947–1974* (collection), 2418
  ★*Atlantic Vocal Groups, 1951–1963* (collection), 2320
  Deep Sea Ball: The Best of Clyde McPhatter, 2279.1
  Lover Please: The Complete MGM and Mercury Singles, 2279.2
  Night Train to Nashville: Music City Rhythm and Blues, 1945–1970, Vol. 2 (collection), 2378
  ★*The R&B Box* (collection), 2239
McRae, Carmen
  ★*American Popular Song: Six Decades of Songwriters and Singers* (collection), 1059
  Carmen Sings Monk, 794.1
  The Definitive Collection (songwriter collection), 1101.1
  Duke Ellington (songwriter collection), 1099.1
  E. Y. Harburg (songwriter collection), 1103
  The Great American Songbook, 794.2
  Hoagy Carmichael (songwriter collection), 1097.2
  ★*The Jazz Singers: A Smithsonian Collection of Jazz Vocals from 1919–1994* (collection), 766
  Jingle Bell Jazz (collection), 3314
  Richard Whiting (songwriter collection), 1116
  Rodgers / Hart (songwriter collection), 1109.1
  Sings Lover Man, 794.3

  The Very Best of Cole Porter (songwriter collection), 1108.3
McShann, Jay
  An Anthology of Big Band Swing (collection), 528
  Big Band Renaissance: The Evolution of the Jazz Orchestra (collection), 739
  Blues from Kansas City, 556
  The Real Kansas City of the '20s, '30s, and '40s (collection), 552
  ★*The Vee-Jay Story: Celebrating 40 Years of Classic Hits* (collection), 2431
McTell, Blind Willie
  ★*The Blues: A Smithsonian Collection of Classic Blues Singers* (collection), 145
  The Classic Years, 249.1
  The Definitive Blind Willie McTell, 249.2
  ★*Legends of the Blues, Vol. 1* (collection), 150
  News and the Blues: Telling It Like It Is (collection), 156
  The Roots of Rap: Classic Recordings of the 1920's and 30's (collection), 157
  The Roots of Rock (collection), 368
  Statesboro Blues, 249.3
  ★*The Story of the Blues* (collection), 158
  When the Sun Goes Down 2: The First Time I Met the Blues (collection), 160
McVea, Jack. *The Big Horn: The History of the Honkin' and Screamin' Saxophone* (collection), 2314
MDC. *American Hardcore* (collection), 1977
Meat Puppets. *Meat Puppets II,* 2149
Medeski, Martin, and Wood
  Combustication, 828
  Icons among Us (collection), 934
meditation music, 1330–1333
  ★*Inside the Taj Mahal, I and II* (Horn), 1331
  ★*Music for Zen Meditation* (Scott), 1332
  Nirvana Road (Deuter), 1330
  Tibetan Bells II (Wolff), 1333
Meditation Singers. *Good News,* 3046
Megadeth. *Peace Sells . . . But Who's Buying?,* 2150
Megginson Female Quartette. *The Half Ain't Never Been Told, Vols. 1 and 2* (collection), 2956
Mehldau, Brad. *Art of the Trio, Vol. 1,* 994
Mekons. *No Thanks! The '70s Punk Rebellion* (collection), 2003
Mel and Tim
  Muscle Shoals Sound (collection), 2605
  Top of the Stax, Vol. 1: Twenty Greatest Hits (collection), 2611

Melanie
  Have a Nice Decade: The '70s Pop Culture Box (collection), 1240
  70s Greatest Hits (collection), 1243
Melford, Myra. *Even the Sounds Shine,* 995
Mellencamp, John. *Scarecrow,* 2080
★Mello-Kings. *The Doo-Wop Box* (collection), 2322
Mello-Moods. *The Doo-Wop Box II* (collection), 2323
Mellow Man Ace. *Escape from Havana,* 2866
Mellows. *The Doo-Wop Box II* (collection), 2323
Meloairs. *Southern Rhythm 'n' Rock: The Best of Excello Records, Vol. 22* (collection), 2427
Melvin, Harold and the Bluenotes
  ★*Love Train: The Sound of Philadelphia* (collection), 2552
  The Essential Harold Melvin and the Blue Notes, 2555
Memphis and St. Louis blues, 229–235
  Blues Masters, Vol. 12: Memphis Blues (collection), 229
  collections, 229–233
  I Ain't Gonna Be Worried No More (Estes), 234
  Masters of Memphis Blues (collection), 230
  ★*Memphis Masters: Early American Blues Classics* (collection), 231
  The Original Rolling Stone (Wilkins), 235
  St. Louis Blues: The Depression (collection), 232
  Wild About My Lovin': Beale Street Blues, 1928–30 (collection), 233
Memphis Jug Band
  Before the Blues: The Early American Black Music Scene; Classic Recordings from the 1920's and 30's, Vols. 1–3 (collection), 183
  The Best Of . . . , 198.1
  Blues Masters, Vol. 12: Memphis Blues (collection), 229
  ★*The Blues: A Smithsonian Collection of Classic Blues Singers* (collection), 145
  Good Time Blues: Harmonicas, Kazoos, Washboards, and Cow-Bells (collection), 268
  Memphis Jug Band with Cannon's Jug Stompers, 198.2
  ★*Memphis Masters: Early American Blues Classics* (collection), 231
  Memphis Shakedown: More Jug Band Classics (collection), 186
  The Roots of Rap: Classic Recordings of the 1920's and 30's (collection), 157

Ruckus Juice and Chittlins: The Great Jug Bands—Classic Recordings of the 1920s and '30s, Vol. 1 (collection), 188

★*The Story of the Blues* (collection), 158

Violin, Sing the Blues for Me: African-American Fiddlers (collection), 192

When the Sun Goes Down 2: The First Time I Met the Blues (collection), 160

Wild About My Lovin': Beale Street Blues, 1928–30 (collection), 233

Memphis Minnie
  ★*Blues Classics* (collection), 146
  Blues Masters, Vol. 12: Memphis Blues (collection), 229
  ★*The Blues: A Smithsonian Collection of Classic Blues Singers* (collection), 145
  ★*Chess Blues* (collection), 287
  The Great Depression: American Music in the '30s (collection), 1066
  ★*Hoodoo Lady*, 277.1
  ★*I Can't Be Satisfied: Early American Women Blues Singers, Vol. 1: Country* (collection), 149
  ★*Legends of the Blues, Vol. 1* (collection), 150
  ★*Memphis Masters: Early American Blues Classics* (collection), 231
  News and the Blues: Telling It Like It Is (collection), 156
  Queen of the Country Blues, 277.2
  The Roots of Rap: Classic Recordings of the 1920's and 30's (collection), 157
  The Roots of Rock (collection), 368
  ★*The Story of the Blues* (collection), 158

Memphis Slim
  ★*Blues Classics* (collection), 146
  Blues in the Mississippi Night (collection), 214
  ★*The Blues: A Smithsonian Collection of Classic Blues Singers* (collection), 145
  Grinder Man Blues: Masters of the Blues Piano (collection), 252
  Memphis Slim and Sonny Boy Williamson: Live in Europe (Memphis Slim and Sonny Boy Williamson), 403
  Messin' Around with the Blues: The Very Best of Memphis Slim (Memphis Slim), 301
  Rockin' This House: Chicago Blues Piano (collection), 257, 306
  When the Sun Goes Down 4: That's All Right (collection), 271

Memphis soul
  The Best of Rufus Thomas: Do the Funky Somethin', 2561

Gee Whiz: The Best of Carla Thomas, 2560

Men at Work. *80's Pop Hits* (collection), 1238

Mengelberg, Misha
  Four in One, 854.1
  ICP Orchestra: Oh My Dog, 854.2

Mercer, Johnny
  Hoagy Carmichael (songwriter collection), 1097.2
  Johnny Mercer, 1214
  Johnny Mercer Centennial Sheet Music Collection (songwriter collection), 1107.2
  Johnny Mercer (songwriter collection), 1107.1
  ★*Sentimental Journey: Pop Vocal Classics, Vol. 1* (collection), 1081
  Too Marvelous for Words: Capitol Sings Johnny Mercer (songwriter collection), 1107.3

Mercer, Mabel
  Alec Wilder (songwriter collection), 1117.1
  ★*American Popular Song: Six Decades of Songwriters and Singers* (collection), 1059
  Cole Porter (songwriter collection), 1108.1
  Cy Coleman (songwriter collection), 1098.2
  Dorothy Fields (songwriter collection), 1100
  Frank Loesser (songwriter collection), 1106.1
  George Gershwin (songwriter collection), 1101.3
  Harold Arlen (songwriter collection), 1095.1
  Jerome Kern (songwriter collection), 1104.1
  Mabel Mercer Sings Cole Porter, 1215
  Oscar Hammerstein II (songwriter collection), 1102

Mercy Dee
  One Room Country Shack, 323.1
  Troublesome Mind, 323.2

Merman, Ethel
  American Music Icon, 1142.1
  ★*An Earful of Music*, 1142.2
  Cole Porter (songwriter collection), 1108.1
  Dorothy Fields (songwriter collection), 1100
  The Flapper Box (collection), 1064
  Harold Arlen (songwriter collection), 1095.1
  Irving Berlin (songwriter collection), 1096.1
  Jule Styne (songwriter collection), 1111.1

Mary Martin and Ethel Merman: Their Legendary Appearance on the Ford 50th Anniversary Show, 1142.3
  Richard Whiting (songwriter collection), 1116
  This Is Art Deco (collection), 1090

Merrill, Helen
  Alec Wilder (songwriter collection), 1117.1
  Arthur Schwartz (songwriter collection), 1110.2
  The Definitive Collection (songwriter collection), 1101.1
  Helen Merrill, 795
  The Very Best of Cole Porter (songwriter collection), 1108.3
  Waller / Razaf (songwriter collection), 1113.2

Merriweather, Big Maceo
  The Bluebird Recordings, Vol. 1: Chicago, 1941–1942, 262
  ★*The Blues: A Smithsonian Collection of Classic Blues Singers* (collection), 145
  Chicago Is Just That Way (collection), 289
  Detroit Blues: Blues from the Motor City (collection), 291
  Grinder Man Blues: Masters of the Blues Piano (collection), 252
  ★*Mean Old World: The Blues from 1940–1994* (collection), 154
  When the Sun Goes Down 4: That's All Right (collection), 271

Merry, Allan "Death." *Eccentric Soul: The Young Disciples* (collection), 2562

Mesney, Dorothy. *The Parlour Piano: American Popular Songs of the 1800s*, 119

Metallica
  Master of Puppets, 2081.1
  Metallica, 2081.2

The Meters
  Beg, Scream, and Shout! The Big Ol' Box of '60s Soul (collection), 2433
  The Meters Anthology: Funkify Your Life, 2366
  ★*What It Is! Funky Soul and Rare Grooves* (collection), 2615

Metheny, Pat
  80/81, 829.1
  Offramp, 829.2
  Pat Metheny Group, 829.3
  Progressions: 100 Years of Jazz Guitar (collection), 481

Method Man. *Tical*, 2867

MF Doom
  Born Like This, 2868.1
  Mm . . . Food?, 2868.2

MFSB
  Love Is the Message: The Best of MFSB, 2556

MFSB (cont.)
  ★*Love Train: The Sound of Philadelphia*
    (collection), 2552
  ★*Saturday Night Fever,* 2658
Miami soul. *Eccentric Soul: The Outskirts
    of Deep City* (collection), 2565
Michel Petrucciani Trio with Jim Hall.
    Live from the Village Vanguard
    (collection), 935
Microscopic Septet. *Seven Men in
    Neckties: History of the Micros,
    Vol. 1,* 996
Micus, Stephen. *On the Wing,* 1363
Midler, Bette
  The Divine Bette Midler, 1289.1
  Experience the Divine: Greatest Hits,
    1289.2
Midnight Oil. *Diesel and Dust,* 2151
Midnighters. *King R&B Box Set*
    (collection), 2424
Mighty Clouds of Joy
  The Best of Mighty Clouds of Joy,
    3022
  Gospel (collection), 2962
  *Living Legends of Gospel: The Quartets,
    Vols. 1 and 2* (collection), 3010
  Testify! The Gospel Box (collection),
    2974
Mighty Hannibal. *The Best of Loma
    Records: The Rise and Fall of a
    1960's Soul Label* (collection),
    2590
Milburn, Amos
  *The Complete Aladdin Recordings of
    Amos Milburn,* 2280.1
  *Crescent City Soul: The Sound of New
    Orleans, 1947–1974* (collection),
    2564
  Let's Have a Party: The Aladdin
    Recordings, 2280.2
  ★*Mean Old World: The Blues from
    1940–1994* (collection), 154
  ★*The R&B Box* (collection), 2239
  The Roots of Rock 'n' Roll, 1946–1954
    (collection), 1755
  ★*Texas Music, Vol. 1: Postwar Blues
    Combos* (collection), 316
Milem, Percy
  The Complete Goldwax Singles, Vol. 2
    (collection), 2592
  The Complete Goldwax Singles, Vol. 3
    (collection), 2593
Millinder, Lucky
  Apollo Jump, 2319.1
  The Very Best of Lucky Millinder,
    2319.2
Millang, Steve. *Holidays and Special
    Times,* 3250
Miller, Buddy. *Best of the Hightone Years,*
    1707
Miller, Effie. *Twenty First Street Stomp:
    Piano Blues of St. Louis* (collection),
    259

Miller, Emmett
  *Good for What Ails You: Music of the
    Medicine Shows* (collection), 184
  The Minstrel Man from Georgia, 1143
Miller, Gene "Bowlegs"
  The Complete Goldwax Singles, Vol. 1
    (collection), 2591
  The Complete Goldwax Singles, Vol. 2
    (collection), 2592
Miller, George. *The Mercury New
    Orleans Sessions 1950 and 1953*
    (collection), 2361
Miller, Glenn
  ★*Big Band Jazz: From the Beginnings to
    the Fifties* (collection), 529
  ★*Brother, Can You Spare a Dime?
    American Song during the Great
    Depression* (collection), 1061
  ★*Essential Glenn Miller* (Miller), 1144
  Harry Warren (songwriter collection),
    1114
  Jule Styne (songwriter collection),
    1111.1
  ★*Nipper's Greatest Hits: The 30's, Vol. 1*
    (collection), 1072
  ★*Nipper's Greatest Hits: The 40's, Vol. 1*
    (collection), 1073
  *Songs That Got Us through World
    War II, Vol. 2* (collection), 1086
  ★*Swing Time! The Fabulous Big Band
    Era* (collection), 1089
Miller, Mitch
  Sing Along with Mitch, 1216
  *16 Most Requested Songs: The 1950s,
    Vol. 1* (collection), 1171
Miller, Polk. *Polk Miller and His Old South
    Quartette,* 1416
Miller, Punch. *New Orleans Jazz*
    (collection), 503
★Miller, Red. *Nashville Jumps: Blues and
    Rhythm on Nashville Independent
    Labels 1945–1955* (collection),
    2376
Miller, Roger
  ★*All Time Greatest Hits,* 1516.1
  *King of the Road: The Genius of Roger
    Miller,* 1516.2
Miller, Ronnie (and the Pips). *The Fire
    / Fury Records Story* (collection),
    2422
Miller, Steve
  The Best of Steve Miller, 1968–1973,
    1840
  Greatest Hits, 1974–1978, 1916
  *Texas Music, Vol. 3: Garage Bands and
    Psychedelia* (collection), 1830
Millinder, Lucky
  An Anthology of Big Band Swing
    (collection), 528
  *Songs That Got Us through World
    War II, Vol. 2* (collection), 1086
Millionaires. *The Complete Goldwax
    Singles, Vol. 1* (collection), 2591

Mills Blues Rhythm Band. *An Anthology
    of Big Band Swing* (collection), 528
The Mills Brothers
  Alec Wilder (songwriter collection),
    1117.1
  The Anthology, 1145
  The Classic Hoagy Carmichael
    (songwriter collection), 1097.1
  Dorothy Fields (songwriter collection),
    1100
  Hit Parade, 1943 (collection), 1157
  Hoagy Carmichael (songwriter
    collection), 1097.2
  Johnny Mercer (songwriter collection),
    1107.1
  *Sentimental Journey: Pop Vocal
    Classics, Vol. 1* (collection), 1167
  ★*Sentimental Journey: Pop Vocal
    Classics, Vol. 1* (collection), 1081
  *Songs That Got Us through World
    War II* (collection), 1085
  Stars of the Apollo (collection), 2240
  This Is Art Deco (collection), 1090
  25 Sweethearts of Yesteryear
    (collection), 1092
Mills, Kerry. *Phono-Cylinders, Vols. 1
    and 2* (collection), 1074
Mills, Stephanie
  Gold, 2281.1
  The Ultimate Collection, 2281.2
Milnes, Sherrill. *Music of the American
    Revolution: The Birth of Liberty*
    (collection), 46
Milsap, Ronnie
  The Scepter Records Story (collection),
    2426
  Ultimate Ronnie Milsap, 1668
Milton, Roy
  *Blue Yule: Christmas Blues and R&B
    Classics* (collection), 3295
  ★*Central Avenue Sounds: Jazz in Los
    Angeles* (collection), 471
  Roy Milton and His Solid Senders, 2282
  ★*The R&B Box* (collection), 2239
  The Roots of Rock 'n' Roll, 1946–1954
    (collection), 1755
  ★*The Specialty Story* (collection), 2428
Mimms, Garnet
  *Beg, Scream, and Shout! The Big Ol'
    Box of '60s Soul* (collection), 2433
  Birth of Soul, 4 Vols. (collection), 2434
  Cry Baby: The Best of Garnet Mimms,
    2498
  *Dave Godin's Deep Soul Treasures,
    Vols. 1–4* (collection), 2435
Mims, Charles. *Kwanzaa for Young People
    (and Everyone Else!),* 3242, 3352
Mingus Big Band. *Live in Time,* 759
Mingus, Charles, 675
  ★*The Birth of the Third Stream*
    (collection), 1030
  The Black Saint and the Sinner Lady,
    675.1

★*Central Avenue Sounds: Jazz in Los Angeles* (collection), 471

Charles "Baron" Mingus: West Coast, 1945–1949, 675.2

Charles Mingus, 648

Charles Mingus: Live in '64, 675.3

Charles Mingus: More Than a Fake Book, 675.4

Charles Mingus: Triumph of the Underdog, 675.5

The Great Concert of Charles Mingus, 675.6

Harlem in Vogue: The Poetry and Jazz of Langston Hughes (collection), 811

★*Ken Burns Jazz Collection: Charles Mingus,* 675.7

★*Ken Burns Jazz: The Story of America's Music* (collection), 478

Let My Children Hear Music, 675.8

★*Mingus Ah Um,* 675.9

Mingus Dynasty, 675.10

★*Pithecanthropus Erectus,* 675.11

Tijuana Moods, 675.12

Ministry. *The Land of Rape and Honey,* 2152

Mink

D.I.Y. Blank Generation: The New York Scene (collection), 1978

No Thanks! The '70s Punk Rebellion (collection), 2003

Minnelli, Liza

Cy Coleman (songwriter collection), 1098.2

Liza Minnelli at Carnegie Hall (Highlights), 1290

Vincent Youmans (songwriter collection), 1118

Minor Threat

American Hardcore (collection), 1977

Complete Discography, 1992

Mint Condition. *The Collection, 1991–1998,* 2391

Minton, Phil. *Doughnut in One Hand,* 855

Minutemen

Double Nickels on the Dime, 2153.1

We Jam Econo, 2153.2

The Miracles. *See also* Robinson, Smokey and the Miracles

Best of Chess R&B, Vols. 1 and 2 (collection), 2420

Dave Godin's Deep Soul Treasures, Vols. 1–4 (collection), 2435

Disco Box (collection), 2644

The Doo-Wop Box II (collection), 2323

Hitsville USA: The Motown Singles Collection (collection), 2603

Motown around the World (collection), 2437

★*The R&B Box* (collection), 2239

Mirowitz, Sheldon. *Piano Solos: Narada Artists* (collection), 1370

Missing Persons. *Like Omigod! The 80s Pop Culture Box (Totally)* (collection), 1241

Mission of Burma. *Vs (the Definitive Edition plus Bonus DVD),* 1993

Missionary Quartet. *Classic African American Gospel from Smithsonian Folkways* (collection), 2959

Mississippi Delta blues, 211–228

Acoustic Country Blues Guitar: Delta Blues before Robert Johnson (collection), 211

Back to the Crossroads: The Roots of Robert Johnson (collection), 212

★*The Best of* Charlie Patton (Patton), 226.1

Big Joe Williams and the Stars of Mississippi Blues (collection), 213

Blues in the Mississippi Night (collection), 214

Blues Masters, Vol. 8: Mississippi Delta Blues (collection), 215

Canned Heat Blues: Masters of Delta Blues (collection), 216

★*The Centennial Collection* (Johnson), 225.1

collections, 211–221

Complete Early Recordings (James), 224.1

Complete Recordings (Patton), 226.2

The Complete Bukka White (White), 228

The Complete Plantation Recordings: The Historic 1941–42 Library of Congress Field Recordings (Waters), 227

Country Blues Guitar in Open Tunings (Grossman), 222.1

Deep Blues (collection), 217

Delta Blues (Grossman), 222.2

Delta Blues Guitar (Grossman), 222.3

Delta Blues: The Original Library of Congress Sessions (House), 223

King of the Delta Blues Singers (Johnson), 225.2

Legends of Country Blues (collection), 218

Masters of the Country Blues: Son House and Bukka White (collection), 219

★*Masters of the Delta Blues: The Friends of Charlie Patton* (collection), 220

The New Transcriptions (Johnson), 225.3

The Road to Robert Johnson and Beyond (collection), 221

Robert Johnson, King of the Delta Blues (Johnson), 225.4

The Search for Robert Johnson (Johnson), 225.5

The Skip James Collection (James), 224.2

Mississippi Mass Choir

It Remains to Be Seen . . ., 3069.2

The First Twenty Years, 3069.1

Mississippi Sheiks

Back to the Crossroads: The Roots of Robert Johnson (collection), 212

★*The Blues: A Smithsonian Collection of Classic Blues Singers* (collection), 145

Honey Babe Let the Deal Go Down: Best of the Mississippi Sheiks, 199.1

Raunchy Business: Hot Nuts and Lollypops (collection), 269

Stop and Listen, 199.2

Violin, Sing the Blues for Me: African-American Fiddlers (collection), 192

When the Sun Goes Down 2: The First Time I Met the Blues (collection), 160

★Missourians. *Big Band Jazz: From the Beginnings to the Fifties* (collection), 529

Missy Dee and the Melody Crew. *Don't Stop: Recording Tap* (collection), 2657

Mist. *Eccentric Soul: Twinight's Lunar Rotation* (collection), 2568

Mitchell, Blue. *The Thing to Do,* 649

Mitchell, Elizabeth. *You Are My Little Bird,* 3222

Mitchell, Freddie. *The Big Horn: The History of the Honkin' and Screamin' Saxophone* (collection), 2314

Mitchell, Guy

★*Sentimental Journey: Pop Vocal Classics, Vol. 3* (collection), 1169

16 Most Requested Songs: The 1950s, Vol. 1 (collection), 1171

Mitchell, Joni

Blue, 1291.1, 1893.1

★*Court and Spark,* 1291.2, 1893.2

Hijera, 1893.3

Hits, 1247, 1291.3

Ladies of the Canyon, 1291.4

Mitchell, Little Anthony. *Boddie Recording Company Cleveland, Ohio* (collection), 2569

Mitchell, Mitchell. *Eccentric Soul: The Prix Label* (collection), 2601

Mitchell, Phillip. *The Spring Story: Essential 70s Soul* (collection), 2608

Mitchell, Roscoe. *Sound,* 927.1

Mitchell, Willie

Poppa Willie: The Hi Years, 1962–74, 2283

The Hi Records Story (collection), 2423

Mitchell's Christian Singers

★*Good News: 100 Gospel Greats* (collection), 2961

Mitchell's Christian Singers (cont.)
  Gospel: Negro Spirituals / Gospel Songs, 1926–1942 (collection), 2963
  ★The Gospel Sound (collection), 2964
  The Gospel Tradition: The Roots and the Branches, Vol. 1 (collection), 2955
Mix Master Mike. Anti-Theft Device, 2869
Mobb Deep
  Hell on Earth, 2870.1
  The Infamous . . . ., 2870.2
Mobley, Hank. Soul Station, 650
Moby
  For the Kids Three! (collection), 3209
  Go: The Very Best of Moby, Deluxe Ed., 2224.1
  Moby, 2224.2
  Play, 2224.3
Moby Grape. Vintage: The Very Best of Moby Grape, 1841
modern blues, 336–366
  All My Life (Brown), 350
  Anthology (King), 354.1
  Anthology (Little Milton), 356.1
  Art of the Shuffle, for Guitar: An Exploration of Shuffle, Boogie, and Swing Rhythms (Rubin), 360.1
  Attack of the Atomic Guitar (Wilson), 365
  B. B. King Anthology (King), 354.3
  B. B. King: The King of the Blues (King), 354.2
  ★The Best of Duke-Peacock Blues (collection), 336
  The Best of Albert King, 353.1
  Blue Flames: A Sun Blues Collection (collection), 337
  Blue Guitar: The Chief and Age Sessions (Hooker), 352.1
  Blues Masters, Vol. 1: Urban Blues (collection), 338
  ★Bobby "Blue" Bland: The Anthology, 349.1
  Bottom of the Top (Walker), 364
  The Cobra Records Story: Chicago Rock and Blues (collection), 339
  collections, 336–347
  The Collection (Parker), 359.1
  The Complete King and Bobbin Recordings (King), 353.2
  Electric Blues Guitar Giants (Sokolow and Schiff), 362
  ★The Essential Otis Rush: Classic Cobra Recordings (Rush), 361
  The Freddie King Collection, 355.1
  Gold (King), 354.4
  Good Stuff (McCain), 358
  Greatest Hits (Little Milton), 356.2
  Greatest Hits (Taylor), 363
  Greatest Hits, Vol. 1 (Bland), 349.2
  How Blue Can You Get? Classic Live Performances (King), 354.5
  Inside the Blues, 1942–1982 (Rubin), 360.2

An Introduction to Earl Hooker (Hooker), 352.2
The Jewel / Paula Records Story: The Blues, Rhythm and Blues, and Soul Recordings (collection), 340
Johnny Ace Memorial Album, 348
Junior's Blues: The Duke Recordings, Vol. 1 (Parker), 359.2
★King of the Blues Guitar (King), 353.3
★Live at the Regal (King), 354.6
Live Wire / Blues Power (King), 353.4
Memphis Blues: Important Postwar Recordings (collection), 341
Mighty Man (Young), 366
The Modern Records Blues Story (collection), 342
More Big Blues (King), 353.5
Original Greatest Hits (King), 354.7
Soul Shots, Vol. 4: Urban Blues (collection), 343
Sun Records Harmonica Classics (collection), 346
Sun Records: The Ultimate Blues Collection (collection), 345
The Sun Blues Years (collection), 344
Superblues: All-Time Classic Blues Hits, Vol. 1 (collection), 347
Two Bugs and a Roach (Hooker), 352.3
Two Steps from the Blues (Bland), 349.3
Ultimate Collection (King), 355.2
The Ultimate Collection (King), 353.6, 354.8
The Very Best of Albert King [1999], 353.7
The Very Best of Albert King [2002], 353.8
★The Very Best of Buddy Guy, 351
The Very Best of Freddy King, Vol. 1, 355.3
Welcome to the Club: The Essential Chess Recordings (Little Milton), 356.3
★West Side Soul (Magic Sam), 357.1
. . . With a Feeling! (Magic Sam), 357.2
Modern Detergents. Boddie Recording Company Cleveland, Ohio (collection), 2569, 2570
Modern Jazz Quartet
  Concorde, 618.1
  Dedicated to Connie, 618.2
  ★Django, 618.3
  ★Ken Burns Jazz: The Story of America's Music (collection), 478
  No Sun in Venice, 618.4
  Odds against Tomorrow [1990] (Lewis and Modern Jazz Quartet), 1055.1
  Odds against Tomorrow [2003] (Lewis and Modern Jazz Quartet), 1055.2
  Third Stream Music, 1042
Modern Lovers. No Thanks! The '70s Punk Rebellion (collection), 2003

modern mainstream: 1970s, 869–900
  Alone Together (Hall), 881
  Art Pepper: Notes from a Jazz Survivor (Pepper), 888.1
  Blues to Africa (Weston), 899.1
  Body and Soul (Cohn), 873
  Coast to Coast (Blakey), 871
  Conjuration: Fat Tuesday's Session (Adams), 869
  Dizzy Gillespie's Big 4 (Gillespie), 878
  Don't Stop the Carnival (Rollins), 891.1
  Echoes of a Friend (Tyner), 897.1
  Endgame Brilliance: Constellation & Tune Up (Stitt), 896
  Enlightenment (Tyner), 897.2
  Harlem Bush Music (Bartz), 870
  Here's to My Lady (Woods), 900.1
  Homecoming: Live at the Village Vanguard (Gordon), 879
  If I'm Lucky (Sims), 895
  In My Life (McPartland), 884
  Intuition (Evans), 874.1
  Jimmy Rowles / Ray Brown: The Duo Sessions (Rowles), 892
  Landscape (Pepper), 888.2
  Live at Blues Alley (Roach), 889
  Live at Maybeck Recital Hall, Vol. 16 (Jones), 883
  Moody's Party: Live at the Blue Note (Moody), 885
  Nights at the Vanguard (Flanagan), 876.1
  The Paris Concert: Edition One (Evans), 874.2
  Pure Getz (Getz), 877
  The Quintet: V.S.O.P. (V.S.O.P.), 898
  Reflections (Morgan), 886
  Return of the Griffin (Griffin), 880
  Road Shows, Vol. 1 (Rollins), 891.2
  Rosewood (Shaw), 893.1
  Solid (Shaw), 893.2
  Something to Live For: The Music of Billy Strayhorn (Farmer), 875
  Spirits of Our Ancestors (Weston), 899.2
  Sunshine of My Soul: Live at the Keystone Korner (Byard), 872
  Then and Now (Rodney), 890
  ★Three for All (Woods), 900.2
  Tommy Flanagan Trio '77 (Flanagan), 876.2
  Virtuoso (Pass), 887
  Wayne Shorter Live at Montreux 1996 (Shorter), 894
  You or Me (Heath), 882
Mogwai. Young Team, 2237
Momps. D.I.Y. Blank Generation: The New York Scene (collection), 1978
Monae, Janelle. ArchAndroid, 1292
Monarchs. The Doo-Wop Box II (collection), 2323
Moncur, Graehan, III. Evolution, 693

Mondy, Alma. *The Mercury New Orleans Sessions 1950 and 1953* (collection), 2361

Monk, T. S. *Monk on Monk*, 997

Monk, Thelonious, 674
  At the Five Spot, 674.1
  Best of Thelonious Monk, 674.2
  Brilliant Corners, 674.3
  The Complete Blue Note Recordings of Thelonious Monk, 674.4
  ★*Jazz on a Summer's Day* (collection), 664
  ★*Ken Burns Jazz Collection: Thelonious Monk*, 674.5
  ★*Ken Burns Jazz: The Story of America's Music* (collection), 478
  Monk's Dream, 674.6
  Monk's Music, 674.7
  Piano Legends (collection), 480
  ★*The Smithsonian Collection of Classic Jazz* (collection), 486
  ★*Sound of Jazz* (collection), 487
  Thelonious Monk, 674.8
  Thelonious Monk: American Composer, 674.9
  ★*Thelonious Monk Orchestra at Town Hall*, 674.10
  ★*Thelonious Monk Quartet with John Coltrane at Carnegie Hall*, 674.11
  Thelonious Monk with John Coltrane, 674.12

The Monkees
  Casey Kasem Presents America's Top Ten through the Years: The Sixties (collection), 1156
  Greatest Hits, 1815
  Nuggets: A Classic Collection from the Psychedelic Sixties (collection), 1809
  ★*Nuggets: Artifacts of the First Psychedelic Era* (collection), 1808
  Pure 60's: The #1 Hits (collection), 1165
  25 All-Time Greatest Bubblegum Hits (collection), 1811

The Monotones
  ★*The Doo-Wop Box* (collection), 2322
  The Golden Era of Rock 'n' Roll (collection), 1748

Monroe, Bill
  Appalachian Stomp: Bluegrass Classics (collection), 1560
  Blue Grass, 1959–1969, 1596.2
  Blue Grass, 1970–1979, 1596.3
  ★*Blue Grass, 1950–1958*, 1596.1
  ★*Blue Moon of Kentucky, 1936–1949*, 1596.4
  Jubilation! Great Gospel Performances, Vol. 3: Country Gospel (collection), 3112
  The Music of Bill Monroe from 1936 to 1994, 1596.5

My Last Days on Earth, Blue Grass, 1981–1994, 1596.6
★*16 Gems*, 1596.7

Monroe Brothers
  ★*Anthology of American Folk Music, Vol. 4* (collection), 1387
  ★*Something Got a Hold of Me: A Treasury of Sacred Music* (collection), 3114

Monroe, Marilyn. *Hoagy Carmichael* (songwriter collection), 1097.2

Monroe Tucker Band. *The Swing Time Records Story: R&B, Blues, and Gospel, 1946–1952* (collection), 2430

Monroe, Vaughn
  ★*Nipper's Greatest Hits: The 40's, Vol. 1* (collection), 1073
  ★*Sentimental Journey: Pop Vocal Classics, Vol. 1* (collection), 1081
  ★*Sentimental Journey: Pop Vocal Classics, Vol. 2* (collection), 1168
  Songs That Got Us through World War II (collection), 1085
  Songs That Got Us through World War II, Vol. 2 (collection), 1086
  Waller / Razaf (songwriter collection), 1113.2

Montana, Patsy
  ★*Best of Patsy Montana*, 1417
  Classic Country Music: A Smithsonian Collection (collection), 1382
  Western Swing: 40 Bootstompers from the Golden Age (collection), 1433

Montgomery, Little Brother
  ★*The Blues: A Smithsonian Collection of Classic Blues Singers* (collection), 145
  Classic African American Gospel from Smithsonian Folkways (collection), 2959
  Conversation with the Blues (collection), 148
  Grinder Man Blues: Masters of the Blues Piano (collection), 252
  ★*Juke Joint Saturday Night: Piano Blues, Rags and Stomps; Classic Recordings from the 1920s and '30s* (collection), 255
  When the Sun Goes Down 2: The First Time I Met the Blues (collection), 160

Montgomery, Wes
  Impressions: The Verve Jazz Sides, 651.1
  ★*The Incredible Jazz Guitar of Wes Montgomery*, 651.2
  Jazz Lullaby (collection), 3264
  Progressions: 100 Years of Jazz Guitar (collection), 481
  Wes Montgomery Live in '65, 651.3

Montoliu, Tete. *Tete!*, 856

Montreux
  Solace: A Windham Hill Collection (collection), 1373
  Windham Hill: The First Ten Years (collection), 1377

Moody Blues. *The Best of the Moody Blues*, 1928

Moody, James
  Moody's Mood for Blues, 652
  Moody's Party: Live at the Blue Note, 885

Mooney, Hal and His Orchestra. *The Definitive Collection* (songwriter collection), 1101.1

Mooney, John. *Telephone King*, 453

The Moonglows
  Best of Chess R&B, Vols. 1 and 2 (collection), 2420
  Best of Doo Wop Ballads (collection), 1743
  Blue Velvet: The Ultimate Collection, 2349.1
  ★*The Doo Wop Box: 101 Vocal Group Gems from the Golden Age of Rock 'n' Roll* (collection), 1745
  ★*The Doo-Wop Box* (collection), 2322
  The Doo-Wop Box II (collection), 2323
  The Golden Era of Rock 'n' Roll (collection), 1748
  The Moonglows, 2349.2
  ★*The R&B Box* (collection), 2239
  Street Corner Serenade: The Greatest Doo-Wop Hits of the '50s and '60s (collection), 1756

Moore, Bobby and the Rhythm Aces
  Beg, Scream, and Shout! The Big Ol' Box of '60s Soul (collection), 2433
  Best of Chess R&B, Vols. 1 and 2 (collection), 2420

★Moore, Gatemouth. *Stompin' at the Savoy: The Original Indie Label, 1944–1961* (collection), 2429

Moore, Herbert. *The Mercury New Orleans Sessions 1950 and 1953* (collection), 2361

★Moore, Jackie. *Atlantic Soul, 1959–1975* (collection), 2589

Moore, Johnny
  ★*Central Avenue Sounds: Jazz in Los Angeles* (collection), 471
  ★*The R&B Box* (collection), 2239

Moore, Johnny B. *Live at Blue Chicago*, 454

Moore, LaVel. *Eccentric Soul: The Young Disciples* (collection), 2562

Moore, Mandy. *90's Pop Hits* (collection), 1242

Moore, Melba
  The Sweetest Feeling: A Van McCoy Songbook (collection), 2447
  This Is It: The Best of Melba Moore, 2284

Moore, Patsy. *Kwanzaa for Young People (and Everyone Else!),* 3352

Moore, Robert. *Crash of Thunder: Boss Soul, Funk, and R&B Sides from the Vaults of the King, Federal, and Deluxe Labels* (collection), 2596

★Moore, Scotty. *Legends of Guitar: Rock The '50s,* Vol. 2 (collection), 1750

Moore, Vaughn. *Hit Parade, 1943* (collection), 1157

Moore, Wild Bill. *The Big Horn: The History of the Honkin' and Screamin' Saxophone* (collection), 2314

★Moore, William. *Guitar Wizards* (collection), 243

Moovers. *Eccentric Soul: The Deep City Label* (collection), 2600

M.O.P. *Warriorz,* 2852

Moran, Jason
Jason Moran Presents the Bandwagon, 998.1
Modernistic, 998.2

Morath, Max
Don't Give the Name a Bad Place: Types and Stereotypes in American Musical Theater, 1870–1900 (collection), 1063
Irving Berlin (songwriter collection), 1096.1
Max Morath Plays the Best of Scott Joplin and Other Rag Classics, 137.1
Ragtime Women, 137.2

Morello, Joe. *Rudimental Jazz: A Musical Application of Rudiments to the Drumset,* 494

Morgan, Frank. *Reflections,* 886

Morgan, Helen
★*American Popular Song: Six Decades of Songwriters and Singers* (collection), 1059
Flappers, Vamps, and Sweet Young Things (collection), 1065
Jerome Kern (songwriter collection), 1104.1
★*Sophisticated Ladies* (collection), 1087

Morgan, Lee
★*Best of Lee Morgan,* 653.1
Sidewinder, 653.3
Sidewinder [1963], 653.2

Morgan, Rocky, and His Triple R Boys. *Swingbillies: Hillbilly and Western Swing on Modern/Colonial/Flair, 1947–1952* (collection), 1431

Morgan, Russ. *Russ Morgan and His Orchestra Play: 22 Original Big Band Recordings,* 1146

Morganfield, McKinley. *See* Muddy Waters

Morisette, Johnnie. *Sam Cooke's SAR Records Story* (collection), 2606

Morissette, Alanis. *Jagged Little Pill,* 2154

Mormon Tabernacle Choir
God Bless America, 3377
The Joy of Christmas, 3281
Songs of the Civil War and Stephen Foster Favorites, 75

Morning Sun Singers. *The Civil War Music Collector's Edition* (collection), 61

Morris Brown Quartet. *I Hear Music in the Air: A Treasury of Gospel Music* (collection), 3008

Morris, Joan
After the Ball: A Treasury of Turn-of-the-Century Popular Songs; Highlights from Vaudeville, 120.1
Moonlight Bay: Songs as Is and Songs as Was, 120.2

★Morris, Joe. *Atlantic R&B, 1947–1974* (collection), 2418

Morris, Keith. *American Hardcore* (collection), 1977

Morrison, Van
★*Astral Weeks,* 1894.1
Moondance, 1894.2
★*Nuggets II: Original Artifacts from the British Empire and Beyond* (collection), 1791
Van Morrison Guitar Songbook, 1894.3

Morse, Ella Mae. *Ella Mae Morse,* 1217

Morse, Robert. *Frank Loesser* (songwriter collection), 1106.1

Morton, Bishop Paul S. *Going Up Yonder: The Best of the Gospel Choirs* (collection), 3051

Morton, Bishop Paul. *We Offer Christ,* 3070

Morton, Jelly Roll
Birth of the Hot: The Classic Chicago "Red Hot Peppers" Sessions, 501.1
★*Central Avenue Sounds: Jazz in Los Angeles* (collection), 471
Collected Piano Music, 501.2
★*The Commodore Story* (collection), 561
The Greatest Ragtime of the Century (collection), 125
★*Jelly Roll Morton,* 501.3
Jelly Roll Morton: The Complete Library of. Congress Recordings by Alan Lomax, 501.4
★*Ken Burns Jazz: The Story of America's Music* (collection), 478
The New Orleans Rhythm Kings and Jelly Roll Morton (collection), 497
Piano Legends (collection), 480
Riverside History of Classic Jazz (collection), 499

Mos Def
Black on Both Sides, 2871.1
The Ecstatic, 2871.2
★Mos Def and Talib Kweli. *Mos Def and Talib Kweli Are Black Star,* 2872

Moses, Lee. *Dave Godin's Deep Soul Treasures, Vols. 1–4* (collection), 2435

Moses, Oral. *Songs of America,* 41

Moss, Bill. *Eccentric Soul: The Capsoul Label* (collection), 2599

Moss, Buddy. *Good Time Blues: Harmonicas, Kazoos, Washboards, and Cow-Bells* (collection), 268

Moss, J. *J Moss Project,* 3093

Moten, Bennie
Bennie Moten's Kansas City Orchestra, 557
★*Big Band Jazz: From the Beginnings to the Fifties* (collection), 529
★*Ken Burns Jazz: The Story of America's Music* (collection), 478
The Real Kansas City of the '20s, '30s, and '40s (collection), 552
★*The Smithsonian Collection of Classic Jazz* (collection), 486

Motian, Paul. *It Should Have Happened a Long Time Ago,* 999

Motorhead. *No Remorse,* 2155

Mott the Hoople. *Old Records Never Die,* 1877

Mottola, Tony. *Frank Sinatra: Concert Collection,* 1224.3

Mountain Singers Male Quartette. *How Can I Keep from Singing: Early American Religious Music and Song, Vols. 1 and 2* (collection), 2957

Move
The Best of the Move, 1799
★*Nuggets II: Original Artifacts from the British Empire and Beyond* (collection), 1791

Mozart, Wolfgang Amadeus
Baby Mozart Music Festival, 3259.1
The Magic Flute Story: An Opera Fantasy, 3259.2

Mr. Lif. *I Phantom,* 2873

Mr. Mister. *Like Omigod! The 80s Pop Culture Box (Totally)* (collection), 1241

★Mr. Swing. *Nashville Jumps: Blues and Rhythm on Nashville Independent Labels 1945–1955* (collection), 2376

Mr. T Experience. *Greasy Kid Stuff* (collection), 3210

Muddy Waters
Afro-American Blues and Game Songs (collection), 169
★*The Anthology,* 308.1
★*Blues Classics* (collection), 146
Blues Masters, Vol. 6: Blues Originals (collection), 367
Blues Masters, Vol. 8: Mississippi Delta Blues (collection), 215
Blues Masters, Vol. 2: Postwar Chicago Blues (collection), 285

The Blues: A Smithsonian Collection of Classic Blues Singers (collection), 145

Chess Blues (collection), 287

The Chess Box, 308.2

Chicago Is Just That Way (collection), 289

The Complete Plantation Recordings: The Historic 1941–42 Library of Congress Field Recordings, 227

Deep Blues, 308.3

Mean Old World: The Blues from 1940–1994 (collection), 154

Muddy "Mississippi" Waters Live, 308.5

Muddy Waters: The Definitive Collection, 308.4

Newport Folk Festival: Best of the Blues, 1959–68 (collection), 392

The Road to Robert Johnson and Beyond (collection), 221

Rock and Roll: The Early Days (collection), 1752

The Roots of Rock 'n' Roll, 1946–1954 (collection), 1755

Muldaur, Maria. *Maria Muldaur*, 2054

Mullican, Moon

   All-Time Country and Western Hits (collection), 1449

   Moonshine Jamboree, 1517

Mulligan, Gerry

   The Best of the Gerry Mulligan Quartet with Chet Baker, 619.1

   Big Band Renaissance: The Evolution of the Jazz Orchestra (collection), 739

   The Birth of the Cool, Vol. 2 (collection), 604

   Jazz Masters: Vintage Collection, 1958–1961 (collection), 477

   Jazz on a Summer's Day (collection), 664

   Ken Burns Jazz: The Story of America's Music (collection), 478

   The Original Sextet: Complete Studio Masters, 619.2

Mullins, Rich. *CCM Top 100: Greatest Songs in Christian Music, Vol. 1* (collection), 3136

multicultural children's music, 3226–3236

   African American Folk Songs and Rhythms (Jenkins), 3234.1

   Animal Playground (collection), 3226

   Baby Loves Salsa Presents Salsa for Kittens and Puppies (collection), 3227

   collections, 3226–3230

   It Takes the Whole Village (African Children's Choir), 3231

   Le Hoogie Boogie: Louisiana French Music for Children (Doucet), 3233

   Multi-Cultural Children's Songs (Jenkins), 3234.2

   The Planet Sleeps (collection), 3228

Seal Maiden: A Celtic Musical (Casey), 3232

Sesame Street Playground (collection), 3229

Songs about Native Americans (Skiera-Zucek), 3235

Songs in French for Children (Vernay), 3236

World Playground: A Musical Adventure for Kids (collection), 3230

Munizzi, Martha. *No Limits—Live*, 3154

Murcell, Raymond. *Angels' Visits and Other Vocal Gems of Victorian America* (collection), 93

Murphey, Michael Martin. *Cowboy Songs*, 1669

Murphy, Mark

   Rah, 796.1

   Timeless, 796.2

Murphy, Spud. *An Anthology of Big Band Swing* (collection), 528

Murphy, Walter and the Big Apple Band. *Disco Box* (collection), 2644

Murray, Billy

   American Popular Song: Six Decades of Songwriters and Singers (collection), 1059

   The Billy Murray Anthology: The Denver Nightingale, 1147

   Phono-Cylinders, Vols. 1 and 2 (collection), 1074

   The Phonographic Yearbook, 1907: Dear Old Golden Rule Days (collection), 1075

   The Phonographic Yearbook, 1908: Take Me Out with the Crowd (collection), 1076

   The Phonographic Yearbook, 1912: Waitin' on the Levee (collection), 1077

Murray, Clarence. *Action Speaks Louder Than Words: The Best of SSS International* (collection), 2588

Murray, David

   Conjure: Music for the Texts of Ishmael Reed (collection), 810

   Deep River, 928.1

   Live from the Village Vanguard (collection), 935

   3D Family, 928.2

Murray, Mickey. *Crash of Thunder: Boss Soul, Funk, and R&B Sides from the Vaults of the King, Federal, and Deluxe Labels* (collection), 2596

Murs. *Murs 3:16: The 9th Edition*, 2875

music in politics. *See* political music

*Music Machine. *Nuggets: Artifacts of the First Psychedelic Era* (collection), 1808

Musiq Soulchild. *Juslisen*, 2385

Musique. *Disco Box* (collection), 2644

Musselwhite, Charlie

   The Harmonica according to Charlie Musselwhite, 376.1

   Stand Back! Here Comes Charley Musselwhite's South Side Band, 376.2

Mvula, Laura. *The Dreaming Room*, 2413

My Bloody Valentine

   Isn't Anything, 2156.1

   Loveless, 2156.2

Myers, Sam. *The Fire / Fury Records Story* (collection), 2422

*The Mystics. *The Doo-Wop Box* (collection), 2322

The Mystiques. *Eccentric Soul: Twinight's Lunar Rotation* (collection), 2568

N

Nakai, R. Carlos. *Sundance Season*, 1335

Napalm Death. *Scum*, 2157

Nas

   God's Son, 2878.1

   Illmatic, 2878.2

   It Was Written, 2878.3

   Stillmatic, 2878.4

Nash, Johnny. *Birth of Soul, 4 Vols.* (collection), 2434

Nashville Bluegrass Band

   Blue Ribbon Bluegrass (collection), 1563

   The Boys Are Back in Town, 1597

   Hand-Picked: 25 Years of Bluegrass on Rounder Records (collection), 1564

   Top of the Hill Bluegrass (collection), 1567

Nashville Mandolin Ensemble. *All the Rage: Mandolin Ensemble Music from 1897–1924*, 121

Nashville rhythm and blues

   Nashville Jumps: Blues and Rhythm on Nashville Independent Labels 1945–1955 (collection), 2376

   Night Train to Nashville: Music City Rhythm and Blues, 1945–1970, Vol. 1 (collection), 2377

   Night Train to Nashville: Music City Rhythm and Blues, 1945–1970, Vol. 2 (collection), 2378

Nasty Dog Catchers. *Eccentric Soul: The Outskirts of Deep City* (collection), 2565

Nathan Hale Ancient Fifes and Drums. *Music of the American Revolution: The Sounds of Ancient Fifes and Drums*, 57

Nathan, Syd. *King R&B Box Set* (collection), 2424

national anthems and patriotic music, 3373–3381

   Battle Cry of Freedom (Robert Shaw Chorale), 3380

national anthems and patriotic music (cont.)
  ★*Collections of National Anthems,
    Vol. 1* (Regimental Band of the
    Coldstream Guards), 3379.1
  ★*Collections of National Anthems,
    Vol. 2* (Regimental Band of the
    Coldstream Guards), 3379.2
  ★*Complete National Anthems of the
    World* (Breiner), 3374
  Encyclopedia of National Anthems
    (Hang), 3376
  God Bless America (Mormon
    Tabernacle Choir), 3377
  *National Anthems from around the
    World* (collection), 3373
  National Anthems of the World (Reed
    and Bristow), 3378
  National Anthems of the World (Vienna
    State Opera Orchestra), 3381
  National Anthems, Vols. 1–4 (Guthrie),
    3375
Native American new age, 1334–1335
  In Medicine River (Oldman), 1334
  Sundance Season (Nakai), 1335
Naughty by Nature. *Naughty by Nature,*
  2879
Navarro, Fats
  *The Complete Blue Note and Capitol
    Recordings of Fats Navarro and
    Tadd Dameron,* 599.1
  Goin' to Minton's, 599.2
NdegéOcello, Me'Shell. *Standing in the
  Shadows of Motown* (collection),
  2445
Neal, Kenny
  Blues Fest: Modern Blues of the '80s
    (collection), 409
  Walking on Fire, 455
Neely, Bill. *16 Down Home Country
  Classics* (collection), 1385
Negro spirituals. *See* spirituals
Nelly
  The Emancipation of Mimi (Carey),
    1256.1
  Nellyville, 2880
★Nelson, Henry. *Sacred Steel: The Steel
  Guitar Tradition of the House of God
  Churches* (collection), 2980
Nelson, Oliver
  Alfie [1997] (Rollins and Nelson),
    1044.1
  Alfie [2000] (Rollins and Nelson),
    1044.2
  *Big Band Renaissance: The Evolution of
    the Jazz Orchestra* (collection), 739
  Blues and the Abstract Truth, 654
Nelson, Prince Rogers. *See* Prince
Nelson, Rick
  The Golden Era of Rock 'n' Roll
    (collection), 1748
  Greatest Hits, 1778
Nelson Riddle Orchestra. *Hit Parade,
  1956* (collection), 1158

Nelson, Romeo. *Shake Your Wicked
  Knees: Rent Parties and Good Times*
  (collection), 258
Nelson, Sandy. *Let There Be Drums, Vol. 1:
  The '50s* (collection), 1751
Nelson, Tracy. *The Best of Tracy Nelson /
  Mother Earth,* 1842
Nelson, Willie
  Classic Country: Kings of Country
    (collection), 1381
  *Classic Country Music: A Smithsonian
    Collection* (collection), 1382
  ★*Legends of Guitar: Rock–The '50s,
    Vol. 2* (collection), 1750
  *Nite Life: Greatest Hits and Rare Tracks,
    1959–1971,* 1518.1
  Phases and Stages, 1518.2
  Pretty Paper, 3336
  ★*Red Headed Stranger,* 1518.3
★Nelstone's Hawaiians. *Anthology of
  American Folk Music, Vols. 1–3*
  (collection), 1386
★Nelville, Aaron. *The R&B Box*
  (collection), 2239
Nena. *Like Omigod! The 80s Pop Culture
  Box (Totally)* (collection), 1241
neo-soul, 2379–2387, 2585–2586
  Acoustic Soul (India.Arie), 2383.1
  After Hours (Patterson), 2386
  Alicia Keys Unplugged, 2384.1
  Back to Black (Winehouse), 2586.1
  *Beautifully Human: Words and Sounds,
    Vol. 2* (Scott), 2387.1
  *I Told You I Was Trouble: Live in
    London* (Winehouse), 2586.2
  Juslisen (Musiq Soulchild), 2385
  Live in Paris (Scott), 2387.2
  Mama's Gun (Badu), 2380.1
  ★*The Miseducation of Lauryn Hill,*
    2382
  *New Amerykah, Part One: 4th World
    War* (Badu), 2380.2
  A Night of Rapture (Baker), 2381
  Songs in A Minor (Keys), 2384.2
  The Soul Sessions (Stone), 2585
  Voyage to India (India.Arie), 2383.2
  *Who Is Jill Scott? Words and Sounds,
    Vol. 1,* 2387.3
Neptunes. *Night Train to Nashville: Music
  City Rhythm and Blues, 1945–1970,
  Vol. 2* (collection), 2378
N.E.R.D. *In Search of . . .,* 2876
Neu!. *Neu!,* 1963
Neutral Milk Hotel. *In the Aeroplane over
  the Sea,* 2225
Neville, Aaron
  *Beg, Scream, and Shout! The Big Ol'
    Box of '60s Soul* (collection), 2433
  *Crescent City Soul: The Sound of New
    Orleans, 1947–1974* (collection),
    2564
  *Finger Poppin' and Stompin' Feet: 20
    Classic Allen Toussaint Productions*

  for Minit Records, 1960–1962
    (collection), 2359
  Ultimate Collection, 2367
  The Very Best of Cole Porter
    (songwriter collection), 1108.3
Neville, Art. *Art Neville: His Specialty
  Recordings, 1956-58,* 2368
★Neville, Cyril. *What It Is! Funky Soul and
  Rare Grooves* (collection), 2615
The Neville Brothers
  Fiyo on the Bayou, 2369.1
  Gold, 2369.2
  Make It Funky! (collection), 2360
  Tell It Like It Is, 2369.3
  Uptown Rulin': The Best of the Neville
    Brothers, 2369.4
  The Very Best of the Neville Brothers,
    2369.5
  Yellow Moon, 2369.6
new acoustic (new age), 1324–1325
  The Music of Leo Kottke (Kottke),
    1325.1
  Passage (Ackerman), 1324.1
  ★*A Shout toward Noon* (Kottke),
    1325.2
  The William Ackerman Collection
    (Ackerman), 1324.2
new age
  ambient, 1320–1323
  East/West, 1313–1315
  electronic/computer, 1316–1319
  jazz/fusion, 1326–1329
  meditation music, 1330–1333
  Native American, 1334–1335
  new acoustic, 1324–1325
  progressive, 1336–1345
  samplers and concept albums,
    1366–1378
  solo instrumental, 1346–1353
  sound health music, 1354
  space music, 1355–1358
  world music, 1359–1365
New Birth. *The Very Best of New Birth,
  Inc,* 2636
New Edition
  Gold, 2285.1
  Hits, 2285.2
New England Ragtime Ensemble. *The Art
  of the Rag,* 138
New England Voices. *The River of Love:
  Music of the Shakers and Based on
  Shaker Theme,* 19
New Grass Revival
  *Fly through the Country / When the
    Storm Is Over,* 1598.1
  Live, 1598.2
  Top of the Hill Bluegrass (collection),
    1567
New Grove Dictionary of Jazz
  (Kernfeld), p3
new jack swing, 2388–2392
  *The Best of Keith Sweat: Make You
    Sweat,* 2392.1

The Collection, 1991–1998 (Mint Condition), 2391
Groove Me: The Very Best of Guy, 2390
Legacy: The Greatest Hits Collection, Deluxe ed. (Boyz II Men), 2388
Sweat Hotel Live (Sweat), 2392.2
Ultimate Collection (Gill), 2389
New Jersey Mass Choir. *Greatest Gospel Choirs* (collection), 3052
New Kids on the Block. *80's Pop Hits* (collection), 1238
New Life Community Choir. *Stand Up: A Collection of America's Great Gospel Choirs* (collection), 3053
New Order. *International,* 2158
New Orleans Rag Time Orchestra. *New Orleans Jazz* (collection), 503
New Orleans revival and traditional styles, 503–509
  collections, 503
  George Lewis with Kid Shots (Lewis), 508
  ★*Kid Ory's Creole Jazz Band 1944–45* (Ory), 509
  The King of the Blues (Johnson), 507
  New Orleans Funeral and Parade (Eureka Brass Band), 505
  New Orleans Jazz Styles: Complete (Gillock), 506
  Talking and Drum Solos / Country Brass Bands (Baby Dodds), 504
New Orleans rhythm and blues
  The Allen Toussaint Collection, 2374.1
  Art Neville: His Specialty Recordings, 1956-58, 2368
  Come On: The Complete Imperial Recordings (King), 2365.1
  ★*Crawfish Fiesta* (Professor Longhair), 2370.1
  ★*Dr. John's Gumbo,* 2364.1
  Earl's Pearls: The Very Best of Earl King, 2365.2
  Fess: The Professor Longhair Anthology, 2370.2
  Finger Poppin' and Stompin' Feet: 20 Classic Allen Toussaint Productions for Minit Records, 1960–1962 (collection), 2359
  Fiyo on the Bayou (Neville Brothers), 2369.1
  general collections, 2359–2361
  Gold (Neville Brothers), 2369.2
  Gris-Gris (Dr. John), 2364.2
  Having a Good Time with Huey "Piano" Smith and His Clowns, 2372
  The Legends of New Orleans: The Music of Fats Domino, 2362.2
  Make It Funky! (collection), 2360
  The Mercury New Orleans Sessions 1950 and 1953 (collection). `, 2361
  The Meters Anthology: Funkify Your Life, 2366

Mos' Scocious: The Dr. John Anthology, 2364.3
New Orleans Piano (Professor Longhair), 2370.3
★*Out of New Orleans* (Domino), 2362.1
Rock 'n' Roll Gumbo (Professor Longhair), 2370.4
Shirley and Lee (Legendary Masters Series, Vol. 1), 2371.1
Simply the Best: Live (Thomas), 2373.1
Sweet Soul Queen of New Orleans: The Irma Thomas Collection, 2373.2
The Sweethearts of the Blues (Shirley and Lee), 2371.2
Tell It Like It Is (Neville Brothers), 2369.3
Ultimate Collection (Neville), 2367
Uptown Rulin': The Best of the Neville Brothers, 2369.4
The Very Best of the Neville Brothers, 2369.5
Walking to New Orleans (Domino), 2362.3
What Is Success? The Scepter and Bell Recordings (Toussaint), 2374.2
Wheelin' and Dealin': The Definitive Collection (Dorsey), 2363
The Wild Tchoupitoulas, 2375
Yellow Moon (Neville Brothers), 2369.6
New Orleans Rhythm Kings
  The New Orleans Rhythm Kings and Jelly Roll Morton (collection), 497
  Riverside History of Classic Jazz (collection), 499
New Orleans soul. *Crescent City Soul: The Sound of New Orleans, 1947–1974* (collection), 2564
New Pornographers. *Electric Version,* 2159
new wave and punk: U.K. *See* punk and new wave: U.K.
new wave and punk: U.S. *See* punk and new wave: U.S.
New York Art Quartet. *New York Art Quartet,* 694
New York Dolls
  New York Dolls, 1878
  No Thanks! The '70s Punk Rebellion (collection), 2003
  Punk: Attitude (collection), 1980
★New York Philharmonic. *Bernstein Favorites: Children's Classics* (collection), 3252
Newbern, Hambone Willie
  Acoustic Country Blues Guitar: Delta Blues before Robert Johnson (collection), 211
  A Richer Tradition: Country Blues and String Band Music (collection), 187
Newborn, Phineas, Jr. *A World of Piano,* 655

Newcombe, Anton and the Brian Jonestown Massacre. *Dig!* (collection), 2092
Newlyweds. *Eccentric Soul: Mighty Mike Lenaburg* (collection), 2563
Newman, Jeanne. *The Complete Goldwax Singles, Vol. 2* (collection), 2592
Newman, Randy
  The Best of Randy Newman, 1908.1
  Sail Away, 1908.2
Newsome, Bobby. *The Spring Story: Essential 70s Soul* (collection), 2608
Newton, James
  African Flower, 1000
  Echo Canyon, 1351
Newton, Wayne. *Have a Nice Decade: The '70s Pop Culture Box* (collection), 1240
Newton-John, Olivia. *Back to Basics: The Essential Collection,* 1293
Ne-Yo. *Good Girl Gone Bad* (Rihanna), 1300
Nichols, Herbie. *Complete Blue Note Recordings,* 656
Nichols, Red
  The First of the Singer Songwriters: Key Cuts (Carmichael), 1124
  Red Nichols and Miff Mole, 1925–1927, 516
  ★*The Smithsonian Collection of Classic Jazz* (collection), 486
★Nightcrawlers. *Nuggets: Artifacts of the First Psychedelic Era* (collection), 1808
Nighthawk, Robert
  ★*Blues Classics* (collection), 146
  Bricks in My Pillow, 302
  ★*Chess Blues* (collection), 287
  Drop Down Mama (collection), 292
Nightingale, J. P. *Chanukah at Home* (collection), 3238
Nightingale Jubalaires. *The Swing Time Records Story: R&B, Blues, and Gospel, 1946–1952* (collection), 2430
Nightingales. *The Best of King Gospel* (collection), 3031
Nightnoise
  Solace: A Windham Hill Collection (collection), 1373
  Windham Hill: The First Ten Years (collection), 1377
Niles, Abbe. *Blues: An Anthology,* 163
Nilsson, Harry. *Personal Best: The Harry Nilsson Anthology,* 1294
Nine Inch Nails
  And All That Could Have Been, 2160.1
  The Downward Spiral, 2160.2
The 1950s and 1960s: cool jazz and the West Coast, 604–625
  ★*Art Pepper Meets the Rhythm Section* (Pepper), 621.1

The 1950s and 1960s (cont.)
> *Art Pepper Plus Eleven: Modern Jazz Classics* (Pepper), 621.2
> *Best of the West Coast Sessions* (Getz), 611.1
> ★*The Best of the Gerry Mulligan Quartet with Chet Baker* (Mulligan), 619.1
> *The Best of Chet Baker Plays* (Baker), 606.1
> *The Birth of the Cool, Vol. 2* (collection), 604
> *Blue Serge* (Chaloff), 608
> *Brazilliance, Vol. 1* (Almeida), 605
> *Chet Baker Live in '64 and '79,* 606.2
> collections, 604
> ★*Complete Birth of the Cool* (Davis), 610
> *The Complete Roost Recordings* (Getz), 611.2
> *Concorde* (Modern Jazz Quartet), 618.1
> *Dave Brubeck Live in '64 and '66,* 607.1
> *Dedicated to Connie* (Modern Jazz Quartet), 618.2
> ★*Django* (Modern Jazz Quartet), 618.3
> *Focus* (Getz), 611.3
> *Gongs East / Three Faces of Chico* (Hamilton), 612.1
> ★*Intuition* (Tristano), 625.1
> *Jazz at Oberlin* (Brubeck), 607.2
> ★*Konitz Meets Mulligan* (Konitz), 615.1
> *The Modern Red Norvo* (Norvo), 620
> *Monterey Concerts* (Tjader), 624
> *Moonlight in Vermont* (Smith), 623
> *No Sun in Venice* (Modern Jazz Quartet), 618.4
> *The Original Sextet: Complete Studio Masters* (Mulligan), 619.2
> *The Poll Winners* (Kessel), 614
> *Quartets* (Getz), 611.4
> *Shelly Manne and His Men, Vol. 1: The West Coast Sound* (Manne), 617.1
> *Shorty Rogers, Vol. 1: West Coast Trumpet* (Rogers), 622
> *Stan Getz and J. J. Johnson at the Opera House* (Getz), 611.5
> *Subconscious Lee* (Konitz), 615.2
> *"The Three" and "The Two"* (Manne), 617.2
> *Three Classic Albums Plus* (Hamilton), 612.2
> *The Trio, Vol. 1* (Hawes), 613
> *2 Degrees East, 3 Degrees West* (Lewis), 616
> *You Get More Bounce with Curtis Counce* (Counce), 609
1970s rock, 1891–2030
1910 Fruitgum Co. *25 All-Time Greatest Bubblegum Hits* (collection), 1811
97th Regimental String Band. *Songs of the Civil War: Battlefields and Campfires,* 76

Nirvana
> *In Utero,* 2161.1
> *Live! Tonight! Sold Out!!,* 2161.2
> ★*Nevermind,* 2161.3
Nite Owls. *Western Swing: 40 Bootstompers from the Golden Age* (collection), 1433
Nix, Reverend A. W.
> *A First-Time Buyer's Guide to American Negro Spirituals* (collection), 32
> *Songsters and Saints: Vocal Traditions on Race Records, Vol. 1* (collection), 190
Nix, Willie. *Blues Masters, Vol. 12: Memphis Blues* (collection), 229
No Doubt. *Rock Steady,* 2162
Noble, Ray
> ★*Swing Time! The Fabulous Big Band Era* (collection), 1089
> *Waller / Razaf* (songwriter collection), 1113.2
Noble, Reginald. *See* Redman
Noel, Fats. *The Big Horn: The History of the Honkin' and Screamin' Saxophone* (collection), 2314
Nomads. *The Complete Goldwax Singles, Vol. 3* (collection), 2593
Noone, Jimmie
> *Chicago Rhythm, Apex Blues,* 517
> ★*The Smithsonian Collection of Classic Jazz* (collection), 486
Nordine, Ken. *You're Getting Better: The Word Jazz Dot Masters,* 814
Norfolk Jubilee Quartet
> *Gospel: Negro Spirituals / Gospel Songs, 1926–1942* (collection), 2963
> ★*A Warrior on the Battlefield: A Cappella Trail Blazers* (collection), 3011
Norful, Smokie
> *Life Changing,* 3094
> *Wow Gospel #1s* (collection), 3074
Norman, Jessye. *Spirituals in Concert,* 42
Norman, Larry
> *Best of Christian Rock (1970–1986), Vol. 1* (collection), 3135
> *Rebel Poet, Jukebox Balladeer: The Anthology,* 3155.1
> *Upon This Rock, Coll. Ed,* 3155.2
North Carolina Mass Choir. *Greatest Gospel Choirs* (collection), 3052
North, Freddie. *Night Train to Nashville: Music City Rhythm and Blues, 1945–1970, Vol. 2* (collection), 2378
North Mississippi All-Stars. *Polaris,* 377
North, Penny. *Boddie Recording Company Cleveland, Ohio* (collection), 2569, 2570
North Wind Of Cleveland, OH. *Boddie Recording Company Cleveland, Ohio* (collection), 2569, 2570

Norumbega Harmony. *Sweet Seraphic Fire: New England Singing-School Music from the Norumbega Harmony,* 20
Norvells. *Eccentric Soul: The Nickel and Penny Labels* (collection), 2567
Norvo, Red
> *Dance of the Octopus,* 581
> *The Great Depression: American Music in the '30s* (collection), 1066
> *The Modern Red Norvo,* 620
> ★*The Smithsonian Collection of Classic Jazz* (collection), 486
Norwood, Dorothy
> *Live,* 3071
> *The Rough Guide to Gospel* (collection), 2970
Notations. *Eccentric Soul: Twinight's Lunar Rotation* (collection), 2568
Notorious B.I.G.
> *Life after Death,* 2881.1
> ★*Ready to Die: The Remaster,* 2881.2
NRBQ. *Peek-a-Boo: The Best of* NRBQ, 1879
Nugent, Ted. *Great Gonzos: The Best of* Ted Nugent, 1950
Numan, Gary. *Like Omigod! The 80s Pop Culture Box (Totally)* (collection), 1241
Nutley Brass. *Greasy Kid Stuff* (collection), 3210
★*The Nutmegs. ★*The Doo-Wop Box* (collection), 2322
N.W.A.
> *Efil4zaggin [Niggaz4life],* 2877.1
> ★*Straight Outta Compton,* 2877.2
Nye, Hermes. *Ballads of the Civil War, 1831–1865,* 77
Nyro, Laura. *Stoned Soul Picnic: The Best of* Laura Nyro, 1895

O

O. C. *Word . . . Life,* 2882
The Oak Ridge Boys
> *Gold,* 1670
> *The Gospel Sessions,* 3128
Oasis
> *Definitely Maybe,* 2163.1
> *Whatever: The '90s Pop and Culture Box* (collection), 1244
> *(What's the Story) Morning Glory?,* 2163.2
★*Oates, John. Atlantic Soul, 1959–1975* (collection), 2589
O'Brien, Mary Isobel Catherine Bernadette. *See* Springfield, Dusty
O'Brien, Tim
> *Red on Blonde,* 1599
> *Top of the Hill Bluegrass* (collection), 1567
Ocean, Billy. *Ultimate Collection,* 2286
Ocean, Frank. *Channel Orange,* 2414

Ocean. *Have a Nice Decade: The '70s Pop Culture Box* (collection), 1240

Ochs, Phil. *Songs of Protest* (collection), 1820

O'Connell, Helen
  Johnny Mercer (songwriter collection), 1107.1
  Legendary Big Band Singers (collection), 767
  Sentimental Journey: Capitol's Great Ladies of Song (collection), 1166

O'Connor, Mark. *Liberty,* 58

O'Connor, Sinead. *I Do Not Want What I Haven't Got,* 2055

O'Daniel, W. Lee, and His Hillbilly Boys. *Western Swing: 40 Bootstompers from the Golden Age* (collection), 1433

O'Day, Anita
  Anita O'Day, 797.1
  Anita O'Day Live in '63 and '70, 797.2
  ★*Jazz on a Summer's Day* (collection), 664
  ★*The Jazz Singers: A Smithsonian Collection of Jazz Vocals from 1919–1994* (collection), 766
  Sentimental Journey: Capitol's Great Ladies of Song (collection), 1166
  The Very Best of Cole Porter (songwriter collection), 1108.3

O'Day, Molly
  Hank Williams Songbook (collection), 1450
  Molly O'Day and the Cumberland Mountain Folks, 1519

★Oden, St. Louis Jimmy. *Nashville Jumps: Blues and Rhythm on Nashville Independent Labels 1945–1955* (collection), 2376

★ODJB. *Ken Burns Jazz: The Story of America's Music* (collection), 478

Of Montreal. *For the Kids Three!* (collection), 3209

★O'Farrell, Chico. *The Original Mambo Kings: An Afro-Cubop Anthology* (collection), 592

Offitt, Lillian
  The Best of Excello Records (collection), 327
  Night Train to Nashville: Music City Rhythm and Blues, 1945–1970, Vol. 2 (collection), 2378
  Southern Rhythm 'n' Rock: The Best of Excello Records, Vol. 22 (collection), 2427

OFS Unlimited. *Eccentric Soul: The Prix Label* (collection), 2601

O'Hearn, Patrick. *The World of Private Music* (collection), 1378

Ohio Express. *25 All-Time Greatest Bubblegum Hits* (collection), 1811

Ohio Players. *Funk on Fire: The Mercury Anthology,* 2637

The O'Jays
  Beg, Scream, and Shout! The Big Ol' Box of '60s Soul (collection), 2433
  ★*Love Train: The Sound of Philadelphia* (collection), 2552
  The Ultimate O'Jays, 2557

Okun, Milton. *Great Songs . . . For Weddings* (collection), 3362

Ol' Dirty Bastard
  #1s (Carey), 1256.2
  Return to the 36 Chambers: The Dirty Version, 2883

Old and in the Way. *Old and in the Way,* 1600

Old and New Dreams. *Playing,* 1001

Old Harp Singers of Eastern Tennessee. *Old Harp Singing,* 3129.1, 3129.2

Old 78's. *Old Time Fiddle Rags, Classic and Minstrel Banjo,* 139

Old South Quartette. *The Earliest Negro Vocal Quartets, 1894–1928* (collection), 3006

Old Town School of Folk Music. *Wiggleworms Love You,* 3189

★Oldfield, Mike. *Tubular Bells,* 1340

Oldman, Coyote. *In Medicine River,* 1334

★Oliphant, Grassella. *What It Is! Funky Soul and Rare Grooves* (collection), 2615

Oliver, King
  ★*Ken Burns Jazz: The Story of America's Music* (collection), 478
  ★*Off the Record: The Complete 1923 Jazz Band Recordings* (collection), 498
  Riverside History of Classic Jazz (collection), 499
  ★*The Smithsonian Collection of Classic Jazz* (collection), 486

Oliver, Rev. George. *This May Be My Last Time Singing: Raw African-American Gospel on 45rpm* (collection), 2982

Oliver, Sy. *Legendary Big Band Singers* (collection), 767

Olson, Phil. *Don't Give the Name a Bad Place: Types and Stereotypes in American Musical Theater, 1870–1900* (collection), 1063

Olympics
  The Best of Loma Records: The Rise and Fall of a 1960's Soul Label (collection), 2590
  Doin' the Hully Gully / Dance by the Light of the Moon / Party Time, 2350.1
  The Very Best of the Olympics, 2350.2

O'Mahoney, Terry. *Jazz Drumming Transitions,* 495

Omartian, Michael. *White Horse / Adam Again,* 3156

O'Neal Twins
  ★*Say Amen, Somebody* (collection), 2971
  Testify! The Gospel Box (collection), 2974

116Clique. *The Compilation Album,* 3179

Ono, Yoko
  A Story, 2056.1
  Walking on Thin Ice, 2056.2

Onyx. *Bacdafucup,* 2884

Orb. *The Orb's Adventures beyond the Ultraworld,* 2226

Orbison, Roy
  16 Biggest Hits, 1779
  ★*Sun Records' Greatest Hits* (collection), 1741

Oregon. *The Essential Oregon,* 1327

Oregon State University Choir. *Make a Joyful Noise: Mainstreams and Backstreams of American Psalmody, 1770–1840* (Oregon State University Choir), 21

Organized Konfusion
  Organized Konfusion, 2885.1
  Stress: The Extinction Agenda, 2885.2

Original Dixieland Jazz Band. *75th Anniversary,* 502

★Original Gospel Harmonettes. *Good News: 100 Gospel Greats* (collection), 2961

Originals. *Heaven Must Have Sent You: The Holland/Dozier/Holland Story* (collection), 2436

The Orioles
  ★*The Doo Wop Box: 101 Vocal Group Gems from the Golden Age of Rock 'n' Roll* (collection), 1745
  ★*The Doo-Wop Box* (collection), 2322
  Jubilee Recordings, 2351.1
  The Orioles Sing Their Greatest Hits, 2351.2
  ★*The R&B Box* (collection), 2239
  The Roots of Rock 'n' Roll, 1946–1954 (collection), 1755

Orishas. *A Lo Cubano,* 2886

Orlando, Tony. *70s Greatest Hits* (collection), 1243

Ory, Kid
  ★*Central Avenue Sounds: Jazz in Los Angeles* (collection), 471
  ★*Kid Ory's Creole Jazz Band 1944–45* (Ory), 509

★Os Mutantes. *Nuggets II: Original Artifacts from the British Empire and Beyond* (collection), 1791

Osborne, Jeffrey. *Ultimate Collection,* 2287

Osborne, Joan. *Standing in the Shadows of Motown* (collection), 2445

The Osbourne Brothers
  The Best of Bluegrass, Vol. 1: Standards (collection), 1561
  Country Bluegrass, 1601.1

The Osbourne Brothers (cont.)
  The Osborne Brothers, 1956–1968,
    1601.2
  The Osborne Brothers, 1968–1974,
    1601.3
Osby, Greg. *Channel Three,* 1002
Oscar Peterson Trio. *The Definitive
    Collection* (songwriter collection),
    1101.1
★The Ospreys. *Atlantic Vocal Groups,
    1951–1963* (collection), 2320
O'Sullivan, Gilbert. *Have a Nice
    Decade: The '70s Pop Culture Box*
    (collection), 1240
Otis, Johnny
  Blues Masters, Vol. 1: Urban Blues
    (collection), 338
  The Capitol Years, 2288.1
  ★*Central Avenue Sounds: Jazz in Los
    Angeles* (collection), 471
  *The Johnny Otis Rhythm and Blues
    Caravan,* 2288.2
  ★*The R&B Box* (collection), 2239
  *Rock Me Baby: The Mercury and
    Peacock Sides 1951–55,* 2288.3
  ★*Stompin' at the Savoy: The
    Original Indie Label, 1944–1961*
    (collection), 2429
OutKast
  Aquemini, 2887.1
  Atliens, 2887.2
  Southernplayalisticadillacmuzik, 2887.3
  Speakerboxxx. The Love Below, 2887.4
  Stankonia, 2887.5
Outlaws. *Wanted: The Outlaws,* 1520
out-of-print items, p3
The Ovations
  The Complete Goldwax Singles, Vol. 1
    (collection), 2591
  The Complete Goldwax Singles, Vol. 2
    (collection), 2592
  The Complete Goldwax Singles, Vol. 3
    (collection), 2593
Over the Rhine. *For the Kids Three!*
    (collection), 3209
Overstreet, Louis. *Fire in My Bones: Raw,
    Rare and Otherworldy African-
    American Gospel* (collection), 2960
Owens, Bobby and the Diplomats.
    *Eccentric Soul: The Tragar and Note
    Labels* (collection), 2602
Owens, Buck
  *The American Roots of the British
    Invasion* (collection), 1786
  ★*The Buck Owens Collection,
    1959–1990,* 1521.1
  Classic Country: Kings of Country
    (collection), 1381
  Very Best of Buck Owens, Vol. 1,
    1521.2
Owens, Dana Elaine. *See* Queen Latifah
Owens, Jack. *Deep Blues* (collection), 217
Ozomatli. *Ozomatli,* 2888

P
P. M. Dawn. *Of the Heart, of the Soul,
    and of the Cross: The Utopian
    Experience,* 2889
Pace Jubilee Singers. *The Half Ain't
    Never Been Told, Vols. 1 and 2*
    (collection), 2956
Padgett, Betty. *Betty Padgett,* 2499
Page, Hot Lips
  ★*The Jazz Singers: A Smithsonian
    Collection of Jazz Vocals from
    1919–1994* (collection), 766
  Stars of the Apollo (collection),
    2240
  ★*Stompin' at the Savoy: The
    Original Indie Label, 1944–1961*
    (collection), 2429
Page, Jimmy. *Stroll On: An Immediate
    Blues Collection* (collection), 369
Page, Patti
  Hit Parade, 1956 (collection), 1158
  *Moments to Remember: The Golden Hits
    of the 50s and 60s Live* (collection),
    1162
  *Sentimental Journey: Pop Vocal
    Classics, Vol. 4* (collection), 1170
  ★*Sentimental Journey: Pop Vocal
    Classics, Vol. 2* (collection), 1168
  16 Most Requested Songs, 1218
Page, Walter. *The Real Kansas City of the
    '20s, '30s, and '40s* (collection),
    552
Paisley, Brad
  Time Well Wasted, 1671.1
  Who Needs Pictures, 1671.2
Palmer, Earl. *Make It Funky!* (collection),
    2360
Palmer, Hap
  Baby Songs Original, 3190
  Hap Palmer's Holiday Magic, 3247
  Sally the Swinging Snake, 3203.1
  ★*Walter the Waltzing Worm,* 3203.2
Parable. *Best of Christian Rock
    (1970–1986), Vol. 1* (collection),
    3135
Paradons. *The Doo-Wop Box II*
    (collection), 2323
Paragon Ragtime Orchestra
  *Black Manhattan: Theater and Dance
    Music of James Reese Europe, Will
    Marion Cook, and Members of the
    Legendary Clef Club* (collection),
    140.1, 1060
  *That Demon Rag: American Popular
    Music from the Ragtime Era,* 140.4
  *Knockout Drops: American Popular
    Music from the Ragtime Era,* 140.2
  *The Paragon Orchestra (Finally) Plays
    "The Entertainer,"* 140.3
The Paragons
  ★*The Doo-Wop Box* (collection), 2322
  The Doo-Wop Box II (collection), 2323
Paris. *Sleeping with the Enemy,* 2890

Paris, Twila. *CCM Top 100: Greatest
    Songs in Christian Music, Vol. 1*
    (collection), 3136
Parker, Charlie
  All "Bird," 603.1
  ★*Best of the Complete Savoy and Dial
    Studio Recordings,* 603.2
  Bird, 1048
  *Celebrating Bird: The Triumph of
    Charlie Parker,* 603.3
  ★*Central Avenue Sounds: Jazz in Los
    Angeles* (collection), 471
  Charlie Parker Omnibook, 603.4
  *The Complete Savoy and Dial Studio
    Recordings,* 603.5
  ★*Confirmation: Best of the Verve Years,*
    603.6
  Diz 'n' Bird at Carnegie Hall, 603.7
  ★*Jazz at Massey Hall,* 603.8
  *Ken Burns Jazz Collection: Charlie
    Parker,* 603.9
  ★*Ken Burns Jazz: The Story of
    America's Music* (collection),
    478
  ★*The Original Mambo Kings: An
    Afro-Cubop Anthology* (collection),
    592
  ★*The Smithsonian Collection of Classic
    Jazz* (collection), 486
  *Town Hall, New York City, June 22,
    1945,* 603.10
★Parker, Chubby. *Anthology of American
    Folk Music, Vols. 1–3* (collection),
    1386
Parker, Evan. *Process and Reality,* 857
Parker, Graham. *Heat Treatment,* 2019
Parker, Junior
  ★*The Best of Duke-Peacock Blues*
    (collection), 336
  ★*Blues Classics* (collection), 146
  Blues Masters, Vol. 12: Memphis Blues
    (collection), 229
  Blues Masters, Vol. 1: Urban Blues
    (collection), 338
  ★*The Blues: A Smithsonian Collection
    of Classic Blues Singers* (collection),
    145
  The Collection, 359.1
  Duke-Peacock's Greatest Hits
    (collection), 2421
  *Junior's Blues: The Duke Recordings,
    Vol. 1,* 359.2
  *Memphis Blues: Important Postwar
    Recordings* (collection), 341
  Soul Shots, Vol. 4: Urban Blues
    (collection), 343
  The Sun Blues Years (collection),
    344
Parker, Little Junior. *Blue Flames: A Sun
    Blues Collection* (collection), 337
Parker, Ray, Jr.
  Greatest Hits, 2289
  ★*Halloween Hits* (collection), 3347

Parker, Robert
   *Action Speaks Louder Than Words:
      The Best of SSS International*
      (collection), 2588
   *Beg, Scream, and Shout! The Big Ol'
      Box of '60s Soul* (collection), 2433
Parker, Weasel. *The Big Horn: The History
   of the Honkin' and Screamin'
   Saxophone* (collection), 2314
Parker, Winfield. *The Spring Story:
   Essential 70s Soul* (collection),
   2608
Parks, Van Dyke. *Song Cycle,* 1968
Parliament
   *The Best of Parliament: Give up the
      Funk,* 2638.1
   The Clones of Dr. Funkenstein,
      2638.2
   *Funkentelechy vs. the Placebo
      Syndrome,* 2638.3
   Gold, 2638.4
   ★*Mothership Connection,* 2638.5
   The Mothership Connection—Live 1976,
      2638.6
Parsons, Gram
   *Classic Country Music: A Smithsonian
      Collection* (collection), 1382
   GP / Grievous Angel, 1522, 1880
Parton, Dolly
   *Classic Country Music: A Smithsonian
      Collection* (collection), 1382
   Dolly Parton Live and Well, 1523
   ★*Essential Dolly Parton,* 1672.1
   The Essential Porter and Dolly, 1549
   *Like Omigod! The 80s Pop Culture Box
      (Totally)* (collection), 1241
   Mission Chapel Memories 1971–1975,
      1672.2
   Trio, 1673
   Ultimate Dolly Parton, 1672.3
Pass, Joe
   Progressions: 100 Years of Jazz Guitar
      (collection), 481
   Virtuoso, 887
Passions
   ★*The Doo-Wop Box* (collection), 2322
   The Doo-Wop Box II (collection), 2323
Pastorius, Jaco
   Jaco Pastorius [1976], 830.1
   Jaco Pastorius [2010], 830.2
patriotic music. *See* national anthems and
   patriotic music
Patterson, Bobby. *Beg, Scream, and
   Shout! The Big Ol' Box of '60s Soul*
   (collection), 2433
Patterson, Rahsaan. *After Hours,* 2386
Pattersonaires. *Happy in the Service of
   the Lord: Memphis Gospel Quartet
   Heritage, the 1980s, Vols. 1 and 2*
   (collection), 3007
Patti Smith Group. *D.I.Y. Blank
   Generation: The New York Scene*
   (collection), 1978

Patton, Charley
   *Acoustic Country Blues Guitar: Delta
      Blues before Robert Johnson*
      (collection), 211
   *American Primitive, Vol. 1: Raw
      Pre-War Gospel* (collection),
      2976
   *Back to the Crossroads: The Roots of
      Robert Johnson* (collection), 212
   *Before the Blues: The Early American
      Black Music Scene; Classic
      Recordings from the 1920's and
      30's, Vols. 1–3* (collection), 183
   ★*The Best of Charlie Patton,* 226.1
   *Blues Masters, Vol. 8: Mississippi Delta
      Blues* (collection), 215
   ★*The Blues: A Smithsonian Collection
      of Classic Blues Singers* (collection),
      145
   Complete Recordings, 226.2
   *The Half Ain't Never Been Told,
      Vols. 1 and 2* (collection), 2956
   ★*Legends of the Blues, Vol. 1*
      (collection), 150
   News and the Blues: Telling It Like It Is
      (collection), 156
   *The Road to Robert Johnson and
      Beyond* (collection), 221
   The Roots of Rock (collection), 368
   *Songsters and Saints: Vocal Traditions
      on Race Records, Vol. 1* (collection),
      190
   ★*The Story of the Blues* (collection),
      158
Patty, Sandi
   *CCM Top 100: Greatest Songs in
      Christian Music, Vol. 1* (collection),
      3136
   Finest Moments, 3157
★Paul, Billy. *Love Train: The Sound of
   Philadelphia* (collection), 2552
Paul, Les
   The Best *of the Capitol Masters: 90th
      Birthday Edition,* 1219.1
   Chasing Sound, 1219.2
   ★*Legends of Guitar: Rock–The '50s,
      Vol. 1* (collection), 1749
   The Legend and the Legacy, 1219.3
   Les Paul Live in New York, 729
   Progressions: 100 Years of Jazz Guitar
      (collection), 481
   ★*Sentimental Journey: Pop Vocal
      Classics, Vol. 3* (collection), 1169
Paulsen, Harald. *From Berlin to Broadway:
   A Selection* (songwriter collection),
   1115.2
Pavarotti, Luciano. *O Holy Night,* 3282
Pavement
   Brighten the Corners, 2164.1
   Crooked Rain, Crooked Rain, 2164.2
   Slanted and Enchanted, 2164.3
   Slow Century, 2164.4
Paycheck, Jimmy. *16 Biggest Hits,* 1524

Payne, Cecil. *The Big Horn: The History
   of the Honkin' and Screamin'
   Saxophone* (collection), 2314
Payne, Freda. *Heaven Must Have Sent
   You: The Holland/Dozier/Holland
   Story* (collection), 2436
Payne, Leon. *I Love You Because,* 1525
Payton, Nicholas. *Icons among Us*
   (collection), 934
Peaches and Herb
   Billboard #1s: The '70s (collection),
      1235
   Disco Box (collection), 2644
Peacock, Charlie
   *CCM Top 100: Greatest Songs in
      Christian Music, Vol. 1* (collection),
      3136
   Love Life, 3158
Peanut Butter Wolf
   My Vinyl Weighs a Ton, 2891.1
   *[Peanut Butter Wolf Presents] Stones
      Throw Ten Years,* 2891.2
Pearl Jam
   Pearl Jam: Touring Band 2000,
      2165.1
   Ten, 2165.2
★Pearlettes. *The Vee-Jay Story:
   Celebrating 40 Years of Classic Hits*
   (collection), 2431
★Pearls. *Atlantic Vocal Groups,
   1951–1963* (collection), 2320
Pearson, Duke. *Big Band Renaissance:
   The Evolution of the Jazz Orchestra*
   (collection), 739
Peebles, Ann
   Blues Fest: Modern Blues of the '70s
      (collection), 408
   *The Complete Ann Peebles on Hi
      Records, Vols. 1 and 2,* 2500
   The Hi Records Story (collection),
      2423
Peerless Quartet
   *The Phonographic Yearbook, 1922: An
      Angel's Voice I Hear* (collection),
      1078
   *The Phonographic Yearbook, 1908:
      Take Me Out with the Crowd*
      (collection), 1076
   ★*Praise the Lord and Pass the
      Ammunition: Songs of World Wars I
      and II* (collection), 1079
Pegdon, Elmer. *Mountain Music Bluegrass
   Style* (collection), 1566
Pendergrass, Teddy
   The Essential Teddy Pendergrass,
      2501.1
   ★*Love Train: The Sound of Philadelphia*
      (collection), 2552
   Teddy, Live in '79, 2290
   The Very Best of Teddy Pendergrass,
      2501.2
Penguin Cafe Orchestra. *Penguin Cafe
   Orchestra,* 1323

The Penguins
  ★*Atlantic Vocal Groups, 1951–1963* (collection), 2320
  Best of Doo Wop Ballads (collection), 1743
  ★*The Doo Wop Box: 101 Vocal Group Gems from the Golden Age of Rock 'n' Roll* (collection), 1745
  ★*The Doo-Wop Box* (collection), 2322
  The Doo-Wop Box II (collection), 2323
  ★*The R&B Box* (collection), 2239
  Street Corner Serenade: The Greatest Doo-Wop Hits of the '50s and '60s (collection), 1756
Penn, Dan. *Do Right Man,* 2502
Penner, Fred. *Christmastime,* 3248
Pennies from Heaven: The American Popular Music Business in the Twentieth Century (Sanjek and Sanjek), 3
Penniman, Richard Wayne. *See* Little Richard
Penny and the Quarters. *Eccentric Soul: The Prix Label* (collection), 2601
Penny, Hank
  Doughboys, Playboys, and Cowboys: The Golden Years of Western Swing (collection), 1428
  Flamin' Mamie, 1938–1941, 1444
  Heroes of Country Music, Vol. 1: Legends of Western Swing (collection), 1429
  Western Swing: 40 Bootstompers from the Golden Age (collection), 1433
Pentagons. *The Doo-Wop Box II* (collection), 2323
The Pentangle
  Early Classics, 1856.1
  Light Flight: The Anthology, 1856.2
  Sweet Child, 1856.3
Peoples, Dottie. *On Time God,* 3095
Peplowski, Ken. *Noir Blue,* 1003
Pepper, Art
  ★*Art Pepper Meets the Rhythm Section,* 621.1
  Art Pepper: Notes from a Jazz Survivor, 888.1
  Art Pepper Plus Eleven: Modern Jazz Classics, 621.2
  Landscape, 888.2
Perceptionists. *Black Dialogue,* 2892
Pere Ubu
  The Modern Dance, 1994.1
  No Thanks! The '70s Punk Rebellion (collection), 2003
  Straight Outta Cleveland (collection), 1888
  The Tenement Year [Remastered & Expanded], 1994.2
  Terminal Tower: An Archival Collection, 1994.3
Perez, Danilo. *Icons among Us* (collection), 934

Perfections. *Eccentric Soul: Twinight's Lunar Rotation* (collection), 2568
Performers. *Eccentric Soul: The Big Mack Label* (collection), 2598
periodicals for up-to-date CD notices and reviews for popular music, list of suggested, p3
Perkins, Carl
  The American Roots of the British Invasion (collection), 1786
  Hit Parade, 1956 (collection), 1158
  ★*Legends of Guitar: Rock–The '50s, Vol. 1* (collection), 1749
  ★*Original Sun Greatest Hits,* 1736
  Rock and Roll: The Early Days (collection), 1752
  ★*Sun Records' Greatest Hits* (collection), 1741
Perkins, Jerry. *The Civil War Music Collector's Edition* (collection), 61
Perkins, Pinetop
  Blues Routes (collection), 413
  Living Chicago Blues, Vol. 2 (collection), 416
  Memphis Blues: Important Postwar Recordings (collection), 341
  The Sun Blues Years (collection), 344
  Sweet Black Angel, 303
Perkins, Velma. *Eccentric Soul: Twinight's Lunar Rotation* (collection), 2568
Perry, Barbara. *The Complete Goldwax Singles, Vol. 2* (collection), 2592
Perry, Katy. *Teenage Dream,* 1295
Perry, Lee "Scratch"
  Essential Lee Perry: The Ultimate Upsetter, 2227.1
  The Ultimate Upsetter, 2227.2
Perryman, Rufus George. *See* Speckled Red
Perryman, Willie Lee. *See* Piano Red
Persuaders. ★*Atlantic Soul, 1959–1975* (collection), 2589
The Persuasions
  Chirpin', 2352.1
  Street Corner Symphony, 2352.2
Pet Shop Boys. *Discography: The Complete Singles Collection,* 2166
Peterson, Lucky. *Blues Fest: Modern Blues of the '90s* (collection), 410
Peterson, Oscar
  ★*At the Stratford Shakespeare Festival,* 730.1
  The Definitive Collection (songwriter collection), 1101.1
  Harold Arlen (songwriter collection), 1095.1
  Oscar Peterson Live in '63, '64, and '65, 730.2
  Oscar Peterson: The Life of a Legend, 708
  Piano Legends (collection), 480
  Trio Plus One, 730.3
Peterson, Ralph, Jr. *Fo'tet Plays Monk,* 1004

Petra
  Best of Christian Rock (1970–1986), Vol. 1 (collection), 3135
  CCM Top 100: Greatest Songs in Christian Music, Vol. 1 (collection), 3136
  Farewell, 3159.1
  Petra, 3159.2
  Ultimate Collection, 3159.3
Pettiford, Oscar. *The Complete Big Band Studio Recordings,* 760
Petty, Tom and the Heartbreakers. *Greatest Hits,* 2086
Petway, Robert. *Big Joe Williams and the Stars of Mississippi Blues* (collection), 213
Peyroux, Madeleine. *Careless Love,* 1296
Phantom Surfers. *Greasy Kid Stuff* (collection), 3210
Pharcyde. *Bizarre Ride II the Pharcyde,* 2893
Pharoahe Monch
  Desire, 2894.1
  Internal Affairs, 2894.2
Philadelphia Brass Ensemble. *A Festival of Carols in Brass,* 3283
Philadelphia soul
  The Best of the Stylistics, 2558
  The Essential Harold Melvin and the Blue Notes, 2555
  La-la Means I Love You: The Definitive Collection (Delfonics), 2553
  Love Is the Message: The Best of MFSB, 2556
  ★*Love Train: The Sound of Philadelphia* (collection), 2552
  Sweet Talking Soul, 1965–1990 (Manhattans), 2554
  The Ultimate O'Jays, 2557
Phillip and Faithfuls. *The Complete Goldwax Singles, Vol. 1* (collection), 2591
Phillips, Esther
  ★*Atlantic R&B, 1947–1974* (collection), 2418
  ★*Atlantic Soul, 1959–1975* (collection), 2589
  Beg, Scream, and Shout! The Big Ol' Box of '60s Soul (collection), 2433
  Esther: The Best of Esther Phillips, 2291
  Night Train to Nashville: Music City Rhythm and Blues, 1945–1970, Vol. 2 (collection), 2378
  The Sweetest Feeling: A Van McCoy Songbook (collection), 2447
★Phillips, Flip. *The Original Mambo Kings: An Afro-Cubop Anthology* (collection), 592
Phillips, Nat. *Dave Godin's Deep Soul Treasures, Vols. 1–4* (collection), 2435
Phillips, Stacy. *The Dobro Book,* 1384

Phillips, Todd. *The Bluegrass Album, Vol. 1* (collection), 1562

Phillips, Washington
A First-Time Buyer's Guide to American Negro Spirituals (collection), 32
Gospel: Negro Spirituals / Gospel Songs, 1926–1942 (collection), 2963
The Gospel Tradition: The Roots and the Branches, Vol. 1 (collection), 2955
The Half Ain't Never Been Told, Vols. 1 and 2 (collection), 2956
I Am Born to Preach the Gospel, 2985
Mountain Gospel: The Sacred Roots of Country Music (collection), 3113
Preachin' the Gospel: Holy Blues (collection), 2979
Songsters and Saints: Vocal Traditions on Race Records, Vol. 1 (collection), 190
Spreading the Word: Early Gospel Recordings (collection), 2972

Phipps, Ernest
The Half Ain't Never Been Told, Vols. 1 and 2 (collection), 2956
Mountain Gospel: The Sacred Roots of Country Music (collection), 3113

Phoenix soul. *Eccentric Soul: Mighty Mike Lenaburg* (collection), 2563

piano blues, 250–265
Barrelhouse Boogie (collection), 250
Best of Blues Piano (Lowry, Wiegratz, Boduch, McGirr and Schroedl), 261
The Bluebird Recordings, Vol. 1: Chicago, 1941–1942 (Merriweather), 262
Blues from the Gutter (Dupree), 260.1
Blues Piano: The Complete Guide with CD (collection), 253
collections, 250–259
★*Cuttin' the Boogie: Piano Blues and Boogie Woogie* (collection), 251
Grinder Man Blues: Masters of the Blues Piano (collection), 252
Hey! Piano Man (collection), 254
★*Juke Joint Saturday Night: Piano Blues, Rags and Stomps; Classic Recordings from the 1920s and '30s* (collection), 255
Mama Don't Allow No Easy Riders Here: Strutting the Dozens; Classic Piano Rags, Blues, and Stomps (collection), 256
The Ma Grinder (Shaw), 263
New Orleans Barrelhouse Boogie (Dupree), 260.2
Otis Spann Is the Blues (Spann), 264.1
Rockin' This House: Chicago Blues Piano (collection), 257
Roosevelt Sykes (Sykes), 265
Shake Your Wicked Knees: Rent Parties and Good Times (collection), 258

Twenty First Street Stomp: Piano Blues of St. Louis (collection), 259
Walking the Blues (Spann), 264.2

piano in the 1960s, 701–710
Bill Evans at Town Hall, Vol. 1 (Evans), 704.2
Bill Evans (Evans), 704.1
Bill Evans Live, '64–'75 (Evans), 704.3
Blues for Smoke (Byard), 702.1
Cecil Taylor: All the Notes (Taylor), 709.1
Cecil Taylor Unit / Roswell Rudd Sextet: Mixed (Taylor), 709.2
Closer (Bley), 701
Conquistador! (Taylor), 709.3
Conversations with Myself (Evans), 704.4
Empyrean Isles (Hancock), 706.1
Erroll Garner Live in '63 and '64 (Garner), 705
Everybody Digs Bill Evans (Evans), 704.5
★*Ken Burns Jazz Collection: Herbie Hancock* (Hancock), 706.2
Magnificent! (Harris), 707
Maiden Voyage (Hancock), 706.3
Nefertiti, the Beautiful One Has Come (Taylor), 709.4
Now He Sings, Now He Sobs (Corea), 703
Oscar Peterson: The Life of a Legend (Peterson), 708
Portrait in Jazz (Evans), 704.6
The Real McCoy (Tyner), 710
Solo / Strings (Byard), 702.2
★*Sunday at the Village Vanguard* (Evans), 704.7
★*Unit Structures* (Taylor), 709.5
★*Waltz for Debby* (Evans), 704.8
The World of Cecil Taylor (Taylor), 709.6

Piano Red
Night Train to Nashville: Music City Rhythm and Blues, 1945–1970, Vol. 2 (collection), 2378
When the Sun Goes Down 4: That's All Right (collection), 271

★Pickett, Bobby Boris. *Halloween Hits* (collection), 3347

Pickett, Wilson
★*Atlantic R&B, 1947–1974* (collection), 2418
★*Atlantic Soul, 1959–1975* (collection), 2589
Beg, Scream, and Shout! The Big Ol' Box of '60s Soul (collection), 2433
★*Funky Midnight Mover: The Atlantic Studio Recordings*, 2503.1
★*Love Train: The Sound of Philadelphia* (collection), 2552
A Man and a Half: The Best of Wilson Pickett, 2503.2
Muscle Shoals Sound (collection), 2605

Respect: Aretha's Influences and Inspiration (collection), 2440
Soul to Soul (collection), 2444
★*The R&B Box* (collection), 2239
The Very Best of Wilson Pickett, 2503.3
★*What It Is! Funky Soul and Rare Grooves* (collection), 2615

Pickow, Peter. *The Library of Ragtime and Early Blues Piano*, 126

P.I.D. *The Chosen Ones*, 3180

Pied Pipers. *Songs That Got Us through World War II, Vol. 2* (collection), 1086

Pierce, Billie
Blues Masters, Vol. 11: Classic Blues Women (collection), 203
New Orleans Jazz (collection), 503

Pierce, Dede. *New Orleans Jazz* (collection), 503

Pierce, Webb
Classic Country: Kings of Country (collection), 1381
Country Style, U.S.A. (collection), 1473
King of the Honky-Tonk, 1526

Pighee, Frankie. *Boddie Recording Company Cleveland, Ohio* (collection), 2569, 2570

Pilgrim Singers. *Powerhouse Gospel on Independent Labels* (collection), 3038

Pilgrim Travelers
The Best of the Pilgrim Travelers, 3023
★*Good News: 100 Gospel Greats* (collection), 2961
Greatest Gospel Gems (collection), 3035
The Great 1955 Shrine Concert (collection), 3034
★*Jubilation! Great Gospel Performances, Vol. 1: Black Gospel* (collection), 2966
Kings of the Gospel Highway: The Golden Age of Gospel Quartets (collection), 3009

Pinchback, Sidney
Eccentric Soul: The Nickel and Penny Labels (collection), 2567
Eccentric Soul: Twinight's Lunar Rotation (collection), 2568

Pink Floyd
★*Dark Side of the Moon*, 1929.1
Saucerful of Secrets, 1800.1
The Wall, 1929.2
Works, 1800.2

Pink Martini. *Hang on Little Tomato*, 1297

Pinza, Ezio. *Oscar Hammerstein II* (songwriter collection), 1102

Pitchford, Lonnie. *Blues Fest: Modern Blues of the '90s* (collection), 410

Pitney, Gene
The American Roots of the British Invasion (collection), 1786

Pitney, Gene (cont.)
Anthology, 1780
The Look of Love: The Burt Bacharach Collection (collection), 1161
Pixies
Doolittle, 2167.1
Surfer Rosa, 2167.2
Plasmatics. *The Tomorrow Show with Tom Snyder: Punk and New Wave* (collection), 1981
★Plater, Bobby. *Nashville Jumps: Blues and Rhythm on Nashville Independent Labels 1945–1955* (collection), 2376
The Platters
All-Time Greatest Hits, 1768.1
★*The Doo Wop Box: 101 Vocal Group Gems from the Golden Age of Rock 'n' Roll* (collection), 1745
★*The Doo-Wop Box* (collection), 2322
The Doo-Wop Box II (collection), 2323
The Magic Touch: An Anthology, 1768.2
Moments to Remember: The Golden Hits of the '50s and '60s Live (collection), 1162
Street Corner Serenade: The Greatest Doo-Wop Hits of the '50s and '60s (collection), 1756
Playboy Five. *The Complete Goldwax Singles, Vol. 1* (collection), 2591
★Playboys. *Atlantic Vocal Groups, 1951–1963* (collection), 2320
Pleasant, Edward. *Black Manhattan: Theater and Dance Music of James Reese Europe, Will Marion Cook, and Members of the Legendary Clef Club* (collection), 1060
Plunkett, Rick. *12-Bar Blues,* 168
The Pogues
If I Should Fall from Grace with God Remastered, 2168.1
Rum, Sodomy, and the Lash, 2168.2
Poindexter, Annette and the Pieces of Peace. *Eccentric Soul: Twinight's Lunar Rotation* (collection), 2568
The Pointer Sisters
The Best of the Pointer Sisters, 2544.1
Like Omigod! The 80s Pop Culture Box (Totally) (collection), 1241
70s Greatest Hits (collection), 1243
Yes We Can Can: The Best of the Blue Thumb Recordings, 2544.2
★The Police. *Every Breath You Take: The Classics,* 2020
political music
Civil War period, 59–80
Revolutionary War period, 44–58
Politicians. *Heaven Must Have Sent You: The Holland/Dozier/Holland Story* (collection), 2436
★Pollack, Ben. *Swing Time! The Fabulous Big Band Era* (collection), 1089

Pomeroy, Herb. *Big Band Renaissance: The Evolution of the Jazz Orchestra* (collection), 739
★Pomus, Doc. *Stompin' at the Savoy: The Original Indie Label, 1944–1961* (collection), 2429
Ponty, Jean-Luc. *Le Voyage: The Jean-Luc Ponty Anthology,* 907
Poole, Charlie
Good for What Ails You: Music of the Medicine Shows (collection), 184
★*Old-Time Songs,* 1418
White Country Blues: A Lighter Shade of Blues, 1427
Poor Righteous Teachers. *Holy Intellect,* 2895
pop. *See* surf, bubblegum, garage bands, and pop
Pop, Iggy
★*Raw Power,* 1881
The Tomorrow Show with Tom Snyder: Punk and New Wave (collection), 1981
Pope, Odean. *Locked and Loaded: Live at the Blue Note,* 1005
Popol Vuh
In Den Gärten Pharoas, 1341.1
Tantric Songs/Hosianna Mantra, 1341.2
popular Christmas music
American Folk Songs for Christmas (Seeger), 3338
Best Christmas Songs Ever (collection), 3291
Best in Christmas Sheet Music (collection), 3292
The Best of James Brown: The Christmas Collection, 3325
★*Billboard Greatest Christmas Hits, 1935–1954* (collection), 3293
Blue Yule: Christmas Blues and R&B Classics (collection), 3295
A Charlie Brown Christmas (Guaraldi), 3329
Christian Christmas Hits (collection), 3296
Christian Christmas Songbook (collection), 3297
The Christmas Caroling Songbook (collection), 3298
Christmas Carols from around the World: A Celebration of International Carols and Regional Traditions (collection), 3299
Christmas Hits Sheet Music Playlist (collection), 3301
Christmas Sheet Music Hits (collection), 3302
The Christmas Songs Big Book (collection), 3303
The Christmas Song (Cole), 3326
Christmas Time Is Here (collection), 3304

Christmas with the Beach Boys, 3324
A Christmas Album (Streisand), 3342
A Christmas Gift for You from Phil Spector (collection), 3300
collections, 3291–3323
The Complete Christmas Music Collection (collection), 3305
The Definitive Christmas Collection (collection), 3306
Dr. Demento Presents: The Greatest Christmas Novelty CD of All Time (collection), 3307
Ella Wishes You a Swinging Christmas (Fitzgerald), 3328
Enchanted Carols: A Feast of Christmas Music with Victorian Music Boxes, Handbells, Church Bells, Barrel Organs, Street Pianos, Handbell Choirs, and Brass Bands (collection), 3308
Essential Songs: Christmas (collection), 3309
Genuine Houserockin' Christmas (collection), 3310
Give Love at Christmas (Temptations), 3344.1
Handel's Messiah: A Soulful Celebration (collection), 3311
The Hilarious Holiday Songbook (collection), 3312
Hipsters' Holiday: Vocal Jazz and R&B Classics (collection), 3313
It's a Spike Jones Christmas, 3334
Jackson 5 Christmas Album, 3332
Jingle Bell Jazz (collection), 3314
Light of the Stable: The Christmas Album (Harris), 3330
Love That Christmas Music: Over 60 of the Best-Loved Christmas Songs (collection), 3315
Mannheim Steamroller Christmas, 3335
Merry Christmas (Supremes), 3343
120 Best-Known Christmas Songs (collection), 3316
The Original Soul Christmas (collection), 3317
Pretty Paper (Nelson), 3336
A Romantic Christmas (collection), 3318
Santa's Greatest Hits (collection), 3319
★*Silent Night* (Jackson), 3333
The Sinatra Christmas Album, 3340
Songs of Christmas (collection), 3320
The Temptations Christmas Card, 3344.2
Traditional Christmas Carols (Seeger), 3339
The 25th Day of December (Staple Singers), 3341
25 Contemporary Christmas Hits (Inman), 3331
We Three Kings (Roches), 3337
A Winter's Solstice (collection), 3321

Wintersong (Winter), 3345

The World's Greatest Christmas Songs for Piano and Voice: 73 Best-Loved Christmas Songs and Seasonal Favorites (Edison), 3327

The World's Most Beloved Christmas Songs (collection), 3322

Yule Struttin': A Blue Note Christmas (collection), 3323

popular jazz of the 1950s and 1960s, 664–673

The Best of Herbie Mann (Mann), 671

★*But Not for Me: Live at the Pershing* (Jamal), 669

collections, 664

Dave Brubeck: In Your Own Sweet Way (Brubeck), 665.1

George Shearing (Shearing), 673

Getz / Gilberto (Getz), 667

Greatest Hits (Guaraldi), 668

★*Jazz on a Summer's Day* (collection), 664

The Original Misty (Garner), 666

Ramsey Lewis' Finest Hour (Lewis), 670

Swiss Movement (McCann), 672

★*Time Out* (Brubeck), 665.2

popular music

evolution of, p1–3

out-of-print items, p3

overview, p1–3

periodicals for up-to-date CD notices and reviews, list of suggested, p3

reference sources and advanced readings, selective list of, p3

popular vocal and instrumental music, 91–123

After the Ball: A Treasury of Turn-of-the-Century Popular Songs; Highlights from Vaudeville (Morris), 120.1

All the Rage: Mandolin Ensemble Music from 1897–1924 (Nashville Mandolin Ensemble), 121

American Dreamer (Foster), 111.1

American Dreamer: Heart Songs (Danton), 107

The American Song Treasury: 100 Favorites (Raph), 122

An American Idyll: American Songs from 1800–1860 (McCabe), 118

Angels' Visits and Other Vocal Gems of Victorian America (collection), 93

Battle Pieces (Shirley), 123

Beautiful Dreamer: Robert White Sings Stephen Foster (Foster), 111.2

collections, 91–101

Colonial America (Hesperus), 115

Come and Trip It: Instrumental Dance Music, 1780s–1920s (collection), 94

Coney Island Baby: The Society for the Preservation and Encouragement of Barber Shop Quartet Singing in

America; 1990 Top Twenty Barber Shop Quartets(collection), 95

★*Dream Faces* (Gale), 113

The Early Minstrel Show (collection), 96

The 1890s, Vol. 2: Wear Yer Bran' New Gown (collection), 92

The 1890s, Vol. 1: Wipe Him Off the Land (collection), 91

English Country Dances: From Playford's Dancing Master, 1651–1703 (collection), 97

Favorite Songs of the Nineties; Complete Original Sheet Music for 89 Songs (Fremont), 112

The Gateway West (Cohen), 106

The Hand That Holds the Bread: Progress and Protest in the Gilded Age (Songs from the Civil War to the Columbian Exposition) (Cincinnati's University Singers), 105.1

Homespun America: Music for Brass Band, Social Orchestra and Choral Groups from the Mid-19th Century (Eastman Wind Ensemble), 108

"I Wants to Be a Actor Lady" and Other Hits from Early Musical Comedies (Cincinnati's University Singers), 105.2

John Playford's Popular Tunes (Broadside Band), 103

Lost Sounds: Blacks and the Birth of the Recording Industry, 1891–1922 (collection), 98

Love Songs of the Civil War (Erbsen), 109

Minstrel Banjo Style (Flesher), 110

Moonlight Bay: Songs as Is and Songs as Was, 120.2

Music of the Gilded Age (collection), 99

Over the Hills and Far Away: Being a Collection of Music from 18th-Century Annapolis (collection), 100

The Parlour Piano: American Popular Songs of the 1800s (Mesney), 119

Pa's Fiddle (Ingalls), 116

The Sidewalks of New York: Tin Pan Alley (Caine), 104

Songs: Foster, Griffes, Copland (collection), 101

Songs My Grandmother Taught Me (Jacobs-Bond), 117

Songs of Stephen Foster (1972) [Foster], 111.3

Songs of Stephen Foster (1998) [Foster], 111.5

Songs of Stephen Foster (2008) [Foster], 111.4

Songs of the Santa Fe Trail and the Far West (Gardner), 114

Sons of the Pioneers Sing the Stephen Foster Songbook (Foster), 111.6

Stephen Foster Song Book: Original Sheet Music of 40 Songs (Foster), 111.8

Stephen Foster Songs (Foster), 111.9

The Stephen Foster Collection: Stephen Foster in Contrast (Foster), 111.7

The Voices That Are Gone (Foster), 111.10

Where Home Is: Life in Nineteenth-Century Cincinnati, Crossroads of the East and West (Aler), 102

Porter, Bobby. *The Fire / Fury Records Story* (collection), 2422

Porter, Cole

Cole Porter (songwriter collection), 1108.1

A Musical Anthology (songwriter collection), 1108.2

The Very Best of Cole Porter (songwriter collection), 1108.3

★Porter, Roy. *Central Avenue Sounds: Jazz in Los Angeles* (collection), 471

Portishead. *Dummy,* 2169

post-1967 mainstream popular, 1235–1312

All the Way: A Decade of Song and Video (Dion), 1265.1

Anthology (Simone), 1302

ArchAndroid (Monae), 1292

Back to Basics: The Essential Collection (Newton-John), 1293

Back to Black (Winehouse), 1311

Barbara Cook at Carnegie Hall (Cook), 1261

The Barry Manilow Anthology (Manilow), 1246

Best of Bread (Bread), 1253

Best of Chris Isaak (Isaak), 1275

The Best of Bonnie Raitt on Capitol, 1989–2003, 1298.1

The Best of Diane Schuur, 1301

The Best of INXS, 1274

The Best of Kirsty MacColl, 1283

Billboard #1s: The '70s (collection), 1235

Billboard #1s: The '80s (collection), 1236

Blue (Mitchell), 1291.1

Brand New Day (Sting), 1306

Careless Love (Peyroux), 1296

Cleo's Choice (Laine), 1282

Closer: The Best of Sarah McLachlan (McLachlan), 1288

Come Away with Me (Jones), 1278

Complete Introduction to Disco (collection), 1237

The Concerts (Streisand), 1307.1

Country Roads Collection (Denver), 1263.1

Court and Spark (Mitchell), 1291.2

Definitive Hits (Alpert), 1250

The Divine Bette Midler (Midler), 1289.1

post-1967 mainstream popular (cont.)

Duets: An American Classic (Bennett), 1251.1

Dusty in Memphis (Springfield), 1305

80's Pop Hits (collection), 1238

The Emancipation of Mimi (Carey), 1256.1

Escondida (Holland), 1272

Essential Neil Diamond (Diamond), 1264

The Essential Video Collection (Joel), 1277.1

Experience the Divine: Greatest Hits (Midler), 1289.2

The Fame (Lady Gaga), 1281

Fearless (Swift), 1308.1

Futuresex/Lovesounds (Timberlake), 1309.1

general collections, 1235–1244

Get Away from Me (McKay), 1287

Girl Singer (Clooney), 1259.1

Glee: The Music—Journey to Regionals (collection), 1239

Gold: Greatest Hits (ABBA), 1248

Golden Hits (Mantovani), 1286

Good Girl Gone Bad (Rihanna), 1300

Greatest Hits (Denver), 1263.2

Greatest Hits (Easton), 1267

Greatest Hits (Fogelberg), 1270

Greatest Hits on Earth (5th Dimension), 1269

★*Greatest Hits* (Streisand), 1307.2

★*Greatest Hits, Vol. 2* (Streisand), 1307.3

★*Greatest Hits, Vols. 1 and 2* (Joel), 1277.2

The Greatest (Duran Duran), 1266

The Greatest Hits (Houston), 1273.1

Hang on Little Tomato (Pink Martini), 1297

Have a Nice Decade: The '70s Pop Culture Box (collection), 1240

Highlights from "Just for the Record" (Streisand), 1307.4

Hits (Mitchell), 1247, 1291.3

In the Lonely Hour (Smith), 1303

Justified (Timberlake), 1309.2

Ladies of the Canyon (Mitchell), 1291.4

Like Omigod! The 80s Pop Culture Box (Totally) (collection), 1241

Liza Minnelli at Carnegie Hall (Highlights) (Minnelli), 1290

Michael Bublé (Bublé), 1254

My Lives (Joel), 1245

My Love: Ultimate Essential Collection (Dion), 1265.2

My Very Best (Farrell), 1268

My World 2.0 (Bieber), 1252

Nick of Time (Raitt), 1298.2

19 (Adele), 1249.1

1989 (Swift), 1308.2

90's Pop Hits (collection), 1242

#1s (Carey), 1256.2

Only You: In Concert (Connick), 1260.1

Oops! . . . I Did It Again (Spears), 1304

Painted from Memory (Costello), 1262

Personal Best: The Harry Nilsson Anthology (Nilsson), 1294

Pieces of You (Jewel), 1276

Reloaded: Greatest Hits (Jones), 1279

70s Greatest Hits (collection), 1243

★*The Singles* (Carpenters), 1257

Sings the Lyrics of Johnny Mercer (Clooney), 1259.2

songwriter collections, 1245–1247

Swing (Manhattan Transfer), 1284.1

Teenage Dream (Perry), 1295

The Tony Bennett / Bill Evans Album (Bennett), 1251.2

25 (Adele), 1249.3

twentyfive (Connick), 1260.2

21 (Adele), 1249.2

Ultimate Collection: The Complete Hits (Captain and Tennille), 1255

The Ultimate Kenny G (G), 1271

Ultimate Manilow (Manilow), 1285

The Ultimate Petula Clark (Clark), 1258

The Ultimate Video Collection (Yankovic), 1312.1

The Very Best of Manhattan Transfer (Manhattan Transfer), 1284.2

Want One (Wainwright), 1310

"Weird Al" Yankovic's Greatest Hits (Yankovic), 1312.2

Whatever: The '90s Pop and Culture Box (collection), 1244

When I Look in Your Eyes (Krall), 1280

Whitney Houston (Houston), 1273.2

The Woman I Am: The Definitive Collection (Reddy), 1299

Postma, Tineke. *Icons among Us* (collection), 934

post-punk rock, 2031–2039

A Brief History of the Twentieth Century (Gang of Four), 2033.1

Chairs Missing (Wire), 2039.1

Closer (Joy Division), 2035.1

Cut (Slits), 2037

Entertainment! (Gang of Four), 2033.2

Grotesque (after Gramme) (The Fall), 2032.1

House Tornado / the Fat Skier (Throwing Muses), 2038.1

In a Doghouse (Throwing Muses), 2038.2

Junkyard (Birthday Party), 2031.1

Live at the Witch Trials (The Fall), 2032.2

Pink Flag (Wire), 2039.2

Pleasure Heads Must Burn (Birthday Party), 2031.2

Prayers on Fire (Birthday Party), 2031.3

Second Edition (Metal Box) (Public Image Ltd.), 2036

The Very Best of the Human League, 2034

This Nation's Saving Grace (The Fall), 2032.3

★*Unknown Pleasures* (Joy Division), 2035.2

post-rock, 2233–2238

Born into Trouble as the Sparks Fly Upward (Silver Mt. Zion), 2238

For Respect (Caballero), 2233

The For Carnation (For Carnation), 2235

Internal Wrangler (Clinic), 2234

Lift Your Skinny Fists Like Antennas to Heaven (Godspeed You Black Emperor), 2236

Young Team (Mogwai), 2237

postwar midwestern blues, 285–310

★*The Anthology* (Waters), 308.1

Blues Hit Big Town (Wells), 309.1

Blues Masters, Vol. 4: Harmonica Classics (collection), 286

Blues Masters, Vol. 2: Postwar Chicago Blues (collection), 285

The Blues World of Little Walter (Little Walter), 300.1

Bricks in My Pillow (Nighthawk), 302

★*Chess Blues* (collection), 287

The Chess Box (Dixon), 295.1

The Chess Box (Howlin' Wolf), 297.1

The Chess Box (Waters), 308.2

Chicago Blues: 15 Electric Blues Guitar Classics . . . Plus the Story Behind Five Generations of Blues in the Windy City (collection), 288

Chicago Is Just That Way (collection), 289

★*Chicago: The Blues Today!* (collection), 290

Classic Early Years (Hooker), 296.1

collections, 285–292

Deep Blues (Waters), 308.3

Deep in the Blues (Cotton), 294

Detroit Blues: Blues from the Motor City (collection), 291

Don't Turn Me from Your Door (Hooker), 296.2

Drop Down Mama (collection), 292

Dust My Broom (Shines), 307.1

Elmore James: Master of the Electric Slide Guitar (James), 298.1

The Essential Little Walter (Little Walter), 300.2

The Essential Sonny Boy Williamson (Williamson), 310.1

★*His Best* (Howlin' Wolf), 297.2

★*His Best* (Little Walter), 300.3

★*His Best* (Williamson), 310.2

★*Hoodoo Man Blues* (Wells), 309.2

Howlin' Wolf Featuring Hubert Sumlin on Guitar (Howlin' Wolf), 297.3

The Howlin' Wolf Story (Howlin' Wolf), 297.4

An Introduction to Snooky Pryor (Pryor), 304

J. B. Lenoir (Lenoir), 299

John Lee Hooker: A Blues Legend (Hooker), 296.3

★*King Biscuit Time* (Williamson), 310.3

The Legendary Modern Recordings (Hooker), 296.4

Messin' Around with the Blues: The Very Best of Memphis Slim (Memphis Slim), 301

Muddy "Mississippi" Waters Live (Waters), 308.5

Muddy Waters: The Definitive Collection (Waters), 308.4

Rockin' This House: Chicago Blues Piano (collection), 306

The Sky Is Crying: The History of Elmore James (James), 298.2

Somebody Loan Me a Dime (Robinson), 305

Sweet Black Angel (Perkins), 303

Sweet Home Chicago: The J.O.B. Sessions (Shines), 307.2

Swinging the Blues (Anderson), 293

★*The Ultimate Collection* (Hooker), 296.5

Willie Dixon: The Master Blues Composer, 1915–1992 (Dixon), 295.2

post-World War II through 1967 mainstream popular, 1155–1234

After Midnight: Complete Session (Cole), 1184.1

After the Lights Go Down Low (Hibbler), 1200

All-Time Greatest Hits (Vinton), 1228

American Caruso (Lanza), 1205.1

American Classic (Bennett), 1179.1

At His Very Best (Jones), 1202.1

★*Best of Lena Horne* (Horne), 1201

★*Best of the Capitol Years* (Sinatra), 1224.1

The Best of Jackie Gleason (Gleason), 1198

The Best of Jimmie Rodgers (Rodgers), 1221

The Best of Martin Denny's Exotica (Denny), 1189

The Best of Miss Peggy Lee (Lee), 1206.1

The Best of Roger Williams (Williams), 1233

The Best of Sammy Davis, Jr. Live (Davis), 1187.1

The Best of Teresa Brewer (Brewer), 1181

The Best of the Capitol Masters: 90th Birthday Edition (Paul), 1219.1

Biggest Hits (Welk), 1231

The Billy Vaughn Collection (Vaughn), 1227

Blue Rose (Clooney), 1183.1

Calypso (Belafonte), 1178.1

Casey Kasem Presents America's Top Ten through the Years: The Doo-Wop Years, 1950s (collection), 1155

Casey Kasem Presents America's Top Ten through the Years: The Sixties (collection), 1156

Chasing Sound (Paul), 1219.2

Come Fly with Me (Sinatra), 1224.2

The Complete Flanders and Swann (Flanders and Swann), 1193.1

Daydreaming: The Very Best of Doris Day (Day), 1188.1

Dean Martin (Martin), 1211.1

The Definitive Collection (Davis), 1187.2

★*Dionne Warwick Collection* (Warwick), 1229.1

Ella Mae Morse (Morse), 1217

Esquivel! Space Age Bachelor Pad Music (Esquivel), 1190

Essential Johnny Mathis (Mathis), 1212.1

The Essential Mario Lanza (Lanza), 1205.2

The Essential Ray Conniff (Conniff), 1186

An Evening with Andy Williams: Live from the Royal Albert Hall, 1978 (Williams), 1232.1

An Evening with Harry Belafonte and Friends (Belafonte), 1178.2

Fever: The Music of Peggy Lee (Lee), 1206.2

50 Years: The Artistry of Tony Bennett (Bennett), 1179.2

The Four Aces Greatest Hits (Four Aces), 1194

★*The Four Freshmen* (Four Freshmen), 1195

Frank Sinatra: Concert Collection (Sinatra), 1224.3

Frank Sinatra Sings for Only the Lonely (Sinatra), 1224.4

general collections, 1155–1172

Golden Girl: Columbia Recordings 1944-1966 (Day), 1188.2

Golden Greats (Laine), 1204

Golden Years of Dick Haymes (Haymes), 1199

★*Greatest Hits* (Como), 1185

Greatest Hits (Faith), 1191

Greatest Hits (McGuire Sisters), 1213

Heavenly (Mathis), 1212.2

Here's to Romance (Clark), 1182

Hit Parade, 1943 (collection), 1157

Hit Parade, 1956 (collection), 1158

The Hits (Fisher), 1192

In the Beginning: The Complete Recordings, 1949–1954 (King), 1203

In the Wee Small Hours (Sinatra), 1224.5

Incredibly Strange Music, Vol. 1 (collection), 1159

Incredibly Strange Music, Vol. 2 (collection), 1160

★*Jo Stafford* (Stafford), 1225

Johnny Mercer (Mercer), 1214

Judy at Carnegie Hall (Garland), 1197

Jump, Jive, an' Wail: The Essential Louis Prima (Prima), 1220.1

★*Jumpin' at Capitol* (Cole), 1184.2

Kay Starr (Starr), 1226

The Legendary Crooners: Frank Sinatra, Dean Martin, Bing Crosby, Nat King Cole, Perry Como (collection), 1207

The Legend and the Legacy (Paul), 1219.3

The Leroy Anderson Collection (Anderson), 1176

The Leroy Anderson Songbook: A Centennial Celebration (songwriter collection), 1173

Live at the Café Carlyle (Short), 1223

Live in Concert (Warwick), 1229.2

The Look of Love: The Burt Bacharach Collection (collection), 1161

Mabel Mercer Sings Cole Porter (Mercer), 1215

A Man and His Music (Sinatra), 1224.6

Midnight, Moonlight, and Magic: The Very Best of Henry Mancini (Mancini), 1210

Moments to Remember: The Golden Hits of the '50s and '60s Live (collection), 1162

Neil Diamond Anthology (songwriter collection), 1175

Nice 'n' Easy (Sinatra), 1224.7

Nipper's Greatest Hits: The 50's, Vol. 2 (collection), 1164

★*Nipper's Greatest Hits: The 50's, Vol. 1* (collection), 1163

Pat Boone (Boone), 1180

Pure 60's: The #1 Hits (collection), 1165

The Remains of Tom Lehrer (Lehrer), 1208.1

Sentimental Journey: Capitol's Great Ladies of Song (collection), 1166

Sentimental Journey: Pop Vocal Classics, Vol. 1 (collection), 1167

Sentimental Journey: Pop Vocal Classics, Vol. 4 (collection), 1170

★*Sentimental Journey: Pop Vocal Classics, Vol. 2* (collection), 1168

★*Sentimental Journey: Pop Vocal Classics, Vol. 3* (collection), 1169

Sing Along with Mitch (Miller), 1216

16 Biggest Hits (Clooney), 1183.2

16 Most Requested Songs (Bennett), 1179.3

post-World War II through 1967 (cont.)
  16 Most Requested Songs (Four Lads),
    1196
  16 Most Requested Songs (Page), 1218
  *16 Most Requested Songs: The 1950s,
    Vol. 1* (collection), 1171
  Sixteen Biggest Hits (Williams), 1232.2
  Sixteen Most Requested Songs
    (Williams), 1232.3
  ★*Songs for Swingin' Lovers* (Sinatra),
    1224.8
  Songs for Young Lovers / Swing Easy
    (Sinatra), 1224.9
  *Songs from the Girl Singer: A Musical
    Autobiography* (Clooney), 1183.3
  The Songs of Bacharach and David
    (songwriter collection), 1174
  *The Songs of Michael Flanders and
    Donald Swann* (Flanders and
    Swann), 1193.2
  songwriter collections, 1173–1175
  The Spike Jones Story (Jones), 1202.2
  *Sweet and Lovely: Capitol's Great Ladies
    of Song* (collection), 1172
  ★*That's Amore* (Martin), 1211.2
  *30th Anniversary Collection: His All
    Time Greatest Hits* (Anka), 1177
  Too Many Songs by Tom Lehrer
    (Lehrer), 1208.2
  The Ultimate Dinah Shore (Shore), 1222
  Very Best of Harry Belafonte
    (Belafonte), 1178.3
  ★*The Very Best of Dinah Washington*
    (Washington), 1230
  The Very Best of Julie London
    (London), 1209
  The Very Best of Nat King Cole (Cole),
    1184.3
  ★*The Very Good Years* (Sinatra),
    1224.10
  The Voice in Time: 1939–1952
    (Sinatra), 1224.11
  The Wildest (Prima), 1220.2
  The World of Nat King Cole (Cole),
    1184.4
  Yesterday's Love Songs, Today's Blues
    (Wilson), 1234
Poulenc, Francis. *Babar the Elephant,*
  3260
Powell, Baden. *Pioneers of the New Age*
  (collection), 1371
Powell, Bud
  ★*The Amazing Bud Powell, Vol. 1,*
    600.1
  ★*The Amazing Bud Powell, Vol. 2,*
    600.2
  Bud Powell Real Book, 600.3
  Jazz Giant, 600.4
  ★*Ken Burns Jazz: The Story of
    America's Music* (collection), 478
  Piano Legends (collection), 480
  ★*The Smithsonian Collection of Classic
    Jazz* (collection), 486

★Powell, Chris. *The Okeh Rhythm and
    Blues Story* (collection), 2425
Powell, Dick
  ★*Brother, Can You Spare a Dime?
    American Song during the Great
    Depression* (collection), 1061
  Harry Warren (songwriter collection),
    1114
  Richard Whiting (songwriter
    collection), 1116
Prado, Perez. *Nipper's Greatest Hits: The
    50's, Vol. 2* (collection), 1164
Prefuse 73. *Vocal Studies + Uprock
    Narratives,* 2228, 2896
preschool children's music, 3191–3207
  ★*Animal Crackers* (Wee Hairy
    Beasties), 3207
  ★*Bob's Favorite Street Songs*
    (McGrath), 3202.1
  *The Bottle Let Me Down: Songs for Bumpy
    Wagon Rides* (collection), 3191
  Children's Songs (collection), 3192
  collections, 3191–3194
  *Colours Are Brighter: Songs for Children
    and Grown Ups Too* (collection),
    3193
  Early, Early Childhood Songs (Jenkins),
    3200
  High Five, 3199
  The Library Boogie (Knight), 3201
  ★*Miss Ella's Playhouse* (Fitzgerald),
    3198
  Mommy Says No! (Asylum Street
    Spankers), 3195
  More Singable Songs (Raffi), 3204.1
  ★*No!* (They Might Be Giants), 3206
  100 Kids' Songs (collection), 3194
  Raffi in Concert, 3204.2
  Rise and Shine (Raffi), 3204.3
  Sally the Swinging Snake (Palmer),
    3203.1
  Sing Me a Story (McGrath), 3202.2
  Singable Songs for the Very Young
    (Raffi), 3204.4
  ★*Snack Time!* (Barenaked Ladies),
    3196
  Stories and Songs for Little Children
    (Seeger), 3205
  ★*Walter the Waltzing Worm* (Palmer),
    3203.2
  Whaddaya Think of That? (Berkner),
    3197
Presidents. *Crash of Thunder: Boss Soul,
    Funk, and R&B Sides from the
    Vaults of the King, Federal, and
    Deluxe Labels* (collection), 2596
Presidents of the United States of
    America. *90's Pop Hits* (collection),
    1242
Presley, Elvis. *See also* Elvis Presley and
    rockabilly
  ★*Billboard Greatest Christmas Hits,
    1955–1983* (collection), 3294

  Elvis '68 Comeback, 1737.4
  Elvis, from Nashville to Memphis,
    1737.2
  *Elvis Gospel 1957–1971: Known Only
    to Him,* 3130.1
  ★*Elvis: 30 #1 Hits,* 1737.1
  Elvis Presley, 1737.3
  The Guitars of Elvis, 1737.5
  Hit Parade, 1956 (collection), 1158
  I Believe: The Gospel Masters, 3130.2
  *The King of Rock 'n' Roll: The
    Complete 50's Masters,* 1737.6
  Nipper's Greatest Hits: The 50's, Vol. 2
    (collection), 1164
  ★*Nipper's Greatest Hits: The 50's, Vol. 1*
    (collection), 1163
  Rock and Roll: The Early Days
    (collection), 1752
  ★*Sun Records' Greatest Hits*
    (collection), 1741
Preston, Billy
  Encouraging Words, 2504.1
  Ultimate Collection, 2504.2
Pretenders
  No Thanks! The '70s Punk Rebellion
    (collection), 2003
  ★*The Singles,* 2170
★Pretty Things. *Nuggets II: Original
    Artifacts from the British Empire and
    Beyond* (collection), 1791
pre–World War II country and western,
    1386–1427
  Altamont: Black Stringband Music,
    1394
  ★*Anthology of American Folk Music,
    Vol. 4* (collection), 1387
  ★*Anthology of American Folk Music,
    Vols. 1–3* (collection), 1386
  Beginning Old-Time Fiddle (Kaufman),
    1389
  ★*Best of Patsy Montana,* 1417
  Biggest Hits/Country Barn Dance
    (King), 1411
  Blues Yodeler and Steel Guitar Wizard
    (Carlisle), 1401
  The Blue Sky Boys, 1398.1
  Brown's Ferry Blues (Delmore
    Brothers), 1407.1
  *The Carter Family, 1927–1934: A. P.,
    Sara, Maybelle,* 1403.2
  ★*The Carter Family: Country Music Hall
    of Fame,* 1403.1
  *The Carter Family on Border Radio,
    Vol. 1,* 1403.4
  The Carter Family, 1935–1941, Vol. 2,
    1403.3
  *The Chattanooga Boys: Complete
    Recorded Works in Chronological
    Order, Vol. 1, 1927–1930* (Allen
    Brothers), 1393
  Classic Cuts (Delmore Brothers),
    1407.2
  Classic Sides (Macon), 1413.1

★*Complete Recorded Works, 1926–1934, in Chronological Order* (McGee), 1415

The Complete Recorded Works, Vol. 1 (Carson), 1402

Darby and Tarlton: Complete Recordings, 1405

Definitive Hoosier Hotshots Collection, 1410

Ernest V. Stoneman: The Unsung Father of Country Music, 1425

★*The Essential Gene Autry,* 1396.1

★*The Essential Jimmie Rodgers,* 1421.1

★*The Essential Roy Acuff,* 1392.1

Fiddlin' Arthur Smith and His Dixieliners, 1423

★*Go Long Mule* (Macon), 1413.2

Greatest Hits, Finest Performances (Davis), 1406

Greenback Dollar (Ashley), 1395

Happy Trails: The Roy Rogers Collection, 1937–1990, 1422

His Twelve Original Recordings (Boggs), 1399

Home, Sweet Home on the Prairie: 25 Cowboy Classics (Robison), 1420

In Concert, 1964 (Blue Sky Boys), 1398.2

In the Shadow of Clinch Mountain (Carter Family), 1403.5

Inducted into the Hall of Fame, 1981 (Dalhart), 1404

Keep My Skillet Good and Greasy (Macon), 1413.3

King of the Hillbillies, Vol. 1: The First 100 Commercial Sides, Some Never before Reissued (Acuff), 1392.2

Last Letter (Griffin), 1409

The Legendary DeFord Bailey: Country Music's First Black Star, 1397

1935–1939: The Early Years (Mainer), 1414

Old-Time Country Guitar: An Instruction Guide to Old-Timey Solo Fingerpicking Guitar (Cicchetti and Bredenberg), 1388

Old-Time Fiddle Tunes and Songs from North Georgia (Tanner and the Skillet Lickers), 1426

Old-Time Mountain Ballads (collection), 1390

Old-Time Mountain Guitar (collection), 1391

★*Old-Time Songs* (Poole), 1418

Old-Time Texas Fiddler (Robertson), 1419

Polk Miller and His Old South Quartette, 1416

RCA Years (Britt), 1400

Recordings of Grayson and Whitter, 1408

Recordings, 1927–1933 (Rodgers), 1421.2

The Singing Brakeman (Rodgers), 1421.3

Sons of the Pioneers: Country Music Hall of Fame, 1424.1

The Sunny Side of Life (Blue Sky Boys), 1398.3

Sweethearts of Country Music (Lulu Belle and Scotty), 1412

That Silver Haired Daddy of Mine (Autry), 1396.2

Ultimate Collection (Sons of the Pioneers), 1424.2

White Country Blues: A Lighter Shade of Blues (collection), 1427

pre-World War II mainstream popular

Alan Jay Lerner (songwriter collection), 1105.1

Alec Wilder Song Collection (songwriter collection), 1117.2

Alec Wilder (songwriter collection), 1117.1

All Time Favorite Dietz and Schwartz Songs (songwriter collection), 1110.1

American Music Icon (Merman), 1142.1

★*American Popular Song: Six Decades of Songwriters and Singers* (collection), 1059

The Anthology (Mills Brothers), 1145

Arthur Schwartz (songwriter collection), 1110.2

Best of Lerner and Loewe (songwriter collection), 1105.2

★*Best of the Big Bands* (James), 1136.1

Best of Will Bradley with Ray McKinley: Eight to the Bar (Bradley), 1122

★*The Best of Al Jolson* (Jolson), 1137.1

The Best of Eddie Cantor: A Centennial Celebration (Cantor), 1123.1

The Best of Hal Kemp and His Orchestra (Kemp), 1138.1

Big Spender, Witchcraft, and Other Cy Coleman Favorites (songwriter collection), 1098.1

The Billy Murray Anthology: The Denver Nightingale (Murray), 1147

Bing Crosby and Some Jazz Friends (Crosby), 1125.2

Bing: His Legendary Years (Crosby), 1125.1

Bing's Gold Records (Crosby), 1125.3

Black Manhattan: Theater and Dance Music of James Reese Europe, Will Marion Cook, and Members of the Legendary Clef Club (collection), 1060

Broadway and Hollywood (songwriter collection), 1115.1

★*Brother, Can You Spare a Dime? American Song during the Great Depression* (collection), 1061

Centennial Anthology (Crosby), 1125.4

★*A Centennial Anthology of His Decca Recordings* (Crosby), 1125.5

★*Classic Judy Garland: The Capitol Years, 1955–1965* (Garland), 1134.1

The Classic Hoagy Carmichael (songwriter collection), 1097.1

Cole Porter (songwriter collection), 1108.1

The Columbia Years (Cantor), 1123.2

The Complete Recordings Nineteen Thirty-Nine: Featuring Frank Sinatra (James), 1136.2

★*The Crooners* (collection), 1062

Cy Coleman (songwriter collection), 1098.2

The Definitive Collection (songwriter collection), 1101.1

Don't Give the Name a Bad Place: Types and Stereotypes in American Musical Theater, 1870–1900 (collection), 1063

Dorothy Fields (songwriter collection), 1100

Duke Ellington Anthology (songwriter collection), 1099.2

Duke Ellington (songwriter collection), 1099.1

E. Y. Harburg (songwriter collection), 1103

★*An Earful of Music* (Merman), 1142.2

The Eddy Duchin Story: 24 Vintage Tracks (Duchin), 1130

Essential Collection: God Bless America (Smith), 1149

Essential Fred Astaire (Astaire), 1120.1

★*Essential Glenn Miller* (Miller), 1144

Fascinating Rhythm: George Gershwin (songwriter collection), 1101.2

★*Favourite Songs of Ethel Waters* (Waters), 1151.1

★*50th Anniversary Collection, Vol. 1* (Andrews Sisters), 1119

The First of the Singer Songwriters: Key Cuts (Carmichael), 1124

Flappers, Vamps, and Sweet Young Things (collection), 1065

The Flapper Box (collection), 1064

Frank Loesser Songbook (songwriter collection), 1106.2

Frank Loesser (songwriter collection), 1106.1

From Berlin to Broadway: A Selection (songwriter collection), 1115.2

Gay Caballero (Crumit), 1126

general collections, 1059–1094

The Genius of Thomas "Fats" Waller (songwriter collection), 1113.1

George Gershwin (songwriter collection), 1101.3

Got a Date with an Angel (Kemp), 1138.2

pre-World War II mainstream popular (cont.)
  Great American Songbook (Astaire), 1120.2
  Greatest Hits (Dorsey), 1128.1, 1129.1
  The Great Depression: American Music in the '30s (collection), 1066
  Harold Arlen Songbook (songwriter collection), 1095.2
  Harold Arlen (songwriter collection), 1095.1
  Harry Warren (songwriter collection), 1114
  Heart and Soul: The Life and Music of Frank Loesser (songwriter collection), 1106.3
  Hoagy Carmichael Centennial Collection (songwriter collection), 1097.3
  Hoagy Carmichael (songwriter collection), 1097.2
  "I Wants to Be a Actor Lady" and Other Hits from Early Musical Comedies (collection), 1067
  If I Had a Talking Picture of You, Vol. 1 (Whiteman), 1153.1
  If You Got to Ask, You Ain't Got It! (Waller), 1133
  The Incomparable Ethel Waters (Waters), 1151.2
  ★Instant Classics (Ink Spots), 1135
  Irving Berlin: A Hundred Years (songwriter collection), 1096.3
  Irving Berlin Anthology (songwriter collection), 1096.2
  Irving Berlin (songwriter collection), 1096.1
  ★It Had to Be You: Popular Keyboard from the Days of the Speakeasy to the Television Era (collection), 1068
  It's Easy to Remember (Crosby), 1125.6
  James Reese Europe Featuring Noble Sissle (Europe), 1132
  James Van Heusen (songwriter collection), 1112.1
  The Jazz Singer (Jolson), 1137.2
  Jerome Kern Collection (songwriter collection), 1104.2
  Jerome Kern (songwriter collection), 1104.1
  Jimmy Dorsey and His Orchestra Play: 22 Original Recordings (Dorsey), 1128.2
  Joe Franklin Presents . . . The Roaring '20s Roar Again (collection), 1069
  Johnny Mercer Centennial Sheet Music Collection (songwriter collection), 1107.2
  Johnny Mercer (songwriter collection), 1107.1
  The Judy Garland Collection (Garland), 1134.2
  Jule Styne (songwriter collection), 1111.1

Just Gershwin Real Book (songwriter collection), 1101.4
Kollege of Musical Knowledge (Kyser), 1139.1
Kurt Weill: American Songbook Series (Weill), 1152
Life Is Just a Bowl of Cherries (Vallee), 1150.1
Makin' Whoopee, Vol. 2 (Whiteman), 1153.2
Makin' Whoopee with "Banjo Eyes" (Cantor), 1123.3
Mary Martin and Ethel Merman: Their Legendary Appearance on the Ford 50th Anniversary Show (Merman), 1142.3
The Middle Years (Williams), 1154
The Minstrel Man from Georgia (Miller), 1143
A Musical Anthology (songwriter collection), 1108.2
★The Music Goes Round and Around: The Golden Years of Tin Pan Alley, 1930–1939 (collection), 1070
1929-1939 (Waters), 1151.3
★Nipper's Greatest Hits: The 20's (collection), 1071
★Nipper's Greatest Hits: The 30's, Vol. 1 (collection), 1072
★Nipper's Greatest Hits: The 40's, Vol. 1 (collection), 1073
★On Stage and Screen (Waters), 1151.4
The Original Latin Dance King (Cugat), 1127
Oscar Hammerstein II (songwriter collection), 1102
Over There! Songs from America's Wars (Marlborough Singers and Chamber Players, tenor John English, and piano Rob Carriker), 1141
Phono-Cylinders, Vols. 1 and 2 (collection), 1074
The Phonographic Yearbook, 1922: An Angel's Voice I Hear (collection), 1078
The Phonographic Yearbook, 1907: Dear Old Golden Rule Days (collection), 1075
The Phonographic Yearbook, 1908: Take Me Out with the Crowd (collection), 1076
The Phonographic Yearbook, 1912: Waitin' on the Levee (collection), 1077
★Praise the Lord and Pass the Ammunition: Songs of World Wars I and II (collection), 1079
Reckless Nights and Turkish Twilights: The Music of Raymond Scott (Scott), 1148
Richard Whiting (songwriter collection), 1116

The Roaring 'Twenties (collection), 1080
Rodgers and Hammerstein Collection (songwriter collection), 1109.2
Rodgers and Hart: A Musical Anthology (songwriter collection), 1109.3
Rodgers / Hart (songwriter collection), 1109.1
Russ Morgan and His Orchestra Play: 22 Original Big Band Recordings (Morgan), 1146
★Sentimental Journey: Pop Vocal Classics, Vol. 1 (collection), 1081
16 Most Requested Songs of the 1940s, Vol. 1 (collection), 1082
16 Most Requested Songs of the 1940s, Vol. 2 (collection), 1083
It's Easy to Remember (Crosby), 1125.7
Songs of Burke and Van Heusen (songwriter collection), 1112.2
Songs of WWI: From Original Recordings 1914–1926 (collection), 1084
Songs That Got Us through World War II (collection), 1085
Songs That Got Us through World War II, Vol. 2 (collection), 1086
songwriter collections, 1095–1118
★Sophisticated Ladies (collection), 1087
Stomp and Swerve: American Music Gets Hot (collection), 1088
Stop, Look, and Listen (Dorsey), 1129.2
Strict Education in Music: 50 of the Best (Kyser), 1139.2
★Sweetest Music This Side of Heaven (Lombardo), 1140
★Swing Time! The Fabulous Big Band Era (collection), 1089
Ten Cents a Dance (Etting), 1131
★That's How Rhythm Was Born (Boswell Sisters), 1121
This Is Art Deco (collection), 1090
Times Ain't What They Used to Be: Early Rural and Popular Music from Rare Original Film Masters (collection), 1091
Too Marvelous for Words: Capitol Sings Johnny Mercer (songwriter collection), 1107.3
Top Hat: Hits from Hollywood (Astaire), 1120.3
25 Sweethearts of Yesteryear (collection), 1092
20th Century Masters: The Best of Judy Garland (Garland), 1134.3
Vagabond Lover (Vallee), 1150.2
The Very Best of Cole Porter (songwriter collection), 1108.3
Vincent Youmans (songwriter collection), 1118
Waller / Razaf (songwriter collection), 1113.2

Whiteman Stomp (Whiteman), 1153.3
With My Little Ukulele in My Hand (collection), 1093
★*Yes, Sir, That's My Baby: The Golden Years of Tin Pan Alley* (collection), 1094
Price, Lloyd
    Lawdy!, 2292.1
    Lloyd Price, Vol. 2: Heavy Dreams, 2292.2
    ★*The R&B Box* (collection), 2239
    The Roots of Rock 'n' Roll, 1946–1954 (collection), 1755
    ★*The Specialty Story* (collection), 2428
Price, Ray
    Classic Country: Kings of Country (collection), 1381
    Hank Williams Songbook (collection), 1450
    The Essential Ray Price, 1527
Price, Sammy
    Blues Routes (collection), 413
    ★*Stompin' at the Savoy: The Original Indie Label, 1944–1961* (collection), 2429
★Price, Zella Jackson. *Say Amen, Somebody* (collection), 2971
Pride, Charley
    Charley Pride, 1528.1
    ★*Essential Charley Pride,* 1528.2
    Grand Ole Opry at Carnegie Hall (collection), 1619
Pridgett, Gertrude Malissa Nix. *See* Rainey, Ma
Prima, Louis
    Jump, Jive, an' Wail: The Essential Louis Prima, 1220.1
    ★*Swing Time! The Fabulous Big Band Era* (collection), 1089
    The Wildest, 1220.2
Primal Scream. *Screamadelica,* 2171
Prince
    Dirty Mind, 2639.2
    The Hits Collection, 2293
    The Hits / the B-Sides, 2639.3
    1999, 2639.1
    Prince: Live in Las Vegas, 2639.4
    ★*Purple Rain: Music from the Motion Picture,* 2639.5
    Sign "O" the Times, 2639.6
    The Very Best of Prince, 2639.7
★Prince, Bobby. *Nashville Jumps: Blues and Rhythm on Nashville Independent Labels 1945–1955* (collection), 2376
Prince Gabe. *The Complete Goldwax Singles, Vol. 1* (collection), 2591
Prince Paul. *A Prince among Thieves,* 2897
Princely Players. *The Civil War Music Collector's Edition* (collection), 61
Prisoners. *Night Train to Nashville: Music City Rhythm and Blues, 1945–1970, Vol. 1* (collection), 2377

Procol Harum. *Greatest Hits,* 1801
Prodigy
    The Fat of the Land, 2172.1
    Music for the Jilted Generation, 2172.2
progressive new age, 1336–1345
    Behind the Gardens, behind the Wall, under the Tree (Vollenweider), 1344.1
    Caverna Magica (Vollenweider), 1344.2
    ★*Fresh Aire* (Mannheim Steamroller), 1339
    In Den Gärten Pharoas (Popol Vuh), 1341.1
    New Age Piano (Ciani), 1336.1
    Nouveau Flamenco (Liebert), 1338
    Selected Recordings (Rypdal), 1342
    Tantric Songs/Hosianna Mantra (Popol Vuh), 1341.2
    ★*Tubular Bells* (Oldfield), 1340
    Vapor Drawings (Isham), 1337
    The Velocity of Love (Ciani), 1336.2
    The Very Best of Yanni (Yanni), 1345
    Yr (Tibbetts), 1343
Pryor, Arthur. *Arthur Pryor: Trombone Soloist of the Sousa Band,* 88
Pryor Band. *Early Syncopated Dance Music: Cakewalks, Two-Steps, Trots and Glides* (collection), 124
Pryor, Snooky
    Chicago Is Just That Way (collection), 289
    An Introduction to Snooky Pryor, 304
Prysock, Arthur. *Legendary Big Band Singers* (collection), 767
Prysock, Red. *The Big Horn: The History of the Honkin' and Screamin' Saxophone* (collection), 2314
The Psychedelic Furs
    All of This and Nothing, 2173
    80's Pop Hits (collection), 1238
P'tits Loups du Jazz. *Animal Playground* (collection), 3226
Public Enemy
    Apocalypse 91 . . . The Enemy Strikes Black, 2898.1
    ★*Fear of a Black Planet,* 2898.2
    ★*It Takes a Nation of Millions to Hold Us Back,* 2898.3
    Yo! Bum Rush the Show, 2898.4
Public Image Ltd. *Second Edition (Metal Box),* 2036
Puckett, Riley. *White Country Blues: A Lighter Shade of Blues,* 1427
Puff Daddy and the Family. *No Way Out,* 2899
Pullen, Don. *New Beginnings,* 1006
★Pullman Porters Quartette. *A Warrior on the Battlefield: A Cappella Trail Blazers* (collection), 3011
Pullum, Joe. *The Swing Time Records Story: R&B, Blues, and Gospel, 1946–1952* (collection), 2430

Pulp. *Different Class,* 2174
punk and new wave: U.K., 2003–2030
    American Hardcore (collection), 1977
    Basher: The Best of Nick Lowe, 2018
    Beat This! The Best of the English Beat, 2013
    The Best of Elvis Costello: The First 10 Years, 2010.1
    ★*The Clash,* 2009.1
    Crossing the Red Sea with the Adverts, 2006
    Cut (Slits), 2026
    D.I.Y. Blank Generation: The New York Scene (collection), 1978
    ★*Every Breath You Take: The Classics* (Police), 2020
    Feeding of the 5000 (Crass), 2011
    The Filth and the Fury (Sex Pistols), 2023.1
    Generation X, 2014
    Heat Treatment (Parker), 2019
    I'm Stranded (Saints), 2022
    The Image Has Cracked (Alternative TV), 2007
    In the City (Jam), 2016.1
    Inflammable Material (Stiff Little Fingers), 2028
    Let's Submerge: The Anthology (X-Ray Spex), 2030
    LiLiPUT, 2017
    London Calling (Clash), 2009.2
    MIA: The Complete Anthology (Germs), 2015
    ★*My Aim Is True* (Costello), 2010.2
    ★*Never Mind the Bollocks Here's the Sex Pistols,* 2023.2
    No New York (collection), 1979
    No Thanks! The '70s Punk Rebellion (collection), 2003
    Once upon a Time: The Singles (Siouxsie and the Banshees), 2025
    Punk: Attitude (collection), 1980
    The Raincoats, 2021
    Searching for the Young Soul Rebels (Dexys Midnight Runners), 2012
    Singles Going Steady (Buzzcocks), 2008
    The Sound of the Jam, 2016.2
    The Specials, 2027
    Stiff, Stiffer, Stiffest: A Stiff Records Collection (collection), 2004
    Tell Us the Truth (Sham 69), 2024
    This Year's Model (Costello), 2010.3
    The Tomorrow Show with Tom Snyder: Punk and New Wave (collection), 1981
    Too Much Two Tone, 2005
    The Undertones, 2029
punk and new wave: U.S., 1977–2002
    Blank Generation (Richard Hell and the Voidoids), 1989
    Can't Stand the Rezillos: The (Almost) Complete Rezillos, 1996

punk and new wave (cont.)
    Complete Discography (Minor Threat),
      1992
    Complete Greatest Hits (Cars), 1984.1
    Damaged (Black Flag), 1982
    Fear of Music (Talking Heads), 1999.1
    Fresh Fruit for Rotting Vegetables (Dead
      Kennedys), 1986
    Greatest Hits (Blondie), 1983
    Greatest Hits (Cars), 1984.2
    ★*Horses* (Smith), 1997
    L.A.M.F. (Johnny Thunders and the
      Heartbreakers), 1990
    Marquee Moon (Television), 2000
    MIA: The Complete Anthology (Germs),
      1988
    The Modern Dance (Pere Ubu), 1994.1
    Q: Are We Not Men? A: We Are Devo,
      1987
    Queen of Siam (Lunch), 1991
    ★*Ramones,* 1995.1
    Remain in Light (Talking Heads),
      1999.2
    Rocket to Russia (Ramones), 1995.2
    Stop Making Sense [1983] (Talking
      Heads), 1999.3
    Stop Making Sense [1984] (Talking
      Heads), 1999.4
    Suicide: The First Album, 1998
    The Tenement Year [Remastered &
      Expanded] (Pere Ubu), 1994.2
    Terminal Tower: An Archival Collection
      (Pere Ubu), 1994.3
    Vs (the Definitive Edition plus Bonus
      DVD) (Mission of Burma), 1993
    Weird World, Vol. 1: 1977–1981
      (Weirdos), 2001
    Wipers Box Set: Is This Real?/Youth of
      America/Over the Edge, 2002
    Young, Loud and Snotty (Dead Boys),
      1985
Purify, James and Bobby. *Soul Shots: A*
    Collection of Sixties Soul Classics
    (collection), 2443

Q
Quartetto Cetra. *Animal Playground*
    (collection), 3226
Quartz. *The Best of T. K. Disco*
    (collection), 2656
Quasimoto. *The Unseen,* 2900
Quebec, Ike. *Blue and Sentimental,* 731
Queen
    Billboard #1s: The '80s (collection),
      1236
    Greatest Hits, 1930
    Like Omigod! The 80s Pop Culture Box
      (Totally) (collection), 1241
Queen Latifah. *All Hail the Queen,* 2901
Queensryche. *Heavy Metal: The First 20*
    Years (collection), 1938
Quicksilver Messenger Service
    Happy Trails, 1843.1

    Quicksilver Messenger Service, 1843.2
    San Francisco Nights (collection), 1829
    Sons of Mercury, 1843.3
Quink. *Carols around the World,* 3284
★Quotations. *The Doo-Wop Box*
    (collection), 2322

R
Rabbitt, Eddie. *Like Omigod! The 80s Pop*
    Culture Box (Totally) (collection),
    1241
★Rachell, Yank. *Let's Get Loose: Folk*
    and Popular Blues Styles from
    the Beginning to the Early 1940s
    (collection), 152
Racy Brothers. *Living Legends of Gospel:*
    The Quartets, Vols. 1 and 2
    (collection), 3010
The Radiants
    Best of Chess R&B, Vols. 1 and 2
      (collection), 2420
    Birth of Soul: Special Chicago Edition
      (collection), 2566
    Eccentric Soul: Twinight's Lunar
      Rotation (collection), 2568
Radio Four. *The Best of Nashboro Gospel*
    (collection), 3032
Radiohead
    The Bends, 2176.1
    Hail to the Thief, 2176.2
    Meeting People Is Easy, 2176.3
    ★*OK Computer,* 2176.4
Raeburn, Boyd
    ★*Big Band Jazz: From the Beginnings to*
      the Fifties (collection), 529
    Big Band Renaissance: The Evolution of
      the Jazz Orchestra (collection), 739
    Boyd Meets Stravinsky, 546
Raekwon. *Only Built 4 Cuban Linx,* 2902
Raffi
    More Singable Songs, 3204.1
    Raffi in Concert, 3204.2
    Raffi's Christmas Album, 3249
    Rise and Shine, 3204.3
    Singable Songs for the Very Young,
      3204.4
rag music. *See* ragtime
Rage against the Machine. *Rage against*
    the Machine, 2177
Ragin, Derek Lee. *Negro Spirituals,* 43
ragtime, 124–144
    American Beauties: The Rags of Joseph
      Lamb (Lamb), 136.1
    American Beauty: A Ragtime Bouquet
      (Smart), 142
    The Art of the Rag (New England
      Ragtime Ensemble), 138
    Black Manhattan: Theater and Dance
      Music of James Reese Europe, Will
      Marion Cook, and Members of
      the Legendary Clef Club (Paragon
      Ragtime Orchestra), 140.1
    Breakin' Notes (Wright), 144

    ★*Classic Piano Rags: Complete Original*
      Music for 81 Rags (Blesh), 130
    Classic Ragtime from Rare Piano Rolls
      (Joplin), 135.1
    Classic Ragtime from Rare Piano Rolls
      (Scott), 141
    collections, 124–125
    Complete Piano Rags (Joplin), 135.2
    The Complete Rags, Marches and
      Waltzes (Joplin), 135.3
    Dick Hyman's Century of Jazz Piano
      (Hyman), 134
    Early Syncopated Dance Music:
      Cakewalks, Two-Steps, Trots and
      Glides (collection), 124
    Elite Syncopations: Classic Ragtime
      from Rare Piano Rolls 1899–1918
      (Joplin), 135.4
    Elite Syncopations: Classic Ragtime
      from Rare Piano Rolls, 1899–1917
      (Joplin), 135.5
    Euphonic Sounds: The Music of Scott
      Joplin (Joplin), 135.6
    Greatest Hits (Joplin), 135.7
    The Greatest Ragtime of the Century
      (collection), 125
    I'll Dance Till de Sun Breaks Through:
      Ragtime, Cakewalks and Stomps
      (Europe, Victor Minstrels, Sousa's
      Band, Collins, Conway's Orchestra
      and Six Brown Brothers), 133
    Knockout Drops: American Popular
      Music from the Ragtime Era
      (Paragon Ragtime Orchestra),
      140.2
    The Library of Ragtime and Early Blues
      Piano (Appleby and Pickow), 126
    Magnetic Rags: Ragtime for Brass
      (Avatar Brass Quintet), 128
    Max Morath Plays the Best of Scott
      Joplin and Other Rag Classics
      (Morath), 137.1
    Memories of You (Blake), 129.1
    Old Time Fiddle Rags, Classic and
      Minstrel Banjo (Old 78's), 139
    On a Circular Staircase (Swanson), 143
    The Paragon Orchestra (Finally)
      Plays "The Entertainer" (Paragon
      Ragtime Orchestra), 140.3
    Piano Rags (Joplin), 135.8
    Piano Works, 1899–1904 (Joplin),
      135.9
    Rags and Waltzes (Joplin), 135.10
    Rags to Riches: The Essential Hits
      (Joplin), 135.11
    Rag-Time Music (Joplin), 135.13
    Ragtime: The Music of Scott Joplin
      (Joplin), 135.12
    Ragtime Women (Morath), 137.2
    The Red Back Book: Elite Syncopations
      (Joplin), 135.14
    Scott Joplin: His Complete Works
      (Joplin), 135.15

Scott Joplin: King of Ragtime Writers from Classic Piano Rolls (Joplin), 135.16

Sincerely, Eubie Blake: Nine Original Compositions for Piano Solo (Blake), 129.2

A Study in Classic Ragtime (Lamb), 136.2

That Demon Rag: American Popular Music from the Ragtime Era (Paragon Ragtime Orchestra), 140.4

That's Ragtime! (Blake), 129.3

William Appling Plays Scott Joplin & J. S. Bach (Appling), 127

World's Greatest Piano Rags (Dowling), 132

You're a Grand Old Rag (Cohan), 131

Rah Digga. *Dirty Harriet,* 2903

Rainbow. *Heavy Metal: The First 20 Years* (collection), 1938

★Rainbows. *The Doo-Wop Box* (collection), 2322

Raincoats. *The Raincoats,* 2021

Rainey, Ma
    Blues Masters, Vol. 11: Classic Blues Women (collection), 203
    ★*The Blues: A Smithsonian Collection of Classic Blues Singers* (collection), 145
    ★*I Can't Be Satisfied: Early American Women Blues Singers, Vol. 2: Town* (collection), 204
    Ma Rainey's Black Bottom, 209.1
    Mother of the Blues, 209.2
    The Road to Robert Johnson and Beyond (collection), 221

Raitt, Bonnie
    The Best of Bonnie Raitt on Capitol, 1989–2003, 1298.1
    Give It Up, 2057.1
    Make It Funky! (collection), 2360
    Nick of Time, 1298.2, 2057.2

Raitt, John
    Alan Jay Lerner (songwriter collection), 1105.1
    Oscar Hammerstein II (songwriter collection), 1102
    Vincent Youmans (songwriter collection), 1118

Rakim. *The 18th Letter,* 2904

Ramey, Troy and the Soul Searchers. *Living Legends of Gospel: The Quartets, Vols. 1 and 2* (collection), 3010

Ramones
    D.I.Y. Blank Generation: The New York Scene (collection), 1978
    No Thanks! The '70s Punk Rebellion (collection), 2003
    Punk: Attitude (collection), 1980
    ★*Ramones,* 1995.1
    Rocket to Russia, 1995.2

The Tomorrow Show with Tom Snyder: Punk and New Wave (collection), 1981

Rampal, Jean-Pierre. *Pioneers of the New Age* (collection), 1371

Ramsey Lewis Trio
    Best of Chess R&B, Vols. 1 and 2 (collection), 2420
    Soul Shots: A Collection of Sixties Soul Classics (collection), 2443

★Ran-Dells. *Halloween Hits* (collection), 3347

★Randolph, Robert. *Sacred Steel: The Steel Guitar Tradition of the House of God Churches* (collection), 2980

Randy and the Rainbows
    ★*The Doo Wop Box: 101 Vocal Group Gems from the Golden Age of Rock 'n' Roll* (collection), 1745
    ★*The Doo-Wop Box* (collection), 2322

Raney, Jimmy. *Progressions: 100 Years of Jazz Guitar* (collection), 481

Raney, Wayne
    All-Time Country and Western Hits (collection), 1449
    Favorite Sacred Songs (collection), 3109

Rankin, Leroy Batman. *The Big Horn: The History of the Honkin' and Screamin' Saxophone* (collection), 2314

rap and hip-hop, 153–2951
    A Lo Cubano (Orishas), 2886
    The Ablist (Swift), 2928
    Africa Raps (collection), 2659
    African Rap (collection), 2660
    The Album (Latyrx), 2840
    The Album (Mantronix), 2858
    All Balls Don't Bounce, Revisited (Aceyalone), 2699.1
    ★*All Eyez on Me* (2Pac), 2935.1
    All Hail the Queen (Queen Latifah), 2901
    All Meat No Filler! The Best of Fat Boys, 2788.1
    ★*Amerikkka's Most Wanted* (Ice Cube), 2819.1
    And Now the Legacy Begins (Drake), 2776
    Anticon Presents Music for the Advancement of Hip Hop (collection), 2661
    Anti-Theft Device (Mix Master Mike), 2869
    Apocalypse 91 . . . The Enemy Strikes Black (Public Enemy), 2898.1
    Aquemin (OutKast), 2887.1
    Arrhythmia (Anitipop Consortium), 2702
    As Nasty as They Wanna Be (2 Live Crew), 2934.1
    Atliens (OutKast), 2887.2

    Attack of the Attacking Things: The Dirty Mixes (Grae), 2807
    Bacdafucup (Onyx), 2884
    Banned in the USA (2 Live Crew), 2934.2
    Based on a True Story (Mack 10), 2853
    Beat Konducta, Vols. 1 and 2 (Madlib), 2854
    The Beatnuts [Street Level], 2711
    Beef (collection), 2662
    Behind the Front (Black Eyed Peas), 2716
    Beneath the Surface (Genius), 2801.1
    Best of the Sugarhill Gang, 2926
    The Best of Cold Chillin': Goin' Off + The Biz Never Sleeps (Biz Markie), 2715
    The Best of Cold Chillin' (Kool G Rap and DJ Polo), 2835
    The Best of Cold Chillin' (Masta Ace), 2860
    The Best of Enjoy! Records (collection), 2663
    ★*The Best of Grandmaster Flash, Melle Mel, and the Furious Five: Message from Beat Street,* 2809
    The Best of Kurtis Blow, 2721.1
    Better Dayz (2Pac), 2935.2
    Big Tyme (Heavy D and the Boyz), 2814.1
    Big Willie Style (Smith), 2921
    Bizarre Ride II the Pharcyde, 2893
    Black Dialogue (Perceptionists), 2892
    Black Elvis/Lost in Space (Kool Keith), 2836
    Black Mafia Life (Above the Law), 2698.1
    Black on Both Sides (Mos Def), 2871.1
    Black Sunday (Cypress Hill), 2747.1
    Blacks' Magic (Salt-n-Pepa), 2915.1
    The Black Album (Jay Z), 2823.1
    Blazing Arrow (Blackalicious), 2719.1
    Blowout Comb (Digable Planets), 2760.1
    ★*The Blueprint* (Jay Z), 2823.2
    Body Count, 2722
    A Book of Human Language (Aceyalone), 2699.2
    Born Like This (MF Doom), 2868.1
    Born to Mack (Too Short), 2932.1
    Both Sides of the Brain (Del Tha Funkee Homosapien), 2757.1
    Bow Down (Westside Connection), 2943
    Boy in Da Corner (Dizzee Rascal), 2765
    Brazilian Hip-Hop (collection), 2664
    Breaking Atoms (Main Source), 2856
    The Breakin' DVD Collection (collection), 2665
    Buhloone Mindstate (De La Soul), 2754.1

rap and hip-hop (cont.)

Business as Usual (EPMD), 2784.1

Business Never Personal (EPMD), 2784.2

By All Means Necessary (Boogie Down Productions), 2724.1

The Cactus Album (3rd Bass), 2930

Can-I-Bus (Canibus), 2732

Capital Punishment (Big Punisher), 2713

The Carnival (Jean), 2824

Carpal Tunnel Syndrome (Kid Koala), 2834

Cee-Lo Green and His Perfect Imperfections, 2811.1

Cee-Lo Green . . . Is the Soul Machine, 2811.2

Certified (Banner), 2706

Check Your Head (Beastie Boys), 2709.1

The Chosen Few (Boot Camp Clik), 2725

Christian rap, 3167–3183

★*The Chronic* (Dr. Dre), 2773.2

The Cold Vein (Cannibal Ox), 2733

collections, 2659–2697

The Collection, Vol. 1 (Bone Thugs-n-Harmony), 2723.1

The College Dropout (West), 2942.1

Comin' out Hard (Eightball and MJG), 2780.1

Connected (Foreign Exchange), 2793

Cosmogramma (Flying Lotus), 2792

★*Criminal Minded* (Boogie Down Productions), 2724.2

Critical Beatdown (Ultramagnetic MC's), 2937

Cypress Hill, 2747.2

Dah Shinin' (Smif-n-Wessun), 2920

Daily Operation (Gang Starr), 2800.1

De La Soul Is Dead, 2754.2

Dead Serious (Das EFX), 2751

Deadringer (rjd2), 2908

Death Certificate (Ice Cube), 2819.2

★*Def Jam Music Group, Inc.: 10th Year Anniversary* (collection), 2666

Def Jux Presents . . . (collection), 2667

Definitive Jux Presents II (collection), 2668

Deltron 3030, 2758

Demon Days (Gorillaz), 2806

Desire (Pharoahe Monch), 2894.1

The Diary (Scarface), 2916.2

Dirty Harriet (Rah Digga), 2903

The Documentary (Game), 2799

Dogg Food (Tha Dogg Pound), 2772

★*Doggystyle* (Snoop Dogg), 2922.2

Don Cartagena (Fat Joe), 2789

Done by the Forces of Nature (Jungle Brothers), 2826.1

The Don Killuminati: The 7 Day Theory (Makaveli), 2857

Donuts (J Dilla), 2822

Dr. Octagonecologyst (Dr. Dre), 2774

E. 1999 Eternal (Bone Thugs-n-Harmony), 2723.2

East Side's Most Wanted, Vol. 1 (collection), 2669

East Side's Most Wanted, Vol. 2 (collection), 2670

Eazy-Duz-It (EazyOE), 2778.1

The Ecstatic (Mos Def), 2871.2

Edutainment (Boogie Down Productions), 2724.3

Efil4zaggin [Niggaz4life] (N.W.A.), 2877.1

Ego Trip's the Big Playback, 2779

The 18th Letter (Rakim), 2904

The Eminem Show, 2783.1

Endtroducing . . . . (DJ Shadow), 2770

Enta da Stage (Black Moon), 2717

★*Enter the Wu-Tang: 36 Chambers,* 2946.1

Escape from Havana (Mellow Man Ace), 2866

Eternal E: Gangsta Memorial Edition (Eazy-E), 2778.2

Extinction Level Event: The Final World Front (Rhymes), 2907.1

Eyes on This (MC Lyte), 2863.1

Fat Boys, 2788.2

Fear Itself (Casual), 2736

★*Fear of a Black Planet* (Public Enemy), 2898.2

15 Years on Death Row (collection), 2671

Flesh of My Flesh, Blood of My Blood (DMX), 2771.1

Float (Aesop Rock), 2700.1

Follow the Leader (Eric B. and Rakim), 2785.1

Food and Liquor (Fiasco), 2790

40 Dayz and 40 Nightz (Xzibit), 2948

400 Degreez (Juvenile), 2828

Freestyle: The Art of Rhyme (collection), 2672

Fresh, Wild, Fly, and Bold (Cold Crush Brothers), 2739

The Freshest Kids, 2797

Full Circle (Hieroglyphics), 2816.1

Funcrusherplus (Company Flow), 2742

Funky Beat: The Best of Whodini, 2944

Funky Technician (Lord Finesse and DJ Mike Smooth), 2849

A Future without a Past (Leaders of the New School), 2841

Game Theory (Roots), 2911.1

Gangsta's Paradise (Coolio), 2744

general collections, 2659–2697

Genocide and Juice (Coup), 2746.1

Get Rich or Die Tryin' (50 Cent), 2791.1

The Geto Boys, 2802.1

Ghetto D (Master P), 2861

Ghetto Music: The Blueprint of Hip Hop (Boogie Down Productions), 2724.4

Global Hip Hop, 2804

Godlovesugly (Atmosphere), 2704.1

God's Son (Nas), 2878.1

Graffiti Rock (collection), 2673

Gravity (Da Bush Babees), 2729

Greatest Hits (Dee), 2756

The Great Adventures of Slick Rick, 2919

The Grind Date (De La Soul), 2754.3

Guerillas in Tha Mist (Da Lench Mob), 2842

Hard Core (Lil' Kim), 2845

Hard Knock Life, Vol. 2 (Jay Z), 2823.3

Headshots: Se7en (Atmosphere), 2704.2

Heavy Hitz (Heavy D and the Boyz), 2814.2

Hell Hath No Fury (Clipse), 2738

Hell on Earth (Mobb Deep), 2870.1

Hell's Winter (Cage), 2730

He's the DJ, I'm the Rapper (DJ Jazzy Jeff and the Fresh Prince), 2767

Hip Hop Essentials, 1979–1991 (collection), 2675

★*Hip Hop Greats [Classic Raps]* (collection), 2676

Hip Hop Immortals: We Got Your Kids (collection), 2677

The Hip Hop Box (collection), 2674

Hispanic Causing Panic (Kid Frost), 2833

Holy Intellect (Poor Righteous Teachers), 2895

Home (Spearhead), 2924

Hot, Cool and Vicious (Salt-n-Pepa), 2915.2

Hot Sauce Committee Part Two (Beastie Boys), 2709.2

House of Pain, 2818

House Party (collection), 2678

Hypocrisy Is the Greatest Luxury (Disposable Heroes of Hiphoprisy), 2763

I Phantom (Mr. Lif), 2873

I Wish My Brother George Was Here (Del Tha Funkee Homosapien), 2757.2

★*The Iceberg: Freedom of Speech . . . Just Watch What You Say* (Ice-T), 2820.1

Ill Communication (Beastie Boys), 2709.3

Ill Na Na (Brown), 2728

I'll Sleep When You're Dead (El-P.), 2782

Illadelph Halflife (Roots), 2911.2

★*Illmatic* (Nas), 2878.2

In Full Gear (Stetasonic), 2925

In God We Trust (Brand Nubian), 2726.1

In Our Lifetime (Eightball and MJG), 2780.2

In Search of . . . (N.E.R.D.), 2876
individuals and groups, 2698–295
The Infamous . . . . (Mobb Deep), 2870.2
Innercity Griots (Freestyle Fellowship), 2795.1
Internal Affairs (Pharoahe Monch), 2894.2
Ironman (Ghostface Killah), 2803.1
★*It Takes a Nation of Millions to Hold Us Back* (Public Enemy), 2898.3
It Takes Two (Base and DJ E-Z Rock), 2708
It Was Written (Nas), 2878.3
It's a Big Daddy Thing (Kane), 2830.1
It's Dark and Hell Is Hot (DMX), 2771.2
Jazzmatazz, Vol. 1 (Guru), 2812
Jermaine Dupri Presents Life in 1472: The Original Soundtrack, 2777
The Jive Collection, Vol. 3 (Schooly D), 2917
King of Rock (Run-D.M.C.), 2913.1
King (T. I.), 2929
Kings of Crunk (Lil' Jon and the East Side Boyz), 2844
Kkkill the Fetus: The Album (Esham), 2786
Krush Groove, 2837
Kurtis Blow, 2721.2
Kurtis Blow Presents the History of Rap, Vol. 2: The Birth of the Rap Record (collection), 2680
Kurtis Blow Presents the History of Rap, Vol. 1: The Genesis (collection), 2679
Kurtis Blow Presents the History of Rap, Vol. 3: The Golden Age (collection), 2681
Labor Days (Aesop Rock), 2700.2
The Lady Killer (Green), 2811.3
Late Registration (West), 2942.2
Let's Get Free (Dead Prez), 2755.1
Let's Get It: Thug Motivation 101 (Young Jeezy), 2949
Licensed to Ill (Beastie Boys), 2709.4
Life after Death (Notorious B.I.G.), 2881.1
Life Is . . . Too Short, 2932.2
Lifestylez ov da Poor and Dangerous (Big L), 2712
Like Water for Chocolate (Common), 2741.1
Liquid Swords (Genius), 2801.2
Livin' Like Hustlers (Above the Law), 2698.2
Loc-Ed after Dark (Tone-Loc), 2931
Long Live the Kane, 2830.2
★*Looking for the Perfect Beat, 1980–1985* (Afrika Bambaataa), 2705
The Lost Freestyle Files (Supernatural), 2927
★*The Low End Theory* (A Tribe Called Quest), 2933.1

Lyricist Lounge: Dirty States of America (collection), 2683
Lyricist Lounge, Vol. 1 (collection), 2682
Lyte as a Rock (MC Lyte), 2863.2
Madvillainy (Madvillain), 2855
The Main Ingredient (Rock and Smooth), 2910.1
Mama Said Knock You Out (LL Cool J), 2847.1
Man on the Moon: The End of the Day (Kid Cudi), 2832
Man or Myth? (DJ Faust), 2766
Marley Marl's House of Hits, 2859
The Marshall Mathers LP (Eminem), 2783.2
The Massacre (50 Cent), 2791.2
Masters of the Universe (Binary Stary), 2714
Me against the World (2Pac), 2935.3
★*Mecca and the Soul Brother* (Rock and Smooth), 2910.2
Midnight Marauders (A Tribe Called Quest), 2933.2
Mind over Matter (Zion I), 2951
The Minstrel Show (Little Brother), 2846
★*The Miseducation of Lauryn Hill,* 2817
Mm . . . Food? (MF Doom), 2868.2
★*Mos Def and Talib Kweli Are Black Star,* 2872
The Mouse and the Mask (Danger Doom), 2750
Mr. Scarface Is Back, 2916.1
A Much Better Tomorrow (Can the Automator), 2749
Muddy Waters (Redman), 2906.1
Murder Was the Case: The Soundtrack, 2874
Murs 3:16: The 9th Edition, 2875
Music to Driveby (Compton's Most Wanted), 2873
My Beautiful Dark Twisted Fantasy (West), 2942.3
My Vinyl Weighs a Ton (Peanut Butter Wolf), 2891.1
Naughty by Nature, 2879
Nellyville (Nelly), 2880
Neva Again (Kam), 2829
Nia (Blackalicious), 2719.2
93 'til Infinity (Souls of Mischief), 2923
No One Can Do It Better (D.O.C.), 2748
No Way Out (Puff Daddy and the Family), 2899
Nocturnal (Heltah Skeltah), 2815
Of the Heart, of the Soul, and of the Cross: The Utopian Experience (P. M. Dawn), 2889
O.G.: Original Gangster (Ice-T), 2820.2
One A.M. (Diverse), 2764

One Day It'll All Make Sense (Common), 2741.2
One for All (Brand Nubian), 2726.2
Only Built 4 Cuban Linx (Raekwon), 2902
Organized Konfusion, 2885.1
overview, p153
The Ownerz (Gang Starr), 2800.3
Ozomatli, 2888
★*Paid in Full* (Eric B. and Rakim), 2785.2
★*Paul's Boutique* (Beastie Boys), 2709.5
[Peanut Butter Wolf Presents] Stones Throw Ten Years, 2891.2
People's Instinctive Travels and the Paths of Rhythm (A Tribe Called Quest), 2933.3
Personal Journals (Francis), 2794
Petestrumentals (Rock), 2909
Phrenology (Roots), 2911.3
The Pillage (Cappadonna), 2735
The Platform (Dilated Peoples), 2762
Please Hammer, Don't Hurt 'Em (M.C. [MC] Hammer), 2862
Power (Ice-T), 2820.3
Power in Numbers (Jurassic 5), 2827.1
The Predator (Ice Cube), 2819.3
A Prince among Thieves (Prince Paul), 2897
Prose Combat (MC Solaar), 2865
Quality Control (Jurassic 5), 2827.2
Quality (Kweli), 2838
Quik Is the Name (Dj Quik), 2769.1
Radio (LL Cool J), 2847.2
★*Raising Hell* (Run-D.M.C.), 2913.2
Rawkus Presents Soundbombing II, 2905
RBG: Revolutionary but Gangsta (Dead Prez), 2755.2
Reachin' (A New Refutation of Time and Space) (Digable Planets), 2760.2
★*Ready to Die: The Remaster* (Notorious B.I.G.), 2881.2
The Realness (Cormega), 2745
Reasonable Doubt (Jay Z), 2823.4
Reel to Reel (Grand Puba), 2808
Reflection Eternal [Train of Thought] (Kweil and Hi Tek), 2839
Regulate . . . G Funk Era (Warren G.), 2941
Relax (Das Rascist), 2752
Resurrection (Common Sense), 2740
Retaliation, Revenge and Get Back (Daz Dillinger), 2753
Return of the DJ, Vol. 1 (collection), 2684
Return of the DJ, Vol. 2 (collection), 2685
Return to the 36 Chambers: The Dirty Version (Ol' Dirty Bastard), 2883
Rhyme and Reason (collection), 2686

rap and hip-hop (cont.)

Ridin' Dirty (UGK), 2936

Ruff Ryder's First Lady (Eve), 2787

Run-D.M.C, 2913.3

The RZA Hits, 2914

Safe + Sound (Dj Quik), 2769.2

Same !@#$ Different Day (Lyrics Born), 2851

★*The Score* (Fugees), 2798

Scratch, 2918

Sex Packets (Digital Underground), 2761

Shadows on the Sun (Brother Ali), 2727

The Shiggar Fraggar Show! Vol. 1 (Invisibl Skratch Pikla), 2821.1

The Shiggar Fraggar Show! Vol. 2 (Invisibl Skratch Pikla), 2821.2

Shock of the Hour (MC Lyte), 2864

6 Feet Deep (Gravediggaz), 2810

Sleeping with the Enemy (Paris), 2890

The Slim Shady LP (Eminem), 2783.3

So . . . How's Your Girl? (Handsome Boy Modeling School), 2813

Solesides: Greatest Bumps (collection), 2687

Soul Food (Goodie Mob), 2805.1

Soundbombing: The Ultimate Guide to Under- ground Hip-Hop (collection), 2688

Soundpieces: Da Antidote! (Lootpack), 2848

soundtracks, 2952–2953

Southernplayalisticadillacmuzik (OutKast), 2887.3

Speakerboxxx. The Love Below (OutKast), 2887.4

St. Elsewhere (Barkley), 2707

Stakes Is High (De La Soul), 2754.4

Stankonia (OutKast), 2887.5

Steal This Double Album (Coup), 2746.2

★*Step in the Arena* (Gang Starr), 2800.2

Still Standing (Goodie Mob), 2805.2

Stillmatic (Nas), 2878.4

Stone Cold Rhymin' (Young MC), 2950

Stones Throw 101 (collection), 2689

★*Straight out the Jungle* (Jungle Brothers), 2826.2

★*Straight Outta Compton* (N.W.A.), 2877.2

Street Jams: Hip-Hop from the Top, Part 1 (collection), 2690

Street Jams: Hip-Hop from the Top, Part 2 (collection), 2691

Street Jams: Hip-Hop from the Top, Part 3 (collection), 2692

Street Jams: Hip-Hop from the Top, Part 4 (collection), 2693

Stress: The Extinction Agenda (Organized Konfusion), 2885.2

★*Strictly Business* (EPMD), 2784.3

Strictly 4 My N.I.G.G.A.Z. (2Pac), 2935.4

Stunts, Blunts, and Hip Hop (Diamond and the Psychotic Neurotics), 2759

Style Wars (collection), 2694

★*The Sugar Hill Records Story* (collection), 2695

The Sun Rises in the East (Jeru the Damaja), 2825.1

Supa Dupa Fly (Elliott), 2781

Supreme Clientele (Ghostface Killah), 2803.2

Tha Carter (Lil Wayne), 2843

Tha Doggfather (Snoop Dogg), 2922.1

Thank Me Later (Drake), 2775

★*Things Fall Apart* (Roots), 2911.4

3rd Eye Vision (Hieroglyphics), 2816.2

★*3 Feet High and Rising* (De La Soul), 2754.4

3 Years, 5 Months, and 2 Days in the Life of . . . (Arrested Development), 2703

Tical (Method Man), 2867

To the East, Blackwards (X-Clan), 2947

To the Extreme (Vanilla Ice), 2939

To Whom It May Concern . . . (Freestyle Fellowship), 2795.2

★*Tommy Boy Greatest Beats: The First Fifteen Years, 1981–1996* (collection), 2696

Tougher Than Leather (Run-D.M.C.), 2913.4

21 and Over (Tha Alkaholiks), 2701

2 Hype (Kid 'n' Play), 2831

2pacalypse Now (2Pac), 2935.5

2001 (Dr. Dre), 2773.1

Ultimate Victory (Chamillionaire), 2737

Undun (Roots), 2911.5

Unfinished Business (EPMD), 2784.4

The Unseen (Quasimoto), 2900

Uptown Saturday Night (Camp Lo), 2731

Utfo, 2938

Vaudeville Villain (Vaughn), 2940

Venni Vetti Vecci (Rule), 2912

Vocal Studies + Uprock Narratives (Prefuse 73), 2896

Warriorz (M.O.P.), 2852

The War Report (Capone-n-Noreaga), 2734

Wave Twisters: Episode 7 Million Sonic Wars within the Protons (DJ Qbert), 2768

We Can't Be Stopped (Geto Boys), 2802.2

What's the 411? (Blige), 2720

When Disaster Strikes . . . (Rhymes), 2907.2

Whut? Thee Album (Redman), 2906.2

★*Wild Style* (collection), 2697

Wild Style: Original Motion Picture Soundtrack, 2945

A Wolf in Sheep's Clothing (Black Sheep), 2718

Word . . . Life (O. C.), 2882

Word of Mouf (Ludacris), 2850

The World Famous Beat Junkies, Vol. 1, 2710.1

The World Famous Beat Junkies, Vol. 2, 2710.2

The World's Greatest Entertainer (Doug E. Fresh and the Get Fresh Crew), 2796

Wrath of the Math (Jer the Damaja), 2825.2

Wu-Tang Forever, 2946.2

Yo! Bum Rush the Show (Public Enemy), 2898.4

rap and hip-hop soundtracks

Above the Rim: The Soundtrack, 2952

Wild Style: Original Motion Picture Soundtrack, 2953

Raph, Theodore. *The American Song Treasury: 100 Favorites,* 122

rappers, early. *See* early rappers

The Rascals

Casey Kasem Presents America's Top Ten through the Years: The Sixties (collection), 1156

Songs of Protest (collection), 1820

The Very Best of the Rascals, 1816

Raspberries

The Raspberries, 1882

Straight Outta Cleveland (collection), 1888

Rasputina. *Colours Are Brighter: Songs for Children and Grown Ups Too* (collection), 3193

Rauhouse, Jon. *The Bottle Let Me Down: Songs for Bumpy Wagon Rides* (collection), 3191

The Ravens

★*The Doo Wop Box: 101 Vocal Group Gems from the Golden Age of Rock 'n' Roll* (collection), 1745

★*The Doo-Wop Box* (collection), 2322

★*The Okeh Rhythm and Blues Story* (collection), 2425

★*The R&B Box* (collection), 2239

★*The Roots of Rock 'n' Roll, 1946–1954* (collection), 1755

★*Stompin' at the Savoy: The Original Indie Label, 1944–1961* (collection), 2429

Their Complete National Recordings, 1947–1950, 2353

Rawls, Lou

Beg, Scream, and Shout! The Big Ol' Box of '60s Soul (collection), 2433

The Essential Lou Rawls, 2505.1

The Jazz Channel Presents Lou Rawls, 2505.2

Living Legends of Gospel: The Quartets, Vols. 1 and 2 (collection), 3010

★*Love Train: The Sound of Philadelphia* (collection), 2552

Soul Shots: A Collection of Sixties Soul Classics (collection), 2443

Yule Struttin': A Blue Note Christmas (collection), 3323

Ray, Eddie. *Eccentric Soul: The Prix Label* (collection), 2601

Ray, Johnnie [Johnny]

    The Roots of Rock 'n' Roll, 1946–1954 (collection), 1755

    ★*Sentimental Journey: Pop Vocal Classics, Vol. 3* (collection), 1169

    16 Most Requested Songs: The 1950s, Vol. 1 (collection), 1171

★Raye, Martha. *The Music Goes Round and Around: The Golden Years of Tin Pan Alley, 1930–1939* (collection), 1070

Razaf, Andy. *Waller / Razaf* (songwriter collection), 1113.2

Read, Bob. *Piano Solos: Narada Artists* (collection), 1370

Rebennack, Malcolm John "Mac." See Dr. John

Rebirth Brass Band. *Kickin' It Live: The Glass House,* 1007

Red, Boogie Woogie. *Conversation with the Blues* (collection), 148

Red Callender Combo. *The Swing Time Records Story: R&B, Blues, and Gospel, 1946–1952* (collection), 2430

Red Hot Chili Peppers. *Bloodsugarsexmagik,* 2178

Red Krayola. *God Bless the Red Krayola and All Who Sail with It,* 1964

Redding, Otis

    ★*Atlantic R&B, 1947–1974* (collection), 2418

    ★*Atlantic Soul, 1959–1975* (collection), 2589

    Beg, Scream, and Shout! The Big Ol' Box of '60s Soul (collection), 2433

    Birth of Soul, 4 Vols. (collection), 2434

    The Complete Stax/Volt Singles 1959–1968 (collection), 2594

    Dave Godin's Deep Soul Treasures, Vols. 1–4 (collection), 2435

    The Dock of the Bay, 2506.1

    Dreams to Remember: The Legacy of Otis Redding, 2506.2

    Dreams to Remember: The Otis Redding Anthology, 2506.3

    Greatest Hits, 2506.4

    Live on the Sunset Strip, 2506.5

    Muscle Shoals Sound (collection), 2605

    Otis Blue: Otis Redding Sings Soul, 2506.7

    ★*Otis! The Definitive Otis Redding,* 2506.6

    The Otis Redding Dictionary of Soul: Complete and Unbelievable, 2506.8

★*The R&B Box* (collection), 2239

Respect: Aretha's Influences and Inspiration (collection), 2440

Stax/Volt Revue: Live in London, Vols. 1 and 2 (collection), 2609

Stax/Volt Revue: Live in Norway 1967 (collection), 2446

Top of the Stax, Vol. 1: Twenty Greatest Hits (collection), 2611

Top of the Stax, Vol. 2: Twenty Greatest Hits (collection), 2612

Reddy, Helen. *The Woman I Am: The Definitive Collection,* 1299

Redman

    Muddy Waters, 2906.1

    Whut? Thee Album, 2906.2

Redman, Don

    An Anthology of Big Band Swing (collection), 528

    Stars of the Apollo (collection), 2240

Redman, Joshua

    Back East, 1008.1

    Wish, 1008.2

Redmond, Roy. *The Best of Loma Records: The Rise and Fall of a 1960's Soul Label* (collection), 2590

Reed, A. C. *Living Chicago Blues, Vol. 3* (collection), 417

★Reed, Bill and Belle. *Anthology of American Folk Music, Vols. 1–3* (collection), 1386

Reed, Blind Alfred

    Old-Time Mountain Ballads (collection), 1390

    ★*Something Got a Hold of Me: A Treasury of Sacred Music* (collection), 3114

Reed, Dock. *Negro Religious Songs and Services* (collection), 2977

Reed, Jerry. *Essential Jerry Reed,* 1529

Reed, Jimmy

    Blues Masters, Vol. 2: Postwar Chicago Blues (collection), 285

    ★*The Blues: A Smithsonian Collection of Classic Blues Singers* (collection), 145

    ★*Mean Old World: The Blues from 1940–1994* (collection), 154

    Superblues: All-Time Classic Blues Hits, Vol. 1 (collection), 347

    ★*The Vee-Jay Story: Celebrating 40 Years of Classic Hits* (collection), 2431

Reed, Lou

    Animal Serenade, 1965.1

    NYC Man: The Collections, 1965.2

    Walk on the Wild Side: The Best of Lou Reed, 1965.3

Reed, W. L. *National Anthems of the World,* 3378

Reese, Della

    Birth of Soul, 4 Vols. (collection), 2434

Nipper's Greatest Hits: The 50's, Vol. 2 (collection), 1164

Reeves, Dianne

    Best of Dianne Reeves, 798

    Icons among Us (collection), 934

Reeves, Jim

    Classic Country: Kings of Country (collection), 1381

    Country Style, U.S.A. (collection), 1473

    Essential Jim Reeves, 1530

    Nipper's Greatest Hits: The 50's, Vol. 2 (collection), 1164

    ★*Nipper's Greatest Hits: The 50's, Vol. 1* (collection), 1163

Reeves, Martha and the Vandellas

    Gold, 2543.1

    Motown around the World (collection), 2437

    The Ultimate Collection, 2543.2

reference sources and advanced readings for popular music, selective list of, p3

★*The Regals. Atlantic Vocal Groups, 1951–1963* (collection), 2320

Regents

    ★*The Doo-Wop Box* (collection), 2322

    The Doo-Wop Box II (collection), 2323

Regimental Band of the Coldstream Guards

    ★*Collections of National Anthems, Vol. 1,* 3379.1

    ★*Collections of National Anthems, Vol. 2,* 3379.2

regional rhythm and blues styles, 2359–2378

regional soul styles, 2552–2570

Reid, Clarence

    Eccentric Soul: The Outskirts of Deep City (collection), 2565

    ★*What It Is! Funky Soul and Rare Grooves* (collection), 2615

Reinhardt, Django

    ★*The Best of Django Reinhardt,* 582.1

    Django Reinhardt: Gypsy Jazz, 582.2

    ★*Ken Burns Jazz: The Story of America's Music* (collection), 478

    Progressions: 100 Years of Jazz Guitar (collection), 481

    ★*The Smithsonian Collection of Classic Jazz* (collection), 486

★Reisman, Leo. *Nipper's Greatest Hits: The 30's, Vol. 1* (collection), 1072

religious and holiday children's music, 3237–3251

    All Aboard the Holiday Express (collection), 3237

    Chanukah at Home (collection), 3238

    Charlie Brown's Holiday Hits (Guaraldi), 3244

    Christmas Sing Along (McGrath), 3246

    Christmastime (Penner), 3248

    collections, 3237–3241

religious and holiday children's
music (cont.)
Festive Songs for the Jewish Holidays
(collection), 3239
Hanukkah and Chinese New Year
(collection), 3240
Hap Palmer's Holiday Magic, 3247
Holiday Fun (collection), 3241
*Holiday Times: Songs, Stories, Rhymes
and Chants for Christmas, Kwaanza,
Hanukkah, Chinese New Year, and
St. Patrick's Day* (Jenkins), 3245
Holidays and Special Times (Scelsa and
Millang), 3250
Jewish Holiday Songs for Children
(Buchman), 3243
*Kwanzaa for Young People (and
Everyone Else!)* (Bonna, Fuller, and
Mims), 3242
Merry Christmas (Scruggs), 3251
Raffi's Christmas Album, 3249
religious music, 1–31
Alleluia: An American Hymnal (Kansas
City Chorale), 15
American Angels (Anonymous), 6.1
*The American Vocalist: Spirituals and
Folk Hymns, 1850-1870* (Boston
Camerata), 8.1
*An American Journey: Bound for
the Promised Land* (Waverly
Consort), 27
And Glory Shone Around (Rose
Ensemble), 22
*Awake, My Soul: The Story of "The
Sacred Harp"* (collection), 1
children's music, religious and
holiday, 3237–3251
collections, 1–5
The Complete Works of William Billings
(Billings), 7.1
*The Continental Harmonist: Hymns and
Fuging Tunes* (Billings), 7.2
*Desire for Piety: Songs from the B. F.
White "Sacred Harp"* (Wiregrass
Sacred Harp Singers), 30
Early American Choral Music (His
Majestie's Clerkes), 14.1
Early Shaker Spirituals (collection), 2
evangelists and other traditional
performers, 2976–2986
*Fasola: Fifty-Three Shape Note Folk
Hymns* (collection), 3
Gentle Words: Shaker Songs (Tudor
Choir [Seattle]), 25.1
*Glory to Him Who Is the Resurrection:
A Moravian Music Sampler*
(collection), 4
Gloryland (Anonymous), 6.2
*Home to Thanksgiving: Songs of Thanks
and Praise* (His Majestie's Clerkes),
14.2
I Am Filled with Heavenly Treasures
(Enfield Shaker Singers), 10

★*I Am the Rose of Sharon: Early
American Vocal Music* (Western
Wind), 28
*A Land of Pure Delight: Anthems and
Fuging Tunes* (Billings), 7.3
*Lost Music of Early America: Music
of the Moravians* (Boston
Camerata), 8.2
*Make a Joyful Noise: Mainstreams and
Backstreams of American Psalmody,
1770–1840* (Oregon State
University Choir), 21
★*Music in America: An Anthology from
the Landing of the Pilgrims to the
Close of the Civil War, 1620–1865*
(Marrocco and Gleason), 16
Music of the Shakers (Smith College
Glee Club), 23
*The New England Harmony: A
Collection of American Choral Music*
(Sturbridge Singers), 24
*Old-Time Gospel Favorites: 14 Gospel
Classics with Harmony and Old-
Time Instruments* (Erbsen), 12
Our American Journey
(Chanticleer), 9.1
periodicals for up-to-date CD notices
and reviews, suggested, p3
*Rivers of Delight: American Folk Hymns
from the Sacred Harp Tradition*
(Word of Mouth Chorus), 31
*The River of Love: Music of the Shakers
and Based on Shaker Theme* (New
England Voices), 19
*Rose of Sharon: 100 Years of American
Music, 1770-1870* (Ensemble
Phoenix Munich), 11
The Sacred Harp (White), 29
The Shapenote Album (Tudor Choir
[Seattle]), 25.2
*Simple Gifts: Shaker Chants and
Spirituals* (Boston Camerata), 8.3
*The Social Harp: Early American Shape-
Note Songs* (McGraw), 18
★*The Social Harp* (McCurry), 17
Southern Harmony, Excerpts (Walker),
26.2
Southern Harmony (Gregg Smith
Singers), 13
southern white religious styles,
3106–3134
★*The Southern Harmony* (Walker),
26.1
*Sweet Seraphic Fire: New England
Singing-School Music from the
Norumbega Harmony* (Norumbega
Harmony), 20
★*Ten Sacred Songs for Soprano,
Strings, and Organ: Music of the
Moravians in America from the
Archives of the Moravian Church
at Bethlehem, Pennsylvania*
(collection), 5

*Trav'ling Home: American Spirituals,
1770-1870* (Boston Camerata), 8.4
Wake Ev'ry Breath (Billings), 7.4
Where the Sun Will Never Go Down
(Chanticleer), 9.2
R.E.M.
Automatic for the People, 2175.1
Document, 2175.2
★*Eponymous*, 2175.3
Murmur, 2175.4
*Whatever: The '90s Pop and Culture
Box* (collection), 1244
Ren, MC. *Shock of the Hour*, 2864
Renfro, Jessie Mae
★*The Gospel Sound of Spirit Feel*
(collection), 2965
*Gospel Warriors: Over 50 Years
of Great Solo Performances*
(collection), 2987
Reno, Don and Smiley, Red
All-Time Country and Western Hits
(collection), 1449
*Don Reno and Red Smiley and the
Tennessee Cut–Ups, 1959–1963*,
1602.1
*Sweethearts in Heaven: The Complete
Dot Recordings 1957–1964*, 1602.2
REO Speedwagon
80's Pop Hits (collection), 1238
The Hits, 2082
The Replacements. *Let It Be*, 2179
The Residents
Eskimo, 1966.1
Icky Flix, 1966.2
The Residents' Commercial Album,
1966.3
Resurrection Band. *Best of Christian Rock
(1970–1986), Vol. 1* (collection),
3135
Revard, Jimmie and His Oklahoma
Playboys. *Western Swing: 40
Bootstompers from the Golden Age*
(collection), 1433
Revelli, William D. *41 Great College
Victory Songs*, 3372
Revels Company. *Christmas Day in the
Morning: A Revels Celebration of the
Winter Solstice*, 3285
Revere, Paul. *Greatest Hits*, 1817
Revolutionary Ensemble. *Vietnam*, 929
Revolutionary War period political
music, 44–58
*American Songs of Revolutionary
Times and the Civil War Era*
(collection), 44
Andrew Jackson: The Atrocious Saint
(Hedge), 52
*Authentic Songs of the American
Revolution and the Civil War Era*
(collection), 45
Ballads of the Revolution (House), 53.1
Ballads of the War of 1812 (House),
53.2

collections, 44–47

The 18th Century American Overture (Jyväskylä Sinfonia), 55

Liberty (O'Connor, Mark), 58

The Liberty Tree: Early American Music (Boston Camerata), 48

Music of the American Revolution: The Birth of Liberty (collection), 46

Music of the American Revolution: The Sounds of Ancient Fifes and Drums (Nathan Hale Ancient Fifes and Drums), 57

Music of the Federal Era (Federal Music Society), 50

Presidential Campaign Songs, 1789–1996 (Brand), 49

Songs and Ballads of American History and of the Assassination of Presidents (collection), 47

The War That Made America (Keane), 56

Winners and Losers: Campaign Songs from the Critical Elections in American History, Vols. 1 and 2 (Janovsky), 54

The World Turned Upside Down: Music from the Yorktown Battlefield (Fifes and Drums of Williamsburg), 51

Reynolds, Debbie. *Sentimental Journey: Pop Vocal Classics, Vol. 4* (collection), 1170

Reynolds, Margaret. *The Best of T. K. Disco* (collection), 2656

The Rezillos

    Can't Stand the Rezillos: The (Almost) Complete Rezillos, 1996

    No Thanks! The '70s Punk Rebellion (collection), 2003

Rhodes, Dusty. *Swingbillies: Hillbilly and Western Swing on Modern/Colonial/Flair, 1947–1952* (collection), 1431

Rhodes, Todd. *Blues for the Red Boy: The Early Sensation Recordings,* 2294

rhythm and blues

    Anthology (Hamilton), 2258

    Anthology (Maze), 2278.1

    At Last! (James), 2266.1

    Bad Boy (Williams), 2301

    The Best of LeVert, 2275

    The Best of Marv Johnson: You've Got What It Takes, 2271

    The Best of Nellie Lutcher, 2277.1

    Bloodshot Eyes: The Best of Wynonie Harris, 2259.1

    blues, 2303–2311

    Blues for the Red Boy: The Early Sensation Recordings (Rhodes), 2294

    Blues with a Beat (Griffin Brothers), 2256

    Buddy and Ella Johnson: 1953–1964, 2270.1

Burnin' Down the House (Etta James and the Roots Band), 2267

The Capitol Years (Otis), 2288.1

Chess King of New Orleans: The Chess Years (Gayten), 2254

★*The Chess Box* (James), 2266.2

The Complete Aladdin Recordings of Amos Milburn, 2280.1

★*The Complete Aladdin Recordings of Charles Brown,* 2248

contemporary, 2393–2417

Control (Jackson), 2263.1

Cow Fingers and Mosquito Pie (Hawkins), 2260

Deep Sea Ball: The Best of Clyde McPhatter, 2279.1

Design of a Decade, 1986/1996 (Jackson), 2263.2

The EP Collection (Doggett), 2252.1

The Essential Etta James, 2266.3

The Essential Michael Jackson, 2264.1

Esther: The Best of Esther Phillips, 2291

Etta James Rocks the House, 2266.4

★*Fever: The Best of Little Willie John,* 2269.1

From Janet to Damita Jo: The Videos, 2263.3

general collections, 2239–2240

general styles, 2239–2302

Gold (Mills), 2281.1

Gold (New Edition), 2285.1

Good Rocking Tonight: The Best of Roy Brown, 2249

Greatest Hits: History, Vol. 1 (Jackson), 2264.2

Greatest Hits (Maze), 2278.2

Greatest Hits (Parker), 2289

Haven't You Heard: The Best of Patrice Rushen, 2296

Hello Stranger: The Best of Barbara Lewis, 2276

High Times: Singles, 1992–2006 (Jamiroquai), 2268

His R&B Recordings 1949–1956: The Sun Years, Plus (Thomas), 2297

Hits (New Edition), 2285.2

The Hits Collection (Prince), 2293

I Like It Like That: Golden Classics (Kenner), 2272

I Remember Chuck Willis/the King of the Stroll, 2302.1

I'm Gonna Shake It! (Gordon), 2255

In the '50s: Hit, Git, and Split (Baker), 2246

Janet Jackon's Rhythm Nation 1814, 2263.4

jazz, 2312–2313

The Johnny Otis Rhythm and Blues Caravan, 2288.2

jump blues, 2314–2319

label overview, 2418–2431

Lawdy! (Price), 2292.1

The Legends Ike and Tina Turner Live in '71, 2299

Let's Have a Party: The Aladdin Recordings (Milburn), 2280.2

Let's Jump Tonight!: The Best of Chuck Willis from 1951–56, 2302.2

Lionel Richie Collection, 2295

Lloyd Price, Vol. 2: Heavy Dreams, 2292.2

Lover Please: The Complete MGM and Mercury Singles (McPhatter), 2279.2

Marshall, Texas Is My Home (Dixon), 2251

Michael Jackson Live in Bucharest: The Dangerous Tour, 2264.3

Miss Rhythm: Greatest Hits and More (Brown), 2250

Nashville rhythm and blues, 2376–2378

Nellie Lutcher and Her Rhythm, 2277.2

neo-soul, 2379–2387

new jack swing, 2388–2392

New Orleans rhythm and blues, 2359–2375

1944–1945 (Gant), 2253

Off the Wall (Jackson), 2264.4

One Last Time Live in Concert (Turner), 2300.1

overview, p126

periodicals for up-to-date CD notices and reviews, suggested, p3

Poppa Willie: The Hi Years, 1962–74 (Mitchell), 2283

Rapture (Baker), 2244

★*The R&B Box* (collection), 2239

regional styles, 2359–2378

Rock Me Baby: The Mercury and Peacock Sides 1951–55 (Otis), 2288.3

Roy Milton and His Solid Senders, 2282

Sexy Ways: The Best of Hank Ballard and the Midnighters, 2247

Since I Met You Baby: The Best of Ivory Joe Hunter, 2261.1

Soul on Fire: The Best of LaVern Baker, 2245

Stars of the Apollo (collection), 2240

Stroll On: The Chuck Willis Collection, 2302.3

The Sun Sessions (Turner), 2298

Teddy, Live in '79 (Pendergrass), 2290

Tell Mama: The Complete Muscle Shoals Sessions (James), 2266.5

This Is It: The Best of Melba Moore, 2284

★*Thriller* (Jackson), 2264.5

Tina: All the Best: The Live Collection (Turner), 2300.2

Tiny Grimes, 1944–1949, 2257.1

Tiny Grimes, 1949–1951, 2257.2

Tiny Grimes, 1951–1954, 2257.3

rhythm and blues (cont.)
  Totally Unrestricted: The Millie Jackson Anthology, 2265.1
  21 of the Best, *1971–1983* (Jackson), 2265.2
  Ultimate Collection (Ocean), 2286
  Ultimate Collection (Osborne), 2287
  The Ultimate Collection (Mills), 2281.2
  The Velvet Rope Tour Live in Concert / Live in Hawaii (Jackson), 2263.5
  The Very Best of Bill Doggett: Honky Tonk, 2252.2
  The Very Best of Bull Moose Jackson: Big Ten-Inch Record, 2262
  The Very Best of Little Willie John, 2269.2
  The Very Best of Major Lance, 2273
  The Very Best of Millie Jackson, 2265.3
  The Very Best of Stacy Lattisaw, 2274
  ★*The Very Best of Wynonie Harris: Good Rockin'* Tonight, 2259.2
  Video Greatest Hits: History (Jackson), 2264.6
  vocal groups, 2320–2358
  Walk 'Em: The Decca Sessions (Johnson), 2270.2
  Woo Wee!: The King and Deluxe Acetate Series (Hunter), 2261.2
rhythm and blues label overview
  ★*Atlantic R&B, 1947–1974* (collection), 2418
  Best of Ace Records, Vol. 2: The R&B Hits (collection), 2419
  Best of Chess R&B, Vols. 1 and 2 (collection), 2420
  Duke-Peacock's Greatest Hits (collection), 2421
  The Fire / Fury Records Story (collection), 2422
  The Hi Records Story (collection), 2423
  King R&B Box Set (collection), 2424
  ★*The Okeh Rhythm and Blues Story* (collection), 2425
  The Scepter Records Story (collection), 2426
  Southern Rhythm 'n' Rock: The Best of Excello Records, Vol. 22 (collection), 2427
  ★*The Specialty Story* (collection), 2428
  ★*Stompin' at the Savoy: The Original Indie Label, 1944–1961* (collection), 2429
  The Swing Time Records Story: R&B, Blues, and Gospel, 1946–1952 (collection), 2430
  ★*The Vee-Jay Story: Celebrating 40 Years of Classic Hits* (collection), 2431
rhythm and blues vocal groups
  ★*All Time Greatest Hits and More* (Drifters), 2335.1
  Anthology (Commodores), 2330

Anthology (Dells), 2332
Anthology: 50th Anniversary (Four Tops), 2341.1
★*Atlantic Vocal Groups, 1951–1963* (collection), 2320
The Best of Earl Lewis and the Channels: New York's Finest, 2345
The Best of Little Anthony and the Imperials, 2347
The Best of the Cadillacs, 2325.1
The Best of the Chantels, 2326
The Best of the Crystals, 2331
The Best of the Emotions: Best of My Love, 2336
The Best of the Flamingos, 2340.1
The Best of the Girl Groups, Vols. 1 and 2 (collection), 2321
The Best of the Ronettes, 2355
Blue Velvet: The Ultimate Collection (Moonglows), 2349.1
Chirpin' (Persuasions), 2352.1
Complete Chess Masters Plus (Flamingos), 2340.2
The Complete Josie Sessions (Cadillacs), 2325.2
Doin' the Hully Gully / Dance by the Light of the Moon / Party Time (Olympics), 2350.1
The Doo-Wop Box II (collection), 2323
50th Anniversary: The Singles Collection, 1961–1971 (Four Tops), 2341.2
50th Anniversary: The Singles Collection, 1961–1969 (Ross), 2356
40th Anniversary, 1953–1993 (Spaniels), 2358
Fourever (Four Tops), 2341.3
general collections, 2320–2324
Gold (Jackson 5), 2343.1
Heaven and Paradise (Don Julian and the Meadowlarks), 2344
I Must Be Dreamin': The Robins on RCA, Crown, and Spark, 1953–55, 2354
It's Hard but It's Fair: King Hits and Rarities ("5" Royales), 2338.1
Jubilee Recordings (Orioles), 2351.1
Life Could Be a Dream: The Doo-Wop Sound, 2346
Live at the Forum (Jackson 5), 2343.2
Lost and Found: Lost without You 1963–1970 (Four Tops), 2341.4
★*Monkey Hips and Rice: The "5" Royales Anthology,* 2338.2
The Moonglows, 2349.2
#1's (Destiny's Child), 2333
Old Town Doo-Wop, Vols. 1–3 (collection), 2324
The Original Master Tapes Collection, Vol. 1 (Five Satins), 2339.1
The Original Master Tapes Collection, Vol. 2 (Five Satins), 2339.2

The Orioles Sing Their Greatest Hits, 2351.2
Rockin' and Driftin' (Drifters), 2335.2
Rocking and Crying the Blues, 1951–1957 (Five Keys), 2337
The Shirelles 25 All-Time Greatest Hits, 2357
Street Corner Symphony (Persuasions), 2352.2
Summer Breeze: Greatest Hits, Live (Isley Brothers), 2342
Their Complete National Recordings, 1947–1950 (Ravens), 2353
★*There's a Riot Goin' On: The Coasters on ATCO,* 2329
The Ultimate Collection (Cleftones), 2327
The Ultimate Collection (Jackson 5), 2343.3
The Very Best of Billy Ward and Dominoes, 2334
The Very Best of Frankie Lymon and the Teenagers, 2348
The Very Best of the Olympics, 2350.2
Your Cash Ain't Nothin But Trash: Their Greatest Hits, 1951–55 (Clovers), 2328
Ribot, Marc. *Spiritual Unity,* 1009
★Rice, Mack. *Atlantic Soul, 1959–1975* (collection), 2589
Rice, Tony
  Blue Ribbon Bluegrass (collection), 1563
  The Bluegrass Album, Vol. 1 (collection), 1562
  58957: The Bluegrass Guitar Collection, 1603.1
  Hand-Picked: 25 Years of Bluegrass on Rounder Records (collection), 1564
  Manzanita, 1603.2
Rich, Buddy
  Big Band Renaissance: The Evolution of the Jazz Orchestra (collection), 739
  Buddy Rich: Holland 1978, 761.1
  Frank Sinatra: Concert Collection, 1224.3
  Swingin' New Big Band, 761.2
Rich, Charlie
  Classic Country: Kings of Country (collection), 1381
  Feel Like Going Home: The Essential Charlie Rich, 1531.1
  The Hi Records Story (collection), 2423
  Ultimate Collection, 1531.2
Richards, Ada. *Good God! Born Again Funk* (collection), 2614
Richards, Johnny. *Big Band Renaissance: The Evolution of the Jazz Orchestra* (collection), 739
Richie, Lionel
  The Definitive Collection, 2507
  Hitsville USA: The Motown Singles Collection, Vol. 2 (collection), 2604
  Lionel Richie Collection, 2295

Richman, Jonathan
    Colours Are Brighter: Songs for Children
        and Grown Ups Too (collection),
        3193
    The Modern Lovers, 1883
Richmond, June. Legendary Big Band
    Singers (collection), 767
★Ricks, Jimmy. Atlantic Soul, 1959–1975
    (collection), 2589
Ride. Nowhere, 2180
Riders in the Sky. Best of the West, 1445
Ridley, Sharon. The Sweetest Feeling: A
    Van McCoy Songbook (collection),
    2447
Righteous Brothers. The Very Best of
    the Righteous Brothers: Unchained
    Melody, 1818
Rihanna. Good Girl Gone Bad, 1300
Riley, Billy Lee
    ★Legends of Guitar: Rock—The '50s,
        Vol. 2 (collection), 1750
    ★Sun Records' Greatest Hits
        (collection), 1741
    Sun Rockabilly: The Classic Recordings
        (collection), 1742
Riley, Terry. Pioneers of the New Age
    (collection), 1371
Rimes, LeAnn. Blue, 1674
Rios, Christopher Lee. See Big Punisher
Rising Sun. Eccentric Soul: The Outskirts of
    Deep City (collection), 2565
Ritchie Family. Disco Box (collection),
    2644
Ritter, Tex. High Noon, 1532.1, 1532.2
Rivers, Earl. "I Wants to Be a Actor Lady"
    and Other Hits from Early Musical
    Comedies (collection), 1067
Rivers, Sam
    Sam Rivers / Dave Holland, Vols. 1
        and 2, 930
    Sam Rivers' Rivbea All-Star Orchestra:
        Inspiration, 762
Rivileers. The Doo-Wop Box II
    (collection), 2323
RJD2. Deadringer, 2908
Roach, Max
    ★Ken Burns Jazz: The Story of
        America's Music (collection), 478
    Live at Blues Alley, 889
    ★Percussion Bitter Suite, 696.1
    We Insist: Freedom Now Suite, 696.2
Roach, Steve
    Dreamtime Return, 1357
    Starflight 1 (collection), 1374
Robbins, Marty
    Classic Country: Kings of Country
        (collection), 1381
    The Essential Marty Robbins, 1533
    Hank Williams Songbook (collection),
        1450
Robert Shaw Chorale
    A Festival of Carols, 3286
    Battle Cry of Freedom, 3380

Roberta Martin Singers. The Best of the
    Roberta Martin Singers, 3047
Roberts, Bob. The Phonographic Yearbook,
    1912: Waitin' on the Levee
    (collection), 1077
Roberts, Joan. Oscar Hammerstein II
    (songwriter collection), 1102
Roberts, Luckey. Luckey and the Lion, 524
★Robertson, Dick. Praise the Lord and Pass
    the Ammunition: Songs of World
    Wars I and II (collection), 1079
Robertson, Eck
    Before the Blues: The Early American
        Black Music Scene; Classic
        Recordings from the 1920's and
        30's, Vols. 1–3 (collection), 183
    Old-Time Texas Fiddler, 1419
Robeson, Paul
    A First-Time Buyer's Guide to American
        Negro Spirituals (collection), 32
    Jerome Kern (songwriter collection),
        1104.1
    Vintage Children's Favorites (collection),
        3211
    When the Sun Goes Down 1: Walk Right
        In (collection), 159
Robillard, Duke. Living with the Blues, 378
The Robins
    ★Atlantic R&B, 1947–1974 (collection),
        2418
    I Must Be Dreamin': The Robins on
        RCA, Crown, and Spark, 1953–55,
        2354
    ★Stompin' at the Savoy: The
        Original Indie Label, 1944–1961
        (collection), 2429
    The Doo-Wop Box II (collection), 2323
★Robinson, Alvin. Atlantic Soul,
    1959–1975 (collection), 2589
Robinson, Bill "Bojangles"
    ★At the Jazz Band Ball: Early Hot Jazz,
        Song, and Dance (collection), 470
    Stars of the Apollo (collection), 2240
Robinson, Candi Sue. Disco Box
    (collection), 2644
Robinson, Cleophus. Someone to Care: The
    Battle Sessions, 3002
Robinson, Fenton
    ★Blues Classics (collection), 146
    Somebody Loan Me a Dime, 305
Robinson, Smokey and the Miracles
    Beg, Scream, and Shout! The Big Ol'
        Box of '60s Soul (collection), 2433
    Definitive Performances, 1963–1987,
        2545.1
    Heaven Must Have Sent You: The
        Holland/Dozier/Holland Story
        (collection), 2436
    Hitsville USA: The Motown Singles
        Collection, Vol. 2 (collection), 2604
    Motown around the World (collection),
        2437
    Rejoice and Shout (collection), 2969

    The Solo Albums, Vol. 2, 2508.1
    Solo Anthology, 2508.2
    35th Anniversary Collection, 2545.2
    ★The Ultimate Collection, 2545.3
Robison, Carson. Home, Sweet Home on
    the Prairie: 25 Cowboy Classics,
    1420
★Robison, Willard. The Crooners
    (collection), 1062
★Rob-Roys. The Doo-Wop Box
    (collection), 2322
Roches. We Three Kings, 3337
rock
    Acoustic Guitar Bible (collection), 1715
    Acoustic Guitar Tab White Pages
        (collection), 1716
    Acoustic Rock Guitar Bible (collection),
        1717
    Bass Tab White Pages (collection),
        1718
    blues and rock, 367–385
    British folk-rock, 1851–1859
    British invasion, 1786–1807
    Classic Rock Guitar Bible (collection),
        1719
    dance music, electronica, etc.,
        2214–2232
    Disco Guitar Bible (collection), 1721
    early rock 'n' roll, 1743–1770
    Elvis Presley and rockabilly,
        1735–1742
    Folk-Rock Guitar Bible (collection),
        1722
    general collections, 1715–1734
    Grunge Guitar Bible (collection), 1723
    guitar heroes, 1860–1869
    Guitar Tab White Pages (collection),
        1724
    Guitar Tab White Pages, Vol. 2
        (collection), 1725
    Guitar Tab White Pages, Vol. 3
        (collection), 1726
    Hard Rock Bass Bible (collection),
        1727
    Hard Rock Guitar Bible (collection),
        1728
    influences on the 1980s: 1960s and
        1970s bands, 1870–1890
    Los Angeles rock, 1901–1912
    mainstream rock, 2064–2090
    the 1970s, 1891–2030
    overview, p102–103
    periodicals for up-to-date CD notices
        and reviews, suggested, p3
    Pop/Rock Bass Bible (collection), 1729
    Pop/Rock Guitar Bible (collection),
        1730
    post-punk, 2031–2039
    post-rock, 2233–2238
    Rock Bass Bible (collection), 1731
    Rock Guitar Bible (collection), 1733
    rock: the 1980s and beyond,
        2064–2213

rock (cont.)
  Rock-Blues Guitar Bible (collection),
    1732
  Southern Rock Guitar Bible
    (collection), 1734
  teen idols, instrumentals, and dance
    hits, 1771–1785
  The Colossal Guitar Songbook
    (collection), 1720
  U.S. rock scene in the sixties,
    1808–1850
  women in rock since in the 1970s,
    2040–2063
Rock, Pete and C. L. Smooth
  The Main Ingredient, 2910.1
  ★*Mecca and the Soul Brother*, 2910.2
Rock, Pete. *Petestrumentals*, 2909
rock: the 1980s and beyond, 2064–2213
  alternative, 2091–2213
  mainstream, 2064–2090
rock theater. *See* art rock and rock
    theater
rockabilly and Elvis Presley. *See* Elvis
    Presley and rockabilly
Rodgers, Jimmie
  ★*American Roots Music* (collection),
    1379
  The Best of Jimmie Rodgers, 1221
  *Classic Country Music: A Smithsonian
    Collection* (collection), 1382
  ★*The Essential Jimmie Rodgers*, 1421.1
  Recordings, 1927–1933, 1421.2
  The Singing Brakeman, 1421.3
  *Times Ain't What They Used to Be:
    Early Rural and Popular Music
    from Rare Original Film Masters*
    (collection), 1091
  *When the Sun Goes Down 2: The First
    Time I Met the Blues* (collection),
    160
  With My Little Ukulele in My Hand
    (collection), 1093
Rodgers, Lucy "Sister Soul." *Good God!
    Born Again Funk* (collection),
    2614
Rodgers, Richard
  Rodgers and Hammerstein Collection
    (songwriter collection), 1109.2
  Rodgers and Hart: A Musical Anthology
    (songwriter collection), 1109.3
  Rodgers / Hart (songwriter collection),
    1109.1
Rodney, Red. *Then and Now*, 890
Roe, Tommy. *25 All-Time Greatest
    Bubblegum Hits* (collection), 1811
Rogers, Ginger. *Harry Warren* (songwriter
    collection), 1114
Rogers, Jimmy
  ★*Blues Classics* (collection), 146
  ★*Chess Blues* (collection), 287
  Chicago Is Just That Way (collection),
    289
Rogers, Kenny. *Ten Years of Gold*, 1675

Rogers, Lee. *Beg, Scream, and Shout!
    The Big Ol' Box of '60s Soul*
    (collection), 2433
Rogers, Lon, & the Soul Blenders.
    *Eccentric Soul: Mighty Mike
    Lenaburg* (collection), 2563
Rogers, Roy
  Blues Fest: Modern Blues of the '80s
    (collection), 409
  *Happy Trails: The Roy Rogers
    Collection, 1937–1990*, 1422
  *Songs That Got Us through World
    War II, Vol. 2* (collection), 1086
Rogers, Shorty
  The Birth of the Cool, Vol. 2 (collection),
    604
  *Shorty Rogers, Vol. 1: West Coast
    Trumpet*, 622
Roland, Walter
  ★*Legends of the Blues, Vol. 2*
    (collection), 151
  ★*Let's Get Loose: Folk and Popular
    Blues Styles from the Beginning to
    the Early 1940s* (collection), 152
Rollers. *Eccentric Soul: The Outskirts of
    Deep City* (collection), 2565
The Rolling Stones
  Aftermath, 1802.1
  ★*Beggars Banquet*, 1802.2
  ★*Exile on Main St.*, 1931.1
  ★*Hot Rocks*, 1802.3
  *Jump Back: The Best of the Rolling
    Stones, '71–'93*, 1931.2
  Let It Bleed, 1802.4
  Out of Our Heads, 1802.5
  The Rolling Stones Guitar Anthology,
    1802.6
  The Rolling Stones, Now!, 1802.7
  Singles Collection: The London Years,
    1802.8
  Some Girls, 1931.3
  Sticky Fingers, 1931.4
  Sucking in the Seventies, 1931.5
Rollins Band. *End of Silence*, 2181
Rollins, Henry. *American Hardcore*
    (collection), 1977
Rollins, Sonny
  Alfie [1997] (Rollins and Nelson),
    1044.1
  Alfie [2000] (Rollins and Nelson),
    1044.2
  The Bridge, 657.1
  Don't Stop the Carnival, 891.1
  East Broadway Rundown, 697.1
  *Four Tenors: John Coltrane, Charles
    Lloyd, Sonny Rollins and Ben
    Webster* (collection), 627
  Jazz Style of Sonny Rollins, 657.2
  ★*Ken Burns Jazz Collection: Sonny
    Rollins*, 657.3
  ★*Ken Burns Jazz: The Story of
    America's Music* (collection), 478
  ★*A Night at the Village Vanguard*, 657.4

Our Man in Jazz, 697.2
  Road Shows, Vol. 1, 891.2
  Saxophone Colossus, 657.6
  Saxophone Colossus [1956], 657.5
  Sonny Rollins, 657.7
  ★*Way Out West*, 657.8
The Romantics. *80's Pop Hits* (collection),
    1238
★Romeos. *Atlantic Vocal Groups,
    1951–1963* (collection), 2320
The Ronettes
  The Best of the Ronettes, 2355
  *A Christmas Gift for You from Phil
    Spector* (collection), 3300
Roney, Wallace. *No Room for Argument*,
    1010
Ronstadt, Linda
  Greatest Hits I and II, 1909.1
  Heart Like a Wheel, 1909.2
  The Very Best of Linda Ronstadt, 1534,
    1909.3
  Trio, 1673
Roomful of Blues. *Blues Fest: Modern
    Blues of the '70s* (collection), 408
roots, 169–182
  Afro-American Blues and Game Songs
    (collection), 169
  *Afro-American Folk Music from Tate
    and Panola Counties, Mississippi*
    (collection), 170
  *Afro-American Spirituals, Work Songs,
    and Ballads* (collection), 171
  *American Primitive, Vol. 2: Pre-War
    Revenants* (collection), 173
  *American Primitive, Vol. 1: Raw
    Pre-War Gospel* (collection), 172
  ★*Avalon Blues* (Hurt), 196
  Best Of . . . (Stokes), 200
  The Best of Cannon's Jug Stompers, 193
  The Best Of . . . (Memphis Jug Band),
    198.1
  Big Brazos (Deep River of Song)
    (collection), 174
  Blues Masters, Vol. 10: Blues Roots
    (Charters), 175
  collections, 169–181
  Everybody Hollerin' Goat (Turner),
    182
  Gospel, Blues, and Street Songs (Davis),
    194
  *Honey Babe Let the Deal Go Down: Best
    of the Mississippi Sheiks* (Mississippi
    Sheiks), 199.1
  Huddie Ledbetter's Best (Leadbelly),
    197.1
  King of the 12-String Guitar
    (Leadbelly), 197.2
  Lead Belly's Last Sessions (Leadbelly),
    197.3
  *The Library of Congress Recordings,
    Vols. 4–6* (Leadbelly), 197.5
  ★*The Library of Congress Recordings,
    Vols. 1–3* (Leadbelly), 197.4

Memphis Jug Band with Cannon's Jug Stompers, 198.2

★*Negro Blues and Hollers* (collection), 178

Negro Prison Camp Worksongs (collection), 179

Negro Work Songs and Calls (collection), 180

Prison Songs, Vol. 1: Murderous Home (collection), 181

Ragtime Blues (Grossman), 195

★*The Roots of the Blues* (Lomax), 177

Ruckus Juice and Chittlins: The Great Jug Bands—Classic Recordings of the 1920s and '30s, Vol. 1 (collection), 188

Ruckus Juice and Chittlins: The Great Jug Bands—Classic Recordings of the 1920s and '30s, Vol. 2 (collection), 189

Songsters and Saints: Vocal Traditions on Race Records, Vol. 1 (collection), 190

Songsters and Saints: Vocal Traditions on Race Records, Vol. 2 (collection), 191

Stop and Listen (Mississippi Sheiks), 199.2

★*Texas Worried Blues: Complete Recorded Works* (Thomas), 201

Violin, Sing the Blues for Me: African-American Fiddlers (collection), 192

Wake Up Dead Man: Black Convict Worksongs from Texas Prisons (Jackson), 176

The Roots
    Game Theory, 2911.1
    Illadelph Halflife, 2911.2
    Phrenology, 2911.3
    ★*Things Fall Apart,* 2911.4
    Undun, 2911.5

★Rose, David. *Nipper's Greatest Hits: The 40's, Vol. 1* (collection), 1073

Rose Ensemble. *And Glory Shone Around,* 22

Rose Royce
    Disco Box (collection), 2644
    The Very Best of Rose Royce, 2651

Rosnes, Renee. *As We Are Now,* 1011

Ross, Annie. *The Bebop Singers* (collection), 765

Ross, Diana
    Complete Introduction to Disco (collection), 1237
    The Definitive Collection, 2509.2
    Diana Ross Live: Stolen Moments—The Lady Sings . . . Jazz and Blues, 2509.1
    50th Anniversary: The Singles Collection, 1961–1969, 2546
    50th Anniversary: The Singles Collection, 1961–1969, 2356

Hitsville USA: The Motown Singles Collection, Vol. 2 (collection), 2604

The Motown Anthology, 2509.3

Ross, Diana and the Supremes
    ★*Gold,* 2547.1
    The No. 1's, 2547.2

Ross, Doctor
    Blue Flames: A Sun Blues Collection (collection), 337
    Memphis Blues: Important Postwar Recordings (collection), 341
    Sun Records Harmonica Classics (collection), 346

Ross, Jackie. *Best of Chess R&B, Vols. 1 and 2* (collection), 2420

Ross, Shirley. *The Classic Hoagy Carmichael* (songwriter collection), 1097.1

Ross, Sonia. *Eccentric Soul: The Tragar and Note Labels* (collection), 2602

Roswell Sacred Harp Quartet. *Mountain Gospel: The Sacred Roots of Country Music* (collection), 3113

Roswell Sacred Harp Singers. *I Belong to This Band: Eighty-Five Years of Sacred Harp Recordings* (collection), 3111

Rova Saxophone Quartet. *Beat Kennel,* 1012

Rowan, Peter
    All on a Rising Day, 1604
    Top of the Hill Bluegrass (collection), 1567

Rowles, Jimmy. *Jimmy Rowles / Ray Brown: The Duo Sessions,* 892

Royal Esquires. *Eccentric Soul: The Prix Label* (collection), 2601

★*Royal Jokers. Atlantic Vocal Groups, 1951–1963* (collection), 2320

Royal Kings. *Boddie Recording Company Cleveland, Ohio* (collection), 2569, 2570

Royal Philharmonic Orchestra. *The Runaway Bunny, Paddington Bear's First Concert, Tubby the Tuba* (collection), 3254

Royal Teens. *The Doo-Wop Box II* (collection), 2323

Royaltones. *Old Town Doo-Wop, Vols. 1–3* (collection), 2324

Rubin, Dave
    Art of the Shuffle, for Guitar: An Exploration of Shuffle, Boogie, and Swing Rhythms, 360.1
    Beginning Blues Guitar: A Guide to the Essential Chords, Licks, Techniques, and Concepts, 167.1
    The Best of R&B: A Step-by-Step Breakdown of the Guitar Styles and Techniques, 456
    Inside the Blues, 1942–1982, 360.2
    Open Tunings for Blues Guitar, 167.2

Solo Blues Guitar, 167.3
12-Bar Blues, 168

Ruby and The Romantics. *The Sweetest Feeling: A Van McCoy Songbook* (collection), 2447

★Ruckles, Charles. *Nashville Jumps: Blues and Rhythm on Nashville Independent Labels 1945–1955* (collection), 2376

Rudd, Roswell. *Regeneration,* 1013

Ruffin, David
    Beg, Scream, and Shout! The Big Ol' Box of '60s Soul (collection), 2433
    The Great David Ruffin: The Motown Solo Albums, Vol. 1, 2510.1
    The Great David Ruffin: The Motown Solo Albums, Vol. 2, 2510.2
    The Ultimate Collection, 2510.3

Ruffin, Jimmy
    Birth of Soul, 4 Vols. (collection), 2434
    Motown around the World (collection), 2437
    The Ultimate Motown Collection, 2511

Rufus. *The Very Best of Rufus, Featuring Chaka Khan,* 2512

Rule, Ja. *Venni Vetti Vecci,* 2912

Rumbel, Nancy. *Piano Solos: Narada Artists* (collection), 1370

The Runaways
    The Best of the Runaways, 2058
    No Thanks! The '70s Punk Rebellion (collection), 2003

Rundgren, Todd. *The Very Best of Todd Rundgren,* 1884

Run-D.M.C.
    King of Rock, 2913.1
    ★*Raising Hell,* 2913.2
    Run-D.M.C, 2913.3
    Tougher Than Leather, 2913.4

Rush, Bobby
    Blues Fest: Modern Blues of the '70s (collection), 408
    Bobby Rush Live at Ground Zero Blues Club, 457

Rush. *Chronicles Deluxe Ed,* 2083

Rush, Otis
    All Your Love I Miss Loving: Live at the Wise Fools Pub, Chicago, 458.1
    ★*The Best of Duke-Peacock Blues* (collection), 336
    Blues Masters, Vol. 6: Blues Originals (collection), 367
    Blues Masters, Vol. 2: Postwar Chicago Blues (collection), 285
    Blues Masters, Vol. 1: Urban Blues (collection), 338
    ★*The Blues: A Smithsonian Collection of Classic Blues Singers* (collection), 145
    ★*Chicago: The Blues Today!* (collection), 290
    The Cobra Records Story: Chicago Rock and Blues (collection), 339

Rush, Otis (cont.)
  ★*The Essential Otis Rush: Classic Cobra
    Recordings,* 361
  ★*Mean Old World: The Blues from
    1940–1994* (collection), 154
  Right Place, Wrong Time, 458.2
  Soul Shots, Vol. 4: Urban Blues
    (collection), 343
Rushen, Patrice
  Disco Box (collection), 2644
  *Haven't You Heard: The Best of Patrice
    Rushen,* 2296
Rushing, Jimmy
  ★*The Blues: A Smithsonian Collection
    of Classic Blues Singers* (collection),
    145
  The Essential Jimmy Rushing, 799
  ★*The Jazz Singers: A Smithsonian
    Collection of Jazz Vocals from
    1919–1994* (collection), 766
  Legendary Big Band Singers
    (collection), 767
  Stars of the Apollo (collection),
    2240
★Russell, Andy. *Sentimental Journey: Pop
    Vocal Classics, Vol. 1* (collection),
    1081
Russell, George
  *Big Band Renaissance: The Evolution
    of the Jazz Orchestra* (collection),
    739
  ★*The Birth of the Third Stream*
    (collection), 1030
  The 80th Birthday Concert, 1043.2
  Ezz-Thetics, 1043.1
  Jazz in the Space Age, 1043.3
  The Jazz Workshop, 1043.4
Russell, Jackie. *Boddie Recording
    Company Cleveland, Ohio*
    (collection), 2569, 2570
Russell, Jane. *Fascinating Rhythm: George
    Gershwin* (songwriter collection),
    1101.2
Russell, Luis
  An Anthology of Big Band Swing
    (collection), 528
  ★*Big Band Jazz: From the Beginnings to
    the Fifties* (collection), 529
  The Luis Russell Story, 547
Russell, Pee Wee
  ★*The Commodore Story* (collection),
    561
  Jazz Reunion, 732.1
  The Land of Jazz, 583
  *Lost Chords: White Musicians and Their
    Contributions to Jazz* (collection),
    479
  ★*Swingin' with Pee Wee,* 732.2
★Rutherford, Leonard. *Anthology of
    American Folk Music, Vols. 1–3*
    (collection), 1386
Ryder, Mitch. *Rev Up: The Best of Mitch
    Ryder and the Detroit Wheels,* 1819

Rypdal, Terje
  Odyssey, 858
  Selected Recordings, 1342
RZA. *The RZA Hits,* 2914

S
S. F. Seals. *Greasy Kid Stuff* (collection),
    3210
Saadiq, Raphael
  Stone Rollin', 2513.1
  The Way I See It, 2513.2
Sacred Four. *Good God! Born Again Funk*
    (collection), 2614
sacred music. *See* religious music
Saddler, J. D. *Boddie Recording Company
    Cleveland, Ohio* (collection), 2569,
    2570
Saffire—The Uppity Blues Women.
    Cleaning House, 459
Safka, Melanie. *See* Melanie
Sahm, Doug. *The Best of Doug Sahm and
    the Sir Douglas Quintet,* 1844
Saints
  I'm Stranded, 2022
  No Thanks! The '70s Punk Rebellion
    (collection), 2003
Sallie Martin Singers. *Throw out the
    Lifeline,* 3048
Salt-n-Pepa
  Blacks' Magic, 2915.1
  Hot, Cool and Vicious, 2915.2
Saluzzi, Dino. *Cité de la Musique,* 859
Sam and Dave
  ★*Atlantic R&B, 1947–1974*
    (collection), 2418
  ★*Atlantic Soul, 1959–1975*
    (collection), 2589
  *Beg, Scream, and Shout! The Big Ol'
    Box of '60s Soul* (collection),
    2433
  *The Complete Stax/Volt Singles
    1959–1968* (collection), 2594
  ★*The Definitive Soul Collection,*
    2514.1
  The Original Soul Men, 2514.2
  ★*The R&B Box* (collection), 2239
  *Stax/Volt Revue: Live in London,
    Vols. 1 and 2* (collection), 2609
  Stax/Volt Revue: Live in Norway 1967
    (collection), 2446
  *Top of the Stax, Vol. 1: Twenty Greatest
    Hits* (collection), 2611
  The Very Best of Sam and Dave,
    2514.3
Sam the Sham. *Texas Music, Vol. 3:
    Garage Bands and Psychedelia*
    (collection), 1830
Samba Salad. *Animal Playground*
    (collection), 3226
Sample, Missionary Mamie. *This May
    Be My Last Time Singing: Raw
    African- American Gospel on 45rpm*
    (collection), 2982

samplers and concept albums (new age),
    1366–1378
  *Magnum Mysterium: A Special 2-1/2
    Hour Collection of Sacred Music
    Classics* (collection), 1366
  *Narada Decade: The Anniversary
    Collection* (collection), 1367
  Narada Wilderness Collection
    (collection), 1368
  New Age Piano Sampler (collection),
    1369
  Piano Solos: Narada Artists (collection),
    1370
  Pioneers of the New Age (collection),
    1371
  *A Quiet Revolution: 30 Years of
    Windham Hill* (collection), 1372
  Solace: A Windham Hill Collection
    (collection), 1373
  Starflight 1 (collection), 1374
  Sunday Morning Coffee (collection),
    1375
  Ultimate New Age (collection),
    1376
  Windham Hill: The First Ten Years
    (collection), 1377
  The World of Private Music
    (collection), 1378
Sanborn, David
  The Best of David Sanborn, 908
  Songs, 831
Sanders, Felicia. *Alan Jay Lerner*
    (songwriter collection), 1105.1
Sanders, Pharoah
  Karma, 698.1
  Tauhid, 698.2
★Santamaria, Mongo. *What It Is! Funky
    Soul and Rare Grooves* (collection),
    2615
Santana
  Abraxas, 1845.1
  ★*Santana,* 1845.2
  Santana's Greatest Hits, 1845.3
  Soul to Soul (collection), 2444
  Viva Santana!, 1845.4
Santana, Carlos
  *Dreamland: World Lullabies and
    Soothing Songs* (collection),
    3263
  Pioneers of the New Age (collection),
    1371
★Santo and Johnny. *Legends of Guitar:
    Rock—The '50s, Vol. 2* (collection),
    1750
Sapp, Marvin. *Here I Am,* 3096
★Saunders, Red. *The Okeh Rhythm and
    Blues Story* (collection), 2425
Sauter-Finegan. *Big Band Renaissance:
    The Evolution of the Jazz Orchestra*
    (collection), 739
★Savitt, Jan. *Swing Time! The Fabulous Big
    Band Era* (collection), 1089
Scaggs, Boz. *Silk Degrees,* 1917

Scaggs, Ricky. *Jubilation! Great Gospel Performances, Vol. 3: Country Gospel* (collection), 3112

★Scales, Harvey. *Atlantic Soul, 1959–1975* (collection), 2589

Scarface
  Mr. Scarface Is Back, 2916.1
  The Diary, 2916.2

Scarlets. *The Doo-Wop Box II* (collection), 2323

Scelsa, Greg. *Holidays and Special Times*, 3250

Schiff, Ronny S.
  Electric Blues Guitar Giants (Sokolow and Schiff), 362
  Stevie Ray Vaughan, Lightnin' Blues, 1983–1987 (Vaughan, Tapella, Sokolow and Schiff), 383

Schlippenback, Alexander von
  Elf Bagatellen, 866.1
  Monk's Casino, 866.2

Schneider, Maria. *Evanescence*, 763

school age or all ages children's music, 3208–3225
  All around the Kitchen! Crazy Videos and Concert Songs! (Zanes), 3225.1
  Alphabutt (Dawson), 3214
  collections, 3208–3211
  Disney's Greatest Hits, Vol. 1 (collection), 3208
  Eat Every Bean and Pea on Your Plate (Boydston), 3212
  Family Dance (Zanes), 3225.2
  Fascinating Creatures (England), 3216
  For the Kids Three! (collection), 3209
  Free to Be . . . You and Me (Thomas), 3223
  Greasy Kid Stuff (collection), 3210
  Mine! (Trout Fishing in America), 3224
  Not for Kids Only (Garcia and Grisman), 3217
  Rhinoceros Tap (Boynton), 3213
  Schoolhouse Rock! (Dorough), 3215
  Sing-a-Longs and Lullabies for the Film Curious George (Johnson), 3220
  The Sunny Side of the Street (Lithgow), 3221
  ★*The Tragic Treasury: Songs from a Series of Unfortunate Events* (Gothic Archies), 3218
  Vintage Children's Favorites (collection), 3211
  You Are My Little Bird (Mitchell), 3222
  ★*You'll Sing a Song and I'll Sing a Song* (Jenkins), 3219

★Schoolboys. *The Doo-Wop Box* (collection), 2322

Schooly D. *The Jive Collection, Vol. 3*, 2917

Schroedl, Scott. *Best of Blues Piano* (Lowry, Wiegratz, Boduch, McGirr and Schroedl), 261

Schueneman, B. *College Fight Songs: An Anthology*, 3371

★Schuller, Gunther. *The Birth of the Third Stream* (collection), 1030

Schuur, Diane
  The Best of Diane Schuur, 1301
  The Definitive Collection (songwriter collection), 1101.1

Schwartz, Arthur
  All Time Favorite Dietz and Schwartz Songs (songwriter collection), 1110.1
  Arthur Schwartz (songwriter collection), 1110.2

Schwarz, Gerard
  Come and Trip It: Instrumental Dance Music, 1780s–1920s (collection), 94
  Cornet Favorites; Highlights from Cousins (Schwartz), 89

Schweizer, Irene. *Piano Solo, Vol. 1*, 860

Scofield, John
  Enroute: John Scofield Trio Live, 1014.1
  Icons among Us (collection), 934
  Progressions: 100 Years of Jazz Guitar (collection), 481
  Time on My Hands, 1014.2

Scorpions. *Heavy Metal: The First 20 Years* (collection), 1938

Scott, Carl. *Times Ain't What They Used to Be: Early Rural and Popular Music from Rare Original Film Masters* (collection), 1091

Scott, Darrell. *Aloha from Nashville*, 1708

Scott, Freddie
  Beg, Scream, and Shout! The Big Ol' Box of '60s Soul (collection), 2433
  Birth of Soul, 4 Vols. (collection), 2434

Scott, Hazel. *Fascinating Rhythm: George Gershwin* (songwriter collection), 1101.2

Scott, James. *Classic Ragtime from Rare Piano Rolls*, 141

Scott, Jill
  Beautifully Human: Words and Sounds, Vol. 2, 2387.1
  Live in Paris, 2387.2
  Who Is Jill Scott? Words and Sounds, Vol. 1, 2387.3

★Scott, Little Jimmy
  All the Way, 800.1
  Falling in Love Is Wonderful, 800.2
  Stompin' at the Savoy: The Original Indie Label, 1944–1961 (collection), 2429

Scott, Mabel
  Hipsters' Holiday: Vocal Jazz and R&B Classics (collection), 3313
  ★*The R&B Box* (collection), 2239

★Scott, Marilyn. *Stompin' at the Savoy: The Original Indie Label, 1944–1961* (collection), 2429

★Scott, Myrtle. *All God's Sons and Daughters: Chicago's Gospel Legends* (collection), 3030

Scott, Raymond. *Reckless Nights and Turkish Twilights: The Music of Raymond Scott*, 1148

★Scott, Tony. *Music for Zen Meditation*, 1332

Scott-Heron, Gil
  The Revolution Will Not Be Televised, 815
  Small Talk at 125th and Lenox, 1974

Scotty and the Rib Tips. *Living Chicago Blues, Vol. 3* (collection), 417

Scruggs, Earl. *See also* Flatt, Lester and Scruggs, Earl
  American Roots Music [CDs] (collection), 1380
  ★*American Roots Music* [DVDs] (collection), 1379
  Best of the Flatt and Scruggs TV Show: Classic Bluegrass from 1956 to 1962, 1583.1
  ★*The Complete Mercury Sessions*, 1583.2
  Earl Scruggs and the 5-String Banjo, 1605.1
  Essential Earl Scruggs, 1605.2
  ★*The Essential Flatt and Scruggs: 'Tis Sweet to Be Remembered*, 1583.3
  Flatt and Scruggs, 1948–1959, 1583.4
  Flatt and Scruggs, 1959–1963, 1583.5
  ★*Will the Circle Be Unbroken?* (collection), 1452

Scruggs, Joe. *Merry Christmas*, 3251

Scruggs, Uncle John. *Times Ain't What They Used to Be: Early Rural and Popular Music from Rare Original Film Masters* (collection), 1091

Seals, Son
  Bad Axe Blues (Seals and Whitehill), 461
  Blues Fest: Modern Blues of the '70s (collection), 408
  Blues Masters, Vol. 9: Postmodern Blues (collection), 412
  ★*Midnight Son*, 460

Searchers. *25 Hits from the British Invasion* (collection), 1792

Sears, Al. *The Big Horn: The History of the Honkin' and Screamin' Saxophone* (collection), 2314

★Seatrain. *What It Is! Funky Soul and Rare Grooves* (collection), 2615

2nd Chapter of Acts. *20*, 3160

2nd South Carolina String Band
  Dulcem Melodies: Favorite Campfire Songs of the Civil War Era, 78.1
  Far, Far from Home, 78.2
  In High Cotton: Favorite Camp Songs of the Civil War, 78.3
  Lightning in a Jar: An Evening of Civil War Music, 78.4

Sedaka, Neil
    All Time Greatest Hits, 1781
    Have a Nice Decade: The '70s Pop Culture Box (collection), 1240
    Nipper's Greatest Hits: The 50's, Vol. 2 (collection), 1164
    ★*Nipper's Greatest Hits: The 50's, Vol. 1* (collection), 1163
Seeds
    Nuggets: A Classic Collection from the Psychedelic Sixties (collection), 1809
    ★*Nuggets: Artifacts of the First Psychedelic Era* (collection), 1808
Seeger, Mike
    American Folk Songs for Christmas, 3338
    Mountain Music Bluegrass Style (collection), 1566
Seeger, Pete
    Pete Seeger's Rainbow Quest, 1606
    Stories and Songs for Little Children, 3205
    Traditional Christmas Carols, 3339
Seeley, Blossom
    Flappers, Vamps, and Sweet Young Things (collection), 1065
    Joe Franklin Presents . . . The Roaring '20s Roar Again (collection), 1069
    ★*Yes, Sir, That's My Baby: The Golden Years of Tin Pan Alley* (collection), 1094
Seger, Bob
    Greatest Hits, 1918.1
    Live Bullet, 1918.2
Selah Jubilee Singers
    Gospel: Negro Spirituals / Gospel Songs, 1926–1942 (collection), 2963
    Jesus Put a Song in My Soul (collection), 3036
Seldom Scene
    Act 3, 1607.1
    Old Train, 1607.2
    Recorded Live at the Cellar Door, 1607.3
    Top of the Hill Bluegrass (collection), 1567
Selvin, Ben. *Irving Berlin: A Hundred Years* (songwriter collection), 1096.3
Sensational Five Singing Sons
    Good God! Born Again Funk (collection), 2614
The Sensational Nightingales
    The Best of the Sensational Nightingales, 3024
    ★*The Gospel Sound of Spirit Feel* (collection), 2965
    Kings of the Gospel Highway: The Golden Age of Gospel Quartets (collection), 3009
★Sensations. *Atlantic Vocal Groups, 1951–1963* (collection), 2320
Sequence. *Hip Hop Essentials, 1979–1991* (collection), 2675

Seven Revelators. *Boddie Recording Company Cleveland, Ohio* (collection), 2569, 2570
7 Seconds. *American Hardcore* (collection), 1977
Sex Pistols
    The Filth and the Fury, 2023.1
    ★*Never Mind the Bollocks Here's the Sex Pistols,* 2023.2
    Punk: Attitude (collection), 1980
Shadowfax
    Shadowfax, 1328
    Solace: A Windham Hill Collection (collection), 1373
    Ultimate New Age (collection), 1376
    Windham Hill: The First Ten Years (collection), 1377
Shadows. *Legends of Guitar: Rock—The '60s, Vol. 1* (collection), 1860
★Shadows of Knight. *Nuggets: Artifacts of the First Psychedelic Era* (collection), 1808
Shafferman, Jean Anne. *Carols for Two,* 3287
Shaggs. *Philosophy of the World,* 1885
Shakti
    Pioneers of the New Age (collection), 1371
    Shakti with John McLaughlin, 861
Shakur, Tupac Amaru. See 2Pac
Shalamar, Sugar Pie. *Heaven Must Have Sent You: The Holland/Dozier/Holland Story* (collection), 2436
Sham 69
    No Thanks! The '70s Punk Rebellion (collection), 2003
    Tell Us the Truth, 2024
Shan, MC. *Hip Hop Essentials, 1979–1991* (collection), 2675
The Shangri Las. *The Best of the Girl Groups, Vols. 1 and 2* (collection), 2321
★Shankar, Ananda. *What It Is! Funky Soul and Rare Grooves* (collection), 2615
Shannon, Del
    Greatest Hits, 1782.1
    Pure 60's: The #1 Hits (collection), 1165
    25 All-Time Greatest Hits, 1782.2
Shante, Roxanne. *Hip Hop Essentials, 1979–1991* (collection), 2675
Sharrock, Sonny. *Progressions: 100 Years of Jazz Guitar* (collection), 481
Shaver, Billy Joe. *Old Five and Dimers Like Me,* 1535
Shaw, Artie
    ★*Big Band Jazz: From the Beginnings to the Fifties* (collection), 529
    Big Band Renaissance: The Evolution of the Jazz Orchestra (collection), 739
    Cole Porter (songwriter collection), 1108.1

    The Complete Gramercy Five Sessions, 584
    ★*The Essential Artie Shaw,* 548
    The Great Depression: American Music in the '30s (collection), 1066
    ★*Ken Burns Jazz: The Story of America's Music* (collection), 478
    ★*Nipper's Greatest Hits: The 40's, Vol. 1* (collection), 1073
Shaw, Eddie
    Blues Fest: Modern Blues of the '70s (collection), 408
    Living Chicago Blues, Vol. 1 (collection), 415
Shaw, Robert. *The Ma Grinder,* 263
Shaw, Sister Rosa. *Powerhouse Gospel on Independent Labels* (collection), 3038
Shaw, Woody
    Rosewood, 893.1
    Solid, 893.2
★Sh-Booms. *Atlantic Vocal Groups, 1951–1963* (collection), 2320
Sheard, Kierra Kiki. *Wow Gospel #1s* (collection), 3074
Shearing, George
    George Shearing, 673
    ★*Jazz on a Summer's Day* (collection), 664
★Sheiks. *Atlantic Vocal Groups, 1951–1963* (collection), 2320
Shellac. *At Action Park,* 2182
Shelley, Michael. *Greasy Kid Stuff* (collection), 3210
★Shells. *The Doo-Wop Box* (collection), 2322
Shelton, B. F.
    Before the Blues: The Early American Black Music Scene; Classic Recordings from the 1920's and 30's, Vols. 1–3 (collection), 183
    Old-Time Mountain Ballads (collection), 1390
Shelton, Roscoe
    Night Train to Nashville: Music City Rhythm and Blues, 1945–1970, Vol. 1 (collection), 2377
    Night Train to Nashville: Music City Rhythm and Blues, 1945–1970, Vol. 2 (collection), 2378
Shelton, Ted, and His Bryan County Boys. *Swingbillies: Hillbilly and Western Swing on Modern/Colonial/Flair, 1947–1952* (collection), 1431
★Shep and the Limelites. *The Doo-Wop Box* (collection), 2322
Shepard, Jean
    Jean Shepard, Honky–Tonk Heroine: Classic Capitol Recordings, 1952–1964, 1536.1
    Melody Ranch Girl, 1536.2
Shepherd, Kenny Wayne. *Ledbetter Heights,* 379

Shepp, Archie
  Four for Trane, 699.1
  The New York Contemporary Five, 699.2
  On This Night, 699.3
The Sheppards
  Birth of Soul: Special Chicago Edition (collection), 2566
  The Doo-Wop Box II (collection), 2323
  ★*The Vee-Jay Story: Celebrating 40 Years of Classic Hits* (collection), 2431
★Sheriff and the Ravels. *The Vee-Jay Story: Celebrating 40 Years of Classic Hits* (collection), 2431
Sherman, Allan. *Dr. Demento Presents: The Greatest Christmas Novelty CD of All Time* (collection), 3307
Sherwood, Adrian. *Never Trust a Hippy*, 2229
★Shilkret, Nat. *Nipper's Greatest Hits: The 20's* (collection), 1071
Shines, Johnny
  Chicago Is Just That Way (collection), 289
  ★*Chicago: The Blues Today!* (collection), 290
  Drop Down Mama (collection), 292
  Dust My Broom, 307.1
  The Road to Robert Johnson and Beyond (collection), 221
  ★*The Story of the Blues* (collection), 158
  Sweet Home Chicago: The J.O.B. Sessions, 307.2
The Shins. *Chutes Too Narrow*, 2183
The Shirelles
  The Best of the Girl Groups, Vols. 1 and 2 (collection), 2321
  The Look of Love: The Burt Bacharach Collection (collection), 1161
  The American Roots of the British Invasion (collection), 1786
  The Doo-Wop Box II (collection), 2323
  The Scepter Records Story (collection), 2426
  The Shirelles 25 All-Time Greatest Hits, 2357
Shirley and Company. *Disco Box* (collection), 2644
Shirley and Lee
  Crescent City Soul: The Sound of New Orleans, 1947–1974 (collection), 2564
  ★*The R&B Box* (collection), 2239
  Shirley and Lee (Legendary Masters Series, Vol. 1), 2371.1
  The Sweethearts of the Blues, 2371.2
Shirley, George. *Battle Pieces*, 123
Shirley Jean and the Relations. *Gimme Your Hand, J-B!* (collection), 2613
Shocked, Michelle. *Mercury Poise: 1988–1995*, 2059

Shocking Blue. *Have a Nice Decade: The '70s Pop Culture Box* (collection), 1240
Shore, Dinah
  ★*American Popular Song: Six Decades of Songwriters and Singers* (collection), 1059
  Arthur Schwartz (songwriter collection), 1110.2
  Duke Ellington (songwriter collection), 1099.1
  Fascinating Rhythm: George Gershwin (songwriter collection), 1101.2
  Frank Loesser (songwriter collection), 1106.1
  Hit Parade, 1943 (collection), 1157
  Irving Berlin: A Hundred Years (songwriter collection), 1096.3
  Irving Berlin (songwriter collection), 1096.1
  James Van Heusen (songwriter collection), 1112.1
  Johnny Mercer (songwriter collection), 1107.1
  Jule Styne (songwriter collection), 1111.1
  ★*Nipper's Greatest Hits: The 40's, Vol. 1* (collection), 1073
  ★*Nipper's Greatest Hits: The 50's, Vol. 1* (collection), 1163
  Sentimental Journey: Capitol's Great Ladies of Song (collection), 1166
  Sentimental Journey: Pop Vocal Classics, Vol. 1 (collection), 1167
  ★*Sentimental Journey: Pop Vocal Classics, Vol. 1* (collection), 1081
  ★*Sentimental Journey: Pop Vocal Classics, Vol. 2* (collection), 1168
  16 Most Requested Songs of the 1940s, Vol. 1 (collection), 1082
  16 Most Requested Songs of the 1940s, Vol. 2 (collection), 1083
  Songs That Got Us through World War II, Vol. 2 (collection), 1086
  25 Sweethearts of Yesteryear (collection), 1092
  The Ultimate Dinah Shore, 1222
  Vincent Youmans (songwriter collection), 1118
Shore, Howard
  Naked Lunch [2003] (Coleman and Shore), 1053.1
  Naked Lunch [2005] (Coleman and Shore), 1053.2
Short, Bobby
  Cole Porter (songwriter collection), 1108.1
  E. Y. Harburg (songwriter collection), 1103
  George Gershwin (songwriter collection), 1101.3
  Harold Arlen (songwriter collection), 1095.1

  Jerome Kern (songwriter collection), 1104.1
  Live at the Café Carlyle, 1223
  Rodgers / Hart (songwriter collection), 1109.1
Shorter, Wayne
  Adam's Apple, 700.1
  Icons among Us (collection), 934
  Night Dreamer, 700.2
  Wayne Shorter: Jazz Classics, 658
  Wayne Shorter Live at Montreux 1996, 894
Show Tunes: The Songs, Shows, and Careers of Broadway's Major Composers (Suskin), 3
Showmen. *Finger Poppin' and Stompin' Feet: 20 Classic Allen Toussaint Productions for Minit Records, 1960–1962* (collection), 2359
Shy Guy Douglas
  ★*Nashville Jumps: Blues and Rhythm on Nashville Independent Labels 1945–1955* (collection), 2376
  Night Train to Nashville: Music City Rhythm and Blues, 1945–1970, Vol. 1 (collection), 2377
  Southern Rhythm 'n' Rock: The Best of Excello Records, Vol. 22 (collection), 2427
Silber, Irwin. *Score of the Civil War*, 79
Silberry, Jane. *When I Was a Boy*, 2060
The Silhouettes
  Best of Doo Wop Uptempo (collection), 1744
  Casey Kasem Presents America's Top Ten through the Years: The Doo-Wop Years, 1950s (collection), 1155
  ★*The Doo Wop Box: 101 Vocal Group Gems from the Golden Age of Rock 'n' Roll* (collection), 1745
  ★*The Doo-Wop Box* (collection), 2322
  Street Corner Serenade: The Greatest Doo-Wop Hits of the '50s and '60s (collection), 1756
Silver Apples. *Silver Apples*, 1886
Silver Convention. *Disco Box* (collection), 2644
Silver Harpes. *This May Be My Last Time Singing: Raw African- American Gospel on 45rpm* (collection), 2982
Silver, Horace
  ★*The Best of Horace Silver, Vol. 1*, 659.1
  ★*The Best of Horace Silver, Vol. 2*, 659.2
  Horace Silver, 659.3
  ★*Ken Burns Jazz: The Story of America's Music* (collection), 478
  Piano Legends (collection), 480
  ★*The Smithsonian Collection of Classic Jazz* (collection), 486
Silver Kings. *Boddie Recording Company Cleveland, Ohio* (collection), 2569, 2570

★Silver Leaf Quartet. *A Warrior on the Battlefield: A Cappella Trail Blazers* (collection), 3011

Silver Mt. Zion. *Born into Trouble as the Sparks Fly Upward.,* 2238

Silverman, Jerry. *Score of the Civil War,* 79

Silvertone Quintet. *Powerhouse Gospel on Independent Labels* (collection), 3038

Silvertone Singers. *The Mercury New Orleans Sessions 1950 and 1953* (collection), 2361

Simmons, Gene. *The Hi Records Story* (collection), 2423

★Simmons, Jumpin' Gene. *Halloween Hits* (collection), 3347

★Simms, Ginny. *Sophisticated Ladies* (collection), 1087

Simms Twins. *Sam Cooke's* SAR Records Story (collection), 2606

Simon and Garfunkel
  Bridge over Troubled Water, 1826.1
  ★*Greatest Hits,* 1826.2

Simon, Carly
  The Best of Carly Simon, 1896
  Billboard #1s: The '70s (collection), 1235
  Have a Nice Decade: The '70s Pop Culture Box (collection), 1240

Simon, Joe
  Beg, Scream, and Shout! The Big Ol' Box of '60s Soul (collection), 2433
  The Chokin' Kind: Golden Classics, 2515.1
  Greatest Hits: The Spring Years, 1970–1977, 2515.2
  ★*Love Train: The Sound of Philadelphia* (collection), 2552
  Night Train to Nashville: Music City Rhythm and Blues, 1945–1970, Vol. 1 (collection), 2377
  Night Train to Nashville: Music City Rhythm and Blues, 1945–1970, Vol. 2 (collection), 2378
  The Spring Story: Essential 70s Soul (collection), 2608
  ★*The Vee-Jay Story: Celebrating 40 Years of Classic Hits* (collection), 2431

Simon, Paul. *See also* Simon and Garfunkel
  The Essential Paul Simon, 1897.1
  Graceland, 2084
  Negotiations and Love Songs, 1897.2

Simon, Pazuzza. *The Big Horn: The History of the Honkin' and Screamin' Saxophone* (collection), 2314

Simone, Nina
  Anthology, 1302
  ★*The Jazz Singers: A Smithsonian Collection of Jazz Vocals from 1919–1994* (collection), 766

Nina Simone Live in '65 and '68, 801
  Respect: Aretha's Influences and Inspiration (collection), 2440
  The Sweetest Feeling: A Van McCoy Songbook (collection), 2447

Simply Red. *Heaven Must Have Sent You: The Holland/Dozier/Holland Story* (collection), 2436

★Sims, Frankie Lee. *Texas Music, Vol. 1: Postwar Blues Combos* (collection), 316

Sims, Gerald. *Birth of Soul: Special Chicago Edition* (collection), 2566

Sims, Zoot
  If I'm Lucky, 895
  The Jack Kerouac Collection (collection), 812

Sinatra, Frank
  Alec Wilder (songwriter collection), 1117.1
  ★*American Popular Song: Six Decades of Songwriters and Singers* (collection), 1059
  ★*Best of the Capitol Years,* 1224.1
  The Classic Hoagy Carmichael (songwriter collection), 1097.1
  Come Fly with Me, 1224.2
  ★*The Crooners* (collection), 1062
  Duke Ellington (songwriter collection), 1099.1
  E. Y. Harburg (songwriter collection), 1103
  Frank Sinatra: Concert Collection, 1224.3
  Frank Sinatra Sings for Only the Lonely, 1224.4
  Hoagy Carmichael (songwriter collection), 1097.2
  In the Wee Small Hours, 1224.5
  James Van Heusen (songwriter collection), 1112.1
  ★*The Jazz Singers: A Smithsonian Collection of Jazz Vocals from 1919–1994* (collection), 766
  Jerome Kern (songwriter collection), 1104.1
  Jule Styne (songwriter collection), 1111.1
  The Legendary Crooners: Frank Sinatra, Dean Martin, Bing Crosby, Nat King Cole, Perry Como (collection), 1207
  A Man and His Music, 1224.6
  Nice 'n' Easy, 1224.7
  ★*Nipper's Greatest Hits: The 40's, Vol. 1* (collection), 1073
  Sentimental Journey: Pop Vocal Classics, Vol. 1 (collection), 1167
  ★*Sentimental Journey: Pop Vocal Classics, Vol. 1* (collection), 1081
  ★*Songs for Swingin' Lovers,* 1224.8
  Songs for Young Lovers / Swing Easy, 1224.9

Songs That Got Us through World War II (collection), 1085
  The Sinatra Christmas Album, 3340
  25 Sweethearts of Yesteryear (collection), 1092
  ★*The Very Good Years,* 1224.10
  Vincent Youmans (songwriter collection), 1118
  The Voice in Time: 1939–1952, 1224.11

Sinatra, Nancy. *Frank Sinatra: Concert Collection,* 1224.3

Singer, Hal
  ★*Stompin' at the Savoy: The Original Indie Label, 1944–1961* (collection), 2429
  The Big Horn: The History of the Honkin' and Screamin' Saxophone (collection), 2314

singers, jazz. *See* jazz singers

Singers Unlimited. *Jazz Lullaby* (collection), 3264

singer-songwriters, 1891–1900
  ★*Astral Weeks* (Morrison), 1894.1
  The Best of Carly Simon, 1896
  Blue (Mitchell), 1893.1
  ★*Court and Spark* (Mitchell), 1893.2
  The Essential Paul Simon, 1897.1
  Ghost Writer / American Boy and Girl (Jeffreys), 1891
  Greatest Hits (Stevens), 1899
  Hijera (Mitchell), 1893.3
  James Taylor's Greatest Hits, 1900.1
  Moondance (Morrison), 1894.2
  Negotiations and Love Songs (Simon), 1897.2
  Stoned Soul Picnic: The Best of Laura Nyro, 1895
  ★*Sweet Baby James* (Taylor), 1900.2
  ★*Tapestry* (King), 1892
  Van Morrison Guitar Songbook, 1894.3
  The Very Best of Phoebe Snow, 1898

Singing Dogs. *Dr. Demento Presents: The Greatest Christmas Novelty CD of All Time* (collection), 3307

Singleton, Claude. *The Big Horn: The History of the Honkin' and Screamin' Saxophone* (collection), 2314

Siouxsie and the Banshees
  No Thanks! The '70s Punk Rebellion (collection), 2003
  Once upon a Time: The Singles, 2025
  Punk: Attitude (collection), 1980

Sir Douglas Quintet. *Texas Music, Vol. 3: Garage Bands and Psychedelia* (collection), 1830

Sister Sledge
  The Best of Sister Sledge (1973–1985), 2652
  Complete Introduction to Disco (collection), 1237
  Disco Box (collection), 2644

Six Brown Brothers. *I'll Dance Till de Sun Breaks Through: Ragtime, Cakewalks and Stomps,* 133

Size, Roni, and Reprazement. *New Forms,* 2230

Skaggs, Ricky
Blue Ribbon Bluegrass (collection), 1563
Grand Ole Opry at Carnegie Hall (collection), 1619
Hand-Picked: 25 Years of Bluegrass on Rounder Records (collection), 1564
Top of the Hill Bluegrass (collection), 1567
Waitin' for the Sun to Shine / Highways and Heartaches, 1676

Skerik. *Icons among Us* (collection), 934

Skiera-Zucek, Lois. *Songs about Native Americans,* 3235

The Skyliners
★*Atlantic Vocal Groups, 1951–1963* (collection), 2320
★*The Doo Wop Box: 101 Vocal Group Gems from the Golden Age of Rock 'n' Roll* (collection), 1745
★*The Doo-Wop Box* (collection), 2322
The Doo-Wop Box II (collection), 2323

Slack, Freddy. *Songs That Got Us through World War II, Vol. 2* (collection), 1086

Slayer. *Reign in Blood,* 2184

Sleater-Kinney
Call the Doctor, 2185.1
Dig Me Out, 2185.2
The Hot Rock, 2185.3

Sledge, Percy
★*Atlantic Soul, 1959–1975* (collection), 2589
★*The Atlantic Recordings,* 2516.1
Beg, Scream, and Shout! The Big Ol' Box of '60s Soul (collection), 2433
It Tears Me Up: The Best of Percy Sledge, 2516.2
Muscle Shoals Sound (collection), 2605
★*The R&B Box* (collection), 2239

Sleepwalkers. *Eccentric Soul: The Big Mack Label* (collection), 2598

Slick Rick. *The Great Adventures of Slick Rick,* 2919

Slick, Sly, and Wounded. *Gimme Your Hand, J-B!* (collection), 2613

Slint
Spiderland, 2186.1
Tweez, 2186.2

The Slits
Cut, 2026, 2037
No Thanks! The '70s Punk Rebellion (collection), 2003
Punk: Attitude (collection), 1980

Sly and the Family Stone
Complete Introduction to Disco (collection), 1237

The Essential Sly and the Family Stone, 1846.1, 2640.1
Greatest Hits, 2640.2
★*Greatest Hits,* 1846.2
San Francisco Nights (collection), 1829
★*Stand!,* 2640.3
There's a Riot Goin' On, 2640.4

Small Faces
The British Invasion (collection), 1788
★*Nuggets II: Original Artifacts from the British Empire and Beyond* (collection), 1791
25 Hits from the British Invasion (collection), 1792

Small Paul. *Eccentric Soul: Mighty Mike Lenaburg* (collection), 2563

Smallwood, Richard. *The Praise and Worship Songs of Richard Smallwood,* 3097

Smart, Gary. *American Beauty: A Ragtime Bouquet,* 142

Smashing Pumpkins. *Siamese Dream,* 2187

Smeck, Roy. *With My Little Ukulele in My Hand* (collection), 1093

Smif-n-Wessun. *Dah Shinin',* 2920

Smiley, Red
Don Reno and Red Smiley and the Tennessee Cut–Ups, 1959–1963, 1602.1
Sweethearts in Heaven: The Complete Dot Recordings 1957–1964, 1602.2

Smith, Arthur "Guitar Boogie." *Here Comes the Boogie Man,* 1537

Smith, Bessie
★*American Popular Song: Six Decades of Songwriters and Singers* (collection), 1059
★*At the Jazz Band Ball: Early Hot Jazz, Song, and Dance* (collection), 470
Bessie Smith Songbook, 210.1
Blues Masters, Vol. 11: Classic Blues Women (collection), 203
★*The Blues: A Smithsonian Collection of Classic Blues Singers* (collection), 145
The Complete Recordings, Vols. 1–5, 210.2
The Complete Recordings, Vols. 1–8, 210.3
Empress of the Blues, Vol. 2, 210.4
★*The Essential Bessie Smith,* 210.5
A First-Time Buyer's Guide to American Negro Spirituals (collection), 32
★*The Jazz Singers: A Smithsonian Collection of Jazz Vocals from 1919–1994* (collection), 766
★*Ken Burns Jazz: The Story of America's Music* (collection), 478
★*Legends of the Blues, Vol. 1* (collection), 150
News and the Blues: Telling It Like It Is (collection), 156
Queen of the Blues, Vol. 1, 210.6

★*The Smithsonian Collection of Classic Jazz* (collection), 486
Stars of the Apollo (collection), 2240
★*The Story of the Blues* (collection), 158

Smith, Carl. *The Essential Carl Smith,* 1538

Smith, Clara
★*I Can't Be Satisfied: Early American Women Blues Singers, Vol. 2: Town* (collection), 204
★*Let's Get Loose: Folk and Popular Blues Styles from the Beginning to the Early 1940s* (collection), 152

Smith College Glee Club. *Music of the Shakers,* 23

Smith, Connie. *The Essential Connie Smith,* 1539

Smith, Doug. *Sunday Morning Coffee* (collection), 1375

Smith, Elliott
Either/Or, 2188.1
Elliott Smith, 2188.2

Smith, Eugene
★*All God's Sons and Daughters: Chicago's Gospel Legends* (collection), 3030
The Great Gospel Men (collection), 2988

Smith, Fiddlin' Arthur. *Fiddlin' Arthur Smith and His Dixieliners,* 1423

Smith, Helene
Eccentric Soul: The Deep City Label (collection), 2600
Eccentric Soul: The Outskirts of Deep City (collection), 2565

Smith, Huey "Piano"
Best of Ace Records, Vol. 2: The R&B Hits (collection), 2419
Crescent City Soul: The Sound of New Orleans, 1947–1974 (collection), 2564
Having a Good Time with Huey "Piano" Smith and His Clowns, 2372
★*The R&B Box* (collection), 2239

Smith, Jabbo. *Jabbo Smith, 1929–1938,* 518

★Smith, Jack. *Yes, Sir, That's My Baby: The Golden Years of Tin Pan Alley* (collection), 1094

Smith, Jimmy
Best of the Blue Note Years, 660.1
Jimmy Smith Live in '69, 660.2
Walk on the Wild Side: Best of the Verve Years, 660.3

Smith, Johnny. *Moonlight in Vermont,* 623

Smith, Kate
The Classic Hoagy Carmichael (songwriter collection), 1097.1
Essential Collection: God Bless America, 1149
Flappers, Vamps, and Sweet Young Things (collection), 1065

Smith, Kate (cont.)
Irving Berlin (songwriter collection),
1096.1
Jerome Kern (songwriter collection),
1104.1
★Nipper's Greatest Hits: The 30's, Vol. 1
(collection), 1072
Richard Whiting (songwriter
collection), 1116
Smith, Keely. Sweet and Lovely: Capitol's
Great Ladies of Song (collection),
1172
Smith, Mabel Louise. See Big Maybelle
Smith, Mamie
Blues Masters, Vol. 11: Classic Blues
Women (collection), 203
Stars of the Apollo (collection), 2240
Smith, Marvin. The Story of Brunswick:
The Classic Sound of Chicago Soul
(collection), 2610
Smith, Michael W.
CCM Top 100: Greatest Songs in
Christian Music, Vol. 1 (collection),
3136
The First Decade, 3161.1
The Second Decade, 3161.2
Smith, O. C. The Very Best of O. C. Smith,
2517
Smith, Patti
★Horses, 1997
No Thanks! The '70s Punk Rebellion
(collection), 2003
Punk: Attitude (collection), 1980
The Tomorrow Show with Tom Snyder:
Punk and New Wave (collection),
1981
Smith, Pine Top. Shake Your Wicked
Knees: Rent Parties and Good Times
(collection), 258
Smith, Roger. The Early Minstrel Show
(collection), 96
Smith, Ruby. Stars of the Apollo
(collection), 2240
Smith, Sam. In the Lonely Hour, 1303
Smith, Six Cylinder. See Taggart, Blind
Joe
Smith, Trevor George, Jr. See Busta Rhymes
Smith, Trixie. Blues Masters, Vol. 11:
Classic Blues Women (collection),
203
Smith, Utah. Fire in My Bones: Raw, Rare
and Otherworldy African-American
Gospel (collection), 2960
Smith, (Wadada) Leo. Kabell Years, 931
★Smith, Walter "Tang." Nashville Jumps:
Blues and Rhythm on Nashville
Independent Labels 1945–1955
(collection), 2376
Smith, Warren. Sun Rockabilly: The
Classic Recordings (collection),
1742
Smith, Whispering Jack. The Roaring
'Twenties (collection), 1080

Smith, Will
Big Willie Style, 2921
90's Pop Hits (collection), 1242
Smith, Willie Mae Ford
★The Great Gospel Women (collection),
2989
Mother Smith and Her Children
(collection), 2991
★Say Amen, Somebody (collection),
2971
Smith, Willie "The Lion"
★The Commodore Story (collection),
561
The Lion and the Lamb (Smith), 525
Piano Legends (collection), 480
Smith, Wilson "Thunder." Texas Blues:
Bill Quinn's Gold Star Recordings
(collection), 314
Smithrim, Katharine. Songs and Games for
Toddlers, 3188
★The Smiths. Best, Vol. 1, 2189
★Smokey Hogg. Nashville Jumps:
Blues and Rhythm on Nashville
Independent Labels 1945–1955
(collection), 2376
Snoop Dogg
★Doggystyle, 2922.2
The Emancipation of Mimi (Carey),
1256.1
Tha Doggfather, 2922.1
Snow, Hank
Classic Country: Kings of Country
(collection), 1381
The Essential Hank Snow, 1540
Snow Patrol. Colours Are Brighter: Songs
for Children and Grown Ups Too
(collection), 3193
Snow, Phoebe. The Very Best of Phoebe
Snow, 1898
Social Distortion. Whatever: The '90s Pop
and Culture Box (collection), 1244
Soft Boys. No Thanks! The '70s Punk
Rebellion (collection), 2003
Soft Machine
Man in a Deaf Corner: Anthology,
1963–1970, 1967.1
Third, 1967.2
Sokoloff, Alan. Don't Give the Name
a Bad Place: Types and Stereotypes
in American Musical Theater,
1870–1900 (collection), 1063
Sokolow, Fred
Chanukah at Home (collection), 3238
Electric Blues Guitar Giants (Sokolow
and Schiff), 362
Stevie Ray Vaughan, Lightnin' Blues,
1983–1987 (Vaughan, Tapella,
Sokolow and Schiff), 383
Solaar, MC. Prose Combat, 2865
Solal, Martial. Bluesine, 862
The Solitaires
Old Town Doo-Wop, Vols. 1–3
(collection), 2324

★The Doo-Wop Box (collection), 2322
The Doo-Wop Box II (collection), 2323
solo instrumental (new age), 1346–1353
★Aerial Boundaries (Hedges), 1348
Alex de Grassi: A Windham Hill
Retrospective (De Grassi), 1347
★Autumn: 20th Anniversary Edition
(Winston), 1353.1
Cristofori's Dream (Lanz), 1350
December: 20th Anniversary Edition
(Winston), 1353.3
Echo Canyon (Newton), 1351
High Plains (Aaberg), 1346
Narada Guitar Sampler (Tingstad),
1352.1
Pastorale: Music of Nature and Grace
(Tingstad), 1352.2
Piano Solos (Winston), 1353.2
Pianoscapes: Deluxe Edition (Jones),
1349.1
Solos and Sketches for New Age Piano
(Jones), 1349.2
songsters, string bands, and jug bands,
183–201
Before the Blues: The Early American
Black Music Scene; Classic
Recordings from the 1920's and
30's, Vols. 1–3 (collection), 183
collections, 183–192
Good for What Ails You: Music of the
Medicine Shows (collection), 184
Harmonica Blues: Great Harmonica
Performances of the 1920s and '30s
(collection), 185
Memphis Shakedown: More Jug Band
Classics (collection), 186
A Richer Tradition: Country Blues and
String Band Music (collection), 187
songwriter collections
post-1967 mainstream popular,
1245–1247
post-World War II through 1967
mainstream popular, 1173–1175
pre-World War II mainstream
popular, 1095–1118
songwriter-singers. See singer-songwriters
Sonic Realm. Halloween Horrorscape, 3351
Sonic Youth
Bad Moon Rising, 2190.1
Corporate Ghost: The Videos,
1990–2002, 2190.2
Daydream Nation, 2190.3
Sister, 2190.4
Sonny and Cher
Casey Kasem Presents America's Top
Ten through the Years: The Sixties
(collection), 1156
The Beat Goes On: The Best of Sonny
and Cher, 1827
Sons of Blues
Living Chicago Blues, Vol. 3
(collection), 417
The New Bluebloods (collection), 419

Sons of the Pioneers
    *Classic Country Music: A Smithsonian
        Collection* (collection), 1382
    *Sons of the Pioneers: Country Music
        Hall of Fame,* 1424.1
    Ultimate Collection, 1424.2
Sotomayor, Rene Francisco. *See* T-Bone
soul
    Advanced Funk Studies (Latham), 2493
    All-Time Greatest Hits (White), 2529.1
    Anthology (Womack), 2533.1
    ★*The Anthology* (Mayfield), 2497.1
    Aretha Franklin: Queen of Soul, 2473.1
    Aretha, the Queen of Soul (Franklin),
        2473.2
    At the Close of a Century (Wonder),
        2534.1
    Atlantic Soul Classics (collection),
        2432
    ★*The Atlantic Recordings* (Sledge),
        2516.1
    *Beg, Scream, and Shout! The Big Ol'
        Box of '60s Soul* (collection), 2433
    Best of Jimmy Hughes, 2484.1
    Best of the Friends of Distinction
        (Franklin), 2475
    The Best of Al Green, 2477.1
    *The Best of Bobby Womack: The Soul
        Years,* 2533.2
    *The Best of Clarence Carter: The Dr.'s
        Greatest Prescriptions,* 2462.1
    The Best of Jerry Butler, 2460.1
    The Best of the Bar-Kays, 2450
    The Best of Thelma Houston, 2483
    The Best of William Bell, 2452.1
    The Best Soul Songs Ever, 2454
    Betty Padgett, 2499
    The Big Book of Motown, 2455
    The Big Book of Soul, 2456
    Birth of Soul, 4 Vols. (collection), 2434
    blues, 2587
    The Bravest Man in the Universe
        (Womack), 2533.3
    *Brenda Holloway: Greatest Hits and
        Rare Classics,* 2482
    Call Me (Green), 2477.2
    A Change Is Gonna Come (Burke),
        2459.1
    Chicago soul, 2566–2568
    The Chokin' Kind: Golden Classics
        (Simon), 2515.1
    *Come On and See Me: The Complete
        Solo Collection* (Terrell), 2521
    ★*Complete Mythology* (Johnson),
        2488.1
    Complete Otis Clay on Hi Records, 2466
    *The Complete Ann Peebles on Hi
        Records, Vols. 1 and 2,* 2500
    *The Complete Country and Western
        Recordings, 1959–1986* (Charles),
        2463.1
    The Complete Goldwax Singles (Carr),
        2461

    *The Complete O. V. Wright on Hi Records,
        Vol. 1: In the Studio,* 2536.1
    *The Complete O. V. Wright on Hi
        Records, Vol. 2: On Stage (Live in
        Japan),* 2536.2
    *The Complete Syl Johnson on Hi
        Records,* 2488.2
    contemporary, 2582–2584
    *Cowboys to Girls: The Best of the
        Intruders,* 2486
    Cry Baby: The Best of Garnet Mimms,
        2498
    Curtis Mayfield Live at Montreux, 1987,
        2497.3
    The Curtis Mayfield Guitar Songbook,
        2497.2
    *Dave Godin's Deep Soul Treasures,
        Vols. 1–4* (collection), 2435
    The Definitive Collection (Richie), 2507
    The Definitive Collection (Ross), 2509.2
    The Definitive Collection (Wonder),
        2534.2
    The Definitive Greatest Hits (Green),
        2477.3
    ★*The Definitive Soul Collection* (Sam
        and Dave), 2514.1
    *Diana Ross Live: Stolen Moments—The
        Lady Sings . . . Jazz and Blues,*
        2509.1
    *The Dionne Warwick Collection: Her
        All-Time Greatest Hits,* 2526.1
    Do Right Man (Penn), 2502
    Do Your Duty (Lavette), 2494.1
    The Dock of the Bay (Redding), 2506.1
    A Donny Hathaway Collection, 2478.1
    Don't Give Up on Me (Burke), 2459.2
    *Don't Sell Your Soul: The Complete
        Story of Mike* (Kirkland), 2492
    The Down Home Soul of Z. Z. Hill, 2480
    *Dreams to Remember: The Legacy of
        Otis Redding,* 2506.2
    *Dreams to Remember: The Otis Redding
        Anthology,* 2506.3
    Encouraging Words (Preston), 2504.1
    The Essential Lou Rawls, 2505.1
    The Essential Teddy Pendergrass, 2501.1
    *Everybody Plays the Fool: The Best of
        Main Ingredient,* 2495
    ★*Everything Is Everything* (Hathaway),
        2478.2
    Extensions of a Man (Hathaway),
        2478.3
    First Take (Flack), 2472.1
    Forty Greatest Hits (Benton), 2453
    ★*Funky Midnight Mover: The Atlantic
        Studio Recordings* (Pickett), 2503.1
    general collections, 2432–2447
    general style, 2432–2537
    *Get It While You Can: The Complete
        Legendary Verve Sessions* (Tate),
        2519
    Gold (Gaye), 2476.1
    The Goldwax Years (Wiggins), 2530

    gospel, 2578–2581
    Greatest Hits (Redding), 2506.4
    *Greatest Hits: The Spring Years,
        1970–1977* (Simon), 2515.2
    *The Great David Ruffin: The Motown
        Solo Albums, Vol. 1,* 2510.1
    *The Great David Ruffin: The Motown
        Solo Albums, Vol. 2,* 2510.2
    *Heaven Must Have Sent You: The
        Holland/Dozier/Holland Story*
        (collection), 2436
    His Greatest Hits, Vols. 1 and 2
        (Charles), 2463.2
    ★*Home in Your Heart: The Best of
        Solomon Burke,* 2459.3
    ★*Hot Buttered Soul* (Hayes), 2479.1
    ★*I Never Loved a Man the Way I Loved
        You* (Franklin), 2473.3
    Iceman: The Mercury Years (Butler),
        2460.2
    *If Loving You Is Wrong, I Don't Want to
        Be Right: The Best of Luther Ingram,*
        2485
    *The Ike and Tina Turner Story,
        1960–1975,* 2523.2
    ★*The Immortal Soul of Al Green,*
        2477.4
    *In Concert Classics Featuring Dionne
        Warwick,* 2526.2
    *In Memphis, 1972–77: The Sounds
        of Memphis and Xl Recordings*
        (Jackson), 2487
    ★*Innervisions* (Wonder), 2534.3
    instrumental and soundtracks,
        2571–2577
    Isaac Hayes: Live at Montreux, 2005,
        2479.2
    It Tears Me Up: The Best of Percy
        Sledge, 2516.2
    I've Got My Own Hell to Raise
        (Lavette), 2494.2
    *The Jazz Channel Presents Bobby
        Womack,* 2533.4
    The Jazz Channel Presents Lou Rawls,
        2505.2
    ★*Just for You* (White), 2529.2
    *Keep What You Get: The Rare &
        Unissued Ronn Recordings* (Taylor),
        2520
    label overview, 2588–2612
    ★*Lady Soul* (Franklin), 2473.4
    *Let the Music Play: The Barry White
        Story,* 2529.3
    Let's Get It On (Gaye), 2476.2
    Let's Stay Together (Green), 2477.5
    Live at Fillmore West (Franklin),
        2473.5
    ★*Live at the Apollo* (Brown), 2457.1
    Live at the Apollo, Vol. 2 (Brown),
        2457.2
    Live at the Garden (Brown), 2457.3
    Live at the Montreux Jazz Festival
        (Charles), 2463.3

soul (cont.)

Live on the Sunset Strip (Redding), 2506.5

Lonely Just Like Me: The Final Chapter (Alexander), 2448.1

A Man and a Half: The Best of Wilson Pickett, 2503.2

A Man and His Soul (Charles), 2463.4

★*The Man Who Invented Soul* (Cooke), 2468.1

Marvin Gaye: Behind the Legend, 2476.3

Marvin Gaye—The Real Thing: In Performance, 1964–1981, 2476.4

★*The Master, 1961–1984* (Gaye), 2476.5

Memphis soul, 2560–2561

Mercy, Mercy! The Definitive Don Covay, 2469

Motown around the World (collection), 2437

Motown 45th Anniversary Songbook (collection), 2438

Motown's First: The Ultimate Selection of Soul (collection), 2439

The Motown Anthology (Ross), 2509.3

The Motown Solo Albums, Vol. 1: Keep on Truckin' (Kendricks), 2490.1

The Motown Solo Albums, Vol. 2: The Thin Man (Kendricks), 2490.2

★*Mr. Excitement!* (Wilson), 2531.1

Nashville (Burke), 2459.4

neo-soul, 2379–2387, 2585–2586

O-Genio Ray Charles, 1963: Live in Brazil, 2463.5

100 Days, 100 Nights (Jones), 2489

One More Time: The Chess Years (Stewart), 2518

One Night Stand: Sam Cooke Live at the Harlem Square Club, 1963, 2468.2

The Original Musiquarium I (Wonder), 2534.4

The Original Soul Men (Sam and Dave), 2514.2

Otis Blue: Otis Redding Sings Soul, 2506.7

★*Otis! The Definitive Otis Redding,* 2506.6

The Otis Redding Dictionary of Soul: Complete and Unbelievable, 2506.8

periodicals for up-to-date CD notices and reviews, suggested, p3

Philadelphia soul, 2552–2558

Piece of Her Heart: The Epic and Shout Years (Franklin), 2474

The Platinum Collection (Conley), 2467

The Platinum Collection (Wright), 2535

Portrait of a Legend (Cooke), 2468.3

Proud Mary: The Best of Ike and Tina Turner, 2523.1

★*Pure Genius: The Complete Atlantic Recordings, 1952–1959* (Charles), 2463.6

Rainbow Road: The Warner Brothers Recordings (Alexander), 2448.2

regional styles, 2552–2570

Rescued: The Best of Fontella Bass, 2451

Respect: Aretha's Influences and Inspiration (collection), 2440

Respect Yourself: The Stax Records Story (collection), 2441

★*Roots of a Revolution* (Brown), 2457.4

Sam Cooke, Legend, 2468.4

Shaft (Hayes), 2479.3

Simply the Best (Turner), 2524

Singles A's and B's, Vol. 1: 1960–1964 (Tex), 2522.1

Singles A's and B's, Vol. 2: 1967–1968 (Tex), 2522.2

Singles A's and B's, Vol. 3: 1969–1972 (Tex), 2522.3

Singles A's and B's, Vol. 4: 1973–1976 (Tex), 2522.4

The Singles, Vol. 2: 1960–1963 (Brown), 2457.6

The Singles, Vol. 3: 1964–1965 (Brown), 2457.7

The Singles, Vol. 4: 1966–1967 (Brown), 2457.8

The Singles, Vol. 5: 1967–1969 (Brown), 2457.9

The Singles, Vol. 6: 1969–1970 (Brown), 2457.10

The Singles, Vol. 7: 1970–1972 (Brown), 2457.11

The Singles, Vol. 8: 1972–1973 (Brown), 2457.12

The Singles, Vol. 9: 1973–1975 (Brown), 2457.13

The Singles, Vol. 10: 1975–1979 (Brown), 2457.14

The Singles, Vol. 11: 1979–1981 (Brown), 2457.15

The Singles, Vol. 1: The Federal Years, 1956–1960 (Brown), 2457.5

Singular Genius: The Complete ABC Singles (Charles), 2463.7

Snatchin' It Back: The Best of Clarence Carter, 2462.2

Solo Anthology (Robinson), 2508.2

The Solo Albums, Vol. 2 (Robinson), 2508.1

Something Extra Special: The Complete Volt Recordings 1968–1971 (Hughes), 2484.2

★*Songs in the Key of Life* (Wonder), 2534.5

Soul Alive! (Burke), 2459.5

Soul Classics (collection), 2442

Soul Shots: A Collection of Sixties Soul Classics (collection), 2443

Soul to Soul (collection), 2444

The Soul of a Bell (Bell), 2452.2

The Soul of O. V. Wright, 2536.3

Spirit in the Dark (Franklin), 2473.6

Standing in the Shadows of Motown (collection), 2445

Star Time (Brown), 2457.16

Stax/Volt Revue: Live in Norway 1967 (collection), 2446

Steal Away: The Early Fame Recordings, Vol. 1 (Hughes), 2484.3

Stevie Wonder Anthology, 2534.6

Stone Rollin' (Saadiq), 2513.1

The Sweetest Feeling: A Van McCoy Songbook (collection), 2447

Take a Look: Complete on Columbia (Franklin), 2473.7

Talking Book (Wonder), 2534.7

Telling the Truth (Wright), 2537

These Songs for You, Live! (Hathaway), 2478.4

20 Greatest Hits (Chi-Lites), 2464

20 Greatest Hits (Davis), 2470

25 All-Time Greatest Hits (Brown), 2458

Ultimate Collection (Marvelettes), 2496

Ultimate Collection (Preston), 2504.2

Ultimate Soul Guitar Collection, 2525

The Ultimate Arthur Alexander, 2448.3

The Ultimate Collection (Kendricks), 2490.3

The Ultimate Collection (Ruffin), 2510.3

The Ultimate Collection (Wells), 2528

The Ultimate Isaac Hayes: Can You Dig It?, 2479.4

The Ultimate Motown Collection (Ruffin), 2511

Unforgettable: A Tribute to Dinah Washington (Franklin), 2473.8

Very Extremely Dangerous (Hinton), 2481

The Very Best of Ben E. King, 2491

The Very Best of Bill Withers, 2532

The Very Best of Curtis Mayfield, 2497.4

The Very Best of Isaac Hayes, 2479.5

The Very Best of Jackie Wilson, 2531.2

The Very Best of O. C. Smith, 2517

The Very Best of Patti Austin: The Singles, 1969–1986, 2449

The Very Best of Roberta Flack, 2472.2

The Very Best of Rufus, Featuring Chaka Khan, 2512

The Very Best of Sam and Dave, 2514.3

The Very Best of Teddy Pendergrass, 2501.2

The Very Best of Wilson Pickett, 2503.3

vocal groups, 2538–2551

Wattstax: 30th Anniversary Special Edition, 2527

The Way I See It (Saadiq), 2513.2

★*What's Going On* (Gaye), 2476.6

Who's Gonna Save the World (Father's Children), 2471

Why Not Tonight? The Fame Recordings, Vol. 2 (Hughes), 2484.4

You Can Run but You Can't Hide (Burke), 2459.6

Young, Gifted, and Black (Franklin), 2473.9

You're Looking Good / Hold On, It's Dee Clark, 2465

Soul Asylum. *Whatever: The '90s Pop and Culture Box* (collection), 1244

Soul, Billy "T." *The Sweetest Feeling: A Van McCoy Songbook* (collection), 2447

Soul Blenders. *Eccentric Soul: Mighty Mike Lenaburg* (collection), 2563

★Soul Brothers Six. *Atlantic Soul, 1959–1975* (collection), 2589

Soul Children
   Chronicle, 2548
   Top of the Stax, Vol. 1: Twenty Greatest Hits (collection), 2611
   Top of the Stax, Vol. 2: Twenty Greatest Hits (collection), 2612

Soul Ensemble. *Eccentric Soul: The Prix Label* (collection), 2601

Soul Expressions. *The Story of Brunswick: The Classic Sound of Chicago Soul* (collection), 2610

soul label overview
   Action Speaks Louder Than Words: The Best of SSS International (collection), 2588
   ★*Atlantic Soul, 1959–1975* (collection), 2589
   The Best of Loma Records: The Rise and Fall of a 1960's Soul Label (collection), 2590
   The Complete Goldwax Singles, Vol. 1 (collection), 2591
   The Complete Goldwax Singles, Vol. 2 (collection), 2592
   The Complete Goldwax Singles, Vol. 3 (collection), 2593
   The Complete Stax/Volt Singles 1959–1968 (collection), 2594
   The Complete Stax/Volt Soul Singles, Vol. 2: 1968–1971 (collection), 2595
   Crash of Thunder: Boss Soul, Funk, and R&B Sides from the Vaults of the King, Federal, and Deluxe Labels (collection), 2596
   Eccentric Soul: The Bandit Label (collection), 2597
   Eccentric Soul: The Big Mack Label (collection), 2598
   Eccentric Soul: The Capsoul Label (collection), 2599
   Eccentric Soul: The Deep City Label (collection), 2600
   Eccentric Soul: The Prix Label (collection), 2601
   Eccentric Soul: The Tragar and Note Labels (collection), 2602

Hitsville USA: The Motown Singles Collection (collection), 2603

Muscle Shoals Sound (collection), 2605

Sam Cooke's SAR Records Story, 1959–1965, 2607

Sam Cooke's SAR Records Story (collection), 2606

The Spring Story: Essential 70s Soul (collection), 2608

Stax/Volt Revue: Live in London, Vols. 1 and 2 (collection), 2609

The Story of Brunswick: The Classic Sound of Chicago Soul (collection), 2610

Top of the Stax, Vol. 1: Twenty Greatest Hits (collection), 2611

Top of the Stax, Vol. 2: Twenty Greatest Hits (collection), 2612

Soul President. *Eccentric Soul: The Big Mack Label* (collection), 2598

Soul Satisfiers of Philadelphia. *Powerhouse Gospel on Independent Labels* (collection), 3038

The Soul Stirrers
   All of My Appointed Time: Forty Years of a Cappella Gospel Singing (collection), 2958
   ★*Good News: 100 Gospel Greats* (collection), 2961
   ★*The Gospel Sound of Spirit Feel* (collection), 2965
   Greatest Gospel Gems (collection), 3035
   The Great 1955 Shrine Concert (collection), 3034
   ★*Jubilation! Great Gospel Performances, Vol. 1: Black Gospel* (collection), 2966
   ★*Jubilation! Great Gospel Performances, Vol. 2: More Black Gospel* (collection), 2967
   Kings of the Gospel Highway: The Golden Age of Gospel Quartets (collection), 3009
   Living Legends of Gospel: The Quartets, Vols. 1 and 2 (collection), 3010
   None but the Righteous: Chess Gospel Greats (collection), 3037
   ★*Sam Cooke with the Soul Stirrers: The Complete Specialty Records Recordings,* 3025.1
   Sam Cooke's SAR Records Story (collection), 2606
   Shine on Me, 3025.2
   ★*The Specialty Story* (collection), 2428

★Soul Survivors. *Love Train: The Sound of Philadelphia* (collection), 2552

soul vocal groups
   ★*Anthology* (Temptations), 2551.1
   Best of the Isley Brothers, 2542.1
   The Best of the Pointer Sisters, 2544.1
   Chronicle (Soul Children), 2548
   Definitive Performances, 1963–1987

(Smokey Robinson and the Miracles), 2545.1

The Definitive Soul Collection (Spinners), 2549.1

Emperors of Soul (Temptations), 2551.2

Essential Collection (Gladys Knight and the Pips), 2541.1

★*50th Anniversary: The Singles Collection, 1961–1971* (Four Tops), 2539

50th Anniversary: The Singles Collection, 1961–1969 (Ross), 2546

Get Ready: Definitive Performances, 1965–1972 (Temptations), 2551.3

Gladys Knight and the Pips and Ray Charles Live at the Greek Theatre, 2541.2

Gold (Gladys Knight and the Pips), 2541.3

Gold (Martha Reeves and the Vandellas), 2543.1

★*Gold* (Ross), 2547.1

The Isleys Live, 2542.2

★*It's Your Thing: The Story of the Isley Brothers,* 2542.3

Magnificent: The Complete Studio Duets (Supremes), 2550.1

Meet the Supremes, 2550.2

Movin' On Up: The Music and Message of Curtis Mayfield and the Impressions, 2538

The No. 1's (Ross), 2547.2

Reach Out (Four Tops), 2540

Reflections: Definitive Performances, 1964–1969 (Supremes), 2550.3

35th Anniversary Collection (Smokey Robinson and the Miracles), 2545.2

3 + 3 (Isley Brothers), 2542.4

The Ultimate Collection (Martha Reeves and the Vandellas), 2543.2

★*The Ultimate Collection* (Smokey Robinson and the Miracles), 2545.3

The Ultimate Collection (Temptations), 2551.4

The Ultimate Isley Brothers, 2542.5

The Very Best of the Spinners, 2549.2

Yes We Can Can: The Best of the Blue Thumb Recordings (Pointer Sisters), 2544.2

Soulettes. *Boddie Recording Company Cleveland, Ohio* (collection), 2569, 2570

Souls of Mischief. *93 'til Infinity,* 2923

Soulsations. *Eccentric Soul: Mighty Mike Lenaburg* (collection), 2563

sound effects, 3382–3383
   Authentic Sound Effects, Vols. 1–3, 3382
   1000 Sound Effects, 3383

sound health music (new age), 1354

Sound Of Soul. *Boddie Recording Company Cleveland, Ohio* (collection), 2569, 2570

Soundgarden. *Superunknown*, 2191

Sounds of Blackness. *Testify! The Gospel Box* (collection), 2974

soundtracks
    disco, 2658
    rap and hip-hop, 2952–2953
    soul instrumental and soundtracks, 2571–2577

Sousa, John Philip
    A Grand Sousa Concert, 90.1
    Music for Wind Band, Vols. 1–15, 90.2
    The Original All-American Sousa!, 90.3
    Sousa Marches Recorded by the Sousa Bans, 90.4
    Sousa's Great Marches in Piano Transcription: Original Sheet Music of 23 Works, 90.5
    The United States Marine Band Performs Sousa Marches, 90.6

Sousa's Band
    Early Syncopated Dance Music: Cakewalks, Two-Steps, Trots and Glides (collection), 124
    I'll Dance Till de Sun Breaks Through: Ragtime, Cakewalks and Stomps, 133

South Georgia Highballers. *Old-Time Mountain Guitar* (collection), 1391

South Shore Commission. *Eccentric Soul: The Nickel and Penny Labels* (collection), 2567

South Suburban Electric Strings. *Eccentric Soul: The Nickel and Penny Labels* (collection), 2567

Southern, Jeri
    Alec Wilder (songwriter collection), 1117.1
    Cole Porter (songwriter collection), 1108.1
    E. Y. Harburg (songwriter collection), 1103
    Richard Whiting (songwriter collection), 1116
    The Very Best of Cole Porter (songwriter collection), 1108.3

Southern rock, 1934–1937
    All Time Greatest Hits (Lynyrd Skynyrd), 1936
    Anthology: The First 30 Years (Marshall Tucker Band), 1937
    Dreams (Allman Brothers), 1935.1
    ★*Live at Fillmore East* (Allman Brothers), 1935.2
    Southern Rock Gold (collection), 1934

Southern Sanctified Singers. *Spreading the Word: Early Gospel Recordings* (collection), 2972

Southern Sons
    Gospel: Negro Spirituals / Gospel Songs, 1926–1942 (collection), 2963
    I Hear Music in the Air: A Treasury of Gospel Music (collection), 3008

Testify! The Gospel Box (collection), 2974

southern white religious styles, 3106–3134
    All Time Favorites (Kingsmen), 3127
    Awake My Soul: The Story of the Sacred Harp (collection), 3106
    ★*The Blackwoods*, 3118
    Cathedral Classics (Cathedral Quartet), 3120
    Children of the Heav'nly King: Religious Expression in the Central Blue Ridge (collection), 3107
    Close Harmony: A History of Southern Gospel Music, Vol. 1 (collection), 3108
    Country Gospel Classics, Vol. 1 (Ford), 3123
    The Early Works (Gaithers), 3124
    Elvis Gospel 1957–1971: Known Only to Him (Presley), 3130.1
    Favorite Gospel Songs (West), 3134
    Favorite Sacred Songs (collection), 3109
    First Family of Gospel (Speer Family), 3131
    45 Songs of Faith (Florida Boys), 3122
    The Goodmans Greatest Hits (Happy Goodman Family), 3125
    The Gospel Music of Johnny Cash, 3119
    The Gospel Sessions (Oak Ridge Boys), 3128
    ★*The Gospel Ship: Baptist Hymns and White Spirituals from the Southern Mountains* (collection), 3110
    Hovie Lister and the Statesmen, 3132
    I Believe: The Gospel Masters (Presley), 3130.2
    I Belong to This Band: Eighty-Five Years of Sacred Harp Recordings (collection), 3111
    I'll Fly Away (Chuck Wagon Gang), 3121
    Jubilation! Great Gospel Performances, Vol. 3: Country Gospel (collection), 3112
    Mountain Gospel: The Sacred Roots of Country Music (collection), 3113
    Old Harp Singing (Old Harp Singers of Eastern Tennessee), 3129.1, 3129.2
    ★*Something Got a Hold of Me: A Treasury of Sacred Music* (collection), 3114
    Songs of the Faith (Isaacs), 3126
    Songs of the Old Regular Baptists: Lined-out Hymnody from Southeastern Kentucky (collection), 3115
    Southern Gospel's Top 20 Songs of the Century (collection), 3116
    Three Wooden Crosses: The Inspirational Hits of Randy Travis, 3133

White Spirituals from the Sacred Harp: The Alabama Sacred Harp Convention, 3117

Soxx, Bob B., and the Blue Jeans. *A Christmas Gift for You from Phil Spector* (collection), 3300

space music (new age), 1355–1358
    Deep Breakfast (Lynch), 1356
    Dreamtime Return (Roach), 1357
    Novus Magnificat (Demby), 1355
    ★*Stratosfear* (Tangerine Dream), 1358

Spalding, Esperanza
    Icons among Us (collection), 934
    Radio Music Society, 1015

Spand, Charlie
    Favorite Country Blues: Guitar-Piano Duets (collection), 267
    ★*Legends of the Blues, Vol. 2* (collection), 151

The Spaniels
    Best of Doo Wop Ballads (collection), 1743
    ★*The Doo Wop Box: 101 Vocal Group Gems from the Golden Age of Rock 'n' Roll* (collection), 1745
    ★*The Doo-Wop Box* (collection), 2322
    The Doo-Wop Box II (collection), 2323
    40th Anniversary, 1953–1993, 2358
    Life Could Be a Dream: The Doo-Wop Sound, 2346
    ★*The R&B Box* (collection), 2239
    ★*The Vee-Jay Story: Celebrating 40 Years of Classic Hits* (collection), 2431

Spanier, Muggsy. *Ragtime Band Sessions*, 585

Spann, Otis
    Conversation with the Blues (collection), 148
    Otis Spann Is the Blues, 264.1
    ★*The Story of the Blues* (collection), 158
    Walking the Blues, 264.2

Sparks Brothers. *Twenty First Street Stomp: Piano Blues of St. Louis* (collection), 259

Sparks, Larry
    Classic Bluegrass, 1608.1
    Last Suit You Wear, 1608.1

Spearhead. *Home*, 2924

Spears, Britney. *Oops! . . . I Did It Again*, 1304

special occasions
    overview, p185
    sport and college songs, 3369–3372
    weddings, 3355–3368

Specials. *The Specials*, 2027

Speckled Red
    Mama Don't Allow No Easy Riders Here: Strutting the Dozens; Classic Piano Rags, Blues, and Stomps (collection), 256

The Roots of Rap: Classic Recordings of the 1920's and 30's (collection), 157

When the Sun Goes Down 3: That's Chicago's South Side (collection), 270

Speer Family
Close Harmony: A History of Southern Gospel Music, Vol. 1 (collection), 3108
First Family of Gospel, 3131

The Spellbinders. *The Sweetest Feeling: A Van McCoy Songbook* (collection), 2447

Spellman, Benny
Birth of Soul, 4 Vols. (collection), 2434
Crescent City Soul: The Sound of New Orleans, 1947–1974 (collection), 2564
Finger Poppin' and Stompin' Feet: 20 Classic Allen Toussaint Productions for Minit Records, 1960–1962 (collection), 2359

Spencer Davis Group. *The Best of the Spencer Davis Group,* 1803

Spencer, Elvin. *Eccentric Soul: Twinight's Lunar Rotation* (collection), 2568

Spencer, Len. *Phono-Cylinders, Vols. 1 and 2* (collection), 1074

Spheeris, Chris. *The Best of Chris Spheeris, 1990–2000,* 1364

Spidells. *Night Train to Nashville: Music City Rhythm and Blues, 1945–1970, Vol. 2* (collection), 2378

Spin Doctors
90's Pop Hits (collection), 1242
Whatever: The '90s Pop and Culture Box (collection), 1244

The Spinners
★*Atlantic R&B, 1947–1974* (collection), 2418
★*Atlantic Soul, 1959–1975* (collection), 2589
The Definitive Soul Collection, 2549.1
★*Love Train: The Sound of Philadelphia* (collection), 2552
The Very Best of the Spinners, 2549.2

Spires, Arthur "Big Boy." *Drop Down Mama* (collection), 292

Spirit of Memphis
The Best of King Gospel (collection), 3031
★*The Gospel Sound of Spirit Feel* (collection), 2965
Happy in the Service of the Lord: Memphis Gospel Quartet Heritage, the 1980s, Vols. 1 and 2 (collection), 3007
Kings of the Gospel Highway: The Golden Age of Gospel Quartets (collection), 3009

Spirit. *Time Circle,* 1847

Spiritual Believers. *Boddie Recording Company Cleveland, Ohio* (collection), 2569, 2570

Spiritualaires of Columbia. *Powerhouse Gospel on Independent Labels* (collection), 3038

Spiritualized. *Ladies and Gentlemen We Are Floating in Space,* 2192

spirituals, 32–43
collection, 32
A First-Time Buyer's Guide to American Negro Spirituals (collection), 32
Give Me Jesus: Spirituals (Hendricks), 39
Let Me Fly: Music of Struggle, Solace and Survival in Black America (Counterpoint), 37
Negro Spirituals (Ragin), 43
Sisters of Freedom (Harlem Spiritual Ensemble), 38
Slave Songs of the United States: The Complete 1867 Collection of Slave Songs (Allen), 33
Songs of America (Moses), 41
Songs of the American Negro Slaves (Larue), 40
Spirituals (Anderson), 35
Spirituals for Solo Singers: 11 Spirituals Arranged for Solo Voice and Piano; for Recitals, Concerts and Contests (Althouse), 34
Spirituals for Solo Singers, Vol. 2: 10 Spirituals Arranged for Solo Voice and Piano; for Recitals, Concerts, and Contests (Beck), 36
Spirituals in Concert (Norman), 42

Spivey, Victoria
Better Boot That Thing: Great Women Blues Singers of the 1920's (collection), 202
Blues Masters, Vol. 11: Classic Blues Women (collection), 203
The Great Depression: American Music in the '30s (collection), 1066
★*I Can't Be Satisfied: Early American Women Blues Singers, Vol. 2: Town* (collection), 204
★*Legends of the Blues, Vol. 2* (collection), 151
News and the Blues: Telling It Like It Is (collection), 156
When the Sun Goes Down 2: The First Time I Met the Blues (collection), 160

Spoon. *Girls Can Tell,* 2193

Spoonie Gee. *The Best of* Enjoy! Records (collection), 2663

sport and college songs, 3369–3372
The Best of College Football Fight Songs (collection), 3370
College Fight Songs: An Anthology (Studwell and Schueneman), 3371
41 Great College Victory Songs (University of Michigan Band/Revelli), 3372

34 Hit Parade Extras: College Songs (collection), 3369

Springfield, Dusty
The British Invasion (collection), 1788
Dusty in Memphis, 1305, 2061
Heaven Must Have Sent You: The Holland/Dozier/Holland Story (collection), 2436
The Look of Love: The Burt Bacharach Collection (collection), 1161

Springfield, Rick. *Like Omigod! The 80s Pop Culture Box (Totally)* (collection), 1241

Springsteen Bruce
★*Born in the USA,* 2085.1
★*Born to Run,* 1919
The Essential Bruce Springsteen, 2085.2

Sprott, Horace. *Classic African American Gospel from Smithsonian Folkways* (collection), 2959

Spruill, Wild Jimmy. *The Fire / Fury Records Story* (collection), 2422

Spurling, Charles. *Crash of Thunder: Boss Soul, Funk, and R&B Sides from the Vaults of the King, Federal, and Deluxe Labels* (collection), 2596

Spyro Gyra. *The Very Best of Spyro Gyra,* 909

Squeeze. *Singles: 45s and under Remastered,* 2194

Squier, Billy. *Like Omigod! The 80s Pop Culture Box (Totally)* (collection), 1241

SSD. *American Hardcore* (collection), 1977

St. Louis blues. *See* Memphis and St. Louis blues

St. Luke COGIC Youth Choir. *Good God! Born Again Funk* (collection), 2614

Stacy, Jess
★*The Commodore Story* (collection), 561
Ec-Stacy: 25 Great Piano Performances, 586

Stafford, Jo
Alec Wilder (songwriter collection), 1117.1
★*American Popular Song: Six Decades of Songwriters and Singers* (collection), 1059
The Classic Hoagy Carmichael (songwriter collection), 1097.1
Duke Ellington (songwriter collection), 1099.1
The Flapper Box (collection), 1064
Harry Warren (songwriter collection), 1114
★*Jo Stafford,* 1225
Johnny Mercer (songwriter collection), 1107.1
Jule Styne (songwriter collection), 1111.1
Oscar Hammerstein II (songwriter collection), 1102

Stafford, Jo (cont.)
    ★Sentimental Journey: Pop Vocal
        Classics, Vol. 1 (collection), 1081
    ★Sentimental Journey: Pop Vocal
        Classics, Vol. 3 (collection), 1169
    Songs That Got Us through World
        War II (collection), 1085
    Songs That Got Us through World
        War II, Vol. 2 (collection), 1086
Stamps-Baxter Quartet. Close Harmony:
        A History of Southern Gospel Music,
        Vol. 1 (collection), 3108
Standells
    Nuggets: A Classic Collection from the
        Psychedelic Sixties (collection),
        1809
    ★Nuggets: Artifacts of the First
        Psychedelic Era (collection), 1808
Stanko, Tomasz. Balladyna, 863
The Stanley Brothers
    The Best of Bluegrass, Vol. 1: Standards
        (collection), 1561
    ★The Complete Columbia Stanley
        Brothers, 1609.1
    ★The Complete Mercury Recordings,
        1609.2
    Earliest Recordings: The Complete
        Rich-RTone 78s, 1609.3
    The Early Starday-King Years,
        1958–1961, 1609.4
    Riding That Midnight Train: The
        Starday-King Years, 1958–1961,
        1609.5
Stanley, Michael. Straight Outta Cleveland
        (collection), 1888
Stanley, Ralph
    Clinch Mountain Country, 1610.1
    Saturday Night; Sunday Morning, 1610.2
Staple, Mavis
    Rejoice and Shout (collection), 2969
    You Are Not Alone, 2581
The Staple Singers
    The Best of the Staple Singers, 2580
    The Best of the Vee-Jay Years, 3049.2
    The Complete Stax/Volt Soul Singles,
        Vol. 2: 1968–1971 (collection),
        2595
    Freedom Highway, 3049.1
    Good News: 22 Gospel Greats
        (collection), 3033
    ★The Gospel Sound (collection), 2964
    ★Jubilation! Great Gospel Performances,
        Vol. 2: More Black Gospel
        (collection), 2967
    Muscle Shoals Sound (collection),
        2605
    The Rough Guide to Gospel (collection),
        2970
    Soul to Soul (collection), 2444
    Testify! The Gospel Box (collection),
        2974
    Top of the Stax, Vol. 1: Twenty Greatest
        Hits (collection), 2611

Top of the Stax, Vol. 2: Twenty Greatest
        Hits (collection), 2612
The 25th Day of December, 3341
Stardusters. The Swing Time Records Story:
        R&B, Blues, and Gospel, 1946–1952
        (collection), 2430
Starlight Gospel Singers. Classic African
        American Gospel from Smithsonian
        Folkways (collection), 2959
Starlites. The Doo-Wop Box II (collection),
        2323
Starr, Edwin
    Beg, Scream, and Shout! The Big Ol'
        Box of '60s Soul (collection), 2433
    Disco Box (collection), 2644
    Hitsville USA: The Motown Singles
        Collection (collection), 2603
    Motown around the World (collection),
        2437
    Songs of Protest (collection), 1820
Starr, Kay
    Hit Parade, 1956 (collection), 1158
    Kay Starr, 1226
    Legendary Big Band Singers
        (collection), 767
    ★Nipper's Greatest Hits: The 50's, Vol. 1
        (collection), 1163
    ★Sentimental Journey: Pop Vocal
        Classics, Vol. 3 (collection), 1169
    Sweet and Lovely: Capitol's Great Ladies
        of Song (collection), 1172
Stars of Faith. God and Me, 3050
Stars of Harmony. The Swing Time
        Records Story: R&B, Blues, and
        Gospel, 1946–1952 (collection),
        2430
Statesmen Quartet. Hovie Lister and the
        Statesmen, 3132
The Statler Brothers
    Best of the Statler Brothers, Vol. 1, 1541.1
    Definitive Collection, 1541.2
Staton, Candi
    The Best of Candi Staton, 2653
    Disco Box (collection), 2644
Staton, Dakota
    ★The Jazz Singers: A Smithsonian
        Collection of Jazz Vocals from
        1919–1994 (collection), 766
    Sweet and Lovely: Capitol's Great Ladies
        of Song (collection), 1172
★Status Quo. Nuggets II: Original Artifacts
        from the British Empire and Beyond
        (collection), 1791
Steadman, Frances
    Gospel Warriors: Over 50 Years
        of Great Solo Performances
        (collection), 2987
    ★The Great Gospel Women (collection),
        2989
Steeleye Span. Spanning the Years, 1857
Steely Dan. The Definitive Collection, 1910
Stein, Ira. Piano Solos: Narada Artists
        (collection), 1370

Steppenwolf. All Time Greatest Hits, 1848
Stereolab. Emperor Tomato Ketchup, 2195
Stereos. The Doo-Wop Box II (collection),
        2323
Sterling Jubilee Singers. Jesus Hits Like
        the Atom Bomb, 3026
Stetsasonic. In Full Gear, 2925
Stevens, Cat
    Greatest Hits, 1899
    Have a Nice Decade: The '70s Pop
        Culture Box (collection), 1240
Stewart, Amii. Disco Box (collection),
        2644
Stewart, Billy
    Beg, Scream, and Shout! The Big Ol'
        Box of '60s Soul (collection), 2433
    Best of Chess R&B, Vols. 1 and 2
        (collection), 2420
    One More Time: The Chess Years, 2518
    Soul Shots: A Collection of Sixties Soul
        Classics (collection), 2443
Stewart, Gary. Out of Hand; Your Place or
        Mine, 1677
Stewart, Jeb. The Complete Goldwax
        Singles, Vol. 1 (collection), 2591
Stewart, Rex
    The Duke's Men: Small Groups, Vol. 1
        (collection), 562
    The Duke's Men: Small Groups, Vol. 2
        (collection), 563
Stewart, Rod
    Billboard #1s: The '80s (collection),
        1236
    Downtown Train: Selections from the
        Storyteller Anthology, 1932.1
    Every Picture Tells a Story, 1932.2
    Have a Nice Decade: The '70s Pop
        Culture Box (collection), 1240
    Stroll On: An Immediate Blues
        Collection (collection), 369
Stewart, Wynn. Very Best of Wynn Stewart
        1958–1962, 1542
Stiff Little Fingers
    Inflammable Material, 2028
    No Thanks! The '70s Punk Rebellion
        (collection), 2003
Sting. Brand New Day, 1306
Stitt, Sonny
    Endgame Brilliance: Constellation &
        Tune Up, 896
    ★Jazz on a Summer's Day (collection),
        664
    Sonny Stitt / Bud Powell / J. J. Johnson,
        601
Stivell, Alan. Renaissance of the Celtic
        Harp, 1365
Stokes, Frank. See also Beale Street Sheiks
    Best Of . . ., 200
    Blues Masters, Vol. 12: Memphis Blues
        (collection), 229
    ★The Blues: A Smithsonian Collection
        of Classic Blues Singers (collection),
        145

Good for What Ails You: Music of the Medicine Shows (collection), 184

Masters of Memphis Blues (collection), 230

★*Memphis Masters: Early American Blues Classics* (collection), 231

Songsters and Saints: Vocal Traditions on Race Records, Vol. 2 (collection), 191

Violin, Sing the Blues for Me: African-American Fiddlers (collection), 192

When the Sun Goes Down 2: The First Time I Met the Blues (collection), 160

Wild About My Lovin': Beale Street Blues, 1928–30 (collection), 233

Stoll, George. *It's Easy to Remember* (Crosby), 1125.6

Stone, Jesse

    ★*Big Band Jazz: From the Beginnings to the Fifties* (collection), 529

    The Real Kansas City of the '20s, '30s, and '40s (collection), 552

Stone, Joss. *The Soul Sessions,* 2585

Stone Roses. *The Stone Roses,* 2196

Stonehill, Randy. *First Love: A Historic Gathering of Jesus Music Pioneers* (collection), 3137

Stoneman, Ernest

    Ernest V. Stoneman: The Unsung Father of Country Music, 1425

    Mountain Gospel: The Sacred Roots of Country Music (collection), 3113

    Old-Time Mountain Ballads (collection), 1390

The Stooges

    Fun House, 1887.1

    Punk: Attitude (collection), 1980

    The Stooges, 1887.2

★Storm, Billy. *Atlantic Vocal Groups, 1951–1963* (collection), 2320

Stormy. *Eccentric Soul: Twinight's Lunar Rotation* (collection), 2568

Story, Carl

    The Best of Bluegrass, Vol. 1: Standards (collection), 1561

    Bluegrass Gospel Collection, 1611

Story, Liz

    A Quiet Revolution: 30 Years of Windham Hill (collection), 1372

    Solace: A Windham Hill Collection (collection), 1373

    Windham Hill: The First Ten Years (collection), 1377

    A Winter's Solstice (collection), 3321

Stoudemire, Jackie. *Don't Stop: Recording Tap* (collection), 2657

Stovepipe, Daddy

    Good for What Ails You: Music of the Medicine Shows (collection), 184

    A Richer Tradition: Country Blues and String Band Music (collection), 187

Stover, Don. *Mountain Music Bluegrass Style* (collection), 1566

Straight Street Holiness Group. *Fire in My Bones: Raw, Rare and Otherworldy African-American Gospel* (collection), 2960

★Strait, George. *Greatest Hits,* 1678

Stranglers. *No Thanks! The '70s Punk Rebellion* (collection), 2003

★Strawberry Alarm Clock. *Nuggets: Artifacts of the First Psychedelic Era* (collection), 1808

Strayhorn, Billy. *Lush Life,* 559

Street People. *The Spring Story: Essential 70s Soul* (collection), 2608

Streets. *Original Pirate Material,* 2231

Strehli, Angela. *Blues Fest: Modern Blues of the '90s* (collection), 410

Streisand, Barbra

    Alan Jay Lerner (songwriter collection), 1105.1

    ★*American Popular Song: Six Decades of Songwriters and Singers* (collection), 1059

    A Christmas Album, 3342

    The Concerts, 1307.1

    Cy Coleman (songwriter collection), 1098.2

    Duets: An American Classic (Bennett), 1251.1

    ★*Greatest Hits,* 1307.2

    ★*Greatest Hits, Vol. 2,* 1307.3

    Highlights from "Just for the Record," 1307.4

    Jule Styne (songwriter collection), 1111.1

Strength in Numbers. *The Telluride Sessions,* 1612

Strich, Elaine

    Rodgers / Hart (songwriter collection), 1109.1

    Vincent Youmans (songwriter collection), 1118

string bands. *See* songsters, string bands, and jug bands

Strothers, Blind Jimmie. *Negro Religious Songs and Services* (collection), 2977

Stuart, Jeb. *Crash of Thunder: Boss Soul, Funk, and R&B Sides from the Vaults of the King, Federal, and Deluxe Labels* (collection), 2596

Stuart, Jerry. *Mountain Music Bluegrass Style* (collection), 1566

Stuart, Marty. *Let There Be Country,* 1679

Studwell, W. *College Fight Songs: An Anthology,* 3371

Sturbridge Singers. *The New England Harmony: A Collection of American Choral Music,* 24

Sturdivant, Bozie. *Negro Religious Songs and Services* (collection), 2977

The Stylistics

    The Best of the Stylistics, 2558

    ★*Love Train: The Sound of Philadelphia* (collection), 2552

Styne, Jule. *Jule Styne* (songwriter collection), 1111

Styx. *Have a Nice Decade: The '70s Pop Culture Box* (collection), 1240

Sublime

    Sublime, 2197

    Whatever: The '90s Pop and Culture Box (collection), 1244

The Sugarhill Gang. *Best of the Sugarhill Gang,* 2926

Sugarloaf. *Have a Nice Decade: The '70s Pop Culture Box* (collection), 1240

Suicide

    D.I.Y. Blank Generation: The New York Scene (collection), 1978

    No Thanks! The '70s Punk Rebellion (collection), 2003

    Suicide: The First Album, 1998

★Sullivan, Joe. *The Commodore Story* (collection), 561

Sullivan, Maxine

    Close as Pages in a Book, 802

    Harry Warren (songwriter collection), 1114

    Jule Styne (songwriter collection), 1111.1

    ★*Sophisticated Ladies* (collection), 1087

    Stars of the Apollo (collection), 2240

    Waller / Razaf (songwriter collection), 1113.2

Summer, Donna

    Bad Girls, 2654.1

    Billboard #1s: The '70s (collection), 1235

    Complete Introduction to Disco (collection), 1237

    Disco Box (collection), 2644

    Donna Summer Live and More Encore!, 2654.2

    The Journey: The Very Best of Donna Summer, 2654.3

Summers, Bill. *The Essence of Kwanzaa,* 3353

Sun Ra

    Big Band Renaissance: The Evolution of the Jazz Orchestra (collection), 739

    Cosmic Tones for Mental Therapy / Art Forms of Dimensions Tomorrow, 695.1

    ★*Heliocentric Worlds,* 695.2

    Sun Ra: A Joyful Noise, 695.3

The Sundays. *Whatever: The '90s Pop and Culture Box* (collection), 1244

Sunnyland Slim

    Chicago Is Just That Way (collection), 289

    The Cobra Records Story: Chicago Rock and Blues (collection), 339

Sunnyland Slim (cont.)
　★*Nashville Jumps: Blues and Rhythm on Nashville Independent Labels 1945–1955* (collection), 2376
　When the Sun Goes Down 4: That's All Right (collection), 271
★Superiors. *Atlantic Vocal Groups, 1951–1963* (collection), 2320
Supernatural. *The Lost Freestyle Files,* 2927
superstars, British. *See* British superstars
Supreme Angels. *The Best of Nashboro Gospel* (collection), 3032
The Supremes. *See also* Ross, Diana and the Supremes
　Beg, Scream, and Shout! The Big Ol' Box of '60s Soul (collection), 2433
　Casey Kasem Presents America's Top Ten through the Years: The Sixties (collection), 1156
　Heaven Must Have Sent You: The Holland/Dozier/Holland Story (collection), 2436
　Hitsville USA: The Motown Singles Collection (collection), 2603
　Hitsville USA: The Motown Singles Collection, Vol. 2 (collection), 2604
　Magnificent: The Complete Studio Duets, 2550.1
　Meet the Supremes, 2550.2
　Merry Christmas, 3343
　Motown around the World (collection), 2437
　Pure 60's: The #1 Hits (collection), 1165
　Reflections: Definitive Performances, 1964–1969, 2550.3
surf, bubblegum, garage bands, and pop, 1808–1819
　Anthology (James), 1813
　Greatest Hits (Monkees), 1815
　Greatest Hits (Revere), 1817
　Nuggets: A Classic Collection from the Psychedelic Sixties (collection), 1809
　★*Nuggets: Artifacts of the First Psychedelic Era* (collection), 1808
　★*Pet Sounds* (Beach Boys), 1812.1
　Rev Up: The Best of Mitch Ryder and the Detroit Wheels, 1819
　★*The Sounds of Summer: The Very Best of the Beach Boys,* 1812.2
　Surf City: The Best of Jan and Dean, 1814
　★*Surfin' Hits* (collection), 1810
　25 All-Time Greatest Bubblegum Hits (collection), 1811
　The Very Best of the Rascals, 1816
　The Very Best of the Righteous Brothers: Unchained Melody, 1818
Surf Riders. *Southern Rhythm 'n' Rock: The Best of Excello Records, Vol. 22* (collection), 2427
★Surfaris. *Surfin' Hits* (collection), 1810

Surman, John. *The Amazing Adventures of Simon Simon,* 864
Sutton, Ralph
　At Cafe des Copains, 733
　★*The Commodore Story* (collection), 561
Swallow, Steve. *Conjure: Music for the Texts of Ishmael Reed* (collection), 810
The Swan Silvertones
　The Best of King Gospel (collection), 3031
　Good News: 22 Gospel Greats (collection), 3033
　Greatest Gospel Gems (collection), 3035
　★*Jubilation! Great Gospel Performances, Vol. 1: Black Gospel* (collection), 2966
　★*Jubilation! Great Gospel Performances, Vol. 2: More Black Gospel* (collection), 2967
　Kings of the Gospel Highway: The Golden Age of Gospel Quartets (collection), 3009
　Love Lifted Me / My Rock, 3027.1
　Pray for Me / Let's Go to Church Together, 3027.2
　Swan Silvertones, 1946–1951, 3027.3
　Testify! The Gospel Box (collection), 2974
Swanee Nightingales. *Boddie Recording Company Cleveland, Ohio* (collection), 2569, 2570
Swanee Quintet
　The Best of Nashboro Gospel (collection), 3032
　The Best of Swanee Quintet, 3028
　Living Legends of Gospel: The Quartets, Vols. 1 and 2 (collection), 3010
Swanee River Boys. *Favorite Sacred Songs* (collection), 3109
Swann, Bettye
　★*Atlantic Soul, 1959–1975* (collection), 2589
　Beg, Scream, and Shout! The Big Ol' Box of '60s Soul (collection), 2433
Swann, Donald
　The Complete Flanders and Swann (Flanders and Swann), 1193.1
　The Songs of Michael Flanders and Donald Swann (Flanders and Swann), 1193.2
Swans. *Children of God / World of Skin,* 2198
Swanson, Adam. *On a Circular Staircase,* 143
Sweat, Keith
　The Best of Keith Sweat: Make You Sweat, 2392.1
　Sweat Hotel Live, 2392.2
Sweeney, Jimmy
　★*Nashville Jumps: Blues and Rhythm on Nashville Independent Labels 1945–1955* (collection), 2376

Night Train to Nashville: Music City Rhythm and Blues, 1945–1970, Vol. 2 (collection), 2378
Sweet Inspirations
　★*Atlantic Soul, 1959–1975* (collection), 2589
　Beg, Scream, and Shout! The Big Ol' Box of '60s Soul (collection), 2433
Sweet, Matthew. *Whatever: The '90s Pop and Culture Box* (collection), 1244
Sweet, Rachel. *Straight Outta Cleveland* (collection), 1888
Swell Maps. *Jane from Occupied Europe,* 2199
Swift, Joe. *The Swing Time Records Story: R&B, Blues, and Gospel, 1946–1952* (collection), 2430
Swift, Rob. *The Ablist,* 2928
Swift, Taylor
　Fearless, 1308.1
　1989, 1308.2
swing era. *See* big bands and the swing era
swing mainstream since 1950, 711–738
　After Midnight: The Complete Session (Cole), 718
　At Cafe des Copains (Sutton), 733
　★*At the Stratford Shakespeare Festival* (Peterson), 730.1
　Back to Back (Ellington), 720.1
　Blue and Sentimental (Quebec), 731
　Complete Legendary Jam Sessions Master Takes (Clayton), 717
　Complete Studio Recordings (Terry), 734
　Concert by the Sea (Garner), 721
　Count Basie Jam: Montreux '77 (Basie), 713.1
　Dancing in the Dark (McKenna), 728
　Duets and Solos (Cheatham), 716
　Earl Hines Plays Duke Ellington (Hines), 726
　For the First Time (Basie), 713.2
　Free Spirits (Williams), 737
　Further Definitions (Carter), 715.1
　The Great Summit: Master Takes (Armstrong), 712.1
　The High and Mighty Hawk (Hawkins), 725
　Jazz in Paris: Improvisations (Grappelli), 722.1
　Jazz Masters, Vol. 11: Stephane Grappelli (Grappelli), 722.2
　Jazz Reunion (Russell), 732.1
　Les Paul Live in New York (Paul), 729
　Lionel Hampton with Oscar Peterson (Hampton), 724
　Little Jazz: The Best of the Verve Years (Eldridge), 719.1
　Louis Armstrong Plays W. C. Handy (Armstrong), 712.2
　Lucky Strikes (Thompson), 735.1
　Lucky Thompson Meets Oscar Pettiford (Thompson), 735.2
　Money Jungle (Ellington), 720.2

Montreux '77 (Carter), 715.2

Oscar Peterson Live in '63, '64, and '65 (Peterson), 730.2

Over the Rainbow (Carter), 715.3

Pres and Teddy (Young), 738

Roy and Diz (Eldridge), 719.2

A Sailboat in the Moonlight (Braff), 714

Satch Plays Fats (Armstrong), 712.3

Satchmo: A Musical Autobiography (Armstrong), 712.4

★*Soulville* (Webster), 736.1

★*Swingin' with Pee Wee* (Russell), 732.2

Take Your Pick (Alden), 711

Tenor Sax Legend: Live and Intimate (Webster), 736.2

Tribute to the Greats (Hodes), 727

Trio Plus One (Peterson), 730.3

Two Classic Albums from Bobby Hackett and Jack Teagarden: Jazz Ultimate / Coast Concert (Hackett), 723

swing soloists and combos, 560–591

After Hours: Charlie Christian, Jazz Immortal / Dizzy Gillespie, 1941 (collection), 560

★*After You've Gone* (Eldridge), 573

Benny Goodman Sextet Featuring Charlie Christian (Goodman), 576.1

Best of the Nat King Cole Trio: Instrumental Classics (Cole), 570

★*The Best of Django Reinhardt* (Reinhardt), 582.1

★*The Best of the Complete Pablo Solo Masterpieces* (Tatum), 587.1

Body and Soul (Hawkins), 579.1

Chicago Style (Condon), 571

★*Classic Early Solos* (Tatum), 587.2

Classic Tenors (Hawkins), 579.2

collections, 560–564

The Commodore Master Takes (Davison), 572

★*The Commodore Story* (collection), 561

Complete American Small Group Recordings (Byas), 568.1

Complete Columbia and RCA Victor Recordings (Kirby), 580

Complete 1946–1951 European Small Group Master Takes (Byas), 568.2

The Complete Aladdin Sessions (Young), 591.1

The Complete Capitol Trios (Goodman), 576.2

The Complete Gramercy Five Sessions (Shaw), 584

The Complete RCA Victor Small Group Recordings (Goodman), 576.3

The Complete Recorded Works, Vol. 2: A Handful of Keys (Waller), 588.1

The Complete Savoy and Dial Master Takes (Garner), 575

Dance of the Octopus (Norvo), 581

Django Reinhardt: Gypsy Jazz (Reinhardt), 582.2

The Duke's Men: Small Groups, Vol. 1 (collection), 562

The Duke's Men: Small Groups, Vol. 2 (collection), 563

Ec-Stacy: 25 Great Piano Performances (Stacy), 586

The First Day (Ammons), 566

★*From Spirituals to Swing: The Legendary 1938 and 1939 Carnegie Hall Concerts Produced by John Hammond* (collection), 564

Genius of Art Tatum (Tatum), 587.3

★*The Genius of the Electric Guitar* (Christian), 569.1

★*Handful of Keys* (Waller), 588.2

The "Kansas City" Sessions (Young), 591.2

★*Ken Burns Jazz Collection: Coleman Hawkins* (Hawkins), 579.3

★*Ken Burns Jazz Collection: Lester Young* (Young), 591.3

The Land of Jazz (Russell), 583

The Noble Art of Teddy Wilson (Wilson), 590

Original Guitar Hero (Christian), 569.2

Piano Starts Here (Tatum), 587.4

The Pied Piper (Berigan), 567

Ragtime Band Sessions (Spanier), 585

Ride, Red, Ride (Allen), 565

Ring Dem Bells (Hampton), 578

Solos (Tatum), 587.5

Stéphane Grappelli (Grappelli), 577

Swingin' with "The Eel" (Freeman), 574

Timeless (Young), 591.4

Zodiac Suite (Williams), 589

swing, western. *See* western swing

Swinging Seven. *Crash of Thunder: Boss Soul, Funk, and R&B Sides from the Vaults of the King, Federal, and Deluxe Labels* (collection), 2596

Switch. *Hitsville USA: The Motown Singles Collection, Vol. 2* (collection), 2604

Switchfoot. *The Beautiful Letdown,* 3162

Swoboda, Alice. *Eccentric Soul: The Tragar and Note Labels* (collection), 2602

Sykes, Roosevelt

★*Blues Classics* (collection), 146

★*The Blues: A Smithsonian Collection of Classic Blues Singers* (collection), 145

Chicago Is Just That Way (collection), 289

Conversation with the Blues (collection), 148

Favorite Country Blues: Guitar-Piano Duets (collection), 267

★*Juke Joint Saturday Night: Piano Blues, Rags and Stomps; Classic Recordings from the 1920s and '30s* (collection), 255

★*Legends of the Blues, Vol. 2* (collection), 151

★*Nashville Jumps: Blues and Rhythm on Nashville Independent Labels 1945–1955* (collection), 2376

Rockin' This House: Chicago Blues Piano (collection), 257, 306

Roosevelt Sykes, 265

Twenty First Street Stomp: Piano Blues of St. Louis (collection), 259

When the Sun Goes Down 4: That's All Right (collection), 271

When the Sun Goes Down 3: That's Chicago's South Side (collection), 270

Sylvers. *Disco Box* (collection), 2644

Sylvester

Disco Box (collection), 2644

The Original Hits, 2655

Symbols. *Old Town Doo-Wop, Vols. 1–3* (collection), 2324

Syms, Sylvia

Cy Coleman (songwriter collection), 1098.2

Dorothy Fields (songwriter collection), 1100

Syndicate of Sound

Nuggets: A Classic Collection from the Psychedelic Sixties (collection), 1809

★*Nuggets: Artifacts of the First Psychedelic Era* (collection), 1808

T

T. I. *King,* 2929

T. Rex. *Electric Warrior,* 1933

Tadlock, Cheryl G. *Classics for Christmas,* 3288

Taff, Russ

The Best of Russ Taff, 3163.1

The Way Home, 3163

Taggart, Blind Joe

American Primitive, Vol. 1: Raw Pre-War Gospel (collection), 2976

The Blues of Texas, Arkansas, and Louisiana (collection), 236

Gospel: Negro Spirituals / Gospel Songs, 1926–1942 (collection), 2963

The Half Ain't Never Been Told, Vols. 1 and 2 (collection), 2956

Songsters and Saints: Vocal Traditions on Race Records, Vol. 2 (collection), 191

Takahashi, Masanori. *See* Kitaro

Take 6. *Take 6,* 3098

Talking Heads

Fear of Music, 1999.1

No Thanks! The '70s Punk Rebellion (collection), 2003

Remain in Light, 1999.2

Stop Making Sense, 1999.3, 1999.4

Tampa Red

The Bluebird Recordings, 1936–1938, 278.1

★*Blues Classics* (collection), 146

Tampa Red (cont.)
  ★*The Blues: A Smithsonian Collection of Classic Blues Singers* (collection), 145
  Chicago Is Just That Way (collection), 289
  The Complete Bluebird Recordings, Vol. 1, 278.2
  ★*Guitar Wizards* (collection), 243
  The Guitar Wizard, 278.3
  ★*Legends of the Blues, Vol. 2* (collection), 151
  ★*Mean Old World: The Blues from 1940–1994* (collection), 154
  When the Sun Goes Down 4: That's All Right (collection), 271
  When the Sun Goes Down 3: That's Chicago's South Side (collection), 270
★Tangerine Dream. *Stratosfear,* 1358
Tanner, Gid
  Classic Country Music: A Smithsonian Collection (collection), 1382
  Good for What Ails You: Music of the Medicine Shows (collection), 184
  Old-Time Fiddle Tunes and Songs from North Georgia, 1426
Tapella, John. *Stevie Ray Vaughan, Lightnin' Blues, 1983–1987* (Vaughan, Tapella, Sokolow and Schiff), 383
Tapscott, Horace. *The Dark Tree,* 1016
Tarheel Slim
  The Fire / Fury Records Story (collection), 2422
  Play My Juke-Box: East Coast Blues (collection), 244
Tarlton, Jimmie
  Darby and Tarlton: Complete Recordings, 1405
  White Country Blues: A Lighter Shade of Blues, 1427
Taste of Honey. *Disco Box* (collection), 2644
Tate, Buddy. *The Big Horn: The History of the Honkin' and Screamin' Saxophone* (collection), 2314
Tate, Howard
  ★*Atlantic Soul, 1959–1975* (collection), 2589
  Beg, Scream, and Shout! The Big Ol' Box of '60s Soul (collection), 2433
  Get It While You Can: The Complete Legendary Verve Sessions, 2519
  Respect: Aretha's Influences and Inspiration (collection), 2440
  ★*What It Is! Funky Soul and Rare Grooves* (collection), 2615
Tatum, Art
  ★*The Best of the Complete Pablo Solo Masterpieces,* 587.1
  ★*Central Avenue Sounds: Jazz in Los Angeles* (collection), 471

  ★*Classic Early Solos,* 587.2
  Genius of Art Tatum, 587.3
  ★*Ken Burns Jazz: The Story of America's Music* (collection), 478
  Piano Legends (collection), 480
  Piano Starts Here, 587.4
  ★*The Smithsonian Collection of Classic Jazz* (collection), 486
  Solos, 587.5
Tavares
  Disco Box (collection), 2644
  ★*Saturday Night Fever,* 2658
★Taylor, Carmen and the Boleros. *Atlantic Vocal Groups, 1951–1963* (collection), 2320
Taylor, Carmol
  The Complete Goldwax Singles, Vol. 2 (collection), 2592
  The Complete Goldwax Singles, Vol. 3 (collection), 2593
Taylor, Cecil
  Cecil Taylor: All the Notes, 709.1
  Cecil Taylor Unit / Roswell Rudd Sextet: Mixed, 709.2
  Conquistador!, 709.3
  ★*Ken Burns Jazz: The Story of America's Music* (collection), 478
  Nefertiti, the Beautiful One Has Come, 709.4
  Piano Legends (collection), 480
  Silent Tongues, 1017.1
  ★*The Smithsonian Collection of Classic Jazz* (collection), 486
  3 Phasis, 1017.2
  ★*Unit Structures,* 709.5
  Willisau Concert, 1017.3
  The World of Cecil Taylor, 709.6
Taylor, Courtney and the Dandy Warhols. *Dig!* (collection), 2092
Taylor, Earl and the Stoney Mountain Boys. *Mountain Music Bluegrass Style* (collection), 1566
Taylor, Earl. *Mountain Music Bluegrass Style* (collection), 1566
★Taylor, Eddie. *The Vee-Jay Story: Celebrating 40 Years of Classic Hits* (collection), 2431
Taylor, Gloria. *Action Speaks Louder Than Words: The Best of SSS International* (collection), 2588
Taylor, Hound Dog
  Blues Fest: Modern Blues of the '70s (collection), 408
  Hound Dog Taylor and the Houserockers, 462
Taylor, James
  Duets: An American Classic (Bennett), 1251.1
  Have a Nice Decade: The '70s Pop Culture Box (collection), 1240
  James Taylor's Greatest Hits, 1900.1
  ★*Sweet Baby James,* 1900.2

Taylor, Johnnie
  Beg, Scream, and Shout! The Big Ol' Box of '60s Soul (collection), 2433
  Chronicle: The 20 Greatest Hits, 2587.1
  The Complete Stax/Volt Singles 1959–1968 (collection), 2594
  The Complete Stax/Volt Soul Singles, Vol. 2: 1968–1971 (collection), 2595
  Rated X-Traordinaire: The Best of Johnnie Taylor, 2587.2
  Top of the Stax, Vol. 1: Twenty Greatest Hits (collection), 2611
  Top of the Stax, Vol. 2: Twenty Greatest Hits (collection), 2612
Taylor, Johnny. *The Blues Is Alright, Vol. 1* (collection), 411
Taylor, Josephine. *Eccentric Soul: Twinight's Lunar Rotation* (collection), 2568
Taylor, Koko
  ★*Blues Classics* (collection), 146
  Blues Fest: Modern Blues of the '70s (collection), 408
  Blues Masters, Vol. 9: Postmodern Blues (collection), 412
  ★*I Got What It Takes,* 463
  Superblues: All-Time Classic Blues Hits, Vol. 1 (collection), 347
Taylor, Little Johnny
  Birth of Soul, 4 Vols. (collection), 2434
  Blues Masters, Vol. 1: Urban Blues (collection), 338
  Greatest Hits, 363
  Superblues: All-Time Classic Blues Hits, Vol. 1 (collection), 347
Taylor, Montana. *Shake Your Wicked Knees: Rent Parties and Good Times* (collection), 258
Taylor, Otis. *White African,* 464
Taylor, Ronnie. *Eccentric Soul: The Capsoul Label* (collection), 2599
Taylor, Rose. *Angels' Visits and Other Vocal Gems of Victorian America* (collection), 93
Taylor, Sam "The Man." *The Big Horn: The History of the Honkin' and Screamin' Saxophone* (collection), 2314
Taylor, Steve. *Best of Christian Rock (1970–1986), Vol. 1* (collection), 3135
Taylor, Ted. *Keep What You Get: The Rare & Unissued Ronn Recordings,* 2520
T-Bone
  Bone-a-Fide, 3181.1
  Tha Life of a Hoodlum, 3181.2
★T.C.I. Women's Four. *A Warrior on the Battlefield: A Cappella Trail Blazers* (collection), 3011
Teagarden, Jack
  An Anthology of Big Band Swing (collection), 528

Bing Crosby and Some Jazz Friends (Crosby), 1125.2

★*The Commodore Story* (collection), 561

★*The Crooners* (collection), 1062

Harold Arlen (songwriter collection), 1095.1

★*Jazz on a Summer's Day* (collection), 664

King of the Blues Trombone, 519

Legendary Big Band Singers (collection), 767

Lost Chords: White Musicians and Their Contributions to Jazz (collection), 479

Waller / Razaf (songwriter collection), 1113.2

Tears for Fears. *Like Omigod! The 80s Pop Culture Box (Totally)* (collection), 1241

Tedashii. *Blacklight,* 3182

Tedeschi, Susan. *Just Won't Burn,* 380

Tee, Willie

Beg, Scream, and Shout! The Big Ol' Box of '60s Soul (collection), 2433

Birth of Soul, 4 Vols. (collection), 2434

teen idols, instrumentals, and dance hits, 1771–1785

All Time Greatest Hits (Sedaka), 1781

Anthology (Pitney), 1780

Gold (Francis), 1777

Greatest Hits (Dion), 1774

Greatest Hits (Nelson), 1778

Greatest Hits (Shannon), 1782.1

In Season: Frankie Valli and the Four Seasons Anthology, 1776.1

Rock Instrumental Classics, Vol. 2: The 60s (collection), 1771

Rumble! The Best of Link Wray, 1785

16 Biggest Hits (Orbison), 1779

Twang Thang: The Duane Eddy Anthology, 1775

25 All-Time Greatest Hits (Shannon), 1782.2

25 Rockin Instrumentals (collection), 1772

The Ultimate Bobby Darin, 1773

The Very Best of Bobby Vee, 1783

The Very Best of Frankie Valli and the Four Seasons, 1776.2

Walk Don't Run: The Best of the Ventures, 1784

Teen Queens. *The Doo-Wop Box II* (collection), 2323

Teen Turbans. *The Best of Loma Records: The Rise and Fall of a 1960's Soul Label* (collection), 2590

Teenage Jesus and the Jerks. *No New York* (collection), 1979

The Teenagers

★*The Doo Wop Box: 101 Vocal Group Gems from the Golden Age of Rock 'n' Roll* (collection), 1745

Life Could Be a Dream: The Doo-Wop Sound, 2346

Street Corner Serenade: The Greatest Doo-Wop Hits of the '50s and '60s (collection), 1756

Tel Fi Demo. *Eccentric Soul: The Nickel and Penny Labels* (collection), 2567

Television

D.I.Y. Blank Generation: The New York Scene (collection), 1978

Marquee Moon, 2000

No Thanks! The '70s Punk Rebellion (collection), 2003

Tempest Trio. *The Best of T. K. Disco* (collection), 2656

Temple, Johnny. *Acoustic Country Blues Guitar: Delta Blues before Robert Johnson* (collection), 211

Temple, Shirley

★*Brother, Can You Spare a Dime? American Song during the Great Depression* (collection), 1061

Richard Whiting (songwriter collection), 1116

Temprees. *Top of the Stax, Vol. 2: Twenty Greatest Hits* (collection), 2612

The Temptations

★*Anthology,* 2551.1

Beg, Scream, and Shout! The Big Ol' Box of '60s Soul (collection), 2433

Complete Introduction to Disco (collection), 1237

The Doo-Wop Box II (collection), 2323

Emperors of Soul, 2551.2

Get Ready: Definitive Performances, 1965–1972, 2551.3

Give Love at Christmas, 3344.1

Hitsville USA: The Motown Singles Collection (collection), 2603

Hitsville USA: The Motown Singles Collection, Vol. 2 (collection), 2604

Motown around the World (collection), 2437

★*The R&B Box* (collection), 2239

Songs of Protest (collection), 1820

The Temptations Christmas Card, 3344.2

The Ultimate Collection, 2551.4

Ten Years After. *The Essential Ten Years After,* 1869

Tennessee Mountaineers. *How Can I Keep from Singing: Early American Religious Music and Song, Vols. 1 and 2* (collection), 2957

Teo, Roy. *Southern Rhythm 'n' Rock: The Best of Excello Records, Vol. 22* (collection), 2427

Terrell, Pha

Legendary Big Band Singers (collection), 767

★*The Music Goes Round and Around: The Golden Years of Tin Pan Alley, 1930–1939* (collection), 1070

Terrell, Sister O. M. *Preachin' the Gospel: Holy Blues* (collection), 2979

Terrell, Tammi. *Come On and See Me: The Complete Solo Collection,* 2521

Terry, Clark. *Complete Studio Recordings,* 734

Terry, Richard. *Eccentric Soul: The Nickel and Penny Labels* (collection), 2567

Terry, Sonny

Afro-American Blues and Game Songs (collection), 169

★*Brownie McGhee and Sonny Terry Sing* (Terry and McGhee), 404

Classic African American Gospel from Smithsonian Folkways (collection), 2959

Country Blues Troubadours, 1938–1948 (Terry and McGhee), 280

Good Time Blues: Harmonicas, Kazoos, Washboards, and Cow-Bells (collection), 268

Hometown Blues, 279.1

Newport Folk Festival: Best of the Blues, 1959–68 (collection), 392

Sonny Terry's Country Blues Harmonica, 279.2

When the Sun Goes Down 4: That's All Right (collection), 271

The Terry's. *The Complete Goldwax Singles, Vol. 2* (collection), 2592

Tesh, John. *Ultimate New Age* (collection), 1376

Tex, Joe

★*Atlantic R&B, 1947–1974* (collection), 2418

Beg, Scream, and Shout! The Big Ol' Box of '60s Soul (collection), 2433

Night Train to Nashville: Music City Rhythm and Blues, 1945–1970, Vol. 1 (collection), 2377

★*The R&B Box* (collection), 2239

Singles A's and B's, Vol. 1: 1960–1964, 2522.1

Singles A's and B's, Vol. 2: 1967–1968, 2522.2

Singles A's and B's, Vol. 3: 1969–1972, 2522.3

Singles A's and B's, Vol. 4: 1973–1976, 2522.4

Texas and West coast blues, 311–326

All the Classics, 1946–1951 (Hopkins), 321.1

Ball 'n' Chain (Thornton), 324.1

Blues Masters, Vol. 3: Texas Blues (collection), 311

Boogie Uproar: Texas Blues and R&B (collection), 312

collections, 311–316

Complete Aladdin Recordings (Hopkins), 321.2

The Complete Capitol / Black and White Recordings (Walker), 325.1

Texas and West coast blues (cont.)
  The Complete Imperial Recordings
    (Walker), 325.2
  ★*Gold Star Sessions, Vols. 1 and 2*
    (Hopkins), 321.3
  Hound Dog: The Peacock Recordings
    (Thornton), 324.2
  Hung Down Head (Fulson), 320.1
  Lil' Son Jackson, Vols. 1 and 2, 322
  Lowell Fulson, 1946 to 1953, 320.2
  *Mojo Hand: The Lightnin' Hopkins
    Anthology*, 321.4
  One Room Country Shack (Mercy Dee),
    323.1
  The Original Peacock Recordings
    (Brown), 317
  The Original Source (Walker), 325.3
  San Francisco Bay Blues (Fuller), 319
  *The Swingtime Records Story: R&B,
    Blues, and Gospel* (collection), 313
  T-Bone Blues (Walker), 325.4
  *The T-Bone Walker Collection: 20
    Great Tunes from a Blues Legend*,
    325.5
  *Texas Blues: Bill Quinn's Gold Star
    Recordings* (collection), 314
  *Texas Blues: Oak Anthology of Blues
    Guitar* (collection), 315
  ★*Texas Music, Vol. 1: Postwar Blues
    Combos* (collection), 316
  Tramp / Soul (Fulson), 320.3
  Troublesome Mind (Mercy Dee), 323.2
  Truckin' with Albert Collins, 318
  Very Best of Johnny "Guitar" Watson,
    326.1
  Very Best of Lightnin' Hopkins, 321.5
  ★*Very Best of T-Bone Walker*, 325.6
  *The Very Best of Johnny "Guitar"
    Watson: In Loving Memory*, 326.2
Texas, Arkansas, and Louisiana blues,
    236–239. *See also* Louisiana blues
  All the Classic Sides (Jefferson), 239.1
  Best of Blind Lemon Jefferson
    (Jefferson), 239.2
  *The Blues of Texas, Arkansas, and
    Louisiana* (collection), 236
  collections, 236–237
  *Texas Blues: Early Blues Masters from
    the Lone Star State* (collection),
    237
  Texas Blues (Grossman), 238
Texas Jubilee Singers. *Spreading the
    Word: Early Gospel Recordings*
    (collection), 2972
Texas rock. *See* West coast and Texas
    rock
Texas Tornadoes. *Texas Tornadoes*, 1680
Tharpe, Sister Rosetta
  ★*Blues Classics* (collection), 146
  ★*From Spirituals to Swing: The
    Legendary 1938 and 1939 Carnegie
    Hall Concerts Produced by John
    Hammond* (collection), 564

★*Good News: 100 Gospel Greats*
    (collection), 2961
★*Goodbye Babylon* (collection), 2954
*Gospel: Negro Spirituals / Gospel Songs,
    1926–1942* (collection), 2963
*Gospel Warriors: Over 50 Years
    of Great Solo Performances*
    (collection), 2987
★*The Gospel Sound of Spirit Feel*
    (collection), 2965
★*The Great Gospel Women* (collection),
    2989
The Great Gospel Women, Vol. 2
    (collection), 2990
Legendary Big Band Singers (collection),
    767
★*Original Soul Sister*, 3003
The Roots of Rock 'n' Roll, 1946–1954
    (collection), 1755
Story of Gospel Music (collection),
    2973
Thelonious Monk Trio. *Jazz Masters:
    Vintage Collection, 1958–1961*
    (collection), 477
Them Two. *Eccentric Soul: The Deep City
    Label* (collection), 2600
They Might Be Giants
  ★*No!*, 3206
  *Whatever: The '90s Pop and Culture
    Box* (collection), 1244
Third Day
  *CCM Top 100: Greatest Songs in
    Christian Music, Vol. 1* (collection),
    3136
  Chronology, Vol. 1, 3164
  Chronology, Vol. 2, 3165
Third Flight. *Eccentric Soul: The Young
    Disciples* (collection), 2562
3rd Bass. *The Cactus Album*, 2930
13th Floor Elevators
  Easter Everywhere, 1849
  *Texas Music, Vol. 3: Garage Bands and
    Psychedelia* (collection), 1830
.38 Special. *Like Omigod! The 80s Pop
    Culture Box (Totally)* (collection),
    1241
Thomas, B. J.
  *The Look of Love: The Burt Bacharach
    Collection* (collection), 1161
  The Scepter Records Story (collection),
    2426
Thomas, Carla
  ★*Atlantic Soul, 1959–1975*
    (collection), 2589
  *Beg, Scream, and Shout! The Big Ol'
    Box of '60s Soul* (collection), 2433
  *The Complete Stax/Volt Singles
    1959–1968* (collection), 2594
  *The Complete Stax/Volt Soul Singles,
    Vol. 2: 1968–1971* (collection),
    2595
  *Dave Godin's Deep Soul Treasures,
    Vols. 1–4* (collection), 2435

Gee Whiz: The Best of Carla Thomas,
    2560
*Stax/Volt Revue: Live in London,
    Vols. 1 and 2* (collection), 2609
*Top of the Stax, Vol. 1: Twenty Greatest
    Hits* (collection), 2611
*Top of the Stax, Vol. 2: Twenty Greatest
    Hits* (collection), 2612
Thomas, Eddie. *Times Ain't What They
    Used to Be: Early Rural and Popular
    Music from Rare Original Film
    Masters* (collection), 1091
Thomas, Franciene. *Eccentric Soul: The
    Tragar and Note Labels* (collection),
    2602
Thomas, Henry
  Blues Masters, Vol. 6: Blues Originals
    (collection), 367
  ★*The Blues: A Smithsonian Collection
    of Classic Blues Singers* (collection),
    145
  *The Blues of Texas, Arkansas, and
    Louisiana* (collection), 236
  *Good for What Ails You: Music of the
    Medicine Shows* (collection), 184
  *The Road to Robert Johnson and
    Beyond* (collection), 221
  The Roots of Rock (collection), 368
  *Songsters and Saints: Vocal Traditions
    on Race Records, Vol. 2* (collection),
    191
  *Texas Blues: Early Blues Masters from
    the Lone Star State* (collection),
    237
  ★*Texas Worried Blues: Complete
    Recorded Works*, 201
Thomas, Irma
  *Beg, Scream, and Shout! The Big Ol'
    Box of '60s Soul* (collection), 2433
  *Crescent City Soul: The Sound of New
    Orleans, 1947–1974* (collection),
    2564
  *Dave Godin's Deep Soul Treasures,
    Vols. 1–4* (collection), 2435
  *Finger Poppin' and Stompin' Feet: 20
    Classic Allen Toussaint Productions
    for Minit Records, 1960–1962*
    (collection), 2359
  Make It Funky! (collection), 2360
  Simply the Best: Live, 2373.1
  *Sweet Soul Queen of New Orleans: The
    Irma Thomas Collection*, 2373.2
  *The Sweetest Feeling: A Van McCoy
    Songbook* (collection), 2447
Thomas, Jessie. *The Swing Time Records
    Story: R&B, Blues, and Gospel,
    1946–1952* (collection), 2430
Thomas, Joe
  The Best of T. K. Disco (collection),
    2656
  *The Big Horn: The History of the
    Honkin' and Screamin' Saxophone*
    (collection), 2314

Thomas, Kid. *New Orleans Jazz* (collection), 503

Thomas, Marlo, and Friends. *Free to Be . . . You and Me,* 3223

Thomas, Michael Tilson. *Songs: Foster, Griffes, Copland* (collection), 101

Thomas, Playboy. *The Swing Time Records Story: R&B, Blues, and Gospel, 1946–1952* (collection), 2430

Thomas, Ramblin'. *Texas Blues: Early Blues Masters from the Lone Star State* (collection), 237

Thomas, Rufus
  ★*Atlantic R&B, 1947–1974* (collection), 2418
  Beg, Scream, and Shout! The Big Ol' Box of '60s Soul (collection), 2433
  The Best of Rufus Thomas: Do the Funky Somethin', 2561
  Blue Flames: A Sun Blues Collection (collection), 337
  Blues Masters, Vol. 12: Memphis Blues (collection), 229
  The Complete Stax/Volt Soul Singles, Vol. 2: 1968–1971 (collection), 2595
  His R&B Recordings 1949–1956: The Sun Years, Plus, 2297
  Memphis Blues: Important Postwar Recordings (collection), 341
  ★*Sun Records' Greatest Hits* (collection), 1741
  The Sun Blues Years (collection), 344
  Top of the Stax, Vol. 1: Twenty Greatest Hits (collection), 2611
  Top of the Stax, Vol. 2: Twenty Greatest Hits (collection), 2612
  ★*What It Is! Funky Soul and Rare Grooves* (collection), 2615

Thomas, Timmy. *The Complete Goldwax Singles, Vol. 2* (collection), 2592

Thompson, Hank
  Doughboys, Playboys, and Cowboys: The Golden Years of Western Swing (collection), 1428
  ★*Hank Thompson,* 1446
  Heroes of Country Music, Vol. 1: Legends of Western Swing (collection), 1429
  Texas Music, Vol. 2: Western Swing and Honky Tonk (collection), 1432

Thompson, Lucky
  Lucky Strikes, 735.1
  Lucky Thompson Meets Oscar Pettiford, 735.2

Thompson, Richard
  Shoot Out the Lights, 1858
  Walking on a Wire: 1968–2009, 1859

Thompson, Suzi and Eric. *16 Down Home Country Classics* (collection), 1385

★Thorne, Del. *Nashville Jumps: Blues and Rhythm on Nashville Independent Labels 1945–1955* (collection), 2376

Thornhill, Claude
  Best of the Big Bands, 549
  ★*Big Band Jazz: From the Beginnings to the Fifties* (collection), 529
  Stars of the Apollo (collection), 2240
  ★*Swing Time! The Fabulous Big Band Era* (collection), 1089

Thornton, Big Mama
  Ball 'n' Chain, 324.1
  ★*The Best of Duke-Peacock Blues* (collection), 336
  ★*Blues Classics* (collection), 146
  Blues Masters, Vol. 3: Texas Blues (collection), 311
  ★*The Blues: A Smithsonian Collection of Classic Blues Singers* (collection), 145
  Duke-Peacock's Greatest Hits (collection), 2421
  Hound Dog: The Peacock Recordings, 324.2
  Rock and Roll: The Early Days (collection), 1752
  The Roots of Rock 'n' Roll, 1946–1954 (collection), 1755

Thornton, Teri. *The Sweetest Feeling: A Van McCoy Songbook* (collection), 2447

Thorogood, George. *Anthology,* 381

Threadgill, Henry
  Just the Facts and Pass the Bucket, 932.1
  Up Popped the Two Lips, 932.2
  Where's Your Cup?, 932.3
  You Know the Number, 932.4

The Three Degrees
  The Best of Loma Records: The Rise and Fall of a 1960's Soul Label (collection), 2590
  ★*Love Train: The Sound of Philadelphia* (collection), 2552

Three Dog Night. *The Complete Hit Singles,* 1920

Three Musketeers. *The Swing Time Records Story: R&B, Blues, and Gospel, 1946–1952* (collection), 2430

Throbbing Gristle
  The Second Annual Report of Throbbing Gristle, 2200.1
  Throbbing Gristle Bring You 20 Jazz Funk Greats, 2200.2

Throwing Muses
  Anthology, 2201
  House Tornado / the Fat Skier, 2038.1
  In a Doghouse, 2038.2

Thunders, Johnny. *No Thanks! The '70s Punk Rebellion* (collection), 2003

Tibbetts, Steve. *Yr,* 1343

'Til Tuesday. *80's Pop Hits* (collection), 1238

Tillis, Mel. *Hitsides! 1970–1980,* 1543

Tillman, Floyd
  The Best of Floyd Tillman, 1544

Texas Music, Vol. 2: Western Swing and Honky Tonk (collection), 1432

★Tilton, Martha. *Sentimental Journey: Pop Vocal Classics, Vol. 1* (collection), 1081

Timberlake, Justin
  Futuresex/Lovesounds, 1309.1
  Justified, 1309.2

★Time Tones. *Atlantic Vocal Groups, 1951–1963* (collection), 2320

Tingstad and Rumbel. *Narada Wilderness Collection* (collection), 1368

Tingstad, Eric
  Narada Guitar Sampler, 1352.1
  Pastorale: Music of Nature and Grace, 1352.2

Tjader, Cal. *Monterey Concerts,* 624

TLC. *Now and Forever: The Hits,* 2415

Toad the Wet Sprocket. *90's Pop Hits* (collection), 1242

TobyMac
  Momentum, 3183.1
  Welcome to Diverse City, 3183.2

toddlers' music. *See* babies' and toddlers' music

★Tokens. *The Doo-Wop Box* (collection), 2322

Tom Robinson Band. *No Thanks! The '70s Punk Rebellion* (collection), 2003

★Tomlin, Pinky. *The Crooners* (collection), 1062

Tone-Loc. *Loc-Ed after Dark,* 2931

Tonéx. *Out the Box,* 3099

Too Short
  Born to Mack, 2932.1
  Life Is . . . Too Short, 2932.2

★Top Notes. *Atlantic Vocal Groups, 1951–1963* (collection), 2320

Tormé, Mel
  ★*American Popular Song: Six Decades of Songwriters and Singers* (collection), 1059
  Arthur Schwartz (songwriter collection), 1110.2
  Cy Coleman (songwriter collection), 1098.2
  Duke Ellington (songwriter collection), 1099.1
  George Gershwin (songwriter collection), 1101.3
  Harold Arlen (songwriter collection), 1095.1
  Harry Warren (songwriter collection), 1114
  Irving Berlin (songwriter collection), 1096.1
  Jazz Lullaby (collection), 3264
  Johnny Mercer (songwriter collection), 1107.1
  Mel Torme: The Best of the Concord Years, 803.1

Tormé, Mel (cont.)
  Mel Torme Swings Shubert Alley, 803.2
  Oscar Hammerstein II (songwriter collection), 1102
  Richard Whiting (songwriter collection), 1116
  Rodgers / Hart (songwriter collection), 1109.1
  ★*Sentimental Journey: Pop Vocal Classics, Vol. 2* (collection), 1168
  The Very Best of Cole Porter (songwriter collection), 1108.3
The Tornadoes
  Rock Instrumental Classics, Vol. 2: The 60s (collection), 1771
  25 Hits from the British Invasion (collection), 1792
Tortoise. *Millions Now Living Will Never Die*, 2202
Toto. *80's Pop Hits* (collection), 1238
Toussaint, Allen
  Conjure: Music for the Texts of Ishmael Reed (collection), 810
  Make It Funky! (collection), 2360
  The Allen Toussaint Collection, 2374.1
  What Is Success? The Scepter and Bell Recordings, 2374.2
  ★*What It Is! Funky Soul and Rare Grooves* (collection), 2615
Tower of Power. *The Very Best of Tower of Power: The Warner Years*, 2641
Townes, Jerry. *Eccentric Soul: The Nickel and Penny Labels* (collection), 2567
Townsend, Henry
  Big Joe Williams and the Stars of Mississippi Blues (collection), 213
  Conversation with the Blues (collection), 148
  St. Louis Blues: The Depression (collection), 232
Townsend, Pete. *Like Omigod! The 80s Pop Culture Box (Totally)* (collection), 1241
traditional Christmas music
  ★*An Old World Christmas: Holiday Favorites from Europe* (collection), 3270
  Big Book of Christmas Songs (collection), 3267
  Carols around the World (Quink), 3284
  Carols for Two (Shafferman), 3287
traditional Christmas music (cont.)
  Christmas Day in the Morning: A Revels Celebration of the Winter Solstice (Revels Company/Langstaff), 3285
  Christmas for Solo Singers (Althouse), 3273
  Christmas for Two (collection), 3268
  Christmas Solos for All Ages (Boytim), 3276
  Christmas Solos for Kids (Lerch), 3280
  Christmas with the Vienna Boys Choir, 3289

The Christmas Collection (Walters), 3290.1
Classical Carols (Walters), 3290.2
Classical Singer's Christmas Album (collection), 3269
Classics for Christmas (Tadlock), 3288
collections, 3267–3272
A Festival of Carols in Brass (Philadelphia Brass Ensemble), 3283
A Festival of Carols (Robert Shaw Chorale), 3286
International Book of Christmas Carols (Ehret and Evans), 3278
The Joy of Christmas (Mormon Tabernacle Choir/Bernstein), 3281
A Little Christmas Music (King's Singers), 3279
Noel, Noel! French Christmas Music, 1200–1600 (Boston Camerata), 3275.1
O Holy Night (Pavarotti), 3282
100 Great Christmas Songs, 3271
170 Christmas Songs and Carols (Cuellar), 3277
★*Sing We Noel: Christmas Music from England and Early America* (Boston Camerata), 3275.2
Thys Yool: A Medieval Christmas (Best), 3274
12 Christmas Favorites (collection), 3272
Traffic
  ★*Mr. Fantasy*, 1804.1
  Smiling Phases, 1804.2
  Traffic, 1804.3
The Trammps
  ★*Atlantic Soul, 1959–1975* (collection), 2589
  Disco Box (collection), 2644
  ★*Saturday Night Fever*, 2658
Traum, Harry. *Bluegrass Guitar*, 1613
Travelers, Jordan. *Good God! Born Again Funk* (collection), 2614
Travis, Merle
  Best of Merle Travis: Sweet Temptation 1946–1953, 1545.1
  Guitar Rags and a Too Fast Past, 1545.2
  The Roots of Rock 'n' Roll, 1946–1954 (collection), 1755
  ★*Will the Circle Be Unbroken?* (collection), 1452
Travis, Randy
  I Told You So: The Ultimate Hits of Randy Travis, 1681.1
  ★*Storms of Life*, 1681.2
  Three Wooden Crosses: The Inspirational Hits of Randy Travis, 3133
Treacherous Three
  The Best of Enjoy! Records (collection), 2663
  Hip Hop Essentials, 1979–1991 (collection), 2675

★Treniers. *The Okeh Rhythm and Blues Story* (collection), 2425
Tribbett, Tye, and G.A. *Wow Gospel #1s* (collection), 3074
Tribbett, Tye. *Victory Live!*, 3100
A Tribe Called Quest
  ★*The Low End Theory*, 2933.1
  Midnight Marauders, 2933.2
  People's Instinctive Travels and the Paths of Rhythm, 2933.3
Tricky. *Maxinquaye*, 2232
Trillium. *Crossing the Stream*, 80
Trin-I-Tee 5:7. *Holla: The Best of Trin-I-Tee 5:7*, 3101
Trischka, Tony. *Hand-Picked: 25 Years of Bluegrass on Rounder Records* (collection), 1564
Tristano, Lennie
  ★*Intuition*, 625.1
  Piano Legends (collection), 480
  ★*The Smithsonian Collection of Classic Jazz* (collection), 486
Tritt, Travis. *Very Best of Travis Tritt*, 1682
The Troggs
  Nuggets: A Classic Collection from the Psychedelic Sixties (collection), 1809
  ★*Nuggets: Artifacts of the First Psychedelic Era* (collection), 1808
  ★*Nuggets II: Original Artifacts from the British Empire and Beyond* (collection), 1791
  Pure 60's: The #1 Hits (collection), 1165
Trotter, John Scott. *It's Easy to Remember* (Crosby), 1125.6
Trout Fishing in America. *Mine!*, 3224
Troy, Doris
  ★*Atlantic Soul, 1959–1975* (collection), 2589
  Beg, Scream, and Shout! The Big Ol' Box of '60s Soul (collection), 2433
Trucks, Derek. *Joyful Noise*, 382
The Trumpeteers
  The Best of King Gospel (collection), 3031
  ★*Good News: 100 Gospel Greats* (collection), 2961
  Testify! The Gospel Box (collection), 2974
Tru-Tones. *Old Town Doo-Wop, Vols. 1–3* (collection), 2324
Tubb, Ernest
  Classic Country: Kings of Country (collection), 1381
  Classic Country Music: A Smithsonian Collection (collection), 1382
  The Complete Live 1965 Show, 1546.1
  Country Style, U.S.A. (collection), 1473
  Jubilation! Great Gospel Performances, Vol. 3: Country Gospel (collection), 3112

Texas Music, Vol. 2: Western Swing and Honky Tonk (collection), 1432

★*The Texas Troubadour,* 1546.2

The Tubes. *Billboard #1s: The '80s* (collection), 1236

Tuck and Patti. *Solace: A Windham Hill Collection* (collection), 1373

Tucker, Bessie

Better Boot That Thing: Great Women Blues Singers of the 1920's (collection), 202

★*I Can't Be Satisfied: Early American Women Blues Singers, Vol. 1: Country* (collection), 149

Tucker, Ira. *Rejoice and Shout* (collection), 2969

Tucker, Jack. *Swingbillies: Hillbilly and Western Swing on Modern/Colonial/ Flair, 1947–1952* (collection), 1431

Tucker, Sophie

★*American Popular Song: Six Decades of Songwriters and Singers* (collection), 1059

Flappers, Vamps, and Sweet Young Things (collection), 1065

This Is Art Deco (collection), 1090

★*Yes, Sir, That's My Baby: The Golden Years of Tin Pan Alley* (collection), 1094

Tucker, Tanya. *Greatest Hits,* 1547

Tudor Choir

Gentle Words: Shaker Songs, 25.1

The Shapenote Album, 25.2

Tuff Darts. *D.I.Y. Blank Generation: The New York Scene* (collection), 1978

Tufo, Vincent. *The Early Minstrel Show* (collection), 96

The Tune Wranglers

Doughboys, Playboys, and Cowboys: The Golden Years of Western Swing (collection), 1428

Western Swing: 40 Bootstompers from the Golden Age (collection), 1433

Turbans

★*The Doo Wop Box: 101 Vocal Group Gems from the Golden Age of Rock 'n' Roll* (collection), 1745

★*The Doo-Wop Box* (collection), 2322

Turner, Big Joe

★*Stompin' at the Savoy: The Original Indie Label, 1944–1961* (collection), 2429

The Swing Time Records Story: R&B, Blues, and Gospel, 1946–1952 (collection), 2430

Turner, Ike. *See also* Turner, Ike and Tina

The Cobra Records Story: Chicago Rock and Blues (collection), 339

★*Legends of Guitar: Rock–The '50s, Vol. 2* (collection), 1750

Memphis Blues: Important Postwar Recordings (collection), 341

The Modern Records Blues Story (collection), 342

Rhythm Rockin' Blues: The Legendary Modern Recordings, 2309

The Sun Sessions, 2298

Turner, Ike and Tina

Beg, Scream, and Shout! The Big Ol' Box of '60s Soul (collection), 2433

The Best of Loma Records: The Rise and Fall of a 1960's Soul Label (collection), 2590

Birth of Soul, 4 Vols. (collection), 2434

The Ike and Tina Turner Story, 1960–1975, 2523.2

The Legends Ike and Tina Turner Live in '71, 2299

Proud Mary: The Best of Ike and Tina Turner, 2523.1

★*The R&B Box* (collection), 2239

Soul to Soul (collection), 2444

Turner, Joe

★*Atlantic R&B, 1947–1974* (collection), 2418

Big, Bad, and Blue: The Big Joe Turner Anthology, 2310.1, 2310.2

★*Blues Classics* (collection), 146

Blues Masters, Vol. 1: Urban Blues (collection), 338

★*The Blues: A Smithsonian Collection of Classic Blues Singers* (collection), 145

★*From Spirituals to Swing: The Legendary 1938 and 1939 Carnegie Hall Concerts Produced by John Hammond* (collection), 564

The Golden Era of Rock 'n' Roll (collection), 1748

I've Been to Kansas City, Vol. 1 (Turner), 281.1

★*The Jazz Singers: A Smithsonian Collection of Jazz Vocals from 1919–1994* (collection), 766

★*Mean Old World: The Blues from 1940–1994* (collection), 154

★*The R&B Box* (collection), 2239

Rock and Roll: The Early Days (collection), 1752

The Roots of Rock 'n' Roll, 1946–1954 (collection), 1755

Shout, Rattle, and Roll, 281.2

★*The Story of the Blues* (collection), 158

The Swingtime Records Story: R&B, Blues, and Gospel (collection), 313

The Very Best of Big Joe Turner, 2310.3

Turner, Othar. *Everybody Hollerin' Goat* (Turner), 182

Turner, Tina. *See also* Turner, Ike and Tina

One Last Time Live in Concert, 2300.1

Private Dancer, 2062, 2583

Simply the Best, 2524

Tina: All the Best—The Live Collection, 2300.2

Turner, Titus

The Fire / Fury Records Story (collection), 2422

★*The Okeh Rhythm and Blues Story* (collection), 2425

Turrentine, Stanley. *The Best of Stanley Turrentine,* 661

The Turtles

Casey Kasem Presents America's Top Ten through the Years: The Sixties (collection), 1156

Pure 60's: The #1 Hits (collection), 1165

Save the Turtles: The Turtles Greatest Hits, 1828

Songs of Protest (collection), 1820

Tutone, Tommy. *Like Omigod! The 80s Pop Culture Box (Totally)* (collection), 1241

Twain, Shania. *Greatest Hits,* 1683

29th Street Saxophone Quartet. *The Real Deal,* 1018

Twista. *The Emancipation of Mimi* (Carey), 1256.1

Twitty, Conway

The Best of Conway Twitty and Loretta Lynn, 1512

Classic Country: Kings of Country (collection), 1381

Gold, 1548.1

Silver Anniversary Collection, 1548.2

Two Gospel Keys

Classic African American Gospel from Smithsonian Folkways (collection), 2959

Fire in My Bones: Raw, Rare and Otherworldy African-American Gospel (collection), 2960

2 Live Crew

As Nasty as They Wanna Be, 2934.1

Banned in the USA, 2934.2

2Pac

★*All Eyez on Me,* 2935.1

Better Dayz, 2935.2

Me against the World, 2935.3

2pacalypse Now, 2935.5

Strictly 4 My N.I.G.G.A.Z., 2935.4

Tyler, Alvin "Red." *Best of Ace Records, Vol. 2: The R&B Hits* (collection), 2419

Tyler, Bonnie. *80's Pop Hits* (collection), 1238

Tyner, McCoy

Echoes of a Friend, 897.1

Enlightenment, 897.2

Jingle Bell Jazz (collection), 3314

Piano Legends (collection), 480

The Real McCoy, 710

U

U2

Achtung Baby, 2087.1

Elevation 2001: U2 Live from Boston, 2087.2

U2 (cont.)
  90's Pop Hits (collection), 1242
  ★*The Joshua Tree,* 2087.3
  U218 Singles, 2087.4
  War, 2087.5
UGK. *Ridin' Dirty,* 2936
Ulmer, James Blood
  Are You Glad to Be in America?,
    1019
  Progressions: 100 Years of Jazz Guitar
    (collection), 481
Ultramagnetic MC's. *Critical Beatdown,*
  2937
Ultravox!. *No Thanks! The '70s Punk
  Rebellion* (collection), 2003
Uncle Louie. *The Best of T. K. Disco*
  (collection), 2656
Uncle Tupelo
  89/93: An Anthology, 1709.1
  No Depression, 1709.2
The Undertones
  No Thanks! The '70s Punk Rebellion
    (collection), 2003
  The Undertones, 2029
United States to 1900. *See* U.S. to 1900
University of Michigan Band. *41 Great
  College Victory Songs,* 3372
The Untouchables
  ★*Atlantic Soul, 1959–1975*
    (collection), 2589
  *Dave Godin's Deep Soul Treasures,
    Vols. 1–4* (collection), 2435
Upsetters. *The Fire / Fury Records Story*
  (collection), 2422
U-Roy. *Dread in Babylon,* 1975
U.S. hitmakers, 1913–1920
  ★*Born to Run* (Springsteen), 1919
  Chicago IX: Greatest Hits, 1914
  Child Is Father to the Man (Blood,
    Sweat, and Tears), 1913.1
  The Complete Hit Singles (Three Dog
    Night), 1920
  Greatest Hits, 1974–1978 (Miller),
    1916
  Greatest Hits (Seger), 1918.1
  Live Bullet (Seger), 1918.2
  Silk Degrees (Scaggs), 1917
  *The Very Best of Daryl Hall and John
    Oates,* 1915
  *What Goes Up: Best of Blood, Sweat,
    and Tears,* 1913.2
U.S. rock scene in the sixties, 1808–1850
U.S. to 1900
  band music, 81–90.6
  overview, p5–6
  periodicals for up-to-date CD notices
    and reviews, suggested, p3
  political music
    Civil War period, 59–80
    Revolutionary War period, 44–58
  popular vocal and instrumental
    music, 91–123
  ragtime, 124–144

  religious music, 1–31
  spirituals, 32–43
USA European Connection. *The Best of
  T. K. Disco* (collection), 2656
UTFO. *Utfo,* 2938
Utica Institute Jubilee Singers. *The Half
  Ain't Never Been Told, Vols. 1 and 2*
  (collection), 2956

V

Vaerieteers. *Night Train to Nashville: Music
  City Rhythm and Blues, 1945–1970,
  Vol. 1* (collection), 2377
Valdelar, Pat. *The Mercury New
  Orleans Sessions 1950 and 1953*
  (collection), 2361
Valdes, Chucho. *Bele Bele en la Habana,*
  865
Valens, Ritchie
  La Bamba and Other Hits, 1769
  ★*Legends of Guitar: Rock–The '50s,
    Vol. 2* (collection), 1750
Valentine, Thomas. *See* Thomas, Kid
The Valentines
  ★*The Doo-Wop Box* (collection),
    2322
  The Doo-Wop Box II (collection),
    2323
  *Night Train to Nashville: Music City
    Rhythm and Blues, 1945–1970,
    Vol. 1* (collection), 2377
  Old Town Doo-Wop, Vols. 1–3
    (collection), 2324
The Valentinos
  ★*Atlantic Soul, 1959–1975*
    (collection), 2589
  Sam Cooke's SAR Records Story
    (collection), 2606
Valesquez, Jaci. *Mi Corazón,* 3166
Vallee, Rudy
  ★*Brother, Can You Spare a Dime?
    American Song during the Great
    Depression* (collection), 1061
  *The Great Depression: American Music
    in the '30s* (collection), 1066
  Life Is Just a Bowl of Cherries, 1150.1
  Richard Whiting (songwriter
    collection), 1116
  Vagabond Lover, 1150.2
  Vincent Youmans (songwriter
    collection), 1118
  ★*Yes, Sir, That's My Baby: The Golden
    Years of Tin Pan Alley* (collection),
    1094
Van Halen
  The Best of Van Halen, Vol. 1, 2088.1
  1984, 2088.2
  ★*Van Halen,* 2088.3
Van Heusen, Jimmy
  James Van Heusen (songwriter
    collection), 1112.1
  Songs of Burke and Van Heusen
    (songwriter collection), 1112.2

Van Keersbilck, David. *The Early Minstrel
  Show* (collection), 96
Van Shelton, Ricky. *16 Biggest Hits,* 1685
Van Zandt, Townes. *Anthology
  1968–1979,* 1710
Vance, Al. *The Complete Goldwax Singles,
  Vol. 1* (collection), 2591
Vandermark, Ken
  School Days: Crossing Division, 1020.1
  Vandermark 5: Simpatico, 1020.2
Vandross, Luther
  Any Love, 2416.1
  80's Pop Hits (collection), 1238
  ★*The Essential Luther Vandross,* 2416.2
  From Luther, with Love: The Videos,
    2584.1
  Love, Luther, 2416.3
  *Luther Vandross Live at Radio City
    Music Hall, 2003,* 2416.4
  Luther Vandross Live at Wembley,
    2584.2
Vangelis
  Antarctica: Music from the Soundtrack,
    1319.1
  ★*China,* 1319.2
  Opera Sauvage, 1319.3
  Ultimate New Age (collection), 1376
Vanilla Ice. *To the Extreme,* 2939
The Vapors. *Like Omigod! The 80s Pop
  Culture Box (Totally)* (collection),
  1241
Varner, Tom. *Second Communion,* 1021
vaudeville or classic blues, 202–210.6
  Bessie Smith Songbook (Smith), 210.1
  *Better Boot That Thing: Great Women
    Blues Singers of the 1920's*
    (collection), 202
  *Blues Masters, Vol. 11: Classic Blues
    Women* (collection), 203
  collections, 202–205
  Complete Recorded Works, Vol. 1
    (Butterbeans and Susie), 206
  The Complete Recordings, Vols. 1–5
    (Smith), 210.2
  The Complete Recordings, Vols. 1–8
    (Smith), 210.3
  Empress of the Blues, Vol. 2 (Smith),
    210.4
  ★*The Essential Bessie Smith* (Smith),
    210.5
  ★*I Can't Be Satisfied: Early American
    Women Blues Singers, Vol. 2: Town*
    (collection), 204
  Ma Rainey's Black Bottom (Rainey),
    209.1
  *Mean Mothers: Independent Womens'
    Blues, Vol. 1* (collection), 205
  Mother of the Blues (Rainey), 209.2
  Queen of the Blues, Vol. 1 (Smith),
    210.6
  The Uncrowned Queen of the Blues
    (Cox), 207
  Young Alberta Hunter (Hunter), 208

Vaughan, Sarah
  Alec Wilder (songwriter collection), 1117.1
  ★*American Popular Song: Six Decades of Songwriters and Singers* (collection), 1059
  The Classic Hoagy Carmichael (songwriter collection), 1097.1
  Cy Coleman (songwriter collection), 1098.2
  The Definitive Collection (songwriter collection), 1101.1
  E. Y. Harburg (songwriter collection), 1103
  Frank Loesser (songwriter collection), 1106.1
  George Gershwin (songwriter collection), 1101.3
  Hoagy Carmichael (songwriter collection), 1097.2
  How Long Has This Been Going On?, 804.1
  James Van Heusen (songwriter collection), 1112.1
  ★*The Jazz Singers: A Smithsonian Collection of Jazz Vocals from 1919–1994* (collection), 766
  Jerome Kern (songwriter collection), 1104.1
  ★*Ken Burns Jazz Collection: Sarah Vaughan*, 804.2
  ★*Ken Burns Jazz: The Story of America's Music* (collection), 478
  Rodgers / Hart (songwriter collection), 1109.1
  Sarah Vaughan, 804.3
  Sarah Vaughan Live in '58 and '64, 804.5
  Sarah Vaughan: The Divine One, 804.4
  Sings the George Gershwin Songbook, 804.6
  ★*The Smithsonian Collection of Classic Jazz* (collection), 486
  Stars of the Apollo (collection), 2240
  Swingin' Easy, 804.7
  The Very Best of Cole Porter (songwriter collection), 1108.3
  Waller / Razaf (songwriter collection), 1113.2
Vaughan, Stevie Ray
  Blues Fest: Modern Blues of the '80s (collection), 409
  Blues Masters, Vol. 9: Postmodern Blues (collection), 412
  Blues Masters, Vol. 3: Texas Blues (collection), 311
  The Essential Stevie Ray Vaughan and Double Trouble, 465.1
  The Sky Is Crying, 465.2
  Stevie Ray Vaughan, Lightnin' Blues, 1983–1987 (Vaughan, Tapella, Sokolow and Schiff), 383

Vaughn, Billy. *The Billy Vaughn Collection*, 1227
Vaughn, Viktor. *Vaudeville Villain*, 2940
Vee, Bobby. *The Very Best of Bobby Vee*, 1783
Vel Tones. *The Complete Goldwax Singles, Vol. 1* (collection), 2591
Velours. *The Doo-Wop Box II* (collection), 2323
Velvelettes. *Motown around the World* (collection), 2437
Velvet Underground
  Loaded, 1889.
  Peel Slowly and See, 1889.2
  The Velvet Underground, 1889.3
  ★*The Velvet Underground and Nico*, 1889.4
Velvetones. *The Doo-Wop Box II* (collection), 2323
★Velvets. *The Doo-Wop Box* (collection), 2322
The Ventures
  Legends of Guitar: Rock–The '60s, Vol. 1 (collection), 1860
  Rock Instrumental Classics, Vol. 2: The 60s (collection), 1771
  Walk Don't Run: The Best of the Ventures, 1784
Venuti, Joe
  Lost Chords: White Musicians and Their Contributions to Jazz (collection), 479
  Stringing the Blues, 520
★Vera, Billy. *Atlantic Soul, 1959–1975* (collection), 2589
Verdon, Gwen
  Cy Coleman (songwriter collection), 1098.2
  Dorothy Fields (songwriter collection), 1100
Vernay, Lucienne. *Songs in French for Children*, 3236
★Versatones. *Atlantic Vocal Groups, 1951–1963* (collection), 2320
★Verson, Vivian. *Nashville Jumps: Blues and Rhythm on Nashville Independent Labels 1945–1955* (collection), 2376
★Vibraharps. *Atlantic Vocal Groups, 1951–1963* (collection), 2320
The Vibrations
  ★*Atlantic Soul, 1959–1975* (collection), 2589
  Best of Chess R&B, Vols. 1 and 2 (collection), 2420
Vibrators. *No Thanks! The '70s Punk Rebellion* (collection), 2003
Victor Minstrels. *I'll Dance Till de Sun Breaks Through: Ragtime, Cakewalks and Stomps*, 133
Victory 5. *Boddie Recording Company Cleveland, Ohio* (collection), 2569, 2570

Victory Travelers. *Good God! Born Again Funk* (collection), 2614
Vienna Boys Choir. *Christmas with the Vienna Boys Choir*, 3289
Vienna State Opera Orchestra. *National Anthems of the World*, 3381
Village People. *Disco Box* (collection), 2644
Vincent, Gene
  Gene Vincent, 1770
  ★*Legends of Guitar: Rock–The '50s, Vol. 1* (collection), 1749
  ★*Legends of Guitar: Rock–The '50s, Vol. 2* (collection), 1750
Vincent, Rhonda
  Angels Are Singing: A Women's Bluegrass Gospel Collection, 1559
  One Step Ahead, 1614
Vinison, Eddie "Cleanhead"
  Blues Masters, Vol. 1: Urban Blues (collection), 338
  ★*The Blues: A Smithsonian Collection of Classic Blues Singers* (collection), 145
  Stars of the Apollo (collection), 2240
Vinton, Bobby. *All-Time Greatest Hits*, 1228
Violent Femmes. *Violent Femmes*, 2203
Violinaires. *None but the Righteous: Chess Gospel Greats* (collection), 3037
Virginia Dandies
  The Half Ain't Never Been Told, Vols. 1 and 2 (collection), 2956
  Mountain Gospel: The Sacred Roots of Country Music (collection), 3113
★Vito and the Salutations. *The Doo-Wop Box* (collection), 2322
Vivaldi, Antonio. *Vivaldi's Ring of Mystery*, 3261
vocal and instrumental music, popular. *See* popular vocal and instrumental music
vocal groups
  rhythm and blues, 2320–2358
  soul, 2538–2551
The Vocaleers
  The Doo-Wop Box II (collection), 2323
  Old Town Doo-Wop, Vols. 1–3 (collection), 2324
Voices of East Harlem. *Soul to Soul* (collection), 2444
Voidoids. *D.I.Y. Blank Generation: The New York Scene* (collection), 1978
Voigt, Deborah. *Songs: Foster, Griffes, Copland* (collection), 101
Vollenweider, Andreas
  Behind the Gardens, behind the Wall, under the Tree, 1344.1
  Caverna Magica, 1344.2
Volumes. *The Doo-Wop Box II* (collection), 2323

Von Streeter, James. *The Big Horn: The History of the Honkin' and Screamin' Saxophone* (collection), 2314

V.S.O.P. *The Quintet: V.S.O.P.,* 898

W

Waco Brothers
Greasy Kid Stuff (collection), 3210
The Bottle Let Me Down: Songs for Bumpy Wagon Rides (collection), 3191

Wagoner, Porter
Classic Country: Kings of Country (collection), 1381
The Essential Porter and Dolly, 1549

★Wain, Bea. *The Music Goes Round and Around: The Golden Years of Tin Pan Alley, 1930–1939* (collection), 1070

Wainwright, Rufus. *Want One,* 1310

Waits, Tom. *Rain Dogs,* 2204

Wakefiled, Frank. *Folkways Years, 1964–1983,* 1568

Walcott, Collin. *Codona,* 867

Walden, Narada Michael. *Disco Box* (collection), 2644

Waldron, Mal
Piano Legends (collection), 480
Sempre Amore, 1022

Walker, Albertina
Please Be Patient with Me, 3004
The Rough Guide to Gospel (collection), 2970

Walker, Charles "Wigg" and the Daffodils. *Night Train to Nashville: Music City Rhythm and Blues, 1945–1970, Vol. 2* (collection), 2378

Walker, Hezekiah. *The Essential Hezekiah Walker,* 3072

Walker, Jerry Jeff
Ultimate Collection, 1551.1
Viva Terlingua!, 1551.2

Walker, Joe Louis
Blue Soul, 466.1
The Gift, 466.2

Walker, Johnny "Big Moose." *Living Chicago Blues, Vol. 2* (collection), 416

Walker, Jr. and the All Stars
Beg, Scream, and Shout! The Big Ol' Box of '60s Soul (collection), 2433
Heaven Must Have Sent You: The Holland/Dozier/Holland Story (collection), 2436
Hitsville USA: The Motown Singles Collection (collection), 2603
The Ultimate Collection, 2577

Walker, Nancy. *George Gershwin* (songwriter collection), 1101.3

Walker, Philip. *Bottom of the Top,* 364

Walker, Ronnie. *The Spring Story: Essential 70s Soul* (collection), 2608

Walker, Scott. *Scott 4,* 1969

Walker, T-Bone
Blues Masters, Vol. 3: Texas Blues (collection), 311
Blues Masters, Vol. 1: Urban Blues (collection), 338
★*The Blues: A Smithsonian Collection of Classic Blues Singers* (collection), 145
★*Central Avenue Sounds: Jazz in Los Angeles* (collection), 471
The Complete Capitol / Black and White Recordings, 325.1
The Complete Imperial Recordings, 325.2
★*Mean Old World: The Blues from 1940–1994* (collection), 154
New Orleans Guitar (collection), 330
The Original Source, 325.3
Soul Shots, Vol. 4: Urban Blues (collection), 343
T-Bone Blues, 325.4
The T-Bone Walker Collection: 20 Great Tunes from a Blues Legend, 325.5
★*Texas Music, Vol. 1: Postwar Blues Combos* (collection), 316
The Roots of Rock 'n' Roll, 1946–1954 (collection), 1755
★*Very Best of T-Bone Walker,* 325.6

Walker, William
Southern Harmony, Excerpts, 26.2
★*The Southern Harmony,* 26.1

Walker, Willie. *The Complete Goldwax Singles, Vol. 3* (collection), 2593

Wallace, Bennie. *Bennie Wallace Plays Monk,* 1023

Wallace, Sippie
Blues Masters, Vol. 11: Classic Blues Women (collection), 203
★*The Blues: A Smithsonian Collection of Classic Blues Singers* (collection), 145
★*I Can't Be Satisfied: Early American Women Blues Singers, Vol. 2: Town* (collection), 204
When the Sun Goes Down 2: The First Time I Met the Blues (collection), 160
Women Be Wise, 405

Waller, Fats
★*Complete Victor Piano Solos,* 526
The Complete Recorded Works, Vol. 2: A Handful of Keys, 588.1
The First of the Singer Songwriters: Key Cuts (Carmichael), 1124
The Genius of Thomas "Fats" Waller (songwriter collection), 1113.1
The Greatest Ragtime of the Century (collection), 125
★*Handful of Keys,* 588.2

If You Got to Ask, You Ain't Got It!, 1133
★*The Jazz Singers: A Smithsonian Collection of Jazz Vocals from 1919–1994* (collection), 766
★*Nipper's Greatest Hits: The 30's, Vol. 1* (collection), 1072
Piano Legends (collection), 480
★*The Smithsonian Collection of Classic Jazz* (collection), 486
Stormy Weather [1999] (Waller, Calloway, Horn, and others), 1057.1
Stormy Weather [2005] (Waller, Calloway, Horn, and others), 1057.2
25 Sweethearts of Yesteryear (collection), 1092
Waller / Razaf (songwriter collection), 1113.2

Wallington, George. *The George Wallington Trios,* 602

Walter B. Rogers Band. *Early Syncopated Dance Music: Cakewalks, Two-Steps, Trots and Glides* (collection), 124

Walters, Richard
Classical Carols, 3290.2
The Christmas Collection, 3290.1

War
All Day Music, 2642.1
Anthology, 1970–1994, 2642.2
Have a Nice Decade: The '70s Pop Culture Box (collection), 1240
The World Is a Ghetto, 2642.3

Ward, Anita. *Disco Box* (collection), 2644

Ward, Billy. *King R&B Box Set* (collection), 2424

Ward, Clara
Gospel Warriors: Over 50 Years of Great Solo Performances (collection), 2987
★*The Gospel Sound of Spirit Feel* (collection), 2965
★*The Great Gospel Women* (collection), 2989
The Great Gospel Women, Vol. 2 (collection), 2990
★*Jubilation! Great Gospel Performances, Vol. 1: Black Gospel* (collection), 2966
Respect: Aretha's Influences and Inspiration (collection), 2440
Testify! The Gospel Box (collection), 2974

Ward, Helen
Johnny Mercer (songwriter collection), 1107.1
★*Sophisticated Ladies* (collection), 1087

Ward, Matthew. *First Love: A Historic Gathering of Jesus Music Pioneers* (collection), 3137

Ward, Robert
    Blues Fest: Modern Blues of the '90s
        (collection), 410
    Fear No Evil, 467
Ware, David S. *Wisdom of Uncertainty,*
    1024
Waring, Fred and His Pennsylvanians
    ★*Nipper's Greatest Hits: The 20's*
        (collection), 1071
    The Roaring 'Twenties (collection),
        1080
    ★*Yes, Sir, That's My Baby: The Golden
        Years of Tin Pan Alley* (collection),
        1094
Warren, Baby Boy. *Detroit Blues: Blues
    from the Motor City* (collection),
    291
Warren G. *Regulate . . . G Funk Era,* 2941
Warren, Harry. *Harry Warren* (songwriter
    collection), 1114
Warrington, Tom. *Essential Styles for
    the Drummer and Bassist: A Cross
    Section of Styles as Played by
    Today's Top Artists* (Houghton and
    Warrington), 493
Wartts, Andrew. *Good God! Born Again
    Funk* (collection), 2614
Warwick, Dionne
    *Beg, Scream, and Shout! The Big Ol'
        Box of '60s Soul* (collection),
        2433
    ★*Dionne Warwick Collection,* 1229.1
    *The Dionne Warwick Collection: Her
        All-Time Greatest Hits,* 2526.1
    *In Concert Classics Featuring Dionne
        Warwick,* 2526.2
    Live in Concert, 1229.2
    *The Look of Love: The Burt Bacharach
        Collection* (collection), 1161
    *Respect: Aretha's Influences and
        Inspiration* (collection), 2440
    The Scepter Records Story (collection),
        2426
Was (Not Was). *Boo!,* 2205
Washboard Sam
    ★*The Blues: A Smithsonian Collection
        of Classic Blues Singers* (collection),
        145
    Rockin' My Blues Away, 282.1
    Washboard Sam 1936–1947, 282.2
    *When the Sun Goes Down 3: That's
        Chicago's South Side* (collection),
        270
★Washington, Baby. *Atlantic Soul,
    1959–1975* (collection), 2589
Washington, Dinah
    After Hours with Miss D, 2313.1
    Alec Wilder (songwriter collection),
        1117.1
    Back to the Blues, 2313.2
    ★*Blues Classics* (collection), 146
    Blues Masters, Vol. 1: Urban Blues
        (collection), 338

*The Complete Roulette Dinah
    Washington Sessions,* 2313.3
The Definitive Collection (songwriter
    collection), 1101.1
The Definitive Dinah Washington,
    2313.4
Dinah Jams, 2313.5
Dinah Sings Bessie Smith, 2313.6
E. Y. Harburg (songwriter collection),
    1103
★*The Fabulous Miss D! The Keynote,
    Decca, and Mercury Singles
    1943–1953,* 2313.7
*First Issue: The Dinah Washington
    Story: The Original Recordings,*
    2313.8
Frank Loesser (songwriter collection),
    1106.1
Gold, 2313.9
★*Jazz on a Summer's Day* (collection),
    664
★*The Jazz Singers: A Smithsonian
    Collection of Jazz Vocals from
    1919–1994* (collection), 766
Legendary Big Band Singers (collection),
    767
★*Mean Old World: The Blues from
    1940–1994* (collection), 154
★*The R&B Box* (collection), 2239
*Respect: Aretha's Influences and
    Inspiration* (collection), 2440
*Sentimental Journey: Pop Vocal
    Classics, Vol. 4* (collection), 1170
The Very Best of Cole Porter
    (songwriter collection), 1108.3
★*The Very Best of Dinah Washington,*
    1230
Waller / Razaf (songwriter collection),
    1113.2
What a Diff'rence a Day Makes, 2313.10
Washington, Grover
    ★*Ken Burns Jazz: The Story of
        America's Music* (collection), 478
    Mister Magic, 910.1
    Winelight, 910.2
Washington, Sister Ernestine
    *Classic African American Gospel from
        Smithsonian Folkways* (collection),
        2959
    ★*Good News: 100 Gospel Greats*
        (collection), 2961
    ★*The Gospel Sound of Spirit Feel*
        (collection), 2965
    The Great Gospel Women, Vol. 2
        (collection), 2990
Waters, Ethel
    ★*American Popular Song: Six Decades
        of Songwriters and Singers*
        (collection), 1059
    Arthur Schwartz (songwriter
        collection), 1110.2
    The Classic Hoagy Carmichael
        (songwriter collection), 1097.1

Cole Porter (songwriter collection),
    1108.1
★*Favourite Songs of Ethel Waters,* 1151.1
*The First of the Singer Songwriters: Key
    Cuts* (Carmichael), 1124
Hoagy Carmichael (songwriter
    collection), 1097.2
The Incomparable Ethel Waters, 1151.2
Irving Berlin: A Hundred Years
    (songwriter collection), 1096.3
★*The Jazz Singers: A Smithsonian
    Collection of Jazz Vocals from
    1919–1994* (collection), 766
    1929–1939, 1151.3
★*On Stage and Screen,* 1151.4
★*Sophisticated Ladies* (collection),
    1087
Waller / Razaf (songwriter collection),
    1113.2
★*Yes, Sir, That's My Baby: The Golden
    Years of Tin Pan Alley* (collection),
    1094
Waters, Muddy. *See* Muddy Waters
Watson, Bobby
    Love Remains, 1025
    Yule Struttin': A Blue Note Christmas
        (collection), 3323
Watson, Dale. *Cheatin' Heart Attack,* 1711
Watson, Doc
    American Roots Music (collection),
        1380
    Black Mountain Rag, 1552.1
    Doc and the Boys/Live and Pickin',
        1552.2
    Essential Doc Watson, 1552.3
    Southbound, 1552.3
    The Songs of Doc Watson, 1615
    Top of the Hill Bluegrass (collection),
        1567
    ★*Will the Circle Be Unbroken?*
        (collection), 1452
Watson, Gene. *Greatest Hits,* 1686
Watson, Johnny "Guitar"
    Very Best of Johnny "Guitar" Watson,
        326.1
    *The Very Best of Johnny "Guitar"
        Watson: In Loving Memory,* 326.2
Watson, Johnny. *Soul Shots: A Collection
    of Sixties Soul Classics* (collection),
    2443
Watson, Merle
    Black Mountain Rag, 1552.1
    Doc and the Boys/Live and Pickin',
        1552.2
    Essential Doc Watson, 1552.3
    Southbound, 1552.3
Watts, Noble "Thin Man." *The Fire / Fury
    Records Story* (collection), 2422
The Watts Prophets. *Things Gonna Get
    Greater,* 1976
Watts 103rd St. Rhythm Band. ★*What It
    Is! Funky Soul and Rare Grooves*
    (collection), 2615

Waverly Consort. *An American Journey: Bound for the Promised Land,* 27

The Way. *Best of Christian Rock (1970–1986), Vol. 1* (collection), 3135

Wayne, David. *E. Y. Harburg* (songwriter collection), 1103

Wayne, Frances. *Harold Arlen* (songwriter collection), 1095.1

We the People. *Eccentric Soul: Mighty Mike Lenaburg* (collection), 2563

Weather Girls. *Disco Box* (collection), 2644

Weather Report
★*I Sing the Body Electric,* 832.1
★*Ken Burns Jazz: The Story of America's Music* (collection), 478
Mysterious Traveller, 832.2
Pioneers of the New Age (collection), 1371

Weathers, Oscar. *The Sweetest Feeling: A Van McCoy Songbook* (collection), 2447

Weaver, Curley
Atlanta Blues: Big City Blues from the Heartland (collection), 241
Good Time Blues: Harmonicas, Kazoos, Washboards, and Cow-Bells (collection), 268
Play My Juke-Box: East Coast Blues (collection), 244

Weaver, Sylvester
The Georgia Blues (collection), 242
A Richer Tradition: Country Blues and String Band Music (collection), 187

Webb, Chick
★*Big Band Jazz: From the Beginnings to the Fifties* (collection), 529
★*Ken Burns Jazz: The Story of America's Music* (collection), 478
★*Spinnin' the Webb,* 550
★*Swing Time! The Fabulous Big Band Era* (collection), 1089

Webb, Jody, and His Round Up Boys. *Swingbillies: Hillbilly and Western Swing on Modern/Colonial/Flair, 1947–1952* (collection), 1431

Weber, Eberhard. *The Colors of Chloe,* 868

Weber, Joan. *Sentimental Journey: Pop Vocal Classics, Vol. 4* (collection), 1170

Webster, Ben
Four Tenors: John Coltrane, Charles Lloyd, Sonny Rollins and Ben Webster (collection), 627
Jazz Lullaby (collection), 3264
Jazz Masters: Vintage Collection, 1958–1961 (collection), 477
★*Soulville,* 736.1
★*Sound of Jazz* (collection), 487
Tenor Sax Legend: Live and Intimate, 736.2

Webster, Katie
Blues Fest: Modern Blues of the '80s (collection), 409
Swamp Boogie Queen, 468

wedding songs, 3355–3368
Amazing Wedding Songs (collection), 3355
The Best Wedding Songs Ever (collection), 3356
The Bride's Guide to Wedding Music: A Complete Resource including 65 Musical Selections in All Styles Plus an Article on Planning the Music for Your Wedding Ceremony (collection), 3357
The Collection of Wedding Music (collection), 3358
Contemporary Wedding Favorites (collection), 3360
Essential Songs: Wedding (collection), 3359
Great Songs . . . For Weddings (collection), 3362
The Knot Collection of Ceremony and Wedding Music Selected by the Knot's Carley Roney (collection), 3361
Rockin' and Rollin' Wedding Songs, Vol. 1 (collection), 3363
Rockin' and Rollin' Wedding Songs, Vol. 2 (collection), 3364
Songs for a Christian Wedding (collection), 3365
Traditional and Popular Wedding Music (collection), 3366
25 Wedding Favorites (collection), 3367
Wedding Songs Big Book (collection), 3368

Wee Hairy Beasties
★*Animal Crackers,* 3207
Animal Playground (collection), 3226

Ween. *Whatever: The '90s Pop and Culture Box* (collection), 1244

Weezer
Weezer, 2206
Whatever: The '90s Pop and Culture Box (collection), 1244

Weill, Kurt
Broadway and Hollywood (songwriter collection), 1115.1
From Berlin to Broadway: A Selection (songwriter collection), 1115.2
Kurt Weill: American Songbook Series, 1152

Weirdos. *Weird World, Vol. 1: 1977–1981,* 2001

Welch, Gillian. *Revival,* 1712

Weldon, Casey Bill. *Bottleneck Trendsetters of the 1930s* (collection), 266

Welk, Lawrence. *Biggest Hits,* 1231

Weller, Paul. *The Tomorrow Show with Tom Snyder: Punk and New Wave* (collection), 1981

Wellington, Valerie
Million Dollar Secret, 469
The New Bluebloods (collection), 419

★Wellman, Charlie. *At the Jazz Band Ball: Early Hot Jazz, Song, and Dance* (collection), 470

Wells, Jean
Dave Godin's Deep Soul Treasures, Vols. 1–4 (collection), 2435
Respect: Aretha's Influences and Inspiration (collection), 2440

Wells, Junior
Blues Hit Big Town, 309.1
Blues Masters, Vol. 4: Harmonica Classics (collection), 286
★*The Blues: A Smithsonian Collection of Classic Blues Singers* (collection), 145
★*Chicago: The Blues Today!* (collection), 290
★*Hoodoo Man Blues,* 309.2
★*Mean Old World: The Blues from 1940–1994* (collection), 154

Wells, Kitty
Essential Recordings, 1553
Jubilation! Great Gospel Performances, Vol. 3: Country Gospel (collection), 3112

Wells, Mary
★*Atlantic Soul, 1959–1975* (collection), 2589
Beg, Scream, and Shout! The Big Ol' Box of '60s Soul (collection), 2433
Heaven Must Have Sent You: The Holland/Dozier/Holland Story (collection), 2436
Hitsville USA: The Motown Singles Collection (collection), 2603
★*The R&B Box* (collection), 2239
The Ultimate Collection, 2528

Wernick, Peter
Bluegrass Banjo, 1616.1
Bluegrass Songbook, 1616.2

★Wesley, Fred. *What It Is! Funky Soul and Rare Grooves* (collection), 2615

West Angeles Church of God in Christ Mass Choir and Congregation. *Saints in Praise: Their Very Best,* 3073

West coast and Texas rock, 1829–1850
Abraxas (Santana), 1845.1
Absolutely Free (Zappa), 1850.1
All Time Greatest Hits (Steppenwolf), 1848
American Beauty (Grateful Dead), 1837.1
The Best of Doug Sahm and the Sir Douglas Quintet, 1844
The Best of Steve Miller, 1968–1973, 1840
The Best of Tracy Nelson / Mother Earth, 1842
Buffalo Springfield Again, 1832.1

Cheap Thrills (Big Brother and the Holding Company), 1831

★*Chronicle* (Creedence Clearwater Revival), 1834

The Collected Country Joe and the Fish, 1833

The Doors, 1835.1

The Doors Essential Guitar Collection, 1835.2

The Doors Legacy: The Absolute Best, 1835.3

Easter Everywhere (13th Floor Elevators), 1849

The Essential Sly and the Family Stone, 1846.1

Freak Out! (Zappa), 1850.2

★*Greatest Hits* (Sly and the Family Stone), 1846.2

Happy Trails (Quicksilver Messenger Service), 1843.1

Hot Burritos! The Flying Burrito Brothers Anthology, 1836

Hot Rats (Zappa), 1850.3

Jefferson Airplane Loves You, 1838.1

Ladies and Gentlemen . . . The Grateful Dead: Fillmore East, April 1971, 1837.2

★*Live Dead* (Grateful Dead), 1837.3

Pearl (Joplin), 1839

Quicksilver Messenger Service, 1843.2

★*Retrospective: The Best of Buffalo Springfield*, 1832.2

San Francisco Nights (collection), 1829

★*Santana*, 1845.2

Santana's Greatest Hits, 1845.3

Sons of Mercury (Quicksilver Messenger Service), 1843.3

Strictly Commercial: The Best of Frank Zappa, 1850.4

★*Surrealistic Pillow* (Jefferson Airplane), 1838.2

Texas Music, Vol. 3: Garage Bands and Psychedelia (collection), 1830

Time Circle (Spirit), 1847

The Very Best of the Doors, 1835.4

Vintage: The Very Best of Moby Grape, 1841

Viva Santana!, 1845.4

★*We're Only in It for the Money* (Zappa), 1850.5

Workingman's Dead (Grateful Dead), 1837.4

West coast blues. *See* Texas and West coast blues

West, Dottie. *Dottie West*, 1554

West, Harry. *Favorite Gospel Songs*, 3134

West, Kanye
  The College Dropout, 2942.1
  Late Registration, 2942.2
  My Beautiful Dark Twisted Fantasy, 2942.3

West, Mae
  ★*Nipper's Greatest Hits: The 30's, Vol. 1* (collection), 1072
  This Is Art Deco (collection), 1090

West, Wesley W. "Speedy." *Stratosphere Boogie: The Flaming Guitars of Speedy West and Jimmy Bryant*, 1555

western swing, 1428–1448
  Anthology (Wills), 1448.1
  Best of the West (Riders in the Sky), 1445
  Cliff Bruner and His Texas Wanderers, 1437
  Coming' Right at Ya / Texas Gold (Asleep at the Wheel), 1434.1
  ★*Complete Recordings of the Father of Western Swing, 1932–1937* (Brown), 1436.1
  Doughboys, Playboys, and Cowboys: The Golden Years of Western Swing (collection), 1428
  Flamin' Mamie, 1938–1941 (Penny), 1444
  ★*Hank Thompson*, 1446
  Heroes of Country Music, Vol. 1: Legends of Western Swing (collection), 1429
  Legends of Western Swing Guitar (collection), 1430
  Light Crust Doughboys, 1936–1941, 1442
  Lost in the Ozone (Commander Cody and His Lost Planet Airmen), 1438
  Saturday Night Rag (Boyd), 1435
  Shame on You (Cooley), 1439
  Smoke! Smoke! Smoke! (Williams), 1447
  South Texas Swing (Hofner), 1441
  Swingbillies: Hillbilly and Western Swing on Modern/Colonial/Flair, 1947–1952 (collection), 1431
  Take It Away the Leon Way! (McAuliffe), 1443
  Texas Moon (Duncan), 1440
  Texas Music, Vol. 2: Western Swing and Honky Tonk (collection), 1432
  Western Swing: 40 Bootstompers from the Golden Age (Asleep at the Wheel), 1434.2
  Western Swing: 40 Bootstompers from the Golden Age (collection), 1433
  Western Swing Chronicles, Vol. 1 (Brown), 1436.2

★Western Wind. *I Am the Rose of Sharon: Early American Vocal Music*, 28

Weston, Kim
  Beg, Scream, and Shout! The Big Ol' Box of '60s Soul (collection), 2433
  Heaven Must Have Sent You: The Holland/Dozier/Holland Story (collection), 2436
  Hitsville USA: The Motown Singles Collection (collection), 2603

Weston, Ollie. *Exploring Jazz Clarinet*, 496

Weston, Paul
  Hit Parade, 1943 (collection), 1157
  ★*Sentimental Journey: Pop Vocal Classics, Vol. 1* (collection), 1081

Weston, Randy
  African Cookbook, 662
  Blues to Africa, 899.1
  Spirits of Our Ancestors, 899.2

Westside Connection. *Bow Down*, 2943

Wham!
  80's Pop Hits (collection), 1238
  Make It Big, 2089

Wheatstraw, Peetie
  Acoustic Country Blues Guitar: Delta Blues before Robert Johnson (collection), 211
  Back to the Crossroads: The Roots of Robert Johnson (collection), 212
  ★*Blues Classics* (collection), 146
  ★*The Blues: A Smithsonian Collection of Classic Blues Singers* (collection), 145
  The Devil's Son in Law, 283
  ★*Legends of the Blues, Vol. 1* (collection), 150
  The Road to Robert Johnson and Beyond (collection), 221
  St. Louis Blues: The Depression (collection), 232
  ★*The Story of the Blues* (collection), 158
  When the Sun Goes Down 3: That's Chicago's South Side (collection), 270

Wheeler, Kenny. *Deer Wan*, 1026

Wheeler, Mary. *Respect: Aretha's Influences and Inspiration* (collection), 2440

Whiskeytown
  Faithless Street, 1713.1
  Strangers Almanac, 1713.2

Whistler. *Violin, Sing the Blues for Me: African-American Fiddlers* (collection), 192

Whitcomb, Ian. *25 Hits from the British Invasion* (collection), 1792

White, Barry
  All-Time Greatest Hits, 2529.1
  ★*Just for You*, 2529.2
  Let the Music Play: The Barry White Story, 2529.3

White, B.F. *The Sacred Harp*, 29

White, Bryan. *Greatest Hits*, 1687

White, Bukka
  Acoustic Country Blues Guitar: Delta Blues before Robert Johnson (collection), 211
  American Primitive, Vol. 1: Raw Pre-War Gospel (collection), 2976
  ★*The Blues: A Smithsonian Collection of Classic Blues Singers* (collection), 145

White, Bukka (cont.)

The Complete Bukka White (White), 228

Legends of Country Blues (collection), 218

★*Legends of the Blues, Vol. 1* (collection), 150

Masters of the Country Blues: Son House and Bukka White (collection), 219

★*Masters of the Delta Blues: The Friends of Charlie Patton* (collection), 220

Newport Folk Festival: Best of the Blues, 1959–68 (collection), 392

News and the Blues: Telling It Like It Is (collection), 156

The Roots of Rock (collection), 368

★*The Story of the Blues* (collection), 158

When the Sun Goes Down 1: Walk Right In (collection), 159

★White, Georgia. *Blues Classics* (collection), 146

White Heart. *CCM Top 100: Greatest Songs in Christian Music, Vol. 1* (collection), 3136

White, Jack

Blunderbuss, 2207.1

Lazaretto, 2207.2

White, Josh. *Preachin' the Gospel: Holy Blues* (collection), 2979

The White Stripes

De Stijl, 2208.1

Elephant, 2208.2

White Blood Cells, 2208.3

Whitehead, Ronnie. *Eccentric Soul: Mighty Mike Lenaburg* (collection), 2563

Whiteheart. *Best of Christian Rock (1970–1986), Vol. 1* (collection), 3135

Whitehill, David. *Bad Axe Blues* (Seals and Whitehill), 461

Whiteman, Paul

★*At the Jazz Band Ball: Early Hot Jazz, Song, and Dance* (collection), 470

★*Big Band Jazz: From the Beginnings to the Fifties* (collection), 529

Bing Crosby and Some Jazz Friends (Crosby), 1125.2

The Classic Hoagy Carmichael (songwriter collection), 1097.1

The First of the Singer Songwriters: Key Cuts (Carmichael), 1124

George Gershwin (songwriter collection), 1101.3

If I Had a Talking Picture of You, Vol. 1, 1153.1

It's Easy to Remember (Crosby), 1125.6

James Van Heusen (songwriter collection), 1112.1

Makin' Whoopee, Vol. 2, 1153.2

★*Nipper's Greatest Hits: The 20's* (collection), 1071

The Phonographic Yearbook, 1922: An Angel's Voice I Hear (collection), 1078

The Roaring 'Twenties (collection), 1080

★*Swing Time! The Fabulous Big Band Era* (collection), 1089

Whiteman Stomp, 1153.3

★*Yes, Sir, That's My Baby: The Golden Years of Tin Pan Alley* (collection), 1094

Whitfield, Weslia. *Arthur Schwartz* (songwriter collection), 1110.2

Whiting, Margaret

★*American Popular Song: Six Decades of Songwriters and Singers* (collection), 1059

Arthur Schwartz (songwriter collection), 1110.2

The Classic Hoagy Carmichael (songwriter collection), 1097.1

Dorothy Fields (songwriter collection), 1100

E. Y. Harburg (songwriter collection), 1103

Frank Loesser (songwriter collection), 1106.1

Harold Arlen (songwriter collection), 1095.1

James Van Heusen (songwriter collection), 1112.1

Jerome Kern (songwriter collection), 1104.1

Johnny Mercer (songwriter collection), 1107.1

Oscar Hammerstein II (songwriter collection), 1102

Richard Whiting (songwriter collection), 1116

Rodgers / Hart (songwriter collection), 1109.1

★*Sentimental Journey: Pop Vocal Classics, Vol. 1* (collection), 1081

★*Sentimental Journey: Pop Vocal Classics, Vol. 2* (collection), 1168

Sweet and Lovely: Capitol's Great Ladies of Song (collection), 1172

Whiting, Richard. *Richard Whiting* (songwriter collection), 1116

Whitley, Keith. *Keith Whitley*, 1688

Whitman, Walt and the Soul Children of Chicago. *Going Up Yonder: The Best of the Gospel Choirs* (collection), 3051

Whitney, Mary Lee. *The Best of Loma Records: The Rise and Fall of a 1960's Soul Label* (collection), 2590

Whittaker, Hudson. *See* Tampa Red

Whitter, Henry. *Recordings of Grayson and Whitter*, 1408

The Who

Best of the Who, 1805.1

Live at Leeds, 1805.3

The British Invasion (collection), 1788

The Kids Are Alright, 1805.2

30 Years of Maximum R&B, 1805.4

Tommy, 1805.5

Who's Next, 1805.6

★*Who's Next (Deluxe Edition)*, 1805.7

Whodini. *Funky Beat: The Best of Whodini*, 2944

Wichita soul. *Boddie Recording Company Cleveland, Ohio* (collection), 2569

Wiegratz, Warren. *Best of Blues Piano (Lowry, Wiegratz, Boduch, McGirr and Schroedl)*, 261

★Wiggins, James. *Juke Joint Saturday Night: Piano Blues, Rags and Stomps; Classic Recordings from the 1920s and '30s* (collection), 255

Wiggins, Jay. *Beg, Scream, and Shout! The Big Ol' Box of '60s Soul* (collection), 2433

Wiggins, Phil. *Blues Routes* (collection), 413

Wiggins, Spencer

The Complete Goldwax Singles, Vol. 1 (collection), 2591

The Complete Goldwax Singles, Vol. 2 (collection), 2592

The Complete Goldwax Singles, Vol. 3 (collection), 2593

The Goldwax Years, 2530

★Wilber, Bob. *The Commodore Story* (collection), 561

Wilco

Summer Teeth, 2209.1

Yankee Hotel Foxtrot, 2209.2

Wild Cherry. *Disco Box* (collection), 2644

Wild Tchoupitoulas. *The Wild Tchoupitoulas*, 2375

Wilder, Alec

Alec Wilder Song Collection (songwriter collection), 1117.2

Alec Wilder (songwriter collection), 1117.1

Wilder, Chuck. *Eccentric Soul: The Tragar and Note Labels* (collection), 2602

★Wiley, Doc. *Nashville Jumps: Blues and Rhythm on Nashville Independent Labels 1945–1955* (collection), 2376

Wiley, Lee

Alec Wilder (songwriter collection), 1117.1

Bing Crosby and Some Jazz Friends (Crosby), 1125.2

Cole Porter (songwriter collection), 1108.1

★*The Commodore Story* (collection), 561

George Gershwin (songwriter collection), 1101.3

Lee Wiley Sings the Songs of Rodgers and Hart and Harold Arlen, 805

Richard Whiting (songwriter
    collection), 1116
Rodgers / Hart (songwriter collection),
    1109.1
★Sophisticated Ladies (collection), 1087
Vincent Youmans (songwriter
    collection), 1118
Waller / Razaf (songwriter collection),
    1113.2
Wilkes, Nathan. Eccentric Soul: The
    Tragar and Note Labels (collection),
    2602
Wilkins, Robert
    Before the Blues: The Early American
        Black Music Scene; Classic
        Recordings from the 1920s and 30s,
        Vols. 1–3 (collection), 183
    ★Blues Classics (collection), 146
    ★Legends of the Blues, Vol. 2 (collection),
        151
    Masters of Memphis Blues (collection),
        230
    The Original Rolling Stone, 235
    The Roots of Rock (collection), 368
★Williams, Andre. The Okeh Rhythm and
    Blues Story (collection), 2425
Williams, Andrea. Eccentric Soul: The
    Tragar and Note Labels (collection),
    2602
Williams, Andy
    Alan Jay Lerner (songwriter
        collection), 1105.1
    An Evening with Andy Williams: Live
        from the Royal Albert Hall, 1978,
        1232.1
    Johnny Mercer (songwriter collection),
        1107.1
    Sixteen Biggest Hits, 1232.2
    Sixteen Most Requested Songs, 1232.3
Williams, Bert
    The Middle Years, 1154
    The Phonographic Yearbook, 1907:
        Dear Old Golden Rule Days
        (collection), 1075
    This Is Art Deco (collection), 1090
Williams, Big Joe
    ★The Blues: A Smithsonian Collection
        of Classic Blues Singers (collection),
        145
    ★Legends of the Blues, Vol. 1 (collection),
        150
    Masters of the Country Blues: Fred
        McDowell and Big Joe Williams
        (collection), 391
    Shake Your Boogie, 406
    When the Sun Goes Down 1: Walk Right
        In (collection), 159
The Williams Brothers
    Greatest Hits, Vol 1, 3029
    Testify! The Gospel Box (collection),
        2974
Williams, Claude. Blues Routes
    (collection), 413

Williams, Cootie
    The Duke's Men: Small Groups, Vol. 1
        (collection), 562
    The Duke's Men: Small Groups, Vol. 2
        (collection), 563
    Stars of the Apollo (collection), 2240
Williams, Dauphin. Eccentric Soul: The
    Young Disciples (collection), 2562
★Williams, Deniece. Love Train: The
    Sound of Philadelphia (collection),
    2552
Williams, Don. The Best of Don Williams,
    Vol. 1, 1689
Williams, Dorothy. The Complete Goldwax
    Singles, Vol. 1 (collection), 2591
Williams, Eddie. The Swing Time Records
    Story: R&B, Blues, and Gospel,
    1946–1952 (collection), 2430
Williams, Frank and the Rocketeers
    Eccentric Soul: The Deep City Label
        (collection), 2600
    Eccentric Soul: The Outskirts of Deep
        City (collection), 2565
Williams, Hank
    Classic Country: Kings of Country
        (collection), 1381
    Classic Country Music: A Smithsonian
        Collection (collection), 1382
    ★Complete Hank Williams, 1556.1
    40 Greatest Hits, 1556.2
    Hank Williams: Honky Tonk Blues,
        1556.3
    Jubilation! Great Gospel Performances,
        Vol. 3: Country Gospel (collection),
        3112
    The Original Singles Collection—Plus,
        1556.4
    The Roots of Rock 'n' Roll, 1946–1954
        (collection), 1755
Williams, Hank, Jr.
    ★Hank Williams Jr.'s Greatest Hits,
        1690.1
    Whiskey Bent and Hell Bound, 1690.2
★Williams, Jabo. Juke Joint Saturday
    Night: Piano Blues, Rags and
    Stomps; Classic Recordings from
    the 1920s and '30s (collection),
    255
Williams, Jessica. The Best of Jessica
    Williams on Jazz Focus, Vol. 1,
    1027
Williams, Joe
    ★American Popular Song: Six Decades
        of Songwriters and Singers
        (collection), 1059
    The Definitive Collection (songwriter
        collection), 1101.1
    Dorothy Fields (songwriter collection),
        1100
    Duke Ellington (songwriter collection),
        1099.1
    Every Day: The Best of the Verve
        Years, 806.1

Harold Arlen (songwriter collection),
    1095.1
James Van Heusen (songwriter
    collection), 1112.1
★The Jazz Singers: A Smithsonian
    Collection of Jazz Vocals from
    1919–1994 (collection), 766
★Nashville Jumps: Blues and Rhythm
    on Nashville Independent Labels
    1945–1955 (collection), 2376
Nothin' but the Blues, 806.2
Rodgers / Hart (songwriter collection),
    1109.1
Williams, Johnny. Eccentric Soul:
    Twinight's Lunar Rotation
    (collection), 2568
Williams, Joyce. Eccentric Soul: The Nickel
    and Penny Labels (collection), 2567
Williams, Kathryn. Colours Are Brighter:
    Songs for Children and Grown Ups
    Too (collection), 3193
Williams, L. C. Texas Blues: Bill Quinn's
    Gold Star Recordings (collection),
    314
Williams, Larry
    The American Roots of the British
        Invasion (collection), 1786
    Bad Boy, 2301
    Soul Shots: A Collection of Sixties Soul
        Classics (collection), 2443
    ★The Specialty Story (collection), 2428
Williams, Lee and the Spiritual QC's. Tell
    the Angels: Live in Memphis, 3021
Williams, Lester
    Boogie Uproar: Texas Blues and R&B
        (collection), 312
    ★Texas Music, Vol. 1: Postwar Blues
        Combos (collection), 316
Williams, Lil' Ed. Blues Fest: Modern Blues
    of the '80s (collection), 409. See
    also Lil' Ed and the Blues Imperials
Williams, Little Jerry. The Best of Loma
    Records: The Rise and Fall of a
    1960's Soul Label (collection),
    2590
Williams, Loretta. Dave Godin's Deep Soul
    Treasures, Vols. 1–4 (collection),
    2435
Williams, Lucinda
    Car Wheels on a Gravel Road, 1714.1,
        2063.1
    Sweet Old World, 1714.2, 2063.2
Williams, Lynn. Eccentric Soul: The
    Outskirts of Deep City (collection),
    2565
Williams, Marion
    All of My Appointed Time: Forty
        Years of a Cappella Gospel Singing
        (collection), 2958
    Gospel Warriors: Over 50 Years
        of Great Solo Performances
        (collection), 2987
    ★The Gospel Sound (collection), 2964

Williams, Marion (cont.)
  ★*The Gospel Sound of Spirit Feel*
    (collection), 2965
  ★*The Great Gospel Women* (collection),
    2989
  The Great Gospel Women, Vol. 2
    (collection), 2990
  ★*My Soul Looks Back: The Genius of
    Marion Williams,* 3005
  ★*Precious Lord: Recordings of the Great
    Gospel Songs of Thomas A. Dorsey*
    (collection), 2968
  Testify! The Gospel Box (collection),
    2974
Williams, Mary Lou
  Free Spirits, 737
  Piano Legends (collection), 480
  *The Real Kansas City of the '20s, '30s,
    and '40s* (collection), 552
  Zodiac Suite, 589
Williams, Mason. *Rock Instrumental
    Classics, Vol. 2: The 60s*
    (collection), 1771
Williams, Maurice, and the Zodiacs. ★*The
    Doo-Wop Box* (collection), 2322
Williams, Paul
  *The Big Horn: The History of the
    Honkin' and Screamin' Saxophone*
    (collection), 2314
  ★*The R&B Box* (collection), 2239
Williams, Pharrell. *GIRL,* 2417
Williams, Robert Pete. *I'm Blue as a Man
    Can Be,* 407
Williams, Roger
  The Best of Roger Williams, 1233
  ★*It Had to Be You: Popular Keyboard
    from the Days of the Speakeasy
    to the Television Era* (collection),
    1068
  *Moments to Remember: The Golden
    Hits of the '50s and '60s Live*
    (collection), 1162
Williams, Sam and the Harris Singers.
    *This May Be My Last Time Singing:
    Raw African- American Gospel on
    45rpm* (collection), 2982
★Williams, Sherman. *Nashville Jumps:
    Blues and Rhythm on Nashville
    Independent Labels 1945-1955*
    (collection), 2376
Williams, Tex
  *Doughboys, Playboys, and Cowboys:
    The Golden Years of Western Swing*
    (collection), 1428
  *Heroes of Country Music, Vol. 1: Legends
    of Western Swing* (collection), 1429
  Smoke! Smoke! Smoke!, 1447
★Williamson Brothers and Curry.
    *Anthology of American Folk Music,
    Vols. 1-3* (collection), 1386
Williamson, Sonny Boy (Aleck Miller)
  *Blue Yule: Christmas Blues and R&B
    Classics* (collection), 3295

Blues Masters, Vol. 6: Blues Originals
    (collection), 367
*Blues Masters, Vol. 4: Harmonica
    Classics* (collection), 286
*Blues Masters, Vol. 2: Postwar Chicago
    Blues* (collection), 285
★*Chess Blues* (collection), 287
The Essential Sonny Boy Williamson,
    310.1
★*His Best,* 310.2
★*King Biscuit Time,* 310.3
*Memphis Slim and Sonny Boy
    Williamson: Live in Europe*
    (Memphis Slim and Sonny Boy
    Williamson), 403
*The Original Sonny Boy Williamson,
    Vol. 1* (Williamson), 284.1
The Original Sonny Boy Williamson
    (Williamson), 284.2
Williamson, Sonny Boy (John Lee Curtis)
  ★*Blues Classics* (collection), 146
  Blues in the Mississippi Night
    (collection), 214
  ★*The Blues: A Smithsonian Collection
    of Classic Blues Singers* (collection),
    145
  ★*Let's Get Loose: Folk and Popular
    Blues Styles from the Beginning to
    the Early 1940s* (collection), 152
  ★*Mean Old World: The Blues from
    1940-1994* (collection), 154
  *When the Sun Goes Down 3: That's
    Chicago's South Side* (collection),
    270
★Willie Tee. *Atlantic Soul, 1959-1975*
    (collection), 2589
Willis, Betty. *Birth of Soul, 4 Vols.*
    (collection), 2434
Willis, Chip, and Double Exposure.
    Eccentric Soul: The Prix Label
    (collection), 2601
Willis, Chuck
  ★*Atlantic R&B, 1947-1974* (collection),
    2418
  *I Remember Chuck Willis/the King of
    the Stroll,* 2302.1
  *Let's Jump Tonight!: The Best of Chuck
    Willis from 1951-56,* 2302.2
  ★*The Okeh Rhythm and Blues Story*
    (collection), 2425
  ★*The R&B Box* (collection), 2239
  The Roots of Rock 'n' Roll, 1946-1954
    (collection), 1755
  Stroll On: The Chuck Willis Collection,
    2302.3
★Willows. *The Doo-Wop Box* (collection),
    2322
Wills, Bob
  American Roots Music (collection),
    1380
  Anthology, 1448.1
  *Classic Country Music: A Smithsonian
    Collection* (collection), 1382

*Doughboys, Playboys, and Cowboys:
    The Golden Years of Western Swing*
    (collection), 1428
  ★*The Essential Bob Wills,* 1448.2
  *Heroes of Country Music, Vol. 1: Legends
    of Western Swing* (collection), 1429
  ★*San Antonio Rose,* 1448.3
  ★*San Antonio Rose* (Wills), 1448.3
  *Texas Music, Vol. 2: Western Swing and
    Honky Tonk* (collection), 1432
Wills, Bob and His Texas Playboys
  *Times Ain't What They Used to Be:
    Early Rural and Popular Music
    from Rare Original Film Masters*
    (collection), 1091
  *Western Swing: 40 Bootstompers from
    the Golden Age* (collection), 1433
Wills, Johnnie Lee
  *Heroes of Country Music, Vol. 1: Legends
    of Western Swing* (collection), 1429
  *Western Swing: 40 Bootstompers from
    the Golden Age* (collection), 1433
Wilner, Hal. *Amarcord Nino Rota*
    (collection), 809
Wilson, Cassandra
  ★*Blue Light 'til Dawn,* 807
  ★*The Jazz Singers: A Smithsonian
    Collection of Jazz Vocals from
    1919-1994* (collection), 766
  ★*Ken Burns Jazz: The Story of
    America's Music* (collection), 478
Wilson, Gerald
  *Big Band Renaissance: The Evolution of
    the Jazz Orchestra* (collection), 739
  ★*Central Avenue Sounds: Jazz in Los
    Angeles* (collection), 471
  Moment of Truth, 764
Wilson, Jackie
  *Beg, Scream, and Shout! The Big Ol'
    Box of '60s Soul* (collection), 2433
  ★*Mr. Excitement!,* 2531.1
  ★*The R&B Box* (collection), 2239
  *Respect: Aretha's Influences and
    Inspiration* (collection), 2440
  *The Story of Brunswick: The Classic
    Sound of Chicago Soul* (collection),
    2610
  *The Sweetest Feeling: A Van McCoy
    Songbook* (collection), 2447
  The Very Best of Jackie Wilson, 2531.2
Wilson, Matt. *Smile,* 1028
Wilson, Nancy
  ★*The Jazz Singers: A Smithsonian
    Collection of Jazz Vocals from
    1919-1994* (collection), 766
  Nancy Wilson / Cannonball Adderley,
    808
  *Sweet and Lovely: Capitol's Great Ladies
    of Song* (collection), 1172
  *The Sweetest Feeling: A Van McCoy
    Songbook* (collection), 2447
  Yesterday's Love Songs, Today's Blues,
    1234

Wilson, Teddy
   The Noble Art of Teddy Wilson, 590
   Piano Legends (collection), 480
   Piano Solos, 527.1
   Storyville Presents Teddy Wilson: The Original Piano Transcriptions, 527.2
Wilson, U. P. *Attack of the Atomic Guitar,* 365
Winans, BeBe. *Heaven,* 3103
Winans, CeCe
   Everlasting Love, 3104.1
   Purified, 3104.2
Winans, Robert. *The Early Minstrel Show* (collection), 96
The Winans
   The Definitive Original Greatest Hits, 3102
   Testify! The Gospel Box (collection), 2974
Winans, Vickie
   Be Encouraged, 3105.1
   How I Got Over, 3105.2
Windy City Four. *None but the Righteous: Chess Gospel Greats* (collection), 3037
Winehouse, Amy
   Back to Black, 1311, 2586.1
   I Told You I Was Trouble: Live in London, 2586.2
Wings of Faith Juniors of Grand Rapids, MI
   Boddie Recording Company Cleveland, Ohio (collection), 2569
   Boddie Recording Company Cleveland, Ohio (collection), 2570
Winston, George
   ★*Autumn: 20th Anniversary Edition,* 1353.1
   December: 20th Anniversary Edition, 1353.3
   Piano Solos, 1353.2
   A Quiet Revolution: 30 Years of Windham Hill (collection), 1372
   Solace: A Windham Hill Collection (collection), 1373
   Ultimate New Age (collection), 1376
   Windham Hill: The First Ten Years (collection), 1377
Winter, Johnny
   Best of Johnny Winter, 384.1
   Blues Masters, Vol. 9: Postmodern Blues (collection), 412
   Scorchin' Blues, 384.2
   Texas Music, Vol. 3: Garage Bands and Psychedelia (collection), 1830
Winter, Lois. *Don't Give the Name a Bad Place: Types and Stereotypes in American Musical Theater, 1870–1900* (collection), 1063
Winter, Paul
   Canyon, 1329.1
   Icarus, 1329.2

Pioneers of the New Age (collection), 1371
Wintersong, 3345
Wolf Eyes: A Retrospective, 1329.3
Winwood, Steve. *Chronicles,* 2090
Wipers. *Wipers Box Set: Is This Real?/ Youth of America/Over the Edge,* 2002
Wire
   Chairs Missing, 2039.1
   No Thanks! The '70s Punk Rebellion (collection), 2003
   Pink Flag, 2039.2
Wiregrass Sacred Harp Singers
   Desire for Piety: Songs from the B. F. White "Sacred Harp," 30
   The Colored Sacred Harp, 2986
Wiseman, Mac
   Early Dot Recordings, Vol. 3, 1617.1
   Mac Wiseman Story, 1617.2
Wison, Teddy. *Stars of the Apollo* (collection), 2240
Withers, Bill
   Respect: Aretha's Influences and Inspiration (collection), 2440
   The Very Best of Bill Withers, 2532
Witherspoon, Jimmy
   The Best of Jimmy Witherspoon: Jazz Me Blues, 2311.1
   Blowin' in from Kansas City, 2311.2
   Blues Masters, Vol. 1: Urban Blues (collection), 338
   ★*The Blues: A Smithsonian Collection of Classic Blues Singers* (collection), 145
   ★*Central Avenue Sounds: Jazz in Los Angeles* (collection), 471
   ★*The Jazz Singers: A Smithsonian Collection of Jazz Vocals from 1919–1994* (collection), 766
   Live at the 1972 Monterey Jazz Festival, 2311.3
   ★*Mean Old World: The Blues from 1940–1994* (collection), 154
   The Modern Records Blues Story (collection), 342
   The 'Spoon Concerts, 2311.4
   The Swing Time Records Story: R&B, Blues, and Gospel, 1946–1952 (collection), 2430
   The Swingtime Records Story: R&B, Blues, and Gospel (collection), 313
   ★*The Vee-Jay Story: Celebrating 40 Years of Classic Hits* (collection), 2431
   Urban Blues Singing Legend, 2311.5
Wolff, Henry. *Tibetan Bells II,* 1333
Womack, Bobby
   Anthology, 2533.1
   Beg, Scream, and Shout! The Big Ol' Box of '60s Soul (collection), 2433
   The Best of Bobby Womack: The Soul Years, 2533.2

The Bravest Man in the Universe, 2533.3
Dave Godin's Deep Soul Treasures, Vols. 1–4 (collection), 2435
The Jazz Channel Presents Bobby Womack, 2533.4
Respect: Aretha's Influences and Inspiration (collection), 2440
Womack Brothers. *Sam Cooke's SAR Records Story* (collection), 2606
women in rock since in the 1970s, 2040–2063
   The Best of the Runaways, 2058
   Broken English (Faithfull), 2046
   Car Wheels on a Gravel Road (Williams), 2063.1
   Dusty in Memphis (Springfield), 2061
   Fanny, 2047
   Fit to Be Tied: Great Hits by Joan Jett and the Blackhearts, 2050.1
   Give It Up (Raitt), 2057.1
   Greatest Hits (Armatrading), 2040
   Greatest Hits (Bangles), 2041
   Greatest Hits (Heart), 2049.1
   Greatest Hits, 1985–1995 (Heart), 2049.2
   I Do Not Want What I Haven't Got (O'Connor), 2055
   I Love Rock 'N' Roll (Jett), 2050.2
   ★*The Immaculate Collection* (Madonna), 2053
   Maria Muldaur, 2054
   Mercury Poise: 1988–1995 (Shocked), 2059
   Nick of Time (Raitt), 2057.2
   Private Dancer (Turner), 2062
   Raw Like Sushi (Cherry), 2044
   Return to the Valley of the Go-Go's, 2048
   Rickie Lee Jones, 2051
   She's So Unusual (Lauper), 2052
   A Story (Ono), 2056.1
   Sweet Old World (Williams), 2063.2
   Ultimate Collection (Benatar), 2042
   Viva! La Woman (Cibo Matto), 2045
   Walking on Thin Ice (Ono), 2056.2
   When I Was a Boy (Silberry), 2060
   The Whole Story (Bush), 2043
Women of the Calabash. *The Kwanzaa Album,* 3354
Wonder, Stevie
   At the Close of a Century, 2534.1
   Beg, Scream, and Shout! The Big Ol' Box of '60s Soul (collection), 2433
   The Definitive Collection, 2534.2
   Duets: An American Classic (Bennett), 1251.1
   Hitsville USA: The Motown Singles Collection (collection), 2603
   Hitsville USA: The Motown Singles Collection, Vol. 2 (collection), 2604
   ★*Innervisions,* 2534.3

Wonder, Stevie (cont.)
  Motown around the World (collection),
    2437
  The Original Musiquarium I, 2534.4
  ★Songs in the Key of Life, 2534.5
  Stevie Wonder Anthology, 2534.6
  Talking Book, 2534.7
Wonders, Thrasher. Classic African
    American Gospel from Smithsonian
    Folkways (collection), 2959
Wood, Brenton. Beg, Scream, and Shout!
    The Big Ol' Box of '60s Soul
    (collection), 2433
Woodbridge, Hudson. See Tampa Red
Woods, Bill, and His Orange Blossom
    Playboys. Swingbillies: Hillbilly and
    Western Swing on Modern/Colonial/
    Flair, 1947–1952 (collection),
    1431
Woods, Maceo. Testify! The Gospel Box
    (collection), 2974
Woods, Oscar. Texas Blues: Early Blues
    Masters from the Lone Star State
    (collection), 237
Woods, Phil
  Here's to My Lady, 900.1
  Phil Woods, 663
  ★Three for All, 900.2
★Wooley, Sheb. Halloween Hits
    (collection), 3347
Word of Mouth Chorus. Rivers of Delight:
    American Folk Hymns from the
    Sacred Harp Tradition, 31
world music (new age), 1359–1365
  The Best of Chris Spheeris, 1990–2000,
    1364
  Celtic Themes: Very Best of Clannad,
    1360
  The Mask and the Mirror (McKennitt),
    1362.1
  Natural Rhythms (Ancient Future),
    1359
  On the Wing (Micus), 1363
  Renaissance of the Celtic Harp (Stivell),
    1365
  The Visit (McKennitt), 1362.2
  ★Watermark (Enya), 1361
World Saxophone Quartet
  Revue, 933.1
  ★The Smithsonian Collection of Classic
    Jazz (collection), 486
  ★Steppin' with the World Saxophone
    Quartet, 933.2
  W.S.Q., 933.3
Wray, Link
  ★Legends of Guitar: Rock–The '50s,
    Vol. 1 (collection), 1749
  Rumble! The Best of Link Wray, 1785
★Wrens. The Doo-Wop Box (collection),
    2322
Wright, Betty
  Eccentric Soul: The Deep City Label
    (collection), 2600

Eccentric Soul: The Outskirts of Deep
    City (collection), 2565
  The Platinum Collection, 2535
Wright, Bill. Eccentric Soul: The Tragar
    and Note Labels (collection),
    2602
★Wright, Billy. Stompin' at the Savoy: The
    Original Indie Label, 1944–1961
    (collection), 2429
Wright Brothers Gospel Singers. I Hear
    Music in the Air: A Treasury of
    Gospel Music (collection), 3008
Wright, Bryan Sheldon. Breakin' Notes,
    144
Wright, Charles and the Watts 103rd St.
    Rhythm Band. Express Yourself,
    2643
★Wright, Charles. What It Is! Funky Soul
    and Rare Grooves (collection),
    2615
Wright, O. V.
  Beg, Scream, and Shout! The Big Ol'
    Box of '60s Soul (collection), 2433
  The Complete Goldwax Singles, Vol. 1
    (collection), 2591
  The Complete O. V. Wright on Hi
    Records, Vol. 1: In the Studio,
    2536.1
  The Complete O. V. Wright on Hi
    Records, Vol. 2: On Stage (Live in
    Japan), 2536.2
  Duke-Peacock's Greatest Hits
    (collection), 2421
  The Hi Records Story (collection),
    2423
  The Soul of O. V. Wright, 2536.3
Wright, Willie. Telling the Truth, 2537
Wu-Tang Clan
  ★Enter the Wu-Tang: 36 Chambers,
    2946.1
  Wu-Tang Forever, 2946.2
Wyatt, Robert. Rock Bottom, 1970
Wyble, Jimmy. Legends of Western Swing
    Guitar (collection), 1430
Wynette, Tammy
  Anniversary, 20 Years of Hits: The First
    Lady of Country Music, 1557
  The Hee Haw Collection, Vol. 3
    (collection), 1451
Wynn, Big Slim. The Big Horn: The History
    of the Honkin' and Screamin'
    Saxophone (collection), 2314
★Wynn, Nan. Sophisticated Ladies
    (collection), 1087

X

X
  Beyond and Back: The X Anthology,
    2210.1
  No Thanks! The '70s Punk Rebellion
    (collection), 2003
  X: The Unheard Music, 2210.2
X-Clan. To the East, Blackwards, 2947

X-Ray Spex
  Let's Submerge: The Anthology, 2030
  No Thanks! The '70s Punk Rebellion
    (collection), 2003
  Punk: Attitude (collection), 1980
XTC. Compact XTC: The Singles,
    1978–1985, 2211
Xzibit. 40 Dayz and 40 Nightz, 2948

Y

Yancey, Jimmy
  Barrelhouse Boogie (collection), 250,
    521
  ★The Blues: A Smithsonian Collection
    of Classic Blues Singers (collection),
    145
  Hey! Piano Man (collection), 254
  Shake Your Wicked Knees: Rent
    Parties and Good Times
    (collection), 258
Yankovic, Weird Al
  The Ultimate Video Collection, 1312.1
  "Weird Al" Yankovic's Greatest Hits,
    1312.2
Yanni
  New Age Piano Sampler (collection),
    1369
  Solace: A Windham Hill Collection
    (collection), 1373
  The Very Best of Yanni, 1345
  The World of Private Music
    (collection), 1378
The Yardbirds
  Casey Kasem Presents America's Top
    Ten through the Years: The Sixties
    (collection), 1156
  Five Live Yardbirds, 385
  Legends of Guitar: Rock–The '60s,
    Vol. 1 (collection), 1860
  Stroll On: An Immediate Blues
    Collection (collection), 369
  25 Hits from the British Invasion
    (collection), 1792
  ★Ultimate!, 1806
Yeah Yeah Yeahs. Fever to Tell, 2212
Yearwood, Trisha
  Grand Ole Opry at Carnegie Hall
    (collection), 1619
  Hearts in Armor, 1691
Yellin, Bob. Mountain Music Bluegrass
    Style (collection), 1566
Yellowjackets. Best of the Yellowjackets,
    911
Yellvington, Malcolm. Sun Rockabilly:
    The Classic Recordings (collection),
    1742
Yes
  Billboard #1s: The '80s (collection),
    1236
  Fragile, 1971
Yo La Tengo
  Electr-O-Pura, 2213.1
  Greasy Kid Stuff (collection), 3210

I Can Hear the Heart Beating as One,
2213.2
Yo Yo's. *The Complete Goldwax Singles,*
Vol. 2 (collection), 2592
Yoakam, Dwight
Guitars, Cadillacs, Etc., Etc., 1692.1
This Time, 1692.2
Yorgesson, Yogi. *Dr. Demento Presents:*
The Greatest Christmas Novelty CD
of All Time (collection), 3307
Yoshizawa, Masakazu. *Kyori*
(Innervisions), 1315
Youmans, Vincent. *Vincent Youmans*
(songwriter collection), 1118
Young and Company. *Disco Box*
(collection), 2644
Young, Andre Romelle. *See* Dre, Dr.
Young Disciples Co. *Eccentric Soul: The*
Young Disciples (collection), 2562
Young Divines. *Eccentric Soul: The*
Tragar and Note Labels (collection),
2602
Young, Faron
The Best of Faron Young, 1558.1
Classic Country: Kings of Country
(collection), 1381
Country Style, U.S.A. (collection),
1473
The Hee Haw Collection, Vol. 3
(collection), 1451
Live Fast, Love Hard: Original Capitol
Recordings 1952–1962, 1558.2
Young Jeezy. *Let's Get It: Thug Motivation*
101, 2949
Young, Karen. *Disco Box* (collection),
2644
Young, Lester
★*Central Avenue Sounds: Jazz in Los*
Angeles (collection), 471
★*The Commodore Story* (collection),
561
The Complete Aladdin Sessions, 591.1
★*From Spirituals to Swing: The*
Legendary 1938 and 1939 Carnegie
Hall Concerts Produced by John
Hammond (collection), 564
Jazz Masters: Vintage Collection,
1958–1961 (collection), 477
The "Kansas City" Sessions, 591.2
★*Ken Burns Jazz Collection: Lester*
Young, 591.3

Pres and Teddy, 738
The Real Kansas City of the '20s, '30s,
and '40s (collection), 552
★*The Smithsonian Collection of Classic*
Jazz (collection), 486
★*Sound of Jazz* (collection), 487
Timeless, 591.4
Young, Mae. *Eccentric Soul: The Big Mack*
Label (collection), 2598
Young Marble Giants. *Colossal Youth,*
1890
Young MC. *Stone Cold Rhymin',* 2950
Young, Mighty Joe
Mighty Man, 366
The Fire / Fury Records Story
(collection), 2422
Young, Neil
★*Decade,* 1911.1
Ragged Glory, 1911.2
Rust Never Sleeps, 1911.3
Tonight's the Night, 1911.4
★Young, Preston. *Anthology of American*
Folk Music, Vols. 1–3 (collection),
1386
Young, Victor
The Definitive Collection (songwriter
collection), 1101.1
Irving Berlin: A Hundred Years
(songwriter collection), 1096.3
It's Easy to Remember (Crosby), 1125.6
Youngblood, Lonnie. *The Best of Loma*
Records: The Rise and Fall of a
1960's Soul Label (collection),
2590
Youngbloods. *San Francisco Nights*
(collection), 1829
Young-Holt Trio
Beg, Scream, and Shout! The Big Ol'
Box of '60s Soul (collection), 2433
The Story of Brunswick: The Classic
Sound of Chicago Soul (collection),
2610
★Young-Holt Unlimited. ★*What It Is!*
Funky Soul and Rare Grooves
(collection), 2615
Youth for Christ Choir. *Good God! Born*
Again Funk (collection), 2614

Z
Zacherle, John. *Halloween Hootenanny*
(collection), 3348

Zanes, Dan, and Friends
All around the Kitchen! Crazy Videos
and Concert Songs!, 3225.1
Family Dance, 3225.2
Zappa, Frank
Absolutely Free, 1850.1
Freak Out!, 1850.2
Hot Rats, 1850.3
Legends of Guitar: Rock–The '60s,
Vol. 1 (collection), 1860
Like Omigod! The 80s Pop Culture Box
(Totally) (collection), 1241
Strictly Commercial: The Best of Frank
Zappa, 1850.4
★*We're Only in It for the Money,* 1850.5
Zawinul, Joe
Joe Zawinul, 833.1
Zawinul, 833.2
Zeger, Brian. *Songs: Foster, Griffes,*
Copland (collection), 101
Zevon, Warren. *A Quiet Normal Life: The*
Best of Warren Zevon, 1912
Zimmerman, Robert Allen. *See* Dylan, Bob
Zion Harmonizers. *Jesus Put a Song in My*
Soul (collection), 3036
Zion I. *Mind over Matter,* 2951
★Zodiacs. *The Doo Wop Box: 101 Vocal*
Group Gems from the Golden Age of
Rock 'n' Roll (collection), 1745
Zombie, Rob. *Halloween Hootenanny*
(collection), 3348
The Zombies
★*Odyssey and Oracle,* 1807
25 Hits from the British Invasion
(collection), 1792
Zonophone Concert Band. *Early*
Syncopated Dance Music:
Cakewalks, Two-Steps, Trots and
Glides (collection), 124
Zorn, John
★*Masada: Live at Tonic,* 1029.1
News for Lulu, 1029.2
ZZ Top
Billboard #1s: The '80s (collection),
1236
Greatest Hits, 1951